The Mark Twain Encyclopedia

Garland Reference Library of the Humanities

(Vol. 1249)

Advisory Board

The
MARK TWAIN
Encyclopedia

EDITORS

J.R. LeMaster
BAYLOR UNIVERSITY

James D. Wilson
UNIVERSITY OF SOUTHWESTERN LOUISIANA

Editorial and Research Assistant
Christie Graves Hamric

GARLAND PUBLISHING, INC.
New York & London
1993

Library of Congress Cataloging-in-Publication Data

The Mark Twain encyclopedia / editors, J.R. LeMaster, James D. Wilson ; editorial and research assistant, Christie Graves Hamric.
    p. cm. — (Garland reference library of the humanities ; vol. 1249)
    Includes bibliographical references and index.
    ISBN 0-8240-7212-X (alk. paper)
    1. Twain, Mark, 1835–1910—Encyclopedias. 2. Authors, American—19th century—Biography—Encyclopedias. I. LeMaster, J.R., 1934– . II. Wilson, James D. (James Darrell), 1946– . III. Hamric, Christie Graves. IV. Series.
PS1330.M37 1993
818'.409—dc20
[B]

92-45662
CIP

Printed on acid-free, 250-year-life paper
Manufactured in the United States of America

In memory of E. Hudson Long
(1908–1990)

Contents

Preface

The Mark Twain Encyclopedia is a reference guide designed for anyone interested in Samuel L. Clemens. The approximately 740 entries, arranged alphabetically, are in fact a collection of articles, ranging significantly in length and covering a variety of topics pertaining to this major American author's life, intellectual milieu, literary career, and achievements. Because so much of Mark Twain's writing (travel narratives, essays, letters, sketches, autobiography, journalism, and fiction) reflects Samuel Clemens's personal experience, particular attention has been given to the delicate interstices between art and life, that is, between imaginative reconstructions and their factual sources of inspiration. Each entry is accompanied by selective bibliography to guide readers to sources that provide more detailed information.

The Mark Twain Encyclopedia is designed to offer the general reader convenient access to basic and reliable biographical information: the author's childhood in Missouri and apprenticeship as riverboat pilot; his early career as journalist in Nevada and California; his world travels; his friendships with or relationships to patriarchs and matriarchs of genteel culture; his reading and education; his family life; his career as businessman—in short, the names, dates, places, and events germane to an understanding of Clemens's life and career. Biography, however, is but one aspect of the encyclopedia. Mark Twain's novels and travel narratives, and most of his short stories, sketches, burlesques, and essays receive individual attention in articles that provide a general introduction to the primary work, that identify major critical approaches and points of scholarly controversy, and that furnish a list of suggested supplementary readings. Significant characters, places, and landmarks—especially those that appear in the major fiction or recur in several works—are treated in shorter entries that identify the item and comment succinctly on its importance. Longer and more general articles treat recurring themes or concepts that loom large in Mark Twain studies: for example, Mark Twain's humor; his use of language; his attitudes on race, war, religion, politics, imperialism, art, science; point of view; imagery; sources; and influences. Some entries break new ground and suggest areas where additional research or investigation is needed. Others synthesize information to provide convenient access to material treated in a variety of disparate sources. Hence *The Mark Twain Encyclopedia* serves the general reader or student as a handy, accessible source of basic information and a launching point for more sustained investigation. At the same time, it serves the more advanced researcher or teacher as a succinct, reliable guide to a wide array of subjects and a review of the current status of Mark Twain scholarship.

In a volume of this scope, proportioning and arranging material to make information readily accessible and usable poses editorial challenges. We have arranged entries alphabetically. The process of assigning titles to entries and determining how to alphabetize them requires a compromise between an editor's penchant for consistency and symmetry on the one hand and a reader's expectations concerning clarity and ease of access on the other. Primary works are alphabetized by the first word in the title, articles excluded: e.g., *Adventures of Huckleberry Finn*; *Connecticut Yankee in King Arthur's Court, A*; "Man That Corrupted Hadleyburg, The." Public figures are listed by surname, regardless of gender. Fictional characters, too, are also listed by surname, except when the reader would likely be more familiar with the given name: e.g., Finn, Huckleberry; Sawyer, Sid; Douglas, Widow; but Angelo and Luigi (Cappello); Jim; Joan of Arc. When there is an entry on an individual who commonly employed a pseudonym, the editors had to decide by which name that individual is more commonly known: e.g., Ward, Artemus; but Clemens, Samuel Langhorne. A similar and more perplexing dilemma is posed by primary works with alternative titles. In his lifetime, Clemens frequently republished his stories, sketches, and novels in different formats and often provided new titles for the same or slightly revised work; after his death, editors excerpted portions of longer works and supplied titles, or they assigned titles to posthumously published manuscripts, frequently fragmentary and untitled. As editors, we simply listed these works by their commonly known titles: e.g., "Jim Smiley and His Jumping Frog" and "The Notorious Jumping Frog of Calaveras County" are listed as "Celebrated Jumping Frog of Calaveras County, The"; *The Tragedy of Pudd'nhead Wilson* as *Pudd'nhead Wilson*; the various manuscripts that compose *The Mysterious Stranger* are all discussed in a single entry, *Mysterious Stranger, The*—although the entry distinguishes among them. Because of the intrinsic difficulties posed by an alphabetical arrangement, the reader should make extensive use of the "see also" references provided with most entries—which specifically direct the reader to other, related, entries—and the index, which provides a listing of all entries that contain a significant discussion of the subject. Virtually all individual entries contain selective bibliographies that direct the reader to those sources deemed most pertinent to further research.

We are grateful to our advisory editors for their suggestions and support in planning this project. Each reviewed our list of proposed topics, called our attention to subjects that should be included in a project of this scope, gave suggestions about organizing the volume, and recommended appropriate scholars to write on particular subjects. Their work, coupled with the enthusiastic, insightful, and meticulous effort of some 180 individual contributors have made this encyclopedia truly a communal endeavor. The diversity of critical approaches reflects the diversity in contemporary American literary scholarship. The editors prize this diversity and have therefore consciously avoided imposing or sanctioning any particular methodology or approach over another; in fact, many controversial subjects and major primary texts receive attention from several different scholars who approach their subjects from widely divergent points of view. We have edited entries to achieve consistency of format, to tighten and improve cogency, to verify accuracy of factual details, and to avoid needless duplication of information provided in related entries. At the same time, we have tried not to interfere with the voices (styles) or distinctive approaches of our individual contributors. Each entry is signed and expresses the judgments and opinions of its author. As general editors, however, we are responsible for any factual errors, and we hope that readers of this encyclopedia will call our attention to such errors so that they may be rectified in subsequent editions.

Despite the size of this volume, and the number of people involved in its production, we are going to press on schedule; we are able to do so because of the conscientious efforts and generous support of the many individuals who have rendered valuable assistance during the course of this project. Our contributors, of course, made the encyclopedia possible. We are grateful to them not only for their excellent work but for their cooperation in meeting deadlines, fulfilling commitments, and making revisions when necessary. We wish to acknowledge the dedicated work of our research assistants— Geraldine Behnke, Trevor J. Morgan, Lisa Calhoun, Patricia Hicks, and Christie Graves Hamric—who contributed in various capacities throughout the duration of the project. We are grateful to our chairs, James Barcus and Doris Meriwether, whose tangible support and encouragement greatly facilitated our work, and to Baylor University and the University of Southwestern Louisiana for the released time, grant support, computer space and equipment, secretarial and research assistance that made possible the timely completion of our tasks. We are grateful to Gary Kuris and his staff at Garland Publishing for their initial faith in the project and the valuable assistance they have provided at every stage. And lastly, we are grateful to our colleagues and families, who persevered while we devoted our time and energy to compiling a reference book on Mark Twain.

J.R. LeMaster and James D. Wilson

Chronology

1835	Samuel Langhorne Clemens born 30 November at Florida, Missouri.
1839	Clemens family moved to Hannibal, Missouri.
1847	Father, John Marshall Clemens, died of pneumonia 24 March at age forty-eight; four surviving children.
1849–1851	Apprentice to Joseph P. Ament, printer; set type for the Hannibal *Courier*.
1850–1852	Brother, Orion, returned to Hannibal in September 1850 to start a Whig newspaper, the *Western Union*. In spring of 1851, Orion purchased the *Weekly Dollar Journal* and combined it with his own paper to form the *Western Union and Hannibal Journal*, which became the *Journal* in February 1852. Sam worked with Orion as "Assistant Editor."
1852	Sketch, "The Dandy Frightening the Squatter," in May issue of the *Carpet-Bag*.
1853	Sam left Hannibal for St. Louis in June. Spent August in New York and visited Philadelphia during the winter. Corresponded for the Muscatine (Iowa) *Journal*.
1854	Visited Washington, D.C., in February. Spent the summer with his mother and Orion in Muscatine, Iowa, where he worked on the *Journal*.
1855	Winter and spring in St. Louis. Joined Orion in Keokuk, Iowa, in the summer, where he worked on the *Daily Post* until fall 1856.
1856–1857	Left Keokuk for St. Louis in the fall of 1856. Began Thomas Jefferson Snodgrass letters for the Keokuk *Daily Post* on 18 October. Moved from St. Louis to Cincinnati, where he lived during the winter and reportedly met the Scotsman named Macfarlane. In April 1857, boarded the *Paul Jones* for New

Orleans, intending to go to South America. Instead, met Horace Bixby, who agreed to teach him the river.

1858–1859	Learned the river as a "cub" and piloted freighters. Brother Henry killed in a steamboat explosion near Memphis in June 1858. Received his pilot license 9 April 1859.
1859	"Sergeant Fathom" published in New Orleans *Crescent* (May).
1861	"Quintus Curtius Snodgrass" letters (authorship disputed) published in New Orleans *Crescent* (21 January-30 March).
1861	Outbreak of the Civil War ended career as riverboat pilot. After the short "Campaign That Failed" stint in the Confederate Army in June, accompanied Orion on a twenty-one day stagecoach journey to Carson City, Nevada, in late July and early August.
1862	"Josh" letters published in Virginia City *Territorial Enterprise* (February-July).
	Joined staff of the *Territorial Enterprise* in August; remained there until May 1864. During November and December, reported on the Second Territorial Legislature of Nevada from Carson City for the *Enterprise*.
	"The Petrified Man" hoax printed in *Territorial Enterprise* (5 October); rpt. San Francisco *Daily Evening Bulletin* (15 October).
1863	2 February, in a dispatch to the *Enterprise* from Carson City, first assumed the name "Mark Twain." In early summer, made his first visit to San Francisco, in company of newspaperman Clement T. Rice (the Unreliable). Met Artemus Ward at Virginia City in December.
	"The Empire City Massacre," *Territorial Enterprise* (28 October).

1864

In January, elected "Governor" of the Third House by fellow newspapermen at Carson City. In May, became involved in a controversy with a rival editor resulting in a proposed duel, in violation of Nevada law. Left for San Francisco, where he worked through the fall as a reporter for the *Morning Call*. Became friends with Bret Harte, Charles Henry Webb, and other members of the San Francisco literary community; contributed burlesques and sketches to the *Golden Era* and the *Californian*.

"Those Blasted Children," New York *Sunday Mercury* (21 February); rpt. in San Francisco's *Golden Era* (27 March).

1864–1865

His investigative reporting of municipal corruption led to Twain's hasty departure from San Francisco to the Tuolumne Hills in the Mother Lode country, 4 December 1864. Stayed with Jim Gillis at Jackass Hill and at nearby Angel's Camp; heard Ben Coon tell the "Jumping Frog" story. Returned to San Francisco, 25 February 1865. Wrote his version of Coon's story, "Jim Smiley and His Jumping Frog."

1865

"Jim Smiley and His Jumping Frog," New York *Saturday Press* (18 November).

1866

7 March, sailed for the Sandwich Islands to write a series of travel letters for the Sacramento *Union*. Remained in Hawaii until early July; wrote special dispatch on the burning of the clipper ship *Hornet* at sea, 25 June. Embarked on the lecture circuit, 2 October, talking on the Sandwich Islands at the San Francisco Academy of Music.

1866–1867

Left San Francisco in December 1866, sailing for New York via the Isthmus of Panama. Wrote travel letters for the *Alta California*, which were subsequently collected and known as *Mark Twain's Travels with Mr. Brown*. Arrived in New York January 1867, continuing the *Alta* corres-pondence with a series of letters recording his impressions of life in New York. March and April, visited St. Louis, Hannibal, and Keokuk. Lectured successfully at Cooper Union in New York on 6 May.

The Celebrated Jumping Frog of Calaveras County and Other Sketches. New York: C.H. Webb (May 1867).

8 June 1867, sailed on the *Quaker City* for Europe and the Holy Land as a correspondent for the *Alta California*; letters would subsequently become *The Innocents Abroad*. Returned to New York, 19 November. Served briefly as private secretary to Nevada Senator William M. Stewart in Washington, D.C. First met Olivia Langdon, 27 December.

1868

2 or 3 January, first date with Olivia, to hear Charles Dickens read. Journeyed to California to secure publishing rights to his *Alta* correspondence in March. Lectured in San Francisco during spring and summer before leaving for New York on 6 July. In August, made his first visit to the Langdon family home in Elmira, New York. Conducted strenuous lecture tour of the Midwest in November and December.

1869

4 February, became engaged to marry Olivia. In August, purchased a partnership in the Buffalo (New York) *Express* with a $25,000 loan from Olivia's father, Jervis Langdon.

The Innocents Abroad. Hartford, Conn.: American Publishing (July).

Under management of James Redpath, engaged in strenuous lecture tour from November 1869 through January 1870.

1870

2 February, married Olivia Langdon, in Elmira, New York. Settled in Buffalo, New York. In March began writing sketches for the *Galaxy*; continued to do so until April 1871.

Made hasty trip to Washington in early July, where he was photographed by Matthew Brady and met General Ulysses S. Grant.

6 August, father-in-law, Jervis Langdon, died.

7 November, first child and only son, Langdon Clemens, born prematurely in Buffalo.

1871

Mark Twain's (Burlesque) Autobiography and First Romance. New York: Sheldon (February).

Spring and summer, Clemens family vacationed at Quarry Farm, in Elmira, which became their favorite summer retreat. In October, liquidated his interest in the Buffalo *Express* and moved to Hartford, Connecticut, where the family rented a house at Nook Farm. Began a lecture tour (November 1871–February 1872) to pay debts caused by sacrifice of Buffalo interests.

1872

Roughing It. Hartford, Conn.: American Publishing (February).

19 March, daughter Olivia Susan (Susy) born.

2 June, Langdon Clemens died of pneumonia.

In August, family sailed for England where on 9 November Twain was honored at Lord Mayor's dinner in London.

1873   Summer spent in England and Europe with family; lectured throughout Britain in November and December.

The Gilded Age (with Charles Dudley Warner). Hartford, Conn.: American Publishing (December).

1874   January, sailed home from England.

8 June, daughter Clara born.

Mark Twain's Sketches, Number One. New York: American News.

Dramatized version of *The Gilded Age* opened in New York (September).

1875   "Old Times on the Mississippi" appeared serially in *Atlantic Monthly* (January-June and August).

Mark Twain's Sketches, New and Old. Hartford, Conn.: American Publishing (July).

1876   *The Adventures of Tom Sawyer.* Hartford, Conn.: American Publishing (December).

1877   April, production of the play *Ah Sin!* in collaboration with Bret Harte; opened in Washington 7 May.

16 May, sailed for Bermuda with Reverend Joseph Twichell.

A True Story and the Recent Carnival of Crime. Boston: James R. Osgood (September).

17 December, made Whittier Birthday Dinner Speech in Boston.

1878–1879   *Punch, Brothers, Punch! and Other Sketches.* New York: Slote, Woodman (March 1878).

Lived abroad in Germany and Italy. August 1878, made walking tour with Twichell through the Black Forest.

1880   *A Tramp Abroad.* Hartford, Conn.: American Publishing (March).

1601, or Conversation as It Was by the Social Fireside in the Time of the Tudors. Cleveland edition (June); West Point edition (1882).

26 July, daughter Jean born.

1881   November, visited Canada for a fortnight.

1882   *The Prince and the Pauper.* Boston: James R. Osgood (January).

April–May, made trip down the Mississippi River to New Orleans, where he met George Washington Cable and Joel Chandler Harris. Returned up river with Horace Bixby.

The Stolen White Elephant, Etc. Boston: James R. Osgood (June).

1883   May, brief visit to Canada.

Life on the Mississippi. Boston: James R. Osgood (May).

1884   Summer, campaigned for Grover Cleveland. November, began lecture tour with G.W. Cable, which lasted until February 1885.

1885   *Adventures of Huckleberry Finn.* New York: Charles L. Webster (February).

Fall, published *Personal Memoirs of U.S. Grant.*

1888   Master of Arts degree from Yale University (honorary).

1889   *A Connecticut Yankee in King Arthur's Court.* New York: Charles L. Webster (December).

1890   Summer, engrossed in Paige typesetting machine. Susy entered Bryn Mawr in the fall.

27 October, mother, Jane Lampton Clemens, died.

1891   June, family closed Hartford home and went to Europe.

1892   Winter of 1891–1892 in Berlin, Germany.

Merry Tales. New York: Charles L. Webster (March).

The American Claimant. New York: Charles L. Webster (May).

1893   *The £1,000,000 Bank-Note and Other New Stories.* New York: Charles L. Webster (February).

Spring, family in Italy. Twain made trips to the United States to stave off failure of the Paige typesetting machine.

1894   18 April, Charles L. Webster and Company executed assignment papers, carrying Clemens into bankruptcy with it.

Summer, family remained in France; Twain visited the United States in July and August. Returned to France to be with family until May 1895.

The Tragedy of Pudd'nhead Wilson and the Comedy Those Extraordinary Twins. Hartford, Conn.: American Publishing (November).

1895   Returned to the United States in May; spent early summer at Quarry Farm. In mid-July, began the lecture tour to Australia, New Zealand, India, and South Africa that produced *Following the Equator*.

1896   *Personal Recollections of Joan of Arc*. New York: Harper (May).

18 August, daughter Susy died of meningitis.

Tom Sawyer Abroad, Tom Sawyer, Detective, and Other Stories. New York: Harper (November).

Winter in London.

1897   *How to Tell a Story and Other Essays*. New York: Harper (March).

Following the Equator. Hartford, Conn.: American Publishing (November).

1898   Last debts paid in full during the winter.

1900   *The Man That Corrupted Hadleyburg and Other Stories and Essays*. New York: Harper (June).

English as She Is Taught. Boston: Mutual Book (October).

Autumn, returned to the United States to a national welcome. Took a house at 14 West Tenth Street, New York.

1901   *To the Person Sitting in Darkness*. New York: Anti-Imperialist League (February).

Summer on Saranac Lake, New York; fall cruise to Nova Scotia on H.H. Rogers's yacht, the *Kanawha*.

October, moved to Riverdale-on-the-Hudson, New York.

1902   Sailed with H.H. Rogers on the *Kanawha* through the Caribbean (13 March–9 April).

A Double-Barreled Detective Story. New York: Harper (April).

June, traveled to Missouri; visited Hannibal for the last time; University of Missouri conferred Litt.D. degree (honorary).

Summer at York Harbor, Maine; daughter Jean suffered two epileptic seizures; Olivia suffered a major nervous collapse on 12 August, and another in November.

November, returned to Riverdale.

1903   *My Debut as a Literary Person and Other Essays and Stories*. New York: American Publishing (April).

October, family settled in Italy for Olivia's health; lived in Florence at the Villa Quarto, then at the Villa Collarini.

1904   *Extracts from Adam's Diary*. New York: Harper (April).

5 June, Olivia Langdon Clemens died in Italy, near Florence.

Family returned to New York City, taking residence at 21 Fifth Avenue.

A Dog's Tale. New York: Harper (September).

1905   Summer in Dublin, New Hampshire; returned to New York 21 October.

King Leopold's Soliloquy. Boston: R.P. Warren (September).

1906   *The $30,000 Bequest and Other Stories*. New York: Harper.

Summer in Dublin, New Hampshire.

What Is Man? published anonymously at the De Vinne Press (August).

Eve's Diary. New York: Harper.

1907   January, made trip to Bermuda with Joseph Twichell.

Christian Science. New York: Harper (February).

16–21 March, brief trip to Bermuda.

8 June, sailed to England; Oxford University conferred Litt.D. degree (honorary).

Summer in Tuxedo Park, New York.

A Horse's Tale. New York: Harper (October).

1908   18 June, moved into "Stormfield" home in Redding, Connecticut.

1909   25 January–6 February, 27 February–11 April, vacations in Bermuda.

Is Shakespeare Dead? New York: Harper (April).

Extract from Captain Stormfield's Visit to Heaven. New York: Harper.

August, suffered "sunstroke" at funeral of Samuel Moffett.

6 October, Clara married Ossip Gabrilowitsch.

18 November–20 December in Bermuda with Albert Bigelow Paine; returned to Redding for Christmas.

24 December, daughter Jean died.

1910   January, returned to Bermuda; returned with Paine to the United States on 12 April.

21 April, Samuel L. Clemens died; buried at Elmira, New York.

Posthumous Publications

1910   *Mark Twain's Speeches*. New York: Harper.

1916   *The Mysterious Stranger*. New York: Harper.

1917   *Mark Twain's Letters*. Ed. Albert B. Paine. 2 vols. New York: Harper.

    "What Is Man?" and Other Essays. New York: Harper.

1919   *The Curious Republic of Gondour and Other Whimsical Sketches*. New York: Boni and Liveright.

1923   *Europe and Elsewhere*. New York: Harper.

1924   *Mark Twain's Autobiography*. Ed. Albert B. Paine. 2 vols. New York: Harper.

1926   *Sketches of the Sixties* (with Bret Harte). San Francisco: J. Howell.

1928   *The Adventures of Thomas Jefferson Snodgrass*. Ed. Charles Honce. Chicago: Pascal Covici.

1935   *Mark Twain's Notebooks*. Ed. Albert B. Paine. New York: Harper.

    Slovenly Peter (Der Struwwelpeter). Trans. Mark Twain. New York: Limited Editions Club.

1938   *Mark Twain's Letters from the Sandwich Islands*. Ed. G. Ezra Dane. Stanford, Calif.: Stanford UP.

    The Washoe Giant in San Francisco. Ed. Franklin Walker. San Francisco: George Fields.

1939   *Letters from Honolulu*. Ed. Thomas Nickerson. Honolulu: Thomas Nickerson.

1940   *Mark Twain in Eruption*. Ed. Bernard DeVoto. New York: Harper.

    Mark Twain's Travels with Mr. Brown. Ed. Franklin Walker and G. Ezra Dane. New York: Knopf.

1941   *Mark Twain's Letters to Will Bowen*. Ed. Theodore Hornberger. Austin: U of Texas P.

    Republican Letters. Ed. Cyril Clemens. Webster Groves, Mo.: International Mark Twain Society.

1942   *Mark Twain's Letters in the Muscatine Journal*. Ed. Edgar M. Branch. Chicago: Mark Twain Association of America.

1943   *Washington in 1868*. Ed. Cyril Clemens. Webster Groves, Mo.: International Mark Twain Society.

1946   *The Letters of Quintus Curtius Snodgrass*. Ed. Ernest E. Leisy. Dallas: Southern Methodist UP (Twain authorship disputed).

1948   *Mark Twain in Three Moods*. Ed. Dixon Wecter. San Marino, Calif.: Huntington Library.

1949   *The Love Letters of Mark Twain*. Ed. Dixon Wecter. New York: Harper.

    Mark Twain to Mrs. Fairbanks. Ed. Dixon Wecter. San Marino: Huntington Library.

1952   *Report from Paradise*. Ed. Dixon Wecter. New York: Harper.

1957   *Mark Twain of the "Enterprise": Newspaper Articles and Other Documents, 1862–1864*. Ed. Henry Nash Smith and Frederick Anderson. Berkeley: U of California P.

    Mark Twain: San Francisco Correspondent. Selections from His Letters to the "Territorial Enterprise": 1865–1866. Ed. Henry Nash Smith and Frederick Anderson. San Francisco: Book Club of California.

1958   *Traveling with the Innocents Abroad*. Ed. Daniel M. McKeithan. Norman: U of Oklahoma P.

1959   *The Autobiography of Mark Twain*. Ed. Charles Neider. New York: Harper.

1960   *Mark Twain and the Government*. Comp. Sven Peterson. Caldwell, Idaho: Caxton.

    Mark Twain-Howells Letters: The Correspondence of Samuel L. Clemens and William D. Howells, 1872–1910. Ed. Henry Nash Smith and William M. Gibson. 2 vols. Cambridge, Mass.: Harvard UP.

1961   *"Ah Sin," A Dramatic Work by Mark Twain and Bret Harte* (with Bret Harte). Ed. Frederick Anderson. San Francisco: Book Club of California.

    Contributions to "The Galaxy" 1868–1871. Ed. Bruce McElderry. Gainesville, Fla.: Scholars Facsimiles and Reprints.

    Life as I Find It. Ed. Charles Neider. Garden City, N.Y.: Hanover House.

    Mark Twain's Letters to Mary. Ed. Lewis Leary. New York: Columbia UP.

    The Pattern for Mark Twain's "Roughing It": Letters from Nevada by Samuel and Orion Clemens, 1861–1862. Ed. Franklin R. Rogers. Berkeley: U of California P.

1962   *Letters from the Earth*. Ed. Bernard DeVoto. New York: Harper & Row.

    Mark Twain on the Damned Human Race. Ed. Janet Smith. New York: Hill and Wang.

1963   *Simon Wheeler, Detective.* Ed. Franklin R. Rogers. New York: New York Public Library.

1966   *The Birds and Beasts of Mark Twain.* Ed. Minnie M. Brashear and Robert M. Rodney. Norman: U of Oklahoma P.

1967   *Mark Twain's Letters to His Publishers, 1867–1894.* Ed. Hamlin Hill. Berkeley: U of California P.

       Mark Twain's Satires & Burlesques. Ed. Franklin R. Rogers. Berkeley: U of California P.

       Mark Twain's "Which Was the Dream?" and Other Symbolic Writings of the Later Years. Ed. John S. Tuckey. Berkeley: U of California P.

1969   *Clemens of the "Call": Mark Twain in San Francisco.* Ed. Edgar M. Branch. Berkeley: U of California P.

       Mark Twain's Correspondence with Henry Huttleston Rogers, 1893–1909. Ed. Lewis Leary. Berkeley: U of California P.

       Mark Twain's Hannibal, Huck & Tom. Ed. Walter Blair. Berkeley: U of California P.

       Mark Twain's Mysterious Stranger Manuscripts. Ed. William M. Gibson. Berkeley: U of California P.

1970   *Mark Twain's Quarrel with Heaven: "Captain Stormfield's Visit to Heaven" and Other Sketches.* Ed. Ray B. Browne. New Haven, Conn.: College and UP.

1972   *Mark Twain's Fables of Man.* Ed. John S. Tuckey. Berkeley: U of California P.

       A Pen Warmed-Up in Hell. Ed. Frederick Anderson. New York: Harper & Row.

1973   *"What Is Man?" and Other Philosophical Writings.* Ed. Paul Baender. Berkeley: U of California P.

1975   *Mark Twain's Notebooks & Journals, Volume I (1855–1873).* Ed. Frederick Anderson, Michael B. Frank, and Kenneth M. Sanderson. Berkeley: U of California P.

       Mark Twain's Notebooks & Journals, Volume II (1877–1883). Ed. Frederick Anderson, Lin Salamo, and Bernard L. Stein. Berkeley: U of California P.

1979   *Mark Twain's Notebooks & Journals, Volume III (1883–1891).* Ed. Robert Pack Browning, Michael B. Frank, and Lin Salamo. Berkeley: U of California P.

       The Works of Mark Twain: Early Tales & Sketches, Volume 1 (1851–1864). Ed. Edgar M. Branch and Robert H. Hirst. Berkeley: U of California P.

1980   *The Devil's Race-Track: Mark Twain's Great Dark Writings.* Ed. John S. Tuckey. Berkeley: U of California P.

1981   *The Works of Mark Twain: Early Tales & Sketches, Volume 2 (1864–1865).* Ed. Edgar M. Branch and Robert H. Hirst. Berkeley: U of California P.

1988   *Mark Twain's Letters, Volume 1 (1853–1866).* Ed. Edgar M. Branch, Michael B. Frank, and Kenneth M. Sanderson. Berkeley: U of California P.

1990   *Mark Twain's Letters, Volume 2 (1867–1868).* Ed. Harriet Elinor Smith and Richard Bucci. Berkeley: U of California P.

       Mark Twain's Own Autobiography: The Chapters from the "North American Review." Ed. Michael J. Kiskis. Madison: U of Wisconsin P.

Contributors

JANET L. ABSHIRE
SUNY, Binghamton
"Adventures of Thomas Jefferson
Snodgrass, The"
Snodgrass, Thomas Jefferson

CRAIG ALBIN
Southwest Missouri State University, West Plains
"Luck"
Talmage, T. Dewitt
Watts-Dunton, Theodore
"You've Been a Dam Fool Mary. You
Always Was!"

A. LYNN ALTENBERND
University of Illinois (Emeritus)
Beecher, Henry Ward
"Belated Russian Passport, The"
Personal Memoirs of U.S. Grant
Taylor, Bayard
Warner, Charles Dudley

JOSEPH ANDRIANO
University of Southwestern Louisiana
Cooper, James Fenimore
Eseldorf
*Extract from Captain Stormfield's Visit to
Heaven*
"Fenimore Cooper's Literary Offenses"
Halley's Comet
"To My Missionary Critics"

ST. GEORGE TUCKER ARNOLD, JR.
Florida International University
Animals
Baker, Jim

LISA ASHER
Baylor University
Wecter, Dixon

HAROLD ASPIZ
California State University, Long Beach
Death
Phrenology

MARY MINOR AUSTIN
University of Southwestern Louisiana
Free Thought
Ingersoll, Robert Green

HOWARD G. BAETZHOLD
Butler University (Emeritus)
"Adam's Soliloquy"
American Claimant, The
Arnold, Matthew
Ball, Charles
Breen, Henry Hegart
Brown, John, M.D.
Burrough, J.H.
Carlyle, Thomas
"Carson Fossil-Footprints, The"
Connecticut Yankee in King Arthur's Court, A
"Curious Republic of Gondour, The"
Dolby, George
"Double-Barreled Detective Story, A"
"Eve Speaks"
Forum
Hirst, Robert H.
Kennan, George
Kipling, (Joseph) Rudyard
Letters of Quintus Curtius Snodgrass
"Monument to Adam, A"
"Shem's Diary"
Snodgrass, Quintus Curtius
"That Day in Eden"
"Those Annual Bills"
"What Is Happiness?"
Wright, Laura M.

J. MARK BAGGETT
Samford University
Bankruptcy

Butters, Henry
Censorship
Copyright
"Evidence in the Case of Smith vs. Jones,
	The"
Hall, Fred
"Trial, A"

JAMES E. BARCUS
Baylor University

Rogers, Henry Huttleston

DAVID BARROW
University of Northern Illinois

Coon, Ben
Lecturer
Orality

DARRYL BASKIN
Elmira College

Elmira College Center for Mark Twain
	Studies at Quarry Farm

MARGARET D. BAUER
University of Tennessee, Knoxville

Browning, Elizabeth Barrett
Clarence
"Little Bessie"
Loftus, Mrs.
"Lucretia Smith's Soldier"

CHARLES FRANKLYN BEACH
Baylor University

Aix-Les-Bains, France
Freemasonry
"Holy Children, The"
Occult
Routledge and Sons, George
"Those Blasted Children"

PETER G. BEIDLER
Lehigh University

Faux, William
Raftsmen's Passage (In *Huckleberry Finn*)
Schultz, Christian, Jr.

PHILIP D. BEIDLER
University of Alabama

Australia
Following the Equator
"Jim Baker's Blue Jay Yarn"
Rhodes, Cecil
Satire

LAWRENCE I. BERKOVE
University of Michigan, Dearborn

Angel's Camp, California
Daggett, Rollin Mallory
De Quille, Dan

Doten, Alfred R.
Free Man of Color
Freedom
Gillis, James N. (Jim)
Gillis, Steve
Golden Era
Goldsmith, Oliver
"Goldsmith's Friend Abroad Again"
Goodman, Joseph Thompson
Goodwin, Charles Carroll
Nevada
Slavery
Townsend, James
Virginia City *Territorial Enterprise*

ANTHONY J. BERRET
St. Joseph's University

England
"Is Shakespeare Dead?"
"Royal Nonesuch, The"
Shakespeare, William

JOHN BIRD
Converse College

"Cannibalism in the Cars"
"Czar's Soliloquy, The"
"Loves of Alonzo Fitz Clarence and
	Rosannah Ethelton, The"
"Mammoth Cod, The"
Paige, James W.
Scatology
1601
"Some Thoughts on the Science of
	Onanism"

MARY BOEWE
Louisville, Kentucky

Fay, Morgan le
"Horse's Tale, A"
Landon, Melville D.
Lecky, W.E.H.
Merlin
Moffett, Pamela
Sandy
Watterson, Henry
Webster, Jean

THOMAS BONNER, JR.
Xavier University of New Orleans

"Facts Concerning the Recent
	Resignation"
"French and the Comanches, The"
Harper's Magazine
New Orleans, Louisiana
Profanity

EARL F. BRIDEN
Bryant College

Conscience
Dueling
Foster, Saladin and Electra
Hadleyburg
Halliday, Jack
Law
"Man That Corrupted Hadleyburg, The"
Richards, Edward and Mary
"$30,000 Bequest, The"

WESLEY A. BRITTON
University of North Texas

Dickens, Charles
Fiske, Minnie Maddern
Keller, Helen Adams
Media Interpretations of Mark Twain's Life
    and Works
Paine, Thomas
Trumbull, James Hammond
Wilde, Oscar

STANLEY BRODWIN
Hofstra University

"Aix, the Paradise of the Rheumatics"
"Extracts From Adam's Diary"
Pudd'nhead Wilson, The Tragedy of

LOUIS J. BUDD
Duke University

Impersonators
Interviews
Mark Twain Circle of America

MARIA BURKE
Louisiana State University, Baton Rouge

"Facts in the Case of the Great Beef
    Contract, The"

JOHN A. BURRISON
Georgia State University

"Golden Arm, The"

STANLEY W. CAMPBELL
Baylor University

History

JAMES E. CARON
University of Hawaii, Manoa

Clemens, Orion
Letters from the Sandwich Islands
Hawaii

EVERETT CARTER
University of California, Davis

Douglas, Widow
Finn, Huckleberry
Grangerfords, The

Innocence
Watson, Miss

NANCY L. CHINN
Baylor University

"Aurelia's Unfortunate Young Man"
Austen, Jane
Condensed Novels
"In Defense of Harriet Shelley"
"Legend of the Capitoline Venus, The"

WILLIAM BEDFORD CLARK
Texas A&M University

Cable, George Washington
Miscegenation
Page, Thomas Nelson

MARY S. COMFORT
Lehigh University

Nook Farm

NANCY COOK
University of Montana

Burke, Edmund
Fenians
Punch, Brothers, Punch!
Riverdale, New York
Ticknor, Caroline
Webster, Charles L.
Whitmore, Franklin Gray

JOHN S. COOLEY
Western Michigan University

Angel Fish and Aquarium Club
Childhood

PASCAL COVICI, JR.
Southern Methodist University

Blaine, Jim
Briggs, Scotty
"Buck Fanshaw's Funeral"
Deadpan
Hoax
"How to Tell a Story"
Humor
Roughing It
Vernacular

RICHARD H. CRACROFT
Brigham Young University

Ireland, Irish, Irishmen
"Reflections on Religion"
Stevenson, Robert Louis

LESTER CROSSMAN

Illustrators

CHARLES L. CROW
Bowling Green State University
"Death Disk, The"
DeVoto, Bernard Augustine
"Five Boons of Life, The"
"Invalid's Story, The"
"Medieval Romance, A"
Medievalism
£1,000,000 Bank-Note, The"
"Victims, The"

JOHN W. CROWLEY
Syracuse University
Atlantic Monthly
Howells, William Dean

SHERWOOD CUMMINGS
California State University, Fullerton
Abolition
Darwin, Charles
Evolution
Science
Spencer, Herbert
Taine, Hippolyte

BEVERLY R. DAVID
Western Michigan University
Beach, Emeline
Beach, Moses S.
Cutter, Bloodgood Haviland
Duncan, Charles C.
Illustrators
Slote, Daniel

JOHN H. DAVIS
Chowan College
"Curious Dream: Containing a Moral, A"
"Curious Experience, A"
"Dog's Tale, A"
"Experience of the McWilliamses with Membranous Croup"
"Indiantown"
"McWilliamses and the Burglar Alarm, The"
"Mrs. McWilliams and the Lightning"
"My Boyhood Dreams"
"Singular Episode, A"
"Story Without an End, A"
"Strange Dream, A"
"Which Was It?"
"Which Was the Dream?"

PATRICK DENEEN
Rutgers University
Boxer Rebellion, The
Grant, Ulysses Simpson
Imperialism
Tweed, William Marcy ("Boss")

LEON T. DICKINSON
University of Missouri, Columbia (Emeritus)
Harte, Francis Bret
Innocents Abroad, The
Pilgrims
Prime, William C.
Sphinx

CARL DOLMETSCH
College of William and Mary
Austria (Austria-Hungary)
Berlin, Germany
Freud, Sigmund
Jews
Switzerland

VICTOR A. DOYNO
SUNY, Buffalo
"As Concerns Interpreting the Deity"
"Damned Human Race, The"
"Emperor-God Satire, The"
"Great Dark, The"
Sketches, New and Old

MARK DRAPER
University of Charleston
Blanc, Marie-Thérèse
Campbell, Alexander
Christian Science
Christian Science
Eddy, Mary Baker
Parker, Edwin P.

EVERETT EMERSON
University of North Carolina, Chapel Hill
Emerson, Ralph Waldo
"Eve's Diary"
Life on the Mississippi
Religion

ALLISON R. ENSOR
University of Tennessee, Knoxville
"Bible Teaching and Religious Practice"
Gainesboro, Tennessee
"How I Edited an Agricultural Paper Once"
Jamestown, Tennessee
"Journalism in Tennessee"
Memphis, Tennessee
Music
Pall Mall, Tennessee
Tennessee Land

HERBERT V. FACKLER
University of Southwestern Louisiana
Slade, Joseph A. ("Jack")

JOHN W. FERSTEL
University of Southwestern Louisiana
> Canada

VICTOR A. FISCHER
University of California, Berkeley
> Manuscript Collections
> Mark Twain Project

SHELLEY FISHER FISHKIN
University of Texas, Austin
> Journalism
> Newspapers
> Racial Attitudes

ANTHONY FONSECA
University of Southwestern Louisiana
> "Bloody Massacre near Carson, A"

ANN M. FOX
Indiana University
> "Corn-Pone Opinions"

MICHAEL B. FRANK
University of California, Berkeley
> Anderson, Frederick
> Correspondence (Mark Twain as Letter
> Writer)

LILIAN R. FURST
University of North Carolina, Chapel Hill
> Naturalism
> Realism

JANET A. GABLER-HOVER
Georgia State University
> Bellamy, Edward
> Finn, Pap
> Hooker, Isabella Beecher
> Hooker, John
> James, Henry
> James, William
> Wilks Family

GREG T. GARRETT
Baylor University
> "Extract from Methuselah's Diary"
> "Letter from the Recording Angel"
> Notebooks and Journals
> "War Prayer, The"

PAULA GARRETT
Baylor University
> *Letters from the Earth*
> Novel

RICHARD GAUGHRAN
Lehigh University
> Bellows, Henry Whitney

Hotten, John Camden
Osgood, James Ripley
Smiley, Jim
"Was It Heaven? Or Hell?"

CAROLYN GAY
Baylor University
> Driscoll, Judge York Leicester
> Driscoll, Tom
> Roxana

DORIS K. GELENCSER
SUNY, Buffalo
> *Meisterschaft*

JOHN C. GERBER
University of Iowa (Emeritus)
> *Adventures of Tom Sawyer, The*
> Clemens, Samuel Langhorne
> Comic Poses
> "Huck Finn and Tom Sawyer Among the
> Indians"
> *Tom Sawyer Abroad*
> *Tom Sawyer, Detective*
> "Tom Sawyer's Conspiracy"

SANDRA GRAVITT
Baylor University
> American Bible Society
> "Petrified Man, The"
> "Professor's Yarn, The"
> Stedman, Arthur
> York Harbor, Maine

ALAN GRIBBEN
Auburn University, Montgomery
> "Age—A Rubáiyát"
> Browning, Robert
> Clemens, Henry
> Conferences
> Reading
> Scholarship, Trends in Mark Twain
> Tuckey, John S.

DESIREE GUZETTA
California State University, Fullerton
> Darwin, Charles

KEVIN HADDUCK
Baylor University
> Brownell, Edward
> Trollope, Frances
> Vanderbilt, Cornelius

DAVID HAINES, JR.
Baylor University
> Duke and the Dauphin, The
> Polly, Aunt
> Shepherdson Family

CHRISTIE GRAVES HAMRIC
Baylor University
"Cecil Rhodes and the Shark"
"Story of Mamie Grant, the Child-Missionary, The"

MAVERICK MARVIN HARRIS
East Texas Baptist University
Chatto and Windus
China
Kellgren, Jonas Henrik
New Zealand
"Word of Encouragement for Our Blushing Exiles, A"

SUSAN K. HARRIS
Pennsylvania State University
Alcott, Louisa May
Dreams
Mental Telepathy/Extrasensory Perception
Phelps, Elizabeth Stuart (Ward)
Sentimentality
Stowe, Harriet Beecher

HUNT HAWKINS
Florida State University
Boer War
"Defense of General Funston, A"
King Leopold's Soliloquy
"Queen Victoria's Jubilee"
Spanish-American War, The
"To the Person Sitting in Darkness"

HAMLIN HILL
Texas A&M University
American Publishing Company, The
Ashcroft, Ralph
"Ashcroft-Lyon Manuscript"
Bliss, Elisha
Lyon, Isabel
Subscription Publication
"Wapping Alice"

RICHARD HILL
Lakeland College
Government
Washington, D.C.

ANDREW JAY HOFFMAN
Brown University
"Facts Concerning the Recent Carnival of Crime in Connecticut, The"
"My Debut as a Literary Person"
Representation
Style, Mark Twain's

DONALD R. HOLLIDAY
Southwest Missouri State University
French Revolution

Providence
Putnam & Sons, G.P.

OLIVER HOWARD AND GOLDENA HOWARD
Blankenship, Thomas Woodson
Clemens, John Marshall
Florida, Missouri
Hannibal, Missouri
Johnson, John Moorman
Mark Twain Research Foundation
Millet, Francis Davis
Quarles, John Adams
Quarles Farm
St. Louis, Missouri

PATRICIA A. HUNT
CUNY
Beecher, Lyman
Bliss, Frank
Macaulay, Thomas Babington, Lord
Monday Evening Club of Hartford
Ollendorff and Mr. Ballou
Social Reform
Welsh, James

M. THOMAS INGE
Randolph-Macon College
Beard, Daniel Carter
Comics
Harris, George Washington

MARCIA JACOBSON
Auburn University
"Advice for Good Little Boys"
"Advice for Good Little Girls"
Aldrich, Thomas Bailey
Boy Books
"Boy's Manuscript"

HUGO D. JOHNSON
Baylor University
Labor
War

SHOLOM J. KAHN
Hebrew University
Holy Land, The
Jerusalem
Mysterious Stranger, The

NICK KARANOVICH
Fort Wayne, Indiana
Paine, Albert Bigelow
Photographs

STUART KENNY
Baylor University
Cosmopolitan

Keokuk, Iowa
St. Petersburg
Shaw, George Bernard
"Stupendous Procession, The"

DAVID B. KESTERSON
University of North Texas
Billings, Josh
Derby, George H.
Literary Comedians
Meine, Franklin J.
Nye, Bill
Regionalism
Stoddard, Charles Warren
Thompson, William Tappan

J.C.B. KINCH
Edinboro University of Pennsylvania
"Around the World" Letters
Europe and Elsewhere
France
"Is He Living or Is He Dead?"
Paris, France

MICHAEL J. KISKIS
Empire State College, SUNY
Autobiographical Dictations
Autobiography
Bowen, Will
"Chapters from My Autobiography"
North American Review
"Salutation Speech from the Nineteenth
    Century to the Twentieth, A"

HAROLD H. KOLB, JR.
University of Virginia
Adventures of Huckleberry Finn

LELAND KRAUTH
University of Colorado
Biographers
Fairbanks, Mary Mason
Family Life
Genteel Tradition

HORST H. KRUSE
Westfälische Wilhelms-Universität, Münster
Germany
Mississippi River
"Open Letter to the American People, An"
Tramp Abroad, A
Webster, Annie Moffett

TIMOTHY J. LAMBRECHT
SUNY, Buffalo
"About All Kinds of Ships"

LUCIUS M. LAMPTON
School of Medicine, University of Mississippi
Genealogy
Lambton Family of Durham
Lampton, James J.
Leathers, Jesse M.
Raymond, John T.
Sellers, Colonel

FRANK H. LEAVELL
Baylor University
Belgian Congo
Blakely, Captain Ned
"Dandy Frightening the Squatter, The"
"Jim Wolf and the Cats"
"Political Economy"

JUDITH YAROSS LEE
Ohio University
"Adventure in Remote Seas, An"
Imagery
Phelps, Silas
Sawyer, Tom
"True Story, A"

KATHRYN KALIN LEE
Baylor University
"Old Times on the Mississippi"

J.R. LEMASTER
Baylor University
Driscoll, Judge York Leicester
Driscoll, Tom
Duke and the Dauphin, The
Estate of Samuel L. Clemens
Mark Twain Company
Mark Twain Papers
"Old Times on the Mississippi"
Polly, Aunt
Roxana
Shepherdson Family
Wecter, Dixon

JAMES S. LEONARD
The Citadel
Blackwood's Magazine
Editions
Russia
Scott, Walter
Spiritualism

JOAN V. LINDQUIST
Temple University
Mark Twain's Study

CHRISTINA LINENFELSER
SUNY, Buffalo
"Turning Point of My Life, The"

ERIC CARL LINK
Southwest Missouri State University

> "Early Rising as Regards Excursions to the Cliff House"

SANDRA K. LITTLETON-UETZ
Purdue University, Calumet

> Anthony, Susan B.
> "Autobiography of a Damned Fool"
> "Burlesque Autobiography"
> "Fable, A"
> "Hellfire Hotchkiss"
> "My Platonic Sweetheart"
> Shelley, Harriet

ROBERT LOWREY
University of Central Arkansas

> "Does the Race of Man Love a Lord?"
> Fischer, Theodor
> Forty-Four
> "International Lightning Trust: A Kind of Love Story, The"
> "Second Advent, The"
> Traum, Philip

KEVIN MAC DONNELL
Austin, Texas

> Auctions
> Forgeries
> Harrison, Katharine I.
> Rare Books

RUTH K. MACDONALD
Purdue University, Calumet

> "Edward Mills and George Benton: A Tale"
> Sawyer, Sid
> "Story of the Bad Little Boy Who Didn't Come to Grief, The"
> "Story of the Good Little Boy Who Did Not Prosper, The"
> Thatcher, Becky

THOMAS A. MAIK
University of Wisconsin, La Crosse

> Cauchon, Pierre
> *Personal Recollections of Joan of Arc*

SUSAN MATTHEWSON
California State University, Fullerton

> "Lowest Animal, The"

CHARLOTTE S. MCCLURE
Georgia State University

> Aphorisms
> Bierce, Ambrose
> Holmes, Oliver Wendell
> Lowell, James Russell
> Whittier, John Greenleaf

JOSEPH B. MCCULLOUGH
University of Nevada, Las Vegas

> "Mental Telegraphy" and "Mental Telegraphy Again"

WILLIAM T. MCDONALD
Baylor University

> Indians
> Joe, Injun
> Macfarlane
> "Mexican Plug, The"

SUSAN G. MCFATTER
University of New Mexico

> *Carpet-Bag*
> *Hawaiian Gazette*
> Keokuk (Iowa) *Gate-City*
> New York *Saturday Press*
> San Andreas *Independent*
> San Francisco *Alta California*
> San Francisco *Call*
> Springfield *Republican*

WILSON CAREY MCWILLIAMS
Rutgers University

> Cleveland, Grover
> Machiavelli
> Malory, Sir Thomas
> Politics

EILEEN NIXON MEREDITH
Morehouse College

> Rhetorical Forms

BRUCE MICHELSON
University of Illinois

> Azores
> Baalbec
> Morgan, Hank
> Travel Writings

DAVID G. MILLER
Mississippi College

> Burlingame, Anson
> "Playing Courier"
> Ragsdale, Bill
> "Unbiased Criticism, An"

ERIC L. MONTENYOHL
University of Southwestern Louisiana

> Folklore
> Harris, Joel Chandler
> Lang, Andrew

ANDY J. MOORE
Baylor University

> "Californian's Tale, The"
> Doyle, Arthur Conan
> Melodrama
> Pinkerton, Allan

SCOTT H. MOORE
Baylor University

Bermuda
Californian
Galaxy

TREVOR J. MORGAN
Baylor University

Athens, Greece
Brownell, George Hiram
"General Grant's Grammar"
Quaker City
Smythe, Carlyle and R.S.

SRIMATI MUKHERJEE
University of New Orleans

India

CAMERON C. NICKELS
James Madison University

Arthur, King
Bacon, Francis
Education
"Some Rambling Notes of an Idle
Excursion"
Wilson, David

DON L.F. NILSEN
Arizona State University

Cap'n Simon Wheeler, the Amateur Detective
Detective Fiction
Holmes, Sherlock
Mark Twain's Travels with Mr. Brown
Wheeler, Simon

JUDE NIXON
Baylor University

God
Social Philosophy

DEBORAH O'CONNELL-BROWN
SUNY, Potsdam

Gabrilowitsch, Nina Clemens
Samossoud, Clara Clemens

L. TERRY OGGEL
Virginia Commonwealth University

American Board of Foreign Missions
Century Magazine
Matthews, J. Brander
Missionaries
Pond, James
Redpath, James
Reid, Whitelaw
Sherman, William Tecumseh
Smarr, Sam

JARRELL A. O'KELLEY
The Defiance College

"As Regards Patriotism"
Briggs, John
"Letters to the *Muscatine Journal*"
Napoleon, Arkansas
Sanitary Commission
Smoking

LAWRENCE J. OLIVER
Texas A&M University

Art
"My First Lie, and How I Got Out of It"
"Riley—Newspaper Correspondent"

DONNA ONEBANE
University of Southwestern Louisiana

Potter, Muff
"Some Learned Fables for Good Old Boys
and Girls"

TOM Z. PARRISH
Baylor University

Barnum, Phineas Taylor
Carnegie, Andrew
Civil War

SANFORD PINSKER
Franklin and Marshall College

Legacy

TIMOTHY C. POLAND
Radford University

FitzGerald, Edward
"Great Revolution in Pitcairn, The"
"Stolen White Elephant, The"
"United States of Lyncherdom, The"

STAN POOLE
Louisiana College

Cincinnati, Ohio
Philosophy
"Sold to Satan"
Washoe Wits
"Was the World Made for Man?"

TOM QUIRK
University of Missouri, Columbia

Determinism
Jim

BURTON RAFFEL
University of Southwestern Louisiana

Cervantes Saavedra, Miguel De
Picaresque
Rabelais, François

JENNIFER L. RAFFERTY
University of Connecticut
"Answers to Correspondents"
Clergy
Kingsley, Charles
Short Story
Stewart, William M.

JOHN REES
University of Southwestern Louisiana
Business

JEANNE CAMPBELL REESMAN
University of Texas, San Antonio
Clemens, Molly Stotts
Day, Alice Hooker
Jackson's Island
Scott, Walter
Sherburn, Colonel
Walter Scott
"What Paul Bourget Thinks of Us"

ROBERT REGAN
University of Pennsylvania
Heroism

THOMAS J. REIGSTAD
Buffalo State College
Buffalo, New York
Buffalo *Express*
"Facts in the Great Landslide Case, The"
"Ghost Story, A"

IRA ROYALS, JR.
Baylor University
Egypt
Glyn, Elinor
Teller, Charlotte

RICHARD DILWORTH RUST
University of North Carolina, Chapel Hill
"Awful German Language, The"
German Language
Longfellow, Henry Wadsworth
Mormons

ROGER B. SALOMON
Case Western Reserve University
Gothic

ROBERT D. SATTELMEYER
Georgia State University
Bixby, Horace E.
Dawson's Landing
"Murder, a Mystery, and a Marriage, A"
Paige Typesetting Machine
Piloting
"Those Extraordinary Twins"
Wakeman, Edgar

GARY F. SCHARNHORST
University of New Mexico
Clemens, Cyril
"Enchanted Sea-Wilderness, The"
Fanshaw, Buck
"Great Prize Fight, The"
Human Nature
Whittier's Birthday Dinner Speech

SUSAN SCHNEIDER
Southwest Missouri State University
Rogers, Ben and Billy

DAVID R. SEWELL
University of Rochester
Dialect
French Language
Gilded Age, The
Language
"Refuge of the Derelicts, The"

PATRICIA SEXTON
California State University, Fullerton
Spencer, Herbert

GRETCHEN E. SHARLOW
Elmira College
Beecher, Julia Jones
Beecher, Thomas Kinnicut
Crane, Susan
Crane, Theodore W.
Park Church, The

LEWIS P. SIMPSON
Louisiana State University, Baton Rouge
Smith, Henry Nash
South, Mark Twain and the

LAURA E. SKANDERA
SUNY, Potsdam
Dickinson, Anna Elizabeth
Gabrilowitsch, Ossip
Gleason, Rachel Brooks, M.D.
King, Grace
Samossoud, Clara Clemens

DAVID E.E. SLOANE
University of New Haven
Edison, Thomas Alva
Ward, Artemus (Charles Farrar Browne)

JOHN DANIEL STAHL
Virginia Polytechnic Institute
Europe
Prince and the Pauper, The
Sexuality

JAMES D. WILSON
University of Southwestern Louisiana
> Allen, Helen
> Angelo and Luigi (Cappello)
> Bibliographies
> Business
> Catholicism
> Cord, Mary Ann ("Auntie")
> "Esquimau Maiden's Romance, The"
> Estate of Samuel L. Clemens
> Gluck, James Fraser
> "Jim Blaine and His Grandfather's Ram"
> Journals
> Mark Twain Company
> Mark Twain Papers
> Rachel, Aunt
> Twichell, Joseph Hopkins

MARY ANN WILSON
University of Southwestern Louisiana
> Italy
> Moore, Julia A.
> Shelley, Mary Godwin

MARY ANN WIMSATT
University of South Carolina
> Blair, Walter
> Local Color
> Thorpe, Thomas Bangs

HERBERT A. WISBEY, JR.
Elmira College
> Clemens, Jane Lampton (Jean)

> Clemens, Langdon
> Clemens, Olivia Susan
> Eastman, Samuel Elijah
> Elmira, New York
> Leary, Katy
> Lewis, John T.
> Nye, Emma

PAUL W. WITKOWSKY
Radford University
> Bricksville
> Criticism
> Dan'l, Uncle
> "Man Who Put Up at Gadsby's, The"

HENRY B. WONHAM
University of Virginia
> "Burning Shame, The"
> Harper and Brothers
> McDougal's Cave
> Point of View
> "Tournament in A.D. 1870, The"
> Webster and Company, Charles L.

P.M. ZALL
Huntington Library, San Marino, California
> "Angel's Camp Constable"
> California
> Comstock Lode
> Jackass Hill
> San Francisco, California
> Webb, Charles Henry

The Mark Twain Encyclopedia

Abolition

Samuel Clemens's attitude toward slavery by the time the Civil War began in 1861, when Clemens was twenty-five, was one of an unexamined acceptance of an institution that had been part of the society he was born and raised in. During the war, however, he rethought his position, and his satirizing Copperheads as a political reporter for the San Francisco *Call* in 1864 indicates at least a political revision. His moving to New York in 1867 continued his indoctrination. Here he mingled with post-abolitionists, wrote for the *Tribune* with its abolitionist history, and shortly thereafter began a lifelong friendship with William Dean Howells (1837–1920), son of an abolitionist. His uniquely ambivalent experience qualified him to write some of the most probing reconsiderations of slavery and abolition in literature, especially in *Huckleberry Finn* (1885) and *A Connecticut Yankee* (1889).

From the vantage point of his earlier Hartford years (1874–1882), Mark Twain looked back on his boyhood and young manhood, when he had taken slavery for granted, as ruled by "ignorance, intolerance, . . . and a pathetic unconsciousness of it all." He became, in Howells's word, "desouthernized," an assessment supported by Twain's enthusiastic participation in the reunion celebrated in 1879 by veterans of General U.S. Grant's Army of the Tennessee. At a deeper level, however, he was nourished by an aspect of his boyhood in a slave state. During his long summers on his uncle John Quarles's farm, near Florida, Missouri, young Sam played with and made "comrades" of the farm's slave children and went to middle-aged slave "Uncle Dan'l" for affection and advice. He had the privilege in his formative years of knowing without restraint persons of another race and class, an experience not always afforded in the North. His move north had introduced him to abolitionist principles; in exchange he had something to say about bridging the gulf between peoples of different races and classes through human understanding. Indeed, the discovery of the humanness of other peoples is a major theme of his writing in this period, from "A True Story" (1874) through the first sixteen chapters of *Huckleberry Finn* (written in 1876), and *The Prince and the Pauper* (1882).

Twain's trip into the post-Reconstruction South in 1882 upset the balance that his north-south views had settled into. He found to his surprise that Southerners were still rehearsing the Civil War; and civil-rights activist George Washington Cable informed him that Southerners were bent on restoring "the old South with merely the substitution of negro tenantry for negro slaves." Twain must also have realized that fact while he had been rehearsing abolitionist principles with a complacent willingness to let the South manage its own social problems. His response to his discoveries was troubled and complex and changed the course of his thinking and writing. The northern chauvinism he had expressed in response to the reunion of Grant's veterans was replaced, in *Life on the Mississippi* (1883), with indignation over Grant's "invasion" of the South and his siege of Vicksburg. At the same time, he railed at Southerners for their "Walter Scottism"—their glorying in rank and privilege. A deeper conflict was on the one hand that he regarded slavery as "a bald, grotesque and unwarrantable usurpation" and on the other that he had known good people who kept slaves. There was the case of his two "uncles." He admired and loved both his Uncle John and Uncle Dan'l. He presented the paradox in *Huckleberry Finn* (1885), where the slaveholding Wilks girls are the gentlest and most sympathetic of creatures and where Uncle Silas and Aunt Sally are "as kind as they could be" to Jim, the runaway slave they have captured and imprisoned. The paradox of benevolence and slavery continued to trouble him until in *A Connecticut Yankee* (1889) he pushed it to a logical extreme (a favorite ploy) to achieve a kind of resolution: "Kindhearted people" complacently witness the beating of a young slave woman. The Boss winces as the whip descends, but he chooses not to interfere, nor will he summarily abolish slavery,

though it is in his power to do so. When people are ready, slavery will be abolished "by command of the nation." Having seen the imperfect results of abolition in his own country, Twain, like Huck before him, did not want to be mistaken for an abolitionist.

Sherwood Cummings

BIBLIOGRAPHY

Budd, Louis J. *Mark Twain: Social Philosopher.* Bloomington: Indiana UP, 1962.

Clemens, Samuel L. *Mark Twain's Autobiography.* Ed. Albert B. Paine. 2 vols. New York: Harper, 1924.

Cummings, Sherwood. *Mark Twain and Science: Adventures of a Mind.* Baton Rouge: Louisiana State UP, 1988.

Wecter, Dixon. *Sam Clemens of Hannibal.* Boston: Houghton Mifflin, 1952.

See also: Adventures of Huckleberry Finn; Racial Attitudes; Slavery

"About All Kinds of Ships"
(1893)

The short story was first published in *The £1,000,000 Bank-Note* in 1893 by Charles L. Webster and Company of New York. "About All Kinds of Ships" is ostensibly a typical Twain effort, consistent with his previous writings in relying upon humor and a tall tale for its effect. The authorial persona recounts his recent transatlantic voyage on a modern luxury liner and notes the many changes that have occurred in maritime travel since his first ocean journey a generation earlier. After marveling at the various conveniences of the newer vessels, Twain then imaginatively recalls, for the sake of contrast, the voyages of two historical personages—Noah and Christopher Columbus—before ending the work with a patented tall tale about stasis.

Beneath the facade of humor, however, the story suggests much more. With a mixed, lifelike tone of gentle sarcasm and genuine reflection, the author concludes that just as nautical technology improves, the romance once offered by the sea decreases. (This concept echoes the reflection on reading the river in *Life on the Mississippi* [1883].) Moreover, Twain suggests by way of analogy that as humanity itself continues to evolve, the poetic element decreases proportionally, a price that is, for him perhaps, too dear. Even in this minor and occasional piece, Twain manages fluently to combine humor and philosophy.

Timothy J. Lambrecht

BIBLIOGRAPHY

Clemens, Samuel L. *The £1,000,000 Bank-Note and Other New Stories.* New York: Charles L. Webster, 1893.

See also: Life on the Mississippi

"Adam's Soliloquy"

(1923)

Written in late February 1905, "Adam's Soliloquy" remained unpublished until Albert Bigelow Paine included it in *Europe and Elsewhere* (1923). In this piece Mark Twain transported Adam (in spirit, though visible to human beings) to contemporary New York City.

Deeply impressed by a dinosaur skeleton in the Museum of Natural History, Adam recalls a recent conversation in which an embarrassed Noah, explaining how the several huge species had been left off the ark, blamed the "carelessness" of his "youthful" sons (then in their early 100s), who had also inadvertently allowed a number of "nuisance" creatures aboard—flies, mosquitoes, snakes, cholera germs, rats, and the like.

Noah's further discourse upon why other useful animals were lost while none of the pests perished finally leads Adam to comment that though people initially were awed at meeting so renowned a being, the patriarch's garrulity and argumentativeness inevitably made them wish that "something had happened to the ark."

A second section, set in adjoining Central Park, finds Adam musing upon the vast expansion of population since the early days and enjoying the idea that all are his relatives.

Observing a young mother and her baby, he is charmed by the fact that her expression exactly repeats that worn by Eve when gazing at her first child some 300,000 years earlier. Further conversation involves the young woman's attempts to discover who Adam really is, byplay about how frightening it would be to meet the original Adam, and his assurances that one should not fear to meet a relative.

"Adam's Soliloquy" reflects Mark Twain's longtime interest in our earliest ancestors, which he had expressed more fully in "Extracts from Adam's Diary" (1893) and in the "Autobiography of Eve" (written in the early 1900s) and originally intended to include in "That Day in Eden," and "Eve Speaks," pieces that Paine also published in *Europe and Elsewhere*. In the summer of 1905, also, Twain would write Eve's story anew in "Eve's Diary."

The treatment of Noah adds an additional fragmentary portrait of the pre-Deluge patriarch to those in "About All Kinds of Ships" (1893), "Extract from Shem's Diary," and "Extracts from Methuselah's Diary" (both first published in part in *Letters from the Earth*, 1962). Moreover, Noah's explanation of how harmful creatures like flies, cholera germs, etc., came to be preserved reveals in an ironically humorous way a concern that elsewhere—especially in the 1906 autobiographical dictations published as "Reflections on Religion" (*Hudson Review* 16 [Autumn 1963]: 329–352) and in "Letters from the Earth" (1909)—would take the form of serious railing at a God who would bestow diseases and other calamities on mankind.

Howard G. Baetzhold

BIBLIOGRAPHY

Clemens, Samuel L. *Europe and Elsewhere.* Ed. Albert B. Paine. New York: Harper, 1923.

Ensor, Allison. *Mark Twain and the Bible.* Lexington: UP of Kentucky, 1969.

See also: "Extracts from Adam's Diary"; God; Religion

"Adventure in Remote Seas, An"
(1967)

Although not published until 1967, the fragmentary "An Adventure in Remote Seas" (Mark Twain Papers 59)—one of several unpublished narratives of disastrous sea journeys first published in *Mark Twain's Which Was the Dream?*—was probably composed 24 May 1898 or 4 June 1898 (Tuckey 14). Twain first sketched out a marooned crew's "life in the interior of an iceberg" (*MTNJ* 3:54) in 1883, but his working notes date from 1897 (Tuckey 87).

The two chapters of George Parker's narrative follow a sealing expedition in 1878 from Australia to an island in the Antarctic Sea, where total success proves totally disastrous. With seal hunting as easy as "murdering children" (92), Parker expects to earn $1,000 from the voyage, but the skins seem worthless compared to the 120 tons of Spanish gold discovered in the island's abandoned house. The men lose track of their ship while sorting through this fortune, however, and are apparently doomed.

"An Adventure in Remote Seas" reiterates Twain's most familiar themes—problems caused by sudden wealth (as in "The Man That Corrupted Hadleyburg" [1899]), confusion over dreamlike reality (as in *Connecticut Yankee* [1889]), and the voyage of personal growth (*Huckleberry Finn* [1885]). It also exemplifies the despair running throughout his late work, though stranded ships symbolized despair as early as the *Smyrniote* incident in *Roughing It* (1872). The story is problematic as a narrative, despite the suggestiveness of a captain named Hardy and a crew representing the world in microcosm because the disaster implied by the existing chapters precludes the narrator's survival.

Judith Yaross Lee

BIBLIOGRAPHY

Clemens, Samuel L. *Mark Twain's Notebooks & Journals, Volume III (1883–1891)*. Ed. Robert Pack Browning, Michael B. Frank, and Lin Salamo. Berkeley: U of California P, 1979.

———. *Mark Twain's "Which Was the Dream?" and Other Symbolic Writings of the Later Years*. Ed. John S. Tuckey. Berkeley: U of California P, 1967.

Jones, Daryl. "Mark Twain's Symbols of Despair: A Relevant Letter." *American Literary Realism, 1870–1910* 15.2 (1982): 266–268.

See also: "Great Dark, The"; "Which Was the Dream?"

Adventures of Huckleberry Finn
(1885)

First published under the title *The Adventures of Huckleberry Finn* in England (December 1884), *Adventures of Huckleberry Finn* is Mark Twain's masterpiece. His tale of an outcast boy and a runaway slave, rafting down the Mississippi, has floated into the world's imagination, selling an estimated 20 million copies in more than fifty languages. Though controversial in Twain's time and our own, *Huckleberry Finn* seems likely to remain on that short list of fictional works whose narrative interest and stylistic power will enlighten, entertain, and disturb readers indefinitely.

Published in America in 1885, when Twain was forty-nine, the novel stands at the chronological center and artistic apogee of his career. The author's early works were largely journalistic reports, even if dramatized and humorized, of recent events. As he matured from reporter to travel writer to novelist, Twain reached further and further back into his life and deeper into his imagination for his subjects, moving from *Innocents Abroad* (1869, based on his 1867 *Quaker City* trip to Europe and the Holy Land) to *Roughing It* (1872, recounting his earlier western experiences of 1861–1867) to "Old Times on the Mississippi" (1875, concerning his four years as steamboat pilot that preceded the trip west) to *The Adventures of Tom Sawyer* (1876, which unlocked memories of his childhood in Hannibal in the 1840s).

Sensing a new opportunity as he finished *Tom Sawyer* in 1875, Twain wrote to W.D.

Howells that "by and by I shall take a boy of twelve and run him on through life (in the first person) but not Tom Sawyer—he would not be a good character for it." During the summer of the following year at Quarry Farm in Elmira—"as quiet and peaceful as a South-sea island"—Twain wrote 400 manuscript pages, about fourteen chapters, of what he called "Huck Finn's Autobiography," in which Huck is placed at the center of the narrative, telling the story from his perspective and in his own words. This stunning change in point of view, reflecting what Twain had learned from his lecturing career and from his recent success in creating a naive young narrator in "Old Times on the Mississippi," can be seen in contrasting the last chapter of *Tom Sawyer* and the first chapter of *Huckleberry Finn*.

Huck's first-person narration removes the sometimes sentimental and always superior omniscient narrator; it provides a continually ironic and humorous structure, since the reader's comprehension reaches beyond Huck's; and it demonstrates Mark Twain's solution to the problem of the vernacular that had vexed a generation of American writers. Attempting to introduce democratically common characters and to loosen up book talk with what Wordsworth called the "language really used by men," American authors such as George Washington Harris stumbled into phonetic and orthographic swamps: "I tell yu she wer a tarin gal enyhow. Luved kissin, wrastlin, an' biled cabbige, an' hated tite clothes, hot weather, an' suckit-riders." Mark Twain solved this problem by creating a symbolic vernacular that has the heft of spoken language—run-on rhythms and repetitions, simple connections, occasional lapses of grammar, colloquialisms, and home-grown metaphors and neologisms—while observing enough of the conventions of written English to make it readable.

Initially, Mark Twain seemed not to recognize the power of his new novel, and he wrote to Howells that "I like it only tolerably well, as far as I have got, and may possibly pigeonhole or burn the MS when it is done."

Twain pigeonholed the manuscript repeatedly over the next seven years, working on sections "by fits and starts" until the summer of 1883, when, in two months at Quarry Farm, he revised the earlier sections and wrote the final twenty-one chapters, this time telling Howells that "I haven't piled up MS so in years . . . and *I* shall *like* it, whether anybody else does or not." The book that Mark Twain liked was issued in America in February 1885 by his newly established publishing company, ghost-directed by his nephew-in-law Charles Webster, who reported sales of 42,000 copies in the first month.

The novel's episodic adventures, held together by the steady current of the river highway, fall into three sections. The first, roughly a quarter of the text, continues the spirit and action of *Tom Sawyer* with a description of Huck's "cramped-up" life at the Widow Douglas's, a midnight meeting of Tom's robber gang, and a raid on a Sunday school picnic. The changed point of view, however, invests these burlesques with a new vividness and freshness, since they are given in Huck's language and governed by his naively insightful point of view:

> Then Miss Watson she took me in the closet and prayed, but nothing come of it. She told me to pray every day, and whatever I asked for I would get it. But it warn't so. I tried it. Once I got a fish-line, but no hooks. It warn't any good to me without hooks.

With the introduction of Pap, who nearly murders Huck in an alcoholic rage, and the slave Jim, who fears being sold down the river, the novel moves out to deeper waters. Fleeing father and owner, civilization and slavery, Huck and Jim push off together on a raft for the extraordinary middle chapters of the novel that constitute Mark Twain's finest achievement. Drifting down the river and by the towns that Twain had known as a pilot and that he had revisited in 1882, the runaways plan to sell their raft at Cairo, Illinois, and take a steamboat "way up the Ohio [river] amongst the free States, and then be out of trouble." This plan fails when they unknowingly pass Cairo in a fog, for Mark Twain, after "fooling over [the book] for seven years," had finally discovered a narrative structure that would allow him to express the ideas that came to dominate his intellectual maturity. Sending his outcasts southward intensified the novel's ironies and expanded the targets of Twain's satire. Trapped on the raft by the King and the Duke, as the invading pair of con artists style themselves, Huck and Jim float ever deeper into slavery, and Twain abandons his burlesque of romanticism and pirate books in order to attack pretentious backwoods aristocrats, boorish town loafers, fickle and cowardly mobs, and unconsciously and uncaringly inhumane slaveholders—an attack that is set off by fleeting moments of calm and beauty on the raft and by the compassionate companionship of a white boy and a black man. The "shackly" one-horse towns along the river that Huck and Jim visit—Pokeville, Bricksville, Pikesville—doze in indolence that periodically explodes into brutality and murder. Their residents are fools whose stupidity and greed make them fair game, deserving victims, of the confidence men who prey on them.

The concluding quarter of the book, anchored ashore at the Phelps plantation where Jim is held captive as a runaway slave, returns Tom Sawyer to the plot along with the tomfoolery that the novel began with. Tom knows but conceals the fact that Jim has been set free by his owner, and he concocts an elaborate plan—bristling with unnecessary saws, rope ladders, prison journals, secret messages, disguises, and a coat of arms—to release Jim from captivity. These final chapters constitute an amusing parody of *The Count of Monte Cristo*, *The Man in the Iron Mask*, and similar works, but Mark Twain seems to have traded in his satiric cannon for a popgun. For some readers, the ending is a lessening of the understanding wrung out of the experiences in the middle section of the novel. Tom's games here are of a different order than those of *The Adventures of Tom Sawyer*, for this time he is playing with a human being; his vicious concealment of

the black man's free status and his wish to "leave Jim to our children" align him with slaveholders and confidence men.

The richness of Twain's picaresque, episodic tale derives in part from its complexities and apparent contradictions. At moments the novel is an idyll of carefree pleasures and natural rhythms that adults like to attribute to childhood, an idyll that has made rafting down the Mississippi part of our national past, though few Americans have ever done it. But these moments are quickly, inevitably punctured by rapacity, cruelty, and death. The story—"a dream full of danger," as Edmund Wilson described Cooper's Leatherstocking Tales—is littered with thirty-four corpses, not including a dozen deaths that flow from Huck's imagination of disaster. Mark Twain's most powerful evocations of a serene landscape ("and next you've got the full day, and everything smiling in the sun, and the song-birds just going it!") and his most exuberant satire ("the old gentleman . . . never charged nothing for his preaching, and it was worth it, too") are presented simultaneously with his grimmest portraits of human behavior ("The boys jumped for the river—both of them hurt—and as they swum down the current the men run along the bank shooting at them and singing out, 'Kill them, kill them!' It made me so sick I most fell out of the tree"). In what is Mark Twain's most humorous, most serious book, stability exists alongside anarchy, the conventional lies next to the nihilistic, and opposites often nest complexly inside one another. The Widow Douglas gives Huck lessons in virtue, which he rejects ("I couldn't see no advantage about it"), and then proceeds to follow. Society preaches the righteousness of slaveholding and promises hell to abolitionists, doctrines that Huck accepts in fact and rejects in action. Powerless, pushed about by conniving individuals and loutish groups, Huck and Jim counter Mark Twain's deeply pessimistic picture of Mississippi valley society by offering the possibility of release through humor and redemption through humanity. Though winning the reader, they lose the story, for Jim, in spite of his freedom, faces an unchanged racist world that still holds his wife and children in bondage; and Huck has no place to go but Indian territory.

Yet, diverse and even contradictory as these elements are, and subversive as the novel is to standard generic expectations, the work is held together by its remarkable harmonies: Huck's integration with the rhythms of nature; the consistently maintained point of view of a fourteen-year-old boy and the deadpan humor it consistently generates; Huck's steady moral vision; the authenticity of the valley setting and the river lore that Mark Twain acquired in his boyhood and steamboating days; and the balanced mixture of insight, criticism, and comedy in the sharpest satiric vignettes in American literature, all filtered through Huck's brilliantly metaphorical yet persuasively homely language. Virtually every aspect of mid-nineteenth-century Mississippi valley culture comes under Mark Twain's fire.

At the height of his powers of invention in the 1880s, Mark Twain was also in a stable middle position between the grab-bag humor of his youth and the invective irony of his old age, between his earlier conventional beliefs and his later fulminations against "the damned human race." Located precisely in the middle of a fifty-year career filled with brilliant yet flawed works, *Adventures of Huckleberry Finn* is as close as its author ever came to a complete, balanced, and unified long work of fiction.

Adventures of Huckleberry Finn has been lavishly praised in the twentieth century as "one of the world's great books and one of the central documents of American culture" (Lionel Trilling), as the book that "all modern American literature comes from" (Hemingway), whose author is "all of our grandfather" (Faulkner), "one of those rare writers who have brought their language up to date, and in so doing, 'purified the dialect of the tribe'" (T.S. Eliot). But from the beginning the novel has been under attack. The Concord Library Committee stumbled into immortality by calling it "the veriest trash. . . . It [is] rough, coarse, and inelegant, dealing with a series of

experiences not elevating." Other nineteenth-century reviewers were less apoplectic, but, complaining of its "irreverence," they often dismissed the book as "mere humor." As twentieth-century readers responded increasingly to what they saw as the book's moral integrity, they began to regard the ending as anticlimactic or even subversive to the lessons of justice and equality exemplified in the middle chapters. Later critics were less disturbed by the absurdity of the ending, which, in their view, is an apt symbol of modern notions of reality. And since the novel was written by a wealthy white male who believed in as well as criticized his generation's drive for technological power and material success and whose humor did not spare minority groups, or anyone else, it comes as no surprise that *Adventures of Huckleberry Finn* has taken its lumps recently in the hands of new historicists, cultural materialists, literary pluralists, feminists, and African-Americanists.

Each criticism of the novel needs to be seen in its context. The Concord Library Committee had both a theory of art (it should uplift) and a theory of written language (it should be genteel) that later generations have found inadequate. Those nineteenth-century readers who dismissed the book as not serious enough did not have the advantage of Freud's *Jokes and Their Relation to the Unconscious*, published in 1905, and they lived in a culture, unlike our own, in which irreverence was not fashionable. The variety of twentieth-century interpretations suggests not so much the fractiousness of critics as the capaciousness of Mark Twain's novel, along with his complicated desire both to believe in and to explode notions of rational and ethical human behavior. And those contemporary critics who see Twain as fatally tempted by nineteenth-century sentimentality, boosterism, and progressivism need to remember that every great artist both is and is not a child of his or her times. It is precisely Twain's amphibian status as insider and outsider that creates the foundation of his humor and the platform from which he can satirize his society even while embedded in it.

Yet of all the criticism directed against *Adventures of Huckleberry Finn*, the most recent—that the book and its author are racist—is the most damaging, and it is likely to endure as long as black Americans have cause to feel insecure or uncomfortable about their cultural status. In terms of the nineteenth century, the charge is unhistorical, and Samuel Clemens's respect, affection, and concern for African-Americans are well documented. In the same year that the novel was published—a year that saw a 50 percent increase in the lynchings of black Americans, which Twain excoriated in "The United States of L`yncherdom" (1923)—the author began to pay the expenses of Warner T. McGuinn, one of the first black students to be accepted at the Yale School of Law, writing to the school's dean that:

> I do not believe I would very cheerfully help a white student who would ask a benevolence of a stranger, but I do not feel so about the other color. We have ground the manhood out of them and the shame is ours, not theirs; and we should pay for it.

The moral argument that Mark Twain embedded in *Adventures of Huckleberry Finn* was recognized immediately by Joel Chandler Harris: "There is not in our fictive literature a more wholesome book than *Huckleberry Finn*. . . . We are taught [by it] the lesson of honesty, justice and mercy." Huck comes to understand the humanity of his raftmate. He identifies with Jim's cause in chapter 11 ("They're after us!"), apologizes to him in chapter 15 ("I didn't do him no more mean tricks, and I wouldn't done that one if I'd a knowed it would make him feel that way"), lies to protect him from slave hunters in chapter 16 ("He's white"), risks the damnation of the religion of his time for not informing on Jim in chapter 31 ("All right, then, I'll *go* to hell"), and attempts, unsuccessfully, to pry Jim loose from Tom's shenanigans in chapter 35 ("Confound it, it's foolish"). Huck never rejects slavery, and he continues to voice the racism of his society, but as Mark Twain wrote in his notebook, Huck's "sound heart" defeats his "diseased conscience."

Times, however, have changed, and our current definitions of racism are more searching, more subtle. Many black readers, offended by the satire at Jim's expense ("Jim was most ruined, for a servant, because he got so stuck up on account of having seen the devil and been rode by witches") are not persuaded by the argument that everyone in the novel is satirized—slaves, poor whites, the "high toned and well born," preachers, the Widow Douglas, Huck himself. These readers wince at the use of the term "Nigger" as well as the passages in which Jim is shown to be superstitious, fearful, and foolish, finding him, as Ralph Ellison put it, "a white man's inadequate portrait of a slave." E.W. Kemble's portraits are judged inadequate as well, and his illustrations of a wide-eyed, thick-lipped Jim seem to derive from nineteenth-century minstrel shows. So do some of Twain's jokes:

> Huck: "What did you speculate in, Jim?"
> Jim: "Well, fust I tackled stock."
> Huck: "What kind of stock?"
> Jim: "Why livestock . . . I put ten dollars in a cow."

The joke was the golden apple for which Mark Twain would always turn aside, and he sometimes sacrifices the long-term demands of his narrative, and Jim's dignity, for the short run opportunities of humor. A novel requires consistency and accumulation. Part of its pleasure derives from the predictability, the inevitability, of the patterns of character and action that govern the miniature world created by the author. Humor, on the other hand, is based on quick splashes rather than long rolling rhythms. It is unpredictable, subversive, amoral, distorting. As a humorist, Twain often pushes his material out to extremes—in Jim's case, extremes of ignorance and superstition—to sharpen the contrasts on which humor thrives. Although he aligns much of his comedy with his plot, it occasionally undercuts the novel's generally sympathetic presentation of Jim.

A final criticism of *Adventures of Huckleberry Finn* derives from the recent debates about the literary canon, which themselves are a product of increasing multiculturalism in the United States. This once subversive book has become approved by the authorities, enshrined in reading lists, and entrenched in school curricula. The sections that offend have been dismissed by white teachers and professors who insist that black readers—in spite of their extensive experience with cultural ironies—do not understand the irony. Insensitive teaching and the introduction of the novel too early in school have compounded the problem. A mother's challenge against the book in the town of State College, Pennsylvania, resulted when a ninth-grade teacher, using *Huckleberry Finn* for exercises in oral reading, insisted that the only black youngster in her class—despite his protest—take the part of Jim.

A nineteenth-century liberal, Mark Twain would approve of the increased sensitivity of the twentieth century to racial injustice: it is a change that he helped to bring about. But yesterday's liberalism often looks like today's conservatism, and it seems wise not to insist that every student, especially every young and black student, read the book as an inevitable part of the American school curriculum.

Curiously, it is the wealth and diversity of the criticism of *Adventures of Huckleberry Finn*, the debates and the passions that it has and will continue to inspire, that provide a persuasive index to its future. Every generation seems to discover a new problem with the book, but every generation continues to read it. Like all great works of art, *Adventures of Huckleberry Finn* has the power to revise and unsettle as well as to define and stabilize. It is a mirror of the reader's dreams and fears, of what we find comic, what we find admirable, and what we find disturbing in human culture—in Huck Finn's time, in Mark Twain's time, and in our own.

Harold H. Kolb, Jr.

BIBLIOGRAPHY

Blair, Walter. *Mark Twain & Huck Finn*. Berkeley: U of California P, 1960.

Budd, Louis J., ed. *New Essays on "Adventures of Huckleberry Finn."* New York: Cambridge UP, 1985.

Clemens, Samuel L. *Adventures of Huckleberry Finn.* Ed. Walter Blair and Victor Fischer. Berkeley: U of California P, 1985.

———. *Mark Twain's Hannibal, Huck & Tom.* Ed. Walter Blair. Berkeley: U of California P, 1969.

Cox, James M. "Remarks on the Sad Initiation of Huckleberry Finn." *Sewanee Review* 62 (1954): 389–405.

Fischer, Victor. "Huck Finn Reviewed: The Reception of *Huckleberry Finn* in the United States, 1885–1897." *American Literary Realism* 16 (Spring 1983): 1–57.

Gerber, John. "The Relation Between Point of View and Style in the Works of Mark Twain." *Style in Prose Fiction, English Institute Essays.* New York: Columbia UP, 1958. 142–171.

Inge, M. Thomas, ed. *Huck Finn Among the Critics.* Frederick, Md.: U Publications of America, 1985.

Marx, Leo. "Mr. Eliot, Mr. Trilling, and Huckleberry Finn." *American Scholar* 22 (Autumn 1953): 423–440.

———. "The Pilot and the Passenger: Landscape Conventions and the Style of *Huckleberry Finn*." *American Literature* 28.2 (May 1956): 129–146.

Sattelmeyer, Robert, and J. Donald Crowley, eds. *One Hundred Years of "Huckleberry Finn."* Columbia: U of Missouri P, 1985.

Smith, Henry Nash. *Mark Twain: The Development of a Writer.* Cambridge, Mass.: Harvard UP, 1962.

Trilling, Lionel. Introduction. *The Adventures of Huckleberry Finn.* By Clemens. New York: Rinehart, 1948. v–xviii.

See also: Douglas, Widow; Duke and the Dauphin, The; Finn, Huckleberry; Grangerfords, The; Jim; Picaresque; Point of View; Racial Attitudes; Sherburn, Colonel; Vernacular; Watson, Miss

"Adventures of Thomas Jefferson Snodgrass, The"
(1856–1857)

These three travel letters, written to the Keokuk *Saturday Post* and the Keokuk *Daily Post* by one Thomas Jefferson Snodgrass as he travels from St. Louis to Cincinnati, are reputed to be the first pieces Twain was commissioned to write for pay. Although late in life Twain maintained that he could not remember writing the letters or being paid for them, Thomas Rees, son of the *Post*'s editor at the time, claimed Twain was paid five dollars per letter. Twain wrote these letters after leaving his brother's employ at the Ben Franklin Book and Job Office to travel to the Amazon. He never made it to the Amazon because he finally got the opportunity to fulfill his dream of becoming a river pilot.

The letters are characterized by heavy dialect, many misspelled words, misused words, and stock situations. Twain utilizes stock incidents as Snodgrass, an unschooled, unsophisticated man, relates his first encounters with the marvels of city life and train travel. The first letter, published 1 November 1856 and bearing a dateline of 18 October 1856 from St. Louis, recounts Snodgrass's foray to the theater. The second letter, dateline 14 November 1856 from Cincinnati (and published 9 November 1856 in the *Daily Post* and 6 December in the *Saturday Post*), describes Snodgrass's train ride from St. Louis to Cincinnati. The last letter, dateline 14 March 1857 from Cincinnati and published 10 April 1857, relates how the innocent and unsuspecting Snodgrass was duped by a city lady who left him with her unwanted child.

The influence of William Tappan Thompson (*Major Jones's Sketches of Travel* [1847]) and other humorists of the time on the content and style of these letters is apparent; the heavy dialect and precarious circumstances in which the unpolished rural personality finds himself are familiar devices of the time. These letters do, however, show the early stages of Twain's effective use of dialect to delineate character.

Another series of ten letters from Quintus Curtius Snodgrass to his friend Charles Augustus Brown, published in the New Orleans *Crescent* in January, February, and March 1861, is sometimes attributed to Twain. Although arguments have been made for both sides of the issue, the evidence for authorship is not conclusive.

Janet L. Abshire

BIBLIOGRAPHY

Benson, Ivan. *Mark Twain's Western Years*. Stanford, Calif.: Stanford UP, 1938.

Branch, Edgar Marquess. *The Literary Apprenticeship of Mark Twain*. Urbana: U of Illinois P, 1950.

Clemens, Samuel L. *The Adventures of Thomas Jefferson Snodgrass*. Ed. Charles Honce. Chicago: Pascal Covici, 1928.

————. *Mark Twain in Eruption*. Ed. Bernard DeVoto. New York: Harper, 1940.

Leisy, Ernest E., ed. *The Letters of Quintus Curtius Snodgrass*. Dallas: Southern Methodist UP, 1946.

McKeithan, D.M. "Mark Twain's Letters of Thomas Jefferson Snodgrass." *Philological Quarterly* 32.4 (1953): 353–365.

See also: Snodgrass, Thomas Jefferson

Adventures of Tom Sawyer, The
(1876)

The Adventures of Tom Sawyer (*TS*) is one of the few books enjoyed by readers of every age. With sales now over 5 million copies, the novel ranks second in popularity among Twain's works, being surpassed only by *Adventures of Huckleberry Finn* (1885). Characteristically, Mark Twain wrote the book in fits and starts. He apparently began it in early January 1873 but soon put it aside to collaborate with Charles Dudley Warner on *The Gilded Age* (1873). Then he picked it up again in the spring and summer of 1874 and wrote, as he said, until his tank ran dry. As Paul Baender has pointed out, paper, ink, pen point, and manner of inscription suggest that the first stop occurred at the end of chapter 4 and the second near the end of chapter 18. Twain finished the story in the spring and early summer of 1875.

With more than usual care, he went back over the first draft and made several hundred changes, principally to sharpen the transitions and make the language more connotative. In addition, he juggled material so that Tom would more consistently grow from a childish scamp to a responsible youth. This done, he had a secretarial copy made of the holograph manuscript and sent it for reactions to his close friend William Dean Howells, editor of the *Atlantic*. The holograph manuscript he sent to his editor, Elisha Bliss of the American Publishing Company in Hartford, Connecticut, so that Bliss could get True Williams started on the illustrations. To Twain's great delight Howells liked the story immensely and returned it with only thirty-one comments penciled in the margins. Acting on these comments, Twain changed certain "off-key" expressions and shortened the sham battle in chapter 3 as well as the episode in chapter 20 in which Tom discovers Becky Thatcher looking at an illustration of a nude figure in the headmaster's anatomy book. Also, he cut the final chapter completely. When the holograph manuscript came back from Bliss, he transferred to it—though rather carelessly—the alterations he had made in the secretarial copy. Then he sent the holograph manuscript back to Bliss, and the secretarial copy to Chatto and Windus in London. Not delaying for illustrations, Chatto and Windus brought out the first English edition on 9 July 1876. From proof sheets of this edition the Belford Brothers in Toronto printed cheap pirated editions with which they flooded the American as well as the Canadian market before the authorized American edition appeared on 8 December. Because of the delay for which Bliss, the engravers, and Twain were all responsible, the appearance of the authorized American edition was not especially newsworthy. The book was not widely reviewed, and sales were slow until the appearance of *Huckleberry Finn* in 1885 brought *TS* fresh attention.

Encouraged by the success of his play titled *Colonel Sellers*, Mark Twain tried to find collaborators to help him dramatize *TS* as early as 1875. Finding none, he dramatized it himself almost ten years later. The copyright for it is dated 1 February 1884. For many good reasons he was unable to find a producer. The play, for example, does not have the structural unity of the novel, the compactness of character, nor the atmosphere. Almost perversely it concentrates on some of the episodes but not necessarily on the most dramatic ones. Finally convinced that he could not dramatize the book, Twain sold the dramatic rights to it in 1885. The play is printed with a detailed introduction and notes by Walter Blair in *Mark Twain's Hannibal, Huck & Tom*.

TS is the most autobiographical of Mark Twain's novels. Physically, St. Petersburg, where the events take place, is Hannibal, Missouri, the town where Sam Clemens spent most of his boyhood. The Mississippi River, Bear Creek, the buildings, the cemetery, and the cave are all as the young Sam knew them. Cardiff Hill is a literary replica of Holliday's Hill and Jackson's Island of Glasscock's Island, since washed away. Although they are altered for humorous and dramatic reasons, the major characters, too, can be traced to Hannibal sources. Tom, Twain later said, is a composite of himself and two companions. Aunt Polly is in part his mother, though more sentimental and ineffective than Mrs. Clemens ever was. Sid is Clemens's younger brother Henry turned into a prissy tattletale. The character of Becky is based on Laura Hawkins, who lived across the street, and Huck on a generous and likable ragamuffin named Tom Blankenship. Twain downgraded Injun Joe from a town loafer to a villain. Despite these autobiographical elements, however, a surprising amount of material reflects Twain's reading. The relation between Tom and Huck, for example, echoes the relationship between Don Quixote and Sancho Panza in Cervantes's *Don Quixote* (1605–1615), one of Twain's favorite books. Similarly, the relation between Aunt Polly and Tom reflects the relation between Mrs. Partington and her son Ike in B.P. Shillaber's Mrs. Partington sketches. Other major sources from Twain's reading include Charles Dickens's *David Copperfield* (1849) and *Tale of Two Cities* (1859), Thomas Bailey Aldrich's *Story of a Bad Boy* (1869), and Edgar Allan Poe's "The Gold Bug." In addition, Twain drew upon pieces he himself had written. He had burlesqued Sunday school stories, for example, in "The Story of the Bad Little Boy Who Didn't Come to Grief" (1865) and "The Story of the Good Little Boy Who Did Not

Prosper" (1870). He had tried to observe events through the eyes of a boy in sections of *The Gilded Age* and of "Old Times on the Mississippi" (1875). His most extensive "rehearsal" for *TS*, however, was a fragment that A.B. Paine, Twain's literary executor, called "Boy's Manuscript." Written about 1868, it tells in diary form the schoolroom antics of a Billy Rogers and of Billy's absurd love affair with an Amy Lawrence. The diary was going nowhere and Twain was wise to stop it, but it proved to be a rich source of material for *TS*.

Despite its off-again, on-again composition, *TS* is Mark Twain's best constructed novel. The structure results from the interweaving of four oppositions (plot seems too imposing a term), each opposition typical of those in a type of fiction popular in the 1870s. The four are as follows: (1) Tom vs. the adult community, a takeoff on the juvenile fiction of the time. Surfacing especially in the first five chapters and then intermittently throughout the book, this opposition results in a genial satire of the juvenile fiction that glorified the Good Boy and piled contumely on the Bad Boy. Twain achieves his satirical effect by making Tom guilty of most of the transgressions of the typical Bad Boy (lying, stealing, smoking, running away from home, and associating with a boy who lacks a Christian upbringing) and yet reaps the rewards customarily reserved for the Good Boy (riches, popular esteem, and the affection of the Good Girl). (2) Tom vs. Becky, a burlesque of romantic fiction. Following the pattern of adult love stories—boy meets girl, boy loses girl, boy gets girl—the puppy antics of Tom and Becky irresistibly call attention to the similarly puppy activities of older lovers. (3) Tom vs. Huck, an adaptation of contemporary local color fiction that depended on talk in the vernacular in part for its effect. This is the strand in *TS* that led directly to *Huckleberry Finn*. (4) Tom vs. Injun Joe, a borrowing from paperback thrillers emphasizing robbery, murder, revenge, treasure hunting, and imminent danger to the hero and heroine. With unusual structural skill, Twain interweaves these oppositions so that

none is forgotten once it is introduced. In the last pages he provides a roundup that resolves all oppositions: Tom becomes one with the community, Tom and Becky adore each other, Tom persuades Huck to join his gang, and Tom triumphs over Injun Joe.

Twain gives his novel further cohesion by having Tom the center of all activity. Other characters are important only in their relation to Tom. Even Huck, as appealing as he is, serves primarily as a foil to show how far Tom is from being a real social rebel—just as Sid and Willie Mufferson serve to show how far he is from being a model boy. At relatively regular intervals Twain pulls Tom and other characters together in a big scene: Tom in Sunday school, for example, Tom at the school graduation services, Tom testifying at the trial of Injun Joe, Tom and his companions attending their own funeral, Tom producing the treasure. In short, *TS* is tightly enough constructed to transcend such palpable weaknesses as the uncertainty of the boys' ages, the vagueness of family relationships, the extraordinary length of the Missouri summer, and the disappearance of Lawyer Thatcher.

As in almost all of Mark Twain's works, the style in *TS* results from the point of view. It is a shifting style because the point of view slides from that of the middle-aged writer to that of the approximately twelve-year-old boy. As the middle-aged author, Twain writes in the conventional, stilted, "literary" manner that characterizes other novels of the period. But when he adopts Tom's point of view, his language immediately freshens. The boy forces him to do what he does best: report concrete happenings in simple pictorial language. In style, therefore, *TS* represents a transition between the mannered discourse in *The Gilded Age* and the vernacular in *Huckleberry Finn*. *TS* gave Mark Twain the character of Huck Finn, and Huck gave him the style that revolutionized American fiction.

Mark Twain once called *TS* "a hymn put into prose to give it a worldly air." For many this definition is sufficient. The story of St. Petersburg, or St. Peter's town, is the story of a heavenly place where, despite anxieties and crimes, a boy can live out his dreams. Yet a closer reading reveals evidences of Twain's growing pessimism. The adult world is far from heavenly. There may be much prating about goodness, and individuals such as Aunt Polly can on occasion be loving and compassionate, but the adults as a group are fickle, vain, materialistic, and bored. Their basic desires are really for economic prosperity and a reputation for respectability. The most unsettling fact in the story is that Tom is surely going to turn out to be just like his elders. At the outset of the book there is nothing he envies so much as Huck Finn's freedom from adult restraints. Yet at the end he is trying to force Huck to accept these very restraints by letting the Widow Douglas adopt him. Tom, in short, has not matured during the course of the narrative but has simply become more like St. Petersburg adults, who are themselves immature. Still, such realization is only the dark underside of the book. Most readers, especially young ones, are amply satisfied with the bright side, the captivating myth of the little town of long ago on the bank of the Great River.

John C. Gerber

BIBLIOGRAPHY

Blair, Walter. *Mark Twain & Huck Finn*. Berkeley: U of California P, 1960.

Clemens, Samuel L. *The Adventures of Tom Sawyer. Facsimile of the Author's Holograph Manuscript with an Introduction by Paul Baender*. Frederick, Md.: U Publications of America, 1982.

―――. *The Adventures of Tom Sawyer, Tom Sawyer Abroad, Tom Sawyer, Detective*. Ed. John C. Gerber, Paul Baender, and Terry Firkins. Berkeley: U of California P, 1980.

―――. *Mark Twain-Howells Letters: The Correspondence of Samuel L. Clemens and William D. Howells, 1872–1910*. Ed. Henry Nash Smith and William M. Gibson. 2 vols. Cambridge, Mass.: Harvard UP, 1960.

DeVoto, Bernard. *Mark Twain at Work*. Cambridge, Mass.: Harvard UP, 1942.

Fetterley, Judith. "The Sanctioned Rebel." *Studies in the Novel* 3 (1971): 293–304.

Hill, Hamlin. "The Composition and Structure of *Tom Sawyer*." *American Literature* 32 (January 1961): 379–392.

McKeithan, D.M. *Court Trials in Mark Twain and Other Essays*. The Hague: Martinus Nijhoff, 1958.

Norton, Charles A. *Writing "Tom Sawyer": The Adventures of a Classic*. Jefferson, N.C.: McFarland, 1983.

Stone, Albert E., Jr. *The Innocent Eye: Childhood in Mark Twain's Imagination*. New Haven, Conn.: Yale UP, 1961.

Wecter, Dixon. *Sam Clemens in Hannibal*. Boston: Houghton Mifflin, 1952.

See also: Adventures of Huckleberry Finn; "Boy's Manuscript"; Heroism; Point of View; Sawyer, Tom; Thatcher, Becky

"Advice for Good Little Boys" (1865)

and

"Advice for Good Little Girls" (1865)

Mark Twain's burlesque advice columns, "Advice for Good Little Boys" and "Advice for Good Little Girls," were first published, either together or in close succession, in 1865, in a nonsectarian family journal, the San Francisco based *Youths' Companion*. The burlesque form of the two pieces suggests the influence of the literary humorists that Twain came into contact with in Nevada and in California. The satirical content offers an early expression of Twain's impatience with the sentimentality in which the genteel culture of the nineteenth century enshrined childhood. It is probably fair to say that these two sketches are germs of *Tom Sawyer* (1876) and *Huckleberry Finn* (1885).

The two sketches do not mirror one another. "Advice for Good Little Girls" is almost half again as long as "Advice for Good Little Boys," and the two pieces do not address parallel subjects. They are based, however, on the same notion of child behavior: that children are naturally mischievous and that particularly trying circumstances make it impossible for a child to keep those mischievous impulses under control. Citing a handful of realistic instances in a child's life, Twain humorously counsels satisfying forms of response. His recommendations range from engaging in minor forms of naughtiness to adopting one or another form of hypocrisy. Twain's use of slang—rather uneven and awkward in these early pieces—and the exaggerated responses to provocation that he sketches out make clear that these pieces are offered as jokes, as burlesques of the kind of moralistic advice a child might find in the Sunday school literature of the day. At the same time, Twain does have a serious point to make. The good child of his titles is neither the child who would be advised nor the child who has been advised; to Twain, a good child is a mischievous child.

Marcia Jacobson

BIBLIOGRAPHY

Branch, Edgar Marquess. *The Literary Apprenticeship of Mark Twain.* Urbana: U of Illinois P, 1950.

Clemens, Samuel L. *The Works of Mark Twain: Early Tales & Sketches.* Ed. Edgar M. Branch and Robert H. Hirst. 2 vols. Berkeley: U of California P, 1979–1981.

Rogers, Franklin R. *Mark Twain's Burlesque Patterns as Seen in the Novels and Narratives, 1855–1885.* Dallas: Southern Methodist UP, 1960.

See also: Adventures of Huckleberry Finn; Adventures of Tom Sawyer, The; Burlesque; Childhood

"AGE—A Rubáiyát"

(1983)

In the autumn of 1898 Mark Twain conceived an irresistible desire to write a burlesque of a poem he much admired, Edward FitzGerald's immensely adulated translation, *The Rubáiyát of Omar Khayyám* (1859). Twain composed five quatrains in Notebook 40 in October 1898, titling them "AGE—A Rubáiyát," then wrote variations of four of these stanzas plus forty-one others on small, numbered leaves of paper. These forty-five

verses combine comical laments about the indignities and frailties of old age with a withering assault on the injustices of humankind's fate. In places the speaker openly compliments and invites death, the "Best Friend of Man" (quatrain 23). Some lines are notably successful at mimicking FitzGerald's poem and reversing his meaning, as when the speaker asks a draught of "kindly Absinth, with its wimpling Sheen/Of dusky half-lights," to "let me drown/The haunting Pathos of the Might-Have-Been" (quatrain 5), or when he urges those who will note his death to "be glad for Me . . . and think/I've found the Voices lost, beyond the Pall" (quatrain 20). Overall, however, the effort often resembles travesty rather than the clever spoof Twain intended.

Certain verses referring to fornication are bawdy beyond the jokes in Twain's *1601 Conversation* (privately printed, 1880), such as where the speaker warms to the topic of "Lechery" (quatrain 40) in terms resembling Twain's lewd "Some Thoughts on the Science of Onanism" (privately printed, 1952, 1964) and "The Mammoth Cod" (privately printed, 1920, 1937, 1976). Two separate, additional quatrains deploring male sexual impotence ("Behold—the Penis mightier than the Sword,/ . . . dreams unmoved of ancient conquests scored") survive in the Beinecke Rare Book and Manuscript Library at Yale University.

On 13 November 1898 Twain wrote from Vienna to propose that Andrew Chatto privately publish a limited edition of the poem, retitled "Omar's Old Age." "Come—is it a wild and vicious scheme?" he asked Chatto. The plan did not proceed, and Twain later extracted twenty verses for inclusion in a sketch titled "My Boyhood Dreams" that appeared in the January 1900 issue of *McClure's Magazine*. The entire sheaf of stanzas became part of biographer Albert Bigelow Paine's personal collection and was eventually published in 1983.

As a commentary on Twain's morose state of mind in 1898, and as a powerfully suggestive indication of his qualms about sexual impotence and old age in general, the burlesque possesses an interest beyond its demonstration of Twain's abilities to copy the style and content of one of the most influential literary works of his day.

Alan Gribben

BIBLIOGRAPHY

Clemens, Samuel L. *Mark Twain's Rubáiyát.* Intro. Alan Gribben. Textual Note by Kevin B. Mac Donnell. Austin, Tex.: Jenkins Publishing, The Karpeles Manuscript Library, 1983.

See also: FitzGerald, Edward; "My Boyhood Dreams"; Scatology

Ah Sin: The Heathen Chinee
(written 1876)

Ah Sin: The Heathen Chinee was written jointly by Mark Twain and Bret Harte in the fall of 1876. On 30 December a contract for production was signed by Twain, Harte, and Charles Parsloe, who played the character Ah Sin. Twain advanced $1,000 toward the production. *Ah Sin* opened 7 May 1877 at the National Theatre in Washington, D.C., for one week. On 31 July the play opened at Daly's Fifth Avenue Theatre in New York. The New York run closed 31 August, and after four weeks on tour, the play was withdrawn and no further productions were mounted.

The idea for the play originated with the critical success of the Chinese character Hop Sing in Harte's *Two Men of Sandy Bar*, which Twain had seen in New York during September 1876. Ah Sin is the name of a similar character in Harte's "Plain Language from Truthful James." The project provided an opportunity for the friends to exploit their western experiences for a public hungry for such material. Harte spent two weeks with Twain in late November and early December working on the play.

The collaborative process Harte and Twain followed was sporadic and uneven. Harte, moody and curt, reflected the formal and stilted

pattern of nineteenth-century theater. Twain, relaxed and casual, consistently revised Harte's work toward more realistic, even burlesque renderings. As a result of this process, the play is often chaotic and the plot incoherent. The characters, except for Ah Sin, are thin and lack clear motivation. However, the most significant dramatic problem derives from an inconsistent mood. Neither Harte nor Twain could decide whether the play should be a tragedy or a melodrama, a comedy or a farce. The inability of Twain and Harte to reconcile their differences precluded proper revisions of the script and led Twain to seize control of the production, excluding Harte. The play failed, and the friendship between the two suffered an irreparable break.

Jerry W. Thomason

BIBLIOGRAPHY

Clemens, Samuel L. *"Ah Sin," A Dramatic Work by Mark Twain and Bret Harte* (with Bret Harte). Ed. Frederick Anderson. San Francisco: Book Club of California, 1961.

———. *Mark Twain-Howells Letters: The Correspondence of Samuel L. Clemens and William D. Howells, 1872–1910.* Ed. Henry Nash Smith and William M. Gibson. 2 vols. Cambridge, Mass.: Harvard UP, 1960.

Goldman, Robert. "Mark Twain as Playwright." *Mark Twain: A Sumptuous Variety.* Ed. Robert Giddings. Totowa, N.J.: Barnes & Noble, 1985. 108–131.

Schirer, Thomas. *Mark Twain and the Theatre.* Nürnberg, Germany: Verlag Hans Carl, 1984.

See also: Dramatist, Mark Twain as; Harte, Francis Bret

"Aix, the Paradise of the Rheumatics"
(1891)

"Aix, The Paradise of the Rheumatics" was first published on 8 November 1891 as one of six letters Mark Twain wrote for the New York *Sun* appearing in installments through 3 April 1892. All but one, "Playing Courier," are ostensibly factual accounts about travel. Burdened by financial problems brought on by the Paige typesetter and his publishing company, Twain traveled to Europe in 1891 in the hope of gathering material for a new travel book as well as to find relief for the rheumatism in his right arm and respite from his difficulties. One of his first stops was at the famous French health resort of Aix-les-Bains, followed by visits to Bayreuth and Marienbad, among other places. Although these pieces—broad mixtures of philosophical reflection, journalistic travel detail, and social commentary laced with satire and humor—were never incorporated or reshaped into a single work, they nevertheless remain significant revelations of Twain's social thought and moods during this period. "Aix, the Paradise of the Rheumatics" is one of the most important of his travel pieces because, in part, it clearly reflects some of the social, theological, and political themes Twain had grappled with in *A Connecticut Yankee in King Arthur's Court* (1889).

The opening paragraphs immediately plunge us into Twain's satiric reflections about the "rabble of nobilities" who come to the resort, including, possibly, "His Satanic Majesty of Russia" (Czar Alexander III), whose "terrible form casts a shadow across the universe like a planet in eclipse. There will be but one absorbing spectacle in this world when we stencil him and start him out." Twain then turns his attention to the geological and historical record of the area in which he sees, in typical Protestant historiographical fashion, the course of civilization represented by the "three symbols" of a Roman arch, a Catholic church, and a telegraph office—"The era of War, the era of Theology, the era of Business." His commentary on those "symbols" embodies a major insight into the way Twain perceived the nature of historical change as it is determined by theological conceptions. Thus, change occurs because of "changes in the Deity—or in men's conception of the Deity. . . ." The "old" God of the "Presbyterians and the rest" has given way to a God of business running his universe in deistic fashion by applying laws necessary to the "successful management of a complex and prodigious es-

tablishment," on an earth now a "mere cork adrift in waters of a shoreless Atlantic," a crucial metaphor for understanding *A Connecticut Yankee* and later, darker works of the 1890s. And yet Twain's basically affirmative response to the new technological-business God ("Mighty has been the advance of the nations and the liberalization of thought") is tempered by the thought that recent Presbyterian synods have again "embarrassed" God by reaffirming the the dogma of infant damnation, a dogma that always enraged Twain. Such reflections tell us much about Twain's tensions and ambivalences as he sought to affirm a modern "liberalized" world while yet recognizing the *residua* of reactionary social theological values that ultimately could not be effaced from the course of "progress."

His philosophical "preamble" over, Twain then returns to his topical matter, a description of the baths, the grounds, the gamblers, the "course" of treatment, all presented with Twain's characteristic stance of skeptical humor, incisive detail and anecdote, information about the wide range of "types" who have come to the baths for their own purposes: ". . . all the nations were there, clothed richly and speaking all the languages. Some of the women were painted and were evidently shaky as to character." Predictably, there is at Aix "a good many liars this year." But Twain's arm does indeed improve—along with every other "important ailment known to medical science"—and so he concludes with a final description of the different excursions available outside of Aix. At Lake Annecy Twain finds a town that is a "revelation," a veritable "dream of the Middle Ages," thus turning Hank Morgan's journey into the past into an experiential fact. He is transported back to a cultivated, picturesque "Eden," his primary image always for peace and serenity. And at the old abbey of Tallories, now an inn, Twain again experiences the romance and bliss of the Middle Ages. The God of business seems distant and forgotten now—as he escapes from the "rush and boom and fret and fever of the nineteenth century" into the "mystery of remote antiquity" where he can imagine a "wandering knight with his tin breeches on" visiting the monks there. Twain ends by remarking that he "could have stayed there a few years and got a solid rest." It seems clear that in this piece Twain is less concerned with his task as a reporter of a famous resort than he is with pondering on those theological and historical issues that engaged his mind and imagination and with finding, as he does, in his contemporary world, "relics" of a blissful Edenic and medieval world impervious to the demystifying satire he occasionally subjected them to in other works.

Stanley Brodwin

BIBLIOGRAPHY

Brodwin, Stanley. "Wandering Between Two Worlds: Theological Realism in Mark Twain's *A Connecticut Yankee.*" *Studies in the Literary Imagination* 16 (Fall 1983): 57–82.

Budd, Louis J. *Mark Twain: Social Philosopher.* Bloomington: Indiana UP, 1962.

Kaplan, Justin. *Mr. Clemens and Mark Twain.* New York: Simon & Schuster, 1966.

Neider, Charles. Introduction. *The Complete Essays of Mark Twain.* By Clemens. Ed. Neider. New York: Doubleday, 1963. xii–xxv.

Salomon, Roger. *Twain and the Image of History.* New Haven, Conn.: Yale UP, 1961.

Tuveson, Ernest Lee. *Redeemer Nation: The Idea of America's Millenial Role.* Chicago: U of Chicago P, 1968.

See also: Aix-les-Bains, France; *Connecticut Yankee in King Arthur's Court, A*; Medievalism; Religion

Aix-les-Bains, France

This village, located eight miles north of Chambéry, is noted for its hot springs and the ruins of a Roman triumphal arch and a temple to Diana.

During the summer of 1891 Twain traveled through Europe, stopping at Aix-les-Bains on the way from Geneva to Bayreuth to rest and enjoy the baths. While there, he began to write accounts of his European journeys for English and American newspapers. In November of that year Twain published an article on "Aix, the Paradise of the Rheumatics" in the *Illustrated London News*. Besides describing the town and his experiences while staying there, Twain comments on the historical progression of man's beliefs about God represented by the juxtaposition of Aix of the ancient (the Roman ruins) with the modern (the telegraph office) and the timeless (the hot springs).

Charles Franklyn Beach

BIBLIOGRAPHY

Clemens, Samuel L. "Aix, the Paradise of the Rheumatics." *Europe and Elsewhere.* By Clemens. New York: Harper, 1923. 94–112.

Paine, Albert Bigelow. *Mark Twain: A Biography.* 3 vols. New York: Harper, 1912.

See also: "Aix, the Paradise of the Rheumatics"

Alcott, Louisa May
(1832–1888)

Writing under her own name and a variety of pseudonyms, (L.M.A., A.M. Berhard, Flora Fairfield, A.M.D. of Amos Bronson, Abba May Alcott), Louisa May Alcott began publishing during the 1850s; throughout her life she produced poetry, tales, essays, fiction, and thrillers. Best known, then and now, are *Little Women* (1868), *Little Men* (1871), and *Jo's Boys* (1886), stories that trace the life of Jo March, central protagonist among the family of women introduced in *Little Women*. *Little Women* was and has continued to be an immensely popular book among women, largely because its protagonist struggles against her culture's gender assumptions and demands. *Little Men* and *Jo's Boys* espouse professional careers for women in addition to marriage, as does *Work: A Story of Experience* (1873).

Mark Twain signed a poem published in the Buffalo *Express* in 1869 "Some of the Little Women" and received a bill for a copy of *Little Women* from a Hartford bookseller in 1889. Coleman O. Parsons suggests that an episode in "The Chronicle of Young Satan" (written 1897–1900), one of the *Mysterious Stranger* manuscripts, may have been stimulated by a similar episode in *Little Men*. Though little direct mention is made of Alcott in Twain's letters or works, it would be surprising if a household of four women, three of them children, did not contain copies of at least the "Little" series. And since one of Twain's great pleasures was reading to his family, it is well within the realm of permissible conjecture to suppose that he read several of Alcott's works.

Susan K. Harris

BIBLIOGRAPHY

Alcott, Louisa May. *The Selected Letters of Louisa May Alcott*. Ed. Joel Myerson and Daniel Shealy. Boston: Little, Brown, 1987.

Gribben, Alan. *Mark Twain's Library: A Reconstruction*. 2 vols. Boston: G.K. Hall, 1980.

Parsons, Coleman O. "The Background of *The Mysterious Stranger*." *American Literature* 32 (March 1960): 55–74.

See also: Women

Aldrich, Thomas Bailey
(1836–1907)

In his own time Thomas Bailey Aldrich was a widely respected man of letters. He filled every aspect of that role: he was a poet, a short-story writer, a novelist, an essayist; he held several editorial positions, the most important of which was that of editor of the *Atlantic Monthly* from 1881 to 1890; and he was a witty and companionable addition to Boston-centered literary life who also maintained life-long friendships with a number of writers, including Mark Twain. Achieving national recognition with his sentimental poem on the death of a child, "The Ballad of Babie Bell" (1855), Aldrich continued writing poetry throughout his life. Like many nineteenth-century writers, he valued his poetry above his other literary achievements; to modern readers, however, the poetry with its gentle

handling of romantic themes seems rather pallid. He was a scrupulous and hard-working editor; but he was also extremely conservative: he took over the *Atlantic* when William Dean Howells left and edited it competently but without the imaginative generosity that had enabled Howells to be receptive to new kinds of writing. He claims our attention today for two works that were admired during his own time as well: an epistolary romance, "Marjorie Daw" (1873), typical of many of his short stories for its light touch and trick ending; and *The Story of a Bad Boy* (1869), a book that Howells praised in his *Atlantic* review as a realistic account of boyhood that must be considered as a central inspiration for Twain's boy books and for the others that followed in the nineteenth century.

The Story of a Bad Boy is a slightly fictionalized account of Aldrich's own boyhood in Portsmouth, New Hampshire. It is narrated in the first person by a speaker whose language is that of an adult but whose point of view conflates both adult and child perspectives. The book opens and closes with a patently contrived fictional frame, while the story consists of mostly humorous sketches that recount a series of events in the life of Tom Bailey. Many of these events are common to all childhoods (or boyhoods) and became the staples of later boy books: the mischievous pranks that cement boyhood friendships, the fight with the school bully, the first love. But Aldrich's book seems to have had a more specific influence on Twain. He had apparently written "Boy's Manuscript" (ca. 1868), the sketch that anticipates *Tom Sawyer* (1876), when he read *The Story of a Bad Boy*. He professed indifference to the book, but as Alan Gribben has argued, there are so many suggestive parallels between Twain's book and Aldrich's that he could hardly have been indifferent (Gribben 1985:153–159, 161–163, 166). With Twain's own book beginning to take shape, Aldrich's book was not quite the catalyst Gribben claims (Gribben accepts the now discredited date of 1870 for "Boy's Manuscript"), but it nevertheless must have had a profound effect on Twain in suggesting ways to expand his boy story beyond the romance with which he began.

Marcia Jacobson

BIBLIOGRAPHY

Aldrich, Thomas Bailey. *The Story of a Bad Boy, The Little Violinist, and Other Sketches.* Vol. 7 of *The Writings of Thomas Bailey Aldrich.* Boston: Houghton Mifflin, 1907.

Greenslet, Ferris. *The Life of Thomas Bailey Aldrich.* Boston: Houghton Mifflin, 1908.

Gribben, Alan. "'I Did Wish Tom Sawyer Was There': Boy-Book Elements in *Tom Sawyer* and *Huckleberry Finn*." *One Hundred Years of "Huckleberry Finn": The Boy, His Book, and American Culture.* Ed. Robert Sattelmeyer and J. Donald Crowley. Columbia: U of Missouri P, 1985. 149–170.

Samuels, Charles E. *Thomas Bailey Aldrich.* New York: Twayne, 1966.

Tomsich, John. *A Genteel Endeavor: American Culture and Politics in the Gilded Age.* Stanford, Calif.: Stanford UP, 1971.

See also: Adventures of Tom Sawyer, The; Atlantic Monthly; Boy Books

Allen, Helen

An Angel Fish and member of Mark Twain's Aquarium Club, Helen Allen was the daughter of William H. Allen, U.S. consul in Bermuda in the early twentieth century. Samuel Clemens spent much of the last six months of his life in Bermuda, arriving there with his biographer Albert B. Paine in November 1909. He made a brief return to New York for the Christmas holidays, where tragedy once again struck the Clemens household: daughter Jean drowned in her bath during an epileptic seizure on the morning of Christmas Eve 1909. Clemens returned to Bermuda in early January 1910 and lived in the Allen household until illness forced his return to New York on 12 April. He died at age seventy-four on 20 April 1910.

Infirm, having outlived his wife and three of his four children, the lonely and disconsolate Clemens took refuge in the Allen household. According to Hamlin Hill, Clemens became obsessed with Helen, who, like most of the Angel Fish, reminded him of his daughter Susy. Helen sat with Clemens, took his dictations, and suffered his sentimental effusions about purity and innocence. Now fifteen years old, however, Helen had begun to focus her interests on young men her own age, and Clemens grew jealous; he did not receive from Helen the adulation and rapt attention he expected from an Angel Fish.

Clemens's relationship with Helen Allen during those last four months in Bermuda has become a matter of scholarly interest and speculation. In *Mark Twain: God's Fool* (1973) Hamlin Hill intimates that Clemens took liberties with the young girl and that her parents, concerned about actual or potential improprieties, summoned Paine to remove Clemens from their household (259–261). The evidence, though speculative, is intriguing and disturbing. There is a cryptic note from an Albert Lee referring to something "terrible . . . unprintable" that happened in Bermuda, and both Paine and Clara Clemens were highly sensitive and secretive about the whole matter of Clemens and his adolescent female admirers. Paine sequestered the Helen Allen manuscripts and noted on Mark Twain's final notebook that it was not to be sold or offered for public perusal for fifty years after Clemens's death.

Yet the Helen Allen manuscripts do survive, and they are now available in John Cooley's edition of the Angel Fish correspondence (1991). Cooley is more reticent than Hill in discussing the matter of Helen Allen: "With the possible exception of Clemens's final visit with the Allen family, restraint and discretion seem to have characterized his relationship with the angelfish" (281). He speculates that Clemens saw himself as Helen's "older friend and protector," the guardian of her innocence and points to Clemens's last written words to Helen: "be cautious, watchful, wary" and avoid becoming "besmirched" (281).

James D. Wilson

BIBLIOGRAPHY

Clemens, Samuel L. *Mark Twain's Aquarium: The Samuel Clemens-Angelfish Correspondence, 1905–1910.* Ed. John Cooley. Athens: U of Georgia P, 1991.

Hill, Hamlin. *Mark Twain: God's Fool.* New York: Harper & Row, 1973.

Quirk, Dorothy. *Enchantment: A Little Girl's Friendship with Mark Twain.* Norman: U of Oklahoma P, 1961.

Stone, Albert E., Jr. *The Innocent Eye: Childhood in Mark Twain's Imagination.* New Haven, Conn.: Yale UP, 1961.

See also: Angel Fish and Aquarium Club; Bermuda; Childhood; Innocence

BIBLIOGRAPHY

Branch, Edgar M. *The Literary Apprenticeship of Mark Twain.* Urbana: U of Illinois P, 1950.

Clemens, Samuel L. *Mark Twain's Autobiography.* Ed. Albert B. Paine. 2 vols. New York: Harper, 1924.

———. *Mark Twain's Letters, Volume 1 (1853–1866).* Ed. Edgar M. Branch, Michael B. Frank, and Kenneth M. Sanderson. Berkeley: U of California P, 1988.

Wecter, Dixon. *Sam Clemens of Hannibal.* Boston: Houghton Mifflin, 1952.

See also: Hannibal, Missouri; Journalism; Newspapers

Ament, Joseph

Born in Tennessee around 1824, Joseph Ament worked as a printer and editor of the Missouri *Courier* in Palmyra, Missouri. In his *Autobiography* (1924), Clemens writes that he started working as Ament's apprentice immediately after John Marshall Clemens, his father, died in 1847. However, his memory had to be faulty, for Ament did not transfer his shop to Hannibal, Missouri, until June 1848. In November 1852 Ament sold the *Courier;* in April 1853 he returned to Palmyra.

Clemens recalls that Ament was extremely stingy. As an apprentice, Clemens was to receive no wages but room and board and two suits a year. According to Clemens, one of the suits "always failed to materialize," the other fit him poorly, and the Aments provided the apprentices scant rations. After leaving Ament's employ, Clemens called his former employer a "diminutive chunk of human meat."

In spite of Clemens's strong criticism of Ament, the man seems to have been generous and brave in some ways, particularly as shown by his rescuing burnable items from Orion Clemens's print shop when it was on fire. Samuel Clemens's apprenticeship to Ament enabled Clemens not to burden his family with financial problems shortly after his father's death. It also provided him with an early opportunity to learn the printing business.

Richard Tuerk

American Bible Society

In one of twenty-six letters for the San Francisco *Alta California*, written before his trip on the *Quaker City*, Mark Twain described a visit to the American Bible Society in the Bible House in New York City. In letter twenty, "For Christians to Read," dated 20 May 1867 and found in *Mark Twain's Travels with Mr. Brown*, Twain wittily blended factual information and personal observations. After listing numerous languages in which the Bibles were translated, giving statistics concerning the number of Bibles printed, speculating on the potential profits of the business, and describing the variety of Bibles in the library, he suggested that he should send the library a copy of his book "so as to make a little variety."

Reverend Franklin S. Rising, a friend of Twain's and a prototype for the minister in *Roughing It* (1872), worked in the Bible House as secretary of the Church Missionary Society of the Episcopal Church.

Sandra Gravitt

BIBLIOGRAPHY

Clemens, Samuel L. *Mark Twain's Notebooks & Journals, Volume I (1855–1873).* Ed. Frederick Anderson, Michael B. Frank, and Kenneth M. Sanderson. Berkeley: U of California P, 1975.

———. *Mark Twain's Travels with Mr. Brown.* Ed. Franklin Walker and G. Ezra Dane. New York: Knopf, 1940.

Ensor, Allison. *Mark Twain and the Bible.* Lexington: UP of Kentucky, 1969.

See also: Bible; *Mark Twain's Travels with Mr. Brown*; San Francisco *Alta California*

American Board of Foreign Missions (American Board of Commissioners for Foreign Missions)

Founded in 1810, the American Board of Commissioners for Foreign Missions was the predominant missionary organization of the century. It had sponsored missionaries in China for seventy years already when, in the summer of 1900, several board missionaries and hundreds of Chinese Christian converts were executed by Boxer rebels in areas outside Peking. In that fall, after the rebellion, one of the board's missionaries, Reverend William S. Ament, and an assistant, Reverend E.G. Tewksbury, escorted by an American cavalry troop searched the countryside for Boxers, collecting indemnities for slain converts, burning peasants' houses, and even asking the soldiers to shoot "suspected Boxers" on the spot. Ament's actions were reported in the New York *Sun* in November and again on Christmas Eve, 1900, in which account Ament was said to have extracted indemnities thirteen times the amount lost. Provoked by Ament's reported conduct as well as by similar American actions elsewhere in the world, Clemens wrote his most important anti-imperialist work, published in February 1901 as "To the Person Sitting in Darkness." It began with a lengthy quotation about Ament from the Christmas Eve *Sun* article. As Clemens anticipated, his satirical essay prompted widespread controversy in America and abroad, both in print and in private correspondence to him. Dr. Judson Smith, corresponding secretary of the board, defended Ament in letters to the New York *Herald* and *Tribune* later in February, questioning the accuracy of the *Sun* dispatch and calling for an apology from Clemens. In a letter in the *Tribune* Clemens replied to Smith by saying that Ament had indicted himself. Not satisfied, Smith repeated his demand for an apology, and in March the New York *Sun* printed an interview with Ament in which he claimed that the indemnity had been only one and a third, not thirteen times, the loss. Clemens's "apology" to Smith and Ament appeared in April as "To My Missionary Critics," using Ament's "clarification" as further evidence of the board's ruthlessness and hypocrisy. This time the reaction was overwhelmingly in Clemens's favor. Ament returned to America in May and continued to give interviews in which he condemned himself until Smith silenced him. Though Smith himself tried a final time to defend the board's missionaries in a May essay, "The Missionaries and Their Critics," it was clear that the board's defense of looting and extortion had fallen apart under the power of Clemens's withering satire.

L. Terry Oggel

BIBLIOGRAPHY

Field, James A., Jr. "Near East Notes and Far East Queries." *The Mission Enterprise in China and America.* Ed. John K. Fairbank. Cambridge, Mass.: Harvard UP, 1974. 23–25.

Foner, Philip S. *Mark Twain: Social Critic.* New York: International Publishers, 1958.

Latourette, Kenneth Scott. *A History of Christian Missions in China.* 1929; rpt. New York: Russell and Russell, 1967.

Miller, Stuart C. "Ends and Means: Missionary Justification of Force in Nineteenth Century China." *The Mission Enterprise in China and America.* Ed. John K. Fairbank. Cambridge, Mass.: Harvard UP, 1974. 249–282.

Rabe, Valentin H. "Evangelical Logistics: Mission Support and Resources to 1920." *The Mission Enterprise in China and America.* Ed. John K. Fairbank. Cambridge, Mass.: Harvard UP, 1974. 56–90.

Schlesinger, Arthur, Jr. "The Missionary Enterprise and Theories of Imperialism." *The Mission Enterprise in China and America.* Ed. John K. Fairbank. Cambridge, Mass.: Harvard UP, 1974. 336–373.

See also: Missionaries; Religion; "To My Missionary Critics"; "To the Person Sitting in Darkness"

American Claimant, The
(1892)

In need of money for expenses connected with the Paige typesetting machine and his family's forthcoming trip to Europe, Mark Twain wrote *The American Claimant* in only seventy-one days, from late February to early May 1891. Syndicated in the New York *Sun* and other newspapers (3 January–30 March 1892) and in *The Idler* (London) from February 1892 to June 1893, it was published in book form by Clemens's own firm, Charles L. Webster and Company, in April 1892 and later the same year by Chatto and Windus in England.

The novel's main character, Colonel Sellers, had appeared earlier in *The Gilded Age* (1873), in *Colonel Sellers* (1874), a play based on that novel, in which his first name was changed from Beriah to Mulberry, and in *Colonel Sellers as a Scientist*, another play, which Twain and William Dean Howells completed in 1883.

For the basic complication of the new book, Mark Twain expanded upon a theme that had long fascinated him—his own family's possible claim, through his mother Jane Lampton, to the earldom of Durham (Rossmore in the novel). The family legend was substantially that outlined in the story—that the eldest Lambton son (and a brother) had immigrated to America during the eighteenth century (presumably changing the spelling of the name to Lampton), whereupon a younger brother took possession of the family lands and subsequent title. Thereafter, from time to time, one of the descendants in America pronounced himself the "rightful heir" and sought (vainly) to establish his claim. In Clemens's own day the claimant was a Jesse M. Leathers (mentioned briefly in the novel as Simon Lathers, whose death makes Colonel Sellers the "rightful heir"). And there is evidence that Clemens was intrigued by the idea that he himself might have a claim to the earldom.

That concept and the treatment of the Colonel's many inventions Twain had already employed to some extent in *Colonel Sellers as a Scientist*, which was performed several times in 1887 as *The American Claimant, or Mulberry Sellers Ten Years Later*. Whereas the play was fundamentally farcical, in the novel the scenes involving the Colonel's inventions and other schemes, though still highly fantastic, are better motivated and integrated into the whole. For the book, also, Mark Twain greatly expanded the role of the current heir to the earldom into a second major theme and the chief vehicle for Clemens's own current political and social ideas.

In that expansion young Viscount Berkeley, inspired by the democratic ideas propounded by a British radical, renounces his claim to the earldom of Rossmore in favor of the American claimant to the title. He travels to the United States to investigate the matter and to observe the workings of democracy at first hand. Believed lost in a hotel fire, Berkeley assumes the name Howard Tracy, seeks work, and after many rebuffs finally is employed to fill in the painted backgrounds of chromo portraits. Totally disillusioned by the violations of democratic principles that he encounters, and the Darwinian "struggle for existence" that he sees in the boardinghouse, he finally decides to heed the advice of his friend Barrow that since he cannot reform the whole aristocratic system, he might just as well enjoy the advantages of his status. Meanwhile he has met Sellers and falls in love with the Colonel's daughter, Sally. Berkeley's father, the present earl, comes to America, is much taken with Sally, and consents to the marriage. At the conclusion, when the family sets off for a visit to England, the Colonel is missing. Off on another grand scheme—to furnish climates to order by control of sun-spots—he concludes the letter explaining his absence with a promise that, with all its hyperbole, embodies not only the genial exuberance, but also the endearing quality of his nature. If successful, he says, he will send them a message: "I will waft a vast sun-spot across the disk like drifting smoke, and you will know it for my love-sign, and will say, 'Mulberry Sellers throws us a kiss across the universe.'"

Hastily and crudely fabricated as it was, *The American Claimant* has generally been regarded as one of Mark Twain's poorer productions. He did manage to convert some of the pointless humor of the play version into meaningful satire and to retain some of Colonel Sellers' original qualities as a good-hearted and lovable visionary, but the projects of the Colonel—his cursing phonograph and his schemes for materialization of the dead, for instance—remain too absurd for any willing suspension of disbelief, though one might conceivably feel sympathy with his desire to materialize departed great statesmen of all ages and countries so as to "furnish this country with a Congress that knows enough to come in out of the rain." The love story is overly sentimental and generally trite, though Sally Sellers does display more "passion" than most of Mark Twain's other female characters.

Nevertheless, the novel represents a significant stage in the development of Clemens's own disillusionment with the idea of progress and the possibilities of democratic reform that had originally inspired *A Connecticut Yankee in King Arthur's Court* (1889). The presentation of young Berkeley's disillusionment with democracy and decision to retain his aristocratic privilege, and the views expressed by his boardinghouse friend, Barrow, may be seen as evidence of a deepened conviction of what Mark Twain ultimately implied in *A Connecticut Yankee*—that the flaws in human nature itself made attempts at reform of people and institutions largely futile. Thus, with all its faults, consideration of this often neglected work is necessary for a full picture of the development of its author's political, social, and philosophical ideas.

Howard G. Baetzhold

BIBLIOGRAPHY

Baetzhold, Howard G. *Mark Twain and John Bull: The British Connection*. Bloomington: Indiana UP, 1970.

Budd, Louis J. *Mark Twain: Social Philosopher*. Bloomington: Indiana UP, 1962.

Grimm, Clyde L. "*The American Claimant*: Reclamation of a Farce." *American Quarterly* 19 (Spring 1967): 86–103.

Regan, Robert. *Unpromising Heroes: Mark Twain and His Characters*. Berkeley: U of California P, 1966.

Salomon, Roger B. *Twain and the Image of History*. New Haven, Conn.: Yale UP, 1961.

Sloane, David E.E. *Mark Twain as a Literary Comedian*. Baton Rouge: Louisiana State UP, 1979.

See also: *Colonel Sellers*; *Colonel Sellers as a Scientist*; *Gilded Age, The*; Sellers, Colonel

American Publishing Company, The

Perhaps the foremost subscription publishing company in the last third of the nineteenth century, the American Publishing Company printed the first six of Mark Twain's major works—*The Innocents Abroad* (1869), *Roughing It* (1872), *The Gilded Age* (1873), *Sketches, New and Old* (1875), *The Adventures of Tom Sawyer* (1876), and *A Tramp Abroad* (1880)—and the final two subscription volumes, *Pudd'nhead Wilson* (1894) and *Following the Equator* (1897). Originally run by Elisha Bliss and then under the control of his two sons, Francis E. and Walter Bliss, the company had branch offices throughout the country to market histories, Civil War commentaries, biblical interpretations, and other factual material until it decided, in 1867, to publish a work of fiction and humor, *The Innocents Abroad*. Encouraged by that volume's success, the American Publishing Company issued volumes by Bret Harte, Dan De Quille, and Marietta Holley. As subscription-book audiences disappeared in the late nineteenth century to urbanization and trade bookstores, the American Publishing Company turned to expensive deluxe editions of authors, including Mark Twain.

Hamlin Hill

BIBLIOGRAPHY

Clemens, Samuel L. *Mark Twain's Letters to His Publishers, 1867–1894.* Ed. Hamlin Hill. Berkeley: U of California P, 1967.

Kaplan, Justin. *Mr. Clemens and Mark Twain.* New York: Simon & Schuster, 1966.

Paine, Albert Bigelow. *Mark Twain: A Biography.* 3 vols. New York: Harper, 1912.

See also: Bliss, Elisha; Subscription Publication

Anderson, Frederick

(1926–1979)

Frederick Anderson was the fifth editor of the Mark Twain Papers. After completing his B.A. at Stanford University in 1948 and his B.L.S. at the University of California at Berkeley in 1950, he became a member of the staff of the Charles F. Doe Library on the Berkeley campus and was subsequently named assistant to Henry Nash Smith, then editor of the Mark Twain Papers. He succeeded Smith in 1964 and held the post until his death.

Anderson was an associate editor and co-editor of several major works: *Mark Twain of the "Enterprise"* (1957), *Mark Twain-Howells Letters* (1960), and three volumes of *Mark Twain's Notebooks & Journals* (1975–1979). Among his other publications were two widely used collections: *Mark Twain: The Critical Heritage* (1971), which gathered contemporary criticism of Mark Twain, and *A Pen Warmed-Up in Hell* (1972), a selection of Mark Twain's most outspoken social criticism.

It was as a general editor, however, that Anderson made his most significant contributions to Mark Twain studies. He expanded and systematized the Mark Twain Papers series of scholarly editions of unpublished literary works, notebooks, and letters, which had been conceived under his predecessor. He provided similar direction for the Works of Mark Twain, the companion series of scholarly editions of previously published works, originally begun at the University of Iowa. These continuing series, both published by the University of California Press, are the primary elements of the editorial program now known as the Mark Twain Project.

Michael B. Frank

BIBLIOGRAPHY

Anderson, Frederick, and Kenneth M. Sanderson, eds. *Mark Twain: The Critical Heritage.* New York: Barnes & Noble, 1971.

Clemens, Samuel L. *"Ah Sin," A Dramatic Work by Mark Twain and Bret Harte* (with Bret Harte). Ed. Frederick Anderson. San Francisco: Book Club of California, 1961.

————. *The Great Landslide Case.* Ed. Frederick Anderson and Edgar M. Branch. Berkeley: Friends of the Bancroft Library, 1972.

————. *Mark Twain-Howells Letters: The Correspondence of Samuel L. Clemens and William D. Howells, 1872–1910.* Ed. Henry Nash Smith and William M. Gibson. 2 vols. Cambridge, Mass.: Harvard UP, 1960.

————. *Mark Twain of the "Enterprise": Newspaper Articles and Other Documents, 1862–1864.* Ed. Henry Nash Smith and Frederick Anderson. Berkeley: U of California P, 1957.

————. *Mark Twain: San Francisco Correspondent. Selections from His Letters to the "Territorial Enterprise": 1865–1866.* Ed. Henry Nash Smith and Frederick Anderson. San Francisco: Book Club of California, 1957.

————. *Mark Twain's Notebooks & Journals, Volume I (1855–1873).* Ed. Frederick Anderson, Michael B. Frank, and Kenneth M. Sanderson. Berkeley: U of California P, 1975. *Volume II (1877–1883).* Ed. Frederick Anderson, Lin Salamo, and Bernard L. Stein. Berkeley: U of California P, 1975. *Volume III (1883–1891).* Ed. Robert Pack Browning, Michael B. Frank, and Lin Salamo. Berkeley: U of California P, 1979.

————. *A Pen Warmed-Up in Hell: Mark Twain in Protest.* Ed. Frederick Anderson. New York: Harper & Row, 1972.

————. *Selected Mark Twain-Howells Letters, 1872–1910.* Ed. Frederick Anderson, William M. Gibson, and Henry Nash Smith. Cambridge, Mass.: Harvard UP, 1967.

See also: Mark Twain Papers; Mark Twain Project; Smith, Henry Nash

Angel's Camp, California

Several of Twain's most famous stories have their origin in his visit, between December

1864 and February 1865, to the cabin of Jim Gillis on Jackass Hill, in Tuolumne County. Twain went there with his good friend, Steve Gillis, who had gotten into trouble with the police over his part in a brawl and decided to leave San Francisco for a while. While they stayed with Steve's brother, Jim, Twain learned how to prospect for pocket mines of gold, but the only treasure he really found was the people he met in the area. From them he picked up both distinctive ways of telling stories and several stories in particular.

The most famous of these tales was "Jim Smiley and His Jumping Frog" (1865). Twain first heard this story from Ben Coon, who lived in Angel's Camp, Calaveras County, a few miles away from Gillis's cabin. Twain was struck with Coon's narration of it, and when he returned to San Francisco at the end of February, Twain committed the story to writing. It was first published in the *Saturday Press* of New York in November 1865. The story became an instant success. Twain revised it into what is now known as "The Celebrated Jumping Frog of Calaveras County," and it became his springboard to fame.

The sentimental "The Californian's Tale" (1893) originated at Angel's Camp, as did "The King's Cameleopard or the Royal Nonesuch" episode from chapters 22 and 23 of *Huckleberry Finn* (1885), much cleaned up from the bawdy original. "Jim Blaine and His Grandfather's Ram" and "Dick Baker and His Cat," both incorporated into *Roughing It* (1872), and "Jim Baker's Blue Jay Yarn," incorporated into *A Tramp Abroad* (1880), are three more stories that came to Twain's attention either at Angel's Camp or at Jackass Hill. These last three may be rooted in American folklore, but Twain's telling of them, far from being a reversion to a primitive oral tradition, is rather a refinement of the oral style into sophisticated literary art.

Lawrence I. Berkove

BIBLIOGRAPHY

Bellamy, Gladys Carmen. *Mark Twain as a Literary Artist*. Norman: U of Oklahoma P, 1950.

Benson, Ivan. *Mark Twain's Western Years*. Stanford, Calif.: Stanford UP, 1938.

Clemens, Samuel L. *Mark Twain's Notebooks & Journals, Volume I (1855–1873)*. Ed. Frederick Anderson, Michael B. Frank, and Kenneth M. Sanderson. Berkeley: U of California P, 1975.

Covici, Pascal, Jr. *Mark Twain's Humor: The Image of a World*. Dallas: Southern Methodist UP, 1962.

Wilson, James D. *A Reader's Guide to the Short Stories of Mark Twain*. Boston: G.K. Hall, 1987.

See also: *Adventures of Huckleberry Finn*; "Celebrated Jumping Frog of Calaveras County, The"; Gillis, Steve; *Roughing It*; *Tramp Abroad, A*

"Angel's Camp Constable"
(1981)

Composed around September or early October 1865, and remaining unpublished among family papers at Vassar College, this draft of a character sketch or episode seems docketed rather than worthy of the title "Angel's Camp Constable." In 1981 it was finally published in *The Works of Mark Twain: Early Tales & Sketches*. It reads like a failed attempt at establishing the artful relationship between narrator-sophisticate and yarn-spinning native eventually perfected in the jumping frog story's final version. Here the first-person narrator obeys the injunction not to laugh as Simon Wheeler unfolds directly, without wandering, a couple of incidents demonstrating his hero, Constable Bilgewater, in action, quelling "insurrections" or "riots," which we are repeatedly assured amount to no more than mere fistfights.

Other than the early use of the names, the sketch's significance lies in showing how Mark Twain tried to capture the style of storytellers at Angel's Camp, especially that of old Ben Coon, who told the frog story, now stressing the style rather than the frame of such yarns. It also shows evolution of the gallery of "pet heroes" who will reappear in the frog story. In these respects, the sketch provides a window into Mark Twain's workshop as he crafts the seemingly artless art of his first famous tale.

P.M. Zall

BIBLIOGRAPHY

Clemens, Samuel L. *The Works of Mark Twain: Early Tales & Sketches, Volume 2 (1864–1865).* Ed. Edgar M. Branch and Robert H. Hirst. Berkeley: U of California P, 1981. 279–281.

Wilson, James D. *A Reader's Guide to the Short Stories of Mark Twain.* Boston: G.K. Hall, 1987.

See also: Angel's Camp, California; "Celebrated Jumping Frog of Calaveras County, The"; Wheeler, Simon

Angel Fish and Aquarium Club

In 1906, at the age of seventy-two, Samuel Clemens began collecting surrogate granddaughters. He expressed this activity in his autobiographical dictations: "as for me, I collect pets: young girls—girls from ten to sixteen years old; girls who are pretty and sweet and naive and innocent. . . ." Clemens was so successful that within a year his collection numbered a dozen young women. In the spring of 1908 he began calling them his Angel Fish and inducting them into the Aquarium Club, an organization he devised to formalize his hobby and to keep the girls in frequent contact. Clemens's correspondence with his angelfish includes approximately 300 known letters, dating from December 1905 to the time of his death in 1910.

Clemens's last years were often dominated by loneliness, illness, and depression, caused in part by the death of his wife Olivia in 1904, limited contact with his surviving daughters, Clara and Jean, and the decline in his health and literary powers. By 1907 Clemens counterbalanced his unhappiness with a number of pleasant diversions that included billiards and card games, a continuous whirl of social engagements, and the friendship of "young girls." His Angel Fish letters were nearly always optimistic, loving, and playful. As Clemens himself expressed it, by 1908 the Aquarium Club had become his "life's chief delight." He extracted numerous visits from the Angel Fish to his rented homes on Fifth Avenue and in Tuxedo Park, New York, and later to his permanent home, Stormfield, in Redding, Connecticut. The Angel Fish attended concerts and plays with him, took walks, and played games, including billiards, canasta, and charades. At the peak of Aquarium Club activity, Clemens received and sent several letters a week to his "fish" and hoped to have at least one Angel Fish visiting every weekend. With the possible exception of Bermuda Angel Fish Helen Allen, Clemens's relationship with the young women was characterized by propriety and discretion, for he was, as he said on many occasions, a protector and defender of schoolgirl innocence.

It is only when the affection, youthfulness, and playfulness of these letters is placed in the literary and autobiographical contexts of Clemens's last decade, a period that produced *The Mysterious Stranger* (1916) and *What Is Man?* (1906) and was clouded by his fatalism and barely contained rage at the "swindle of life," that the Angel Fish period can be fully appreciated—as counterpoint to the prevailing mood of Samuel Clemens's last decade.

John Cooley

BIBLIOGRAPHY

Clemens, Samuel L. *Mark Twain's Aquarium: The Samuel Clemens-Angelfish Correspondence, 1905–1910.* Ed. John Cooley. Athens: U of Georgia P, 1991.

Hill, Hamlin. *Mark Twain: God's Fool.* New York: Harper & Row, 1973.

Quick, Dorothy. *Enchantment: A Little Girl's Friendship with Mark Twain.* Norman: U of Oklahoma P, 1961.

See also: Allen, Helen; Childhood; Innocence

Angelo and Luigi (Cappello)

The Cappellos are the Italian twin brothers who are the central focus of "Those Extraordinary Twins" (1894) ("TET") and who continue to figure prominently, though largely as catalysts to the main action, in *Pudd'nhead Wilson* (1894). The latter has its roots in the former. Mark Twain began writing "TET" intending it to be a "howling farce," only to set it aside to complete "Tom Sawyer Abroad" (1894); when he returned to the manuscript in early 1893, he confessed to Fred Hall that he did so with "a little different plan" (*Letters* 319). He thoroughly recast the characters of David Wilson, Tom Driscoll, and Roxana and began to think of the novel as the story not of the twins but of those three characters who had fired his imagination. By 30 July 1893 he had virtually completed his revision, or transformation, again writing to Hall: "I have pulled the twins apart & made two individuals of them; I have sunk them out of sight, they are mere flitting shadows, now, & of no importance. . . . The whole story is centered on the murder and the trial" (*Letters* 354–355). It is this text, now entitled *Pudd'nhead Wilson*, that began to appear serially in *Century Magazine* in December 1893. When the American Publishing Company published the book form of *PW* in 1894, however, it included with it the excised and abandoned farce of "TET," "refuse matter" Mark Twain had sold to the company for $1,500 (Berger 173–178).

Angelo and Luigi thus derive from the Siamese freak in the earlier farce, a conglomeration of two heads and four arms joined to a single trunk. The brothers are reminiscent of Chang and Eng, the twins who have separate bodies but are joined by a fleshly ligature in Mark Twain's essay "Personal Habits of the Siamese Twins" (1869). In that earlier essay farce results because one twin's allegiance is to the Union, the other's to the Confederacy. The more immediate inspiration for the characters of Angelo and Luigi Cappello comes from the celebrated Italian Siamese twins, Giacomo and Giovanni Tocci, who shared one body but who had distinct and often contradictory personalities and character traits (Gillman 60–61). In all cases, the intriguing questions posed involve identity: do the twins have collective or individual status, and to what

extent can they be held individually responsible for their collective actions? The separation of Angelo and Luigi into discrete, fraternal twins in *PW* has caused critical difficulties because there seems to be a careless carry-over of traits from the Siamese twins that are inappropriate for separate ones, and because their role in the novel seems extraneous, even diversionary. Yet, in fact, the twins assume a similar role in each story, one crucial to the theme of the novel in which, the author claims, they had become "mere flitting shadows." As Gillman points out, the questions they raise pertaining to moral and legal responsibility become all the more pertinent "when applied to a racial context": the twins serve as an analogue of one of the novel's central implications, "that slavery is not simply an abhorrent social institution, but a metaphor for the individual's relationship to himself, to his intimates, and to his society" (Gillman 69). In addition to serving as an analogue for the serious issues the novel raises pertaining to identity, moral responsibility, and social interrelationships, however, the twins also reinforce a complementary theological point germane to an understanding of *PW*.

In "TET" the linked brothers are contrary in personality yet mutually dependent; neither could exist without his opposite. Curiously, the darker of the two (Luigi) reveals to Aunt Patty that in spite of their present Siamese bond, he and his brother are not twins at all: he is six months older than Angelo. Though biologically impossible, Luigi's claim is rich in theological implication. Like Mark Twain's Siamese twins, the biblical Adam (human) is an inextricable cohesion of light and dark forces—the angelic (Angelo) and the satanic or Luciferian (Luigi). Yet Adam was not so at his creation. Prior to his decision to eat the forbidden fruit—the Fall—he had no awareness of evil, though he did have the capacity to reason, to make a choice (to eat the fruit or to obey God). The choice may have been rational or irrational, have had favorable or disastrous consequences, but it was not evil. It is only as Adam assumes the Moral Sense with his choice in the Garden of Eden to eat from the tree of knowledge of good and evil that the forces of evil in the universe, which predate and are separate from Adam, are assimilated. Once fused, however, the angelic (Angelo) and the demonic (Luigi) are co-dependent and inseparable. So too the twins in "TET," initially separate, become inextricably linked, sharing a single pair of legs that each controls for alternate twenty-four hour intervals. When the twins are on trial for kicking Tom Driscoll, diffused responsibility becomes the issue. Because the jury cannot distinguish which twin had control of the legs at the time, both are freed (later, of course, both are hanged): "Our verdict is that justice has been defeated by the dispensation of God" ("TET" 153). Given our dual yet inextricably yoked natures, we as humans are neither entirely innocent nor guilty. If neither side of our divided nature has control over the other, then freedom is a fiction and moral responsibility a theological quagmire resolved not by justice but by God's "dispensation"—the salvation or damnation granted, the Calvinist believed, arbitrarily.

The twins in *PW* are ostensibly separate and have radically different traits: Angelo is fundamentally a good man, moral in his behavior, sympathetic and strong in his religious faith; Luigi is evil in thought and deed, resolute in his denial of God. The initial information we receive—that they are foreign, the connotations of the names Angelo and Luigi, the light and dark complexions, their good and bad dispositions—serves quickly to establish their dichotomous natures. Yet they retain the inextricable interdependence of the original Siamese pair. "We were," Luigi tells Aunt Patsy, "their [his parents] only child" (*PW* 27). Though critics generally attribute this puzzling statement to Twain's carelessness in converting the Siamese twins into separate fraternal ones, the singular "child" in this context may well refer to two natures mutually interdependent or two forces fused into one existence. Later Luigi explains to Wilson that in slaying the thief who attacked his brother

he acted from self-interest: "I saved my own life, you see" (*PW* 52). Tom Driscoll derisively calls the twins a "human philopena"— "let this human philopena snip you out a speech" (*PW* 56)—a change from the analogy to a pair of scissors Tom makes in "TET." Assuming philopena to mean a single nut with two kernels, critics again claim an inconsistent analogy (and mixed metaphor) due to careless editing. The Latin roots of philopena, however, give theological richness to the analogy absent in the original scissors metaphor: "philo" means love, specifically agape love; "poena" means penalty, as in a forfeit. The union of the two in the image of a single nut with two kernels suggests the Miltonic duality of soul, a flawed entity redeemed by love. The word "snip," apparently more appropriate to the initial scissors metaphor, remains pertinent in this enriched context since it means to separate, discriminate—precisely the function of a moral conscience.

Dawson's Landing, however, lacks a moral conscience—the ability to see the world in metaphysical terms, to discern good and evil, let alone to understand that because of their inextricable mutually dependent nature they are present in the hearts of all of us and hence we are all twins. Thus they are blind to the moral implications of Wilson's ironic joke about killing his half of the dog; they know, of course, that if you kill one half of a dog you kill the other half as well, but they never realize that in perpetuating the moral atrocity of chattel slavery they are killing one half of the social body and hence dooming the other half to certain death as well. Angelo and Luigi are the personified moral conscience come to visit Dawson's Landing, and they serve a role similar to that of the ironic stranger in "The Man That Corrupted Hadleyburg" (1899); they "snip" at the character of the town, precipitating the incidents leading to the trial that exposes Tom as an imposter and murderer. They offer the opportunity for self-examination and moral awareness. Yet the upheavals they engender bring no significant changes in the characters' natures or outlooks. Tom's punishment for his crimes underscores the amoral nature of Dawson's Landing, Mark Twain's "waste land." Originally sentenced to life imprisonment, Tom is spared because of his value as a slave; instead, he is sold down river as partial payment on the Driscoll estate. With their perverse materialistic logic, the townspeople reason that if Tom were white and free, he should be punished; but to lock up a valuable slave would mean material loss for the owners. Under a capitalistic ethos value is determined not by metaphysical categories of good and evil but by financial ones of profit and loss. Good becomes goods: "As soon as the Governor understood the case, he pardoned Tom at once, and the creditors sold him down the river" (*PW* 115).

James D. Wilson

BIBLIOGRAPHY

Anderson, Frederick. Introduction. *Pudd'nhead Wilson and Those Extraordinary Twins*. By Clemens. Ed. Frederick Anderson. San Francisco: Chandler, 1968. vii–xxxii.

Berger, Sidney E. "Textual Introductions and Table of Variants." *Pudd'nhead Wilson and Those Extraordinary Twins*. By Clemens. Ed. Sidney E. Berger. Norton crit. ed. New York: Norton, 1980. 171–212.

Clemens, Samuel L. *Mark Twain's Letters to his Publishers, 1867– 1894*. Ed. Hamlin Hill. Berkeley: U of California P, 1967.

———. *Pudd'nhead Wilson and Those Extraordinary Twins*. Ed. Sidney E. Berger. Norton crit. ed. New York: Norton, 1980.

Cox, James M. *Mark Twain: The Fate of Humor*. Princeton, N.J.: Princeton UP, 1966.

Fisher, Marvin, and Michael Elliott. "*Pudd'nhead Wilson*: Half a Dog Is Worse Than None." *Southern Review* 8 (1972): 533–547.

Gillman, Susan. *Dark Twins: Imposture and Identity in Mark Twain's America*. Chicago: U of Chicago P, 1989.

Haines, James B. "Of Dogs and Men: A Symbolic Variation on the Twin Motif in *Pudd'nhead Wilson*." *Mark Twain Journal* 18 (Winter 1976–1977): 3, 14–17.

See also: Law; Miscegenation; *Pudd'nhead Wilson, The Tragedy of*; "Those Extraordinary Twins, The Comedy"

Animals

Mark Twain's lifelong fascination with animals—including his identification with them and his ability to personalize and give them characters quite as richly comic as his humans—makes his animals masterworks of a great comic imagination. Far more than do pets, novelties, or sources of transportation, his birds, dogs, horses, frogs, camels, and insects receive the three-dimensionality—feelings, potential for relationships, even capacity for generating occasional tragic effects—usually assigned humans. Twain inherited from his fellow mid-nineteenth-century humorists of the antebellum deep South—the southwest humorists—a superb set of techniques for picturing the humanized animal, mixed with a curious, contradictory set of traditions as to attitudes in picturing comic animals interacting with the people about them. Twain—the master of the group as well as the most forward-looking—combined, edited, and reshaped the tradition that he inherited. His innovations resulted in Twain's wonderfully comic animal portraiture, funny without being cruel, that leads the reader's imagination to see man in the animal, the animal in man at once, until the creature is suspended between human and beast, resulting in a comic composite that delights as it comments on both parts of the combination.

One group of largely sophisticated, upper-class writers who felt strongly the social divisions of the deep South caste system (poor whites and the landowning elite were not at all the same) used images of animals and figures of speech featuring animals to ridicule the redneck's and backwoodsman's simplicity and to show their cruelty. A second group saw the closeness of man and animal on the frontier as an appealing bond; these writers personified their animals respectfully, affectionately, picturing hunts as conflicts of equals. Twain draws techniques from both groups, but in attitude he shows the style of the animal-admiring humorists. In terms of identifying with the animals, the sources vary from the disdainfulness of Augustus Baldwin Longstreet's gentleman narrator to Thomas

Thorpe's hero-hunter-narrator feeling genuine love and awe for his quarry in "The Big Bear of Arkansas" (1841), a parallel to Twain's total identification with the Indian crow from the late travel sketches. The crow is the ultimate expression of an empathy with animals so complete that it has led a number of modern critics to assert that Twain wrote of animals as if he were one of them.

Some key techniques Twain adopted from other humorists appear in Longstreet's "The Horse-Swap" (1835), where the author pictures Little Bullet, a wretched, earless backwoods nag, as a misarrangement of a horse's parts: "His height was about twelve hands, but, as his shape partook somewhat of that of the giraffe, his haunches stood much lower." Twain will similarly rearrange his animals' parts. Also, Longstreet animates individual features of Little Bullet independently; witness this: "From the root [his tail] dropped into a graceful festoon; then rose in an handsome curve; then resumed its first direction. . . . The whole had a careless and bewitching inclination to the right." "The Horse-Swap" also shows a key Twain technique, the collusion of a man-and-animal team seeking to dupe another such team in a risky swap. Knowing his role, Bullet seems eager to strut, when a rider is found: "Here Bullet bristled up, and looked as if he had been hunting for Bob all day long. . . ." By the time the swap is made, the horse and the flamboyant, boasting frontiersman who owns him, "the *Yellow* Blossom," have struck the reader as wonderfully funny, and appealing, but at the close of the swap we learn that Bullet's sprightly motions result from his having a hideous infected sore under his saddle. Worse, the horse for which Bullet is being swapped turns out to be both deaf and blind. The disgusted gentleman narrator can only mutter his offense at the cruelty of the hicks, leaving the reader with scorn of the inhumanity of the frontiersmen. Surely, Longstreet suggests, such folks can in no sense be permitted to run the country!

Twain escaped an involvement with the gentleman politics and attitudes of the Con-federacy serious enough to mar his art. He writes in "Private History of a Campaign That Failed" (1885) of his brief service, then desertion of a southern guerilla band. While discarding the other comedian's politics, Twain takes from Longstreet his favored techniques of animal depiction, using them with genius. In attitude, however, Twain identified with the work of the animal-admiring humorists, such as Alexander McNutt and Thomas Thorpe. His bond with the creatures, like Thorpe's, went deeper than the attraction of a humorist to a rich source of material; his animal sketches show the kinship Twain the pagan felt for the truer life beneath the human level. They show his admiration for the natural logic guiding the uncomplicated lives spared awareness of man's damnable—to Twain—awareness of "the Moral Sense." In his relations with the beasts, he certainly felt something akin to the emotions of Jim Doggett, the master bear hunter of "Big Bear of Arkansas," as Jim trailed the near mythical big bear, whom he finally found after years of unsuccessful hunts. "Wasn't he a beauty!" Jim cries, as he recalls the big bear, lumbering uphill, unconcernedly flinging Jim's dogs aside; "I loved him like a brother!"

How the inherited techniques and Twain's additions blended appears in Twain's coyote portrait, from *Roughing It* (1872). The best of Longstreet appears in the humanizing of the coyote—he's canine and lamentable human drifter at once. He even suffers civil war between his parts: ". . . even while his exposed teeth are pretending a threat, the rest of his face is apologizing for it." Like Longstreet, Twain uses interanimal comparisons. These especially struck him on his travels, as in the Syrian camel from *Roughing It*: ". . . down on his knees, flat on his breast to receive his load, he looks something like a goose swimming; . . . upright he looks like an ostrich with an extra set of legs."

The man-beast collaboration, a cruel betrayal in "Horse-Swap," is very different in "The Celebrated Jumping Frog of Calaveras County" (1865). Old Simon Wheeler is the reverse of Longstreet's narrator, and the relationship of hick and eastern sophisticate is topsy-turvy. Simon relates the tale of Jim Smiley and his animal partners in a story that defines bonds with all the intensity of human love. Andrew Jackson, the bull pup, never fails his owner in their jointly setting up the betting crowd, and when Smiley fails in his part of the scheme, arranging the match with a dog minus hind legs, the comedy takes on a touch of genuine tragedy. We have been drawn in by Wheeler's reverent characterization of the heroic animal, and this element of pathos applied to a frontier bulldog gives it uniqueness. When Andrew dies of a broken heart, we can only resent the betrayal and mourn a brilliant career cut off in its prime, even while we delight in the idea of perceiving the dog in this way. The dog gets the comic wholeness Longstreet's animals deserve, but are denied.

Twain's bird portraits, and encounters of men and birds, reflect another influence, the lore that child Sam Clemens heard from the old black raconteur Uncle Dan'l on memorable nights in his cabin in Hannibal, as described in his *Autobiography* (1924); this is the same material that Joel Chandler Harris was to make immortal in the narrations of Uncle Remus. Twain, like Harris's narrator, extended his self-image, his life and thoughts, into that part of animal life with which he identified most closely. The raucous bird—journalist, debater, lecturer of the air—must be called Twain's totem, the animal with whom he shares a spirit, as the timid but ingenious and finally victorious rabbit was the slave's totem.

Twain's bird characters regularly project a delight in comic word play and insult, a Tom Sawyer quality that is a key part of Uncle Remus's birds as well. In "Jim Baker's Blue Jay Yarn" (1880), for example, birds reflect western "boom times" frontier society just as Harris's humanized creatures re-create the slave's plantation surroundings and reflect the dialogue there. Twain prided himself on his virtuosity at the profanity, bragging, posturing, exaggerating, and lying that constituted dialogue in the "flush times" of Virginia City,

Nevada, when Twain worked there as a cub reporter. The horde of profane, witty blue jays getting off as many leather-headed opinions as any crowd of humans reflects the comic editorial battles and verbal pyrotechnics shown at the drunken symposiums with which Twain, and co-workers such as Dan De Quille and Artemus Ward, entertained journalist friends on the *Territorial Enterprise*.

The version of Twain's bird totem that shows his most complete identification with any creature, however, is the "Bird of Birds—the Indian Crow." Met on his desperate and overlong final lecture tour, by which he attempted to pay back creditors after he had misinvested his wealth in a typesetting machine that failed, Twain acknowledges his worst traits as those of the bird: "The hardest lot that wears feathers," the crow is similar to our blackbird, but it is superficial. Like the artist describing him, he is "just a rowdy, and is always noisy when awake—always chaffing, scolding, scoffing, laughing, ripping, and cursing." Twain's bird *alter ego* reflects the frontier boor within the would-be eastern gentleman who felt he shocked the New England literary elite when he lampooned Holmes and Emerson in an after-dinner speech. Like his creator, the bird sees all and has an opinion on it, which he voices, "particularly if it is none of his business." The bird's view is always savage, "violent and profane—the presence of ladies does not affect him." The bird suggests its connection to the author who let the Gas Company have it for, ". . . your chuckle-headed Goddamned fashion of shutting your Goddamned gas off without giving any notice to your Goddamned parishoners."

The bird, as he and his friends sit on Twain's Bombay balcony and discuss the lecturer unabashedly, gives Twain hope. The bird is an invention, but the inventor is no longer bungling nature but a divinely inspired artist, an Eastern god who has distilled the bird's comic nature through repeated incarnations: "He has been reincarnated more times than Shiva." To Twain, the bird's progress from incarnation to incarnation, villainy to villainy, is not the expected degradation, but perpetual cheerfulness. "His life is one long thundering ecstasy of happiness, and he will go to his death untroubled, knowing that he will soon turn up again as an author or something." The bird seems a part of the Twain who in one of his darkest hours told himself: "Will I ever be happy again? I will, and soon, for I know my temperament."

Thus, the animals are Twain's self-projections, his friends, some of his key sources of comic inspiration, his reminders to himself to bear up under difficulty, and his delight. Utilizing his inherited traditions from southwest humor and slave literature, plus gatherings from his travels, all underpinned by his own compelling identification with the animals, and willingness to see every animal in human context—human in animal—Twain generates a rich and comic cast of animal characters. He creates for the reader a potent bond between our species and those flying, crawling, swimming, and running about us in the world.

St. George Tucker Arnold, Jr.

BIBLIOGRAPHY

Blair, Walter. *Native American Humor*. San Francisco: Chandler, 1960.

Blair, Walter, and Hamlin Hill. *America's Humor: From Poor Richard to Doonesbury*. New York: Oxford UP, 1978.

Clemens, Samuel L. *Following the Equator*. Hartford, Conn.: American Publishing, 1897.

———. *Roughing It*. Ed. Franklin R. Rogers and Paul Baender. Berkeley: U of California P, 1972.

Cohen, Hennig, and William B. Dillingham, eds. *Humor of the Old Southwest*. Boston: Houghton Mifflin, 1964.

See also: "Celebrated Jumping Frog of Calaveras County, The"; "Jim Baker's Blue Jay Yarn"; Southwestern Humor; Thorpe, Thomas Bangs

"Answers to Correspondents" (1865)

Mark Twain's "Answers to Correspondents" began on 6 June 1865 and continued in six weekly columns in the *Californian*. In 1867 a composite of "Answers to Correspondents" was published in *The Jumping Frog of Calaveras County*.

Twain developed the correspondents' column into a literary form by writing burlesques of conventional advice columns. Rather than relying on the numerous submissions from readers, Twain developed fictional characters and attitudes. In a burlesque communication from "Melton Mowbray, *Dutch Flat*" Twain evaluated a Byron poem as good Dutch Flat poetry. The "absurd squib" was taken in good faith by some Pacific coast editors, and Twain found himself plagued with another misunderstood hoax reminiscent of "A Bloody Massacre near Carson" (1863). Twain's correspondents' column is most significant for the introduction of the character Simon Wheeler, who would remain in the author's literary imagination throughout his career. Wheeler sends in a poem ostensibly written by a gambling parson from Arkansas titled "He Done His Level Best." The poem served as a prelude to Emmeline Grangerford's "Ode to Stephen Dowling Bots" in *Adventures of Huckleberry Finn* (1885).

Mark Twain used the correspondents' column as a forum for self-conscious criticism of the literary journal. Although he made some cautious political criticism in the fourth column, most of the material was aimed at contemporary journalistic practices. He burlesqued literary critics, etiquette columns, and San Francisco theatrical criticism.

Jennifer L. Rafferty

BIBLIOGRAPHY

Clemens, Samuel L. *The Works of Mark Twain: Early Tales & Sketches, Volume 2 (1864–1865)*. Ed. Edgar M. Branch and Robert H. Hirst. Berkeley: U of California P, 1981. 177–232.

See also: Burlesque; Criticism; Journalism

Anthony, Susan B.
(1820–1906)

The second of eight children born to Daniel and Lucy (Read) Anthony, Susan B. Anthony was reared in the Quaker belief that allowed women as well as men to speak in meetings. Her reform activity included temperance, anti-slavery, and her area of greatest personal success, women's suffrage. She joined the Daughters of Temperance in 1848. When denied permission to speak at an 1853 Albany Sons of Temperance rally, she realized the magnitude of social imbalance to be addressed. She was frequently attacked, viciously, in the press. After campaigning tirelessly nationwide for Negro suffrage, she was disheartened to see the Fourteenth Amendment exclude women. In 1869 she helped form the National Woman Suffrage Association, holding the office of president until 1900.

The Beecher family are among the friends Anthony and Twain had in common after he moved his family to Nook Farm, a center for reformist activity. Satiric comments about Anthony appeared in the Buffalo *Express* while under Twain's leadership. His later views on suffrage were more supportive, as evidenced by several speeches and platform appearances he made for the cause. Both Anthony and Twain believed that women voters would bring higher moral standards to politics.

Sandra Littleton-Uetz

BIBLIOGRAPHY

Andrews, Kenneth R. *Nook Farm: Mark Twain's Hartford Circle*. Cambridge, Mass.: Harvard UP, 1950.

Barry, Kathleen. *Susan B. Anthony: A Biography of a Singular Feminist*. New York: New York UP, 1988.

See also: Nook Farm; Social Reform; Women's Rights

Aphorisms

A shrewd observer of life and human nature and a provocative commentator on what he called "the damned human race," Mark Twain recorded in humorous and ironical aphorisms his American experience at home and abroad. His observations of perverse yet compassionate human thought and action produced a variety of terse and cleverly worded statements that not only are scattered throughout his writings but also are used as aphorisms in chapter headings in *Pudd'nhead Wilson* (1894) and *Following the Equator* (1897). Twain identifies them respectively as *Pudd'nhead Wilson's Calendar* and as "The Pudd'nhead Maxims" designed to lure young people toward "high moral altitudes." Selections of Twain's typical humor, wisdom, and aphorisms in *Mark Twain at Your Fingertips* (1948) and *The Art, Humor, and Humanity of Mark Twain* (1959) make many of the scattered statements accessible to the reader.

These aphorisms draw on the conventions of western humor that Twain perfected in his writing and lecturing as well as on a tendency in American speech that is derived from Protestant proverbs. They allow Twain to record his pointed observations, his opinions, and "truths" on types of individuals and society not only with a burlesque humor but also with a satiric depth and stylistic distinction that readers do not expect. Usually, they are expressed in one sentence, sometimes two, so that his philosophizing on people's foibles or on his own disappointments, disillusionments, and despair of humanity is enlightened by his familiar formula for telling a story: an elaboration of situation, a pause, and snapper at the end. The semicolon in a compound sentence and the period between two sentences provide the pause between the pointed observation or "truth" and the snapper with an unexpected, even contradictory, turn or twist.

As the aphorisms with their varied tone and subject matter occur in all of Twain's writings, they reflect his dual personality and world view. His humorous and ironical quips reveal a transition from his earlier more optimistic view of life as in *A Connecticut Yankee in King Arthur's Court* (1889) to his later expressions of despair in *What Is Man?* (1906). Often resembling the sardonic humor of Ambrose Bierce's definitions in *The Devil's Dictionary* (1906), Twain's aphorisms show more distance between the writer and the object of his satire, hence becoming less urgent in their attack. Close attention to Twain's and Bierce's expression of their skepticism about the prevailing ethos of American life and its direction helps to preserve a sense of the American past that consisted of both optimistic and pessimistic views of its future.

Charlotte S. McClure

BIBLIOGRAPHY

Caron, James E. "Pudd'nhead Wilson's Calendar: Tall Tales and a Tragic Figure." *Nineteenth-Century Fiction* 36.4 (March 1982): 452–470.

Clemens, Samuel L. *The Art, Humor, and Humanity of Mark Twain*. Ed. Minnie M. Brashear and Robert M. Rodney. Norman: U of Oklahoma P, 1959.

———. *Following the Equator*. Hartford, Conn.: American Publishing, 1897.

———. *Mark Twain at Your Fingertips*. Ed. Caroline Thomas Harnsberger. New York: Beechhurst P, 1948.

———. *Pudd'nhead Wilson and Those Extraordinary Twins*. Facsimile First Edition 1894. San Francisco: Chandler, 1968.

See also: Bierce, Ambrose

Arnold, Matthew
(1822–1888)

Son of Thomas Arnold, famous headmaster of Rugby, Matthew Arnold, after a rather undistinguished career at Oxford, first became known as a poet, publishing some six volumes of verse from 1849 to 1867 and catching in memorable phrases some of the social and religious turmoil of an era in which he saw himself "wandering between two worlds, one dead, the other powerless to be born." Beginning in the early 1860s he turned more and more to literary, social, and religious criticism, most notably in *Essays in Criticism* (1865; *Second Series*, 1888), *Culture and Anarchy* (1869), *Literature and Dogma* (1873), and *Discourses in America* (1885), which included "Literature and

Science," "Numbers, or The Majority and the Remnant," and "Emerson." His scores of lectures and essays, published in some twenty-two volumes during his lifetime, sought to raise the intellectual and cultural levels of a society that he once characterized as "an upper class materialized, a middle class vulgarized, and a lower class brutalized." In literary criticism, an essential guide to "culture," his lofty goal was to propagate "the best that is known and thought in the world" and to create "a current of true and fresh ideas."

Writing for Arnold was primarily a spare-time occupation, for he led an extremely busy professional life. In 1851, the year of his marriage to Frances Lucy Wightman, he became an inspector of schools and held that demanding position for the next thirty-five years. His extremely productive life ended suddenly on 15 April 1888 as the result of a heart attack, only two weeks after his essay "Civilization in the United States" appeared in the April issue of *Nineteenth Century*.

That essay was to bring vigorous reactions from Mark Twain—after the editor of *Forum*, Lorettus Metcalf, requested a rebuttal of Arnold's criticisms. Clemens earlier may have resented Arnold's comments in "A Word About America" (1882), especially since the critic had specifically mentioned Mark Twain as an exemplar of the rowdy American humor that he found most distasteful. But there is no real evidence to support that conclusion. And when Arnold presented his "Numbers" lecture in Hartford on 15 November 1883 during his American lecture tour (1883–1884), Clemens and he reportedly enjoyed each other's company both at a reception the night before the lecture and the next afternoon when the Clemenses themselves entertained Arnold and his wife and daughter at a tea. Remarking upon the occasion that evening, Joseph Twichell noted in his journal that the Arnolds had made a very favorable impression and that the critic himself seemed more sympathetic and gentler than his works might lead people to think.

Some rumblings of animosity toward Arnold's opinions did surface in the spring of 1887, following the appearance of his review of General Grant's Memoirs (1885–1886) in the *Nineteenth Century* for January and February. Though the review was largely complimentary, Clemens was ruffled by Arnold's criticisms of Grant's grammar and literary style—"an English without charm and without high breeding"—and no doubt also by comments on American boasting, now that the criticism seemed implicitly aimed at Grant. That April Clemens treated the Army and Navy Club of Connecticut to a speech on "General Grant's Grammar," in which he drew upon H.H. Breen's *Modern English Literature: Its Blemishes and Defects* (1857) for "proof" that the general's grammatical faults were no more frequent nor serious than those of many acknowledged literary masters, added an example of awkward construction from Arnold's own review, and concluded with a paean to the soldier-author, who "all untaught by the silken phrase-makers, linked words together with an art surpassing the art of the schoolmen."

Though some have argued otherwise, Arnold's criticisms had only minor influence on the shift to more serious satire that occurred in *A Connecticut Yankee* (1889) in the summer of 1887. But Clemens's reactions to "Civilization in the United States" did provide additional fuel the following year.

In that article Arnold had cited numerous flaws in American "culture," many of which he had mentioned in earlier essays—the unfortunate propensity for boasting, an avidity for "news," the vulgarity and brashness of American journalism, a cultural scene seriously lacking in "interest," an unfortunate "addiction to the 'funny man,'" a need for self-criticism and an excessive sensitivity toward criticism from others, and a particular insensitivity reflected in the ugliness of many place-names.

During the following few months, in reply to Arnold's charges, Twain drafted a half-dozen essays, mostly unfinished, but totaling some 100 manuscript pages. At one point that June he even considered turning the material into a book to be called "English Criticism on America. Letters to an English Friend." For some reason, however, possibly because he ultimately decided that a public attack on the so recently dead Arnold would be inappropriate, he never fulfilled Metcalf's request for the *Forum* article.

In these essays and also in his acceptance of an honorary master's degree from Yale that June, Mark Twain took vigorous exception to Arnold's definition of "civilization" and, above all, his insistence on "a spirit of reverence" as the quintessential element of any truly civilized society. As might be expected, he objected especially strongly to Arnold's charge that America's deplorable lack of that reverence was fostered not only by an irresponsible press but by its "addiction to the 'funny man.'" The Yale degree, he said, was a tribute to all humorists and a timely response to "the late Matthew Arnold's sharp rebuke to the guild of American 'funny men' in his latest literary delicacy." It would remind the world that the humorist's real purpose—"the deriding of shams, the exposure of pretentious falsities, the laughing of stupid superstitions out of existence"—made him "the natural enemy of royalties, nobilities, privileges, and all kindred swindles, and the natural friend of human rights and human liberties." And when he resumed work on *A Connecticut Yankee* shortly thereafter, he began with a direct slap at the foolish "reverence" that characterized British subservience to rank and caste.

Twain would repeat his objections to Arnold's pronouncements several times in works of the next few years. In April 1890 the speech "On Foreign Critics" indirectly refuted Arnold's charges by enumerating the many contributions to freedom provided by the "irreverent" American press. In addition, specifically citing the critic's description of American society as organized chiefly for the benefit of the masses, he argued that such a society was greatly superior to a "civilization" largely restricted to a small "cultivated" upper class.

Again in chapter 10 of *The American Claimant* (1892), Twain drew on the earlier essays for an episode in which Lord Berkeley [Howard Tracy], at a meeting of the Mechanics Club, listens to a speech by an editor of the *Daily Democrat*, who argued that in stressing the importance of "reverence" and charging the American newspaper with killing the "discipline of respect," Arnold had overlooked the fact that the chief virtue of American journalism was "its frank and cheerful irreverence."

In another direction Arnold's essay review of Edward Dowden's *The Life of Percy Bysshe Shelley* (1886) in the *Nineteenth Century* for January 1888 (collected in *Essays in Criticism, Second Series* the same year) inspired two additional critiques. In both of them, Twain took exception to the favorable assessment of the poet's character and deplored Shelley's treatment of his wife, Harriet. In the first, still unpublished, Mark Twain refuted with bitter irony Arnold's final portrait of Shelley as generous, refined, gracious, and considerate. For the second, published as "In Defense of Harriet Shelley" in the *North American Review* (July, August, September 1894), his target was Dowden's biography itself.

Arnold's works thus provided important stimuli for a number of Mark Twain's works. Apparently liking the critic as a person, Twain obviously detested his insistence on "high seriousness" in literature and "reverence" in society. Yet, though their methods were at almost opposite poles, Twain, through his humorous deriding of "shams," sought, like Arnold, to improve the human condition.

Howard G. Baetzhold

BIBLIOGRAPHY

Arnold, Matthew. *The Complete Prose Works of Matthew Arnold.* Ed. R.H. Super. 11 vols. Ann Arbor: U of Michigan P, 1960–1977.

———. *The Poems of Matthew Arnold.* Ed. K. Allot. London: Longmans, 1965.

———. *The Poetical Works of Matthew Arnold.* Ed. C.B. Tinker and H.F. Lowry. London: Oxford UP, 1950.

Baetzhold, Howard G. *Mark Twain and John Bull: The British Connection.* Bloomington: Indiana UP, 1970.

Clemens, Samuel L. *The American Claimant.* New York: Charles L. Webster, 1892.

———. "In Defense of Harriet Shelley." *How to Tell A Story.* By Clemens. New York: Harper, 1897. 15–90.

———. "On Foreign Critics." *Mark Twain Speaking.* By Clemens. Ed. Paul Fatout. Iowa City: U of Iowa P, 1976. 257–260.

Gribben, Alan. *Mark Twain's Library: A Reconstruction.* 2 vols. Boston: G.K. Hall, 1980.

Honan, Park. *Matthew Arnold: A Life.* New York: McGraw-Hill, 1981.

Howells, William Dean. *My Mark Twain: Reminiscences and Criticisms.* New York: Harper, 1910.

McKeithan, D.M. "The Occasion of Mark Twain's Speech 'On Foreign Critics.'" *Philological Quarterly* 27 (July 1948): 276–279.

Paine, Albert Bigelow. *Mark Twain: A Biography.* 3 vols. New York: Harper, 1912.

See also: *American Claimant, The; Connecticut Yankee in King Arthur's Court, A; Criticism; England; "General Grant's Grammar"; "In Defense of Harriet Shelley"*

"Around the World" Letters
(1869–1870)

From 16 October 1869 to 5 March 1870, while Mark Twain was co-owner and co-editor of the Buffalo *Express*, a series comprised of ten "Around the World" travel letters appeared in the *Express*. These items have not been reprinted; however, thanks to the efforts of Martin B. Fried, who had photocopies made from the microfilm of Twain's writings in the Buffalo *Express*, this material is available through the Rare Book Room of the Buffalo and Erie County Public Library or The Mark Twain Papers (University of California, Berkeley).

Twain's intention in publishing these letters was quite novel; he planned to remain at home in Buffalo while gathering material and inspiration by proxy from the correspondence of Professor Darius R. Ford of Elmira College, the actual around-the-world traveler who was accompanied by Charles Langdon (Olivia's brother). Writing in the first person, Twain was to elaborate and embellish these travel accounts with his characteristic humor, thereby giving the letters his own unique literary flavor in the manner of *The Innocents Abroad* (1869). The reality of the situation, however, varied significantly from the initial plan. While awaiting Ford's correspondence, Twain most likely was the exclusive writer of letters numbered 1, 3, 4, 5, 6, and 7, dealing with California and Nevada; these are based on Twain's own earlier travels and experiences in the American West. Examples of Twain's use of southwestern humor are evidenced. These pieces were revised later and used in his 1872 publication, *Roughing It* (consult "Introduction," "Textual Notes," and "Collation" in the 1972 University of California edition of *RI* for additional information). Letter 2, a wholly fictitious sketch about Twain's adventures in Haiti, humorously contrasts the American and Haitian coinage system; Letter 8, "Dining with a Cannibal," is an outlandish account of a cannibal who believes he has eaten a Frenchman, only later to discover that he actually had eaten his own brother. The intended collaborative effort between Ford and Twain failed miserably. The latter complained to the Langdons on 26 March 1870 that in six months Ford had written only two letters—probably number 9, "The Pacific," and number 10, "Japan"—which were signed D.R.F. in the *Express*. Although many of the pieces as they appeared in the *Express* are ephemeral, less than memorable, and largely fragmentary and disjointed in nature, it is interesting to examine initially worked materials for *RI* and Twain's journalistic style during this period.

J.C.B. *Kinch*

BIBLIOGRAPHY

Clemens, Samuel L. "Around the World" Letters. *Letter No. 1*: "The Dead Sea" (16 October 1869); *Letter No. 2*: "Adventures in Hayti" (30 October 1869); *Letter No. 3*: "California—Continued" (13 November 1869); *Letter No. 4*: "California—Continued" (11 December 1869); *Letter No. 5*: "California—Continued" (18 December 1869); *Letter No. 6*: "'Early Days' in Nevada" (8 January 1870); *Letter No. 7*: "Pacific Coast—Concluded" (22 January 1870); *Letter No. 8*: "Dining with a Cannibal" (29 January 1870); *Letter No. 9*: "The Pacific" (12 February 1870); and *Letter No. 10*: "Japan" (5 March 1870—signed D.R.F.). Buffalo *Express*; not reprinted.

———. *The Forgotten Writings of Mark Twain.* Ed. Henry Duskis. New York: Philosophical Library, 1963.

———. *Roughing It.* Ed. Franklin R. Rogers and Paul Baender. Berkeley: U of California P, 1972.

———. *The Works of Mark Twain: Early Tales & Sketches, Volume 1 (1851–1864).* Ed. Edgar M. Branch and Robert H. Hirst. Berkeley: U of California P, 1979.

Emerson, Everett. *The Authentic Mark Twain: A Literary Biography of Samuel L. Clemens.* Philadelphia: U of Pennsylvania P, 1984.

Fried, Martin B. "Mark Twain in Buffalo." *Niagara Frontier* (Winter 1959): 89–110.

McCullough, Joseph B. "A Listing of Mark Twain's Contributions to the Buffalo *Express*, 1869–1871." *American Literary Realism, 1870–1910* 5 (Winter 1972): 61–70.

Steinbrink, Jeffrey. "How Mark Twain Survived Sam Clemens' Reformation." *American Literature* 55 (October 1983): 299–315.

Wilson, James D. *A Reader's Guide to the Short Stories of Mark Twain.* Boston: G.K. Hall, 1987.

See also: Journalism; Travel Writings

Art

More attention has been paid to the art of Mark Twain than to Mark Twain's attitude toward art. Yet, it is impossible to appreciate the former fully without understanding the latter. Though Twain never articulated a theory of aesthetics, and though he enjoyed disparaging cultivated art critics as well as uncultivated amateurs who aped their views, he was deeply interested in painting and other arts. Deprived of formal art instruction, he made sincere efforts in his adult years to educate himself in the subject. Though he was always somewhat insecure about his ability to critique works of art, especially those deemed classics, he nonetheless was often moved to express his views on art and artists.

Attempts by Edward Wagenknecht, Gladys Bellamy, and Sydney Krause to provide a full and accurate assessment of Twain's attitude toward art, or his aesthetic sense, have had to overcome two obstacles: Twain's comments on art are scattered throughout his voluminous writings; and when making those comments, he was usually wearing the mask of the naive fool or of the crusty grumbler, employing such rhetorical devices as understatement and exaggeration. Moreover, Twain was not always consistent in what he admired or detested in a work of art. In general, however, his taste in the fine arts was governed by the same basic principles that governed his taste in literature: put simply, he admired art that could appeal to common people, that was a sincere expression of the artist's vision and emotions, that was logical in its context, and that conveyed a sense of human values; he scorned the esoteric, sensational, idealized, and slavishly imitative.

The starting point for any discussion of Twain's taste in art is *The Innocents Abroad* (1869). During his 1867–1868 grand tour of the Old World, Twain visited and recorded his impressions of the most treasured works of art and architecture of Western culture; *The Innocents Abroad* is thus the richest source of his opinions on art. Many of those opinions, especially in reference to the "Old Masters," have become notorious. As Brander Matthews once wrote (in regard to Twain's well-known disdain for romantic writers like Sir Walter Scott), Twain's most obvious limitation as a literary critic was implacable application of the literary standards of his age to the literature of an earlier one. That limitation is equally obvious in his harsh assessments of the Old Masters. Unable or unwilling to judge their paintings by medieval or Renaissance criteria, he applied nineteenth-century standards. He faulted painters such as Botticelli and Raphael, for example, for their preoccupation with religious themes and figures, for their failure to depict their contemporary times, and for their idealized representations of humans. On the rare occasions when he was charmed by a painting's color and expression, his pleasure gave way to his contempt of the Old Masters'

"cringing spirit" and their "nauseous adulation" of their aristocratic patrons. As such comments suggest, Twain's aesthetic judgments were inextricably connected to his social and political values.

The Innocents Abroad is not without praise for classical art. Twain was enchanted, for example, by the cathedrals of Notre Dame and Milan, comparing the latter to a poem written in marble; he found Versailles a veritable Garden of Eden; and the ruins of Athens overwhelmed him with a sense of history. The majority of his critiques in *The Innocents Abroad*, however, are negative.

During the six months prior to writing the letters that would become *The Innocents Abroad*, Twain had composed a smaller group of letters describing his journey from San Francisco to New York, and several of them provide insights into his developing sense of aesthetics. (Originally published in the *Alta California* during 1866–1867, the letters were reprinted as *Mark Twain's Travels with Mr. Brown* in 1940.) Reporting, from behind his fool's mask, on his visit to New York's Academy of Design, he claims that ignorance is preferable to knowledge when it comes to art, since cultured art critics seem to be able to detect only blemishes in the works they critique. He drops the mask, however, when he insists that a picture should be able to convey its message to the uncultivated observer, and when he condemns the architects of the Academy building for trying to reproduce the romance and charm of antiquity instead of the vibrant rush and clamor of the modern metropolis. Alexander Turner Stewart committed a similar breach of taste in Twain's view by attempting to reproduce an Old World marble palace amidst the elegant brownstones lining Fifth Avenue; the result, Twain snipes, was a pretentious monstrosity that resembled a mausoleum. In a letter on Albert Bierstadt's painting of Yosemite Valley, Twain demands that a painted (and, by implication, a verbal) portrait must be as accurate as possible; Bierstadt's representation of Yosemite, he complains, is too "gorgeous." The moral, some might say prudish, element in Twain's aesthetic standards is clearly projected in his reviews of the *Black Crook*, a melodrama whose bevy of scantily clad young women made it America's first great "girlie" show. Twain indicts the show for being an outrage to modesty and a threat to public morals.

If the *Black Crook* and similar productions were, in Twain's view, the most degraded form of human performance, Negro spirituals were among the most noble. Though he developed an appreciation for Beethoven, Brahms, Chopin, and Schubert, and for *Tannhäuser* and several other operas, he was as little taken by classical music as by classical painting or sculpture. The music created by African-Americans, however, stirred him to his depths. Expressing the heartfelt emotions of those who created them and capable of moving the untutored listener, the spirituals epitomized elegant beauty to Twain.

In later life Twain became somewhat more tolerant of the Old Masters, but not of art critics. His "Instructions in Art" (1903), a madcap account (with illustrations) of his own ventures in sketching, parodies jargon-laden, ostentatious art criticism.

The one creator that never seems to have disappointed or repelled Twain was nature. His novels and nonfiction writings regularly reveal his deep sensitivity toward natural beauty. His last home, Stormfield, was designed to merge into the tranquil settings of pines and cedars; its rooms had no pictures on the walls, Twain explained, because no artist could ever equal the beauty of the surrounding landscape. Twain enjoyed the work of many artists, but nature, as he wrote in *The Innocents Abroad*, was to him the "monarch of all the old masters."

Lawrence J. Oliver

BIBLIOGRAPHY

Bellamy, Gladys Carmen. *Mark Twain as a Literary Artist*. Norman: U of Oklahoma P, 1950.

Clemens, Samuel L. *The Innocents Abroad/Roughing It*. Ed. Guy Cardwell. New York: Library of America, 1984.

———. "Instructions in Art." *Metropolitan Magazine* 18.1, 2 (April–May 1903). Rpt. *Mark Twain at His Best: A Comprehensive Sampler*. By Clemens. Ed Charles Neider. Garden City, N.Y.: Doubleday, 1986. 122–131.

———. *Mark Twain's Travels with Mr. Brown*. Ed. Franklin Walker and G. Ezra Dane. New York: Knopf, 1940.

———. *A Tramp Abroad*. Ed. Charles Neider. New York: Harper & Row, 1977.

Krause, Sydney J. *Mark Twain as Critic*. Baltimore: Johns Hopkins UP, 1967.

Matthews, Brander. "Mark Twain and the Art of Writing." *Essays in English*. By Matthews. New York: Scribner, 1921. 241–268.

Wagenknecht, Edward. *Mark Twain: The Man and His Work*. Rev. ed. Norman: U of Oklahoma P, 1967.

See also: Criticism; *Innocents Abroad, The*; Music

Arthur, King

Historians disagree as to whether King Arthur was in fact a Celt leader who fought against the Saxons in the fifth or sixth century, but he does emerge in British and Continental romances and chronicles of later centuries as a pseudo-historical figure whose round table at Camelot became the starting place for exploits of other knights, such as Galahad, Gawain, and Lancelot. Thomas Malory's *Le Morte D'Arthur* (printed by Thomas Caxton in 1485) represents a conflation of stories from various sources and became the quasi-authoritative text that established the important conventions of the Arthurian legend. Malory's book was one of Mark Twain's favorites, and it provided most of the information about King Arthur for *A Connecticut Yankee in King Arthur's Court* (1889), although Twain adapted it to his own thematic purposes. Early in *CY*, Hank Morgan is as contemptuous of King Arthur as he is of aristocracy in general—an ignorant, even cruel, privileged class whose status has nothing to do with real worth. As Hank and King Arthur travel together disguised, however, the Yankee sees a more human dimension to the king for the first time. When the king, heedless of his own well-being, stays to give comfort to those in the smallpox hut, Hank says, "He was great now, sublimely great." And when the slave driver cannot break the king's spirit with repeated beatings, it proves to Hank that Arthur was "a good deal more than a king; he was a man." The king even vows to end slavery, but Twain does not follow up on that promise after Arthur and Hank are rescued. The book ends rather quickly after the rescue, in fact, and in a long passage taken from Malory, King Arthur dies in mortal combat with Modred.

Cameron C. Nickels

BIBLIOGRAPHY

Clemens, Samuel L. *A Connecticut Yankee in King Arthur's Court.* Ed. Bernard Stein. Berkeley: U of California P, 1979.

See also: *Connecticut Yankee in King Arthur's Court, A*; Malory, Sir Thomas

"As Concerns Interpreting the Deity"

(written 1905)

In this short work Twain uses his arsenal of familiar weapons to attack the notion of interpretation. Twain marshals his awkward drawing ability, his use of "scholarly" sources, his complex tonal variation, and his contrasts of diction to destroy pretentious, authoritative "interpretations" of God's involvement in the world. The reader will enjoy comparing this short, emphatic essay with, for example, the problematical interpretations of the Greeley letter in *Roughing It* (1872) and the Colosseum newsletter and the hotel advertisement in *Innocents Abroad* (1869).

Using examples to develop the point, the text contains a childish, eight-part parodic hieroglyphic, with its own scratched-over cancellation. Four proposed "interpretations" or translations qualify one another. They each agree upon the final element, "upon pain of death," but disagree completely about the beginning and middle of the "interpretation."

This juxtaposition serves as a mutual qualification, a reciprocal contradiction. Humans will attribute meanings, true or untrue. Whatever is unknowable or unprovable about the Deity will be confidently deciphered and interpreted.

Twain juxtaposes these dreadful drawings with quotations in "interpretations," authoritative explications. The essay pivots upon the contrast between the difficulty of interpreting ancient human communications (part 1) and the apparent ease and certainty of interpreting divine communications (part 2). Accordingly, Twain adopts a great variety of tones: the mock reverential, the sarcastic, the cynical, and a pompously authoritarian voice.

Much of the essay revolves around contrasts. Twain will use a long, additive, convoluted sentence to contrast with an emphatic four-word sentence. Similarly, Twain seems to enjoy using elevated polysyllabic diction that is undercut by common vocabulary of fashion ("Entrails have gone out, now") or of business ("It was dreamed by Caesar Augustus's mother, and interpreted at the usual rates"). The resulting incongruities create humor about human fallibility—inability to understand the obvious combined with certainty about the unknowable.

Twain uses a two-part structure, offering remarks about the hieroglyphics and about augury for interpretation of entrails (divination) to lead into an extended criticism of Christian religious interpreters who can, with assurance, with an unintended mockery of ordinary cause and effect reasoning, confidently interpret punishments from God.

The two-part structure, with examples from different eras, creates a synechdoche for human history: things have not improved; human folly is a constant. A sensitive reader may shudder at the merciless quality of religious vengeance, or chuckle at some animal imagery, but the essay's main value remains in its tonal variety and in the sarcastic argument about the folly of human attempts at interpretations of a Deity. Twain's tonal variations retain a satiric sting, as a duncelike speaker says about one interpreter, "Sometimes I am half persuaded he was only a guesser, and not a good one."

It must be mentioned that the California text is the only reliable text. Paine omitted Twain's powerful final example, and this omission and others render all earlier texts valueless.

Victor Doyno

BIBLIOGRAPHY

Clemens, Samuel L. *"What Is Man?" and Other Philosophical Writings.* Ed. Paul Baender. Berkeley: U of California P, 1973.

See also: Human Nature; Humor; Religion

"As Regards Patriotism"
(1923)

Written about 1900 but published posthumously in 1923, "As Regards Patriotism" distinguishes between two kinds of patriotism. One is the product of individual reason and conscience. The other is the patriotism of the majority, which is acquired "at the public trough." Though the Anglo-American tradition of liberty of conscience makes the former possible, politicians and the press lead most people in the opposite direction. Both types of patriotism result from "training." People in a democratic society are, in fact, trained to fear "independence in political thought." They can also be trained, however, to "manufacture their own patriotism," to forge in their minds and hearts, and to test with their conscience, a private and independent patriotism, as opposed to that which is held "by command."

Jarrell A. O'Kelley

BIBLIOGRAPHY

Clemens, Samuel L. *The Complete Essays of Mark Twain.* Ed. Charles Neider. Garden City, N.Y.: Doubleday, 1963.

See also: Determinism; Politics

Ashcroft, Ralph
(d. 1947)

As the treasurer of the American branch of the Plasmon Company, Ralph Ashcroft, a dapper Liverpudlian, first crossed Clemens's path in 1903. Sympathetic to the Clemens faction in elaborate legal maneuvers, Ashcroft became increasingly involved with Clemens's other legal affairs. He accompanied Clemens to England as a sort of personal secretary in 1907 for the Oxford degree ceremonies; in 1908 he became an officer of the Mark Twain Company, the idea for which he claimed first occurred to him several years earlier.

On 14 November 1908 Clemens signed a comprehensive transfer of all his business matters to Ashcroft and Isabel Lyon. The two business managers married in early 1909, in what Lyon was later to call "part of a deal whereby she would thus legitimize her standing in the household." After Clemens became convinced that the Ashcrofts were guilty of various crimes, he revoked all of their responsibilities, wrote the "Ashcroft-Lyon Manuscript" to protect Clara Clemens from their revenge, and convinced himself that he had been the victim of their duplicity. The couple moved to Montreal in 1913 and separated in the 1920s. Ashcroft remarried in 1927 and died in Canada in 1947.

Hamlin Hill

BIBLIOGRAPHY

Hill, Hamlin. *Mark Twain: God's Fool.* New York: Harper & Row, 1973.

See also: "Ashcroft-Lyon Manuscript"; Lyon, Isabel; Plasmon

"Ashcroft-Lyon Manuscript"
(written 1909)

This is the title of a manuscript that Mark Twain composed between 2 May 1909 and 21 October 1909. Written in the form of a letter to William Dean Howells, it was intended both as a segment in the final method of writing autobiography and also as a document to insure that Ralph Ashcroft and Isabel Lyon would not continue to badger Clara Clemens after her father's death. As Clara said, "He wrote out a full description of their entire story of dishonesty which I was to publish if there was no other way to keep them quiet."

The manuscript begins with a chronological account of Clemens's grievances against the Ashcrofts but loses its coherent order when its author, in recurring bursts of vindictiveness, remembers additional allegations against his deposed business manager and social secretary. Altogether, Mark Twain wrote 429 pages of manuscript, which he supplemented with newspaper clippings, bookkeeping accounts, a statement by Jean, and similar exhibits of the case he was making.

The charges—including that Miss Lyon drank too much Scotch, made pincushions, and was attempting to marry Clemens—degenerate into a discussion of the claims by both Perry and Cook of discovering the North Pole. It is useful for indicating how significantly Mark Twain had lost control over his materials, had been unable to maintain his comic distance from his subject, and had degenerated into petty vindictiveness in the last months of his life.

Hamlin Hill

BIBLIOGRAPHY

Hill, Hamlin. *Mark Twain: God's Fool.* New York: Harper & Row, 1973.

See also: Ashcroft, Ralph; Autobiography; Lyon, Isabel

Athens, Greece

During the 1867 *Quaker City* excursion, the ship's visit to Athens proved to be anticlimactic and disappointing for the majority of the passengers. However, a daring escapade enacted by Twain and three other tourists provided Twain with a wonderful experience, which in turn became one of the more charming episodes in *The Innocents Abroad* (1869).

The *Quaker City* left Italy at a time when a cholera epidemic was raging throughout the country; and when the *Quaker City* approached Athens, the health officer denied the passengers clearance to visit the city. Instead, the passengers were confined to a miserable quarantine aboard the *Quaker City*, which had dropped anchor outside of the harbor. However, Twain, along with three other passengers, stole out in a boat at nightfall and landed in Athens. The four men climbed the hill of the Acropolis and coaxed four guards at the gates of the ancient fortress to allow them entrance. Once inside the Greek ruins, Twain and the others gained a breathtaking view of Athens and the surrounding countryside by moonlight. On the way back to the boat, the four men became encouraged by their success and slipped into boisterous behavior, but fortunately they made it back to the *Quaker City* unmolested.

Trevor J. Morgan

BIBLIOGRAPHY

Budd, Louis J. *Mark Twain: Social Philosopher.* Bloomington: Indiana UP, 1962.

Clemens, Samuel L. *Traveling with the Innocents Abroad.* Ed. Daniel M. McKeithan. Norman: U of Oklahoma P, 1958.

Ganzel, Dewey. *Mark Twain Abroad: The Cruise of the "Quaker City."* Chicago: U of Chicago P, 1968.

Long, E. Hudson. *Mark Twain Handbook.* New York: Hendricks House, 1957.

See also: Innocents Abroad, The

Atlantic Monthly

Devoted to literature, art, and politics, the magazine the *Atlantic Monthly* was founded in 1857 in Boston by a group of prominent New Englanders. The first issue included (anonymous) contributions by Ralph Waldo Emerson, Oliver Wendell Holmes (who named the magazine), Henry Wadsworth Longfellow, James Russell Lowell (the first editor), Harriet Beecher Stowe, and John Greenleaf Whittier. Purchased in 1859 by Ticknor and Fields, publisher of most of these writers, the *Atlantic* became not only the organ of the New England establishment but also the national standard of literary excellence.

James T. Fields, who became editor in 1861, hired William Dean Howells as his assistant in 1866. Upon succeeding Fields as editor, Howells expanded the range of the *Atlantic* by adding new departments and soliciting work from writers outside New England. Among them was Mark Twain, who met Howells in 1869 at the magazine's offices (124 Tremont Street) after the latter had published his favorable notice of *The Innocents Abroad* (1869). Howells continued to review Mark Twain's books and to print his work in the *Atlantic* until his resignation in 1881.

Twain's first appearances in the *Atlantic* were "A True Story" (November 1874) and "Old Times on the Mississippi" (January to July 1875); ten other pieces followed, the last of which was "Mrs. McWilliams and the Lightning" (September 1880). On Howells's invitation, Twain attended the *Atlantic's* birthday dinner for Whittier on 17 December 1877. His speech, a burlesque of Emerson, Holmes, and Longfellow, was perceived by Howells as lese majesty. Mark Twain, who was also mortified, had no deep affinities to the *Atlantic* circle, but he continued to regard Howells as his close friend and literary adviser.

John W. Crowley

BIBLIOGRAPHY

Howells, William Dean. *My Mark Twain: Reminiscences and Criticisms*. New York: Harper, 1910.

Lynn, Kenneth S. *William Dean Howells: An American Life*. New York: Harcourt Brace Jovanovich, 1971.

Paine, Albert Bigelow. *Mark Twain: A Biography*. 3 vols. New York: Harper, 1912.

See also: Howells, William Dean; Whittier Birthday Dinner Speech

Auctions

The dispersal of Twain's belongings began before his death in 1910. As the Clemens family moved from one home to another in their endless travels, they left behind or gave away to neighbors and servants pieces of furniture, books, and manuscripts. The founding of the Mark Twain Library at Redding, Connecticut, in 1908 resulted in a donation of 1,751 books directly from Twain, and records indicate that Clara Clemens may have donated as many as 2,500 books after her father's death.

Concerned with copyright protection of his writings, Twain formed the Mark Twain Company, which resulted in the preservation of many of his manuscripts and personal papers, now housed at the University of California at Berkeley. The bulk of the estate passed to his daughter Clara.

In February 1911, at Clara's wishes, the first formal sale of Twain's estate took place, and some 500 lots of books and manuscripts were sold, together with 56 lots at the end of the sale that included bric-a-brac in the form of pottery vases, brass and irons, bronze statues, a wooden cigar holder, and various framed etchings and paintings. Prices were modest, and an anticipated second sale was never held.

Meanwhile, Twain's Hartford home had been sold in 1903 to a family that completely redecorated the interior, removing most of the original Tiffany fixtures. The furniture was removed and sold at auction. By 1929 the home had served as a school, an apartment, and a storage warehouse. In that year it was purchased for preservation as a museum, and the work of locating lost fixtures, furniture, and even windows has continued ever since. Considering the neglect and the passing of time, an astonishing number of relics have been recovered. The great Scottish mantel from the library was found in a nearby Redding barn, and descendants of the 1903 auction buyers have generously returned important pieces of furniture over the years.

In 1937 the Twain letters and manuscripts from the estate of his official biographer, Albert Bigelow Paine, were sold, and in 1951 Clara held a poorly managed sale of her belongings at her home in Los Angeles, where more than 350 lots of books and furniture were sold amidst a circuslike atmosphere, mostly at bargain prices. One of Mark Twain's desks sold at that sale surfaced in the 1970s and has finally found its way into a private Twain collection. From time to time, monogram silverware from the Twain estate appears in the market, as do other relics of dubious origins. Clara sold or gave away relics from time to time, and since her death in 1962, other relics, including articles of her clothing, have entered the market, all finding eager buyers.

Books from Twain's library have surfaced steadily over the years, mostly from the 1911 and 1951 sales, but many originate with the Mark Twain Library in Redding, which disposed of many volumes in the 1940s and early 1950s before their importance was recognized. Today, more than 800 volumes from Twain's library are located in public and private collections.

Kevin Mac Donnell

BIBLIOGRAPHY

American Art Association. *First Editions, Autograph Letters, Manuscripts . . . Manuscripts and Letters by Samuel L. Clemens, The Collection of Albert Bigelow Paine.* New York: Anderson Galleries, 1937.

Anderson Auction Company. *Catalogue of the Library and Manuscripts of Samuel L. Clemens.* New York: Anderson Auction, 1911.

Christie, Manson, and Woods International, Inc. *The Estelle Doheny Collection.* 7 vols. New York: Christie, Manson, and Woods, 1987–1988.

Faude, Wilson H. *The Renaissance of Mark Twain's House.* Larchmont, N.Y.: Queens House, 1978.

Gabrilowitsch, Clara Clemens. *Mark Twain Library Auction.* Los Angeles: E.F. Whitman and F.B. O'Connor, 1951.

Gribben, Alan. *Mark Twain's Library: A Reconstruction.* 2 vols. Boston: G.K. Hall, 1980.

Leab, Katharine, and Daniel Leab, eds. *American Book Prices Current.* 95 vols. New York: Bancroft-Parkman, 1895–1990. Various places, various publishers.

See also: Manuscript Collections; Rare Books

"Aurelia's Unfortunate Young Man"

(1864)

"Aurelia's Unfortunate Young Man" was first published as "Whereas" in the 22 October 1864 issue of the *Californian*, edited at the time by Bret Harte. Subsequent editions of this story were much abridged and used the longer, more descriptive title. The original version begins with the narrator's description of "Love's Bakery," a place according to the narrator in which hearts, not bread, are kneaded. This introduces Aurelia's story where love is threatened by her fiancé's physical afflictions. Beginning with scars from small pox, Williamson Breckinridge Caruthers subsequently loses a leg, an arm (to a Fourth of July cannon), then the other (to a carding machine), the use of an eye, his other leg, and finally his scalp. Having postponed and rescheduled their wedding after each of these unfortunate losses, Aurelia is writing to the story's narrator for advice. Even though she still loves Caruthers, for obvious reasons her parents are now against their marrying. The narrator's advice is for Aurelia to equip Caruthers with wooden appendages, a glass eye, and a wig and to give him a ninety-day test period to see if he breaks his neck. If he does not, she should marry him. Neither the narrator nor Aurelia ever shows real sympathy for Caruthers, and both see Caruthers's misfortunes only in terms of the difficulties they present for her.

Obviously satirizing contemporary portrayals of romantic love and the irrational devotion common in sentimental romances, Twain created an entertaining black comedy that is also a parody of the popular newspaper advice columns of that time. Twain's editor, Charles Henry Webb, is probably responsible for condensing the story and renaming it. Twain himself kept rewriting and reprinting it until the last revision appeared in *Sketches, New and Old* (1875).

For several reasons the sketch is important in its various versions. When it first appeared in the *Californian*, Twain was in a period in which he could devote himself to his writing, and for two months he published daily pieces on a variety of subjects, fictional and factual. Everett Emerson asserts that "Aurelia's Unfortunate Young Man" is "one of Twain's freshest and most original" sketches and deserves more attention as an example of Twain's "comic artistry." For Franklin R. Rogers this sketch shows a "new consciousness in [Twain's] use of language." In particular he notes Twain's use of rhythmic, alliterative sentences. In discussing Twain's use of comedy, John C. Gerber notes Twain's complicated use of the pose of moralist. "Aurelia's Unfortunate Young Man" provides an example of using this pose to ridicule moralism itself.

Nancy Chinn

BIBLIOGRAPHY

Clemens, Samuel L. "Aurelia's Unfortunate Young Man." *Sketches, New and Old*. By Clemens. New York: Harper, 1903. 334–338.

———. "Whereas." *The Works of Mark Twain: Early Tales & Sketches, Volume 2 (1864–1865)*. By Clemens. Ed. Edgar M. Branch and Robert H. Hirst. Berkeley: U of California P, 1981. 88–93.

Emerson, Everett. *The Authentic Mark Twain: A Literary Biography of Samuel L. Clemens*. Philadelphia: U of Pennsylvania P, 1984.

Gerber, John C. "Mark Twain's Use of the Comic Pose." *Critical Essays on Mark Twain, 1910–1980*. Ed. Louis J. Budd. Boston: G.K. Hall, 1983. 131–143.

Rogers, Franklin R. *Mark Twain's Burlesque Patterns as Seen in the Novels and Narratives, 1855–1885*. Dallas: Southern Methodist UP, 1960.

See also: Californian; Comic Poses; Condensed Novels

Austen, Jane
(1775–1817)

Satirist and social critic, Jane Austen wrote English novels of manners in the nineteenth century. Her major works include *Sense and Sensibility* (1811), *Pride and Prejudice* (1813), *Mansfield Park* (1814), *Emma* (1816), *Northanger Abbey*, and *Persuasion* (1818). Austen, who never married, lived and wrote in the midst of an active and affectionate family.

Mark Twain did not write an essay on Jane Austen but did comment on her work in letters and journals. These comments reveal a surprising degree of hostility toward her writing. The earliest reference is in a December 1895 entry in a journal kept on board the *Mararoa* while sailing in the Indian Ocean. He calls Austen (and Goldsmith) "[t]horoughly artificial." A few months later he finds the ship's library good because it does not contain any Austen novels: "That one omission alone would make a fairly good library out of a library that hadn't a book in it." This is the source for Twain's chapter in *Following the Equator* (1897) on Austen's lack of literary merit. In his biography Paine quotes Twain saying that on reading *Pride and Prejudice* or *Sense and Sensibility*, "I feel like a barkeeper entering the kingdom of heaven." And in a letter to a close friend, Twain reveals his most strident response to Austen: "Every time I read *Pride and Prejudice* I want to dig her up and beat her over the skull with her own shin-bone." "Every time I read" is as significant as his response because his distaste did not keep him from going back to "Austin's" novels. (Twain persistently misspells her name.) Twain, like Austen, began writing burlesques and moved to forms combining burlesque and original fiction before writing independent works. Austen joined other major authors Twain detested such as Scott, Eliot, Cooper, James, and Poe.

Critics have not agreed on or completely explained the reasons for Twain's hostility. In 1920 Van Wyck Brooks interpreted Twain's dislike as "an act of revenge on Howells, who also wrote novels." Brander Matthews is probably closer to the truth when he states that Austen's artistic vision was too restricted for Twain and his distaste was a response to her "placid and complacent acceptance of a semi-feudal social organization, stratified like a chocolate layer-cake, with petty human fossils in its lower formations." In "Transatlantic Configurations: Mark Twain and Jane

Austen," Richard Poirer suggests that "Austen's satire has behind it a confidence that English society gives everyone a chance, as the society in *Huckleberry Finn* does not, to find a place that can be called 'natural.'" Analyzing Twain's comments on the characters in *Sense and Sensibility*, Alan Gribben finds that Twain's "critical standard required the creation of at least one character with whom he might identify and sympathize." Clearly, Twain was never able to bridge the gap between his American world of adventure and Austen's restrained interiors.

Nancy Chinn

BIBLIOGRAPHY

Brooks, Van Wyck. *The Ordeal of Mark Twain*. Rev. ed. New York: E.P. Dutton, 1933.

Clemens, Samuel L. *Following the Equator*. Hartford, Conn.: American Publishing, 1897.

———. *Mark Twain's Notebook*. Ed. Albert B. Paine. New York: Harper, 1935.

DeVoto, Bernard. *Mark Twain's America*. Boston: Little, Brown, 1932.

Ferguson, DeLancey. *Mark Twain: Man and Legend*. Indianapolis: Bobbs Merrill, 1943.

Gribben, Alan. *Mark Twain's Library: A Reconstruction*. 2 vols. Boston: G.K. Hall, 1980.

Krause, Sydney J. *Mark Twain as Critic*. Baltimore: Johns Hopkins UP, 1967.

Matthews, Brander. *Essays on English*. New York: Scribner, 1921.

Paine, Albert Bigelow. *Mark Twain: A Biography*. 3 vols. New York: Harper, 1912.

Poirer, Richard. *A World Elsewhere: The Place of Style in American Literature*. New York: Oxford UP, 1966.

Rogers, Franklin R. *Mark Twain's Burlesque Patterns as Seen in the Novels and Narratives, 1855–1885*. Dallas: Southern Methodist UP, 1960.

See also: Condensed Novels; Criticism

Australia

As the title of a recent study suggests, the place of Australia in Twain's writing is best contemplated under the broader appellation of Australasia. That is what he called it, more or less interchangeably with its modern name, along with neighboring New Zealand, during his fifteen-week visit there in 1895, and what is depicted in the record of that visit came to fill most of the first half of his final travel book, known to Americans as *Following the Equator* (1897) and to English and Australasian audiences as *More Tramps Abroad* (1897).

One is surprised that Twain, one of the most prolific literary travelers in our history, did not get to Australia sooner. With the colorful circumstances of its settlement by a bona fide criminal class, not to mention the legendary fauna that would have made such lively additions to the Mark Twain bestiary, the place seems literally invented for his writing imagination. More is the surprise, therefore, at how pedestrian he managed to make it seem once he finally got there. A chief reason for this—well known from biography and correspondence—was that the travel and the travel writing were both being done on salary as part of a desperate post-bankruptcy lecture tour. Still, to Twain's credit and that of his hosts, it should be said that the Australasian sojourn, if short on the exotica of Ceylon and India that followed, seems to have been rather more genial than the season in hell he generally made the trip out to be. This did little, however, to cure the ordinariness in the resultant writing. Twain, in fact, in regard to both Australia and New Zealand, turns out to be pretty much the kind of travel writer the author of *The Innocents Abroad* (1869) or *Roughing It* (1872) would have warned us about. He writes about harbors, climate, agriculture, transportation, and principal cities, often resorting to the kinds of chamber of commerce observations that would themselves have earlier been the meat of self-satire. Memphis and Little Rock become crude bench marks for the climates of corresponding southern latitudes and Nevada for dust storms; Syndey and Melbourne look "English with American trimmings." In reverse emphasis, their inhabitants are described as essentially American Englishmen.

As to the possibilities for cross–cultural observation, such commonplaces of perspective seem to have taken the edge off Twain's eye.

In a phrase, familiarity seems to have bred familiarity. The Twain writing here, of course, is at the height of his anti-imperial fulmination. Hence, on behalf of aboriginal peoples, there are ritual laments against depredations conducted in the name of "the white man's notion that he is less savage than the savages." As to comedy, one must settle for a specious anecdote about Cecil Rhodes, the natural curiosity of a railroad that changes gauges on the New South Wales-Victoria frontier, and a parting sally against Julia A. Moore, the Sweet Singer of Michigan. Even animal jokes are in short supply, with the author seizing occasion to claim only, "I myself am the last marsupial." In so doing, he was attempting humor about his own empty pockets and large penury. As to the work of his writing, however, it seems to signal a sense of himself as a truly endangered species, the traveling humorist for whom, increasingly, nothing in the world seemed curious enough to be funny.

Philip D. Beidler

BIBLIOGRAPHY

Clemens, Samuel L. *Following the Equator*. Hartford, Conn.: American Publishing, 1897.

————. *More Tramps Abroad*. London: Chatto and Windus: 1897.

Shillingsburg, Miriam Jones. *At Home Abroad: Mark Twain in Australasia*. Jackson: UP of Mississippi, 1988.

See also: Following the Equator; New Zealand; Travel Writings

Austria (Austria-Hungary)

Samuel L. Clemens sojourned in the dual monarchy then customarily but unofficially called Austria-Hungary with his wife, their daughters, and their housekeeper, Katy Leary, on three separate occasions during the 1890s. The Clemenses divided most of August 1891 between two spas, Marianske Lazne (Marienbad) and Frantiskovy Lazne (Franzensbad), in the Austrian crown land of Bohemia, since 1918 part of Czechoslovakia. His experiences there provided Mark Twain

material for a satirical travel article, "Marienbad—A Health Factory," he contributed to the New York *Sun* and McClure's Syndicate (reprinted in *Europe and Elsewhere* 1923). Clemens's second visit in Austria was a brief stopover in Innsbruck, 21–24 June 1893, en route from Florence to Berlin.

On 19 September 1897 the Clemens family set out by train from Weggis, Switzerland, where they spent the previous two months, and after stopping three days in Innsbruck and four in Salzburg, they reached the Austrian capital, Vienna, on 27 September. Next day they engaged an eight-room suite at the Hotel Metropole, where they remained until 20 May 1898. From then until the following 14 October they rented a furnished villa (then Paulhof, now Sonnenhof at Karlsgasse 3) in rural Kaltenleutgeben, a hydrotheraphy resort twelve miles southwest of Vienna. When they returned to the city that autumn, the family took a spacious apartment in the Hotel Krantz (now Ambassador) where they remained until departing on 26 May 1899 for Prague, where they spent a long weekend en route to England.

Other places in the Habsburg empire visited by Clemens include Bad Ischl and Hallstatt in the Salzkammergut, where the family vacationed from 16 to 27 August 1898, and Budapest, where they spent 23–29 March 1899 as guests of "Otthon," the Hungarian press club. While there, Twain delivered a banquet speech to "Otthon" (although not the one called "German for Hungarians" assigned to this occasion in Paine's collection, *Mark Twain's Speeches*), gave a public reading, and made a phonographic recording that has since been lost.

Clara Clemens's desire to study piano with the renowned piano teacher Theodor Leschetizky (1830–1915) and later to take voice lessons from the Wagnerian contralto Marianne Brandt (1842–1921) was the reason for her family's long residence in Vienna and its environs. As a result, Clemens himself was thrust into the vortex of Viennese musical circles, becoming personally acquainted there with such composers and concert virtuosi as Johann Strauss the Younger (1825–1899), Hans Richter (1843–1916), Gustav Mahler (1860–1911), Karl Goldmark (1830–1915), Antonin Dvorak (1841–1904), Fritz Kreisler (1875–1962), Alfred Grünfeld (1852–1924), and Ossip Gabrilowitsch (1878–1936), who married Clara Clemens in 1909.

By 1897 Twain was probably America's most famous public figure and celebrity-mad Vienna lionized him. He was taken up in the social circles of the eccentric dowager Furstin (Princess) Pauline Metternich (1836–1921), which included among others Grafin (Countess) Misa Wydenbruck-Esterházy, Grafin (Countess) Emily De Lowszowska (who dedicated her "erotic" novel to him), and Erzherzogin (Archduchess) Maria Theresa, stepmother of Franz Ferdinand (1863–1914), the heir to the Habsburg crowns whose murder at Sarajevo (28 June 1914) touched off World War I. Twain was also feted in Vienna's large diplomatic community, especially by American envoy Charlemagne Tower (1848–1923) and his British counterpart, Sir Horace Rumbold. As a result, he gave several public readings for charities sponsored by his aristocratic hosts, at the first of which, on 1 February 1898 in the Bösendorfer Saal, Dr. Sigmund Freud (1856–1939) was a member of the audience. Twain also made platform appearances at pacifist rallies organized in support of the first Hague Conference (May-June 1899) by Freifrau (Baroness) Bertha Kinsky von Suttner (1843–1914), founder and guiding spirit of the Oesterreichische Friedensfreunde (Austrian Friends of Peace).

Upon arriving in Vienna, Twain was beseiged by interviewers from many of the city's forty-five newspapers, and he thereupon formed a wide acquaintanceship among local journalists. The popular dialect humorist of *Neues Wiener Tagblatt*, Eduard Poetzl (1851–1914), became his closest friend in Vienna. Other journalist friends there included the novelist Bettina Wirth (1849–1917), translator of Bret Harte and Vienna correspondent for the London *Daily News*, and Ferdinand

Gross (1840–1904), editor of *Fremden-Blatt* who was also president of "Concordia," the liberal Austrian press club. Gross invited Twain to address the club at a *Festkneipe* (festive drinking party) on 31 October 1897. His brief speech in German, "Die Schrecken der deutschen Sprache" ("The Horrors of the German Language," not to be confused with the earlier and lengthier "Awful German Language" in *A Tramp Abroad* [1880]), delivered before an illustrious gathering, was one of the high points of his twenty-month Viennese sojourn.

Siegmund Schlesinger (1832–1916), a well-known Viennese playwright-journalist and one of Twain's first interviewers, prevailed upon him in January 1898 to collaborate in writing two comedies—*Die Goldgräberin* (The Lady Goldminer), to be set in the Klondike, and *Der Gegenkandidat, oder die Frauen Politiker* (The Opposition Candidate, or Women Politicians), on the topic of women's suffrage—purportedly for performance at the k.k. Hofburgtheater (Imperial-Royal Court Theatre) with Katerina von Schratt, the emperor's mistress, in leading roles. The collaboration, in which Twain was to supply plot situations and characters while Schlesinger wrote the German dialogue, dragged on throughout the next sixteen months without resulting in a stageworthy piece, and the manuscripts have been lost.

At the same time (January–March 1898) Twain undertook to translate two theatrical hits of the 1897–1898 Vienna season—a naturalistic "social problem" drama, *Bartel Turaser*, by Phillipp Langmann (1862–1920) and a farce, *Im Fegefeuer* (In Purgatory), by Ernst Gettke (1870–1914) and Alexander Engel (1868–1930)—for the New York or London stages without finding a producer willing to risk them. The manuscripts of Twain's translations are also apparently not extant. In early April 1898 he commenced but was discouraged from completing a translation of Theodor Herzl's drama, *Das Neue Ghetto* (The New Ghetto), the premiere of which he had attended (with Sigmund Freud) on 5 January 1898. An original farce of his own, *Is He Dead?*, adapted from his earlier story about the painter Francois Millet ("Is He Living or Is He Dead?" [1893]), completed in three weeks in late January–early February 1898, was similarly unsuccessful in finding a producer, although its unpublished manuscript survives in the Mark Twain Papers at Berkeley.

As these abortive efforts suggest, Twain's lifelong fascination with the theater and his ambitions as a dramatist were greatly stimulated in Vienna, where he attended theatrical as well as operatic performances with unusual frequency and became acquainted with such prominent theatrical personalities as the actors Alexander Girardi and Adolf von Sonnenthal and impresarios as Baron Alfred von Berger, Dr. Max Burckhardt, and Dr. Paul Schlenther. One play in the Hofburgtheater repertory, Adolf von Wilbrandt's *Der Meister von Palmyra*, a ponderous five-act *dramatische Dichtung* (poetic drama), impressed him enormously. He saw it repeatedly and made it the subject of "About Play-Acting," a serious article of dramatic criticism published in *The Forum* magazine (October 1898) and collected in *The Man That Corrupted Hadleyburg & Other Stories and Sketches* (1900). This play has been cited by many scholars as a major source of themes and ideas Twain expressed in "The Chronicle of Young Satan" (1969), on which he was working at that time.

The Austro-Hungarian empire was deep in a constitutional crisis when Clemens arrived in Vienna, and during his first two months there he witnessed anarchic upheavals in the Reichsrat (parliament) that eventuated in the fall of the moderate regime of Count Kasimir Badeni (1846–1909), the most violent public demonstrations and riots in the realm since 1848 and the effective end of Austrian political liberalism. These events became the subject of "Stirring Times in Austria," one of Twain's best pieces of political reportage, published in *Harper's Monthly* in February 1898 and in his collected works. A caustic sequel to this, titled "Government By Article 14," remains in manuscript in the Mark Twain Papers.

In the heated partisan debates that erupted when Badeni tried to win support among the young Czech deputies for renewing the *Ausgleich* (the arrangement whereby Austria and Hungary had been confederated under a single monarch since 1867) by granting the Czech language equal status with German in the Bohemian judicial system, the prime minister was challenged by and fought a duel with the leader of the opposition. The incident prompted Twain's polemical essay, "Dueling," posthumously published in *Europe and Elsewhere*.

On 10 September 1898 the Austrian empress was assassinated in Geneva, Switzerland, by an Italian anarchist. Clemens was outraged at what seemed, on the one hand, a senseless murder and, on the other, a harbinger of the coming disintegration of European order that Karl Kraus called in his epic drama "The Last Days of Mankind." On 17 September he took his family from Kaltenleutgeben to a balcony of the Hotel Krantz to view the procession accompanying the empress's bier to the Habsburg crypt in the Capuchin Church, one of the most extravagant displays of funereal pomp ever seen in the history of European royalty. He described the ceremonial in elaborate detail in a piece of vivid reportage, "The Memorable Assassination," posthumously published with *What Is Man?* (1917).

On 16 March 1898 Clemens met a gifted young Polish schoolteacher, Jan Szczepanik (pron. "Shte-pan-ick," 1872–1926), who had invented a machine called a *Raster* for electrically transfiguring photographic images into perforations on jacquard loom cards used in weaving carpets and other textiles, and a primitive form of closed-circuit television called *Fernseher*. This "Austrian Edison," as Twain dubbed the inventor, had been established in a laboratory in Vienna by Ludwig Kleinberg, an entrepreneur who was then selling foreign rights to Szczepanik's patents. Sensing a chance for a bonanza for the owner of the American rights to the *Raster*, Clemens took a two-month option on both inventions for an offer of $1.5

million and then tried strenuously to persuade his New York financial adviser, Henry Huttleston Rogers, to provide the money to conclude the contract. Ultimately, Rogers vetoed the investment, since there was insufficient growth in industrial weaving in the United States to recoup more than the payment for the rights.

Although disappointed in his efforts, Twain nevertheless put his experiences with Szczepanik to good literary use in a sketch about the absurd bureaucratic ruse whereby the inventor had avoided military conscription, "The Austrian Edison Keeping School Again," and a satirical short piece of science fiction, "From the 'London Times' of 1904," making imaginative use of Szczepanik and his *Fernseher* to "solve" a presumed murder and to lampoon perverse "French justice" in the second trial of Captain Alfred Dreyfus.

The Dreyfus Affair and the anti-Semitic turn rioting took in several Austrian cities after Count Badeni's dismissal provided Twain an overt rationale for the polemical essay he completed in late July 1898, "Concerning the Jews," published in *Harper's Monthly* in October 1899 and included in his collected works. In reality, attacks upon him in Vienna's anti-Semitic opposition press for his close association with Jewish journalists and philo-Semites of Vienna's dominant liberal press (e.g., *Neue Freie Presse, Neues Wiener Tagblatt*, et al.) were what prompted him to organize and express his views about the Jews and anti-Jewish prejudices and persecutions in an essay that, despite being factually flawed and perhaps somewhat myopic, is one of his best organized and most cogently argued. Such attacks on "the Jew Mark Twain" increased in scurrility and frequency in *Reichspost* and other newspapers during his Vienna sojourn and were joined in April 1899 by the celebrated Viennese satirist Karl Kraus (1874–1936) in the third number of Kraus's influential magazine, *Die Fackel*.

The Clemenses' frantic but vain search for effective treatments for their youngest daughter Jean's increasingly frequent epileptic seizures while in the city brought the writer into

contact with many illustrious members of Vienna's medical profession. Among the eminent physicians Clemens consulted were the neuropathologist Heinrich Obersteiner (1847–1922), the psychiatrist Richard von Krafft-Ebing (1840–1902), senior colleagues at the University of Vienna of Sigmund Freud, whom he may also have consulted, the pioneering pediatrician Alexander von Huettenbrenner (1842–1905), and the founder of Austrian hydrotherapy, Wilhelm Winternitz (1834–1917), to whose rigorous "cold water cures" Olivia Clemens and her daughters submitted themselves throughout the summer of 1898 without much apparent benefit.

Opportunities for frequent social contact and conversation with these and other leaders in scientific, literary, and artistic circles at that intellectually charged "golden moment" of the Viennese *fin de siècle* when much of what the present century has called "modern" was being created there stimulated his mind and art to an extraordinary degree. In sum, Vienna acted upon Twain as a tonic, shaking him from the despondency and torpor into which he had fallen after his series of personal misfortunes in the 1890s, reawakening dormant interests, and stimulating new ideas or new variants of old ones. Twain's development and expression during the final phase of his long, richly varied career cannot be understood except against the background of his Viennese experiences.

Twain accomplished more writing during his twenty months in Vienna and Kaltenleutgeben than in almost any other comparable period of his career. Among the most significant literary products of this sojourn are his Socratic dialogue, *What Is Man?* (1906), the first part of his book, *Christian Science* (1907), the "Early Days" section of his *Autobiography* (1924), and above all his most powerful short story, "The Man That Corrupted Hadleyburg" (1899), and two of the three "Mysterious Stranger" manuscripts ("The Chronicle of Young Satan" and "Schoolhouse Hill" [1969]).

Altogether more than thirty works issued whole or in part from his pen during this period. Several, such as "My Platonic Sweetheart," "Wapping Alice," the fragmentary "Which Was the Dream?," "The Great Dark," and "Mysterious Stranger" sequence, have been posthumously published. Other completed pieces, such as "Government By Article 14" (a sequel to "Stirring Times in Austria"), "American Representation in Austria" (a lampoon on the United States ambassador, Addison C. Harris), and the farce, *Is He Dead?*, remain in manuscript in the Mark Twain Papers at Berkeley along with a fragmentary humorous sketch, "Kaltenleutgeben," about a loquacious housemaid at Villa Paulhof Twain nicknamed Wuthering Heights, and two essay fragments, "In Defense of Royalty and Nobility" and "The New War Scare."

On 25 May 1899, the day before his departure from Vienna, Clemens was invited to a short private audience with Franz Joseph I (1830–1916) of Habsburg-Lorraine, Emperor of Austria, Apostolic King of Hungary, etc., at the Hofburg. At a press conference with Viennese reporters after the audience, he made flattering remarks about both the monarch and the city, saying that he had been made to feel "at home" in Vienna and that anyone who lived there a couple of years would never "completely go away." Although the writer never physically returned to the Danube city, these words proved metaphorically prophetic.

Carl Dolmetsch

BIBLIOGRAPHY

Dolmetsch, Carl. *"Our Famous Guest": Mark Twain in Vienna.* Athens: U of Georgia P, 1992.

See also: Dramatist, Mark Twain as; Europe; Freud, Sigmund; German Language; Jews; Music

Autobiographical Dictations
(1885–1909)

Mark Twain's autobiographical dictations include the Grant dictations (1885), the dictations begun in Florence, Italy (1904), and the final dictations composed between January 1906 and 1909. Typescripts are in the Bancroft Library, University of California, Berkeley.

The Grant dictations are Twain's record of his relationship with Ulysses S. Grant (1822–1885). They describe their first meeting, Twain's arrangements as publisher of Grant's *Memoirs* (1885), and Grant's method of dictating. The Florence dictations focus on life at Villa Quarto, comparisons between Florence in 1904 and the family's 1892 experience in Italy, and remembrances of friends and books. Olivia Clemens's death in June 1904 ended the dictating. The final dictations began as a way for Albert Bigelow Paine to collect materials for a biography. Twain believed that the rambling conversation would generate memories and that the informal setting and congenial audience would prompt him to speak openly. He spins yarns of Hannibal, the Mississippi, his careers as miner, reporter, lecturer, and his success as a writer—many are seasoned with opinions on politics, government, business, family life, and literature. Twain completed 252 dictations between 1906 and 1909: 134 in 1906, 70 in 1907, 34 in 1908, and 14 in 1909. They total some half million words.

Twain used dictations for sections of "Chapters from My Autobiography" (*North American Review*, 1906–1907). Paine used them as his primary source for *Mark Twain: A Biography* (1912); he used the Grant and Florence dictations for *Mark Twain's Autobiography* (1924). Bernard DeVoto and Charles Neider shaped editions of Twain's autobiography from the dictations. All of the autobiographical dictations have not yet been published. The amount and scope of the material is daunting (Twain wove newspaper clippings, letters, and full manuscripts into the dictations); the editorial problems are myriad.

Michael J. Kiskis

BIBLIOGRAPHY

Clemens, Samuel L. "Chapters from My Autobiography." *North American Review* 183 (1906); 184, 185, 186 (1907): various issues.

————. *Mark Twain's Autobiography*. Ed. Albert B. Paine. 2 vols. New York: Harper, 1924.

————. *Mark Twain in Eruption*. Ed. Bernard DeVoto. New York: Harper, 1940.

————. *Mark Twain's Own Autobiography: The Chapters from the "North American Review."* Ed. Michael J. Kiskis. Madison: U of Wisconsin P, 1990.

Paine, Albert Bigelow. *Mark Twain: A Biography*. 3 vols. New York: Harper, 1912.

See also: Autobiography; "Chapters from My Autobiography"

Autobiography
(1870–1909)

Mark Twain composed his autobiography over a forty-year period from 1870 to 1910. He experimented with a variety of methods and forms: from autobiographical sketches to childhood memories, from commentary on contemporary events to reflections on his life experiences to carefully sculpted eulogies for family and friends. He shaped these fragments when he prepared "Chapters from My Autobiography" for the *North American Review* in 1906 and 1907. However, since his death in 1910, several editors have returned to the autobiographical manuscripts and have given their own design to Twain's autobiography: Albert Bigelow Paine published *Mark Twain's Autobiography* (1924), Bernard DeVoto presented *Mark Twain in Eruption* (1940), Charles Neider edited *The Autobiography of Mark Twain* (1959), and Michael J. Kiskis collected the *North American Review* chapters for a single edition (1990). About a third of Twain's autobiographical manuscripts remain unpublished. The manuscripts are part of the Mark Twain Project based at the University of California at Berkeley.

Autobiography and first-person narrative are intimately related. Twain's mastery of first-person narrative underlies the critical and popular success of his novels *Adventures of Huckleberry Finn* (1885), *A Connecticut Yankee in King Arthur's Court* (1889), and *Personal Recollections of Joan of Arc* (1896), and his travel books include *The Innocents Abroad* (1869),

Roughing It (1872), *A Tramp Abroad* (1880), and *Following the Equator* (1897). It is easy to see how closely his first-person narratives are related to autobiography: at one time Twain himself proposed that a reader need only set the books in sequence to form an autobiography. That view still persists for many readers who interpret *The Adventures of Tom Sawyer* (1876), *Life on the Mississippi* (1883), and *Adventures of Huckleberry Finn* as an autobiographical trilogy. The problem is that Twain often uses reality to spark fiction—as in *Life on the Mississippi* when he deliberately adjusts life to sharpen the image of the cub pilot. In the end Twain's first-person narratives are his link to the storytelling tradition of the Southwest, a tradition energized by the tall tale, as well as his link to the oral tradition of slave kitchens and childhood ghost stories. All of this influenced Twain's approach to autobiography.

Twain did not begin to write autobiography with any plan to publish a separate volume. His early, rather tentative explorations are related to his fiction: "The Tennessee Land" (1870) and "Early Years in Florida, Missouri" (1877), for example, were written when Twain was occupied with reclaiming his Mississippi experience for *The Gilded Age* (1873), "Old Times on the Mississippi" (1875), *The Adventures of Tom Sawyer*, and the early sections of *Adventures of Huckleberry Finn*.

With the Grant dictations in 1885, Twain began to compose autobiography intentionally to preserve events from his adult life in the East: it would not be used to enhance his fiction. The anecdotes focusing on Grant, Twain's activity on the general's behalf, and the growth of their mutually satisfying relationship thrust Twain in a new direction. He saved these experiences because of their inherent worth. They were important highlights of Twain's career as a publisher and examples of his status as a public figure.

The separation between fiction and autobiography grew clearer as Twain continued his experiments. After some years he returned to autobiography in a series of character sketches that were prompted by Jane Lampton

Clemens's death in 1890 and the variety of disasters connected to the Paige typesetter. Twain wrote about the influence of these events on his life. While he reached toward autobiography to explore his relationships and to record his reactions, his emphasis was not on self—on Twain—but on the other. He was gradually moving from using memory as fodder for fiction to using personal relationships as the bases for occasional sketches.

Twain's move to self-reflection was prompted by the trauma and resulting pressure of bankruptcy compounded by the shock of his daughter Susy's death from spinal meningitis in 1896. While in Europe during 1897–1899, Twain turned to autobiography with "Early Days," a mix of commentary on his experiences in Europe as well as a reflection on his past. In effect, Twain was now using the autobiography not as a way to stimulate fiction or as a repository for anecdotes about particular friends but as a balm for his wounded spirit. "Early Days" becomes the centerpiece of Twain's autobiographical compositions because of its series of reminiscences of Quarles Farm and of Twain's childhood in the midst of peace and plenty. Long portions recover singular childhood experiences: Twain's carefully drawn images and precise use of language transport him back to the farm and to innocence and joy; he overloads paragraphs with explicit descriptions of the farm, of the idyllic life that revolved around the kitchen and the table; he conjures up feelings of safety; he moves gracefully between an idyllic past and a troubled present. The idyll carries the day, and Twain resurrects a sense of peace and well-being not available in the empty present. For the first time, Twain uses autobiography to find peace and to reintegrate himself with the world. Just as the Grant dictations moved Twain to use autobiography as a record of his experience and relationship, "Early Days" allowed him to use autobiography to reclaim the best of times and to compose a eulogy for his past. And that eulogy allowed him to face the present more energetically.

Eulogies become even more prominent when Twain again returned to autobiography in Florence in 1904. The Florence dictations mark the beginning of Twain's final attempt to combine recollections and commentary as autobiography, an attempt he continued in the final series of dictations that began in 1906. Throughout the dictations Twain holds court as past events and people parade by. In Florence he focuses on place as he describes the Villa Quarto, and he explores the relationship of place to time by introducing entries from his notebooks composed during the family's earlier visit to Italy during the 1890s. As his interest in the juxtaposition falters, he moves on to compose memories of friends as well as of early writings. The Florence experiments came to an end with Olivia's death in June 1904.

During these years of experiment Twain thought little of offering a full autobiography to the public. Even when Albert Bigelow Paine entered the picture and the two began their series of conversations known as the final autobiographical dictations, Twain thought of the project as a source for the biography that Paine would produce. His thoughts of an autobiography did not take shape until well after they had begun their sessions. The prospect became clear when George Harvey, editor of the *North American Review*, approached Twain with a proposal to publish installments of the autobiography. That proposal led to the twenty-five installments titled "Chapters from My Autobiography."

Twain's interest in the autobiography was highest during the early months of the dictations, but his fire for the project dimmed as time passed: little work was done after 1907; 1909 saw only a handful of dictating sessions. The swing in Twain's interest is not surprising given his long practice of "pigeonholing" manuscripts when he had reached an impasse: when the "well" ran dry, he would set aside the work and wait for his tank to fill up again. No tale, however, was put aside as frequently as his autobiography. And no tale caused as much frustration as he tried to find the best way to tell his story. As he became less enamored of dictating, Twain returned to the pen in a search for a new and more effective autobiographical method. He attempted to write letters to friends—letters in which he believed he could be even more frank than in the dictations. The "Ashcroft-Lyon Manuscript" was the first and last attempt with the letter format: the text quickly degenerated into an outlet for frustrations and feelings of betrayal.

Ultimately, Twain seems to have decided to leave the manuscripts and commentaries to his editors. In his mind his autobiography came to a halt with still another tragic death: that of his youngest daughter, Jean, who was found dead on the morning of Christmas Eve 1909. In a pattern reminiscent of Twain's actions after the deaths of Susy, Jane Lampton Clemens, Olivia Clemens, and Henry Huttleston Rogers, he took up the pen to find solace. In the days immediately after Jean's death he penned "The Death of Jean," which was published in *Harper's* in 1910. He told Paine the piece was the final chapter of his autobiography. He did not begin another.

There has been relatively little critical work done relating to the autobiography. Part of the difficulty stems from the chaotic collection of manuscripts that is identified as the autobiography. Critics have devoted time to molding these materials into acceptable narrative shapes or have paid attention to self-contained pieces within the manuscripts, both to make the range of materials more accessible to critical analysis and to preserve Twain's reputation as a fine teller of focused tales. The wealth of material has supported Twain's own statements that the autobiography will never be completed; the nonchronological and association-driven sequence of Twain's thoughts have made it difficult to see the manuscripts as a single, clear, integrated, coherent tale. There is also the problem of truth: Twain was well aware of his weakness for a good story, and he was quite willing to adjust the record to enhance the tale.

The excerpts in Paine's, DeVoto's, and Neider's highly edited volumes offer a peculiar picture of Twain: Paine's Twain is the literary experimenter and self-conscious satirist, DeVoto's is the social and political commentator, Neider's is the narrative genius. Each editor has provided the frame within which Twain's portrait hangs. In the end, however, Twain himself left a coherent tale. He also left a tale loaded with truth. The most coherent of Twain's autobiographies is the one he himself planned and shaped and published in the *North American Review*—"Chapters from My Autobiography." From its opening statement of the problems inherent in autobiography to its closing tall tale and comment on truth, the whole vibrates with the clear and unmistakable and unifying voice of Mark Twain. His voice gives this tale its coherence; his constancy gives it its truth.

Michael J. Kiskis

BIBLIOGRAPHY

Clemens, Samuel L. *The Autobiography of Mark Twain.* Ed. Charles Neider. New York: Harper, 1959.

———. "Chapters from My Autobiography." *North American Review* 183 (1906); 184, 185, 186 (1907): various issues.

———. *Mark Twain-Howells Letters: The Correspondence of Samuel L. Clemens and William D. Howells.* Ed. Henry Nash Smith and William M. Gibson. 2 Vols. Cambridge, Mass.: Harvard UP, 1960.

———. *Mark Twain in Eruption.* Ed. Bernard DeVoto. New York: Harper, 1940.

———. *Mark Twain's Autobiography.* Ed. Albert B. Paine. 2 vols. New York: Harper, 1924.

———. *Mark Twain's Own Autobiography: The Chapters from the "North American Review."* Ed. Michael J. Kiskis. Madison: U of Wisconsin P, 1990.

Cox, James M. *Mark Twain: The Fate of Humor.* Princeton, N.J.: Princeton UP, 1966.

Emerson, Everett. *The Authentic Mark Twain: A Literary Biography of Samuel L. Clemens.* Philadelphia: U of Pennsylvania P, 1984.

Hill, Hamlin. *Mark Twain: God's Fool.* New York: Harper & Row, 1973.

Kaplan, Justin. *Mr. Clemens and Mark Twain.* New York: Simon & Schuster, 1966.

Macnaughton, William R. *Mark Twain's Last Years as a Writer.* Columbia: U of Missouri P, 1979.

Paine, Albert Bigelow. *Mark Twain: A Biography.* 3 vols. New York: Harper, 1912.

See also: Autobiographical Dictations; "Chapters from My Autobiography"; *North American Review*

"Autobiography of a Damned Fool"
(1967)

This title was supplied by Albert B. Paine. Having begun composition in March 1877, Twain referred to it only as "Orion's autobiography." It was published in 1967 along with a sequence of material linked together by Twain's attempts to work his brother's quicksilver temperament into a fictional character, among them "Affeland" and "Hellfire Hotchkiss" (*Satires & Burlesques* 134–174). He tried to interest others in taking up the subject. Howells declined, and when Orion himself attempted one in 1880, it was not what Twain wanted after all.

The working notes for the Hannibal version of the *Mysterious Stranger* show a character named Oliver Hotchkiss, whose weathervane-type mind causes him continually to shift religions and opinions. This characteristic was drawn from the real-life Orion's basic nature, which Twain analyzed in an early notebook entry (1:28). By making the main character, Bolivar, an eighteen-year-old printer's apprentice, "Autobiography of a Damned Fool" could represent Twain's search for a way to continue *Tom Sawyer* (1876) (Hill 123). On the other hand, it is possible that the material from "Autobiography" was used to expand the framework of *Huckleberry Finn* (1885) with a burlesque of temperance literature (*Mark Twain's Burlesque Patterns* 128). Though he put the manuscript of "Autobiography" away in 1877 unable to finish it after only two months, it influenced his major writings.

Sandra Littleton-Uetz

BIBLIOGRAPHY

Clemens, Samuel L. "Autobiography of a Damned Fool." *Mark Twain's Satires & Burlesques.* By Clemens. Ed. Franklin R. Rogers. Berkeley: U of California P, 1967. 134–161.

———. *Mark Twain's Notebooks & Journals, Volume I (1855–1873).* Ed. Frederick Anderson, Michael B. Frank, and Kenneth M. Sanderson. Berkeley: U of California P, 1975.

Hill, Hamlin. *Mark Twain and Elisha Bliss.* Columbia: U of Missouri P, 1964.

Rogers, Franklin R. *Mark Twain's Burlesque Patterns as Seen in the Novels and Narratives, 1855–1885.* Dallas: Southern Methodist UP, 1960.

See also: Clemens, Orion; "Hellfire Hotchkiss"

"Awful German Language, The"
(1880)

An Appendix (D) to *A Tramp Abroad* (1880), "The Awful German Language" is Mark Twain's summary of his frustrations with learning the German language. It ends with eight humorous suggestions for reform of the language, with the objection that if German is not changed, "it ought to be gently and reverently set aside among the dead languages, for only the dead have time to learn it."

This burlesque supports Mark Twain's complaint in his notebook that in early times "some sufferer had to sit up with a toothache, and he put in the time inventing the German language."

The main problems with the language, as Mark Twain illustrates them in "The Awful German Language," are confusing cases, parenthetical expressions (especially those found in a German newspaper), separable verbs, declension of adjectives, and the confusing genders of nouns in which "a fish is *he*, his scales are *she*, but a fishwife is neither." This last point forms the impetus for Mark Twain's hilarious anecdote "Tale of the Fishwife and Its Sad Fate."

Mark Twain had a playful interest in great, long compounded German words. He uses one of these, *Freundschaftsbezeigungenstadtverordnetenversammlungenfamilieneigenthümlichkeiten*, in the piece that ends "The

Awful German Language," "A Fourth of July Oration in the German Tongue, Delivered at a Banquet of the Anglo-American Club of Students by the Author of this Book." His main humorous device in this closing part is to intermix English and German indiscriminately. ("Sie mussen so freundlich sein, und verzeih mich die interlarding von ein oder zwei Englischer Worte, hie und da, denn ich finde dass die deutsche is not a very copious language, and so when you've really got anything to say, you've got to draw on a language that can stand the strain.")

Mark Twain reworked similar material in a speech to the Vienna Press Club (1897) titled "Die Schrecken der Deutschen Sprache"—which literally translated into "English" as "The Horrors of the German Language"—and he used "The Awful German Language" in lecture appearances into the twentieth century.

Richard Dilworth Rust

BIBLIOGRAPHY

Clemens, Samuel L. *A Tramp Abroad*. Hartford, Conn.: American Publishing, 1880.

———. *Mark Twain's Speeches*. New York: Harper, 1923.

See also: German Language

Azores

On 21 June 1867, the steamship *Quaker City* arrived in the waters off Corvo, in the Azores group. A few hours later the passengers disembarked at Horta, and the next two days brought Mark Twain his first immediate experience of European life. Mark Twain's adventures in the Azores, as chronicled in chapters 5 and 6 of *The Innocents Abroad* (1869), are not fondly described: much of the space is given over to complaint about the laziness, greed, technological stasis, and Roman Catholicism of the native Portuguese population. Twain does muster some enthusiasm, however, for the roads and stonework in the towns of Horta and Fayal and for careening around the countryside on exuberant donkeys.

Bruce Michelson

BIBLIOGRAPHY

Ganzel, Dewey. *Mark Twain Abroad: The Cruise of the "Quaker City."* Chicago: U of Chicago P, 1968.

See also: Europe; *Innocents Abroad, The*

B

Baalbec

Baalbec is a city in southern Lebanon, legendary for the extensive and somewhat mysterious ruined metropolis nearby. With a small group, Mark Twain visited Baalbec on a horseback trip from Damascus, as the *Quaker City* party made scattered and zigzagging progress from Ephesus through Syria to the Holy Land. Chapter 43 of *The Innocents Abroad* (1869) describes the tour of the ruins, which appear in three illustrations in the first edition. The Baalbec chapter stands out in the last third of the book as an instance in which Mark Twain's prose shows rare enthusiasm about a Middle Eastern site. Unharassed, for the time being, by beggars, guides, and religious pilgrims, Twain could contemplate a colossal wreck that had not yet been extensively excavated, or incorporated into the itinerary of hordes of ordinary visitors. Though he makes no mention here of Baalbec's associations with the kingdom of Palmyra and its daring Queen Zenobia (the beautiful, defiant woman favored in nineteenth-century classroom lore), he was apparently awed by the immensity of two temples built during periods of Roman domination, pleased by the imagination-freeing uncertainty of the city's history, and impressed by the uncommon immediacy and relative privacy of his experience.

Bruce Michelson

See also: Holy Land, The; *Innocents Abroad, The*

Bacon, Francis
(1561–1626)

Politician, statesman, essayist, and philosopher, Francis Bacon had a secondary advisory role in the court of Queen Elizabeth, but he prospered in the reign of her successor, James I, rising to the highest legal appointment in the kingdom, lord chancellor, in 1618. In 1621, however, upon pleading guilty to taking bribes, he retired from public life and spent his remaining years writing on philosophy in the broadest sense. "I have taken all knowledge to be my province," he asserted. Although critical of earlier methods of determining truth, particularly Aristotelian logic and medieval scholasticism, Bacon was not the father of modern science as Voltaire and Diderot, among others, claimed, but his philosophical writing did encourage the scientific method of finding truths by inductive reasoning from observable facts and experiments. Mark Twain probably did not read the work of Bacon himself, but he knew well the history of the period and had studied Thomas Macaulay's essay on the philosopher. Lord Bacon appeared in *1601* (1876) as one of the intimates of Queen Elizabeth, along with Sir Walter Raleigh, Ben Jonson, and William Shakespeare. In *Is Shakespeare Dead?* (1909), Twain argued with relentless inductive reasoning against what he called the "superstition" that William Shakespeare had written the plays attributed to him. Twain, well read in the controversy, considered the better-educated and more cosmopolitan Francis Bacon a better candidate.

Cameron C. Nickels

BIBLIOGRAPHY

Clemens, Samuel L. *Is Shakespeare Dead?* New York: Harper, 1909.

————. *[Date, 1601] Conversation, As It Was By the Social Fireside in the Time of the Tudors.* Ed. Franklin J. Meine. Chicago: n.p., 1939. Rpt. New York: Lyle Stuart, 1961.

See also: Is Shakespeare Dead?

Baker, Jim

("Tom Quartz," or "Tom Quartz, the Dynamite Cat," from *Roughing It*, 1872. "Jim Baker's Blue Jay Yarn," or "What Stumped the Blue Jays," from *A Tramp Abroad*, 1880.) Jim Baker is the "middle-aged, simple-hearted" California gold-rush pocket miner Mark Twain features in sketches in two of his travelogues who has had limited success as a prospector but has shown masterful accomplishment as animal-tall-tale storyteller. Jim has remained in the gold fields after the great rush has ended, and the mother lode exhausted, seeking the rare remaining "pockets." His tales show Twain at his best, in short sketch form, in picturing the slightly mentally distorted narrator and the personalized animal.

Mildly addled by his long-term lack of human society, Jim humanizes imaginatively his only animate, vocal neighbors, the birds and the beasts. The character Jim Baker grew from real-life Jim Gillis, with whom Twain bunked in the California gold diggings—the temporary miners' cities of Angel's Camp and Jackass Hill, from 4 December 1864 to 25 February 1865. When inspired, Gillis invented, ad-libbing on the spot, marvelous fantasies featuring his rarely speaking partner, Jim Stoker, and humanized animals. Jim Baker resembles his original in being "gray as a rat, earnest, thoughtful, slenderly educated, slouchily dressed and clay-soiled." But for Twain, Gillis's "style and bearing could make any costume regal." Jim Baker affects us similarly. Sure, the miner is a bit "touched"—Twain solemnly validates that Jim understands blue jay speech because "[He] told me so himself." He similarly authenticates Jim's grasp of a cat's inner mental life. But we are all the more kindly drawn to Jim as he sketches eavesdropping on blue jays or recalls his bond to Tom Quartz, his brilliant mining cat, sorrowing over the time that the cat was accidentally blown up in a quartz mining explosion.

The cat survives, yet Jim fears their empathy is damaged. Twain notes his original for Tom Quartz lived only in Gillis's imagination; the intricacy of feeling Jim Baker holds for Tom Quartz, assigning the cat rare insight for prospectors' geological indications, shows Baker transforming the usual insatiable cat curiosity into a rare gift of mining intuition. Tom is endowed, too, with *all* human possibilities for genius and emotional intricacy; resentment, dignity, and aloofness suggest the lonely narrator's mental oddity.

The blue jays certainly suggest how Jim sees in the disputative—often leather-headed jays—all the racket and argument carried on by joyous, irony-loving, miner humans. Jim creates, in his account of the birds' "speech," all the joyous, uninformed debate, and good-humored delight in satirizing the main jay's sucker-error—trying to fill the unfillable knot-hole—that marks frontier human society. "Don't try to tell me a jay hasn't got a sense of humor," says Jim, "'cause I know better."

St. *George Tucker Arnold*

BIBLIOGRAPHY

Blair, Walter, and Hamlin Hill. "Mark Twain's Chestnuts." *America's Humor: From Poor Richard to Doonesbury.* New York: Oxford UP, 1978. 303–348.

Clemens, Samuel L. *Roughing It.* Ed. Franklin R. Rogers and Paul Baender. Berkeley: U of California P, 1972.

———. *A Tramp Abroad.* Hartford, Conn.: American Publishing, 1880.

See also: Animals; "Jim Baker's Blue Jay Yarn"

Baldwin, Joseph Glover
(1815–1864)

Lawyer, editor, politician, writer, and judge, Joseph Glover Baldwin is best known for his highly successful collection of humorous sketches and biographies celebrating the boom times on the old southwestern frontier titled *The Flush Times of Alabama and Mississippi* (1853). Combined with his urbane wit and elegant style, his classic character creations such as Ovid Bolus, Esq., and Simon Suggs, Jr., won him large audiences during the years preceding the Civil War.

Baldwin was born, reared, and trained in the law in Virginia, where he developed conservative affinities for Whig politics and Episcopal worship before migrating to the frontier areas of Mississippi (1836) and Alabama (1837). He finally transplanted to California (1845), where he became a leading attorney and an associate justice of the California Supreme Court (1859–1861). His career as a genteel, amateur writer began in 1851 when he composed a series of sketches based on his experi-

ences as a lawyer in the inflated, unsettled world of the southwestern frontier.

A number of these sketches appeared in the *Southern Literary Messenger* (1852–1853) before Baldwin revised, added to, and collected them for book publication as *Flush Times* (1853). They are authentic and unusually vivid pictures of the people and places Baldwin had come to know: charming con artists and rascally villains are interspersed with more serious portraits of his colorful but respectable legal colleagues. Though Baldwin does not employ much vernacular in his writings, he does render raucous frontier life with all its roughness and merriment in a realistic fashion. As Kenneth Lynn has pointed out, there is also a "Gentleman" as the salvation of the South underlying Baldwin's humor (114–124).

Mark Twain was familiar with the standard popular books of southwestern humor, including *Flush Times.* In it he encountered a successful kindred talent with remarkable ability to create lifelike portraits of picaresque characters and "the reign of humbug, and wholesale insanity" of the times. He also probably recognized something of a kindred spirit in Baldwin whose humorous sketches are tinged with an underlying pessimism that sometimes belies their overt hilarity.

W. *Craig Turner*

BIBLIOGRAPHY

Blair, Walter. *Native American Humor.* New York: American Publishing, 1937. Rpt. San Francisco: Chandler, 1960.

Lynn, Kenneth S. *Mark Twain and Southwestern Humor.* Boston: Little, Brown, 1959.

See also: Southwestern Humor

Ball, Charles

Charles Ball (dates unknown) was an escaped slave whose story, as told to Isaac Fisher, went through at least six editions between 1836 and 1859. Titled *Slavery in the United States: A Narrative of the Life and Adventures of Charles Ball, A Black Man* (1836), it also appeared in

1859, somewhat abridged, as *Fifty Years in Chains: or, The Life of an American Slave*. Mark Twain was fascinated with this vivid account of slave life and borrowed many details for his portraits of the slave bands in *A Connecticut Yankee* (1889).

Howard G. Baetzhold

BIBLIOGRAPHY

Baetzhold, Howard G. *Mark Twain and John Bull: The British Connection*. Bloomington: Indiana UP, 1970.

Ball, Charles. *Slavery in the United States: A Narrative of the Life and Adventures of Charles Ball, A Black Man*. Lewiston, Pa.: John W. Shugert, 1836. Rpt. *Fifty Years in Chains: or, The Life of an American Slave*. Indianapolis: Dayton and Asher, 1859. Rpt. *Fifty Years in Chains*. Intro. Philip Foner. New York: Negro UP, 1969.

Gribben, Alan. *Mark Twain's Library: A Reconstruction*. 2 vols. Boston: G.K. Hall, 1980.

Nichols, Charles Harold. *Many Thousand Gone: The Ex-Slaves' Account of Their Bondage and Freedom*. Bloomington: Indiana UP, 1969.

See also: Connecticut Yankee in King Arthur's Court, A; Slavery

Bankruptcy

(1894)

Mark Twain entered voluntary bankruptcy in 1894 as a result of the failure of Charles L. Webster and Company, the publishing firm of which he was a partner. At the time he assigned the debt, Mark Twain owned approximately two-thirds interest in the company, and his wife was the company's largest creditor. By eventually paying his creditors in full even though they agreed to accept a 50 percent settlement, Mark Twain won international praise.

There were two major sources of Twain's indebtedness: the publishing business itself and his investment in the Paige typesetter machine. The publishing company, which Webster managed and Twain funded, achieved a few successes, most notably the publication of General Grant's *Memoirs*. But even before Webster, the husband of Mark Twain's niece,

sold his share of the business to Fred Hall, the typesetting investment was draining the firm's assets. The typesetting investment was ill-conceived from the outset. Acting on the claim of Paige that the machine would revolutionize the publishing industry, Twain sunk almost $200,000 into the machine, up to $3,000 a month, ever optimistic that its production would make him a millionaire.

On 18 April 1894 the bank foreclosed on its loan, and the firm's assets were assigned to Bainbridge Colby, a receiver, to determine assets, liabilities, and creditors. All but a few creditors agreed to accept fifty cents for every dollar of their claim. Olivia Langdon Clemens, the major creditor, never filed a claim, though she was given the copyrights to Twain's books. During this time Twain also relied on the financial advice of Henry H. Rogers, a Standard Oil executive, who negotiated Mrs. Clemens's preferred treatment with creditors.

Like his father before him, Mark Twain vowed to pay his remaining debts, citing a moral obligation to do so. He left on a worldwide speaking tour in August 1895, and the money from the tour and the royalties from *Following the Equator* (1897) enabled him to satisfy his creditors by 1898. But the tour forced him to leave his daughter Susy in Elmira, where she died suddenly on 18 August 1896. Mark Twain's bankruptcy chastened him and destroyed his lifelong dream of financial independence. Yet even after his experience with the typesetter, he still entertained the possibility of investing in equally risky enterprises.

J. Mark Baggett

BIBLIOGRAPHY

Clemens, Samuel L. *Mark Twain-Howells Letters: The Correspondence of Samuel L. Clemens and William D. Howells, 1872–1910*. Ed. Henry Nash Smith and William M. Gibson. 2 vols. Cambridge, Mass.: Harvard UP, 1960.

———. *Mark Twain's Autobiography*. Ed. Albert B. Paine. 2 vols. New York: Harper, 1924.

"Examining Mark Twain's Assets." New York *Times*, 12 July 1895, 9.

Leary, Lewis. "The Bankruptcy of Mark Twain." *Carrell* 9 (1968): 13–20.

Webster, Samuel Charles. *Mark Twain, Business Man.* Boston: Little, Brown, 1946.

See also: Business; Paige Typesetting Machine; Webster and Company, Charles L.

Barnum, Phineas Taylor
(1810–1891)

In 1835, the year Mark Twain was born, P.T. Barnum burst on the New York scene with a sensational hoax that signaled the advent of a new era in American public entertainment. For Barnum, a twenty-five-year-old Connecticut yankee, it all began with an exhibition of Joice Heth, a wizened Negro woman alleged to be 161 years old and to have been George Washington's nurse. This successful test of public credulity ended the struggles of a petty grocer and set Barnum on the road to fame and fortune. In 1842 he opened his American Museum in New York City, attracting a steady stream of spectators with a menagerie, a legitimate collection of curios, and a succession of fantastic freaks, including the incredible Fiji mermaid, the bearded lady, and two authentic giants. His most famous attraction was General Tom Thumb, a twenty-eight-inch midget discovered by Barnum in upper New York State and presented to the public as a recent arrival from England. Displaying his genius for promotion and advertisement, Barnum promoted Jenny Lind's concert tour of America in 1850 into a financial triumph. His last major venture, a circus billed as "The Greatest Show on Earth," opened in New York in 1871. Ten years later he united forces with his chief competitor and thereafter presented the circus as Barnum and Bailey, a show that featured the celebrated elephant Jumbo, advertised as the "Last Mastadon on Earth."

Barnum took great delight in Mark Twain's public lectures. For gilded splendor, Barnum's house at Bridgeport, Connecticut, surpassed Mark Twain's home at Hartford. After hearing a recording of Barnum's voice, Professor William Lyon Phelps called Barnum "the Shakespeare of Advertising and the greatest practical psychologist who ever lived." Remembered as "the fabulous showman," Barnum's success symbolized the spirit of America's Gilded Age. It is reasonable to assume that Mark Twain's flair for self-promotion drew inspiration from Barnum's example.

Tom Z. Parrish

BIBLIOGRAPHY

Barnum, Phineas Taylor. *Barnum's Own Story.* Ed. Waldo R. Browne. New York: Viking, 1927.

Bradford, Gamaliel. *Damaged Souls.* Boston: Houghton Mifflin, 1923.

Wallace, Irving. *The Fabulous Showman: The Life and Times of P.T. Barnum.* New York: Knopf, 1959.

Beach, Emeline

Daughter of Moses S. Beach and, like her father, a passenger on the *Quaker City* Holy Land excursion, Miss Emeline Beach became a friend of Samuel Clemens during the voyage. Later, when Mark Twain was revising his *Alta California* letters for publication in *Innocents Abroad* (1869), he appealed to Emeline Beach to "refresh his memory" on the "Old Masters" and their pictures. Beach replied, offering information on the various classical artists, and urging Clemens to use the utmost discretion in his handling of all material concerning art and artists.

Beverly David

BIBLIOGRAPHY

Booth, Bradford. "Mark Twain's Friendship with Emeline Beach." *American Literature* 19 (November 1947): 119–130.

Clemens, Samuel L. *Mark Twain's Letters, Volume 2 (1867–1868).* Ed. Harriet Elinor Smith and Richard Bucci. Berkeley: U of California P, 1990.

See also: Art; *Quaker City*

Beach, Moses S.

The editor of the New York *Sun*, Moses S. Beach was a fellow passenger on the *Quaker*

City excursion described by Mark Twain in *The Innocents Abroad* (1869). Besides being a tourist on the Holy Land cruise, Beach had hired a photographer, William James, to sail with the *Quaker City* and produce stereopticon slides of interesting scenes. Beach also had saved tourist-card photographs of the passengers. Many of these slides and cards provided images used as models by the illustrators for various prints in the pages of *Innocents Abroad*. Beach's portrait appears in the first edition (615).

Beverly David

BIBLIOGRAPHY

Clemens, Samuel L. *The Innocents Abroad*. Hartford, Conn.: American Publishing, 1869.

Hirst, Robert, and Brandt Rowles. "William E. James's Stereoptic Views of the *Quaker City* Excursion." *Mark Twain Journal* 22 (Spring 1984): 15–33.

See also: Illustrators; *Quaker City*

Beard, Daniel Carter
(1850–1941)

Now best known as a founder of the Boy Scouts of America, Daniel Carter Beard first came to know Mark Twain as the illustrator for *A Connecticut Yankee in King Arthur's Court* (1889). Born in Cincinnati, Ohio, son of the painter James Henry Beard, young Dan experienced the boisterous life of a frontier town and found the rigors of backwoods life essential to the strength of the American character. After graduating in civil engineering from Worrall's Academy in Covington, Kentucky, in 1869, Beard surveyed and prepared maps throughout the eastern United States for nine years. In 1878 he decided to follow an earlier inclination for drawing and joined his father and two brothers, James Carter Beard and Thomas Francis Beard, all popular illustrators in New York. Soon his illustrations and cartoons were appearing in *Cosmopolitan*, *Life*, *St. Nicholas*, and many of the widely circulated periodicals of the time. In New York he also began to write and illustrate a series of popular handicraft books about outdoor activities for boys, beginning with *What to Do and How to Do It: The American Boy's Handy Book* (1882).

Beard's illustrations for *Cosmopolitan* captured Twain's interest, and Beard was commissioned to illustrate *A Connecticut Yankee* in June of 1889. Twain was so delighted with the drawings that he gave Beard a free hand to interpret the text according to his own ideas, which were then under the influence of Henry George and his single-tax theories. Beard incorporated many prominent personalities of the period into his drawings, and in a quarter of them Beard either expanded on Twain's expressed thoughts or included ideas not found in the text at all. Since Twain enthusiastically approved every drawing in the novel, it should be read as a full collaboration between the author and artist. The pictures are as essential to an understanding of the work as are the words. Beard went on to illustrate other works by Twain, such as *The American Claimant* (1892), *The £1,000,000 Bank-Note* (1893), *Tom Sawyer Abroad* (1894), and *Following the Equator* (1897), but none inspired the collaborative magic that occurred with *A Connecticut Yankee*.

Beard wrote and illustrated his own utopian novel based on the theories of Henry George called *Moonblight* (1892). After the turn of the century he devoted most of his time to organizing youth development groups such as the Sons of Daniel Boone (1905) and the Boy Pioneers of America (1909), which merged with the Boy Scout movement in 1910. Through his columns for *Boys' Life* magazine, his boys' camps in Pennsylvania, and his public appearances dressed in buckskin, "Uncle Dan" became a folk hero in the popular mind. He remained close friends with Twain throughout his life and was proud to be known as "the Mark Twain of art." There is no substantial biography of Beard, but one can use with caution the anecdotal autobiography *Hardly a Man Is Now Alive* (1939) and the biography by Cyril Clemens and Carroll Sibley, *Uncle Dan* (1938).

M. Thomas Inge

BIBLIOGRAPHY

Beard, Daniel Carter. *Hardly a Man Is Now Alive: The Autobiography of Dan Beard.* New York: Doubleday, Doran, 1939. 334–350.

———. "Mark Twain, the Man, as Dan Beard Knew." *San Francisco Examiner,* 25 April 1910, 16.

Clemens, Cyril, and Carroll Sibley. *Uncle Dan: The Life Story of Dan Beard.* New York: Crowell, 1938.

See also: Connecticut Yankee in King Arthur's Court, A; Illustrators

Beecher, Henry Ward
(1813–1887)

During his tenure as pastor of the Plymouth (Congregational) Church in Brooklyn, New York (1847–1887), Henry Ward Beecher was perhaps the most influential clergyman on the American scene. As editor of the *Independent* and as prolific contributor to it and other religious periodicals, Beecher served a vast audience beyond the large congregation he quickly developed. His sermons and other papers regularly appeared in book form: *Star Papers, or Experiences of Art and Nature* (1855); *Sermons by Henry Ward Beecher* (2 vols., 1868); *The Life of Jesus the Christ* (2 vols., 1872, 1874); *Yale Lectures on Preaching* (1872–1874); *Evolution and Religion* (1885).

An oratorical style that mingled sentiment, humor, and passion was an apt vehicle for a subject matter that blended politics, current social issues, and a dulcified theology little resembling the staunch Calvinism of his father, Lyman Beecher. Initially moderate on abolition, he became a leader in the movement after the denomination endorsed it. He was also an advocate of Darwinian evolution at a time when most of his peers denounced it. Throughout his career he advocated the realization of God's purpose in love—love of God and of one's fellows.

Mark Twain met Beecher in Brooklyn (January 1868) immediately after the conclusion of the *Quaker City* cruise. (Beecher had been advertised as one of the attractions of the journey but had withdrawn just before sailing.) The older man advised Twain on his dealings with Elisha Bliss of the American Publishing Company, who had proposed that Twain make a book of his travel letters. When Twain became a resident of Nook Farm (October 1871) he also became a neighbor of two sisters and a half-sister of Beecher. The clergyman was a frequent visitor to the colony. When Beecher was tried in 1874 on a charge of adultery with Elizabeth Tilton, wife of a colleague, Twain was not convinced of Beecher's innocence despite the adjournment of the trial and exoneration by a panel of Congregational ministers subsequently convened by Beecher's church. Yet, at the time of Beecher's death Twain commended Joseph H. Twichell's sermon praising Beecher's life and work.

Lynn Altenbernd

BIBLIOGRAPHY

Abbott, Lyman. *Henry Ward Beecher.* Cambridge, Mass: Riverside P, 1904.

Beecher, Henry Ward. *Autobiographical Reminiscences of Henry Ward Beecher.* Ed. T.J. Ellinwood. New York: Frederick A. Stokes, 1898.

Clark, Clifford E. *Henry Ward Beecher: Spokesman for a Middle-Class America.* Urbana: U of Illinois P, 1978.

Hibben, Paxton. *Henry Ward Beecher: An American Portrait.* New York: Doran, 1927.

McLoughlin, William Gerald. *The Meaning of Henry Ward Beecher: An Essay on the Shifting Values of Mid-Victorian America, 1840–1870.* New York: Knopf, 1970.

Rourke, Constance. *Trumpets of Jubilee: Henry Ward Beecher, Harriet Beecher Stowe, Lyman Beecher, Horace Greeley, P.T. Barnum.* Intro. Kenneth S. Lynn. New York: Harcourt Brace, 1927.

See also: Clergy; Hooker, Isabella Beecher; Nook Farm; Stowe, Harriet Beecher

Beecher, Julia Jones
(1826–1905)

Frances Juliana Jones, known as Julia, married Thomas K. Beecher, the minister of The Park

Church, Elmira, New York, in 1857, after the death of his first wife, Julia's cousin, Olivia Day. The marriage was acknowledged as platonic, based on a kindred love for Day. Twain critically noted the relationship in a letter to Olivia Langdon, 17 May 1869. Working together in the church ministry, the Beechers developed a renowned Sunday school, which Livy joined in 1858. Beecher was an intimate friend of the Langdons. The Clemenses often visited her home near Quarry Farm.

Beecher was artistic, making rag baby dolls and peculiar creatures from twisted roots as fund raisers for missions. Twain named the creatures "jabberwoks" and served as auctioneer to sell them in Hartford. The Elmira College Mark Twain Archives houses three stones containing a contract written by Twain 2 July 1895 pledging apology should he meet Beecher in heaven and thus prove correct her belief in immortality.

Twain and Beecher were friends. Firm in her faith, the witty and intelligent Beecher relished challenging conversations with Twain.

Gretchen E. Sharlow

BIBLIOGRAPHY

Eastman, Annis F. *A Flower of Puritanism: Julia Jones Beecher*. Elmira, New York: Snyder, 1905.

Eastman, Max. *Enjoyment of Living*. New York: Harper, 1948.

Rugoff, Milton. *The Beechers: An American Family in the Nineteenth Century*. New York: Harper & Row, 1981.

Stowe, Lyman Beecher. *Saints, Sinners and Beechers*. New York: Blue Ribbon Books, 1934.

Taylor, Eva. *A History of The Park Church*. Elmira, New York: The Park Church, 1946.

See also: Beecher, Thomas Kinnicut; Park Church, The

Beecher, Lyman
(1775–1863)

An influential Congregationalist minister and theologian, Lyman Beecher fathered a remarkable set of children, many of whom Mark Twain knew well. Thomas Kinnicut Beecher

(1824–1900) was Olivia Langdon's pastor at The Park Church (Congregational) of Elmira, New York, and officiated at her marriage to Twain. Olivia Langdon's mother was a close friend of Isabella Beecher Hooker (1822–1907), and Olivia was friends with Isabella's daughter, Alice. Harriet Beecher Stowe (1811–1896) was Twain's neighbor at Nook Farm in Hartford, Connecticut. Beecher's thirteen children also included author and educator Catharine Beecher and the famous preacher Henry Ward Beecher. Twain's meeting Beecher's children marks his transition from western ruffian to East Coast literary lion.

Patricia Hunt

BIBLIOGRAPHY

Andrews, Kenneth R. *Nook Farm: Mark Twain's Hartford Circle*. Cambridge, Mass.: Harvard UP, 1950.

Paine, Albert Bigelow. *Mark Twain: A Biography*. 3 vols. New York: Harper, 1912.

See also: Beecher, Henry Ward; Beecher, Thomas Kinnicut; Nook Farm; Stowe, Harriet Beecher

Beecher, Thomas Kinnicut
(1824–1900)

From 1854 to 1900 Thomas Kinnicut Beecher was the minister of The Park Church (Congregational) in Elmira, New York. Beecher was an adviser, teacher, and close friend of the Langdon family. In unpublished dictation for his Autobiography, 1 March 1907, Twain declared Beecher "one of the best men" he had ever known (Microfilm Collection, Elmira College, #1800, MTP, Berkeley). Beecher was involved in the life of the entire community, active in school administration, politics, planning bridges, even providing everyday chores for the needy such as cutting wood and painting houses. After his death, he was lauded as Elmira's First Citizen, and the city erected a statue in his honor. Beecher distinguished himself by his independent nonsectarian approach to religion. He expressed progressive, sometimes controversial, ideas in a local weekly newspaper column, *Miscellany*, and in a collection of ecumenical lectures, *Our Seven Churches* (1870), dedicated to his mentor, Horace Bushnell. Along with the Reverend Joseph Twichell, Beecher officiated at the wedding of Samuel Clemens and Olivia Langdon, 2 February 1870. He and his wife Julia were with the party accompanying the newlyweds by train to their home in Buffalo, New York, the following evening. On 23 August 1896, it was Beecher who conducted the funeral of Olivia Susan Clemens in the Langdon home.

Beecher was a member of the famous and influential Lyman Beecher family. Like others in his celebrated family, Beecher was often characterized as brilliant, unconventional, and eccentric. He helped found an Elmira Academy of Sciences and corresponded with Darwin and other leading scientists. Twain's story "Monument to Adam," in *The $30,000 Bequest and Other Stories* (1917), recounts the 1879 hoax when Twain and Beecher responded in jest to the growing acceptance of Darwin's theory of evolution. Beecher chose to maintain his position at the Elmira church without a contract, on a monthly basis, preferring the title "teacher of the gospel" to "pastor." He often dressed in shabby work clothes with a distinctive cap, made for him by Susan Crane, and rode an oversized tricycle that he had designed for rough roads. He played baseball and billiards, brewed beer, and enjoyed the company of friends, including Twain, at Klapproth's Saloon. After the unorthodox Beecher had been expelled from the local ministerial union for moving services from the overcrowded church to the Opera House, Twain rallied to his defense in the Elmira *Weekly Advertiser*, 17 April 1869. Twain chided the "little congress of congregationless clergymen . . . who have crushed a famous BEECHER and reduced his audiences from fifteen hundred down to fourteen hundred and seventy-five in one fell blow!" In the July 1871 issue of the *American Publisher*, Twain humorously endorsed his plan for a larger

building with an article "The New Beecher Church."

Beecher designed and built his own house, which was near Twain's summer home, Quarry Farm, which Beecher had named. Twain respected Beecher as an eloquent preacher and enjoyed him as a neighbor, an interesting conversationalist, and an intimate friend.

Gretchen E. Sharlow

BIBLIOGRAPHY

Caskey, Marie. *Chariot of Fire: Religion and the Beecher Family*. New Haven, Conn.: Yale UP, 1978.

Eastman, Max. *Enjoyment of Living*. New York: Harper, 1948.

Rugoff, Milton. *The Beechers: An American Family in the Nineteenth Century*. New York: Harper & Row, 1981.

Stowe, Lyman Beecher. *Saints, Sinners and Beechers*. New York: Blue Ribbon Books, 1934.

Taylor, Eva. *A History of The Park Church*. Elmira: The Park Church, 1946.

See also: Clergy; Park Church, The

"Belated Russian Passport, The"

(1902)

Twain wrote "The Belated Russian Passport" during 1902 and published it in *Harper's Weekly* for 6 December 1902. The piece, of about 7,000 words, was subsequently reprinted in Harper's Uniform Edition and its successors, but not in the Stormfield Edition.

Alfred Parrish, lonesome and homesick in a Berlin beer saloon, is challenged by his lively American fellow-students to perk up and at least see St. Petersburg before he leaves Europe. Accosted by the "brisk and businesslike" Major Jackson, who urges him to reconsider his homeward journey and to start for the Russian metropolis forthwith, Parrish puts himself into the hands of the stranger. Soon he is not sure whether the man he has entrusted with his rail tickets and all his funds is a sharper or a lunatic.

Failing in efforts to secure a passport for Parrish, the oddly matched pair travel toward Russia. Employing a blend of trickery and effrontery, Jackson attempts to secure the passport at the frontier, then in St. Petersburg, then from the general of the secret police, and finally from the U.S. legation. The secretary there protests, "There's no way in the world of identifying him," but when Parrish cries out, "It's the last of earth for Alfred Parrish," the secretary relents and begins a line of questioning about Parrish's origins in New Haven. The crucial bit of evidence is a painting in his home that Parrish quotes his father as describing as "the hell-firedest nightmare he ever struck." "Saved!" cries the secretary; "*I* identify you; I've lived in the house, and I painted the picture myself."

The work is a slight sketch, apparently intended as a satire on bureaucracy and as a small-world story. Though it includes some amusing touches, such as the dependable frontier-humor device of a comic list cataloging the furnishings of a typical U.S. legation, it is marred by the anticlimactic ending, which gives the effect of a shaggy-dog story. William Dean Howells, writing from Kittery Point, Maine, on 27 September 1902, said, "This is great, but the goat's-tail ending was an awful thing to do to me: I did want it to go on so." Howells was characteristically generous.

Lynn Altenbernd

BIBLIOGRAPHY

Clemens, Samuel L. "The Belated Russian Passport." *Harper's Weekly* 46 (6 December 1902): 4–5, 8–9.

————. *Mark Twain-Howells Letters: The Correspondence of Samuel L. Clemens and William D. Howells, 1872–1910.* Ed. Henry Nash Smith and William M. Gibson. 2 vols. Cambridge, Mass: Harvard UP, 1960. 2:745–746.

Wilson, James D. *A Reader's Guide to the Short Stories of Mark Twain.* Boston: G.K. Hall, 1987.

Belgian Congo

Mark Twain never visited the Congo. The closest he came were his visits to Morocco and Egypt, related in *The Innocents Abroad* (1869), and Madagascar and South Africa, related in *Following the Equator* (1897). The Belgian Congo (now Zaire) is a land of over 900,000 square miles largely in the basin of the Congo River in central Africa. Twain's interest in the Congo was stimulated by the atrocities that King Leopold II of Belgium committed against the people of that region.

Playing one country against another, Leopold persuaded the Berlin Conference on Africa (1884–1885) to declare that this land be called the Congo Free State with King Leopold II as its sovereign ("Belgian Congo"). Under this license, granted by the white European and American powers, for twenty years Leopold exploited the wealth of the Congo and caused one of the most horrible persecutions in the history of the world.

To harvest the rubber, ivory, and minerals, the king sent European agents to the Congo, who in turn recruited black armies from hostile tribes to terrorize the natives into working. If the natives did not produce enough rubber, they were murdered, or their hands were cut off, or other atrocities were rained upon them. Although Leopold did not set out to slaughter and maim those blacks, he obviously cared more for the wealth than for the people, and he was responsible for the corrupt system that encouraged the sores to fester. An estimated 5 to 8 million blacks were slaughtered during Leopold's reign.

These horrors remained unknown outside of Africa for many years, but finally the stories began to leak out through missionaries and others. The growing world outrage finally came to a focus in the Congo Reform Association, founded by E.D. Morel in 1904.

When Morel asked Mark Twain to write something for the crusade, Twain was eager. His hatred for any kind of oppression had been growing since his youth, and his opposition to imperialism was well known. Both his bitterness and his powers of satire were now at their peak. Furthermore, he had already warmed up with an unpublished curse on Leopold and America called "Thanksgiving

Sentiment." He now wrote an invective satire, *King Leopold's Soliloquy,* in which the king reviews the horrors and condemns himself by his own defense. The article attacks Leopold personally for his crimes, the United States for endorsing the project, and the entire human race for ignoring the atrocities. Finding the article too severe for the magazines, Twain gave it to the Congo Reform Association, who printed it as a pamphlet in 1905.

Boosted by Twain's pamphlet, the Congo Reform Association was one of the forces that persuaded the Belgian parliament to wrest the Congo from the king. In 1908 the parliament annexed the region as a colony named the Belgian Congo.

Frank H. Leavell

BIBLIOGRAPHY

Clemens, Samuel L. *King Leopold's Soliloquy.* Berlin: Seven Seas, 1961.

Conrad, Joseph. *Heart of Darkness.* New York: Washington Square, 1967.

Giddings, Robert. "Mark Twain and *King* Leopold of the Belgians." *Mark Twain: A Sumptuous Variety.* Ed. Giddings. Totowa, N.J.: Barnes & Noble, 1985. 199–221.

Paine, Albert Bigelow. *Mark Twain: A Biography.* 3 vols. New York: Harper, 1912.

Slade, Ruth M. *King Leopold's Congo.* 1962; rpt. Westport, Conn.: Greenwood P, 1974.

See also: King Leopold's Soliloquy; Leopold II, King of the Belgians

Bellamy, Edward

(1850–1898)

American author Edward Bellamy was famous for his utopian novel *Looking Backward* (1888), which encouraged other utopian novels such as Howells's *A Traveller from Altruria* (1894). It also spawned a nationalist political movement linked loosely to Populism and influenced union activities and counter-Marxist movements of social reform in America well into the 1930s. Bellamy's other works include "Religion of Solidarity" (1873), *The Blindman's World and Other Stories* (1898), *Dr. Heidenhoff's Process* (1880), *Mrs. Ludington's Sister* (1884), and *Equality* (1897).

Bellamy was born in the industrial town of Chicopee Falls, Massachusetts, the son of a Baptist minister. His social conscience was his directive force. Although he passed the Massachusetts bar examination with distinction (1871), he closed his law office after only one case involving the eviction of a widow. Bellamy died of tuberculosis at forty-eight.

The nearly simultaneous publication of two utopian fictions, Mark Twain's *A Connecticut Yankee in King Arthur's Court* (1889) and Bellamy's *Looking Backward,* seems remarkable. Mark Twain conceived of *CY* in late 1884. Bellamy's idea came in the fall or winter of 1886. Mark Twain called *LB* "the latest and best of all the Bibles." There are startling affinities between the Bellamy and Twain works. Both involve time travel; Hank Morgan travels back to Arthurian England and Bellamy's Julian West to 2000 A.D. Both Twain and Bellamy were interested in the world of the somnolent and the notion of dual selves; hence, their heroes' methods of transporting through time. Both hated aristocracy and advocated social equalization through technology in their utopias. Mark Twain's optimism wavers in his inverse utopia, as does his concept of his own time as the perfect world. Bellamy's faith in progress is unequivocal. Universal equality will naturally evolve through industrialization premised on democratic principles.

The simultaneity of *CY* and *LB* defines a time of social turbulence in Gilded Age America when agrarian ideals and the ethos of democracy became difficult to reconcile with the prevailing social injustice.

Janet Gabler-Hover

BIBLIOGRAPHY

Bellamy, Edward. *The Blindman's World and Other Stories.* Boston: Houghton Mifflin, 1898.

———. *Looking Backward 2000–1887.* Ed. John L. Thomas. Cambridge, Mass: Harvard UP, 1967.

Bowman, Sylvia E. *Edward Bellamy.* Boston: Twayne, 1986.

Morgan, Arthur E. *Edward Bellamy.* New York: Columbia UP, 1944.

Smith, Henry Nash. *Mark Twain: The Development of a Writer.* Cambridge, Mass: Harvard UP, 1962.

See also: Connecticut Yankee in King Arthur's Court, A; Morgan, Hank; Technology, Mark Twain and

Bellows, Henry Whitney
(1814–1882)

Unitarian minister, author, and humanitarian, Henry Whitney Bellows founded the United States Sanitary Commission in 1861, organized to supervise and supply medical relief on Civil War battlefields (Wilbur 467–468). A popular and eloquent speaker, Bellows befriended Twain in 1864 while the author was reporting for San Francisco's *Daily Morning Call* and the minister was raising funds for the commission and preaching at the city's First Unitarian Church.

Bellows evidently attracted Twain with his wit and humor, which the minister considered necessary for the health of heart and mind (Clemens, *Letters* 308 n4). Twain also praised the minister for the genuineness of his Christianity, reporting about him favorably, even flatteringly, on occasion (Clemens, *Call* 67–68; 257–258).

Richard Gaughran

BIBLIOGRAPHY

Clemens, Samuel L. *Clemens of the "Call": Mark Twain in San Francisco.* Ed. Edgar M. Branch. Berkeley: U of California P, 1969.

———. *Mark Twain's Letters, Volume 1 (1853–1866).* Ed. Edgar M. Branch, Michael B. Frank, and Kenneth M. Sanderson. Berkeley: U of California P, 1988.

Wilbur, Earl Morse. *A History of Unitarianism.* Boston: Beacon P, 1945.

See also: Sanitary Commission

Berlin, Germany

The capital of the kingdom of Prussia and after 1871 also capital, cultural hub, and largest city of the German empire, with an 1890 population of nearly 2.5 million (including suburbs), Berlin was the Clemens family residence from 15 October 1891 until 1 March 1892. The family also visited Berlin for a fortnight in late May and early June 1892 en route to their summer sojourn in Bad Nauheim, and again briefly from 28 June to 1 July 1893. They settled first near the city center in a ground-floor flat at Koernerstrasse 7 that Olivia Clemens and her sister, Susan Crane, had rented on a brief house-hunting excursion while the Clemenses were in Marienbad. While Clemens was absent on business in New York and Hartford for six weeks (November–December 1891), Olivia discovered the neighborhood to be somewhat inelegant and unfashionable, if not disreputable. So, near the end of December 1891 the family moved to Hotel Royal, on Unter den Linden, for the remainder of their stay.

The elder Clemenses spent 4–12 January 1892 as guests of a Pastor Obermann at the health resort of Ilsenburg in the Harz Mountains, where, ironically, Clemens contracted influenza and bronchial pneumonia that kept him abed for a month after his return to the city and permanently damaged one of his lungs.

Already an international celebrity in 1891 whose works were widely read throughout Germany, especially after the publication of *A Tramp Abroad* (1880), Mark Twain was lionized during his winter in Berlin as he had not been in previous European sojourns. Sought after by newspaper interviewers and feted socially by the United States minister to the Hohenzollern court, William Walter Phelps, he had the opportunity to mingle with such luminaries of Germany's intellectual establishment as the physicist Hermann von Helmholtz (1821–1894), the historian Theodor Mommsen (1817–1903), and the pathologist Rudolf Virchow (1821–1902). While browsing in the Royal Library, Twain was permitted to peruse some of the manuscripts of Frederick the Great (1712–1786) and his sister, the Margravine of Bayreuth (1709–1758), and of the illustrious philosopher Arthur Schopenhauer (1788–1860), among others.

Twain gave two public readings in Berlin in mid-January 1892 at the Gewerbehaus and Y.M.C.A. Hall, respectively, and a third at the Congregational Chapel on 25 May 1892 when he was passing through the city. There is apparently no record of what he read at these performances.

He attended numerous public and cultural events, state dinners, and other society functions while in Berlin, but, socially speaking, the high point of Twain's sojourn occurred on 20 February 1892 at the home of his St. Louis-born cousin, Mollie Clemens von Versen, whose husband was a general in the Prussian army and member of the imperial general staff. Emperor Wilhelm II (1859–1941) had requested the von Versens to host a dinner party for him to meet the author privately and informally. Among a dozen other table guests were the emperor's brother Prince Heinrich, the imperial chamberlain Prince Radolin, Friedrich Rottenburg and Rudolf Lindau of the German foreign ministry, and several high-ranking military and naval officers. The after-dinner "smoking parialiament," as Twain called the postprandial beer and cigars, lasted until the emperor rose to leave at midnight. Perhaps it was because the emperor monopolized the conversation on this occasion, as well as his dismissal a year earlier of the "Iron Chancellor," Otto von Bismarck (1815–1898), whose political perspicacity Twain admired, that the author wrote Howells he thought Wilhelm II "a cockahoop sovereign."

Twain accomplished little writing in Berlin. In October 1891, preparing for a short trip to the United States, he spent three sleepless days and nights frantically translating Dr. Heinrich Hoffmann's German nursery classic, *Der Struwelpeter* (1842), in the vain hope of publishing it back home with Hoffmann's original illustrations as a Christmas gift book. It had to wait, however, until 1935 when Harper's posthumously published it as *Slovenly Peter*.

Shortly after his February dinner with the emperor, Twain finished "The German Chi-

cago," the last of six travel articles he had contracted to write at $1,000 apiece for the New York *Sun* and S.S. McClure's Syndicate. The implied comparison of Berlin with Chicago was apt since both cities had mushroomed from provincial towns to metropolises in less than two generations. Unlike older European capitals, Berlin had a sense of newness, energy, and modernity akin to what one felt in America's second city, and Twain dwelt on this atmosphere and other aspects he admired, stressing cleanliness, orderliness, and efficiency in his paean to this bustling German city at the confluence of the Spree and Havel rivers.

Two other essays from his nearly five months in Berlin remain unpublished in the Mark Twain Papers at Berkeley. One is a whimsical travel letter, "Koernerstrasse," satirizing the Clemenses' first place of residence in Berlin and its inhabitants that Olivia prevailed upon him not to publish. ("The German Chicago" was its substitute.) The other is a short serious article, "Postal Service," enviously praising the efficiency of Germany's postal system, especially Berlin's intracity pneumatic tube mail service (*Rohrpost*) and the system's willingness to invite and respond to complaints.

Carl Dolmetsch

BIBLIOGRAPHY

Clemens, Samuel L. "The German Chicago." *Literary Essays*. By Clemens. Vol. 24 of *The Writings of Mark Twain*. New York: Collier, 1918. 244–261.

———. *Mark Twain's Notebook.* Ed. Albert B. Paine. New York: Harper, 1935. 215–243.

———. *Mark Twain's Own Autobiography: The Chapters from the "North American Review."* Ed. Michael J. Kiskis. Madison: U of Wisconsin P, 1990.

———, trans. *Slovenly Peter.* New York: Harper, 1935.

Fisher, Henry W. *Abroad With Mark Twain and Eugene Field: Tales They Told to a Fellow Correspondent.* New York: Nicholas L. Brown, 1922.

Horwitz, Max. "Mark Twain in Berlin." Cited in *Mark Twain's German Critical Reception, 1875–1986.* Comp. J.C.B. Kinch. Westport, Conn.: Greenwood P, 1989. 9–10.

Paine, Albert Bigelow. *Mark Twain: A Biography.* 3 vols. New York: Harper, 1912.

Scott, Arthur L. *Mark Twain at Large.* Chicago: Henry Regnery, 1969.

See also: Austria(Austria-Hungary); Germany

Bermuda

This British colony in the North Atlantic ocean was a favorite vacation spot and retreat for Samuel Clemens in his later years. Clemens first visited Bermuda on his return from the Mediterranean, arriving on the *Quaker City* on 11 November 1867. The ship had planned to dock for a single day, but surprised by the beauty, serenity, and cleanliness of the island, and charmed by their warm reception, the passengers and crew extended their stay for a total of five days (Ganzel 289–293). Clemens's next visit to Bermuda came in May 1877. He was accompanied by his good friend and Hartford minister, Joseph H. Twichell; their experiences and conversations in the course of a walking tour of the island formed the basis of "Some Rambling Notes of an Idle Excursion" (1877). Although Clemens was not to return to Bermuda for thirty years, he made several trips between 1907 and 1910. His most extended stay came during the last six months of his life. With official biographer Albert B. Paine he visited Bermuda from 18 November to 20 December 1909, returning to New York for the Christmas holidays. Clemens was back in Bermuda in early January 1910, this time residing in the household of William H. Allen, the U.S. consul. There he remained until 12 April when Paine, summoned from New York, took the ailing and rapidly fading Clemens back home (Hill 249–261).

Clemens found much to celebrate in Bermuda. Its climate provided a welcome respite from the New York winter, and the warm salt air seemed to help his chronic bronchitis. Clemens was enamored of the island's natural beauty, its cleanliness, and the leisure of his life there. His only complaint, in fact, was that Bermuda was too clean; he is reported to have remarked that the spotless streets and sidewalks forced one to step aside to spit—which

made conversation disjointed. Much to his delight, Clemens found no newspapers in Bermuda, no train stations, no noise, and, best of all, no poverty. The local inhabitants were polite, orderly, and well-educated.

The most complete account of Clemens's experiences in Bermuda is given by Elizabeth Wallace in *Mark Twain and the Happy Island* (1914). Wallace was one of the several adopted granddaughters, christened "Angel Fish," with whom Clemens loved to converse and take long walks or rides in donkey carts around the island. Bermuda, like these new-found friendships, was a source of strength and serenity to the ailing author. To Wallace, Clemens wrote: "I think I could live here always and be contented. You go to Heaven if you want to—I'd druther stay here."

Scott H. Moore

BIBLIOGRAPHY

Ganzel, Dewey. *Mark Twain Abroad: The Cruise of the "Quaker City."* Chicago: U of Chicago P, 1968.

Hill, Hamlin. *Mark Twain: God's Fool.* New York: Harper & Row, 1973.

Paine, Albert Bigelow. *Mark Twain: A Biography.* 3 vols. New York: Harper, 1912.

Scott, Arthur L. *Mark Twain at Large.* Chicago: Henry Regnery, 1969.

Wallace, Elizabeth. *Mark Twain and the Happy Island.* Chicago: A.C. McClurg, 1914.

See also: Allen, Helen; Angel Fish and Aquarium Club; "Some Rambling Notes of an Idle Excursion"

Bible

Samuel Clemens was more faithful to the Bible than he meant to be, using it more often than any other book to spark his own writing. Unable to let go of the humor that resulted from juxtaposing the characters and situations depicted in the Bible with modern life, he exploited it shamelessly. He was also bothered by the Bible and the God it depicted. Until his death he kept his doubts largely private. As early as 1870, he expressed them in correspondence to his wife: "To trust the God of the Bible is to trust an irascible, vindictive, fierce and ever fickle and changeful master" (Paine 1:412). Only in the last twenty years of his career did he begin writing meditations voicing such concerns. Most of these meditations—essays and fiction—he left unpublished at his death.

Clemens's early training undoubtedly had something to do with his acquaintance with the Christian Scriptures. He absorbed the Bible stories during his Presbyterian upbringing and, by his own admission, read the "unexpurgated" Scriptures through in his teen years. This early experience with the Bible never fostered an uncritical love of it, however. Clemens carried on a lifelong battle with the Scriptures. While he occasionally showed affection for them, more often he criticized the Bible's distortions and its "upward of a thousand lies" (*Letters* 14). The distortions included the scriptural assessments of characters like Jacob and Jesus as well as its exaggeration about the virtues of the Promised Land. The lies included the assessment of man as "little lower than the angels" and the representation of God as good.

The Practical Approach

Though he did not credit Ralph Waldo Emerson with suggesting his practical approach to sacred literature or to the people and places depicted in it, Twain used the method Emerson had touted in "The American Scholar" (1837)—he looked through his own eyes rather than through those of tradition. For that reason his pictures of Noah, Jacob, Joshua, St. Paul, Jesus's brothers and sisters, Mary Magdalene, and a host of others are sometimes shocking but always fresh. He scrutinized Scripture through his own eyes; he examined tradition through his own eyes; and most of all, he looked at Palestine with his own eyes.

Nowhere is this method more evident than in written accounts of the *Quaker City* excursion. Now in the guise of Mark Twain, Clemens was one of sixty-five passengers aboard the ship *Quaker City* on a six-month

tour of Europe and the Holy Land in 1868. Readers of the *Alta California*, the New York *Herald*, and the New York *Tribune* saw Twain's dispatches during the journey. Others encountered somewhat milder salvos about biblical sites and characters when they read *Innocents Abroad* (1869), the book commemorating the trip. He used his own slangy style to evoke humor, wishing peace to Lot's wife's sediment, calling Nimrod a "brick," and observing that Joseph's sale to the Israelites came at prevailing rates with "ten percent off for cash," for example.

His assessments go further than applying nineteenth-century language to ancient characters or conditions. They inevitably show thought about matters never noticed by most casual readers of the Bible. For example, the Bible shows a preference for Jacob over Esau; however, Twain examines the biblical stories about the two and thumps for the moral superiority of Esau. He valued Esau's unconditional forgiveness of Jacob even after Jacob had stolen the birthright. Twain says that Jacob, "incapable of comprehending nobility of character" in his brother, "proved his own moral bankruptcy by trying to bribe Esau to get what Esau gave freely" (*IA* 355).

While Twain's unusual critical assessments touch a variety of biblical characters, often staining their reputations, there are no critical judgments of God or of Jesus in *Innocents Abroad*. Perhaps Twain believed the American public would not tolerate irreverence toward those figures. More likely by the time the book was being finished and proofed, he was struggling hard to make himself fit a more traditional Christian mold to please Olivia Langdon, whom he was to marry.

Biblical settings get special consideration in the book. However, they never live up to their billing. Twain remembered a Sunday school picture showing Joshua and the Israelite spies bringing back a bunch of grapes so heavy that several men bearing a single bunch on a pole between them were hardly able to carry the load. The Palestine Twain and the tourists saw had none of that bounty. What it did have was much dust and little arable land. "I must studiously and faithfully unlearn a great many things I have somehow absorbed concerning Palestine," he observed (*IA* 349).

He tried to help his readers unlearn as well, sometimes calling biblical descriptions of places into question. More often, however, he challenged the romantic descriptions of biblical sites given by writers of guidebooks. William C. Grimes and the author of *Life in the Holy Land* describe Genessaret in fetching terms. Twain disputes their descriptions, finding that "no ingenuity could make such a picture beautiful—to one's actual vision" (*IA* 367). If he robbed biblical characters and settings of the magic of romance in *Innocents Abroad*, Twain at least felt that he had given his readers a liberal dose of truth.

Even the most famous of Twain's works include occasional references to the Bible. Almost always they emphasize a practical approach to or observation about life rather than an acceptance of a romanticized view of Scripture. For example, *The Adventures of Tom Sawyer* (1876) contains the delightful memory verse episode. Tom wants to impress the new girl in town, Becky Thatcher. He contrives to trade his boy treasures for colored tickets showing the number of Bible verses memorized, and he presents enough of the tickets to win a Bible. He expects the presentation of the Bible in front of the entire Sunday school to be his moment of glory. He will impress Becky and her parents. That glory fades, however, when Tom is asked to demonstrate his Bible knowledge by naming the twelve disciples and the only biblical names he can think of are David and Goliath.

The emphasis in the story is on the practical use of the Bible to attain a goal. It also shows how the Calvinistic emphasis on the Bible can be distorted by a clever boy. This and other similar references by Twain offer little insight about Twain's attitude toward Scripture itself. Even when he preserves a romanticized view of the Scriptures, like Jim's story of King Solomon in *Adventures of Huckleberry Finn* (1885), he is interested in folk

belief, not in adopting such a view of the Scriptures himself.

The Philosophical Meditations

With the composition of "Bible Teaching and Religious Practice" in 1890, Twain began writing theoretical statements about biblical truth. While they allowed him to express what he had reasoned out but never said elsewhere, they also allowed him to say in a more direct way what he had implied in his early work.

In "Bible Teaching," the Scriptures are called a drugstore "made up of about equal portions of baleful and debilitating poisons, and healing and comforting medicines" (*E&E* 387). In a crude form of homeopathic medicine, the poisons have almost always been chosen as the prescription for human ills. The result is that the Christian religion and the Bible on which it depends have no solid record of improving the condition of humanity. Improvement has only come by practical action, ignoring biblical teaching. Twain offers two examples, slavery and witchcraft. The faithful, citing biblical teaching, kept both alive for centuries. Banishing both slavery and the belief in witchcraft was a practical, not a religious, move.

Twain's pessimism about the Bible in the 1890s and after was not merely theoretical. It was personal. In that regard, it was fundamentally different from his earlier skeptical observations. Perhaps he had realized that he was not immortal or invincible. Mired in the financing of the Paige typesetter and the ownership of a publishing business on its way down, he was, like Adam, beginning to taste defeat. The deaths of family members in the last two decades of his life only added to the pessimism. The God of the Old Testament, that irascible and vengeful creature, became for Twain the real God. He existed and in His existence cared little for man except to torture him. The culmination of this pessimism came in the dialogue *What Is Man?* (1906). While Twain decreed that most of his work attacking biblical truth or religious belief not be published during his lifetime, this piece, years in preparation, he brought out himself in an anonymous edition of 250 copies in 1906 (*What Is Man?* 14). That he was the author was revealed two days after his death in 1910.

Even the essay's title is dependent on the Bible. The question is posed at least three times in Scripture: Job 7:17, 15:14, and Psalms 144:3. In each case, the writer is astounded that man, of such small significance, demands God's attention. Agreeing that man is of small significance, Twain preaches that the human is a machine of limited capabilities. "He is moved, directed, COMMANDED, by exterior influences—*solely*. He *originates nothing*, himself" (*What Is Man?* 128). Adam, unable to invent anything, only gained the idea that it was immodest to go naked from eating the apple (*What Is Man?* 130). God's culpability in this affair is implied. In addition, the essay deals with issues of free will and the nature of instinct and thought as well. Portions of the dialogue Twain rejected for publication dealt with God directly and with the Moral Sense. In that segment about God Twain claims that knowledge of this Being comes by observing His deeds in persons, nature, and, likely, in "His Book" (*What Is Man?* 477). God's goodness is an attribute the Old Man in the dialogue cannot be persuaded exists.

The four mysterious stranger manuscripts, left unpublished at Twain's death, confirm what his nonfictional investigations of morality, sin, suffering, and death meant. A young Satan, an unfallen relative of the fallen angel, discloses secrets of the universe. Among them are mankind's insignificance, the damning nature of the Moral Sense, and God's vengeful character. Even the most exciting of the manuscripts, "No. 44, The Mysterious Stranger," seems more an illustration of the author's philosophical position than an exciting fiction.

Biblical Images

In *Mark Twain and the Bible* Allison Ensor maintains there are three significant biblical images Twain uses to project himself and his

ideas: the prodigal son; the Fall; and Noah and the Flood. Each has special significance in the Twain corpus (Ensor 29–72).

An image cultivated assiduously through the middle of Twain's career is that of the prodigal son. The returning son, guilty of waste and riotous living, can be forgiven all by those who love him. It was an image Twain applied to himself and, according to some, one that helped give Tom Sawyer and Huck Finn their charm. How did Twain apply the image to himself? In letters both to Olivia Langdon before their marriage and Mary Mason Fairbanks, he adopted the role of the prodigal son, returning to the fold. In one letter to Fairbanks on 17 June 1868 he closes with "Your returning Prodigal." The letter also includes the phrase "the Prodigal in a far country chasing of husks."

The first chapters of Genesis were never far from Twain's consideration. Adam was, by all accounts, his favorite biblical character. Twain could identify with a person who had inhabited paradise without understanding it and who understood neither the reason for nor the necessity of banishment from paradise when it came. In the 1870s the humorist proposed building a monument in Elmira, New York, to his venerable ancestor. He presented that idea again in a speech in the 1880s. The stone was never raised, and Twain's lasting memorials to Adam were the sketches he penned about him after 1890. These fictional meditations mixed the kind of good-humored jabbing at biblical material found as early as the *Quaker City* excursion with more probing questions about life, death, and morality.

Adam's Diary (1893) first appeared in *The Niagara Book*, a souvenir of the Buffalo World's Fair. In 1904 Twain published it as a book. In some versions of the *Diary*, Twain embellishes the biblical tale about the first family by setting Eden in the United States with Niagara Falls as part of the garden. Adam complains about his wife's naming the animals before he gets an opportunity to do so. He accepts the view, promulgated by some biblical interpreters, that the animals ate only plants until after the Fall, until death had been introduced into the world. Indeed, Eve eats of the forbidden fruit partly because she believes the animals' diet will be better if they can have meat. A 1905 composition, *Eve's Diary*, is filled with Adam's growing affection for Eve and with her attraction to the Brontosaurus.

In *Europe and Elsewhere* (1923) Albert Bigelow Paine, Twain's literary executor, included several sketches in which the Adam family played a part: "Eve Speaks," "Adam's Soliloquy," and "That Day in Eden." "That Day in Eden" recounts the Fall and the conditions preceding it as told by Satan. He is no villain in this piece but a kind soul, pitying a naive Eve who understands neither the curse of gaining the Moral Sense nor that of death. In the Genesis account God tells the first couple that even touching the fruit of the Tree of the Knowledge of Good and Evil will bring death. The serpent, wily messenger of evil, contradicts God, telling Eve she will not die and tempting her further by telling her that eating of the fruit will make her like God, knowing good and evil.

Twain introduces a number of changes in "That Day in Eden." Satan, not a serpent, appears in the garden. He is not a tempter but a messenger trying to get Eve to avert the disasters eating the fruit will bring. Unlike the serpent, Satan believes that eating the forbidden tree will bring death; and he knows that death is not desirable. The problem is that he cannot convey that message to Eve, though he tries. God has made her without experience of death and therefore unable to understand it. He has also made her without morals or the necessity of them, so she cannot understand what the Tree of the Knowledge of Good and Evil will do to her and her descendants and why it will be bad. She does not eat of the forbidden tree because she has an overwhelming desire to be like God but because she has curiosity. She does not know what the Moral Sense is like and can only find out by acquiring it.

The twist in Twain's thinking is that he takes the Bible quite seriously in some re-

spects: Adam and Eve existed; they ate of the forbidden fruit; and their difficulties as well as those of their ancestors dated from that act. He implies in this piece what he says explicitly in "Letters from the Earth" (1962): God was at fault for the difficulty in Eden. He made Adam and Eve unable to understand the consequences of their actions, and since they could not understand, it was churlish of Him to punish them for the fault. Punish them He did, however. Satan accused God of demanding that His creatures forgive each other "unto seventy times seven" while He Himself failed to forgive Adam and Eve their first indiscretion. He lived up to His name in the Old Testament as a vengeful God, and He punished them as He has continued to punish untold generations of the human race ever since for this single offense.

Because mankind continues to suffer and God seems not to care, Twain concludes that man is an unimportant part of creation. In "The Damned Human Race" (1962), while overtly saying that the earth was made for man, Twain quietly shows that man was at most an afterthought. The humorist-turned-theologian argues that since God pronounced His creation "good," most people feel bound to agree with Him. Our words do agree, but we find ourselves eliminating parts of that creation—the flies and fleas, for example—showing that we, like Twain himself, neither believe nor act as though the creation or the creator is good.

Noah represents the one who has left a world behind and who must make a new, less impressive start. Throughout his career, Twain at times felt that, like Noah, he was the only one who had escaped to tell the tale. From an article written for the Buffalo *Express* under the signature "Hy Slocum" to "About All Kinds of Ships" and "Letters from the Earth," Noah claims a spot in Twain's thinking that no other character could have fit. How does one begin again when his world has been emptied of all that is meaningful?

Pervasive Influence

The Bible was a pervasive influence on Mark Twain's work. Critics have disagreed about whether the writer's style unconsciously preserves the cadence and rhythm of the King James Version of the Scriptures. Ensor and DeLancey Ferguson doubt the style owes much to the Bible; Paine and Edward Wagenknecht find it the source of Twain's style. On the other hand, Stanley Brodwin establishes Twain's reliance on the American preacher for his speaking style, and the preacher's reliance on the English Bible, and particularly on the prophets, is commonly accepted.

No matter how the critics decide this issue of style, the fact remains that Mark Twain's work begins and ends with a consideration of biblical concerns. Twain's argument with the Scriptures attests both to his fun-loving nature and to his concern about philosophical issues facing mankind.

David O. Tomlinson

BIBLIOGRAPHY

Brodwin, Stanley. "Mark Twain in the Pulpit: The Theological Comedy of *Huckleberry Finn*." *One Hundred Years of "Huckleberry Finn."* Ed. Robert Sattelmeyer and J. Donald Crowley. Columbia: U of Missouri P, 1985. 371–385.

———. "The Theology of Mark Twain: Banished Adam and the Bible." *Critical Essays on Mark Twain, 1910–1980*. Ed. Louis J. Budd. Boston: G.K. Hall, 1983. 176–193.

Clemens, Samuel L. *Europe and Elsewhere*. New York: Harper, 1923.

———. *The Innocents Abroad*. New York: New American Library, 1966.

———. *Letters from the Earth*. Ed. Bernard DeVoto. New York: Harper & Row, 1962.

———. *Mark Twain's Mysterious Stranger Manuscripts*. Ed. William M. Gibson. Berkeley: U of California P, 1969.

———. *"What Is Man?" and Other Philosophical Writings*. Ed. Paul Baender. Berkeley: U of California P, 1973.

Ensor, Allison. *Mark Twain and the Bible*. Lexington: UP of Kentucky, 1969.

Hays, John Q. *Mark Twain and Religion: A Mirror of American Eclecticism*. Ed. Fred A. Rodewald. New York: Peter Lang, 1989.

Paine, Albert Bigelow. *Mark Twain: A Biography*. 3 vols. New York: Harper, 1912.

See also: Angelo and Luigi (Cappello); Calvinism; "Eve's Diary"; "Extracts from Adam's Diary"; God; *Letters from the Earth*; Religion

"Bible Teaching and Religious Practice"
(1923)

Twain compares the Christian Bible with a drug store: "Its contents remain the same, but the medical practice changes." He maintains that Christian beliefs, based on the Bible, gradually change over the centuries, the harsher ones being replaced by more enlightened positions, while the Bible itself does not change. Continuing the medical analogy, Twain argues that it is the patient rather than the physician who institutes the change; eventually the physician accepts it in order to be able to continue his practice.

Several examples are cited. For example, Christianity originally preached hell and damnation and approved of slavery and of the persecution of witches, basing its views on biblical texts. With the passage of time the church eventually reversed itself, emphasizing love and compassion, opposing slavery, and recognizing that witches never existed.

Allison R. Ensor

See also: Bible; Religion

Bibliographies

There are two broad categories of bibliographical tools available to the researcher interested in Mark Twain: bibliographies of primary documents (i.e., books, stories, essays, sketches, speeches, letters, etc.) written by Samuel Clemens; and listings, annotations, and evaluations of secondary scholarship concerned with Clemens and his writings.

In the first category the starting point is Merle Johnson's *A Bibliography of the Works of Mark Twain* (1935), to be supplemented by the other reference sources cited below. Virtually every year new Mark Twain material surfaces: previously unpublished letters, neglected newspaper sketches, manuscripts suppressed or thought lost. Major posthumously published works—both complete and fragmentary—have first seen print since Johnson's pioneering bibliography. Most notable among these are Bernard DeVoto's edition of *Letters from the Earth* (1962) and the numerous volumes published by the Mark Twain Project. Indeed, one is reminded of Mark Twain's 1893 story "Is He Living or Is He Dead?" in which he tells of a hoax perpetrated by four French artists who spread the rumor that one of their number is dead, thus inflating his reputation and the value of his work. Perhaps Mark Twain, like Francois Millet, is alive out there somewhere cranking out the primary materials that feed the Mark Twain industry and add to his legendary status.

There are several significant collections of Mark Twain manuscript material open to inspection by researchers. A general guide to the major repositories is J. Albert Robbins, *American Literary Manuscripts* (rev. ed., Athens: U of Georgia P, 1977). Several of the collections have published descriptive listings of their specialized holdings: Lucile Adams, *"Huckleberry Finn": A Descriptive Bibliography of the "Huckleberry Finn" Collection at the Buffalo Public Library* (published by the Buffalo (N.Y.) Public Library, 1950); William M. McBride, *Mark Twain: A Bibliography of the Collections of the Mark Twain Memorial and the Stowe-Day Foundation* (Hartford, Conn.: McBride, 1984); Alan Simpson, *Mark Twain Goes Back to Vassar* (Poughkeepsie, N.Y.: Vassar College, 1977). Alan Gribben's two volume *Mark Twain's Library: A Reconstruction* (Boston: G.K. Hall, 1980) is an invaluable guide to Mark Twain's reading, the marginal comments he recorded in his books, and the present location of those books.

The indispensable volume in the second category is Thomas A. Tenney's *Mark Twain: A Reference Guide* (1977), an annotated listing, by year, of virtually everything written about Samuel L. Clemens. The problem with any bibliography or checklist of secondary material is that it is dated as soon as it is compiled. To keep current, the researcher must peruse a few annual publications. From 1977 to 1983 Tenney published annual supplements to his reference guide in the journal *American Literary Realism*; since 1984 these supplements have appeared in the *Mark Twain Circular*. Another very useful source is *American Literary Scholarship: An Annual*, published by Duke University Press since 1963. Each annual volume in this series devotes a chapter to a review of Mark Twain scholarship; the reviews, written over the years by such distinguished and seasoned Mark Twain scholars as John C. Gerber, Louis J. Budd, Hamlin Hill, and Robert Sattelmeyer, provide an authoritative analysis of the state of Mark Twain studies. More comprehensive, though not annotated or evaluative, is the *International Bibliography of Books and Articles on the Modern Languages and Literatures*; published annually by the Modern Language Association, this bibliography includes doctoral dissertations and materials published outside the United States. Other current listings of scholarship appear in *American Literature* and in the "Checklist of Scholarship on Southern Literature" that is included annually in the spring issue of the *Mississippi Quarterly*. The *Mark Twain Circular*, published quarterly by the Mark Twain Circle of America, offers reviews of recent books and articles about Mark Twain, and contains the most up-to-date announcements of interest to the Mark Twain enthusiast. Perhaps the most current of all sources of information about new books on Mark Twain are the many publishers' advertisements that fill the annual convention issue (November) of *PMLA*.

The bibliography of bibliographies that follows offers a comprehensive sampling of research materials available in most academic libraries.

James D. Wilson

BIBLIOGRAPHY

Primary

Benson, Ivan. "Periodical Bibliography: Bibliography of the Writings of Mark Twain in the Newspapers and Magazines of Nevada and California, 1861–1866." *Mark Twain's Western Years.* By Benson. Stanford, Calif.: Stanford UP, 1938. 165–174.

Blanck, Jacob. *Bibliography of American Literature.* Vol. 2. New Haven, Conn.: Yale UP, 1957. 173–254.

Branch, Edgar M. "A Chronological Bibliography of the Writings of Samuel Clemens to June 8, 1867." *American Literature* 18 (May 1946): 104–159.

Brashear, Minnie M. "Mark Twain's Juvenilia." *American Literature* 2 (March 1930): 25–53.

Budd, Louis J. "A Listing of and Selection from Newspaper and Magazine Interviews with Samuel L. Clemens, 1874–1910." *American Literary Realism* 10 (Winter 1977): i–100.

Cooley, John. "A Calendar of Letters." *Mark Twain's Aquarium: The Samuel Clemens-Angelfish Correspondence 1905–1910.* By Clemens. Ed. Cooley. Athens: U of Georgia P, 1991. 285–293.

Fatout, Paul. "A Chronology." *Mark Twain Speaking.* By Clemens. Ed. Fatout. Iowa City: U of Iowa P, 1976. 647–680.

Johnson, Merle D. *A Bibliography of the Works of Mark Twain, Samuel Langhorne Clemens: A List of First Editions in Book Form and of First Printings in Periodicals and Occasional Publications of His Various Literary Activities.* Rev. ed. New York: Harper, 1935.

Kiskis, Michael J. "Appendix B: Mark Twain's Experiments in Autobiography"; "Appendix C: The Editions and the Chronology of Composition." *Mark Twain's Own Autobiography: The Chapters from the "North American Review."* By Clemens. Ed. Kiskis. Madison: U of Wisconsin P, 1990. 253–257.

Machlis, Paul, ed. *Union Catalog of Clemens Letters.* Berkeley: U of California P, 1986.

McCullough, Joseph B. "A Listing of Mark Twain's Contributions to the *Buffalo Express,* 1869–1871." *American Literary Realism* 5 (Winter 1972): 61–70.

Mobley, Lawrence E. "Mark Twain and the *Golden Era.*" *Publications of the Bibliographical Society of America* 58.1 (1964): 8–23.

Smith, Henry Nash, ed. *Mark Twain of the "Enterprise": Newspaper Articles and Other Documents, 1862–1864.* Berkeley: U of California P, 1957. 209–234.

Secondary

Andrews, William L., and Jack D. Wages. "Southern Literary Culture: 1969–1975." *Mississippi Quarterly* 32 (1979): 33–42.

Asselineau, Roger. *The Literary Reputation of Mark Twain from 1910–1950: A Critical Essay and a Bibliography.* Paris: Didier, 1954. 67–226.

Beebe, Maurice, and John Feaster. "Criticism of Mark Twain: A Selected Checklist." *Modern Fiction Studies* 14.1 (Spring 1968): 93–139.

Branch, Edgar M. "Mark Twain Scholarship: Two Decades." *"Adventures of Huckleberry Finn" with Abstracts of Twenty Years of Criticism.* Ed. James Bowen and Richard VanDerBeets. Glenview, Ill.: Scott, Foresman, 1970. 344–349.

Budd, Louis J. "Samuel Langhorne Clemens (1835–1910)." *A Bibliographical Guide to the Study of Southern Literature.* Ed. Louis D. Rubin, Jr. Baton Rouge: Louisiana State UP, 1969. 175–179.

Clark, Henry Hayden, J.C. Mathews, and Howard G. Baetzhold. "Mark Twain." *Eight American Authors: A Review of Research and Criticism.* Ed. James Woodress. New York: Norton, 1971. 273–320.

Consigio, Carla. "Nota bibliografica su la fortuna di Mark Twain in Italia." *Studi Americani* 4 (1958): 198–208.

Dolmetsch, Carl. "Huck Finn's First Century: A Bibliographical Survey." *American Studies International* 22.2 (1984): 79–121.

Gerstenberger, Donna, and George Hendrick. *The American Novel, 1789–1959. A Checklist of Twentieth Century Criticism.* Denver: Swallow, 1961. 236–250.

Gribben, Alan. "Removing Mark Twain's Mask: A Decade of Criticism and Scholarship." *Emerson Society Quarterly* 26.2–3 (1980): 100–108, 149–171.

Hemminghaus, Edgar Hugo. *Mark Twain in Germany.* New York: Columbia UP, 1939. 147–164.

Hill, Hamlin. "Who Killed Mark Twain?" *American Literary Realism* 7 (1974): 119–124.

Kiell, Norman. *Psychoanalysis, Psychology, and Literature: A Bibliography.* Metuchen, N.J.: Scarecrow P, 1982.

Kinch, J.C.B. *Mark Twain's German Critical Reception 1875–1986.* Westport, Conn.: Greenwood P, 1989.

Kirby, David K. *American Fiction to 1900: A Guide to Information Sources.* Detroit: Gale Research, 1975. 59–70.

Leary, Lewis. *Articles on American Literature 1900–1950.* Durham, N.C.: Duke UP, 1954. 43–55.

Leary, Lewis, and John Auchard. *Articles on American Literature, 1950–1967.* Durham, N.C.: Duke UP, 1970. 56–77.

————. *Articles on American Literature, 1968–1975.* Durham, N.C.: Duke UP, 1978. 72–86.

Long, E. Hudson. *Mark Twain Handbook.* New York: Hendricks House, 1957.

Long, E. Hudson, and J.R. LeMaster. *The New Mark Twain Handbook.* New York: Garland, 1985.

Oggel, L. Terry, and William Nelles. *Index to Volumes 1–21 of the "Mark Twain Journal" 1936–1983 (formerly "Mark Twain Quarterly" 1936–1953).* Special issue. *Mark Twain Journal* (1985): i–28.

Rodney, Robert M. *Mark Twain International: A Bibliography and Interpretation of His Worldwide Popularity.* Westport, Conn.: Greenwood P, 1982.

Taylor, Paul. "Selected Bibliography of Criticism 1968–1983." *One Hundred Years of "Huckleberry Finn": The Boy, His Book, and American Culture.* Ed. Robert Sattelmeyer and J. Donald Crowley. Columbia: U of Missouri P, 1985. 405–417.

Tenney, Thomas A. "An Annotated Checklist of Criticism on *Adventures of Huckleberry Finn,* 1884–1984." *Huck Finn Among the Critics: A Centennial Selection.* Ed. M. Thomas Inge. Frederick, Md.: University Publications of America, 1985. 317–465.

————. *Mark Twain: A Reference Guide.* Boston: G.K. Hall, 1977.

Williams, Jerry T., ed. *Southern Literature 1968–1975: A Checklist of Scholarship.* Boston: G.K. Hall, 1978. 57–78.

Wilson, James D. *A Reader's Guide to the Short Stories of Mark Twain.* Boston: G.K. Hall, 1987.

See also: Biographers; Comics; Correspondence; Editions; Illustrators; Journals; Manuscript Collections; Mark Twain Papers; Mark Twain Project; Media Interpretations; Scholarship, Trends in Mark Twain

Bierce, Ambrose
(1842–1914?)

Ambrose Bierce, Civil War soldier, journalist, and writer of fiction, essays, fables, satires, epigrams, and verse, is most recognized for his short stories. Not only did he contribute to the development of American short stories with a technique that M.E. Grenander calls "ironical terror," but he was also instrumental in the development of the German short story. Once judged by traditional critical standards as a personality, a failed realist or naturalist in his time, Bierce actually established aesthetic standards of language and literature that move toward the modern. Bierce's fiction offers the critic today the opportunity to study him as an experimentalist in the dislocation of linear plot lines and in the characterization of perceptions of time and point of view. He practiced an invective type of journalism and put the "real war" in which he had fought into his columns and later in a collection titled *In the Midst of Life—Tales of Soldiers and Civilians* (1898). A cynic with a mordant sense of humor and a fierce need to express the truth of the human condition, Bierce mastered the art of witty epigrams in *The Devil's Dictionary* (1906) and the gothic treatment of insanity and the supernatural in *Can Such Things Be?* (1893).

Born in Ohio, Bierce, as a youth of nineteen without formal education and with a mind already formed by wide reading, volunteered and served throughout the Civil War, discovering historical experience to be an exciting as well as a horrible highlight of his life. A freelance journalist in San Francisco until 1872, he married Mary Eleanor Day, daughter of a Nevada miner; he then went to London, where between 1872 and 1877 he published three books and continued his friendship with fellow journalist Mark Twain as a member of the famous White Friars' Club. Back in San Francisco between 1877 and 1896, Bierce wrote the column "Prattle" for the *Argonaut,* the *WASP,* and the San Francisco *Examiner* in which some of his war stories appeared along with his comically invective writing. His short stories of the 1880s, rejected by magazine editors as "revolting," were published as *Tales of Soldiers and Civilians* (1892) and *Can Such Things Be?* (1893). Between 1909 and 1912 he collected and had his works published in twelve volumes, an effort that is disorganized and incomplete. A war correspondent in 1896 and again in 1914, Bierce disappeared in Mexico in the latter year.

Ambrose Bierce's humor was in the mainstream of American humor although his humor had classical and satirical roots. His writings are filled with epigrams that, because of their civilized wit and satiric intensity, meant to abuse their object, are similar to but better than Mark Twain's aphorisms. Two of his short stories—"An Occurrence at Owl Creek Bridge" and "Parker Adderson, Philosopher"—have been made into films. "Moxon's Master" and "The Man and the Snake" show his skepticism about the self-affirming propositions of science as well as anticipate computers and robots. Full critical assessment of Bierce's writings still awaits a definitive and annotated edition of his stories, as complete a collection of his letters as possible, and publication of more of his journalistic work.

Charlotte S. McClure

BIBLIOGRAPHY

Bierce, Ambrose. *Can Such Things Be?* New York: Cassell, 1893.

———. *The Collected Works of Ambrose Bierce, 1909–1912.* 12 vols. New York: Neale, 1909–1912.

———. *The Cynic's Word Book.* New York: Doubleday, Page, 1906.

———. *In the Midst of Life; Tales of Soldiers and Civilians.* New York: Putnam, 1898.

———. *The Letters of Ambrose Bierce.* Ed. Bertha Clark Pope. San Francisco: Book Club of California, 1922.

———. *Skepticism and Dissent: Selected Journalism from 1898–1901.* Ed. Lawrence I. Berkove. Ann Arbor, Mich.: Delmas, 1980.

Davidson, Cathy N. *Critical Essays on Ambrose Bierce.* Boston: G.K. Hall, 1982.

———. *The Experimental Fictions of Ambrose Bierce: Structuring the Ineffable.* Lincoln: U of Nebraska P, 1984.

Grenander, M.E. *Ambrose Bierce.* Boston: Twayne, 1971.

McWilliams, Carey. *Ambrose Bierce: A Biography.* New York: Albert and Charles Boni, 1929.

Billings, Josh
(1818–1885)

Among the literary comedians Josh Billings (pen name of Henry Wheeler Shaw) was the major "Crackerbox philosopher." His forte, both in his essays and his platform lectures, was the witty, pithy aphorism. Much like Twain's early success with "The Celebrated Jumping Frog of Calaveras County" (1865), Billings rode to fame on the coattails of his "Essa on the Mule" (1864), a piece making use of Billings's characteristic comic misspellings and grammatical improprieties. His major books of essays and sayings are *Josh Billings, Hiz Sayings* (1865), *Josh Billings on Ice* (1868), and *Everybody's Friend* (1874). From 1869 to 1879 he produced the famous *Josh Billings' Old Farmer's Allminax,* which became one of the most popular publications in America at the time. Billings's first pseudonym was "Efrem Billings" (from 1859 into the early 1860s), and when contributing to the *Century Magazine* (beginning in 1884), he used the name "Uncle Esek."

Billings was born in Lanesboro, Massachusetts, and educated at Hamilton College in Clinton, New York. His father was a Massachusetts legislator and U.S. congressman. Billings married Zilpha Bradford in 1845, a marriage that produced two daughters. Before he became a literary man at age forty-five, he worked as farmer, auctioneer, coal mine operator, alderman, real estate agent, and steamboatman. It was in the 1860s that his short comic essays and witty sayings began to attract attention in regional newspapers. Artemus Ward was instrumental in getting *Josh Billings, Hiz Sayings* into print in 1865, and that book launched a literary career that consisted of eight more books, two major columns (the most famous being for the *New York Weekly* from 1867 to 1885), the popular *Allminax,* and one of the most successful comic lecturing routines of the nineteenth century.

Billings and Mark Twain met on the lecture circuit in 1869 and often passed time together, usually in company with Petroleum V. Nasby (David Ross Locke). Billings frequently mentioned Twain in his writings and lectures, usually in a spirit of playfulness but with obvious admiration. Shaw's art was closest to Twain's in the use of the aphorism, the finely honed sayings that became Billings's trademark and that Twain occasionally borrowed and fashioned as his own. Billings's lectures and essays often consisted of strings of aphorisms either woven around a central theme or rambling and diverse. Using the phonetic spellings and other verbal tricks of the literary comedians, he addressed a host of topics from animal life, to human types, to morality, to personal and social foibles of the human race. In the tradition of the crackerbox philosopher he commented on practically everything. His sayings were fresh and surprising in their turns of phrase, often conveying deep wisdom.

Billings is seen by modern readers largely as a literary curiosity, mainly because of the misspellings and other verbal tricks. Nevertheless, many of his essays still read well, his aphorisms are enjoyable, and the burlesque *Allminax* is informative and entertaining.

David B. Kesterson

BIBLIOGRAPHY

Billings, Josh. *The Complete Works of Josh Billings.* New York: G.W. Dillingham, 1888.

Clemens, Cyril. *Josh Billings, Yankee Humorist.* Webster Groves, Mo.: International Mark Twain Society, 1932.

Jones, Joseph. "Josh Billings: Some Yankee Notions on Humor." *Studies in English.* Austin: U of Texas P, 1943. 148–161.

Kesterson, David B. *Josh Billings.* New York: Twayne, 1973.

———. "The Mark Twain-Josh Billings Friendship." *Mark Twain Journal* 18 (Winter 1975–1976): 5–9.

See also: Aphorisms; Literary Comedians

Biographers
(1899–1991)

With characteristic exaggeration Mark Twain once observed that all his works were "autobiographies" (Clemens xxvii). Despite, or perhaps because of, the presence of the life in the writings, scholars have repeatedly attempted to capture the life of Samuel Clemens, the man who was Mark Twain.

Biographical commentaries on Clemens are too numerous to treat comprehensively. (A useful guide is *The Mark Twain Handbook,*

supplemented by the annual review of Twain scholarship in *American Literary Scholarship*.) Besides direct biographies, almost every critical study contains biographical observation or material. Here, with one exception, only book-length studies will be considered. Some studies, not strictly biographies, will be included because they have set the terms for subsequent biographies. In short, this is a review of significant works in the history of Clemens biography rather than a complete survey.

For *The Writings of Mark Twain* (1899–1907) Samuel E. Moffett provided a biographical sketch partly ghostwritten by Twain himself. It called attention to these issues that have surfaced in later biographies: Clemens's regional identity, his notable family lineage, his education in life rather than schools, his exemplary family life, his significant contributions to literature, his importance as a philosopher of humanity, his successful business affairs, his status as a man of honor, his deep humanitarianism, and his inveterate humor (Moffett 22:387–405). In brief this is Clemens's own self-portrait against which later biographies have played.

The most accurate and informative overall picture of Clemens can be seen by consulting four indispensable, complementary works: Dixon Wecter's *Sam Clemens of Hannibal* (1952), Albert Bigelow Paine's *Mark Twain: A Biography* (1912), Justin Kaplan's *Mr. Clemens and Mark Twain* (1966), and Hamlin Hill's *Mark Twain: God's Fool* (1973).

Wecter's study follows Clemens only through his eighteenth year (it was the first volume of a projected series), but it gives more reliable information than any other for this formative period. As literary executor of the Clemens estate, Wecter based his work solidly on unpublished as well as published family materials, on documentary records, and on historical sources. It is a thorough account of the Clemens family that gives a sense of the Hannibal milieu as well as a glimpse into the emotional life of young Sam. Sensible, judicious, scholarly, it establishes solid ground for the early years.

Although published two years after Clemens's death, Paine's three-volume *Mark Twain: A Biography* is the official biography authorized by Clemens. To write it, Paine became Clemens's secretary and companion during the final four years of his life, ultimately moving in to live with and care for him. It is the only biography that covers the entire life in detail, making use of original materials and personal contacts. The book is a treasure house of information, anecdote, and evaluation. One must enter it with care, however, since Paine was openly partisan, admiring Clemens almost without reservation, and thoroughly Victorian. He shaped the life to fit his own sense of propriety—a sense that Clemens most often shared (though Twain would often spoof it). Some parts of the life narrated by Paine are so heavily edited as to be misrepresented; others are out-and-out fiction. Yet the exhaustive story is alive with a strong sense of Clemens's family, with a firsthand knowledge of the times and with an indelible if laudatory view of Clemens himself. This Victorian three-decker stands as a monument to Clemens and yet still delivers an essential sense of the man.

In a sense Justin Kaplan's Pulitzer Prize winning *Mr. Clemens and Mark Twain* gives the side of the man Paine left out. Where Paine found sweetness and light, Kaplan finds bitterness and dark. Beginning, unfortunately, when Clemens is thirty-one, Kaplan locates, tracks, and documents a divided man. Deftly grounding his story in Clemens's turbulent era, he plays the public man off against the private. While he probes the psyche of Clemens/Twain, he does so with caution and restraint, always couching his analysis in apt and lucid language. While Paine concentrates on the family life and public activities, slighting the literature, Kaplan offers provocative assessments of the major works as expressions of the lived life. He is neither sensational nor protective; within the truncated time frame of his study he strikes a balanced view. His biography teeter-totters in keeping with the steady swings of Clemens and Twain. This is a solid, reliable, insightful modern account, a turbo-charged car in comparison to Paine's horse and buggy.

Just as Wecter provides an excellent account of Clemens's early years, so Hill gives the best version of the final decade. His is not a cheerful view. Drawing on new materials, *Mark Twain: God's Fool* reveals—and indeed at times seems to revel in—the tensions that divided Clemens's household and the strains that tormented the man. Exploding Paine's idyll of a beneficent man and loving family, Hill exposes Clemens's rage, his paranoia, his pettiness, and his maniacal self-absorption at the same time that he shows the deep conflicts and rivalries shattering first the family and then the staff with whom Clemens surrounded himself. The biography traces effectively both the outer and inner lives of Clemens, giving special attention to his sexual prudery and prurient interests. (This is a long way from Paine's pristine genius.) Although it deals only with the last ten years, Hill's study raises issues that reverberate back through the whole of Clemens's life. Future biographies must reckon with his insights.

There are four relatively brief biographies that attempt with considerable success to assay the entire life in a single volume. Early and brief as it is, Archibald Henderson's *Mark Twain* (1911) offers an interesting appraisal that paradoxically emphasized Clemens's southern roots and his cosmopolitan position. Edward Wagenknecht's *Mark Twain: The Man and His Work* (1935, revised 1967) is a sometimes thin account of the life that rightly stresses the histrionic Twain and richly examines the personal performances in the literature. He argues that Twain the pessimist is born of Twain the idealist. DeLancey Ferguson's *Mark Twain: Man and Legend* (1943) draws the line between the mythic and the real with acuity and good sense. The biography is marred by a lack of documentation and starred by its extraordinary lucidity and reasonableness, especially in its assessments of the literature. Most recently, John Lauber has created in *The Inventions of Mark Twain* (1990) an up-to-date popular biography, with commentary on major works, that provides a sensible overview.

Almost all accounts of Clemens's life written after 1920 contend in one way or another with the thesis first set forth by Van Wyck Brooks in *The Ordeal of Mark Twain* (1920, revised 1933). Brooks argued with forceful prose and little evidence that Twain was an artist thwarted first by his western environment and then by an effete eastern culture. For Brooks, Clemens wed himself to mediocrity when he married Olivia Langdon and aligned himself with the genteel culture she embodied, and he then further emasculated his talent by flirting with the bitch-goddess, success. Bernard DeVoto's *Mark Twain's America* (1935) is a powerful refutation, richly detailed. Less biography than cultural analysis, it makes the case for the West as the source of Twain's greatness. While most biographies are haunted by the specter of the Brooks-DeVoto controversy, the ghost may at last have been laid to rest by Guy Cardwell's fine study, *The Man Who Was Mark Twain* (1990). Cardwell debunks the idea of Twain as a genius of the frontier and sees instead the allure—and the empowerment—of the East for Twain.

Two areas of Clemens's biography, both narrow and restricted, remain problematical yet important. The first is the western period. Although the Mark Twain Project has published authoritative editions of the early tales and sketches as well as the letters from this time, there is currently no full, detailed, reliable account of these formative years. Five studies with varying focuses provide useful information and analysis: Minnie M. Brashear, *Mark Twain, Son of Missouri* (1934); Ivan Benson, *Mark Twain's Western Years* (1938); Effie Mona Mack, *Mark Twain in Nevada* (1947); Edgar Marquess Branch, *The Literary Apprenticeship of Mark Twain* (1950); and Paul Fatout, *Mark Twain in Virginia City* (1964). The two recent biographies that do attempt to recount the western years more comprehensively both fail. Nigey Lennon's *The Sagebrush Bohemian: Mark Twain in California* (1991), though informed by recent scholarship, is

undocumented and sometimes misconstrues facts and misinterprets Twain. And Margaret Sanborn's *Mark Twain: The Bachelor Years* (1990), while in touch with essential information, popularizes the life, seeing, for instance, Clemens's all too real struggles for survival as mere adventures. The period up to 1870 awaits synthesis and interpretation.

The second area of biography that calls for reassessment is Clemens's family life. Family accounts such as Susy Clemens's biography of "Papa" (written in 1885, published in 1985) and Clara's *My Father, Mark Twain* (1931) provide intimate but favorably biased insights into this crucial dimension of Clemens. Caroline Thomas Harnsberger's *Mark Twain, Family Man* (1960) and Edith Colgate Salsbury's *Susy and Mark Twain: Family Dialogues* (1965), general renderings of the domestic Clemens, are also largely approving, as is Mary Lawton's version of Katy Leary's recollections of her domestic service, *A Lifetime with Mark Twain* (1925). What is missing is a biography emphasizing the family life that sees through the sentimental image fostered by Clemens, Livy, and their daughters.

In an odd way, a sort of biography is emerging in the excellent introductions and annotations provided by the editors of the Mark Twain Project to Twain's notebooks, journals, and letters. Without question, theirs is the most reliable factual information available. Yet if the task of biography is the twofold one of giving information and of interpreting it, then the objectivity of the Mark Twain Project often leaves the life that emerges through the various volumes largely unexplained. Piecemeal as these commentaries are, they are always worth consulting.

Finally, one of the most intriguing and fruitful developments in the area of Clemens biography is the appearance of several books tracing the life through some special facet of Twain's creative performances. Three of these unconventional "biographies" deserve attention.

Louis J. Budd's *Our Mark Twain: The Making of His Public Personality* (1983) is a meticulously researched study of Clemens's public life as Mark Twain. Chock-full of shrewd insights, Budd's work reveals the machinery of Twain's lifelong self-mythologizing as well as the myths it engendered. It illuminates brilliantly the Clemens who lived in the public eye and so complements, and sometimes challenges, conventional biographies of the private man. It is an indispensable work for understanding Clemens/Twain. In *The Authentic Mark Twain* (1984) Everett Emerson offers up a literary biography of Clemens that traces his life through the writings as well as the lived events. Although the definition of the authentic Twain is somewhat restricted, Emerson's account of the life in letters is well documented, usefully chronological, and unusually comprehensive. It is also freely evaluative, making copious judgments on the quality of the literature and not a few on the man who lived and wrote it into existence. Emerson's view of Clemens/Twain is rather conventional, but his careful, detailed exploration of the man in and out of the literature is sound scholarship and is often based on unpublished materials. *The Authentic Mark Twain* (1984) is an excellent point of departure for considering the life embedded in the literature. Finally, like Emerson, Jeffery Steinbrink is concerned in *Getting To Be Mark Twain* (1991) with the interrelationship of Clemens's private life and Twain's public writings. Focusing on the short but important period, 1868–1871, he examines both the constraints Clemens felt in his life and the strategies by which he transcended them as Mark Twain in his writing. Although the study considers only a small fragment of Clemens's long life, it is an illuminating account of that moment and of Clemens's creative self.

These three recent studies suggest that much can be learned about Clemens's life through new angles of approach. To judge from these three works, Twain was right: his books are autobiographies, and the story of the life they contain, the life of Clemens the man and Twain the artist, is still unfolding.

Leland Krauth

BIBLIOGRAPHY

Benson, Ivan. *Mark Twain's Western Years.* Stanford, Calif.: Stanford UP, 1938.

Branch, Edgar Marquess. *The Literary Apprenticeship of Mark Twain.* Urbana: U of Illinois P, 1950.

Brashear, Minnie M. *Mark Twain: Son of Missouri.* Chapel Hill: U of North Carolina P, 1934.

Brooks, Van Wyck. *The Ordeal of Mark Twain.* Rev. ed. New York: Dutton, 1933.

Budd, Louis J. *Our Mark Twain: The Making of His Public Personality.* Philadelphia: U of Pennsylvania P, 1983.

Cardwell, Guy. *The Man Who Was Mark Twain: Images and Ideologies.* New Haven, Conn.: Yale UP, 1991.

Clemens, Clara. *My Father, Mark Twain.* New York: Harper, 1931.

Clemens, Olivia Susan. *Papa: An Intimate Biography of Mark Twain.* Ed. Charles Neider. Garden City, N.Y.: Doubleday, 1985.

Clemens, Samuel L. *Mark Twain's Own Autobiography: The Chapters from the "North American Review."* Ed. Michael J. Kiskis. Madison: U of Wisconsin P, 1990.

———. *The Writings of Mark Twain.* Author's National Edition. 25 vols. New York: Harper, 1899–1907.

DeVoto, Bernard. *Mark Twain's America.* Boston: Little, Brown, 1932.

Emerson, Everett. *The Authentic Mark Twain: A Literary Biography of Samuel L. Clemens.* Philadelphia: U of Pennsylvania P, 1984.

Fatout, Paul. *Mark Twain in Virginia City.* Bloomington: Indiana UP, 1964.

Ferguson, DeLancey. *Mark Twain: Man and Legend.* Indianapolis: Bobbs-Merrill, 1943.

Harnsberger, Caroline Thomas. *Mark Twain, Family Man.* New York: Citadel P, 1960.

Henderson, Archibald. *Mark Twain.* New York: Stokes, 1911.

Hill Hamlin. *Mark Twain: God's Fool.* New York: Harper & Row, 1973.

Kaplan, Justin. *Mr. Clemens and Mark Twain.* New York: Simon & Schuster, 1966.

Lauber, John. *The Inventions of Mark Twain.* New York: Hill and Wang, 1990.

Lawton, Mary. *A Lifetime with Mark Twain.* New York: Harcourt Brace, 1925.

Lennon, Nigey. *The Sagebrush Bohemian: Mark Twain in California.* New York: Paragon House, 1990.

Long, E. Hudson, and J.R. LeMaster. *The New Mark Twain Handbook.* New York: Garland, 1985.

Mack, Effie Mona. *Mark Twain in Nevada.* New York: Scribner, 1947.

Paine, Albert Bigelow. *Mark Twain: A Biography.* 3 vols. New York: Harper, 1912.

Salsbury, Edith Colgate. *Susy and Mark Twain: Family Dialogues.* New York: Harper & Row, 1965.

Sanborn, Margaret. *Mark Twain: The Bachelor Years.* New York: Doubleday, 1990.

Steinbrink, Jeffery. *Getting To Be Mark Twain.* Berkeley: U of California P, 1991.

Wagenknecht, Edward. *Mark Twain: The Man and His Work.* New Haven, Conn.: Yale UP, 1935.

Wecter, Dixon. *Sam Clemens of Hannibal.* Boston: Houghton Mifflin, 1952.

See also: Autobiography; Brooks, Van Wyck; Clemens, Samuel Langhorne; Correspondence; Family Life; Paine, Albert Bigelow; Wecter, Dixon

Bixby, Horace E.
(1826–1912)

Horace Bixby was the pilot of the steamboat *Paul Jones* who in April 1857 agreed for $500 to take on Samuel Clemens as an apprentice or "cub" pilot and teach him the river and his trade. Clemens served as Bixby's cub (with several interruptions) for two years, until he received his own pilot's license in April 1859.

Originally from upstate New York, Bixby spent sixty-six years in the western steamboat trade, rising from "mud clerk" to hold licenses to pilot on the Ohio, Mississippi, and Missouri rivers. He served with distinction as pilot of a Union gunboat and as a chief in the Union River Service during the Civil War and remained active during the long economic decline of steamboats after the war. His fame, however, was due to Mark Twain's portrait of him as the profane, irascible, and consummately skilled "lightning pilot" of "Old Times on the Mississippi" (1875) and *Life on the Mississippi* (1883). In both, Bixby is a demanding taskmaster who exposes the cub pilot's ignorance and puts him through a series of grueling and humiliating lessons before he can begin to master his craft. Although Mark Twain exaggerates his own youth and naiveté in this portrayal, his depiction of Bixby appears to

have been accurate in the main, for they were cordially reunited in 1882 when Twain revisited the Mississippi, and newspaper interviews with Bixby in 1882 and in 1910 (after Mark Twain's death) essentially corroborate Twain's account of their relationship. Bixby was apparently too busy to write his own memoirs of life on the Mississippi, remaining active as a pilot until the year of his death, 1912.

Robert Sattelmeyer

BIBLIOGRAPHY

Bates, Allan. "Mark Twain and the Mississippi River." Ph.D. diss., U of Chicago, 1968.

Clemens, Samuel L. *Life on the Mississippi.* Boston: James R. Osgood, 1883.

———. *Mark Twain's Letters, Volume 1 (1853–1866).* Ed. Edgar M. Branch, Michael B. Frank, and Kenneth M. Sanderson. Berkeley: U of California P, 1988.

See also: Life on the Mississippi; "Old Times on the Mississippi"; Piloting

Blackwood's Magazine

Blackwood's Magazine—or *The Edinburgh Monthly Magazine* (1817), or *Blackwood's Monthly Magazine* (1817–1905)—was a literary monthly originally conceived by its founder, William Blackwood, as a Tory response to the Whiggish *Edinburgh Review*. It gained popularity by sensationalism, including vitriolic attacks on what it called "the Cockney School of Poetry," but also published fiction by such notables as Sir Walter Scott, George Eliot, and Joseph Conrad. Excerpts from *Blackwood's* (and other literary magazines) were published in the Hannibal newspapers during Mark Twain's childhood. In the early 1880s *Blackwood's* forays against Twain's friends Charles Dudley Warner and William Dean Howells (and against American literature in general) incited a counterattack by Twain in an essay that remained unpublished but may have provided the germ to anti-British elements of *A Connecticut Yankee in King Arthur's Court* (1889). A 1907 *Blackwood's* essay by Charles Whibley, while acknowledging Twain's talent, called *A Connecticut Yankee* "a masterpiece of vulgarity," criticized Twain for his lack of respect for cultural monuments and traditions, and deplored his popularity as a public figure. Twain mentions *Blackwood's* (in passing) in one published writing: *A Tramp Abroad* (1880:chapter 43).

James S. Leonard

BIBLIOGRAPHY

Baetzhold, Howard G. *Mark Twain and John Bull: The British Connection*. Bloomington: Indiana UP, 1970.

Gribben, Alan. *Mark Twain's Library: A Reconstruction*. Vol. 1. Boston: G.K. Hall, 1980.

Clemens, Samuel L. *A Tramp Abroad*. Hartford, Conn.: American Publishing, 1880.

Whibley, Charles. "Mustangs without Method." *Blackwood's Magazine* 182 (August 1907): 279–286. Rpt. *Mark Twain: The Critical Heritage*. Ed. Frederick Anderson. New York: Barnes & Noble, 1971. 271–276.

See also: Connecticut Yankee in King Arthur's Court, A; England

Blaine, Jim

Appearing in chapter 53 of *Roughing It* (1872) as the teller of "His Grandfather's Ram," Jim Blaine, the alcoholic miner with the compulsively associative and unselective memory, returned to help Twain out on the lecture platform, both in 1884, during his tour of readings with George Washington Cable and then during his world tour of 1895–1896. The story itself shows Twain in the stance he so often adopted, that of an ignorant greenhorn duped by the initiated. In *Roughing It* "the boys" silently weep tears of laughter to see him so taken in by the promise of a story that never gets beyond its opening sentence. Blaine, finally in drunkenly perfect condition to tell his wonderful story, mentions the ram once and never returns to the creature again. Instead, he wanders down the byways of memory, giving the family history of people connected first to Grandfather, then to the ram's first owner, and then to no one quite knows whom. When Blaine falls asleep midway through a sentence, Twain's narrator notices the tears and "perceived that [he] was 'sold.'"

Years later, dictating his autobiography, Twain remembered how he altered the telling of the story for use on the lecture circuit. Its alleged "point" became that of illustrating "certain bad effects of a good memory." Twain, that is, cajoled his audiences into reenacting the very role that, long ago, he himself had played. One pictures those lecture audiences, sitting expectantly, waiting to hear what happens to the ram and—a new detail—to the seat of Grandfather's trousers. As with Twain in *Roughing It*, however, the auditors are buried by the irrelevant details dredged up from Blaine's memory. Of special interest to today's reader, telling the story aloud led to considerable revision of the written version. Anyone concerned with the requirements of oral as opposed to written narrative can profitably contrast the version in the book with the lecture version in *Mark Twain in Eruption* (1940).

Pascal Covici, Jr.

BIBLIOGRAPHY

Clemens, Samuel L. *Mark Twain in Eruption*. Ed. Bernard DeVoto. New York: Harper, 1940.

Covici, Pascal, Jr. *Mark Twain's Humor: The Image of a World*. Dallas: Southern Methodist UP, 1962.

Feinstein, George. "Mark Twain's Idea of Story Structure." *American Literature* 18 (1946): 160–163.

Hollenback, John W. "Mark Twain, Story-Teller, at Work." *College English* 7 (1946): 303–312.

See also: Autobiography; "Jim Blaine and His Grandfather's Ram"; *Roughing It*

Blair, Walter

(1900–)

A force in American literary scholarship for more than five decades, Walter Blair is the preeminent student of American humor and a major figure in Mark Twain studies. With such books as *Native American Humor* (1937) and *Horse Sense in American Humor* (1942), he in effect created the field of humor studies, and his labors in that field qualified him well for his extensive work on Twain. Blair has written seminal studies of Twain, has edited volumes in the University of California edition of Twain, and has helped to edit and write important volumes dealing with American literature. The record of Blair's life and work forms a valuable index to several major strains in American literary scholarship during the second half of the twentieth century.

Blair was born in Spokane, Washington, in 1900; he was educated at Yale University and at the University of Chicago, from which he received his Ph.D. in 1931. Virtually all of his academic career was spent at Chicago, where he taught American literature from 1929 to 1968, chairing the department during 1951–1960. He served on the editorial boards of two major scholarly journals, *American Literature* (1943–1951) and *Publications of the Modern Language Association* (1945–1951). For his numerous publications and professional activities, in 1974 he received the prestigious Jay B. Hubbell medallion awarded by the American Literature Section of the Modern Language Association for distinguished service to the professional study of American letters.

Many of Blair's best-known publications center on humor: the ground-breaking *Native American Humor: Tall Tale America* (1944), which went through twenty-six printings, and (with Franklin J. Meine), *Half Horse-Half Alligator: The Growth of the Mike Fink Legend* (1956). Blair's years of scholarship in this vein of American literature culminated in two volumes: *American Humor: From Poor Richard to Doonesbury* (1978), a book he wrote with Hamlin Hill, and *The Mirth of a Nation: America's Great Dialect Humor* (1983), edited with the late Raven I. McDavid, Jr. Blair's valuable studies of Twain include *Mark Twain & Huck Finn* (1960); *The Art of Huckleberry Finn* (1962), with Hamlin Hill; and volumes in the California Twain edition: *Mark Twain's*

Hannibal, Huck & Tom (1969), and *Adventures of Huckleberry Finn* (1985), with Victor Fischer. Blair's influential role in American literary scholarship is demonstrated by the widely used anthology *The Literature of the United States* (1947), which he edited with Theodore Hornberger and Randall Stewart, and by the companion volume *American Literature: A Brief History* (1964), which he wrote with Hornberger, Stewart, and James E. Miller, Jr.

In these and other books Blair shows a wide-ranging knowledge of history, biography, and popular culture as well as European and American literary traditions. He brings this knowledge skillfully to bear on discussions of his subject, whether it be southwestern humor or Mark Twain. He is equally deft at blending popular and serious approaches to academic topics. Scholarship in American literature would be much poorer without the pioneering investigations, the engaging style, the urbane humor, and the imaginative energy of Walter Blair.

Mary Ann Wimsatt

BIBLIOGRAPHY

Blair, Walter. *Horse Sense in American Humor.* Chicago: U of Chicago P, 1942.

———. *Mark Twain & Huck Finn.* Berkeley: U of California P, 1960.

———. *Native American Humor.* New York: American Publishing, 1937. Rev. ed. San Francisco: Chandler, 1960.

———. *Tall Tale America: A Legendary History of Our Humorous Heroes.* New York: Coward-McCann, 1944.

Blair, Walter, and Hamlin Hill. *American Humor: From Poor Richard to Doonesbury.* New York: Oxford UP, 1978.

———, eds. *The Art of Huckleberry Finn.* San Francisco: Chandler, 1962.

Blair, Walter, Theodore Hornberger, and Randall Stewart, eds. *American Literature: A Brief History.* New York: Scott, Foresman, 1964.

———. *The Literature of the United States.* 2 vols. New York: Scott, Foresman, 1947. 3rd ed. 1966.

Blair, Walter, and Raven I. McDavid, Jr., eds. *The Mirth of a Nation: America's Great Dialect Humor.* Minneapolis: U of Minnesota P, 1983.

Blair, Walter, and Franklin J. Meine, eds. *Half Horse-Half Alligator: The Growth of the Mike Fink Legend.* Chicago: U of Chicago P, 1956.

Clemens, Samuel L. *Adventures of Huckleberry Finn.* Ed. Walter Blair and Victor Fischer. Berkeley: U of California P, 1985.

————. *Mark Twain's Hannibal, Huck & Tom.* Ed. Walter Blair. Berkeley: U of California P, 1969.

See also: Scholarship, Trends in Mark Twain; Southwestern Humor

Blakely, Captain Ned

Mark Twain tells the story of Captain Ned Blakely and Bill Noakes in *Roughing It* (1872). The story goes that Captain Blakely, "a rough, honest creature, full of pluck and . . . simplicity," sailed from San Francisco to the Chincha Islands, a desolate cluster just west of Peru. In port one Bill Noakes, a bully and a mate of another ship, came aboard Blakely's ship and challenged him to prove who was the better man, whereupon the captain obliged by beating him to a pulp and throwing him overboard.

A favorite among Blakely's crew was a Negro mate. A week later, to relieve his frustration, Noakes shot the Negro mate in the back before half a dozen witnesses. Defying Noakes's threats, Blakely boarded Noakes's ship that night and took him prisoner.

The next morning the captain invited the other captains on the island to come aboard and attend the hanging. Horrified, they insisted that the prisoner must first be given a fair trial. Although Blakely could see no point in trying a man who was obviously guilty, he grudgingly permitted the formality. After the verdict of guilty, the captain invited the assembly to come along and watch him hang the culprit. Meanwhile, back in California the news endeared Captain Blakely to the citizens who appreciated such simple and primitive justice.

Twain inserts this digression into *Roughing It* in the context of frontier justice in Nevada and California. It invites comparison with many other trials in Twain's works (McKeithan). Furthermore, the colorful bravery of Captain Blakely anticipates such later characters as Colonel Sherburn of *Adventures of Huckleberry Finn* (1885) and Captain Stormfield.

Frank H. Leavell

BIBLIOGRAPHY

Clemens, Samuel L. *Roughing It.* Ed. Franklin R. Rogers and Paul Baender. Berkeley: U of California P, 1972.

McKeithan, Daniel M. *Court Trials in Mark Twain and Other Essays.* The Hague: Martinus Nijhoff, 1958.

See also: Roughing It; "Trial, A"

Blanc, Marie-Thérèse

The first European critic to give Mark Twain serious critical attention, Marie-Thérèse Blanc ("Theodore Bentzon") was for many years the critic for the *Revue des Deux Mondes.* The championess of the Gallic genteel tradition, she was, despite her brilliance, profoundly incapable of understanding Twain's deadpan humor. She made a minutely precise translation of his "Jumping Frog" story (the first in French), but its point sailed over her head. She was equally incapable of comprehending the fictional first person narrative of *Innocents Abroad* (1869), and similarly the charm of Colonel Sellers in *The Gilded Age* (1873) eluded her. She encouraged Twain's antagonism toward the French, but did introduce him to the European literary community.

Mark Draper

BIBLIOGRAPHY

Anderson, Frederick, and Kenneth M. Sanderson, eds. *Mark Twain: The Critical Heritage.* New York: Barnes & Noble, 1971.

Blair, Walter. *Mark Twain & Huck Finn.* Berkeley: U of California P, 1960.

Henderson, Archibald. "The International Fame of Mark Twain." *North American Review* 192 (December 1910): 805–815.

Wilson, Mark K. "Mr. Clemens and Madame Blanc: Mark Twain's First French Critic." *American Literature* 45 (January 1974): 537–556.

See also: "Celebrated Jumping Frog of Calaveras County, The"; France

Blankenship, Thomas Woodson

In his *Autobiography* (1924) Mark Twain reveals that his most celebrated literary character, Huck Finn, was modeled after Clemens's childhood Hannibal companion, Tom Blankenship (dates unknown), "exactly as he was": "ignorant, unwashed, insufficiently fed, but he had as good a heart as ever any boy had." Tom lived with both parents and seven siblings in what Dixon Wecter calls "a ramshackle old barn of a house" (147) adjacent to Clemens's boyhood home on Hill Street. His companionship was forbidden to children of "respectable" families, which of course made him all the more attractive.

Woodson Blankenship, Tom's father, came originally from South Carolina; he is listed among the seventy-eight pioneers of Ralls County, Missouri, having voted in the first election in New London in 1822. In the 1830s he worked as a cooper for Benjamin Spalding and owned land along the Salt River. By 1840 Woodson had moved his growing family to Hannibal and apparently had begun to experience financial difficulty. In 1845 Woodson Blankenship appeared on the roll of tax delinquents; Clemens remembers the parents as "paupers and drunkards."

Hannibal in the 1840s and 1850s was a difficult place to live for a man past fifty who could no longer manage arduous labor in the sawmills, rope walks, and meat-packing houses where work was available. Hard pressed to support his large family, Woodson Blankenship, unless he had affluent relatives who lived nearby, would have indeed been in danger of becoming a pauper. The neighboring Clemens family, with an ailing but proud father who died in 1847, might well have fallen into a situation similar to the Blankenships—had there not been fewer children and many relatives who regularly supplied them with food and cash. Young Sam Clemens clearly was drawn to his "outlaw" friend Tom Blankenship and had sympathy and admiration for the boy who went barefoot all the time, defied concerted attempts to "civilize" him, received his only education from the woods and streets, and with his "good heart" and lively imagination led the other children in their unsupervised play.

Oliver Howard and Goldena Howard

BIBLIOGRAPHY

Bacon, Thomas H. *A Mirror of Hannibal*. Hannibal, Mo.: C.P. Greene, 1905.

Blair, Walter. *Mark Twain & Huck Finn*. Berkeley: U of California P, 1960.

Clemens, Samuel L. *Mark Twain's Autobiography*. Ed. Albert B. Paine. 2 vols. New York: Harper, 1924.

Wecter, Dixon. *Sam Clemens of Hannibal*. Boston: Houghton Mifflin, 1952.

See also: Clemens, John Marshall; Hannibal, Missouri

Bliss, Elisha
(1822–1880)

Born in Springfield, Massachusetts, Elisha Bliss became the secretary of the American Publishing Company in 1867 and alternated that office with the one of president until his death on 28 September 1880. In his official position, Bliss wrote Clemens on 21 November 1867, proposing that the humorist consider writing a book for subscription publication. Clemens agreed to the terms and became an American Publishing Company author for the entire decade of the 1870s.

An astute businessman in a semi-reputable profession, Bliss obtained contracts for not only *The Innocents Abroad* (1869) but also *Roughing It* (1872), *The Gilded Age* (1873), *Sketches, New and Old* (1875), *The Adventures of Tom Sawyer* (1876), and *A Tramp Abroad* (1880). Although Clemens became increasingly conversant with the mechanics of subscription publication, it was Elisha Bliss who engineered the advertising, promotion, and sales mechanics of those books whose publication he oversaw. His decision to chance a work of humor with his company was a bold one, but his instinct that Mark Twain had a ready-made audience among the purchasers of subscription books proved accurate and enormously profitable.

Indeed, Mark Twain decided that some of Bliss's profits rightfully belonged to him as author and moved in the late 1870s toward, first, his publishing arrangement with James R. Osgood and, finally, to the establishment of Charles L. Webster and Company.

Although Mark Twain's lifelong enmity toward Bliss erupted as late as his autobiographical dictation of 21 February 1906, when he labeled Bliss a "bastard monkey," Bliss can claim the credit for recognizing Mark Twain's proper audience, placing his literature in the hands of that audience, and educating his apprentice author in the mechanics of subscription publication. His influence lurks at least dimly behind Mark Twain's ultimate bankruptcy, but even more important, behind the humorist's self-definition of his role as the "People's Author" and the spokesman for "the mighty mass of the uncultivated," the "Belly and Members," as he expressed it in his famous 1890 letter to Andrew Lang.

Hamlin Hill

BIBLIOGRAPHY

Clemens, Samuel L. *Mark Twain's Letters to His Publishers, 1867–1894.* Ed. Hamlin Hill. Berkeley: U of California P, 1967.

Hill, Hamlin. *Mark Twain and Elisha Bliss.* Columbia: U of Missouri P, 1964.

See also: American Publishing Company; Subscription Publication

Bliss, Frank

Frank Bliss (dates unknown) was the treasurer and later manager of the American Publishing Company. He inherited the top post from his father, Elisha Bliss, Jr. (1822–1880), who was Mark Twain's first subscription publisher.

Twain's dealings with the elder Bliss were constantly troubled. Twain blamed Elisha for delays in bringing out *The Adventures of Tom Sawyer* (1876) and contracted independently with Frank in 1878 for an original manuscript. After Frank's company published one book (not Twain's), Frank returned to the American Publishing Company, which issued *A Tramp Abroad* in early 1880. Elisha died that fall, Frank succeeding him, but Twain was arranging a subscription plan with James R. Osgood. Twain's own firm, Charles L. Webster, went bankrupt in 1894, and Bliss then published *Pudd'nhead Wilson* (1894), *Following the Equator* (1897), and *Mark Twain's Complete Works in Uniform Edition* (1899).

Frank Bliss corresponded regularly with Twain concerning manuscripts, illustrations, and business particulars. Clemens had little faith in Frank, often feeling he was being taken advantage of or outright cheated, as he thought he had been by Elisha.

Patricia Hunt

BIBLIOGRAPHY

Clemens, Samuel L. *The Autobiography of Mark Twain.* Ed. Charles Neider. New York: Harper, 1959.

———. *Mark Twain's Letters.* Ed. Albert B. Paine. 2 vols. New York: Harper, 1917.

———. *Mark Twain's Letters to His Publishers, 1867–1894.* Ed. Hamlin Hill. Berkeley: U of California P, 1967.

———. *Mark Twain's Notebook.* Ed. Albert B. Paine. New York: Harper, 1935.

Emerson, Everett. *The Authentic Mark Twain: A Literary Biography of Samuel L. Clemens.* Philadelphia: U of Pennsylvania P, 1984.

Hill, Hamlin. *Mark Twain and Elisha Bliss.* Columbia: U of Missouri P, 1964.

Kaplan, Justin. *Mr. Clemens and Mark Twain.* New York: Simon & Schuster, 1966.

Paine, Albert Bigelow. *Mark Twain: A Biography.* 3 vols. New York: Harper, 1912.

See also: American Publishing Company; Bliss, Elisha

"Bloody Massacre near Carson, A"
(1863)

Initially appearing as a news release in the Virginia City *Territorial Enterprise* on 28 October 1863, this sketch is referred to variously as "The Latest Sensation," "Empire City Massacre," "Dutch-Nick Massacre," and "My

Bloody Massacre." No copy of the original *Enterprise* article is extant. Branch and Hirst reproduce the story from copies in the Gold Hill *News*, the Sacramento *Union*, and the San Francisco *Evening Bulletin*.

"A Bloody Massacre near Carson" is a hoax, prompted by a remark by fellow *Territorial Enterprise* employee C.A.V. Putnam that San Francisco newspapers were shamefully ignoring a "dividend cooking" scheme perpetrated by the Spring Valley Water Company to defraud unsuspecting, independent investors. To capture the public's attention, Mark Twain embeds the fraud within a sensational story of a fictionalized massacre: P. Hopkins, a stockholder who lived somewhere between Empire City and Dutch Nick, apparently went insane after losing his money in the dividend cooking schemes of the Daney Gold and Silver Mining and the Spring Valley Water companies; as a consequence, he went on a murderous rampage, killing his wife and seven of his nine children with an axe, a knife, and a blunt instrument. After slitting his own throat, Hopkins rode five miles on horseback to Carson City, where he collapsed and died in the Magnolia Saloon. The article concludes with a satirical jab at the water company, whose illegal practice engendered Hopkins's murderous behavior, and the San Francisco newspapers, who had ignored the water company's fraudulent scheme.

It was common practice among the *Territorial Enterprise* editors to publish satirical, quasi-fictionalized stories (or hoaxes), but the sensational "A Bloody Massacre near Carson" generated unusual controversy. Although Mark Twain had carefully woven clues throughout his sketch to alert readers to its fictionality and satiric intent, newspapers throughout Nevada and California were taken in by the hoax and reprinted the article as fact. Mark Twain immediately published a retraction (entitled, "I Take It All Back"), but red-faced editors in San Francisco and Sacramento were not so easily appeased. They demanded his resignation and called into question both the integrity of the *Territorial Enterprise* and the reliabil-

ity of anything it published. Fearing he had done irreparable damage to the paper's reputation, Mark Twain offered to resign; he was dissuaded, however, by his editor and good friend Joseph Goodman.

In addition to the Spring Valley Water Company and its practice of "dividend cooking," the story satirizes the San Francisco newspapers, a reading public that responded only to sensationalism, and Peter Hopkins, owner of the Magnolia Saloon, who was infamous for his "forty-rod" whiskey. Ivan Benson suggests that the hoax reveals Mark Twain's persistent fascination with gory violence.

Anthony Fonseca

BIBLIOGRAPHY

Benson, Ivan. *Mark Twain's Western Years*. Stanford, Calif.: Stanford UP, 1938.

Clemens, Samuel L. *The Works of Mark Twain: Early Tales & Sketches, Volume 1 (1851–1864)*. Ed. Edgar M. Branch and Robert H. Hirst. Berkeley: U of California P, 1979. 320–326.

Fatout, Paul. *Mark Twain in Virginia City*. Bloomington: Indiana UP, 1964.

Miller, William C. "Mark Twain's Source for 'The Latest Sensational' Hoax?" *American Literature* 32 (March 1960): 75–78.

See also: Hoax; Journalism; Nevada

Boer War
(1899–1902)

In this war Great Britain defeated the Boers, descendants of Dutch settlers, to gain control of their mineral-rich republics, the Orange Free State and Transvaal. These territories were later combined with the British Cape Colony and Natal to form the Union of South Africa. Mark Twain's interest in the Boer War stemmed from his three-month visit to South Africa in 1896 during his around-the-world lecture tour described in *Following the Equator* (1897). On this trip Twain conceived his first systematic anti-imperialist opinions.

Mark Twain arrived in South Africa in May, slightly more than four months after the Jameson Raid, a precursor to the Boer War.

Twain took a keen interest in the episode, even visiting some of the raiders in jail in Pretoria. Prompted by Cecil Rhodes, who was the premier of Cape Colony, Dr. Leander Starr Jameson had led some 600 men in an attack on the Transvaal, hoping to stir up a revolt among the *uitlanders* (non-Boers) and to provoke intervention by Great Britain. The raid failed when Jameson and his men were captured after only four days.

In South Africa Twain's primary sympathies were with the Africans, exploited by Boer and Briton alike. Between the Boers and the Britons, however, Twain sided with the former, seeing them as underdogs against a mighty imperial power. When the Boer War finally broke out, Twain wrote in his notebook that it was the responsibility of Rhodes and Joseph Chamberlain, Britain's pro-imperialist colonial secretary. He partially suppressed his impulse to protest when he realized, as he wrote his friend William Dean Howells, that on the international scene a defeat of Britain would strengthen the autocracies in Germany and Russia. Twain did, however, deliver incidental blows to Britain in "A Salutation Speech from the Nineteenth Century to the Twentieth" (1900) and "To the Person Sitting in Darkness" (1901).

Hunt Hawkins

BIBLIOGRAPHY

Budd, Louis J. *Mark Twain: Social Philosopher.* Bloomington: Indiana UP, 1962.

Clemens, Samuel L. *Mark Twain's Notebook.* Ed. Albert B. Paine. New York: Harper, 1935.

Foner, Philip S. *Mark Twain: Social Critic.* New York: International Publishers, 1958.

Koss, Stephen E., ed. *The Anatomy of an Anti-War Movement: The Pro-Boers.* Chicago: U of Chicago P, 1973.

Pakenham, Thomas. *The Boer War.* New York: Random House, 1979.

See also: Imperialism; "Salutation Speech from the Nineteenth Century to the Twentieth, A"; "To the Person Sitting in Darkness"

Bowen, Will
(1836–1893)

William "Will" Bowen was perhaps Mark Twain's closest childhood friend in Hannibal. Bowen's father and brothers were steamboat pilots; Bowen himself served as a pilot with Twain on three boats: the *Alfred T. Lacey*, *A.B. Chambers,* and the *Alonzo Child.* In 1868 he left the river to work in the insurance business. Twain and Bowen corresponded until a couple of years before Bowen's death.

While their friendship was sometimes rocky because of Bowen's politics—he piloted for the North during the Civil War—and because of a misunderstanding over a $200 loan Twain made to Bowen while they were both still piloting, their early years were filled with Tom Sawyer-like adventure: when Bowen was ill with measles, Twain crawled into bed with him to catch the disease and become the center of attention; their gang rolled a huge bolder down Holliday's Hill in an attempt to frighten a passing slave (the bolder crashed into a cooper's shed); they accidentally discovered the body of a drowned runaway slave; they hid playing cards in a preacher's "baptizing robe" to avoid being punished (the cards floated to the surface when the preacher immersed new converts); they tormented a louse with a pin until caught by their teacher, Mr. Dawson.

Twain used Bowen as the model for Joe Harper in *The Adventures of Tom Sawyer* (1876) and *Adventures of Huckleberry Finn* (1885) and used their escapades as the grist for many episodes featuring Tom and Huck. More importantly, Twain's exchanges with Bowen often sparked memories that found their way into both Twain's fiction and his autobiography.

Michael J. Kiskis

BIBLIOGRAPHY

Clemens, Samuel L. "Chapters from My Autobiography." *North American Review* 183 (1906); 184, 185, 186 (1907): various issues.

———. *Mark Twain's Hannibal, Huck & Tom.* Ed. Walter Blair. Berkeley: U of California P, 1969.

———. *Mark Twain's Letters, Volume 1 (1853–1866).*
Ed. Edgar M. Branch, Michael B. Frank, and
Kenneth M. Sanderson. Berkeley: U of Califor-
nia P, 1988.

———. *Mark Twain's Letters, Volume 2 (1867–1868).*
Ed. Harriet Elinor Smith and Richard Bucci.
Berkeley: U of California P, 1990.

———. *Mark Twain's Own Autobiography: The Chapters from the "North American Review."* Ed. Michael
J. Kiskis. Madison: U of Wisconsin P, 1990.

Paine, Albert Bigelow. *Mark Twain: A Biography.* 3
vols. New York: Harper, 1912.

Wecter, Dixon. *Sam Clemens of Hannibal.* Boston:
Houghton Mifflin, 1952.

See also: Adventures of Huckleberry Finn;
Adventures of Tom Sawyer, The

Boxer Rebellion, The
(1899–1902)

Between 1898 and 1899 a growing movement of anti-foreign, pro-dynastic Chinese
intellectuals and peasants succeeded in attacking the lodgings and technologies of Chinese
and European Christians; they eventually entered and occupied Peking in June 1900. Their
victory, however, was short-lived; the Boxers
were eventually routed by a combination of
European and American forces in August 1900,
who then actively punished the rebels and
imposed heavy indemnities on even innocent
Chinese.

Mark Twain expressed an intense identification with the failed Chinese rebellion, reasoning that Americans would be as justified in
reacting against foreign occupation as had the
Boxers. Twain admired the patriotism of the
Chinese and concluded that inasmuch as "the
Boxer believed in driving us out of his country . . . , I am a Boxer, too, for I believe in
driving him out of our country." By appealing to native American animosity toward the
Chinese in America—perhaps his own included—Twain sought to demonstrate the
mutual sentiment of "patriotism" shared by
both the Boxers and the Americans and
through inexorable logic to foster sympathy
for the Boxers' actions.

Twain also held a profound contempt for
the Christian missionaries in China who, following the rebellion's demise, imposed heavy
and indiscriminate indemnities. In his essays
"To the Person Sitting in Darkness" (1901)
and "To My Missionary Critics" (1901) Twain
cogently attacked the immoral and unchristian underpinnings of these unjust punishments, suggesting that "for a century to come,
Chinese converts will consider looting and
vengeance Christian virtues."

Patrick Deneen

BIBLIOGRAPHY

Clemens, Samuel L. "To My Missionary Critics."
The Complete Essays of Mark Twain. By Clemens.
Ed. Charles Neider. Garden City, N.Y.:
Doubleday, 1963. 296–310.

———. "To the Person Sitting in Darkness." *The
Complete Essays of Mark Twain.* By Clemens. Ed.
Charles Neider. Garden City, N.Y.: Doubleday,
1963. 282–296.

See also: China; Imperialism; Missionaries

Boy Books

Thomas Bailey Aldrich's *The Story of a Bad
Boy* (1869) is usually acknowledged as the first
boy book. William Dean Howells praised it in
his review in the *Atlantic* as a book that portrayed boy life as it is, not as moralists would
have it be; he noted its autobiographical aspect; he recommended the book to both children and adults (boys and men, to be precise);
and he foresaw that similar books would follow. In praising its realism, Howells distinguished the book from the didactic stories
about children that were standard in the juvenile literature of the period. In noting its autobiographical nature, he recognized that here
was the sustained story of a single boy's life—
something that distinguished it from the stories of mischievous boys that had earlier appeared in the work of such humorists as George
Washington Harris or Benjamin P. Shillaber.
In recognizing the appeal of the book to both
children and adults, he acknowledged its sheer
fun and its appealing evocation of the past.

And finally, he was as percipient as usual in recognizing that Aldrich's book would be followed by others. The genre Aldrich initiated proved extremely durable, spanning the years between the end of the Civil War and World War I and appealing to both major and minor writers.

It was above all a nostalgic genre, one of many escapist responses to the extraordinary changes America underwent in the second half of the nineteenth century as the country recovered from the Civil War and moved toward world leadership and changed from an agrarian, rural nation to an industrialized and urbanized one (Lears). Some of the boy books are relatively straightforward accounts of the author's experience of change: Joel Chandler Harris's *On the Plantation* (1892), Edward Everett Hale's *A New England Boyhood* (1893), and Hamlin Garland's *Boy Life on the Prairie* (1899) are examples. Others, while essentially autobiographical, depersonalize the author's experience to generalize about the nature of boyhood in that vanished past: Charles Dudley Warner's *Being a Boy* (1877) and Howells's *A Boy's Town* (1890) follow this strategy. And still others, by far the majority, freely embroider the author's past to create a blend of fiction and autobiography. Aldrich's book fits this category, as do Mark Twain's *The Adventures of Tom Sawyer* (1876) and *Adventures of Huckleberry Finn* (1885), Stephen Crane's *Whilomville Stories* (1900), Howells's *The Flight of Pony Baker* (1902), Booth Tarkington's *Penrod* (1914) and a host of others by now forgotten authors.

In their appeal to adults as well as children, these books enjoyed a different segment of the literary market than did the juvenile adventure series of the period or the didactic Horatio Alger books. Their real competitors were the works of Robert Louis Stevenson, Rudyard Kipling, Kenneth Grahame, and James Barrie—authors who were as widely read by adults as by children. What set the boy books apart, aside from their realistic American settings, was the developmental notion of boyhood that informed them. The boy-book writers all accepted the notion that the development of the individual recapitulates the development of the species, that the growing boy, therefore, is a savage who will evolve into a civilized man (Cady 96–97, 100–101; Gould 135–143). (The growing girl was thought to miss this stage because women evolve from homemakers, not hunters.) This recapitulation theory is acknowledged in a variety of ways in the boy books, ranging from authorial intrusion to suggestive metaphor to an emphasis on competitive or quarrelsome boy activity.

The notion that boyhood is naturally set apart from manhood by the course of human development would have been reinforced by the experience of profound social change that set the boy-book writers' adult lives apart from their boyhood; the inevitable result was the treatment of boyhood as a self-enclosed time. Many of the boy books call attention to this by the word "boy" in their titles or subtitles; they are not books about growing up as is the parallel girls' genre, which focuses on the continuity between girlhood and womanhood and is best represented by a book whose title tells all: Louisa May Alcott's *Little Women* (1868). The notion that boyhood is characterized by savagery accounts for the emphasis on "badness" in the boy book. Boy-book boys are not wicked; they are simply rambunctious, mischievous, or, to use one of the words of the period, "lively." Peck's bad boy in George W. Peck's book of that title (1883) is the one boy who goes beyond acceptable boy behavior in his viciousness. But Peck was writing in the tradition of the early humorists (and taking advantage of the market created by the boy-book writers) rather than in the autobiographical and semi-autobiographical mode initiated by Aldrich. The boy books deal with many of the same events—imaginative games that enliven small town or farm life for a boy, pranks that pit boys against authority figures, first romances that challenge a boy's self assurance—for these are the staples of every boy's experience. These are also events that allow the author to reveal and to revel in the boy protagonist's disruptive behavior. They would have provided a special delight for the nineteenth-century child reader for whom characters in books were often lessons personified, and they would have reminded the adult reader of what he once was and perhaps under that layer of adult manners still was, the recapitulation theory to the contrary.

Each of the books named above has much to offer the modern reader who is interested in small-town and rural life in the nineteenth century, the forces that shaped male behavior, and the strategies employed by the writers of boyhood autobiography. Each book contributed something new to the genre. Mark Twain, of course, remains the best known and most widely read of the boy-book writers. His humor, his imagination, and his insight into boy psychology all distinguish his boy books. More specifically, in the characters of Huck and Tom, Twain introduced the boy pals to the genre, close friends whose different personalities and values would provide a commentary on each other and on their society. In *Huck Finn* he took the audacious step of letting the boy protagonist tell his own story, and since he chose a boy whose vision was not distorted by education, he had a narrator who could describe the life around him as it really was. Much of *Huck Finn*, in fact, leaves the world of boyish activity to become a picaresque examination of the evils of society. In doing this, Twain was acknowledging that the recapitulation theory, which confined savagery to boyhood, was only a pretty myth, that savagery, in fact, was the human condition. Such recognition would ultimately make writing boy books as the nineteenth century knew them impossible. But Twain was not quite ready to give up the escapism the boy book offered, and he tried it again and again. A series of abortive attempts yielded only *Tom Sawyer Abroad* (1894) and *Tom Sawyer, Detective* (1896), disappointing, derivative books that took advantage of the market for boy books but, missing the autobiographical core of Twain's first two boy books, lacked real investment on the part of the author. If Twain

was not ready to give up boy books, neither was his culture. It would take the widespread destruction of World War I to undermine seriously the comfortable belief in boyhood savagery on which so many entertaining books were based.

Marcia Jacobson

BIBLIOGRAPHY

Cady, Edwin H. *The Light of Common Day: Realism in American Fiction.* Bloomington: Indiana UP, 1971.

Gould, Stephen Jay. *Ontogeny and Phylogeny.* Cambridge, Mass: Harvard UP, 1977.

Howells, W.D. "Review of Thomas Bailey Aldrich's *The Story of a Bad Boy.*" *Atlantic Monthly* 25 (January 1870): 124–125.

Lears, T.J. Jackson. *No Place of Grace: Antimodernism and the Transformation of American Culture 1880–1920.* New York: Pantheon, 1981.

Stone, Albert E., Jr. *The Innocent Eye: Childhood in Mark Twain's Imagination.* New Haven, Conn: Yale UP, 1961.

See also: Adventures of Huckleberry Finn; Adventures of Tom Sawyer, The; Aldrich, Thomas Bailey; Childhood

"Boy's Manuscript"
(written ca. 1868)

The Adventures of Tom Sawyer (1876) had a long genesis that began with a sketch in the form of a diary kept by its boy protagonist. Albert Bigelow Paine found the manuscript among Twain's unpublished papers, titled it "Boy's Manuscript," and dated it tentatively 1870; Bernard DeVoto published it for the first time in *Mark Twain at Work* (1942) with a helpful commentary pointing to links between the manuscript and the novel; the volume of unfinished Huck Finn and Tom Sawyer stories in the University of California's paperback Mark Twain Library reprints the piece and corrects the date of composition.

Although the first two pages of "Boy's Manuscript" are missing, it was evidently a finished piece that comes to about twenty printed pages. In the form of an intermittently kept diary covering five weeks, it recounts young Billy Rogers's courtship of Amy—an affair of the heart that burlesques Twain's own courtship of Olivia Langdon and rehearses many of the tribulations that Tom Sawyer and Becky Thatcher will experience but that comes to an end here with a silly quarrel and the appearance of a new girl, a nineteen-year-old sophisticate. With its emphasis on romance, the tale necessarily briefly sketches other boy life experiences and makes them secondary to the main theme. In the novel many of these will be expanded to carry as much weight as the romance itself. The first-person narrative, however, will have to wait for *Huckleberry Finn* (1885). Billy Rogers's voice is not convincingly that of a child: he is too self-aware, and he inconsistently uses both literary language and a loosely rendered backwoods speech. In setting "Boy's Manuscript" aside, Twain rightly recognized that it did not realize the potential of its material. Yet the piece deserves attention: as DeVoto observed in presenting it to the world, it was Twain's first attempt to write an extended piece of fiction and it was his first attempt to make use of material from his Hannibal boyhood (DeVoto 8).

Marcia Jacobson

BIBLIOGRAPHY

Clemens, Samuel L. *Huck Finn and Tom Sawyer Among the Indians and Other Unfinished Stories.* Foreword and Notes by Dahlia Armon and Walter Blair. Berkeley: U of California P, 1989.

DeVoto, Bernard. *Mark Twain at Work.* Cambridge, Mass.: Harvard UP, 1942.

See also: Adventures of Tom Sawyer, The

Breen, H[enry] H[egart]
(1835–1882)

British author H.H. Breen wrote one of the books Mark Twain treasured most—*Modern English Literature: Its Blemishes and Defects* (London, 1857). Acquired in 1876, apparently after a bookseller had "ransacked" England searching for a copy, the much annotated volume, now in the Mark Twain Papers, several times furnished Twain ammunition, most notably for a speech at the Army and Navy Club of Connecticut in April 1887. Titled "General Grant's Grammar" by A.B. Paine in *Mark Twain's Speeches* (1923), the address invoked Breen's book in attacking Matthew Arnold's review of the *Personal Memoirs of U.S. Grant* (New York, 1885) that had appeared in *Murray's* magazine for January and February 1887.

Howard G. Baetzhold

BIBLIOGRAPHY

Blair, Walter. *Mark Twain & Huck Finn.* Berkeley: U of California P, 1960.

Clemens, Samuel L. *Mark Twain Speaking.* Ed. Paul Fatout. Iowa City: U of Iowa P, 1976. 226–227.

———. *Samuel L. Clemens, Some Reminiscences and Some Excerpts from Letters and Unpublished Manuscripts.* Ed. Jervis Langdon. n.p., n.d. (dedication dated 7 October 1938). Pamphlet.

Gribben, Alan. *Mark Twain's Library: A Reconstruction.* 2 vols. Boston: G.K. Hall, 1980.

See also: "General Grant's Grammar"

Bricksville

The fictional town of Bricksville, Arkansas, appears in chapters 21–23 of *Adventures of Huckleberry Finn* (1885). It is the scene of the Sherburn-Boggs episode, of the circus where Huck is fooled by the "drunk" trick rider, and of the performances by the King and the Duke as Shakespeareans and as "The Royal Nonesuch." The town is not named, however, until chapter 28, when Huck leaves a note for Mary Jane Wilks with the words "*Royal Nonesuch, Bricksville*" on it.

Aside from common sources for his descriptions of a one-horse southern town and a circus, Twain drew on various specific sources for his portrait of Bricksville. According to Walter Blair, the town is based on Napolean, Arkansas, a town at the confluence of the Arkansas and Mississippi rivers that had been washed away by the time Twain wrote about it in *Life on the Mississippi* (1883). Twain himself identified the source of the Sherburn-Boggs episode as the 1845 Owsley-Smarr shooting in Hannibal, and "The Royal Nonesuch" is based on a tale that he heard in a California mining camp in 1865.

Twain's depiction of the town and of its residents is entirely unflattering. The citizens are lazy in their daily life, insensitive in their response to Boggs's death, cowardly in their abortive attempt to lynch Colonel Sherburn, and gullible, selfish, and stupid in their response to "The Royal Nonesuch." Arthur G. Pettit and Kenneth S. Lynn attribute this treatment to Twain's jaundiced view of the South, particularly after his 1882 return to the Mississippi River. It may be equally useful, however, to see it as signaling his increasingly bitter view of human nature in general and as prefiguring his later, darker writings.

Paul Witkowsky

BIBLIOGRAPHY

Blair, Walter. *Mark Twain & Huck Finn*. Berkeley: U of California P, 1960.

Clemens, Samuel L. *Adventures of Huckleberry Finn*. Ed. Walter Blair and Victor Fischer. Berkeley: U of California P, 1985.

Lynn, Kenneth S. *Mark Twain and Southwestern Humor*. Boston: Little, Brown, 1959.

Pettit, Arthur G. *Mark Twain and the South*. Lexington: UP of Kentucky, 1974.

See also: *Adventures of Huckleberry Finn*;
    "Royal Nonesuch, The";
    Sherburn, Colonel

Briggs, John

Samuel Clemens's boyhood friend John Briggs (dates unknown) served as a model, along with Clemens himself, for Tom Sawyer and also for Joe Harper. With Briggs, Sam saw a man shot by a widow whom he was harassing. Together the two boys frightened people on their way to church by rolling rocks down Holliday's Hill, dug for treasure with Tom Blankenship, and found the drowned body of a runaway slave who had been befriended by Ben Blankenship as Huck Finn was to befriend Jim. A prosperous farmer in later life,

Briggs last met his friend when Clemens visited Hannibal in 1902.

Jarrell A. O'Kelley

BIBLIOGRAPHY

Clemens, Samuel L. *The Autobiography of Mark Twain*. Ed. Charles Neider. New York: Harper, 1959.

Paine, Albert Bigelow. *Mark Twain: A Biography*. 3 vols. New York: Harper, 1912.

See also: Blankenship, Thomas Woodson;
    Hannibal, Missouri

Briggs, Scotty

Miner, rough-neck, and, above all, honest man, Scotty Briggs confounds an eastern minister with western slang in chapter 47 of *Roughing It* (1872). Representing the lingo and manners of Virginia City's vast underclass, Briggs arranges for "Buck Fanshaw's Funeral" in lively vernacular that repeatedly forces a frail fugitive from an eastern theological school to request that Briggs rephrase his incomprehensible remarks. He repeatedly acknowledges his own failure to comprehend the euphemistic—and euphuistic—circumlocutions of the genteel East and strives manfully to confine his grief-stricken utterance to language less colorful and profane than he finds normal. Throughout the exchange readers wonder at the minister's pomposity and at what seems to be almost a deliberate refusal to understand Briggs.

Twain presents the exchange as a sample of western slang and as an effort to understand an important stratum of boomtown silver-mining society. He then concludes the chapter on a curious note indeed: Briggs turns out to be "the only convert to religion that was ever gathered from the Virginia roughs." He falls victim to the East, even though he besmirches (with the western "violence" of his slang) the Old Testament tales that he tells to his Sunday school classes. The patronizing tone of the suddenly genteel narrative voice raises to a reader's consciousness the conflict, alive throughout Twain's career, between accommodation to and rebellion against eastern propriety.

Pascal Covici, Jr.

BIBLIOGRAPHY

Covici, Pascal, Jr. *Mark Twain's Humor: The Image of a World*. Dallas: Southern Methodist UP, 1962.

Gibson, William M. *The Art of Mark Twain*. New York: Oxford UP, 1976.

Lynn, Kenneth S. *Mark Twain and Southwestern Humor*. Boston: Little, Brown, 1959.

Mack, Effie Mona. *Mark Twain in Nevada*. New York: Scribner, 1947.

Smith, Henry Nash. *Mark Twain: The Development of a Writer*. Cambridge, Mass.: Harvard UP, 1962.

See also: "Buck Fanshaw's Funeral"; *Roughing It*

Brooks, Van Wyck
(1886–1963)

Born in 1886 in Plainfield, New Jersey, to Charles Edward Brooks and Sarah Bailey Ames Brooks, Van Wyck Brooks graduated Phi Beta Kappa from Harvard in 1907. Although he later received honorary doctorates from Harvard and Columbia, among others, and was awarded the Pulitzer Prize for history (1936), his importance to Mark Twain scholarship rests in his *The Ordeal of Mark Twain* (1920, revised ed., 1933), the controversial first volume in a trilogy including volumes on Henry James and Ralph Waldo Emerson. Brooks died 2 May 1963 in Bridgewater, Connecticut, but the controversy over his thesis—that Mark Twain's genius was stultified by the forces of Puritanism, the frontier, and the genteel influences of his age—continues unabated.

Brooks argues that Twain, trapped in the ugly reality of the material world, betrayed his artistic spirit by capitulating to social and financial enticements. Brooks viewed Twain as a "victim of arrested development" who was essentially emasculated by his mother, Jane Lampton Clemens, and his wife, Olivia Langdon Clemens; by the genteel values of Hannibal, Elmira, and Hartford; and by the

influence of such friends as William Dean Howells. Brooks reached his thesis by drawing heavily on Herbert Croly's *The Promise of American Life* (1909) and Bernard Hart's *The Psychology of Insanity* (1912). Believing that not repressed sex but repressed artistry and creativity damaged Twain, Brooks saw in him a dual personality that first manifested itself in his boyhood somnambulism.

Brooks's book stirred such controversy that it inspired a passionate refutation by Bernard DeVoto, entitled *Mark Twain's America* (1932). DeVoto assaulted Brooks thoroughly. Furthermore, since then he has been challenged by numerous other critics, some of whom charge him with thesis mongering and failure to ground his ideas in textual argument and analysis. No Twain enthusiast should ignore the critical debate fueled by Brooks's book. A very useful summary of the controversy, replete with reprints of early critical reactions, is Lewis Leary's *A Casebook on Mark Twain's Wound*.

Although Brooks may not have been correct about the causes, his thesis is highly provocative, and much modern criticism continues to explore and to validate his belief in Twain's dual personality. Brooks was the first to note the frequent recurrence of twins and all types of doubleness; the importance of the Mississippi to Twain's creativity; the usefulness of psychoanalytic terms to explore a significant author's personality; and the fusion of the historical and Freudian perspectives. Ultimately, the heated debate introduced by Brooks provides a vital and integral strand of Twain scholarship.

Abby H.P. Werlock

BIBLIOGRAPHY

Brooks, Van Wyck. *The Ordeal of Mark Twain*. New York: Dutton, 1920.

Clemens, Samuel L. *Mark Twain's Autobiography*. Vol. 1. Ed. Albert B. Paine. New York: Harper, 1924.

———. *Mark Twain's Hannibal, Huck & Tom*. Ed. Walter Blair. Berkeley: U of California P, 1969.

Cowley, Malcolm. "Brooks's Mark Twain: Thirty-Five Years After." *New Republic* 132 (20 June 1955): 18.

DeVoto, Bernard. *Mark Twain's America*. Boston: Little, Brown, 1932.

Hoopes, James. *Van Wyck Brooks: In Search of American Culture*. Amherst: U of Massachusetts P, 1977.

Kaplan, Justin. *Mr. Clemens and Mark Twain*. New York: Simon & Schuster, 1966.

Leary, Lewis, ed. *A Casebook on Mark Twain's Wound*. New York: Crowell, 1962.

Vitelli, James R. *Van Wyck Brooks*. New York: Twayne, 1969.

Wasserstrom, William. *The Legacy of Van Wyck Brooks: A Study of Maladies and Motives*. Carbondale: Southern Illinois UP, 1971.

———, ed. *Van Wyck Brooks: The Critic and His Critics*. Port Washington, N.Y.: Kennikat, 1979.

See also: Biographers; Clemens, Samuel Langhorne; DeVoto, Bernard; Scholarship, Trends in Mark Twain

Brown, John, M.D.
(1810–1882)

Much beloved as a physician, John Brown, M.D., won wider fame with his writings, especially the sentimental dog story *Rab and His Friends* (1859). During their visit to Edinburgh in 1873, the Clemens family became close friends with Brown, later corresponding with him until his death and with his son Jock thereafter. Enthusiastic about *Rab*, and even more so about Brown's sketch of the precocious Marjorie Fleming, Mark Twain later wrote his own sketch, "Marjorie Fleming, the Wonder Child" (*Harper's Bazaar*, November 1909).

Howard G. Baetzhold

BIBLIOGRAPHY

Brown, John. *Marjorie Fleming: A Sketch*. Edinburgh, 1863. Reprinted from the *North British Review*.

———. *Rab and His Friends*. Boston: Ticknor and Fields, 1859.

Clemens, Samuel L. *Mark Twain's Autobiography*. Vol. 2. Ed. Albert B. Paine. New York: Harper, 1924.

Gribben, Alan. *Mark Twain's Library: A Reconstruction*. Vol. 2. Boston: G.K. Hall, 1980.

See also: "Marjorie Fleming, the Wonder Child"

Brownell, Edward

During his stay in Keokuk, Iowa, Edward Brownell (dates unknown) clerked in the bookstore on the ground floor of the building in which Samuel Clemens worked and lived. Brownell joined Samuel, Henry, and a friend, Dick Hingham, for social evenings in the third-floor office of Orion Clemens. Clemens once boasted to Brownell that he could write a funnier book than the one he happened to be reading, to which Brownell replied that Clemens was too lazy for such a venture. Years later, during his "Sandwich Island" lecture in Keokuk, Clemens identified Brownell as one of the greatest liars in the world (the other being the king of the Sandwich Islands).

Kevin Hadduck

BIBLIOGRAPHY

Clemens, Samuel L. *The Art, Humor, and Humanity of Mark Twain*. Ed. Minnie Brashear and Robert M. Rodney. Norman: U of Oklahoma P, 1959.

Paine, Albert Bigelow. *Mark Twain: A Biography*. 3 vols. New York: Harper, 1912.

See also: Keokuk, Iowa

Brownell, George Hiram
(1875–1950)

George Hiram Brownell was a recognized Mark Twain expert who made numerous contributions in the field of Mark Twain scholarship. Brownell was born in Janesville, Wisconsin, in 1875, and he died seventy-five years later in Fort Lauderdale, Florida. Brownell's work in Mark Twain studies was extensive. He was involved in the Mark Twain Research Foundation, serving as both secretary and director of research for the foundation. He is also recognized for his editorial work on the staff of the *Twainian*.

Brownell contributed many articles to the *Twainian* and other periodicals. He accumulated an enormous amount of information concerning the life, works, and critical studies of Mark Twain; according to the notice of his death in the New York *Times*, Brownell had collected an index of over 8,000 cards concerning Mark Twain. Brownell also possessed many first editions of Twain's works and books concerning the famous humorist.

Trevor J. Morgan

BIBLIOGRAPHY

"George H. Brownell, Mark Twain Expert." New York *Times*, 2 June 1950, late ed., sec. L, p. 23.

Long, E. Hudson. *Mark Twain Handbook*. New York: Hendricks House, 1957.

See also: Journals; Mark Twain Research Foundation

Browning, Elizabeth Barrett
(1806–1861)

In a letter written to Olivia Langdon on 18 October 1868, Clemens refers to Elizabeth Barrett Browning's *Aurora Leigh* (1857) as a work that puzzles him. Evidently, Olivia had been helping Clemens understand this poem, a favorite of hers, for on 30 October, when Clemens refers to it again, he writes that he is ready for more "lessons" (*Letters* 268, 274). At the end of this year, while on a lecture circuit, Clemens continues to complain about *Aurora Leigh*'s obscurity in his correspondence with his fiancée (*Love Letters* 34). Olivia, retaliating playfully in a letter to Mrs. Fairbanks dated 13 February 1870, writes that when Mrs. Fairbanks visits, they will have Clemens read to them from Elizabeth Barrett Browning (*Fairbanks* 126). Finally, in a letter to Olivia in which Clemens responds indignantly to a reviewer's inability to appreciate his humor in *Roughing It* (1872), he refers to the poor choice he himself would make to review the poetry of Elizabeth Barrett Browning (*My Father* 47).

In a letter written to Olivia on 17 May 1869, mocking a memoir being written about an acquaintance of the Langdons who had recently died, Clemens proposes to write the tribute himself. Among other sentimental poetry, he will include in it "some dark and bloody mystery out of the Widow Browning" (*Love Letters* 96). This reference is in-cluded under Alan Gribben's entry on Barrett Browning in his *Mark Twain's Library*. More likely, Clemens was referring to Robert Browning in this case. Since Elizabeth Barrett Browning died in 1861, it is Robert Browning who was widowed at this time; furthermore, his *The Ring and the Book*, published in 1868, tells of a violent murder.

Margaret D. Bauer

BIBLIOGRAPHY

Clemens, Clara. *My Father, Mark Twain*. New York: Harper, 1931.

Clemens, Samuel L. *The Love Letters of Mark Twain*. Ed. Dixon Wecter. New York: Harper, 1949.

———. *Mark Twain to Mrs. Fairbanks*. Ed. Dixon Wecter. San Marino, Calif.: Huntington Library, 1949.

———. *Mark Twain's Letters, Volume 2 (1867–1868)*. Ed. Harriet Elinor Smith and Richard Bucci. Berkeley: U of California P, 1990.

Gribben, Alan. *Mark Twain's Library: A Reconstruction*. Vol. 1. Boston: G.K. Hall, 1980.

See also: Browning, Robert

Browning, Robert
(1812–1889)

Samuel Clemens's adulation of Robert Browning's poetry has been accepted for many years, but supplemental documentation of the enormity of this admiration and the extent of Clemens's acquaintance with Browning's work continues to multiply. In 1886 and 1887 Clemens led a weekly Browning study class for women in the library of the Clemenses' Hartford house. "They say the poetry never gets obscure till I begin to explain it," he informed Mary Hallock Foote on 2 December 1887. "So I've stopped being expounder, and thrown my heft on the reading." The moral for teachers should be evident, he added: "Don't explain your author, read him right and he explains himself" (De Casseres 7). Mary Bushnell Cheney reported that Clemens's "reading was not oratorical and aimed at no effects of cadence. Free from self-consciousness, attempting only to let those sentences speak for themselves as the author meant them, mastering in the easiest way the parenthetical style so habitual with Browning, sentence within sentence conveying the thought, Mr. Clemens . . . let him interpret himself with no intrusion of his own personality" (Cheney 6). Dramatic monologues were especially effective in Clemens's treatment.

Many Browning volumes survive from Clemens's library (in addition to copies he annotated in the library of Susan and Theodore Crane at Quarry Farm), and these reveal an elaborate system of pencil markings that Clemens devised "in order to give the eye instant help in placing & shading emphases— a very necessary precaution when one reads Browning aloud" (comment written in *Dramatis Personae, Dramatic Romances and Lyrics* [1884], Mark Twain Project at Berkeley).

Among the poems that Clemens read to appreciative groups in informal as well as scheduled oral performances were "Up at a Villa— Down in the City," "Muleykeh," "Clive," "Andrea del Sarto," "Abt Vogler," "Rabbi Ben Ezra," "Before" and "After," "How They Brought the Good News from Ghent to Aix," "Old Pictures in Florence," "With Daniel Bartoli," "Tray," and "Christmas-Eve." Like his affection for such works as William Morris's "Shameful Death" and the verse of Rudyard Kipling, which Clemens also read orally with much frequency, his immersion in the poetry of Robert Browning testified to Clemens's quest for intellectual challenge and aesthetic gratification as well as to his perennial search for materials that could be effective in oral performance.

Alan Gribben

BIBLIOGRAPHY

Cheney, Mary Bushnell. "Mark Twain as a Reader." *Harper's Weekly* 55 (7 January 1911): 6.

Clemens, Samuel L. *When Huck Finn Went Highbrow.* Ed. Benjamin De Casseres. New York: Thomas F. Madigan, 1934.

Gribben, Alan. "'It Is Unsatisfactory to Read One's Self': Mark Twain's Informal Readings." *Quarterly Journal of Speech* 62 (February 1976): 49–56.

———. *Mark Twain's Library: A Reconstruction.* Vol. 1. Boston: G.K. Hall, 1987.

———. "'A Splendor of Stars & Suns': Twain as a Reader of Browning's Poems." *Browning Institute Studies* 6 (1978): 87–103.

See also: Lecturer; Reading

"Buck Fanshaw's Funeral"
(1872)

The anthologized version of the popular chapter 47 from *Roughing It* (1872) distorts meaning while preserving hilarity. Without its first and last paragraphs, the account of Scotty Briggs's efforts to procure the services of a newly arrived eastern minister beautifully illustrates the slang of the Nevada silver fields, a slang rich, "copious," and "infinitely varied." A quick reading of the delicious episode might seem to confirm that a linguistic intent provides the story's principal focus. Taking his lingo from games of chance—poker, monte, pool, faro, whist—as well as from everywhere else, Scotty Briggs bombards the minister with language that he cannot understand. Buck "has gone up the flume . . . throwed up the sponge . . . kicked the bucket." When the minister concludes that perhaps Scotty means to say that his friend "has departed to that mysterious country from whose bourne no traveler returns," Briggs wonders at the minister's ignorance: "Return! I reckon not. Why pard, he's *dead!*"

Almost the whole story consists of the slang-obstructed conversation between western miner and eastern minister. Only two short paragraphs summarize the funeral, Briggs's brief response to which is itself slang, "without apparent relevancy" to the occasion, except that, as he has said, it was Buck Fanshaw's "word" upon many an occasion: "No Irish need apply." Slang, whether rationally communicative or not, says Twain, was the manner of speaking in the Nevada silver fields of the 1860s.

But the story embodies a great deal more than this local-color interest in mining-town speech habits, as its context in *Roughing It* makes clear. In the first paragraph Twain (or his narrative voice: sometimes the distinction has considerable significance; sometimes not) has a serious sociological purpose. Having heard that to understand a community one must observe the funerals of its leading citizens, he infers a need to detail funerals of both "the distinguished public benefactor" and "the distinguished rough." These two extremes made up the types most highly honored in Virginia City, the citizens buried "with most eclat," and Buck had few equals as "rough." Throughout the book, and most explicitly in the chapters following the funeral, the social implications of western lawlessness receive horrified attention. What seemed at first a delighted sojourn into a free-and-easy land of laissez faire, an escape from the city and from eastern civilization, becomes an embroilment in insecurity, violence, fear, and chaos. The fun of Scotty's way of speaking and the fun of the eastern minister's impossibly opaque obtuseness underline the shift from immediate pleasure to deep-seated repulsion: we can enjoy the verbally fantastic preparations for Buck's funeral, but grim reality lies ahead.

With this in mind, the last paragraph provides an index to ambivalences extremely important for an understanding of Mark Twain and Sam Clemens, artist and human being. In language dripping with the smugness of eastern propriety at its most genteel, the narrator recounts that Scotty Briggs, "in after days," became the only Virginia City rough who converted to Christianity. "He talked to his pioneer small-fry in language they understood!" The narrator had the "large privilege" of hearing Briggs present—"a month before he died"—a slang version of "the beautiful story of Joseph." Note that Twain had told it in similar style in one of his letters to the *Alta California*, a letter omitted from *The Innocents Abroad* (1969) because Mrs. Fairbanks was appalled by Twain's disrespect for the sacred. Here, without repeating his earlier newspaper piece, Twain's narrator simply "leave[s] it to the reader" to imagine it, "as it fell, riddled

with slang, from the lips of that grave earnest teacher," who, like "his little learners," was "unconscious . . . that any violence was being done to the sacred proprieties!"

Twain, or his narrator, patronizes the crudities of western efforts to become civilized. Twain also parodies the eastern gentility that he will so ambivalently reject in the Whittier Birthday Dinner Speech of 1877. At the same time, he may be trying to be "good," trying to appropriate the attitudes that his wife still wanted him to acquire. Certainly he is reminding himself of the harsh facts, as well as of the freedoms, of life in his "good old days" of less than ten years earlier. Celebrating wild western slang as it becomes an eastern tool of domestication, Twain here fashions a wonderfully successful linguistic tour de force and a comprehensive, albeit brief, survey of attitudes and values that will concern him for the rest of his writing life.

Pascal Covici, Jr.

BIBLIOGRAPHY

Clemens, Samuel L. *Roughing It*. Ed. Franklin R. Rogers and Paul Baender. Berkeley: U of California P, 1972.

Covici, Pascal, Jr. *Mark Twain's Humor: The Image of a World*. Dallas: Southern Methodist UP, 1962.

Gibson, William M. *The Art of Mark Twain*. New York: Oxford UP, 1976.

Lynn, Kenneth S. *Mark Twain and Southwestern Humor*. Boston: Little, Brown, 1959.

Mack, Effie Mona. *Mark Twain in Nevada*. New York: Scribner, 1947.

Smith, Henry Nash. *Mark Twain: The Development of a Writer*. Cambridge, Mass.: Harvard UP, 1962.

See also: Briggs, Scotty; Genteel Tradition; *Roughing It*; Vernacular; Whittier Birthday Dinner Speech

Buffalo, New York

Mark Twain lived in Buffalo, a city on the shore of Lake Erie in western New York, from early August 1869 to mid-March 1871. While there, he co-owned and edited the *Express*, a daily newspaper, and began his family life as husband and father. In 1870 Buffalo was a bustling commercial center with a population of 118,000.

The period spent in Buffalo is pivotal in Twain's career. It marked his final attempt at the daily grind of full-time journalism; after Buffalo, he shifted to become a man of letters in Hartford, Connecticut. He came to Buffalo as a thirty-four-year-old bachelor at the recommendation of his wealthy prospective father-in-law, Jervis Langdon, who lent Twain the money to become a one-third partner in the *Express*. For the first couple of months he rented a room in a boardinghouse at 39 East Swan Street just steps from his newspaper office. After he and Olivia Langdon married, he settled into a handsome, fully furnished, and well-staffed house at 472 Delaware Street, a wedding gift from his father-in-law. Although the house was demolished in 1963, a weekly business newspaper now operates at the site and has preserved the carriage house and the mansion's original foundation.

Twain made several lifelong friends in Buffalo, most notably David Gray (editor of the rival *Daily Courier*) and Charles M. Underhill (a Langdon coal company official), both of whom he and his wife often visited during the 1870s and 1880s. Twain's time in Buffalo was productive—he wrote several early chapters of *Roughing It* (1872) in his upstairs den, he contributed columns to the *Express* and *Galaxy* magazine, and his son Langdon was born in November 1870. But the period is forever associated with a string of tragedies. Jervis Langdon died and Olivia became bedridden with grief. A family friend, Emma Nye, who visited Olivia, died of typhoid fever in their master bedroom. Olivia never fully recovered in Buffalo after her difficult pregnancy.

In 1871 Twain severed his ties with the *Express*, moved his family temporarily to Elmira, and sold the grand house at a loss of $1,000. Nook Farm and the Hartford literati beckoned.

Thomas J. Reigstad

BIBLIOGRAPHY

Buffalo City Directory for 1871. Buffalo: Warren, Johnson, 1871.

Clemens, Samuel L. *The Love Letters of Mark Twain.* Ed. Dixon Wecter. New York: Harper, 1949.

———. *Mark Twain to Mrs. Fairbanks.* Ed. Dixon Wecter. San Marino, Calif.: Huntington Library, 1949.

Fried, Martin J. "Mark Twain in Buffalo." *Niagara Frontier* (Winter 1959): 89–110.

Kaplan, Justin. *Mr. Clemens and Mark Twain.* New York: Simon & Schuster, 1966.

Reigstad, Tom. "Twain's Langdon-appointed Guardian Angels in Buffalo: 'Mac,' 'Fletch,' and 'Dombrowski.'" *Mark Twain Society Bulletin* (July 1989): 1–8.

See also: Buffalo *Express*; Family Life; Langdon, Jervis

Buffalo *Express*

In 1869 Mark Twain borrowed $25,000 from his future father-in-law Jervis Langdon to buy a one-third share of the Republican-oriented *Express* in Buffalo, New York. He left the business end to his partner Colonel George H. Selkirk and most political matters to partner and co-editor Josephus N. Larned. He worked diligently for the first two months, scanning newspaper exchanges, coaching reporters, writing articles, and revamping the graphic design.

The *Express* was located in a four-story brick building at 14 East Swan Street in Buffalo. Twain smoked cigars constantly in his third-floor office, sometimes sitting at a comfortable yellow chair with a writing board hinged onto the arm, other times writing at a desk opposite Larned, with whom he occasionally shared manuscripts in progress.

From October 1869 to January 1870 he lectured throughout the Northeast, faithfully mailing stories to the *Express*. After returning to Buffalo as a newlywed in February 1870, his commitment to the daily newspaper grind slipped. Although he supplied stories regularly through 1870 and early 1871, Twain seldom showed up at the *Express*, often making editorial decisions and sending directives to his staff from his Delaware Street home.

Twain's *Express* contributions include sixty feature stories, thirty-one editorials, and thirty brief entries in a "People and Things" column. Some stories focused on local issues, such as greedy coroners, deteriorating graveyards, dusty street conditions, and incompetent postmasters. Some of the ten stories in his "Around the World" series were incorporated into *Roughing It* (1872).

Nearly twenty *Express* stories appeared in *Galaxy* magazine. Several were later reprinted in *Sketches, New and Old* (1875). But the quality of Twain's *Express* writing is uneven; many pieces have never been reprinted. Twain left Buffalo and the *Express* for the literary pastures of Hartford, Connecticut, early in 1871. Eventually he sold his interest in the *Express* at a huge $10,000 loss.

Thomas J. Reigstad

BIBLIOGRAPHY

Berry, Earl D. "Mark Twain as a Newspaperman." Buffalo *Express*, 11 November 1917.

Clemens, Samuel L. *The Love Letters of Mark Twain.* Ed. Dixon Wecter. New York: Harper, 1949.

———. *Roughing It.* Ed. Franklin R. Rogers and Paul Baender. Berkeley: U of California P, 1972.

Kaplan, Justin. *Mr. Clemens and Mark Twain.* New York: Simon & Schuster, 1966.

McCullough, Joseph B. "A Listing of Mark Twain's Contributions to the Buffalo *Express*, 1869–1871." *American Literary Realism, 1870–1910* 5 (Winter 1972): 61–70.

See also: "Around the World" Letters; Buffalo, New York; Journalism

Buntline, Ned
(1823–1886)

Ned Buntline is the pseudonym for Edward Zane Carroll Judson, author, adventurer, and political agitator. Judson served in both the navy and the army, from which latter service he was cashiered for drunkenness. He once served a year in a New York jail for organizing a political riot and later helped to establish the Know-Nothing Party (1854). He authored 400 dime novels, of which literary genre he is said to be the originator. In 1869 Buntline nicknamed and helped to promote William F. Cody as "Buffalo Bill" by writing several novels about his exploits as well as a play, in some productions of which he persuaded Cody to act the part of himself.

Mark Twain used the title of a Ned Buntline novel—*The Black Avenger of the Spanish Main*—in two of his works: *The Adventures of Tom Sawyer* (1876) and an early undated essay entitled "Jul'us Caesar."

Fred Weldon

BIBLIOGRAPHY

Gribben, Alan. *Mark Twain's Library: A Reconstruction.* 2 vols. Boston: G.K. Hall, 1980.

Monaghan, Jay. *The Great Rascal: The Life and Adventures of Ned Buntline.* Boston: Little, Brown, 1952.

Rogers, Franklin R. *Mark Twain's Burlesque Patterns as Seen in the Novels and Narratives, 1855–1885.* Dallas: Southern Methodist UP, 1960.

Burke, Edmund
(1729–1797)

A great British political writer and statesman, Edmund Burke was born in Dublin, the son of a Catholic mother and a Protestant father. He was educated at Trinity College, Dublin, then moved to London, where he studied law. Preferring literature to the law, Burke moved in literary circles and made a small living from his writing. In 1756 he married. He returned to Dublin in 1759, and by 1766 he was elected to parliament.

Burke published works on a wide variety of subjects, though his political writing remains best known. In 1770 he published *Thoughts on the Cause of the Present Discontents,* a justification of the value of political parties. Though himself a Protestant, Burke defended disenfranchised Catholics and the persecuted Irish, as well as the American colonies. Burke spent fourteen years on the impeachment of Warren Hastings, first governor of British India. Although Hastings was acquitted in 1795, Burke's efforts spurred reform. It is to this last work that Mark Twain turns for his attack on corruption in New York City politics.

In the 1901 mayoral campaign in New York, Twain backed Seth Low on the Fusion ticket against Edward M. Shepard, the Tammany Hall candidate. On 17 October 1901 Twain spoke at a dinner for the Acorns, a society in opposition to Tammany Hall politics. The speech was "Edmund Burke on Croker and Tammany" (Fatout 404–413). In this unusually serious speech, Twain delivered a set of extracts from Burke's impeachment of Hastings, substituting the name of Tammany Hall boss Richard Croker for that of Warren Hastings and comparing Croker's abuses in New York with Hastings's abuses in India.

Twain's use of Burke added historical significance to the mayoral election as well as elevated his own stature as a political thinker. Moreover, the use of Burke, a defender of the Irish, might have gained some Irish supporters in the attack on Croker. The speech quickly was published as a supplement to *Harper's Weekly*, then reprinted as a pamphlet by the Acorns. Hundreds of thousands of copies were circulated before the election, and Twain considered himself largely responsible for Shepard's defeat.

Nancy Cook

BIBLIOGRAPHY

Burke, Edmund. *The Works of Edmund Burke.* 12 vols. Boston: Little, Brown, 1865–1871.

———. *Selected Writings and Speeches.* Ed. Peter J. Stanlis. Gloucester, Mass.: Peter Smith, 1968.

Clemens, Samuel L. "Edmund Burke on Croker and Tammany." *Harper's Weekly* Supplement 45.2339 (19 October 1901): 1602.

———. *Edmund Burke on Croker and Tammany.* New York: Economist P, 1901.

———. *Mark Twain Speaking.* Ed. Paul Fatout. Iowa City: U of Iowa P, 1976.

See also: Ireland, Irish, Irishmen; New York, New York; Politics

Burlesque

Burlesque is a type of humor characterized by imitation and exaggeration. It is usually distinguished by ridiculous distortion and seeks to amuse rather than to correct. When used exclusively to imitate and exaggerate character, burlesque is often labeled caricature, and when directed against style, it is frequently called parody. Typically, burlesque involves a large discrepancy between subject matter and style.

Twain's western literary apprenticeship was largely given over to writing burlesques. While the frontier humor that he knew so well employed burlesque techniques, Twain's associations in Nevada and California with Bohemians such as Orpheus C. Kerr, Artemus Ward, Dan De Quille, and Bret Harte gave him firsthand knowledge of the burlesque novel form that was so popular among that group. These associations led him to devalue the southwestern humor mode and to cultivate their more pervasive and self-consciously sophisticated burlesque attitudes.

Twain's first condensed burlesque novel appeared in 1863, and for the next eight years more than half of the fifty-three short humorous pieces that he wrote were either burlesques or used burlesque as a primary device. While some commentators have seen this as at best an elementary stage in or at worst a detour that delayed Twain's development as a literary artist, Franklin R. Rogers has argued insistently that the period of 1855 to 1885 was an experimental one for Twain during which he learned invaluable lessons in the art of structure from his use of burlesque.

While many may not agree with Rogers that this apprenticeship in burlesque was the major shaping influence on Twain's career as novelist, certainly Twain made heavy use of burlesque forms and techniques throughout his career and found its inherent exaggeration and anti-romanticism congenial with his themes and talents.

W. Craig Turner

BIBLIOGRAPHY

Long, E. Hudson, and J.R. LeMaster. *The New Mark Twain Handbook.* New York: Garland, 1985.

Rogers, Franklin R. *Mark Twain's Burlesque Patterns as Seen in the Novels and Narratives, 1855–1885.* Dallas: Southern Methodist UP, 1960.

See also: Condensed Novels; Exaggeration

"Burlesque Autobiography"
(1871)

Published first as a book in 1871 as *Mark Twain's (Burlesque) Autobiography and First Romance*, the story was put out by Sheldon and Company in violation of Twain's contract with Elisha Bliss. The "Autobiography" had not been issued before it was joined with "The First Romance" to make a small book. "The Romance" had appeared as the "Awful, Terrible Medieval Romance" earlier, in the *Express* (1870). It has since been anthologized under this first title. In addition to the two texts, there was a running series of cartoon caricatures of the scandalous Erie Railroad Ring. *Mark Twain's (Burlesque) Autobiography* later appeared in 1906 as "A Burlesque Biography" in *The $30,000 Bequest and Other Stories.* Twain bought the plates of the original combined publication, out of dissatisfaction with his writing, but the texts have survived in other forms (Johnson 12–13).

Written around the time of his courtship of Olivia Langdon, the text of "Burlesque Autobiography" may be viewed as Twain's playful treatment of the ordeal he underwent when Olivia's father, Jervis Langdon, asked him for character references. Treated as the author's attempt to make light of his predicament, "Burlesque Autobiography" gains a context in which Twain's use of euphemism appears as funny as most of his frontier humor.

Sandra Littleton-Uetz

BIBLIOGRAPHY

Bellamy, Gladys C. *Mark Twain as a Literary Artist.* Norman: U of Oklahoma P, 1950.

Clemens, Samuel L. "A Burlesque Biography." *The $30,000 Bequest and Other Stories.* By Clemens. New York: Harper, 1906. 254–262.

Johnson, Merle. *A Bibliography of the Works of Mark Twain.* 1935; rpt. Westport, Conn.: Greenwood P, 1972.

See also: Autobiography; Langdon, Jervis

Burlingame, Anson
(1820–1870)

From 1861 to 1868 Anson Burlingame was the United States minister to China. Then the Chinese government enlisted him for the first diplomatic mission by China to foreign powers. That mission resulted in the Burlingame Treaty of 1868 between the United States and China. Burlingame died in St. Petersburg, Russia, trying to obtain similar treaties.

Mark Twain first met Burlingame in Hawaii (June 1866), where Twain was writing for the Sacramento *Union.* The two men developed an immediate friendship. Twain presented the minister with many of his tales and sketches and received an enthusiastic response.

In his *Autobiography* (1924) Twain calls Burlingame a "great citizen and diplomat" and a "charming man." Burlingame and Twain shared many experiences and ideas. The minister was a son of the frontier, coming of age in many of the kinds of towns and camps that Twain wrote about. He was also a member of the Know-Nothing Party early in his political career and probably shared many of Twain's views on politics.

David G. Miller

BIBLIOGRAPHY

Clemens, Samuel L. *Mark Twain's Autobiography.* Ed. Albert B. Paine. 2 vols. New York: Harper, 1924.

Concise Dictionary of American Biography. 2nd ed. New York: Scribner, 1977.

Lanman, Charles. *Biographical Annals of the Civil Government of The United States During Its First Century.* Washington, D.C.: James Anglim, 1876.

"Burning Shame, The"

During one of the long, rainy days at Angel's Camp in 1865, Jim Gillis entertained Mark Twain with the story of how a wandering tragedian hoaxed some small-town folks with an obscene performance at the local playhouse. According to Twain's recollection, Gillis's "pard," Dick Stoker, augmented the narrative by acting out the part of "Rinaldo," the sham tragedian who shocks his backwater audience by performing a bizarre phallic dance (*Eruption* 361).

In 1877 Twain made notes for incorporating "The Burning Shame" into a novel about Orion Clemens's life, the "Autobiography of a Damned Fool," but when the novel bogged down, he decided instead to use the tale in another manuscript he was working on at the same time. In chapter 23 of the California edition of *Adventures of Huckleberry Finn* (1885), Huck describes how the king stuns an audience full of "greenhorns" and "flatheads" in Bricksville, Arkansas, by performing "The King's Cameleopard or the Royal Nonesuch," a version of Dick Stoker's obscene dance. While the episode is one of the most memorable in the novel, Twain lamented that in preparing Gillis's raunchy tale for publication he was forced to "modify it considerably," and this he felt "was a great damage" to the original (*Eruption* 361).

Henry B. Wonham

BIBLIOGRAPHY

Blair, Walter. *Mark Twain & Huck Finn*. Berkeley: U of California P, 1960.

Clemens, Samuel L. *Adventures of Huckleberry Finn*. Ed. Walter Blair and Victor Fischer. Berkeley: U of California P, 1985.

———. *Mark Twain in Eruption*. Ed. Bernard DeVoto. New York: Harper, 1940.

Paine, Albert Bigelow. *Mark Twain: A Biography*. 3 vols. New York: Harper, 1912.

See also: Gillis, Jim; "Royal Nonesuch, The"

Burrough, J[acob] H.
(1825–1883)

In later years a lawyer and judge in Cape Girardeau, Missouri, J.H. Burrough earlier had been a journeyman chairmaker and roomed with Samuel Clemens, then a journeyman printer, in a St. Louis boardinghouse in late 1854 and early 1855. As Clemens later remarked in a letter to Burrough's son Frank (15 December 1900), he was impressed by Burrough's wide reading and keen literary judgments, and they became close friends. Given Burrough's occupation and intellectual interests, he was almost certainly the model for Barrow, the journeyman chairmaker and boardinghouse friend of Howard Tracy in *The American Claimant* (1892).

Howard G. Baetzhold

BIBLIOGRAPHY

Baetzhold, Howard G. *Mark Twain and John Bull: The British Connection*. Bloomington: Indiana UP, 1970.

Clemens, Samuel L. Letter to J.H. Burrough, 1 November 1876. *The Portable Mark Twain*. By Clemens. Ed. Bernard DeVoto. New York: Viking, 1946. 749–752.

———. Letter to Frank E. Burrough, 15 December 1900. Southeast Missouri State College, Cape Girardeau. Mark Twain Papers.

———. *Mark Twain's Notebooks & Journals, Volume I (1855–1873)*. Ed. Frederick Anderson, Michael B. Frank, and Kenneth M. Sanderson. Berkeley: U of California P, 1975.

———. *Mark Twain's Notebooks & Journals, Volume II (1877–1883)*. Ed. Frederick Anderson, Lin Salamo, and Bernard L. Stein. Berkeley: U of California P, 1975.

Business

The life and art of Samuel L. Clemens are intertwined with the broad world of business in nineteenth-century America. He was born on the Missouri frontier in 1835 to a family of modest means, and his father's premature death in 1847 forced Clemens to work at an early age. His family's dreams of wealth from Tennessee land investments never having materialized, and the opportunities for advancement without capital in the antebellum South severely limited, Clemens nevertheless refused to resign himself to poverty. The lure of Nevada with its illusions of quick fortune beckoned him as the Civil War brought an end to his ambitions as a cub pilot on the Mississippi; and though he saw in the West that the victims of illusion proved far more numerous than those who actually "struck it rich," Clemens was determined to make the system work for him. Hard work, ingenuity, and luck were the passport to upward mobility in an America free of the class restrictions of decadent Europe. Marrying the daughter of a wealthy eastern industrialist in February 1870, settling in Hartford and raising a family during the boom years of Reconstruction, and becoming a valued member of the genteel Nook Farm community, Clemens in mid-life assumed the perspectives and optimism of the upper-middle class. Later in life he would prove sympathetic to the plight of the working class, lending his support to various labor reform causes, but unlike William Dean Howells he never became a socialist. Entrepreneur, showman, inventor, investor, publisher, and editor as well as author, Samuel Clemens was intoxicated with dreams of wealth in an age of laissez-faire capitalism.

From October 1861 until August 1862, Clemens raised capital, procured inventory, and worked as a laborer, foremen, treasurer, and corresponding secretary for a business that followed the path of most American enterprises before and since: it failed in the first twelve months. The history of Clemens's first business venture is found in the letters he wrote as a Nevada prospector. The tone of these letters establishes a pattern that would recur through most of Clemens's business correspondence: visions of limitless profit give way to bitter disappointment, followed by a remarkable resiliency of spirit as Clemens begins anew his quest for fortune. After admonishing himself in October 1861 to "tell everything (about the mining business) as it is—no better, and no worse" (*Letters* 132), Clemens

calmly predicted that a man with $3,000 could turn it into $100,000 in six months. Six months later, however, Clemens revealed to his brother Orion that things had not worked out as planned and requested that his brother send "$40.00 or $50.00—by mail—immediately" (*Letters* 186). A mere two months later, Clemens sought his pleasures in less tangible areas: "if the ledges prove worthless, it will be a pleasant reflection to know that others were beaten worse than ourselves." By July he was getting desperate, and implored Orion to write the Sacramento *Union* to tell them he would write as many letters as they wanted for $10 a month (*Letters* 229). In August, broke, he walked the 130 miles across the mountains to join the staff of the *Territorial Enterprise* in Virginia City.

From 1863 through 1868 Clemens managed to avoid the speculating world of commerce altogether. Instead of digging holes in the ground and writing letters detailing the few months remaining until he and his partners would realize millions, he wrote the newspaper articles, sketches, and travel letters and delivered the lectures that would establish him as one of the leading humorists of the decade. But Clemens feared he was merely running in place, drifting, not going anywhere financially; he needed a profession. Rubbing shoulders with the monied elite on board the *Quaker City* on a voyage to Europe, Palestine, and Egypt in 1867, he envisioned his opportunity. He would gather his travel letters, written for and owned by the *Daily Alta*, and market them as a book through Elisha Bliss. He had first to travel to San Francisco to pressure the *Alta* to release what they had bought and paid for; but Clemens, sold on the idea of subscription publication, was convinced that this was the way to market his literary talent—his only capital—and make his way into genteel, monied society as a bona fide man of letters.

The siren of the American dream of ownership beckoned again as Clemens prepared to settle down into a respectable marriage. Using $25,000 borrowed from his prospective father-in-law, Clemens purchased one-third interest in the Buffalo *Express*. For a short time he actually behaved like a proprietor, working long hours to turn out articles, sketches, and editorials. But in October 1869, only two months after he had started work on the *Express*, he took a leave of absence to return to the lecture circuit; he needed the quick money and calculated that his public appearances would help sales of his new book, *The Innocents Abroad* (1869). Clemens never returned to the *Express* with his full attention, calculating at one point during the spring of 1870 that his obligations to the *Express* and to the New York-based *Galaxy* would require only six days of his attention each month. Domestic obligations, however, claimed most of the rest of his time, and Clemens decided to move from Buffalo, first to his wife's hometown to Elmira, then to Hartford, Connecticut. In the spring of 1871 he sold his share of the *Express* at a loss of $10,000.

Clemens's next business disaster began as a mere speculation when he decided to invest $2,000 in the Paige typesetter, a machine described to him over a billiard table in 1880. Over the next five years he invested an additional $11,000; the real disaster, however, did not begin until 1886, when James Paige sold Clemens half-ownership of the machine for a promise that he would bankroll the redesign, production, and promotion. "I can get a thousand men worth a million apiece to go in with me if I can get a perfect machine," Clemens claimed, ignoring the prophetic warning of his business adviser, Franklin G. Whitmore, that the support he had so rashly promised could bankrupt him.

By this time Clemens's fourth business venture—Charles L. Webster and Company, Publishers—was achieving reasonable success, and had he not constantly drained its profits to feed the typesetter, it is possible that the company would still be publishing today. It was started in 1884 when, generally dissatisfied with his publishers and the return on his work, Clemens decided to publish his own books. His nephew, Charles L. Webster, who was already managing Clemens's business affairs,

became president of the company. Under his direction the company offered its first book to the public in February 1885: *Adventures of Huckleberry Finn*, which would eventually sell over 10 million copies. It sold 50,000 in the first three months after its release and insured the financial strength for marketing the firm's next big project, the *Personal Memoirs of U.S. Grant,* which paid to Grant's widow the largest royalties known up to that time.

Although these early successes were not repeated—not with *Diversions of a Diplomat in Turkey,* nor with *Life of Pope Leo XIII* (which Clemens foolishly thought would be required reading for every Catholic in America), nor with *The Genesis of the Civil War*—the death of Charles L. Webster and Company can be traced directly to the Paige typesetter. Perhaps had he owned the "perfect machine," Clemens may have been able to attract a thousand men with a million dollars; in retrospect, however, it is astonishing that Clemens thought the "perfect machine" was even attainable. By 1887 his $13,000 investment had swollen to a $50,000 commitment, and he was bankrolling his partner at $3,000 a month. By 1894, when he was finally rid of the typesetter, Clemens had spent over $200,000 on the then outmoded machine, at least $10,000 of it borrowed from his wife's mother. Paige's machine forced Clemens to file for personal bankruptcy and forced him to undertake a world lecture tour to struggle clear of debt, but it had never completed a single task.

One would have thought Clemens had learned his lesson. Yet even after Henry Huttleston Rogers, one of the principal architects of the Standard Oil Trust and a sharp negotiator, had managed the author's financial reconstruction, Clemens was bit again. This time the lure was plasmon, a British health food product that he was convinced would instantly alleviate famine in India. Clemens became interested in plasmon while in Vienna in 1898. His initial investment in the British company proved modestly successful, but a subsequent $25,000 investment in an American branch of the company (under the direction of Henry Butters) proved disastrous. Now solvent, and free of the Hartford house that had become a financial albatross, Clemens could this time withstand the monetary loss. But he could ill afford the psychological strain; it left him full of bitter recriminations—against Butters, against the capitalistic system, against God—and aggravated the anguish he felt over his rapidly deteriorating family life.

Mounting medical expenses, high living costs, disappointing book sales, anxieties over declining artistic creativity, fears of being swindled by financial advisers and associates fostered Clemens's continuing preoccupation with money in late life. Indeed, much of his artistic effort from the early 1890s until his death in 1910 sprang from his desperation to satisfy creditors. The corrupting force of illusory, instantaneous wealth is a central theme of "The Man That Corrupted Hadleyburg" (1899). Scholars see anxieties about money as the primary inspiration for "The $30,000 Bequest" (1904), a thinly veiled autobiographical story in which Clemens accepts responsibility for the catastrophes that ensued from his chronic infatuation with illusory wealth in the late 1880s. On his death bed, Saladin Foster articulates the lesson he has learned and voices hope that his fate, now sealed, might at least serve as a cautionary tale: "Vast wealth, acquired by sudden and unwholesome means, is a snare. It did us no good, transient were its feverish pleasures; yet for its sake we threw away our sweet and simple and happy life— let others take warning by us" (*Short Stories* 522).

More optimistic, and equally as germane, is the story "The £1,000,000 Bank-Note" (1893), written in late 1892 and reflecting "the author's need for credit as he was facing bankruptcy" (Emerson 188). The story tells of one Henry Adams, a twenty-seven year old mining broker's clerk from San Francisco who, "alone in the world, and . . . nothing to depend on but my wits and clean reputation," arrives in London "ragged and shabby" with a single dollar in his pocket. He is given a million pound bank note as an interest-free loan for thirty days; his benefactors are two wealthy old gentlemen who select him to settle a wager between them. The note, Adams discovers, has no controvertible cash value because he cannot cash it (how could he ever explain its origin?); he cannot even give it away. The resourceful Adams, however, is able to parlay the unnegotiable note into a fortune: he rises to social prominence, gains prosperity, even wins the love of a beautiful heiress—all without cashing the note that he returns, intact, at the appointed hour.

Samuel Clemens's million-pound note was his talent, which he marketed with remarkable skill and success in America's Gilded Age. Without a patron, without an inherited legacy, Clemens came eastward from San Francisco, like Adams, with "nothing to depend on but [his] wits"; he created, packaged, and sold Mark Twain—as celebrity, platform lecturer, newspaper correspondent, and author. Rarely has any writer taken so absorbing an interest in promoting, distributing, and copyrighting his material; few have more astutely gauged the market. Mark Twain brought Samuel Clemens fame, money, and influence—all, one might argue, without diminishing his initial capital. His subsidiary business ventures may have been failures and may have created havoc in his life, but in his ultimate business venture, inventing and marketing himself, he was a consummate success.

James D. Wilson and John Rees

BIBLIOGRAPHY

Budd. Louis J. *Our Mark Twain: The Making of His Public Personality.* Philadelphia: U of Pennsylvania P, 1983.

Clemens, Samuel L. *The Complete Short Stories of Mark Twain.* Ed. Charles Neider. Garden City, N.Y.: Hanover House, 1957.

———. *Mark Twain's Correspondence with Henry Huttleston Rogers, 1893–1909.* Ed. Lewis Leary. Berkeley: U of California P, 1969.

———. *Mark Twain's Letters, Volume 1 (1853–1866).* Ed. Edgar M. Branch, Michael B. Frank, and Kenneth M. Sanderson. Berkeley: U of California P, 1988.

Emerson, Everett. *The Authentic Mark Twain: A Literary Biography of Samuel L. Clemens*. Philadelphia: U of Pennsylvania P, 1984.

Geismar, Maxwell. *Mark Twain: An American Prophet*. Boston: Houghton Mifflin, 1970.

Hill, Hamlin. *Mark Twain: God's Fool*. New York: Harper & Row, 1973.

Kaplan, Justin. *Mr. Clemens and Mark Twain*. New York: Simon & Schuster, 1966.

Paine, Albert Bigelow. *Mark Twain: A Biography*. 3 vols. New York: Harper, 1912.

Webster, Samuel C. *Mark Twain, Business Man*. Boston: Little, Brown, 1946.

See also: Bankruptcy; *Gilded Age, The*; Paige Typesetting Machine; Plasmon; Sellers, Colonel; Webster and Company, Charles L.

Butters, Henry

Henry A. Butters was an associate of Mark Twain in promoting the sale of plasmon, a nutritional meat substitute that became another of Twain's ill-fated investments. In 1900 Twain purchased a one-sixth share in a syndicate designed to market plasmon, a health food powder created in Germany. The syndicate sold the American rights to Butters, who was part of an American syndicate (Webster 440). In a letter to his wife in 1904, Twain accused Butters of stealing 250 shares of stock from the company (*Correspondence* 557–559), and later branded Butters "the meanest white and the most degraded in spirit and contemptible in character I have ever known" (*Eruption* 356).

J. Mark Baggett

BIBLIOGRAPHY

Clemens, Samuel L. *Mark Twain in Eruption*. Ed. Bernard DeVoto. New York: Harper, 1940.

———. *Mark Twain's Correspondence with Henry Huttleston Rogers, 1893–1909*. Ed. Lewis Leary. Berkeley: U of California P, 1969.

Webster, Samuel Charles. *Mark Twain, Business Man*. Boston: Little, Brown, 1946.

See also: Business; Plasmon

C

Cable, George Washington
(1844–1925)

A bedraggled veteran of the Confederate cavalry, George Washington Cable returned to his native New Orleans at the close of the Civil War and by the mid-1870s was publishing the stories of Louisiana Creole life that were to make him famous. Assembled in *Old Creole Days* (1879), Cable's early tales were more than conventional local color fiction. Already they revealed the moral zeal and penetrating powers of social analysis that would inform his first novel, *The Grandissimes* (1880). Some twenty volumes of varied length would follow, works of fiction and nonfiction alike, but Cable's first two books are still regarded as his most lasting achievement. Students of southern literature often point to *The Grandissimes* as the first "modern" southern novel, a tribute to Cable's courage and skill in addressing the tragic role slavery and racism played in his region's history.

A man of profoundly religious sensibilities, Cable, in essays like "The Freedman's Case in Equity" (1885) and "The Negro Question in the United States" (1888), became at once celebrated and notorious as a spokesman for the rights of black Americans in the post-Reconstruction era. Cable appealed to what he called a "Silent South" of decent whites who, like him, were burdened with guilt over the former Confederacy's heritage of racial wrongs. Nevertheless, he deemed it necessary to expatriate himself, settling in Northampton, Massachusetts, in 1885. His literary powers (though not his output) may have declined after 1890, but his commitment to social reform and Christian renewal persisted, gradually expressing itself in a less confrontational and controversial fashion.

Cable knew and admired Mark Twain's writing from the early 1870s on, and in *Life on the Mississippi* (1883) Twain honored Cable as "the South's finest literary genius," a "masterly delineator of its interior life and history." Fond of each other's company, the two had a chance to become better acquainted when

Cable fell ill while a house guest of the Clemens family in Hartford. Twain resented the inconvenience, but their rapport was such that he recruited Cable to accompany him on the reading circuit during the 1884–1885 season. Billed as "Twins of Genius," they were for the most part complementary platform performers, with the relatively diminutive and lively Cable contrasting in an effective way with Twain the shuffling *eiron*. In the course of their tour, certain predictable tensions arose, though Twain seems to have experienced more than his share of irritation. Cable apparently upstaged Twain on more than one occasion, and this may have been a factor in Twain's growing disaffection with his partner. In any event, in private communications Twain assembled a bill of particulars against the New Orleanian, faulting Cable for his parsimony and abuse of expense claims and for what Twain saw as Cable's insufferable piety. To Twain's annoyance, Cable neither drank, nor smoked, nor swore, and he refused to travel on the Sabbath, preferring to attend multiple church services. Twain wrote William Dean Howells that Cable had caused him to "abhor and detest" the biblical day of rest "and hunt up new and troublesome ways to dishonor it." Cable likely never knew the degree to which he was an object of Twain's derision, though reports of trouble between the two did appear in the press. Nevertheless, the conclusion of their lecture tour marked the end of their intimate association, but by no means the end of their mutual expressions of admiration and respect. Cable was among those who participated in the Carnegie Hall memorial service for Twain in 1910.

Cable's views on the race question were indeed remarkable for his time. Even a progressive Southerner like Henry W. Grady found them shockingly radical. The extent to which Cable's ideas may have influenced Twain's thinking and writing on the subject remains a matter of speculation. As a troubled Southerner, Twain did indeed share Cable's sense of guilt—personal and collective over slavery. To be sure, Cable, building in part upon the tradition of abolitionist fiction that had preceded him, had dared to treat race relations in the South in a most uncompromising and courageous way, thus breaking new and fertile ground for the southern literary imagination. It is also worth noting that it was Cable who first introduced Twain to the *Morte D'Arthur*; in so doing he became (in Twain's words) "the godfather" of *A Connecticut Yankee in King Arthur's Court* (1889), a novel that obliquely, but forcefully, conveys Twain's indictment of the antebellum South and its peculiar institution.

William Bedford Clark

BIBLIOGRAPHY

Butcher, Philip. *George W. Cable*. New York: Twayne, 1962.

Cable, George W. *Mark Twain and G.W. Cable: The Record of a Literary Friendship*. Ed. Arlin Turner. East Lansing: Michigan State UP, 1960.

Cardwell, Guy Adams. *Twins of Genius*. East Lansing: Michigan State College P, 1953.

Rubin, Louis D., Jr. *George W. Cable: The Life and Times of a Southern Heretic*. New York: Pegasus, 1969.

Turner, Arlin. *George W. Cable: A Biography*. Baton Rouge: Louisiana State UP, 1966.

———, ed. *Critical Essays on George W. Cable*. Boston: G.K. Hall, 1980.

See also: Abolition; Lecturer; Slavery; South, Mark Twain and the

California

Before seeing it, Mark Twain envisioned California as a region and state of mind connected with wild claims of easy fortune and eternal spring—"the Garden of Eden reproduced." Contrasted to Nevada, so it was, for here he found among tailings of the old gold fields a new species of childlike free spirits spinning the kind of California stories about blue jays and jumping frogs that would become the hallmark of his own.

Promoters had long sung of growing wheat with seven heads to the stalk, 120 bushels to the acre, and about the 102–year-old man tired of living, taken across the border to die and then, on being carried back for burial, reviving. Such stories became so common that for three months newspapers treated discovery of gold in 1848 at Sutter's Mill with skepticism.

But when the government published official reports of gold strikes, the whole Western world rushed in, willingly suspending disbelief for the greater good of greed. Typically, the best-selling book of the thirty suddenly published that winter of 1848–1849, *Four Months Among the Gold-Finders in California*, was written by *Punch* illustrator Henry Vizetelly, who never left London.

Newspapers, too, created the illusion of a fabulous El Dorado with news of nuggets from Wood Creek at 75 ounces and from Sierra City at 141 ounces, along with stories about the wife of one returned miner who retrieved his cast-off clothes, shook them out, and recovered gold dust worth $23,000. Printers succumbed to their own lure until, by the mid-fifties, San Francisco boasted more newspapers than London.

Though sometimes out of necessity printed on the cheapest paper, the California press was surprisingly sophisticated. The leading San Francisco *Golden Era*, with peak circulation of about 20,000 (at a time when newspapers were read aloud), ran serializations of Dickens's novels and the then avant-garde verse of Samuel Taylor Coleridge. Newspapers catered to cultured tastes.

Harvard President Edward Everett had sent off his boys to California admonishing them to carry "the Bible in one hand and your New England civilization in the other." That civilization soon submerged into a heady brew compounded of cultures from all over the country, the continent, and the world—Australia, South America, China, Europe. Culture carried you so far.

Working in the gold fields, a miner could, on luckier days, earn perhaps $10 or even $50 a day when bread sold at one dollar a slice, two dollars buttered, and shovels at $50. Some were placer miners, standing in mud or bone-chilling streams washing gold flakes from the sand. When streams were exhausted, they would turn to quartz mining, breaking ribbons of gold out of solid rock.

As even surface quartz mines depleted, shafts had to be dug deeper and deeper, as deep as 9,000 feet, meaning that large companies had to move in with large machinery, displacing the ruggedly independent partnerships of the earlier fifties. A similar displacement was happening on the land as homesteaders found their claims contested and wrested from them by large developers.

Homesteaders or miners, those who could afford to, sucked up their pride and went back home. Others moved north to Oregon and Washington, the miners following every rumor about new strikes in British Columbia, eventually Alaska. The unlucky ones forced to remain where they were in the coastal frontier formed a new underclass, huddling among the tailings of the coastal frontier.

They realized the futility of reworking the old claims, left off working with their hands, and sat around patiently waiting for something to turn up—living in rotting cabins left behind by luckier folks, even their blankets and books. These folks were not illiterate hulks. They evolved a new culture to fit circumstances. Far from the paths trod by wandering actors or musicians, they created their own entertainment.

They would play a kind of "actuality" charades with studied straight faces. One community formed a fictional corporation to import smoke in pound packages from downriver. They concocted a plot on the part of the treasurer to embezzle funds (a dime a day for whiskey) and sent down to Stockton for two mule teams of lawyers to come up and try the case—all fictional, of course, but true to their imaginations and ingeniously consistent with nature.

Tiring of that game, one of the group, writer Prentice Mulford, chose the option of running for the state legislature and luckily lost. For in those days California politics could be deadly. From statehood in 1850, Democrats ruled the legislature. In 1857 Senator David

C. Broderick split the party when he urged an anti-slavery stand. He was assassinated. This was no game.

On the eve of the Civil War the Democrats were talking secession. In the race for president Californians went for Lincoln by a mere 1,000 votes out of a population of 379,994. A Republican legislature rode in on his coattails. And another direct result of his election was the naming of Orion Clemens, Samuel's brother, to be Nevada's territorial secretary and consequent coming of Mark Twain on what was supposed to be a three-month jaunt.

For three roustabout years he aimlessly ambled along the Nevada-California border seeking treasure or aim in life, rescued at last by San Francisco's *Morning Call* to come down and serve as general assignment reporter. This enabled him to put up at the posh Occidental Hotel, in his words, "Heaven on the half-shell," positioning himself at last to make a choice of California life.

His coming to San Francisco coincided with the beginning of a new literary newspaper called "the best weekly literary paper in the United States," the *Californian*, a lodestone for local literati, among them Bret Harte, Prentice Mulford, Charles Stoddard, Ina Coolbrith, and with such true professional journalists as Noah Brooks—all practicing the kind of serious culture Mark Twain aspired to.

Moonlighting from his various journalism jobs, Twain joined them in October 1864 at "$50 a month for one article a week." In a couple of months, however, he left the metropolis for a three-month hibernation in the Mother Lode country. During December and January he dwelt in a cabin with Jim and Steve Gillis and Jim's partner Dick Stoker. Now he would meet the California counterculture.

Winters on the hill could be brutally bone chilling from the incessant rains that formed an island of mud and manure. In the cabin four men who could not bathe clustered for warmth, their beds wood planks, their wool blankets always damp, infested with fleas. Dick Stoker had a menagerie of a learned pig, a jay, a deodorized skunk, and a cat called Tom Quartz. Jim Gillis kept a dog named Guess in case anyone asked.

Gillis also kept a library of good books, a godsend for someone with Mark Twain's nervous energy confined to a narrow cabin. For additional recreation he had the endless chain of tales told by his hosts and their visitors, many of them from the underclass the Gold Rush left behind. He found even more when his hosts took him over to Angel's Camp, about nine miles northwest. Named not for its inhabitants but for the man who set up the first trading post, the camp had a tavern that sheltered the visitors with a roof and dishwater-bean soup. Jim Gillis said they had to put up with the weather but ". . . we *won't* stand the dishwater and beans any longer." Yet the storytelling here taught Mark Twain that the secret of California tales lay in the way they were told.

A half-dozen years later he would remind Jim Gillis how they had "sat around the tavern stove and heard that chap tell about the frog," a tale long familiar on the Pacific slope but now told in such a way as to make them quote "from that yarn" and laugh "over it out there on the hillside."

"Jim Smiley and His Jumping Frog" appeared in the 18 November 1865 issue of New York's *Saturday Press*, but exactly a month earlier another New York literary magazine, the *Round Table*, had hailed Mark Twain as "foremost" among "merry gentlemen of the California press"—praise, he told his brother, that made him "really begin to believe there must be something to it."

Now enriched with new knowledge, he returned to San Francisco journalism until March 1866, when he left on assignment to the Hawaiian (then Sandwich) Islands. There he picked up plenty of materials for lecturing on his travels when he got back. For this new career he billed himself as "the wild humorist of the Pacific slope," touring to popular acclaim through the frontier towns of the Mother Lode and Nevada, telling his tales in a new-found California style.

As if reprising his previous half-dozen years, he made the circuit from Sacramento to Marysville, Grass Valley, Red Dog, You Bet, and the Nevada towns before making a farewell talk in San Francisco, assuring everyone that, though shipping east, he considered California "my new home." He would retrace the whole circuit again two years later, lecturing on *The Innocents Abroad* (1869) and once again giving a farewell lecture—his last one. His comic handbill this time had an admonition from the police chief: "You had better go." And he went—for good.

P.M. Zall

BIBLIOGRAPHY

Koone, Helene. *How Shakespeare Won the West.* Jefferson, N.C.: McFarland, 1989.

Walker, Franklin. *San Francisco's Literary Frontier.* New York: Knopf, 1939.

Wecter, Dixon. "Mark Twain and the West." *Huntington Library Quarterly* 8 (August 1945): 359–377.

See also: Angel's Camp, California; San Francisco, California

Californian

In 1864, while living in San Francisco as a reporter for the *Morning Call*, Mark Twain began publishing a series of sketches in the *Californian*, an established literary journal edited at the time by Bret Harte. In a 25 September 1864 letter to his mother Twain boasted that the *Californian* "circulated among the highest class of the community" and called it "the best weekly literary paper in the United States" (*Letters* 312). Harte's magazine also paid well. For one article a week Twain received $50 a month; his salary at the *Call*, for arduous journalistic reporting, had been $25 a week.

The most distinguished of Mark Twain's contributions to the *Californian* are his two condensed novels: "Whereas" (22 October 1864), later retitled "Aurelia's Unfortunate Young Man"; and "Lucretia Smith's Soldier" (3 December 1864). Both show his developing skills as a satirist and master of literary parody. They are reprinted in *Early Tales & Sketches, Volume 2* (ed. Branch and Hirst, 1981). In 1865 Twain contributed six items for the *Californian*'s new advice columns; one of these contains a poem by "Simon Wheeler." Twain's contributions to the *Californian* mark a period in his career when he first began to use the vernacular language of home-spun characters to advance his skill and reputation as a humorist and ironic moralist.

Scott H. Moore

BIBLIOGRAPHY

Branch, Edgar Marquess. *The Literary Apprenticeship of Mark Twain.* Urbana: U of Illinois P, 1950.

Clemens, Samuel L. *Mark Twain's Letters, Volume 1 (1853–1866).* Ed. Edgar M. Branch, Michael B. Frank, and Kenneth M. Sanderson. Berkeley: U of California P, 1988.

————. *The Works of Mark Twain: Early Tales & Sketches, Volume 2 (1864–1865).* Ed. Edgar M. Branch and Robert H. Hirst. Berkeley: U of California P, 1981.

Emerson, Everett. *The Authentic Mark Twain: A Literary Biography of Samuel L. Clemens.* Philadelphia: U of Pennsylvania P, 1984.

See also: "Aurelia's Unfortunate Young Man"; Condensed Novels; Journalism; "Lucretia Smith's Soldier"

"Californian's Tale, The"
(1893)

Written in 1892, "The Californian's Tale" was first published a year later by Arthur Stedman in a volume entitled *The First Book of the Author's Club, Liber Scriptorium.* It was subsequently included in *The $30,000 Bequest and other Stories* (1906). The story seems to come from an earlier experience Mark Twain had had during his days with Jim Gillis at Angel's Camp during the winter of 1864. He recorded in his notebook then that he had happened upon a poor fellow at Tuttleville and that this poor fellow talked constantly and enthusiastically about going to the next village to meet his wife, who had been absent for a week. To

Mark Twain's astonishment, he found out later that this deranged man had been making this journey regularly over the twenty-three years following her death. Twain remembered this episode and chose to incorporate the basic facts into "The Californian's Tale."

In this story a narrator is traveling through an old deserted mining area. He comes upon a cozy rose-clad cottage and finds Henry, its owner, standing at the gate. After being invited in, the narrator is struck by the neatness of the home, evident touches that only a woman could keep up. Every room in the cottage has the same pattern of neatness, and Henry replies often that it is "All her work; she did it all herself—every bit!" Henry persuades the stranger to stay with him a few days until her return on Saturday so that he can meet her. Before the scheduled arrival time, friends of Henry (Tom, Joe, and Charly) come by and set up everything for a festive homecoming. They repeatedly drink to the wife's health until Henry passes out, after which they undress him and tuck him into his bed. In astonishment the narrator then learns that these dear friends have gone through this ritual every year for the nineteen years since his wife had disappeared after being captured by Indians.

Although Mark Twain maintained a lifelong attack against sentimentality in fiction, with this story he does depart from his usual sardonic pose. James D. Wilson maintains that Twain wrote this story about a man's lifelong affection for his wife only after getting medical reports that Livy did not have a heart disease, that she indeed would be well again (Wilson 12).

Andy J. Moore

BIBLIOGRAPHY

Benson, Ivan. *Mark Twain's Western Years*. Stanford, Calif.: Stanford UP, 1938.

Emerson, Everett. *The Authentic Mark Twain: A Literary Biography of Samuel L. Clemens*. Philadelphia: U of Pennsylvania P, 1984.

Paine, Albert Bigelow. *Mark Twain: A Biography*. 3 vols. New York: Harper, 1912.

Wilson, James D. *A Reader's Guide to the Short Stories of Mark Twain*. Boston: G.K. Hall, 1987.

See also: Sentimentality

Calvinism

Calvinism is that formulation of Christian religious beliefs and practices originating with the reformer John Calvin (1509–1564). It influenced numerous sixteenth- and seventeenth-century religious groups, and most American bodies in the free church tradition, including the Congregational, Presbyterian, the Methodist, and Baptist, have Calvinistic theology at their base. Though in a different tradition, Anglicanism has shown the influence of both its Roman Catholic background and of Calvinist reforms from the outset. Among the Anglicans, those who felt Calvinist reforms should replace Roman traditions entirely become known as Puritans.

Sam Clemens's acquaintance with Calvinism came early. The two churches in the Hannibal of his youth were Presbyterian and Methodist. At various times his mother was a member of each. Both Sam's home and his early church experiences put him in touch with the smothering practical Calvinism of the small town and backwoods. He was never comfortable with it. Understandably, since both the churches he knew well shared the same theological base, young Sam identified Calvinism with Christianity itself. Even in adulthood as Mark Twain, he was rarely able to view Christianity apart from the hated Calvinistic interpretation of it.

Calvin's *Institutes of the Christian Religion* was his most complete treatment of the faith. A slim volume in 1536, the *Institutes* grew to over 1,500 pages with Calvin's final revision in 1559. It details, among other things, doctrinal positions on the Scriptures, God's omnipotence, sin, and predestination—all doctrines that drew fire from Mark Twain.

The *Genevan Confession* of 1536, written by Calvin and Farel, presents a digest of Calvin's theology. Its twenty-one provisions included the following: the declaration of Scripture as the sole determinant of faith and practice, the assertion that there was only one God, the belief that the law of God is alike for all, the belief that man is by nature blind and sinful, the belief that God makes all good, and the belief that faith makes the gifts of God available. The *Confession* contained both provisions peculiar to Calvinism and the radical reformers—the Scripture as sole determinant of faith and practice, for example—and those shared with all Christians—the assertion that there was only one God, for example.

When Dutch Reformed theologians met at the Synod of Dort (1618–1619), they listed the Five Points of Calvinism. The points reemphasized some of the tenets of the *Genevan Confession*, but they gave new prominence to predestination and election, doctrines found in the *Institutes* but virtually ignored in the *Confession*. The points were humans are fettered by sin, God unconditionally elects or predetermines those who will be saved, Christ's salvation is limited to the elect, God's grace is irresistible, and those elected are saved forever.

Mark Twain on the *Genevan Confession*

Twain never issued a point-by-point refutation of the tenets of Calvinism, but over the half century of his career as a writer he had something to say about most of them. Following is a digest of his opinions about the listed six points of the *Genevan Confession*:

1. Scripture. By asserting that the Scripture was the only authority for faith and practice, Calvin denied the distorting role tradition had played in Roman Catholicism and the authority of the Roman hierarchy. Popes had made the church a place to satisfy political ambitions and personal appetites, not a place of serious worship.

He went a step further, encouraging only a plain and literal interpretation of Scripture. That is, Calvin denied the efficacy of allegorical and anagogical interpretations commonly used in the Roman church. Writers, used to

depending on levels of interpretation beyond the literal, understandably chafed at this limitation. Mark Twain was no exception.

By the mid-nineteenth century, American churches made practical moves to establish scriptural authority. They tried to instill a knowledge and a love of the Bible beginning in childhood. Mark Twain reported being compelled to read "an unexpurgated Bible" before he was fifteen; according to his *Autobiography* (1924), he eagerly sought the rewards usually given for memorizing Scripture. Indeed, the rewards meant more to him than the Scripture did. When he found that he could repeat the same verses about the wise and foolish virgins (Matthew 25) each week for repeated credit, he was overjoyed.

Tom Sawyer pulled similar shenanigans, trading childhood treasures for colored tickets, the receipts for memorizing verses. Tom's aim was not so much the Bible that he would receive as a reward but his recognition as a paragon of virtue in front of Becky Thatcher and her parents. The ardently sought recognition turned sour when Tom, quizzed about his Bible knowledge, listed David and Goliath among the disciples.

The anecdotes highlight one shortcoming Twain saw in the practice of American Protestant churches: they did not really encourage respect for the Scripture. They invited, almost encouraged, corruption, though Calvin and his cohorts had chosen Scripture as the solid basis for the faith to avoid corruption.

Twain's criticism of Scripture went further. He parodied the literal interpretation of the Bible, thus creating comedy. The stories, particularly those of his favorite biblical book, Genesis, interpreted literally, violated logic and the human spirit. In addition, while preserving God's power, they often showed Him as an unreasonable tyrant.

Letter III in "Letters from the Earth" features comments on God's failure to forgive Adam and Eve's first transgression. God failed to show the couple what the difference between good and evil was before facing them with a choice. The couple could not choose meaningfully. In addition, God punished them without mercy for choosing badly. The Scriptures, as Twain saw them, depict God as a bully: "He has one code of morals for himself and quite another for his children." While God required his children to forgive an offender to seventy times seven, He Himself did not forgive the first offense.

The first large audience Twain gathered for his humorous renditions of biblical stories read them in *Innocents Abroad* (1869). Such stories popped up constantly in his work, however. Allison Ensor has noted that Twain referred to Adam, Christ, Noah, the Prodigal Son, Eve, Solomon, and Moses more often than to any other biblical figures, devoting more than twenty passages to each. He refers to a broad range of biblical characters and stories, however, showing that the early biblical training gave him more than a passing knowledge of the Scriptures.

2. There is only one God. At times in his life, particularly during the courtship of Olivia, Twain seemed ready to support Christian monotheism. More often, he delighted in showing his contemporaries the fragile gods they worshiped while they thought that they believed only in the God of the Bible.

The Gilded Age (1873) exhibits the unworthy gods men worship, money and success prominent among them. In Twain's later work additional gods are not merely a matter of man's misperception—accepting the transient as ultimate. Satan himself becomes a second god, independent and kinder than the God of Christian worship. The most striking presentation of this viewpoint comes in "No. 44, The Mysterious Stranger" (1969).

3. The law of God is alike for all. Calvin wanted people to recognize that Christianity was not a religion of privilege. Twain sometimes caught Christians assuming privilege. Much of the fun of *Innocents Abroad* comes at the expense of those serious religious pilgrims who, like the captain, assume their moral superiority grants them immunity from the laws of God and man.

4. Man is by nature blind and sinful. "In Adam's fall, we sinned all," the American Puritans taught. Like Calvin they blamed man's imperfect nature on Adam's original sin as Genesis 2 depicts it.

Twain accepted mankind's frailties. Indeed, he often gloried in them. His humor features shortsighted con men, overly sentimental girls, ignorant townspeople, and bungling villains. All his characters had warts. When they had insight about their own condition, it was usually an accidental flash. When they tried to be wise, they most often acted foolishly. When these misguided souls interacted with one another, ignoring the imperfections Twain's readers could see so clearly, comedy resulted.

Blindness is sometimes the basic motif in his novels. *The Prince and the Pauper* (1882) works because neither the king nor his court can tell a gutter snipe in a royal clothing from the real prince.

The blindness was often more than physical, however. For Twain there was a moral dimension as well. "The Celebrated Jumping Frog of Calaveras County" (1865), Twain's first widely successful story, is built on moral blindness. Jim Smiley hopes to win a bet by cheating a stranger. Twain's twist is showing us that moral scruples have less of a hold on mankind than we might at first believe. The stranger cheats more outrageously than Smiley and wins the bet. Neither Smiley nor the stranger has a moral conscience; they sin boldly.

Adventures of Huckleberry Finn (1885) illustrates another facet of the moral blindness of humans. Huck befriends the runaway slave Jim. Jim wants to join his wife and family. Huck aids him in his plans to escape, not only defying community standards and national law but, as he understood it, God's law. Huck is willing to risk hell to uphold moral correctness, however. He can see the right even when others cannot. His action expresses the unsophisticated belief that the Moral Sense, not law, is the best guide to action. Unlike Jim Smiley, Huck Finn has a conscience; and Twain's message is that it will guide him to correct action even if that action defies transient interpretations of God's will.

The heartwarming belief in basic human goodness did not last. In several stories, "The Man That Corrupted Hadleyburg" (1899) being the most important, Twain illustrates the frailty of the Moral Sense. He asserts the belief that "every man has his price."

Twain's sympathy for man's condition surfaced when he looked at the Fall. First, he found the Creator's expectations for man unrealistic. He, the Creator, made an imperfect being and then demanded perfect performance from it. Second, Twain blamed the Fall on the Creator. Had He properly acquainted his creatures with the differences between good and evil and with the meaning of the consequences of their actions, the outcome might have been different.

5. God makes all good. In *Innocents Abroad* and the early letters to Livy, Twain did not seriously question God's goodness. After meeting life's disappointments—the death of a daughter and bankruptcy—he had insistent questions about the Creator. He began to examine both God's role as malicious torturer and Satan's giving mankind warnings about God's mischief. Finally, he could not see God as good to Adam or to himself.

6. Faith makes the gifts of God available. Twain did not have faith. He proclaimed that he would have been a wonderful minister but for one shortcoming—he had no religion. Unable to attest to the wonders of faith himself, he looked critically at those who did believe, often uncovering their hypocrisy and their inconsistencies. He was never so unfriendly to the faith or the faithful that he refused to associate with them. As late as 1907, he gave a lecture to benefit a church, for example. His closest friend for many years was Joseph Twichell, a minister in Hartford. In spite of these things, he never found much solace in the Christian faith; and as we have already seen, he found much to disturb him about it.

One of the most interesting and troublesome doctrines of Calvinism was the view that individuals were predestined by God either for eternal salvation or for damnation. Twain's early Christian training in this doctrine may have prepared him to accept deterministic views of another sort, however. In 1856, while working as a printer in Cincinnati, Twain met a forty-year-old Scotsman named Macfarlane. In his *Autobiography* (1924) the writer tells that Macfarlane saw creation evolving into higher and more perfect forms until man was reached. There the scheme broke down. Man's structure determined that he would have the base emotions of malice, envy, vindictiveness, and hatred. If human beings believed they were capable of good, then they were being misled. The writer thought that the Moral Sense was the final trick played on humans by a cruel creator. Twain talked of "the damned human race" because he thought there was no salvation for the race at all. God had predestined every human for damnation. Calvinism provided some hope that an individual might be included with the elect. Twain provided none.

Mark Twain was no Calvinist. His reactions to Calvinism are, however, at the heart of both his humor and his bitterness.

David O. Tomlinson

BIBLIOGRAPHY

Calvin, John. *Institutes of the Christian Religion.* Trans. Ford Lewis Battles. 2 vols. Philadelphia: Westminster, 1960.

Clemens, Samuel L. *The Innocents Abroad.* Hartford, Conn.: American Publishing, 1869.

———. *Letters from the Earth.* Ed. Bernard DeVoto. New York: Harper & Row, 1962.

———. *Mark Twain's Autobiography.* Ed. Albert B. Paine. 2 vols. New York: Harper, 1924.

———. *Mark Twain's Mysterious Stranger Manuscripts.* Ed. William M. Gibson. Berkeley: U of California P, 1969.

———. *A Pen Warmed-Up in Hell: Mark Twain in Protest.* Ed. Frederick Anderson. New York: Harper & Row, 1972.

Ensor, Allison. *Mark Twain and the Bible.* Lexington: UP of Kentucky, 1969.

Manschreck, Clyde L., ed. *A History of Christianity: Readings in the History of the Church from the Reformation to the Present.* Englewood Cliffs, N.J.: Prentice-Hall, 1964.

Wolterstorff, Nicholas. "John Calvin." *The Encyclopedia of Philosophy.* Vol. 2. Ed. Paul Edwards. New York: Macmillan, 1967. 7–9.

See also: Bible; Determinism; Religion

Campbell, Alexander

(1788–1866)

One of the founders of the church known as the Disciples of Christ, Alexander Campbell was an Irish-born theologian and writer on religious subjects. With his father he founded a new society, originally known as the "Campbellites," whose theology was to be based solely on the Bible. He traveled throughout the South and Southwest, preaching to large crowds. The founder of Bethany College in Virginia, and author of many works on Christian subjects, he was also one of the few clergyman with whom Twain did not have an entirely amiable relationship. About 1847 Campbell delivered a sermon in the Hannibal public square; the order for reprints was given to the Hannibal *Courier* where Clemens was at the time a printer's apprentice. When, with another apprentice, Wales McCormick, Clemens set all sixteen pages in type, two words were inadvertently omitted. To avoid resetting three entire pages, the words "Jesus Christ" were abbreviated to J.C. Soon, Campbell appeared and delivered a stern lecture on the evils of diminishing the Savior's name. When the pages were reset, that name had been augmented to Jesus H. Christ, a typographical emendation Twain ascribed to his fellow apprentice.

Mark Draper

BIBLIOGRAPHY

Clemens, Samuel L. *Mark Twain's Autobiography.* Ed. Albert B. Paine. 2 vols. New York: Harper, 1924.

Dole, Nathan, Forrest Morgan, and Caroline Ticknor. *The Bibliophile Library of Literature, Art, and Rare Manuscripts.* New York: International Bibliophile Society, 1904.

Harris, William, and Judith S. Levey, eds. *The New Columbia Encyclopedia.* New York: Columbia UP, 1975.

Hart, J.D. *The Oxford Companion to American Literature.* 2nd ed. New York: Oxford UP, 1948.

Canada

Twain's attitude toward North America's largest country was typically that of a United States citizen in that he took Canada for granted and generally considered it lacking any major national distinctiveness. His only preoccupation with Canada involved the Toronto publishers who frequently pirated his new works, leading him several times to visit Canada to protect his copyrights. His only other contacts with Canada involved his speaking tours, which allowed him occasional opportunities to visit Canadian cities. Not surprisingly, the influence of Canada on Twain remained slight with only his oblique use of the Canadian landscape in a couple of stories.

Twain visited Windsor, Ontario, briefly, in 1871 but actually claimed as his first a trip to Montreal in 1881 to stave off threats to his copyright for his newly published *The Prince and the Pauper* (1881). At a public dinner held for Twain, Louis Frechette, the brother of William D. Howells's son-in-law, read a special poem in his honor. Twain experienced a similar welcome in 1883 in Ottawa and later traveled to Canada on a lecture tour that included Winnipeg, Vancouver, and Victoria.

Notable links to Canada in Twain's fiction are relatively few. His short story, "The Esquimau Maiden's Romance" (1893), with its mention of the Aurora Borealis, presumably takes place in the Canadian North. In addition, Twain's early burlesque, "A Day at Niagara" (1869), describes the Canadian side of the great falls.

The fledgling Canadian literary culture of the nineteenth century clearly made only a slight impact on Twain. Although he had read Thomas Chandler Haliburton's *The Clockmaker*

(1837) as a boy, the links between Haliburton's and Twain's works remain rather elusive. The rather modest case for Haliburton's influence on Twain usually focuses on Huck Finn, Hank in *A Connecticut Yankee in King Arthur's Court* (1889), and *Innocents Abroad* (1869).

Noteworthy is Twain's own influence on Canadian humorist Stephen Leacock, whose admiration for Twain and whose enthusiasm for *A Connecticut Yankee in King Arthur's Court* can be seen in his *Arcadian Adventures with the Idle Rich* (1914). In fact, Leacock himself wrote in his essay "Mark Twain and Canada" (1935) that Twain had traveled considerably more to distant British places than he ever had to the United States's next door neighbor.

John W. Ferstel

BIBLIOGRAPHY

Clemens, Samuel L. *Mark Twain's Letters to His Publishers, 1867–1894.* Ed. Hamlin Hill. Berkeley: U of California P, 1967.

———. *Mark Twain's Notebooks & Journals, Volume II (1877–1883).* Ed. Frederick Anderson, Lin Salamo, and Bernard L. Stein. Berkeley: U of California P, 1975.

Leacock, Stephen. "Mark Twain and Canada." *Queen's Quarterly* 42 (Spring 1935): 68–81.

Pond, Major J.B. *Eccentricity of Genius: Memories of Famous Men and Women of the Platform and Stage.* New York: G.W. Dillingham, 1900.

See also: Copyright; Pond, James

"Cannibalism in the Cars"

(1868)

Mark Twain's "Cannibalism in the Cars" is a short humorous sketch detailing an outbreak of cannibalism among a trainload of snow-bound congressmen. Twain wrote the sketch in either 1867 or early 1868; it was first published in November 1868 in George Routledge and Sons' magazine *Broadway* and then collected in *Sketches, New and Old* (1875).

The sketch is a frame tale, with the narrator Mark Twain describing his meeting with a middle-aged gentleman on a train trip to St. Louis. The two strike up a conversation; after hearing that Mark Twain has just come from Washington, the stranger asks about various congressmen, then relates to Mark Twain a "secret chapter of his life" (340). The narrative concerns a trip from St. Louis to Chicago in 1853, with twenty-four passengers, all adult males, becoming snowbound. After all attempts at extrication fail, they sit for a week before finally taking action: forming legislative committees, making motions and resolutions, then nominating two candidates, one for dinner and the other for breakfast (others had been rejected for toughness or lack of bulk). They elect two more meals each day, then another train finally comes. At this point in the story the stranger departs the train, leaving a stunned and horrified Mark Twain, who finds out from the conductor that the man had been a member of Congress who became frostbitten while snowbound and now buttonholes strangers to tell them his story. Edgar M. Branch proposes as a source for the story a piece in Orion Clemens's Muscatine *Tri-Weekly Journal* published in 1855 (586).

Stylistically, the story follows the frame technique Twain used in many of his sketches, but instead of a vernacular narrator has a narrator who uses parliamentary terms and procedures. Indeed, much of the humor of the piece arises from the incongruity of parliamentary language being used to decide on the order in which men will cannibalize each other. As David E.E. Sloane has observed, the parliamentary rhetoric makes the tale increasingly more grotesque, heightening Twain's satire of Congress (94). The framework technique, the inflated rhetoric, and the humor all serve to distance the reader from the grisly events of the story, a distance that further sharpens the satire. This satire takes Congress as its major target but, in a wider sense, exposes some of the hidden cruelties of "civilized" behavior.

"Cannibalism" is certainly a minor piece, but perhaps one that deserves more attention. Branch calls it a tour de force (585); Sloane compares the congressional narrator to Simon Wheeler for his use of digression and deadpan

(94), and notes the completeness of the Mark Twain persona (95). Overall, the piece has the raucous humor characteristic of Twain's early work.

John Bird

BIBLIOGRAPHY

Branch, Edgar M. "Mark Twain: Newspaper Reading and the Writer's Creativity." *Nineteenth-Century Fiction* 37 (March 1983): 576–603.

Clemens, Samuel L. *The Complete Short Stories of Mark Twain.* Ed. Charles Neider. Garden City, N.Y.: Hanover House, 1957. 9–16.

Sloane, David E.E. *Mark Twain as a Literary Comedian.* Baton Rouge: Louisiana State UP, 1979.

See also: Government; Washington, D.C.

"Canvasser's Tale, The"
(1876)

First published in the *Atlantic Monthly* for December 1876, "The Canvasser's Tale" was later published as "The Echo That Didn't Answer" in *Beeton's Christmas Annual* (1877). This little-known tale uses techniques of some of Twain's famous works. Like "The Celebrated Jumping Frog of Calaveras County" (1865), this story consists of a narrative within a narrative and draws on elements of the tall tale. Like *Roughing It* (1872), it parodies high literary style.

The story contains a joke within a joke. A canvasser selling echoes tells the narrator about his uncle's attempts to purchase all worthwhile echoes in the country. He buys one hill of the Mountain of Repetitions but discovers another collector owns the other. They become embroiled in a lawsuit that results in neither being allowed to use the echo. The uncle dies with the property "tied up and unsalable." Consequently, the canvasser inherits great debts and a large collection of echoes. The English earl whose daughter the canvasser is about to marry cancels the wedding. The narrator vows he will never buy an echo but ends up buying "two-barreled echoes in

good condition" and receives for free a third that "only spoke German."

Richard Tuerk

BIBLIOGRAPHY

Clemens, Samuel L. "The Canvasser's Tale." *Atlantic Monthly* 38 (December 1876): 673–676.

———. *Tom Sawyer Abroad, Tom Sawyer, Detective, and Other Stories, Etc. Etc.* New York: Harper, 1896. 363–370.

Wilson, James D. *A Reader's Guide to the Short Stories of Mark Twain.* Boston: G.K. Hall, 1987.

Cap'n Simon Wheeler, the Amateur Detective
(1967)

Clemens toyed with the idea of an extended fictional work featuring Simon Wheeler as early as 1873, but he had difficulty securing a suitable forum for developing the character. In 1876 Clemens tried to interest Charles Reade in producing a proposed play about Simon Wheeler. Reade responded that the project, though "full of Brains," did not cater enough to popular taste to be feasible on stage. Later that year Clemens presented a revised plot to Chandos Fulton, who, on 12 March 1877, urged the author to fill out his outline and submit the play for production. Encouraged by Fulton's note, Clemens wrote *Cap'n Simon Wheeler, the Amateur Detective* (*CSW*) at Quarry Farm between 27 June and 11 July 1877; the entire play was conceived, plotted, and written in two weeks of dedicated energy and enthusiasm (Rogers 216–217). Clemens wrote to Howells on 6 July that he had finished his play and remarked that he had never had so much fun in his life as he had in writing this farce.

The play survives in two forms, the holograph manuscript and an amanuensis copy prepared in late 1877 or early 1878. Rogers reproduces the holograph manuscript in his edition of *Satires & Burlesques* (1967), though his text incorporates the italicizations and stage directions of the amanuensis copy.

Called by Clemens "a light tragedy," *CSW* burlesques the methods of detective Allan Pinkerton as they are demonstrated in Pinkerton's books *The Expressman and the Detectives, Mississippi Outlaws and the Detectives*, and *Poisoner and the Detectives*. The plot of Clemens's play is ridiculous and its dialogue absurd. *CSW* introduces three New York Pinkerton detectives and Simon Wheeler, all of whom try to discover the identity of a murderer. Twain, of course, had used the character Simon Wheeler earlier as the vernacular narrator of the story of "Jim Smiley and His Jumping Frog" (1865). Wheeler's associative process of thought and garrulous personality would seem to make him incapable of pursuing an idea or hypothesis to its logical conclusion; hence, he would seem the antithesis of the logical thinking machine the Pinkerton detective often becomes. Humor in *CSW* results from the outlandish theories suggested by the "logical" detectives: one believes the murder weapon to be a hymn book and so collects as evidence all hymnals he can locate. As it turns out, the murder victim (Hugh Burnside) has not been murdered at all; in fact, he attends his own funeral in disguise. There has been a killing, however, though it was accidental. The victim is a desperate villain named Jack Bilford.

Clemens appropriately labeled his play a farce. Rogers suggests that as Clemens's spontaneity increased so his critical powers decreased. Wheeler's antics, however, allowed the author to escape from the irksome world of reality and enter the world of fantasy, where laws of probability are suspended and only the villains suffer (Rogers 12).

Howells convinced his friend to rewrite *CSW* as a novel, and in the fall and winter of 1877–1878 Clemens attempted to do so, though he abandoned the project before he was half through it. The manuscript, titled *Simon Wheeler, Detective*, is included in the Rogers text (312–444). Everett Emerson claims that the unfinished novel is much more interesting than the play from which it was cast, in large part because of Clemens's inherent abilities as a novelist. The Missouri settings are vivid, and the plot concerns two families (one from Kentucky, the other from Virginia) who are embroiled in a feud that foreshadows the Grangerford-Shepherdson feud in *Adventures of Huckleberry Finn* (1885). There are other parallels to later works as well: Judge Griswold anticipates Colonel Grangerford, Hugh Burnside is a sentimental poet in the school of Emmeline Grangerford, and Cap'n Simon Wheeler, like Captain Wakeman, has a dream that foreshadows "Captain Stormfield's Visit to Heaven" (Emerson 95–96).

Although Dion Boucicault, a leading New York playwright and actor, thought *CSW* a better play than *Ah Sin* (1876), Clemens was unable to find a producer, and his play was never staged.

Don L.F. Nilsen

BIBLIOGRAPHY

Clemens, Samuel L. *Mark Twain's Satires & Burlesques.* Ed. Franklin R. Rogers. Berkeley: U of California P, 1967. 220–289.

Emerson, Everett. *The Authentic Mark Twain: A Literary Biography of Samuel L. Clemens.* Philadelphia: U of Pennsylvania P, 1984.

Long, E. Hudson. *Mark Twain Handbook.* New York: Hendricks House, 1957.

See also: Burlesque; Detective Fiction; Dramatist, Mark Twain as; Wheeler, Simon

Cardiff Hill

Fictional location of much of *The Adventures of Tom Sawyer* (1876), Cardiff Hill was Mark Twain's imaginative name for Holliday's Hill, which rises nearly 300 feet above the Mississippi for two miles northward of Hannibal, Missouri, where Twain spent his boyhood. Near its crest lived Mrs. Holliday and her husband Captain Richard Holliday, who before his death had served with Judge Clemens as justice of the peace. His widow is the model for the Widow Douglas of *Tom Sawyer*. Some years after the publication of the novel, Twain visited the site of the Holliday mansion (which burned down in 1894) and told its occupant that the hill had reminded him of a similar one in Cardiff, South Wales. References to Cardiff Hill recur throughout the novel, with lyrical, romantic descriptions appearing in chapters 2, 7, and 8.

Tom Sawyer, sometimes alone, sometimes with Joe Harper and Huck Finn, escapes the confinement of town and classroom by climbing Cardiff Hill, which comes to represent the idyllic life of action and imagination as opposed to the restrictive reality of home and work. It also evokes the nostalgia of lost childhood: just as Twain had played Robin Hood with boyhood friend Will Bowen in the woods on Holliday's Hill, Tom and his companions prefer being outlaws in the Sherwood Forest-like woods of Cardiff Hill to being president of the United States.

Although Twain has been criticized for deliberately romanticizing his boyhood haunts, Cardiff Hill could be the scene of dark happenings, too. Injun Joe's revenge plot against the Widow, and its defeat when Huck summons help, has roots in an actual incident in which men threatened a respectable widow and her daughter; the widow shot and killed one of the men and was acquitted (Wecter 159–160). Typically, however, Cardiff Hill, seen through a haze of misty purples and soft greens, fragrant with blossoms, is the "Delectable Land" that beckons the youthful characters of *Tom Sawyer* (chapters 2, 46).

Abby H.P. Werlock

BIBLIOGRAPHY

Allen, Jerry. "Tom Sawyer's Town." *National Geographic* 110 (July 1956): 120–140.

Clemens, Samuel L. *The Adventures of Tom Sawyer, Tom Sawyer Abroad, Tom Sawyer, Detective.* Ed. John C. Gerber, Paul Baender, and Terry Firkins. Berkeley: U of California P, 1980.

Dunsmoor, Kathryn. "Land of Tom and Huck." *Scholastic* 27 (23 November 1935): 11–12.

Interview with Mrs. R.E. Ireland, *Hannibal Courier-Post,* 6 March 1935.

Wecter, Dixon. *Sam Clemens of Hannibal.* Boston: Houghton Mifflin, 1952.

See also: Adventures of Tom Sawyer, The; Hannibal, Missouri

Carlyle, Thomas
(1795–1881)

Born in Ecclefechan, Scotland, and educated at the University of Edinburgh (which he left in 1814 without taking a degree), Thomas Carlyle gained fame during his lifetime and thereafter as an individualistic, highly controversial writer, whose works—biography, history, literary comment, and economic and social criticism—ultimately filled thirty volumes in the Centenary Edition (1896–1899).

After marriage to Jane Welsh in 1826, Carlyle lived from 1828 until 1834 at Craigenputtock, where he wrote his spiritual autobiography *Sartor Resartus* (1833–1834) and most of the works later collected in *Critical and Miscellaneous Essays* (1839). In 1834 the Carlyles moved to the still memorialized London address, 5 Cheyne Walk, Chelsea, where they lived for the remainder of their lives. There Carlyle produced many of the works for which he is most famous—*The French Revolution: A History* (1838); *On Heroes, Hero-Worship, and the Heroic in History* (1841), which specifically set forth his belief that history was determined by great individuals; his development of economic theories in *Chartism* (1839), *Past and Present* (1843), and *Latter-Day Pamphlets* (1850); *Oliver Cromwell's Letters and Speeches* (1845); and the great biographies, *The Life of John Sterling* (1851) and the *History of Frederick II of Prussia, Called Frederick the Great* (1858–1865). Running through all his works is an emphasis on spiritual values over the material and on the importance of the individual over the mass of mankind.

Carlyle was obviously one of Clemens's favorite authors. Ultimately, Clemens owned later editions of most of the works mentioned above, except perhaps for *Chartism* and *Latter-Day Pamphlets.* In addition, his library contained James Anthony Froude's four-volume *Thomas Carlyle: A History of the First Forty Years of His Life* (1882) and the two-volume *Thomas Carlyle: A History of His Life in London, 1834–1881* (1884). When it appeared in 1883, he also read Froude's edition of *Letters and Memorials of Jane Welsh Carlyle, Prepared for Publication by Thomas Carlyle* and probably also acquired Charles Eliot Norton's edition of *The Correspondence of Thomas Carlyle and Ralph Waldo Emerson* (1883). And Carlyle's writings provided important stimuli for Mark Twain's works and ideas from at least the early 1870s. Of the Scotsman's extensive influence, this account can touch only the surface.

By far the most important to Mark Twain was Carlyle's vivid history of the French Revolution—"one of the greatest creations that ever flowed from a pen"—which, after his first encounter about 1871, he read and reread throughout the rest of his life. Though he was to change his position during the composition of *A Connecticut Yankee in King Arthur's Court* (1889), the first readings, as he himself later said, aligned him with the Girondins, the moderate republicans whom Carlyle also favored. The historian's picture of the "howling Sansculottic earthquake" doubtless supplemented Twain's deep distrust of the masses during the 1870s. Moreover, Twain's denunciations of legislative bodies and journalistic irresponsibilities during these years almost echo some of Carlyle's blasts at the inefficiency of the French National Assembly and his scorn for the "Fourth Estate."

While in Paris during the European trip of 1878–1879 the Clemenses used Carlyle's history as one of their principal guidebooks to scenes made memorable by the French Revolution and Reign of Terror. It is easy to see agreement with Carlyle's opinions underlying Mark Twain's comments on the French and the revolution in *A Tramp Abroad* (1880) and even more clearly in passages ultimately omitted from the volume, like "The French and the Comanches" (first published in *Letters from the Earth* 1962). His horror at the atrocities perpetrated by the revolutionaries, his scorn for the vacillations of Louis XVI, and his implied admiration for Napoleon closely parallel those of Carlyle. Carlyle's view of history as largely the influence of individuals probably enhanced Twain's similar propensity, though he was considerably more capricious than Carlyle in blaming individuals for group or national faults, as when he charged Louis XVI and Marie Antoinette with responsibility for the revolution and later suggested (in *Life on the Mississippi* [1883]) that the romantic ideas of Sir Walter Scott had caused the Civil War.

Touches from *The French Revolution* may also be found in *Huckleberry Finn* (1885), especially in the depiction of the mob in the aftermath of the Sherburn-Boggs incident and more specifically in details of the "Evasion" in the latter chapters. And a few years later, Mark Twain would continue to draw heavily on incidents and ideas from this favorite book for *A Connecticut Yankee*.

Meanwhile, beginning in 1882, he added many additional volumes of Carlyle to his library, including *Sartor Resartus, On Heroes, Hero-Worship and the Heroic in History*, and *The Letters and Speeches of Oliver Cromwell*. If *On Heroes, Hero-Worship and the Heroic in History* did not create Twain's admiration for Napoleon and Cromwell, it doubtless enhanced it. Moreover, from *The Letters and Speeches of Oliver Cromwell* he made note of an incident involving Cromwell's treatment of certain mutinous colonels, which he ultimately adapted for a short story, "The Death Disk" (1901), and sometime later for a play, *The Death Wafer* (still unpublished).

During the summer of 1887, while drawing upon details from *The French Revolution*, Taine's *Ancient Regime* (1876), and Saint-Simon's *Memoirs* (trans. 1822–1859) for his descriptions of the sad plight of Arthurian peasants, Twain told his friend Howells that he no longer favored Carlyle's moderate position, but was now a "Sansculotte," a radical revolutionary. Still *A Connecticut Yankee* reveals other agreements with Carlyle. Hank Morgan, both in his own person and in his several statements stressing the importance of basic "manhood," surely reflects Carlyle's theory of the superiority of individuals as directors of the course of history—even though he ultimately fails. And echoes of Carlyle's clothes philosophy, apparent in his *French Revolution* though much more fully developed in *Sartor Resartus*, are specifically found in the Yankee's tirade against the worship of the "rags" of nobility and aristocracy in chapter 20.

The French Revolution also furnished specific details for other episodes. The destruction of Merlin's tower (chapter 5) borrows from Carlyle's description of the Feast of Pikes. "A Competitive Examination" (chapter 25) draws upon Carlyle's discussion of the distinction between "old" and "new" nobility and the "four-generation" rule for determining qualifications. And "The Battle of the Sand Belt" (chapter 43) closely reflects elements of Carlyle's vivid recreation of the march on Versailles during the "Insurrection of Women."

In 1904, whether consciously or unconsciously, Twain again called upon Carlyle's clothes philosophy in "The Czar's Soliloquy" (1905), in which Nicholas II explains at length how his power depended upon the people's worship of external appearances, the clothes he wore.

Finally, *Sartor* played an important role among the influences on "No. 44, The Mysterious Stranger." Among other possible sources, its emphasis on the transcendental nature of the universe was a major stimulus for the solipsistic dream ending, written the same year as "The Czar's Soliloquy."

On Heroes, Hero-Worship and the Heroic in History too, may have played a part. Lecture one, "The Hero as Divinity," also touched upon existence as a dream and quoted the beginning of one of Clemens's favorite passages from Shakespeare's *The Tempest*—Prospero's "We are such stuff as dreams are made on." In *Sartor* Carlyle also invokes Prospero's message several times while tailoring the clothes philosophy to fit his vision of the unreality of the world of the senses and the symbolic nature of the universe. Carlyle's influence on Mark Twain thus was almost lifelong. And one might find an appropriate

final tribute in the fact that on the very morning of the day Carlyle died, Clemens turned again to his much-worn copy of the *History of the French Revolution*.

Howard G. Baetzhold

BIBLIOGRAPHY

Baetzhold, Howard G. *Mark Twain and John Bull: The British Connection.* Bloomington: Indiana UP, 1970.

Blair, Walter. *Mark Twain & Huck Finn.* Berkeley: U of California P, 1960.

———. "The French Revolution and *Huckleberry Finn.*" *Modern Philology* 55 (August 1957): 21–35.

Campbell, Ian. *Thomas Carlyle.* London: Hamilton, 1974.

Carlyle, Thomas. *The Works of Thomas Carlyle.* Ed. H.D. Traill. Centenary ed. 30 vols. London: Chapman and Hall, 1896–1899; New York: Scribner, 1896–1901.

Froude, James Anthony. *Thomas Carlyle: A History of the First Forty Years of His Life, 1795–1835.* London: Longmans, Green, 1882.

———. *Thomas Carlyle: A History of His Life in London, 1834–1881.* 2 vols. London: Longmans, Green, 1884.

Gribben, Alan. *Mark Twain's Library: A Reconstruction.* 2 vols. Boston: G.K. Hall, 1980.

Kaplan, Fred. *Thomas Carlyle.* Ithaca, N.Y.: Cornell UP, 1983.

"Thomas Carlyle." *Dictionary of Literary Biography.* Vol. 55. *Victorian Prose Writers Before 1867.* Detroit: Gale Research, 1987. 46–64.

See also: Connecticut Yankee in King Arthur's Court, A; French Revolution; Heroism; Reading; Taine, Hippolyte

Carnegie, Andrew
(1835–1919)

If Horatio Alger successfully idealized the story of a boy's rise from rags to riches, Andrew Carnegie, his contemporary, acted it out in real life on a scale that no fiction writer would have dared to imagine. Son of a Scottish handloom weaver and grandson of Thomas Morrison, a dynamic agitator for social and political reform in Great Britain, Carnegie came with his family to Allegheny, Pennsylvania, in 1848. There he went to work as a bobbin boy in a cotton factory. His spare time was spent in self-education by reading. Employed as a messenger in a Pittsburgh telegraph office, he soon taught himself the skills of an operator. Recognizing young Carnegie's energy and initiative, Thomas Scott of the Pennsylvania Railroad employed him as a personal calligrapher and private secretary. While with the railroad (1853–1865), Carnegie took his first steps as a capitalist. He introduced the use of Pullman sleeping cars and acquired an eighth interest in the Woodruff Company, original holders of the Pullman patents. By 1863 his ventures produced an annual income of $45,460. He was also active in the transportation of troops during the Civil War and organized the military telegraph department.

In 1865, at the age of thirty, Carnegie turned all his energies to the iron industry. His Keystone Bridge Company succeeded by virtue of his organizing ability and salesmanship. Success in oil operations and as a salesman of railroad securities abroad laid the foundations for his success as an entrepreneur. By 1868 he owned securities and partnership interests that produced nearly $60,000 per year. In 1873 he committed all his profits to what was a new American industry—steel. His announced policy of "putting all his eggs in one basket and watching the basket" so delighted Mark Twain that he adopted it for his story *Pudd'nhead Wilson* (1894).

Building a staff of expert managers, Carnegie introduced into his company a rational operating structure. He gave unceasing attention to cost accounting and low operating cost, always insisting on up-to-date machinery, for which he made immense outlays during times of depression. His company, until shortly before its absorption into the U.S. Steel Corporation in 1901, was never a corporation; it remained a limited partnership, every share held by his business associates, with Carnegie himself owning the majority interest. By 1889 American steel production had passed that of Great Britain and Carnegie had established himself as the world's foremost manufacturer. Throughout his life Carnegie cultivated friendship with the literary and political world, counting among his intimate acquaintances William E. Gladstone, James Bryce, Theodore Roosevelt, and Mark Twain. From 1889 to 1910 his closest friend was the scholar John Morley.

In an article entitled "Wealth" (*North American Review*, 1889) Andrew Carnegie announced his concept of stewardship, or the responsibility of rich men to hold their wealth in trust for the public interest. When he sold the Carnegie company to the newly founded U.S. Steel in 1901, he began to put his philosophy of stewardship into practice. He disposed of some $350,000,000 in many public benefactions, which included the erection of public library buildings, the encouragement of scientific research, and the furtherance of international peace. His well-known essay "The Gospel of Wealth" celebrated a universe of force not unlike the social Darwinism of Jack London.

Tom Z. Parrish

BIBLIOGRAPHY

Livesay, Harold C. *Andrew Carnegie and the Rise of Big Business.* Ed. Oscar Handlin. Boston: Little, Brown, 1975.

Wall, Joseph Frazier. *Andrew Carnegie.* New York: Oxford UP, 1970.

Carpet-Bag

The Boston *Carpet-Bag*, a weekly magazine published by B.P. Shillaber from 1852 to 1853, was one of the many humor journals popular during the mid-nineteenth century. The *Carpet-Bag* was one of the out-of-town exchanges that came to Orion Clemens's Hannibal *Journal*, at which Sam Clemens was employed as a cub reporter. On 1 May 1852 a short sketch by Clemens entitled "The Dandy Frightening the Squatter" appeared in the *Carpet-Bag*. The tale is a variation of a well-known anecdote of which at least one other version had previously been published. The story, signed "S.L.C.," is Clemens's first recorded published literary work.

Susan McFatter

BIBLIOGRAPHY

Benson, Ivan. *Mark Twain's Western Years*. Stanford, Calif.: Stanford UP, 1938.

Branch, Edgar M. *The Literary Apprenticeship of Mark Twain*. Urbana: U of Illinois P, 1950.

Emerson, Everett. *The Authentic Mark Twain: A Literary Biography of Samuel L. Clemens*. Philadelphia: U of Pennsylvania P, 1984.

See also: "Dandy Frightening the Squatter, The"

"Carson Fossil-Footprints, The"

(1884)

Refusing at first when an old San Francisco friend, Joseph Goodman, in mid-December 1883, solicited a contribution for a new periodical that he and others were establishing, Mark Twain finally relented and, late in January, hastily wrote and sent "The Carson Fossil-Footprints," which appeared as the lead article in Volume 1, Number 1 of the *San Franciscan* for 16 February 1884. The piece was reprinted in at least two other newspapers, the Sacramento *Daily Record-Union* (25 March 1885) and San Francisco *Examiner* (1892 or 1893), in the bibliography items listed below and will be first collected in the Iowa-California Edition of *The Writings of Mark Twain* in *Middle Tales & Sketches, 1874–1895*.

In the sketch Mark Twain presents the "cold facts" about the controversy currently raging between noted scientists as to whether the mysterious set of larger-than-human footprints found during excavations for the prison grounds at Carson City, Nevada, were those of a giant species of prehistoric man or of a giant ground sloth, the Mylodon or Morotherium. Claiming authority as an eyewitness, and incorporating many contemporary allusions to persons and events from his days in Nevada, he explains in careful detail how the large tracks and those of other varieties accompanying them were actually made by inebriated members of the Nevada legislature, celebrating the adjournment of that body after an unusual rain shower had muddied the dry alkali flat.

The style of "The Carson Fossil-Footprints" closely resembles Mark Twain's earlier burlesques of scientific inquiry like "A Full and Reliable Account of the Extraordinary Meteoric Shower of Last Saturday Night" in the *Californian* of 19 November 1864 (*Early Tales & Sketches* 2:116–124). It is interesting, therefore, both as a reminiscence of the Nevada days and, especially in view of how hastily it was written, as an example of its author's skill in reproducing the sort of piece that first made him popular.

Howard G. Baetzhold

BIBLIOGRAPHY

Brownell, George H. "Much Mystery Still Surrounds Twain Tale of 'Carson Footprints.'" *Twainian* 8 (May-June 1948): 1–3.

Clemens, Samuel L. *The Works of Mark Twain: Early Tales & Sketches, Volume 2 (1864–1865)*. Ed. Edgar M. Branch and Robert H. Hirst. Berkeley: U of California P, 1981.

Emerson, Everett. "A Send-Off for Joe Goodman: Mark Twain's 'The Carson Fossil-Footprints.'" *Resources for American Literary Study* 10 (1980): 71–78.

Catholicism

Like many nineteenth-century Americans raised in the Calvinist churches on the southwest frontier, Samuel Clemens harbored deeply rooted prejudices against the Roman Catholic Church and its adherents. As an adolescent printer's apprentice and newspaper typesetter in Hannibal, his first contact with Catholicism was limited to the Irish, French, and German immigrants who came first to St. Louis and then began to fan out through the upper Mississippi valley. The immigrants, largely poor, were perceived by the more firmly settled, primarily Anglo-Saxon Protestant, population as unwanted economic competition. From the pulpits of fundamentalist and "high-brow" Protestant churches alike came vehement denunciations of the Roman church. Ministers called into question the patriotism of the new "invaders," raising the phobia of "foreign" domination and exacerbating the insecurities of congregations already suspicious of the heterodox customs, languages, religious rituals, and cultural expectations the immigrants brought with them. Sam's older brother Orion publicly assailed the Catholic convert Orestes Brownson for believing "that the rusty old Pope in Rome has a right to dictate who shall be our Presidents, Governors, Senators, Representatives, etc."; two days later he began an editorial in his Hannibal newspaper, "wherever there is Catholic rule there is blight" (Wecter 230–231). Horace Bushnell, head of a Connecticut Congregationalist church and subsequently mentor to the pastors of Clemens's Nook Farm community, wrote that "Romanism" was the great threat to the West, second only to ignorance and illiteracy (Posey 87). Clemens's early antipathy to Catholicism thus reflected widespread political and cultural forces more than it testified to staunch denominational conviction.

This cultural defensiveness underlies Mark Twain's first extended attack on the Catholic Church, *The Innocents Abroad* (1869), which contrasts the moral energy, democratic principles, pragmatic world view, and industrial might of his Protestant homeland with decadently aesthetic, morally corrupt, largely feudal, and overwhelmingly Catholic Europe: "The Popes have long been the patrons and preservers of art, just as our new, practical Republic is the encourager and upholder of mechanics" (*Innocents Abroad*, chapter 28). The Catholic Church receives Twain's rebuke not for its doctrinal positions but as "an institution which seemed to have abandoned religion in its quest for splendor and power" (Scott 401). The vast discrepancy between rich and poor Twain blames in large part on a church that historically had forged political alliances with the cultured aristocracy to enhance its own power and wealth at the expense of the illiterate, superstitious poor it held in abject servitude. Leslie Fiedler suggests that in *Innocents Abroad* Twain reflects "merely the other side of the old WASP ambivalence, its secular pu-

ritanism: that fear of High Art and High Church worship which the followers of Henry Adams had rejected in favor of the religion of art" (Fiedler 81). Fiedler, however, undervalues the moral basis of Twain's reservations; although at times moved by the aesthetic beauty of Catholic art, intellectually Twain found morally reprehensible the class oppression that made it possible (Ganzel 127).

In *A Connecticut Yankee in King Arthur's Court* (1889) Twain again takes aim against the Catholic Church as the principal obstacle to Hank Morgan's attempted renovation of feudal society. The church thrives on ignorance, fear, and superstition as it rigorously programs its docile followers to do its bidding. Foiled in his attempt to usher in his agenda of egalitarian reform, Hank concedes that the church thoroughly understands human nature, and he uses that understanding to exploit the peasants as it solidifies its terrible power. Yet as many critics have noted, it is difficult to reduce *CY* to a simple formula. The church may well be corrupt and the unjust social order it engenders reprehensible, but Hank, as its adversary, has his own character flaws as he tries to bend an entire civilization to his own singular vision, a civilization that even he admits, at the end, had its own beauty and poetry; the ultimate target of Twain's satire is as much nineteenth-century America as it is feudal, Catholic, Europe.

One of the saints of the Catholic Church serves as Mark Twain's most glorious heroine: Joan of Arc. He acknowledges the validity of the voices she hears and, like the Catholic Church, extols her as a model of religious devotion, moral purity, courage, and self-sacrifice. Yet in his *Personal Recollections of Joan of Arc* (1896), Twain fashions a Joan who is most Protestant in her resistance to church hierarchy and reliance on individual intuition (Spengemann 117). The adversary to Twain's transcendent heroine is the very church that subsequently canonizes her.

Late in life, however, Samuel Clemens apparently freed himself from virulent anti-Catholicism as his antipathy to Protestant fundamentalism intensified. After his daughter Jean entered a convent for treatment of epilepsy, he admitted to daughter Clara that he was "very, very glad Jean is in a convent," and that he would not "be the least bit sorry" if the nuns were to "make a good strong unshakable Catholic of her." Citing Catholicism as "doubtless the most peace giving and restful of all the religions," Clemens makes the startling confession, "If I ever change my religion I shall change to that" (*My Father* 100).

James D. Wilson

BIBLIOGRAPHY

Clemens, Clara. *My Father, Mark Twain*. New York: Harper, 1931.

Clemens, Samuel L. *The Innocents Abroad*. Hartford, Conn.: American Publishing, 1869.

Durocher, Aurele A. "Mark Twain and the Roman Catholic Church." *Journal of the Central Mississippi Valley American Studies Association* 1 (Fall 1960): 32–43.

Fiedler, Leslie. "An American Abroad." *Partisan Review* 33 (Winter 1966): 77–91.

Ganzel, Dewey. *Mark Twain Abroad: The Cruise of the "Quaker City."* Chicago: U of Chicago P, 1968.

Posey, Walter. *Religious Strife on the Southern Frontier*. Baton Rouge: Louisiana State UP, 1965.

Scott, Arthur. "Mark Twain Looks at Europe." *South Atlantic Quarterly* 52 (July 1953): 399–413.

Spengemann, William C. *Mark Twain and the Backwoods Angel: The Matter of Innocence in the Works of Samuel L. Clemens*. Kent, Ohio: Kent State UP, 1966.

Wecter, Dixon. *Sam Clemens of Hannibal*. Boston: Houghton Mifflin, 1952.

Wilson, James D. "In Quest of Redemptive Vision: Mark Twain's *Joan of Arc*." *Texas Studies in Language and Literature* 20 (Summer 1978): 181–198.

———. "Religious and Esthetic Vision in Mark Twain's Early Career." *Canadian Review of American Studies* 17.2 (Summer 1986): 155–172.

See also: *Connecticut Yankee in King Arthur's Court, A*; *Innocents Abroad, The*; *Italy*; *Personal Recollections of Joan of Arc*; *Religion*

Cauchon, Pierre
(d. 1442)

As an historical figure, Pierre Cauchon, Bishop of Beauvais who presides over Joan of Arc's trial, appears only in *Personal Recollections of Joan of Arc* (1896). His elegant dress and importance as he presides over fifty distinguished ecclesiastics are betrayed by his physical appearance: obesity, splotchy complexion, puffing, and wheezing. In short, Cauchon is a fraud.

For the self-aggrandizing Cauchon, success at Joan's trail means appointment as Archbishop of Rouen; consequently, when Joan's impeccable military record leaves no basis for trial, he contrives crimes against religion. Referred to as "bastard of Satan" by the narrator, Cauchon is fitting for such villainy.

Commenting on Cauchon in source marginal notations as "that villain priest," Twain obviously finds him repulsive, echoing sentiments toward Catholicism found in *The Innocents Abroad* (1869) and *A Connecticut Yankee in King Arthur's Court* (1889), among others.

Thomas A. Maik

BIBLIOGRAPHY

Clemens, Samuel L. *Personal Recollections of Joan of Arc*. Westport, Conn.: Greenwood P, 1980.

Gerber, John C. *Mark Twain*. Boston: Twayne, 1988.

Sepet, Marius. *Jeanne D'Arc*. Tours: Alfred Mame Et Fils, 1887.

Stone, Albert E., Jr. *The Innocent Eye: Childhood in Mark Twain's Imagination*. New Haven, Conn.: Yale UP, 1961.

See also: *Personal Recollections of Joan of Arc*

"Cecil Rhodes and the Shark"
(1897)

Written for inclusion in *Following the Equator* and never published otherwise during Twain's lifetime, "Cecil Rhodes and the Shark" tells the story of a young man's traveling to Australia to make his fortune. There he discovers a bit of coveted information via a newspaper swallowed by a shark. Charles Neider, in his introduction to a collection of Twain's short stories, refers to Twain's literary habit of "inserting yarns of pure fiction in a non-fictional work," of which "Cecil Rhodes" is an example in the travel book *Following the Equator* (Neider xi). The short anecdote is based in fantasy and illustrates one young man's manipulations for success.

The basic plot of "Cecil Rhodes" is fairly simple. The young Cecil Rhodes travels to Sidney to make a fortune but fails to find work. When he is out of money and wandering near the water, a fisherman invites him to watch the fishing lines. Cecil catches a shark, inside of which is the remainder of a London newspaper carrying word of the outbreak of war. Since news typically takes fifty days to travel from London to Sidney by ship and since this paper is only ten days old, the information is invaluable. Cecil Rhodes, a capitalizing young man, then goes to the house of a wool merchant to strike a deal with the fortuitous information. When the merchant discovers what Cecil has done to discover the information and to maneuver the situation, he declares the young man to be "remarkable."

As some critics have noted, "Cecil Rhodes" displays some of Twain's later naturalistic beliefs. This is evident at the end of the tale when the wool merchant tells Cecil that men fall into three categories—commonplace, remarkable, and lunatics. Cecil's manipulations cause the man to classify him as remarkable. Wilson sees a stronger link with the naturalistic philosophy, saying that "humans and shark are both predators in a Darwinistic struggle for survival" in a story that "satirizes the machinations of Cecil Rhodes, whose . . . ruthless activity make(s) him the beneficiary of this predatory cycle" (27). "Cecil Rhodes" displays Twain's mind set later in his life, his ear for a good tale, and his ability to communicate that tale—whether fact or fiction.

Christie Graves Hamric

BIBLIOGRAPHY

Clemens, Samuel L. "Cecil Rhodes and the Shark." *The Complete Short Stories of Mark Twain.* By Clemens. Ed. Charles Neider. Garden City, N.Y.: Hanover House, 1957. 334–339.

Neider, Charles. Introduction. *The Complete Short Stories of Mark Twain.* By Clemens. Ed. Neider. Garden City, N.Y.: Hanover House, 1957. xi–xxii.

Wilson, James D. *A Reader's Guide to the Short Stories of Mark Twain.* Boston: G.K. Hall, 1987.

See also: Australia; *Following the Equator*

"Celebrated Jumping Frog of Calaveras County, The"
(1865)

Mark Twain wrote his story of the jumping frog Dan'l Webster and the gambler Jim Smiley at the invitation of Artemus Ward (Charles Farrar Browne), his friend and the most popular American humorist of the day, to help fill out a volume of humorous sketches that Ward was editing. Fortuitously, and fortunately for Twain, the frog story arrived too late for inclusion in Ward's book; it was published instead as "Jim Smiley and His Jumping Frog" in the New York *Saturday Press* on 18 November 1865. It was soon reprinted in newspapers and comic periodicals throughout the nation, was pirated by Beadle's Dime Books, and was later collected with a new title in *The Celebrated Jumping Frog of Calaveras County and Other Sketches* (1867). This humorous short story brought Twain his first popular acclaim and has proven to be his first literary masterpiece. It reveals the literary heritage from which Twain was emerging, and though he was later to refer to it as a "villainous backwoods sketch," it includes the seeds of Twain's best and most characteristic humor techniques.

Perhaps nowhere is Mark Twain's dictum in "How to Tell a Story" that "[t]he humorous story depends for its effect upon the manner of telling" better illustrated than in "The Jumping Frog." Twain went to the hills of California prospecting for gold, but what he found in the winter of 1864–1865 proved to be far more valuable: in places like Jackass Hill and Angel's Camp he heard and sometimes recorded in his notebook frontier stories told by Ben Coon, Jim Gillis, and others from which he was to mine his best early fiction. Twain heard wry old Ben Coon (also known as Ross Coon) drone out the frog story in January 1865, and he recorded its essentials in his notebook: "Coleman with his jumping frog—bet stranger $50—stranger had no frog, and C. got him one:—in the mean time stranger filled C.'s frog full of shot and he couldn't jump. The stranger's frog won." From this small, unpromising nugget Twain refined his first great literary effort. Although the story had been told many times before, Twain was the first to realize its full artistic potential.

At its core, "The Jumping Frog" is a simple tables-turned practical joke story—in the vein of his earlier "The Dandy Frightening the Squatter" (1852)—in which a seemingly innocent outsider appears ready to be duped by the incorrigible gambler Jim Smiley. But the humorous "effect" of the story grows out of Twain's abilities to understand and employ the oral tradition of storytelling that he learned primarily from the southwestern humorists and that had been recalled for him in the California mountains by the tale-telling abilities of Coon and Gillis. The story is a frame narrative that operates on three levels simultaneously: on the first level is Twain's letter to fellow humorist Artemus Ward—the literary frame. This gullible, humorless, but civilized frame narrator describes being tricked into asking old Simon Wheeler about a fictitious Reverend Leonidas W. Smiley, being subsequently blockaded in by Wheeler, and being forced to listen to the history of Jim Smiley. Though he later dropped the pretense of a letter, Twain retained the naive literary narrator.

The second level develops its humor from the deadpan, monotone, meandering storytelling of frontiersman Simon Wheeler and illustrates Twain's belief that "the humorous story . . . may wander around as much as it pleases, and arrive nowhere in particular . . .

the teller does his best to conceal the fact that he even dimly suspects that there is anything funny about it" ("How to Tell as Story"). The final level is the story itself, actually three stories that center on the character of the compulsive gambler Jim Smiley. Smiley will "bet on *any* thing," Wheeler insists, including the destination of straddle-bugs and even the health of Parson Walker's wife, a wager that he offers to the preacher himself.

The three stories that Wheeler focuses on are Smiley's asthmatic horse, nicknamed the fifteen-minute nag; his small but ferocious fighting bull pup named Andrew Jackson; and, of course, his notorious jumping frog Dan'l Webster. Each is a reversal story in which the anticipated outcome is overturned, and the three operate on a climactic scale of increasing length and complexity. The comic mare trails in every race, but always manages—"desperate-like"—to wildly finish a neck in front of her competition. The ornery-looking and more individualized Andrew Jackson is described as a talented canine with "genius" who could have "made a name for hisself" had he not been pitted against a dog with no hind legs. Finally, Dan'l Webster, the educated but modest frog, is presented as more "gifted" than any of his species. He, too, is undefeated until the stranger outwits Jim Smiley and fills Dan'l with quail shot.

The climax of the Smiley stories, which is really an anticlimax, occurs when the obviously not so guileless stranger stops at the door, turns and points to the lead-filled frog, and repeats his earlier observation: "*I* don't see no p'ints about that frog that's any better'n any other frog." In the end, however, Twain rightly returns to his human characters treated in a comic, not pathetic, mode. Thus, the master stroke with which Twain concludes the story is to have the distracted Wheeler buttonhole the frame narrator attempting to escape and begin anew with a story of Smiley's one-eyed stump-tailed cow. The narrator, however, has reached his limit and takes his leave, thus depriving himself—and Twain's readers—of what hints at being the best Smiley story yet.

Twain employs the characteristic frontier-versus-civilization contrast so skillfully developed in the frame narratives of southwestern humorists, the leisurely earthy vernacular of their accomplished tall-tale tellers, and eccentric characterizations not only of Wheeler and Smiley but also of the humanized animals. Somewhat more subtle, perhaps, is his satire in further contrasting the frontier West and the civilized East through the use of two notorious politicians, each appropriate for the personality of the respective animal named after him: Andrew Jackson and Dan'l Webster.

"The Jumping Frog" is the best fiction written by Mark Twain during his western sojourn. It moves beyond the outlandish journalistic hack work, the western burlesques, and the one-dimensional gag sketches that so characterize his early career as a comedian. His accurate reproduction of the speech rhythms and idioms of the frontier setting, his sensitive use of local folklore and native characters, and his dramatic presentation of anecdote not only add a flavor of local color realism, but also point to Twain's growing awareness of the value of aesthetic distance. In this "villainous backwoods sketch" Twain substitutes objectivity for didacticism, character development for extravagant jokes, and pathos for puns. In "The Celebrated Jumping Frog of Calaveras County" Mark Twain brought together in proper proportions his own natural talents and the southwestern humor tradition that best suited them with a regional story worthy of both: he skillfully balances his matter with his manner, and for the first time he reveals the heights of which his artistry was capable.

W. Craig Turner

BIBLIOGRAPHY

Bellamy, Gladys Carmen. *Mark Twain as a Literary Artist.* Norman: U of Oklahoma P, 1950.

Branch, Edgar Marquess. *The Literary Apprenticeship of Mark Twain.* Urbana: U of Illinois P, 1950.

———. "'My Voice Is Still for Setchell': A Background Study of 'Jim Smiley and His Jumping Frog.'" *Publications of the Modern Language Association* 82 (1967): 591–601.

Cox, James M. *Mark Twain: The Fate of Humor.* Princeton, N.J.: Princeton UP, 1966.

Gibson, William M. *The Art of Mark Twain.* New York: Oxford UP, 1976.

Krause, Sydney J. "The Art and Satire of Twain's 'Jumping Frog' Story." *American Quarterly* 16 (Winter 1964): 562–576.

Lewis, Oscar. *The Origin of the Celebrated Jumping Frog of Calaveras County.* San Francisco: Book Club of California, 1931.

Lynn, Kenneth S. *Mark Twain and Southwestern Humor.* Boston: Little, Brown, 1959.

See also: Deadpan; Folklore; "How to Tell a Story"; Smiley, Jim; Southwestern Humor; Wheeler, Simon

Censorship

Adventures of Huckleberry Finn (1885) has been the main target of the censors of Mark Twain's work. From the time of its publication in England in December 1884 (as *The Adventures of Huckleberry Finn*), the novel has been banned in classrooms and libraries and attacked on moral, political, and, in the 1980s, racial grounds. *The Adventures of Tom Sawyer* (1876) has often been a censored companion of Huck's, and yet Twain stories with more daring political and sexual content have not been as controversial.

Huckleberry Finn's reception signaled a public uneasiness with the style and themes of the work. Among the country's major newspapers and magazines, it received scant attention. Of those newspapers that did review it, most dismissed the language as too vulgar for polite literature and compared it to other pulp novels of the time.

Then came the Concord (Massachusetts) Public Library's decision in March 1885 to ban the book from its shelves, a celebrated event that provoked both support and derision. The library committee said the book was unsuitable for impressionable young people; but the action also raises questions about the New England literary establishment's acceptance of Mark Twain (Stavely 1656). Twain reacted with characteristic humor, condemning the committee as "moral icebergs" and joking in a letter to his publisher that the decision would sell thousands of books (*Mark Twain's Letters* 452–453).

The public outcry against *Huckleberry Finn* died down in the early twentieth century, but by the 1960s, when the novel was generally acknowledged to be an American literary masterpiece, schools and libraries began again to censor it. This era of censorship, which continues to the present day, has concentrated its objections on the racial implications of the book. Critics charge that the use of the word "nigger" and the depiction of Jim reinforce insulting racial stereotypes.

Annually, *Huckleberry Finn* is ranked near the top of the list of censored books by library and publishing organizations (Woods 83; Karolides 2). Studies have documented accounts of its being removed from the curriculum of schools in New York City, in Miami, in Denver, in Houston, in Davenport, Iowa, as well as in England, Germany, and Russia (Downs 53).

The culminating irony of Mark Twain censorship occurred in 1982, when a black administrator at the Mark Twain Intermediate School in Fairfax, Virginia, called the book "racist" and sought to ban it from the school's curriculum (Fields 18). As it did in 1885, this public censorship of the book resulted primarily in a defense by literary experts and observers who praised the sensitive treatment of racial themes. The controversy also produced several bowdlerized versions and an allegorical novel, *The Day They Came to Arrest the Book*, by Nat Hentoff.

The Adventures of Tom Sawyer has not received the same prominent censorship, but it was banned long before *Huck Finn* by the Brooklyn (N.Y.) Library, which found it too coarse for young readers. Other works that might have been more logical targets for censors—*1601*, "To the Person Sitting in Darkness," and "The Mammoth Cod"—have escaped largely because they have avoided the commercial mainstream. Not surprisingly, the anti-British sentiments in *A Connecticut Yankee in King Arthur's Court* (1889) and *Following the Equator* (1897) provoked mild attempts at censorship in England. The Soviet Union, labeling Mark Twain a bourgeois writer, at times confiscated his books (Haight 50).

To some degree, Mark Twain undoubtedly subjected his books to the editing of a group of friends, especially his wife, William Dean Howells, and, to some extent, Mary Mason Fairbanks. Whether he compromised his artistic integrity in allowing them to censor his work, or whether their revisions were cosmetic is the subject of much debate. Recently published Mark Twain manuscripts suggest that he refused to allow some inflammatory material to be published (Cardwell 175). More likely, Mark Twain wrote with self-prescribed limits in mind, declaring that his most vitriolic sentiments were written privately, for "relief."

J. Mark Baggett

BIBLIOGRAPHY

Cardwell, Guy A. "Mark Twain: A Self-Emasculated Hero." *Emerson Society Quarterly* 23 (1977): 173–187.

Fields, Howard. "Principal in Fairfax County, Va., Recommends Restriction of *Huckleberry Finn*." *Publishers Weekly* (23 April 1982): 18.

Haight, Anne Lyon, and Chandler B. Grannis. *Banned Books: 387 B.C. to 1978 A.D.* 4th ed. New York: Bowker, 1978.

Hentoff, Nat. *The Day They Came to Arrest the Book.* New York: Dell, 1983.

Hoffman, Frank. *Intellectual Freedom and Censorship: An Annotated Bibliography.* Metuchen, N.J.: Scarecrow P, 1989.

Karolides, Nicholas J., and Lee Burress, eds. *Celebrating Censored Books.* Racine: Wisconsin Council of Teachers of English, 1985.

Meltzer, Milton. "Hughes, Twain, Child, and Sanger: Four Who Locked Horns with the Censors." *Wilson Library Bulletin* 44 (1969): 278–286.

Stavely, Keith, and Lani Gerson. "We Didn't Wait for the Censor: Intellectual Freedom at the Watertown Public Library." *Library Journal* 108 (1983): 1654–1658.

Vogelback, Arthur L. "The Publication and Reception of *Huckleberry Finn* in America." *American Literature* 11 (1939): 260–272.

Woods, L.B. *A Decade of Censorship in America: The Threat to Classrooms and Libraries, 1966–1975.* Metuchen, N.J.: Scarecrow P, 1979.

See also: Adventures of Huckleberry Finn;
Adventures of Tom Sawyer, The;
Genteel Tradition; Racial Attitudes

Century Magazine

Century Illustrated Monthly Magazine began in 1881 as a continuation of *Scribner's Monthly.* Richard Watson Gilder (1844–1909), who had been associate editor of *Scribner's Monthly*, was its editor until his death. Under his leadership *Century* became noted for superior illustrations, serialized fiction, and biography by the best writers of the day. Its circulation during the late 1880s climbed to more than 200,000. The February 1885 issue was a high-water mark in American journalism, for it contained installments of Howells's *The Rise of Silas Lapham*, James's *The Bostonians*, and Twain's *Huckleberry Finn*. Gilder's *Century* showed Clemens particular favor not only by regularly reviewing his books, but also by publishing eight pieces about him (including items by Howells and George Ade) and by publishing twenty-three selections by him (including "The Private History of a Campaign That Failed" [1885] and installments of *Huckleberry Finn* [1885], *Connecticut Yankee* [1889], and *Pudd'nhead Wilson* [1894]). With Clemens's "full consent," Gilder edited the installments of *Huck Finn* to meet the expectations of *Century*'s refined audience. He was nevertheless obliged to defend Clemens against charges of immorality, which he did with courage and force.

L. Terry Oggel

BIBLIOGRAPHY

DeVoto, Bernard. *Mark Twain's America.* Boston: Little, Brown, 1932.

Gilder, Richard Watson. *Letters of Richard Watson Gilder.* Ed. Rosamond Gilder. Boston: Houghton Mifflin, 1916.

Mott, Frank Luther. *A History of American Magazines, 1741–1930.* 5 vols. Cambridge, Mass.: Harvard UP, 1930–1968.

Cervantes Saavedra, Miguel de
(1547–1616)

Spain's most famous novelist, Miguel de Cervantes Saavedra was the son of a poor apothecary surgeon. His grandfather had been a prominent lawyer, but the family had fallen on hard times. Reasonably well educated by the Jesuits but scholarly neither by temperament nor by training, Cervantes's youthful escapades forced him to become a soldier in foreign wars, fighting gallantly and losing the use of his left hand after the Battle of Lepanto (1571) and being imprisoned and held for ransom in Algiers (1575–1580). A troubled petty bureaucrat and unsuccessful writer for most of the rest of his life, he turned out poems, many plays, stories, and one early novel; as a government official he was constantly in difficulties and not seldom in jail, usually for failure to keep his accounts in balance. Cervantes finally won literary success in 1605 with the first part of *Don Quixote*. Part two appeared in 1615, hastened by a spurious and inferior part two that had appeared anonymously in 1614.

La Galatea (1585), Cervantes's first novel, was never finished (though he spoke to the last about a long-promised sequel). It is a pastoral romance, composed of loosely structured episodes, some in verse; much of the material is reworked from traditional sources. The style is capable but distinctly ornate. The novel that he completed just before his death, *Persiles and Sigismunda* (1617), is a complex moral fantasy extraordinarily different from (but at first even more popular than) the poignant realism and dazzling psychological perception, and the witty mock heroism, of his and Spanish literature's greatest novel, *Don Quixote*.

An immensely long book of roughly half a million words, *Don Quixote* sweeps its self-enchanted hero through a series of strange and wonderful adventures at once tender and brutal. The novel is written in a style simultaneously passionate and blessed with Olympian objectivity, fiercely realistic, and yearningly romantic. In the style of the time, there are many narrative discursions, especially in part one. But the book's central relationships are (1) the half mad, half brilliantly sane conflict in the hero's mind between decayed, immoral modernity and the noble, chivalric past celebrated in song and story and (2) the interplay between the wildly idealistic, impractical hero, who frequently cannot see (and does not want to see) as far as the nose on his face, and his worldly, intensely practical page, Sancho Panza. Cervantes deploys these powerfully opposing forces much as Jonathan Swift uses the stark, basic oppositions in *Gulliver's Travels* (though without Swift's withering contempt and cynicism) and with a warm humor rich in worldly experience. The novel is full of sharply etched, unforgettable scenes in which differing perceptions of reality are whirled about with sometimes cyclonic rapidity: Don Quixote madly attacking a windmill, believing it to be one among a crowd of wicked giants; his half-sleeping battle with an innkeeper's wineskins, which the madly dreaming knight believes to be wicked monsters; and, toward the end of the book, genuine battles with would-be rescuers, determined to save the magnificently lovable old man from his dangerous wandering. Don Quixote (and frequently Sancho with him) is constantly beaten and battered—but no reality except death itself is strong enough to render him conventionally sane. The long, delightful conversations between Don Quixote and Sancho Panza beautifully heighten this perpetual, unresolvable quarrel about the nature of reality. Far-ranging, immensely wise, and wonderfully funny, these masterfully written dialogues keep the novel's pulse quick and, set as they are between more active episodes, also serve to keep the reader devotedly turning pages.

Twain, who had read Cervantes as early as 1860 and at one point discussed with William Dean Howells the possibility of turning *Don Quixote* into a play, correctly ranked Cervantes with Shakespeare.

Burton Raffel

BIBLIOGRAPHY

Byron, William. *Cervantes, A Biography*. Garden City, N.Y.: Doubleday, 1978.

Cervantes, Miguel de. *Don Quixote*. Trans. C.A. Jones. Harmondsworth (England): Penguin, 1972.

———. *Exemplary Stories*. Ed. and trans. C.A. Jones. Harmondsworth (England): Penguin, 1950.

———. *Interludes*. Trans. E. Honig. New York: Signet, 1964.

———. *Persiles and Sigismunda*. Trans. Celia R. Weller and Clark A. Colahan. Berkeley: U of California P, 1989.

El Saffar, Ruth. *Distance and Control in "Don Quixote": A Study in Narrative Technique*. Chapel Hill: U of North Carolina P, 1975.

Gribben, Alan. *Mark Twain's Library: A Reconstruction*. 2 vols. Boston: G.K. Hall, 1980.

Madariaga, Salvador de. *Don Quixote: An Introductory Essay in Psychology*. Oxford: Oxford UP, 1935.

Ortega y Gasset, Jose. *Meditations on Quixote*. New York: Norton, 1963.

Riley, Edward Calverley. *Cervantes's Theory of the Novel*. Oxford: Clarendon, 1962.

Unamuno, Miguel de. *The Life of Don Quixote and Sancho According to Miguel de Cervantes Saavedra*. New York: Knopf, 1927.

Wilson, Diana de Armas. *Allegories of Love: Cervantes's "Persiles and Sigismunda."* Princeton, N.J.: Princeton UP, 1991.

See also: Picaresque

"Chapters from My Autobiography"
(1906–1907)

The *North American Review* published "Chapters from My Autobiography" in twenty-five installments between 7 September 1906 and December 1907. George Harvey (1864–1928), publisher of the *North American Review*, paid Twain $30,000; the money went toward the construction of Twain's house in Redding, Connecticut.

Using a loose chronological arrangement, Twain wove together material that he composed between 1870 and 1907: some from his autobiographical dictations, some from earlier writings that described his youth in Hannibal. Twain spins yarns of his days reporting for the Virginia City *Territorial Enterprise*; he offers memories of his courtship of Olivia Langdon (1845–1904), their life in Hartford, and their summers in Elmira; he delivers heartfelt eulogies for Livy, Langdon Clemens (1870–1872), Susy Clemens (1872–1896), Orion Clemens (1825–1897), Henry Clemens (1838–1858), and Jane Lampton Clemens (1803–1890). Especially intriguing is Twain's practice of incorporating selections from the biography of him that Susy wrote at age thirteen.

Though Twain prepared the series, which makes it valuable to any study of Twain's approach to autobiography and storytelling, "Chapters" has been overshadowed by Albert Bigelow Paine's *Mark Twain's Autobiography* (1924), Bernard DeVoto's *Mark Twain in Eruption* (1940), and Charles Neider's *The Autobiography of Mark Twain* (1959). In *Mark Twain's Own Autobiography* (1990) Michael J. Kiskis unites the installments in a single volume and argues that "Chapters" should be read as a unified, coherent tale and appreciated as the "authorized" text of Twain's autobiography.

Michael J. Kiskis

BIBLIOGRAPHY

Clemens, Samuel L. *The Autobiography of Mark Twain*. Ed. Charles Neider. New York: Harper, 1959.

———. "Chapters from My Autobiography." *North American Review* 183 (1906); 184, 185, 186 (1907): various issues.

———. *Mark Twain in Eruption*. Ed. Bernard DeVoto. New York: Harper, 1940.

———. *Mark Twain's Autobiography*. Ed. Albert B. Paine. 2 vols. New York: Harper, 1924.

———. *Mark Twain's Own Autobiography: The Chapters from the "North American Review."* Ed. Michael J. Kiskis. Madison: U of Wisconsin P, 1990.

See also: Autobiography

Chatto and Windus

Founded in 1855 by John Camden Hotten, the British publishing firm that in 1873 took on the name of its chief partners, Andrew Chatto and W.E. Windus, has continued to publish books of distinction by noted English and American authors. In the nineteenth century it introduced many American authors to English readers, notably Mark Twain, Bret Harte, Artemus Ward, Oliver Wendell Holmes, Edgar Allan Poe, Walt Whitman, and Ambrose Bierce. In 1946 the firm took under its management the Hogarth Press (founded in 1917 by Leonard and Virginia Woolf) and in 1969 joined with Jonathan Cape, Ltd.

Although Twain was incensed by Hotten's piracy of some of his earlier works, his fair treatment by the new owners of the firm resulted in a lifelong friendly business relationship that made Chatto and Windus the British publisher of his works. The company has published his works virtually *in toto*. Through their Popular Novels series, Chatto and Windus gained for Twain (and Harte) an enduring popularity in England.

Maverick Marvin Harris

BIBLIOGRAPHY

Clemens, Samuel L. *Mark Twain's Letters to His Publishers 1867–1894*. Ed. Hamlin Hill. Berkeley: U of California P, 1967.

Warner, Oliver. *Chatto & Windus*. London: Chatto and Windus, 1973.

See also: Hotten, John Camden

Childhood

Samuel Clemens practically devoted his career to writing about children; in doing so he continued to relive his own childhood and to revivify the sense of the child within the adult. Significant treatments of childhood appear in five novels, several novellas, and a host of stories, essays, sketches, dictations, and letters. Childhood was probably the central experience of Clemens's life and consequently is one of the richest subjects in his writing. Although Mark Twain wrote almost exclusively about boys and the Mississippi River culture of his adolescence during his most successful years, he turned his attention to teenaged girls during his last decade. While Twain's boy characters crave adventure and experience independence from the adult world, his girl characters are idealized, perfect, maidenly, and usually content with their place in society.

Twain wrote about childhood within a well-established literary context, which generally contrasted the innocence and innate goodness of children with the depravity of the adult world. From Fielding and Dickens, as well as American writers of his own and the preceding generation, Twain inherited the tradition of the good-bad boy protagonist. He adhered to this convention, creating boy heroes who, despite their rebellious misadventures and offenses against polite society, revealed unexpected strength of character and moral integrity. In deference to the propriety of his publishers and readers, Twain's adolescent characters, both male and female, exist in a pre-sexual condition in a seemingly asexual world. Despite his indebtedness to convention, tradition, and taste, Twain wrote the finest adolescent novels of his age, *The Adventures of Tom Sawyer* (1876) and *Adventures of Huckleberry Finn* (1885), in the latter case one of the world's great novels.

The publication of *Tom Sawyer* marked Twain's debut as a writer of boyhood novels. William Dean Howells, novelist and editor of the *Atlantic Monthly*, considered it "the finest boy's story I ever read." The adolescent Samuel Clemens and his home town, Hannibal, Missouri, on the Mississippi River, provided all the material Twain needed for his good-bad boy protagonists and his nostalgic picture of antebellum rural America. Tom exhibits all the reprehensible tricks and pranks one could hope for in a boyhood novel, but with them a craving for independence from the adult world and a resourcefully romantic imagination. In short, Twain created in Tom Sawyer a character recognizable by type yet uniquely individual and sufficiently complex to satisfy adult as well as younger readers.

The themes of independence and escape from family and society into a world apart are even more fully developed in *Huckleberry Finn*. Twain also experimented boldly here with voice, allowing his young protagonist a first-person narrative of his remarkable adventures. In order to gain freedom from his imprisoning "Pap," Huck stages his own "murder" and witnesses his funeral. His voyage down the great river is not only a search for self, as he changes identities in each challenging episode, but also a search for a moral and ethical foundation to his life.

Clemens declared in his autobiography that in creating Huck Finn he drew his childhood friend Tom Blankenship exactly as he was. Tom Blankenship was both ignorant and unwashed, but he "had a good heart" and was to young Clemens the most wonderfully independent person imaginable. The central theme of escape to freedom unites Huck and the runaway slave Jim in their common search for freedom. The novel is also a tableau of antebellum river culture and a biting social satire on the pettiness and malevolence of American life and perhaps of the human condition.

With *The Prince and the Pauper* (1882) Twain abandoned his Mississippi River settings for the London court of Prince Edward and the Offal Court of Tom Canty. A historical romance with a wildly unlikely plot, Twain intended the novel as a "yarn for youth" and dedicated it to his daughters, "those well-mannered and amiable children. . . ." Not only did he use the familiar convention of "switched identities," Twain carefully tested the manuscript by reading it, in progress, to the children of Nook Farm. The result was a commercial success, probably because it conformed to the dictates of the Genteel Age as a suitable book for young readers.

Late in Samuel Clemens's life, as if a necessary counterpoint to his many personal boyhood recollections and portraits of boys, he began to explore a second great childhood subject matter, the adolescent girl. Although it came too late in his creative life to result in great literary achievements, this revival of interest in the schoolgirl in his memory and his imagination represents an important dimension in Clemens's personal and creative life.

When Clemens's three daughters, Susy, Clara, and Jean were children they reminded him of his own childhood and rekindled the child in him as he wrote and staged skits and stories for their entertainment. In a series of losses the happy family that had been the emotional foundation of Clemens's life crumbled away: his favorite daughter, Susy, died in 1896, his wife Olivia died in 1904, daughter Jean was institutionalized with epilepsy, and Clara was seldom in the household after her mother's death. Thus, in the last decade Clemens felt increasingly lost and adrift, and as much as he attempted to make writing the center of his life, he was also losing his literary powers.

Clemens counteracted this "derelict" period as best he could by writing his autobiography, gathering about himself a club of teen-aged girls, and by turning his literary imagination to the adolescent female as an untapped subject. In dictating his autobiography he recalled his youthful sweethearts, Laura Hawkins and Laura Wright. Clemens dictated detailed passages about both girls, but especially about that blue-eyed "charmer" Laura Hawkins who lived in Hannibal and was his source for Tom Sawyer's girlfriend, Becky Thatcher. Clemens possessed a remarkable memory, and so long as it remained sharp, he could relive scenes from his past practically at will. Thus he kept alive vivid memories of his own teenaged sweethearts as well as of his daughters as little girls, loving memories of earlier times to buffer his personal loneliness after his wife's death, and his despairing sense of the human condition.

In both his fictional and autobiographical writing Clemens returned with some frequency to the idea of a "platonic sweetheart," in which a young man longs for and wishes to protect his younger, school-aged sweetheart, from whom he has been separated. This theme is a shaping concept behind his *Personal Recollections of Joan of Arc* (1896), but it is most fully developed in his dream sketch, "My Platonic Sweetheart" (1898). Clemens later admitted that *Joan of Arc* expressed his love for his deceased daughter Susy, as well as for schoolgirl innocence and heroic potential. The Joan of Arc legend probably appealed to Clemens not just because of Joan's idealism and heroism, but because of her legendary purity and lack of sexual development.

In his last decade as a writer Twain turned increasingly to young women as protagonists for his stories, as well as to "schoolgirls" for friendship and correspondence. Among these works are "Eve's Diary" (1905), "A Horse's Tale" (1906), and "Marjorie Fleming, the Wonder Child" (1909). Just as all the teen-aged boys in Twain's fiction are reflections of his own boyhood, so it is possible that the inspiration for his fictional portraits of girls comes from his first girlfriends and from the memory of daughter Susy.

As if to complement his literary portraits of girls, Clemens began to make friends with and write to schoolgirls, starting in 1906. He was so successful in the new childhood venture that by 1908 he had collected thirteen "Angel Fish," as he called them, and he inducted them into the Aquarium Club. Clemens's correspondence with the Angel Fish includes 300 letters, which are nearly always loving, optimistic, and playful.

Mark Twain lived his Hannibal boyhood with particular intensity and relived it the rest of his life. His passionate interest in childhood matched perfectly with the literary tastes of late-nineteenth-century American readers for stories about good-bad boys and innocent maidens. Twain wrote to this genteel readership yet also challenged its conventions. Through the voices of his child protagonists and his universal employment of humor, including sharp-edged social satire, Twain sustained his complex roles as both insider and outsider, entertainer and social critic. For Samuel Clemens and his readership, childhood was a central experience and unforgettable time of life, a coincidence that helped to make him the first American writer to appeal to a broadly democratic and international audience.

John Cooley

BIBLIOGRAPHY

Clemens, Samuel L. *Mark Twain's Aquarium: The Samuel Clemens-Angelfish Correspondence, 1905–1910.* Ed. John Cooley. Athens: U of Georgia P, 1991.

———. *Mark Twain's Autobiography.* Ed. Albert B. Paine. 2 vols. New York: Harper, 1924.

Hill, Hamlin. *Mark Twain: God's Fool.* New York: Harper & Row, 1973.

Quick, Dorothy. *Enchantment: A Little Girl's Friendship with Mark Twain.* Norman: U of Oklahoma P, 1961.

Stone, Albert E. *The Innocent Eye: Childhood in Mark Twain's Imagination.* New Haven, Conn.: Yale UP, 1961.

See also: Angel Fish and Aquarium Club; Boy Books; Hannibal, Missouri; Innocence; Women

China

Early in life Mark Twain developed an interest in China. On 24 January 1869 he wrote his future wife, Livy, that a senator had counseled him "to take the post of United States Minister to China," but he chose instead to pursue a literary career.

His interest had been piqued by Anson Burlingame, then minister to China, whom Twain met in Honolulu and came to admire greatly. Like Burlingame, he respected the Chinese and resented their mistreatment by outsiders. In "A Tribute to Anson Burlingame" (1870) he praised the American diplomat for punishing Americans in China who took advantage of the Chinese (*Complete Essays* 4).

Twain was an outspoken critic of American involvement in the Philippines and China. He was especially incensed by the Reverend Dr. Ament of the American Board of Foreign Missions for collecting indemnities for damages caused by the Boxers. Ament had demanded, and had collected, 300 taels for each

of the 300 murdered Christians, plus full payment for destroyed Christian property. The payment came not from the Boxers but from innocent Chinese citizens—an injustice, Twain claimed, compounded by a fine of one-third of the indemnity as a penalty. The "tainted money" was nothing less than "theft and extortion." He concluded that the missionaries who had gone to China to propagate Christian morals and justice "had adopted pagan morals and justice in their place."

Twain's advocacy of Chinese rights included the welfare of the Chinese in the United States. In 1868 he had praised the Burlingame Treaty with China because it opened the door to the Chinese labor force, but the intent of the Southern Pacific Railroad in 1870 to use a million-dollar subsidy to hire only white labor, thereby excluding Chinese coolies, evoked a sarcastic response to the prejudice and chicanery. "Disgraceful Persecution of a Boy," published May 1870 in the *Galaxy*, likewise expressed his indignation at the mistreatment of the Chinese in California. Again, some years later (1880) Twain attempted, along with General Grant and others, to forestall the closing of the Chinese Educational Mission in Hartford, which provided support for the education of approximately 100 Chinese students in the United States, but unfortunately their efforts could not prevail. The Chinese indeed had a friend in Mark Twain.

Maverick Marvin Harris

BIBLIOGRAPHY

Clemens, Samuel L. *The Complete Essays of Mark Twain.* Ed. Charles Neider. Garden City, N.Y.: Doubleday, 1963.

———. *The Love Letters of Mark Twain.* Ed. Dixon Wecter. New York: Harper, 1949.

———. *Mark Twain's Notebooks & Journals, Volume I (1855–1873).* Ed. Frederick Anderson, Michael B. Frank, and Kenneth M. Sanderson; *Volume II (1877–1883).* Ed. Frederick Anderson, Lin Salamo, and Bernard L. Stein; *Volume III (1883–1891).* Ed. Robert Pack Browning, Michael B. Frank, and Lin Salamo. Berkeley: U of California P, 1975–1979.

See also: Ament, Joseph; American Board of
Foreign Missions; Boxer Rebellion,
The; Missionaries; "To My
Missionary Critics"; "To the
Person Sitting in Darkness"

Christian Science

Christian Science is a religion based upon the principles of divine healing demonstrated in the words and deeds of Jesus Christ as expressed by Mary Baker Eddy and practiced by the Church of Christ, Scientist. The fundamental principle of Christian Science is a denial of the reality of the world of matter, the key point mockingly attacked by Mark Twain in his book *Christian Science* (1907). The Christian Scientist believes that the reality of the physical world is only an illusion, that true reality is spiritual. This affirmation of the underlying reality of spirit guides not only the religious thought of the Christian Scientists, but their everyday behavior as well. To these true believers, all sin, all sickness, is but an apparition, a misconception, and as such can be overcome only by the power of the mind. As a result, they refuse all conventional medical treatment. The origin of the Church of Christ, Scientist lies in the personal experience of Mary Baker Eddy, who in 1866 reported experiencing an immediate healing after reading in the New Testament the story of divine healing by Jesus.

The one authorized textbook of Christian Science is the 1875 book *Science and Health* by Mary Baker Eddy. From among students of these teachings, she recruited disciples, establishing the Church of Christ, Scientist in 1879. In 1892, in Boston, the First Church of Christ, Scientist was founded under her strict control. This is the Mother church, of which all Christian Science churches throughout the world are branches. All these branch churches are self-supporting and self-governing. Nonetheless, all must accept the principles formulated by the founder and laid down in the *Church Manual.*

The churches are without a formal priesthood. Two readers conduct the worship services, one reading from the Scriptures, the other from *Science and Health.* Except for the denial of the reality of matter and the logical consequences of this idea, the teachings of the Church of Christ, Scientist differ little from those of other Christian churches. Studying the same lessons simultaneously, all churches study teachings based on the life and sayings of Jesus Christ. Although found in all countries with a sizeable Protestant population, most Christian Scientists are Americans. The reality of the Church of Christ, Scientist in the 1990s is quite different from the powerful machine Twain feared would come to dominate American life by the 1940s. Today that church is quite ill, suffering from a shrinking number of branch churches, a drop in the number of practitioners healing, an aging congregation, and a steep decline in membership. Twain would undoubtedly be sympathetic.

Despite his religious skepticism, despite his mordantly critical book, Twain disapproved of neither religion nor spiritual healing. His own mother once cured by a faith healer, a Dr. Newton, Twain approved of his daughter Susy's interest in Christian Science, and daughter Clara eventually joined the church. He never opposed Christian Science as a religion; rather, he opposed what he saw as Eddy's personal duplicity and the threat of the church to dominate American political life. Twentieth-century scholarship and history indicate that he was wrong about the latter but correct about the former.

Mark Draper

BIBLIOGRAPHY

Braden, Charles S. *Christian Science Today.* Dallas: Southern Methodist UP, 1958.

Clemens, Samuel L. *Christian Science.* New York: Harper, 1907.

Eddy, Mary Baker. *Science and Health, with Key to the Scriptures.* Boston: First Church of Christ, Scientist, 1971.

Leighman, Thomas L. *Why I Am a Christian Scientist.* New York: Thomas Nelson, 1958.

Peel, Robert. *Christian Science: Its Encounter with American Culture.* New York: Holt, 1977.

See also: Christian Science; Eddy, Mary Baker; Religion

Christian Science
(1907)

In the two volumes constituting this work, which is largely a synthesis of articles previously published in popular magazines, Twain delivers a hilarious and scathing attack on Mary Baker Eddy and the new—and then swiftly growing—church she had recently founded. Although *Christian Science* has received sparse scholarly attention compared to Twain's other works, it is a tour de force of penetrating wit and keen analysis, revealing both his skill in polemics and his disdain for obscure grandiosity and sham spirituality. The work's subject is a natural result of Twain's lifelong fascination with the supernatural, an interest decidedly ambivalent. Scholars have commented on Twain's tendency to scoff publicly, but explore privately, spiritual phenomena, a tendency not unusual in a generation that vacillated between the certainty of the eighteenth century and the doubt and suspicions of the twentieth.

The initial four chapters of Book I are devoted to an amusing narration in which Twain claims to have been mangled in a fall from an Alpine cliff. No physician being available, he is treated by a Christian Science healer—and "widow in the third degree"—whose therapy is based on the principle that injury, pain, and death are all unreal. (However, Twain does have her shriek loudly when she accidentally rakes her hand on an all too apparently real pin in her dress.)

Twain's assault goes directly for the jugular, the essential vulnerability of Christian Science: the conviction of the unreality of the material world. He opposes the wail of a cat to the philosophizing of the resolute healer. In the middle of the practitioner's therapeutic sermon, a cat's tail is stepped on, and when it lets fly "a frenzy of cat profanity," Twain engages the healer in a convoluted discussion about the reality of the cat's pain. Twain reasons that the cat's pain cannot be imaginary for the cat has no mind, hence cannot imagine pain; nor is the cat's pain real, for pain itself, being a physical phenomenon, is itself unreal. Twain wonders then what troubled the cat, concluding that "God in His pity has compensated the cat with some kind of mysterious emotion usable when her tail is trodden on which, for the moment, joins cat and Christian in one common brotherhood . . ." (*Christian Science* 11).

When he recognizes that his broken bones are mere imaginary torture—though he does allow that they could be no more uncomfortable if they were real ones—Twain is miraculously cured: "I heard a dull click inside and knew that the two ends of a fracture had been successfully joined. This muffled clicking and gritting and grinding and rasping continued during the next three hours, and then stopped—the connections had all been made" (*Christian Science* 26). He then turns to a horse doctor to treat his stomachache and head cold. The veterinarian cannot cure these ailments but doses him with bran, turpentine, and axle grease to turn the cold and stomachache into the blind staggers, which he *can* treat. Twain reports that these measures were successful but also expresses the opinion that the Christian Science literature in and of itself would have produced a superior quality of blind staggers.

The remainder of the book comprises a relentless and devastatingly precise assault on Christian Science and especially its founder. Twain assails her spiritual tyranny, love of the dollar, self-involvement, her implied claim to divinity, and most of all the self-contradiction, incoherence, ignorance, and affectation of her writing. Much of the good humor permeating the first part of the book disappears in the mounting intensity of Twain's attack, which includes an insightful questioning of the legitimacy of Mary Baker Eddy's claim to authorship.

The basis of Twain's doubts have been sustained by subsequent scholarship. Powerful evidence exists that Eddy claimed the intellectual property of others as her own. But why did Twain attack Christian Science with such ferocity? First, the great skeptic was deeply interested in true spirituality; he loathed sham, hypocrisy, and fraud, especially of the self-glorifying variety and was ever ready to puncture self-deluded would-be prophets. Twain saw Eddy as "the queen of frauds and hypocrites," a cunning businesswoman amassing power, privilege, and wealth. Third, he feared the rapid expansion of Christian Science then occurring, predicting in the book that the movement would control the U.S. Congress by the 1930s. In this he was wrong, underestimating the skepticism of the American people. But his profound misgivings about Mary Baker Eddy have found considerable scholarly justification in the years since Twain's death.

Mark Draper

BIBLIOGRAPHY

Clemens, Samuel L. *Christian Science*. New York: Harper, 1907.

———. *Mark Twain's Fables of Man*. Ed. John S. Tuckey. Berkeley: U of California P, 1972.

Ensor, Allison. *Mark Twain and the Bible*. Lexington: UP of Kentucky, 1969.

Foner, Philip S. *Mark Twain: Social Critic*. New York: International Publications, 1958.

Gribben, Alan. "'When Other Amusements Fail': Mark Twain and the Occult." *The Haunted Dusk: American Supernatural Fiction, 1820–1920*. Ed. Howard Kerr, John W. Crowley, and Charles L. Crow. Athens: U of Georgia P, 1983. 169–189.

Wilson, James D. "'Monumental Sarcasm of the Ages': Science and Pseudoscience in the Thought of Mark Twain." *South Atlantic Bulletin* 40 (May 1975): 72–82.

See also: Christian Science; Eddy, Mary Baker; Religion

Cincinnati, Ohio

Located on the Ohio River, Cincinnati was a major western publishing center when Mark Twain arrived there in October 1856. Having grown restless at his brother's small printing company in Iowa, Twain moved to Cincinnati hoping to earn enough money to finance a trip to South America. He immediately took a job with a large printing firm and worked there until 15 May 1857, when he boarded the steamer *Paul Jones* bound for New Orleans.

Twain's six months in Cincinnati are some of the least documented of his life, but two travel letters and one sketch published in the Keokuk *Post* during this period suggest that his experiences there both extended his literary aspirations and shaped his philosophy. Adopting the persona of Thomas Jefferson Snodgrass, a country bumpkin on his first trip away from home, Twain experimented in the two travel letters with the comic device of the naive narrator he would later use with such impressive effects.

Twain's most significant experience in Cincinnati was his exposure to the deterministic ideas that eventually came to dominate his late work. In a sketch signed simply "L" (18 November 1856) but attributed to Twain, the author relates a discussion among the occupants of his Cincinnati boardinghouse concerning the influence of heredity and environment upon human behavior. These themes are echoed in a passage Twain wrote for his autobiography in 1898, when he recalled a fellow Cincinnati boarder named Macfarlane who articulated his own evolutionary scheme well before Darwin published *The Descent of Man* in 1871. (Albert Bigelow Paine dates the passage on Macfarlane included in his version of the *Autobiography* as 1898, but in the textual notes to the equivalent passage collected in *"What Is Man?" and Other Philosophical Writings* [591–592], Paul Baender questions Paine's dating and suggests a possible date of 1894 or 1895.) Macfarlane held a similar view of progressive development through ascending species, but he made one qualification. With the advent of man, "the progressive scheme broke pitifully down and went to wreck and ruin!" (*Autobiography* 1:146). Scholars have disagreed about whether Macfarlane was an actual acquaintance (Paine, Baker) or a fictional persona created to articulate Twain's own view of Darwinism (Baender), but Twain clearly associated this major body of ideas with his sojourn in Cincinnati.

Stan Poole

Bibliography

Baender, Paul. "Alias Macfarlane: A Revision of Mark Twain Biography." *American Literature* 38 (1966): 187–197.

Baker, William. "Mark Twain in Cincinnati: A Mystery Most Compelling." *American Literary Realism, 1870–1910* 12.2 (Autumn 1979): 299–315.

Clemens, Samuel L. *The Adventures of Thomas Jefferson Snodgrass.* Ed. Charles Honce. Chicago: Pascal Covici, 1928.

———. "[Cincinnati Boarding House Sketch]." *The Works of Mark Twain: Early Tales & Sketches, Volume 1 (1851–1864).* By Clemens. Ed. Edgar M. Branch and Robert H. Hirst. Berkeley: U of California P, 1979. 382–386.

———. *Mark Twain's Autobiography.* Ed. Albert B. Paine. 2 vols. New York: Harper, 1924.

———. *Mark Twain's Letters, Volume 1 (1853–1866).* Ed. Edgar M. Branch, Michael B. Frank, and Kenneth M. Sanderson. Berkeley: U of California P, 1988.

———. *"What Is Man?" and Other Philosophical Writings.* Ed. Paul Baender. Berkeley: U of California P, 1973.

Paine, Albert Bigelow. *Mark Twain: A Biography.* 3 vols. New York: Harper, 1912.

See also: Macfarlane

Civil War

The year 1885 signaled a turning point in Mark Twain's brilliant career, a year made notable by puzzling contradictions. The past decade had witnessed his greatest achievements as a creative writer. While still relishing his latest triumph, *Huckleberry Finn* (and while royalties from his books were pouring in), his grand lifestyle combined with shaky business investments threatened his financial security.

Added to this ominous sign was an astonishing paradox. Representing his own Charles L. Webster Publishing Company, Twain secured a lucrative contract that made him, a former Confederate volunteer, the publisher of General Ulysses S. Grant's *Personal Memoirs.* Then came an incredible leap that topped all contradictions. At the invitation of *Century Magazine*, Mark Twain undertook to write a piece for the currently popular series called "Battles and Leaders of the Civil War." Realizing that his own war record was suspect, this seemed a daring impertinence. If skeptics, however, reckoned on Mark Twain's love of money, they had misjudged the man. His writing for *Century Magazine*'s "Battles and Leaders" series, reinforced by his frequent contacts with General Grant, had deeply affected the famous humorist.

At the psychological moment, editors at Century Publishing Company had conceived the idea of publishing a series of articles on the principal battles of the Civil War, written by the leaders of both sides. A vast majority of the general officers, North and South, responded positively to *Century*'s invitation. Starting in November 1883 under expert editorial guidance, the series lost no time in winning an enthusiastic readership.

Enriched by illustrations and battlefield maps, "Battles and Leaders" set new production standards for American periodicals. The special features accompanying each article enabled readers to grasp significant battle details in relation to overall military strategy and tactics. The articles gave an illuminating insight into the military mind, while the ordeals of the common soldier emerged primarily by inference. Nothing previously published on the Civil War had excited such widespread interest. By re-creating a fading epoch for a new generation of rising Americans, "Battles and Leaders" doubled *Century Magazine*'s subscription list. Subsequently republished in a handsome four-volume edition, it remains today a primary historical source for Civil War enthusiasts.

When the series "Battles and Leaders" appeared in the early 1880s, Mark Twain stood at the forefront of America's literary establishment. His editors expected him to write, of course, not a standard battle account but an imaginative re-creation of his personal experience in Missouri during the first months of the war. For an odd bedfellow among famous generals, the undertaking presented formidable problems. Mark Twain knew nothing about battle. He had never faced a shower of bullets or charged an exploding cannon. His exposure to war, in fact, had scarcely topped the hardships of a long summer hike. The only fruitful approach to his dilemma lay in the possibilities of humor. Since humor was Mark Twain's forte, it is not surprising that his genius for comic exaggeration met the challenge with a scintillating parody on war that stands high in the estimation of modern critics. "The Private History of a Campaign That Failed," says Bernard DeVoto, "is one of the best things he [Mark Twain] ever wrote."

In early July 1861, nearing the age of twenty-six, Samuel Clemens left a small band of Confederate irregulars called the Marion Rangers. This motley company of raw recruits from Marion County, Missouri, had banded together to defend their state against Union invasion. Numbering in its ranks fifteen young men, it made Sam Clemens second lieutenant, a meaningless rank in a squad of undisciplined individuals. When Sam Clemens slipped his ties to the Marion Rangers, he had no clear goal except to flee from everything that reminded him of military service. Finally, on 18 July, after a two-week stay in St. Louis, he made a decisive break with his past.

Accompanying his older brother, Orion, recently appointed secretary of the Nevada Territory, Sam Clemens set out for the West to face destiny on his own terms. Going by overland stage from Missouri to Nevada, he left behind nothing to regret. For young Sam Clemens, unmarried and uncommitted, his flight gave him a chance for a new beginning.

Blithely ensconced in Nevada during the first three years of the war, Sam Clemens spent his time prospecting for silver, loafing in bohemian ease, and learning the newspaper world of the booming West. In Virginia City he met the popular humorist Artemus Ward, who recognized his talent and sparked his imagination. It was in Nevada also that he took his immortal pen name "Mark Twain." By his flight from Missouri, Mark Twain had elected to stand outside the central experience of nineteenth-century American history. This was a momentous personal decision loaded with the potential of painful repercussions. It was also destiny's favored child gliding unconsciously toward the spirit of the Gilded Age: give me liberty and give me wealth.

Drifting on to California in 1864, Mark Twain continued to enjoy his unregimented life in the West. After a short time as a reporter in San Francisco, he began to write humorous pieces for the coast literary papers the *Californian* and the *Golden Era*. Under the tutelage of Bret Harte, he mastered new skills in writing. Displaying the jaunty air that epitomized his middle years, he accumulated episodes, kept an eye open for his main chance, and cultivated his art of interposing the loaded word between himself and the world. By the end of the war the lecture platform loomed large in his sight. After that, there was no stopping his career.

Westerners respected Mark Twain's neutrality in the nation's sectional conflict. They helped him to scramble in his own way. For a man of his temperament, this encouragement was critical. Emerson had preached self-reliance, Mark Twain pursued self-realization, and the West fed his appetite for recognition and acclaim. His western apprenticeship, which ended in December 1866, profoundly shaped Mark Twain's character and career.

By 1885 the spirit of the Gilded Age had captured its greatest critic, now a national celebrity established in the East. His popularity won for him access to the rich, the famous, and the powerful people of his day. His book royalties and lecture fees reached an unprecedented high for an American author. But extraordinary literary success could not meet the demands of his extravagant lifestyle. To make ends meet, he extended himself into business ventures. With a $25,000 investment in the Charles L. Webster Publishing Company, he became the publisher of his own books. In January 1885 he signed the contract to publish General Grant's *Personal Memoirs*. When *Century Magazine* later in the same year asked Mark Twain to contribute a piece to its "Battles and Leaders" series, the celebrated anti-hero responded with alacrity. When "The Private History of a Campaign That Failed" was published by *Century* in the December 1885 issue, he had a reputation at stake.

"The Private History of a Campaign That Failed" is a good example of how a creative writer can exploit an experience that the ordinary person would want to forget. Trivial, fantastic, and evanescent were the impressions at Mark Twain's immediate recall. What he lacked in solid facts he supplied with his luminous imagination. It is impossible to separate fact from fiction in "The Private History of a Campaign That Failed," but the feeling is that invention took control. One thing is certain: out of a shabby personal experience, brief and inglorious, Mark Twain concocted a rousing artistic success.

The question arises of why Mark Twain, an able-bodied young man, evaded military service in a war that tormented his native state. The slavery issue is conspicuously absent from "The Private History of a Campaign That Failed," but on careful reading an explanation emerges. Not personal disgust with "the herd of cattle" as he dubbed the Marion Rangers, not "the steady trudging that came to be like work," not the early disillusionment so keenly felt, not the paltry equipment issued to him, not the monotony and degradation of daily routine, not even the fear of death weighed heavily in Mark Twain's decision. What settled the matter for him was his lively imagination. The poignant incident in which the unidentified stranger, the symbol of everyman, is mistakenly shot to death in the moonlight draws us closer to Mark Twain's deepest feelings. In the death scene, bearing the similitude of a disturbing dream, Mark Twain recaptures the fellow-creature feeling that characterizes his river waif Huckleberry Finn. What troubled Mark Twain was the idea of taking the life of a man "who had never done him any harm." This was the gravamen of his aversion to war. That the haunting death scene was a creation of Mark Twain's imagination is highly probable. Great fiction feeds on the truth of the heart, not on historical fact.

In his book *Men Against Fire*, Brigadier General S.L.A. Marshall, America's foremost authority on the psychology of men in battle, confirms the ultimate truth that Mark Twain depicted in "The Private History of a Campaign That Failed," which is the extreme difficulty of transforming nonviolent civilians into combat soldiers. Also, a statistical analysis of the ammunition expended in battles, when weighed against the casualties suffered, suggests that countless Civil War soldiers on both sides took their place in the front lines with no intent to kill. They cloaked their horror of killing in the noise of aimless firing. Mark Twain fled while others stood, but many who stood were apparently his brothers under the skin. Perhaps Mark Twain understood what S.L.A. Marshall has documented through interviews of American combat soldiers in three modern wars.

One irony of Mark Twain's piece is that it undercuts the heroic image of war portrayed in the "Battles and Leaders" series. When Century Publishing Company published *Battles and Leaders of the Civil War* in book form, enhanced by additional articles, Mark Twain's "The Private History of a Campaign That Failed" was excluded. The second irony is that Mark Twain's contribution to the original magazine series gives more pleasure today than any war account ever written by a Civil War general.

Tom Z. Parrish

BIBLIOGRAPHY

Aaron, Daniel. *The Unwritten War: American Writers and the Civil War*. New York: Knopf, 1973.

Clemens, Samuel L. *The Portable Mark Twain*. Ed. Bernard DeVoto. New York: Viking P, 1946. 119–142.

Kaplan, Justin. *Mr. Clemens and Mark Twain*. New York: Simon & Schuster, 1966.

Linderman, Gerald. *Embattled Courage: The Experience of Combat in the American Civil War*. New York: Free P, 1987.

Nichols, Roy F., ed. *From Sumter to Shiloh: Battles and Leaders of the Civil War*. New York: Castle Books, 1956.

See also: Century Magazine; Personal Memoirs of U.S. Grant; South, Mark Twain and the; War

Clarence

Clarence is the seemingly simple-minded youth who befriends and aids the imprisoned Hank Morgan in the beginning of *A Connecticut Yankee in King Arthur's Court* (1889). In chapter 10 Morgan reports that twenty-two-year-old Clarence has become his "right hand." Three years later it is Clarence who leaves the manuscript with the sleeping Morgan so that when Morgan wakes in the nineteenth century he will find it beside him.

Initially, Clarence's role in the novel is simply to inform Morgan of public sentiment toward him. His assistance with Morgan's schemes to outwit Merlin supports the credibility of their repeated successes. His help to Morgan develops in significance from merely following directions for the destruction of Merlin's tower and sending the necessary supplies for repairing the holy fountain to initiating the rescue of Morgan and King Arthur by the knights on bicycles. Clarence's behavior upon his appearance at the rescue scene reveals Morgan's influence on him; like his mentor, Clarence has clearly enjoyed the fanfare of the knights' timely arrival.

Clarence's fluency with modern English, noted several times in the closing chapters, reflects his assimilation of Morgan's nineteenth-century view of the world. Similarly, his adoption of Morgan's plans for a republic illustrates his own increasing sophistication, and his witty proposal of a royal family of cats to head the republic reveals a thinking man who understands the difficulty of enforcing radical changes too suddenly.

On Morgan's return to Camelot after the interdict, Clarence resumes his role as informant, but his report of the dissolution of the Round Table demonstrates a keen perception of the situation. He explains that, although Guenevere occasioned the downfall, the end was inevitable; indeed, if not for the queen, Morgan would have been the cause. Exhibiting an understanding of the power of fear, he tells Morgan that they will lose all of the men from their schools and factories when the knights march for the church; shrewdly, therefore, Clarence has selected boys who have only known the reign of The Boss to comprise Morgan's army. Finally, it is Clarence, with his knowledge of both the chivalric and the nineteenth-century mentalities, who advises Morgan to give up the idea of suggesting a truce with chivalry.

Margaret D. Bauer

BIBLIOGRAPHY

Clemens, Samuel L. *A Connecticut Yankee in King Arthur's Court*. Ed. Bernard L. Stein. Berkeley: U of California P, 1979.

See also: Connecticut Yankee in King Arthur's Court, A

Clemens, Cyril Coniston
(1902–)

Born on Bastille Day, 1902, Cyril Clemens has enjoyed a long, useful, and sometimes eccentric career promoting the fame of his cousin Mark Twain. He founded what is now the *Mark Twain Journal*, built an important collection of Twain letters and manuscripts, and shared generously of his time and knowledge. His work has made Cyril vulnerable to unnecessary conflicts with the once fiercely protective Samuel Clemens estate, the postal authorities, and even the Internal Revenue Service, while neither receiving nor seeking to benefit himself.

Of comfortable independent means, Cyril Clemens never exploited his relationship to Mark Twain for profit, as has been charged. And although lawyers for the Samuel Clemens estate called him "a very distant relative who won't keep his distance" and questioned whether he was kin at all, Cyril was never in doubt. His father visited Twain, and occasioned the famous remark: "James Ross Clemens, a cousin of mine, was seriously ill two or three weeks ago, in London, but is well now. The report of my illness grew out of his illness, the report of my death was an exaggeration." This note in Twain's hand appeared in facsimile in *Outlook* in 1910 and in the *Mark Twain Quarterly* in 1947. Isabelle Budd documented the kinship in the fall 1985 issue of the *Mark Twain Journal*: Twain and Cyril are descended from Ezekiel Clemens (1696–ca. 1778) and are third cousins, twice removed.

As a young man, Cyril found his calling as president of the International Mark Twain Society, founded in 1923 (and incorporated in 1936 as the nonprofit Mark Twain Memorial Association). In 1927 he made Benito Mussolini honorary president and in 1930 awarded him the first Mark Twain Gold Medal (as "Great Educator"). In 1935 the grateful Duce donated $200 toward a Mark Twain memorial in St. Louis.

By 1951 some two dozen gold medals had been awarded, chiefly to literary figures and heads of state such as Rudyard Kipling, Willa Cather, Robert Frost, Kemal Ataturk, Winston Churchill, and Franklin Roosevelt (who told Cyril that *A Connecticut Yankee* [1889] gave him the name for the New Deal). Cyril also wrote hundreds of surprised persons (selected from newspaper stories or *Who's Who*) that they had been "unanimously elected" to the distinction of Knight of Mark Twain, Daughter of Mark Twain, or honorary member of the Mark Twain Society. A few refused the honor: Bernard Shaw said if he received

the gold medal he would pawn it, and Don Marquis and Bertrand Russell declined knighthood because they detested Mussolini. But many recipients answered warmly, declaring their lifelong appreciation of Mark Twain and his works. Cyril made some of them committee chairmen on his impressive letterhead (among them Charles de Gaulle, military committee, and King Leopold of Belgium, entomological committee) and dozens of them honorary members (including Clara Clemens, Mary Roberts Rinehart, Mark Clark, and Manuel Quezon).

Cyril collected letters from some prominent personages as thin pamphlets with titles such as *Mark Twain and Winston Churchill* and *Mark Twain and Franklin D. Roosevelt*. He gave copies of these and his other books to libraries and has also given libraries his letters from Roosevelt, Einstein, and others. Major recipients are the Jefferson Memorial in St. Louis and, for Twain letters and manuscripts, the Mark Twain Memorial in Hartford.

He got into trouble with *Mark Twain the Letter Writer* (1932), which the Samuel Clemens estate suppressed for copyright infringement, and *My Cousin Mark Twain* (1939), which the estate attacked on similar grounds but which never sold well anyway. Even his *Mark Twain Quarterly*, begun in 1936 with a number of special issues devoted to celebrated writers such as A.E. Housman, J.M. Barrie, and Robert Frost, had a checkered history. Things fell apart in 1954, when the postal authorities pointed out that the *Quarterly* had never published four issues in a year and in recent times had only published one issue per year; the *Quarterly* had quietly changed its name to the *Mark Twain Journal*. More seriously, there was an attempt that year to deny mailing privileges to the Mark Twain Society as an "unlawful enterprise," with Cyril and his "accomplice" H. Bristol Williams fraudulently soliciting donations. A few weeks later Williams died; it turned out that he had used the impressive letterhead for solicitations of his own and had deposited $31,000 in a secret bank account in the name of the Mark Twain Society over the years 1944–1954, withdrawing $20,000 for personal use. Eventually, the Internal Revenue Service seized what remained of the account for back taxes. Lee Meriwether, then over ninety, came out of retirement to negotiate, and eventually won the return of $4,427. For a time Meriwether served as president of the society, and he edited the 1957 issue of the *Mark Twain Journal* while Cyril and his family vacationed in California. This was an opportunity for Meriwether to publish notes on the vicissitudes of the society.

The society made a good recovery, increasingly becoming Cyril's one-man show; the *Journal* began to grow, with submissions from academics under pressure to publish. Cyril never quite understood that pressure, and when the *Mark Twain Journal* moved to Charleston, South Carolina, in 1983, there was a backlog of some fifty accepted articles (many ten years old and two that had languished for over twenty years). The two 1983 issues were three times the size of previous issues, to fulfill a moral responsibility to bring all these articles into print at last. Since then, the *Mark Twain Journal* has become a more conventional academic publication (the oldest American journal devoted to a single author), emphasizing articles documented from sources in Twain's own lifetime.

Thomas A. Tenney

BIBLIOGRAPHY

Blaise, Bunker. "The Mark Twain Society." *Saturday Review of Literature* 20 (15 July 1939): 11–12.

Blase, Horace. "Ambassador-at-Large to His Cousin Mark Twain." St. Louis *Post-Dispatch*, 1 March 1936, Sunday Magazine, 5.

Budd, Isabelle. "The Relation of Mark Twain to Cyril Clemens." *Mark Twain Journal* 23 (Fall 1985): 2.

Crinklaw, Don. "The Twain Cousin. For Nearly 50 Years, Cyril Clemens Has Had A Great Time Being Related to Mark Twain." *St. Louisan* 7 (June 1975): 42–48.

Frommer, Walter H. "Mark Twain's Living Press Agent." St. Louis *Globe-Democrat*, 15 January 1950, 1F.

Meriwether, Lee. "Me and Mark Twain." *Mark Twain Journal* 10 (Fall–Winter 1957): 17–19.

———. "Our Struggle with the Internal Revenue Service." *Mark Twain Journal* 10 (Fall–Winter 1957): 1–2, 9.

———. "A Short History of the Mark Twain Memorial Association." *Mark Twain Journal* 10 (Fall–Winter 1957): 10–11, 19.

Orthwein, Walter E. "Mark Twain Society Is His Life's Work. Cyril Clemens Has Gathered Vast Collections of Author's Letters and Books." St. Louis *Globe-Democrat*, 27 June 1958, 1F.

See also: Journals; *Twainian, The*

Clemens, Henry
(1838–1858)

The youngest child of John Marshall and Jane Lampton Clemens, Henry was born on 13 June 1838, probably before the Clemens family left Florida, Missouri, for Hannibal. Closer in age to Sam Clemens than their older brother Orion (born in 1825), Henry was Sam's frequent playmate and like him learned the printing trade. Mark Twain acknowledged that Henry was the inspiration for Sid in *The Adventures of Tom Sawyer* (1876) but added that "Henry was a very much finer and better boy than ever Sid was" (Clemens, *Chapters* 5). It was Sam Clemens who got Henry a position as clerk on the ill-fated steamboat *Pennsylvania* in 1858; Sam rushed to Memphis after the vessel exploded on 13 June, only to watch helplessly as his twenty-year-old brother succumbed to ghastly injuries. Henry died on 21 June 1858. Chapter 20 of *Life on the Mississippi* (1883) recounts one version of Henry's death. In an autobiographical passage dictated in 1905 Twain lingers over the pathos of Henry's fate, associating it with an eerie dream of his brother in a coffin with roses on his breast. Several commentators have explored the guilt that Twain's recollections of Hannibal and Florida manifest, speculating about possible connections with this traumatic ordeal of watching Henry's final sufferings.

Alan Gribben

BIBLIOGRAPHY

Clemens, Samuel L. *Mark Twain's Letters, Volume 1 (1853–1866).* Ed. Edgar M. Branch, Michael B. Frank, and Kenneth M. Sanderson. Berkeley: U of California P, 1988.

———. *Mark Twain's Own Autobiography: The Chapters from the "North American Review."* Ed. Michael Kiskis. Madison: U of Wisconsin P, 1990.

Gribben, Alan. "Those Other Thematic Patterns in Mark Twain's Writings." *Studies in American Fiction* 13 (1985): 194–195.

Robinson, Forrest G. *In Bad Faith: The Dynamics of Deception in Mark Twain's America.* Cambridge, Mass.: Harvard UP, 1986.

———. "Why I Killed My Brother: An Essay on Mark Twain." *Literature and Psychology* 30 (1980): 168–181.

Wecter, Dixon. *Sam Clemens of Hannibal.* Boston: Houghton Mifflin, 1952.

See also: Conscience; Piloting

Clemens, Jane Lampton
(1803–1890)

One of two children of Benjamin Lampton and Margaret Montgomery Casey, who had moved from Virginia to Kentucky in 1779, Jane Lampton was born in Adair County, Kentucky, on 18 June 1803. She married John Marshall Clemens on 6 May 1823, but late in life told her son Sam that she had done so only after an uncle thwarted her romance with a man probably named Richard Barrett (Wecter 17–19). She moved with Clemens to Tennessee, then to Missouri, bearing altogether seven children: Orion, Pamela, Margaret May, Pleasant Hannibal, Benjamin, Samuel, and Henry. Samuel was born on 30 November 1835. The severe financial difficulties during her husband's last years compelled Jane to take in boarders. After Clemens's death in 1847, she depended completely on her three surviving children. Sam supported her financially, and she lived first with Pamela in St. Louis and later Fredonia, New York, and then with Orion and his wife Mollie in Keokuk, Iowa, from 1886 until her death on 27 October 1890.

Her role in Twain's life continues to be a source of disagreement. On his father's death,

her well-known declaration that Sam must assume a responsible adult role, and her later extraction of her eighteen-year-old son's promise never to drink or gamble, has prompted such critics as Van Wyck Brooks to accuse her, along with Twain's wife, Olivia Langdon Clemens, of cramping his spirit. Others—Albert Bigelow Paine and Dixon Wecter, for instance—argue that he both admired and felt protective toward her: in a letter to Orion in 1859 Twain admonished him to keep unpleasant news from her so that she would have no cause to worry or grow anxious (*Letters* 24).

Jane Clemens was undoubtedly a vivacious personality: a red-headed beauty who smoked a pipe, she loved dances, parties, and horseback riding. In 1853 Twain wrote "Oh, She Had a Red-Head," a humorous tribute to all who shared his and Jane's hair color. His lifelong humanitarianism and dislike of bullies he almost certainly owes to his mother. Her maternal qualities appear in Aunt Polly in *Tom Sawyer* (1876), and he named his daughter Jane (Jean) Lampton Clemens (1880–1909) after this "soldierly" woman whom he calls his "first and closest friend" (*Autobiography* 1:115). Moreover, at least one critic traces Joan of Arc's temperament to Jane's courageous nature (Blair 42), and several critics suggest that her apparently tomboyish qualities provided a source for women characters in "Hellfire Hotchkiss" (1897) and *The Mysterious Stranger* (1916).

Ultimately, Jane Clemens bequeathed to Twain her storytelling abilities and provided him with rich inspiration. Almost certainly the source of his wit, sense of humor, and eloquence, Twain exclaimed of her one evening in Keokuk, "What books she could have written!" (Kaplan 265).

Abby H.P. Werlock

BIBLIOGRAPHY

Brooks, Van Wyck. *The Ordeal of Mark Twain.* Rev. ed. New York: Dutton, 1933.

Clemens, Samuel L. "Hellfire Hotchkiss." *Mark Twain's Satires & Burlesques.* By Clemens. Ed. Franklin

R. Rogers. Berkeley: U of California P, 1967. 172–203.

———. *Mark Twain's Autobiography.* Ed. Albert B. Paine. 2 vols. New York: Harper, 1924.

———. *Mark Twain's Hannibal, Huck & Tom.* Ed. Walter Blair. Berkeley: U of California P, 1969.

———. "Oh, She Had a Red Head." Hannibal *Daily Journal,* 13 May 1853.

———. *The Selected Letters of Mark Twain.* Ed. Charles Neider. New York: Harper & Row, 1982.

Emerson, Everett. *The Authentic Mark Twain: A Literary Biography of Samuel L. Clemens.* Philadelphia: U of Pennsylvania P, 1984.

Harnsberger, Caroline Thomas. *Mark Twain, Family Man.* New York: Citadel P, 1960.

Kaplan, Justin. *Mr. Clemens and Mark Twain.* New York: Simon & Schuster, 1966.

Webster, Doris, and Charles Webster. "Whitewashing Jane Clemens." *Bookman* 61 (July 1925): 531–535.

Webster, Samuel Charles. *Mark Twain, Business Man.* Boston: Little, Brown, 1946.

Wecter, Dixon. *Sam Clemens of Hannibal.* Boston: Houghton Mifflin, 1952.

See also: Brooks, Van Wyck; Clemens, John Marshall

Clemens, Jane Lampton [Jean]
(1880–1909)

Jane Lampton Clemens, known as Jean, was born in Elmira, New York, on 26 July 1880, and named after her maternal grandmother. Eight years younger than sister Susy, and six years younger than Clara, Jean was the baby of the family though neither as precocious as Susy nor as independent as Clara. She had a passionate love of animals and an aptitude for languages but no other special talents in a highly talented family. She began to have epileptic seizures when she was about sixteen, perhaps an aftermath of scarlet fever, and her parents sought a cure trying different doctors in the United States and abroad, dietary regimes, and even faith healing. Eventually, she was institutionalized, leaving her with a sense of failure and rejection.

After her mother's death, with Clara married and living abroad and her father unhappy with Isabel Lyon, his long-time secretary, Jean joined her father at Stormfield as his secretary. Her death by drowning in her bathtub on the morning before Christmas, 24 December 1909, was the last of several bitter tragedies in Mark Twain's life. His "The Death of Jean" is a moving tribute. She is buried in Woodlawn Cemetery in Elmira.

Herbert A. Wisbey, Jr.

BIBLIOGRAPHY

Harnsberger, Caroline T. *Mark Twain, Family Man.* New York: Citadel P, 1960.

See also: Family Life

Clemens, John Marshall
(1798–1847)

Father of Samuel Langhorne Clemens, John Marshall Clemens was born 11 August 1798 in Campbell County, Virginia, the eldest of the five children of Samuel B. (1770–1805) and Pamela Goggin Clemens (1775–1844). After the accidental death of the father in August 1805, the family moved to Kentucky, where Pamela married Simon Hancock in 1809. John went to work at age eleven as a clerk in an iron mine. Subsequently the boy studied law under the tutelage of a prominent attorney, and at age twenty-one he obtained his license to practice. The same year, however, he was assessed the expenses Hancock had incurred in rearing the Clemens children and the family's slaves. The debt depleted the family estate and, coupled with poor investments in timberland, bequeathed a legacy of genteel poverty from which Clemens was never completely freed.

John married Jane Lampton (1803–1890) on 6 May 1823. The couple settled first in Fentress County, Tennessee, where John opened a law practice and a small general store and served as a county commissioner, circuit clerk, and acting attorney general. In 1831 the family moved to Three Forks on the Wolf River, and John served as U.S. postmaster in nearby Pall Mall, Tennessee (1832–1835). Five children were born to the Clemenses during their twelve-year tenure in Tennessee: Orion (b. 1825 near Gainesboro, d. 1897); Pamela (b. 1827 in Jamestown, d. 1904); Pleasant Hannibal (b. 1828 in Jamestown, d. same year); Margaret (b. 1830 in Jamestown, d. 1839); and Benjamin (b. 1832 in Pall Mall, d. 1842). Jane was pregnant with her sixth child, Samuel Langhorne, when the family moved to Missouri in 1835; he was born two months prematurely on 30 November 1835 in Florida, Missouri, where John had opened a dry goods store. A seventh child, Henry, was born in Hannibal in 1838. He died in 1858 from injuries incurred in a Mississippi River steamboat explosion.

In November 1839 John moved his family from Florida to Hannibal, Missouri. There he opened a law office and small general store in the Virginia Hotel. He also assumed an active role in civic affairs, proving instrumental in establishing the town's first public library, helping to plan the railway line between Hannibal and St. Joseph, serving as justice of the peace, and taking charge of road districting and construction. He was the Whig candidate for the office of Marion County circuit clerk when in the spring of 1847 he contacted pleurisy and then pneumonia that claimed his life on 24 March.

A proud, austere man with aristocratic pretensions, John Clemens presided over a reserved, formal household. Samuel Clemens, in fact, claimed that he could not recall ever having heard or seen his father laugh, and John's death-bed kiss to daughter Pamela was, the author later revealed, the first family kiss he had ever witnessed. Indeed, Samuel Clemens confessed that "my father and I were always on the most distant terms," as the elder Clemens, though he eschewed Calvinist dogma and "never spoke of religious matters," proved to be a stern Puritan moralist who held his male children to a strict ethical code. John clung tenaciously to the illusion of enlightened gentility, frustrated by never realized hopes of wealth from Tennessee timberland and rather primitive conditions on the Missouri frontier. Samuel Clemens's final and most vivid memory of his father is a harrowing one: he reports in his *Autobiography* (1924) that he, as a twelve-year-old boy, peeped through a keyhole to witness the village doctor, at night and by candlelight, dissect John's corpse on the family dining room table in a gruesome postmortem search for the cause of death.

Oliver Howard and Goldena Howard

BIBLIOGRAPHY

Clemens, Samuel L. *Mark Twain's Autobiography*. Ed. Albert B. Paine. 2 vols. New York: Harper, 1924.

Howard, Oliver, and Goldena Howard. *The Mark Twain Book*. New London, Mo.: Ralls County Book, 1985.

Paine, Albert Bigelow. *Mark Twain: A Biography*. 3 vols. New York: Harper, 1912.

Wecter, Dixon. *Sam Clemens of Hannibal*. Boston: Houghton Mifflin, 1952.

See also: Clemens, Jane Lampton; Florida, Missouri

Clemens, Langdon
(1870–1872)

Mark Twain's first child and only son was born in Buffalo, New York, 7 November 1870. His premature birth followed a series of traumatic events including the death of Jervis Langdon, Mrs. Clemens's father, in August and that of a childhood friend, Emma Nye, in the Clemens's home in September. The baby was never robust and died in Hartford on 2 June 1872. He was buried beside his grandfather in Elmira's Woodlawn Cemetery. With characteristic guilt feelings, Mark Twain blamed himself for the child's death, recalling an incident when the infant kicked off his covers and became chilled while on a ride with his father.

Herbert A. Wisbey, Jr.

BIBLIOGRAPHY

Clemens, Samuel L. *Mark Twain's Autobiography*. Ed. Albert B. Paine. 2 vols. New York: Harper, 1924.

Clemens, Mollie Stotts

(1834–1904)

Mary Eleanor "Mollie" Stotts Clemens married Samuel Clemens's brother Orion Clemens (1825–1897) in 1854. Clemens had a close relationship with Mollie and Orion. Clemens briefly went into the printing business with his newly married brother in Keokuk, Iowa, in early 1855. Orion's and Mollie's daughter, Jennie Clemens, born in 1855, died of meningitis in Carson City, Nevada, in 1864, with Clemens among those at her bedside.

One of the earliest existing letters in Clemens's hand (18 June 1858) is to "Dear Sister Mollie." Clemens describes one of the most painful incidents of his life, the death of his brother Henry, who died in Memphis of injuries received in the explosion of the river steamer *Pennsylvania* in 1858. There are several other important letters to Orion and Mollie (*Mark Twain's Letters* 1:80–83 *et passim*; Webster 34–35). Clemens assisted Mollie by absorbing some of the medical expenses of her father, William Stotts, who was gravely ill in Keokuk, Iowa, where Mollie and Orion were living (*Notebooks & Journals* 3:254, 331).

Clemens once noted that "Mollie does up gossip pretty well," and he knew her to be an asset when he wanted to scold Orion, though others characterized her as difficult (Webster 120, 129). Yet Clemens perpetrated a hoax that left her socially ostracized. In May 1864 the Nevada Territory was in the midst of a campaign to raise money for the Sanitary Fund, the Red Cross of the Civil War. The repeated auctioning of a flour sack had created an unfriendly rivalry among various towns. The ladies of Carson City gave a benefit ball on 5 May 1864; Mollie was one of the sponsors. One night in the offices of the Virginia City *Territorial Enterprise*, quite drunk with his friend Dan De Quille (William Wright), Clemens penned a mock column for the *Enterprise* in which he questioned whether the proceeds from the ball would go to the Sanitary Fund or to a Miscegenation Society in the East. After the two friends had put the paper to bed and had decided not to publish the squib, Clemens tossed the item aside and went off to the theater, forgetting that the composing room foreman might think it was copy for the next day's paper. He did, and it appeared in the *Enterprise* on 17 May. A furor erupted. Clemens wrote a letter of apology to the only one of the Carson City ladies who did not include Mollie in her anger, Mrs. W.K. Cutler. He found it impossible to apologize publically, though the rival newspaper, the *Union*, excoriated Clemens in an article and nearly caused him to engage in a duel with its author.

Jeanne Campbell Reesman

BIBLIOGRAPHY

Clemens, Samuel L. *Mark Twain's Letters, Volume 1 (1853–1866)*. Ed. Edgar M. Branch, Michael B. Frank, and Kenneth M. Sanderson. Berkeley: U of California P, 1988.

———. *Mark Twain's Notebooks & Journals, Volume III (1883–1891)*. Ed. Robert Pack Browning, Michael B. Frank, and Lin Salamo. Berkeley: U of California P, 1979.

Fatout, Paul. *Mark Twain in Virginia City*. Bloomington: Indiana UP, 1964.

Ferguson, DeLancey. *Mark Twain: Man and Legend*. Indianapolis: Bobbs-Merrill, 1943.

Webster, Samuel Charles. *Mark Twain, Business Man*. Boston: Little, Brown, 1946.

See also: Clemens, Orion

Clemens, Olivia Langdon

(1845–1904)

Olivia Louise Langdon, born 27 November 1845, was the daughter of Jervis and Olivia Lewis Langdon of Elmira, New York. She had an adopted sister, Susan, nine years her senior, and a younger brother, Charles, born in 1849. At her birth Livy's parents were one of the most recent families to Elmira. By the time she was seventeen, they would be the wealthiest and most prominent, a result of her father's business interests in coal and lumber.

Livy grew up in the largest, most elegant house in Elmira, which she described as "a generous free household." Her parents were pillars of the community and the church. William Lloyd Garrison, Frederick Douglass, and Gerrit Smith were all guests in the Langdon home. When the home was razed in 1939, tunnels between Park Church and the home were discovered, indicating the house was once a stop on the underground railroad.

Livy's education was conventional for a young lady of her social status and time. Her earliest teacher was her mother, who instilled in her a love of reading and learning. Livy attended Elmira Ladies' Seminary until the age of nine and later Elmira Seminary from 1855 until she was sixteen.

At sixteen, according to Mark Twain's autobiography, Livy fell on the ice and suffered a partial paralysis. For two years she was confined in a darkened room unable to walk or sit up without the aid of a tackle suspended from the ceiling. Nothing cured her nervous prostration or neurasthenia until Langdon paid Dr. James Rogers Newton over $2,000 to do it. Twain relates that Newton cured Livy in one session. According to the journals of her mother, however, Livy's cure from Newton and other doctors took three years. In either case, she did walk again.

Twain liked to tell the story in his autobiography. It was also related in Paine's biography that Twain first saw Livy in a miniature that her brother Charles Langdon carried with him on the *Quaker City* cruise in the summer of 1867. He insisted that a glimpse of her was enough to fall in love with her, though he did not meet her until a Christmas reunion of the *Quaker City* passengers. In one week he was in her company three times, but in his letters he does not mention Livy by name; he simply calls her "Charlie Langdon's sister." He did not really get to know her until he visited the Langdons in August 1868.

Within a week of his visit, Twain declared his love for Livy and proposed to her. She promptly refused. At thirty-four, Twain thought he was too old to find someone. At twenty-two, Livy had decided because of her health that she would be the daughter to stay home and care for her parents. Livy was the epitome of the late-nineteenth-century upper-class woman—delicate, idealized, refined—all characteristics that Twain admired. Twain was the most unusual man Livy had met—independent, irreverent, worldly.

Upon her refusal to marry him, Twain began courting Livy by letters. Twain wooed her in the same way he presented himself to all women. He was a flawed man. Would she lecture him and help to reform him? Livy's pet name for him, Youth, reflects his role. Once he won Livy over, he still had to convince her fearful parents. Mr. and Mrs. Langdon allowed them to become engaged, but it would be in secret while Twain had time to remedy his reputation as the "wild humorist of the Pacific slope." He gave up drinking, smoking, swearing, and even attended church for a time.

Livy saw as her new role in life being a helpmate to her future husband. She worked with him on the galleys of *Innocents Abroad* (1869) during their engagement. Livy continued this job as editor throughout their married life. Twain described her as his "faithful, judicious, and painstaking editor" for a "third of a century." Twain did not see her as a censor but trusted her judgment in grammar, style, and what his reading audience would and would not accept. Anything Twain did not want to change in a manuscript, he never did.

Twain and Livy were married 2 February 1870 and set up their first home in Buffalo, New York. The home was purchased and furnished by Jervis Langdon, so his daughter would have the type of lifestyle, complete with fine furnishings and servants, to which she was accustomed. The newlyweds lived in Buffalo for only a year. Jervis Langdon had loaned Twain the money to purchase part of the Buffalo *Express*, but he did not enjoy his editing responsibilities. Livy was depressed over the death of her father on 6 August 1870 and the birth of her sickly son Langdon, who died in 1872.

Livy and Twain next lived in the Nook Farm suburban area of Hartford, Connecticut, first in a rented home and then in a house that Livy helped to design, which they built in 1874 and which they later redecorated in 1881. They spent their summers in Elmira, where their three daughters were born: Susy in 1872, Clara in 1874, and Jean in 1880.

The Clemenses often lived abroad because of the expenses incurred by the Hartford home that Livy saw as a place of entertaining for her famous husband. They lived abroad in 1873 and 1878. When they went abroad in 1891, Livy never dreamed it would be for nine years or that she would never enter her Hartford home again. Twain had invested heavily in the Paige typesetter and in his own Webster Publishing Company. His financial reversals were aggravated by a panic in 1893 when banks failed and creditors called in their debts. Finally, in 1894 Twain had to declare bankruptcy. On their twenty-fifth wedding anniversary Livy and Twain were $100,000 in debt. Through the help of the financier Henry Huttleston Rogers of Standard Oil, Livy was named the chief creditor for the Hartford house and Twain's copyrights were placed in her name.

In order to be free of what Livy called "the bondage of debt," Livy and Twain undertook a round-the-world lecture tour in the fall of 1895. The tour began in Cleveland, crossed the United States to the Pacific, and included Australia, New Zealand, India, and South Africa. Livy calculated that their debts would be paid off in four years. She insisted the debts would be paid in full.

Back in England in 1896, the couple were preparing to return to the United States when they received word that Susy, who had remained behind with Jean, was ill in Hartford.

Immediately, Clara and Livy left for America, but it was too late. Susy died of spinal meningitis while they were still at sea. The death of Susy was a blow from which Livy and the rest of the family never fully recovered. They blamed themselves for not being with her. Unable to return to Hartford where Susy died, Livy and her family continued to live abroad, often partaking of health cures for Livy's increasing ill health and Jean's epilepsy.

In 1900 the Clemenses returned to the United States to live in Riverdale, New York. By 1902 Livy's health had so deteriorated that she had to live in a warmer climate. She and her family moved to the Villa di Quarto near Florence, Italy. She died on 5 June 1904 of a weak heart. Her body was returned to Elmira, where it was buried in Elmira's Woodlawn Cemetery.

Livy's tremendous influence on Mark Twain shows in the difficulty he had in living and writing after her death. His own pet names for her show that she was the center of his life, for he called her "my darling little mentor" and "my dear little gravity." His most poignant tribute to her and their thirty-four years of marriage appears in "Eve's Diary" (1905). Standing at Eve's grave, Adam declares, "Wheresoever she was, there was Eden."

Resa Willis

BIBLIOGRAPHY

Clemens, Samuel L. *The Love Letters of Mark Twain.* Ed. Dixon Wecter. New York: Harper, 1949.

———. *Mark Twain's Autobiography.* Ed. Albert B. Paine. 2 vols. New York: Harper, 1924.

Harnsberger, Caroline Thomas. *Mark Twain, Family Man.* New York: Citadel P, 1960.

Lawton, Mary. *A Lifetime with Mark Twain.* New York: Harcourt, Brace, 1925.

Paine, Albert Bigelow. *Mark Twain: A Biography.* 3 vols. New York: Harper, 1912.

Steinbrink, Jeffrey. "How Mark Twain Survived Sam Clemens' Reformation." *American Literature* 55 (October 1983): 299–315.

Wilson, James D. "Religious and Esthetic Vision in Mark Twain's Early Career." *Canadian Review of American Studies* 17.2 (Summer 1986): 155–172.

Clemens, Olivia Susan

(1872–1896)

Olivia Susan Clemens, known as Susy, was born in Elmira, New York, on 19 March 1872. She was a precocious and sensitive child who was educated at home by governesses and tutors as a cosmopolitan young lady fluent in German and French. Her sister Clara was two years younger but more self-assured and independent. The two girls spent happy summers in Elmira at Quarry Farm owned by their aunt, Susan Crane, after whom Susy was named. Jean, eight years younger than Susy, was too young to share most of their games. All three girls loved animals, enjoyed theatricals, and adored their father and his stories.

When she was fourteen, Susy began a biography of her father, which she continued for about a year. As Susy reached adolescence, she struggled to cope with the demands of an erratic father and a mother in ever precarious health. Although she began college at Bryn Mawr, she dropped out before the year ended. When Mark Twain's financial problems required the family to live abroad for three frugal years in hotel rooms, flats, and rented villas, Susy was bored and unhappy. She did not accompany her parents on the lecture tour around the world in 1895–1896. Shortly before she and Jean were to rejoin the family in England, she became ill and died of spinal meningitis at the Hartford house on 8 August 1896.

Susy's death was a blow from which the family never recovered. Birthdays and holidays became sad occasions, and they never again lived in the Hartford house. Fair-haired Susy was clearly Mark Twain's favorite child. He saw her in Joan of Arc, and, perhaps, his attraction to the virginal young girls he called

"Angel Fish" was an attempt to recall the lost daughter he never ceased to mourn.

Herbert A. Wisbey, Jr.

BIBLIOGRAPHY

Clemens, Susy. *Papa: An Intimate Biography of Mark Twain.* Ed. Charles Neider. Garden City, N.Y.: Doubleday, 1985.

Salisbury, Edith C. *Susy and Mark Twain: Family Dialogues.* New York: Harper & Row, 1965.

Clemens, Orion

(1825–1897)

Orion Clemens was the eldest child of John and Jane Clemens. He was a newspaper editor, reporter, proofreader, inventor, lecturer, farmer, lawyer, writer, entrepreneur, and secretary of the Territory of Nevada, but never successful. His secretaryship was crucial, however, for Orion was accompanied by his brother to Nevada, where Sam turned newspaperman and invented Mark Twain.

Orion married Mary (Mollie) Stotts. They had one child, Jennie, who died in 1864 at age six. Most of Orion's life was spent in Iowa. He was known for his honesty, especially as secretary, but twice his scruples cost him political offices as well as opportunities to sell family land in Tennessee.

Also characteristic of Orion was his inclination to visionary schemes, which, when coupled with chronic inability to sustain his efforts, resulted in a lifetime of failures. Among numerous lifelong efforts to become more than an occasional writer for newspapers was an attempt in the early 1880s, under Sam's ostensible supervision, to write a chronicle of his failures, "The Autobiography of a Crank." That project, too, was abandoned before completion. Visionary scheming ran in the family, for Orion and even Sam at times were as apt a model for Colonel Sellers as was their cousin James Lampton. Orion apparently recognized his faults, referring to himself in his last extant letter to Sam (30 November 1897) as fit to be a fool character.

Sam's relationship to his older brother was complex. Letters from Sam to Orion alternate between being exasperated with Orion's lack of common sense and telling him intimate details of his own business machinations, even tolerating advice from Orion as lawyer. Sam acted as the older brother, giving advice, and as an employer, giving orders. Since Sam virtually supported Orion and Mollie, he may have felt justified in sometimes treating Orion as a lackey. Sam probably saw enough of himself in Orion that his older brother's life may have served as a warning, spurring Sam to constantly market Mark Twain.

James E. Caron

BIBLIOGRAPHY

Kaplan, Justin. *Mr. Clemens and Mark Twain.* New York: Simon & Schuster, 1966.

Lorch, Fred W. "Orion Clemens." *Palimpsest* 10 (October 1929): 353–386.

Mack, Effie Mona. "Orion Clemens, 1825–1897, A Biography." *Nevada Historical Society Quarterly* 4 (July-December 1961): 62–109.

Paine, Albert Bigelow. *Mark Twain: A Biography.* 3 vols. New York: Harper, 1912.

See also: "Autobiography of a Damned Fool"; Clemens, Mollie Stotts; Hannibal, Missouri; Tennessee Land

Clemens, Samuel Langhorne

(1835–1910)

The topic can best be viewed in two parts— "The Man: Samuel L. Clemens" and "The Author: Mark Twain."

The Man: Samuel L. Clemens

Still considered America's premier humorist, Samuel L. Clemens was born 30 November 1835 in Florida, Missouri, a backwoods town with a population of about a hundred. He was the child of John Marshall Clemens, a man of unbending rectitude, and Jane Lampton Clemens, a warm and affectionate woman, apparently a good storyteller. They named the baby Samuel Langhorne after his paternal grandfather and a family friend back in Virginia. Their other children who grew to maturity were Orion (1825–1897), Pamela (1827–1904), and the younger brother Henry (1838–1858), who was scalded to death in a steamboat explosion. In 1839 John Clemens moved his family to Hannibal, Missouri, a fast-growing town on the western bank of the Mississippi. Except for summers spent on his Uncle John Quarles's farm near Florida, Missouri, Sam grew up in Hannibal and absorbed its life so fully that he was later able to make it the setting for *The Adventures of Tom Sawyer* (1876). Shortly after his father died in March 1847, Sam had to drop out of school and go to work. His first jobs were on Hannibal newspapers, notably his brother Orion's Hannibal *Journal,* for which he wrote several of his first sketches. His bent for travel showed up early, for from 1853 to 1857 he set type for newspapers in St. Louis, New York, Philadelphia, Muscatine and Keokuk (Iowa), and Cincinnati. From St. Louis he sent back one and from Cincinnati two "Thomas Jefferson Snodgrass Letters" to the Keokuk *Post,* his earliest attempts at imitating the newspaper sketches of contemporary southwestern humorists.

A new chapter in his life began in 1857 when he persuaded Horace Bixby, a master pilot on the lower Mississippi (St. Louis to New Orleans) to take him on as an apprentice pilot. Two years later on 9 April 1859 he, too, was licensed as a pilot on the lower Mississippi. Records indicate that he worked on eighteen boats without being responsible for any smashups. In the spring of 1861, however, he had to leave the river when federal gunboats closed it to commercial traffic. So his life again changed dramatically.

After about two weeks of "training" in a ragtag group of Confederate volunteers, he joined Orion on a stagecoach trip to Carson City, Nevada, where Orion was to be secretary for the Nevada Territory. Once in Nevada, Clemens tried to make an instant fortune in both timber and gold but failed at both. Some humorous western stories that he signed "Josh," however, gained him a job as reporter and free-lance writer on the Virginia City *Territorial Enterprise*. From Mondays through Fridays he reported straightforwardly the doings of the Nevada legislature, but on Saturdays he ridiculed whatever in Nevada life caught his fancy. For the Saturday issue of the *Enterprise*, 2 February 1863, he first signed himself "Mark Twain." Thereafter it became his habit to sign his imaginative works "Mark Twain" and his legal and business documents "Samuel L. Clemens." On the Mississippi "Mark Twain" was a cry of the leadsman meaning two fathoms (twelve feet) of safe water. But just why he selected this cry is still not known with certainty.

In spring 1864 he left Virginia City to avoid, so the story goes, having to fight an illegal duel with a rival editor. He settled in San Francisco, where he first worked for the *Morning Call* and later contributed to such literary magazines as the *Golden Era* and the *Californian*. The winter of 1864–1865 he spent in Calaveras County, where he first heard the story of the jumping frog he would make so famous. In spring 1866 the Sacramento *Union* sent him to the Sandwich Islands (now the Hawaiian Islands) to report on the life and on business possibilities there. These reports from Hawaii further enriched his reputation as a writer, especially an account of the plight of the survivors of the clipper ship *Hornet* that burned in mid-Pacific. Even the *Atlantic Monthly* carried this account. On his return to San Francisco he was persuaded to give a humorous public lecture on his Hawaiian experiences. It was a huge success, an augury of his subsequent career as a humorous lecturer as well as a humorous writer.

He wrote for the San Francisco *Alta California* when he returned to the East in late 1866, and it was the *Alta California* that in the summer of 1867 sent him to Europe and the Holy Land on the tour ship *Quaker City*, a trip

he celebrated in lectures and in *The Innocents Abroad* (1869). While on the trip, a fellow passenger, Charles Langdon, showed Clemens an ivory miniature of his sister Olivia (Livy). Clemens later said that he fell in love with her immediately. Whether that was true or not, he did marry Livy in February 1870, and the brash Westerner and the reserved well-to-do Easterner from Elmira, New York, settled in Buffalo, where Livy's father helped Clemens acquire a part-interest in the Buffalo *Express*. Less than two years later they moved to Hartford, Connecticut, so that Clemens could be near his publisher, Elisha Bliss, owner of the American Publishing Company, a subscription house that sold its books through door-to-door salesmen rather than through bookstores. The APC did not have the prestige of older and more conventional publishers, but Clemens was drawn to it because it paid higher royalties. In the early seventies the Clemenses built a splendidly eccentric house in Nook Farm, a suburb of Hartford. "Part cathedral, part cuckoo clock" was the way Clemens described it. They lived there until 1891, though they frequently spent their summers at Quarry Farm, the home of Livy's adopted sister, Sue Crane. It was at Quarry Farm just east of Elmira that Clemens wrote substantial portions of his finest novels.

During this period the Clemenses had four children: Langdon, who lived less than two years, 1870–1872; Olivia Susan (Susy), 1872–1896; Clara Langdon, 1874–1962; and Jane Lampton (Jean), 1880–1909. Clara married Ossip Gabrilowitsch in 1909, and the couple had one child, Nina, 1911–1966. Clara later married Jacques Samossoud. There are no direct descendants.

The decades of the 1870s and 1880s were probably Clemens's happiest and certainly his most productive. His books were selling well, and he more than matched the income from his writing by the income from his lecturing. The 1890s and the 1900s, however, were all down hill. As early as 1891 the family moved to Europe, where they could live more economically and where, they hoped, Livy's health would improve. But Clemens lost so much money in poor investments that in 1894 he had to declare bankruptcy. Especially disastrous were his investments in the Paige typesetting machine, in which he lost almost $200,000, and his own publishing firm, Charles L. Webster and Company, named for his nephew whom he first put in charge. Fortunately, Clemens met Henry H. Rogers, a vice president of the Standard Oil Company, who advised him so shrewdly on his financial affairs that by the end of the century he was again a comparatively rich man. But there was not so happy a turn in family affairs. Susy, Clemens's favorite daughter, died of meningitis in 1896 while he was on a round-the-world lecture tour trying to recoup some of his fortune. Livy grew steadily frailer, Clara was in and out of a sanitarium, and Jean developed epilepsy. Livy died in Florence, Italy, in 1904, and Jean died in 1909, the day after she and her father had trimmed the Christmas tree in their home in Redding, Connecticut. Despite the adulation that poured in from every side—Yale, Missouri, and Oxford conferred honorary degrees upon him; he was in constant demand for after-dinner speeches; and newspapers reported his most casual remarks—he became a melancholy and guilt-ridden man. He blamed himself for all the family tragedies. To the end, though, he kept his sense of humor. Angina pectoris finally laid him low, and he died on 21 April 1910. He was buried in the cemetery at Elmira.

The Author: Mark Twain

Mark Twain's earliest writings were principally news accounts, letters, humorous sketches, and burlesques published in Missouri, Iowa, Nevada, and California newspapers and magazines. His first humorous piece, so far as is known, was "A Gallant Fireman" published in Orion's Hannibal *Western Union* on 16 January 1851, and his second was "The Dandy Frightening the Squatter" published in Benjamin P. Shillaber's *Carpet-Bag* (Boston) 1 May 1852. As might be expected, this early work is derivative and overwrought. Only "Jim Smiley

and His Jumping Frog," which appeared first in the New York *Saturday Press* on 18 November 1865 gives clear evidence of what is to come.

Twain's five travel books combine personal experience with material from other sources. They are not so much unified and coherent narratives as compendia of memories, factual reports, stories, jokes, legends, local color sketches, and satires on places and people he encountered, all loosely held together by chronological threads. Twain based *Innocents Abroad* (1869) on his trip to Europe and the Holy Land in 1867 on the *Quaker City*, *Roughing It* (1872) on his trip west in 1861–1866, and *A Tramp Abroad* (1880) primarily on a walking trip he took with Reverend Joseph Twichell through parts of Germany and Switzerland in 1878. *Life on the Mississippi* (1883) resulted chiefly from a recent trip on the Mississippi between New Orleans and St. Paul, though the best chapters (4–17) are those in which he burlesques his days as a cub pilot. These were published originally in five installments as "Old Times on the Mississippi" in the *Atlantic Monthly* in 1875. The fifth travel book, *Following the Equator* (1897), tells of his lecture tour around the world taken two years before. For its relative mastery of both form and content, most readers find *Roughing It* the best of these travel volumes, though particular episodes in others, such as "The Blue Jay Yarn" in *A Tramp Abroad*, deserve places among the best of his humor.

Mark Twain wrote six major novels. The first, *The Gilded Age* (1873), was a collaborative effort with Charles Dudley Warner, which depicts the get-rich-quick fever in post-Civil War days on the frontier and in the nation's capital. The best feature is the character of Beriah Sellers, a backcountry Missourian who constantly expects to make millions though he does not have a dollar in his pocket. *The Adventures of Tom Sawyer* (1876), Twain's second most popular book, fondly spoofs his own boyhood in Hannibal. St. Petersburg, as he calls it, is at one level a heavenly place where a boy's dreams do come true and at another level a river town where adults are conventional and bored and sometimes cruel. Written primarily for young readers, *The Prince and the Pauper* (1882) tells of the dramatic results when Tom Canty, a London ragamuffin, and the prince (Edward VI, to be) exchange clothes. As narrated by Huckleberry Finn, *Adventures of Huckleberry Finn* (1885) is not only Mark Twain's best book but one of the finest novels ever written. The main central section recounts the experiences of Huck and the runaway slave Jim as they drift down the Mississippi from Missouri to Arkansas on a raft. The farcical happenings in the early and late chapters dominated by Tom Sawyer seem almost trivial when compared with the moral and social issues faced by Huck and Jim while on the raft, but they are not trivial enough to weaken seriously the overall impact of the book. *A Connecticut Yankee in King Arthur's Court* (1889) is early science fiction narrated by a New England mechanic who is hit over the head by a crowbar and wakes up in sixth-century England. The juxtaposition of the two cultures gives the author many opportunities to dramatize historical changes, sometimes hilariously, sometimes sardonically. Twain's last major novel, *Pudd'nhead Wilson* (1894), confronts the problem of slavery in Missouri in the middle of the nineteenth century, especially as it involves the mulatto woman Roxy. Weakened by farcical characters and situations, the book nevertheless makes the point strongly that in a slave society both the slaves and their owners are enslaved. Much weaker works are *The American Claimant* (1892), *Tom Sawyer Abroad* (1894), and *Tom Sawyer, Detective* (1896). Twain wrote one biography, *Personal Recollections of Joan of Arc* (1896), and off and on from 1870 to 1909 he wrote and dictated his autobiography.

As Twain grew older and became more and more pessimistic, he found that the best outlet for his feelings was satire in various forms. Principally, he used the satirical essay to attack such diverse phenomena as Western imperialism, lynching in the South, and the writings of James Fenimore Cooper. But also

for satirical purposes, he used such forms as book-length nonfiction (*Christian Science* [1907]), the short story ("The Man That Corrupted Hadleyburg" [1899]), letters (*Letters from the Earth* [1962]), diaries "Extracts from Adam's Diary" [1893], a prayer ("The War Prayer" [1923]), and a fantasy (*The Mysterious Stranger*). He left this last in three fragments, but they all attack the nature of man and of the universe. Life, they make clear, is too insane to be anything but a dream. There was no authoritative edition of these fragments until 1969.

Taken as a whole, Twain's writings show him to be a bundle of contradictions. By turn, for example, he is in the same work, even on the same page, an optimist and a pessimist, an idealist and a materialist, a reformer and a determinist. The proportions, however, do not remain the same. The later works become increasingly more pessimistic, more indignant about human behavior. Despite the evident contradictions and confusions, his writings show a stable moral core. From *Innocents Abroad* in 1869 to his last works such as *The Mysterious Stranger* he displays a hatred for hypocrisy, injustice, and cruelty, and a deep regard for human affection. He calls himself both a humorist and a moralist, and he is right. In fact, his moral perceptions make him the great humorist that he is, for they provide the basis for the exposure in his humor of the dismaying incongruities between the human race's ideals and its behavior. In addition, of course, his works throughout show him to be a master of a colloquial style that gives his writing clarity and immediacy. When he assumes the point of view of a boy and uses the boy's vernacular, the writing becomes nothing less than folk poetry. Admittedly, the works are uneven. Few American novels are more clumsily contrived than *The American Claimant* but few novels in any language are as compelling as *Huckleberry Finn*.

John C. Gerber

BIBLIOGRAPHY

Blair, Walter. *Mark Twain & Huck Finn*. Berkeley: U of California P, 1960.

Budd, Louis J. *Mark Twain: Social Philosopher.* Bloomington: Indiana UP, 1962.

Clemens, Samuel L. *Mark Twain-Howells Letters: The Correspondence of Samuel L. Clemens and William D. Howells, 1872–1910.* Ed. Henry Nash Smith and William M. Gibson. 2 vols. Cambridge, Mass.: Harvard UP, 1960.

Emerson, Everett. *The Authentic Mark Twain: A Literary Biography of Samuel L. Clemens.* Philadelphia: U of Pennsylvania P, 1984.

Fatout, Paul. *Mark Twain on the Lecture Circuit.* Bloomington: Indiana UP, 1960.

Ferguson, DeLancey. *Mark Twain: Man and Legend.* Indianapolis: Bobbs-Merrill, 1943.

Gerber, John C. *Mark Twain.* Boston: Twayne, 1988.

Howells, William Dean. *My Mark Twain: Reminiscences and Criticisms.* New York: Harper, 1910.

Kaplan, Justin. *Mr. Clemens and Mark Twain.* New York: Simon & Schuster, 1966.

Paine, Albert Bigelow. *Mark Twain: A Biography.* 3 vols. New York: Harper, 1912.

Smith, Henry Nash. *Mark Twain: The Development of a Writer.* Cambridge, Mass.: Harvard UP, 1962.

See also: Autobiographical Dictations; Autobiography; Biographers; Clemens, Jane Lampton; Clemens, John Marshall; Estate of Samuel L. Clemens; Family Life; Hannibal, Missouri; Photographs

Clergy

Mark Twain cultivated numerous friendships with members of the clergy beginning in his frontier days and continuing through the Hartford years. He had little regard for the "mush and milk" preachers and missionaries whose travel books he satirized in the Sandwich Island letters to the Sacramento *Union* (1866) and *The Innocents Abroad* (1869). Twain preferred the liberal Henry Ward Beecher's passionate oratory and good Yankee business sense, and he held the reformer Horace Bushnell in high regard. The Reverend Joseph Hopkins Twichell of Hartford, Connecticut, became Twain's closest friend.

In a letter sent to his mother from San Francisco in 1866, Twain made a formidable list of clergymen friends and claimed that whenever anyone offered him a letter of introduction to a preacher, he "snaffled[d] it on the spot" (Branch 368). He found that professional preachers, as long as they were not narrow-minded and bigoted, were the best conversationalists. To his brother Orion, Clemens admitted in October 1865 that becoming a preacher had been one of the two "powerful ambitions" in his life. Claiming that he "lacked the necessary stock in trade, i.e. religion," Clemens asserted that he intended to follow a "call" in another direction as a humorist of a "low order" (Branch 322–324). Although Clemens's letter is filled with irony and self-derision, Twain, nevertheless, later identified himself as a lay preacher and referred to his humor as a sermon. Twain's friend the Reverend Nathaniel Judson Burton, a disciple of Bushnell, lends credence to this claim, for he stated that he felt "a vague kind of moral support" whenever Twain was "anywhere around" (Andrews 43).

In 1868 Twain met Twichell, pastor of the Asylum Hill Congregational Church in Hartford. Twichell preached a "muscular and non-doctrinal Christianity" (Kaplan 82), and he tolerated Mark Twain's irreverence. Twain felt that Twichell "struck twelve" in his sermons. Twichell inspired Twain to write "Old Times on the Mississippi" (1875) and helped him to recognize the literary material in his boyhood idyll. He figures as Twain's traveling companion in "Some Rambling Notes of an Idle Excursion" (1877) and *A Tramp Abroad* (1880). Twain joked that he liked to have a clergyman along on an excursion to serve as a "lightning rod" (Fatout 508).

Twain's fictional clergymen range from the bookish but benevolent minister of "Buck Fanshaw's Funeral" (1872) to the inept orator Reverend Mr. Sprague of *The Adventures of Tom Sawyer* (1876). Twain's clergymen frequently function as foils for the vernacular character in much the same way that the Mr. Twain persona had balanced Brown in Twain's Sandwich Island letters. In keeping with the tradition of southwestern humor, Twain's characterization of the King and the Duke in

Adventures of Huckleberry Finn (1885) is at least partially dependent on a satire of the circuit preachers from his boyhood.

The affinity in Twain's mind between the humorist and the lay preacher may have influenced his story "The Late Reverend Sam Jones's Reception in Heaven" (1891). Here Twain and the Archbishop of Canterbury mistakenly exchange passes aboard a train to the New Jerusalem. The humiliated archbishop is taken for a professional humorist and transported to Sheol while Twain gains admittance to heaven. The anecdote that Twain once masqueraded as Reverend Twain when he was introduced to Captain Charles Duncan provides a humorous picture of the artist on the eve of the *Quaker City* excursion.

In "Bible Teaching and Religious Practice" (1923) Twain refers to clergymen as "ecclesiastical physicians" who drugged their followers and kept them "religion-sick" for centuries. He condemns the Catholic Church for authorizing and practicing slavery long after other Christians had freed their slaves. In the unfinished manuscript "The Chronicle of Young Satan" (1897–1900), Satan exposes the hypocrisies of the Catholic Church but, in a benevolent moment, uses his supernatural powers to "save" the kind Father Peter by making him go mad.

Although in his fiction and polemical essays, Mark Twain often portrays clergymen negatively, in his own life and acquaintance he admired preachers like Thomas K. Beecher of Elmira who retained the "heroism" of the early "Christian character." Twain had only disdain for those who manipulated their followers in the name of religion.

Jennifer L. Rafferty

BIBLIOGRAPHY

Andrews, Kenneth R. *Nook Farm: Mark Twain's Hartford Circle*. Cambridge, Mass.: Harvard UP, 1950.

Brodwin, Stanley. "Mark Twain in the Pulpit: The Theological Comedy of *Huckleberry Finn*." *One Hundred Years of "Huckleberry Finn": The Boy, His Book, and American Culture*. Ed. Robert Sattelmeyer and J. Donald Crowley. Columbia: U of Missouri P, 1985. 371–385.

Clemens, Samuel L. "The Chronicle of Young Satan." *Mark Twain's Mysterious Stranger Manuscripts*. By Clemens. Ed. William M. Gibson. Berkeley: U of California P, 1969. 35–174.

———. *Mark Twain and the Three R's: Race, Religion, Revolution—And Related Matters*. Ed. Maxwell Geismar. Indianapolis: Bobbs–Merrill, 1973.

———. *Mark Twain's Letters, Volume 1 (1853–1866)*. Ed. Edgar M. Branch, Michael B. Frank, and Kenneth M. Sanderson. Berkeley: U of California P, 1988.

———. *Mark Twain's Quarrel with Heaven*. Ed. Ray B. Browne. New Haven, Conn.: College and UP, 1970.

———. "Speech as Presiding Officer at the Public Meeting of the New York State Association for Promoting the Interests of the Blind" (29 March 1906). *Mark Twain Speaking*. By Clemens. Ed. Paul Fatout. Iowa City: U of Iowa P, 1976. 506–511.

Emerson, Everett. *The Authentic Mark Twain: A Literary Biography of Samuel L. Clemens*. Philadelphia: U of Pennsylvania P, 1984.

See also: Beecher, Thomas Kinnicut; Religion; Twichell, Joseph

Cleveland, Grover
(1837–1908)

Grover Cleveland was the twenty-second and twenty-fourth president of the United States (1885–1889, 1893–1897). A supporter of civil service reform, low tariffs, and government austerity, Cleveland opposed imperialism and government intervention in the economy.

To the distress of many of his Republican friends, Mark Twain supported the Democratic Cleveland in 1884. Sharing the distaste of the Mugwumps (independent Republicans, mostly from the genteel classes) for Cleveland's opponent, James G. Blaine, a man of very suspect public integrity, Twain wrote William Dean Howells that his duty to his "conscience and honor" outweighed any loyalty to party, or even to county (*Mark Twain-Howells Letters* 2:508–509). During the campaign it was revealed that Cleveland had carried on an affair with a widow, probably fathering her illegitimate child, inspiring critics to challenge his moral fitness to be president. Twain regarded such notions as a "sham and lie," arguing that a bachelor's "private intercourse with a consenting widow" cast no shadow on Cleveland's public virtues (*Mark Twain-Howells Letters* 2:501).

Twain called on Cleveland in Albany shortly after his election, a visit that virtually coincided with Twain's idea for *A Connecticut Yankee in King Arthur's Court* (1889). Twain also saw Cleveland in Washington in March 1885, an occasion on which, according to Twain, the President told him the "most ancient of all humorous stories," about the humorist whose rural audience could hardly keep from "laughing right out in meetin'" (*Notebooks & Journals* 3:308–309; see also *A Connecticut Yankee in King Arthur's Court*, chapter 9).

Twain's support and admiration for Cleveland deepened with the years. Regarding Cleveland's two terms as the only interruptions in America's decline toward monarchy, Twain praised Cleveland after his death as "a very great President" who, adding dignity to the office, was "all that a President ought to be" (*Mark Twain in Eruption* 347).

Wilson Carey McWilliams

BIBLIOGRAPHY

Blodgett, Geoffrey. *The Gentle Reformers: Massachusetts Democrats in the Cleveland Era*. Cambridge, Mass.: Harvard UP, 1966.

Clemens, Samuel L. *A Connecticut Yankee in King Arthur's Court*. Ed. Bernard Stein. Berkeley: U of California P, 1979.

———. *Mark Twain-Howells Letters: The Correspondence of Samuel L. Clemens and William D. Howells, 1872–1910*. Ed. Henry Nash Smith and William M. Gibson. 2 vols. Cambridge, Mass.: Harvard UP, 1960.

———. *Mark Twain in Eruption*. Ed. Bernard DeVoto. New York: Harper, 1940.

———. *Mark Twain's Notebooks & Journals*. Ed. Frederick Anderson, et al. 3 vols. Berkeley: U of California P, 1975–1979.

Nevins, Alan. *Grover Cleveland: A Study in Courage*. New York: Dodd Mead, 1932.

See also: Politics

Colonel Sellers
(written 1874)

Colonel Sellers is Mark Twain's dramatization of *The Gilded Age* (1873), the novel he co-authored with Charles Dudley Warner. It was written during June–July 1874 and copyrighted 20 July; it was the first work produced in the gazebo at Elmira. The play had been leased to John T. Raymond late in May, before the script was written. It opened at Rochester, New York, on 31 August 1874 for a one-week run, and moved to the Park Theatre in New York on 16 September 1874, where it remained until January 1875. Following the New York run, Raymond toured the play for the next twelve years, generating well over $100,000 in royalties for Twain.

Prior to collaborating with Warner on *Gilded Age*, Twain had already attempted three plays and had displayed considerable interest in drama. Even before the novel was published in December 1873, Twain insisted on a dramatic copyright, which was granted 19 May 1873.

Without Twain's or Warner's knowledge, Gilbert B. Densmore and John T. Raymond presented a dramatic version of *Gilded Age* at the California Theatre, San Francisco, beginning 22 April 1874 and mounting six performances. The play was an immediate success. Warner learned of the event from the San Francisco *Chronicle* and notified Twain, who responded to the news in an unusual manner. Instead of stopping the performances, he asked Warner to renegotiate their copyright, giving Twain sole right to the material Densmore had used. After Warner conceded, Twain enjoined further performances.

In writing a new script, Twain took considerable liberties with the novel, changing names, dates, places, and relationships. He also included material belonging to Warner, contrary to their new agreement. The plot for the drama was based upon Densmore's production, although significant changes were made.

More than any other work by Twain, *Colonel Sellers* reveals his potential as a dramatist.

Had financial pressures been less while he was working on this piece, he might have found the time to realize that dramatic potential.

Jerry W. Thomason

BIBLIOGRAPHY

Clemens, Samuel L. *Mark Twain-Howells Letters: The Correspondence of Samuel L. Clemens and William D. Howells, 1872–1910.* Ed. Henry Nash Smith and William M. Gibson. 2 vols. Cambridge, Mass.: Harvard UP, 1960.

———. *Mark Twain's Letters to His Publishers, 1867–1894.* Ed. Hamlin Hill. Berkeley: U of California P, 1967.

French, Bryant Morey. *Mark Twain and "The Gilded Age": The Book That Named an Era.* Dallas: Southern Methodist UP, 1965.

Goldman, Robert. "Mark Twain as Playwright." *Mark Twain: A Sumptuous Variety.* Ed. Robert Giddings. Totowa, N.J.: Barnes & Noble, 1985. 108–131.

Schirer, Thomas. *Mark Twain and the Theatre.* Nürnberg: Verlag Hans Carl, 1984.

Thomason, Jerry W. "*Colonel Sellers:* The Story of a Play." Ph.D. diss., U of Missouri–Columbia, 1991.

See also: Dramatist, Mark Twain as; *Gilded Age, The*; Raymond, John T.; Warner, Charles Dudley

After two other flirtations with producing the comedy (1886 and 1890), the authors abandoned it. It never played in New York, exhausting itself in a single week of one-night stands around the country. Twain subsequently used some of the material in *The American Claimant* (1892).

Years later Howells could remember, "No dramatists ever got greater joy out of their creations, and when I reflect that the public never had the chance of sharing our joy I pity the public from a full heart."

David O. Tomlinson

BIBLIOGRAPHY

Clemens, Samuel L. *Mark Twain-Howells Letters: The Correspondence of Samuel L. Clemens and William D. Howells, 1872–1910.* Ed. Henry Nash Smith and William M. Gibson. 2 vols. Cambridge, Mass.: Harvard UP, 1960.

Eble, Kenneth. *Old Clemens and W.D.H., The Story of a Remarkable Friendship.* Baton Rouge: Louisiana State UP, 1985.

Howells, William Dean. *My Mark Twain: Reminiscences and Criticisms.* Ed. Marilyn Baldwin. Baton Rouge: Louisiana State UP, 1967.

See also: Dramatist, Mark Twain as; Raymond, John T.

Colonel Sellers as a Scientist

(written 1883)

Though first mentioning this play in 1878, Mark Twain and William Dean Howells did not start serious collaboration until 1883. Successively, they called it *The Steam Generator, Ormes Motor,* and *Colonel Sellers as a Scientist.*

Sellers, a character in *The Gilded Age* (1873), became the center of a successful dramatization of that novel starring John T. Raymond; but Raymond rejected this Twain-Howells sequel in 1884.

Sellers's impulsiveness was modeled partly on that of Twain's own brother Orion. By turns, the play depicted the colonel enthralled with his own inventions, pursuing the rightful title to an earldom, dabbling in spiritualism, and embracing the temperance movement.

Comic Poses

A comic pose is a role that Mark Twain, narrating as "Mark Twain," assumes briefly for the purpose of humor or satire. It is to be distinguished from a narrative persona such as Huckleberry Finn or Hank Morgan that he adopts as narrator for an entire work. Twain uses two types of comic poses, one in which he pretends to be superior to the persons and the life about him and the other in which he pretends to be inferior to them. In both instances he exaggerates the happenings and the style so greatly that there can be no doubt that he is indulging in a comic pose and not writing as the real Mark Twain.

The chief poses of superiority are those of the Gentleman (social superiority), the Sentimentalist (superiority in feeling), and the

Teacher (intellectual superiority). Twain endows his Gentleman with elevated social status, an air of condescension, and a language of formality if not elegance. It was this pose that he assumed in the first piece he signed "Mark Twain." It appeared in the Virginia City *Territorial Enterprise* on 2 February 1863 and lampooned a rival editor as being wholly uncouth, whereas Mark Twain was portrayed as every inch the Gentleman. Hardly original, it was a pose that had been used by A.B. Longstreet, John J. Hooper, T.B. Thorpe, and other southwestern humorists to offset themselves as authors from the rustics they were writing about. In his travel letters from Hawaii and Europe and the Holy Land (1866–1867) Twain keeps himself apart from the gamey Mr. Brown by being the ultra-fastidious Gentleman. Mark Twain's stuffiest Gentleman, however, still remains the visitor from the East in "Jim Smiley and His Jumping Frog" (1865). As the Sentimentalist, Twain poses as a person of deep and exquisite feelings. At the tomb of Adam in *Innocents Abroad* (1869), for example, he bursts into tears because he and Adam never met. The Sentimentalist is a pose he tends to discard in later "Mark Twain" works, but the Teacher is one he continues to use. No travel book is without absurd how-to-do-it explanations delivered with great seriousness. Taken as a whole, though, the poses of superiority, at least of the wild, boisterous kind, appear primarily in his early works. As he grew older and more pessimistic, Twain clearly found it difficult to assume superiority to life, even in a pose.

The most common poses of inferiority are those of the Sufferer (physical inferiority), the Simpleton (intellectual inferiority), and the Tenderfoot (social inferiority). In these the narrator presents himself as the butt of the humor, the person of inexperience in an alien and often malevolent universe. As the Sufferer, Twain endures many familiar misadventures: riding an unruly horse, eating nauseating native food, being victimized by waitresses and clerks. But there are more original ones, such as being thrown over Niagara Falls by a band of Irish Indians and as a newspaper editor in Tennessee being stoned, thrown through a window, and scalped. In such situations the Sufferer becomes either paranoid, and on occasion blames the person making him suffer, or unbelievably calm and stoical, and accepts the torture with formal dignity. Almost as farcical is the role of the Simpleton who believes everything told him, however outrageous. He is convinced, for example, that while in the Holy Land he is shown the center of the earth and the dirt from which God first made man. The most appealing and most lasting of his comic roles is that of the Tenderfoot. This is a role that more clearly grows out of life rather than being imposed on it. In *Roughing It* (1872) and "Old Times on the Mississippi" (1875), Twain stays with the pose long enough to make it an element in the movement of the story. He takes the ultimate step in *Huckleberry Finn* (1885) by giving the role of the Tenderfoot to the narrator of the entire book, thus making the comic pose the narrative persona. When writing as the Tenderfoot, Twain tries to see life as the greenhorn might, with the result that the emphasis is on highly concrete detailing and a careful rendering of the vernacular—and often a poignancy that the other roles do not evoke.

The comic pose brings to Twain's writing a vigor, often a joyousness, that his straight reporting as "Mark Twain" seldom achieves. A role shields Twain, always an insecure person, from reality and gives him a mastery over what often intimidates him. The pose consciousness focuses his imagination and at the same time energizes it.

John C. Gerber

BIBLIOGRAPHY

Blair, Walter. *Horse Sense in American Humor.* Chicago: U of Chicago P, 1942.

Clemens, Samuel L. *Mark Twain of the "Enterprise": Newspaper Articles and Other Documents, 1862–1864.* Ed. Henry Nash Smith and Frederick Anderson. Berkeley: U of California P, 1957.

———. *Mark Twain's Travels with Mr. Brown.* Ed. Franklin Walker and G. Ezra Dane. New York: Knopf, 1940.

Gerber, John C. "Mark Twain's Use of the Comic Pose." *Publications of the Modern Language Association* 77 (June 1962): 297–304.

McKay, Janet Holmgren. *Narration and Discourse in American Realistic Fiction.* Philadelphia: U of Pennsylvania P, 1982.

Rogers, Franklin R. *Mark Twain's Burlesque Patterns as Seen in the Novels and Narratives 1855–1885.* Dallas: Southern Methodist UP, 1960.

Smith, Henry Nash. "Mark Twain as an Interpreter of the Far West: The Structure of *Roughing It.*" *The Frontier in Perspective.* Ed. Walker D. Wyman and Clifton B. Kroeber. Madison: U of Wisconsin P, 1957. 205–228.

See also: Humor; Point of View; Representation

Comics

From his early days as a raucous frontier humorist to his latter years as a white-suited and white-haired patriarch of American literary humor, Mark Twain was a delightful subject for the pens of America's caricaturists and comic artists. His distinct physiognomy, unruly hair, and penchant for striking poses endeared him to those influential cartoonists who portrayed him for the nations periodicals, such as Thomas Nast, Joseph Keppler, John T. McCutcheon, and Richard F. Outcault (the father of the comic strip). On the occasion of Twain's death in 1910, nearly every editorial cartoonist on a major newspaper commented on the loss through a cartoon memorializing the man or his work, an event usually reserved for the deaths of presidents or declarations of war.

Twain's two most popular characters entered the pages of the newspapers in 1918 in the form of a comic strip entitled *Tom Sawyer and Huck Finn.* The syndicate, the McClure Company, began the strip with permission of the author's estate as each installment carried the copyright notice of the Mark Twain Company or the name of Twain's daughter, Clara Clemens Gabrilowitsch. The artist and presumed author of the feature was Clare Victor Dwiggins (1874–1958), who used the pen name "Dwig" and specialized in portraying with nostalgic romanticism the lives of children in rural America in the decades before and after the turn of the century, especially in his popular daily panel series *School Days* (1917–1932). Dwiggins had a loose and sketchy style that invested realistic events with appealing wit and warm caricature, and it lent itself to the depiction of rambunctious children's activities.

He was a suitable choice for *Tom Sawyer and Huck Finn* as an artist, but the story line lacked the satiric edge and critical bite of Twain's fiction and drew little of its content from either Twain novel, except for some additional characters such as Becky Thatcher, Injun Joe, Aunt Polly, the Widow Douglas, and Miss Watson. Conflicts between Huck's independent lifestyle and Tom's traditional mores occasionally were subject matter for the strip's humor, as were Tom's tricks on his peers to get away to fish and yet get his yard work done.

Dwiggins favored at the start single gag strips over extended narrative and employed the type of comedy that was the staple of all the other popular children's strips of the time, such as *Skippy* by Percy Crosby, *Reg'lar Fellers* by Gene Byrnes, and *Out Our Way* by J.R. Williams. Despite several interruptions and changes in title, the strip had a faithful following and probably served to support Twain's reputation as a chronicler of boyhoods past. Dwiggins also used the characters in a series of comic book adventure stories contributed first to *Doc Savage Comics* (1940–1943) and then after 1943 to *Supersnipe Comics* (1942–1949). The feature was concluded when Dwiggins decided to leave the comics for illustration and painting in 1946. A collection of *Tom Sawyer and Huck Finn* Sunday strips appeared in 1925, and a set of the daily strips from 1940 was reprinted in 1990 as *The Adventures of Huckleberry Finn.*

The first adaptation of a Twain work to the comic book appeared in 1942, just nine years after the origin of the medium. This was Oskar Lebeck's *The Complete Story of Tom*

Sawyer, the second number of the Famous Stories Book series issued by Dell Publishing Company. It is a full retelling that includes the major events of the plot, rearranges and abbreviates some of them, and strangely omits the famous fence-painting episode. The art is realistic and vivid. Dell also issued a second more simplified version as *Adventures of Tom Sawyer* in its Dell Junior Treasury series as issue number 10 (October 1957).

In 1941 Albert Kanter began a major publishing project to adapt classic works of literature to the comic book in an effort to draw young readers away from ordinary comic books and lead them to the great books. It was a sign of Twain's standing and reputation that early in the series of Classic Comics (or Classics Illustrated after 1947), issue number 19 (April 1944) was *Huckleberry Finn* with a text adapted by Evelyn Goodman and art by Louis Zansky. Since the intent of the series was to remain as faithful to the text as possible, the adaptation exercised few of the artistic possibilities of the comic book form, and Zansky's art was static and even crude often. The cover depicts Huck and Jim being shot at from the captain's deck of a wrecked steamboat, an action-filled scene that has no counterpart in the novel or the following adaptation. As one would expect, the first-person narrative voice, the American vernacular, and the ingenious use of irony and burlesque—all distinguishing features of the novel—could not be retained. What was left were selected points of dramatic crisis and the swift pace of the narrative as Huck and Jim escape and keep on the move. While much of the basic plot was retained, most of the meaning, especially the social and political implications of the work, was not.

The first version, nevertheless, was so successful among the readers that it went through nine printings, but with the tenth printing a new cover and interior art were provided. This second adaptation, drawn by Frank Giacoia, moved closer to Twain's text in that it used the first-person point of view in narration, attempted an approximation of Huck's language, and included one of the novel's moral crises concerning Jim. The art was more polished and detailed than that of Zansky but approximates the wholesome qualities of book illustration while using effectively perspective and different angles of vision. The second version went through another eleven printings, making it one of only nine titles in the entire Classics series to go beyond twenty printings.

A year after the initial publication of *Huckleberry Finn*, a second Twain title appeared as number 24 (September 1945), *A Connecticut Yankee in King Arthur's Court*, with drawings by Jack Hearne and a text by Ruth Roche and T. Scott. The adaptation focuses on the chivalric conflicts of the novel that have made it popular as a children's book but could not approach Twain's satiric intent to contrast the sixth century with the nineteenth and to ridicule monarchy, the church, vested interest, and Victorian romanticism. Hearne's artwork is striking and especially strong in the use of dramatic facial expressions. After seven printings, a new cover and interior art were provided for an additional eight printings by Jack Sparling, whose mannered and expansive style was much less attractive than that of Hearne. Also, the ending was changed so that Hank Morgan survives, and the plot was shortened.

Classic Comics number 29 (July 1946) was *The Prince and the Pauper*, illustrated by Arnold Hicks and written by Scott Feldman and Jack Bass. This popular tale of switched identities adapts easily to the comic book format and retains its social criticism of man's inhumanity to man, but the crude artwork detracts from its appeal. A horrific cover with the hermit about to stab the prince was quickly changed after the first printing because of concern over public opinion. The title would see fifteen printings but without improved art.

An adaptation of *The Adventures of Tom Sawyer* surprisingly did not appear until August 1948 as number 50 in the series. The artwork of Aldo Rubano is quite innovative in comparison with the other titles. The text retains the principle matters of plot, while Rubano allows his pictures to break free of the conventional panels: characters wander across the pages, and a kind of simultaneous cinematic action is achieved that is possible only in comic book art. This title was one of the most distinctive in the Classics series. Nevertheless, after eight printings, new artwork was prepared for another seven printings, but the uncredited artist for the new version was uninspired and no match for Rubano.

The final Twain adaptation in the Classics series was number 91 (March 1952), *Pudd'nhead Wilson*, with art by Henry C. Kiefer. The major plot elements, including the ambiguities of racial identity (a first in the comic books), were transposed, but Kiefer's penchant for staged tableaus and excessive detail do not make for engaging reading. The title saw only four printings. In a series from the same publisher, The World Around Us, number 27 (November 1960) carried an illustrated text rendition of "The Notorious Jumping Frog of Calaveras County," with drawings by Gray Morrow.

In 1990 the Classics Illustrated series was revived by the Berkeley/First Publishing Company, and number 9 was a new adaptation of *The Adventures of Tom Sawyer* by Michael Ploog. The artist's distinctive style, laced with whimsy and charming caricature, is highly suitable for Twain's text. It is an appealing and faithful introduction to the novel.

The Pendulum Press began to issue in 1973 a set of new adaptations to the comic book format called the Now Age Illustrated series, except they were in black and white and produced in a smaller paperback size. These were done specifically for classroom use, used set type rather than hand lettering, maintained a vocabulary aimed at established grade levels, and included word lists and questions at the back.

Four Twain titles appeared in the series: *Huckleberry Finn* (1973), text by Naunerle Farr and art by Francisco Redondo; *Tom Sawyer* (1973), text by Irwin Shapiro and art by E.R. Cruz; *A Connecticut Yankee in King Arthur's Court* (1977), text by John Norwood Fago and art by Francisco Redondo; and *The Prince and the Pauper* (1978), text by John Norwood Fago and art by E.R. Cruz. Except for the usual plot compression, all are faithful to the originals and are realistically illustrated with careful attention to historical detail for the time and place of each novel. In 1990 Pendulum Press began to reissue the titles in a larger, deluxe, full-color Collector's Edition for the trade market.

When the Marvel Classics Comics series began publication in 1976, the first twelve titles were abbreviated color reprints of Pendulum titles, including *Tom Sawyer* as number 7 (1976). Issue number 33 was an original adaptation of *The Prince and the Pauper* (1978) by writer Don McGregor and several unidentified artists. The style and plot elements are heavily action-oriented in the Marvel comics tradition.

One other version of *The Prince and the Pauper* has been published by Walt Disney Publications, actually an adaptation of the 1990 animated film with text by Scott Saavedra and art by Sergio Asteriti. Featuring Mickey Mouse, Goofy, Pluto, and Donald Duck in the lead roles, neither film nor book bears much relationship to Twain's novel, except for the use of the switch between peasant and prince.

The attraction of Twain for comic book adaptors demonstrates the author's continuing vitality among readers in the twentieth century, even though they tend to overlook the deeper strains of cynicism in Twain's major works that scholars have come to emphasize in the last half of the century. The comics have proven to be a powerful means of communication through words and pictures and undoubtedly have served to keep Twain in the forefront of the minds and imaginations of young and older American readers, many of whom have been led to the original works.

M. Thomas Inge

BIBLIOGRAPHY

Dwiggins, Clare Victor. *The Adventures of Huckleberry Finn*. Newbury Park, Calif.: Malibu Graphics, 1990.

Goulart, Ron, ed. *The Encyclopedia of American Comics*. New York: Facts on File, 1990. 113–114, 190–191.

Malan, Dan. *The Complete Guide to Classics Collectibles. Volume 1: The U.S. Series of Classics Illustrated*. St. Louis: Malan Classical Enterprises, 1991.

Marschall, Rick. "An American Classic and a Classic Comic Strip." *Nemo: The Classic Comics Library* 16 (December 1985): 19–33.

See also: Illustrators; Media Interpretations

Comstock Lode

About 100 miles east of Sacramento, California, in Nevada, and halfway up Mount Davidson, the Comstock Lode was a vein of gold and silver first assayed at $3,876 a ton when $100 a ton was considered a good find. The vein was discovered by a couple of placer miners in a creek owned by Emanuel Penrod and an eccentric character, Henry Page Comstock, who gave it his name. From discovery in mid-June 1859 until the following spring, the lode caused little excitement, but then followed a rush unlike any since that of 1849. Twain arrived in the area with the swell of population and left with the collapse of prosperity from inefficient mining, shaky stock speculation, and limitless lawsuits over claims that profited nobody but lawyers. Nevertheless, the lode capitalized San Francisco, which served as port of entry and site of the mint.

P.M. Zall

BIBLIOGRAPHY

Elliott, Russell R. *History of Nevada*. 2nd. ed. Lincoln: U of Nebraska P, 1987.

Lillard, Richard G. *Desert Challenge*. New York: Knopf, 1942; rpt. Lincoln: U of Nebraska P, 1966.

See also: California; Nevada

Concord Public Library

In March 1885 the Public Library Committee of Concord, Massachusetts, banned *Adventures of Huckleberry Finn* (1885) from the library less than a month after the library bought a subscription copy of the recently published book. Members of the committee condemned *Huckleberry Finn* for being "rough, coarse, and inelegant" and for "dealing with a series of experiences not elevating." They considered the book "more suited to the slums than to intelligent, respectable people" (Boston *Transcript*, 17 March 1885). That same month, in a letter to Frank A. Nichols of the Concord Free Trade Club, Clemens claimed that the library's action had doubled the sales of *Huckleberry Finn* and would prompt those who had bought the book "to read it, out of curiosity, instead of merely intending to do so" (*Letters* 2:876–879).

Roberta Seelinger Trites

BIBLIOGRAPHY

Clemens, Samuel L. *Mark Twain-Howells Letters: The Correspondence of Samuel L. Clemens and William D. Howells, 1872–1910*. Ed. Henry Nash Smith and William M. Gibson. 2 vols. Cambridge, Mass: Harvard UP, 1960.

See also: Adventures of Huckleberry Finn; Censorship

Condensed Novels

The condensed novels are a part of the larger group of writings by Mark Twain that are literary burlesques of familiar nineteenth-century genres. These novels are actually only of story length and are modeled on Thackeray's "Mr. Punch's Prize Novelists." Bret Harte used this form also for his *Condensed Novels and Other Papers* (1867), so he influenced Twain during this period when they were both working for the *Californian*. According to Rogers, the seven works called condensed novels are "Lucretia Smith's Soldier" (1864), "The Story of the Bad Little Boy" (1865), "Who Was He?" (written 1867), "The Story of Mamie Grant, the Child-Missionary" (written 1868), "Burlesque *L'Homme Qui Rit*" (written 1869), "Boy's Manuscript" (written ca. 1868), and "The Story of the Good Little Boy" (1870).

"Lucretia Smith's Soldier" is not a burlesque of a particular novel or novelist, but, according to Twain in his preface to the sketch, "those nice, sickly war stories in *Harper's Weekly*." In addition to the war stories, Twain targets the platitudes of sentimental novels like Pierce Egan's *Such Is Life* (1864) and Mary Elizabeth Braddon's *The Trail of the Serpent* (1863–1864). The novel is composed of four chapters, each only several paragraphs long and ending in a melodramatic climax. Because the time is May 1861, Lucretia Borgia Smith wants her beloved to join the army. Thinking he does not intend to become a soldier, she rejects Reginald de Whittaker. When she finds out that he has gone off to war, she is angry that "[n]o soldier in all the vast armies would breathe her name as he breasted the crimson tide of war!" Even though he never writes, she goes to his bedside when she sees his name on a list of the wounded. After several weeks of devotion at his bedside when his bandages are removed, she learns that the soldier is Richard Dilworthy Whittaker. The unsentimental conclusion is that Lucretia's Whittaker has yet to appear. For Branch and Hirst the story is "a warning to all sentimentalists to get their facts straight, and its ending argues that the sentimental mask cannot really endure a serious misreading of the facts." "Lucretia Smith's Soldier" was reprinted in numerous other papers and very popular. It was next reprinted in *The Celebrated Jumping Frog* (1867), where it was also popular with reviewers. It was reprinted in 1872 and 1874 and considered for *Sketches, New and Old* (1875) but not included in the final selections.

"The Story of the Bad Little Boy" (1865) and "The Story of the Good Little Boy" (1870) parody the familiar good-boy, bad-boy stories of the period. Reprinted together in *Sketches, New and Old* the stories provide complete reversals of the formulas they burlesque. Each story contains a boy with the initials J.B.: Jim Blake is the "bad little boy" and Jacob Blivens the "good little boy." The boys are opposites, and evil triumphs in each story. For Martin, these are the two selves Twain sees himself split between. Gribben puts these stories in the movement that gave rise to the bad-boy book, beginning with Thomas Bailey Aldrich's *The Story of a Bad Boy* (1869). The books in this movement suggest that a rascal may become a more useful adult than a good boy. "The Story of the Bad Little Boy" and *Tom Sawyer* were both popular and closely associated for their similar themes. Also a precursor is "Boy's Manuscript" (written ca. 1868) because it provides the materials that Twain expanded into *Tom Sawyer*, the important step before the boy's book is transformed into the classic *Adventures of Huckleberry Finn* (1885). This episodic story follows the escapades of Billy Rogers.

Mark Twain's Satires & Burlesques (1967) contains the previously unpublished "Who Was He?" (written 1867), an unfinished burlesque of Victor Hugo's *Les Travailleurs de la Mer*; "The Story of Mamie Grant, the Child-Missionary" (written 1868); and "Burlesque *L'Homme Qui Rit*" (written 1869). The first is an excellent parody of the English translation of Hugo's style, but the form is restrictive. In the later burlesques Twain attempts to escape the form's limitations. In "The Story of Mamie Grant" Twain burlesques temperance literature as well as religious tracts and produces, according to Rogers, a condensed novel that has "a dimension and depth, a richness and complexity in ridicule or satire which is rarely found in the burlesque literature of the nineteenth century." The burlesque of Hugo's *L'Homme qui rit* was based on William Young's translation *The Man Who Laughs* (1869). Twain transforms Hugo's story into a political allegory about Andrew Johnson's career, particularly after he succeeds Lincoln as president and reveals his own shifting allegiance against Johnson in particular and Democrats in general.

A reading of these condensed novels clearly shows Twain developing into the author of *Tom Sawyer* and *Huckleberry Finn*.

Nancy Chinn

BIBLIOGRAPHY

Clemens, Samuel L. *Mark Twain's Satires & Burlesques.* Ed. Franklin R. Rogers. Berkeley: U of California P, 1967.

———. *Mark Twain's Sketches, New and Old.* Hartford, Conn.: American Publishing, 1875.

———. *The Works of Mark Twain: Early Tales & Sketches, Volume 2 (1864–1865).* Ed. Edgar M. Branch and Robert H. Hirst. Berkeley: U of California P, 1981.

DeVoto, Bernard. *Mark Twain at Work.* Cambridge, Mass.: Harvard UP, 1942.

Gribben, Alan. "'I Did Wish Tom Sawyer Was There': Boy-book Elements in *Tom Sawyer* and *Huckleberry Finn*." *One Hundred Years of "Huckleberry Finn": The Boy, His Book, and American Culture.* Ed. Robert Sattelmeyer and J. Donald Crowley. Columbia: U of Missouri P, 1985. 149–170.

Martin, Jay. "The Genie in the Bottle: Huckleberry Finn in Mark Twain's Life." *One Hundred Years of "Huckleberry Finn": The Boy, His Book, and American Culture.* Ed. Robert Sattelmeyer and J. Donald Crowley. Columbia: U of Missouri P, 1985. 56–81.

Rogers, Franklin R. *Mark Twain's Burlesque Patterns as Seen in the Novels and Narratives, 1855–1885.* Dallas: Southern Methodist UP, 1960.

See also: Boy Books; "Boy's Manuscript"; Burlesque; "Lucretia Smith's Soldier"; *Sketches, New and Old*; "Story of the Bad Little Boy Who Didn't Come to Grief, The"; "Story of the Good Little Boy Who Did Not Prosper, The"

Conferences

Ever since the inception of American literary studies, Mark Twain's life and writings have occupied a central place in programs offered by the Modern Language Association, its regional affiliates, and such regular conferences as those sponsored by the American Studies Association, the Western American Literature Association, and (since 1989) the American Literature Association. In addition, special conferences in the 1980s and 1990s focused on American humor or on Mark Twain exclusively, and these shaped and accelerated research on him as a literary figure. Several conferences might be specifically noted. The "Conference on American Humor" held in April 1980 at Southwest Texas State University in San Marcos, for example, attracted scholars from across the United States and predictably elicited numerous references to Mark Twain's role in the development of a national humorous literature. Hamlin Hill delivered the keynote address at this conference, which Arlin Turner and Jack Meathenia planned, and J.A. Leo Lemay, John Gerber, and Brom Weber presided at individual sessions.

The Eighth Alabama Symposium on English and American Literature, arranged by the University of Alabama in October 1981, discussed an intriguing subject, "The Mythologizing of Mark Twain." A subsequent volume of that same title, edited by the conference directors Sara deSaussure Davis and Philip D. Beidler, collected eight of the papers and was published by the University of Alabama Press in 1984. Henry Nash Smith, Louis J. Budd, and Stanley Brodwin were among the contributors.

In April 1984 John Bryant and Gus Kolich chaired "The Penn State Conference on American Comedy: One Hundred Years of Huckleberry Finn" in University Park, Pennsylvania. John Barth and Hamlin Hill were featured speakers. The proceedings included an examination of questions surrounding the teaching of *Huckleberry Finn* in the public schools amid calls for censorship owing to its still volatile language and subject matter.

A highly unusual conference on "Dickens and Twain" evolved from the Dickens Project sponsored by the University of California, Santa Cruz, in August 1984. Leslie Fiedler delivered the keynote address and Fred Kaplan, Chris R. Vanden Bossche, Murray Baumgarten, Jonathan Arac, Henry Nash Smith, Forrest Robinson, and Norris Pope moderated sessions, with J. Hillis Miller presenting a closing address. The group also toured the Mark Twain Project in the Bancroft Library at the University of California, Berkeley.

An equally elaborate conference celebrated the one-hundredth anniversary of the publication of Twain's most acclaimed novel. Robert Sattelmeyer and J. Donald Crowley chaired a program dedicated to "Centennial Perspectives on *Huckleberry Finn*: The Boy, His Book, and American Culture" at the University of Missouri, Columbia, in April 1985. John C. Gerber, James M. Cox, David L. Smith, Louis J. Budd, Hamlin Hill, Jay Martin, Tom Quirk, and others presented lectures. Attendees saw a performance of Hal Holbrook's "Mark Twain Tonight" and visited the Mark Twain Shrine and Birthplace Museum at Florida, Missouri, and the Mark Twain Home and Museum in Hannibal. A simultaneously published book—*One Hundred Years of Huckleberry Finn: The Boy, His Book, and American Culture* (U of Missouri P, 1985)—collected conference papers along with additional, related submissions.

Another conference, "Mark Twain and His America," also paid tribute to the anniversary of Twain's masterpiece and published (in 1990) the proceedings of its meeting in December 1985 at Siena College in Loudonville, New York. Henry Nash Smith delivered the keynote address, "Mark Twain: Ritual Clown," and there were papers presented by Sydney Krause, Robert Regan, and others (edited by Mary Fitzgerald-Hoyt and published by Siena Research Institute as *Mark Twain: Ritual Clown* in 1990). Francis V. Madigan, Jr., Douglas Lonnstrom, and Thomas O. Kelly II chaired the event.

Susan K. Gillman and Forrest G. Robinson co-directed a conference emphasizing new critical approaches to *Pudd'nhead Wilson* at the University of California, Santa Cruz, in March 1987. James M. Cox delivered the keynote address. The conferences offered an interdisciplinary approach to Twain's enigmatic novel, with literary critics, historians, political scientists, and anthropologists presenting papers. The proceedings of the conference were published as *Mark Twain's Pudd'nhead Wilson: Race, Conflict, and Culture*, ed. Gillman and Robinson (Duke UP, 1990).

Beginning in 1986 with "Mark Twain and Women," organized by Louis J. Budd, Everett Emerson, and Alan Gribben, the Mark Twain Circle of America (sometimes in conjunction with the American Humor Association) has conducted special sessions on Mark Twain at the annual MLA conventions. In San Francisco in 1987 Louis J. Budd led a session on "Mark Twain and the West" that included Hill, Robert Hirst, Susan K. Gillman, and John Seelye as participants. A program at the 1990 Chicago MLA meeting, organized by Susan K. Harris, treated the topic of "Mark Twain and Money" as interpreted by Susan K. Gillman, Andrew Jay Hoffman, and Sherwood Cummings.

Another influential gathering was sponsored by the Elmira College Center for Mark Twain Studies at Quarry Farm; in August 1989 it presented a program in Elmira, New York, titled "Mark Twain and *A Connecticut Yankee in King Arthur's Court*: American Issues, 1889–1989" that featured addresses by Justin Kaplan, Frederick Crews, W. Carey McWilliams, M. Thomas Inge, Mary Boewe, Howard Baetzhold, John Daniel Stahl, and Cecelia Tichi. Louis J. Budd and Everett Emerson co-chaired the event. The next Elmira College conference is scheduled for August 1993 and has as its topic "The State of Mark Twain Studies." The Mark Twain Memorial in Hartford, Connecticut, has sponsored two annual fall Twain symposia—"New Perspectives on Mark Twain" (October 1990) and "Issues of Race and Prejudice" (October 1991).

Alan Gribben

Connecticut Yankee in King Arthur's Court, A
(1889)

Conceived in December 1884, *A Connecticut Yankee in King Arthur's Court* was written at various periods from 1885 to 1889. It was published first in England by Chatto and

Windus on 6 December 1889, as *A Yankee in the Court of King Arthur* and four days later in the United States by Clemens's own firm, Charles L. Webster and Company. Intended at first to be chiefly humorous, it ultimately embodied some of Mark Twain's most serious political, social, and philosophical concerns.

Discovery of a copy of Sir Thomas Malory's *Morte D'arthur* in a Rochester, New York, bookstore during the reading tour with George Washington Cable (1884–1885) sparked Mark Twain's initial "dream of being a knight-errant in armor in the middle ages" and the attendant difficulties presented by the iron clothing. That "dream," in turn, inspired the intriguing idea of transporting a superintendent of the Colt Arms Factory in Hartford to sixth-century England, and by February 1886 Mark Twain had composed at least the introductory "A Word of Explanation" and the first three chapters.

Twain's early claim that the book was to be a burlesque contrast between modern and ancient times is borne out by his performance in November 1886 at the Military Service Institution on Governor's Island in New York harbor. There, after reading "all that was then written," he provided an "outline" of the remainder of the story. The brash Yankee would outdo the knights in lying about their exploits. Armed with the superior knowledge of the nineteenth century, within two years he would be running the country—at "a modest royalty of forty percent." During that time, also, he would defeat a host of Arthur's enemies at one of the great tournaments by mowing them down with Gatling guns from behind an electrified barbed-wire fence. In three-and-a-half years the "fuss and flummery of romance" would be completely cleared away and the improvement would be complete, with the Northwest Passage replacing the Holy Grail as object of knightly quests and Arthur's 140 knights established as a stock board, with a seat at the Round Table worth $30,000.

The first three chapters accord with the original intention. But when Twain resumed work on the novel in the summer of 1887, his concept of the Yankee's role changed significantly. As work on the novel proceeded that summer, and again in 1888 and part of 1889, the burlesque would continue in various ways, but instead of merely profit for himself and for the king's treasury, the Yankee's goal became the total reform of political and social evils in Arthur's kingdom. Instead of using the Gatling guns and electrified fence against Arthur's enemies, he would turn them against the entire chivalry of England and the values for which they stood. And episode after episode—though the humor continued strong—he would castigate the attitudes bred by the feudal ideal.

Part of the reason for the shift may have been purely practical. As with all his books, Mark Twain was vitally interested in sales. In letters and ultimately in the prospectus of the book, he and the publishers purposely played up the anti-aristocratic elements of the story in order to appeal to the American public.

But there were obviously other and more important considerations—a new sympathy for equalitarian democracy, much different from his "elitist" stance of the 1870s, as reflected in "The Curious Republic of Gondour" (1875); enthusiasm for the activities of the Knights of Labor and for the policies of Grover Cleveland, notably for free trade over protection; and a growing antagonism toward England, derived from his reading (especially of George Standring's "People's History of the English Aristocracy" and, to a much lesser extent, of the criticisms of America by Matthew Arnold) and further fueled by his observation of current political and social events there. These readings and observations brought a new sense that ancient evils fostered by monarchy, aristocracy, and the established church had continued into the present, which, in turn, sparked a number of the more serious concerns that underlie the humor of the novel.

Though the contemporary stimuli were significant, the shift from burlesque "contrast" to more serious satire does not mean that Mark Twain intended *A Connecticut Yankee* solely as an attack upon England and certainly not just on the nineteenth century, as some have suggested, even though Dan Beard's illustrations emphasized certain contemporary political and social concerns. The sources Twain drew upon for ideas, episodes, and specific details indicate a much broader scope. The major ones alone (and there were many more) drew upon most of the ages of Western history from classic antiquity to the time of the novel itself. And Mark Twain's use of his sources to illustrate the people's subjection to the "superstitions" fostered by monarchy, aristocracy, and the church strongly supports the contention that the novel was meant to provide an examination of man's "slavery" to those "superstitions," not only as they had existed in medieval times, but as they had persisted though the centuries into Twain's own age.

One of Mark Twain's most ambitious undertakings, *A Connecticut Yankee* contains numerous elements from his earlier works and some that look forward to later ones. Its basic structure is the "frame story," which he had learned from the southwestern humorists and used in a number of his shorter pieces. Many of the humorous devices, burlesques and otherwise, look back to the earlier writings and Twain's tutelage by some of the so-called literary comedians, who often combined burlesque and social criticism. Like Prince Edward traveling with Miles Hendon through Tudor England in *The Prince and the Pauper* (1882), the Yankee journeys through the realm with King Arthur, observing the people and conditions. As he comments on his experiences, humorously or critically, he also resembles the narrators of *The Innocents Abroad* (1869) and *A Tramp Abroad* (1880) and their confrontations with an alien culture.

From a different perspective, Hank Morgan's journey through time—an early example of science fiction in America, and among the first anywhere to take the traveler back instead of forward in time—foreshadows later strange travels by Twain's characters: in a

drop of water under a microscope in "The Great Dark," in dreams in "My Platonic Sweetheart" (both written 1898), and in the veins of a drunken tramp in "Three Thousand Years Among the Microbes" (written 1905).

As a stranger who manipulates and (for a time) dominates a community, the Yankee is a predecessor of such characters as the perpetrator of the hoax in "The Man That Corrupted Hadleyburg" (1899), Philip Traum in "Chronicle of Young Satan" (written 1897–1900) and the character Forty-Four in "No. 44, The Mysterious Stranger" (written 1902–1905, 1908). Hank's rise and fall also suggests the cyclical theory of history that Mark Twain would promulgate much more fully in "The Secret History of Eddypus" (written 1901–1902) and "Passage from a Lecture" (early 1900s).

In terms of Twain's own career, the work shows a progression from the essentially light-hearted satire of *The Innocents Abroad* (1869) through the more serious touches in *The Prince and the Pauper* (1882) (which was written at a time when Twain still thought that with the right sort of ruler real progress could be achieved) and the deepening pessimism and developing determinism of *Life on the Mississippi* (1883) and *Adventures of Huckleberry Finn* (1885). Whereas Huck's "sound heart" was not quite overmastered by society's training, now the only element in Hank Morgan not governed by his conviction that "training is everything; training is all there is *to* a person" is the "one atom in me that is truly me."

Critics have generally agreed that the works after *A Connecticut Yankee* became more deeply pessimistic. Some have argued that the book marked the *beginnings* of Twain's "later pessimism," which, exacerbated by the failure of his publishing company and the Paige typesetter and by family problems, dominated the 1890s and beyond. Others, however, have correctly placed it rather as one of the final *steps* in a growing disillusionment with human nature and the development of the deterministic philosophy that culminated in *What Is Man?* (1906).

But the dream device employed by the novel, and the Yankee's sense of life as "a pathetic drift amid the eternities," also presages a somewhat contradictory—and potentially more positive—interest in dreams and unfettered "dream-selves" that would emerge most fully in his later years in "My Platonic Sweetheart" and "No. 44, The Mysterious Stranger." At the end of the latter, Forty-Four reveals to August Feldner that all existence is a dream and August himself only a thought "wandering forlorn among the eternities," but at the same time admonishes him to "dream other dreams, and better! . . ."

Initial criticism of *A Connecticut Yankee* in America was generally favorable, with William Dean Howells and others hailing it as a democratic and populist attack on both ancient and modern evils. As might be expected, British critics, for the most part, either took umbrage at the "insult" offered to Tennyson, Malory, and the chivalric ideal or dismissed the book as one whose intended humor did not amuse.

Twentieth-century criticism has been so diverse as to challenge brief summary. In the best treatment of what Mark Twain actually *meant* his novel to be, Everett Carter (using E.D. Hirsch's distinction between "meaning" and "significance") divided contemporary critics and scholars into two groups—the first of which regards the book as an attack upon the sentimentalism and evils of the past and an expression of nineteenth-century faith in technology and the second (and now much more populous) as an attack both on America's faith in material progress and on technology itself.

While those categories are largely valid, they do not suggest the wide variety of treatment the novel has received. It has been studied from historical, social, mythic, political, economic, linguistic, psychological, and theological perspectives. Its sources have been examined for their influence on its ideas. The book's subtexts and the Yankee's actions have been probed from Freudian, Marxist, structuralist,

phenomenological, and other points of view. It has been declared a denunciation of medieval and modern England and of certain nineteenth-century practices in America. Some have argued that though it praises technology, it bemoans the loss of romantic values and early innocence. It has been called the most complete example in American humor of a translation of social commentary into literary burlesque. It has been presented as a reflection of Mark Twain's obsession with the Paige typesetting machine and its ultimate failure.

Much attention has been focused on the character of the Yankee, including discussion of the degree to which Mark Twain should or should not be identified with his protagonist, and of whether the Yankee is a reliable or unreliable narrator. Hank Morgan appears in these deliberations in myriad forms—as an entrepreneur with some flaws, but with a serious desire to create a better world; a Tom Sawyer grown up into a Barnumlike showman; a vernacular hero, a capitalist hero, an American Adam, a new Prometheus attempting to bring enlightenment to a benighted world; a robber baron; an epitome of American individualism; a reformer whose lust for power transforms him into a dictator who coldbloodedly creates a holocaust and whose capacity for violence reveals a fundamental characteristic of American society at large. His experiences, and especially his death, longing for his "lost land" and sixth-century family, have been viewed as an expression of Mark Twain's growing wish to escape from time and so be free of anguish and despair. He has also been declared to be a type rather than an individual, and thus not subject to limits of personality—a traditional hero whose psychological journey in quest of self brings him into conflict with a world that ultimately defeats him and who, seen allegorically, is an avatar of American industrialism and American imperialism.

Contemporary critics have been especially disturbed by the violence and the horror of the destruction of the 25,000–30,000 knights in the Battle of the Sand Belt. The episode is indeed horrible, but in this instance, as in others, some seem to forget that *A Connecticut Yankee* is an adventure story, humorous as well as serious, with many of the exaggerations characteristic of the type. This is not to say that the ending is meant to be humorous, though one passage that Twain deleted at the suggestion of E.C. Stedman does seem to lean in that direction, with its details of mock scientific measurements of the mass of "homogeneous protoplasm" and "alloys of iron and buttons" left by the dynamite explosion. Earlier critics probably regarded the horrific ending either as a type of tall-tale exaggeration or as the hyperbole of the adventure story genre itself. And Twain himself very likely expected the readers' reactions to be much like those of modern audiences to the violence in animated cartoons or in a closer analogy to the cataclysmic endings of James Bond films.

Most critics of recent years have concluded that, artistically, *A Connecticut Yankee* is a failure. Some have argued that it is great despite its faults, but more have declared that the weaknesses significantly outweigh the virtues. Among the most obvious flaws are the inconsistencies of characterization. The Yankee, introduced as a brash entrepreneur, knowledgeable in little but technological skills, soon exhibits an acquaintance with history, politics, and economic theory far beyond what might logically be expected. From a humorously garrulous nuisance, Sandy (the Demoiselle Alisande la Carteloise) suddenly emerges toward the novel's end as devoted wife and mother. Too often direct diatribe replaces dramatization, with Mark Twain's own voice supplanting that of his narrator. In other instances the striving for a laugh destroys a carefully crafted and essentially serious mood. More basically, though the Yankee purports to have instituted major reforms, the novel does not really illustrate the benefits of the new civilization in any significant way.

These flaws, and the presence of elements so disparate as to defy a blending—comedy, burlesque, satire, diatribe, melodrama, sentimentality, parody, pathos, and social commentary—cause serious problems, to be sure. But many of them are also intriguing. If the book is indeed a failure, it is the failure of a great writer. Despite artistic and thematic confusions, it remains a classic, almost unique of its kind, and in various ways continues to delight and instruct. Its adaptation (though considerably revised) for three films, two musicals, and a Bugs Bunny cartoon helps to substantiate its continuing popular appeal.

Moreover, the very variety of scholarly criticism attests to the richness of the work. The humor, even some of the broad burlesque, is often of a high order. If Hank Morgan's vernacular voice sometimes slips into Mark Twain's own, at its best it reveals the same mastery that pervades *Huckleberry Finn*. The serious questions the work touches upon are those that will continue to be addressed by writers and thinkers concerned with the relationship of material and moral progress. Readers not concerned with the niceties of critical theorizing will continue to be fascinated by the Yankee's adventures, will laugh at the humorous touches, and will be touched by the serious elements. Although its analysts have been unable to fit it exactly into established genres, *A Connecticut Yankee* will continue to occupy a truly important place in the canon of American literature.

Howard G. Baetzhold

BIBLIOGRAPHY

Baetzhold, Howard G. "The Course of Composition of *A Connecticut Yankee*: A Reinterpretation." *American Literature* 33 (May 1961): 195–214.

———. *Mark Twain and John Bull: The British Connection.* Bloomington: Indiana UP, 1970.

Boewe, Mary. "Twain on Lecky: Some Marginalia at Quarry Farm." *Mark Twain Society Bulletin* 8.1 (January 1985): 1–6.

Brodwin, Stanley. "Wandering Between Two Gods: Theological Realism in Mark Twain's *A Connecticut Yankee*." *Studies in the Literary Imagination* 16.2 (Fall 1983): 57–82.

Budd, Louis J. *Mark Twain: Social Philosopher.* Bloomington: Indiana UP, 1962.

Carter, Everett. "The Meaning of *A Connecticut Yankee*." *American Literature* 50 (November 1978): 418–440.

Clemens, Samuel L. *A Connecticut Yankee in King Arthur's Court*. Ed. Bernard L. Stein. Berkeley: U of California P, 1979.

Cox, James M. "*A Connecticut Yankee in King Arthur's Court*: The Machinery of Self-Preservation." *Yale Review* 50 (Autumn 1960): 89–102.

Cummings, Sherwood. *Mark Twain and Science: Adventures of a Mind*. Baton Rouge: Louisiana State UP, 1988.

Ensor, Allison, ed. *A Connecticut Yankee in King Arthur's Court*. Norton crit. ed. New York: Norton, 1982.

Fetterly, Judith. "Yankee Showman and Reformer: The Character of Mark Twain's Hank Morgan." *Texas Studies in Language and Literature* 14 (Winter 1973): 667–680.

Harris, Susan K. *Mark Twain's Escape from Time: A Study of Patterns and Images*. Columbia: U of Missouri P, 1982.

Hoffman, Andrew Jay. *Twain's Heroes, Twain's Worlds*. Philadelphia: U of Pennsylvania P, 1988.

Ketterer, David. "Epoch-Eclipse and Apocalypse: Special 'Effects' in *A Connecticut Yankee*." *Publications of the Modern Language Association* 88 (October 1973): 1104–1114.

Regan, Robert. *Unpromising Heroes: Mark Twain and His Characters*. Berkeley: U of California P, 1966.

Salomon, Roger B. *Twain and the Image of History*. New Haven, Conn.: Yale UP, 1961.

Sloane, David E.E. *Mark Twain as a Literary Comedian*. Baton Rouge: Louisiana State UP, 1979.

Smith, Henry Nash. *Mark Twain's Fable of Progress: Political and Economic Ideas in "A Connecticut Yankee."* New Brunswick, N.J.: Rutgers UP, 1964.

Williams, James D. "The Use of History in Mark Twain's *A Connecticut Yankee*." *Publications of the Modern Language Association* 80 (March 1965): 102–110.

See also: Arnold, Matthew; Arthur, King; Beard, Daniel Carter; Carlyle, Thomas; Clarence; Determinism; Malory, Sir Thomas; Medievalism; Merlin; Morgan, Hank; Sandy; Slavery; Taine, Hippolyte; Technology, Mark Twain and

Conscience

Mark Twain's preoccupation with the problems of conscience had its roots in Samuel Clemens's lifelong sense of personal guilt. Though Twain generally interpreted this punitive faculty in secular terms, as a product of "training" and thus relative to human circumstance, he found in the idea of conscience one explanation of man's duality and made the superego the major adversary for a number of his fictional characters.

According to Van Wyck Brooks, Clemens's childhood guilt, and particularly the remorse stimulated by his father's death, lay behind Mark Twain's "ordeal," which permanently crippled his creative spirit. While Brooks's thwarted-genius thesis has been challenged, notably by Bernard DeVoto, there is abundant evidence attesting to young Sam's overactive Presbyterian conscience, which haunted him about events over which he had little or no control. In *Life on the Mississippi* (1883) and the *Autobiography* (1924), Twain recalls his younger self's paroxysms of guilt about Hannibal stabbings, shootings, drownings, and the burning to death of a jailed tramp to whom a charitable Sam had given matches. To the sensitive child, human calamity and natural violence were providential admonitions, expressly designed to bring him to repentance.

Although the mature writer ridiculed all theological appeals to "special Providences," his adult years were punctuated by periods of intense guilt: for his brother Henry's death in a steamboat explosion; for the exposure that, as he told William Dean Howells, "killed" his infant son; for daughter Susy's death from meningitis; and for the pains he had inflicted upon his wife. The outrageous logic of his remorse suggests that he was looking for a crime to which he could plead guilty, as Justin Kaplan contends. For example, he traced his responsibility for Susy's suffering to his failure to oppose his niece Annie Moffett's marriage to Charles L. Webster. The latter had managed Clemens's publishing firm and thus was instrumental in his bankruptcy, which led to his round-the-world lecture tour, which in turn meant leaving Susy behind, "a pauper and an exile" soon to face death.

The conscience theme is found in many of

Twain's narratives. The problem of the over-burdened conscience finds its way into *The Adventures of Tom Sawyer* (1876). Knowing that Muff Potter is innocent, Tom is harried by dreams that point to his undischarged responsibility and terrified by a storm calculated, or so it appears, to make him repent. Critics continue to debate the question of whether Tom grows in moral maturity as a result, in part, of his conscience's badgering. It is clear, however, that such punishments are suffered not only by children: Aunt Polly reproaches herself with biblical injunctions defining her "duty" to discipline Tom.

Twain's treatment of conscience in *Adventures of Huckleberry Finn* (1885) is illuminated by other works, particularly "The Facts Concerning the Recent Carnival of Crime in Connecticut" (1876). A grimly funny allegory in which the narrator murders his conscience, an alter ego embodied as a hideous dwarf, "Carnival of Crime" dramatizes two qualities of conscience experienced by Huck. For the dwarf's business is sadistically to inflict pain out of all proportion to his victim's offenses, and he punishes his victim's every act, virtuous or vicious. Nor is conscience, as Twain argues in "The Character of Man," an essay included in the *Autobiography* (1924), a God-given absolute and thus universal in its correctives. Instead, it is, as he notes in a journal entry of 7 January 1897, entirely a product of training, i.e., of the conditioning one undergoes on the strength of human association, religious instruction, and exposure to time- and space-bound custom and law.

Like the narrator of "Carnival of Crime," Huck is profoundly divided against himself, a division defined in Twain's well-known notebook entry of 23 August 1895 in terms of a morally healthy heart and a grotesquely trained conscience. The moral basis of Huck's decisions has been challenged by critics who point out that Huck resolves his conflicts not by appeal to a coherent ethical scheme but in his choice of a hedonistically comfortable course of action. There is no question, however, that Huck's conscience is an internalized creation

of his slaveholding culture and therefore condemns his loyalty to an escaped slave; and to Huck, as to Tom Sawyer in his tale, conscience is an instrument of Providence. Moreover, as Huck discovers when he hurries to the rescue of the King and Duke and arrives too late, conscience has "no sense" and attacks one for right as well as wrong conduct. It is simply "no good," he concludes, and if it were a yellow dog, he would poison it.

The theme of the burdensome conscience emerges in subsequent narratives. To Hank Morgan, a hero of *A Connecticut Yankee in King Arthur's Court* (1889), conscience is a useless and ponderous "anvil." When he learns that his friend Nikolaus is soon to die, Theodor Fischer, narrator of "The Chronicle of Young Satan" (written between 1897 and 1900), is tormented by memories of the wrongs he has done his comrade. A similar situation develops in "No. 44, The Mysterious Stranger," a product of 1902–1908; believing Forty-Four dead, August Feldner is reproached by his conscience for his failings of love and loyalty.

Pascal Covici points out that young Satan in the "Chronicle" performs an essential function of conscience in his ego-destroying criticism of the human race, which punctures the complacency of his young friends. Sholom Kahn takes a similar view of Forty-Four, whom he describes as a dramatization of the always problematic superego of Twain's fiction. Covici also suggests that Reverend Burgess symbolically functions as the communal conscience in "The Man That Corrupted Hadleyburg" (1899). Unconsciously recognizing that they deserve chastening, the Hadleyburgians embrace the ironic stranger's plan to have Burgess, the hated pariah, chair the town meeting, for they see in Burgess the one person willing and, as master of ceremonies, able to punish them.

In *What Is Man?* (1906), which was drafted in 1898, Twain elevated conscience to the status of the single driving force behind all human action. Man-the-machine, his persona argues, is set in motion by one imperative, the absolute need to gain his own self-approval, a drive that activates his various automatically functioning faculties. And Twain provides a variety of labels for this master passion, including the word *Conscience*.

His Old Man concedes that there is freedom of choice if not of will, a critical ability to ascertain the right and just. It is this perceptual capacity that Twain calls the "Moral Sense" and traces to Adam and Eve's eating of the forbidden fruit. In Twain's view, however, man's pride in the Moral Sense is unwarranted, since, as he argues in *What Is Man?*, "Chronicle of Young Satan," and *Letters from the Earth* (1962), fallen man's intellectual discrimination between right and wrong results mainly in his choice of wrong and thus places him below the animals in the chain of being. As the Old Man explains, all behavior is entirely governed by the master passion, a conscience that is indifferent to right and wrong and is itself determined by one's inborn temperament and training. Furthermore, this "Ruler" is the only "indisputable 'I'" discoverable in a person, and it is a fickle master, repeatedly changing its commands and consequently requiring endless acts of repentance from its helpless human slave.

In the notebook entry of 7 January 1897, the year that he drafted *What Is Man?*, Twain also denied that conscience is man's other self and formulated a dualism involving a waking, workaday self and an autonomous self of dreams. When he came to explore this scheme in "No. 44, The Mysterious Stranger," however, he added a third "self," resulting in a nondeterminist tripartite anatomy comprised of Waking-Self, Dream-Self, and immortal Soul. His development of this scheme in "No. 44" left room for conscience only as a property of the waking-self and a function of the mysterious stranger. More important, the narrative's ending asserts that the conscience-burdened waking-self, along with the stranger, God, and the universe, is only a dream, an illusion of the solitary soul that, like the artist, creates such phenomena out of pure thought.

Interestingly, both the conscience-driven machine of *What Is Man?* and the solitary

Cartesian thinker of "No. 44" are figures liberated from moral responsibility. It might be argued that these figures represent psychological vehicles by which the writer could deny his own guilt by regarding himself either as a mechanism operated by an absolute yet amoral force or a solipsistic fabricator of illusory dream-sins committed by a spectral self. Together they serve to establish, at any rate, that the problem of conscience obsessed Mark Twain at the end as at the beginning of his literary career, even as it comprised the thematic and dramatic center of so many of his works.

Earl F. Briden

BIBLIOGRAPHY

Brooks, Van Wyck. *The Ordeal of Mark Twain*. Rev. ed. New York: Dutton, 1933.

Clemens, Samuel L. *Letters from the Earth*. Ed. Bernard DeVoto. New York: Harper & Row, 1962.

———. *The Love Letters of Mark Twain*. Ed. Dixon Wecter. New York: Harper, 1949.

———. *Mark Twain's Autobiography*. Ed. Albert B. Paine. 2 vols. New York: Harper, 1924.

———. *Mark Twain's Mysterious Stranger Manuscripts*. Ed. William M. Gibson. Berkeley: U of California P, 1969.

———. *"What Is Man?" and Other Philosophical Writings*. Ed. Paul Baender. Berkeley: U of California P, 1973.

Covici, Pascal, Jr. *Mark Twain's Humor: The Image of a World*. Dallas: Southern Methodist UP, 1962.

DeVoto, Bernard. *Mark Twain's America*. Boston: Little, Brown, 1932.

Howells, William Dean. *My Mark Twain: Reminiscences and Criticisms*. New York: Harper, 1910.

Kahn, Sholom J. *Mark Twain's Mysterious Stranger: A Study of the Manuscript Texts*. Columbia: U of Missouri P, 1978.

Kaplan, Justin. *Mr. Clemens and Mark Twain*. New York: Simon & Schuster, 1966.

See also: Dreams; Human Nature

Coon, Ben

First mentioned by Twain in a notebook entry written in Angel's Camp, California, on or around 25 January 1865, Coon is identified only as an Illinois river pilot. He is generally acknowledged as the oral source of the "Jumping Frog" (1865) and the model for the tale's deadpan narrator, Simon Wheeler.

Coon is also apparently the narrator of an earlier sketch, "An Unbiased Criticism" (1865), although there he is called only by his last name and is identified as an "ex-corporal." An excellent discussion of this and other minor confusions that have attached to Coon's identity over the years appears in *Mark Twain's Notebooks & Journals, Volume I (1855–1873)* (21, 75). Whatever the conflations and elaborations Coon underwent in his transformation from mining camp character to fictional narrator of Twain's sketches, he is, nonetheless representative of the western vernacular storyteller whose obliviousness to the humorous implications of his own narrative prefigures the straight-faced Twain of the lecture platform as well as the inadvertent cultural critique voiced by Huckleberry Finn.

David Barrow

BIBLIOGRAPHY

Clemens, Samuel L. *Mark Twain's Notebooks & Journals, Volume I (1855–1873)*. Ed. Frederick Anderson, Michael B. Frank, and Kenneth M. Sanderson. Berkeley: U of California P, 1975.

———. "Private History of the 'Jumping Frog' Story." *North American Review* 158 (April 1894): 446–453.

Wilson, James D. *A Reader's Guide to the Short Stories of Mark Twain*. Boston: G.K. Hall, 1987.

See also: Angel's Camp, California; "Celebrated Jumping Frog of Calaveras County, The"; Vernacular; Wheeler, Simon

Cooper, James Fenimore
(1789–1851)

Mark Twain viewed James Fenimore Cooper in much the same way that he viewed Sir Walter Scott—with consistent contempt for what Twain considered the romancers' dangerously delusive myths. Whether the myth be Scott's chivalry or Cooper's noble savage,

it became a menace when people actually started to believe it.

Practically every reference to Cooper that Twain made, outside the famous lampooning critique "Fenimore Cooper's Literary Offenses," was to his Indians. Twain rarely applied the sense of cultural relativism to Native Americans that he eventually did to blacks and other ethnic groups; his experiences out West in the 1860s cemented in him a notion that Indians were an essentially deplorable and degraded race. (It never occurred to him that the United States was practicing the same kind of imperialism against the Indians that it was practicing against the Filipinos. Moreover, he championed the Boxer Rebellion in China, but he considered the Indians involved in similar uprisings as ignoble and treacherous.)

Cooper had, by his own admission, presented the beau ideal of the Indian; Twain gives us the other extreme. In 1862, in two letters to his mother written from Carson City, Nevada, Sam Clemens attempted to disillusion his mother concerning the Indians by describing their disgusting personal habits and hygiene, none of which could be found in Cooper. Then, in a letter to the *Alta* in 1867, he contrasted "the kind of Indians God made" with those that Cooper made. The latter are dead—"died with their creator." Next, in chapter 19 of *Roughing It* (1872), Twain adopted the persona of "a disciple of Cooper and a worshiper of the Red Man—even of the scholarly savages in the 'Last of the Mohicans.'" He gives up the "mellow moonshine of romance," however, when he discovers that the Goshute Indians are "treacherous, filthy and repulsive" and that all Indians are like the Goshutes. He challenged Cooper again in 1884, this time in the persona of Huck Finn in the aborted tale "Huck Finn and Tom Sawyer Among the Indians." Tom Sawyer, of course, has learned all about the noble red man from Cooper's novels, and like the narrator of *Roughing It* he is disillusioned when he and his friends become the victims of the Indians' treachery.

In every case, Mark Twain used James Fenimore Cooper as the butt of his satire debunking the romantic myth of "the noble Red Man."

Joseph Andriano

BIBLIOGRAPHY

Clemens, Samuel L. *Mark Twain's Hannibal, Huck & Tom*. Ed. Walter Blair. Berkeley: U of California P, 1969. 81–140.

———. *Mark Twain's Letters, Volume 1 (1853–1866)*. Ed. Edgar M. Branch, Michael B. Frank, and Kenneth M. Sanderson. Berkeley: U of California P, 1988.

———. *Mark Twain's Travels with Mr. Brown*. Ed. Franklin Walker and G. Ezra Dane. New York: Knopf, 1940.

———. *Roughing It*. Ed. Franklin R. Rogers and Paul Baender. Berkeley: U of California P, 1972.

Foner, Philip S. *Mark Twain: Social Critic*. New York: International Publishers, 1958.

See also: Criticism; "Fenimore Cooper's Literary Offenses"; Indians; Racial Attitudes; Sentimentality

Copyright

Mark Twain was influential in supporting the copyright legislation of 1909, a precursor of the modern law that offered greater commercial protection to American authors and publishers. Acting on his long interest in a secure copyright, Mark Twain spoke before two congressional committees considering new legislation, once in 1886, and again in 1906. The 1906 hearing paved the way for a favorable bill that became the copyright law of 1909.

Book pirating, especially by Canadian publishers, motivated Mark Twain's persistent attempts to obtain a satisfactory copyright law. During the years when piracy was widespread, 1873 until 1886, Mark Twain even traveled to Canada to protect the copyright on his books, which were often copied, then sold in the United States more cheaply than the copyrighted editions on which he received a royalty. To prevent British publishers from copying American editions of *Adventures of Huckle-berry Finn*, he first published the novel in England in 1884 to secure the copyright; in 1885 he published the book in America.

In 1887 Mark Twain took his objections to court in *Clemens v. Belford*, a case involving copyright that became legal precedent for many later opinions. A publisher had published several previously unpublished Mark Twain sketches, attributing each one to "Mark Twain," but without the author's permission. Twain contended that the use of his *nom de plume* was a copyright violation. However, the judge noted that Mark Twain had not protected the sketches with copyright; thus they were in the public domain. The use of the author's pseudonym was proper because the publisher had given Mark Twain credit. Therefore, the court ruled that the publisher had not violated the copyright law (*Clemens v. Belford*). The case was one of many in which Mark Twain and his heirs filed suit to protect his copyright (e.g., *Clemens v. Estes and Lauriat*).

The first step toward remedying the situation occurred in 1886, when a bill proposing an international copyright law was proposed in Congress in order to allow foreign authors copyright protection in the United States. In an earlier letter to William Dean Howells, Mark Twain had prepared a mock petition to Congress advocating copyright protection for foreign authors, but the petition never reached Congress. Such protection would also provide reciprocal protection to American authors publishing abroad. Mark Twain was one of several authors and publishers solicited by the American Copyright League to present their views on international copyright legislation. His short statement supported the bill in principle, but he advocated an amendment requiring foreign works to be printed in the United States as well. It was not until 1891 that Congress passed the Chace Act, which granted this international copyright protection.

Before he spoke for the last time to Congress, Mark Twain was invited to speak before a committee of the House of Lords in London in 1900. There he advocated a perpetual copyright, an old notion of his by now, which was greeted with amusement by the committee and press.

On a visit to Washington in 1906, Mark Twain was asked again to speak to a congressional committee considering the domestic copyright. His appearance, for the first time publicly in a striking white suit, was more informal as he pronounced himself satisfied with a bill extending copyright fifty years past the author's death. This final advocacy was to bear the most fruit as three years later, a similar law owes its existence to Mark Twain's efforts in lobbying presidents and Congress.

J. Mark Baggett

BIBLIOGRAPHY

Clemens, Samuel L. "Letter To William Dean Howells." 14 September 1875. *Mark Twain-Howells Letters: The Correspondence of Samuel L. Clemens and William D. Howells, 1872–1910.* By Clemens. Ed. Henry Nash Smith and William M. Gibson. Cambridge, Mass.: Harvard UP, 1960. 99–101.

———. "Unmailed letter to H.C. Christiancy, on book piracy," 18 December 1887. *The Selected Letters of Mark Twain.* By Clemens. Ed. Charles Neider. New York: Harper & Row, 1982. 173–175.

Clemens v. Belford, 14 Fed. 728 (N.D. Ill. 1883).

Clemens v. Estes & Lauriat, 22 F. 899 (C.C.D. Mass. 1885).

Paine, Albert Bigelow. *Mark Twain: A Biography.* 3 vols. New York: Harper, 1912.

United States. Senate. "Reports of Committees of the Senate of the United States for the 1st Session of the Congress, 1885–1886." Vol. 7. No. 1188. Washington, 1886, 15–16, 23–25, 48, 60, 129.

United States. Senate and House of Representatives. "Arguments before the Committees on Patents." Washington: GPO, 1906: 116–121.

See also: Canada; Howells, William Dean; Washington, D.C.

Cord, Mary Ann ("Auntie")

The cook and domestic worker for the Crane family at Quarry Farm, Mary Ann Cord is the source of "A True Story" (1874) and model for the character of Aunt Rachel. In an Au-

gust 1877 letter to Howells, Clemens describes her as "Aunty Cord, age 62, turbaned, very tall, very broad, very fine in every way." "A violent Methodist," Cord's heated discussions of religion with fellow black worker John Lewis, "an implacable Dunker-Baptist," proved a source of delight to Clemens during his visits to Quarry Farm.

Cord was born in Virginia and had twice been sold as a slave. One evening in the summer of 1874, Clemens encouraged the then sixty-year-old rotund cook to speak of her experiences before the whole family, assembled on the large front veranda of the Quarry Farm house. Auntie Cord's moving account of her tragic life as a slave, which included separation from all her children, deeply impressed Clemens—as did her poise and natural grace in telling her tale. Later in the summer Clemens reconstructed the evening's experience as "A True Story Repeated Word for Word as I Heard It," and sent the piece to Howells for publication in the *Atlantic Monthly* (4 November 1874). Although he altered the chronology of her tale to improve cogency, Twain worked diligently to capture the speech and heroic demeanor of Auntie Cord in what is a succinct and unsentimental account of black life in the antebellum South.

James D. Wilson

BIBLIOGRAPHY

Bellamy, Gladys. *Mark Twain as a Literary Artist.* Norman: U of Oklahoma P, 1950.

Clemens, Samuel L. *Mark Twain-Howells Letters: The Correspondence of Samuel L. Clemens and William D. Howells, 1872–1910.* Ed. Henry Nash Smith and William M. Gibson. Vol. 1. Cambridge, Mass.: Harvard UP, 1960.

———. *A True Story and the Recent Carnival of Crime.* Boston: James R. Osgood, 1877.

Jerome, Robert D., and Herbert A. Wisbey, Jr., eds. *Mark Twain in Elmira.* Elmira, N.Y.: Mark Twain Society, 1977.

Wilson, James D. *A Reader's Guide to the Short Stories of Mark Twain.* Boston: G.K. Hall, 1987.

Wisbey, Herbert A., Jr. "The True Story of Auntie Cord." *Mark Twain Society Bulletin* 4 (June 1981): 1, 3–4.

See also: Quarry Farm; Rachel, Aunt; Racial Attitudes; "True Story, A"

"Corn-Pone Opinions"
(1923)

The short essay "Corn-Pone Opinions" was written in 1901; its publication came in 1923 in Mark Twain's *Europe and Elsewhere*. The definitive text is in *"What Is Man?" and Other Philosophical Writings* (1973), edited by Paul Baender.

The essay deals with social conformity. Twain asserts that the more negative disposition of the human race to imitate others, mindlessly, consistently overrides humans' ability to reason. He employs various effective literary devices to disarm rather than disassociate the reader.

These devices include the repetition of certain images and irony. The humorous first boyhood lesson in social conformity described ("It was deeply impressed upon me. By my mother. Not upon my memory, but elsewhere.") contrasts with the jaded pessimism of the closing remarks about the same lesson learned. The character "Jerry" and his message also provided an interesting parallel to the author, a less serious depiction that lowers the guard of the reader against its more "legitimate" repetition in the person of Twain and his message. Perhaps it is for these reasons that this opening anecdote exists, for it never becomes a framing tale, although it does provide a source of irony by creating a "catch-22" situation for Twain. He depicts himself as a captive audience to Jerry, his "original" lecturer on conventionality ("You tell me whar a man gits his corn pone, en I'll tell you what his 'pinions is"). "I think Jerry was right," he claims. Is Twain then a conformist? If not, the essay's eventual publication is sure to propagate a whole conforming group of self-proclaimed nonconformists, seemingly qualifying or contradicting its purpose.

Twain continues, however, to strike a balance in "Corn-Pone Opinions" between completely undercutting himself and sounding overly moralistic through his control of structure and imagery. Overtly, the essay is presented as an argument, not a sermon. Rhetorical questions, elevated language, and short, clipped declarations interspersed throughout the text are part of this strategy; Twain also speaks of the problem at hand as a personal one, "ours" rather than "yours." The images Twain uses of social conformity cover the spectrum from the laughable slavishness to clothing styles ("If Eve should come again, in her ripe renown, and reintroduce her quaint styles—well, we know what would happen") to the seriousness of thoughtless commitment to political parties and causes. Interestingly, changing literary fashions lie "caught in the middle" along this continuum of importance.

"Corn-Pone Opinions" remains one of Twain's relatively neglected essays. Although its biting sarcasm may descend into that gloom so characteristic of Twain's later writing, the essay still gives ample evidence of craftsmanship coupled with common sense.

Ann M. Fox

BIBLIOGRAPHY

Clemens, Samuel L. *"What Is Man?" and Other Philosophical Writings.* Ed. Paul Baender. Berkeley: U of California P, 1973. 92–97.

See also: Europe and Elsewhere

Correspondence (Mark Twain as Letter Writer)

Mark Twain's letters have been a primary source of information about his life and career since his death in 1910. Biographers, critics, and editors of his works have made the study of his letters an indispensable part of their endeavors. And general readers, no less than these specialists, have been fascinated and delighted by the keen observation, humor, and verbal brilliance everywhere evident in them.

Some 11,500 letters by Mark Twain are known to survive. Yet this seemingly staggering figure, which is steadily growing as letters continue to be discovered, certainly represents only a small percentage of his correspondence. Extrapolating from his own estimates of his daily output, which at various times ranged between ten and thirty, and even allowing for exaggeration, it is not unlikely that he wrote at least 100,000 letters during his lifetime, and perhaps twice that many. The bulk of his surviving manuscript letters are in publicly accessible collections—most notably the Mark Twain Papers at the Bancroft Library in Berkeley, the Mark Twain Memorial and the Stowe-Day Foundation in Hartford, the Vassar College Library, the Alderman Library at the University of Virginia, the New York Public Library, the Yale University Library, the Houghton Library at Harvard, and the Huntington Library in San Marino, California. Many letters are in private hands, however, for manuscripts by Mark Twain have become prized collectibles, bringing ever escalating prices on the rare book and manuscript market. Letters are now routinely purchased by foreign collectors, reducing the likelihood that they will ever become available to students of Mark Twain. The *Union Catalog of Clemens Letters* (1986), edited by Paul Machlis, is an invaluable guide to the extant documents, giving the date, place of writing, addressee, and location of the manuscript or other most authoritative text for each letter. A similar catalogue of letters received by Clemens is now in preparation.

There have been several efforts to preserve Mark Twain's letters in printed form. Even before Twain's death, Albert Bigelow Paine, his official biographer and literary executor, began gathering the letters that he drew on extensively for *Mark Twain: A Biography* (1912) and afterward included in *Mark Twain's Letters* (1917). Although Paine implied that his edition was "reasonably complete," he in fact published only 500 letters. He silently edited many of their texts, suppressing or altering material that he believed inappropriate to the proper and purified man he wished to present. Nevertheless, his edition remains an important research tool because some of the manu-

scripts he saw have since been lost, making his flawed texts the only remaining record of those originals. Moreover, his personal association with Mark Twain furnished him with unique information that he frequently incorporated into his running commentary.

Like Paine, Samuel C. Webster, in *Mark Twain, Business Man* (1946), linked letter texts with a running commentary, in this case to build a defense of his father, Charles L. Webster, the nephew by marriage and business partner whom Clemens blamed for the failure of his publishing house. Although slanted to show the least favorable aspects of Clemens's personality and dealings, Webster's book remains a significant resource, not only for the letters it published, with tolerable accuracy, but also for its wealth of family information about the circumstances of their writing.

Subsequent editors of letters were more candid and responsible than Paine and more dispassionate than Webster. Dixon Wecter's *Love Letters of Mark Twain* (1949) and *Mark Twain to Mrs. Fairbanks* (1949) isolated Clemens's letters to two of the significant women in his life: Olivia Louise Langdon, whom he married in 1870, and Mary Mason Fairbanks, the friend and adviser he first met in 1867 on the Holy Land excursion he described in *The Innocents Abroad* (1869). Wecter did none of the deliberate bowdlerizing typical of Paine, but rather he strove for textual accuracy and, especially in the letters to Mrs. Fairbanks, moved in the direction of modern scholarly editing by selectively printing and commenting on Mark Twain's cancellations and other revisions and by providing some documentary annotation. Henry Nash Smith, William M. Gibson, and Frederick Anderson, in *Mark Twain-Howells Letters* (1960), gathered the extended literary and personal correspondence between Mark Twain and his friend and critic, William Dean Howells. This edition set a high standard of scholarship and accountability. Editorial policy regarding normalization and regularization of letter texts was clearly stated, cancellations were printed in place whenever recoverable and judged significant, a consistent effort was made to correct the dates of letters misdated by Mark Twain and to supply dates where he omitted them, and the texts were elucidated by meticulous annotation. (A selected edition of these letters was published in 1967.) This editorial methodology was carried forward in the initial two volumes of letters in the Mark Twain Papers series, *Mark Twain's Letters to His Publishers* (1967), edited by Hamlin Hill, and *Mark Twain's Correspondence with Henry Huttleston Rogers* (1969), edited by Lewis Leary. The first of these traced Mark Twain's literary career, with particular emphasis on the business aspects of that career; the second captured his relationship with Henry H. Rogers, the Standard Oil executive who rescued him from bankruptcy and became the closest friend of his later years.

These editions of Mark Twain's letters, useful and admirable in many respects, shared one limitation. Organized topically, they were necessarily partial, in both senses of the word, conveying a fragmented impression of Mark Twain's literary and nonliterary occupations and preoccupations. A reader interested in the full record of any given period had to resort to each volume in turn, at best a frustrating and uncertain process since there was no way of knowing what had *not* found a place in these individual collections. *Mark Twain's Letters, Volume 1 (1853–1866)* (1988), edited by Edgar Marquess Branch, Michael B. Frank, and Kenneth M. Sanderson, and *Volume 2 (1867–1868)* (1990), edited by Harriet Smith, Richard Bucci, and Lin Salamo, initiated a remedy for this situation. The first installments, in the Mark Twain Papers series, for a chronological edition of *all* of Mark Twain's known letters (including those that have been previously published), they were comprehensive in technique as well as content. Their texts derived from the original manuscripts whenever extant (previous scholarly editions frequently depended on photocopy), represented in place all features of the manuscripts, including cancellations and other revisions, and were accompa-

nied by a detailed record of editorial decisions and by extensive documentation that included annotation, illustrations, manuscript facsimiles, and materials such as maps and genealogies as appropriate.

That Mark Twain's letters continue to merit publication and study is beyond question. Samuel L. Clemens arguably was and remains the most important writer yet produced by the United States, an author whose significance was vast during his lifetime and is still growing more than eighty years after his death. Seen even in his own day as the representative *American*, not merely as representative American writer, this Southerner-Northerner-Westerner-Easterner embodied virtually every American impulse and was immersed in virtually every important event of his era. Rooted in the poor, rural, antebellum South, fatherless and a school dropout at the age of eleven, he became, in the course of his restless drive toward success and security an itinerant printer and newspaper contributor; a Mississippi riverboat pilot; a Confederate irregular and Confederate deserter; a gold and silver miner in the Nevada Territory; a newspaper reporter and correspondent in Nevada, San Francisco, and the Sandwich Islands; a world traveler and travel correspondent; a star on the lecture circuit; a newspaper owner and editor; the author of immensely popular short stories, novels, travel books, literary and social criticism, and a voluminous autobiography; a boom-or-bust speculator, businessman, and publisher; an inventor; a devoted husband and father; and an international celebrity whose comings and goings were regularly followed in the world press and whose opinions were sought, and often given in letters, on everything from home maintenance to capital punishment to racial injustice.

The nearly sixty years of this multifaceted and mercurial career are reflected, in intimate detail and with spontaneous wit, in Mark Twain's letters. Inasmuch as he was an unbashedly, even insistently, autobiographical writer, his letters preserve, in its most immediate, least reworked form, the raw material

188 Correspondence (Mark Twain as Letter Writer)

of much of his best literature. They therefore provide a special yardstick by which to size his imagination and take the measure of his literary achievement. And since his correspondence extended far beyond the bounds of family and personal friends to include scores of authors and editors and critics, politicians and other public figures, magnates and social reformers, as well as ordinary readers, these same letters constitute a kind of time capsule of American culture, of the historical, social, and psychological forces that shaped it in the nineteenth century and continue to shape it today. Consequently, no reading of them can be unrewarding.

Michael B. Frank

Clemens, Samuel L. *The Love Letters of Mark Twain.* Ed. Dixon Wecter. New York: Harper, 1949.

———. *Mark Twain-Howells Letters: The Correspondence of Samuel L. Clemens and William D. Howells, 1872–1910.* Ed. Henry Nash Smith and William M. Gibson. 2 vols. Cambridge, Mass.: Harvard UP, 1960.

———. *Mark Twain to Mrs. Fairbanks.* Ed. Dixon Wecter. San Marino, Calif.: Huntington Library, 1949.

———. *Mark Twain's Correspondence with Henry Huttleston Rogers, 1893–1909.* Ed. Lewis Leary. Berkeley: U of California P, 1969.

———. *Mark Twain's Letters.* Ed. Albert B. Paine. 2 vols. New York: Harper, 1917.

———. *Mark Twain's Letters, Volume 1 (1853–1866).* Ed. Edgar M. Branch, Michael B. Frank, and Kenneth M. Sanderson. Berkeley: U of California P, 1988.

———. *Mark Twain's Letters, Volume 2 (1867–1868).* Ed. Harriet Elinor Smith and Richard Bucci. Berkeley: U of California P, 1990.

———. *Mark Twain's Letters to His Publishers, 1867–1894.* Ed. Hamlin Hill. Berkeley: U of California P, 1967.

———. *Selected Mark Twain-Howells Letters, 1872–1910.* Ed. Frederick Anderson, William M. Gibson, and Henry Nash Smith. Cambridge, Mass: Harvard UP, 1967.

———. *Union Catalog of Clemens Letters.* Ed. Paul Machlis. Berkeley: U of California P, 1986.

Paine, Albert Bigelow. *Mark Twain: A Biography.* 3 vols. New York: Harper, 1912.

Webster, Samuel Charles. *Mark Twain, Business Man.* Boston: Little, Brown, 1946.

See also: Manuscript Collections; Mark Twain Papers

Cosmopolitan

In 1893, at a time when he was in desperate financial straits, Mark Twain was offered $5,000 by John Walker, editor of *Cosmopolitan* magazine, for a series of twelve stories. Clemens received $800 for the first, "The Esquimau Maiden's Romance," a satiric story of an ill-fated romance, and also published "Is He Living or Is He Dead?" about an artist who tried to inflate the value of his work by feigning death. Neither story is considered among his best.

Later, in 1899, Twain published a sketch, "At the Appetite Cure," a satiric look at diets, and, more important, he published a series of articles on Christian Science. These were more important in that they became the basis for a later full-length work and were considered by the readers of *Cosmopolitan* to have done a great deal of damage to the reputation of the Christian Science movement.

Stuart Kenny

Emerson, Everett. *The Authentic Mark Twain: A Literary Biography of Samuel L. Clemens.* Philadelphia: U of Pennsylvania P, 1984.

Wilson, James D. *A Reader's Guide to the Short Stories of Mark Twain.* Boston: G.K. Hall, 1987.

See also: Christian Science

Crane, Susan
(1836–1924)

Susan Crane was Olivia Langdon Clemens's older sister and the wife of Theodore Crane. Born in Spencer, New York, she was adopted by Jervis and Olivia Lewis Langdon as a small child, after the deaths of her parents, Elijah and Mary Dean. She was with the Langdons before their 1845 move to Elmira, New York, and the birth of their daughter, Olivia (1845–1904). The sisters had a close, loving relationship which was later shared with their husbands, Theodore Crane and Samuel Clemens. The Clemens family lived with the Cranes during the summers from 1870 to 1903 at their home, Quarry Farm, located on the outskirts of Elmira. In 1874 Crane had a study built at the farm for Twain. Located on a remote high spot overlooking beautiful scenery, the octagonal study provided Twain a comfortable, private place in which to write. Twain was stately the most productive when writing at Quarry Farm, declaring it to be "the home of Huck and Tom, because they were created there." Crane was a leader in Park Church. In 1902 she established the Quarry Farm Dairy, an experimental dairy, the first in the region to be certified for the production of germ-free milk.

Crane referred to her home as "Go As You Please Hall." She was open to new ideas and had a liberal approach to religion, always welcoming and enjoying Twain's unorthodox philosophies. The farm was suited to both work and relaxation. The front porch was a favorite place for family gatherings, where Twain often read his manuscripts aloud. Twain devised a game on the expansive front lawn to help his children learn dates in history while running to the assigned pegs. A playhouse for children, "Ellerslie," stood one hundred yards from the study. On hot nights, the family could sleep outside in a pavilion known as "the tent." Twain's favorite cat, Sour Mash, lived at Quarry Farm.

Mark Twain described the Crane home as a place where one got "a foretaste of heaven." He affectionately referred to his sister-in-law as "Saint Sue." To the Clemens family, she was a constant source of strength, security, and loving sympathy. She was present at the births of all of the Clemens children. Susy (1872), Clara (1874), and Jean (1880) were born at Quarry Farm. When Susy Clemens died (1896), her aunt was with her in Hartford. Crane went to York Harbor, Maine, to care for Livy after her 1902 heart attack. Livy recuperated the following summer at Quarry Farm. In 1905 Twain inscribed a portrait, "To Susy Crane the lady beloved—from 'the Holy Samuel.'"

Gretchen E. Sharlow

BIBLIOGRAPHY

Jerome, Robert D., and Herbert A. Wisbey, Jr., eds. *Mark Twain in Elmira.* Elmira, N.Y.: Mark Twain Society, 1977.

Paine, Albert Bigelow. *Mark Twain: A Biography.* 3 vols. New York: Harper, 1912.

See also: Crane, Theodore W.; Quarry Farm

Crane, Theodore W.
(1831–1889)

Theodore W. Crane was the husband of Olivia Clemens's older sister Susan. The Clemens family lived with the Cranes at their home, Quarry Farm, in Elmira, New York, for many summers during the 1870s and 1880s. Crane was the financial manager of the coal business J. Langdon & Company, and a leader of Park Church, which his family helped establish as an anti-slavery church in 1845.

Although the Cranes had no children of their own, Crane was devoted to his Clemens nieces, all three of whom were born at Quarry Farm. He enriched their summer home with favorite pets and games, a piano, and a fine library. His library included sets of Dickens, Shakespeare, and W.E.H. Lecky. He and Twain enjoyed one another's company especially reading and discussing literature together.

Crane was Twain's beloved brother-in-law and friend. In September 1888 he suffered a stroke followed by months of pain and then death at age fifty-eight. These events saddened Twain and influenced his writing of the final chapters of *A Connecticut Yankee in King Arthur's Court* (1889).

Gretchen E. Sharlow

BIBLIOGRAPHY

Gribben, Alan. *Mark Twain's Library: A Reconstruction.* Vol 1. Boston: G.K. Hall, 1980.

Jerome, Robert D., and Herbert A. Wisbey Jr., eds. *Mark Twain in Elmira*. Elmira, N.Y.: Mark Twain Society, 1977.

Paine, Albert Bigelow. *Mark Twain: A Biography*. 3 vols. New York: Harper, 1912.

See also: Crane, Susan; Reading

Criticism

As a public literary critic, Twain was neither prolific nor systematic; he produced no serious book reviews and relatively few extended literary essays, and in writing or speaking about his own works he was more likely to tell stories than to analyze or to explain. Much of his criticism consisted of ephemeral or private writings: newspaper articles and reviews, satires and burlesques, lectures, marginalia and notebook entries, and letters—especially in his correspondence with William Dean Howells. Some of his longer essays on literary subjects, such as "In Defense of Harriet Shelley" (1894) and *Is Shakespeare Dead?* (1909), are not really works of literary criticism at all. But the criticism that he did write was consistent with his fiction and with his theoretical stance as a realist, and his critical writings are characterized by vigorous and articulate statements of his principles and preferences.

In the only full-length study of Twain's literary criticism, Sydney J. Krause identifies two personas or masks that Twain adopted in his public writings on theater, journalism, art, and literature: the "muggins" or fool in his earlier works and the "grumbler" in his later works. In some cases, in fact, Twain seems more concerned with his masks than with his message; in the Whittier birthday speech (1877), for example, whatever criticism he may have intended of the New England literary establishment seems to be subordinated to his comic development of the miner's persona. But Krause's distinction between the two masks—and between Twain's use of masks and his more straightforward appreciative writings—obscures an essential thematic continuity in Twain's criticism. Whether disguised as muggins or grumbler or speaking in his own voice, Twain never wavered from his commitment to realism and from his rejection of any philosophical or aesthetic system that attempted to impose itself on reality.

In his literary criticism as in his criticism of society, Twain had no use for sentimentality or for artifice. Just as the sentimental piety of Sunday-school texts provoked him to burlesque in "The Story of the Bad Little Boy" (1865) and "The Story of the Good Little Boy" (1870), the sentimental extravagance of popular literature provoked him to parody: Paul Duoir's "My Kingdom," in which the poet's kingdom turns out to be his lover's heart, became "My Ranch" (1865), in which the lover is replaced by a sow; and the poetry of Julia A. Moore, the "Sweet Singer" of Michigan and author of *The Sentimental Song Book*, was transformed in *Adventures of Huckleberry Finn* (1885) into Emmeline Grangerford's maudlin "Ode to Stephen Dowling Bots, Dec'd." The English novel of sensibility elicited a similar reaction: in *Following the Equator* (1897) he compared *The Vicar of Wakefield* (1762) to Julia A. Moore's poetry and described it as having "[n]ot a sincere line in it . . . one long waste-pipe discharge of goody-goody puerilities and dreary moralities." In his notebook he dismissed Goldsmith's novel, and some of Jane Austen's as well, as "thoroughly artificial."

Twain's commitment to realism was absolute. What he demanded in literature—and in criticism—was a rigorous adherence to realism in both form and content: simple and direct language, accuracy in the choice and presentation of material, an appropriate concern for the rules of logic. As early as "Comments on English Diction" (1876), he criticized both Dickens and Sir Walter Scott for wordiness, and in the same year he satirized overblown Victorian rhetoric in the "Compositions by the Young Ladies" in *The Adventures of Tom Sawyer* (1876). In 1884 he wrote a letter to E.W. Howe praising *The Story of a Country Town* for its simple and sincere style and for the accuracy of its portrait of small-town life. And his insistence on logic is clear in his articles on Harriet Shelley and on Shakespeare: in the first essay he uses the rules of logic and evidence to defend the poet's first wife against Edward Dowden's suggestion that she was responsible for the breakup of their marriage; in the second he uses them to prove that the historical Shakespeare could not possibly have written the plays attributed to him.

These principles were inviolate to Twain, especially for the writer of fiction. The writers that he most scorned were the ones who paid insufficient attention to the requirements of realism, whether or not they had even intended to be realists. It is his Procrustean application of these principles that accounts for the venom of his attacks on his two best-known literary targets, James Fenimore Cooper and Sir Walter Scott. And, especially when their friendship disintegrated, there are the same principles that turned him against Bret Harte, whose special and unpardonable offense was violating the principles of a realism that he claimed to be defending.

Twain's assault on Cooper is typical of his inflexible enforcement of the realistic ideal. In "Fenimore Cooper's Literary Offenses" (1895) he scores critical points by applying the principles of late-nineteenth-century realism to early-nineteenth-century romance; the Leatherstocking Tales are an easy target for Twain's contempt, especially since he singles out the two most mythic and least realistic of the tales, *The Pathfinder* (1840) and *The Deerslayer* (1841), for the bulk of his sarcasm. Much of Twain's criticism of Cooper is legitimate even on Cooper's own terms, but the essay as a whole—like the additional material that Bernard DeVoto later published as "Fenimore Cooper's Further Literary Offenses" (1946)—is in many ways less useful as a critique of Cooper than as an exposition of Twain's own critical principles. Cooper's sins as a romantic novelist are sins against realism. His language is inflated and often imprecise; in "Further Offenses" Twain describes Cooper's style as "grand, awful, beautiful" and demonstrates by cutting a hundred unneces-

sary words from a 320–word paragraph. His eye for physical detail is consistently inaccurate—"He saw nearly all things as through a glass eye, darkly"—and his ear for dialect and for the rhythm of ordinary speech is equally poor. His plot inventions frequently violate the rules of nature and of logic—in the Indian raid on Tom Hutter's ark in *The Deerslayer*, for example, and in the shooting-match in *The Pathfinder*.

Much of the criticism of Scott that Twain included in *Life on the Mississippi* (1883) is in fact directed less against Scott himself than against the South for continuing to take Scott's "maudlin Middle-Age romanticism" too seriously. Twain was also capable of admiring at least some of Scott's work; in a 1903 letter to Brander Matthews he praised *Quentin Durward* (1823)—though he pretended to doubt that Scott had written it. But as early as 1876 he wondered in a letter to Howells "by what right old Walter Scott's artificialities shall continue to live," and in another letter to Matthews in 1903 he asked a series of questions about Scott that echo the "rules" that he identifies in "Fenimore Cooper's Literary Offenses." Twain's criticism of Scott's fiction in *Life on the Mississippi* is not nearly so systematic as his criticism of Cooper, but even in blaming the South he manages to blame Scott for his inflated style and his sentimentality, for his obsession "with the sillinesses and emptinesses, sham grandeurs, sham gauds, and sham chivalries of a brainless and worthless long-vanished society," and in general for the anti-realistic model that he established for southern writers. Twain explicitly contrasts the Scott-crippled southern literary establishment with the few "modern," i.e., realistic, southern writers like George Washington Cable and Joel Chandler Harris who have managed to escape the earlier writer's baleful influence.

Of the three most notable targets of Twain's critical scorn, Bret Harte is perhaps the most significant to an understanding of Twain's critical realism. He is the only one who claimed to be a realist himself and thus the only one whose work legitimately could be measured against the same standards that Twain applied to Cooper and to Scott. Twain's criticism of Harte's fiction is complicated by his personal dislike for Harte after their friendship broke up; many of his letters to Howells express his animosity, and much of the extended 1906 dictation on Harte that DeVoto first published in full in *Mark Twain in Eruption* (1940) is devoted to personal rather than literary concerns. But Twain the betrayed friend was also Twain the literary critic, and his criticism of Harte's fiction is consistent with the principles of realism that he embodied in his own work and that he expressed in his writings on Cooper, Scott, and others.

The only thing that Twain seems to have admired in Harte's fiction is his realistic description of the western landscape; on several occasions—in his dictation on Harte, in his letters to Howells, in a "Contributor's Club" essay in the *Atlantic Monthly* in June 1880—he remarked on Harte's accurate eye for scenic detail as the only good thing about his writing. At the same time, however, in his public and private writings and in his marginal comments in his copies of *The Luck of Roaring Camp and Other Sketches* (1870) and *The Twins of Table Mountain*, he criticized Harte for some of the same flaws that he attacked in Cooper and Scott. According to Twain, Harte's version of the California miners' dialect was unbelievable, as was his representation of their way of life. He saw Harte's style as mannered and artificial, and his fiction as sentimental rather than realistic; in his 1906 dictation he accused Harte of imitating his "pathetics" from Dickens and of claiming to have "mastered the art of pumping up the tear of sensibility." He was particularly irritated at the heart-of-gold stereotype that Harte had created for his gamblers, burglars, and whores.

If Harte was a realist who had betrayed realism, the writers that Twain admired were those who had kept the faith. Notable among them were Howells and Emile Zola. His last published essay in literary criticism was an appreciative article on Howells in *Harper's*

Monthly Magazine in 1906; much of it deals with Howells's nonfiction, but his general concern is with the simplicity and felicity of Howells's style and with his ability to re-create reality in his writings. Zola was at first more problematic for Twain, but in the end he helped Twain confirm his own commitment to an unflinching realism; in an essay on *La Terre* that DeVoto included in *Letters from the Earth* (1962), Twain acknowledges that his initial response to Zola's brutal naturalism was disbelief but that he has been convinced by Zola's vision of reality and has in fact integrated it into his own view of nineteenth-century America. It is reasonable to assume that Zola's pessimistic naturalism would have struck a responsive chord in Twain as he moved toward his own bitter final phase (DeVoto dates his reading of *La Terre* as 1905–1909 or slightly earlier; Krause, who sees Zola's influence in Twain's own philosophical shift, dates it as 1888), but what is most significant for Twain as a critic is that Zola's realism was so convincing to Twain that it won him over in spite of himself.

Twain was by no means a great or even an important critic, certainly not remotely comparable to his friend Howells. His criticism was limited in part because his range of reading was limited and in part because he felt unqualified to be a critic; in 1898 he confessed to Joseph Twichell that "I haven't any right to criticize books, and I don't do it except when I hate them." When he did hate books—like Goldsmith's, Austen's, Scott's, Cooper's, Dickens's, Harte's—it was because they violated his vision of literature and of the world, and the criticism that he did write, exaggerated as it may have been at times, can most usefully be read as part of his statement of that vision.

Paul Witkowsky

BIBLIOGRAPHY

Clemens, Samuel L. *Is Shakespeare Dead?* New York: Harper, 1909.

———. *Letters from the Earth*. Ed. Bernard DeVoto. New York: Harper & Row, 1962.

————. *Life on the Mississippi.* Vol. 9 of the Author's National Edition. New York: Harper, 1899.

————. *Literary Essays.* Vol. 22 of the Author's National Edition. New York: Harper, 1899.

————. *Mark Twain-Howells Letters: The Correspondence of Samuel L. Clemens and William D. Howells, 1872–1910.* Ed. Henry Nash Smith and William M. Gibson. 2 vols. Cambridge, Mass.: Harvard UP, 1960.

————. *Mark Twain in Eruption.* Ed. Bernard DeVoto. New York: Harper, 1940.

————. *Mark Twain Speaking.* Ed. Paul Fatout. Iowa City: U of Iowa P, 1976.

————. *Mark Twain's Letters.* Ed. Albert B. Paine. 2 vols. New York: Harper, 1917.

————. *"What Is Man?" and Other Philosophical Writings.* Ed. Paul Baender. Berkeley: U of California P, 1973.

Krause, Sydney J. *Mark Twain as Critic.* Baltimore: Johns Hopkins UP, 1967.

Paine, Albert Bigelow. *Mark Twain: A Biography.* 3 vols. New York: Harper, 1912.

See also: Art; Cooper, James Fenimore; "Fenimore Cooper's Literary Offenses"; Harte, Francis Bret; Realism; Scott, Walter; Sentimentality

Cromwell, Oliver
(1599–1658)

Oliver Cromwell ruled England from 1648 to 1658, a time when Puritan religious dominance was backed by military force. In the nineteenth century he was romanticized as a champion of liberty; in the twentieth he seems a prototype of modern dictators. In any event, Clemens read *Oliver Cromwell's Letters and Speeches,* and the influence on Clemens was substantial. One need only read "The Death Disk" for evidence of that.

Cromwell's family were gentry from Huntingdon. He attended Sidney-Sussex College, Cambridge, a center of Puritan ideas. In religion Cromwell was an independent (Calvinist, but rejecting Presbyterian church government in favor of independent congregations). A man of intense inner struggles, Cromwell was tormented by conscience but regarded himself as a chosen instrument of God whose victories were divine judgments.

Cromwell represented Cambridge in the Long Parliament (1640). After the outbreak of war between Parliament and King Charles I, Cromwell raised a cavalry regiment that earned the name "Ironsides." He participated in Parliament's first major victory (Marston Moor, 1644). Cromwell helped create parliament's professional New Model Army but was able to circumvent the Self-Denying Ordinance that removed members of Parliament from their commands. He was thus second in command at the decisive parliamentary victory at Naseby (1645).

After Naseby, the Long Parliament attempted to negotiate with the imprisoned king to make Presbyterianism the established religion. The king negotiated but ultimately refused to desert the Anglican Church. Cromwell and the New Model Army easily crushed the royalists in a brief second civil war (1648). This conflict convinced Cromwell that King Charles, "that man of blood," would have to be removed. Cromwell and the army, which was dominated by independents, had now quarreled with Parliament over pay, negotiation with the king, and the establishment of Presbyterianism. On 6 December 1648 the army sent Colonel Thomas Pride to arrest army opponents in Parliament. After "Pride's Purge," Cromwell and the army dominated "the Rump" as the remnant of Parliament was called. Proceeding to the king, Cromwell resolved, "We will cut off his head with the crown upon it." The Rump created a special tribunal to try the king. The king refused to recognize this wildly illegal court and was executed on 30 January 1649.

The Rump next sent Cromwell to subdue Ireland, which had been in rebellion during the civil wars. There, Cromwell and the New Model were guilty of terrible massacres at Drogheda and Wexford (1649). The lands of Irish rebels were confiscated, Catholicism was suppressed, and Protestant resettlement was encouraged.

In 1650 Cromwell was recalled to fight the Scots, who now recognized King Charles II. The New Model Army gained more apocalyptic victories, crushing the Scots in the battles of Dunbar (1650) and Worcester (1651). Scotland was annexed to England and placed under military rule.

Both sides in the civil wars had taken arms to defend their interpretation of the law and constitution. Cromwell wanted to rule legally, not as military dictator, but the laws did not support him, and since he regarded opponents as the enemies of God, he constantly reverted to rule by force.

Cromwell quarreled with the Rump and in 1653 replaced it with the "Barebones Parliament," whose radicalism led to immediate dismissal. The generals next drew up the Instrument of Government, a constitution that made Cromwell Lord Protector (1653). Cromwell attempted to live within this "commonwealth" government, but after an abortive rebellion in 1655 he resorted to direct military rule through eleven districts headed by major-generals and backed by a network of spies.

Cromwell waged successful wars against Spain and the Netherlands that made England feared throughout Europe, but the expenses led to more quarrels with the commonwealth parliaments. At home there was religious toleration for Protestants and repression for Roman Catholics and Anglicans. Puritanism suppressed theaters and popular amusements. Holidays, including Christmas, were outlawed except the dreary Puritan sabbath.

Few regretted the death of "Old Noll," as Cromwell was known, on 3 September 1658. Most were eager to restore the old constitution under Charles II, who returned in 1660. Yet, in nineteenth-century America, a Puritan heritage and hatred of monarchy and established churches made Cromwell seem a precursor of our own revolution. The English were more varied in their evaluation of Cromwell, but Mark Twain and his readers would have followed the strongly favorable views of Samuel Rawson Gardiner and other nineteenth-century "Whig" historians whose dramatic and detailed prose reinforced American predilections.

Arthur White

BIBLIOGRAPHY

Ashley, Maurice. *The Greatness of Oliver Cromwell.* New York: Macmillan, 1958.

Cromwell, Oliver. *The Writings and Speeches of Oliver Cromwell.* Ed. W.C. Abbott. 4 vols. Cambridge, Mass.: Harvard UP, 1937–1947.

Fraser, Antonia. *Cromwell, The Lord Protector.* New York: Knopf, 1973.

Gardiner, Samuel R. *History of the Commonwealth and Protectorate (1649–1660).* London: Longmans, Green, 1894–1901.

———. *The History of England from the Accession of James I to the Outbreak of Civil War (1603–1642).* 11 vols. London: Longmans, Green, 1863–1886.

———. *History of the Great Civil War (1642–1649).* 3 vols. London: Longmans, Green, 1886.

———. *Oliver Cromwell.* London: Longmans, Green, 1901.

———. *The King's War, 1641–1647.* London: William Collins, 1958.

See also: Calvinism, "Death Disk, The"

Crystal Palace Exhibition
(1853–1858)

This exhibition was located in the main hall of the Exhibition of the Industry of All Nations at New York's first world's fair. The hall was modeled after the Crystal Palace that had opened in London two years earlier. Built of cast and wrought iron and tinted glass on a cruciform floorplan with a dome at the intersection, it was located at the northern city limits between Fortieth and Forty-second Streets on Sixth Avenue. Fires occurring in 1856 and 1858 totally destroyed the building.

Alluring newspaper publicity about this exposition may have been the proximate cause of Sam Clemens's leaving Hannibal when he did. He described the Crystal Palace in a letter to his sister (3 September 1853), and in what appears to be the beginning of Clemens's "tramp journalism," he described the Crystal Palace and other New York sights in a series of letters written to his brother Orion in Hannibal for publication in the *Journal*.

Fred Weldon

BIBLIOGRAPHY

Clemens, Samuel L. *Mark Twain's Letters, Volume 1 (1853–1866)*. Ed. Edgar M. Branch, Michael B. Frank, and Kenneth M. Sanderson. Berkeley: U of California P, 1988.

Ferguson, DeLancey. *Mark Twain: Man and Legend*. Indianapolis: Bobbs-Merrill, 1943.

Long, E. Hudson. *Mark Twain Handbook*. New York: Hendricks House, 1957.

Paine, Albert Bigelow. *Mark Twain: A Biography*. 3 vols. New York: Harper, 1912.

"Cure for the Blues, A"

(1893)

"A Cure for the Blues" is Mark Twain's satiric essay discussing the obscure novella *The Enemy Conquered, or Love Triumphant* (1845) by Samuel Watson Royston. After hearing portions of the book read aloud by George Washington Cable in 1884, Twain obtained a copy of the novella through his friend Reverend Joseph Twichell and was apparently charmed by those flaws that have guaranteed its obscurity. Twain's essay first appeared in the 1893 edition of *The £1,000,000 Bank-Note and Other New Stories*, accompanied by a reprinted text of *The Enemy Conquered*, which listed the author's name as G. Ragsdale McClintock, a pseudonym that Twain apparently created to replace Royston's name (Cardwell 425–429). "A Cure for the Blues" suggests that the unintentional comic effects of Royston's *The Enemy Conquered*—its usefulness as a "cure for the blues"—derive from the author's apparent innocence of his pamphlet's complete lack of any literary merit. Quoting heavily from the pamphlet, Twain's comic satire of Royston's overblown style is itself unexceptional.

Ginger Thornton

BIBLIOGRAPHY

Cardwell, Guy A. "Mark Twain's Failures in Comedy and *The Enemy Conquered*." *Georgia Review* 13 (1959): 424–436.

Clemens, Samuel L. *A Cure for the Blues, with "The Enemy Conquered, or Love Triumphant" by G. Ragsdale McClintock*. Rutland, Vt.: Charles E. Tuttle, 1964.

See also: Criticism

"Curious Dream: Containing a Moral, A"

(1870)

Initially published in the Buffalo *Express* (30 April, 7 May 1870), then collected in *Mark Twain's Sketches, New and Old* (1875), this sketch is superficially what its title implies: a curiosity with a purpose. That purpose is to expose the woeful neglect of local cemeteries. Because it uses the dream primarily to make a point about a public issue, "A Curious Dream" has little in common with the author's later dream fiction; nevertheless, the story is not ephemeral.

"A Curious Dream" resembles "A Ghost Story" (1870) in its parody of graveyard fiction. Its ostensible focus, however, is social satire. John Baxter Copmanhurst, deceased, appears to the narrator at midnight to lament the neglect of the dead and their graves by relatives squandering their inheritances. Battered headstones, leaking plots, and rotting coffins leave the ghostly cemetery inhabitants to roam Buffalo streets at night, disconsolate over the "neglect of one's posterity." Copmanhurst's reiterated complaint—that the deceased suffer profound discomfort while their living kinfolk luxuriate with inherited money—cultivates guilt, like the later dreams of Tom and Huck. Its purpose is to encourage reform. The story literally shamed Buffalo citizens into making local improvements and inspired national reform movements (Paine 1:402).

Well-crafted entertainment, "A Curious Dream" rises above the level of ephemeral satire. Marshall sees structural and thematic echoes of Dante's *Inferno* in the dreamer's vision of the spiritual world, the appearance of a guide offering an epiphanic moral, and the dreamer's awakening from the supernatural experience chastened and wiser. In its indictment of the corpse's desire for worldly comforts as well as the narrator's sympathy for Copmanhurst's materialism, "A Curious Dream" suggests the Dantean theme that fleshly desires block spiritual insight (Marshall 41–43). Gribben offers a more biographical reading. The story reflects Mark Twain's recurring fascination with the macabre, specifically pain and horror, and with the focus on reanimated corpses testifies to his desperate attempt to confront and overcome death (Gribben 196–197).

John H. Davis

BIBLIOGRAPHY

Budd, Louis J. *Mark Twain: Social Philosopher.* Bloomington: Indiana UP, 1962.

Gribben, Alan. "Those Other Thematic Patterns in Mark Twain's Writing." *Studies in American Fiction* 13.2 (Autumn 1985): 185–200.

Marshall, W. Gerald. "Twain's 'A Curious Dream' and *The Inferno.*" *Mark Twain Journal* 21.3 (Spring 1983): 41–43.

Paine, Albert Bigelow. *Mark Twain: A Biography.* 3 vols. New York: Harper, 1912.

Wilson, James D. *A Reader's Guide to the Short Stories of Mark Twain.* Boston: G.K. Hall, 1987.

See also: Death; Dreams; Gothic

"Curious Experience, A"
(1881)

Written in the spring and published in November 1881, "A Curious Experience" appeared in *Century Magazine.* The $400 lump sum and $30 for each additional page amount to the same payment Mark Twain received for his second *Century* publication, excerpts from *Huckleberry Finn,* in December 1884. An irate nineteenth-century reader protested the story's lack of originality, claiming he had heard an army officer tell it in 1878. The story, however, makes no pretense to originality—as the narrator makes clear at the beginning and the end. Scholars generally have dismissed "ACE" as artless and inconsequential (Emerson 115; Wilson 31). As a result little attention has been given to the story's central themes: the contrast of excessive and empty imagination and the illusionary nature of truth.

"ACE" concerns deception; the story generates curiosity about Robert Wicklow's fiction-based illusions, which provide a case study of a youth's escape from reality. Melding romantic fiction with reality, seeming-spy Wicklow confounds the unsightful military brass, which is unsuccessful in its attempts to connect truth to the myriad of suggestions, details, and facts. Authorities, believing Wicklow's fantasies, conjoin his creations, substantiating "suggestions." The detail-entangled major, after saying to ignore details for gist of meaning, ironically loses the gist. References to truth/partial truth (history, "suggestive facts," rumors, lies, "nearly," "just about") coupled with evocative language play with light/knowledge motifs (Wicklow, Rayburn, Sterne [German "stern" for star], candlelight, "dim light," "pitch darkness") suggest full truth is unknowable.

This historical romance explores the conflict of dreams/reality and highlights a recurring Twainian theme—romanticism as threat to social and moral health. The major's frame narration increases suspense, arouses curiosity, and reveals his responsibility ("I steered the talk . . ." [Neider 165]) for leading us into the shadowy realm of truth/fantasy.

John H. Davis

BIBLIOGRAPHY

Clemens, Samuel L. "A Curious Experience." *The Complete Short Stories of Mark Twain.* By Clemens. Ed. Charles Neider. Garden City, N.Y.: Hanover House, 1957. 163–186.

———. *Mark Twain's Letters to His Publishers, 1867–1894.* Ed. Hamlin Hill. Berkeley: U of California P, 1967.

Emerson, Everett. *The Authentic Mark Twain: A Literary Biography of Samuel L. Clemens.* Philadelphia: U of Pennsylvania P, 1984.

Wagenknecht, Edward. *Mark Twain: The Man and His Work.* 3rd ed. Norman: U of Oklahoma P, 1967.

Wilson, James D. *A Reader's Guide to the Short Stories of Mark Twain.* Boston: G.K. Hall, 1987.

See also: Dreams

"Curious Republic of Gondour, The"
(1875)

Written in 1875, "The Curious Republic of Gondour" appeared in the *Atlantic Monthly* for October and was first collected in *The Curious Republic of Gondour and Other Whimsical Sketches* (1919).

The sketch resulted from some of the same concerns with corruption in government that had produced the humorous satire of *The Gilded Age* (1873). This time Clemens was wholly serious, however, insisting that his article appear anonymously, lest his pen name cause readers to regard the piece merely as humorous whimsy.

Stimulated by his growing conviction that governmental corruption had resulted from control of the ballot box by the ignorant and incompetent, and by his favorable impression of the British system during his several visits of 1872–1874, he embodied his proposals for reform in a Swiftian account of Gondour's solutions to its political and social problems, told from the point of view of an American traveler recently returned from that "curious republic."

To remove control of elections from "the ignorant and non-taxpaying classes" and to establish intellectual qualifications as primary, Gondour maintained its original universal suffrage but added from one to nine additional votes, depending upon the level of education reached. Additional votes could also be gained by the accumulation of property, but care was taken that the educated could always outvote the wealthy and thus protect the rights of the "great lower rank of society."

Under this system Gondour soon found that the governing power passed to those best fitted to exercise it, and further reforms followed swiftly. Candidates for government service now submitted to examinations demanding broad general knowledge as well as familiarity with the specific requirements of the position sought. In the case of civil service appointments, the examinations all but eliminated "cronyism" and nepotism.

Governmental efficiency also increased greatly since experienced minor officials and their staffs continued, even when changes in administration brought appointment of new minsters of chiefs, and salaries were high enough to remove temptations from bribery or other financial inducements.

To further insure continuity, the titular head of state (a position twice held by women) served a twenty-year term, subject, like all public officials, to impeachment and dismissal for misconduct. Most of the real power, however, lay in the hands of the ministers and the parliament.

After describing in some detail the workings and implications of the many reforms, and a conversation with one citizen about the flourishing, totally free educational system, the narrator concluded his account with the ironic observation that "the loving pride of country" exhibited by his companion—a quality long absent from his own land—was most annoying, as was the pervasive presence of patriotic music. "Therefore," he said, "I was glad to leave that country and come back to my dear native land, where one never hears that sort of music."

Though his views would change drastically during the following decade, Clemens would continue to preach the evils of an unrestricted suffrage to friends and acquaintances for the remainder of the 1870s. And his scorn would again find ironic expression in the episode written in 1876 for *Huckleberry Finn* (1885), in which the ignorant, drunken Pap Finn rails against a "govment" that would allow a "Negro"—in this case a highly educated man—to vote.

Howard G. Baetzhold

BIBLIOGRAPHY

Baetzhold, Howard G. "Mark Twain: England's Advocate." *American Literature* 28.3 (November 1956): 328–346.

———. *Mark Twain and John Bull: The British Connection.* Bloomington: Indiana UP, 1970.

Blair, Walter. *Mark Twain & Huck Finn.* Berkeley: U of California P, 1960.

Budd, Louis J. *Mark Twain: Social Philosopher.* Bloomington: Indiana UP, 1962.

Clemens, Samuel L. *The Curious Republic of Gondour and Other Whimsical Sketches.* New York: Boni and Liveright, 1919.

See also: Government; Politics

Cutter, Bloodgood Haviland
(1817–1906)

Cutter was the farmer-poet tourist on the *Quaker City* Holy Land excursion whom Mark Twain later described as the "Poet Lariat." Twenty years after the *Quaker City* voyage Bloodgood Cutter published some collected verse, *The Long Island Farmer's Poems: Lines Written on the "Quaker City" Excursion*, in a vanity press edition. Cutter billed himself on the title page as "Mark Twain's 'Lariat' [*sic*] in 'Innocents Abroad.'"

Beverly David

BIBLIOGRAPHY

Ganzel, Dewey. *Mark Twain Abroad: The Cruise of the "Quaker City."* Chicago: U of Chicago P, 1968.

Winterich, John T. "The Life and Words of Bloodgood Haviland Cutter." *Colophon,* part 2, 30 May 1930.

See also: Innocents Abroad, The; Quaker City

"Czar's Soliloquy, The"
(1905)

Mark Twain's short polemical piece "The Czar's Soliloquy" was written in response to "Bloody Sunday" in Moscow, the 22 January 1905 massacre of over 1,000 men, women, and children. It was published in the *North American Review* in March 1905.

In the piece Twain lets Czar Nicholas II indict himself with his own words as he soliloquizes before a mirror, a premise based on the fact that the Czar was known to meditate for an hour after his morning bath. The piece begins with the Czar contemplating his naked body and making a statement about the power of clothes. He goes on to muse aloud about the various atrocities he has committed on the Russian people and to wonder at what curious animals they are that they do not rise up and overthrow or assassinate him. As the piece ends, Czar Nicholas is preparing to restore his lost respect in the human race and in himself by putting on his clothes, the only symbol of his power. The entire piece is spoken from the Czar's viewpoint, but the Czar speaks many of Twain's political views: the tyranny of monarchy, the necessity and rightness of rebellion, and the cowardice of mobs. The piece is the most extended example of Twain's long history of attacks on Czarist Russia.

Generally, critics have considered the piece to be a powerful statement of political views, but a failure in an artistic sense. Hamlin Hill finds the opening clothes metaphor a tiresome repetition of Hank Morgan in *A Connecticut Yankee in King Arthur's Court* (1889) and the comments on the servility of the masses, assassination, and the training of children too cumbersome to be artful. Linking this piece with *King Leopold's Soliloquy* (1905), as most critics have done, Hill argues that in neither soliloquy does Mark Twain achieve the total suspension of disbelief necessary for full success and that both pieces expose too much anger, an anger that overwhelms the method and the expression (100). William R. Macnaughton disagrees, however, arguing that the soliloquies should be considered separately, that each contains formal as well as polemical merit. He sees in "The Czar's Soliloquy" formal control: a consistent tone, a carefully managed point of view, and a structural unity resulting from the opening and ending clothing metaphor (204–205). In either case, "The Czar's Soliloquy" does have merit as a clear statement of Mark Twain's personal dislike for

Czarist Russia and his overall support for rebellion and revolution, a lifelong support that Philip Foner outlines very well (153–163). Further, it is a clear example of the kind of polemical writing damning the human race that dominated Twain's later writings.

John Bird

BIBLIOGRAPHY

Clemens, Samuel L. *Mark Twain: Life as I Find It.* Ed. Charles Neider. New York: Harper & Row, 1977.

————. *Mark Twain on the Damned Human Race.* Ed. Janet Smith. New York: Hill and Wang, 1962.

Foner, Philip S. *Mark Twain: Social Critic.* 2nd ed. New York: International Publishers, 1966.

Hill, Hamlin. *Mark Twain: God's Fool.* New York: Harper & Row, 1973.

Macnaughton, William R. *Mark Twain's Last Years as a Writer.* Columbia: U of Missouri P, 1979.

See also: King Leopold's Soliloquy; Russia

Daggett, Rollin Mallory
(1831–1901)

Rollin Daggett was one of the colorful and versatile group of men who comprised the early staff of the newspaper *Territorial Enterprise* published in Virginia City, Nevada. Journalist, poet, politician, and author, his other distinctions included service as congressman from Nevada (1879–1881) and minister to Hawaii (1882–1885).

Twain felt comfortable enough with Daggett to banter him in print, e.g., "The Carson Fossil-Footprints" (1884). Nevertheless, by his outspoken and skillful editorial opposition to injustice and corruption, Daggett was a mentor and ally of Twain's. Daggett is credited with having provided Twain a model on how to fight vice in high places. As congressman, Daggett in 1880 supported Twain on copyright law revision. Twain later arranged for his own firm to publish Daggett's book *The Legends and Myths of Hawaii* (1888).

Daggett was a valued and influential friend to Twain for much of his life, and his high spirits, courage, and devotion to principle helped shape Twain during his formative Nevada years.

Lawrence I. Berkove

BIBLIOGRAPHY

Angel, Myron. *History of Nevada*. Oakland: Thompson and West, 1881. Rpt. Berkeley: Howell-North, 1958.

Benson, Ivan. *Mark Twain's Western Years*. Stanford, Calif.: Stanford UP, 1938.

Clemens, Samuel L. *Mark Twain of the "Enterprise": Newspaper Articles and Other Documents, 1862–1864*. Ed. Henry Nash Smith and Frederick Anderson. Berkeley: U of California P, 1957.

Goodwin, Charles C. *As I Remember Them*. Salt Lake City: Salt Lake Commercial Club, 1913.

Weisenburger, Francis Phelps. *Idol of the West: The Fabulous Career of Rollin Mallory Daggett*. Syracuse, N.Y.: Syracuse UP, 1965.

See also: Nevada; Virginia City *Territorial Enterprise*

"Damned Human Race, The"
(1962)

As a title, "The Damned Human Race" refers to five brief, more or less philosophical essays that Bernard DeVoto decided to group (*Letters from the Earth* 209–232) and name as "representative specimens" of Twain's late works. DeVoto justified this decision by mentioning that the essays form a kind of "cumulative annotation" of *What Is Man?* and *The Mysterious Stranger* (203). There is an obvious philosophical congruence with the mocking, trenchant tirades of Twain's later years.

The five essays that DeVoto assembled are "Was the World Made for Man?," "In the Animals' Court," "Zola's *La Terre*," "The Intelligence of God," and "The Lowest Animal."

"Was the World Made for Man?"

(See Baender's *What Is Man?* 101–106.) In this sarcastic essay, composed in 1903, Twain adopts a patient tone to recount how the findings of geological history can be twisted or ignored to make humans believe that all the eons of time and evolutionary development were, utterly unknowingly, leading to the creation of the proper conditions for the grotesquerie man (in the generic sense). For example, the oyster took about 19 million years to make and probably thought the entire evolutionary process was to lead to "oysters," not realizing that someday men would conclude, equally egotistically, that the world was leading up to men. Each creature, in turn, suffers life on earth and wonders, "What it was all for?," a phrase that Susy Clemens used for her philosophical musings. This essay mocks religious explanations of humankind's importance, closing with a rudely vulgar tone.

"In the Animals' Court"

This essay, probably composed in 1905, also may be found, with useful annotation, in Baender's *What Is Man?* (121–123). A court transcript presents a brief criminal charge, defense, and verdict applied to a rabbit, lion, fox, horse, wolf, sheep, and machine. The animals' natural activities are ignored. Oddly enough, the court dismisses the machine's case because the last defendant is only a machine, although the court feels fully able to judge all the others, regardless of their nature.

"Zola's *La Terre*"

Twain's book report proceeds in a concrete, sequential mental style, leading to a generalization that Americans can be despised as much as the French. Twain pretends a grudging respect for Emile Zola's realistic talents, believing that Zola's ability to awaken a sleeping disgust should merit a grudge. In this involuted way, Twain comments on human nature.

"The Intelligence of God"

Baender dates the composition of this essay in 1905 (see *What Is Man?* 107–108) and supplies an accurate text. The essay restates thoughts that appear in many of Twain's later writings, some of which are collected in *Letters from the Earth*.

"The Lowest Animal"

Baender dates the composition of this essay in 1896 and provides a much more accurate text (*What Is Man?* 81–89) than had DeVoto. Apparently DeVoto both named the section and chose wordings for his printing, although Twain's manuscript frequently had pairs of alternative word choices.

Enthusiastic students of Twain must be cautioned that "The Damned Human Race" is an editorial construct by DeVoto, not, as it appears, a consistent but elliptically jumpy argument by Twain.

Victor Doyno

BIBLIOGRAPHY

Clemens, Samuel L. *Letters from the Earth*. Ed. Bernard DeVoto. New York: Harper & Row, 1962.

——. *"What Is Man?" and Other Philosophical Writings*. Ed. Paul Baender. Berkeley: U of California P, 1973.

See also: Evolution; *Letters from the Earth;* *What Is Man?*

Dan'l, Uncle

Uncle Dan'l (dates unknown) was a middle-aged slave belonging to Sam Clemens's uncle John Quarles. Mark Twain recalled him fondly in his *Autobiography* (1924) and traced his "strong liking for his race" to his childhood visits to his uncle's farm.

Uncle Dan'l was especially popular with the children of the family for his nightly storytelling, and the adult Twain remained impressed. In an 1881 letter to Joel Chandler Harris he acknowledged Uncle Dan'l as his source for the ghost story "The Golden Arm," which he used in his platform performances; he later included it as an example of the storyteller's art in "How to Tell a Story" (1897).

Twain also drew on his uncle's slave as a character model. He first used Uncle Dan'l under his own name in chapter 3 of *The Gilded Age* (1873), in which the Hawkinses' slave mistakes an approaching steamboat for God. Later, more significantly, Uncle Dan'l became the principal model for Miss Watson's Jim in *Adventures of Huckleberry Finn* (1885) and in *Tom Sawyer Abroad* (1894).

Paul Witkowsky

BIBLIOGRAPHY

Clemens, Samuel L. *Mark Twain's Autobiography.* Ed. Albert B. Paine. 2 vols. New York: Harper, 1924.

———. *Mark Twain's Letters.* Ed. Albert B. Paine. 2 vols. New York: Harper, 1917.

Wecter, Dixon. *Sam Clemens of Hannibal.* Boston: Houghton Mifflin, 1952.

See also: Jim; Quarles Farm

"Dandy Frightening the Squatter, The"

(1852)

On 1 May 1852 Boston's *Carpet-Bag* carried a funny story entitled "The Dandy Frightening the Squatter." The story was set in Hannibal, Missouri, on the Mississippi River some thirteen years before and was signed S.L.C. The evidence leaves little doubt that the author was sixteen-year-old Samuel Langhorne Clemens, who was then working on his brother Orion's newspaper *Journal and Western Union* in Hannibal. "The Dandy" is probably the first story that Clemens ever published beyond his brother's paper. Bernard DeVoto explains the background of the two newspapers (86–91), but Franklin J. Meine deserves credit for discovering Clemens's first story (*Tall Tales* 446–448).

The story goes that when a steamboat touched at Hannibal to take on wood, a dandy, or city slicker, tried to impress the ladies with a flourish of bravado by scaring a squatter, or backwoodsman, standing on the shore. Armed with a Bowie knife and two pistols, the dandy walked up to the squatter as if he recognized him and intended to kill him, whereupon the rustic knocked the dandy into the river. The dandy was dragged out of the water in shame, but the ladies awarded the weapons to the squatter.

This scrap of frontier humor carries on the eternal conflict between the city slickers and the country hicks. The arrogant fop invades the bumpkin's turf with the intention to outwit and exploit him, but the bumpkin beats him at his own game and sends him scurrying away in humiliation. Simple honesty and justice prevail.

Frank H. Leavell

BIBLIOGRAPHY

Blair, Walter. *Native American Humor (1800–1900).* New York: American, 1973.

Clemens, Samuel L. *The Works of Mark Twain: Early Tales & Sketches, Volume 1 (1851–1864).* Ed. Edgar M. Branch and Robert H. Hirst. Berkeley: U of California P, 1979. 63–65.

DeVoto, Bernard. *Mark Twain's America.* Boston: Little, Brown, 1932.

Eby, Cecil D. "Dandy versus Squatter: An Earlier Round." *Southern Literary Journal* 20.1 (Fall 1987): 33–36.

Meine, Franklin J. *Tall Tales of the Southwest, 1830–1860.* New York: Knopf, 1946.

See also: Carpet-Bag; Southwestern Humor

Darwin, Charles
(1809–1883)

Charles Darwin was born in 1809 in Shrewsbury, England, into a family of some distinction and wealth. His father Robert Darwin (1776–1848) was a successful doctor, and his grandfather Erasmus Darwin (1731–1802), also a doctor, had made a name as an early theorist of evolution. Charles was himself an average student with no settled ambition. He first studied at Edinburgh University to become a doctor and then at Cambridge to become a clergyman. He earned a B.A., without honors, but his intention to take a pulpit was permanently sidetracked in 1831 by a serendipitous event. With little qualification beyond the recommendation of J.S. Henslow, professor of Botany at Cambridge, Darwin was appointed "naturalist" of the five-year-long British expedition setting out to explore the coasts of South America and points west on HMS *Beagle*. Not a trained scientist, young Darwin nevertheless proved to possess a tireless ambition to observe natural evidences, to record them, to take specimens, and to have an endless curiosity about those evidences expressed in experiment, speculation, and theory.

Three years after returning to England he married Emma Wedgwood, and three years after that made his final move, to a house in the village of Down in Kent, where he continued to ruminate upon the geological and biological data he had brought back from the expedition, especially from the Galapagos, where life had precisely adapted itself to the unique conditions of that isolated archipelago. It took more than two decades before, in *Origin of Species* (1859), Darwin was ready to publish his theory of evolution through natural selection and another twelve years before, in *Descent of Man* (1871), he would include man in that evolution.

Now generally accepted by scientists, the idea of natural selection was resisted in Darwin's time because its ruthlessness seemed to deny transcendental design and purpose in nature and in evolution. As such, it gave added

authority to the agnostic world view that had been opening up for more than a century under astronomers' probing into an apparently limitless sidereal universe and geologists' and paleontologists' pushing back the age of the planet, and life on it, millions upon millions of years.

Mark Twain's response to Darwin and his ideas is classic and speaks not only for his generation, in whose time those ideas emerged, but for members of succeeding generations who, nurtured in traditional creeds, later encounter Darwin. "More of a philosopher than anything," in his young daughter Susy's words, Twain was extraordinarily responsive to ideas, especially those that promised larger meanings. As a boy, he was indoctrinated in the fundamentalism of Hannibal's Presbyterian church and Old Ship of Zion Methodist Sunday school. As an ambitious young man, he launched on a program of self-education to supplement his formal schooling, which had ended when he was eleven. He read Thomas Paine's (1737–1809) *Age of Reason* (1794) and astronomies. He reinforced his reading of Charles Lyell (1797–1875) on geology with the practical geology he learned when in 1861–1862 he prospected for silver ore in Nevada. The result of his self-education initiated him into a pre-Darwinian enlightenment.

Twain was thirty-six when, on reading the just published *Descent of Man* in 1871, he first grappled with Darwin's ideas. The numerous underlinings and the earnest tone of the marginalia in his copy are quite different from the sarcasms that more often decorate the margins of books he read. He paid Darwin serious attention; nevertheless, during the next several years his public attitude toward Darwinism, if not Darwin, was humorous and condescending. From the time he briefly met "the great Darwin" in 1879, however, he spoke only in the most respectful terms of "that mighty man" and of his laboring "for the whole human race."

Twain's pessimism and determinism, which tentatively began in response to his river trip into the deep South in 1882, found more frequent expression during the next several years and in 1891 began to take on a darkly Darwinistic tone. Twain ridiculed the naiveté of people who clung to their faiths—"those old theologians never reasoned at all"—and saw men as subject to the same laws as directed animal behavior. Behind his forthright intellectual statements of Darwinism, however, was his nostalgia for his former beliefs, expressed in his returning again and again in his last years to the theme of Adam and Eve and Eden.

Sherwood Cummings and Desiree Guzetta

BIBLIOGRAPHY

Clemens, Samuel L. *Mark Twain Speaking*. Ed. Paul Fatout. Iowa City: U of Iowa P, 1976.

Colp, Ralph, Jr. "Charles Darwin: Man and Scientist." *Centennial Review* 27.2 (Spring 1983): 96–110.

Cummings, Sherwood. *Mark Twain and Science: Adventures of a Mind*. Baton Rouge: Louisiana State UP, 1988.

Gribben, Alan. *Mark Twain's Library: A Reconstruction*. 2 vols. Boston: G.K. Hall, 1980.

Poole, Stan. "In Search of the Missing Link: Mark Twain and Darwinism." *Studies in American Fiction* 13 (1985): 201–215.

See also: Determinism; Evolution; Philosophy; Science

Dauphin, Louis XVII, The
(1785–1795)

Prince Louis-Charles was the second son of Louis XVI of France and Marie Antoinette. He became dauphin, heir to the throne, at the death of his oldest brother in 1789. His life after 1789 was scarred by the terrifying events of the French Revolution.

In August 1792 he was imprisoned with his family in the Temple prison in Paris. His father was executed in January 1793. Royalists now considered the dauphin to be King Louis XVII. A few months later Louis-Charles was taken from his mother and put in the care of a shoemaker, Antoine Simon, who taught him to curse God and to sing revolutionary songs. At his mother's trial in October 1793, her prosecutors produced a document signed by the dauphin accusing Marie Antoinette of sexually abusing her son.

After both parents were guillotined, the tormented child was returned to prison, where he died of tuberculosis on 9 June 1795 at the age of ten. Because of the obscurity and secrecy surrounding his final imprisonment and death, many persons later claimed to be Louis XVII, miraculously escaped from prison. One sees Twain's interest in the story of the dauphin in such works as *The Prince and the Pauper* (1882) and *Joan of Arc* (1896), but in *Adventures of Huckleberry Finn* (1885) he "plays" the story for all it is worth.

Arthur W. White

BIBLIOGRAPHY

Castelot, André. *Louis XVII*. Paris: A. Fayard, 1960.

Hibbert, Christopher. *The Days of the French Revolution*. New York: Morrow Quill, 1981.

Schama, Simon. *Citizens: A Chronicle of the French Revolution*. New York: Knopf, 1989.

See also: Duke and the Dauphin, The; French Revolution

Dawson's Landing

Dawson's Landing is the setting of Mark Twain's novel *Pudd'nhead Wilson* (1894) and the accompanying farce "Those Extraordinary Twins," from which it developed. Like the St. Petersburg of *The Adventures of Tom Sawyer* (1876) and *Adventures of Huckleberry Finn* (1885), Dawson's Landing is modeled on Mark Twain's boyhood home, Hannibal, Missouri. J.D. Dawson was a Hannibal schoolmaster, the original of the teacher Dobbins in *Tom Sawyer*. In contrast to St. Petersburg, which is placed in Hannibal's correct geographic location—approximately 100 miles north of St. Louis—Dawson's Landing is placed roughly the same distance ("half a day's journey, per steamboat") south of St. Louis. This seemingly insignificant geographical change points to the main difference between Dawson's

Landing and the earlier versions of Mark Twain's archetypal small Mississippi River towns. Dawson's Landing is a slaveholding town, geographically on the edge of the Mississippi delta, where the fear of being sold "down the river" haunts the black characters and generates the plot of the novel when the virtually white slave girl Roxy switches her baby with the baby of her master. The leading citizens of Dawson's Landing, carrying burlesque names suggestive of British nobility ("Colonel Cecil Burleigh Essex"), are members of the F.F.V. (First Families of Virginia), further emphasizing the town's southern roots and its residents' commitment to the code of honor that led to feuds, duels, and ultimately (so Twain believed) the Civil War. The principal description of the town that opens the novel is, like the town itself, deceptive, masking these characteristics behind a facade of "whitewashed exteriors . . . almost concealed from sight" by gardens and the mythical attributes of the American small town.

Robert Sattelmeyer

BIBLIOGRAPHY

Clemens, Samuel L. *Pudd'nhead Wilson and Those Extraordinary Twins*. Ed. Sidney E. Berger. Norton crit. ed. New York: Norton, 1980.

Fiedler, Leslie. "As Free as Any Cretur." *Pudd'nhead Wilson and Those Extraordinary Twins*. By Clemens. Ed. Sidney E. Berger. Norton crit. ed. New York: Norton, 1980. 220–229.

Toles, George E. "Mark Twain and *Pudd'nhead Wilson*: A House Divided." *Novel* 16.1 (Fall 1982): 55–75.

See also: Hannibal, Missouri; *Pudd'nhead Wilson, The Tragedy of*; "Those Extraordinary Twins, The Comedy"

Day, Alice Hooker

(1847–1928)

A friend of Olivia Langdon Clemens, Alice Hooker Day was a niece of two prominent clergymen, Henry Ward Beecher and Thomas K. Beecher, and the daughter of Isabella Beecher Hooker and lawyer and real-estate developer John Hooker. As a guest visiting Jervis and Olivia Lewis Langdon, she was present at a New Year's Day 1868 reception at the elegant home in New York City of some friends of the Langdons, Thomas S. and Anna E. Berry. Clemens attended in the company of Charles Langdon in order to call on Miss Langdon, whom he had met only five days earlier. The Hookers were original residents and developers of the Nook Farm community in Hartford, Connecticut, and had become friends with the Langdons through Thomas K. Beecher, pastor of the Park Congregational Church in Elmira, New York, which the Langdons helped found. Clemens wrote to his mother and sister that at the Berrys he and Charles Langdon "sent the old folks home early, . . . and then I just staid and deviled the life out of those girls." Despite the fact that little or no alcohol was served, Clemens stayed from 11:00 A.M. to midnight, so smitten was he by Miss Langdon. Miss Hooker, whom Clemens described as a beautiful girl, appears not to have distracted his attention (*Mark Twain's Letters* 2:144–145). She may, however, be the source of the "Miss Hooker" Twain refers to in *Adventures of Huckleberry Finn* (1885), as in chapter 13 when Huck includes her in a list of persons to be rescued from the wrecked *Walter Scott*.

When Twain was invited to the Hookers's home in Hartford later in January 1868 (as he had previously been invited to visit Henry Ward Beecher), he found out that as at the Berrys, things were quite upright, so much so that Twain wrote to a friend that "I don't dare to smoke after I go to bed, and in fact I don't dare to do *anything* that's comfortable and natural" (*Mark Twain's Letters* 2:166).

In June 1869 Clemens accompanied Miss Langdon and her family to Hartford to the marriage of Alice Hooker to John Calvin Day; Olivia Langdon was one of the bridesmaids, and Henry Ward Beecher performed the ceremony. The affair was quite fashionable and expensive (Kaplan 100). After his own marriage in 1870, Clemens moved to Hartford with his wife and family, renting the Hooker house on Forest Street. He enjoyed his Nook Farm neighbors, relatives, and friends carefully chosen by Hooker, including Harriet Beecher Stowe and her sister Catherine Beecher, an educator and author. For the first time since his Hannibal boyhood Clemens felt part of a stable community, and his wife enjoyed her close contact with her friend Mrs. Day (Kaplan 140–141). After his bankruptcy in 1894, Clemens rented a house he had purchased in Hartford, in which he and his family had lived for many years, to the Days.

Jeanne Campbell Reesman

BIBLIOGRAPHY

Andrews, Kenneth R. *Nook Farm: Mark Twain's Hartford Circle.* Cambridge, Mass.: Harvard UP, 1950.

Clemens, Samuel L. *Mark Twain's Autobiography.* Ed. Albert B. Paine. 2 vols. New York: Harper, 1924.

———. *Mark Twain's Letters, Volume 2 (1867–1868).* Ed. Harriet Elinor Smith and Richard Bucci. Berkeley: U of California P, 1990.

Ferguson, DeLancey. *Mark Twain: Man and Legend.* Indianapolis: Bobbs-Merrill, 1943.

Jerome, Robert D., and Herbert A. Wisbey, Jr., eds. *Mark Twain in Elmira.* Elmira, N.Y.: Mark Twain Society, 1977.

Kaplan, Justin. *Mr. Clemens and Mark Twain.* New York: Simon & Schuster, 1966.

See also: Nook Farm

"Day at Niagara, A"

(1869)

After Samuel Clemens assumed his post as one of the newspaper's proprietors and editors in August 1869, "A Day at Niagara" was the first humorous article under Mark Twain's byline to appear in the Buffalo *Express.* It was published on 21 August, together with an accompanying "Salutory" in which Mark Twain promised his new audience, "I shall always confine myself strictly to the truth, except when it is attended with inconvenience."

"Day at Niagara" tells the story of "Mark Twain's" visit to Niagara Falls, portraying him as a chronic bad boy and the butt of his own humor. In the first of the piece's two principal parts, "Signs and Symbols," he chafes at notices around the falls that forbid exactly those kinds of behavior that appeal to him, from throwing stones over the edge to smoking. At the peak of his frustration he recalls the "honored maxim" that "all signs fail in a dry time" and takes "consolation in the flowing bowl" despite a posted prohibition on drinking. In the second part, "The Noble Red Man," he cites his lifelong romantic fascination with the American Indian as promoting several attempts on his part to strike up conversations with the "Sons of the Forest" he finds hawking souvenirs to Niagara tourists. Each of his Noble Red Men eventually reveals himself to be Irish, and finally all are sufficiently annoyed by his gibberish to break his bones and hurl him over the falls. There he encounters a Canadian coroner who is patiently willing to watch him drown in order to have his business.

To the extent that Mark Twain comes across in these initial Buffalo forays as the Rake Unreformed, he is quite differentiable from Samuel Clemens, who was trying at the time to settle down and prove himself a suitable fiancé for Olivia Langdon. To the extent that "The Noble Red Man" betrays implicit bigotry, it offers an early insight into the complex matter of Clemens's treatment of race.

Jeffrey Steinbrink

BIBLIOGRAPHY

Clemens, Samuel L. "A Day at Niagara." Buffalo *Express,* 21 August 1869.

———. "Salutory." Buffalo *Express,* 21 August 1869.

See also: Buffalo *Express*; Indians; Racial Attitudes

Deadpan

The poker-faced recital of irrelevant or non-sensical material by a narrator or speaker whose attitude suggests that valuable information is being communicated; this "deadpan" discourse, along with its opposite, the asking of an inane question as if in total seriousness, constitutes one of Mark Twain's most delicious skills. It makes possible most of the early hoaxes, which depend mainly upon verbal misguidance (such as "The Empire City Massacre" [1863]) rather than upon mistakes about reality (as in the ending of *Huckleberry Finn* [1885]).

In a tribute to one of his many mentors, Twain credits Artemus Ward (Charles Farrar Browne) with a sentence of deadpan double-talk far too long to quote here ("First Interview with Artemus Ward," written in 1870, three years after Ward's death—in *Sketches, Old and New* [1875]). Ward's presentation of nonsense hides all sense of fun: in what Twain takes to be a sincere effort to explain, Ward leans "far across the table, with determined impressiveness wrought upon his every feature, and fingers prepared to keep tally of each point enumerated."

Similarly, in *The Innocents Abroad* (1869) Twain's travelers wonder if an Egyptian mummy is dead and generally plague their guide with similarly inane questions aimed at denigrating what he shows them and thereby pushing him on to greater efforts. The one who generally asks the questions "can keep his countenance, and look more like an inspired idiot, and throw more imbecility into the tone of his voice than any man that lives." To deaden one's pan, in other words, is to counterfeit, to act a part with such consummate skill that one's real self, as revealed by one's facial and verbal mannerisms, is as if it had never been. With Twain's pen, this device of the poker table both amuses and assaults: when Twain lets readers into the joke, we smile; when Twain takes us in by the joke—when, that is, he makes us the victims of his hoax—initially we squirm. But, finally, Twain always manages to deliver rare pleasure with his two-edged sword.

Pascal Covici, Jr.

BIBLIOGRAPHY

Clemens, Samuel L. *Mark Twain in Eruption.* Ed. Bernard DeVoto. New York: Harper, 1940.

Covici, Pascal, Jr. *Mark Twain's Humor: The Image of a World.* Dallas: Southern Methodist UP, 1962.

Rogers, Franklin R. *Mark Twain's Burlesque Patterns as Seen in the Novels and Narratives, 1855–1885.* Dallas: Southern Methodist UP, 1960.

Smith, Henry Nash. *Mark Twain: The Development of a Writer.* Cambridge, Mass.: Harvard UP, 1962.

See also: Hoax; Humor

Death

Mark Twain's attitudes toward death were conditioned by his reaction to Calvinist doctrines concerning immortality; to the pervasive spiritualism of the era, with its professed triumphs of individual spirits over death and disintegration; and to Darwinian science and secular skepticism, which pointed to the randomness and finality of death. The interplay of the traditional liberal faiths and the new science reinforced Twain's fascination with death, the complex and contradictory nature of his responses, and the countertheology of his later years. A preoccupation with death was also part of the Romantic literary tradition. The newspaper exchanges that young Clemens handled were filled with tales of premature burial; western folklore reveled in the terrors of death. The three major poets of Twain's lifetime—Poe, Whitman, Dickinson—and writers like Elizabeth Stuart Phelps and Harriet Beecher Stowe played elaborate games with death, grief, and resurrection.

Personal tragedies and a sensitive nature also conditioned Twain's outlook. He seemingly inherited his mother's passion for funerals (Wecter 295), a connoisseurship evident in the description of funerals and cemeteries in the novels and travel books. As a child of four, he lost a baby sister; at seven, a ten-year-old brother and his paternal grandfather; at twelve, his father (the secret viewing of whose autopsy continued to haunt him). He witnessed the agonizing death of his younger brother Henry, following a steamboat explosion (a climactic moment in *Life on the Mississippi* [1883], chapter 20). Throughout his adult years obsessive guilt feelings over the deaths of Henry, his infant son Langdon, and his twenty-four-year-old daughter Susy haunted him.

Preoccupation with the theme of death undercuts the comedy of *The Innocents Abroad* (1869) as Twain describes churches, cemeteries, and ruins in Europe and the Holy Land. Classical and biblical sites customarily evoked a sentimental awe of death among tourists and writers; Twain makes them the source of moving prose as well as humor. The Paris city morgue fascinated him; the statue of a skinless man in a Geneva cemetery revived the boyhood trauma of seeing a corpse in his father's office. The book's first half culminates in the hilarious Christopher Columbus "Is he dead?" routine, modeled on a joke by Artemus Ward. The more somber second half, with its haunting descriptions of extinct societies and sacred monuments to death, Twain characterizes as "The Grand Holy Land Funeral Procession" (Bridgman 27).

Roughing It (1872) plays lighthearted games with death: murderous frontiersmen, the desperado Slade, skeletons on the prairie, hints of massacres and cannibalism. (Other death hoaxes, such as "The Petrified Man" [1862] and "Cannibalism in the Cars" [1868], were collected in *Sketches, New and Old* [1875].) *Roughing It* mocks Victorian funerary traditions: Scotty Briggs's colloquial ordering of Buck Fanshaw's funeral, Jim Blaine's Wheeler whose remains were interwoven in a length of carpeting, the shocking burial ceremonies of Princess Victoria. Twain's tale of surviving the snowstorm marks his first use of the "resurrection" motif. A more somber regard for death appears in his reportage of the *Hornet* disaster and his moment of terror staring into the crater of Halekala volcano.

Whether observing murder and grave robbing, contemplating suicide ("Ah, if he could only die *temporarily*"), joining the Cadets of Temperance to walk in a funeral procession, or saving his life by escaping Injun Joe's notice in the haunted house and in McDougal's cave, Tom Sawyer plays elaborate death games mingling fun, showmanship, and terror. Huck Finn, Joe Harper, and Tom are "resurrected" at their own funeral service, eliciting Twain's delighted comment that the grieving townspeople have been "sold." Tom's second "resurrection," after his presumed death in the caves, forms much of the novel's climactic ending. Nevertheless, the novel's ambience of death and Tom's brooding over his self-assumed guilt in the immolation of Muff Potter (Twain suggests that he was guilty of a similar deed in his boyhood) prefigures the darker treatment of death in subsequent works.

Adventures of Huckleberry Finn (1885) depicts a world of violence and murder—thirteen corpses! As an innocent, Huck witnesses, or appears to be complicit in, many deaths. Through many affecting scenes Huck's apparent emotional detachment from death prefigures young Satan's lack of a Moral Sense and Twain's own obsession with the meaninglessness of death. Huck is "resurrected" from his self-staged "execution" into a free and lonesome hero who watches the searchers sound for his "corpse." By not reporting the drowning thieves while aboard the *Walter Scott*, he possibly causes their deaths; by arranging the rendezvous between Sophia Grangerford and Harley Shepherdson, he triggers the blood feud in which his friend Buck dies before his eyes. Noteworthy, too, are the examples of the morbid corpse humor that always intrigued Twain: the deleted tale of Dick Albright's baby (*Life on the Mississippi*, chapter 3) and the mawkish post mortem poetry of Emmeline Grangerford.

The death-ridden tragicomedy of *A Connecticut Yankee* (1889) anticipates Twain's gloomy, often comically bitter, treatment of death in his last two decades. Hank Morgan mocks Malory's deadly jousts, kills Sir Dinadin for telling a stale joke, and watches amused as Morgan le Fay kills a page and a musician. Hank is repeatedly "resurrected": when he forecasts the solar eclipse, when bicycle-mounted knights rescue him from hanging, and in several instances of challenging the armed knights (those "white Indians") and his casual dispatching them with revolver, machine guns, and dynamite. He survives the holocaust of the Sand Belt—where 25,000 knights, "homogeneous protoplasm" whose order he is sworn to destroy, are dispassionately slaughtered and his band of boy defenders dies of miasma—only to be "resurrected," bewildered and despairing, in the nineteenth century. Twain even contemplated having Hank commit suicide at this point (*Notebooks & Journals* 3:216, 415). As savior/destroyer, Hank revels in the mass killings and superweaponry that Twain later deplored on the part of American and foreign imperialism. In moving contrast, Twain treats the deaths of the Arthurian peasantry (by imprisonment, torture, hanging, flaying alive, smallpox) with outrage, tenderness, sympathy, even a Victorian sentimentality.

In the final two decades of Twain's writings, death is often treated as a chance event in a purposeless universe or as an escape from the bitterness of existence: "the compassionate, the healer of hearts, man's only friend" (*Fables of Man* 201–202). The tone grows darker, but violence, sentimentality, resurrection games, and morbid jokes still flourish in the writings and notebooks. Twain ridiculed Victorian antinominalism, which held that suffering, empathy, and atonement assured one's salvation in a paradise premised on an idealized earthy existence. Nature, he asserted, "does not even vaguely indicate a future life" (Macnaughton 99). He also rejected history and causality in a world in which the individual life or death seemed not to matter. Thus, the character of young Satan, like a capricious and unfeeling God, makes and unmakes human beings and destroys and resurrects himself. In a notable trope (developed in "No. 44, The Mysterious Stranger," "The Great Dark," and elsewhere) life and death are movingly imagined as a dream that shades off into nightmare. Still, a glimmer of traditional hope remains. Twain describes death as a boon "that steeps in dreamless and enduring sleep the pains that persecute the body, and the shame and grief that eat the mind and heart" ("Five

Boons" 222). And on his wife's tomb he inscribed, "*Gott sei dir gnädig, mein' Wonne.*"

Harold Aspiz

BIBLIOGRAPHY

Bridgman, Richard. *Traveling in Mark Twain.* Berkeley: U of California P, 1987.

Clemens, Samuel L. "The Five Boons of Life." *The $30,000 Bequest and Other Stories.* By Clemens. New York: Harper, 1906. 218–223.

———. *Mark Twain's Fables of Man.* Ed. John S. Tuckey. Berkeley: U of California P, 1972.

———. *Mark Twain's Notebooks & Journals, Volume III (1883–1891).* Ed. Robert Pack Browning, Michael B. Frank, and Lin Salamo. Berkeley: U of California P, 1979.

Macnaughton, William R. *Mark Twain's Last Years as a Writer.* Columbia: U of Missouri P, 1979.

Pettit, Arthur G. *Mark Twain and the South.* Lexington: UP of Kentucky, 1974.

Robinson, Forrest G. *In Bad Faith: The Dynamics of Deception in Mark Twain's America.* Cambridge, Mass: Harvard UP, 1986.

St. Armand, Barton Levi. *Emily Dickinson and Her Culture: The Soul's Society.* New York: Cambridge UP, 1984.

Sanborn, Margaret. *Mark Twain: The Bachelor Years.* New York: Doubleday, 1990.

Wecter, Dixon. *Sam Clemens of Hannibal.* Boston: Houghton Mifflin, 1952.

See also: Calvinism; Dreams; Gothic; Religion

"Death Disk, The"
(1901)

This story is based on an incident in *Oliver Cromwell's Letters and Speeches*, which Clemens discovered in 1883. In December of that year he wrote to Howells, describing a play he intended to make of the incident. However, the material became a short story, which Clemens composed in London in October 1899 and published in *Harper's Monthly Magazine* in December 1901. It was collected in *A Double-Barreled Detective Story* (1902) and in *My Debut as a Literary Person* (1903).

The story retains the dramatic structure of its planned original version and may be envisioned in three scenes: Abbey's home, Oliver Cromwell's headquarters in the tower of London, and another room in the tower. In the first, Abbey's parents conceal from her that her father, one of Cromwell's colonels, is to be executed, with two others, for exceeding their orders in a battle (though victorious); in the second, Cromwell decides that only one of the colonels will be chosen by lot to be executed. The lot will be chosen by the first child passing by. The child, naturally, is Abbey, who naively charms Cromwell and receives from him a promise of obedience. In the third scene, Abbey gives the fatal lot, the death disk (which is the prettiest), to her own father. With everyone weeping, including Cromwell, the Lord Protector is reminded of his promise to obey Abbey, and the prisoner is released unharmed.

The story expresses Clemens's grief for his lost daughter Susy and helps us to understand his affection for other little girls in his old age, including the Angel Fish Club of adoring Susy substitutes. Nonetheless, most present-day readers find the story unbearably sentimental. James Cox calls it frankly nauseating. In its own time, however, the story was admired: probably no fact more clearly indicates the difference between turn-of-the century tastes and our own. Upon Clemens's death one eulogy singled out "Death Disk" as the highest of his achievements.

Charles L. Crow

BIBLIOGRAPHY

Baetzhold, Howard G. *Mark Twain and John Bull: The British Connection.* Bloomington: Indiana UP, 1970.

Cox, James M. *Mark Twain: The Fate of Humor.* Princeton, N.J.: Princeton UP, 1966.

Wilson, James D. *A Reader's Guide to the Short Stories of Mark Twain.* Boston: G.K. Hall, 1987.

See also: Cromwell, Oliver; Sentimentality

"Defense of General Funston, A"

(1902)

This article by Mark Twain concerns General Frederick Funston's capture of the Filipino independence leader Emilio Aguinaldo on 23 March 1901. That capture essentially ended the two-year war during which the United States wrested control of the Philippines from its inhabitants after having nominally gotten the colony from Spain in the December 1898 Treaty of Paris concluding the Spanish-American War. The article appeared in the May 1902 issue of the *North American Review*, more than a year after the capture but responding more immediately to a bragging speech by Funston at the Lotus Club on 8 March 1902.

In the article Twain is extremely bitter about Funston's method. After having intercepted a request by Aguinaldo for reinforcements, Funston disguised some Macabebe Filipinos as the relief force and himself and four other Americans as their prisoners. When they safely reached the hideout, they opened fire on Aguinaldo's men. Twain especially condemned the fact that the starving Funston had accepted food from Aguinaldo while en route.

Twain's "defense" of Funston is that he was not really responsible for his actions because they were determined by his inborn disposition and training. This defense may be read ironically, as Philip Foner insists (378), but the irony is strained because Twain here uses the same deterministic philosophy presented quite seriously in his *What Is Man?* (1906). Thus it seems more accurate to read the article as an instance where Twain's deepening pessimism began to undercut his anti-imperialism.

Hunt Hawkins

BIBLIOGRAPHY

Bain, David H. *Sitting in Darkness: Americans in the Philippines.* Boston: Houghton Mifflin, 1984.

Budd, Louis J. *Mark Twain: Social Philosopher.* Bloomington: Indiana UP, 1962.

Foner, Philip S. *Mark Twain: Social Critic.* New York: International Publishers, 1958.

Wildman, Edwin. *Aguinaldo: A Narrative of Filipino Ambitions.* Boston: Lothrop, 1901.

See also: Imperialism; Spanish–American War

De Quille, Dan
(1829–1898)

In his time, Dan De Quille was the most popular writer in the Comstock Lode region after gold was discovered in 1859. He was a nationally known author, journalist, and humorist. A year after De Quille began reporting for the Virginia City *Territorial Enterprise* in 1861, Mark Twain joined the paper and the two men became fast friends and roommates as well as colleagues. The slightly older and more experienced De Quille served as a friendly mentor to Twain, but Twain developed so rapidly that influence soon flowed in both directions. Despite the relative brevity of their personal contact (1862–1864, 1875), their association was so intense that evidence of their mutual influence continued to appear in their respective works until the 1890s.

Born William Wright on a farm near Fredericktown, Ohio, De Quille moved with his family in 1847 to another farm near West Liberty, Iowa. He married in 1853 but left behind his wife and three surviving children in 1857 to seek his fortune in the West as a prospector. He discovered in four years that he was more successful as a writer than a miner and spent the next thirty-six years in the West, mostly in Virginia City, pursuing overlapping but separate literary and journalistic careers.

De Quille came to know his part of the Old West probably more thoroughly than any other author, and Twain learned much from him. De Quille was also one of the great masters of the hoax, which he and Twain practiced imaginatively and wittily in pretended rivalry with each other in the *Territorial Enterprise.* Twain's "The Petrified Man" (1862) must have inspired De Quille's "The Silver Man" (1865), a more scientifically elaborate hoax.

And De Quille's "The Fighting Horse of the Stanislaus" (1874) has some striking, although probably coincidental, resemblances to "The Celebrated Jumping Frog of Calaveras County" (1865).

In 1861 De Quille wrote a series of articles for the *Golden Era* and the Cedar Falls *Gazette* (Indiana) entitled "Washoe Rambles," reporting his travels through the mining areas of western Nevada. Some of these articles were later incorporated into his most well-known work, *The Big Bonanza* (1876), the classic contemporary account of the Comstock Lode. This material was largely factual, but it was embellished by some humorous fictional episodes. Twain very likely drew ideas from the original series for *Roughing It* (1872) and almost certainly adapted some of its episodes for *Huckleberry Finn* (1885).

De Quille in January 1875 published "Pilot Wylie," a fictionalized sketch based on Twain's piloting days that preceded by five months Twain's use of the same material in the June 1875 installment of "Old Times on the Mississippi," serialized in the *Atlantic Monthly.* It is possible that Twain read the sketch before he completed the June piece. Twain's article on "Mental Telegraphy" in *Harper's Magazine* (December 1891) was based in part on a true event in 1875 when he and De Quille shared a telepathic experience. Again, De Quille in a newspaper column of January 1889 preceded Twain in reporting this incident.

Informative memoirs and anecdotes of Twain occur in De Quille's columns throughout his entire newspaper career. Occasionally, De Quille attempted to imitate Twain in some of his fictional and humorous sketches, but he eventually established his own literary voice and wrote some noteworthy fiction. De Quille is one of the most important of that circle of writers who helped create the literary environment that nurtured and shaped Twain in his western years and started him on his career.

Lawrence I. Berkove

BIBLIOGRAPHY

Berkove, Lawrence I. "Dan De Quille and 'Old Times on the Mississippi' [Includes 'Pilot Wylie']." *Mark Twain Journal* 24.2 (Fall 1986): 28–35.

Branch, Edgar M. *The Literary Apprenticeship of Mark Twain.* Urbana: U of Illinois P, 1950.

Clemens, Samuel L. *Mark Twain of the "Enterprise": Newspaper Articles and Other Documents, 1862–1864.* Ed. Henry Nash Smith and Frederick Anderson. Berkeley: U of California P, 1957.

De Quille, Dan. *The Big Bonanza.* Ed. Oscar Lewis. New York: Crowell, 1947.

———. *Dan De Quille of the Big Bonanza.* Ed. James J. Rawls. San Francisco: Book Club of California, 1980.

———. *Dives and Lazarus.* Ed. Lawrence I. Berkove. Ann Arbor, Mich.: Ardis, 1988.

———. *The Fighting Horse of the Stanislaus: Stories and Essays by Dan De Quille.* Ed. Lawrence I. Berkove. Iowa City: U of Iowa P, 1990.

———. *Washoe Rambles.* Ed. Richard E. Lingenfelter. Los Angeles: Westernlore, 1963.

Lewis, Oscar, ed. *The Life and Times of the Virginia City Territorial Enterprise.* Ashland, Oreg.: Lewis Osborne, 1971.

Loomis, C. Grant. "The Tall Tales of Dan De Quille." *California Folklore Quarterly* 5 (January 1946): 26–71.

See also: Hoax; Literary Comedians; Nevada; Virginia City *Territorial Enterprise*

Derby, George H.
(1823–1861)

One of the earliest literary comedians, George Horatio Derby wrote under two main pseudonyms, John Phoenix and (John P.) Squibob. Derby's satiric essays and sketches were collected in *Phoenixiana* (1856) and *The Squibob Papers* (1859).

Born in Dedham, Massachusetts, son of John Barton and Mary (Townsend) Derby, Derby graduated from West Point in 1846 and remained in the U.S. Army thereafter, serving primarily in the topographical engineers. He was cited for gallantry in the Mexican-American War. Derby married Mary Ann Coons of St. Louis in the early 1850s.

Derby began contributing humorous sketches to area newspapers and magazines in 1850 while surveying for the corps of engineers in California. His specialty was inane burlesques and nonsense humor covering a wide range of topics from scientists and technology to language study, music, and literature. He was undoubtedly the most brilliant of the literary comedians and made numerous allusions in his works to his many fields of learning. The tone of his essays is good-natured, lacking Twain's venom. Derby's techniques, many of which influenced Twain, included the deadpan telling of humorous incidents, the use of irreverence and exaggeration, witty aphorisms, playful irony, puns, and other verbal tricks. Absurdity reigns supreme in his writings.

Derby's short career bloomed so early that he influenced almost all the literary comedians to follow, including mainstay Artemus Ward. Derby's humor can be read appreciatively by a modern audience. His satire and irony offer a commingling of exaggerated humor of the West with the urbane wit of the neoclassical period. His often nonsensical humor has been echoed in such twentieth-century publications as the *New Yorker*.

David B. Kesterson

BIBLIOGRAPHY

Bellamy, Gladys Carmen. "Mark Twain's Indebtedness to John Phoenix." *American Literature* 13 (1941): 29–43.

Stewart, George R. *John Phoenix Esq., The Veritable Squibob: A Life of Captain George H. Derby, U.S.A.* New York: Holt, 1937.

See also: Literary Comedians

Detective Fiction

Much of Mark Twain's detective fiction consists of conscious, and perhaps overwrought, parody or burlesque of the genre. "What a curious thing a 'detective' story is," Twain confessed in 1896, "And was there ever one that the author needn't be ashamed of, except

[Poe's] 'Murders in the Rue Morgue'" (Rogers, *Simon Wheeler* xii). His unproduced play *Cap'n Simon Wheeler, the Amateur Detective* (written 1877) and the aborted novelistic adaptation *Simon Wheeler, Detective* (written 1877–1898), his novellas *Tom Sawyer, Detective* (1896) and *Tom Sawyer's Conspiracy* (written 1897–1900), and his short stories "The Stolen White Elephant" (1882) and "A Double-Barreled Detective Story" (1902) parody the formula writing characteristic of the genre and in doing so satirize the sentimentality and romantic expectations of readers of detective fiction generally. Burlesque is the prevalent mode of these farcical pieces that expose the absurdity of detectives and their methods—both actual, historical ones, such as Allan Pinkerton and his agency, and fictional ones, such as Arthur Conan Doyle's Sherlock Holmes. Twain's spoof of English detective fiction in particular mirrors his more general dismissal of European manners, artifacts, and culture. Detective elements, however, play a major role in some of Twain's more serious and accomplished fiction as well. *Pudd'nhead Wilson* (1894), *Personal Recollections of Joan of Arc* (1896), "The Man That Corrupted Hadleyburg" (1899), and "The Chronicle of Young Satan" version of *The Mysterious Stranger Manuscripts* (1969) all involve crime detection and/or dramatic courtroom scenes. The prominent role of trial scenes and public revelations of guilt in Twain's late fiction substantiates Howard Baetzhold's claim that the author looked on detectives and detective methods with mixed emotions (*John Bull* 298).

Mark Twain wrote "The Stolen White Elephant" in November or December 1878, less than a year after his aesthetically unsuccessful attempts with Simon Wheeler in the detective role. Inspired by a newspaper account of a bizarre grave robbery in which a corpse was stolen from a family crypt and the almost farcical attempts of New York detectives to locate the missing cadaver, "SWE" is a burlesque tale of a former Indian civil servant charged with the responsibility of pre-

senting a royal gift—a white elephant—from the King of Siam to the Queen of England. Unfortunately, the elephant is stolen in Jersey City, and the "celebrated Inspector Blunt" assumes the tasks of solving the crime and locating the hardly inconspicuous cargo. Humor results from the absurd situation and deadpan narration; neither the Indian narrator nor Inspector Blunt sees anything unusual about the case. To Mark Twain, the detectives' theories, methods, and actions in this farce are no more absurd than those of their real life counterparts. The claims of infallibility of the Pinkerton Agency Mark Twain thought ridiculous, and both "SWE" and the earlier Simon Wheeler pieces lampoon detectives' pretensions to certainty (Baldanza 100). In an expression, these first pieces of detective fiction burlesque "the spectacular detective."

"A Double-Barreled Detective Story" is a literary parody inspired primarily by Arthur Conan Doyle's very popular *A Study in Scarlet* (1887), which Joseph Twichell had lent Clemens to read. James D. Wilson points out that both the Doyle novel and Twain's parody are "double-barreled," although the barrels are reversed in the two stories both in structure and theme (56). In the first half of his story Twain parodies melodrama while in the second half he lampoons detective fiction. Where nothing is superfluous in Doyle's carefully constructed novel, everything is a series of accidents in Twain's parody. Though impressed with Doyle's writing and fascinated by detectives and courtroom drama, Clemens was suspicious of the fictional detective's arrogant claim that he could solve any mystery and was critical of his methods. William Macnaughton believes that "A Double-Barreled Detective Story" is one of the worst examples of Mark Twain's fiction because it lacks subtlety (169). Wilson, however, points out that the story is structured like *Pudd'nhead Wilson* in that it blends, in admittedly burlesque fashion, two contradictory genres—a dark revenge tragedy and a parody of Sherlock Holmes (56), whose "spectacular" detective skills are throughout exaggerated and parodied and who, at the end, is hanged. Wells-Fargo Ferguson describes the event: "They hung him in San Bernardino last week, whilst he was searching around after you [Fetlock Jones]. Mistook him for another man. They're sorry, but they can't help it now" (Neider 464).

"A Double-Barreled Detective Story" appeared initially in two installments in *Harper's Monthly Magazine* in 1902; when later that year Harper and Brothers published the story in book form, Clemens published in the midst of his story a number of letters from puzzled readers of the magazine who inquired about his reference to a "solitary esophagus" in the passage that opens chapter four. Clemens responds to these letters, explaining that there is nothing unusual about the reference to the "solitary esophagus" since the entire passage is nonsense and written as a burlesque. The reference reinforces the story's conscious attempt at literary parody, for as numerous critics have noted, the "esophagus" passage parallels Doyle's description in *A Study in Scarlet* of Utah's "great alkali plain," parallels that include not only language and visual imagery but also style, plot, and characterization (Kraus 12; Baetzhold, *John Bull* 299–304; Ritunnano 10–14; Wilson 54). Rogers points out that the use of inappropriate technical terms or foreign expressions is a common device of literary parody and suggests a source for the "esophagus" in Charles Henry Webb's burlesque *St. Tivel'mo* (1867), which refers to "chirurgeons who have passed beyond the stormy esophagus of science" (*Satires & Burlesques* 24).

Mark Twain was greatly influenced by Arthur Conan Doyle, whose work he both glamorized and satirized. What Twain targeted especially in his parodies of detective fiction were the melodrama, the formulaic writing, the implausibility, the sentimentality, and the superhuman abilities of the detectives themselves, who tended to rely inflexibly on their scientific methods of investigation even in situations where these methods were patently absurd. Doyle's success, however, highlighted

the dramatic power of detective quests and public revelations of guilt, and in the last fifteen years of his career Mark Twain incorporated these elements into his best work. Most notable in this context is *Pudd'nhead Wilson*, a novel that grew out of the original farce "Those Extraordinary Twins" (1894) but which emerges as a provocative and tragic study of racial identity, guilt, and communal moral responsibility. The detective, David Wilson, uses the then novel science of fingerprinting to unravel a crime and establish identity only to leave unsettled the more serious questions of environmental determinism, moral responsibility, and social justice.

Don L. F. Nilsen

BIBLIOGRAPHY

Baetzhold, Howard G. *Mark Twain and John Bull: The British Connection.* Bloomington: Indiana UP, 1970.

———. "Of Detectives and Their Derring-Do: The Genesis of Mark Twain's 'The Stolen White Elephant.'" *Studies in American Humor* 2.3 (January 1976): 183–195.

Baldanza, Frank. *Mark Twain: An Introduction and Interpretation.* New York: Barnes & Noble, 1961.

Clemens, Samuel L. "A Double-Barreled Detective Story." *The Complete Short Stories of Mark Twain.* By Clemens. Ed. Charles Neider. Garden City, N.Y.: Hanover House, 1957. 423–469.

———. *Mark Twain's Satires & Burlesques.* Ed. Franklin R. Rogers. Berkeley: U of California P, 1967.

———. *Pudd'nhead Wilson and Those Extraordinary Twins.* Ed. Sidney E. Berger. Norton crit. ed. New York: Norton, 1980.

———. *Simon Wheeler, Detective.* Ed. Franklin R. Rogers. New York: New York Public Library, 1963.

———. *The Stolen White Elephant, Etc.* Boston: James R. Osgood, 1882.

Kraus, W. Keith. "Mark Twain's 'A Double-Barreled Detective Story': A Source for the Solitary Oesophagus." *Mark Twain Journal* 16.3 (Summer 1972): 10–12.

Macnaughton, William R. *Mark Twain's Last Years as a Writer.* Columbia: U of Missouri P, 1979.

Ritunnano, Jeanne. "Mark Twain vs. Arthur Conan Doyle on Detective Fiction." *Mark Twain Journal* 16.1 (Winter 1971–1972): 10–14.

Wilson, James D. *A Reader's Guide to the Short Stories of Mark Twain.* Boston: G.K. Hall, 1987.

See also: Burlesque; *Cap'n Simon Wheeler, the Amateur Detective*; "Double-Barreled Detective Story, A"; Doyle, Arthur Conan; "Stolen White Elephant, The"

Determinism

The concept (which here is to be considered as a conclusion of nineteenth-century scientific materialism and to be distinguished from related notions of Providence, design, fatalism, or even the comprehensive "preforeordestination") probably entered actively into Twain's thinking sometime in the late 1870s or early 1880s. It had settled sufficiently into an utterable personal conviction by 19 February 1883, if not before, when he announced to the Monday Evening Club that man is "merely a machine automatically functioning" and that he gets all his inspiration from the "outside." From that point on, some form of Twain's "gospel" entered, one way or another, into virtually everything he wrote. It is present, for example, in his contemplation of the effects of training and inheritance in *A Connecticut Yankee in King Arthur's Court* (1889), *Pudd'nhead Wilson* (1894), and *The Mysterious Stranger* (1916). It enters negatively into Twain's lament in *Life on the Mississippi* (1883) that in childhood the events of life were "not the natural and logical results of great general laws, but of special orders"; didactically in *Huckleberry Finn* (1885) when Jim explains that the behavior of Solomon is due to the way he was "raised"; and autobiographically in "The Turning Point of My Life" (1910) when Twain elaborates on the links in his "life-chain" and concludes that he is in the literary profession because he had measles when he was twelve years old. It has the force of moral parable in "The Man That Corrupted Hadleyburg" (1899), and it is expressed rather grandly by "Mark Twain" (as the heretical Bishop of New Jersey of a thousand years past) in "The Secret History of Eddypus" (1972): "Evolution is a blind giant who rolls a snowball down a hill. The ball is made of flakes—*circumstances*." But Twain's determinism is most conspicuously and deliberately rendered in his dialogue between an Old Man and a Young Man in *What Is Man?* (1906). There, through the voice of the Old Man, Twain sets forth his major deterministic ideas: that thought is merely the mechanical putting together of sense impressions, that animals too have the reasoning faculty, that our capacity differs from theirs only in degree, that we are ruled by an interior master or conscience who commands us to gratify it, that all our ideas are attributable to heredity and temperament or to environment and training, that no one—not even a Shakespeare or an Edison—has the capacity to originate anything, and that instinct is merely petrified thought passed on from generation to generation as inherited habit. These are the most salient features of Twain's determinism.

The sum and substance of Twain's thoughts on determinism are nicely captured in a syllogism supplied by Sherwood Cummings: major premise—the universe is governed by an immutable system of laws; minor premise—the human animal is as much a part of nature as any other species; conclusion—human beings are likewise governed, in every particular of their being, by natural law. As Cummings also points out, Twain was never so unwavering or, for that matter, so logical in the expression of his gospel. Incompatibilities, contradictions, paradoxes, and inconsistencies are as pervasive in his thinking as is his insistence that man is a machine and that "Training is everything." Twain's thoughts on determinism may or may not attain to a full-fledged, fully articulated philosophical position of some interest. Certainly their author thought they did, and that was how Paul Carus, the editor of the respected philosophical journal *The Monist*, treated *What Is Man?* in 1913. Carus found that the document agreed with the "facts" of science and psychology and that Twain's argument is quite sound. He did note a "peculiarity" in Twain's reasoning, however. Mark Twain appears to believe that the mind is somehow separable from its mechanical operations. And John Tuckey focused on this same point in his "Mark Twain's Dialogue," noting that in his later writings Twain displays a resistance to his own deterministic bias disclosed by the retention of the "me" as an entity apart from and strangely independent of the machinery that is man. So tenacious is that desire that "The Mysterious Stranger," which early displays typical deterministic elements, abandons that position for the concluding affirmation of the "I" (albeit a solipsistic one), a "vagrant thought" that is "wandering among the empty eternities."

This inconsistency in Twain's position, along with others, may be taken in several ways: that Twain is a sloppy thinker, an amateur philosopher who is not apt to detect the logical contradictions inherent in his reasoning; or, more generously, that Twain is an earnest "Truth-Seeker" like the Old Man in *What Is Man?* but unlike him, never completely convinced by the philosophy he recommends and therefore relentlessly testing his own convictions against alternative possibilities and searching for some ground of faith; or, finally, that Twain had other motives, probably unknown to himself, that led him to his gospel and that a desire for self-absolution, not logical rigor, charted the course of his speculations. There has been at least as much interest in Twain's motivation for adopting a deterministic philosophy as in the content of the philosophy itself.

Critics such as Carl Van Doren, Edward Wagenknecht, and Bernard DeVoto have found in Twain's embrace of determinism the attempt to create an antidote to the claims of his own troubled conscience. If one's life is entirely the result of external circumstance, then one cannot be held accountable for cowardice, cruelty, or failure; one may as well blame a sewing machine for poor stitches or a typewriter for bad writing. This was a supremely rationalized way of keeping clean and blameless. Alexander E. Jones and, more recently, William R. Macnaughton have argued that Twain had a literary as well as a personal motive for advocating his determinism, that he wished to puncture the pretensions of an overprideful human race. *What Is Man?*, especially, attacks smugness and self-satisfaction and does so by revealing that virtue and heroism can no way attach to a creature whose acts are engendered by circumstance and training. These two points of view are not contradictory, of course; nothing is quite so prideful as a guilty conscience.

Every village must have its atheist, and to some extent Twain plays that role in his later years—nay-sayer, gadfly, cynic. His heretical philosophy of determinism probably owes its origins to a double allegiance—first, to sincere conviction, however modified by personal motive and, second, to its capacity to scandalize and to rupture provincial self-satisfaction and to challenge national pieties. Regardless, Twain's gospel, his own comments notwithstanding, was neither so iconoclastic nor so outrageous as he liked to believe, and its tent meetings were pitched on solid and august footings. Twain may have believed that he scandalized his Hartford neighbors when he gave his talk "What Is Happiness?" and he thought *What Is Man?* so heretical that he published it anonymously and even refused to have the copyright in his own name. But the intellectual ground he meant to occupy was familiar and respectable enough, and Paul Baender has shown that when the authorship of *What Is Man?* became generally known, few indeed experienced the shock or the intellectual enlightenment intended. Still, to the extent that it provided him with a literary point of view and convinced him that he had something to say, Twain's determinism contributed something to his literary productivity in his later years. We have come to recognize in Mark Twain's late writings an imaginative flexibility and a formal variety that are never so mechanical as the philosophy he would have us adopt.

Tom Quirk

BIBLIOGRAPHY

Baender, Paul. Introduction. *The Works of Mark Twain: "What Is Man?" and Other Philosophical Writings.* By Clemens. Ed. Paul Baender. Berkeley: U of California P, 1973. 1–34.

Boller, Paul F. "Mark Twain's Mechanistic Determinism." *Freedom and Fate in American Thought: From Edwards to Dewey.* By Boller. Dallas: Southern Methodist UP, 1978. 188–216.

[Carus, Paul]. "Mark Twain's Philosophy." *Monist* 23 (April 1913): 181–223.

Cummings, Sherwood. *Mark Twain and Science: Adventures of a Mind.* Baton Rouge: Louisiana State UP, 1988.

DeVoto, Bernard. *Mark Twain at Work.* Cambridge, Mass.: Harvard UP, 1942.

Jones, Alexander E. "Mark Twain and the Determinism of *What Is Man?*" *American Literature* 29 (March 1957): 1–17.

Macnaughton, William R. *Mark Twain's Last Years as a Writer.* Columbia: U of Missouri P, 1979.

Tuckey, John. "Mark Twain's Later Dialogue: The 'Me' and the Machine." *American Literature* 41 (January 1970): 532–542.

Van Doren, Carl. *The American Novel, 1789–1939.* New York: Macmillan, 1940.

Wagenknecht, Edward. *Mark Twain: The Man and His Work.* New Haven, Conn.: Yale UP, 1935.

Waggoner, Hyatt H. "Science in the Thought of Mark Twain." *American Literature* 8 (1937): 357–370.

See also: Human Nature; Philosophy; *Pudd'nhead Wilson, The Tragedy of;* Science; *What Is Man?*

DeVoto, Bernard Augustine
(1897–1955)

Bernard DeVoto was an editor, historian, teacher, journalist, conservationist, and writer of fiction. He was second editor (after Albert Bigelow Paine) of the Mark Twain Papers (1938–1946). His works include *Mark Twain's America* (1932), *Mark Twain in Eruption* (1940), *Mark Twain at Work* (1942), *Letters from the Earth* (completed 1939, published 1962); *The Course of Empire* (1952), *Across the Wide Missouri* (1947), *Year of Decision, 1846* (1943) (histories); *The Journals of Lewis and Clark* (1953); and fiction, some under the pen name of John

August. He was for eighteen months (September 1935–March 1938) editor of the *Saturday Review of Literature,* and from 1935 until his death he wrote "The Editor's Easy Chair" column at *Harper's,* a forum once held by William Dean Howells.

A native of Utah, son of an apostate Mormon mother and an apostate Catholic father (as he liked to say), DeVoto remained defiantly a Westerner in outlook and scholarly interests, though much of his career was spent near the Harvard Yard. It was as a Westerner that he wrote *Mark Twain's America* (1932), a spirited rebuttal of Van Wyck Brooks's *The Ordeal of Mark Twain* (1920). Brooks's largely Freudian reading saw Clemens as emotionally starved and warped by the frontier, a culturally barren region peopled by repressed puritans. DeVoto's frontier, in contrast, was richly diverse, with a folk tradition of music and storytelling that nourished the young artist.

In his clash with Brooks, as in his years as editor of the Mark Twain Papers, DeVoto helped set the agenda of Mark Twain scholarship. Critics still find fruitful questions such as the relationship between Clemens the private man and his persona Mark Twain, the sources and "fate" of his humor, and the crisis of his mature years—all issues raised by the Brooks-DeVoto dialogue. DeVoto himself continued the debate in "The Symbols of Despair" (in *Mark Twain at Work*), an attempt to construct a psychological study of the artist in his old age, which, in contrast to what he considered Brooks's too facile theorizing, was based on study of the late manuscripts in the Mark Twain Papers. As editor of the Mark Twain Papers, DeVoto for the first time made the collection available to qualified scholars. As far as the trustees of the estate, the Doubleday editors, and Clara Clemens allowed, DeVoto tried to correct the public image of Mark Twain as a genial humorist, an image that had been carefully nurtured by Paine and Frederick Duneka. In *Letters from the Earth* DeVoto proposed to give readers their first glimpse of some of the most cynical of Twain's unpublished satires and of his late experiments in symbolic narrative (as represented by "The Great Dark"). Unfortunately, publication of the volume was blocked by Clara Clemens, and it was not to appear until 1962, with a preface by Henry Nash Smith, which was in part a tribute to his pioneering predecessor.

Charles L. Crow

BIBLIOGRAPHY

Brooks, Van Wyck. *The Ordeal of Mark Twain*. Rev. ed. New York: Dutton, 1933.

Clemens, Samuel L. *Letters from the Earth*. Ed. Bernard DeVoto. New York: Harper & Row, 1962.

———. *Mark Twain in Eruption*. Ed. Bernard DeVoto. New York: Harper, 1940.

DeVoto, Bernard. *The Letters of Bernard DeVoto*. Ed. Wallace Stegner. Garden City, N.Y.: Doubleday, 1975.

———. *Mark Twain at Work*. Cambridge, Mass.: Harvard UP, 1942.

———. *Mark Twain's America*. Boston: Little, Brown, 1932.

Sawey, Orlan. *Bernard DeVoto*. New York: Twayne, 1969.

Smith, Henry Nash. Preface. *Letters from the Earth*. By Clemens. Ed. Bernard DeVoto. New York: Harper & Row, 1962. vii-ix.

Stegner, Wallace. *The Uneasy Chair: A Biography of Bernard DeVoto*. Garden City, N.Y.: Doubleday, 1974.

See also: Letters from the Earth; Mark Twain Papers

Dialect

For Mark Twain and his contemporaries, "dialect" usually meant what one would today call "regional" (rather than "class" or "occupational") dialect, the characteristic speech of a province or back country region as opposed to the standard language of a political, cultural, or educational center. A "dialect writer" was an author chiefly known for representing a particular dialect, such as the southern black speech of Joel Chandler Harris's tales or the Yankee vernacular of James Russell Lowell's *Biglow Papers*. Important as Twain's mastery of dialect was in individual works, his literary range clearly places him beyond the strict confines of that label.

Attitudes toward dialect were in flux during the nineteenth century. The romantics had elevated its status by associating it with rural virtue, while academic philology was beginning to break down the hierarchical distinctions between standard languages and dialects. A conservative distrust of dialect, however, remained strong: grammarians spoke of it as "lawless," literally without rules, and as late as 1898 Henry James would dismiss dialect as the "complete debasement" of colloquial language. In both England and America dialect in literature was used largely for comic purposes until mid-century, and in the American tradition before Twain it had most often been "framed" by a genteel, educated narrator who introduced dialect speakers. Writers felt simultaneous pressure to capture dialect accurately and to distance themselves from its users. As many critics have noted, Twain's innovation in *Huckleberry Finn* (1885) was to assign entire narrative responsibility to Huck's dialect voice. Yet Twain remained sensitive to dialect's social stigma, noting at the end of *Pudd'nhead Wilson* (1894) that the former slave Valet de Chambre is barred from polite society because he speaks "the basest dialect of the negro quarter."

Twain's main conscious concern as a dialect writer was accuracy. Pleased when William D. Howells praised the black dialect in "A True Story" (1874), he explained, "I amend dialect stuff by talking & talking & *talking* it till it sounds right" (Smith 26). A writer like Bret Harte, whom Twain judged to have a tin ear for dialect, was a frequent target for his scorn: "no human being, living or dead, ever had experience of the dialect which [Harte] puts into his people's mouths" ("Contributor's Club" 850).

Most scholarly attention to dialect in Twain's work has focused on *Huckleberry Finn* and Twain's assertion in his "Explanatory" note that the novel carefully depicts seven distinct dialects. David Carkeet's definitive study, the most sensitive to both literary and linguistic issues, concludes that his claim is largely valid and that it accurately mirrors his serious intention to create realistic dialogue. Walter Blair provides a useful introduction to Twain's place in the tradition of American dialect humor.

David R. Sewell

BIBLIOGRAPHY

Blair, Walter. *Native American Humor.* New York: Harper & Row, 1960.

Carkeet, David. "The Dialects in *Huckleberry Finn.*" *American Literature* 51 (1979): 315–332.

[Clemens, Samuel L.] "The Contributor's Club." *Atlantic Monthly* 45 (1880): 850–852.

———. *Mark Twain-Howells Letters: The Correspondence of Samuel L. Clemens and William D. Howells, 1872–1910.* Ed. Henry Nash Smith and William M. Gibson. 2 vols. Cambridge, Mass.: Harvard UP, 1960.

———. *Pudd'nhead Wilson and Those Extraordinary Twins.* Vol. 14 of the Author's National Edition. New York: Harper, 1917.

Ives, Sumner. "A Theory of Literary Dialect." *Tulane Studies in English* 2 (1950): 137–182.

James, Henry. "The Novel of Dialect." *Literature* 3.1 (9 July 1898): 17–18.

Pederson, Lee A. "Negro Speech in the *Adventures of Huckleberry Finn.*" *Mark Twain Journal* 13 (Winter 1965): 1–4.

See also: Harte, Francis Bret; Language; Southwestern Humor

Dickens, Charles
(1812–1870)

A popular British Victorian novelist, Charles Dickens grew up in poverty in circumstances similar to those about which he later wrote in *David Copperfield* (1849). In 1835 Dickens reported debates in the House of Commons to the *Morning Chronicle,* and from 1835 to 1837 he wrote sketches for various periodicals under the pen name "Boz." His subsequent novels and six annual Christmas stories brought him prosperity in both earnings and public good will. His most important works include *Oliver Twist* (1837), *Nicholas Nickleby* (1838),

The Old Curiosity Shop (1841), *Bleak House* (1858), *Little Dorrit* (1857), and *Great Expectations* (1861). Dickens's fiction was characterized by child characters, his keen interest in social conditions, and his descriptive writing style. His comic sketches and observations, as in *Hard Times* (1854) and *American Notes* (1842), influenced American humorists in both subject matter and style, Dickens using both low characters and vernacular language and dialects.

Twain wrote that Dickens was a popular novelist in Hannibal, and the early "Boz" sketches were community favorites. Twain's reading of Dickens included *The Life and Adventures of Martin Chuzzlewit* (1843), which he read on the river in 1860. In December 1861 he took *Dombey and Son* (1848) with him to Humbolt County. He likely read even more of the Dickens canon; there are echoes in Twain's early sketches of *The Pickwick Papers* (1836), *A Tale of Two Cities* ([1859], a novel Twain read repeatedly), and *David Copperfield.*

In California in the 1860s Twain's interest in Dickens began to wane, criticizing authors who were "ambitiously and undisguisedly imitating Dickens," particularly Bret Harte. Twain's antipathy for romantic sentimentality was one reason for this change of heart; another was the increasing frequency of published comparisons of the two writers. Twain, wanting to be a "great original," was rankled by any suggestion of literary influence. Still, their careers overlapped in a variety of ways.

On 19 November 1867 Dickens arrived in Boston harbor to begin his final American lecturing tour; Twain, on board the *Quaker City,* arrived in New York the same day, shortly to begin his first professional lecture series. Twain bemusedly wrote his mother from New York in November 1867, "You bet you when Charles Dickens sleeps in this room next week it will be a gratification to him to know that I slept in it also." Twain saw Dickens that season when his friend Charles Langdon invited him to dine with his family and to see Dickens. On New Year's Eve 1867 Clemens accompanied Olivia

Langdon to the reading at Steinway Hall in New York. Twain was disappointed with Dickens's performance, calling the passages from *David Copperfield* "monotonous, the pathos was purely verbal . . . with no heart."

While most of Twain's reading of Dickens took place before 1870, around 1868 he finished a precursor of *Tom Sawyer* (1876), "Boy's Manuscript," a possible burlesque of *David Copperfield*. He read *Barnaby Rudge* (1841) in 1878. The entire Clemens family read *A Tale of Two Cities* in Paris in 1879, using the novel as a guidebook.

In his later years Twain routinely complained about Dickens's romanticism, saying in his 1876 "Comments on English Diction" that Dickens used "too many words." Twain's Hartford friend Joseph Twichell was surprised to learn in 1896 that Twain "did not relish Dickens." Finally, Twain attempted in 1909 to distance himself from "Boz" by telling Albert Bigelow Paine that he had not read or become interested in Dickens. Despite this cantankerous claim, the evidence is that Dickens was a strong influence on Mark Twain and, ultimately, that the two will share similar positions in popular and literary lexicons.

Wesley Britton

BIBLIOGRAPHY

Dickens, Charles. *The Letters of Charles Dickens.* Vol. 2. Pilgrim ed. Ed. Madeline House, et al. Oxford: Oxford UP, 1969

Forster, John. *Life of Charles Dickens.* London: Chapman and Hall, 1872.

Johnson, Edgar. *Charles Dickens: His Tragedy and Triumph.* 2 vols. New York: Simon & Schuster, 1952.

See also: England; Reading

Dickinson, Anna Elizabeth

(1842–1932)

Anna Elizabeth Dickinson, a well-known suffragette of her day, toured with Samuel Clemens during the early 1870s and was known as the "Queen of the Lecture Circuit." Clemens remembered her as a compel-

ling attraction, and in 1872 she grossed over $20,000. In her memoirs, *A Ragged Register (of People, Places, and Opinions)* (1879), Dickinson wrote about her famous friends and life on the lyceum circuit. Dickinson was an avowed feminist (although she never joined any of the various groups), and on 24 March 1863 she electrified Isabella Beecher Hooker with her stage presence when she lectured in Hartford. (She was the first woman to deliver a public address there.) Dickinson and Beecher quickly became acquainted, and, shortly thereafter, Dickinson was introduced to the Langdons. Dickinson and Olivia Langdon Clemens became friends, and Dickinson stayed with the Langdon family during March 1867 while lecturing in the Elmira area. Dickinson had an immense influence upon Olivia Clemens, and in a letter written during their engagement, Olivia, citing Dickinson as an inspiration, questioned Clemens about what her role should be within the women's movement.

Dickinson's lecture subjects primarily concerned suffragette matters and Negro rights; in 1870 Dickinson began delivering her most popular lecture, a tribute to Joan of Arc. She became so closely identified with the figure of Joan that she was hailed by the press as the juvenile Joan of Arc. Dickinson's career gradually waned, although she attempted several comebacks and for a short time tried acting. In her heyday, from 1864 until the mid-seventies, Dickinson was an important national figure; in April 1864 she was invited to speak before Congress and one month later she had a private audience with President Lincoln. Dickinson must be credited with being an important role model for Olivia Langdon, and she functioned as Olivia's mentor in introducing her to suffragette matters.

Laura E. Skandera

BIBLIOGRAPHY

Chester, Giraud. *Embattled Maiden: The Life of Anna Dickinson.* New York: Putnam, 1951.

Clemens, Samuel L. Autobiographical Dictation. Microfilm. 12 October, 1907. No. 69, Mark Twain Papers.

————. Letter to Olivia Langdon Clemens regarding Anna Dickinson. 22 January 1869, Mark Twain Papers.

Dickinson, Anna Elizabeth. *A Ragged Register.* New York: Harper, 1879.

James, Edward T., ed. *Notable American Women, 1607–1950: A Biographical Dictionary.* 3 vols. Cambridge, Mass.: Harvard UP, 1973.

See also: Clemens, Olivia Langdon; Women's Rights

Disraeli, Benjamin
(1804–1881)

Benjamin Disraeli was born in London in 1804 to Jewish parents who converted to the Church of England in 1816. Disraeli left school at fifteen and worked for a newspaper before suffering a nervous collapse at age twenty-one. In 1830 a tour of the Middle East restored his mental state.

On his return he entered Conservative politics. Elected to parliament in 1837, he followed Sir Robert Peel's leadership. In the early forties he led a group known as "Young England" preaching "Tory Democracy," which meant paternalistic measures for the poor. In this period Disraeli wrote the novels *Coningsby* (1844), *Sybil* (1845), and *Tancred* (1847). He eventually produced twelve novels.

In 1845 Disraeli broke with Peel over the Corn Laws. He became a leader in the Protectionist Party led by the Earl of Derby. He was chancellor of the exchequer in the brief Derby government of 1852.

In 1866 an ailing Derby returned to office, but Disraeli led his government. Disraeli's Reform Bill of 1866 gave urban workers the vote to attach them to the Conservative Party. In 1868 Disraeli succeeded Derby as prime minister for ten months before losing office to William E. Gladstone and the liberals.

In 1874 the Conservatives beat Gladstone and returned Disraeli as prime minister. Disraeli legalized trade unions (1875), made primary education compulsory (1876), acquired shares in the Suez Company (1875), and made Victoria Empress of India (1876). In 1878 the Congress of Berlin resolved Balkan disputes in England's favor. By 1879 the country was bogged down in expensive Afghan and Zulu wars. Disraeli's leadership was faltering due to ill health and his promotion to the House of Lords as Earl of Beaconsfield in 1876. After losing the election of 1880 to Gladstone, Disraeli seemed to rebound as a vigorous opposition leader until he suddenly succumbed to bronchitis on 19 April 1881.

Gladstone and other opponents regarded Disraeli as an ambitious opportunist, made more sinister by brilliance, charm, and an exotic origin. Queen Victoria, however, grateful for his deference to her and her new imperial title, judged him the best of her ministers. In his novels, where ideals emerge untrammeled by political expediency, Disraeli shows a vision of an organic society where monarch, aristocracy, and other classes live in a harmony of deference and paternalism. Efforts to balance these romantic views and the hardheaded politician have bedeviled evaluations of Disraeli from his day to the present.

It is precisely this matter of balancing the romantic views with those of the hardheaded politician that accounts for Twain's fascination with Disraeli. He fluctuated greatly concerning political leaders and government. He did the same concerning labor unions. Although he wanted to believe in democracy and the masses, they always disappointed him. At the same time he found the monarchies of Europe repugnant. For convincing evidence of the contradiction between Twain's romantic views or idealism and his mechanistic views of hardheaded politics, one needs to read such sources as *The Prince and the Pauper* (1882), *A Connecticut Yankee in King Arthur's Court* (1889), and "Refuge of the Derelicts" (1906).

Arthur W. White

BIBLIOGRAPHY

Blake, Robert. Lord. *The Conservative Party from Peel to Churchill.* London: Eyre and Spottiswoode, 1970.

————. *Disraeli.* London: Eyre and Spottiswoode, 1966.

Feuchtwanger, E.J. *Disraeli, Democracy and the Tory Party; Conservative Leadership and Organization After the Second Reform Bill.* Oxford: Clarendon P, 1968.

Froude, James A. *The Life of the Earl of Beaconsfield.* London: J.M. Dent, 1931.

Levine, Richard A. *Benjamin Disraeli.* New York: Twayne, 1968.

Maurois, André. *Disraeli, A Picture of the Victorian Age.* Trans. Hamish Miles. New York: Appleton, 1928.

Smith, Paul. *Disraelian Conservatism and Social Reform.* Toronto: Toronto UP, 1967.

See also: England; Government; Politics

"Does the Race of Man Love a Lord?"

(1902)

In the form of a personal essay turning on variations on "loving a lord"—that is, on the "human race's fondness for contact with power and distinctions"—Mark Twain's essay asserts that we envy those we believe possess greater or more conspicuous power, whether we be kings or junior clerks. It was first published in the *North American Review* (April 1902).

Like most of Mark Twain's later writings, "Love a Lord" preaches the deterministic "gospel" of *What Is Man?* (1906) when he maintains that everyone is driven by his associations and training to envy those who are known to possess more power or conspicuousness. But he is also mindful of man's propensity to embrace concepts that he does not, in fact, believe. For example, man asserts that he is the noblest work of God but carefully avoids thinking about the ramifications of that statement, given slavery, despotism, etc.: "We do not deal much in fact when we are contemplating ourselves," says Mark Twain.

The ultimate irony of the piece is that even though Englishmen *and* Americans love a lord, so too lords love kings, minor kings love major ones, and so on, even though, really, "There is no variety in the human race": without their clothes neither the junior clerk nor

the major king have distinctions over any other human.

Robert E. Lowrey

BIBLIOGRAPHY

Clemens, Samuel L. "Does the Race of Man Love a Lord?" *North American Review* 174 (1902): 433–444.

Cox, James M. *Mark Twain: The Fate of Humor.* Princeton, N.J.: Princeton UP, 1966.

Emerson, Everett. *The Authentic Mark Twain: A Literary Biography of Samuel L. Clemens.* Philadelphia: U of Pennsylvania P, 1984.

Hill, Hamlin. *Mark Twain: God's Fool.* New York: Harper & Row, 1973.

Macnaughton, William R. *Mark Twain's Last Years As a Writer.* Columbia: U of Missouri P, 1979.

Spengemann, William C. *Mark Twain and the Backwoods Angel: The Matter of Innocence in the Works of Samuel L. Clemens.* Kent, Ohio: Kent State UP, 1966.

See also: Determinism; *What Is Man?*

"Dog's Tale, A"

(1903)

First published in the Christmas issue of *Harper's Monthly Magazine* (December 1903), "A Dog's Tale" was Mark Twain's last work completed at Quarry Farm and all that he wrote in the summer of 1903 before leaving with Olivia for Florence, Italy. The story was written largely to please daughter Jean, who had been outspoken in support of anti-vivisectionist causes. A British organization, The National Anti-Vivisectionist Society, distributed pamphlets containing the story in London in 1904; in September of the same year Harper and Brothers published a deluxe edition, illustrated by W.T. Smedley. The story is collected in *The $30,000 Bequest and Other Stories* (1906).

Written in the tradition of Aesop's fables, "A Dog's Tale" specifically echoes Robert Browning's poem "Tray," though as Baetzhold points out, Twain's story lacks Browning's authorial detachment and as a result becomes more maudlin (292–293). As the title implies, the narrator of "Dog's Tale" is an heroic dog with a young puppy. The dog rescues her master's daughter from a nursery fire and receives praise from her master for her courage and loyalty. The master's friends and colleagues, however, insist that the dog acted not nobly but instinctively. For dubious "humanitarian" causes, the master subjects the dog's pup to vivisection while the mother watches her pup's agonizing death. Whereas most story variants end with the rescuer dog's death preceding discovery of its true heroism, Twain's tale carefully individualizes both humans and animals as it intensifies irony with the puppy's slow, painful death, and pathos with the dog mother's starving herself while fruitlessly awaiting the pup's rebirth.

Too close identification of author and animal protagonist renders "A Dog's Tale" aesthetically less successful than such classic Twain animal stories as "The Celebrated Jumping Frog" (1865) and "Jim Baker's Blue Jay Yarn" (1880). Yet the polemical nature of the narrative and the experimental point of view clarify certain significant themes. Depicting language as "gone to the dogs," Twain attacks its social misuse to impress or to trivialize; ironically, the narrator dog's actions are more authentic and noble than the scientist humans' imposing but empty rhetoric. The servility of the dogs affords Twain an opportunity to explore as well the human institution of slavery: the animals parody human slaves' family separations, docile servitude, losses of identity, and roles as children's playthings and guardians. The most focused target of the story's wrath, however, is "frosty" science or, more specifically, the abuses of abstract scientific theory manifested in rhetorical defenses of vivisection. The human master's compassionless science stands juxtaposed to the dog's profound empathy for human loss and suffering.

Despite its sentimentality, which links it to "A Horse's Tale" (1906), "A Dog's Tale" remains a powerful indictment of cruelty to animals.

John H. Davis

BIBLIOGRAPHY

Baetzhold, Howard G. *Mark Twain and John Bull: The British Connection.* Bloomington: Indiana UP, 1970.

Campbell, Killis. "From Aesop to Mark Twain." *Sewanee Review* 19 (January 1911): 43–49.

Clemens, Samuel L. "A Dog's Tale." *The $30,000 Bequest and Other Stories.* By Clemens. 1906. Rpt. New York: Harper, 1917. 48–64.

Emerson, Everett. *The Authentic Mark Twain: A Literary Biography of Samuel L. Clemens.* Philadelphia: U of Pennsylvania P, 1984.

Herzberg, Gay S. "'A Dog's Tale': An Expanded View." *Mark Twain Journal* 19 (1977–1978): 20.

Wilson, James D. *A Reader's Guide to the Short Stories of Mark Twain.* Boston: G.K. Hall, 1987.

See also: Animals; "Horse's Tale, A"; Sentimentality

Dolby, George

George Dolby (dates unknown), the British impresario who managed Dickens's last reading tours, including that to the United States, was also agent for Mark Twain's very successful English lectures in 1873–1874. Twain later remembered him as convivial company in after-lecture chats—"large and ruddy, . . . a tireless and energetic talker, and always overflowing with good nature and bursting with jollity . . . [a] gladsome gorilla" (*Autobiography* 1:140).

Howard G. Baetzhold

BIBLIOGRAPHY

Clemens, Samuel L. *Mark Twain's Autobiography.* Ed. Albert B. Paine. 2 vols. New York: Harper, 1924.

Dolby, George. *Charles Dickens as I Knew Him.* New York: Scribner, 1912.

See also: England

Doten, Alfred R.
(1829–1903)

Alf Doten, an original "forty-niner" and a Nevada pioneer, was one of the outstanding journalists and principal chroniclers of the

Comstock region. He worked for such early papers as the Como *Sentinel*, the Virginia City *Daily Union*, and the *Territorial Enterprise*, where he was Twain's colleague and friend.

His main contribution to Comstock journalism was as reporter, editor, and, later, owner and publisher of the Gold Hill *Evening News*, where he kept a loaded revolver in his desk to defend himself against disgruntled readers. He, therefore, along with Joseph Goodman may have been one of the models for Twain's "Journalism in Tennessee" (1869) which, despite its title, reflects the feistiness of Comstock journalism and the hazards faced by its practitioners.

Doten is of interest to Twain scholars both as a possible influence on Twain and as an important source of historical information. Doten's diary, published in 1973 as *The Journals of Alfred Doten* (including his series of three articles on "Early Journalism of Nevada" for the *Nevada Monthly* magazine of 1899), is a valuable record of Comstock life and personalities.

Lawrence I. Berkove

BIBLIOGRAPHY

Angel, Myron. *History of Nevada*. Oakland: Thompson & West, 1881. Rpt. Berkeley: Howell-North, 1958.

Doten, Alfred. *The Journals of Alfred Doten 1849–1903*. Ed. Walter Van Tilburg Clark. 3 vols. Reno: U of Nevada P, 1973.

Drury, Wells. *An Editor on the Comstock Lode*. Reno: U of Nevada P, 1984.

See also: "Journalism in Tennessee"; Nevada; Virginia City *Territorial Enterprise*

"Double-Barreled Detective Story, A"

(1902)

On 6 September 1901 Mark Twain delightedly reported to Henry H. Rogers that he had worked all that day revising a story begun on 29 August, "a burlesque of Sherlock Holmes," and would add a final chapter on the seventh. Published first in *Harper's Monthly* for January and February 1902, and as a Harper book the following April, "A Double-Barreled Detective Story" was first collected in a volume of the same name (Leipzig: Bernhard Tauchnitz, 1902), then in *My Debut as a Literary Person with Other Essays and Stories* (Hartford, Conn.: American Publishing, 1903), and later by Harper and Brothers in *The Man That Corrupted Hadleyburg* (Author's National Edition, Vol. 23).

This tale, employing many of the burlesque devices Mark Twain had learned in his San Francisco days, notably the "condensed novel" form, was the latest expression of his longtime love-hate relationship with detective stories.

In the story the barrels of Twain's literary shotgun are aimed at melodramatic literature in general and at detective fiction and Sir Arthur Conan Doyle's Sherlock Holmes in particular. His immediate stimulus was probably *The Hound of the Baskervilles*, the first installment of which appeared in the *Strand* magazine in August 1901, but the chief inspiration and target, from which he borrowed both theme and structure, was Doyle's *A Study in Scarlet* (1887).

In the overmelodramatic first section of Twain's story, Jacob Fuller, angered by his aristocratic father-in-law's sneering attempts to prevent his marriage, decides to avenge the insults by mistreating his wife, hoping that her tales of suffering will break the old man's heart. After three months, furious at her proud refusal to complain to her parent, even though she is now pregnant, Fuller ties her to a roadside tree, sets his bloodhounds on her, and when they have stripped off her clothes, leaves her to be found by passers-by the following day. After the birth of her child and the death of her father, she moves away, assumes the name Stillman, and plans her own revenge. Her son, Archy, whose prenatal experience has left him with the "gift of the bloodhound"—a supersensitive sense of smell—will, when grown, track Fuller down and hound him to his self-destruction.

Archy pursues his quarry for some two months from Denver to Mexico before discovering that he has followed the wrong man, a cousin of Fuller's with the same name. Catching the "scent" again, he tracks the real Fuller to Australia, India, and back without ever catching up with him, and finally, three-and-a-half years later, he loses the trail completely near Hope Canyon, a silver-mining area in California.

The second section, like that in Doyle's *A Study in Scarlet*, begins with an elaborate description of the scene, as if it were a totally new piece. A parody both of Doyle's passage and of overblown Victorian "word-painting," the passage traps the unwary reader with the picture of "lilacs and laburnums, lit with the glory-fires of autumn" that hang "burning and flashing in the upper air" and other elaborate details. So skillfully is it done that on first reading one probably does not realize the hoax until the culminating image of a "solitary oesophagus" sleeping "upon motionless wing." And some contemporary readers missed even the "oesophagus," or, accepting the other details, requested information about the nature of that creature.

This second barrel then takes specific aim at Sherlock Holmes and his methods. In the Hope Canyon mining camp young Fetlock Jones (later revealed as the great detective's nephew) plans the murder of his abusive master Flint Buckner. Sherlock Holmes (unexplainedly) arrives in Hope Canyon just in time to investigate the explosion that kills Buckner. Much parody follows as the miners remark upon the elaborate "scientific" means by which the "Extraordinary Man" (as Dr. Watson, too, so often called Holmes) mistakenly deduces that Sammy Hillyer is the culprit. It then remains for Archy Stillman to provide his own analysis and bring about Fetlock Jones's confession.

Next day the innocent Jacob Fuller, whom Archy had earlier hounded, arrives in town, half-crazed and believing that it was Sherlock

Holmes who had been tracking him. A lynch mob forms to punish Holmes for harassing Fuller, but Sheriff Jack Fairfax arrives in time to face down the mob and apologize to the famous detective. Archy then learns that Fetlock Jones had escaped, and the miners agree to let his Uncle Sherlock "track him out" if he wished to do so, since "it is in his line." Finally, Archy's quest reaches its anticlimactic conclusion when Sammy Hillyer informs him that the murdered Flint Buckner was the real Jacob Fuller.

For some critics the absurdities and confusions of "A Double-Barreled Detective Story" make it one of Mark Twain's least successful works. The story is certainly extravagant and ridiculous, full of coincidences and unexplained details. But it is, of course, intentionally so. Moreover, the tale gains considerable interest in its relationship to *A Study in Scarlet*, which, at least to Twain, provided a unifying element, and in its echoing of a number of Doyle's other stories. One of the truly humorous touches, in its burlesque of the almost supernatural skills with which Doyle endowed his sleuth, occurs when Wells-Fargo Ferguson describes in detail for the boys at the tavern how Holmes would have handled a particular investigation, and murmurs, in reverent awe, "I wonder if God made him?" Whereupon Ham Sandwich solemnly remarks, "Not all at one time, I reckon."

With all its flaws, "A Double-Barreled Detective Story" is notable also for its adaptation of a number of important elements of Mark Twain's earlier writings. Besides its "condensed novel" form, employed in such works as "Aurelia's Unfortunate Young Man" (1864) and "Lucretia Smith's Soldier" (1864), and its spoof of detectives, as in the play and novel versions of *Simon Wheeler, Detective* (written in 1877–1878) and "The Stolen White Elephant" (1882), the story also reflects Twain's portrayals of California mining camps in works like "Jim Smiley and His Jumping Frog" (1865) and *Roughing It* (1872). Like *Huckleberry Finn* (1885) it features the gullibility of the townspeople and the ridiculousness of the southern notion of a revenge mob when faced by a brave man like Colonel Sherburn. Moreover, a major theme of most of the writings of Twain's late years is suggested by Archy's comment at one point that the laws of nature were "blind and unreasoning and arbitrary."

Howard G. Baetzhold

BIBLIOGRAPHY

Baetzhold, Howard G. *Mark Twain and John Bull: The British Connection.* Bloomington: Indiana UP, 1970.

Cooper, Lane. "Mark Twain's Lilacs and Laburnums." *Modern Language Notes* 47 (February 1932): 85–87.

Gribben, Alan. *Mark Twain's Library: A Reconstruction.* 2 vols. Boston: G.K. Hall, 1980.

Hill, Hamlin. *Mark Twain: God's Fool.* New York: Harper & Row, 1973.

Kraus, W. Keith. "Mark Twain's 'A Double-Barreled Detective Story': A Source for the Solitary Oesophagus." *Mark Twain Journal* 16.2 (Summer 1972): 10–12.

Macnaughton, William R. *Mark Twain's Last Years as a Writer.* Columbia: U of Missouri P, 1979.

Ritunnano, Jeanne. "Mark Twain vs. Arthur Conan Doyle on Detective Fiction." *Mark Twain Journal* 16.1 (Winter 1971–1972): 10–14.

Wilson, James D. *A Reader's Guide to the Short Stories of Mark Twain.* Boston: G.K. Hall, 1987.

See also: Burlesque; Condensed Novel; Detective Fiction

Douglas, Widow

Modeled after Mrs. Richard T. Holliday of Holliday's Hill in Hannibal, the Widow Douglas is the kind lady of Cardiff Hill in the St. Petersburg of the Tom Sawyer–Huck Finn narratives who in *The Adventures of Tom Sawyer* (1876) adopts the homeless Huck Finn and who continues to make a home for him in the subsequent tales. She provides the occasion for Huck Finn's first exercise of muted heroism, a heroism always accompanied by the picaro's wily instincts for self-preservation, when he alerts Welshman to Injun Joe's intentions to mutilate her. In *The Adventures of Tom Sawyer* Twain identifies her as "fair, smart,

and forty, a generous, good-hearted soul," a characterization that continues to be true of her in *Adventures of Huckleberry Finn* (1885) and in her brief mentions in *Tom Sawyer Abroad* (1894), "Huck Finn and Tom Sawyer Among the Indians" (1969), and "Tom Sawyer's Conspiracy" (1969). The exception to this description is the passing allusion in *Life on the Mississippi* (1883) where she is characterized as a "persecuting good widow who wished to make a nice, truth-telling, respectable boy" of Huck, thereby generating, despite the obviously comic tone of this characterization, a good deal of serious evaluation of her as the representative of the debilitating repressions of civilization. When he wrote *Adventures of Huckleberry Finn*, Twain made sure to spare the widow this oppressive role by introducing Miss Watson who becomes the rigidly unpleasant persecutor of Huck and the betrayer of Jim. In contrast to Miss Watson, the widow is uniformly benevolent, continues to be Huck's good friend, and gives him a home under her roof. While Miss Watson worked him hard, the widow "made her ease up"; while Miss Watson's Providence held no attractions for Huck, "a poor chap would stand considerable show with the widow's Providence." Huck resolves to "belong to the widow's Providence."

Everett Carter

BIBLIOGRAPHY

Branch, Edgar M. "The Two Providences: Thematic Form in 'Huckleberry Finn.'" *College English* 11 (January 1950): 188–195.

Clemens, Samuel L. *Adventures of Huckleberry Finn.* Ed. Walter Blair and Victor Fischer. Berkeley: U of California P, 1985.

———. *The Adventures of Tom Sawyer.* Ed. John C. Gerber and Paul Baender. Berkeley: U of California P, 1982.

———. *Life on the Mississippi.* Boston: James R. Osgood, 1883.

Pettit, Arthur G. *Mark Twain and the South.* Lexington: UP of Kentucky, 1974.

See also: *Adventures of Huckleberry Finn*; *Adventures of Tom Sawyer, The*; Watson, Miss

Doyle, Arthur Conan
(1859–1930)

In 1891 this English novelist emerged as one of the world's best-known detective writers with publication of *The Adventures of Sherlock Holmes*. Doyle's famous detective, however, made his first appearance in Doyle's *A Study in Scarlet* (1887). This ingenious detective reappeared in Doyle's *The Memoirs of Sherlock Holmes* (1893), *The Hound of the Baskervilles* (1902), and *The Return of Sherlock Holmes* (1905). Doyle provided Sherlock Holmes with a fictional home at 221B Baker Street, London, and a good-natured but bungling associate, Dr. Watson. Late in his life he embarked on a worldwide crusade for spiritualism and wrote a two-volume *History of Spiritualism* (1926).

Apparently under the influence of Doyle's *A Study in Scarlet*, Mark Twain wrote "A Double-Barreled Detective Story" in 1902, the very year that Doyle was knighted. Doyle's famous detective even appears in Twain's story. The result is burlesque and parody, a satiric take off on Doyle's new detective fiction. Mark Twain seemed to have had little affection for Doyle's new genre and for Sherlock Holmes's "cheap & ineffectual ingenuities" (Emerson 239). Mark Twain may have disparaged this new genre, but some of his later fiction—*Pudd'nhead Wilson* (1894) and *Tom Sawyer, Detective* (1896), the trial scenes in *Joan of Arc* (1896), and "The Man That Corrupted Hadleyburg" (1899)—did employ detectives and ingenious courtroom tactics, perhaps inspired by Doyle's very popular fiction.

Andy J. Moore

BIBLIOGRAPHY

Baetzhold, Howard G. *Mark Twain and John Bull: The British Connection.* Bloomington: Indiana UP, 1970.

Emerson, Everett. *The Authentic Mark Twain: A Literary Biography of Samuel L. Clemens.* Philadelphia: U of Pennsylvania P, 1984.

Long, E. Hudson. *Mark Twain Handbook.* New York: Hendricks House, 1957.

Ritunnano, Jeanne. "Mark Twain vs. Arthur Conan Doyle on Detective Fiction." *Mark Twain Journal* 16.1 (Winter 1971): 10–14.

Rogers, Franklin R. *Mark Twain's Burlesque Patterns as Seen in the Novels and Narratives, 1855–1885.* Dallas: Southern Methodist UP, 1960.

Wilson, James D. *A Reader's Guide to the Short Stories of Mark Twain.* Boston: G.K. Hall, 1987.

See also: Detective Fiction; "Double-Barreled Detective Story, A"

Dramatist, Mark Twain as

The dramatic work of Mark Twain deserves recognition as an essential element in his literary career. He collaborated on ten plays, translated three from German into English, and individually authored eleven more, with *Colonel Sellers* becoming one of the most successful pieces of the 1870s. Several prose works—*Innocents Abroad* (1869), *Roughing It* (1872), *The Adventures of Tom Sawyer* (1876), *The Prince and the Pauper* (1882), and *The American Claimant* (1892)—began as dramatic scripts; while six of his prose works—*The Adventures of Tom Sawyer*, *Adventures of Huckleberry Finn* (1885), *The Prince and the Pauper*, *A Connecticut Yankee* (1889), *Pudd'nhead Wilson* (1894), and *Joan of Arc* (1896)—were dramatized under his supervision.

Twain became professionally involved in theater as a critic for the Virginia City *Territorial Enterprise* in 1862. By 1863 he was known as "The Great Eastern Slope theatrical critic." His flair for burlesque and a thorough knowledge of the theater made his reviews popular and led to his first play. While working for the San Francisco *Morning Call*, he attended a weak production of *Il Trovatore* at Maguire's Opera House. Twain responded with a four-act burlesque, *Il Trovatore* (1866).

In 1872–1873 Twain was at work on two theatrical pieces, including a burlesque based upon Shakespeare's *Hamlet* and bearing the same name. The other piece, a dramatic version of *Tom Sawyer*, was copyrighted in 1875. There is no evidence that either script was produced. However, Twain revised *Tom Sawyer* periodically over a period of twenty years.

Twain maintained a heightened interest in producing dramatic material throughout the 1870s. He and Charles Dudley Warner secured a dramatic copyright for *The Gilded Age* on 19 May 1873, seven months before the novel was published. In April 1874 Gilbert Densmore, of the San Francisco *Golden Era*, dramatized and produced a version of *The Gilded Age*. The copyright was invoked, and further use of the material stopped. Twain then negotiated with Warner for separate copyrights, wrote his own script titled *Colonel Sellers*, and leased the work to John T. Raymond. It was an immediate success and remained popular for thirteen years.

The financial success of *Colonel Sellers* made Twain eager to continue dramatic work. After a failed attempt to collaborate on a book with English novelist Charles Reade, Twain sent him a plot for a drama in 1875. Receiving a rejection from Reade, Twain sent the material to Chandos Fulton in New York. With Fulton's encouragement, Twain finished the script which he called *Cap'n Simon Wheeler, the Amateur Detective* (1877).

In September 1876 Twain was approached by Bret Harte for the purpose of collaborating on a play built around the Chinaman from Harte's "Plain Language from Truthful James." Despite a less than comfortable relationship, Twain and Harte produced a rough script in under three months and launched *Ah Sin* (1876) with minimal revisions and little success.

Twain's dramatic collaboration with William D. Howells began in 1875 when Twain approached Howells with a request that he dramatize *The Adventures of Tom Sawyer*. Howells rejected the idea. However, after several failed projects Twain and Howells finally produced *Colonel Sellers as a Scientist* (1883). The play, originally conceived in the spring of 1878 as *Orme's Motor*, then *The Steam Generator*, finally reached the stage as *The American Claimant* (1887) with Twain himself providing the financing. The effort was another disappointment.

Collaborations with other authors did not satisfy Twain's appetite for drama. With encouragement from Augustine Daly, the most prominent producer of the time, he wrote a new drama titled *The Prince and the Pauper* (1886), revived *Tom Sawyer*, and offered them as part of a package with *Colonel Sellers as a Scientist* to M.H. Mallory, instead of negotiating for *Colonel Sellers* alone as he had promised Howells.

Twain wrote *Meisterschaft* (1887), containing both English and German dialogue, as an illustration for a German class that met in his home. While in Vienna a decade later, he extended his work in German by joining with Siegmund Schlesinger to co-author *Der Gegenkandidat, or Women in Politics* (1898) and to lay out a plot for *Die Goldgraeberin, or The Woman Gold-Miner* (1898).

Twain never became an accomplished dramatist, but some of his strongest attributes as a writer were enhanced by his dramatic work. His mastery of dialogue can be attributed in part to his experience with the demands of writing for the stage. His early involvement with the living characters of the theater sharpened his sensitivity for the subtleties of character so necessary to the creation of a Huckleberry Finn. Moreover, Twain never lost the desire to write plays, for even on the trip home from Bermuda in 1910 he told Albert Bigelow Paine of a dream about a play he had in mind.

Jerry W. Thomason

BIBLIOGRAPHY

Clemens, Samuel L. *Mark Twain–Howells Letters: The Correspondence of Samuel L. Clemens and William D. Howells, 1872–1910.* Ed. Henry Nash Smith and William M. Gibson. 2 vols. Cambridge, Mass.: Harvard UP, 1960.

————. *Mark Twain's Letters to His Publishers, 1867–1894.* Ed. Hamlin Hill. Berkeley: U of California P, 1967.

————. *Mark Twain's Satires & Burlesques.* Ed. Franklin R. Rogers. Berkeley: U of California P, 1967.

Goldman, Robert. "Mark Twain as Playwright." *Mark Twain: A Sumptuous Variety.* Ed. Robert

Giddings. Totowa, N.J.: Barnes & Noble, 1985. 108–131.

Schirer, Thomas. *Mark Twain and the Theatre.* Nürnberg: Verlag Hans Carl, 1984.

See also: Ah Sin: The Heathen Chinee; Austria (Austria-Hungary); *Colonel Sellers*; Raymond, John T.

Dreams

Mark Twain had a lifelong fascination with dreams. From his apparent dream premonition of his brother's death in 1858 to his many late manuscripts, diary entries, and other references to dreams, Twain indicates that the idea of a separate, independent existence in a "dream-life" may have provided him with an imaginable alternative to the actual life that became increasingly painful and frustrating.

Twain's dreams fall into roughly four categories: the dream as premonition, the dream as nightmare, the dream as escape from morality, and the dream as creative principle. The first category includes "serious" references to his own and other documented premonitory dreams, but it primarily appears in his fiction within the vernacular frame as a comic device, often used by the "dreamer" to explain apparently bizarre behavior (Jim's "dream" at the beginning of *Huckleberry Finn* [1885]; Jim's later "dream" as a moral lesson on the raft). The second category, the dream as nightmare, probably begins around the time of composition of *A Connecticut Yankee in King Arthur's Court* (1889) and provides one framework for understanding that text. Twain's best-known "nightmare" texts, however, have been collected by John S. Tuckey under the title of *Mark Twain's "Which Was the Dream?" and Other Symbolic Writings of the Later Years* (1967). The dates of composition of most of these manuscripts coincide with Twain's personal misfortunes, especially his bankruptcy and his daughter Susy's death. In these nightmare texts dreamers, generally happy successful men, fall asleep and experience nightmares of financial reversals, familial deaths, and the failure of

personal nerve. At the conclusion of the "dream" the protagonist discovers that it, in fact, is the reality and his "happy" life the dream.

The third category, dreams as escape, is best represented by Twain's late sketch, "My Platonic Sweetheart" (*Harper's Magazine*, 1912). Here the narrator records a series of dreams, experienced at intervals over the course of his life, in which his adolescent self meets with a dream sweetheart and experiences various adventures that inevitably end with the girl's apparent, but nontragic, death. Each new sequence, however, sees her alive again: "It may be that she had often died before, and knew there was nothing lasting about it" (301), the narrator concludes. "My Platonic Sweetheart" ends with Twain's most explicit statement of belief in an alternate existence that, significantly, is freed from the restrictions of time and space: "In our dreams . . . ," the narrator avers, "we do make the journeys we seem to make; we do see the things we seem to see; . . . they [our Dream Selves] are real, not chimeras; and they are immortal and indestructible. They go whither they will; they visit all resorts, all points of interest, even the twinkling suns that wander in the wastes of space . . . . We know this because there is no other place" (303).

Twain's nightmare dreams and his escape dreams unite in his most extended exploration of the relationship between dreams and waking life: *The Mysterious Stranger* manuscripts. (*Note*: All references are to William M. Gibson's edition of the manuscripts, published by the University of California Press in 1969.) Though generally failing as humor, most of *The Mysterious Stranger* manuscripts were nevertheless cast in a comic mode. August Feldner, the narrator of "No. 44, The Mysterious Stranger," the most nearly complete of the manuscripts, presents his double, Philip Traum, as the nihilistic alternative to his own essentially obedient and unquestioning personality. Twain's distribution of characteristics between his doubles, however, is not simple: August may be dour and his dream self gay; August may be frightened and law abiding, while his double is unintimitable and iconoclastic, but August is also humane and pitying, while Philip is incapable of sympathy. "The Mysterious Stranger" culminates in Philip Traum's solipsistic revelation that the world—both actual and dream—does not exist independently of the mind of the dreamer, and that the narrator's—the writer of the story—is the mind that dreams. Twain's conviction of immortality, his sense that the dreaming self is the true creative principle, his horror at the spectacle of human (and universal) cruelty, and his search for an escape from the human condition, come together in an implicit theory of creative solipsism, his sense that the mind of the creative artist is the God who creates and destroys the perceptible world but, alas, cannot destroy itself.

Susan K. Harris

BIBLIOGRAPHY

Cummings, Sherwood. *Mark Twain and Science: Adventures of a Mind.* Baton Rouge: Louisiana State UP, 1988.

Davis, John H. "The Dream as Reality: Structure and Meaning in Mark Twain's 'The Great Dark.'" *Mississippi Quarterly* 35 (Fall 1982): 407–426.

Gillman, Susan. *Dark Twins: Imposture and Identity in Mark Twain's America.* Chicago: U of Chicago P, 1989.

Harris, Susan K. *Mark Twain's Escape from Time: A Study of Patterns and Images.* Columbia: U of Missouri P, 1982.

Salvaggio, Ruth. "Twain's Later Phase Reconsidered: Duality and the Mind." *American Literary Realism, 1870–1910* 12 (1979): 322–329.

See also: Mental Telepathy/Extrasensory Perception; *Mysterious Stranger, The;* "Which Was the Dream?"

Driscoll, Judge York Leicester

In Mark Twain's *Pudd'nhead Wilson* (1894) Judge York Leicester Driscoll is the county judge of Dawson's Landing. He is forty years old and is greatly revered in the community. He and his wife adopt Tom, Percy Driscoll's son. The judge is a freethinker, which he can well afford to be because of the freedom his position in the community allows him.

The judge represents true Virginian ancestry. His manners and his rigid adherence to the "social code" retain his forefathers' tradition of aristocracy. He is a pillar of the community, and extremely proud of his position. Judge Driscoll treats "Tom," really Roxy's baby, as his heir; he treats "Chambers," his true nephew, as a slave. His life's ambition is to be a gentleman without stain or blemish. He is horrified when Tom breaks the unwritten code by refusing to fight in a duel. The judge fights in the duel for Tom. Because of this incident, compounded with accumulated gambling debts, Tom falls out of his uncle's graces. Knowing his uncle will probably not give him money to pay for his debts, Tom attempts to steal money from his sleeping uncle. The judge awakens while Tom is robbing him, and Tom murders him.

For Twain, Judge Driscoll represents all that is static and stationary about southern culture. His is the mind set that allowed slavery to continue for so long. Judge Driscoll represents social caste, law, and order; Tom, his antithesis, murders him.

J.R. LeMaster and Carolyn Gay

BIBLIOGRAPHY

Brashear, Minie M., and Robert M. Rodney. *The Art, Humor, and Humanity of Mark Twain.* Norman: U of Oklahoma P, 1959.

Budd, Louis J. *Our Mark Twain: The Making of His Public Personality.* Philadelphia: U of Pennsylvania P, 1983.

DeVoto, Bernard. *Mark Twain's America.* Boston: Little, Brown, 1932.

Geismar, Maxwell. *Mark Twain: An American Prophet.* New York: McGraw-Hill, 1970.

Leavis, F.R. "The Moral Astringency of Pudd'nhead Wilson." *Discussions of Mark Twain.* Ed. Guy A. Cardwell. Boston: D.C. Heath, 1963. 82–91

Pettit, Arthur G. *Mark Twain and the South.* Lexington: UP of Kentucky, 1974.

See also: Driscoll, Tom; *Pudd'nhead Wilson, The Tragedy of*

Driscoll, Tom

Mark Twain's *Pudd'nhead Wilson* (1894) traces Tom Driscoll's life from infancy to the time he is sent down the river as a slave. Tom Driscoll, really Valet de Chambre, is the usurping heir of Judge Driscoll. Valet de Chambre is born to twenty-year-old Roxy, a one-sixteenth black slave of Percy Northumberland Driscoll. Chambre's father, the deceased Colonel Essex, was white. Although Roxy's baby is one thirty-second black, he is a slave. Roxy also nurses Thomas à Becket Driscoll, Percy Driscoll's son. The two boys look very similar; in fact, only Roxy can tell them apart. When the babies are seven months old, Roxy dresses her baby in Thomas à Becket's clothes, and puts Chambre's clothes on Tom. She then puts her baby in the Driscoll cradle and places the true heir to the Driscoll estate in her son's cradle. No one suspects the switch. Roxy's plan to rescue her son from slavery backfires. Because of the training "Tom" receives in childhood, he becomes a gambler, a thief, a liar, and eventually a murderer.

The babies' temperaments are identical until Roxy switches them. Tom's coddling as a youngster ruins his character. It is not, as Roxy assumes, his black blood that destroys him. Immediately after Roxy changes the babies, Tom begins to assert his unpleasant personality. Tom is a troublesome child. He cries without reason; he hits or claws anyone who comes near him; he screams until his desires are met. Tom is petted and indulged in every whim by his mother, by Roxy, and by "Chambers." Tom is merciless toward Chambers and Roxy and hateful to practically everyone else. Chambers fights Tom's battles, pulls his sled, obeys his commands, and is rewarded with blows and rebukes.

As a young man, Tom is kicked by Luigi Cappello and then backs out of a duel. His uncle, Judge York Leicester Driscoll, who had adopted him, is repulsed by Tom's cowardice. The judge has already lost patience with Tom for the gambling debts Tom has accumulated in St. Louis. To attempt to pay his debts, Tom dresses as a woman and steals his neighbors' valuables. A jewel-encrusted knife stolen from the Italian twins is of little use since anyone returning the knife for a reward will be arrested. Tom's financial troubles mount steadily.

When Roxy is thirty-five, she is freed, and she takes a job as a chambermaid on a steamboat. She works for eight years and then returns to Dawson's Landing. The penniless Roxy approaches Tom obsequiously, hoping Tom will be kind to her. Tom is horrified. Suddenly, their roles are reversed. Through her knowledge of the precariousness of his situation, Roxy now controls Tom's financial affairs. Tom's gambling debts secret, and his inheritance safe, Roxy tells him to sell her into slavery, pay off his debts, and then buy her back within a year. Tom sells her down the river and thinks he is rid of his trouble. Roxy escapes and returns to Dawson's Landing. She demands that Tom confess his crimes to his uncle and that he ask for the money to buy her back from her owners. Tom decides to steal the money from the sleeping Judge Driscoll. His uncle awakens, and Tom kills him with a stolen Indian knife. Tom is unmasked in court by Pudd'nhead Wilson and is sold down the river as a slave.

Before Tom knows of his heritage, he focuses his hatred upon the family's slaves. When Tom learns that his "mammy" is actually his mother, he suffers from an agonizing crisis of identity. Now he is an outcast, just as those he had treated cruelly all of his life. When he discovers that he is in fact a slave, he directs his malice toward his fellowmen. For Tom, Judge Driscoll had represented old Virginia aristocracy, law, and order: everything Tom is not and consequently hates.

Tom demonstrates Mark Twain's belief that "training is all." It is not Tom's black heritage that ruins his character, but rather his childhood training. Since Tom is a product of his society, he represents the inherent evil of slavery and of all mankind. He depicts the duplicitous nature of a society that privately tolerates miscegenation and then despises its victims.

J.R. LeMaster and Carolyn Gay

BIBLIOGRAPHY

Budd, Louis J. *Our Mark Twain: The Making of His Public Personality*. Philadelphia: U of Pennsylvania P, 1983.

Geismar, Maxwell. *Mark Twain: An American Prophet*. New York: McGraw-Hill, 1970.

Kaplan, Justin. *Mark Twain and His World*. New York: Simon & Schuster, 1974.

Pettit, Arthur G. *Mark Twain and the South*. Lexington: UP of Kentucky, 1974.

See also: Miscegenation; *Pudd'nhead Wilson, The Tragedy of*; Slavery

Dublin, New Hampshire

Samuel Clemens spent the summers of 1905 and 1906 on Monadnock, a mountain near Dublin, a town in southern New Hampshire. At the time, Dublin had an approximate population of 600.

The summer of 1905 Clemens lived in Love Tree Hill, the home of Henry Copley Greene. While there, he worked on "Three Thousand Years Among the Microbes" and finished "Eve's Diary" (1905). He also wrote "A Horse's Tale" (1906) at the request of Minnie Maddern Fiske and an essay about free speech, "The Privilege of the Grave."

While staying at the Upton House the summer of 1906, Clemens dictated material to Josephine Hobby for the Paine biography. Clemens wrote Howells that he had decided to publish *Extract from Captain Stormfield's Visit to Heaven* (1909) and gave George Harvey permission to publish selections from the *Autobiography* in the *North American Review*.

Still grieving for his wife's death two years earlier, Clemens complained that the only problem with Dublin was loneliness.

Roberta Seelinger Trites

BIBLIOGRAPHY

Clemens, Samuel L. *Mark Twain's Autobiography*. Ed. Albert B. Paine. 2 vols. New York: Harper, 1924.

Paine, Albert Bigelow. *Mark Twain: A Biography*. 4 vols. New York: Harper, 1912.

Dueling

Though he had a dangerous brush with the *code duello* in the 1860s, Mark Twain exploited the duel as a comic and satiric resource throughout his literary career. In general, he treated the code as a senseless anachronism in the nineteenth century, a vivid example of the drag of custom on legal and social progress.

In May 1864 when he was acting editor of the Virginia City *Territorial Enterprise*, Twain became embroiled with a rival editor, James L. Laird, and violated Nevada law by challenging him. Fortunately, no fighting occurred, and Twain left the territory for California. There is no evidence to corroborate his story of the pistol-practice session that induced Laird to decline the combat. A work, apparently, of Twain's comic imagination, "How I Escaped Being Killed in a Duel" appeared in *Every Saturday* on 21 December 1872 and was retold in lectures, the *Autobiography* (1924), and Paine's *Mark Twain: A Biography* (1912).

In the late 1870s Twain pressed dueling into the service of social satire. The *Atlantic Monthly* for February 1879 published "The Recent Great French Duel," an attack directed less at the code than at the French, always one of Twain's favorite targets. A farcical account of a contest between members of the National Assembly, Gambetta and Fourtou, the sketch emphasizes the theatricality and cowardice Twain imputed to the French. The piece became chapter 8 of *A Tramp Abroad* (1880) and is juxtaposed with chapters describing student duels in Germany, where, Twain implies, ancient, bloody custom prevails over law. A similar contrast, now between the French duel and its deadly Austrian counterpart, is developed at the beginning of "Dueling," a product, according to Paine, of 1898. First published in *Europe and Elsewhere* (1923), the essay takes a serious turn, however, cataloguing a number of tragedies that have resulted from trifling offenses against gentlemanly honor and contending that the code's victims are not its adherents but their families. Thus a law requiring that loved ones attend their kinsmen's combats would induce truly honorable men to stop dueling.

In his characterization of the American South, Twain again points to the duel as an example of a culture's entrapment in outworn traditions. In *Life on the Mississippi* (1883) dueling is cited as a sign of the region's Walter Scott medievalism; and in chapter 40 an extended footnote enumerating reports of duels serves to undercut the South's claim to enjoy a civilization of the "highest type." In *Pudd'nhead Wilson* (1894) and "Those Extraordinary Twins" (1894), however, Twain is ambivalent in his attitude toward his Dawson's Landing aristocrats, who are sticklers for the niceties of honor. As scholars note, he evidently modeled his two proud descendants of the First Families of Virginia after his father and respected their integrity and nobility. Yet Twain ironically establishes that Judge Driscoll and his lawyer friend Pembroke Howard place their honor above the law and, in Howard's case, above religion too. Moreover, the duels in these two works have markedly farcical features and open the way to Twain's ridicule of sensation-hungry villagers who confer social and political eminence on lawbreakers.

In two stories of the late 1890s the duelist has Twain's whole-hearted endorsement. First published by John Tuckey in *Mark Twain's Fables of Man* (1972), "Newhouse's Jew Story" and its expanded version, which Tuckey called "Randall's Jew Story," satirize anti-Semitism by dramatizing the benevolence and courage of a Jewish hero. In both tales the protagonist saves an old Southerner and his daughter from the ignominious loss of their slave by using the code's compulsions to rid the river of a dissolute gambler. Thus the duel, which these stories hold up as a vicious practice in itself, also serves to reveal genuine strength of character and attack prejudice.

An index to Mark Twain's development from intemperate journalist to inventive comedian and humane satirist, the duel also functions in his literary works as a significant gauge of a culture's historical progress and its human products.

Earl F. Briden

BIBLIOGRAPHY

Clemens, Samuel L. *Europe and Elsewhere.* New York: Harper, 1923.

————. *Mark Twain of the "Enterprise": Newspaper Articles and Other Documents, 1862–1864.* Ed. Henry Nash Smith and Frederick Anderson. Berkeley: U of California P, 1957.

————. *Mark Twain's Autobiography.* Ed. Albert B. Paine. 2 vols. New York: Harper, 1924.

————. *Mark Twain's Fables of Man.* Ed. John S. Tuckey. Berkeley: U of California P, 1972.

————. *Pudd'nhead Wilson and Those Extraordinary Twins.* Ed. Sidney E. Berger. Norton crit. ed. New York: Norton, 1980.

Fatout, Paul. *Mark Twain in Virginia City.* Bloomington: Indiana UP, 1964.

Paine, Albert Bigelow. *Mark Twain: A Biography.* 3 vols. New York: Harper, 1912.

See also: Pudd'nhead Wilson, The Tragedy of

Duke and the Dauphin, The

In chapters 19 through 33 of *Adventures of Huckleberry Finn* (1885), the Duke and the Dauphin play a significant role. Introducing themselves as the Duke of Bridgewater and "Looy" (Louis) XVII, Dauphin of France, these two rapscallions board the raft a few days after Huck and Jim leave the Grangerford plantation. The Dauphin, perhaps seventy years old, is bald with gray whiskers. The Duke is approximately thirty years old.

These two confidence men exploit Huck and Jim as a means of escaping pursuit, deceiving townsfolk, and obtaining money. Although both tell Huck they are of royal descent, Huck is not duped into believing their schemes. The Duke claims to be a Shakespearean actor, a medicine man, a circuit lecturer, and a schoolteacher. The Dauphin reads fortunes, performs faith healings, and preaches. Partially out of fear, partially out of pity, Huck lies to people about the pair to protect them from harm, although he would prefer to desert the swindlers upon the first opportunity. For example, Huck hurriedly leaves the graveyard as the townsfolk exhume a coffin containing gold he has hidden therein. Fearing discovery, Huck flees for the raft without rejoining the Duke and the Dauphin, but the con artists catch up with Huck, angry because he has attempted to leave them.

In Pikesville the Dauphin sells Jim as a runaway slave. Huck manages to lose them here but informs them of the citizens' intent to run them out of town. He is too late, however, and the two are tarred, feathered, and ridden out on a rail.

Literally, the Duke and Dauphin represent the type of sharpers who infested the shores of the Mississippi in the nineteenth century. Symbolically, they represent that vile class that feeds on honest people. In assigning them titles, Twain satirizes royalty. Royalty's uselessness and cruelty figures into other Twain novels such as *Innocents Abroad* (1869), *The Prince and the Pauper* (1882), *A Connecticut Yankee in King Arthur's Court* (1889), and *Personal Recollections of Joan of Arc* (1896). Twain also uses these two comic figures to poke fun at the decadent South. Unkempt yet ostentatious, the Duke and the Dauphin symbolize the gauche appearance and values of many Southerners in Twain's day. In the end, they are recognized for the frauds they actually are, just as Twain seeks to prove the postbellum South to be the veneered semblance of what it pretends to be.

Twain's sources for the characters of the Duke and the Dauphin can be traced with considerable accuracy. For example, Louis XVII's ambiguous death inspired rumors concerning his whereabouts in the Louisiana region of the Mississippi River. Possible precursors to the Dauphin include a fraudulent Mohawk Indian named Eleazar Williams turned Christian missionary, an English impostor named Tichborne falsely laying claim to a great estate, and Captain Duncan of the sailing vessel *Quaker City* in *Innocents Abroad*. In addition, Twain's own mother boasted a claim to the earlship of Durham through her Lampton ancestors. Both the Duke and the Dauphin represent a mixture of actual and fictitious characters combined to create a rich composite of various levels in American society. In his unique way of manipulating satire, Twain creates two of his most memorable characters.

J.R. LeMaster and David Haines, Jr.

BIBLIOGRAPHY

Baldanza, Frank. *Mark Twain: An Introduction and Interpretation.* New York: Barnes & Noble, 1961.

Blair, Walter. *Mark Twain & Huck Finn.* Berkeley: U of California P, 1960.

DeVoto, Bernard. *Mark Twain's America.* Boston: Little, Brown, 1932.

Paine, Albert Bigelow. "Huck Finn Comes into His Own." *Huck Finn and His Critics.* Ed. Richard Lettis, Robert F. McDonnell, and William E. Morris. New York: Macmillan, 1962. 278–283.

See also: Adventures of Huckleberry Finn;
Dauphin, Louis XVII, The

Duncan, Charles C.

During Mark Twain's Holy Land excursion aboard the *Quaker City* Charles C. Duncan was the ship's captain. Later he served as shipping commissioner of the port of New York. In Twain's eyes, Duncan was a pious hypocrite. In 1877, in a column published in the New York *World*, Twain called him merely the "head waiter of the Holy Land cruise." Twain's remarks were in response to Duncan's being accused of misappropriation of the ship's funds. Duncan sued Clemens twice; both suits were settled out of court. Captain Duncan's portrait appears in the first edition of *Innocents Abroad* (641).

Beverly David

BIBLIOGRAPHY

Clemens, Samuel L. *The Innocents Abroad.* Hartford, Conn.: American Publishing, 1869.

———. *Mark Twain's Notebooks & Journals, Volume III (1883–1891).* Ed. Robert Pack Browning, Michael B. Frank, and Lin Salamo. Berkeley: U of California P, 1979.

See also: Innocents Abroad, The; Quaker City

Duneka, Frederick A.
(d. 1919)

In 1900 Frederick A. Duneka left the New York *World* and became general manager and secretary of Harper and Brothers. Four years before his death in 1919 he became vice president.

While at Harper's he edited Twain's "Chapters from My Autobiography" published in the *North American Review* in 1906–1907 and helped Albert Bigelow Paine assemble the 1916 edition of *The Mysterious Stranger* that Paine fraudulently claimed represented Clemens's final intentions.

Twain's main interaction with Duneka involved monetary matters. Suspicious of all publishers, Twain did not trust Duneka. He was especially upset by Duneka's handling of the 1906 version of *Mark Twain's Library of Humor*. In letters to Henry Huttleston Rogers written in 1906 Twain calls Duneka "that Jesuit," "slippery beyond imagination," and "a sacred enemy." Nonetheless, in 1938 Isabel Lyon recalled that Duneka was always "gentle and tactful" in his dealings with Twain.

Richard Tuerk

BIBLIOGRAPHY

Clemens, Samuel L. *Mark Twain's Correspondence with Henry Huttleston Rogers: 1893–1909*. Ed. Lewis Leary. Berkeley: U of California P, 1969.

"Frederick A. Duneka Dead." New York *Times*, 25 January 1919, 11.

Hill, Hamlin. *Mark Twain: God's Fool*. New York: Harper & Row, 1973.

See also: Harper and Brothers; Paine, Albert Bigelow

E

"Early Rising as Regards Excursions to the Cliff House"
(1864)

"Early Rising as Regards Excursions to the Cliff House" first appeared in San Francisco's *Golden Era* on 3 July 1864. This literary vignette grew out of Twain's work as a reporter for the San Francisco *Daily Morning Call*, for which Twain was, in his words, "*the* reporter" from 7 June to 11 October 1864. On 25 June 1864 the *Daily Morning Call* published "A Trip to the Cliff House." "Early Rising," which appeared only eight days later, is a condemnation, not of the Cliff House, but of an early morning carriage ride that took him there.

Thematically, "Early Rising" seems to be Twain's satiric response to both the sentimentalism of Lisle Lester's "Morning Rides," which recommended early morning pilgrimages to the Cliff House, and the maxims of Benjamin Franklin, specifically "Early to bed, early to rise, makes a man healthy, wealthy and wise," which appears as an epigraph at the beginning of "Early Rising."

While predictable through its formulaic parallelism, "Early Rising" is notable in that it shows how Twain's comic genius was developing during the early days of his career, and it also paves the way for such sketches as "The Late Benjamin Franklin," a piece that appeared in the *Galaxy* in July 1870, in which Twain points out at some length his distaste for Franklin's aphorisms.

Eric Carl Link

BIBLIOGRAPHY

Clemens, Samuel L. *Clemens of the "Call": Mark Twain in San Francisco.* Ed. Edgar M. Branch. Berkeley: U of California P, 1969.

———. *Contributions to "The Galaxy" 1868–1871.* Ed. Bruce R. McElderry, Jr. Gainesville, Fla.: Scholars' Facsimiles and Reprints, 1961.

———. *The Works of Mark Twain: Early Tales & Sketches, Volume 2 (1864–1865).* Ed. Edgar M. Branch and Robert H. Hirst. Berkeley: U of California P, 1981. 24–30.

See also: Journalism; San Francisco *Morning Call*

Eastman, Samuel Elijah
(d. 1925)

The Reverend Samuel E. Eastman and his wife, the Reverend Annis Ford Eastman, went to Elmira, New York, in 1894 as assistant ministers of Park Church (Independent Congregational) and became co-pastors after the death of the Reverend Thomas K. Beecher in 1900. Their liberal ideas were reflected in the lives of their children, Crystal Eastman and Max Eastman, intellectuals and reformers of national significance. Mrs. Eastman wrote the funeral sermon for Mark Twain, although it was read by her husband because of illness. Mrs. Eastman died in 1910 and her husband in 1925.

Herbert A. Wisbey, Jr.

BIBLIOGRAPHY

Eastman, Max. *Heroes I Have Known.* New York: Simon & Schuster, 1942.

See also: Park Church, The

Eddy, Mary Baker
(1821–1910)

The founder of the Christian Science religion, Mary Baker Eddy was one of the most remarkable—and controversial—of nineteenth-century women. Born in Bow, New Hampshire, in 1821 of Calvinist ancestry, she showed little early sign of becoming an important personage in religion. In 1843 she married George Glover. Six months later, she was a widow and pregnant. On 12 September 1844 she gave birth to a son. Unable to care for him, she gave him to a former family servant, and when that family moved to Minnesota, her son went with them. Thus, although subsequently called "Mother" by many thousands, Eddy was, ironically, never a mother to her own son.

A second marriage, to Daniel Patterson, a dentist, proved unhappy. Mrs. Patterson (Eddy) became interested in spiritualism and mesmerism (hypnotism), popular subjects in New England at the time. Afflicted since childhood with an undisclosed spinal ailment, she heard of mental cures being effected by Phineas P. Quimby. She wrote Quimby asking him to visit her. When he did not respond, she went to him, seeing him on 10 October 1862, when she was forty-one. She believed herself cured by her contact with him. From this time, healing became her major preoccupation. Her correspondence with Quimby makes it clear that she sought to follow his methods. For some time she was his enthusiastic disciple, adopting his idea that the Bible contained a science to solve all of life's problems. Soon after, she delivered a public lecture on "Phineas P. Quimby's special Science healing disease." At first, she believed, like Quimby, that the healer actually took on a sufferer's ailment and then threw it off. This doctrine of transference lingered for many years in her teaching.

Separated from Dr. Patterson, estranged from her sister, and suffering from a return of her spinal illness, she subsequently took refuge in a series of private homes.

In January 1866 Quimby died. Two weeks later, Eddy fell on an icy pavement, and it is from her recovery from her injuries after reading of Jesus's healing ministry that the beginnings of Christian Science are dated. She subsequently proclaimed that before the spontaneous disappearance of her symptoms, her condition had been "pronounced fatal by the physician." However, this pronouncement was denied emphatically by the attending physician, Dr. Alvin W. Cushing. Quoting from his notes made at the time of treatment, Dr. Cushing asserted that he never pronounced her case serious, much less grave. Six months after her fall and miraculous recovery, his records show that Eddy, despite her discovery of personal healing power, had Dr. Cushing treat her for a bad cough.

Those who accept Eddy's tale must also explain the existence of a letter in Eddy's own handwriting dated 14 February 1866 addressed to Julius Dresser, a former Quimby patient, saying that "[t]wo weeks ago I fell" and pleading for healing help. That same year, Eddy was separated from her husband. Seven years later she divorced him. He died in the poorhouse while she, ironically, was enjoying great riches and comfort.

After the separation, she lived for several years in rented rooms, never long at one place, well received at first, then forced to move. There are many stories of her envy, bigotry, personal rancor, and narrowness.

In 1883, when she was accused of plagiarizing from Phineas Quimby, she portrayed him as being more of a hindrance that help to her, characterizing him as an illiterate mesmerist. She claimed to be the only and original discoverer of the principles of spiritual healing. However, there exists overwhelming evidence that she plagiarized large parts of her manuscript, including the very nucleus of her well-known "scientific statement of being" from a manuscript prepared by one Francis Lieber on Hegelian metaphysics. A comparison of parallel pages of her work and that of Lieber's earlier work reveals a similarity that is very difficult to question. The board of directors of the First Church of Christ, Scientist claim to have in their files indisputable evidence refuting the charge of plagiarism, but they have thus far been unwilling to make this public.

Objective scholarship about Mary Baker Eddy is hampered by the nature of material available, the overwhelming bulk of which is either unrelentingly laudatory or unreservedly hostile. She can hardly be the saint her followers portray, yet her detractors, usually those hostile to the very idea of valid religious experience, must deal with the many accounts of inexplicable healing based on her teachings, accounts both more challenging and more convincing than the miraculous healing she reported.

Mark Twain's skepticism often caused him to attack religious beliefs, and in *Innocents Abroad* (1869) and *Joan of Arc* (1896) he attacks the duplicity of the church. This is also the case in the selections Bernard DeVoto chose for the first two sections of *Letters from the Earth* (1962). As for Eddy, Twain saw her as "an old swindler" in a history of swindlers hiding behind the cloak of the church. His *Christian Science* (1907) is another of his attempts to come to terms with what he saw as the ongoing duplicity of the church.

Mark Draper

BIBLIOGRAPHY

Dakin, Edwin P. *Mrs. Eddy*. New York: Scribner, 1929.

Eddy, Mary Baker. *Science and Health, with Key to the Scriptures*. Boston: First Church of Christ, Scientist, 1971.

Haushalter, Walter M. *Mrs. Eddy Purloins from Hegel*. Boston: Beauchamp, 1936.

Peel, Robert. *Mary Baker Eddy*. 3 vols. New York: Holt, 1977.

See also: Christian Science; *Christian Science*; Religion

Edinburgh, Scotland

Edinburgh is the capital of Scotland. Twain, his wife Livy, and his daughter Susy, fourteen months old at the time, visited Edinburgh in 1873. In his *Autobiography* (1924) Twain writes that they came "from London, fleeing thither for rest and refuge" after a grueling schedule of "six weeks of daily lunches, teas and dinners away from home." While there, they stayed in Veitch's family hotel. They left Edinburgh and went to Ireland at the end of August.

In Ireland Livy became ill. On their return to Edinburgh, Twain became friends with the physician and author John Brown (1810–1882), who treated Livy for her illness. Biographer of Marjorie Fleming, Brown told Twain about the Scottish child whose life and works fascinated Twain so much that in 1901 he wrote "Marjorie Fleming, the Wonder Child."

When Twain visited Edinburgh, it had slightly over 240,000 inhabitants and many stately monuments and buildings. He bought and shipped to America a carved oak mantlepiece taken from one of the city's castles for his home at Nook Farm. Still, for him the most important results of the visit were his friendship with Dr. Brown and his learning about Marjorie Fleming.

Richard Tuerk

BIBLIOGRAPHY

Clemens, Samuel L. "Marjorie Fleming, the Wonder Child." *Harper's Bazaar* 43 (December 1909): 1182–1183.

———. *Mark Twain's Autobiography.* Ed. Albert B. Paine. 2 vols. New York: Harper, 1924.

Gillies, James B. *Edinburgh: Past and Present.* Edinburgh: Oliphant, Andersen and Ferrier, 1886.

Kaplan, Justin. *Mr. Clemens and Mark Twain.* New York: Simon & Schuster, 1966.

Salsbury, Edith Colgate, ed. *Susy and Mark Twain: Family Dialogues.* New York: Harper & Row, 1965.

See also: Brown, John, M.D.; "Marjorie Fleming, the Wonder Child"

Edison, Thomas Alva
(1847–1931)

As the "Wizard of Menlo Park" and "the genius who spat on the floor," Thomas Alva Edison became the foremost symbol of the American pragmatic thinker-doer in the great age of industrial invention stretching from the Civil War through the turn of the century. Beginning with major advances in telegraphic apparatus in the 1870s, Edison pioneered the electric light (1879), power distribution networks (1882), the phonograph (1877), and the moving picture (1891), among other significant achievements. Given credit as the man who illuminated the world, he was awarded over 4,000 patents in his lifetime, and made and lost several fortunes in the course of his career as inventor entrepreneur.

Throughout his life Edison was a frequent teller of comic and somewhat salty stories. He was also a clever publicist of his inventions in the Barnum-Twain mode fictionalized in Twain's Connecticut Yankee, Hank Morgan.

Unlike Hank Morgan, however, Edison's exuberance was held back by the conservative financial interests that controlled many of the industries he created. Although he seems to have cherished a Victorian home life, Edison was a relentless worker and spent most of his time at his laboratory; throughout his life he insisted that inspiration was 99 percent perspiration.

On meeting Madeleine Edison, the inventor's daughter, on a cruise about 1907, Twain said to her in his characteristic comic drawl: "I think your father is a gre-a-t man, and he—he thinks *I* am a great man."

David E.E. Sloane

BIBLIOGRAPHY

Dyer, Frank Lewis, Thomas Martin, and William Meadowcroft. *Edison, His Life and Inventions.* New York: Harper, 1929.

Josephson, Matthew. *Edison, a Biography.* New York: McGraw-Hill, 1959.

Sloane, Madeleine Edison. Personal reminiscence.

Editions

Mark Twain's immense popularity, in the United States and worldwide, has resulted to date (extrapolating from Robert M. Rodney's 1982 *Mark Twain International*) in roughly 7,000 single editions of his various works and approximately 75 collected editions. About 22 of the single editions have been produced in the United States, 13 percent are English-language editions produced outside the United States, and 65 percent are foreign-language editions (especially German, Spanish, and Russian). About half of the collected editions are domestic and half are foreign.

Most of Twain's important works were originally published by the American Publishing Company, of which he became a director and part owner, and Charles L. Webster and Company, which he established for his nephew (Charles Webster) in the early 1880s but later abandoned as part of his bankruptcy proceedings in 1894. Two notable exceptions were *The Prince and the Pauper* (1882) and *Life on the*

Mississippi (1883), both of which were published by James R. Osgood (Boston) during the transition from American Publishing to Webster. The course of Twain's associations with his publishers ran generally as follows: American Publishing, 1869–1880 and 1894–1902; Osgood, 1882–1883; Webster, 1882–1894; Harper and Brothers, 1896–1910. The major works were published mainly by subscription, which proved a very lucrative method for Twain, and were copiously illustrated. Twain's principal English publisher was Chatto and Windus, but his works were also printed in numerous pirated editions in England and Canada. The authorized English editions usually preceded the American for copyright purposes, and the pirated editions followed almost instantly. Aside from the three-volume "New Holiday Edition" of *Mark Twain's Works* published by Webster in 1891, the first collected edition was the twenty-five-volume *Mark Twain's Works in Uniform Edition*, published by American Publishing in 1899. By the time of Twain's death in 1910, American Publishing and Harper and Brothers had completed or had in process a total of fifteen editions of the collected works.

The problem of identifying the best available editions of Twain's works and papers has been greatly simplified during the past quarter-century thanks to the threefold yield of the Mark Twain Project (headquartered at the Bancroft Library, University of California, Berkeley): the Mark Twain Papers, the Works of Mark Twain (in cooperation with the Iowa Center for Textual Studies, University of Iowa), and the Mark Twain Library. Each volume in these series has been prepared using the best available materials and in consultation with top scholars in the field. Although much of the projected output remains to be achieved, the results to date have established the Mark Twain Project's work as the likely last word in Twain scholarship ahead of scholarship for most other major American authors.

The Mark Twain Papers series publishes previously unpublished works, letters, notebooks, and other Twainiana, accompanied by descriptions of texts and sources, discussions of textual questions, and abundant annotations concerning the biographical and literary contexts of the items reproduced. The titles to date are *Letters to His Publishers, 1867–1894* (1967); *Satires & Burlesques* (1967); *"Which Was the Dream?" and Other Symbolic Writings of the Later Years* (1967); *Hannibal, Huck, and Tom* (1969); *Mysterious Stranger Manuscripts* (1969); *Correspondence with Henry Huttleston Rogers, 1893–1909* (1969); *Fables of Man* (1972); *Notebooks & Journals, Volume I (1855–1873)* (1975), *Volume II (1877–1883)* (1975), and *Volume III (1883–1891)* (1979); *Letters, Volume 1 (1853–1866)* (1988) and *Volume 2 (1867–1868)* (1990). The three *Notebooks & Journals* volumes comprise a completed set (although they do not completely reprint Twain's notebooks and journals), but additional *Letters* volumes are forthcoming. Besides making available previously unpublished material, the Mark Twain Papers publications have made considerable progress toward sorting out confusions about Twain's later writings, especially about the false closure of *The Mysterious Stranger*, and have provided important background for major published works such as *Huckleberry Finn* and *Tom Sawyer*.

The Works of Mark Twain (also known as the Iowa-California editions) bring current scholarship to bear on novels, sketches, etc., published during Twain's lifetime. The text for each work is carefully substantiated, and its republication is supported by description of original texts, discussion of their textual authority, and reproduction of materials deemed relevant to determinations of authorial intention. The following titles have appeared: *Roughing It* (1972), *"What Is Man?" and Other Philosophical Writings* (1973), *A Connecticut Yankee in King Arthur's Court* (1979), *The Prince and the Pauper* (1979), *Early Tales & Sketches, Volume 1 (1851–1864)* (1979) and *Volume 2 (1864–1865)* (1981), *The Adventures of Tom Sawyer, Tom Sawyer Abroad, Tom Sawyer, Detective* (1980), and *Adventures of Huckleberry Finn* (1985).

The detailed discussions of early editions of the Works of Mark Twain series make its volumes a valuable bibliographic resource. And both the Works of Mark Twain volumes and those in the Mark Twain Papers series are good reference sources regarding manuscript versions of the works, fragments, or papers they include. For a more general bibliographic overview, each annual installment of *American Literary Scholarship* (1962–date) contains a review of Mark Twain scholarship for the subject year, including listings of significant new editions and evaluation of their strengths and weaknesses.

One criticism leveled at the Works of Mark Twain series concerns the failure in some of the early volumes, notably *Roughing It* and *Tom Sawyer*, to reproduce the original illustrations.

The Mark Twain Library series uses texts established for the works and papers series as a basis for inexpensive clothbound and paperback editions, omitting the textual apparatus of the works volumes but incorporating all the original illustrations. Titles to date are *A Connecticut Yankee in King Arthur's Court* (1983), *The Prince and the Pauper* (1983), and *Adventures of Huckleberry Finn* (1985). They directly correspond to volumes in the works series; the three-pronged Tom Sawyer volume in the works series is divided into *The Adventures of Tom Sawyer* (1982) and *Tom Sawyer Abroad, Tom Sawyer Detective* (1982); *No. 44, The Mysterious Stranger* (1982) derives from the *Mysterious Stranger Manuscripts* volume of the papers; and *Huck Finn and Tom Sawyer Among the Indians, and Other Unfinished Stories* (1989) corresponds to the papers' *Mark Twain's Hannibal, Huck & Tom*.

An additional volume issuing from the Mark Twain Project but not officially included in any of the three series is *The Devil's Race-Track: Mark Twain's Great Dark Writings: The Best from "Which Was the Dream?" and "Fables of Man"* (1980), which offers (as the title indicates) a selection drawn from two of the papers volumes. These low-priced editions have been produced with classroom use in mind and serve that purpose well.

The Norton Critical Editions series includes paperback editions of three Twain novels: *Adventures of Huckleberry Finn, A Connecticut Yankee in King Arthur's Court*, and *Pudd'nhead Wilson and Those Extraordinary Twins*. These editions provide reasonably reliable texts (although not up to the standards of the Mark Twain Library editions), some information on textual problems and controversies, background material on sources and indications of authorial intention, and a sampling of major criticism. These are especially useful as a starting point for independent research on the novels, and for that reason (plus a relatively low price) they make good college-level texts.

Two moderately priced cloth-bound volumes from the Library of America offer another source for reliable editions of Twain's works. *The Mississippi Writings* volume (1982) contains *Tom Sawyer, Life on the Mississippi, Huckleberry Finn*, and *Pudd'nhead Wilson*; the second volume (1987) consists of *The Innocents Abroad* and *Roughing It*. The combination of modest price and sound scholarship makes these volumes suitable for both library and private collections. Since *The Innocents Abroad* has not been issued as yet in the Works of Mark Twain or the Mark Twain Library, the Library of America edition is (by default, one might say) the best available edition.

Important collections of Twain's correspondence prior to the Mark Twain Papers volumes include Albert Bigelow Paine's two-volume edition of *Mark Twain's Letters* (Harper and Brothers, 1917), *Mark Twain and George Washington Cable: A Record of a Literary Friendship* (Michigan State University Press, 1960), and *Mark Twain–Howells Letters: The Correspondence of Samuel L. Clemens and William D. Howells, 1872–1910* (Harvard University Press, 1960). The "Notebooks" volumes were preceded by the 1935 *Mark Twain's Notebook* (Harper and Brothers), also edited by Paine. *The Mysterious Stranger* volumes replace the notorious 1916 version in which Paine and

Frederick Duneka "finished" Twain's unfinished text(s).

Facsimile reproductions make the first editions of *Huckleberry Finn* (Harper & Row, 1987) and *Pudd'nhead Wilson* (Chandler, 1968) generally available, and there are well-done reproductions of two important holograph manuscripts: *The Adventures of Tom Sawyer* (University Publications/ Georgetown University Press, 1982) and *The Adventures of Huckleberry Finn (Tom Sawyer's Comrade): A Facsimile of the Manuscript* (Gale, 1983). The *Huckleberry Finn* manuscript is, of course, partial, covering about 60 percent of the novel, and the price for holograph reproduction is high. Selections of Twain's poetry can be found in *On the Poetry of Mark Twain with Selections from His Verse* (Arthur L. Scott, University of Illinois Press, 1966) and *Mark Twain's Rubáiyát* (Alan Gribben, Jenkins, 1983).

James S. Leonard

BIBLIOGRAPHY

Blanck, Jacob, comp. *Bibliography of American Literature.* New Haven, Conn.: Yale UP, 1955. 173–254.

Johnson, Merle. *A Bibliography of the Works of Mark Twain.* New York: Harper, 1935.

McBride, William M., comp. *Mark Twain: A Bibliography of the Collections of the Mark Twain Memorial and the Stowe-Day Foundation.* Hartford, Conn.: McBride, 1984.

Parker, Herschel. [Review of five volumes of Works of Mark Twain and Mark Twain Papers.] *Journal of English and Germanic Philology* 81 (October 1982): 596–604.

Rodney, Robert M., ed. and comp. *Mark Twain International: A Bibliography and Interpretation of His Worldwide Popularity.* Westport, Conn.: Greenwood P, 1982.

See also: Bibliographies; Correspondence; Manuscript Collections; Mark Twain Papers; Mark Twain Project

Education

Mark Twain's formal education was brief and had little to do with his literary career except as a source of humor for his early novels, but as an adult he valued learning, read widely, had a working knowledge of three foreign languages, and received honorary degrees from three universities, including a doctorate from Oxford.

His schooling began at four-and-a-half in Hannibal "dame" schools, where each day began with a prayer and a chapter from the New Testament. Older, he moved on to "common" schools, taught by men. Lessons, no doubt, were taught from the standard school texts of the time, such as Webster's spellers and McGuffey's readers. Some sense of the type of schooling he received and his reaction to it can be found in *Tom Sawyer* (1876) and *Huckleberry Finn* (1885). Like Samuel Clemens, Tom Sawyer had a quick and inventive mind, but neither was a conscientious scholar, and the liberal application of the switch could not reform them. Both, however, prided themselves on their one academic achievement, winning consistently the medal given weekly for spelling, which they sometimes would trade for the medal for conduct consistently won by the good boy of the class.

Clemens's formal education ended sometime after his father's death in March 1847, when he was apprenticed to a Hannibal printer and subsequently served as editorial assistant for his brother Orion's newspaper. Abraham Lincoln once called the printing office "the poor boy's college," and so it was for the adolescent Samuel Clemens. The exchange system among newspapers put him in touch with not only the news of the day but also the literature, the lasting and the ephemeral, in particular native American humor, which inspired his first published literary efforts in Hannibal newspapers. Twain would later recall that his interest in "serious" reading also began at this time when he came upon a stray page from a history of Joan of Arc blowing along the street, which led to his first efforts to learn foreign languages as well as to his lifelong interest in that historical heroine in particular and history in general. All of his life he read avidly and widely, although he usually preferred nonfiction to belles lettres.

Twain's school days provided him with much of the humor of *Tom Sawyer* and *Huckleberry Finn*, but he was critical of the educational methods of his time, which stressed rote memorization and enforced learning with punishment. Twain demonstrated his theories with the method he devised to teach his children about the history he loved. Together, they lined their driveway with stakes identifying the history of English monarchs and spaced proportionately to represent the length of their reigns. Other stakes identified the history of other nations, of science, and of literature. History could thus be visualized and associated with familiar landmarks—and the exercise was beneficial as well, he said.

Twain's philosophy of education is closely related to his concept of "training," by which he meant not merely "study, instruction, lectures, sermons" but "*all* the outside influences" that determine what people believe and how they act, for good and for ill, he wrote in *What Is Man?* (1906). He believed that "[t]raining toward higher and higher, ever higher ideals is worth any man's thought and labor and diligence," but the impulse for change must come from the outside. He explored that philosophy in *A Connecticut Yankee in King Arthur's Court* (1889) with Hank Morgan's secret "man factories," schools that would turn out enlightened citizens whose minds would not be enslaved by the church and state. The Yankee's utopian dream of reform proves a failure, however, when the church asserts its power with an interdict, and all but fifty-two of the "students" go over to the enemy. "Did you think you had educated the superstitions out of them?" Clarence asks, a conclusion suggesting Twain's ultimate despair about the damned human race.

Cameron C. Nickels

BIBLIOGRAPHY

Clemens, Samuel L. *Mark Twain's Autobiography*. Ed. Albert B. Paine. 2 vols. New York: Harper, 1924.

Gribben, Alan. *Mark Twain's Library: A Reconstruction*. 2 vols. Boston: G.K. Hall, 1980.

Paine, Albert Bigelow. *Mark Twain: A Biography*. 3 vols. Harper, 1912.

Wecter, Dixon. *Sam Clemens of Hannibal*. Boston: Houghton Mifflin, 1952.

See also: *Connecticut Yankee in King Arthur's Court, A*; Hannibal, Missouri; Reading; *What Is Man?*

"Edward Mills and George Benton: A Tale"
(1880)

First published in the *Atlantic Monthly* in August 1880 and reprinted in *The $30,000 Bequest* (1906), this short story carries on Twain's sardonic criticism of sentimental women; simple-minded religion, including Sunday school stories; and glib aphorisms, including the work ethic, as guides to the conduct of life. The title characters are foster brothers, adopted by a couple who teach them, "Be pure, honest, sober, industrious, considerate, and you will never lack friends."

Edward Mills follows their precept and is killed by his brother, leaving his family destitute. George Benton breaks laws, enjoys himself, and dies at the gallows, with crowds of women begging for a pardon and his family dutifully supported by a charitable organization. This story has received virtually no critical commentary, being a more complicated joke on the heroes than earlier stories but still underdeveloped in plot and character.

Ruth K. MacDonald

BIBLIOGRAPHY

Clemens, Samuel L. *The $30,000 Bequest and Other Stories*. New York: Harper, 1906. 129–138.

Wilson, James D. *A Reader's Guide to the Short Stories of Mark Twain*. Boston: G.K. Hall, 1987.

See also: Boy Books

Edward VII
(1841–1910)

Edward VII of England, eldest son of Queen Victoria and Prince Albert, became king at age sixty after a frustrating life of exclusion from any role in his mother's court or government. Victoria and Albert's exalted expectations for their heir overpowered the prince, who consoled himself with clothes, race horses, yachting, gambling, and women. While intervening in Edward's college escapades, Prince Albert caught a chill from which he died in 1861. The desolated widow never forgave her son.

After marrying the beautiful Alexandra of Denmark, Edward became the leader of society's "fast set," which included Jewish financiers and Edward's mistresses, Alice Keppel and actress Lily Langtree. The prince traveled restlessly, visiting the United States in 1860 and venturing to Russia, Turkey, and India. He frequented Paris and fashionable continental spas.

In his brief reign (1901–1910) Edward was the last European monarch to succeed at family diplomacy. He loathed his nephew Kaiser Wilhelm II of Germany but used their relationship to control tensions between their countries. His popularity in France contributed to the *Entente Cordiale* of 1904. Edward was progressive at home and helped steer the country through the Budget Crisis of 1910. He died on 9 May 1910. The eight reigning monarchs and other royalty at his funeral constituted one of the last pageants of the prewar world. Edward was the symbol of the Edwardian age, its elegance, its discreet dissipations, and its worldly amiability as Victorian rectitude mellowed in the last days before the Great War.

Twain's interest in the theme of the heir apparent occurs in a number of his works, most specifically in *The Prince and the Pauper* (1882), set in sixteenth-century England. But Twain knew Edward VII, even dined with him at Bad Nauheim, Germany. The meeting was not a success because Twain insisted on being the center of attention, a fact that seemed not to impress Edward. Ironically, they died in the same year.

Arthur W. White

BIBLIOGRAPHY

Lee, Sir Sidney. *King Edward VII*. 2 vols. New York: Macmillan, 1925.

Magnus, Philip. *King Edward the Seventh*. New York: Dutton, 1964.

St. Aubyn, Giles. *Edward VII, Prince and King*. New York: Atheneum, 1979.

See also: England

Egypt

Samuel Clemens and his party on the ship *Quaker City*, described in *The Innocents Abroad* (1869), stopped at Egypt on their return trip from the Holy Land. They arrived 2 October 1867 at the Egyptian seaport of Alexandria after a two-day voyage from Joppa. They traveled inland by train and, on donkeys, toured Cairo and the pyramids at Giza before returning to the ship on 6 October and leaving the following day. Accompanying them to Egypt as deck passengers were about forty members of the unsuccessful Adams Colony, who were seeking free passage back home to the state of Maine.

Clemens said Alexandria at night with its commercial buildings and gas lighting reminded him of Paris or a European city. By contrast, Cairo was the complete Oriental capital, with camels, dark-skinned inhabitants, costumes, and winding streets. He judged the Nile at Cairo narrower than the Mississippi, but the great pyramid of Cheops was taller than the highest bluff on the river between St. Louis and New Orleans—480 versus 413 feet.

Looking at Egypt from the top of the great pyramid, Clemens described seeing an enchanted green Eden in one direction and "a mighty sea of yellow sand" in the other. Up close, the faces of Egyptian guides, beggars, and children tortured travelers with appeals for money. At the pyramids Clemens hired an Arab to drive away the crowd of beggars. He was similarly annoyed by the souvenir hunting of fellow travelers, who with hammers and sledges chipped away at Cleopatra's

Needle, Pompey's Pillar, and even the face of the Sphinx itself.

Clemens was moved by the age, loneliness, and magnitude of the 5,000-year-old Egyptian antiquities. He praised ancient Egypt as "the mother of civilization—which taught Greece her letters." Clemens said Egypt developed a concept of eternal life before the children of Israel did, had glass and glass painting 3,000 years before England, knew lost techniques of medicine and surgery just now being rediscovered, made paper, operated public schools, embalmed the dead, and left enduring evidence of culture and intelligence to outlast all scoffers.

Ira Royals, Jr.

BIBLIOGRAPHY

Clemens, Samuel L. *The Innocents Abroad.* Hartford, Conn.: American Publishing, 1869.

Ganzel, Dewey. *Mark Twain Abroad: The Cruise of the "Quaker City."* Chicago: U of Chicago P, 1968.

See also: Innocents Abroad, The

Elmira, New York

Mark Twain first came to Elmira in 1869 to court Olivia Langdon, the sister of Charles Langdon, a fellow passenger on the *Quaker City* cruise made famous by the book *The Innocents Abroad* (1869). Livy was the daughter of wealthy businessman Jervis Langdon, and her marriage to the young author two years later began one of the most celebrated love stories in American literary history. For the next forty years Elmira played a major role in the life of the author and his family, until his death in 1910.

The city of Elmira, with a population of about 16,000 in 1870, was the county seat of Chemung County, New York. Through railroads and a canal it had access to the great bituminous and anthracite coal regions of Pennsylvania. It was a station on the Underground Railroad before the Civil War and the site of a prison camp during the war. Elmira

Female College, opened in 1855, was a pioneer in higher education for women.

For the Clemens family, Elmira meant Quarry Farm, located on East Hill about two and a half miles from the Langdon family home downtown. It was purchased as a summer home in 1869, and when Jervis Langdon died the following year, the farm was left to the oldest Langdon daughter, Susan L. Crane. It was to Quarry Farm that Mark Twain and Livy came on their way to a new home in Hartford after an unhappy interlude in Buffalo. For most of the summers in the 1870s and 1880s, the Clemens family came back to Elmira where their three daughters—Susy, Clara, and Jean—were born.

Mark Twain completed *Roughing It* (1872) in Elmira, and in subsequent summers he wrote major portions of *The Adventures of Tom Sawyer* (1876), *Adventures of Huckleberry Finn* (1885), *The Prince and the Pauper* (1882), *A Tramp Abroad* (1880), *Life on the Mississippi* (1883), *A Connecticut Yankee in King Arthur's Court* (1889), and other works. Free from the interruptions of his Hartford home, he worked in an octagonal study built for him in 1874. Elmira became well known as Mark Twain's summer home. Visitors purchased postcards of Quarry Farm and reporters, including young Rudyard Kipling who came on his way home from India, climbed the hill to interview the literary celebrity.

Mark Twain often walked to town, where he found many sources of congenial companionship. The Elmira Watercure and the home of Thomas K. and Julia Beecher were frequent stopping-off places. The Elmira Reformatory, opened in 1876, provided Mark Twain with a captive audience to try out his lectures, and a friend in the person of its pioneering superintendent, Zebulon R. Brockway.

Literary critics once argued about the influence of Livy and Elmira on Mark Twain's writing. Most now agree with the assessment of Max Eastman, whose parents served a joint ministry at Park Church. After describing the cultural atmosphere he experienced as a youth, he concluded that "the Elmira influence was a vitally liberating one to Mark Twain." Park Church was central to the life of the Langdon family, and its charismatic pastor, Thomas Beecher, provided intellectual stimulus for Mark Twain.

Visits to Elmira became less frequent after financial difficulties made it necessary for the Clemens family to live abroad. Yet it was from Elmira that Mark Twain left on his lecture tour around the world that resulted in the book *Following the Equator* (1897). When Susy Clemens died of spinal meningitis in Hartford, her body was brought back to Elmira to join that of her infant brother. The last summer the family spent at Quarry Farm was in 1903. Mark Twain, concerned for Livy's health, did little writing there. Livy died the next year in Florence, Italy. She was buried beside Susy in Elmira's Woodlawn Cemetery, to be joined by Jean in 1909 and by Mark Twain himself in 1910. Clara and her husband Ossip Gabrilowitsch, and daughter, Nina, are also buried there—all of the direct descendants of Mark Twain.

Quarry Farm remained in the Langdon family until 1982 when it was given to Elmira College and became the home of the Center for Mark Twain Studies at Quarry Farm. Mark Twain's study, an earlier gift, was moved to the Elmira College campus in 1952. Various city landmarks such as the Mark Twain Riverfront Park, the Clemens Performing Arts Center on the Clemens Center Parkway, and Katy Leary Park commemorate the author's association with Elmira. The Mark Twain Society, incorporated in 1975, has published *Mark Twain in Elmira* and publishes a biannual bulletin. Scholars have discovered the resources of the Mark Twain Archives in the Gannett-Tripp Learning Center of Elmira College. Quarry Farm still has a good view of the Chemung River and the hills stretching into Pennsylvania that inspired Mark Twain to write.

Herbert A. Wisbey, Jr.

BIBLIOGRAPHY

Jerome, Robert D., and Herbert A. Wisbey, Jr., eds. *Mark Twain in Elmira.* Elmira, N.Y.: Mark Twain Society, 1977.
Cotton, Michelle. *Mark Twain's Elmira, 1870–1910.* Elmira, N.Y.: Chemung County Historical Society, 1985.

See also: Elmira College Center for Mark Twain Studies at Quarry Farm; Mark Twain's Study; Quarry Farm

Elmira College Center for Mark Twain Studies at Quarry Farm

(1983–)

The Elmira College Center for Mark Twain Studies at Quarry Farm was established at the outset of 1983 to provide Mark Twain scholars with the same temporary residence Samuel L. Clemens found so congenial to his own creative efforts. Here, throughout the 1870s and 1880s, the Clemens family summered as guests of Clemens's in-laws, Susan and Theodore Crane; and here, as well, Clemens wrote the major portions of his chief works of this same period. In addition to its program of fellowships-in-residence, the center sponsors a number of other activities intended to foster and support Mark Twain studies.

The facilities of the center are located three miles outside Elmira on an idyllic six-and-a-half-acre hilltop site overlooking the Chemung River valley. At the close of 1982 Clemens's grandnephew, Jervis Langdon, Jr., gave the site and the structures located on it as a gift to Elmira College with the stipulation that the grounds and buildings be preserved and utilized as a Center for Mark Twain Studies. The facilities of the center include a fine Victorian house with period furnishings and paintings; a small conference center in renovated structures that once housed a laundry, woodshed, and sleeping quarters for the household staff; and a large Victorian barn renovated to accommodate larger audiences for center-sponsored events in the temperate portion of the year. Also occupying the center's grounds is the original site of the famous octagonal study where Twain wrote when summering at Quarry Farm. (The study was removed to the Elmira College campus in 1952.) The farm setting is removed and quiet, and the view, especially from the great porch of the main house, where Twain often read his day's work to a varying assembly of family, friends, neighborhood children, and household staff, is panoramic.

The main house, with a fully equipped kitchen, is reserved as a residence for visiting scholars; center offices are located in the small conference cottage behind the main house; and caretakers are in residence in a wing adjacent to the main house.

Center fellows-in-residence at Quarry Farm enjoy access to the Langdon-Crane Library, the John S. Tuckey Memorial Library, and the Mark Twain Archive of the college's Gannett-Tripp Library. The first two of these libraries are located in the main house at Quarry Farm, while the latter is on the Elmira College campus. The 1,800-volume Langdon-Crane Library consists of classic works of nineteenth- and early-twentieth-century American and European literature and history. The John S. Tuckey Memorial Library consists of 200 standard titles of biography and criticism in the field of Mark Twain studies. The Mark Twain Archive of the college's Gannett-Tripp Library contains works with Twain marginalia, an extensive collection of Mark Twain first editions, original Twain notes, letters and photos, and microfilm portions of the major Twain collections at Berkeley, Vassar, and Hartford. An exhaustive collection of all the talks sponsored by the center is available both in the main house at Quarry Farm and at the college's Gannett-Tripp Library. The collection includes the talks given by Henry Nash Smith and John S. Tuckey, subsequently published as the first two *Quarry Farm Papers*, as well as talks by other distinguished academic visitors to the center, Quarry Farm fellows, and presenters at center conferences.

Fellowships-in-residence at Quarry Farm usually run from two weeks to two months. They include free lodging at Quarry Farm and sometimes a stipend in exchange for a public talk on work in progress. In addition to these Quarry Farm fellowships-in-residence, the center also awards named fellowships in recognition of distinguished service to the center, lasting contributions to the field of Mark Twain studies, or some combination of these.

Other center programs include a distinguished academic visitors series; public talks and chamber theater; special presentations for community and school groups; summer graduate courses, seminars, or institutes for school teachers; colloquia and conferences; and publications.

In addition to a newsletter, *Dear Friends*, published for the Friends of the Center, the center also publishes the above-mentioned occasional series of *Quarry Farm Papers*, which make available in print talks of the first importance to Mark Twain studies given by visitors to the center.

The center's staff, consisting of a director, associate director, curator, Mark Twain archivist, and a photo-librarian, is aided by a community advisory board and a distinguished national committee of academic advisers.

Darryl Baskin

See also: Journals; Quarry Farm

Emerson, Ralph Waldo
(1803–1882)

In Mark Twain's time Ralph Waldo Emerson, essayist, poet, and lecturer, was widely recognized as a great man. After leaving the ministry in 1832, he became a leader of the Transcendentalist movement. On his lecture tours he brought his striking personality as well as ideas to a wide audience. His essays were widely read, his difficult poetry much less well known.

Although Emerson was more than thirty years Clemens's senior, it was inevitable that they should encounter one another, especially after Clemens settled in New England and was introduced to its distinguished writers in Boston. Apparently as early as his Hannibal days Clemens identified Emerson as an important literary figure. In 1906 he recalled in an autobiographical dictation that in 1853 his brother Orion had asked several celebrated writers, including Emerson, to write an original story for his newspaper. The next reference to Emerson in Clemens's writings can be found in "Concerning the Answer to That Conundrum" (8 July 1864), where he refers to "the great law of compensation," which Emerson had made famous with his essay on the subject. In another column for the *Californian*, dated 17 June 1865, "Answers to Correspondents," Mark Twain explains how to become a literary connoisseur. One part of his advice is to ascribe to Emerson "all the poetry you can't understand."

In April 1867 Mark Twain lectured in Keokuk, Iowa, and Quincy, Illinois, to large crowds only three months after Emerson had lectured in the same towns. When Mark Twain lectured in St. Louis on the same tour, the local newspaper compared the two and reported that Mark Twain had succeeded in interesting and amusing "a large and promiscuous audience" as Emerson had failed to do.

Alan Gribben has identified three volumes of Emerson's writings that Mark Twain owned: *Essays, Selections from the Writings of Ralph Waldo Emerson,* and *Parnassus,* an anthology of poems that Emerson edited. The fireplace of the Clemens Hartford house was (and is) decorated with a brass engraving of a quotation from Emerson's essay "Domestic Life": "The ornament of a house is the friends who frequent it." One who knew Mark Twain remembered that he had called Emerson a great man who "valued impressions and ideas above everything." Gribben quotes Isabel Lyon's journal for 16 May 1906, reporting that Mark Twain had sat one evening before and after dinner with Emerson's poems and read many

of them aloud. That same year at a congressional committee hearing on patents Mark Twain identified Emerson as one of the few writers of nineteenth-century America whose books had lasted forty-two years.

Mark Twain's most famous reference to Emerson came in his celebrated Whittier birthday speech, made in Emerson's presence on 17 December 1877. Mark Twain had been introduced into the Boston literary scene in 1871, when William Dean Howells had taken him to dine at the Saturday Club, of which Emerson, Holmes, and Longfellow were members. At the Whittier dinner Mark Twain told amusingly of a miner who reported having been visited by three men who identified themselves as Henry Wadsworth Longfellow, Oliver Wendell Holmes, and Ralph Waldo Emerson. The man who represented himself as Emerson was described as "a seedy little bit of a chap" (Emerson was a tall, commanding figure); he was said to have quoted from five of Emerson's poems: "Mithridates," "Concord Hymn," "Brahma," "Song of Nature," and "Monadnoc." Afterward, when with encouragement from Howells Mark Twain wrote letters of apology to the three writers, Emerson's daughter Ellen replied to Mrs. Clemens that her father had not been able to hear the speech but was amused when it was read to him the next day. She added that the Emersons had enjoyed many of Mark Twain's works and identified *The Innocents Abroad* (1869) as a special favorite of her father's. At the same time Mark Twain also wrote to Mary Mason Fairbanks that in his Whittier birthday speech he had no intention of hurting "those great poets' feelings." Emerson was also present at an 1879 birthday celebration honoring Oliver Wendell Holmes when Mark Twain spoke again, but this time he made no mention of Emerson.

In April 1882, shortly before his trip to the Mississippi River, Mark Twain went with Howells to Concord to pay his respects to Emerson; that evening they went back to the house and stood outside, reverently. Later, while he was in New Orleans, Mark Twain heard that the great man had died on 27 April and recorded in his notebook, "So glad I visited him two or three weeks ago."

It cannot be said that Emerson was a significant influence on Mark Twain and certainly not vice versa. Rather, Emerson was a presence in Mark Twain's life as an important representative of New England high culture.

Everett Emerson

BIBLIOGRAPHY

Gribben, Alan. *Mark Twain's Library: A Reconstruction.* 2 vols. Boston: G.K. Hall, 1980.

Rusk, Ralph L. *The Life of Ralph Waldo Emerson.* New York: Scribner, 1949.

See also: Whittier Birthday Dinner Speech

"Emperor-God Satire, The"
(1972)

This piece commands attention because in it Mark Twain attempts to work out some of his recurrent themes in a relatively systematic way. Bernard DeVoto titled this short manuscript; John S. Tuckey dated the composition to the 1870s based on a similarity of its paper to that used for "The Propositions of God," which Albert B. Paine had earlier dated to the 1870s. First publication of the fable came in *Mark Twain's Fables of Man* (1972).

DeVoto's title seems quite appropriate because in this brief, fantastic fable Twain explores the beliefs about the Emperor-God who lives in a fictional place called Unyumi (i.e., "un-you-mi" or "not you me" or "not you and I"). The attributes of a God and of an emperor seem similar; both are elevated, honored, controlling personalities who can be capricious, willful, mean, and conscienceless, yet still be worshiped by the people. Thus this satire also reflects badly, by implication, upon the followers, all those humans who worship or support an emperor or God.

In this transparently clear story Twain develops his ideas systematically. He uses the setting or geography to correspond to cultural distinctions; the more civilized or more sophisticated believers live inland, and the God consistently ignores their prayers (Twain uses for these people a deistic conception of a distant, uninvolved God). In contrast, the less civilized, savage tribes live near the sea, and the same God inconsistently involves himself in their lives, frequently with disastrous results. He will be irascible, moody, killing one tribal king and favoring another, reversing the moon, changing the tides, and drowning many people. This God even supervises with great detail the tribes' sexual practices and their baking of sacrificial animals. This God is active, interventionist, temperamental, but not really helpful.

Throughout his career Twain pondered the morality or folly of people praying to a God for personal interests even though other humans would be harmed (see *Innocents Abroad* [1869] or "The Second Advent" [1972]). Similarly, Twain's ideas of reincarnation, repetition, and historical cycles surface because this Emperor-God has ruled for over 11,000 years by using the bodies of 1,246 priests, not suitably embalmed. Thus this satire can apply to many levels of civilization and to a large portion of history.

Twain's artistic skill shows even in this minor work. He deftly sharpens the satire with surgical skill. For example, the priests of the sophisticated believers have the duty of transporting gifts to the God, but they only deliver a "tolerable" amount of the gifts. Twain, however, revised the phrasing so that only "a small percentage of the gifts" are delivered, subtly implying the priests' greed, generation after generation. The tone of this satire is careful, detailed, patient, and explanatory. The reader realizes the intellectual power of the satire only when considering the resemblance to the known monarchial and religious practices of this planet. But readers should not worry because this dreadful God is the Emperor of "Unyumi" ('not you and/or me')!

Victor Doyno

BIBLIOGRAPHY

Clemens, Samuel L. *Mark Twain's Fables of Man*. Ed. John S. Tuckey. Berkeley: U of California P, 1972. 116–120.

See also: God; Religion

"Enchanted Sea-Wilderness, The"
(1967)

A discarded section of *Following the Equator* (1897), "The Enchanted Sea-Wilderness" is the first of three "voyage of disaster" fragments Twain wrote during the late 1890s. This initial version of the tale, composed in late 1896 and broadly modeled upon Samuel Coleridge's "The Rime of the Ancient Mariner," was originally published in *Mark Twain's "Which Was the Dream?"* (1967). It is narrated by a "bronzed and gray sailor" who somehow survived the voyage of the vessel *Mabel Thorpe* en route to Australia in 1853. A friendly St. Bernard, the crew's pet, saves their lives by warning of a fire, but at the captain's orders he is left behind when they abandon ship. The captain, who "had an idea he was born lucky," is cursed for his heartlessness. The sailors drift in the lifeboat into "the Devil's Race Track," the great circle of currents between the Cape of Good Hope and the South Pole, then into the utter calm of "the Everlasting Sunday" at its center. Months later, they spy a fleet of wrecked ships manned by "leathery shriveled-up effigies," corpses preserved for years in the dry, cold climate. The fragment is of particular interest as a rehearsal for "The Great Dark."

Gary Scharnhorst

BIBLIOGRAPHY

Clemens, Samuel L. *Mark Twain's "Which Was the Dream?" and Other Symbolic Writings of the Later Years*. Ed. John S. Tuckey. Berkeley: U of California P, 1967. 76–86.

Jones, Daryl. "Mark Twain's Symbols of Despair: A Relevant Letter." *American Literary Realism 1870–1910* 15.2 (Autumn 1982): 266–268.

Marotti, Maria Ornella. *The Duplicating Imagination: Twain and the Twain Papers*. University Park: Penn State UP, 1990.

See also: Dreams; "Great Dark, The"

England

In *Turn West, Turn East* (1951) Henry Seidel Canby contrasts Mark Twain's turn toward the West of newness and imagination with Henry James's turn toward the East of tradition and reflection. Yet Twain also turned often toward the East, to Europe and England especially, for a variety of reasons and with great benefits to his creativity. His approaches to England will be discussed under five headings: ancestry, travel, arrangements for publishing and marketing his works, subjects for writing, and literary influences.

During his career Twain often showed both playful and wishful interests in English noble ancestry. He liked to think that his father was a descendant of Gregory Clement, one of the judges who condemned King Charles I to execution, and he procured a copy of the warrant with Clement's signature and an engraving of his picture. He also heard that his mother, Jane Lampton, came from the Lambtons of Durham. However, when Jesse Leathers, a distant cousin of hers, claimed that he was the rightful Earl of Durham and asked for money to contest his case, Twain refused, although he later worked this incident into his play *Colonel Sellers as a Scientist* (written 1883) and his novel *The American Claimant* (1892). While in England during 1873 he followed the Tichborne trial and had a friend save newspaper reports of it. This concerned the butcher, Arthur Orton, who tried to prove that he was Sir Roger Tichborne, the long lost son of Lady Tichborne. Many of Twain's most colorful characters—Colonel Sellers, the King and the Duke, Young Satan, even Shakespeare—are "claimants" to titles and fortunes, and they reflect both a scorn and a fondness for nobility on Twain's part.

Twain first traveled to England in the fall of 1872. He wanted to advertise himself to English readers, arrange for a faithful and profitable publication of his books there, and gather notes as a tourist for a satirical book on England. During his stay, however, he realized that he was already known and liked there as a humorist. He was invited to speak at clubs and banquets, met several authors—Charles Kingsley, Charles Reade, Thomas Hood, Robert Browning—and felt quite at home in this respectable company. The following May 1873 he returned with his wife and his daughter Susy. Again he toured and met famous people—Herbert Spencer, Anthony Trollope, Lewis Carroll—but he also began giving public lectures, first on the Sandwich Islands and then on the American West. Although he wrote some sketches of English travel (for example, "A Memorable Midnight Experience" [1874], on his visit to Westminster Abbey) he held off on a satirical book, perhaps because he was too charmed by English life and society. After leaving England in January 1874, he did not return until the summer of 1879, having just spent over a year in Germany and France compiling material for *A Tramp Abroad* (1880). This time he met Charles Darwin and American expatriates Henry James and James Whistler. He also researched and visited scenes that he would use in *The Prince and the Pauper* (1882). In the summer of 1894 he stopped in England again after a three-year stay on the Continent, and he lived in England for a year, July 1896 to July 1897, after his world lecture tour of the English provinces. There he wrote his book on that tour, *Following the Equator* (1897), in which he generally approved of British rule in India, yet criticized some of their practices in South Africa. He visited England to receive an honorary degree from Oxford University along with Auguste Rodin, Camille Saint-Saëns, and Rudyard Kipling. This time he met King Edward VII.

As mentioned, one reason Twain made trips to England was to oversee publication of his books there, and Dennis Welland gives a thorough and detailed account of these transactions. In 1870 English copyright for a book could be acquired only by first publishing the book in England. Since Twain's early books were first published in the United States, English publishers printed and sold them, along with collections of his newspaper sketches, without his permission and usually without paying him. By letters, and then by a visit to England in 1872, Twain arranged with Routledge and Sons to publish his books with his own prefaces, revisions, and with fair payment. In 1876 he switched to Chatto and Windus, probably because of their higher royalties and more aggressive marketing, and they became his English publishers for the next twenty years. Moncure Conway, an American expatriate in England, acted as Twain's literary agent, helping with negotiations, writing reviews, and even reading early samples of his forthcoming books in public lectures. Still, problems occurred that aroused Twain's ire. *The Adventures of Tom Sawyer* (1876), for instance, was supposed to be published in England one day ahead of its American publication, to gain English copyright. However, since the American edition was delayed, a Canadian publisher printed the English edition and distributed it in the United States with no profit for Twain. Sometimes an English edition had to appear first without illustrations in order to meet its deadline. Through the 1880s, however, timing and communications improved, and Twain profited well from English sales. In England, by the way, his books sold through bookstores, not by subscription as in America.

Rather than travel or business, however, it was the reading of English authors, and the influence that this reading had on his own writing, especially on his books about England, that brought Twain closest to English culture and ideas. Howard Baetzhold has analyzed the influences of English authors on Twain's general views of England and on many of his particular themes and techniques.

Baetzhold divides Twain's views on England into three periods. In the first period, the 1870s and early 1880s, Twain was attracted to English tradition and aristocracy. Although he blamed Sir Walter Scott for reviving feudalism in *Ivanhoe* (1819), he appreciated Scott's historical realism in *Quentin Durward* (1823), and he found in Thomas Carlyle's *The French Revolution* (1837) and Charles Dickens's *A Tale of Two Cities* (1859) valid descriptions of social problems in his own time. He especially agreed with Carlyle's fear of rule by the masses and his search for strong individual leaders. In his own historical novel, *The Prince and the Pauper*, Twain put Prince Edward through an ordeal that would train him to be such a leader. He relied heavily on W.E.H. Lecky's *A History of European Morals* (1869) for the concept of moral training. In the second period, the mid-1880s to the early 1890s, Twain shifted to a strong democratic stance. He bitterly satirized humanity's subjection to the superstitions of religion, aristocracy, law, education, and romance. *A Connecticut Yankee in King Arthur's Court* (1889) expressed his views during this period. Although it was directed against the superstitions of universal humanity, its setting in England and its occasional references to contemporary English institutions, the established church, for example, made the novel also a criticism of England. Again Twain used Carlyle, but now he opposed Carlyle's moderate royalist stance, and he also burlesqued the notion of "reverence" discussed in recent articles by Matthew Arnold. From the mid-1890s on, however, Twain became reconciled to English culture. In his lecture tour of the English colonies, described in *Following the Equator*, he generally supported the civilizing influence of English rule in India and, with some exceptions, in South Africa. In this his views resembled those of his good friend, Rudyard Kipling.

Besides these influences on Twain's general reactions toward England, Baetzhold examines influences of English authors on specific themes and techniques. Twain often considered the early English authors (Chaucer and Shakespeare, Samuel Pepys, and the eighteenth-century novelists Fielding, Sterne, and Smollett) to be coarse in content and style, yet he found in them an honesty, freedom, and robustness that would have enlivened Victo-

rian literature. English books of travel, both real and imaginary, such as *Gulliver's Travels* (1726), *Robinson Crusoe* (1719), Goldsmith's *Citizen of the World* (1762), and Byron's *Childe Harold's Pilgrimage* (1812–1818) helped Twain develop techniques of movement, perspective, and satire in his travel books and episodic novels. Dickens, whom he saw at a reading in New York in December 1867, was a strong personal and literary influence. Both writers came from humble origins, advanced by self-education and journalism, and appealed to a popular readership through humor and social criticism. Their boyhood stories especially hold much in common. Baetzhold traces direct links between *David Copperfield* (1850), Twain's burlesque "Boy's Manuscript" (written ca. 1868), and *Tom Sawyer* (1876). Finally, Charles Darwin's *The Descent of Man* (1871) and Edward FitzGerald's *Rubáiyát of Omar Khayyám* (1859) contributed to Twain's later theories of natural determinism. It should also be mentioned that Twain read Robert Browning to a group of young women on Saturday mornings at his Hartford home for about three years, beginning in 1886.

Except for occasional accusations of vulgarity, the English critics were almost unanimous in praising Twain's humor and realism. It was when he tried to become serious that their opinions divided. Some found the romance and morality in *The Prince and the Pauper* too dull and wished that he had stayed with pure humor, while others praised his mixture of humor with human perceptiveness and pathos in that novel. Several English reviewers objected to Twain's rough treatment of the Arthurian tales in *A Connecticut Yankee* as an insult to Sir Thomas Malory's *Morte D'Arthur* (1485) and Alfred Lord Tennyson's recent *Idylls of the King* (1859). It seems that what Twain wanted most was to be accepted by the English as more than just a humorist, as a serious and profound writer, and he cherished the few articles that responded to him in this way.

A. Berret

BIBLIOGRAPHY

Baetzhold, Howard G. "Mark Twain and Dickens: Why the Denial?" *Dickens Studies Annual* 16 (1987): 189–219.

———. *Mark Twain and John Bull: The British Connection*. Bloomington: Indiana UP, 1970.

Gillman, Susan K., and Robert L. Patten. "Dickens: Doubles:: Twain: Twins." *Nineteenth Century Fiction* 39.4 (March 1985): 441–458.

Lorch, Fred W. "Mark Twain's Public Lectures in England in 1873." *American Literature* 29 (November 1957): 297–304.

Passon, Richard. "Twain and Eighteenth-Century Satire: The Ingenue Narrator in *Huckleberry Finn*." *Mark Twain Journal* 21.4 (Fall 1983): 33–36.

Poole, Stan. "In Search of the Missing Link: Mark Twain and Darwinism." *Studies in American Fiction* 13.2 (Autumn 1985): 201–215.

Regan, Robert. "'English Notes': A Book Mark Twain Abandoned." *Studies in American Humor* 2 (January 1976): 157–170.

———. "Mark Twain, 'The Doctor' and a Guidebook by Dickens." *American Studies* 22.1 (Spring 1981): 35–55.

Sargent, Mark L. "A Connecticut Yankee in Jane Lampton's South: Mark Twain and the Regicide." *Mississippi Quarterly* 40.1 (Winter 1986–1987): 21–31.

Weintraub, Stanley. *The London Yankees: Portraits of American Writers and Artists in England 1894–1914*. New York: Harcourt Brace Jovanovich, 1979.

Welland, Dennis. *Mark Twain in England*. London: Chatto and Windus, 1978.

See also: Arnold, Matthew; Chatto and Windus; *Connecticut Yankee in King Arthur's Court, A*; Copyright; Darwin, Charles; Dickens, Charles; Europe; *Following the Equator*; Imperialism

Eseldorf

A fictional Austrian village, Eseldorf is the setting for two of the *Mysterious Stranger* manuscripts: "The Chronicle of Young Satan" (written 1897–1900) and "No. 44, The Mysterious Stranger" (written 1902–1908). German for "Assville" or "Donkeytown," Eseldorf is less a realistically sketched village than a locus for Twain's satire against Christianity (especially Catholicism) and small town narrowmindedness.

Although these two versions of *The Mysterious Stranger* are set in different centuries, Eseldorf does not change significantly between the 1702 of "Chronicle" and the 1490 of "No. 44." Even though the printing press has just been invented in the latter, and "The Age of Reason" is soon to replace "The Age of Faith" in the former, Austria is still "asleep" in the Middle Ages. Moreover, Eseldorf is in the "middle of that sleep, being in the middle of Austria." The repetition of the word "middle" in both versions emphasizes Twain's point that he has set his satirical fable in the heart of Europe, both spatially and temporally. Much of the villagers' cruelty and inhumanity described in the tale is a consequence of the "disastrous Moral Sense" promulgated by Judeo-Christian scripture and the Catholic Church.

Scholars have noticed a similarity between Eseldorf and St. Petersburg/Hannibal. Bernard DeVoto and Henry Nash Smith actually equate Eseldorf with Hannibal, since Twain calls both a paradise for boys (though for different reasons) and the boys as well as some of the villagers bear at least superficial resemblances to Huck, Tom, and some of the people in St. Petersburg. John Tuckey, however, convincingly argues that Twain used his notebook descriptions of the Swiss village of Weggis to create not only the visual image of Eseldorf but also its character. Twain resided in Weggis from late summer to early fall of 1897, when he recorded impressions of the lethargic town on Lake Lucerne, located in the heart of Europe. Juxtaposing these descriptions with the ones in "Chronicle" and "No. 44," Tuckey clearly demonstrates that Twain found such small European hamlets—whether the year was 1897, 1702, or 1490—to be paradises only for the poor, the ignorant, and the unthinkingly pious.

As an imagined fusion of Hannibal and Weggis, Eseldorf ties the New World together with the Old: both are bound by their common origins. Rather than equate Eseldorf with either Hannibal or Weggis, Twain imagined a place where witch burning, stoning, and lynching all could occur and where the people are kept in ignorant superstition and cowed reverence for their priests, ministers, and monarchs. That such a town should be in Austria made sense to Twain, who noticed that even in 1897 the Austrian parliament was still as repressive as the prince in "Chronicle" and "No. 44." In his essay "Stirring Times in Austria" (1898) he mentioned the collusion between the parliament and the church, whose priests teach the Austrians "to be docile and obedient and to be diligent in acquiring ignorance about things here below." As Walter Grunzweig points out, this comment is strikingly similar to remarks in the beginning of "Chronicle" and "No. 44," when Twain first describes Eseldorf and its inhabitants.

To Mark Twain, then, the Village of Asses is peculiar to no one particular time or place. It may be found wherever oppression and repression flourish under the auspices of church and state.

Joseph Andriano

BIBLIOGRAPHY

Clemens, Samuel L. *Mark Twain's Mysterious Stranger Manuscripts.* Ed. William M. Gibson. Berkeley: U of California P, 1969.

DeVoto, Bernard. *Mark Twain at Work.* Cambridge, Mass.: Harvard UP, 1942.

Grunzweig, Walter. "Commanches in the Austrian Parliament: Austria as a Metaphor for Mark Twain's Disillusionment with Democracy." *Mark Twain Journal* 23.2 (Fall 1985): 3–9.

Macnaughton, William C. *Mark Twain's Last Years as a Writer.* Columbia: U of Missouri P, 1979.

Smith, Henry Nash. "Mark Twain's Images of Hannibal: From St. Petersburg to Eseldorf." *University of Texas Studies in English* 37 (1958): 3–23.

Tuckey, John. "Hannibal, Weggis, and Mark Twain's Eseldorf." *American Literature* 42.2 (1970): 235–240.

See also: Austria; Catholicism; Fischer, Theodor; *Mysterious Stranger, The*

"Esquimau Maiden's Romance, The"
(1893)

Written in response to John Brisben Walker's offer of $5,000 for twelve original stories for publication in *Cosmopolitan Magazine*, "The Esquimau Maiden's Romance" appeared in that magazine in late 1893. It was subsequently reprinted in *The Man That Corrupted Hadleyburg and Other Stories and Essays* (1900). Like "The Loves of Alonzo Fitz Clarence and Rosannah Ethelton" (1878) and the condensed novel "Aurelia's Unfortunate Young Man" (1864), the story burlesques the conventional love story so popular with genteel nineteenth-century readers.

Burlesque is certainly the dominant mode of this implausible romance that consists of two interwoven stories. The first concerns the plight of the young Eskimo princess Lasca—unequaled among the girls who feed "at her father's hospitable trough" (198)—whose lover is falsely accused of pilfering one of twenty-two fishhooks given Lasca by her fabulously wealthy father. In this Arctic community Mark Twain tells us, the fishhooks "represent the same financial supremacy" as a hundred million dollars in New York. The outraged community executes the suspected thief, but subsequently, while giving her hair its annual brushing, Lasca discovers the missing hook embedded in her locks and is devastated in her bereavement. A frame story encloses Lasca's account of her ordeal, consisting of the interaction and conversation between this primitive Eskimo girl and the narrator, Mark Twain, who represents nineteenth-century genteel culture.

It is through the frame that the story's more serious themes emerge. The contrast between the image of the young princess's "scraping blubber-grease from her cheeks" (197) and the narrator's genteel description of the Aurora Borealis, "a spectacle of almost intolerable splendor and beauty" (197), prefigures the radical incongruity between their respective social and cultural realms. The narrator appears humorously condescending when he remarks that Lasca is "a beautiful creature from the Esquimaux point of view. Others would have thought her a trifle over-plump" (197–198) or when he notes that "not even the richest man in the city of New York has two slop-tubs in his drawing-room" (201). Yet when the bereaved princess laments the moral deterioration of her tribe, she introduces the theme that unites two apparently dissimilar cultures: that of money and its corrupting influence in a society of otherwise principled and happy individuals. "Once plain, simple folk" content with the modest, utilitarian "bone fish-hooks of their fathers," her community is "now eaten up with avarice and would sacrifice every sentiment of honor and honesty" in pursuit of their concept of wealth, "the debasing iron fish-hooks of the foreigner" (213). Her observation, of course, anticipates the more bitter treatment of the same theme in "The $30,000 Bequest" (1904) and "The Man That Corrupted Hadleyburg" (1899)—the title story of the volume in which this burlesque romance reappears: money destroys innocence and subverts human affection in any community; indeed, it destroys the very idea of community as individuals neglect human relationships in pursuit of fatuous dreams.

Written specifically for money at a time when Clemens was suffering from the acute financial pressures that would lead him to bankruptcy a year later, "The Esquimau Maiden's Romance," Geismar argues, is a story "concerned with the meaning of money as romance, fairy tale, delusion, disease, and nightmare" (Geismar 199). This burlesque romance of an Eskimo girl's ill-fated love thus brings into stark relief the deficiencies of any culture that places a higher premium on material wealth than it does on human love and trust.

James D. Wilson

BIBLIOGRAPHY

Clemens, Samuel L. *The Man That Corrupted Hadleyburg and Other Stories and Essays*. New York: Harper, 1900. 197–224.

Covici, Pascal, Jr. *Mark Twain's Humor: The Image of a World*. Dallas: Southern Methodist UP, 1962.

Geismar, Maxwell. *Mark Twain: An American Prophet*. Boston: Houghton Mifflin, 1970.

Wilson, James D. *A Reader's Guide to the Short Stories of Mark Twain*. Boston: G.K. Hall, 1987.

See also: Bankruptcy; Burlesque; Business; "Man That Corrupted Hadleyburg, The"; "$30,000 Bequest, The"

Estate of Samuel L. Clemens (1910–1964)

Six months after his death, Samuel Clemens's estate was appraised at $541,136, later reduced to $471,136 when accepted by the probate court on 14 July 1911. The executors were Edward Eugene Loomis (1864–1937), Jervis Langdon II (1875–1952), and Zoheth Sparrow Freeman (b. 1875). Clara Clemens Gabrilowitsch (later Samossoud) was the sole beneficiary. The principal assets included fifty shares of the Mark Twain Company, valued at $200,000; shares in American Telephone and Telegraph, Anaconda Copper, J. Langdon & Company, Union Pacific, United Fruit, and Utah Consolidated Mining, valued at $181,795; the Redding house and property, valued at $70,000; and various literary manuscripts and documents, known ultimately as the Mark Twain Papers, on which no value was set. The will gave Clara the income from these assets, held in trust, but allowed her to dispose of them only upon her own death. Through the Mark Twain Company (which owned all of Clemens's literary property) the executors, who were often also directors of the company, vigorously pursued their fiduciary responsibility to derive income for the estate both from existing and from future copyrights. An indirect consequence of their efforts was to keep the Mark Twain Papers largely intact, but inaccessible, until Albert Bigelow Paine was succeeded by Bernard DeVoto in 1938. The estate was formally closed on 21 February 1964 when its assets of $928,565 were transferred to the Clara Clemens Samossoud Trust, created at her death in 1962. Clara bequeathed the manuscripts from her father's estate to the University of California, while the income from the remainder went first to her second husband, Jacques Samossoud (1894–1966), then to Dr. William E. Seiler (1909–1978). Upon the latter's death, Clara's estate was itself transformed into the Mark Twain Foundation, a nonprofit, charitable trust.

J.R. LeMaster and James D. Wilson

BIBLIOGRAPHY

Budd, Isabelle. "Clara Samossoud's Will." *Mark Twain Journal* 25 (Spring 1987): 17–30.

———. "Twain's Will Be Done." *Mark Twain Journal* 22 (Spring 1984): 34–39.

"Mark Twain Estate about Half Million." New York *Times*, 15 July 1911, 7.

"Mark Twain Left Daughter $611,136." New York *Times*, 27 October 1910, 1.

"Twain and Hemingway: Accounting of 2 Estates." New York *Times*, 22 February 1964, 1, 18.

See also: DeVoto, Bernard; Samossoud, Clara Clemens; Mark Twain Company; Mark Twain Papers; Paine, Albert Bigelow

Europe

Mark Twain is arguably the first major American author to approach Europe with a thoroughly American attitude, that is to say, without the idea that Europe is a superior culture from which Americans must derive their customs, ideas, and values, though he stands in a long line of American authors who have sought to define their cultural identity by writing about Europe, including Emerson, Cooper, Adams, Hawthorne, Howells, and Henry James. *The Innocents Abroad* (1869), with its irreverent humor, freshness, and energy, did for American travel writing what *Adventures of Huckleberry Finn* (1885) did for the American novel: it introduced a new, vivid, engaging colloquial voice and its corresponding persona. Europe provided the youthful Mark Twain with a stage for zestful spoofing and burlesque, as well as sometimes ironic, sometimes sincere encounters with history. His later

novels set in Europe (*The Prince and the Pauper* [1882], *A Connecticut Yankee in King Arthur's Court* [1889], and *Personal Recollections of Joan of Arc* [1896]) gave Mark Twain the material with which to represent his American social and political ideas in fictional form.

Mark Twain's views of Europe are not easily summarized because Twain wrote so much about it and because his attitudes evolved, sometimes in complex ways, throughout his lifetime. What Henry Nash Smith aptly called "the Matter of Europe" forms an important counterpart to "the Matter of Hannibal" in Mark Twain's works. Not only did Samuel Clemens live in Europe for more than ten years of his life, his imaginative engagement with European culture, people, places, and symbols forms a major strand of his work. Europe, in his imagination, underwent a metamorphosis from being the exotic backdrop against which he staged his youthful escapades, to representing symbolically the evils and attractions of Western history, to embodying a timeless metaphor for the human condition.

In *Innocents Abroad* he staged a comic assault on the prestige of Europe by parodying the conventions of the "European Tour." By turns admiring, naive, enraged, and critical, Mark Twain diminished the authority of European culture by making himself, ostensibly a representative American, the central subject of his narrative. He condemned the "Old Masters" for their obsequiousness to their patrons and the Catholic Church in Italy for its prosperity in the midst of poverty, but he also envied the leisurely public life of European society. He took his revenge against subservient yet condescending tour guides by calling them all Ferguson, railing against them, and making them the butt of jokes, such as asking, about a mummy that a guide showed them with particular pride, "Is—is he dead?"

In *A Tramp Abroad* (1880) he represented Europe as a realm of ritual activity: tourism with Baedeker as its Bible, and he parodied the rituals by pretending to "pedestrianize" all over the Continent but actually riding every conveyance possible and by pretending to study

German and art. Being educated into European culture was an arcane discipline, as Mark Twain represented it, which he alternately poked fun at and espoused. The target of his satire was slavish admiration of Europe much more than Europe itself, though the remoteness, authority, and difficulty of European high culture did arouse his resentment.

Sam Clemens was both attracted to and repelled by the glamor, the power, and the trappings of monarchy and aristocracy. Rank and privilege aroused his democratic ire but also his ambitious imagination. Thus Europe in his fiction became the scene in which he staged many variations on the conflict between the abuse of aristocratic power and its potential for self-fulfillment and self-aggrandizement. One of the more subtle variations on this theme was his accusation that the "Sir Walter Scott disease" contributed to causing the Civil War. Another was his satire on chivalry in Tom Sawyer's high jinks in *Huckleberry Finn*. In *The Prince and the Pauper* he explored the romantic attractions of the social extremes of Elizabethan England, with an eye to the political evils of monarchy, aristocracy, and the established church. *The Prince and the Pauper* is the first of several fictions in which Old World slavery alludes to slavery in the New World, in which the issue of social rank in Europe becomes a metaphor for questions of parentage and identity, and in which ridicule and condemnation of European customs mingle with undisguised fascination with the color, ritual, and ceremony of ancient traditions.

Samuel Clemens's views of different European nations changed as his personal experiences evolved. His first impression of France was very favorable: everything seemed orderly and well run in France. But soon disillusionment set in, and Mark Twain came to see France as the embodiment of effeminacy, moral (especially sexual) corruption, and cowardly brutality, and thereafter he never wavered in condemning the French in the most vituperative terms. By comparison, he loved Germany and the Germans, though not necessarily the German language, which he struggled to learn,

used for years in his private notebooks and letters, and facetiously offered to improve in his very funny essay "The Awful German Language" (first published as an appendix to *A Tramp Abroad*). He liked what he perceived as the warmth, dignity, and ease of German public life, and his feelings about Germany were certainly not unfavorably influenced by the fact that Baron von Tauchnitz, his German publisher, voluntarily paid him royalties at a time when international copyright protections did not yet exist. Though he satirized Alpine climbing in *Tramp Abroad* and criticized the Swiss for cheating and rudeness, he eulogized Switzerland as "The Cradle of Liberty" and showed great appreciation for its natural beauty. He had a prejudice against the Portuguese; he mocked the citizens of the Azores as ignorant and backward, and even in as late a work as *The Mysterious Stranger* the hateful imperialist is Portuguese. Italy was tainted as the "home of priestcraft" and the oppressive presence of the "Old Masters," but in time he came to feel a deep affection for Italy, especially Florence, and he and Olivia settled there for what turned out to be the last period of her life.

The nation with which he had the most passionate engagement, however, the one he had the most fierce disagreements with and the most profound attraction for, is England. Not only is Samuel Clemens's debt to British literature very great, the history of his quarrels with Britain virtually constitutes the history of his political evolution. In 1872 he visited England and took notes for what he projected as a satirical book about the nation. However, he liked England too much at this time to satirize it, and the book was never finished. His main source of outrage at that time was a British pirate publisher named Hotten, but in general British customs and government aroused his admiration and intensified his criticisms of the United States.

In the late 1880s, however, Mark Twain began to attack Britain, partly in response to Matthew Arnold's criticism of American culture as lacking reverence. Twain criticized aristocracy and monarchy, calling them piracy and fraud. In *Connecticut Yankee* he found a fictional outlet for his increasing animus against British history and society. Arthurian England became the vehicle for Mark Twain's attacks on feudal superstitions, cruelties, and exploitations. Chivalry and the established church are represented as the enemies of progress, common sense, and the self-respect of ordinary people.

In the 1890s his animosity toward Britain decreased as his general disillusionment with humanity increased. Though he condemned European (and American) imperialism, he thought British rule had brought many benefits to India, and his friendship with Rudyard Kipling reinforced his sympathies for British law. In *The American Claimant* (1892) he contrasted the snobberies and inequalities of American society unfavorably with the nobility of character of an English aristocrat. As his condemnation of humanity for its cowardice and cruelty became more universal, Europe ceased to be the exclusive site of specific abuses and increasingly became the means by which he metaphorically represented human corruption in general. In *Joan of Arc* (1896) Mark Twain's target was no longer the French specifically or even the Catholic Church so much as the qualities of greed and brutality that inhabit institutions in all societies.

Mark Twain observed the Austrian parliament in one of its periods of fierce debate and wrote about it as a political journalist, in "Stirring Times in Austria" (1898), but in his fiction Austria served, in two of the drafts of his Mysterious Stranger manuscripts, as an allegorical backdrop for his increasingly metaphysical criticisms. Eseldorf, the Austrian village, and Hannibal became contiguous if not synonymous in Mark Twain's imagination. Samuel Clemens had become a citizen of the world; as such, he was a fierce, cynical enemy of oppression and "sham" in the abstract. However, he was quite comfortable in his friendships with aristocrats and royalty, since he considered himself a member of the aristocracy of talent. His democratic sentiments,

which had often caused him to skewer fictionalized (and sometimes highly imaginary) versions of European history, were increasingly undermined by his contempt for what he regarded as the weakness and cowardice of the common man, which he found in America as much as in Europe or anywhere else in the world.

Still, as from the beginning of his career, European characters, events, and places furnished him with vivid literary materials with which to explore his themes imaginatively. He lived his life, in his later years, on a world stage, and Europe was central to that stage. In the early 1890s he fled to Europe as a refuge from extravagant expenditure and from memories of an era of his life in Hartford; he sought out Europe as a place that offered both celebrity and a measure of isolation when he wanted it; and he cared passionately about his European audience, even when he was antagonistic toward it. His honorary degree from Oxford in 1907 was the culmination of a lifelong aspiration and of a history of lionization that contributed immeasurably to the achievement of his ambitions as a public figure at home and abroad.

John Daniel Stahl

BIBLIOGRAPHY

Baetzhold, Howard G. *Mark Twain and John Bull: The British Connection.* Bloomington: Indiana UP, 1970.

Bridgman, Richard. *Traveling in Mark Twain.* Berkeley: U of California P, 1987.

Clemens, Samuel L. *Mark Twain's Travels with Mr. Brown.* Ed. Franklin Walker and G. Ezra Dane. New York: Knopf, 1940.

Ganzel, Dewey. *Mark Twain Abroad: The Cruise of the "Quaker City."* Chicago: U of Chicago P, 1968.

Hemminghaus, Edgar H. *Mark Twain in Germany.* New York: Columbia UP, 1939.

Krumpelmann, John T. *Mark Twain and the German Language.* Baton Rouge: Louisiana State UP, 1953.

Regan, Robert. "'English Notes': A Book Mark Twain Abandoned." *Studies in American Humor* 2 (1976): 157–170.

Salomon, Roger B. *Twain and the Image of History.* New Haven, Conn.: Yale UP, 1961.

Scott, Arthur L. *Mark Twain at Large.* Chicago: Henry Regnery, 1969.

Smith, Henry Nash. *Mark Twain: The Development of a Writer.* Cambridge, Mass.: Harvard UP, 1962.

————. *Mark Twain's Fable of Progress: Political and Economic Ideas in "A Connecticut Yankee."* New Brunswick, N.J.: Rutgers UP, 1964.

See also: Austria (Austria-Hungary); Catholicism; England; France; Germany; *Innocents Abroad, The*; Italy; Switzerland; Travel Writings

Europe and Elsewhere
(1923)

Europe and Elsewhere (*EE*) includes a total of thirty-five essays, letters, travel pieces, and newspaper articles—all of which were first published or reprinted in the United States in book form. The volume was compiled posthumously by Twain's literary executor, Albert Bigelow Paine, who also contributed an introduction. Included in the prefatory materials is Brander Matthews's "An Appreciation"; this "Biographical Criticism" also introduced the Uniform Edition of *Mark Twain's Works* (1899).

While this eclectic collection exhibits no unifying theme as such, it does demonstrate Twain's wide-ranging interests, concerns, and views, as well as his sense of despair and alienation. Although there are examples of Twain's uniquely brilliant humor exhibited in some of the travel pieces included herein, most critics seem to concur that these later travel accounts never quite measure up to *The Innocents Abroad* (1869). A number of reasons might account for this decline: the pressure of deadlines, an increasing pessimism, a greater reliance on printed sources for materials, and a lack of the freshness that had been evidenced during his first European trip. The collection also exhibits a pervasive sense that Twain viewed human history and culture from a the-more-some-things-change-the-more-they-remain-the-same point of view: a nostalgia for those things that have changed, but not for the bet-

ter; a despair over those things that have not changed, but should have; and a thankful and tender musing over those things that have never changed and hopefully never will. Twain did not have the "Corn-Pone Opinions" (1900) he believed were held by most of the human race. Utilizing irony, satire, humor, and parody to level stinging social criticism, Twain analyzed with wit and viewed with the cynical eye of a true independent thinker such broadly defined human institutions and forms of behavior as slavery, religion, patriotism, imperialism, and mass public opinion.

Also collected in *EE* are some of Twain's occasional essays: two editorials from the Buffalo *Express*, a piece about the temperance crusade and women's rights, and a lengthy series of letters written during June 1873 for the New York *Herald* about the lavish British reception for the Shah of Persia. Many of the diverse pieces in *EE*, such as "Aix, the Paradise of the Rheumatics" and "Marienbad—A Health Factory," were the products of experiences and observations gathered during Twain's European travels and his periods of residence there during the years 1878–1879 and 1891–1895. Some of these pieces were false starts or fragments of intended larger projects that, for one reason or another, were aborted. For example, the descriptive sketch of a nighttime visit to Westminster Abbey entitled "A Memorable Midnight Experience" (1872) was part of a would-be novel on England. Although Twain initially planned another book, entitled *The Innocents Adrift*, broadly based on his ten-day adventures on the Rhône, he never completed the manuscript; however, Paine—perhaps rather unjudiciously and without informing the reader—edited and deleted almost half of Twain's original 174 manuscript pages to produce "Down the Rhône" (1891) as it appears in *EE*.

Two pieces linked to "Eve's Autobiography"—"That Day in Eden" and "Eve Speaks" (both written around 1905–1906)—are part of what Bernard DeVoto in *Letters from the Earth* (1962) labeled "Papers of the Adam Family." In the former essay, a reflection on the Edenic Fall, Satan recounts Adam's and Eve's inability to understand abstract concepts such as good, evil, death, pain, fear, and the Moral Sense prior to their having eaten from the tree of knowledge. In the latter essay, Eve bitterly recollects man's expulsion from the garden and Adam's and her initial discovery of death and sorrow.

EE also includes excellent examples of Twain's knowledge and interest in both history and contemporary social issues; most of his attacks against perceived injustices were lodged in the form of satire or ironic commentary. This radical social criticism and moral outrage characterize many of his later writings. "A Word of Encouragement for Our Blushing Exiles" (1898) is an admission that during the Spanish-American War American intervention in the liberation of Cuba was done "under a sham humanitarian pretext"; Twain compared modern American imperialism to a catalogue of brutish European imperialistic exploits. Outraged by his own nation's racism, in "The United States of Lyncherdom" (written 1901) he attacked the moral ineptitude that allowed lynching—the product of mob instinct; Twain, well aware of the ironically charged and controversial nature of this essay, chose not to publish it during his life. "To the Person Sitting in Darkness" (1901) created a national sensation as well as a savage debate between Twain and the American Board of Foreign Missions; it is a masterful and satiric polemic condemning imperialism and the West for military intervention in China, South Africa, and the Philippines. "To My Missionary Critics" (1901) recapitulates the charges mounted against Reverend William Ament in "To the Person Sitting in Darkness" and underscores Twain's contempt for the American-Christian missionaries' role in imperialism; both of these works first appeared in the *North American Review*. In "As Regards Patriotism" (written ca. 1900), Twain considers patriotism a "trained" behavior, or the product of social conditioning, that is "furnished, cut and dry, to the citizen by the poli-

tician and the newspaper"; he concludes this essay by suggesting that individuals also "can be trained to manufacture their own Patriotism" by relying on their own minds, hearts, and consciences to make their own morally correct decisions. "Dr. Loeb's Incredible Discovery" also censures mass opinion as does "Paralyzing Consensus of Opinion" even from the scientific experts. Riddled with wit and cynicism is an essay in the form of a dialogue entitled "The Dervish and the Offensive Stranger"; it is a treatise on moral and immoral acts perpetrated throughout history.

The interjection of his singular type of humor, which ranges from gentle to blatant, as well as his exceptional descriptions of both scenery and people, characteristically occupies most of Twain's writings throughout the collection. However uneven the quality of the individual works may be, or as in the case with many of the selections in the volume where substance is not necessarily a primary criterion for inclusion, the value of these pieces to contemporary Twain studies lies in their reflection of the author's political, social, and religious attitudes.

J.C.B. Kinch

BIBLIOGRAPHY

Baldanza, Frank. *Mark Twain: An Introduction and Interpretation.* New York: Barnes & Noble, 1961.

Clemens, Samuel L. *Europe and Elsewhere.* New York: Harper, 1923.

Foner, Philip S. *Mark Twain: Social Critic.* New York: International Publishers, 1958.

Geismar, Maxwell. *Mark Twain: An American Prophet.* Boston: Houghton Mifflin, 1970.

Macnaughton, William R. *Mark Twain's Last Years as a Writer.* Columbia: U of Missouri P, 1979.

Scott, Arthur L. "*The Innocents Adrift* Edited by Mark Twain's Official Biographer." *Publications of the Modern Language Association* 78 (June 1963): 230–237.

See also: Europe; Religion; Satire; Social Reform; Travel Writings

Eve

The character of Eve is prominent in a number of short pieces, two of which were published before Twain's death: "Extracts from Adam's Diary" (1893) and "Eve's Diary" (1905). They were published separately and then together in *The $30,000 Bequest* (1906) and in a volume called *Eve's Diary*, also in 1906. The latter contains an expanded version of "Adam's Diary." Eve appears also in the posthumously published "That Day in Eden" and "Eve Speaks," both of which were written around 1900 and published in 1923 in *Europe and Elsewhere*. She is the narrator of "Eve's Autobiography," written in 1905–1906, and is described by Satan in "Letters from the Earth," both of which were first published in *Letters from the Earth* in 1962.

In all of the stories Eve is the mate of Adam and the "founding mother" of the human race. In "Eve Speaks" she is the mother of Cain and Abel, and in "Eve's Autobiography" she has nine children, including Cain, Abel, Gladys, and Edwina. In both of these stories her children are born before the Fall. In "That Day in Eden," "Extracts from Adam's Diary," and "Eve's Diary," her prelapsarian innocence includes ignorance of sex, and her children are not conceived until after the Fall. In the stories that include a description of the Fall, Eve eats of the forbidden fruit before Adam, but she does not tempt him into eating it; Twain portrays both of them as childlike in their innocence. In "Extracts from Adam's Diary" Twain suggests humorously that Eve acts partly from compassion to bring death into the world in order to provide meat for the carnivores. In Twain's posthumous works the Fall is not treated so lightly. Twain emphasizes the bitter concept of the cruelty of God's commandment. As Satan observes in "That Day in Eden" and "Letters from the Earth," it was cruel of God to forbid Adam and Eve to eat of the fruit and then punish them for doing so when their total ignorance prevents them from understanding the consequences. God is portrayed as the guilty one.

In other posthumous stories it is Eve (rather than Adam) who articulates Twain's criticism of God. In "Eve's Autobiography" Eve notes that she and Adam do not know the meaning of the words God uses—death, good, and evil—because the words are outside their experience; in order to know what they mean, they will have to eat the forbidden fruit. In "Eve Speaks" she says that God's command is ridiculous. Without a Moral Sense they cannot understand what God's command means; yet they will not gain a Moral Sense until they eat of the forbidden fruit. "It would have been fairer and kinder to have given us the Moral Sense first," Eve comments. "Then we could have been blamed if we disobeyed" (*Works* 20:347).

In all of the Eve stories, Eve is intelligent, though ignorant and innocent. In three of the works Eve speaks in her own voice, one of the few women in Twain's work who tells her own story. Yet although Eve is speaking, she cannot be said to have an independent existence. Susan K. Harris characterizes Eve as Twain's ideal woman, pointing out that her principal function is to humanize Adam (123–124). Yet this ideal woman exists not for herself, but only in relation to her husband. Eve's world revolves around Adam. In "Eve's Diary" she says "I want to learn to like everything he is interested in" (*Works* 18:379). In "Extracts from Adam's Diary" and "Eve's Diary" Adam at first resists her, complaining that she talks too much or that she has an annoying habit of naming things. Eve, on the other hand, loves Adam unquestioningly. She protects him and encourages him: "I do not let him see that I am aware of his defect," she says in "Eve's Diary" of his inability to name things (*Works* 18:364–365). Her life is dedicated to making him happy. In "Eve's Diary" she tries to obtain some of the forbidden apples for Adam because she thinks they will please him: "So I come to harm through pleasing him, why shall I care for that harm?" (*Works* 18:365–366).

Eve's function in several of the stories is to provide dialogue and language for the primal Adam, whom she forces out of solipsism and teaches to say "we" (Sewell 11–12). Stanley Brodwin notes that Twain creates irony in the Adamic stories by writing about mythic characters in an absurdly realistic way (*Humor* 52–53). "Eve's Diary" was written soon after Livy died, and it is believed that Eve, as she is represented in this work, reflects Twain's attitude toward his wife (e.g., Paine 3:1225; Hill 112; Emerson 258). The stories have also been associated with Twain's domestic life at Hartford (Baldanza 128). At the end of "Eve's Diary" when Eve is dead, Adam says, "Wheresoever she was, *there* was Eden" (*Works* 18:381), which suggests the loss that Twain felt after Livy's death.

Joyce W. Warren

BIBLIOGRAPHY

Baldanza, Frank. *Mark Twain: An Introduction and Interpretation.* New York: Barnes & Noble, 1961.

Brodwin, Stanley. "The Humor of the Absurd: Mark Twain's Adamic Diaries." *Criticism* 14 (1972): 49–64.

————. "Mark Twain's Masks of Satan: The Final Phase." *American Literature* 45 (May 1973): 206–227.

Clemens, Samuel L. *Europe and Elsewhere.* Vol. 20 of *The Complete Works of Mark Twain.* New York: Harper, 1923.

————. *Letters from the Earth.* Ed. Bernard DeVoto. New York: Harper & Row, 1962.

————. *The $30,000 Bequest and Other Stories.* Vol. 18 of *The Complete Works of Mark Twain.* New York: Harper, 1923.

Emerson, Everett. *The Authentic Mark Twain: A Literary Biography of Samuel L. Clemens.* Philadelphia: U of Pennsylvania P, 1984.

Ensor, Allison. *Mark Twain and the Bible.* Lexington: UP of Kentucky, 1969.

Harris, Susan K. *Mark Twain's Escape from Time: A Study of Patterns and Images.* Columbia: U of Missouri P, 1982.

Hill, Hamlin. *Mark Twain: God's Fool.* New York: Harper & Row, 1973.

Macnaughton, William R. *Mark Twain's Last Years as a Writer.* Columbia: U of Missouri P, 1979.

Paine, Albert Bigelow. *Mark Twain: A Biography.* Vol. 3. New York: Harper, 1912.

Sewell, David R. *Mark Twain's Languages: Discourse, Dialogue, and Linguistic Variety.* Berkeley: U of California P, 1987.

Wilson, James D. *A Reader's Guide to the Short Stories of Mark Twain.* Boston: G.K. Hall, 1987.

See also: "Eve Speaks"; "Eve's Autobiography"; "Eve's Diary"; "Extracts from Adam's Diary"; "That Day in Eden"

"Eve Speaks"
(1923)

Written sometime during the early 1900s, "Eve Speaks" was first published in *Europe and Elsewhere* (1923) by Albert Bigelow Paine, who furnished the new title for what Mark Twain originally called "Passage from Eve's Diary." A sequel to "That Day in Eden" (also Paine's title), the sketch was originally intended, with its companion piece, for inclusion in a longer work, parts of which Bernard DeVoto published as "Papers of the Adam Family" in *Letters from the Earth* (1962). Details in the manuscript show that it was meant to precede the segment that DeVoto titled "Passage from Eve's Autobiography, Year of the World 920."

Here, three months after the expulsion from the Garden of Eden, Eve elaborates on some of the points made by Satan in "That Day in Eden." She, too, speaks of unfairness, on the grounds that as innocents she and Adam simply had not known the meaning of right and wrong and hence had not understood the implications of or consequences of disobeying God's command. And even though they had experienced hunger, cold, pain, hate, and remorse, they still had not understood what death is. That mystery is soon solved, however, when they find Abel drenched in blood, cannot wake him, and conclude that this is indeed death, from which he will *never* wake.

In this piece, as in "That Day in Eden," and especially in Eve's conclusion it would have been fairer if the Moral Sense had been bestowed beforehand so that she and Adam could have known right from wrong and hence would rightfully have been blamed for their disobedience, Twain again castigates the injustice, if not the stupidity, of the Deity. And he has Satan provide a coda "From Satan's Diary": "Death has entered the world . . .; the product of the Moral Sense is complete. . . ."

As with "That Day in Eden," if Mark Twain thought of publication at all, he doubtless decided that blaming the Fall on God, rather than man, was too strong for the tastes of the reading public. He would attack the Bible story even more vigorously in autobiographical dictations of June 1906 (see "Reflections on Religion") and in "Letters from the Earth" (written 1909), but these, too, would not be published until long after his death.

Howard G. Baetzhold

BIBLIOGRAPHY

Clemens, Samuel L. *Europe and Elsewhere.* New York: Harper, 1923.

————. "Letters from the Earth." *Letters from the Earth.* By Clemens. Ed. Bernard DeVoto. New York: Harper & Row, 1962. 1–33.

————. "Reflections on Religion." Ed. Charles Neider. *Hudson Review* 16.3 (Autumn 1963): 329–352.

Ensor, Allison. *Mark Twain and the Bible.* Lexington: UP of Kentucky, 1969.

See also: Eve; *Letters from the Earth*; "Reflections on Religion"; "That Day in Eden"

"Eve's Autobiography"

(1962)

Extracts from this work were published posthumously in *Letters from the Earth*, edited by Bernard DeVoto and first published in 1962. DeVoto concludes that "Eve's Autobiography" was written in 1905–1906 after "Eve's Diary" (1905). He includes sections of it in "Papers of the Adam Family," material purporting to be translated from the "adamic" by Mark Twain.

The humor in the autobiography derives from the description of the ignorant Adam and Eve attempting to make sense of their surroundings. Eve describes Adam and herself as scientists. Some of their conclusions are accurate; some erroneous. Adam discovers that

water runs downhill, and Eve "discovers" that cows make milk by absorbing it from the atmosphere. Contained within the autobiography is an extract purportedly from "Eve's Diary" in which further scientific discoveries are made. Eve discovers that lions and many other animals are carnivores, and she and Adam attempt to see if all fish will develop legs as did the "fish" (tadpoles) in the pond. When Adam is away, Cain is born. At first Eve does not know what the creature is, but soon she feels a great love for the child and longs to share her joy with Adam. For some time, however, Adam does not understand what the child is, and his scientific experiments attempting to learn what kind of bird or reptile it is cause Eve great distress. Before they leave Eden, Adam and Eve have nine children. This is similar to the situation in "Eve Speaks" (1923), where Cain and Abel are born while Adam and Eve are still in Eden, but it differs from Twain's portrayal of the Adam and Eve story in other works. In "Extracts from Adam's Diary" (1893) and "Eve's Diary" they have no children until after the Fall, and in "Letters from the Earth" the principal result of the Fall is the knowledge of the "art and mystery of sexual intercourse" (*Letters* 23, 25).

Throughout the autobiography, Eve has a discreetly protective attitude toward Adam, praising him for his discoveries and maintaining a dictionary for him so that the "poor boy" will not be humiliated by his inability to spell. Adam is "a good deal inflated" by his discovery that water runs downhill; he is piqued if others do not mention it, and he is devastated when another scientist receives credit for the discovery. Eve consoles him, telling him that no one can take away the honor of being the first man and insisting that one day he will regain recognition as the discoverer of the law that water runs downhill.

As Allison Ensor has noted, "Eve's Autobiography" contains both the lighter humor of the earlier "Extracts from Adam's Diary" and "Eve's Diary" and the seriousness of the posthumously published "That Day in Eden" (written 1900), "Letters from the Earth," and

"Eve Speaks" (written 1900) (59–60). Eve's comments about the incomprehensibility of God's command look forward to the bitter condemnation in the posthumous works. At one point Adam and Eve hear the voice of the Lord of the Garden, which tells them that they will die if they eat the fruit of the tree that will give them a knowledge of good and evil. Since they have no experience with any of these words, Eve concludes it is unreasonable to expect either of them to have any conception of what the words mean. They are about to eat the apple in order to find out what the words mean when they are distracted by a new creature—a dinosaur—which they take home with them. The other serious note comes at the end of the autobiography. Eve expresses astonishment that she and Adam were instrumental in "the most conspicuous and stupendous event which would happen in the universe for a thousand years—the founding of the human race!" (*Letters* 81). As Stanley Brodwin points out, the irony contained in this comment is evident in its being immediately followed by an extract from a newspaper article on overpopulation, which concludes that war is the only way that the planet can be saved (*Letters* 61).

Joyce W. Warren

BIBLIOGRAPHY

Brodwin, Stanley. "The Humor of the Absurd: Mark Twain's Adamic Diaries." *Criticism* 14 (1972): 49–64.

Clemens, Samuel L. *Letters from the Earth.* Ed. Bernard DeVoto. New York: Harper & Row, 1962.

Ensor, Allison. *Mark Twain and the Bible.* Lexington: UP of Kentucky, 1969.

Macnaughton, William R. *Mark Twain's Last Years as a Writer.* Columbia: U of Missouri P, 1979.

See also: Eve; "Eve's Diary"; "Extracts from Adam's Diary"

"Eve's Diary"

(1905)

"Eve's Diary," a sequel to "Extracts from Adam's Diary" (1893) and in some sense a tribute to Olivia Clemens, was written in July 1905, a year after Olivia's death, while Clemens, his daughter Jean, and Isabel Lyon were summering at Dublin, New Hampshire, near Mount Monadnock. Clemens had been working on "No. 44, The Mysterious Stranger" but dropped it when Frederick Duneka of *Harper's Magazine* requested contributions. To write "Eve's Diary" he turned to "Extracts from Adam's Diary," written twelve years before; the earlier work was to serve as Eve's text. Like Olivia, Eve is described as having died before her husband; Adam's tribute at Eve's grave may be understood as Clemens's tribute to his wife: "Wheresoever she was, *there* was Eden." (This observation resembles what he wrote to Joseph Twichell in 1904, "Wherever Livy was, that was my country.") "Eve's Diary" was published in the Christmas issue of *Harper's*, and the next year, 1906, it was made into a book with many illustrations. It also appeared in *Their Husbands' Wives*, edited by William Dean Howells and Henry Mills Alden (the editor of *Harper's*), in 1906.

Eve begins her diary the day after her creation. She is unaware of Adam but recognizes that she is only part of an experiment. Eve greatly admires the beauty of the world that has just been finished; she recognizes in herself "a passion for the beautiful." When she is unable to knock down some stars, she cries, as she says, naturally. At last she finds the "other Experiment" (Adam), which she finds to lack compassion, though in time she enjoys his company. She experiences pain and fire, which become destructive and introduce her to fear. She has much to learn. There is no account of the Fall in "Eve's Diary," though Eve has some sense of foreboding.

Innocence is a major theme in Mark Twain's writings, but since it is rarely found in his last works, it is a pleasure to find it an important theme in "Eve's Diary." Unlike accounts of innocence accompanied by its loss, such as the famous one in "Old Times on the Mississippi" (1875), this time there is no loss, for the Fall merely causes Eve to recognize that expulsion from Eden is insignificant since she retains Adam. She asks herself why she loves him and answers, "Merely because he is masculine, I think." She cannot stop loving him and explains, "It is a matter of sex, I think."

Returning to "Adam's Diary" in order to write "Eve's Diary," Clemens included a passage in the new work that he labeled "Extract from Adam's Diary," though neither he nor subsequent editors have included it in editions of "Adam's Diary," where it belongs. He also supplemented "Eve's Diary" with a new chapter of "Adam's Diary" that was first published in 1984 by Everett Emerson in *The Authentic Mark Twain* (259–260).

Also related to "Eve's Diary" is the only partially published "Eve's Autobiography," which shows Eve reviewing her 900 years of life and quoting from her diary descriptions of the events before the Fall. This time Adam and Eve are presented as scientists. There are also other related posthumous works: "That Day in Eden (Passage from Satan's Diary)," in which Eve and Adam age immediately following the Fall, and "Eve Speaks," which emphasizes the losses suffered as the result of the Fall. In writing these three presentations of Eve, Clemens was in a much less gentle and sentimental mood.

A 1989 presentation by the Public Broadcasting Service of a drama that combined "Adam's Diary" and "Eve's Diary" demonstrated that Mark Twain's attitude toward men and women was distinctly Victorian. Much of the amusement it provides came from its contrast of that view with the attitudes of late-twentieth-century viewers. "Eve's Diary" is notable for its good humor and lack of the pessimism so often found in Mark Twain's later writings.

Everett Emerson

BIBLIOGRAPHY

Emerson, Everett. *The Authentic Mark Twain: A Literary Biography of Samuel M. Clemens.* Philadelphia: U of Pennsylvania P, 1984.

Hill, Hamlin. *Mark Twain: God's Fool.* New York: Harper & Row, 1973.

Macnaughton, William R. *Mark Twain's Last Years as a Writer.* Columbia: U of Missouri P, 1979.

See also: Eve; "Eve Speaks"; "Eve's Autobiography"; "Extracts from Adam's Diary"; Innocence

"Evidence in the Case of Smith vs. Jones, The"
(1864)

"The Evidence in the Case of Smith vs. Jones" is Mark Twain's mock account of a police court trial, first published in San Francisco's *Golden Era* on 26 June 1864. It was one of two sketches that Mark Twain sold to the *Golden Era*, a literary magazine, and was based on similar court trials he attended as reporter for the San Francisco *Morning Call*.

The sketch is a burlesque, as the narrator elaborately adopts a pose of high seriousness, appealing to the "People" to resolve the question of innocence or guilt. Although the two parties, Smith and Jones, are never introduced, the narrator recounts the sharp differences in their testimonies. Then a parade of colorful witnesses is called to the stand, each giving a contradictory account of what appears to have been a barroom brawl. Each one's banter with the stoical judge and the increasingly frustrated prosecuting attorney degenerates into a perplexing series of charges and countercharges. Judge Shepheard, a real figure in the city's police court, finally postpones the case.

In format, the sketch mingles dramatic dialogue with the narrator's intrusive comment. As an early sketch, the treatment is heavy-handed, but it does show Mark Twain experimenting with the clash of speech patterns, in this case western vernacular and stilted legalese; and it does represent a stage of development of his burlesque style, in which his attempt to incorporate humor into the narrative is less than successful.

J. Mark Baggett

BIBLIOGRAPHY

Clemens, Samuel L. "The Evidence in the Case of Smith vs. Jones." *The Works of Mark Twain: Early Tales & Sketches, Volume 2 (1864–1865)*. By Clemens. Ed. Edgar M. Branch and Robert H. Hirst. Berkeley: U of California P, 1981. 13–21.

See also: Burlesque; Vernacular

Evolution

For Western people who had lived during the century before the publication of Charles Darwin's (1809–1882) *Origin of Species* in 1859, the idea of evolution had been sufficiently disturbing. Evolutionists Comte Georges de Buffon (1707–1788), Erasmus Darwin (1731–1802), Jean Baptiste de Lamarck (1744–1829), and geologist Charles Lyell (1797–1875) had shown not only that the earth and its creatures had undergone great changes since the creation, but also that the creation was vastly older than the few thousand years ascribed to it by Archbishop James Ussher's (1581–1656) Bible-based chronology. In adjusting to this developing view, deists, who were the heirs of the Enlightenment, fared best. Scorning religious "superstition," dedicated to reason and to a belief in a reasonable Creator, they were encouraged by the reasonable (but incorrect) assumption that underlay early evolutionary theory. That assumption was that the adaptations of one generation were inheritable by succeeding generations, for example, that a camel is born with knee calluses because previous generations had developed them through kneeling or that the elephant's trunk had lengthened through generational stretchings after food. Even though the enlightened citizen could no longer think of the creation as a single, complete, and relatively recent event, that person could see evolution as further evidence of the Deity's design.

Darwin's "natural selection" explained evolution in a quite different way, and because it appeared to take the holiness out of nature, it was strongly resisted, by layman and scientist alike, for some decades. Natural selection is based on the premises that there is infinite variation among life forms, both animal and plant; that many more life forms come into being than can survive; and that nature "selects" those forms whose variations make them best adapted to their particular environments. At any given moment, unimaginable numbers of creatures are doomed to die before reproducing themselves, terminating genetic chains stretching back through unimaginable generations, thus modifying (though the phrase was not in Darwin's vocabulary) the gene pool.

Mark Twain was deeply involved in and vividly responded to his culture's successive crises over evolution and in the process recapitulated three centuries of Western intellectual experience. Indoctrinated in Hannibal's Protestant fundamentalism, he feared thunderstorms as a boy, taking them as signs of divine wrath, just as he took the drowning of a playmate as a "special judgment" on someone "loaded with sin." As a young man on his own in eastern cities, he widened his horizons through reading, in particular, Lyell's *Principles of Geology* (1830–1833), and through conversations with an amateur intellectual named Macfarlane who had concocted his own theory of evolution. As cub pilot, he came across Thomas Paine's (1737–1809) *Age of Reason* (1794), which he read "with fear and hesitation, but marveling at its fearlessness and wonderful power." Such was the impact of the *Age of Reason* on Twain's mind that he became, and for some thirty years remained, a deist and as such continued to accommodate himself to a pre-Darwinian concept of evolution.

Twain appears to have paid little attention to the first appearance of Darwin's *Origin of Species* in 1859 (the date of the copy he owned is 1884) but did study Darwin's *Descent of Man* (1871) in the year of its publication. The underlinings and marginal comments in his copy of *Descent* (of volume 1; volume 2 has not been located) showed that he read with utmost attention; nevertheless, the effect of this early reading was, if anything, only subliminally erosive of his faith in a purposeful evolution. It was, apparently, an accumulation of evidence and no particular crisis that precipitated his conversion to a darkly Darwinistic view of evolution in 1891. From that time on he casually referred to the eons that passed before "primeval man" emerged a hundred thousand years ago; he saw God and nature as caring "not a rap for us"; and he made stark statements of social Darwinism. Only in brilliant but brief moments, as in "The Secret History of Eddypus" (1902), did he hark back to the "wonderful all-clarifying law of Evolution" that he had been pleased to contemplate.

Sherwood Cummings

BIBLIOGRAPHY

Cummings, Sherwood. *Mark Twain and Science: Adventures of a Mind*. Baton Rouge: Louisiana State UP, 1988

Gribben, Alan. *Mark Twain's Library: A Reconstruction*. 2 vols. Boston: G.K. Hall, 1980.

Waggoner, Hyatt Howe. "Science in the Thought of Mark Twain." *American Literature* 8 (1937): 357–370

See also: Darwin, Charles; Macfarlane; Science

Exaggeration

In Henri Bergson's classic treatise on comedy, the French philosopher comments that exaggeration only succeeds as comedy when it appears to be a means to an end, for the process of distortion rather than the distortion itself evokes laughter (Bergson 77–78). Distortion is so basic to Clemens's comedy that James M. Cox considers exaggeration to be the characterizing style of the Twain persona who shapes all of Clemens's humor (22). Exaggeration works as humor for Clemens because the process of identifying the distortion engages his reader's intellectual vanity.

Developed from the tradition of exaggeration in southwestern humor, Clemens's paradigmatic exaggeration involves a narrator telling a story to an audience who may be distinct from the reader. For example, in the third chapter of *A Tramp Abroad* (1880) Twain recalls Jim Baker's description of a blue jay who has been unable to fill a hole in the side of a vacant house with acorns. Jim Baker plays the role of the narrator; Twain is his audience. A framing device further complicates this exaggeration: Twain, ostensibly the audience of the original tale, becomes the character who actually relates the blue jay story to the reader. The same process occurs when the narrator of "The Celebrated Jumping Frog of Calaveras County" (1865) listens to Simon Wheeler's story about Jim Smiley's trained animals and then retells the story to the reader.

Shifting the source of the narration emphasizes the distortion process. The more the story is retold, the further the reader is removed from the truth. The comedy lies in the reader's knowledge of the truth despite the exaggerator's attempts to obscure it.

Whether elaborating on a fact or embellishing a tale, each of Clemens's exaggerators relies on the gullibility of others, but the reader's knowledge ultimately foils the exaggeration. Whoever reads Jim Baker's story laughs because he or she knows that the blue jay is incapable of having dropped "not any less than two tons" of acorns into the house (Clemens 1:21). The reader's knowledge is therefore essential to Clemens's humor, for anyone who believes that blue jays would fly "from all over the United States to look down that hole, every summer for three years" would be unable to laugh at Baker's exaggeration.

Thus, Clemens's style of exaggeration manipulates the reader into a process of discovering the truth. As the reader recognizes the truth that is being distorted by whichever of Clemens's characters is exaggerating, the reader becomes aware of his or her own knowledge. Feeling the sense of intellectual superiority that Bergson defines as a prerequisite to laughter, the reader can then laugh.

Roberta Seelinger Trites

BIBLIOGRAPHY

Bergson, Henri. "Laughter." *Comedy*. Ed. and trans. Wylie Sypher. Garden City, N.Y.: Doubleday, 1956. 61–190.

Clemens, Samuel L. *A Tramp Abroad*. 2 vols. New York: Harper, 1921.

Covici, Pascal, Jr. *Mark Twain's Humor: The Image of a World*. Dallas: Southern Methodist UP, 1962.

Cox, James M. *Mark Twain: The Fate of Humor*. Princeton, N.J.: Princeton UP, 1966.

Kolb, Harold H., Jr. "Mark Twain and the Myth of the West." *The Mythologizing of Mark Twain*. Ed. Sara deSaussure Davis and Philip D. Beidler. University: U of Alabama P, 1984. 119–135.

Lynn, Kenneth S. *Mark Twain and Southwestern Humor*. Boston: Little, Brown, 1959.

See also: Burlesque; "Celebrated Jumping Frog of Calaveras County, The"; "Jim Baker's Blue Jay Yarn"

"Experience of the McWilliamses with Membranous Croup"
(1875)

The first of three stories concerning comic tribulations of a middle-class married couple, "Experience of the McWilliamses with Membranous Croup" appeared among Twain's best short fiction in *Mark Twain's Sketches, New and Old* (1875). Although later notes about scarlet-fever illnesses of daughters Jean and Susy and W.D. Howells's son John recalling "Experience of the McWilliamses with Membranous Croup" never became stories, Twain transformed similar comments about the croup following a mid-January 1875 family encounter, affirming Clemens's home life as the basis of McWilliams's adventures.

Convinced by her child's slight coughing not only of Penelope's impending death from membranous croup but also that Penelope would fatally infect her baby sibling, Caroline McWilliams keeps husband Mortimer awake all night: moving the crib back and forth, turning the temperature up and down, shortening intervals and increasing dosages of medicines, applying poultice layers and extra clothing, and finally dragging their ill physician from bed because Penelope perspires. All along Caroline ignores Mortimer's protestations, ironies, sarcasms, and attempted reasonings only

to learn, to Mortimer's joy and her disdain, that the cough results from a swallowed pine splinter. Caroline (Evangeline in later stories) earlier had assured him chewing on pine is healthful. A fourth-paragraph reference particularizing wives and the final paragraph applying Mortimer's experience to that of other husbands identify "Experience" as domestic comedy, its sexist overtones redeemed by the husband narrator's irony and self-deprecating humor.

Critics, however, dispute degrees of redemption and humor. Alfred Habegger dubs "Experience" classic and unfunny in treating the genre of the humorless mother, in which the common-sensical husband acquiesces to the unreasonable wife in child care. Emerson, saying "Experience" may be the author husband's subtle revenge, approaches Habegger's general assertion that irony is the husband's revenge on the demanding wife, but it is closer to the tone of Howells's belief that "Experience" reveals secret feelings of all husband fathers, which is in implicit agreement with Twain's ironic postscript suggesting the universality of the story. Mortimer represents everyone's impotence before irrationality, and the domestic problems in these too neglected stories—forming a unit with Adam and Eve's diaries—extend their appeal beyond the Clemenses (Wilson 76).

Some think Twain turns in new directions with "Experience." Rather than sexist, Van Wyck Brooks views the McWilliams stories as emasculating; they reflect the author's break with the West to join wife Olivia's eastern, middle-class domesticity. While claiming that the *Sketches* volume mainly represents Twain's past, Everett Emerson notes sharp differences between pieces extolling western outlooks, often attacking eastern ways, and "Experience," the latter emphasizing through exaggerating domestic life of socially refined, wealthy New England people, with Twain as "the typical American male," not the western bohemian comically reflecting problems of growing middle-class America (Wilson 80). Another shift occurs in technique and subtlety.

Abandoning the frame contrasting educated outside and uneducated inside narrators typical of southwestern humorists, these McWilliams stories employ identical frameworks—a traveler telling a fellow passenger his wife's latest whimsicality—with a self-aware narrator resigned to his ineffectuality in absurd marital situations reconciling himself to readers with insightful irony and deadpan humor (Covici 46). The perspective of the frame affords McWilliams subtle characterization, generates sympathy, amusement, even respect; with third-person narration, McWilliams might appear ridiculous, pitiful, and pitiable, patronized rather than respected, whereas this frame coaxes smiling identification with him. Exaggeration places common human foibles in perspective, reminding readers of a larger, vulnerable, human community (Wilson 80).

This "subtle artistry," improved over earlier blunter narrative techniques, is one Twain refinement announced by "Experience." Despite scholars' scant interest in Twain's "'domestic' phase," "Experience" introduces it, a break with the West, middle-class backdrops, shifts in characterization and technique, and a fresh source of humor and subject matter later found, in addition to McWilliams's adventures, in works as diverse as the Adam-Eve diaries, "Hadleyburg" (1899), "Indiantown" (written ca. 1899), and "The $30,000 Bequest" (1904). In "Experience" Twain brings humor home.

                                        John H. Davis

BIBLIOGRAPHY

Brooks, Van Wyck. *The Ordeal of Mark Twain*. Rev. ed. New York: Dutton, 1933.

Clemens, Samuel L. "Experience of the McWilliamses with Membranous Croup." *Sketches New and Old*. By Clemens. Hartford, Conn.: American Publishing, 1893. 86–97.

———. *Mark Twain-Howells Letters: The Correspondence of Samuel L. Clemens and William D. Howells, 1872–1910*. Ed. Henry Nash Smith and William M. Gibson. Vol. 2. Cambridge, Mass.: Harvard UP, 1960.

Covici, Pascal, Jr. *Mark Twain's Humor: The Image of a World*. Dallas: Southern Methodist UP, 1962.

Emerson, Everett. *The Authentic Mark Twain: A Literary Biography of Samuel L. Clemens*. Philadelphia: U of Pennsylvania P, 1984.

Gibson, William M. *The Art of Mark Twain*. New York: Oxford UP, 1976.

Habegger, Alfred. "Nineteenth-Century American Humor: Easygoing Males, Anxious Ladies, and Penelope Lapham." *Publications of the Modern Language Association* 91 (October 1976): 884–899.

Howells, William Dean. *My Mark Twain: Reminiscences and Criticisms*. Ed. Marilyn Baldwin. Baton Rouge: Louisiana State UP, 1967.

Wilson, James D. *A Reader's Guide to the Short Stories of Mark Twain*. Boston: G.K. Hall, 1987.

See also: Family Life; McWilliams, Mortimer and Caroline (Evangeline); "McWilliamses and the Burglar Alarm, The"; "Mrs. McWilliams and the Lightning"

Extract from Captain Stormfield's Visit to Heaven
(1909)

The last book by Mark Twain published in his lifetime was an unfinished satirical fable titled *Extract from Captain Stormfield's Visit to Heaven*, appearing six months before he died. About two-thirds of it had been serialized in *Harper's Monthly Magazine* (December 1907–January 1908) and helped pay for part of Twain's final residence in Connecticut, which Clara Clemens therefore renamed "Stormfield." Twain worked on the book sporadically for forty years; it was first conceived in 1868. He "often thought of finishing it" but ended up writing only six chapters, the first four of which were published. In his *Autobiography* (1906) Twain claimed that he got the idea for the book from Captain Ned Wakeman, on whose ship he traveled, but as Ray Browne points out (21), Twain made no mention, in the notebooks written at the time, of Wakeman's dream vision of heaven. Twain's notebook entries are otherwise very detailed concerning the character of this impressive captain (who would reappear as Ned Blakely in *Roughing It* [1872]). It seems unlikely that Twain would have omitted a remarkable celestial dream supposedly recounted to him by Wakeman.

Stormfield's character is probably based in part on Wakeman, but the vision of heaven itself is more likely a complex response to orthodox Christian ideas about the celestial afterlife that go back at least to *Pilgrim's Progress* (1678). "Bunyan's heaven," Twain wrote in his notebook (*Stormfield* 101, n. 16), is one of several "old abandoned heavens." Another was the heaven imagined by Elizabeth Stuart Phelps in *The Gates Ajar* (1868), of which Twain considered *Stormfield* a good-natured burlesque. When he mentions Phelps in his *Autobiography* (1924), he imperfectly recalls that she had created "a mean little ten-cent heaven about the size of Rhode Island"—a narrow vision he believed he had broadened in *Stormfield*. But as Robert Rees and William Gibson have shown, Twain borrowed rather liberally from Phelps, whose character Aunt Winifred ridicules people's simple-minded misconceptions about heaven—not to the extent of Twain's satire, of course, but enough to indicate that Twain was later unfair to Phelps.

Since Twain worked on *Stormfield* at several different periods of his career, its tone varies from light satire to bitter sarcasm. If there is a thread that ties the work together, it is the thwarting of expectation concerning what the afterlife will be like. When Captain Stormfield dies, he assumes he is "booked" for hell. He does indeed descend into a "blinding fire," but it turns out to be the sun. Stormfield realizes that he is traveling at the speed of light through physical space. The journey to heaven is a star trek, complete with a race with a huge comet that turns out to be a brimstone-fueled cargo ship (with a crew of a hundred billion souls from a hundred thousand different worlds) bound for hell. When Stormfield arrives at heaven, he discovers that he is in the wrong district: his decision to race the comet put him off course. The head clerk has never even heard of earth, much less San Francisco. Later, Stormfield discovers that earth is referred to as "the Wart" in heaven.

Expectations are thwarted on almost every page. A mother who has lost her little girl consoles herself that they will be reunited in heaven. Years later when the mother arrives expecting to see her two-year-old daughter, she discovers the girl has grown up, has acquired formidable scientific learning, and has nothing in common with her mother. But, like Captain Stormfield, she adapts. People must *adapt* to the new environment called heaven—and to the idea that in heaven earthly rank is of no consequence. People unheralded on earth are of the highest rank in heaven—if their earthly deeds were good. A sausage maker from Hoboken who gave all his extra meat to the poor is a lord in heaven; a "common tailor from Tennessee" who wrote poetry unappreciated in his lifetime is in heaven ranked higher than Shakespeare. Nothing is as Stormfield expected.

Like "Letters from the Earth," "Chronicle of Young Satan," and other works from his late years, *Stormfield* is Mark Twain's lesson in cultural and cosmic relativism. The journey itself and the later conversation Stormfield has with Sandy are calculated to broaden the ethnocentric and heliocentric reader's perspective. As Stormfield soars away at the speed of light, he meets other "spiritualized bodies," including Solomon Goldstein, who also thinks he is bound for hell. When Stormfield sees him crying, he (Stormfield) assumes it is because the Jew has died before foisting a cheap coat off on some unsuspecting "hayseed." As a Christian, Stormfield has been "trained" to be anti-Semitic, but he learns his lesson when he discovers that Goldstein is crying because he believes he will never see his little daughter again. Stormfield is humbled further when he later learns that there are very few white angels in heaven—"mud colored" and red angels far outnumber them. And human beings are outnumbered by creatures from other worlds—worlds that make Jupiter look like a "mustard-seed."

Stormfield was not Twain's last word on heaven; for that consult *Letters from the Earth* (Letter II), in which he slaughters the sacred cow already kicked by *Stormfield*. For Twain, the conception of heaven as a place where everyone sings and plays harps—and where everyone is white and Christian (Christ is only briefly alluded to in *Stormfield*)—has not "a rag of intellectuality" about it (*Letters* 19). *Stormfield* is Twain's imagination of a more intelligent heaven, a deistic heaven, informed by nineteenth-century science's latest discoveries about the scale of the universe. The last two chapters of the manuscript, weakest in fictional technique because they are mainly philosophical conversations between Sandy and Stormfield, are nonetheless worth reading for their cosmic perspective. Twain probably wrote chapter 5, "Captain Stormfield Resumes," around 1909, when he did calculations in his notebook converting light years to miles. Stormfield is staggered by the vast emptiness of space when he learns that a light-year is equivalent to 6 billion miles (actually 6 trillion—Twain later corrected the mistake in his notebook [Paine 1510]). Sandy slyly hints to Stormfield that the vastness of space is necessary in part to keep the various Christian sects in heaven out of range from one another—they are all at least 5,000 light-years apart.

At its best, *Stormfield* is an awe-inspiring and humbling experience. The vision of souls leaving earth and traveling like a "flock of glow-worms" in the blackness of space at the speed of light toward an unimaginably distant heaven is as hopeful as Christian's progress toward the celestial city, but it is not just for the redeemed. Twain's heaven includes "cannibals, Presbyterians, pariahs, politicians, teetotalers, Turks, and Tramps." It also includes extraterrestrials, who constantly remind us that we are not the center of the universe; our solar system is "one of the little new systems" in a sparsely populated area that the clerk mistakes for a "flyspeck" on the map of the cosmos.

This astronomical perspective on the afterlife has inspired at least one major American science-fiction writer, Philip Jose Farmer, whose *Riverworld* series is in part an elaboration on Twain's vision. In volume 2 of the series, *The Fabulous Riverboat*, the protagonist is Samuel Clemens in an afterlife in which all the human beings who ever died find themselves reincarnated along a great river. He builds a paddleboat and (along with Sir Richard Burton) in volume 3 (*The Dark Design*) seeks the source of the river and an answer to the mystery of the afterlife. Twain's panoramic landscape of an extraterrestrial heaven as a natural environment to which our "spiritualized bodies" would have to adapt was an attempt to provide the modern age with a Darwinian, deistic heaven. It is appropriate that the vision would have its reincarnation in modern science fiction.

Joseph Andriano

BIBLIOGRAPHY

Browne, Ray B. Introduction. *Mark Twain's Quarrel with Heaven.* By Clemens. Ed. Ray B. Browne. New Haven, Conn.: College and University P, 1970. 11–37.

Clemens, Samuel L. "Captain Stormfield's Visit to Heaven." *Mark Twain's Quarrel with Heaven.* By Clemens. Ed. Ray B. Browne. New Haven, Conn.: College and University P, 1970. 39–110.

———. *The Science Fiction of Mark Twain.* Ed. David Ketterer. Hamden, Conn.: Archon, 1984.

Gibson, William M. *The Art of Mark Twain.* New York: Oxford UP, 1976.

McMahan, Elizabeth, ed. *Critical Approaches to Mark Twain's Short Stories.* Port Washington, N.Y.: Kennikat, 1981.

Paine, Albert Bigelow. *Mark Twain: A Biography.* 3 vols. New York: Harper, 1912.

Rees, Robert A. "'Captain Stormfield's Visit to Heaven' and *The Gates Ajar.*" *English Language Notes* 7 (March 1970): 197–202.

Wecter, Dixon. Introduction. *Report from Paradise.* By Clemens. New York: Harper, 1952. ix–xxv.

See also: Letters from the Earth; Religion; Science; Wakeman, Edgar

"Extract from Methuselah's Diary"

(1962)

Among the thousands of pages of Mark Twain's writing left unpublished at his death were many satirical writings concerning biblical history and characters such as Adam, Eve, Satan, Shem, and Methuselah. Twain wrote "Extract from Methuselah's Diary" in the late 1870s. After Twain's death, "Extract" was collected by editor Bernard DeVoto as part of a larger group, "Papers of the Adam Family," and was ready for publication as early as 1939, but Twain's daughter Clara raised objections that delayed the project until 1962, when she gave her consent to publish the volume called *Letters from the Earth*, in which "Extract" appears.

In "Extract" Twain uses Methuselah's diary to critique institutions such as slavery and contemporary issues that interested him, such as official policy toward Native Americans. Twain's belief in the correspondence of human behavior throughout history allowed him to create his satiric effect by having Methuselah raise questions about the human behavior he observes. Methuselah is not yet the thoroughgoing skeptic Twain was, but he is, at the time of this extract, still only sixty years old; considerable time remains to develop his critical sensibilities. Twain's notes indicate that he intended further explorations of Methuselah's world but, with the exception of a short "Later Extract from Methuselah's Diary," never got around to writing them.

The two extracts that have been published, however, give us a unique perspective on human foolishness through the consciousness of that human who would have the greatest opportunity to observe it, Methuselah.

Greg Garrett

BIBLIOGRAPHY

Clemens, Samuel L. *Letters from the Earth*. Ed. Bernard DeVoto. New York: Harper & Row, 1962. 62–67.

See also: Letters from the Earth

"Extracts from Adam's Diary"

(1893)

Originally appearing as a souvenir item for the Buffalo World's Fair in 1893 in *The Niagara Book*, "Adam's Diary" was the first of a small number of published works exploring in seriocomic fashion, but with clear autobiographical implications, the impressions, emotional relationships, and experiences of the first couple in Eden. Shortened by 750 words, it appeared in *Tom Sawyer, Detective* (London, 1897) and then as a separate work with illustrations by E. Strothman, published by Harper and Brothers in 1904. Twain again slightly revised this work in 1905, adding some 650 words in an attempt to improve its literary quality. It was published with "Eve's Diary" in *The $30,000 Bequest and Other Stories* in 1906. (This volume should not be confused with the volume by the same name in the Author's National Edition, in which both works also appeared.) "Eve's Diary" was published in 1905 by *Harper's Magazine*, a year after Olivia Clemens's death, and again in a collection of stories called *Their Husbands' Wives* in 1906 with illustrations by Lester Ralph. Other significant additions to this Adamic complex are "That Day in Eden" and "Eve Speaks," both written ca. 1900 and published in *Europe and Elsewhere* (1923). "Eve's Autobiography," a large section from the "Papers from the Adam Family," was composed, according to Bernard DeVoto, ca. 1905–1906, and emphasizes postlapsarian life in sharply satirical form. Parts of these "Papers" and "Autobiography" were included by DeVoto in *Letters from the Earth* (1962).

Unquestionably, Mark Twain's fascination (indeed, preoccupation) with Adam, Eve, Satan, and other characters in Genesis such as Noah and his sons, began during his Sunday school days in Hannibal and continued throughout his life, at last finding full expression in these pieces and fully justifying Minnie Brashear's statement, "No one used Bible stories as mythology to the extent that Mark Twain has." Twain's "joke" that he was "kin" to Adam and, later, Satan is only a superficial comic mask for exploring those considerably deeper experiential and theological considerations embedded in the "kinship" that ultimately reaches to the primal situation of Eden and the Fall itself.

Twain exploited the comic and burlesque possibilities of treating Adam anachronistically or with different modes of incongruity (as in the visit to Adam's tomb in *Innocents Abroad* [1869]) in order to satirize contemporary values and behavior. In the course of his artistic and intellectual development, his "identification" with the Adamic myth and its characters provided him with a familiar but powerful trope through which he could reinterpret his attitudes about God, good and evil, belief and skepticism, spiritual alienation and affirmation, even the theological nature of humor inherent in the very idea of a fallen world. When, in a letter of 1887, Twain referred to himself as a "banished Adam who is revisiting his half-forgotten Paradise and wondering how the arid outside world could ever have seemed green and fair to him," he revealed a spiritual perception that, especially in his later years, lurked beneath the wide range of thematic patterns and seriocomic tonalities in a number of his novels and stories.

The Adamic diaries are, in form and tone, sophisticated folktales, and they embody a major strand in Twain's complex tapestry of artistic devices, patterns, and "mythic" imagery. They serve not only as seemingly naive (or radically innocent) commentaries on one of the most influential stories in Western literature and religion, but also supply an imaginatively instructive alternative for his readers to the Sunday school Bible images that Twain had rejected as he gradually emancipated himself from the Presbyterian fundamentalism of his youth. Thus, in "Adam's Diary," myth and reality are placed in comic tension by giving Adam and Eve character traits that ring psychologically true while maintaining the mythic roles in Eden. In a clever revision of his original scheme Twain calls Eden "Niagara Falls," thereby comically developing the im-

plications of the pun throughout. Here, Eve is no fatal temptress; rather, she is a "new" and playful creature who annoys Adam because she talks too much, names everything herself, and cries when Adam objects. The conditions for a postlapsarian world are foreshadowed by the presence of carnivores and a buzzard who, as it were, are waiting to fulfill their true natures. During the comic interplay of Adam and Eve's confrontation with the inexplicable forces and natural laws of their world, the Fall is being prepared. Adam ruefully notes Eve's friendship with a serpent and later eats the apples Eve brings him although he has already watched the disturbing fact of the animals eating each other. He learns from an accusing Eve that, according to the serpent, it was a "chestnut" that causes this. Unlike Eve who does not know that a "chestnut" is a "moldy" joke, Adam realizes that he has committed the fatal chestnut by thinking that Niagara Falls would have been more wonderful if it flowed upward. This is the First Chestnut and "coeval" with creation, and so humor itself is implicated in the Fall, a fact that the "guilty" Adam must accept. Yet this Adam and Eve suffer no profound agonies of expulsion, nor does Twain dramatize the anger of a punishing Deity. Indeed, the most radical theological element in this diary lies in God's "hidden" and unstated presence and intervention. The inference is that God either indifferently watches these events or has maliciously caused the Fall, being outraged by Adam's innocent "joke," descriptions consonant with Twain's stated beliefs about the cruelty of the biblical Deity.

There is more psychological comedy in the first couple's confusion about their children's identity as human and in their innocent curiosity creating (and parodying) scientific inquiry. But in the end they affirm the "chestnut" that brought them together, for Adam knows that it is "better to live outside the Garden with her than inside it without her." Whether read as a personal fantasy or truth of his marriage, Twain affirms the universal wisdom that human relationships, with all their foibles and irritations, remain the basis for a meaningful life in a fallen world, a significant statement considering this period when Twain's pessimistic determinism and later nightmare/dream visions would pervade his art.

"Eve's Diary" maintains the same moods and techniques as "Adam's Diary," although Twain offers variations and new insights into his characters. As Adam notes (in an interpolated extract from his diary), Eve is "all interest, eagerness, vivacity, the world to her is a . . . joy." She is the experimenter who learns that "*The burnt Experiment shuns the fire.*" It is her love of God's world and her desire to discover its secrets that define her character. The Fall takes place only because she wishes to please Adam by getting him the forbidden apples and she accepts the "harm" that comes from doing this. After the Fall, she looks back on what seems to have been a "dream" and yet finds consolation in her love for Adam. As she grows older and nears death, she has discovered her universal purpose as the "first wife, and in the last wife I shall be repeated." At Eve's grave Adam elegiacally says, "Wheresoever she was, *there* was Eden." (The reader will note several Miltonic echoes throughout these diaries.) Thus, their love transcends the Fall, indeed, turns it into a salvational *felix culpa.*

Twain's treatment of the Adamic myth takes on a darker perspective in "That Day in Eden" and "Eve Speaks" as he dramatizes the causes for the expulsion and recognition of death itself. As a sympathetic Satan observes in "That Day in Eden," the "command of refrain had meant nothing to them . . . and [they] could not understand untried things and verbal abstractions which stood for matters outside their little world and . . . experience." Adam and Eve acquire the Moral Sense after innocently tasting the forbidden fruit, that innate capacity to distinguish good from evil that Twain had come to regard as the very cause of guilt and suffering and evil in the world, put into humanity's heart by God, who is the only responsible agent for a fallen world. Adam and Eve are guiltless, victims of an incomprehensible prohibition by an incomprehensible (and therefore cruel) Deity. Evil is necessary, Satan knows, for "no one can do wrong without knowing how to distinguish between right and wrong." With the murder of Abel, Adam and Eve begin to understand death and to grieve, but as Satan writes in his diary postscript, "The Family think ill of death—they will change their minds." Death, and not love, now becomes the consolation of the fortunate Fall. Taken as a whole, these diaries offer the comic-pathetic irony that the fall derives from the first couple's loving and innocently curious natures. Only their hearts and wit and intellectual innocence betray them before a God whose creation is beautiful, but whose best gift is death. The diaries are therefore not only splendid examples of Twain's folk art (in spite of odd inconsistencies of plot and motivation), but also a crucial demonstration of his theological interpretation of life, which all his secularism could not efface or provide a compensating alternative.

Stanley Brodwin

BIBLIOGRAPHY

Brodwin, Stanley. "The Humor of the Absurd: Mark Twain's Adamic Diaries." *Criticism* 14 (1972): 49–64.

———. "Mark Twain's Masks of Satan: The Final Phase." *American Literature* 45 (1973): 202–227.

———. "The Theology of Mark Twain: Banished Adam and the Bible." *Mississippi Quarterly* 29 (1976): 167–189.

Ensor, Allison. *Mark Twain and the Bible.* Lexington: UP of Kentucky, 1969.

Macnaughton, William R. *Mark Twain's Last Years as a Writer.* Columbia: U of Missouri P, 1979.

Parsons, Coleman O. "The Devil and Samuel Clemens." *Virginia Quarterly Review* 23 (1947): 582–606.

Werge, Thomas. "Mark Twain and the Fall of Adam." *Mark Twain Journal* 15.2 (1970): 5–13.

See also: "Adam's Soliloquy"; Bible; Eve; "Eve Speaks"; "Eve's Diary"; "Monument to Adam, A"; Religion; "That Day in Eden"

F

"Fable, A"

(1909)

First published in the December 1909 *Harper's Magazine*, "A Fable" later appeared in *The Mysterious Stranger and Other Stories* (1922). Twain wrote it in June while at his summer retreat in Dublin, New Hampshire, where among other projects he worked on his autobiography.

In the tradition of Aesop, Twain's gentle satire involves a cast of animal characters who take turns looking into a mirror and searching for a beautiful piece of art reflected in it. They only see themselves because they do not know where they "ought to stand" (*Mysterious Stranger* 282).

The one study done on this tale endows it with a lesson on educational methodology, but unconvincingly (Prince 7–8). Ironically, the writer seems to have missed the moral of the tale: "You can find in a text whatever you bring, if you will stand between it and the mirror of your imagination. You will not see your ears, but they will be there" (*Mysterious Stranger* 284).

Twain composed many dark pieces during this period. However, this fable stands as an indication of Twain's recurrent humorous situation similar to the 1880 "Jim Baker's Blue Jay Yarn." Animals and their behavior were a source of pleasure for Twain. Significantly, the main character, the house cat, whose report of what he has seen motivates the others, turns out to be the only one who could see the work of art. Other characters have names borrowed from Rudyard Kipling's *Jungle Book* stories (1894–1895). Twain admired Kipling, so he would be unlikely to use Hathi, the elephant, and Baloo, the bear, in a negative fashion.

The moral at the end of "A Fable" is similar in comedic nature to the preface in *Huckleberry Finn* (1885). A June 1906 letter to Henry Huttleston Rogers reveals that Twain first thought of publishing part of the autobiography at this time (*Correspondence* 611). Perhaps he sketched "A Fable" as a potential preface. He had had the concept of mirror text in mind since the 4 April 1906 dictation: "The autobiography of mine is a mirror, and I am looking at myself in it all the time" (*Mark Twain's Autobiography* 2:312).

Sandra Littleton-Uetz

BIBLIOGRAPHY

Clemens, Samuel L. "A Fable." *The Mysterious Stranger and Other Stories*. By Clemens. New York: Harper, 1922. 281–284.

———. *Mark Twain's Autobiography*. Ed. Albert B. Paine. 2 vols. New York: Harper, 1924.

———. *Mark Twain's Correspondence with Henry Huttleston Rogers, 1893–1909*. Ed. Lewis Leary. Berkeley: U of California P, 1969. 611–612.

Gibson, William M. *The Art of Mark Twain*. New York: Oxford UP, 1976.

Prince, Gilbert. "Mark Twain's 'A Fable': The Teacher as Jackass." *Mark Twain Journal* 17.4 (Winter 1974): 7–8.

Wilson, James D. *A Reader's Guide to the Short Stories of Mark Twain*. Boston: G.K. Hall, 1987.

See also: Animals

"Facts Concerning the Recent Carnival of Crime in Connecticut, The"

(1876)

Mark Twain first presented "The Facts Concerning the Recent Carnival of Crime in Connecticut" ("CCC") at a meeting of the Monday Evening Club, held at his Hartford home on 24 January 1876. William Dean Howells shared the club's enthusiasm for the story and published it in the June 1876 *Atlantic Monthly*. Popular reaction to the tale has been mixed, but critics agree that in the surprisingly autobiographical "CCC" Twain gave his first strong fictional image of a man divided against himself, an image that he explored in a commanding portion of his subsequent writing.

The nameless narrator—seemingly Twain himself—begins "CCC" sitting in his study,

"feeling blithe, almost jocund." He has reached a point in his life where guilt no longer mitigates the satisfaction he derives from even his worst habits, such as smoking. A letter arrives promising a visit from his esteemed and high-moraled Aunt Mary, and in his joyful mood he wishes his "most pitiless enemy" would appear before him so he could bring peace between them.

Immediately, a mold-covered and deformed dwarf strolls in. Despite the dwarf's nauseating appearance, the narrator perceives similarities between the dwarf and himself, as though the dwarf's looks, manner, and speech are caricatures of his own. After some offensive prattle the dwarf rudely berates the narrator for lying to a beggar, mistreating an aspiring author, and contributing to his brother's sickliness and death—all internal conflicts that grated Twain personally—and at last confesses to being his conscience.

The narrator joyfully leaps to kill the dwarf, but this conscience, reflecting the narrator's light-hearted approach to murder, soars to the top of a bookcase. The narrator's hurled missiles miss their lofty mark, and he sits down exhausted. The narrator/slave then interviews his conscience/lord-and-master on the nature of his work. Consciences are "merely disinterested agents . . . appointed by authority, . . . [and] we leave the consequences where they belong." Consciences have no moral compass; they simply harass people for the pleasure of it and therefore make them repent every action: feeding a tramp or turning him away, giving him work or killing him. As a result, consciences, invisible to all but their slaves (and then only rarely), grow in stature and beauty—or in deformity and noxiousness—as their slaves react to their needling. This accounts for the dwarf's appearance. The narrator's conscience played the tobacco "card a little too long, and I lost." Now any chastisement of the narrator's smoking, by anyone, just puts conscience to sleep.

Aunt Mary arrives and sets right to work producing guilt in the narrator. The conscience tumbles heavily from his perch, and the narrator eyes him malevolently. Aunt Mary trembles at the look, which the narrator ascribes to excessive smoking. Now the conscience is done for. Aunt Mary pleads with the narrator "to crush out that fatal habit," and the conscience slips into deep slumber. "With an exultant shout," the narrator claims, "I sprang past my aunt." He tears his conscience to bits, sends his nagging aunt on her way, and contentedly begins his carnival of crime. This formerly benign man kills tramps and old enemies, swindles widows, and burns a house that obstructs his view. He sells corpses "by the gross, by cord measurement, or per ton." At last, he is truly happy, albeit thoroughly antisocial.

This simple allegory exposes the conflict Twain later mined with striking result. Huck's willingness to go to hell in chapter 31 of *Adventures of Huckleberry Finn* (1885) differs very little from the narrator's destruction of his conscience. Huck does not side with good in that moving chapter; he only refuses conscience of any kind. Hank Morgan's self-exploration in *A Connecticut Yankee in King Arthur's Court* (1889) reaches its apotheosis in the final separation between his soul and his corporeal self, a separation that in the end kills him. Theodor Fischer/August Feldner's dream self—a self finally indifferent to acts of saving destruction in "The Mysterious Stranger" (1969)—owes its fictional origin to the death of the nauseating dwarf.

"CCC" is the seminal and comic fictional expression of what grew to become Twain's most dark and dominant theme. In his 7 January 1897 notebook entry, Twain concluded that his approach to conscience in "CCC" was wrong and that the conscious self and the separate interior one must always be strangers to one another.

Andrew Jay Hoffman

BIBLIOGRAPHY

Blues, Thomas. *Mark Twain & the Community.* Lexington: UP of Kentucky, 1970.

Covici, Pascal, Jr. *Mark Twain's Humor: The Image of a World.* Dallas: Southern Methodist UP, 1962.

Gibson, William M. *The Art of Mark Twain.* New York: Oxford UP, 1976.

Johnson, James L. *Mark Twain and the Limits of Power: Emerson's God in Ruins.* Knoxville: U of Tennessee P, 1982.

Kaplan, Justin. *Mr. Clemens and Mark Twain.* New York: Simon & Schuster, 1966.

Lynn, Kenneth S. *Mark Twain and Southwestern Humor.* Boston: Little, Brown, 1959.

See also: Conscience

"Facts Concerning the Recent Resignation"
(1868)

In the preface to the 1875 *Sketches, New and Old* Mark Twain indicates blithely that some of the material is included because it "seemed instructive." Among the sketches, "Facts Concerning the Recent Resignation," which first appeared in the New York *Tribune* on 13 February 1868, satirized his brief experiences as a private secretary to Senator William M. Stewart. Albert B. Paine reported that it was "impossible to conceive of Mark Twain as anybody's secretary."

Stewart and Twain lampooned each other, and the rift has been the subject of commentary. A companion to "My Late Senatorial Secretaryship" (1868), the sketch "Washington, Dec. 2, 1867" details the narrator's resignation as clerk of the Senate Committee on Conchology, a position held for six days and one that limited his "voice in the counsels of the nation." Twain describes unsuccessful attempts to correct three cabinet officers. In the attempts to offer good advice to the government, the secretary invades a cabinet meeting at the White House and confronts the President. When he returns to his clerical post, the committee members assault him for their not being able to locate him for their own tasks. He resigns with Patrick Henry's cry of liberty or death, bills the government for his consultations with cabinet members, and blasts the practice of congressional appointments of clerks.

This two-month interlude as a congressional secretary, designed to give Twain the time to write, actually gave him a subject as he expanded his efforts to publish in the East.

Thomas Bonner, Jr.

BIBLIOGRAPHY

Clemens, Samuel L. *The Writings of Mark Twain*. Ed. Albert B. Paine. 37 vols. New York: Wells, 1922–1925.

French, Bryant Morey. *Mark Twain and "The Gilded Age."* Dallas: Southern Methodist UP, 1965.

Kaplan, Justin. *Mr. Clemens and Mark Twain*. New York: Simon & Schuster, 1966.

Paine, Albert Bigelow. *Mark Twain: A Biography*. 3 vols. New York: Harper, 1912.

See also: Politics; *Sketches, New and Old*; Washington, D.C.

"Facts in the Case of the Great Beef Contract, The"

(1870)

"The Facts in the Case of the Great Beef Contract" ("GBC") first appeared in the "Memoranda" section of the May 1870 *Galaxy*. It was Clemens's first contribution as head of the humor department of the New York–based literary magazine, a position he held while simultaneously serving as editor of the Buffalo *Express*. The sketch was anthologized in the "Memoranda" pamphlet of 1871, in *Public and Parlor Reader* (1871), *Sketches Number One* (1874), and *Sketches, New and Old* (1875).

With heavy doses of hyperbole and farce, "GBC" satirizes governmental procedures and lack of communication between U.S. agencies. The story focuses on the insurmountable difficulties of the frustrated narrator (Twain) to settle accounts between John Wilson Mackenzie, deceased, and the U.S. government for thirty barrels of beef that Mackenzie was to have delivered to General Sherman during the Civil War. Tracking the course of the beef and establishing responsibility for payment becomes a hilarious exposure of governmental bureaucracy and evasion that reflects Clemens's personal frustration experi-

enced as a secretary in Washington, D.C., under William Stewart.

Maria Burke

BIBLIOGRAPHY

Sloane, David E.E. "Mark Twain's Comedy: The 1870s." *Studies in American Humor* 2 (January 1976): 146–156.

Wilson, James D. *A Reader's Guide to the Short Stories of Mark Twain*. Boston: G.K. Hall, 1987.

See also: Galaxy; Government; Washington, D.C.

"Facts in the Great Landslide Case, The"

(1870)

One of Twain's special Saturday features for the Buffalo *Express*, "The Facts in the Great Landslide Case" ("FGLC") appeared on 2 April 1870. It is the second of three versions of the story that Twain published.

The seed for the *Express* piece is a straightforward report of a real practical joke played on the attorney general of the Nevada Territory, Benjamin Bunker. Twain published the factual account in the San Francisco *Daily Morning Call* on 30 August 1863. He revised it into a well-developed sketch for the *Express*. "FGLC" contains ingredients of the comic "dandy versus squatter" confrontation, with Nevada ranchers outwitting and contriving an elaborate courtroom hoax on an educated Easterner, the overconfident blowhard of an attorney general. Bunker, whose name is changed to General Buncombe, is duped into defending rancher Dick Sides, who tearfully claims that a neighbor's ranch slid down a mountainside, completely covering his property. The two ranchers orchestrate a trial, each claiming to own the land. The judge, a party to the joke, listens to the naive Buncombe's eloquently bombastic defense and eventually renders an amusingly absurd decision: Sides can keep his ranch as long as he can dig it out. The judge's distorted logic and Buncombe's failure to recognize that he is the butt of ridicule are masterful strokes of humor; they are typical of Twain's "inspired idiot" characterizations.

Twain reconsidered "FGLC" a third time for inclusion, with minor revisions of the *Express* version, in chapter 34 of *Roughing It* (1872). In *Roughing It* the plaintiff's name is changed to Dick Hyde, and in order to make the judge's ruling even more ridiculous, Twain increased the depth under which the plaintiff's ranch is buried from six feet to thirty-eight feet. Effie Mona Mack's identification of the real-life practical-joking ranchers has been disputed (Rogers and Baender 580–581).

Thomas J. Reigstad

BIBLIOGRAPHY

Blair, Walter. *Native American Humor.* San Francisco: Chandler, 1960.

Branch, Edgar M. *The Literary Apprenticeship of Mark Twain.* Urbana: U of Illinois P, 1950.

Clemens, Samuel L. *Roughing It.* Ed. Franklin R. Rogers and Paul Baender. Berkeley: U of California P, 1972.

Mack, Effie M. *Mark Twain in Nevada.* New York: Scribner, 1947.

See also: Buffalo *Express*; Law; *Roughing It*

Fairbanks, Mary Mason
(1828–1898)

A refined woman, a graduate of Emma Willard's Female Seminary, Mary Mason taught school before marrying Abel W. Fairbanks and becoming the mother of two children. She was a writer of travel letters and occasional pieces for her husband's newspaper, the Cleveland *Herald*. She met Samuel Clemens on the *Quaker City* excursion and remained his friend for thirty-two years.

Fairbanks's writing, sometimes under the anagramic pseudonym "Myra," was that of the cultivated amateur rather than professional. Commentators differ on the quality of her prose, some finding it precise but dull (Kaplan 43), others seeing it as a work of grace and charm (Ganzel 18). During the *Quaker City* cruise Fairbanks and Clemens formed a friendship crucial to Clemens's future and rewarding for her own life. Clemens declared that Fairbanks was "the most refined, intelligent, & cultivated lady in the ship" (Webster 97). She edited some of the travel letters he wrote for the *Alta California*, letters that formed the seedbed for *The Innocents Abroad* (1869), bringing them more into line with conventional standards of diction and taste. Largely at Clemens's invitation she assumed the roles of mentor in the social graces, adviser on literary matters, and confidant of personal affairs. To his wayward son, she played guiding mother. The roles were mutually satisfying: she enjoyed scolding him over his personal habits and making suggestions for his professional development; he enjoyed provoking the chiding, submitting to her preachment, and then ignoring her advice. Both realized that, as Fairbanks put it, "my apron string is no check to you" (Wecter xxx).

For Clemens, Fairbanks embodied the genteel tradition. While as Mark Twain he would laugh at the narrow morality, obsessive refinement, and rigid proprieties of the genteel class, as Samuel Clemens he was careful to honor these to secure a position in America's social and financial structures. The pivotal event in this difficult navigation was Clemens's courtship of Olivia Langdon, and his relationship to Fairbanks was a kind of rehearsal for that courtship (Cox 67–72). In giving Fairbanks the task of reforming the rough edges of his character while affirming the worth of its core, he created a stratagem that he would use in his marriage suit, as he transferred Fairbanks's role to Livy. Fairbanks herself furthered the courtship by testifying to the worried Langdons that Clemens was at bottom a man of reliable character.

A person of enterprise, as well as cultivation, Fairbanks is one of several women manipulated by Clemens to serve his own psychic and social ends (Warren 149–185). He used her as surrogate mother not only to woo the genteel but also to bolster his own sense of self-worth. Such a mechanism of self-validation was central to Clemens's self-creation. It was also crucial to Mark Twain's comic art, for Twain seized the boundaries of propriety established by Fairbanks (and others) as the limits his humor would transgress.

There was, however, reciprocity in the Fairbanks-Clemens friendship. She used her tie to Clemens to seek professional advancement for her children; she used Mark Twain as copy for her writing; she obtained money from him when her husband faced bankruptcy; and she warmed herself through the years in the sun of Clemens's fame. Long after the mother-son dynamic had lost whatever energy it had for them both, their correspondence demonstrated an abiding loyalty and affection.

Leland Krauth

BIBLIOGRAPHY

Clemens, Samuel L. *Mark Twain to Mrs. Fairbanks.* Ed. Dixon Wecter. San Marino, Calif.: Huntington Library, 1949.

Cox, James M. *Mark Twain: The Fate of Humor.* Princeton, N.J.: Princeton UP, 1966.

Ganzel, Dewey. *Mark Twain Abroad: The Cruise of the "Quaker City."* Chicago: U of Chicago P, 1968.

Kaplan, Justin. *Mr. Clemens and Mark Twain.* New York: Simon & Schuster, 1966.

Warren, Joyce W. *The American Narcissus: Individualism and Women in Nineteenth-Century American Fiction.* New Brunswick, N.J.: Rutgers UP, 1984.

Webster, Samuel Charles. *Mark Twain, Business Man.* Boston: Little, Brown, 1946.

See also: Genteel Tradition; *Innocents Abroad, The*; Women

Family Life

(1870–1910)

"We are a very happy family!" Susy Clemens exclaimed at age fourteen as she began the biography of her father that was also to become a chronicle of the family (Susy Clemens 83). Susy was partly right. Samuel Clemens's family life was happy, but it was also often filled with tension and conflict. While there is disagreement over the tenor of family life, there is general recognition that it was central to Clemens and to Mark Twain.

Clemens's family life began soon after his marriage to Olivia, with the birth of their first child, Langdon, in November 1870. Although Langdon died in 1872, the family grew steadily with the births of Susy in March of 1872, of Clara in June of 1874, and of Jean in July of 1880. Clemens, Livy, and their three daughters lived two family lives—one real, the other imagined. The first was often vexed by volatile personal temperaments and domestic difficulties; the second was always idyllic. Clemens's family life can best be considered in three periods: the years in Hartford, 1870–1891; the years in exile, 1891–1900; and the final years in America, 1900–1910.

The Years in Hartford (1870–1891)

These were in many ways the most important years for the family. During this formative period Clemens and Livy discovered their marital roles; the children grew into distinct personalities; the family worked out its habitual relations; and the myth of a perfect, joyous home life was created.

The Clemenses's early family life transpired under conditions of phenomenal affluence. The ostentatious home Clemens built at 351 Farmington Avenue in the midst of the genteel Nook Farm writers colony was staffed by servants, some of whom, like the maid, Katy Leary, the butler, George Griffin, and the coachman, Patrick McAleer, were to become virtual members of the family, though members who always knew their place. Livy assumed the duties of the traditional middle-class Victorian lady: she ran the household, keeping track of all domestic affairs and overseeing the education of the children, which was conducted chiefly through a series of nursemaids, governesses, and eventually chaperons. Clemens pursued his literary endeavors and business ventures, often away from home.

The home life was consummately social. As Clemens and Livy settled into their Hartford home, they became good friends with such neighbors as the Warners, the Stowes, the Hookers, and the Gillettes, holding and attending lavish dinners. On Fridays Clemens would often have men in for billiards, while Livy served tea for their wives. Clemens attended the Monday Evening Club and the Saturday Morning Club, and at times he conducted literary study groups in his home. As Mark Twain's fame grew, the family received a seemingly endless series of house guests, ranging from the beloved William Dean Howells to the barely tolerated George Washington Cable. The burden of their elaborate entertaining fell disproportionately on Livy, but both Livy and Clemens considered their friends a part of their daughters' education. "All trainers of the family," Clemens remarked (Harnsberger 20).

Although Clemens and Livy tacitly accepted the conventional separation of the two spheres, the private for the woman, the public for the man, their home life was actually dominated by Clemens. His desires were indulged; his moods were respected. (Livy's word was law, but she seldom uttered it.) When he was not working or was away on business, Clemens was an attentive father who created an atmosphere of unpredictable play. He read to his girls, drew cartoons for them, told them endless stories, and romped with them. There were "jungle" hunts in the library, and excursions outside—skating on the nearby pond, tobogganing, carriage and pony rides. The family enjoyed such communal entertainments as charades and home theatricals (most memorably a dramatic performance of *The Prince and the Pauper* [1882]). They nursed and frolicked with a series of pets—cats, dogs, ponies, and even a cow. One of the constant pastimes was "dusting papa off," that is, correcting his dress, manners and speech, and reminding him to be on his best behavior at varied official functions. Memories of this idyllic family life were recorded in two unpublished documents, "A Family Sketch" and "The Children's Record."

This family life took place in Hartford for eight or nine months and then in Elmira for three to four as the family usually moved to Quarry Farm, home of Livy's sister, Sue Crane, each summer. Though somewhat more bucolic, the activities, minus the house guests and formal dinners, were much the same. It was during the summer interlude, however, that Mark Twain did most of his writing.

While there was unmistakable mutual love and affection in the Clemens home life, there was also tension. Clemens was both a doting, generous, indulgent father and a tyrant. His moods and whims dominated the home. His anger often made it a place of terror. (His daughters were afraid to be in a room alone with him.) Livy was occasionally overwhelmed by her responsibilities and sometimes smothered by her husband's insatiable ego. Illness, both physical and emotional, was frequent in the family. As the girls grew, the home life became taut with conflicts over independence, propriety, romantic attachments, careers, money, and even sex. Early biographers emphasized the idyllic side of the home (Susy Clemens, Paine, Clara Clemens, Harnsberger, Salsbury, Lawton), while more recent commentaries have underscored the tortured aspect of the family life (Kaplan, Hill, Cardwell). Both existed, and the task for future studies is to discover the just balance.

The Years in Exile (1891–1900)
When Clemens closed the Hartford home in June 1891 to go abroad to conserve money, the family life changed decisively. For the next nine years the family was really without a home, moving from country to country— Germany, France, Italy, Austria, England— from city to city, and from house to house. They were adrift. Though less opulent than life in Hartford, the years of exile were still privileged. The Clemenses generally lived abroad as aristocrats and were treated as celebrities, since Mark Twain's fame was by then worldwide. Increasingly, they lived apart, however. Clara was often in schools or training for a musical career; Jean was often in sanitariums or at health spas; Susy was eventually back at Elmira for her health; and Clemens himself often left his family to return to the United States to oversee his failing finances. Paradoxi-

cally, their separations seemed only to increase the tensions latent in the family life. Neither Clemens nor Livy was ready to release their daughters into the world. Livy worried over Clara's conduct without her "checking influence," and Clemens instructed her to adhere strictly to all canons of "perfect breeding." The more the family grew apart, the more the parents insisted on its behaving as if it were together.

The Final Years (1900–1910)

The death of Susy in 1896 was a fateful prelude to the final dissolution of the family. First secluding themselves to grieve in a rented home in England and then moving to live for two restorative years in Vienna, Clemens, Livy, Clara, and Jean were a family knit together chiefly by striated finances, grief, a remembered past, and an uncertain future. Increasingly, Clemens seemed to live outside the home in the social world of his fame. Their triumphant return to the United States in 1900 ushered in a time of illness for both daughters and for Livy, one that reached its nadir in Livy's death in June 1904. After that, the family no longer had a family life to speak of. Clara and Jean spent much time in sanitariums, rest homes, and asylums (to escape their father as much as to recover their health), while Clemens escaped to banquets, to Bermuda, and into alcohol and billiards (Hill 179–262). The daughters avoided their father, and he neglected Jean and overdirected Clara. For a time Clara did assume the role of hectoring mother, once fulfilled to Clemens's delight by Livy, but the family was one in name more than anything else. The marriage of Clara to Ossip Gabrilowitsch in October 1909 and the death of Jean in December of the same year marked the end of family life for Clemens.

The importance of the early family life for the aged Clemens is suggested by his rather pathetic efforts to recreate in his gathering of little girls, his Angel Fish, as he called them, some echo of the idyllic times with the young Susy, Clara, and Jean. But those times were beyond recall. His family life was the stabilizing center without which Clemens was less and less able to control his personal disorders—his despair, his rage, his fear—and without which Mark Twain was less and less likely to write. The home was the core of existence for Mark Twain as well as for Sam Clemens. Family life formed the sanctuary that restored Clemens, strengthened him, and empowered him both to contend with the world and to create.

Leland Krauth

BIBLIOGRAPHY

Andrews, Kenneth R. *Nook Farm: Mark Twain's Hartford Circle.* Cambridge, Mass.: Harvard UP, 1950.

Cardwell, Guy. *The Man Who Was Mark Twain.* New Haven, Conn.: Yale UP, 1991.

Clemens, Clara. *My Father, Mark Twain.* New York: Harper, 1931.

Clemens, Samuel L. *Mark Twain's Aquarium: The Samuel Clemens–Angelfish Correspondence 1905–1910.* Ed. John Cooley. Athens: U of Georgia P, 1991.

Clemens, Susy. *Papa: An Intimate Biography of Mark Twain.* Ed. Charles Neider. Garden City, N.Y.: Doubleday, 1985.

Harnsberger, Caroline T. *Mark Twain, Family Man.* New York: Citadel P, 1960.

Harris, Susan K. *Mark Twain's Escape from Time: A Study of Patterns and Images.* Columbia: U of Missouri P, 1982.

Hill, Hamlin. *Mark Twain: God's Fool.* New York: Harper & Row, 1973.

Kaplan, Justin. *Mr. Clemens and Mark Twain.* New York: Simon & Schuster, 1966.

Lawton, Mary. *A Lifetime with Mark Twain.* New York: Harcourt, Brace, 1925.

Paine, Albert Bigelow. *Mark Twain: A Biography.* 4 vols. New York: Harper, 1912.

Salsbury, Edith Colgate, ed. *Susy and Mark Twain: Family Dialogues.* New York: Harper & Row, 1965.

See also: Biographers; Clemens, Olivia Langdon; Clemens, Olivia Susan; Clemens, Samuel Langhorne; Nook Farm; Quarry Farm; Samossoud, Clara Clemens

Fanshaw, Buck

The funeral for Buck Fanshaw, a saloon-keeper and "representative citizen" of Virginia City who committed suicide "in the delirium of a wasting typhoid fever," is described in chapter 47 of *Roughing It* (1872). His friend Scotty Briggs, a "stalwart rough," arranges the "obsequies" with a minister, the recent graduate of an eastern seminary, in a conversation that illustrates the difference between colloquial and genteel language. In the end, Fanshaw's funeral—complete with "plumed hearse," brass bands, and processions of secret societies, political officials, and military battalions—sets the local standard for such ceremonies. For "years afterward," as Twain writes, "the degree of grandeur attained by any civic display in Virginia was determined by comparison with Buck Fanshaw's funeral." The anecdote is often cited to suggest the narrative shift from sympathy for "the boys" in the first half of *Roughing It* to irony and subtle condescension toward them in the second half. In "after days it was worth something to hear the minister tell" this story, Twain reports—a crucial suggestion he identified with the polite classes in the latter chapters of the text.

Gary Scharnhorst

BIBLIOGRAPHY

Beidler, Philip D. "Realistic Style and the Problem of Context in *The Innocents Abroad* and *Roughing It*." *American Literature* 52 (March 1980): 33–49.

Clemens, Samuel L. *Roughing It*. Ed. Franklin R. Rogers and Paul Baender. Berkeley: U of California P, 1972.

Smith, Henry Nash. *Mark Twain: The Development of a Writer*. Cambridge, Mass.: Harvard UP, 1962.

See also: Briggs, Scotty; "Buck Fanshaw's Funeral"; *Roughing It*

Faux, William

(b. 1785)

English William Faux published in 1823 a travel book called *Memorable Days in America*. The book describes Faux's journey from England to America in 1819–1820 to investigate the opportunities for trade and immigration in what was then the western part of America (now Ohio, Indiana, Kentucky, and Illinois). The book contains many descriptions of America and Americans, as well as much social commentary—particularly about the crassness of Americans and their immoral practice of slavery.

There is some evidence that Faux's book may have influenced Twain's *Adventures of Huckleberry Finn* (1885). The specific parallels are inexact, but it is important to remember that in 1882, when Twain was working to complete *Life on the Mississippi* (1883), he wrote to his publisher James R. Osgood asking for a book by a writer named "Fawkes." The context of the request suggests that "Fawkes" was an early travel writer who had visited the Mississippi valley. No such book by a writer named "Fawkes," however, has ever been identified. Whether or not Twain actually consulted *Memorable Days in America*, there can be little doubt that his "Fawkes" was a misspelling, or a variant spelling, of "Faux," and that this was the book that he wanted Osgood to send him.

Peter G. Beidler

BIBLIOGRAPHY

Beidler, Peter G. "'Fawkes' Identified: A New Source for *Huckleberry Finn*?" *English Language Notes* 29(1991): 54–60.

Faux, William. *Memorable Days in America 1819–1820*. London: W. Simpkin and R. Marshall, 1823. Rpt. New York, AMS P, 1966.

See also: *Adventures of Huckleberry Finn*; Bricksville

Fay, Morgan le

Sister of King Arthur and wife of King Uriens, redheaded Queen Morgan le Fay is variously described by the Connecticut Yankee as "a silky smooth hellion," "a Vesuvius," and "fresh and young as a Vassar pullet." In Mark Twain's *A Connecticut Yankee in King Arthur's Court* (1889) she dominates only three chapters (16–

18) and is briefly mentioned in a fourth (19). Then she disappears, her erratic malevolence having served its narrative purpose.

A legendary figure of ancient and evil origin, le Fay ("the fairy," i.e., a supernatural being) descended from three Celtic deities; in medieval literature this sorceress is mistress of black magic, in contrast to the white magic of Merlin. In Malory's *Morte D'Arthur* (1485) she has degenerated into a licentious mortal whose wickedness is generally ineffectual.

In *CY* the Yankee is in nervous awe of "Mrs. le Fay," who imprisons or murders her victims at will and is "loaded to the eye-lids with cold malice"; it is Sandy who frightens the wicked queen with threats of the Yankee's retaliation. Mark Twain's Morgan le Fay (portrayed by illustrator Beard as an angelic matron on a demonic throne) is pure humbug. The female counterpart of Hank Morgan, she is allied to him in more than name, for both are fast-talking pretenders, without true magical prowess, and both are abusers of power—destroyers of the chivalric world of King Arthur.

Mary Boewe

BIBLIOGRAPHY

Clemens, Samuel L. *A Connecticut Yankee in King Arthur's Court.* Ed. Bernard L. Stein. Berkeley: U of California P, 1979.

Morgan, Henry Grady. "The Role of Morgan le Fay in Malory's *Morte Darthur.*" *Southern Quarterly* 2 (January 1964): 150–168.

See also: *Connecticut Yankee in King Arthur's Court, A*; Malory, Sir Thomas; Sandy

Fenians

Founded in 1856 in both Ireland and America, the Fenian movement was a secret revolutionary society that hoped to win Irish independence from England by violent means. The movement made spectacular progress in post-Civil War America, with Fenians active in most parts of the country, including Califor-

nia. Mark Twain, who frequently voiced anti-Irish sentiments, published a humorous piece, "Bearding the Fenian in His Lair," in the *Territorial Enterprise* 28 January 1866. That piece survives as "Among the Fenians," included in *The Celebrated Jumping Frog of Calaveras County and Other Sketches* (1867). In it Twain attempts to converse in Gaelic cliches with Dennis McCarthy, the editor of the San Francisco edition of the Fenian journal, *The Irish People.*

Nancy Cook

BIBLIOGRAPHY

Budd, Louis J. *Mark Twain: Social Philosopher.* Bloomington: Indiana UP, 1962.

Clemens, Samuel L. *The Celebrated Jumping Frog of Calaveras County and Other Sketches.* Ed. John Paul. New York: Webb, 1867. 58–59.

Ó Broin, Leon. *Fenian Fever: An Anglo-American Dilemma.* London: Chatto and Windus, 1971.

See also: Ireland, Irish, Irishmen

"Fenimore Cooper's Literary Offenses"
(1895)

Mark Twain's most famous literary essay is both outrageous in its lampooning jibes at Cooper's *Leatherstocking Tales* and instructive in its delineation of the rules and aesthetics of realism. Published in the *North American Review* in 1895, "Fenimore Cooper's Literary Offenses" was originally conceived as the first of several lectures in a series for which Twain's persona was to be "Professor of Belles Lettres in the Veterinary College of Arizona." Although he dropped all specific references to this voice, it served not only to burlesque academic literary criticism, but also to provide the reader with some horse sense on the extravagances of romanticism.

Early readers of the essay (e.g., D.L. Maulsby in 1897) immediately recognized that Twain deliberately imposed the standards of realism on romance, although he claimed that his "nineteen rules governing literary art" were in "the domain of romantic fiction." Some of the rules, of course, apply to all writing—e.g., "eschew surplusage" and "use the right word, not its second cousin." But many of them pertain only to a realist aesthetic—e.g., plausibility of plot (rule nine) and authenticity of dialogue (rule five). The humor of the essay, which is often hilarious, derived chiefly from Twain's misapplication of the rules; he imposes them on Cooper's texts, particularly *Deerslayer* (1841) and *Pathfinder* (1840), in a deliberately preposterous fashion, as when he lists about thirty different examples of Cooper's failure to write *le mot juste*—without giving the context or the precise source of any of the examples.

Because Cooper was "satisfied with the approximate word," and had no ear for "word music," his style was, to Twain, slovenly and unartistic. Furthermore, Cooper was a poor observer of human conversation and behavior (whether Anglo or Native American), and even of the frontier itself, which Twain in his pose as a Westerner knows firsthand. Taken out of context, the passages Twain offers as evidence are indeed execrable, but as Sydney Krause has shown, he often alters Cooper's texts to make them appear more inept. For example, in his apparent paraphrase of the scene depicting the ambush of the ark in *Deerslayer*, Twain creates his own fiction, a caricature of the original text. Krause demonstrates that Twain's principal technique in the essay is to juxtapose overstatement (e.g., "Cooper has scored 114 offenses against literary art out of a possible 115") with understatement (e.g., "the difference between a Cooper Indian and the Indian that stands in front of the cigar shop is not spacious").

Twain's most cogent criticism is of Cooper's style—especially his redundancy and prolixity, what Twain calls "surplusage" (e.g., "Mental imbecility"). Also convincing are the examples of indecorous diction, as when Natty Bumppo alternates his speech patterns between "the showiest kind of book-talk . . . and the basest of base dialects." Twain must have realized that he was on stronger ground when attacking style than when ridiculing plot, for

he continued the assault in "Cooper's Prose Style" (a.k.a. "Fenimore Cooper's Further Literary Offenses"), which is redundant from the first essay, though it contains some very funny jibes. Cooper's use of the words "fragments" and "digestible sustenance" to describe hunks of raw venison grates on Twain's "fastidious ear" as he deconstructs a passage from *The Last of the Mohicans* (1826) that is especially fraught with prolix sentences "not suited to the transportation of raw meat."

What Twain deliberately ignores in both essays, however, is that Cooper's tales are greater than the telling. As many readers have realized, what is most compelling about *The Leatherstocking Tales* is the grand design: the myth of Natty Bumppo as the American Adam; we remember symbolic and archetypal scenes, like his death facing west at the end of *The Prairie* (1827), long after we have forgotten Cooper's infelicitous phrases.

Several critics have attempted to test whether Twain practiced in his own literary texts what he preached in "Offenses." Richard Peck and Craig Cotora apply Twain's rules to *Huckleberry Finn* (1885) and *Connecticut Yankee* (1889), respectively, demonstrating that, taken out of context, any text can be shown to violate some of the rules.

Since it contains some persuasive critiques of Cooper's style and provides an effective summation of realist aesthetics, "Offenses" is more than a mere lampoon. Nevertheless, it remains one of the funniest pieces Mark Twain ever wrote.

Joseph Andriano

BIBLIOGRAPHY

Clemens, Samuel L. "Cooper's Prose Style." *Letters from the Earth.* By Clemens. Ed. Bernard DeVoto. New York: Harper & Row, 1962. 117–124.

———. "Fenimore Cooper's Literary Offenses." *Literary Essays.* Vol. 22 of *Mark Twain's Works.* By Clemens. New York: Harper, 1897. 78–96.

Cotora, Craig. "Mark Twain's Literary Offenses; or, The Revenge of Fenimore Cooper." *Mark Twain Journal* 21.3 (Spring 1983): 19–20.

DeVoto, Bernard. Editor's Notes. *Letters from the Earth*. By Clemens. Ed. Bernard DeVoto. New York: Harper & Row, 1962. 289–302.

Hazuka, Tom. "Cooper Was No Architect: Mark Twain as Literary Craftsman." *South Dakota Review* 25.2 (1987): 35–46.

Krause, Sydney J. *Mark Twain as Critic*. Baltimore: Johns Hopkins UP, 1967.

Maulsby, D.L. "Fenimore Cooper and Mark Twain." *Dial* 22 (16 February 1897): 107–109.

Peck, Richard E. "A Mark Twain 'Literary Offence.'" *Mark Twain Journal* 14.3 (1968): 7–9.

See also: Cooper, James Fenimore; Criticism; Realism

Fields, James T.
(1817–1881)

James Fields was an American book publisher, editor, and author. He was a founding partner of the Boston firm that published the foremost British and American authors and poets of the period. He succeeded James Russell Lowell as editor of the *Atlantic Monthly* (1862), upon his retirement from which in 1870 he began writing and lecturing. His most respected literary work is *Yesterdays with Authors* (1872). Clemens included two of Fields's poems in his anthology *Mark Twain's Library of Humor* (1888).

It was in Fields's office at the *Atlantic* in 1869 that Clemens first met William Dean Howells, who was then an assistant to Fields. Clemens relished frequent literary luncheon meetings with his circle of close friends, including Howells, Fields, and Bret Harte.

Fred Weldon

BIBLIOGRAPHY

Gribben, Alan. *Mark Twain's Library: A Reconstruction*. 2 vols. Boston: G.K. Hall, 1980.

Howells, William Dean. *My Mark Twain: Reminiscences and Criticisms*. New York: Harper, 1910.

Long, E. Hudson. *Mark Twain Handbook*. New York: Hendricks House, 1957.

Paine, Albert Bigelow. *Mark Twain: A Biography*. 3 vols. New York: Harper, 1912.

See also: Atlantic Monthly

Finn, Huckleberry

Fashioned in the likeness of Tom Blankenship, the son of one of Hannibal's two town derelicts, and taking his last name from Jimmy Finn, another town drunkard, Huckleberry Finn, the best-known character in Mark Twain's fiction, makes his celebrated reappearance as the fourteen-year-old vernacular narrator of *Adventures of Huckleberry Finn* (1885). In *Life on the Mississippi* (1883) he narrates a chapter drawn from but not republished in the work in progress that would become *Adventures of Huckleberry Finn*. He reappears as the narrator of "Huck Finn and Tom Sawyer Among the Indians" (1969), *Tom Sawyer Abroad* (1894), *Tom Sawyer, Detective* (1896), the fragments "Doughface" (1969), "Tom Sawyer's Gang Plans a Naval Battle" (1969), and "Tom Sawyer's Conspiracy" (1969); he also appears in the unproduced play *Tom Sawyer* (1969). He is briefly mentioned in the "Mysterious Stranger" fragment "Schoolhouse Hill" (1969).

The origin of his unusual and unusually apt first name is mysterious; Twain reports only that "there was something about that name that suited"; it carries with it a freight of associations: simplicity, homeliness, earthiness, directness, virtues that are part of the constitution of this ingratiating adolescent. Embryonic in *The Adventures of Tom Sawyer* (1876), where he makes possible the rescue of the Widow Douglas from injury at the hands of Injun Joe, and where his hard-headed common sense is contrasted with Tom Sawyer's romanticism, his instinctive humanitarian decency becomes a salient part of his character, together with a feeling of loneliness and a longing for the solace of a family, a longing that alternates with his comic rebellion against the constrictions of genteel behavior. In *Adventures of Huckleberry Finn* he assumes the role of narrator with the voice of a boy of the American Southwest. The dialect is not always consistent, and there are several intrusions of sophisticated authorial diction, but his speech is close enough to the rhythms and tone of the vernacular to earn it Ernest

Hemingway's oft quoted praise as the model for subsequent American literature.

The manipulation of Huck's character by the author results in an irony that transforms the comedy into a satiric criticism of the shortcomings of southern society both before and after the Civil War. While he learns to respect Jim's friendship and loyalty, Huck remains to the end a southern boy with unyielding social prejudices. His famous decision to "go to hell" when he decides to transgress his society's code to aid Jim to escape is the supreme example of Twain's use of Huck's character to produce a condemnation of the racial intolerance that can cause the struggle between a "sound heart" and a socially induced "conscience." More than in *The Adventures of Tom Sawyer*, Huck in *Adventures of Huckleberry Finn* is the embodiment of a national faith in the trustworthiness of experience as the test of value, a champion of the empirical pragmatism that is contrasted with the irresponsible, if occasionally engaging, romantic foolishness of Tom Sawyer. The contrast between Huck's pragmatism and Tom's romanticism is sounded early, kept alive in the middle chapters, and becomes the reason for the extended and often criticized farcical ending.

Except for his role in "Tom Sawyer's Conspiracy," where he shows some of the qualities he exhibited in the earlier works, Huck becomes more and more recessive until in "Schoolhouse Hill" he is reduced to a single mention as one of Tom Sawyer's friends. In each of the sequels he is described as having returned to St. Petersburg and to the home of the Widow Douglas, homecomings that place in proper comic perspective his often quoted rejection, in *Adventures of Huckleberry Finn*, of the Widow's attempt to civilize him.

Critical controversy about Huck's character has centered about his role as an outsider. After rejecting the verdict of some nineteenth-century librarians who banned Huck as an anti-social delinquent, several generations of readers accepted him as a moral character in a genial story. Many modern critics have returned in an inverted way to the stance of the nineteenth-century librarians, revering Huck as a saint of the counterculture, a radically "bad" boy who rejects the norms and values of middle-class American society. Others have countered that the characterization of Huck is the means by which Twain attacked the attitudes of the pre- and post-Civil War slaveholding and unreconstructed South, while implicitly upholding the values of republican America.

Everett Carter

BIBLIOGRAPHY

Blair, Walter. *Mark Twain & Huck Finn*. Berkeley: U of California P, 1960.

Carter, Everett. "The Modernist Ordeal of Huckleberry Finn." *Studies in American Fiction* 13.2 (Autumn 1985): 169–183.

Clemens, Samuel L. *Adventures of Huckleberry Finn*. Ed. Walter Blair and Victor Fischer. Berkeley: U of California P, 1985.

Manieere, W.R. "Huck Finn, Empiricist Member of Society." *Modern Fiction Studies* 14 (Spring 1968): 57–66.

Smith, Henry Nash. *Mark Twain: The Development of a Writer*. Cambridge, Mass.: Harvard UP, 1962.

Thompson, Charles M. "Mark Twain as an Interpreter of American Character." *Atlantic Monthly* 79 (April 1897): 443–450.

Wecter, Dixon. *Sam Clemens of Hannibal*. Boston: Houghton Mifflin, 1952.

See also: Adventures of Huckleberry Finn

Finn, Pap

Pap Finn is Huck Finn's frighteningly abusive father. He is based on Hannibal drunkard Jimmy Finn, whom Judge Clemens once attempted unsuccessfully to reform. Pap is first mentioned in *The Adventures of Tom Sawyer* (1876) along with Huck's mother, in reference to their illiteracy and fighting. Huck also predicts in *Tom Sawyer* that since Pap will just appropriate it, there is no point in finding the treasure. Pap dominates chapters 4 through 7 of *Huckleberry Finn*. He is an illiterate fifty-year-old drunkard who holes up in a hut on the Illinois shore. He ends up mysteriously dead, floating past Huck and Jim on Jackson's

Island in a house, although Jim withholds Pap's identity from Huck until much later.

Pap's ethical bearing on Huck invites a diversity of opinion. Pap is interpreted as a naturalistic entity conjoined with other paeans of institutional force. In his canny exploitation of democratic and religious conventions, Pap inadvertently demonstrates the dark underside of selfishness that resides within caretaking institutions more intent on the appearance of benevolence than its reality. Examples of Pap's rhetoric include his "call this a govment" speech (see J.T. Trowbridge's *Cudjo's Cave*, 1864), a drunken protest against voting privileges of a "mulatter" Ohio professor. Pap also sentimentalizes on temperance, reform, and parenthood, playing on the easy sentiments of a new judge and his wife to give him custody of Huck and his money. Huck stages his own "death" to escape his drunken father. For some, Huck's legacy of abuse gives him empathy that enables his emotional transcendance of social convention.

Other scholars instead conclude that Huck is blighted deterministically by Pap. They argue that Huck inherits Pap's relativistic ethics. Huck never transcends the social logic of self-interest, nor can he ever be truly "free." One's view of Pap's influence on Huck is thus a key to ethics in *Huckleberry Finn*.

Janet Gabler-Hover

BIBLIOGRAPHY

Beaver, Harold. "Huck and Pap." *Huck Finn*. Ed. Harold Bloom. New York: Chelsea House, 1990. 174–183.

Clemens, Samuel L. *Adventures of Huckleberry Finn*. Ed. Walter Blair and Victor Fischer. Berkeley: U of California P, 1985.

DeVoto, Bernard. *Mark Twain at Work*. Cambridge, Mass.: Harvard UP, 1942.

Gabler-Hover, Janet A. *Truth in American Fiction: The Legacy of Rhetorical Idealism*. Athens: U of Georgia P, 1990.

Kastely, James. "The Ethics of Self-Interest: Narrative Logic in *Huckleberry Finn*." *Nineteenth-Century Literature* 40 (March 1986): 412–437.

Sloane, David E.E. *Adventures of Huckleberry Finn: American Comic Vision*. Boston: G.K. Hall, 1988.

See also: Adventures of Huckleberry Finn; Finn, Huckleberry

Fischer, Theodor

Theodor, sixteen-year-old son of the Eseldorf church organist, is the protagonist of "The Chronicle of Young Satan" (written in three periods between 1897 and 1900) and the cobbled and bowdlerized *The Mysterious Stranger: A Romance*, published in 1916 by Mark Twain's literary executor, Albert Bigelow Paine, and Frederick A. Duneka of Harper and Brothers.

Theodor is the reflective narrator of the "Eseldorf" version of Mark Twain's mysterious stranger fragments who learns from young Satan, the nephew of the famous fallen angel, mysteries about life that he would have otherwise never imagined. Although the narrator is a grandfather (*MSM* 148), he narrates from the perspective of an ironic sixteen-year-old storyteller with wise eyes but an innocent tongue, as his description of the fiendish Father Adolf demonstrates: "he was dissolute and profane and malicious, but otherwise a good enough man" (*MSM* 37).

From his experiences with young Satan, Theodor learns that the human Moral Sense not only distinguishes between right and wrong but also allows humankind to commit evil acts, unlike the "higher animals" such as dogs and cats. Like August Feldner in "No. 44, The Mysterious Stranger," Theodor learns the "gospel" of Mark Twain's deterministic *What Is Man?* (1906), the atrocities of human history, and the value of humor to blow a "colossal humbug . . . to rags and atoms at a blast."

Like Huck Finn, Sieur Louis de Conte, Hank Morgan, and others, Theodor Fischer narrates his own journey to awareness, but unlike these other narrators Theodor has a clearer sense of the mysteries of the universe and the limitations of human intellect to understand those mysteries because of his association with the supernatural young Satan.

However, scholars disagree about the value of what Theodor learns; some assert that he is burdened with the nihilistic, solipsistic dark world of a disgruntled ex-moralist (Bellamy 372, Brodwin 189, Cox 286, Smith 188), while others believe that he is liberated from the misconceptions of the popular culture and empowered with a vision that will enable him to enhance humanity through his creativity (Harris 42, Kahn 191, Varisco 749).

Robert E. Lowrey

BIBLIOGRAPHY

Bellamy, Gladys. *Mark Twain as a Literary Artist.* Norman: U of Oklahoma P, 1950.

Brodwin, Stanley. "The Theology of Mark Twain: Banished Adam and the Bible." *Mississippi Quarterly* 29 (1976): 167–189.

Clemens, Samuel L. *Mark Twain's Mysterious Stranger Manuscripts.* Ed. William M. Gibson. Berkeley: U of California P, 1969.

Cox, James M. *Mark Twain: The Fate of Humor.* Princeton, N.J.: Princeton UP, 1966.

Gibson, William M. *The Art of Mark Twain.* New York: Oxford UP, 1976.

Harris, Susan K. *Mark Twain's Escape from Time: A Study of Patterns and Images.* Columbia: U of Missouri P, 1982.

Kahn, Sholom J. *Mark Twain's Mysterious Stranger: A Study of the Manuscript Texts.* Columbia: U of Missouri P, 1978.

Smith, Henry Nash. *Mark Twain: The Development of a Writer.* Cambridge, Mass.: Harvard UP, 1962.

Tuckey, John S. *Mark Twain and Little Satan: The Writing of "The Mysterious Stranger."* West Lafayette, Ind.: Purdue UP, 1963.

Varisco, Raymond. "Divine Foolishness: A Critical Evaluation of Mark Twain's *The Mysterious Stranger.*" *Revista/Review Interamericana* 5 (1975): 741–749.

See also: Eseldorf; *Mysterious Stranger, The*; Traum, Philip

Fiske, Minnie Maddern (Marie Augusta Davey)
(1865–1932)

Born in New Orleans, Minnie Maddern Fiske was a distinguished American actress who began her career at the age of three. Fiske's fa-

ther, Thomas W. Davey, a theatrical manager, put Minnie on the stage under her mother's maiden name, "Little Minnie Maddern." At five, Fiske debuted in New York in *A Sheep in Wolf's Clothing* and appeared later that year as Eva in *Uncle Tom's Cabin.* In 1882 she debuted as an adult actress; in 1892 she married Harrison Grey Fiske, a playwright and theatrical manager. She starred in her husband's 1893 *Hester Crewe*, a modest success. *Tess of the D'Urbervilles* (1897) was her first hit. She began to specialize in Ibsen and Shakespeare plays, including *Hedda Gabler* (1903) and *Rosmersholm* (1907), becoming noted for her roles as Ibsen's heroines.

Before Fiske's marriage, Mark Twain briefly considered managing her. Much later, a letter from Fiske to Twain inspired Twain to write "A Horse's Tale" (1906), an anti-bullfight story. On 18 September 1905 Twain received a letter from Fiske asking for such a story, perhaps inspired by Jean Clemens's letter in *Harper's Weekly* of 1 April, "A Word for the Horses" about the evils of checkreins and martingales.

Wesley Britton

BIBLIOGRAPHY

Binns, Archie. *Mrs. Fiske and the American Theatre.* New York: Crown, 1955.

See also: Clemens, Jane Lampton (Jean); "Horse's Tale, A"

FitzGerald, Edward
(1809–1883)

Edward FitzGerald was the English scholar and translator known for his translation of *The Rubáiyát of Omar Khayyám*, the twelfth-century Persian poem celebrating a deterministic philosophy of *carpe diem.* FitzGerald's *Rubáiyát* first appeared in 1859, becoming enormously popular and going through five editions.

Twain was aware of FitzGerald's translation as early as 1876. By 1879 the poem was Twain's favorite, and he would continue to be charmed by the poem for the remainder of his life. Twain's billiard-playing cronies, the "Friday Evening Club," were often regaled by Twain's recitations from the *Rubáiyát*, much of which he had committed to memory. Twain, in fact, completed twenty stanzas of verse imitative of the *Rubáiyát*, entitled "To the Above Old People."

Clearly, the poem provided a significant influence for Twain's developing determinism. The *Rubáiyát* presents man as a puny being, devoid of a will, trapped in a world of forbidden pleasures to which he cannot help but succumb, yet for which he will be called to account by an insensitive and absurd creator. Therefore, he should indulge in those pleasures without guilt, for soon he will return to dust. Such cynical determinism, disparagement of a beneficent deity, and condemnation of the defects of humanity, especially of the "Moral Sense," are decidedly evident in much of Twain's later work, such as "The Lowest Animal" (1962), *The Mysterious Stranger* (1916), and *What Is Man?* (1906).

Tim Poland

BIBLIOGRAPHY

Baetzhold, Howard G. *Mark Twain and John Bull: The British Connection.* Bloomington: Indiana UP, 1970.

Clemens, Samuel L. *Mark Twain-Howells Letters: The Correspondence of Samuel L. Clemens and William D. Howells, 1872–1910.* Vol. 1. Ed. Henry Nash Smith and William M. Gibson. Cambridge, Mass.: Harvard UP, 1960.

FitzGerald, Edward, trans. *The Rubáiyát of Omar Khayyám.* New York: Crowell, 1921.

Mac Donnell, Kevin, and Alan Gribben, eds. *Mark Twain's Rubáiyát.* Austin, Texas: Jenkins, 1983.

Paine, Albert Bigelow. *Mark Twain: A Biography.* Vol. 2. New York: Harper, 1912.

Terhune, Alfred McKinley. *The Life of Edward FitzGerald.* London: Oxford UP, 1947.

See also: "AGE—A Rubáiyát"; Determinism

"Five Boons of Life, The"
(1902)

Clemens's life entered a dark phase after the death of daughter Susy in 1896, and much of his subsequent writing is introspective, pessimistic, and fragmentary. "The Five Boons" was written in spring 1902, while Clemens lived at Riverdale, on the border of New York City. Unlike most of the writing of this period, it was completed, and published in *Harper's Magazine* in December 1902. Harper and Brothers collected it in *The Mysterious Stranger and Other Stories* (1922).

The five boons are gifts offered by a fairy to a youth. The youth chooses, in succession, Pleasure, Love, Fame, and Power. Each turns to ashes in his experience. Finally—no longer a youth—he asks for Death, but he is told it has been given to a trusting child. Nothing remains but "the wanton insult of Old Age."

"Five Boons" is linked thematically to "The Victims" and other manuscripts of the period collected by John S. Tuckey in *Mark Twain's Fables of Man* (1972). The story has been praised by some readers, especially William Gibson and Everett Emerson, for its simple elegance and classic wisdom. Hamlin Hill, however, finds it only another example of Clemens's waste of his talent in response to the emotionally unstable, sickly atmosphere of his family life in this period.

Charles L. Crow

BIBLIOGRAPHY

Budd, Louis J. *Our Mark Twain: The Making of His Public Personality.* Philadelphia: U of Pennsylvania P, 1984.

Clemens, Samuel L. *Mark Twain's Fables of Man.* Ed. John S. Tuckey. Berkeley: U of California P, 1972.

Emerson, Everett. *The Authentic Mark Twain: A Literary Biography of Samuel L. Clemens.* Philadelphia: U of Pennsylvania P, 1984.

Gibson, William M. *The Art of Mark Twain.* New York: Oxford UP, 1976.

Hill, Hamlin. *Mark Twain: God's Fool.* New York: Harper & Row, 1973.

Wilson, James D. *A Reader's Guide to the Short Stories of Mark Twain.* Boston: G.K. Hall, 1987.

See also: Death; "Victims, The"

Florida, Missouri

Surveyed and platted in the spring of 1831, Florida, Missouri, was built on high ground between the north and south forks of the Salt River in Monroe County. The John Marshall Clemens family moved to Florida in May or June 1835. Jane, pregnant at the time and miserable in St. Louis, wanted to be near her sister, Patsy Lampton Quarles, who lived with her husband John on a farm on the outskirts of Florida. The Clemens family initially lived in a small rented cottage, though in September John Marshall purchased two and three-fourths acres of ground just outside the town's northern boundary and began to build a house. Their son, Samuel Langhorne Clemens, was born in Florida on 30 November 1835.

After the state of Missouri declared the Salt River navigable, John Marshall Clemens helped to form the Salt River Navigation Company in 1837. Its primary purpose was to sell bonds to finance construction of a series of dams to control water levels and open the seventy-mile river to commerce on the Mississippi. The bond sale, however, failed; Florida, never very large, remained a small farming community. John Marshall Clemens moved his family to Hannibal in 1839.

Today the main attraction for visitors is the Mark Twain State Park, adjacent to town. Established in 1924, it was the first state park in north Missouri and the first to be purchased by public subscription. In the park is the Mark Twain Birthplace Memorial Shrine, which contains the cottage in which Samuel Clemens was born, furnished with period pieces. Also part of the shrine are a library, a theater, and a museum area that features furniture from the Hartford, Connecticut, home, the manuscript of *The Adventures of Tom Sawyer* (1876), and numerous family portraits. Other area attractions include the Mark Twain National Forest, with 1.5 million acres of abundant wildlife, and the Mark Twain Lake. Formed by Cannon Dam, this 18,600 acre reservoir furnishes hydroelectric power to the region and offers numerous recreational opportunities.

There is a 1,700-acre waterfowl refuge area. Surrounding lands are open to hunting and trapping, and there are hiking trails and public beaches.

Oliver Howard and Goldena Howard

BIBLIOGRAPHY

Gregory, Ralph. *Mark Twain's First America: Florida, Missouri, 1835–1840*. Florida, Mo.: Friends of Florida, 1965.

Howard, Oliver, and Goldena Howard. *The Mark Twain Book*. New London, Mo.: Ralls County Book, 1985.

See also: Clemens, John Marshall; Quarles Farm

Folklore

Folklore includes those aspects of culture that are spread through informal means and circulate traditionally among members of a group in different versions. It also includes the processes of traditional performance and communication. Folklore therefore subsumes, but is not limited to, (1) oral forms, such as myths, legends, folktales, jokes, proverbs, riddles, curses, oaths, taunts, or tongue twisters; (2) material forms, such as folk arts, folk crafts, folk architecture, folk costume, transportation forms, foodways, and space and property organization; (3) social folk customs, including rites of passage, festivals and celebrations, recreational forms, games, folk medicine, folk religion; and (4) performing folk arts, such as traditional music, dance, and drama. Mark Twain had a profound interest in the informal and traditional aspects of American culture, and his representations of them helped demonstrate the unique aspects of the American from other cultures around the world.

Certainly, the most attention has been given to the American folklore recorded in Twain's corpus. Steven Swann Jones's bibliography cites thirty-seven different authors who have written specifically about the folklore in the works. At times the number and range of folklore items depicted seems overwhelming. In

Tom Sawyer (1876), for example, the first appearance of Huck Finn brings about a discussion of wart cures utilizing dead cats, stump water, and verbal charms (chapter 6). When Tom decides to run away (chapter 8), he turns to pack his most valued possessions—including his marbles. But his belief that burying one marble would cause all his misplaced marbles to gather is frustrated when the others fail to appear. Tom ponders the belief "and finally decided that some witch had interfered and broken the charm." He proceeds to prove this with a test utilizing a doodle-bug. While *Tom Sawyer* contains a sampling of American folklore, the later *Huckleberry Finn* (1885) makes Huck's acquisition and appreciation of folklore its point. That book begins in and with Huck's voice, only one example of the folk speech found in the novel. Huck explicates (chapter 1) the widow's table manners and foodways: "The widow rung a bell for supper, and you had to come on time. When you got to the table you couldn't go right to eating, but you had to wait for the widow to tuck down her head and grumble a little over the victuals, though there warn't really anything the matter with them. That is, nothing only everything was cooked by itself." Chapter 1 also reveals several of the folk beliefs that Huck already knew: "The stars was shining, and the leaves rustled in the woods ever so mournful; and I heard an owl, away off, who-whooing about somebody that was dead, and a whipporwill and a dog crying about somebody that was going to die. . . ." Most significant for the plot is Huck's flipping of the spider into the candle flame, which, in his own words, "was an awful bad sign and would fetch me some bad luck. . . ." Even though he tries several different ways to ward off this bad luck, it is with this that the book's adventures begin. Any number of other examples from the novel can be cited, for the work is truly an account of Huck's education, albeit from Jim and others.

Huckleberry Finn certainly describes many of the informal aspects of American culture, for Huck does his best to avoid formal institutions like church or school. Chapter 11 provides an excellent example of the importance of folklore within the story. Here Huck dons an old gown and bonnet in order to pose as a girl, hoping to mask inquiries about his own disappearance. He is surreptitiously tested several times (threading a needle, throwing objects at rats, and catching objects in his dress) by his hostess and caught. She scolds him, "You do a girl tolerable poor, but you might fool men, maybe." Indeed, Huck has much to learn, but most particularly a blend of Afro-American and Anglo-American folklore. His adventures expose him to folklore as diverse as customs to raise bodies from the river (chapter 8) to traditional folk art ("Shall I Never See Thee More Alas," chapter 17).

Although most of the critical attention has gone to these two novels, there are many other areas still to be studied. For example, Twain's humor sometimes dealt with national stereotypes. Perhaps the best-known example is found in *The Innocents Abroad* (1869) with its description of French guides (chapter 13), its comments on the English-language abilities of Frenchmen (chapter 15), and the description of Italian guides (chapter 27). Twain's comments about other nations (and, by implication, the United States) go far beyond this work to include, for example, his speech "The Horrors of the German Language" and his retranslations from the French of "The Celebrated Jumping Frog of Calaveras County" as "The Frog Jumping of the County of Calaveras." All of these works demonstrate Twain's fine appreciation of regional and national characteristics and their potential for humor.

Less attention has been paid to Twain's personal ties to folklore. For instance, Mark Twain was a charter member of the American Folklore Society when it was created in 1888. Certainly, Twain was not the only writer whose interest in folklore led him to join folklore societies; Joel Chandler Harris and Edward Eggleston also were charter members of the American Folklore Society, and George Washington Cable was an officer of the rival

Chicago Folklore Society. Arguably, these writers, through works such as Twain's *Tom Sawyer* and *Huckleberry Finn* and Harris's *Uncle Remus, His Songs and Sayings* (1880) and *Nights with Uncle Remus* (1883), generated much of the interest in American folklore that led to the creation of the organizations. None of these authors, however, remained in these scholarly societies for more than a few years. Twain also wrote two essays that recount his experiences with mental telegraphy; he also encouraged research by others, especially the famous (English) Society for Psychical Research, into the accounts of all psychic phenomena. While Twain was no folklorist, he did set down a number of particularly valuable works as records of American traditional culture. "How to Tell a Story" (1895), for example, provides an ethnographic account of the performance aspects of a horror legend. Thus, Twain provides a valuable sociocultural record about the performances of "The Golden Arm." "Buck Fanshaw's Funeral" (*Roughing It*, 1872) provides an excellent example of several varieties of American folk speech and the problems any community may face in a relatively simple verbal encounter. Several other stories, including especially "The Celebrated Jumping Frog of Calaveras County" (1865) and "The Story of the Old Ram" (*Roughing It*), have been mentioned as particularly valuable in the study of American humor. Although Twain is rarely considered an ethnographer, his own ties to folklore societies and his writings demonstrate his interest in American culture and folklore, especially narrative forms and humor.

Perhaps the least attention has gone to the folklore about Mark Twain. He was a public figure as author, commentator, and critic, writing about his own experiences in many of his books (e.g., *The Innocents Abroad, Roughing It, A Tramp Abroad* [1880], and *Life on the Mississippi* [1883]) and his speeches, and because of this Twain contributed to his own public persona in no small way. Historians have certainly tried to compare verifiable records against Twain's own accounts (such as

his "The Private History of a Campaign That Failed" [1885]). Such a comparison points out that Twain, like most storytellers, is not so much concerned with historical detail as he is a good narrative. A further measure of Twain's significance in American culture, especially in regard to the folklore about him, is the rich collection of anecdotes concerning Twain in Zall's *Mark Twain Laughing* and in other sources. That work gathers together some of the many traditional stories surrounding Twain and his commentary on contemporary life and culture. Much more could be done with Twain and his role in and impact upon American culture, work similar to that of Mary Ellen Brown on Robert Burns.

Mark Twain's work is significantly richer and more valuable for his attention to folklore. He had the ability to represent American (folk) speech in print, and through this he preserved many other aspects of traditional American culture. Indeed, Twain's success and significance must be partly attributable to his ability to record (and comment upon) American folklore in an appealing and meaningful way.

Eric L. Montenyohl

BIBLIOGRAPHY

Brown, Mary Ellen. *Burns and Tradition*. Urbana: U of Illinois P, 1984.

Dundes, Alan. *Cracking Jokes: Studies of Sick Humor Cycles and Stereotypes*. Berkeley: Ten Speed P, 1987.

Jones, Steven Swann. *Folklore and Literature in the United States: An Annotated Bibliography of Studies of Folklore in American Literature*. New York: Garland, 1984.

Stahl, Sandra K.D. "Studying Folklore and American Literature." *Handbook of American Folklore*. Ed. Richard M. Dorson, et al. Bloomington: Indiana UP, 1983. 422–433.

Zall, Paul M. *Mark Twain Laughing: Humorous Anecdotes by and About Samuel Clemens*. Knoxville: U of Tennessee P, 1985.

See also: "Golden Arm, The"; Harris, Joel Chandler; "How to Tell a Story"; Vernacular

Following the Equator: A Journey Around the World
(1897)

Mark Twain's last, long, literary travel book *Following the Equator* was no doubt intended to suggest a twilight reprise on the old fun of *The Innocents Abroad* (1869) or *Roughing It* (1872). (To capitalize explicitly on a third, earlier "travel" connection, in fact, the English edition was entitled *More Tramps Abroad*.) But the recovery of anything like the early mood is not to be. Instead, we get a last major exercise in the mainly pictorial, anecdotish, often plagiaristic page filling typical of long stretches of *Life on the Mississippi* (1883) or *A Tramp Abroad* (1880). One wished desperately at the very least for *Following the Equator* to have its "moments," as do even the most profusely padded out of the travel narratives. The medium, after all, summoned up Mark Twain in some of his most brilliantly productive moments of narrative invention, including, as various commentators have noted, much of *Huckleberry Finn* (1885). Here, however, we generally get the other side of the travel *and* the account page—Mark Twain, promoter of his disastrously fluctuating fortunes, in one of his commercially most cynical modes of narrative indulgence.

It seems halfhearted and tired, because he was halfhearted and tired. The book, as is well known, was conceived of mainly as a money-maker which grew out of another money-maker, namely, a post-bankruptcy lecture tour in the wake of the twin disasters of the Paige typesetter and the Charles L. Webster publishing company. The 1895–1896 tour (Hawaii, a dear old place of memory, had to be bypassed because of cholera) included Fiji, Australia, New Zealand, Ceylon, India, Mauritius, and South Africa. By the time the 1897 book had been seen through publication, fatigue, old age, ill health, and debt had further been compounded by the crucial disaster of Susy Clemens's death.

Thus, it was really with great truth that Twain wrote to Howells of the text, "I wrote my last travel-book in hell; but I let on, the best I could, that it was an excursion through heaven. Some day I will read it, and if its lying cheerfulness fools me, then I shall believe it fooled the reader. How I did loathe that journey around the world!—except for the sea part and India." In spite of this, the book is, if anything, remarkable in that it transcends all its inclinations to be *merely* cheerful and inoffensive. To be sure, as predicted in the quote, one seems almost appalled at how truly boring Twain manages to make all of Australasia, even down to customary animal stories, of which those regions of the wombat and the platypus should have furnished an original mother lode. The meager ones he gets off tweak Cecil Rhodes, along with Julia A. Moore, "Sweet Singer of Michigan," and P.T. Barnum, all of whom emerge in some bizarre contest of multiple appearances as recurrent subjects of derision in the text. In the first story, Rhodes, opening up the bellies of Australian sharks he has been catching for bounty, is alleged to have come upon information leading to his first fortune in a swallowed communication from London that enables him to corner the world sheep's wool market. In the second, a spuriously footnoted piece of "Marsupial" lore identifies the two principals of that specimen in the Southern Hemisphere, noted for their bulging pouches, as "Mr. Rhodes and the kangaroo," and the "latest," with the largest of empty pockets, as Twain himself, the bankrupt traveling lecturer.

Once Twain achieves India, however, the better hope additionally contained in his assessment emerges in the work's sudden intake of color, interest, and energy. At the very least, it is uncommonly good travel writing, full of the commingled wonder and mystery that has fascinated Western sojourners in that land then and now. Also, increasingly, as the circuit of Twain's wanderings carries him through the sorrowful history of aboriginal race subjected to the latest Anglo-European inventions in genocide and plunder, and despite a somewhat bizarre defense of the benefits of law and social stability promised by the progress of empire, it also builds to an incandescence of anti-colonialist diatribe anticipating such classics as "To the Person Sitting in Darkness" (1901). And in the dimension of humor, it also has classic moments of inspired cross-cultural lunacy: there are long stretches of horseplay involving an Indian manservant peremptorily named Satan that recall the hapless, put-upon Fergusons of *The Innocents Abroad*; in the midst of a Far Eastern railroad encounter with a ludicrous dog of indeterminate breed, we blunder along into a quite literal shaggy-dog reminiscence somehow involving a St. Bernard and a Scotty Briggs-like Irish factotum duped into allowing Twain entrance to the chambers of a reclusive New York impresario; and in a glorious interlude detailing a mountain train ride down from the Himalayas, the author persuades us that we may well have shared descriptively and anecdotally in "the most enjoyable day," he avers, "I have spent on earth."

Once India is passed, however, the rest of the exotic world seems for the most part a barely diverting travail, and South Africa (especially in sections we know to have been last-minute padding to a publisher's specifications) becomes an occasion for invective on the Boer conflicts, the Jameson Raid, and again, of course, Cecil Rhodes, the exemplar of empire, described conclusively as "the marvel of the time, the mystery of the age, an Archangel with wings to half the world, Satan with a tail to the other half."

Perhaps the one explicit feature of distinction *Following the Equator* can claim as a travel book is that it increasingly hankers (like other texts of the later years such as "The Man That Corrupted Hadleyburg" [1899] and the host of dark fragments) toward the pointing of ashen, empty apothegms. A geopolitical one, for instance, contained both within the text and among the host of acerbic, mainly dark epigraphs, ascribed to *Pudd'nhead Wilson's New Calendar*, that have foregrounded all of the book's chapters, is "Get your formalities right—never mind about the moralities." Perhaps the most personally telling of such Wilsonish pearls, however, is the one that occurs rather late in the text at the head of chapter 20. This one reads, "There are two times in a man's life when he should not speculate: when he can't afford it, and when he can." To such wisdom of experience, the author might now have added that of the travel lecturer and the travel writer; and the emergent moral, out of this, the last of Twain's long completed works, would probably read as follows: "Speculate not at all if it means that one may have to circle the girdle of the globe and then write another Mark Twain travel book about it when one is old and tired." That the book resulting here, at the very least, completes the world circuit of culture begun so many years earlier in *The Innocents Abroad* and *Roughing It* is a miracle of resilience and humor set out against the greater darkness of the last years.

Philip D. Beidler

BIBLIOGRAPHY

Bridgman, Richard. *Traveling in Mark Twain*. Berkeley: U of California P, 1987.

Clemens, Samuel L. *Following the Equator*. Hartford, Conn.: American Publishing, 1897.

———. *Mark Twain-Howells Letters: The Correspondence of Samuel L. Clemens and William D. Howells, 1872–1910*. Ed. Henry Nash Smith and William M. Gibson. 2 vols. Cambridge, Mass.: Harvard, UP, 1960.

Kaplan, Justin. *Mr. Clemens and Mark Twain*. New York: Simon & Schuster, 1966.

Macnaughton, William R. *Mark Twain's Last Years as a Writer*. Columbia: U of Missouri P, 1979.

Shillingsburg, Miriam Jones. *At Home Abroad: Mark Twain in Australasia*. Jackson: UP of Mississippi, 1988.

See also: Australia; Imperialism; India; *Tramp Abroad, A*; Travel Writings

Forgeries

Forgers have been the bane of scholars and collectors since ancient times. The typical forger is a person driven by a combination of greed and a carefully concealed and deep-rooted contempt for society. The production and sale of forgeries satisfies such a personality, and the favorite targets of such forgers are famous historical and literary figures. Within fifteen years of his death, Mark Twain became the target of such forgers.

No forgeries can be dated from Twain's lifetime, but one of the first to forge his autograph was the son of Eugene Field, Eugene Field II. In the 1920s Field forged a number of Twain autographs, mostly inscriptions in books supposedly given by Twain to his father (whose autograph he also forged). One of these forged inscriptions in a copy of *Tom Sawyer Abroad* (1894) was sold as a "probable forgery" by Christie's in the Estelle Doheny Collection in 1988 for $308 to a New York antiquarian bookseller, who immediately offered it for sale as genuine in his next catalogue for $5,000. Beginning about 1930, spurious Twain signatures and documents were produced by Joseph Cosey, a forger now more famous for his skillful forgeries of Edgar A. Poe and Abraham Lincoln. Alan Gribben in *Mark Twain's Library: A Reconstruction* (1980) cites several forged Twain inscriptions in books supposedly from his library. The most recent forger of Twain material to be uncovered is Mark Hoffman, the Utah murderer, infamous for his forgeries of Mormon documents, whose forgery sales alone totaled $3 million, mostly to members of the Mormon Church. Ironically, Twain himself was a skillful forger, although with an intent entirely different from those already discussed. *Roughing It* (1872) contains two examples: Twain's illustration of an Indian's signature on a government pay voucher and a facsimile of a letter from Horace Greeley accompanied by Twain's nonsensical transcription of the text. Such humorous and benign forgeries were a feature of several of Twain's own works.

Kevin Mac Donnell

BIBLIOGRAPHY

Christie, Manson, and Woods International, Inc. *The Estelle Doheny Collection.* Part IV. 7 vols. New York: Christie, Manson, and Woods, 1987–1989.

Clemens, Samuel L. *Roughing It.* Hartford, Conn.: American Publishing, 1872.

Gribben, Alan. *Mark Twain's Library: A Reconstruction.* 2 vols. Boston: G.K. Hall, 1980.

Hamilton, Charles. *Great Forgers and Famous Fakes.* New York: Crown, 1980.

Sillitoe, Linda, and Allen Roberts. *Salamander, The Story of the Mormon Forgery Murders.* Salt Lake City: Signature Books, 1988.

See also: Manuscript Collections; Rare Books

Forty-Four

Forty-Four is the name of the mysterious stranger in both the "Schoolhouse Hill" (written 1898) and "The Print Shop" (written 1902–1908) fragments, published for the first time in *The Mysterious Stranger Manuscripts* (1969). The character of the mysterious stranger, however, is quite different in each of the fragments. In "Schoolhouse Hill," set in Hannibal/St. Petersburg, told by an omniscient narrator, and featuring both Tom Sawyer and Huck Finn, Mark Twain intended Forty-Four to be "a good little devil" who astounds the town with feats of memory, various languages, and showy miracles. In "No. 44, The Mysterious Stranger," or "Print Shop" version, set in Austria and told by the reflective narrator August Feldner, Forty-Four retains his miraculous characteristics, the Socratic manner, and ideas from Mark Twain's *What Is Man?* (1906), but in this fragment Forty-Four is never associated with Satan, except in his occupation as a "printer's devil."

The mysterious stranger, in all three fragments, is a complex, supernatural character who is a trickster, in the same sense that Prometheus and Satan are tricksters in their specific mythologies: one of their functions is to challenge and test the limits of order, meaning, and value—God. In Mark Twain's fragments young Satan and Forty-Four test the providential God of seventeenth-century Austria and nineteenth-century America as He is perceived by fallen men. In all three fragments the mysterious strangers function as demons, or personal spirits, to precocious, good-hearted teenagers, similar to Huck Finn, who are on the brink of discovering the paradoxes of the adult world.

Forty-Four in the "Print Shop" fragment is the only stranger who is truly "mysterious" since all of the others are identified in the stories as a nephew of the Deceiver, Satan (Kahn 8). What he reveals to August Feldner, which the other strangers do not, is Mark Twain's understanding of the complexity of human personality and its various limits. Through Forty-Four, August comprehends the differences between his Workaday-Self (fleshy, dull, unimaginative, mechanical), his Dream-Self (exciting, romantic, imaginative), and his Soul-Self (immortal, unfettered, creative).

These revelations allow Mark Twain's youthful reflective narrator to transcend the mechanistic philosophy of *What Is Man?* toward a more optimistic maturity. By the end of "No. 44, The Mysterious Stranger" Mark Twain had developed a character who could understand the paradoxes of his culture and, along with the narrator of "Letters from the Earth" (1962), recognize that the providential God perceived by the Workaday-Self was grotesque and that human capacity for evil was somehow related to that myopic perception. Since "No. 44, The Mysterious Stranger" was never completed, general conclusions are problematic; nevertheless, Mark Twain seems to be closer to reconciling the nature of man with the American myth in this narrative than in *Huckleberry Finn* (1885), *A Connecticut Yankee* (1889), and other novels.

Robert E. Lowrey

BIBLIOGRAPHY

Brodwin, Stanley. "Mark Twain's Masks of Satan: The Final Phase." *American Literature* 45 (1973): 206–227.

Clemens, Samuel L. *Mark Twain's Mysterious Stranger Manuscripts*. Ed. William M. Gibson. Berkeley: U of California P, 1969.

Delaney, Paul. "The Dissolving Self: The Narrators of Mark Twain's *Mysterious Stranger* Fragments." *Journal of Narrative Technique* 6.1 (1976): 50–65.

Gibson, William M. *The Art of Mark Twain*. New York: Oxford UP, 1976.

Kahn, Sholom J. *Mark Twain's Mysterious Stranger: A Study of the Manuscript Texts*. Columbia: U of Missouri P, 1978.

Lowrey, Robert E. "Imagination and Redemption: 44 in the Third Version of *The Mysterious Stranger*." *Southern Review* 18.1 (1982): 100–110.

May, John R. "The Gospel According to Philip Traum: Structural Unity in *The Mysterious Stranger*." *Studies in Short Fiction* 8 (1971): 411–422.

Scrivner, Buford, Jr. "*The Mysterious Stranger*: Mark Twain's New Myth of the Fall." *Mark Twain Journal* 17.4 (1975): 20–21.

Tuckey, John S. *Mark Twain and Little Satan: The Writing of "The Mysterious Stranger."* West Lafayette, Ind.: Purdue UP, 1963.

See also: Fischer, Theodor; *Mysterious Stranger, The*; Traum, Philip

Forum

Founded in 1886 and continuing under several titles until January 1950, *Forum* magazine published two of Mark Twain's essays, "About Play-Acting" (October 1898) and "Diplomatic Play and Clothes" (March 1899). Earlier, its then editor, Lorettus S. Metcalf, invited Twain in April 1888 to write a rebuttal to Matthew Arnold's "Civilization in the United States," which had appeared in that month's issue of the *Nineteenth Century* magazine. Though Mark Twain never fulfilled the request, possibly because Arnold's death that same month would have made an attack inappropriate, several drafts of anti-Arnold (and anti-British) pieces remain in the Mark Twain Papers.

Howard G. Baetzhold

BIBLIOGRAPHY

Baetzhold, Howard G. *Mark Twain and John Bull: The British Connection*. Bloomington: Indiana UP, 1970.

Mott, Frank Luther. *A History of American Magazines, 1885–1905*. Vol. 4. Cambridge, Mass.: Harvard UP, 1957.

See also: Arnold, Matthew; England; Europe

Foster, Saladin and Electra

The main characters of "The $30,000 Bequest" (1904), Saladin and Electra Foster are a young couple whose contented, unpretentious lives are destroyed by fantasies of riches. He is a well-paid bookkeeper, she a loving wife and mother, conventionally pious Christian, and thrifty businesswoman whose modest property investments underpin their security. Both have inherited a penchant for dreaming.

Drawn into fantasy lives by a forthcoming bequest, they define virtually all relationships and roles in economic terms. Aptly called Aleck, the prudential wife becomes their investment-portfolio manager and reveals her cash-nexus religiosity in her conspicuous charities and business transactions with God. The weaker partner, Sally, as he is called, squanders a fortune and leads a secret life of idleness and debauchery. They turn marriage brokers for their daughters. Moral bankrupts whose day-to-day lives are ruined, the Fosters discover the bequest hoax and lose first their sanity and then their lives.

Scholars speculate about the autobiographical overtones of Twain's characterization, agreeing generally that the Fosters are modeled upon the Clemenses and that Saladin dramatizes Samuel Clemens's own money fantasies and business naivete. The Fosters certainly are vehicles for a theme found in many of Twain's later works, i.e., selfish man's liability to temptation in a money-centered civilization.

Earl F. Briden

BIBLIOGRAPHY

Emerson, Everett. *The Authentic Mark Twain: A Literary Biography of Samuel L. Clemens.* Philadelphia: U of Pennsylvania P, 1984.

Geismar, Maxwell. *Mark Twain: An American Prophet.* Boston: Houghton Mifflin, 1970.

Hill, Hamlin. *Mark Twain: God's Fool.* New York: Harper & Row, 1973.

Wilson, James D. *A Reader's Guide to the Short Stories of Mark Twain.* Boston: G.K. Hall, 1987.

See also: "$30,000 Bequest, The"

France

Mark Twain set foot in France for the first time in 1867 while on his *Quaker City* voyage. As evidenced in *The Innocents Abroad* (1869), he was overwhelmed by the sights; he extolled the virtues of the French rail system and was impressed by French precision, neatness, and the beauty of the land, culture, and people. He subsequently made numerous trips to France with extended stays in Paris, La Bourboule-les-Bains, and Étretat. While resting at Aix, he raved about the health rewards of the baths in his "Aix, the Paradise of the Rheumatics" (1891). Fond memories of his ten-day trip on the Rhône River are recorded in "Down the Rhône" (1891).

Political disillusionment in general and the Franco-Prussian War in specific, as well as unfortunate personal experiences, seem to have caused Twain to reassess his initially positive feelings toward France. In his writings he often used France and the French people as subject matter for his humor; his treatment ranged from gentle humor to biting satire and sarcasm. Twain came to admit to having only one prejudice—his dislike of the French. His growing contempt for France—almost a Francophobia—first was confined to his private notebooks and unpublished manuscripts wherein he labeled the country as the "artificial nation" and the people and their language as "sophomoric and theatrical." France, according to Twain, was a nation governed by prostitutes. He abhorred the French attitudes toward sex; he considered France's "filthy-minded" citizens the "disparaged and depreciated link between man and the simian" ("The French and the Comanches" 151). Later in life he openly attacked French "barbarism," morals, and courtship customs. Until about 1900 Twain used France and the French as the scapegoats for much of his pessimism toward mankind in general; thereafter, he no longer seemed to single out the French to bear the sins and shortcomings of all of mankind. Yet, it is ironic that the human being Twain admired most in history was Joan of

Arc, who was not only French but also the national heroine of France. *Personal Recollections of Joan of Arc* (1896) was his tribute to her. Additionally, Twain's political beliefs were affected deeply by the democratic ideals (not the excesses) of the French Revolution.

During his lifetime Twain was never popular in France. French readers of his day did not appreciate his humor because of the specific Americanisms contained therein and the roughness and blatancy of his humor; any artistic success he achieved in France during his lifetime was due to his penetrating observations of life. Since Twain's death, however, there has been renewed interest by French readers and critics.

J.C.B. Kinch

BIBLIOGRAPHY

Asselineau, Roger. *The Literary Reputation of Mark Twain from 1910–1950: A Critical Essay and Bibliography*. Paris: Marcel Didier, 1954.

Bentzon, Th[érèse] (Mme. Marie-Thérèse Blanc). "Les Humoristes américaines: I. Mark Twain." *Revue des Deux Mondes* 100 (July 1872): 313–335.

Clemens, Samuel L. "The French and the Comanches." *Letters from the Earth*. By Clemens. Ed. Bernard DeVoto. New York: Harper & Row, 1962. 146–151.

———. *The Innocents Abroad*. Hartford, Conn.: American Publishing, 1869.

———. *Mark Twain Papers*. Bancroft Library, U of California, Berkeley. Notebooks numbers 13, 14, 21, 31, 32a, and 32b.

———. *Mark Twain's Autobiography*. Ed. Albert B. Paine. New York: Harper, 1924.

———. *Mark Twain's Notebook*. Ed. Albert B. Paine. New York: Harper, 1935.

Henderson, Archibald. "The International Fame of Mark Twain." *North American Review* 192 (December 1910): 805–815.

———. *Mark Twain*. New York: Frederick A. Stokes, 1912.

Kaplan, Justin. *Mr. Clemens and Mark Twain*. New York: Simon & Schuster, 1966.

Long, E. Hudson. *Mark Twain Handbook*. New York: Hendricks House, 1957.

Rodney, Robert M., ed. *Mark Twain International: A Bibliography and Interpretation of His Worldwide Popularity*. Westport, Conn.: Greenwood P, 1982.

Scott, Arthur L. *Mark Twain at Large*. Chicago: Henry Regnery, 1969.

Wagenknecht, Edward. *Mark Twain: The Man and His Work*. Rev. ed. Norman: U of Oklahoma P, 1967.

See also: "Aix, the Paradise of the Rheumatics"; Blanc, Marie-Thérèse; "French and the Comanches, The"; French Language; French Revolution; *Innocents Abroad, The*; Paris, France; *Personal Recollections of Joan of Arc*

Free Man of Color

The free man of color (F.M.C.) was, technically, a manumitted slave in pre-Civil War America. In truth, however, an F.M.C. was not free in the sense that white men were free. He had neither the advantages of protection by law that free men had nor the advantages of protection by owners that slaves had. Mark Twain aptly described the F.M.C. category in *Connecticut Yankee* (1889) as "a sarcasm of law and phrase."

Each state had its own set of laws regarding the F.M.C.s. Generally speaking, the laws of slave states bordering free states were more restrictive than those in the deep South, but the laws everywhere grew more severe as the Civil War approached. F.M.C.s were not allowed to vote or serve in the militia, were usually not allowed to be witnesses in court cases, were stringently limited in their meetings or associations with slaves, were restricted in their occupations, were forbidden to buy or sell liquor, and were almost on a level with slaves in matters of criminal law. In Missouri F.M.C.s had to have a license to live in the state and had to carry it at all times, were required to give a bond in order to travel to another county, and were subject to a $500 fine or imprisonment for one year if they went to a free state or territory and returned.

If the wife of an F.M.C. were still a slave, she could be kept apart from her husband, "married" to another slave, or sold. The child of an F.M.C. and a slave wife belonged to the owner of the wife and could be taken from the couple or sold.

Twain knew about F.M.C.s from his youth in Missouri. Almost certainly, the publication of George Washington Cable's *The Grandissimes* (1880) drove home to Twain the cruel anomaly of the category. The significance of this realization becomes apparent at the end of *Huckleberry Finn* (1885) when Tom Sawyer demands the release of Jim: "Turn him loose! he ain't no slave; he's as free as any creature that walks this earth!" This line is profoundly ironic, for Jim is an F.M.C.; he is not free, nor are his wife and child free. He becomes the victim of a cruel delusion, for his return home will, in effect, mean that he will have to work like a slave to free his family, and his freedom will be precarious. By extension, also, just as Jim is not truly free, Tom's statement implies that no other creature is truly any freer.

Twain next used the F.M.C. category in "Huck Finn and Tom Sawyer Among the Indians," begun after *Huckleberry Finn* but left unfinished. Significantly, one of the reasons that Jim goes with Huck and Tom is to escape the white men in his town who would steal his papers and sell him down the river.

A figurative extension of the F.M.C. category appears in chapter 34 of *Connecticut Yankee* (1889), when Hank and King Arthur are sold into slavery because they could not prove they were free men. Hank reflects that the "same infernal law had existed in our own South in my time" but not until he experienced it himself did he realize it was "hellish."

Twain was not attacking the F.M.C. category per se, for it no longer existed after the Civil War. Like Cable and Joel Chandler Harris, he used it to attack the practical re-enslavement of black freedmen by the Jim Crow laws of the New South. More broadly, however, he used it to question human freedom.

Lawrence I. Berkove

BIBLIOGRAPHY

Basso, Hamilton. *The Light Infantry Ball.* Garden City, N.Y.: Doubleday, 1959.

Berkove, Lawrence I. "The Free Man of Color in *The Grandissimes* and Works by Harris and Mark Twain." *Southern Quarterly* 18.4 (Summer 1980): 60–73. Rpt. *The Grandissimes: Centennial Essays.* Ed. Thos. J. Richardson. Jackson: UP of Mississippi, 1981.

———. "The 'Poor Players' of *Huckleberry Finn*." *Papers of the Michigan Academy of Science, Arts, and Letters* 53 (1968): 291–310.

Cable, George Washington. *The Grandissimes.* New York: Scribner, 1880.

Catteral, Helen Tunicliff, ed. *Judicial Cases Concerning American Slaves and the Negro.* Vols. 3, 5. Washington, D.C.: Carnegie Institute, 1926–1937.

Farnam, Henry W. *Chapters in the History of Social Legislation in the United States to 1860.* Ed. Clive Day. Washington, D.C.: Carnegie Institute, 1938.

Harris, Joel Chandler. *Free Joe and Other Georgian Sketches.* New York: Collier, 1887.

Hogan, William R., and Edwin A. Davis, eds. *William Johnson's Natchez.* Baton Rouge: Louisiana State UP, 1951.

Sterkx, H.E. *The Free Negro in Ante-Bellum Louisiana.* Rutherford, N.J.: Fairleigh Dickinson UP, 1972.

See also: Adventures of Huckleberry Finn; Freedom; Slavery

Freedom

Mark Twain was at odds with himself over the issue of freedom; he was publically committed to it, yet personally he did not believe it existed. At the heart of the matter is the intellectual legacy left him by the Calvinism of his formative years. It is a paradox that a large part of the population of the United States, in the nineteenth century the world's most advanced and militant democracy, believed in Calvinism, whose doctrine of predestination practically negated the idea of freedom. Yet of all nineteenth-century authors, Mark Twain was the one most alive to the contradiction of predestination and freedom. His grappling with this contradiction became increasingly agonized over the course of his lifetime. Ultimately, his struggles with it shaped his literature and endowed it with rich complexity and tragic power.

The contradiction between a belief in Calvinism and freedom may be appreciated once it is understood that predestination means that every occurrence, every act, every word, even every thought of everything created was immutably decreed by God before creation. Nothing happens by chance; all is appointed to occur when and how God decided. Calvinism accepted that an all-powerful and all-knowing God was in full control. Indeed, from the biblical point of view, predestination follows logically from the description of God and from the narrative of His shaping of events; it is free will that is a mystery.

Sam Clemens brooded on this absolute domination of creation all his life. He did not like it; he fought it; he tried to reject it but could not. Even when, in his early manhood, he attempted to replace it with deism or his wife's religion, it made too much sense to be extirpated from his mind. He was left with a tendency to see life as only *seeming* to allow for freedom, and the more he reflected on it, the more convinced he was that life was really a rigged puppet show—only an illusion of freedom. As a consequence, in much of his best work there are conflicting levels of value regarding freedom.

Roughing It (1872), for example, may be read as a humorous blend of anecdotes and biography about the American dream of going west, finding wealth and thereby escaping man's doom to earn his bread by the sweat of his brow, and achieving happy freedom. And it may also be read, more gloomily, as an exposure of the grand illusions of the foredoomed pursuit of liberty, wealth, and happiness. "Silver fever" is described as an illness that blinded miners to reality; because of it, they voluntarily spent their whole lives in solitary, dangerous, and difficult circumstances in the delusion that enormous wealth was just around the corner. The garden "paradise" of Hawaii was similarly not without its serpents: native scorpions and foreign missionaries.

Huckleberry Finn (1885), widely understood as a novel affirming democracy and equality, has a surprisingly different force when attention is given to the pattern of events that inevitably contradict freedom: the drift of the raft southward, ever more deeply into slave territory; the funneling of "coincidences" toward the last ten chapters wherein Huck and Jim are put at the mercy of the arch-romantic Tom Sawyer and revert to what they were at the beginning; and the ironic character of Jim's "freedom" at the end. Jim becomes not a "free" man but an F.M.C.—a free man of color. As such, his status hides the truth of his delusion. By implication, others are also unaware of the extent of their playing a role and are therefore not truly free.

A Connecticut Yankee in King Arthur's Court (1889) may be profitably read as evidence of Twain's political liberalism, anti-authoritarianism, and militantly democratic progressivism. Recent scholarship, however, has tended to see Hank as a despot more terrible than any other in Arthur's England and his "republic" a nightmare of the worst features of modern "civilization." Even the progressive view of the novel regards its conclusion as a tragedy, either because of Hank's misconceptions leading to the defeat of democracy or because of structural flaws in the novel. The predestinarian view sees the Battle of the Sand Belt as inevitable because the entire hope of altering time—the past, present, or future—is only a dream doomed from the first to failure.

There can be no doubt that Mark Twain the public figure lent his prestige and talents to causes that opposed tyranny. Especially in his later years, Twain attacked Western imperialism in China, South Africa, the Congo, and the Philippines; he sardonically mocked the pious pretensions of the rich and powerful; and he supported political causes that ended oppression and privilege and extended democracy. In some of his letters and speeches he projected political optimism. At the same time, such products of his literary and philosophical thought as "The Man That Corrupted Hadleyburg" (1899), the *Mysterious Stranger* manuscripts (1969), "The Great Dark" (1942), *What Is Man?* (1906), *Letters from the Earth* (1962), and "The Damned Human Race" (1962) were unbelievably bleak and pessimistic.

Twain variously called himself a deist, a Christian, and a secular determinist, but the persistent presence in his works of religious contexts in which God, a surrogate with divine powers, or "chance" manipulated the actions and destinies of humans suggests that Twain was never fully successful in freeing himself of Calvinist doctrine. Twain, of course, was heretically Calvinist; he regarded God as omnipotent, omniscient, but malevolent. His hatred of a divine tyrant expressed itself covertly as well as overtly in his efforts to show that God permitted no freedom and that the human race was damned: had been created flawed and was never intended to improve.

Young Sam Clemens could climb the hill back of his house in Hannibal and look across the breadth of the Mississippi at Illinois. Missouri was a slave state, and Illinois was a free state. It must have occurred to him that, despite its laws, the part of Illinois across the Mississippi and south to the Ohio River was pro-slavery; its free status was an illusion. This vision of contradiction could have been a paradigm for Twain, for he saw it repeated everywhere ever after. One part of his mind wished for freedom; another disbelieved its possibility; but his heart entirely yearned for it.

Lawrence I. Berkove

BIBLIOGRAPHY

Berkove, Lawrence I. "The 'Poor Players' of *Huckleberry Finn*." *Papers of the Michigan Academy of Science, Arts, and Letters* 53 (1968): 18–26.

———. "The Reality of the Dream: Structural and Thematic Unity in *A Connecticut Yankee*." *Mark Twain Journal* 22.1 (Spring 1984): 8–14.

Budd, Louis J. *Mark Twain: Social Philosopher.* Bloomington: Indiana UP, 1962.

Cummings, Sherwood. *Mark Twain and Science: Adventures of a Mind.* Baton Rouge: Louisiana State UP, 1989.

Foner, Philip S. *Mark Twain: Social Critic.* New York: International Publishers, 1958.

Hill, Hamlin. *Mark Twain: God's Fool.* New York: Harper & Row, 1973.

Marx, Leo. "Mr. Eliot, Mr. Trilling, and *Huckleberry Finn*." *American Scholar* 22.4 (Autumn 1953): 423–440.

Smith, Henry Nash. *Mark Twain: The Development of a Writer.* Cambridge, Mass.: Harvard UP, 1962.

Wilson, James D. "Religious and Esthetic Vision in Mark Twain's Early Career." *Canadian Review of American Studies* 17.2 (Summer 1986): 155–172.

See also: Calvinism; Determinism; Free Man of Color; Naturalism; Religion

Freemasonry

While residing in St. Louis, Twain became active in the local chapter of the Polar Star Lodge, applying for membership in December 1860 and attaining the third degree by the following July. Twain allowed his membership to lapse during his years in the West, rejoining the lodge in 1867. While traveling in Europe and the Middle East later that year, Twain visited the forest of the Lebanese cedars from which King Solomon is thought to have taken timber for his temple—a symbolic site for any Mason. Twain later presented to his lodge a gavel constructed with wood from this forest.

In 1869, however, he withdrew his membership when he decided to remain permanently in the East. Twain never again became active in the Masonic order, associating instead with less formal groups, such as the Nook Farm community. Alexander E. Jones suggests, however, that Masonic rituals, symbols, and teachings significantly influenced Twain's writing, particularly in the descriptions of Palestine in *The Innocents Abroad* (1869) and in his beliefs about God and the universe.

Charles Franklyn Beach

BIBLIOGRAPHY

Jones, Alexander E. "Mark Twain and Freemasonry." *American Literature* 26 (1954): 363–373.

Strong, Leah A. *Joseph Hopkins Twichell: Mark Twain's Friend and Pastor.* Athens: U of Georgia P, 1966.

Wagenknecht, Edward. *Mark Twain: The Man and His Work.* Rev. ed. Norman: U of Oklahoma P, 1967.

Free Thought

The concept of free thought has existed for as long as there has been organized religion. Depending on the historical context, freethinkers have been called heretics, libertines, skeptics, infidels, atheists, agnostics, and other things. Molyneux first used the term "candid freethinker" in a 1697 letter to John Locke. In 1708 Jonathan Swift characterized freethinkers as "atheists, libertines, [and] despisers of religion."

Free thought reached its zenith in America during the second half of the nineteenth century. Like the protest movement of the 1960s, free thought consisted of an amalgam of loosely defined groups focused on human rights: woman suffrage, abolition of slavery, and anti-war sentiment.

According to Warren, freethinkers were usually characterized by the application of reason and scientific principles to natural law and human existence and by rejecting the idea of divine intervention; often they defied classification: some denounced the "absurdities of theology"; others were interested in elevating science or using "ecclesiastical methods for the advancement of liberal thought" (32).

Influenced by Darwin, Thomas Paine, and Spencer's social Darwinism, Mark Twain's position ultimately resembled his freethinking contemporaries who were interested in criticizing and denouncing absurdities and hypocrisies, especially those evident in Christianity.

While Twain cultivated friendships with leading proponents of the movement whom he genuinely admired—Henry Ward Beecher, Robert G. Ingersoll, and others—his fear of lost income and popularity dictated his public image.

His earlier fiction, while skeptical in nature, displays youthful exuberance. As he grew older, the same lack of faith resulted in what

Doyno calls his "extraordinarily bleak, fragmentary writings" (11). Clearly, what appeared as irreverent innocence in *Huckleberry Finn* (1885) became bitter satire in his later writing, possibly transformed by "undeniable proof of the despondency that could come . . . to a sensitive and unschooled mind from the perception of the gulf fixed between ideals and experience" (Knight 152).

Albert Bigelow Paine, Twain's official biographer, and Twain's daughter Clara concealed entire works or omitted damning passages from Twain's works in an effort to safeguard his popularity. Twain was painfully conscious that "a consensus examines a new thing with its feelings rather oftener than with its mind." A "closet" free-thought sympathizer, Twain spent his life carefully balancing a public career as an American hero with the pressures of the thinking inner-self. There was no real ambivalence and no spiritual hypocrisy; the matter was financial: "[A] man is not independent, and cannot afford views which might interfere with his bread and butter" (qtd. in Doyno 426). And so he insisted that some of his later work "not be exposed to any eye until the edition of A.D. 2046."

Letters from the Earth, finally published in 1962, typifies Twain's wit, satire, and anger toward a system of belief that no longer worked for him. Unwilling to jeopardize his public image, Twain exposed absurdities in his fiction: "In time, the Deity perceived that death was a mistake: . . . A way must be contrived to pursue the dead beyond the tomb. As the gentle savior, [God] was a thousand billion times crueler than he ever was in the Old Testament" (Clemens 45).

It was only after his death that the extent of Twain's affiliation with free thought became known. An article entitled "What was Mark Twain's Religion?" appeared in the free-thought periodical the *Truth Seeker*, 7 May 1910. This article, anonymously authored, suggests various links between Twain and the movement. Further, William Dean Howells provides additional evidence in a *Harper's*

Monthly article: "[Twain] never went back to anything like faith in the Christian theology, or in the notion of life after death . . ." (363).

When placing Twain in the framework of the free-thought "boom" in America, it is essential not to accept outright all connections attributed to him. His sentiments were clearly sympathetic with the movement, and he lacked the religious convictions of his Christian contemporaries. Many scholars believe Twain was ambivalent about religion, but it is clear from his earliest lectures and writings that he held an irreverent position concerning most religious tenets and that the irreverence grew stronger throughout his life. Though "Judge Driscoll could be a freethinker and still hold his place in society," Twain could not risk it (qtd. in Doyno 290).

Mary Minor Austin

BIBLIOGRAPHY

Bray, Robert. "Mark Twain Biography: Entering A New Phase." *Midwest Quarterly* 15.3 (April 1974): 286–301.

Clemens, Samuel L. *Letters from the Earth*. Ed. Bernard DeVoto. New York: Harper & Row, 1962.

———. *Mark Twain, Selected Writings of an American Skeptic*. Ed. Victor Doyno. Buffalo, N.Y.: Prometheus, 1983.

———. *Selected Mark Twain-Howells Letters, 1872–1910*. Ed. Frederick Anderson, William M. Gibson, and Henry Nash Smith. Cambridge, Mass.: Harvard UP, 1967.

Ensor, Allison. *Mark Twain and the Bible*. Lexington: UP of Kentucky, 1969.

Knight, Grant C. *The Critical Period in American Literature*. Chapel Hill: U of North Carolina P, 1951.

Paine, Albert Bigelow. *Mark Twain: A Biography*. 3 vols. New York: Harper, 1912.

Warren, Sidney. *American Freethought, 1860–1914*. New York: Columbia UP, 1943.

See also: Ingersoll, Robert Green; Religion

"French and the Comanches, The"

(1962)

Written in 1879, this essay, originally to be a part of *A Tramp Abroad* (1880), did not appear in print until Bernard DeVoto's edition of *Letters from the Earth* in 1962, a volume he had originally planned to publish in 1939. Twain wrote it as one of several chapters critical of the French in February 1879 while he was ill in Paris. Of this material, only "Paris Notes" (1882) and this item have appeared in print. DeVoto observed that he did not think that the remaining unpublished chapters on the French then in the Twain estate were worth publishing.

Twain satirically compares the French with the Comanches in a motif that had become familiar by the nineteenth century: civilized societies shown at a disadvantage to primitive ones. Twain focuses on their responses to love. He cites a catalogue of French horrors like the St. Bartholomew's Day massacre (1572) and notes the "tiger" in the French that makes them good soldiers. He observes that the French surpass the Chinese but not the Comanches. Finally, he calls on America to send missionaries to the French to lift them up to the brotherhood of humanity.

The process of academic inquiry is Twain's modus operandi here, for he treats his subject as if it were a footnote, a technique incorporating his more characteristic practice of building on stories—one proceeding from the other. The essay, written under less than optimum conditions, simply amplifies Twain's usual dislike of the French.

Thomas Bonner, Jr.

BIBLIOGRAPHY

Clemens, Samuel L. *Letters from the Earth*. Ed. Bernard DeVoto. New York: Harper & Row, 1962.

DeVoto, Bernard. *Mark Twain's America*. Boston: Little, Brown, 1932.

Emerson, Everett. *The Authentic Mark Twain: A Literary Biography of Samuel L. Clemens*. Philadelphia: U of Pennsylvania P, 1984.

See also: Blanc, Marie-Thérèse; DeVoto, Bernard Augustine; France; *Letters from the Earth*; Paris, France

French Language

Mark Twain's scorn for France colored his attitude toward its language. In an 1879 notebook entry naming the French as the connecting link between man and monkey, Twain dismisses French as "a mess of trivial sounds" (*Notebooks* 2:320). Yet the first foreign language Mark Twain studied was indispensable to him when he relied heavily on French sources in researching *Joan of Arc* (1896). He had begun teaching himself French in 1855, filling his first surviving notebook with error-ridden copybook exercises. By 1860 he was reading and transcribing Voltaire, and he continued to read French literature and history throughout his life. But *Innocents Abroad* (1869) records his difficulties with the spoken language, which he would never master despite repeated stays in France. In a letter of 1892 he admits that he catches "only words, not phrases" of French conversation (*Letters* 2:572); in 1900 he told a New York interviewer, recalling his two-years' residence in France, "I did not learn French, and do not yet know how to speak the language" (Budd 81).

Twain's one significant literary treatment of French is "The Jumping Frog" (1875), where he presents a comically literal re-Englishing of a French version of his famous story to prove that its humor has been lost in translation.

David R. Sewell

BIBLIOGRAPHY

Budd, Louis J., ed. "A Listing of and Selection from Newspaper and Magazine Interviews with Samuel L. Clemens, 1874–1910." *American Literary Realism* 10 (1977): i–xii, 1–100.

Clemens, Samuel L. "The Jumping Frog." *Sketches, New and Old.* Vol. 19 of the Author's National Edition. New York: Harper, 1917. 15–34.

————. *Mark Twain's Letters.* Ed. Albert B. Paine. 2 vols. New York: Harper, 1917.

————. *Mark Twain's Notebooks & Journals, Volume II (1877–1883).* Ed. Frederick Anderson, Lin Salamo, and Bernard L. Stein. Berkeley: U of California P, 1975.

See also: Blanc, Marie-Thérèse; France; Language

French Revolution

The French Revolution provided Twain with an enduring fascination. Following 1871 when he first read Thomas Carlyle's *History*, Twain read extensively of French revolutionary history during 1876–1877, 1879, 1882–1883, and 1887. He was reading Carlyle, one of three books kept at his bedside, moments before his death in 1910 (Baetzhold 27–42, 87–113). Twain reflected his consuming interest in the French Revolution in specific scenes—especially in *Tom Sawyer* (1876), *Huckleberry Finn* (1885), and *Connecticut Yankee* (1889) and in evolutionary social and political theme development.

Walter Blair's seminal "The French Revolution and *Huckleberry Finn*" demonstrates Twain's narrative uses of French revolutionary history. In *Tom Sawyer*, Tom's secret codes and gang oaths and etiquette; in *Huck Finn*, the lynch mob and Tom's rescue of Jim; in *Connecticut Yankee*, the Boss's destruction of Merlin's tower and the final battle exemplify Twain's use of the French Revolution in his fiction.

The French Revolution's greatest influence on Twain was on the evolution of his ideas and themes. In 1871 Twain generally concurred with Carlyle's moderate view of both French nobles and commoners; as late as March 1879 he scathingly modified the motto of the revolution: "Liberty (to . . . butcher)—Equality (in bestiality)—Fraternity (of Devils)" (qtd. by Baetzhold 42). By August 1887, however, Twain declared himself a "Sansculotte!—and not a pale, characterless Sansculotte, but a Marat" (Paine 490). Further, in September 1889 he named the revolution the "noblest and holiest thing and the most precious that ever happened . . ." (Paine 514). Early and late, Twain's attitude toward the revolutionary forces is paralleled in his works—from his description of the "savage-looking ruffians" of the Faubourg St. Antoine and his sympathy for "poor Marie Antoinette" in *Innocents Abroad* (chapter 16) to his recognition in *Connecticut Yankee* (chapter 13) of two "Reigns of Terror," the last a "minor . . . momentary Terror" compared to the first, which "lasted a thousand years" under the traditional auspices of church and monarchy.

Donald R. Holliday

BIBLIOGRAPHY

Baetzhold, Howard G. *Mark Twain and John Bull: The British Connection.* Bloomington: Indiana UP, 1970.

Blair, Walter. "The French Revolution and *Huckleberry Finn.*" *Modern Philology* 55 (August 1957): 21–35.

———. *Mark Twain & Huck Finn.* Berkeley: U of California P, 1960.

Clemens, Samuel L. *Mark Twain's Letters.* Ed. Albert B. Paine. 2 vols. New York: Harper, 1917.

Gribben, Alan. "Carlyle, Thomas." *Mark Twain's Library: A Reconstruction.* Vol. 1. Boston: G.K. Hall, 1980. 127–130.

See also: Carlyle, Thomas; France; Politics

Freud, Sigmund

(1856–1939)

The Austrian neurologist and founder of psychoanalysis was, save perhaps only the Viennese newspaper humorist, Eduard Poetzl (1851–1914), Mark Twain's most devoted admirer in Austria during and after the Clemens family's sojourn in Vienna in 1897–1899. In *Civilization and Its Discontents* (1930) Freud described his impressions of a Twain reading he attended at the Boesendorfer Saal on 1 February 1898, and he was probably at other platform appearances by Twain in Vienna during 1898 and early 1899. If they ever met and conversed, neither recorded it. In view of their mutual friendships in Vienna, including Freud's partner at weekly tarok games, Friedrich Eckstein (1860–1938), and his neighbor, Theodor Herzl (1860–1904), the journalist-playwright and Zionist leader, among others, it seems likely they at least shook hands. Clemens sought advice and treatment for his daughter Jean's increasingly frequent epileptic seizures from Freud's colleagues in the Vienna medical faculty, Heinrich Obersteiner (1847–1922), Rob-

ert Gersuny (1844–1924), and Alexander von Huettenbrenner (1842–1905), and he may also have discussed her case with Dr. Freud himself, whose reputation before publishing *The Interpretation of Dreams* (1900) was mainly as a practicing pediatric neuropathologist and an untenured university lecturer.

Whether personally acquainted or not, Freud was sufficiently well versed in Twain's writings to allude to several of them illustratively in five works of his own, the earliest being *The Psychopathology of Everyday Life* (1901). In *Jokes and Their Relation to the Unconscious* (1905) he cites details from *The Innocents Abroad* (1869), *Roughing It* (1872), and *Sketches, New and Old* (1875) to exemplify his axiom that "an economy of pity is one of the most frequent sources of humorous pleasure," and in *A Contribution to a Questionnaire on Reading* (1907) he lists "Mark Twain's *Sketches*" among "ten good books of modern literature," adding that if he could extend the list he would also include *Tom Sawyer* (1876) and *Huckleberry Finn* (1885). Other brief allusions to Twain's works may be found in Freud's *On the History of the Psychoanalytic Movement* (1914) and *The "Uncanny"* (1919). In his remarks about seeing Twain in Vienna in *Civilization and Its Discontents* (1930), Freud mentions Twain's "Morals Lecture" anecdote (which he misnames *The First Melon I Ever Stole*) as an illustration of "enhancing morality as a consequence of ill-luck." McGrath has also suggested that Twain's "Stirring Times in Austria" (1898) may have influenced Freud's dream about Dr. Lecher's twelve-hour speech in the Reichsrat, self-analyzed in *The Interpretation of Dreams.* Finally, when invited to write "A Comment on Anti-Semitism" for a refugee journal (*Die Zukunft*) in 1938, the exiled octogenarian, terminally ill psychiatrist made extensive use of Twain's "Concerning the Jews" (1899), although confessing "I can no longer recall where I read the essay of which I made a precis nor who was its author."

Twain makes no mention of Freud in his works or still unpublished papers, and he was doubtless unaware of Freud's writings inasmuch as even *The Interpretation of Dreams* remained virtually unknown to laymen before 1910. Yet, much of what Twain wrote between 1897 and 1906—notably "Which Was the Dream?," "My Platonic Sweetheart," "Wapping Alice," "The Great Dark," the three *Mysterious Stranger* manuscripts, and sections of *What Is Man?*—embodies themes and ideas analogous to Freud's theories about dreams and their meanings, about the relationship of dreams to reality, and about the tripartite nature of selfhood and identity that Freud denominated *Id*, *Ego*, and *Super-Ego*. Some of these congruencies may be explained by the interest Freud and Twain shared in the psychological writings of Georg Christoph Lichtenberg (1742–1799) and Johann Friedrich Herbart (1776–1841), Twain's attention to the experiments of Jean-Martin Charcot (1825–1893), whose Sorbonne lectures Freud had attended (1885–1886), and his avid reading during the 1890s of reports of the London-based Society for Psychical Research.

Since 1920 numerous literary disciples of Freud in the United States and abroad have made significant, if sometimes hotly controversial contributions, to Twain biography, scholarship, and criticism. Whether the distinction of being Twain's first Freudian interpreter belongs to Gamaliel Bradford or Waldo Frank (*Our America*, 1919) is debatable, but his first Freudian biographer was indisputably Van Wyck Brooks, whose highly influential *The Ordeal of Mark Twain* (1920) polarized Twain studies for a generation after the rebuttal to it offered by Bernard DeVoto in *Mark Twain's America* (1932).

More recently, important applications of "psychography" (Bradford's term) with a Freudian orientation have come from Guy Cardwell, Leslie Fiedler, Justin Kaplan, and Edward Wagenknecht. While Freudians have concentrated mainly on Clemens's private life, especially his alleged domination by women (mother, wife, daughters, Mrs. Fairbanks, his

nymphette "Aquarium," etc.) and his "identity crisis" resulting from his creation of a literary *persona* distinct from his real self, they have also focused on his treatment of women, guilt, sexuality, and homoeroticism in his writings. A thorough study of possible Freudian elements in Twain's late works is Susan Gillman, *Dark Twins: Imposture and Identity in Mark Twain's America* (1989). Maxwell Geismar, in *Mark Twain: An American Prophet* (1970), attempted a cursory refutation of some of Twain's Freudian interpreters, albeit from a Rankian and Marxist perspective.

Carl Dolmetsch

BIBLIOGRAPHY

Brooks, Van Wyck. *The Ordeal of Mark Twain*. Rev. ed. New York: Dutton, 1933.

Cardwell, Guy. *The Man Who Was Mark Twain: Images & Ideologies*. New Haven, Conn.: Yale UP, 1991.

DeVoto, Bernard. *Mark Twain's America*. Boston: Little, Brown, 1932.

Dolmetsch, Carl. "Mark Twain and Sigmund Freud: Vienna's Odd Couple?" *The William and Mary Gazette* 55.1 (Summer 1986): 8–12.

———. *"Our Famous Guest": Mark Twain in Vienna*. Athens: U of Georgia P, 1992.

Freud, Sigmund. *The Standard Edition of the Complete Psychological Works of Sigmund Freud*. Ed. and trans. James Strachey, Anna Freud, et al. 24 vols. London: Hogarth P and the Institute of Psychoanalysis, 1953–1974. 6:236, 8:230–231, 9:245–247, 17:237, 21:126, 23:289–293.

Gay, Peter. *Freud: A Life for Our Time*. New York: Norton, 1988.

Gillman, Susan. *Dark Twins: Imposture and Identity in Mark Twain's America*. Chicago: U of Chicago P, 1989.

McGrath, William J. *Freud's Discovery of Psychoanalysis: The Politics of Hysteria*. Ithaca, N.Y.: Cornell UP, 1986.

Richmond, Marion B. "The Lost Source in Freud's 'Comment on Anti-Semitism': Mark Twain." *Journal of the American Psychoanalytic Association* 28 (1980): 563–574.

See also: Austria(Austria-Hungary); Biographers; Brooks, Van Wyck; Jews

Gabrilowitsch, Nina Clemens
(1910–1966)

Nina Clemens Gabrilowitsch, the sole grandchild of Samuel Clemens, was born at Stormfield in Redding, Connecticut, just four months after her grandfather's death. Clara Clemens Gabrilowitsch, the Clemenses' second oldest daughter, was Nina's mother, and her father was Ossip Gabrilowitsch, an eminent pianist and conductor.

Soon after Nina's birth, the Gabrilowitsches moved to Europe. The family lived in Nymphenburg, Bavaria, until the onset of World War I. When Nina was three, the family returned to the United States. In 1918 Ossip Gabrilowitsch accepted a position as conductor of the Detroit Symphony Orchestra.

Nina was educated at home by her mother, a nurse, and a governess until she was eight, when she was enrolled in the Liggett School, a private academy in Detroit. Nina studied at Barnard College, where she participated in theatrical productions. Upon graduating in 1934, she remained in New York to pursue an acting career. She met with little success. In 1935 she married Carl Rutgers; the marriage lasted less than a year.

After Ossip Gabrilowitsch's death in September 1936, Clara moved to Hollywood, California. Nina soon joined her and once again attempted to enter the creative community. Nina considered photography her greatest talent, although she never received public recognition, and she authored an unpublished autobiography titled *A Life Alone*. Nina suffered from acute alcoholism and drug addiction, and in 1964 she voluntarily appointed conservators to manage her estate. On 16 January 1966 Nina took an overdose of barbiturates and died in a Hollywood hotel across the street from her penthouse. She was fifty-five. Nina is buried at the Clemens family plot in Elmira, New York.

Deborah O'Connell-Brown

BIBLIOGRAPHY

Harnsberger, Caroline Thomas. *Mark Twain, Family Man*. New York: Citadel P, 1960.

"Nina Clemens Gabrilowitsch, 55, Twain's Last Direct Heir, Dies." New York *Times*, 19 January 1966, 41.

"Rites for Mark Twain's Last Descendant Set." Los Angeles *Times*, 19 January 1966, part 2, n.p.

See also: Gabrilowitsch, Ossip; Samossoud, Clara Clemens

Gabrilowitsch, Ossip
(1878–1936)

Ossip Gabrilowitsch was Samuel Clemens's son-in-law. Gabrilowitsch married Clara Clemens in October 1909. Gabrilowitsch was a distinguished musician and conductor, and as a pianist he went on several tours of the United States and Europe. He directed the Konzertverein Orchestra in Meunchen in 1910, and in 1918 he became the first conductor of the Detroit Symphony Orchestra. He remained musical director there until his death in 1935. In 1928 Gabrilowitsch was joint conductor of the Philadelphia Orchestra with Leopold Stokowski.

Gabrilowitsch was born a Russian Jew in St. Petersburg. He was a child prodigy at the piano, and at the age of ten he was admitted to the St. Petersburg Conservatory. He eventually came to study with Theodor Leschetizky. In 1894 Gabrilowitsch, accompanied by his mother, traveled to Vienna, where Leschetizky lived, to begin studying with him. Gabrilowitsch gave his debut in 1896 in Berlin and was enthusiastically received. Gabrilowitsch and Clara Clemens met in Vienna (at the time she was also a pupil of Leschetizky's) and had a romantic relationship lasting for several years. After a serious illness, with Clara nursing Gabrilowitsch back to health, they became engaged. Immediately after their marriage, they left for Europe where they had decided to live. The Gabrilowitsches returned permanently to America in 1914 after the outbreak of World War I, and

Gabrilowitsch became an American citizen in 1921. Clemens was fond of his son-in-law and reputedly his last words were spoken to Gabrilowitsch when he asked for a glass of water.

Laura E. Skandera

BIBLIOGRAPHY

Clemens, Clara. *My Husband Gabrilowitsch*. New York: Harper, 1938.

Saleske, Gdal. *Famous Musicians of Jewish Origin*. New York: Bloch Publishing, 1949.

Zurier, Melvin L. "My Cousin, Mark Twain." *Rhode Island Jewish Historical Notes* 8 (November 1981): 283–299.

See also: Gabrilowitsch, Nina Clemens; Samossoud, Clara Clemens

Gainesboro, Tennessee

Gainesboro is a town on the Cumberland River, east of Nashville, county seat of Jackson County. John Marshall Clemens and Jane Lampton Clemens lived in Gainesboro ca. 1825–1827, soon after their 1823 marriage in Columbia, Kentucky, and before their move to Fentress County, Tennessee. Their oldest child, Orion, was born in Gainesboro (not Jamestown, as stated in Mark Twain's *Autobiography*), 17 July 1825. In the previous month, on 16 June 1825, Jane Clemens's sister Martha Ann ("Patsy") married John A. Quarles in Gainesboro. Orion Clemens paid a visit to Gainesboro shortly after the end of the Civil War and described it in a newspaper letter signed "Cumberland" and dated St. Louis, 11 March 1867.

Allison R. Ensor

BIBLIOGRAPHY

Clemens, Samuel L. *Mark Twain's Autobiography*. Ed. Albert B. Paine. 2 vols. New York: Harper, 1924.

Howard, Oliver, and Goldena Howard. *The Mark Twain Book*. New London, Mo.: Ralls County Book, 1985.

See also: Clemens, Orion; Tennessee Land

Galaxy

Between 1868 and 1871 Mark Twain contributed over eighty articles and essays to the serial publication the *Galaxy*. The New York–based *Galaxy* was for a time a leading national magazine. Established in 1866 by William C. Church, the magazine maintained a wide readership and published a diverse collection of materials including short stories by both Henry James and Ivan Turgenev and military reports from George Armstrong Custer. Though the *Galaxy* reached the height of its popularity in April 1871, publishing more than 22,000 copies, the journal was forced to cease publication by 1878 due to financial difficulties.

Almost all of Twain's contributions to the *Galaxy* were published under the title "Memoranda." Twain requested that this "department" not be advertised as "Humorous." While he promised his readers a serious column, full of "statistics and agriculture," in actuality he delivered a series of satirical essays aimed mostly at deserving personalities and national institutions. He frequently used the *Galaxy* to defend the mistreated Chinese in America or to ridicule hypocritical preachers and their moralisms. Twain's complete *Galaxy* writings have been compiled and published under the title *Contributions to "The Galaxy" 1868–1871*, edited with an introduction by Bruce R. McElderry, Jr.

Scott H. Moore

BIBLIOGRAPHY

Clemens, Samuel L. *Contributions to "The Galaxy" 1868–1871*. Ed. Bruce R. McElderry, Jr. Gainesville, Fla.: Scholars' Facsimiles and Reprints, 1961.

Emerson, Everett. *The Authentic Mark Twain: A Literary Biography of Samuel L. Clemens*. Philadelphia: U of Pennsylvania P, 1984.

Long, E. Hudson. *Mark Twain Handbook*. New York: Hendricks House, 1957.

"General Grant's Grammar"

General Grant's *Memoirs*, published by Charles L. Webster and Company, became financially successful for the firm and was well received by the public. However, Matthew Arnold wrote a scathing critical review of the book, inviting Mark Twain's anger. Speaking at the Army and Navy Club in New York City in 1886, Mark Twain responded to Arnold's attack with "General Grant's Grammar," an address in which Twain finds fault in the grammar of many notable English writers.

Twain begins the address with a tongue-in-cheek reference to "great and honored author, Matthew Arnold" and Arnold's recent verbal attacks on General Grant's book. Twain's main argument in the address is that Grant's grammar is not any worse than that of some of the greatest writers of Western literature. Twain cites many examples of writers with poor grammar, including Shakespeare, Milton, Southey, Lamb, and Scott. Twain even goes as far as to point out grammatical errors within Arnold's critical review of Grant's book.

After exposing the grammatical errors within the works of such famous English writers, Twain praises the simple but effective style and content of Grant's book. Twain encourages his audience to overlook Grant's rough grammar and acknowledge the noble thoughts that Grant attempted to convey in his book. Although passionate about his esteem of General Grant, Twain's response in "General Grant's Grammar" to Arnold's criticism is mild.

Trevor J. Morgan

BIBLIOGRAPHY

Budd, Louis J. *Mark Twain: Social Philosopher*. Bloomington: Indiana UP, 1962.

Clemens, Samuel L. "General Grant's Grammar." *Mark Twain: A Biography*. Vol. 3. By Albert B. Paine. New York: Harper, 1912. 1651–1652.

Long, E. Hudson. *Mark Twain Handbook*. New York: Hendricks House, 1957.

Trilling, Lionel. *Matthew Arnold*. 2nd ed. New York: Columbia UP, 1949.

See also: Arnold, Matthew; Grant, Ulysses S.

Genteel Tradition

First coined as a term in 1911 by George Santayana, the genteel tradition designates a hegemonic influence in American life from the early decades of the nineteenth century to the first decade of the twentieth. The tradition, originating in the East, was constituted by a set of social codes, religious attitudes, moral values, and cultural norms shared by a privileged middle to upper class. A powerful force in American society, the genteel tradition is crucial in understanding Samuel Clemens's life and Mark Twain's art.

What Victorianism was to England, the genteel tradition was to America. The genteel believed in the moral order of the universe, in proper social behavior, and in the power of art to shape and sustain civilization. The genteel celebrated self-cultivation and refinement in the private sphere and ethical conduct in the public. They were cultural imperialists who attempted to impose their concept of high culture on the masses (Brodhead) and to exert political power through moral suasion in behalf of traditional ideals (Tomsich, Sproat). They controlled key instruments of literary production, such as publishing houses and magazines, and they established an exclusive network of social relations. At its most intense the genteel tradition became rigidly prescriptive, narrowly orthodox, excessively delicate, contributing to what has been called the feminization of American culture (Douglas). In the arena of American intellectual and social life the tribe of the genteel was legion. To make his way in society and in literature, Clemens had to come to grips with the genteel tradition.

"Solemnity, decorum, dinner, dominoes, prayers, slander," thus Mark Twain satirized gentility in *The Innocents Abroad* (1869). But by the time his book hit the press Clemens had already begun a lifelong process of acculturation to the genteel tradition. He had married Olivia Langdon, a refined and proper young lady, accepted a respectable position with the Buffalo *Express*, and settled comfortably into the nexus of the East. When he established himself and his family in his ostentatious house at Nook Farm in 1874, where he was to live and work for the most productive period of his life, he occupied a prominent position in one of the citadels of gentility.

Critics are divided over Clemens's alignment with gentility. Some see it as stifling his authentic creativity (Brooks), while others find that it nurtured and refined his talent while tolerating its eccentricity (Andrews). His best biographer has seen him responding with both acquiescence and rebellion (Kaplan), but one judicious recent critic has maintained that he was enamored with the East, anxious to wed himself to its mores and standards (Cardwell). Certainly, the general framework of the tradition was at one with the aristocratic aspirations of Clemens's parents, and it seemed both to satisfy his own innate delicacy and to guide his desire to be a gentleman.

Mark Twain's writings often pivot around the norms of the genteel tradition. His early fame was won partly through his irreverent attacks on genteel attitudes in *The Innocents Abroad*, but he also honors many genteel values in the book. His next travel adventure, *A Tramp Abroad* (1880), is itself a genteel narrative, and his final excursion, *Following the Equator* (1897), is written with an Olympian outlook often adopted by genteel writers. His short stories and essays also vacillate between assault on and acceptance of genteel standards. Asked because of his spreading popularity and seeming respectability to speak at the birthday banquet held in 1877 by the *Atlantic Monthly* for John Greenleaf Whittier, Twain stunned his audience by spoofing the genteel eastern writers. But rather than stand by his irreverent jest, he apologized profusely for its unintended incivility (Smith 92–112).

While *The Prince and the Pauper* (1882) and *Joan of Arc* (1896) are written in the genteel mode, Twain's most significant works are again divided over genteel matters. *Tom Sawyer* (1876) moves largely within the safe precincts of gentility but toys with a violence and a dark sense of human nature at odds with the tradition. However one interprets it, *Huckleberry Finn* (1885) is a radical, subversive book, yet the very norms it undermines are those upheld by the genteel tradition. Under the guise of raucous rebellion, *A Connecticut Yankee* (1889) may in fact articulate conventional attitudes (Cox 198–222), and in a similar way *Pudd'nhead Wilson* (1894) seems to attack slavery by deploying genteel attitudes toward race and sex. What becomes clear is that Twain's imaginings, like Clemens's life, are bounded by the strictures of gentility—whether adhered to or transgressed.

As his fame grew and as the genteel tradition weakened, Clemens was less pressed to conform in his life and writings. When daughter Clara admonished him to "remember proprieties" while in England to receive his honorary doctorate from Oxford, he replied, "They all pattern after me" (Clara Clemens 270). But he was never really free from his sense of genteel decorum. Violating its minor strictures, he upheld its general standards. He lived his life largely in accord with them, and he reared his daughters strictly in terms of them (Hill). He fulfilled the essence of the genteel tradition, while jettisoning its encrustation.

The core of Mark Twain's achievement may lie in his response to facets of the genteel tradition. His humor steadily wars with its orthodoxies (Cox), and his style at its most original deploys a vernacular language in behalf of common rather than genteel values (Smith). Far from confining him, the genteel tradition gave Twain an ideology, a set of social norms, and a style to depart from—from time to time.

Leland Krauth

BIBLIOGRAPHY

Andrews, Kenneth R. *Nook Farm: Mark Twain's Hartford Circle.* Cambridge, Mass.: Harvard UP, 1950.

Brodhead, Richard H. "Literature and Culture." *Columbia Literary History of the United States.* Ed. Emory Elliott. New York: Columbia UP, 1988. 467–481.

Brooks, Van Wyck. *The Ordeal of Mark Twain.* Rev. ed. New York: Dutton, 1933.

Cardwell, Guy. *The Man Who Was Mark Twain.* New Haven, Conn.: Yale UP, 1991.

Clemens, Clara. *My Father, Mark Twain.* New York: Harper, 1931.

Cox, James M. *Mark Twain: The Fate of Humor.* Princeton, N.J.: Princeton UP, 1966.

Douglas, Ann. *The Feminization of American Culture.* New York: Knopf, 1977.

Hill, Hamlin. *Mark Twain: God's Fool.* New York: Harper & Row, 1973.

Kaplan, Justin. *Mr. Clemens and Mark Twain.* New York: Simon & Schuster, 1966.

Santayana, George. *Winds of Doctrine: Studies in Contemporary Opinion.* New York: Harper, 1926.

Smith, Henry Nash. *Mark Twain: The Development of a Writer.* Cambridge, Mass.: Harvard UP, 1962.

Sproat, John G. *"The Best Men": Liberal Reformers in the Gilded Age.* New York: Oxford UP, 1968.

Tomsich, John. *A Genteel Endeavor: American Culture and Politics in the Gilded Age.* Stanford, Calif.: Stanford UP, 1971.

See also: Adventures of Tom Sawyer, The; Innocents Abroad, The; Prince and the Pauper, The; Pudd'nhead Wilson, The Tragedy of

German Language

In "The Awful German Language," appended to *A Tramp Abroad* (1880), Mark Twain laments that although a gifted person ought to learn French in thirty days it would take thirty years to learn German. While never fully mastering the language, even in thirty years, Mark Twain was to put his struggles with it to humorous use in personal anecdotes, speeches, and literary works.

As John T. Krumpelmann shows in *Mark Twain and the German Language*, Mark Twain first tried to learn German as a boy of fifteen, but it was not until he resolved to take his family to Europe for an extended stay beginning in 1878 that he seriously studied German.

Mark Twain's notebooks for that summer tell of his dream that "all bad foreigners went to German Heaven—couldn't talk and wished they had gone to the other place." He avowed that with its four cases and sixteen *thes*, "once the German language gets hold of a cat it's good-bye cat." At a performance in German of *King Lear*, he "[n]ever understood anything but the thunder and lightning."

While Mark Twain made progress in reading German books, he thought that "only God can read a German newspaper." In respect to the quality of his spoken German, in *A Tramp Abroad* Mark Twain tells how while talking in English about some private matters, he was stopped by his friend Joe Twichell, who said, "Speak in German, Mark. Some of these people may understand English."

Mark Twain uses German for humorous effect in "Mrs. McWilliams and the Lightning" (1882), *Meisterschaft: In Three Acts* (1888), and *A Connecticut Yankee in King Arthur's Court* (1889), in which German tongue twisters are part of magical effects. In his speech on "The Horrors of the German Language" (1897), Mark Twain proposed simplifying German so that "when you her for prayer need, One yer yonder-up understands."

Richard Dilworth Rust

Bibliography

Clemens, Samuel L. *Mark Twain's Notebooks & Journals, Volume II (1877–1883)*. Ed. Frederick Anderson, Lin Salamo, and Bernard L. Stein. Berkeley: U of California P, 1975.

———. *Mark Twain's Speeches*. New York: Harper, 1923.

———. *A Tramp Abroad*. Hartford, Conn.: American Publishing, 1880.

Krumpelmann, John T. *Mark Twain and the German Language*. Baton Rouge: Louisiana State UP, 1953.

Sewell, David R. *Mark Twain's Languages: Discourse, Dialogue, and Linguistic Variety*. Berkeley: U of California P, 1987.

See also: Austria(Austria-Hungary); "Awful German Language, The"; Language

Germany

Of Mark Twain's many travels and of his sojourns in Europe, only two took him to Germany. While there is no full account of these stays and no complete record of his experiences in that country, most of his itineraries and his places of residence as well as many of his meetings and the impressions he gathered can be reconstructed from his letters and notebooks, published and unpublished, as well as, to a certain extent, from the literary use he made of these experiences. Their general importance has been recognized in standard biographies and critical studies as well as a number of special investigations (e.g., Holger Kersten, "*A Tramp Abroad*: Mark Twain's Deutschlandbild und seine Voraussetzungen," emphasis in the latter category having fallen on Mark Twain and the German language, e.g., John T. Krumpelmann, *Mark Twain and the German Language*, and many shorter articles by other scholars), and on the publication and reception of the author's work in Germany and the German-speaking countries. Of the various bibliographical studies centering on the response to Mark Twain's writings, Robert M. Rodney, *Mark Twain International: A Bibliography of His Worldwide Popularity* (1982), and J.C.B. Kinch, *Mark Twain's German Critical Reception, 1875–1986: An Annotated Bibliography* (1989), deserve special mention, the latter supplanting a number of previous works in a tradition going back to the year of the author's death. A comprehensive assessment (focusing on and integrating the author's experiences in Germany, his image of Germany and of Germans, and Germany's image of Mark Twain) still remains to be undertaken.

More than a decade apart from each other, Mark Twain's stays in Germany occurred at different stages in his life and his career as a writer, and they were intended to serve different purposes. The first, between April 1878 and February 1879, was motivated by his desire to escape the burden of social and business responsibilities in America as much as by his wish (expressed in a letter of 9 March 1878 to Mary Mason Fairbanks) "to find a German village where nobody knows my name or speaks any English, & shut myself up in a closet two miles from the hotel, and work every day without interruption" to produce a book whose materials were to grow out of the very experiences of the trip. Taking his wife and his two daughters as well as Miss Clara Spaulding of Elmira and a nurse, Mark Twain sailed on the *Holsatia* (together with Germanophile Bayard Taylor en route to Berlin to assume the post of United States minister), landing in Hamburg on 25 April 1878. After a few days in the city (staying at the Hotel Kronprinz, "the best hotel I know") the entourage proceeded to Hanover, Cassel, and Frankfort, eventually arriving in Heidelberg on 6 May, where they took spacious apartments in the Schlosshotel, commanding a spectacular view of Heidelberg Castle, the Neckar River, and the distant valley of the Rhône. Following his original plan, Twain also rented a furnished room in a house on the Königsstuhl high above the hotel and immediately began to work on the manuscript of what became *A Tramp Abroad* (1880), his third travel book. Collecting material and making notes for it ("stuff which has never been in a book," as he wrote the prospective publisher on 13 July), he also made excursions to Mannheim and Worms, and he fully entered into the life of the city, delivering, at the Fourth of July banquet of the Anglo-American Club of Students, an "Oration" that testifies to his delight in turning his moderate knowledge of German to the same kind of comic use that characterizes his shrewd essay on "The Awful German Language," another product of his trip. On 23 July the party proceeded to Baden-Baden at the entrance of the Black Forest, one of the most fashionable German watering places, where on 1 August they were joined by the Reverend Joseph H. Twichell, a good friend of Twain's. After two brief walking tours out of Baden-Baden (to Schloss Favorite on 2 August and to Ebersteinburg and Gernsbach on 4 August), Twain and Twichell on 5 August started on a two-day Black Forest excursion that took them to Ottenhöfen, Allerheiligen, and Oppenau (from where they returned to Baden-Baden by train), and on 8 August the two friends went out again on a three-day Neckar tour to Heidelberg, Wimpfen, Heilbronn, Hirschhorn (by river boat), Neckarsteinach, Dilsberg, Neckargemünd, and back to Baden-Baden via Heidelberg. In modified form, these experiences became part of *A Tramp Abroad*, supplemented by information culled from the Baedeker and other guidebooks that had been of help in planning the route. On 12 August the friends proceeded to Switzerland, from where Twichell departed for home four weeks later.

The Twain party returned to Munich on 15 November to set up their winter quarters in Fräulein Dahlweiner's Pension, Karlstrasse 1a. A few days later, on 19 November, the author again rented a separate room, a mile away, "at 45 Nymphen[burger]strasse—Frau Kratz," and continued to work on his manuscript while the whole family devoted itself to the study of German until, on 27 February 1879, they moved on to Paris; eventually they traveled to England and from there back to New York City. Although upon his arrival on 3 September 1879 Mark Twain expressed great relief at returning home, the eleven weeks he had spent in Heidelberg more or less lived up to his expectations, as did the "mighty good time" with Twichell. This being the part of his journey that went into the manuscript of his book, the impression that *A Tramp Abroad* gives of his first visit to Germany is much more positive than the experience as a whole actually turned out to be. For even though his plan of shutting himself off in a room to work on his book was actually realized in Munich just as it had been in Heidelberg, the writing there for different reasons did not go as well as expected, and various ailments and illnesses that afflicted himself and members of his family further contributed to his negative evaluation of the 1878–1879 European tour as a whole.

Mark Twain's second visit to Germany occurred in 1891–1892 as part of what turned out to be an extended European sojourn because of his wife's health and their attempt to provide musical instruction for their daughters as well as to economize on household expenses. The few months he and his family spent in the capital of Berlin, October 1891 to February 1892, may be said to be the period in which German appreciation of Mark Twain and the recognition of his achievement reached their climax. His response to this experience deserves to be studied in detail. Both before and after the Berlin period his movements were dictated by illness, his own as much as Livy's. After he visited Bayreuth (referred to by the author as the "Shrine of St. Wagner" in a sketch of 1891) to attend its annual festival in August, rheumatism drove him to Marienbad in Bohemia for the second half of the month. Subsequently, he enjoyed "exquisite glimpses" of the ancient city of Nuremberg, and from 2 to 5 September the Clemenses revisited Heidelberg (even taking their old room, no. 40, in the Schlosshotel and walking up the Königsstuhl) before they proceeded to Switzerland, from where Mark Twain started on a boat trip down the Rhône in quest of materials for still another travel book. They spent the winter in Berlin (including a visit to Dresden for a reading with passages from *A Tramp Abroad* as well as eight days in the village of Ilsenburg in the Harz Mountains), and after a spring excursion to Italy and a hurried trip for Mark Twain back to the United States, they lived for a whole three months at Bad Nauheim, where they stayed at the Hotel Kaiserhof while both Twain and Livy were taking the baths. He found the place comfortable as well as inexpensive. Its easy access to Frankfort, Wiesbaden, and Hamburg made up for whatever facilities he found lacking there, and meetings with friends and celebrities such as Chauncey Depew, Joe Twichell, Sir Charles Hall, the English Ambassador to Germany, and, most notably, the Prince of Wales (later King Edward VII) helped to keep up his spirits. When the family left for Florence on 10 September 1892, Twain was able to conclude that Livy was much better and that he himself was healthy and had made excellent progress on two works, *Tom Sawyer Abroad* (1894) and "Those Extraordinary Twins" (1894).

Although Germany as a nation and the Germans as people never ranked first in Mark Twain's estimation, he liked both. They may claim the distinction, moreover, of not having been subject to the vicissitudes of the author's moods, which colored his image of other nations and peoples.

Horst H. Kruse

BIBLIOGRAPHY

Clemens, Samuel L. *Mark Twain's Notebooks & Journals, Volume II (1877–1883)*. Ed. Frederick Anderson, Lin Salamo, and Bernard L. Stein. Berkeley: U of California P, 1975.

Kersten, Holger. "*A Tramp Abroad*: Mark Twains Deutschlandbild und seine Voraussetzungen." Master's thesis, Kiel, 1988.

Kinch, J.C.B. *Mark Twain's German Critical Reception, 1875–1986: An Annotated Bibliography*. Westport, Conn.: Greenwood P, 1989.

Krumpelmann, John T. *Mark Twain and the German Language*. Baton Rouge: Louisiana State UP, 1953.

McKeithan, Daniel M. *A Mark Twain Notebook for 1892*. Essays and Studies on American Language and Literature, 17. Upsala, Sweden: Lundquista-Bokhandeln, 1965.

Michael, D. "Heidelberg als ameikanische 'Love Story': Vor 150 Jahren wurde Mark Twain geboren—Erinnerung an seinen dreimonatigen Aufenthalt im ehemaligen Schlosshotel." *Ruperto Carola* 37 (1985): 88–91.

Peiper, Werner, ed. *Mark Twain: Ein Amerikaner in Heidelberg: Sein Bummel durch Deutschland 1878*. Heidelberg: Grubhofer, 1985.

See also: "Awful German Language, The"; Berlin, Germany; German Language; *Tramp Abroad, A*

"Ghost Story, A"
(1870)

One of Mark Twain's regular humorous installments in the Buffalo *Express* on Saturdays, "A Ghost Story: By the Witness" appeared on 15 January 1870. It is datelined "New York, January" because Twain was on the last leg of his lecture tour before marrying Olivia Langdon in Elmira, New York.

Soon after Twain assumed editorship of the *Express* in August 1869, the Cardiff Giant story broke. After much controversy, this great petrified giant allegedly dug up on a farm in central New York was exposed as a hoax. The statue—and even a fake version of it—went on display, luring large crowds in Albany and New York City. "A Ghost Story" follows his 23 October 1869 *Express* story, "A Capitoline Venus," which alludes to the recent furor over the Cardiff Giant.

In "A Ghost Story" Twain satirizes the materialistic success of the Cardiff Giant swindle. As much a spoof of gothic thrillers as a barbed social commentary, it shows devices typical to Twain's humorous style: an innocently victimized narrator, exaggeration, a slow build-up, and a reversal of expectations. The narrator is haunted in his room by the clumsy ghost of the Cardiff Giant. In a comic twist that piles fraud upon fraud, the ghost, who has come to New York City to gain peace by burying the Cardiff Giant, has himself been duped. The "real" giant is in Albany; only a plaster version is on display in New York.

Twain kept thinking about this celebrated deceit. His June 1870 *Galaxy* column recounts his own "Petrified Man" hoax perpetrated in the "Washoe Joke" story of 1862. "A Ghost Story" was reprinted in *Sketches, New and Old* (1875) without the subtitle, but with an additional footnote explaining the Cardiff Giant.

Thomas J. Reigstad

BIBLIOGRAPHY

Clemens, Samuel L. *Contributions to "The Galaxy" 1868–1871.* Ed. Bruce R. McElderry. Gainesville, Fla.: Scholars' Facsimiles & Reprints, 1961.

———. *Mark Twain's Sketches, New and Old.* Hartford, Conn.: American Publishing, 1875.

See also: Hoax

Gilded Age: A Tale of To-Day, The
(1873)

Mark Twain's first book-length piece of fiction is also the only one he wrote jointly, rendering its status in the Twain canon problematic. Early in 1873 Twain and Charles Dudley Warner, his Hartford neighbor and fellow author, agreed to collaborate on a novel. According to Albert Bigelow Paine's well-known but unverifiable story, the partnership began when the two men, complaining over dinner about the state of American fiction, were challenged by their wives to produce something better. Within three months they had completed a novel in which, they would claim in their preface, "scarcely a chapter . . . does not bear the marks of the two writers." Published in Hartford in December 1873, *The Gilded Age* sold briskly (Twain would later boast that its first two months' sales were the largest ever achieved by an American book). But early reviewers complained that the collaboration was a gimmick; twentieth-century critics have praised the novel's social satire while branding it an artistic failure; and at least one modern editor has sought to salvage the novel by excising Warner's portion altogether (Neider, *Adventures*).

Bryant Morey French subtitles his definitive study of *The Gilded Age*, "The Book That Named an Era." Most modern criticism has focused on the novel as a social document, a critical portrait of a United States suffering in the early 1870s from the corrupt Grant administration and Tammany Hall, land-grabbing railroad companies, unethical lobbyists, shady "wildcat" banks and promoters of get-rich-quick schemes, and a greedy, socially pretentious middle class. The fact that the novel is a thorough roman à clef (French documents meticulously just how many of the characters had well-known real-life counterparts) is doubtless one reason why *Gilded Age* has been read primarily as a realistic reflection of its age. Critics have disagreed widely, however, over the political assumptions underlying Mark Twain's portion of the satire. Vernon Parrington felt that Twain attacked merely the agents of social corruption while ignoring its fundamental source in the capitalist system itself. Other, less doctrinaire readers also detect a basic conservatism in Twain's social philosophy: Kenneth Lynn argues that *Gilded Age* upholds the enlightened republicanism of Nook Farm, while Louis Budd sees Twain as a champion of middle-class liberal values, uninterested in the plight of the common man, and even more conservative than his genteel co-author. But Marxist critic Philip Foner finds in *Gilded Age* a genuinely subversive critique of the three major sources of American social corruption: Wall Street, frontier speculators, and Washington politicos.

Far less has been written about nonpolitical issues in *Gilded Age*. Wayne Mixon usefully historicizes Colonel Sellers as a representative of the New South movement that Twain disdained. David Sewell explores linguistic corruption in the novel; Susan Harris offers an important feminist corrective to earlier readings of Laura Hawkins as a parodic sentimental heroine by showing how she embodies an essentially reactionary view of women's social roles.

Whether or not the collaboration produced a unified novel, Twain's portions of *Gilded Age* are crucially linked in style and matter with his major works of the next decade. *Gilded Age* provides Twain his first extended opportunity to draw upon those memories of the Mississippi valley and his family background that will be crucial in *The Adventures of Tom Sawyer* (1876) and *Adventures of Huckleberry Finn* (1885). It is a testing ground where Twain learns to translate real people into fiction: his father, with the pathetic dream of riches in the Tennessee Land, into Squire Hawkins; his feckless brother Orion into Washington Hawkins; his mother's cousin James Lampton into Colonel Sellers, a portrait from life. (Years later, George Washington Cable, after overhearing Twain in conversation with Lampton, would marvel, "That was Colonel Sellers!" [French 167].)

Most important, the central theme of the gap between appearance and reality—a theme fully shared by Warner—links *Gilded Age* to Twain's other major fiction. From the title, with its echo of whited sepulchers, to Colonel Sellers's cheerful assurance that a tallow candle in a stove is sufficient because "what you want is the *appearance* of heat, not the heat itself" (10:72), *Gilded Age* explores the many ways in which representation can falsify reality—in politics, economics, language, and sexual relationships. Its characters' most common error is to confuse a representation with the thing represented—to believe, for instance, that a map *creates* a territory, as when Colonel Sellers uses forks and spoons to lay out on his kitchen table a diagram of the projected railroad to Stone's Landing, which he gradually begins to speak of as already complete. Twain and Warner suggest that American society as a whole may be founded on such errors: Washington, D.C., itself was built as artificially as Colonel Sellers's proposed town of "Napoleon," as Twain reminds us in describing how the unfinished Washington Monument "towers out of the mud—sacred soil is the customary term" (10:237). In the novel's economic realm, the name for making something out of nothing is "speculation," a term that Twain associates with Squire Hawkins's dream of selling the worthless Land in Tennessee for millions and with all of Colonel Sellers's visionary projects. But Warner, too, blames the "fever of speculation" (11:191) for weakening the moral fiber of Gilded Age America's young men.

In Twain's career *Gilded Age* marks an important transition between two forms of social criticism. In his West Coast and Buffalo journalism Twain had frequently attacked specific abuses: incompetence in the Nevada legislature, police harassment of Chinese in San Francisco, graft in Boss Tweed's New York City. But in *Gilded Age*, for the first time, such ills have become symptoms of a more general social malaise, a development that will continue through *Adventures of Huckleberry Finn* (1885) and later anatomies of human nature like *Pudd'nhead Wilson* (1894) and "The Man That Corrupted Hadleyburg" (1899), where deceitful appearance is seen as the very precondition of society.

David R. Sewell

BIBLIOGRAPHY

Budd, Louis J. *Mark Twain: Social Philosopher.* Bloomington: Indiana UP, 1962.

Clemens, Samuel L. *The Adventures of Colonel Sellers.* Ed. Charles Neider. Garden City, N.Y.: Doubleday, 1965.

Clemens, Samuel L., and Charles Dudley Warner. *The Gilded Age.* Vols. 10 and 11 of the Author's National Edition. New York: Harper, 1915.

Foner, Philip S. *Mark Twain: Social Critic.* New York: International Publishers, 1958.

French, Bryant Morey. *Mark Twain and "The Gilded Age."* Dallas: Southern Methodist UP, 1965.

Harris, Susan K. "Four Ways to Inscribe a Mackerel: Mark Twain and Laura Hawkins." *Studies in the Novel* 21 (1989): 138–153.

Hill, Hamlin. "Toward a Critical Text of *The Gilded Age.*" *Papers of the Bibliographical Society of America* 59 (1965): 142–149.

Lynn, Kenneth S. *Mark Twain and Southwestern Humor.* Boston: Little, Brown, 1959.

Mixon, Wayne. *Southern Writers and the New South Movement, 1865–1913.* Chapel Hill: U of North Carolina P, 1980.

Parrington, Vernon Louis. *Main Currents in American Thought.* New York: Harcourt, Brace, 1930.

Sewell, David. *Mark Twain's Languages: Discourse, Dialogue, and Linguistic Variety.* Berkeley: U of California P, 1987.

See also: Hawkins, Laura; Illustrators; Politics; Representation; Sellers, Colonel; Warner, Charles Dudley; Washington, D.C.

Gillis, James N. (Jim)
(1830–1907)

Jim Gillis, a bachelor brother of Steve Gillis, lived in Angel's Camp, California, and made a living pocket mining for gold. Twain and Steve visited him between December 1864 and February 1865. Jim Gillis made a vivid and lasting impression on Twain, who picked up storytelling techniques from him and also the plots of several tales. One story became the "Dick Baker and His Cat" episode in *Roughing It* (1872); another, "Jim Baker's Blue Jay Yarn" in *A Tramp Abroad* (1880); and a third, "The King's Camelopard or the Royal Nonesuch" episode in chapters 22–23 of *Huckleberry Finn* (1885)—greatly toned down from its original ribald form as "The Tragedy of the Burning Shame." Twain also learned about pocket mining from Gillis, information that was used in *Roughing It.* Gillis might also have served as model for the fictionalized portrait of the failed old miner in chapter 60 of that book and for Jim Baker in *A Tramp Abroad.*

Lawrence I. Berkove

BIBLIOGRAPHY

Bellamy, Gladys Carmen. *Mark Twain as a Literary Artist.* Norman: U of Oklahoma P, 1950.

Berkove, Lawrence I. "Jim Gillis: 'The Thoreau of the Sierras.'" *Mark Twain Circular* 2.3–4 (March–April 1988): 1–2.

Branch, Edgar M. *The Literary Apprenticeship of Mark Twain.* Urbana: U of Illinois P, 1950.

Clemens, Samuel L. *Mark Twain's Autobiography.* Ed. Albert B. Paine. 2 vols. New York: Harper, 1924.

———. *Mark Twain's Notebooks & Journals, Volume I (1855–1873).* Ed. Frederick Anderson, Michael B. Frank, and Kenneth M. Sanderson. Berkeley: U of California P, 1975.

———. *Roughing It.* Ed. Franklin R. Rogers and Paul Baender. Berkeley: U of California P, 1972.

See also: Angel's Camp, California; "Jim Baker's Blue Jay Yarn"; *Roughing It*

Gillis, Steve
(1838–1918)

One of Twain's closest friends, Steve Gillis was a compositor on the Virginia City *Territorial Enterprise.* Gillis had a reputation for being both a practical joker and a ready fighter. Both men remained loyal to each other during times of trouble. The story that Gillis was involved in Twain's "duel" appears to be inaccurate, but Gillis did leave Virginia City with Twain when the latter departed suddenly. Later, when Gillis had to flee San Francisco after a brawl, Twain went with him to Angel's Camp, California, where they stayed with Steve's brother, Jim. Providing the occasion for this trip was one of Gillis's main services to Twain's literary career.

Lawrence I. Berkove

BIBLIOGRAPHY

Clemens, Samuel L. *Mark Twain of the "Enterprise": Newspaper Articles and Other Documents, 1862–1864.* Ed. Henry Nash Smith and Frederick Anderson. Berkeley: U of California P, 1957.

Gillis, William R. "Memories of Mark Twain and Steve Gillis." *Mark Twain's Sojourn in Tuolumne County, California.* Sonora, Calif.: Tuolumne County Historical Society, 1987.

"Mark Twain and the Old Enterprise Gang." [San Francisco]: Grabhorn, 1940.

See also: Gillis, James N. (Jim); Virginia City *Territorial Enterprise*

Gleason, Rachel Brooks, M.D.
(1820–1909)

With her husband, Silas O. Gleason, M.D., Rachel Brooks Gleason opened the Elmira water cure on 1 June 1852. Gleason was among the first women to graduate from medical school in the United States; she received her medical degree in 1851. The Gleasons practiced hydropathic medicine, a system using water as a cure and preventative for disease, and Rachel specialized in the treatment of women's health. She was a popular lecturer and wrote *Talks to My Patients* (1870), which quickly became a best seller with eight editions and had a New York and London publisher. Rachel Gleason was Olivia Langdon Clemens's lifelong physician and delivered all four of her children. In addition to treating Olivia for her gynecological problems, Rachel Gleason treated Isabella Beecher Hooker, Jervis Langdon, and Mollie Clemens (Samuel Clemens's sister-in-law) at the water cure. Clemens is on record as calling her "the almost divine Mrs. Gleason." The Gleason water cure became famous throughout the eastern seaboard and attracted an extensive and well-known clientele including Elizabeth Cady Stanton, Susan B. Anthony, and Emily Dickinson's mother. It is likely that the Clemens's penchant for visiting baths throughout Europe was fostered early on by the family's treatment at the Gleasons' Elmira water cure.

Laura E. Skandera

BIBLIOGRAPHY

Cayleff, Susan. *Wash and Be Healed: The Water Cure Movement and Women's Health.* Philadelphia: Temple UP, 1987.

Donegan, Jane B. *Hydropathic Highway to Health.* Westport, Conn.: Greenwood P, 1986.

Giammichele, Evelyn. "Elmira Water Cure." *Chemung Historical Journal* (December 1966): 1535–1541.

Gleason, Mrs. Rachel Brooks, M.D. *Talks to My Patients.* New York: Wood and Holbrook, 1870.

Gluck, James Fraser
(1852–1897)

Attorney and avid collector of books, manuscripts, and literary memorabilia, James Fraser Gluck was curator of the Buffalo (New York) Public Library when in 1885 he wrote to Samuel Clemens requesting that the author donate one of his manuscripts to the library's collection. Gluck had for some time actively pursued autograph manuscripts and letters; from writers, publishers, agents, and private individuals he had obtained donations or purchased from his own funds a substantial array of letters and manuscripts of major eighteenth- and nineteenth-century British and American writers. Because Clemens had lived in Buffalo for a time after his marriage to Olivia in February 1870, Gluck hoped the now celebrated author might be sympathetic to his request.

Clemens responded immediately by sending the second half of the manuscript of his recently published *Adventures of Huckleberry Finn* (1885); it was, he apologized, all he could locate at the time. The first half of the manuscript Clemens located in 1887 and sent it on to Gluck to complete the donation. Inexplicably, however, the first half of *Huckleberry Finn* never became a part of the Buffalo collection; it simply disappeared—until discovered in a trunk in an attic in Los Angeles in February 1991. Speculation is that Gluck, who donated more than 475 autograph manuscripts and letters to the Buffalo library, had taken this one home to examine; apparently it got misplaced and was forgotten after Gluck's death in 1897.

The recent discovery of the missing half of the *Huckleberry Finn* manuscript has generated a great deal of excitement and controversy over legal rights to possession. Officials of the Buffalo and Erie County Public Library are hopeful that this manuscript will become a permanent part of their substantial collection of Mark Twain resource material.

James D. Wilson

BIBLIOGRAPHY

Clemens, Samuel L. *Adventures of Huckleberry Finn.* Ed. Walter Blair and Victor Fischer. Berkeley: U of California P, 1985.

Reif, Rita. "How 'Huck Finn' Was Rescued." New York *Times*, 17 March 1991, H. 38.

See also: Auctions; Manuscript Collections; Rare Books

Glyn, Elinor

(1864–1943)

An English novelist and later a Hollywood screen writer, Glyn met with Clemens in early 1908. They discussed her most recent novel, *Three Weeks* (1907), a highly romantic tale of an extramarital affair. Clemens admired Glyn, and their meeting became the "damndest conversation" he had ever had with a woman (*Mark Twain in Eruption* 315). He agreed that society's regulation of sexual relations conflicted with higher law, but she wanted Clemens's public support of her view and urged him to speak out. He said he had "a large cargo" of private opinions that were not for print, and while he agreed with her in private, he was not inclined publicly to defend her book (316–318). Glyn later wrote out Clemens's comments and sent them to him. Clemens bluntly replied, "It is a poor literary job" (*Mark Twain's Letters* 2:809).

A flamboyant and beautiful redhead, Glyn began publishing romance novels in 1900. Her husband died in 1905, and she went to Hollywood in 1920, where several of her novels were filmed—including *Three Weeks* and *It*. The latter story with an American setting made

"it" a slang term for personal magnetism. She returned to England in 1929.

Ira Royals, Jr.

BIBLIOGRAPHY

Clemens, Samuel L. *Mark Twain in Eruption.* Ed. Bernard DeVoto. New York: Harper, 1940.

———. *Mark Twain's Letters.* Ed. Albert B. Paine. 2 vols. New York: Harper, 1917.

Glyn, Anthony. *Elinor Glyn: A Biography.* Garden City, N.Y.: Doubleday, 1955.

See also: Sexuality

God

Allison Ensor's *Mark Twain and the Bible* calls our attention to Twain's knowledge of the Bible, his rejection of its inerrancy, his lampooning of its many stories, his consistent satirizing of Christian ideas, his ridicule of the Holy Land and its people, and his identification with such biblical personalities as Adam, Joseph, and Noah. Twain's formal knowledge of God began when he was forced by his "unfaithful guardians," presumably his mother and sister Pamela, to read the Bible "unexpurgated" and in its entirety before he was age fifteen. His father, however, did not exert the same religious influence. Twain recalled his father's never attending church, never speaking of religious matters, and never sharing in the "pious joys" of his Presbyterian family, an indifference that never seemed to have affected him. Consequently, Twain's comments on the Bible reveal a familial mixture of love and irreverence. He often denounced the Bible but was so fond of its stories that he revised them, albeit in radical ways, throughout his writings. Rather than moving "further from the Bible's concepts and characters," as Stanley Brodwin ascertains, Twain "mined them more deeply" (171). His essay "Bible Teaching and Religious Practice" associates the Bible with a "drug store" supervised by quacks who keep their desperate patients "religion sick for eighteen centuries," never allowing them a well day during all that time. One year before he died, Twain expressed this ambiguous view of the Bible: it is "full of interest. It has noble poetry in it; and some clever fables; and some blood-drenched history; and some good morals; and a wealth of obscenity; and upwards of a thousand lies" (*Letters from the Earth* 14). In fact, Twain condemned all Bibles, believing that not only do they blatantly plagiarize from each other but that they exert a pernicious influence on readers.

However, when Twain married Olivia Langdon (1870), he temporarily set aside his religious skepticism and surrendered to her biblical concept of God. They prayed together and read the Bible regularly. Twain did not mind praying, for he always acknowledged a God. But he did not subscribe to the Bible's view that such a God capitulated to human solicitations or could be bargained with. In his *Autobiography* (1924) Twain recalled, not altogether humorously, that his most authentic answer to prayer came when, in response to Mrs. Horr's (his Sunday school teacher) instruction that the Bible endorses answers to prayers, he prayed for gingerbread and received it when his schoolmate Margaret Kooneman, the baker's daughter, carelessly left her gingerbread unattended. "In all my life," said Twain, "I believe I never enjoyed an answer to prayer more than I enjoyed that one." In a just as humorous episode in "Captain Stormfield's Visit to Heaven" (1907–1908), Twain solved the riddle of unanswered prayers by drawing a distinction between human time and providential time: if people accept biblical inerrancy and recognize this time difference, "they'd pray for rain a year before they want it, and then they'd be all right" (109).

But Twain soon grew to resent reading the Bible. He felt that many of its stories, especially in the Old Testament, went against his reason. In *The Innocents Abroad* (1869), for instance, Twain described himself "surprised and hurt" from his Holy Land experiences. The bunch of grapes he saw there seemed smaller than its exaggerated version pictured in his Sunday school books; the Pilgrims' hypocritical devotion to the letter of the Jewish law at the expense of higher moral laws led him to conclude that their "idea of the Savior's religion seems to me distorted"; and the close proximity of places from which "sprang the now flourishing plant of Christianity" was most astonishing to him. To Twain's "logical reasoning mind," says Albert Paine, much of the Bible "seemed absurd: a mass of fables and traditions, mere mythology." He despised theology and the superstition and ignorance connected to it, once stating that the Bible, like most books, shrinks and changes as one matures. He noted that the world, rather than the church, has always corrected the Bible, and he urged humans to revise their "ideas again about God. Most of the scientists have done it already; but most of them don't dare to say so" (Paine, *Biography* 3:1357). Twain dared. He felt that "the world's moral laws" derive from "the world's experiences." Thus, there is no need for a God to come down from heaven to point out human immoralities. Man must be cognizant of these. But to commit immoralities, whatever they are, harms man and not God, for he is beyond moral law; on the contrary, to refrain from committing immoralities does not please God. Thus Twain dismissed the necessity of a hell or a heaven (Paine, *Biography* 4:1583).

Twain's vitriolic attacks on the Bible are based on his belief that the book condones, even sponsors, all sorts of injustices. He was most offended by God's cruelty, which required the death of many innocent people and the slaughter of many ancient tribes, from the slaying of people uninvolved in Onan's sexual offense to the genocide of the Midianites. If God had a motto, said Twain, it would have read: "Let no innocent person escape" (*Letters from the Earth* 49). Twain's unorthodox view of God, then, was inextricably tied not so much to his understanding of the Bible as his disagreements with it.

One such contention was with the character of God, the subject of Twain's first dictation to his biographer, Albert Bigelow Paine. Twain portrayed God as a man "charged and overcharged with evil impulses beyond the human limit." He felt that the Old Testament presents God as perpetually "vindictive," "unjust," "ungenerous," "pitiless and vengeful." God's punishment, Twain felt, is unnecessarily severe: children are punished for the actions of their parents, populations for the action of their leaders, and even livestock for the sins of their owners. Such brutality led Twain to conclude that there has never been a single authentic instance in history of God's mercy. The law of nature is "ferocity," Twain wrote in his *Notebook*, and the law of nature is the law of God. Thus "there is nothing kindly, nothing beneficent, nothing friendly in Nature toward any creature, except by capricious fits, and starts; and that Nature's attitude toward all life is profoundly vicious, treacherous, and malignant" (255–256). Twain even called into question God's fatherly attribute, seeing him daily inflicting upon his children, beginning with the "crime of creating Adam," "a thousandth part of the pains and miseries and cruelties."

The God of the Old Testament and the Christ of the New evoked the most vicious attacks from Twain. He called the incarnation the "Jekyl and Hyde of sacred romance": "God, so atrocious in the Old Testament, so attractive in the New." One half of this divided God remained in heaven to spy into man's behavior on earth, while the other half came as the savior of a small and obscure people. "His sole solicitude was about a handful of truculent nomads," writes Twain. "He worried and fretted over them in a peculiarly and distractingly human way." On the one hand, he fondled them and on the other chastened them mercilessly. But although God "sulked," "cursed," "raged," and "grieved" according to his mood and in response to the Israelites' behavior, his efforts were fruitless; he could not rule them. "To trust the God of the Bible," Twain concluded, "is to trust an irascible, vindictive, fierce and ever fickle and changeful master" (Paine, *Biography* 2:412). What God lacks, Twain said in one of his many maxims, is "conviction—stability of

character. He ought to be a Presbyterian or a Catholic or *something*—not try to be everything" (*Notebook* 344). Indeed, as Browne notes, Twain's hatred toward this God was "absolute and all-pervading" (12).

But Twain drew a distinction between the biblical God, man's "pet invention," and the "true God." The genuine God demands no flatteries and established no "Unforgivable Sin"; he is not vengeful, creates neither a heaven nor a hell, but values kindnesses and spends his time seeking ways to make man happy. Additionally, Twain's God is one who "has uttered no promises, but whose beneficent, exact, and changeless ordering of the machinery of his colossal universe is proof that he is at least steadfast to his purposes"; his "unwritten laws" affect man equally and impartially and so testify to his justness and fairness. Around 1860 he stated his creed: "I believe in God the Almighty." But that God, Twain maintained, has never disclosed himself to man. While his goodness, justice, and mercy are evident in his works, he acts by no special providence. Twain held that the universe is governed by "strict and immutable laws," so that fatalities or fortunes occur "indiscriminately" (Paine, *Biography* 4:1583). Here Twain embraces a deistic view of God, influenced, critics have suggested, by his reading of Thomas Paine's *The Age of Reason* (1794–1796). Alexander Jones, however, has argued that Twain's deism was also influenced by his Freemasonry association. The Mason dogma, similar to that advocated by Paine, states that religious creeds are human inventions and that the Old Testament God is vindictive and malevolent; on the contrary, the Creator God is the archetypal artisan and his creation, once studied, would evoke humility in the contemplative. Twain's view of God was also helped by Hartford's liberal religious environment, a connection cogently treated in Kenneth Andrews's *Nook Farm* (1950).

Twain's philosophical determinism assumed its fullest expression in *What is Man?* (1906). This essay, which Twain called his "Bible," reflects the "permanent" depression that settled over him and Livy after the death of their daughter Susy. "No one who can think," he wrote, "can imagine the universe made by chance. It is too nicely assembled and regulated. There is, of course, a great Master Mind, but it cares nothing for our happiness or our unhappiness." Twain felt that God had "no special consideration for man's welfare or comfort," or else "he would not have created things that beset man." Unknown to God is the "human conception of pity and morality." In his 23 June 1906 dictation he stated that the Creator God made "an unchanging law" that all his creatures "should suffer wanton and unnecessary pains and miseries" all their days. Furthermore, all creatures are involved in that cycle of preying on others more hapless in an "all-comprehensive malice." Following the writing of *What is Man?* Twain's view of God moved slightly away from determinism toward absurdism, tending, as Stanley Brodwin suggests, in the direction of a more "metaphysically acceptable concept of God" (175). Thus by the time Twain arrived at the dream passage that concludes "No. 44, The Mysterious Stranger" (1969, written ca. 1904) we find this denial: "Nothing exists; all is a dream. God—man—the world . . . [T]here is no God, no universe, no human race, no earthly life, no heaven, no hell. It is all a Dream, a grotesque and foolish dream" (404–405).

The tragedies of life, however, shook Twain's belief in a deistic or absurdist God. Not only was he distraught over the death of his daughter, but years earlier when his brother Henry was injured in an 1858 explosion on board the ship *Pennsylvania*, Twain recalled praying as never before that "the great God might let this cup pass from me—that he would strike me to the earth, but spare my brother—from me—that he would pour out the fullness of his just wrath upon my wicked head but have mercy, mercy upon that unoffending boy" (*Letters* 1:40). When Henry died of his wounds a few days later, there seems little doubt that Twain held God accountable if not for the disaster then surely for not sparing his brother. Yet, as Paine suggested, Twain "never

questioned that the wider scheme of the universe was attuned to the immutable law which contemplates nothing less than absolute harmony" (Paine, *Biography* 4:1584).

Twain even admitted harmony in the creation of man. "The human being is a machine. An automatic machine," he wrote in *Letters from the Earth*. "It is composed of thousands of complex and delicate mechanisms, which perform their functions harmoniously and perfectly, in accordance with laws devised for their governance, and over which the man himself has no authority, no mastership, no control." Man also is not immune from that malice. Twain maintained that the Creator planned enemies (disasters, diseases) to beset these mechanisms. Twain also blames Christ— "the earthly half"—for selectively healing, feeding, and raising the dead when, in fact, he possessed the power to heal and feed everyone and even to raise the dead. Thus when Christ mourns over the sufferings of humans, he is in reality hypocritical.

Twain's view of Christ, however, remains equivocal. In his 1871 defense of the actor George Holland, Twain felt that "[a]ll that is great and good in our particular civilization came straight from the hand of Jesus Christ" and that the Church has neglected its responsibility to shape the lives and the conscience of its congregation. Yet he apparently rejected the incarnation, the divinity of Christ, and the atonement. In an 1878 letter to his brother Orion, Twain pointed out that neither he nor Howells believed in hell nor in the divinity of Christ, though he did confess that Christ is "a sacred Personage" (*Letters* 1:323). He held that there is "nothing connected with the atonement scheme that is rational. If Christ was God, He is in the attitude of One whose anger against Adam has grown so uncontrollable in the course of ages that nothing but a sacrifice of life can appease it, and so without noticing how illogical the act is going to be, God condemns Himself to death—commits suicide on the cross, and in this ingenious way wipes off that old score" (*Notebook* 290). Later, in one of his dictations, Twain dismissed the

Gospel account of Christ as a "myth," claiming that "[t]here have always been Saviors in every age of the world. It is all just a fairy tale like the idea of Santa Claus." And when he drew a distinction between God and Christ, he felt that God comes closer to being respected than does "his reformed self . . . guilelessly exposed in the New Testament" who invented Hell; for this Twain noted in *Letters from the Earth*, the "palm for malignity must be granted to Jesus" (45). But Christ's heavenly self, "His Old Testament Self, is sweetness and gentleness and respectability, compared with His reformed earthly self." For though fearful and repulsive, the Old Testament God was at least frank and outspoken and "makes no pretense to the possession of a moral or a virtue of any kind—except with his mouth."

Twain further reasoned that "[i]f Christ was God, then the crucifixion is without dignity. It is merely ridiculous, for to endure several hours' pain is nothing heroic in God." Furthermore, "[f]or a God to take three days on a Cross out of a life of eternal happiness and mastership of the universe is a service which the least among us would be glad to do upon the like terms" (*Notebook* 364). But Twain again contradicted himself, returning to a merciful Christ. He held that Christ exhibited the morals and virtues lacking in his "abandoned, malignant half that abides upon the throne." He portrayed Christ as "just, merciful, charitable, benevolent, forgiving, and full of sympathy for the suffering of mankind and anxious to remove them." In the very next breath, however, Twain faults Christ for creating a hell to punish those who fail to worship him as God, even those generations that preceded him and so had no knowledge of him. This indictment is also directed to God regarding the Fall and Adam's transgression, a "juvenile misdemeanor" in Twain's estimation.

The logic behind Satan's dialogue with Eve in "That Day in Eden" (*Europe and Elsewhere*, 1923) states that God's prohibition could not have been kept by the human pair who were denied the protection necessary to withstand temptation. God failed to give them that vital "Moral Sense," without which wrong does not exist. Adam and Eve are so puzzled over the words "Good," "Evil," and "Death," that when Satan defines the latter as long sleep, Eve desires it unaware of its connotation. "Words referring to things outside of her experience were a foreign language to her, and meaningless," Satan remarked. "Poor ignorant things . . . they were but children, and could not understand untried things and verbal abstractions which stood for matters outside of their little world and narrow experience." For things outside of our experience *"cannot be made comprehensible to us in words."* Twain made a similar claim in his dictation. Adam was by stature a man, but in "knowledge and experience" he was no older than two and therefore could not have known what death meant. Thus the Edenic plot was sinister and to punish the disobedient couple unjust. But while Twain was quite willing to see God the "Author and Inventor of Sin and Author and Inventor of the Vehicle and Appliances for its commission," he also felt that Providence must not be the scapegoat for human shortcomings (*Notebook* 301, 347).

Albert Bigelow Paine contends that Twain's "belief in God, the Creator, was absolute; but it was a God far removed from the Creator of his early teaching. Mark Twain's God was of colossal proportions." But Twain's God resists clear portraiture. That he is not the God of the Bible remains obvious. "It is most difficult to understand the disposition of the Bible God," he once wrote; "it is such a confusion of contradictions; of watery instabilities and iron firmnesses; of goody-goody abstract morals made out of words, and concreted hell-born ones made out of acts; of fleeting kindness repented of in permanent malignities." Paine claimed that Twain "said what he meant." However, as far as God is concerned, Twain's extensive comments are so contradictory that it proves difficult, if not impossible, to derive a comprehensive view of his God. What we are left with—and it would be a sinister joke if Twain deliberately forged it—is an incomprehensible view of God. To that extent, then, Twain is right. For, ultimately, if God could, in human terms, be figured out, then he could not be God.

Jude V. Nixon

BIBLIOGRAPHY

Andrews, Kenneth R. *Nook Farm: Mark Twain's Hartford Circle*. Cambridge, Mass.: Harvard UP, 1950.

Brodwin, Stanley. "The Theology of Mark Twain: Banished Adam and the Bible." *Mississippi Quarterly* 29.2 (1976): 167–189.

Clemens, Cyril. "Mark Twain's Religion." *Commonweal* (28 December 1934): 254–255.

Clemens, Samuel L. "Bible Teaching and Religious Practice." *The Complete Essays of Mark Twain*. By Clemens. Ed. Charles Neider. Garden City, N.Y.: Doubleday, 1963. 568–572.

———. "Captain Stormfield's Visit to Heaven." *Mark Twain's Quarrel with Heaven*. By Clemens. Ed. Ray B. Browne. New Haven, Conn.: College and UP, 1970. 39–110.

———. *The Innocents Abroad*. Hartford, Conn.: American Publishing, 1869.

———. *Letters from the Earth*. Ed. Bernard DeVoto. New York: Harper & Row, 1962.

———. *Mark Twain's Autobiography*. Ed. Albert B. Paine. 2 vols. New York: Harper, 1924.

———. *Mark Twain's Letters*. Ed. Albert B. Paine. 2 vols. New York: Harper, 1917.

———. *Mark Twain's Letters to Mary*. Ed. Lewis Leary. New York: Columbia UP, 1961.

———. *Mark Twain's Mysterious Stranger Manuscripts*. Ed. William M. Gibson. Berkeley: U of California P, 1969.

———. *Mark Twain's Notebook*. Ed. Albert B. Paine. New York: Harper, 1935.

———. "Reflections on Religion." Ed. Charles Neider. *The Hudson Review* 16.3 (1963): 329–352.

———. "That Day in Eden." *The Complete Essays of Mark Twain*. By Clemens. Ed. Charles Neider. Garden City, N.Y.: Doubleday, 1963. 668–672.

Ensor, Allison. *Mark Twain and the Bible*. Lexington: UP of Kentucky, 1969.

Hauck, Richard Boyd. *A Cheerful Nihilism: Confidence and "The Absurd" in American Humorous Fiction*. Bloomington: Indiana UP, 1971. 133–166.

Jones, Alexander E. "Mark Twain and Freemasonry." *American Literature* 26.3 (November 1954): 363–373.

Paine, Albert Bigelow. *Mark Twain: A Biography*. 4 vols. New York: Harper, 1912.

See also: Bible; "Bible Teaching and Religious Practice"; Determinism; Eve; *Extract from Captain Stormfield's Visit to Heaven*; *Letters from the Earth*; Providence; Religion; *What Is Man?*

"Golden Arm, The"
(1888)

In letters written in 1881 to Joel Chandler Harris, Mark Twain discussed a folktale he enjoyed telling on the lecture platform. Printed in an obscure source in 1888, "The Golden Arm" (also known as "Ghost Story") was included in and therefore published as a part of Twain's essay "How to Tell a Story" in *Youth's Companion* (1895) and later in *How to Tell a Story and Other Essays* (1897). This correspondence documents one source of the folklore Twain used in his writings.

"The Golden Arm" is the English form of a European folktale, first published by the Grimm brothers, in which stealing a corpse's gold arm causes the culprit to be haunted. The suspenseful repetition of the ghost's query, "Who's got my golden arm?" culminates in the narrator's jumping at an audience member while shouting, "You've got it!" Southern blacks acquired the story; Twain heard it as a boy in the 1840s from Uncle Dan'l, a slave of his uncle John Quarles (and the model for Jim of *Huckleberry Finn* [1885]), in Florida, Missouri, during Uncle Remus-like plantation storytelling sessions.

It is not surprising, then, that Twain would admire Harris's *Uncle Remus, His Songs and His Sayings* (1880) and initiate correspondence a year before their first meeting at George Washington Cable's home in New Orleans. Twain sent Harris his version of their tale, which he claimed was, among Negroes, "as common & familiar as the Tar Baby" and suggested that the creator of Uncle Remus "work up the atmosphere with your customary skill and it will 'go' in print."

Unfamiliar with the story, Harris inquired about it among his black contacts and found a variant in Atlanta, in which the stolen objects were silver coins placed on the corpse's eyelids. This he published as "A Ghost Story" in *Nights with Uncle Remus* (1881). Twain liked Harris's version so much that he alternated it with his own when performing on the lecture circuit.

Twain incorporated "The Golden Arm" into a collection of essays to illustrate the importance of the pause in oral narration; he acknowledged to Harris that the sound effects that make it such "a lovely story to tell" are "lost in print." But in their correspondence concerning the tale, these two giants of the local color movement shared their love of regional American folklore and confirmed the influence it had on their work.

John A. Burrison

BIBLIOGRAPHY

Burrison, John A. *"The Golden Arm": The Folk Tale and Its Literary Use by Mark Twain and Joel C. Harris.* Atlanta: Georgia State University, Arts and Science Research Papers, No. 19, 1968.

Clemens, Samuel L. *How to Tell a Story and Other Essays.* New York: Harper, 1897.

English, Thomas H., ed. *Mark Twain to Uncle Remus, 1881–1885.* Atlanta: Emory U. Publications, Sources and Reprints, Series 7, No. 3, 1953.

See also: Dan'l, Uncle; Folklore; Harris, Joel Chandler

Golden Era

Founded in San Francisco in 1852 by Rollin Daggett and J. Macdonough Foard, but published from 1860 to 1867 by James Brooks and Joseph E. Lawrence, the *Golden Era* was one of the first West Coast literary journals deliberately to attempt to foster a distinctive literature of the West. Among the writers who contributed to it were Bret Harte, Dan De Quille, Artemus Ward, Charles Warren Stoddard, Adah Isaacs Menken, Ada Claire, and Mark Twain.

Twain had been working for the *Territorial Enterprise* in Virginia City for about a year when he began, in September 1863, to send "literary" articles to the *Golden Era*. He continued to contribute for about a year. Some *Golden Era* pieces were written expressly for it; others were reprinted from the *Enterprise*. Twain quickly became a favorite writer for the journal and received a high compliment in November 1863 when another—and prestigious—*Era* writer, Fitzhugh Ludlow, singled him out for praise and called him the "Washoe Giant." The compliment caught the eye of Artemus Ward, who arrived in Virginia City several weeks later, and Ward reinforced it with his own encouragement.

The *Golden Era* accelerated Twain's transition from journalism to literature. He temporarily discontinued his contributions to it in 1864, when he switched to the *Californian*, a more "high-toned" literary journal, but he returned to it in 1865 and 1866, and his publications in it furthered his career.

Lawrence I. Berkove

BIBLIOGRAPHY

Benson, Ivan. *Mark Twain's Western Years.* Stanford, Calif.: Stanford UP, 1938.

Branch, Edgar M. Introduction. *The Works of Mark Twain: Early Tales & Sketches, Volume 1 (1851–1864).* By Clemens. Ed. Edgar M. Branch and Robert H. Hirst. Berkeley: U of California P, 1979. 1–57.

———. *The Literary Apprenticeship of Mark Twain.* Urbana: U of Illinois P, 1950.

Fatout, Paul. *Mark Twain in Virginia City.* Bloomington: Indiana UP, 1964.

Humphreys, Glenn E. "The *Golden Era*." *American Literary Magazines: The Eighteenth and Nineteenth Centuries.* Ed. Edward E. Chielens. Westport, Conn.: Greenwood, 1986.

See also: San Francisco, California; Virginia City *Territorial Enterprise*

Goldsmith, Oliver
(1728–1774)

Oliver Goldsmith was a neoclassical English author whose works were very popular in Twain's America and were both widely quoted and frequently imitated. Although Goldsmith was capable of sharp satire, as in his poem "The Deserted Village" (1770), which attacked the laws that depopulated English villages in order to expand grazing land, he was best known as a more gentle satirist. Of especial interest to Twain were Goldsmith's "Letters from a Citizen of the World" (1760–1762). These essays purported to be letters from Lien Chi Altangi, a Chinese traveler, describing England to his countrymen back home. Utilizing the Chinese traveler as an innocent and naive observer, Goldsmith pointed up the great disparity between appearance and reality in his society. Twain imitated Goldsmith with his own series, "Goldsmith's Friend Abroad Again" (1870–1871).

Lawrence I. Berkove

BIBLIOGRAPHY

Goldsmith, Oliver. *Collected Works of Oliver Goldsmith*. Vol. 2. Ed. Arthur Friedman. Oxford: Clarendon P, 1966.

Gribben, Alan. *Mark Twain's Library: A Reconstruction*. 2 vols. Boston: G.K. Hall, 1980.

See also: "Goldsmith's Friend Abroad Again"

"Goldsmith's Friend Abroad Again"
(1870–1871)

The West's unjust treatment of Chinese angered Mark Twain, and he attacked it in print as early as 1863. While a reporter in San Francisco in 1865–1866, he witnessed outrages committed against Chinese and assailed them with some bitterness. Twain's most sustained attack on the problem occurred, however, while he lived in Buffalo, New York.

Imitating Oliver Goldsmith's famous essay series, "Letters from a Citizen of the World"

(1760–1761), Twain wrote a short series of his own and published it in three issues of the *Galaxy*: October and November 1870 and January 1871. Using the fictitious Ah Song Hi, a naively idealistic Chinese Americaphile, as a narrator, Twain depicted him as deceived when he was recruited to become a coolie, when he was transported to San Francisco, and when he fell into the clutches of the law. The short series is shockingly realistic in its portrayal of the villainy of California's courts, the brutality of its jails, and the oppression of the underclasses in them.

Lawrence I. Berkove

BIBLIOGRAPHY

Bellamy, Gladys Carmen. *Mark Twain as a Literary Artist*. Norman: U of Oklahoma P, 1950.

Foner, Philip S. *Mark Twain: Social Critic*. New York: International Publishers, 1958.

Gribben, Alan. *Mark Twain's Library: A Reconstruction*. 2 vols. Boston: G.K. Hall, 1980.

See also: Goldsmith, Oliver; Racial Attitudes

Goodman, Joseph Thompson
(1838–1917)

Joseph Goodman was the guiding genius behind the Virginia City *Territorial Enterprise*, the newspaper which gave Mark Twain his start. A highly talented individual himself, Goodman gathered together the remarkable men who comprised the staff of the *Enterprise*. In addition to being an excellent editor, Goodman was also a sage counselor and remained Twain's lifelong and influential friend.

Goodman thrived on challenge. He and Denis McCarthy bought the *Enterprise* in 1861, converted it from a moribund weekly into a successful daily, and began hiring some of the best journalistic talent on the West Coast. Goodman sold the *Enterprise* in 1874; worked for several California periodicals; founded the ambitious but short-lived literary weekly, the *San Franciscan*, in 1884; and then took up the study of Mayan hieroglyphics.

Goodman might well have been a model

whom Twain attempted to emulate, not wisely but too well. Goodman took intrepid stands and once fought a duel, but he spared his opponent's life and converted him into a friend. He gave his writers free rein, provided only that they took personal responsibility for what they wrote. It is worth noting that Twain became unpopular on the Comstock for his sharp criticism and that his departure from Nevada took place as a consequence of his having challenged an opponent to a duel while he was serving as temporary editor of the *Enterprise* in Goodman's absence.

Although slightly older than Goodman, Twain always looked up to him, kept in touch with him, and regarded him with respect. For all his venturesome personality, Goodman was self-possessed, stable, and had good judgment. He steadied Twain and gave him good practical advice. His most important services to Twain, however, took place at the beginning of Twain's literary career: his original recognition of Twain's ability, his sober and steadfast encouragement of the volatile young writer, and his establishing on the *Enterprise* a creative but principled style that shaped Twain for the rest of his life.

Lawrence I. Berkove

BIBLIOGRAPHY

Adams, Eva B. "Joseph T. Goodman: The Man Who Made Mark Twain." Master's thesis, Columbia U, 1936.

Goodman, Joseph. *Heroes, Badmen, and Honest Miners: Joe Goodman's Tales of the Comstock Lode.* Ed. Phillip I. Earl. Reno, Nev.: Great Basin P, 1977.

See also: Nevada; Virginia City *Territorial Enterprise*

Goodwin, Charles Carroll
(1832–1917)

C.C. "Judge" Goodwin was a highly talented and respected editorial writer and sometime editor of the Virginia City *Territorial Enterprise* from the early 1860s until 1880. He left Virginia City for Salt Lake City, where he be-

came owner and editor of the Salt Lake City *Tribune.*

Goodwin was liked for being courteous and gentle although, like the other *Enterprise* writers, he took strong editorial stands on principle and was fearless and tenacious in their behalf. His novel, *The Comstock Club* (1891), is a historically useful, although somewhat romanticized, reflection of many Comstock issues, attitudes, and ideals.

His major contribution to Twain studies is his memoirs, principally *As I Remember Them* (1913), an account of Comstock personalities and events that includes biographical and anecdotal information on Twain and his relationship with his colleagues.

Lawrence I. Berkove

BIBLIOGRAPHY

Angel, Myron. *History of Nevada.* Oakland, Calif.: Thompson and West, 1881. Rpt. Berkeley, Calif.: Howell-North, 1958.

Goodwin, Charles C. *As I Remember Them.* Salt Lake City: Salt Lake Commercial Club, 1913.

Weisenburger, Francis Phelps. *Idol of the West: The Fabulous Career of Rollin Mallory Daggett.* Syracuse, N.Y.: Syracuse UP, 1965.

See also: Nevada; Virginia City *Territorial Enterprise*

Gorky, Maxim
(1868–1936)

Born Aleksei Maksimovich, Maxim Gorky is the writer of the Russian Revolution credited with founding the socialist realism movement in literature.

In April 1906 Gorky visited New York City in an attempt to raise funds for his fellow revolutionaries. Clemens, ever sympathetic to those who opposed royalty, supported Gorky by providing an introduction for the Russian writer one night at a club dinner and by writing a letter on Gorky's behalf that was read to an audience of 3,000 at the Grand Central Palace.

Clemens withdrew his support for Gorky, however, when the press revealed that Gorky was not married to the woman with whom he was living, the Russian actress Maria Andreyeva. Several hotels in New York evicted the couple, and Gorky's fund-raising efforts were foreshortened by the attention the scandal received in newspapers nationwide.

Clemens did not necessarily condemn Gorky's behavior, but he understood that the American public would not contribute money to anyone who disregarded American morality. Clemens wrote of the incident: "Laws can be evaded and punishment escaped, but an openly transgressed custom brings sure punishment" (Paine 4:1285).

Roberta Seelinger Trites

BIBLIOGRAPHY

Paine, Albert Bigelow. *Mark Twain: A Biography*. 4 vols. New York: Harper, 1912.

Gothic

Since the mid-eighteenth century the term "gothic" has been used to describe a subgenre of narrative popular in Europe, in England, and in America. On any given occasion this subgenre is characterized by some or all of the following qualities: a metaphysics of horror with God absent or demonic in an alternative universe of death that inverts or denies any form of rational or moral order; a physical landscape of nightmare, representing the actualization in reality of this alternative world; and, finally, a central experience of catastrophe, some sort of "fall" or otherwise crucial experience that changes life categorically and makes this world of horror suddenly palpable. The gothic protagonist is often a "witness," a visionary, a mad prophet of sorts. While Mark Twain writes very little that can be labeled in its entirety as gothic fiction, he nevertheless incorporates many gothic elements piecemeal into his work and, particularly later in life, responds fully to the thematic implications of these elements.

Twain, first of all, makes a few attempts literally to write a ghost story, attempts un-

derstandable enough both in light of nineteenth-century popular conventions and (more significantly) the context of his roots in southern folk culture. "A Ghost Story" (1870) is undoubtedly parodic, a fraudulent story about a fraudulent figure; as *The Innocents Abroad* (1869) makes clear, Twain had a fine ear for the sentimental and melodramatic absurdities of Victorian style. "A Ghost Story" involves all the conventional paraphernalia: the lonely room in a house, huge, isolated, and unoccupied until the narrator moves in; the shrieking winds outside, the mysterious groans and footfalls within; the narrator's attempt to rationalize what is happening as "simply a hideous dream." But it is, in fact, the spirit of the Cardiff Giant (P.T. Barnum's archaeological fraud) who appears, breaking the narrator's chairs when he tries to sit down and failing to remember in which museum his "real" fraudulent body has been deposited.

Closer to Twain's childhood background but still treated with comic distancing are his two other conventional ghost stories, "The Golden Arm" and the tale of Dick Allbright's involvement with the haunted barrel floating on the Mississippi, related in chapter 3 of *Life on the Mississippi* (1883). In both cases the dark theme of death's intrusion into life is muted in favor of qualities of sheer storytelling. "The Golden Arm," indeed, was incorporated into Twain's instructional essay, "How to Tell a Story" (1895). Alan Gribben's essay "'When Other Amusements Fail': Mark Twain and the Occult," in *The Haunted Dusk* (1983), remains the best survey of this aspect of his work.

More central to the fundamental implications of gothic narrative are episodes of horror and the macabre scattered throughout Twain's work. In *Sam Clemens of Hannibal*, for example, Dixon Wecter notes the recurrence of the experience of death by fire and relates it to the episode from Twain's childhood in which a drunken tramp sets his bed afire in a jail cell, is trapped there, and burns to death in horrible agony. His matches had been supplied as a friendly gesture by young Sam Clemens. Twain gives his own version of this story in chapter 56 of *Life on the Mississippi*, in the first volume of *Mark Twain's Autobiography* (1924), and in the precarious history of the almost doomed Muff Potter in *Tom Sawyer* (1876). This doom is, in effect, ratified in the figure of Tom's antagonist, Injun Joe, trapped in a sealed cave and finally starving to death, a prototypical experience of gothic narrative most commonly associated with the work of Edgar Allan Poe. Gribben notes that burial alive is dealt with passingly in "Villagers of 1840–3" (1897) and in a tale of revenge recorded in chapter 31 of *Life on the Mississippi*.

From a larger perspective, *Tom Sawyer* can stand as representative of Twain's serious use of gothic during the early and middle years of his work. The horrors of the book—labyrinthine cave entrapment, brutal murders in ghoulish places, "devilish" antagonists—are contained in their implications by careful placement within a larger context. A relatively benign and still coherent day world mutes these "nights of horror" (as Twain puts it in a chapter heading), a world in which conventional and traditional sources of order (social, religious, even folkloric) are still intact, if usually absurdly sentimental and often substantially ineffective. Even in *Adventures of Huckleberry Finn* (1885) Twain integrates the vision of a totally murderous world with moments of idyllic peace, the experience of love, hints of freedom, and escape.

Other gothic motifs emerge in the literature of this period and will coalesce and come to full expression in the substantial body of materials, often fragmentary, usually unfinished and unpublished, edited by John Tuckey as *The Devil's Race-Track: Mark Twain's Great Dark Writings* (1980). Twain's sense of brutal, arbitrary, categorical determinism, for example, expresses itself in his fascination with twins: riches and power versus poverty and abject victimization in *The Prince and the Pauper* (1882); black slavery versus white supremacy in *The Tragedy of Pudd'nhead Wilson* (1894). His early experience in a slaveholding society and the Calvinist background of his family undoubtedly both contributed to his growing

sense of a terrible "fall" or fated prior "election" as they have so often influenced other writers in the "American Gothic" tradition. Of more immediate relevance to Twain's steadily darkening mood, critics have often cited his bankruptcy (1894) and the death of his daughter Susy in 1896. *A Connecticut Yankee in King Arthur's Court* (1889) sums up the implications for gothic narrative of this period: the overwhelming degradations of a chattel culture swamp all attempts at rational, orderly change; and the final military conflict generates a wasteland of corpses that reduces the conventional world to mere nostalgic dream.

This landscape of death is central to gothic narrative and powerfully informs much of Twain's final work. Gothic is a literature of absence; life and death alike are robbed of any transcendental or redemptive significance. To be sure, the manuscripts collected in *The Devil's Race-Track* are by and large incomplete. Perhaps Twain was finally daunted by the stylistic demands of gothic narrative insofar as it constitutes a sharp departure from realistic fiction. Or perhaps he refused fully to acknowledge the thematic implications of his own work. Nevertheless, these writings make up an important body of gothic work. Everywhere sudden, appalling catastrophe transports the "happy family" into some alternate landscape characterized by entrapment, emptiness, loss of all meaning and any significant structuring of time and history, a nightmare world of "too many horribles." In "The Enchanted Sea-Wilderness," for example, the narrator is sucked by a maelstrom of wind and water (the "Devil's Race-Track" itself) into a still and silent sea: "the silence of death was everywhere." This is literature reminiscent of such major gothic as Poe's *Narrative of Arthur Gordon Pym* (1838) and communicating the same all-encompasing psychological and metaphysical despair.

In short, Twain's use of gothic explores, in one way or another, the full range of its possibilities.

Roger Salomon

BIBLIOGRAPHY

Clareson, Thomas D. "Mark Twain." *Supernatural Fiction Writers: Fantasy and Horror.* Vol. 2. Ed. Everett Franklin Bleiler. New York: Scribner, 1985. 761–768.

Clemens, Samuel L. *The Devil's Race-Track: Mark Twain's Great Dark Writings.* Ed. John S. Tuckey. Berkeley: U of California P, 1980.

Frank, Frederick S. *Through the Pale Door: A Guide to and through the American Gothic.* Westport, Conn.: Greenwood P, 1990.

Gribben, Alan. "'When Other Amusements Fail': Mark Twain and the Occult." *The Haunted Dusk: American Supernatural Fiction, 1820–1920.* Ed. Howard Kerr, John W. Crowley, and Charles L. Crow. Athens: U of Georgia P, 1983, 171–189.

Wecter, Dixon. *Sam Clemens of Hannibal.* Boston: Houghton Mifflin, 1952.

See also: Death; Dreams; Occult

Government

To propose that Mark Twain was ambivalent toward governments in general and hostile to governments in particular would be stating the case rather too mildly. At various stages of his life he expressed eloquently the tenets of monarchists and anti-monarchists, laissez-faire capitalists and socialists, southern Whigs, New England Republicans, and Mugwump supporters of the Democratic ticket. With friends and enemies in all camps, Mark Twain never wanted for someone to exasperate.

His ambivalence manifested itself early. The Civil War bitterly divided the country for generations, but young Sam Clemens managed to position himself on all sides of the issue. In the autobiographical "Private History of a Campaign That Failed" (1885), Twain recounts being "strong for the Union" one week and in the Confederate Army the next. A few weeks later he deserted both causes for the more primitive politics of the western territories, where, as a journalist in Nevada and California, he was indifferent to the "war news." "If they [the United and Confederate states] will leave us alone," he wrote, "we can get rich." As his newspaper work brought him into contact with the law-making apparatus, he managed to develop a hearty contempt for politicians; and the spectacle of government, whether by the people or otherwise, made up the raw material of his most biting satire. An early story, "Cannibalism in the Cars" (1868), features various senators and congressmen stranded in a snowstorm employing tricks of parliamentary procedure to eat one another. In *Following the Equator* (1897), he called congress "the only distinctly native American criminal class." *The Gilded Age* (1873), his first extended work of fiction, excoriated Washington as a place where senators "with high moral tone" could be bought for $3,000 and an average representative of the people sold for $500.

Twain's growing contempt for government also reached beyond his native shores. *The Prince and the Pauper* (1882) was one of several literary works in which he exposed the cruelty and capriciousness of British royalty. He did not target England alone, however; to Twain all monarchies were equally repugnant, and he insulted the crowned heads of Europe indiscriminately with such public utterances as, "There are no common people except in the highest spheres of society" and "There was never a throne which did not represent a crime."

Though Twain would on occasion praise nationalism, he bitterly opposed what he considered the imperialism of the U.S. and British governments. Referring to the Boer and Spanish-American wars, he remarked to young Winston Churchill in 1900 that the two nations were now "kin in sin." He was also inclined to extend this "sin kin" to practically every government in Europe—France, for instance, who "gave us the reign of terror and sent Dreyfus to a living hell"; and Spain, who "sent half of the harmless West Indians into slavery and the rest to the grave."

Twain's low estimation of humanity in general led to a prediction that the United States would eventually become a monarchy. He felt that this development would be a tragedy; but, paradoxically, he also held the view that democracy was a dangerous mistake. He scorned the concept of one-man, one-vote and advocated (quite vehemently at times) Disraeli's notion of meritocracy, wherein men of demonstrated intelligence, ability, and property would be granted plural votes. In 1875 he proposed this solution in "The Curious Republic of Gondour," an unsigned article in the *Atlantic*, and he was known to belabor his house guests with heated invective against universal suffrage. During one period of his life he would go so far as to announce that he hated "all shades and forms of republican government."

On numerous occasions, usually involving his interest in and championing of an underdog cause, Twain would seem to reverse his anti-populist sentiments. However, these newly embraced "democratic" impulses were usually undermined by his growing sense of misanthropy. In the throes of that affliction, Twain could be as denigrating to the "common man" as to the aristocracy. In *Gilded Age* and *Life on the Mississippi* (1883) he described settlers as vacuous, tobacco-chewing "cattle," and in the former book he described the urban proletariat as people with "low foreheads and heavy faces . . . some had a look of animal cunning, while the most were only stupid."

A similar attitude toward "commoners" can also be seen in *Huckleberry Finn* (1885) and *Connecticut Yankee* (1889), wherein the unsophisticated citizen is as often unsympathetic or even downright mean as otherwise. In *Connecticut Yankee* Twain had Hank Morgan declare that "where every man in a State has a vote, brutal laws are impossible" and there was "plenty good enough material for a republic in the most degraded people that ever existed." But like his author, Hank became disillusioned with the "human muck." Using his elite youth corps, the Connecticut Yankee ended his noble experiment of bringing democracy to medieval England by destroying all but a few of those he had freed from the "monarchist shams" that Twain professed to despise. Overall, *Yankee* was such an ambivalent work that even Albert Bigelow Paine,

Twain's friend and friendly biographer, was critical of its strange combination of pro-and anti-democratic postulations.

William Dean Howells, a closer friend and genteel socialist, hoped to win Twain as noted author to the Cause, and from time to time he chafed Clemens for his lack of staunchness in supporting the political faction then considered synonymous with helping the downtrodden. But though he often shared the charitable impulses of the socialists, Twain usually repudiated socialism, likening Howells's vision that "the government of the future will support and employ every man" to the corrupt welfare-state of Rome in its decline.

Twain also dismissed communism, calling it "idiocy," but when communists fit the bill as underdogs, he could declaim like a bomb-throwing Bolshevik. At various times he advocated the violent overthrow of the Russian government, not only endorsing revolutionists like Gorky, but going so far as to say, publically, that "if such a government [as Russia] cannot be overthrown otherwise than by dynamite, then thank God for dynamite!"

Such strong social criticism, coupled with Twain's antipathy toward organized religion and his coining of "progressive" phrases like "Gilded Age" and "New Deal," has convinced some critics that Twain was a seminal leftist, while others fear that his endorsement of Republican candidates and his creeds against "the people" place him solidly in the right wing. The truth may be that Twain was neither "conservative" nor "liberal" in the accepted senses of the terms, but rather a rare example of that anomaly in political gatherings, the idealist. Because his idealism was ever buffeted by the machinations of human beings whose natures he understood but could not bring himself to accept, he was naturally prone to frustration. Twain spent his life flailing at all that was "just not fair" in the world, but he inevitably disappointed the zealots he seemed to echo, for he dismissed causes as easily as he took them up. Because he was a famous author, his pronouncements on government received wide currency, but he was as liable to self-effacement as he was to vehement exhortation. "My instincts and interests are merely literary," he disclaimed when pursued by the press gangs of various causes. "They rise no higher, and I scatter from one interest to another, lingering nowhere. I am not a bee, I am a lightning bug."

Twain's "lightning" across the firmament of government might give pause to the literati who wish that poets really did legislate the world, but Twain was always true to his own creed of common decency. He has been called the "Lincoln of our literature," and like Lincoln he believed that truth and justice always outweighed expediency. For all his jaded views on human nature and penchant for the tall story, Twain hated half-truths and had no patience with lies. If his ambivalence toward government and politics seems disconcerting, it may be because he was a "Mugwump" to the bone: too much of an honest man and idealist to maintain for long any political stance that demanded unquestioning allegiance.

Richard Hill

BIBLIOGRAPHY

Clemens, Samuel L. *The Complete Short Stories of Mark Twain*. Ed. Charles Neider. Garden City, N.Y.: Hanover House, 1957.

————. *A Connecticut Yankee in King Arthur's Court*. Ed. Bernard Stein. Berkeley: U of California P, 1979.

————. *Mark Twain: Selected Writings of an American Skeptic*. Ed. Victor Doyno. Buffalo, N.Y.: Prometheus, 1983.

————. *Mark Twain and the Government*. Comp. Svend Petersen. Caldwell, Idaho: Caxton, 1960.

————. *Mark Twain at Your Fingertips*. Ed. Caroline Harnsberger. New York: Beechhurst P, 1948.

————. *Mark Twain's Autobiography*. Ed. Albert B. Paine. 2 vols. New York: Harper, 1924.

————. *The Prince and the Pauper*. Ed. Victor Fischer and Lin Salamo. Berkeley: U of California P, 1979.

Clemens, Samuel L., and Charles Dudley Warner. *The Gilded Age*. Hartford, Conn.: American Publishing, 1873.

Foner, Philip. *Mark Twain: Social Critic*. New York: International Publishers, 1958.

Kaplan, Justin. *Mr. Clemens and Mark Twain*. New York: Simon & Schuster, 1966.

Paine, Albert Bigelow. *Mark Twain: A Biography*. 3 vols. New York: Harper, 1912.

Wagenknecht, Edward. *Mark Twain: The Man and His Work*. Rev. ed. Norman: U of Oklahoma P, 1967.

Wilson, James D. *A Reader's Guide to the Short Stories of Mark Twain*. Boston: G.K. Hall, 1987.

See also: Philosophy; Politics

Grangerfords, The

The proud family of planter aristocracy that takes in Huckleberry Finn after the destruction of his raft in *Adventures of Huckleberry Finn* (1885) comprises the patriarch, Colonel Saul, "about sixty," his wife Rachel, six sons, and three daughters—a clan whose feud with the neighboring Shepherdsons provides the occasion for Twain's attack on senseless codes of southern honor and for satire on sentimental literature and false art. Huck's gratitude for the hospitality of this "mighty nice family," and his awed admiration for the handsome, mannerly colonel, "a gentleman all over," expresses the reverse side of Twain's hostility toward the South: his sympathy with the best elements of the plantation culture. The colonel, his eldest surviving son, Bob, his second son, Tom, both "thirty or more" and "all of them fine and handsome," and the youngest son, Buck, "about as old as me" says Huck ("thirteen or fourteen,") are killed in the final paroxysm of the Shepherdson-Grangerford feud that has already claimed the lives of three other unnamed Grangerford sons. The women remain: Rachel, the elder daughter Charlotte, twenty-five and beautiful, and Sophia, twenty, "gentle and sweet like a dove," whom Huck helps to elope with Harney Shepherdson, providing this bitter episode with a promise of a happy ending.

The Grangerford episode also provided Twain with the occasion for one of his free-swinging attacks on sentimentalism. The Grangerford plantation house, much like the "House Beautiful" in *Life on the Mississippi* (1883), is a compilation of middle-class bad taste: sentimental pictures, a showpiece clock that does not tell time, fake fruit in a fake basket, and crayon sketches devoted to suffering and death, sketches whose style impresses Huck but whose subjects give him the "fantods." The art is the work of the remarkable Emmeline Grangerford, the deceased daughter, whose poetry matched her sketches and who pined away before the age of fourteen after failing to find a rhyme for "Whistler." Before her demise, she had completed her masterwork, the "Ode to Stephen Dowling Bots, Dec'd," providing an example of Twain's complex humor: the "pure" humor typical of the Southwest that gives pleasure in relieving fear of danger and death and the satire that ridicules human folly, in this case the sentimentalism of nineteenth-century popular poetry.

Everett Carter

BIBLIOGRAPHY

Clemens, Samuel L. *Adventures of Huckleberry Finn.* Ed. Walter Blair and Victor Fischer. Berkeley: U of California P, 1985.

———. *Life on the Mississippi.* Boston: James R. Osgood, 1883.

———. *Mark Twain's Hannibal, Huck & Tom.* Ed. Walter Blair. Berkeley: U of California P, 1969.

Pettit, Arthur G. *Mark Twain and the South.* Lexington: UP of Kentucky, 1974.

See also: Adventures of Huckleberry Finn; Finn, Huckleberry; Sentimentality; South

Grant, Ulysses Simpson
(1822–1885)

As lieutenant-general of the Army of the Potomac (1863–1866), Ulysses S. Grant commanded the Union forces to victory over the Confederacy in the Civil War and thereafter served for two terms as the eighteenth President of the United States (1869–1877). Though his administration was riddled with corruption and scandal, Grant was nonetheless deemed to be scrupulously honest—perhaps to the point of naiveté—a dubious virtue

that served him better as a military leader than either as president or, later, as a private businessman. On retiring from the presidency, Grant toured the world and was received with esteem and honor abroad and at home; nevertheless, lacking business acumen, and manipulated by a dishonest partner, Grant was nearly penniless in the mid-1800s. To ensure a livelihood for his family, Grant turned to writing his *Memoirs* (2 vols., 1885–1886), which were subsequently published by Mark Twain's publishing house. This last task, finished on his deathbed, culminated a legendary career and a long friendship with Twain.

Twain claimed often to have suggested to Grant as early as 1881 that he write his memoirs. Grant, in financial straits by 1884, and suffering early signs of throat cancer, made an initial agreement with the Century Company to publish the book. Twain intervened and persuaded Grant that he might demand a more lucrative contract elsewhere. Grant subsequently agreed to publish with Twain's own firm, Charles L. Webster and Company, on more favorable terms. The book was enormously successful, and Twain was able to provide Grant's widow with the single largest royalty check up to that time in the amount of $200,000. Twain, for his own part, deemed Grant's *Memoirs* to be "a great, and in its peculiar department, unique and inapproachable literary masterpiece" (*Speeches* 57).

Twain alternately described Grant himself as "an iron man," as "eternal," as "*man*—all over—rounded and complete." Nevertheless, despite his great admiration, Twain also took pleasure in competing with Grant and "defeating" him in personal ways. One of Twain's early conquests of Grant occurred in Chicago in 1879 during a reunion of Civil War heroes. Twain later described with relish how his speech alone broke the general from his solemnity, how he alone "licked" Grant. However, their "competition"—wholly imagined by Twain in most regards—found its most fanciful exposition in Twain's essay "The Private History of a Campaign That Failed" (1885). An embellished reconstruction of

Twain's short service with the Confederate army in 1861, Twain describes the hasty conclusion of his military career when word that a Union colonel named U.S. Grant approached their Missouri camp. Initially entitled "My Campaign Against Grant," Twain intimates that Grant's initial victory, in driving Twain westward and into his literary career, thereby set up the circumstances that would later permit Twain to save Grant late in life as his friend and publisher. Thus was Twain ironically to become savior of his early conqueror.

Patrick Deneen

BIBLIOGRAPHY

Catton, Bruce. *U.S. Grant and the American Military Tradition.* New York: Grosset and Dunlap, 1954.

Clemens, Samuel L. *The Autobiography of Mark Twain.* Ed. Albert B. Paine. 2 vols. New York: Harper, 1924.

———. *Mark Twain's Speeches.* Ed. Albert B. Paine. New York: Harper, 1923.

———. "The Private History of a Campaign That Failed." *A Pen Warmed-Up in Hell: Mark Twain in Protest.* By Clemens. Ed. Frederick Anderson. New York: Harper & Row, 1972. 6–27.

Gerber, John. "Mark Twain's Private Campaign." *Civil War History* 1 (1955): 37–60.

Grant, Ulysses S. *Personal Memoirs of U.S. Grant.* 2 vols. New York: Charles L. Webster, 1885–1886.

Mattson, J. Stanley. "Mark Twain on War and Peace: The Missouri Rebel and 'The Campaign That Failed.'" *American Quarterly* 20 (1968): 783–794.

See also: Civil War; *Personal Memoirs of U.S. Grant*; Politics; Webster and Company, Charles L.

"Great Dark, The"

(1962)

Bernard DeVoto supplied the title for this long fragment, written in the fall of 1898, concerning the Edwards family's "voyage to disaster." Although an excerpt from "The Great Dark" appeared in DeVoto's *Mark Twain at Work* (1942), the complete text of the fragment was not published until 1962 (in *Letters From the Earth* 185–227). The now standard authorita-

tive text is in John Tuckey's edition of *Mark Twain's "Which Was the Dream?" and Other Symbolic Writings of the Later Years* (1967).

"The Great Dark" is one of a complex of fragments Mark Twain began and abandoned during the period 1896–1905, all evolving from a germinal idea the author envisioned as early as 1891: a tale of a prosperous, happily married family man on the verge of a spectacular financial success who experiences sudden reversals and a series of personal and family disasters—only to awaken from his nightmarish dream to discover his life unchanged. By the time this idea began to take shape in the assorted manuscripts, Clemens in his own life had experienced a series of devastating setbacks, most notably the failures of the Paige typesetting machine and Webster Publishing Company that led to his financial collapse in 1894 and the death in Hartford of his favorite daughter Susy in 1896—while Clemens was in England at the conclusion of a taxing around-the-world lecture tour undertaken to struggle clear of debt. Hence it is not surprising that he found the original idea compelling and brought to it many autobiographical elements. It is also not surprising that as the idea evolved it grew increasingly dark in its exploration of the relationship between dream and reality. In two of these related fragments, "Which Was the Dream?" (written May–August 1897) and "Which Was It?" (written 1899–1903), it is the burning of the family home that precipitates the series of disasters. In "The Enchanted Sea-Wilderness" (written spring 1897) Mark Twain turns to the motif of the sea voyage that is the crux of "The Great Dark."

Early scholarly approaches to "The Great Dark" emphasized the obvious autobiographical relevance of the fiction to the author's life. The fictional sea voyage represents the unpredictable confrontations with sea monsters and the consequent terrors of a father powerless to protect his family from disaster. The story uses a double introductory narrative frame, with a short statement by Mrs. Edwards leading to Mr. Edwards's long narrative. The foolish father's self-confidence leads him to permit his family to embark on a sea voyage in a microscopic world, in a drop of water that has been stimulated by a drop of Scotch whiskey. Under the microscope there are large dark areas and a smaller area of intense white light; all around are immense germlike sea monsters that threaten and attack the boat.

The story develops its themes through a series of dualistic contrasts: ship and home; normal size and the microscopic; black and white; frequent shadows, mists, gloom, and infrequent clear vision; familial love and sheer terror before the uncontrollable; apparent wakefulness and dream vision. In a letter about the story Clemens confided to William Dean Howells that he was designing "a tragedy trap"; that is, he was deliberately manipulating the reader's expectations with early comedy, such as the parodies of sea fiction in its reliance on nautical terms or the humor of the invisible Superintendent of Dreams drinking a sailor's coffee. In this comically contrasting context, the philosophical exploration of the uncertainty of relationships between dream or illusion and the supposedly real is engaging but safely abstract. The fragment's "tragedy trap" springs on the unsuspecting reader, however, when the sea monsters threaten the boat and the children are lost. Recent aesthetic and religious approaches to the story add resonances to the biographical readings of a story whose basic imaginative metaphor strikes disturbingly close to home. In the alien, even malevolent, cosmos Mark Twain envisions in his later years, perhaps our only escape is in the deus ex machina device of the dream; but, as the title of another fragment in the series asks, "Which Was the Dream?"

Victor Doyno

BIBLIOGRAPHY

Clemens, Samuel L. "The Great Dark." *Mark Twain's "Which Was the Dream?" and Other Symbolic Writings of the Later Years.* By Clemens. Ed. John S. Tuckey. Berkeley: U of California P, 1967. 102–150.

Davis, John H. "The Dream as Reality: Structure and Meaning in Mark Twain's 'The Great Dark.'" *Mississippi Quarterly* 35.4 (1982): 407–426.

Dennis, Larry. "Mark Twain and the Dark Angel." *Midwest Quarterly* 8 (1967): 181–197.

DeVoto, Bernard. Editor's Notes. *Letters from the Earth.* By Clemens. Ed. DeVoto. New York: Harper & Row, 1962. 231–239.

Jones, Daryl E. "The *Hornet* Disaster: Twain's Adaptation in 'The Great Dark.'" *American Literary Realism* 9 (1976): 243–247.

———. "Mark Twain's Symbols of Despair: A Relevant Letter." *American Literary Realism* 15.2 (1982): 266–268.

Macnaughton, William R. *Mark Twain's Last Years as a Writer.* Columbia: U of Missouri P, 1979.

Welsh, Kathleen. "Rude Awakenings and Swift Recoveries: The Problem of Reality in Mark Twain's 'The Great Dark' and 'Three Thousand Years Among the Microbes.'" *American Literary Realism* 21.1 (Fall 1988): 19–28.

Wilson, James C. "'The Great Dark': Invisible Spheres, Formed in Fright." *Midwest Quarterly* 23.2 (Winter 1982): 229–243.

See also: Dreams; "Which Was the Dream?"

"Great Prize Fight, The"
(1863)

Originally published in the *Golden Era* on 11 October 1863, "The Great Prize Fight" recounts an imaginary boxing match for a purse of $100,000 between Governor Leland Stanford and Governor-elect F.F. Low of California. After training six weeks for the bout, the fighters are represented in their corner by William Stewart, a prominent lawyer from the Washoe district, and Judge Stephen J. Field of the supreme court. Not only does the sketch burlesque the rough-and-tumble of state politics; it also parodies the style of contemporary sports writing. In the early rounds Low "gave Stanford a plaster in the eye" and "busted him in the snoot," while Stanford "replied with an earthquake on Low's bread-basket" and "mashed him in the ear." The principals are gradually dismantled and the ring strewn with their body parts until they look "like shapeless, mutilated, red-shirted firemen." The fight apparently ends in a draw. Then Twain confesses in a postscript that the fight had never occurred, that he is the butt of a hoax perpetrated by a local hosteler who claims to have heard the story from John B. Winters, a local candidate for Congress. With its rollicking political satire, this sketch is characteristic of Twain's early newspaper humor.

Gary Scharnhorst

BIBLIOGRAPHY

Branch, Edgar M. *The Literary Apprenticeship of Mark Twain.* Urbana: U of Illinois P, 1950.

Clemens, Samuel L. *Mark Twain's San Francisco.* Ed. Bernard Taper. New York: McGraw-Hill, 1963.

"Great Revolution in Pitcairn, The"

(1879)

Written in Europe in 1878, "The Great Revolution in Pitcairn" was originally intended as a chapter in *A Tramp Abroad* (1880). However, Twain decided against including the story in that work and instead published it in the March 1879 issue of the *Atlantic Monthly*. Subsequently, Twain included the story in the 1882 volume *The Stolen White Elephant, Etc.* and later in his 1896 collection of short fiction *Tom Sawyer Abroad.*

Twain situates his dystopian tale on the South Pacific island of Pitcairn, which was colonized in 1790 by the mutineers of the celebrated British ship *Bounty* and their Tahitian wives. He draws upon a familiar technique to provide the framework and information for his story—alleged reports of the island brought back by naval vessels that had anchored there and traded with the inhabitants. Those reports speak of an island community of utopian purity, simplicity, and Christian piety. The islanders, the few remaining original settlers and their descendants, live contented, uncomplicated lives in an arcadian community where their "sole occupations . . . were farming and fishing; their sole recreation, religious services."

However, a serpent must, of course, enter this garden. That serpent appears in the form of a conniving American renegade, Butterworth Stavely. He quickly recognizes the community as easy prey for a shrewd manipulator such as himself and immediately sets about sowing the seeds of discontent and corruption. Stavely is so adept at this that he succeeds in having the reigning "magistrate" deposed and himself set up in that position. In rapid order Stavely imposes a Western style of culture on a world where it does not fit, introducing all the usual problematic forms—political and social hierarchy, a military structure (the navy is composed of one whale boat, the only boat on the island), paper currency, and taxation, culminating in having himself crowned Emperor Butterworth I. Eventually, the absurdity of the unwieldly world that Stavely creates becomes evident even to the simple islanders, and they, in turn, depose him and reinstate the old order.

"The Great Revolution in Pitcairn" offers early evidence of Twain's growing cynicism and provides an early discussion of the corruptibility of humanity that would become a more focused theme in later works, such as *A Connecticut Yankee in King Arthur's Court* (1889), "The Man That Corrupted Hadleyburg" (1899), and *The Mysterious Stranger* (1916). For Twain, human nature is so weak and pliable that it becomes child's play for a determined outsider to enter the seemingly stable community and turn it upside down for his own purposes. Clearly, the island of Pitcairn becomes the world in small and Stavely the general forces of corruption that exploit that world.

However, those masses who allow themselves to be exploited are not the only targets of Twain's disdain. "The Great Revolution in Pitcairn" is decidedly also an attack on tyranny and exploitation itself, presenting a vehement condemnation of the Western imperialist ideal that seeks to impose profitable Western political, social, and economic forms on non-Western cultures. Twain saw this imperialism embodied perhaps most firmly in the mentality and strategy of the American missionaries. In this respect, the story can also be seen as an early, indirect attack on the cultural tyranny of those missionaries that Twain would later attack, still indirectly, in "The United States of Lyncherdom" (1901) and, quite directly, in "To the Person Sitting in Darkness" (1901). Interestingly, as Twain rehearses the polemic against the lynch mob of "The United States of Lyncherdom" in the earlier fiction of *Adventures of Huckleberry Finn* (1885), so also does he rehearse the denunciation of Western missionary methods of "To the Person Sitting in Darkness" in the earlier fiction of "The Great Revolution in Pitcairn."

Tim Poland

BIBLIOGRAPHY

Baetzhold, Howard G. *Mark Twain and John Bull: The British Connection.* Bloomington: Indiana UP, 1970.

Bellamy, Gladys C. *Mark Twain as a Literary Artist.* Norman: U of Oklahoma P, 1950.

Blair, Walter. *Mark Twain & Huck Finn.* Berkeley: U of California P, 1960.

Budd, Louis J. *Mark Twain: Social Philosopher.* Bloomington: Indiana UP, 1962.

Clemens, Samuel L. *The Stolen White Elephant, Etc.* Boston: James R. Osgood, 1882.

Covici, Pascal, Jr. *Mark Twain's Humor: The Image of a World.* Dallas: Southern Methodist UP, 1962.

DeVoto, Bernard. *Mark Twain at Work.* Cambridge, Mass.: Harvard UP, 1942.

Wilson, James D. *A Reader's Guide to the Short Stories of Mark Twain.* Boston: G.K. Hall, 1987.

See also: Imperialism; Missionaries

Greeley, Horace
(1811–1872)

Horace Greeley was an author, newspaper editor, and lecturer. By the time young Samuel Clemens reached New York in 1853, Greeley was already well established as the popular crusading and progressive editor of the *Tribune*, the newspaper that he founded. Though Greeley was never successful as a candidate, his political opinions were highly respected and that, coupled with his part in the founding of the Republican Party (1856) and his support of Abraham Lincoln, made Greeley a powerful influence in national politics, a position he held until he broke with the party (1872) and became the presidential nominee of both a rump convention of dissident Republicans and the Democratic Party. He died within weeks after losing the election to Grant.

Clemens met Greeley only once in an unpleasant encounter at the *Tribune* office. He respected Greeley and may have joined in the public's adulation, but he staunchly opposed his presidential candidacy. As a humorous device, Clemens often began his lectures with the repetitive telling of a boring, pointless story about Greeley and a rustic carriage driver named Hank Monk, a version of which appears in chapter 20 of *Roughing It* (1872).

Fred Weldon

BIBLIOGRAPHY

Clemens, Samuel L. *Mark Twain Speaks for Himself.* Ed. Paul Fatout. West Lafayette, Ind.: Purdue UP, 1978.

Fatout, Paul. *Mark Twain on the Lecture Circuit.* Bloomington: Indiana UP, 1960.

Gribben, Alan. *Mark Twain's Library: A Reconstruction.* 2 vols. Boston: G.K. Hall, 1980.

Long, E. Hudson. *Mark Twain's Handbook.* New York: Hendricks House, 1957.

Paine, Albert Bigelow. *Mark Twain: A Biography.* 3 vols. New York: Harper, 1912.

H

Hadleyburg

Located somewhere in the hinterland, Hadleyburg is the fictional version of small-town America presented in "The Man That Corrupted Hadleyburg" (1899). Hadleyburg is morally blind and reverts, following a sensational ritual of self-exposure, to an unreformed and misconceived view of itself. Insular, smug, dominated by an elite oligarchy, the town is edenic only in its vulnerability to temptation and its fall, which is engineered by a satanic stranger. It takes particular pride in its reputation for honesty, on which it trades commercially and in which it trains its citizens from infancy. The principles of honest dealing are enforced less by personal conviction than by tyrannical public opinion, however, and, worse still, are put to no pragmatic test until the stranger's hoax begins its work. Nor is the moral collapse of the town a fortunate fall. In shedding its naiveté, Hadleyburg fails to gain the clear-sighted moral realism that would comprise a basis for its redemption. As James D. Wilson points out, the town instead re- turns to its pride in an honesty that was never more than skin deep and is now fortified merely with a watchful prudence, so that Hadleyburg will not be caught "napping again."

Scholars have proposed that Hadleyburg is modeled after specific places: Oberlin, Ohio; Fredonia, New York; the Hannibal that appears, in various guises, in many of Mark Twain's narratives. More generic than individualized, however, Hadleyburg is a dystopian inversion of the popular, sentimentalized portrait of the American village and is the setting for a human drama universal in its implications.

Earl F. Briden

BIBLIOGRAPHY

Wilson, James D. *A Reader's Guide to the Short Stories of Mark Twain.* Boston: G.K. Hall, 1987.

See also: Dawson's Landing; "Man That Corrupted Hadleyburg, The"

Hall, Fred

Fred J. Hall succeeded Charles Webster in managing Charles L. Webster and Company and was a limited partner with Mark Twain when the firm went bankrupt in 1894. Initially, Mark Twain liked Hall, describing him as a bright, industrious young man (Hill 252, 331); nevertheless, Hall's tireless efforts to manage the business economically could not save the company, whose profits were being drained by Mark Twain's investment in the Paige typesetting machine. After the firm's bankruptcy, in which Hall also incurred liability, Mark Twain's opinion changed; he accused Hall of deception, and even tried to repudiate a personal loan to him (Hill 266). Yet Hall was a valuable sounding board for Mark Twain, and the subject of their earlier letters was often not business but Mark Twain's state of mind.

J. Mark Baggett

BIBLIOGRAPHY

Clemens, Samuel L. *Mark Twain's Letters to his Publishers, 1867–1894.* Ed. Hamlin Hill. Berkeley: U of California P, 1967.

Hall, Fred J. "Fred J. Hall Tells the Story of His Connection with Charles L. Webster and Co." *Twainian* 6 (November–December 1947): 1–3.

———. "Letters from Fred J. Hall to Paine." *Twainian* 26 (July–August 1967): 2.

Kiralis, Karl. "Two More Recently Discovered Letters by S.L. Clemens." *Mark Twain Journal* 16 (Summer 1973): 18–20.

Paine, Albert Bigelow. *Mark Twain: A Biography.* 3 vols. New York: Harper, 1912.

See also: Bankruptcy; Webster and Company, Charles L.

Halley's Comet

One of Mark Twain's most famous anecdotes concerns this most famous of celestial objects. According to Albert Bigelow Paine, Twain remarked (during or just after one of their conversations on astronomy in 1909) that it would be "the greatest disappointment of his life" if he did not "go out with" Halley's Comet in 1910, since he had "come in with" it in 1835.

On 16 November 1835, just two weeks before the birth of Samuel Clemens, the comet was at perihelion; then, remarkably, in 1910, its closest approach was on 20 April, the day before Twain's death. The coincidence has impressed not only astrologers but even skeptical scientists like Fred Whipple and Isaac Asimov.

Twain did not consider the comet a noxious danger or evil omen. He seems instead to have fancied it a sort of cosmic Charon's boat, which had ushered his spirit "in" to earth; now, in 1909, fully aware of his heart disease, he was "looking forward" to the ride "out." Identifying with the comet, he imagined that God viewed it as He viewed him, an "indefinable freak." It is not surprising, then, that he wrote a "Letter from the Comet" (ca. 1885) in which he takes its point of view, puzzled—on its return to earth after seventy-one years—at the disappearance from paradise of Adam, who (the comet assumes) must have "moved."

In chapter 3 of "Captain Stormfield's Visit to Heaven" (written ca. 1870), the dead captain, en route to heaven, encounters Halley's Comet on his way out of the solar system. The comet pales by comparison, however, to others he encounters—and races—in interstellar space. For Twain, then, the comet was not only a means of achieving a cosmic perspective, but also a symbol of cosmic relativism.

Joseph Andriano

BIBLIOGRAPHY

Clemens, Samuel L. "Captain Stormfield's Visit to Heaven." *Mark Twain's Quarrel with Heaven.* By Clemens. Ed. Ray B. Browne. New Haven, Conn.: College and University P, 1970. 39–110.

———. "Letter from the Comet." *Mark Twain's Fables of Man.* By Clemens. Ed. John S. Tuckey. Berkeley: U of California P, 1972. 437–439.

Paine, Albert Bigelow. *Mark Twain: A Biography.* 3 vols. New York: Harper, 1912.

Whipple, Fred L., and Daniel W.E. Green. *The Mystery of Comets.* Washington, D.C.: Smithsonian Institution P, 1985.

Zall, Paul M. *Mark Twain Laughing: Humorous Anecdotes by and About Samuel Clemens*. Knoxville: U of Tennessee P, 1985.

See also: Death; *Extract from Captain Stormfield's Visit to Heaven*

Halliday, Jack

The "no-account" loafer, fisherman, and hunter in "The Man That Corrupted Hadleyburg" (1899), Jack Halliday is a grown-up Huck Finn. A social outsider, he is indifferent to public opinion, has few illusions about his townspeople, and irreverently mocks their moral pretense.

Halliday's role is to offer his town the objectifying perspective of comedy. Going about with his toy camera, he records and laughs at the villagers' absorption in their dreams of wealth, symbolically holding out to them the basis, in laughter, of an unillusioned self-regard. At the story's climax he is appropriately chosen to auction off the bogus gold by a society that needs, as it unconsciously realizes, to find itself funny. As Master of the Revels, he presides over a painful illusion-destroying yet therapeutic ritual of laughter that unfortunately falls short of its full redemptive value.

Thus Halliday figures importantly in the development of a central theme in "Hadleyburg" and other works by Mark Twain: the twofold function of laughter as, on the one hand, an instrument of social tolerance and flexibility, a function evident in *Tom Sawyer* (1876), and, on the other, a powerful, though underused, weapon against humbug, a function argued in "The Chronicle of Young Satan," written between 1897 and 1900.

Earl F. Briden

BIBLIOGRAPHY

Clemens, Samuel L. *Mark Twain's Mysterious Stranger Manuscripts*. Ed. William M. Gibson. Berkeley: U of California P, 1969.

Covici, Pascal, Jr. *Mark Twain's Humor: The Image of a World*. Dallas: Southern Methodist UP, 1962.

Geismar, Maxwell. *Mark Twain: An American Prophet*. Boston: Houghton Mifflin, 1970.

See also: "Man That Corrupted Hadleyburg, The"

Hannibal, Missouri

Platted in 1819, Hannibal is located on the Mississippi River, approximately ninety miles north of St. Louis. The Clemens family moved there from Florida, Missouri, in 1839, when Samuel Langhorne Clemens was almost four years old. The boy grew to maturity in Hannibal. He went to work as an apprentice to printer Joseph P. Ament in 1849, setting type for the Hannibal *Courier*. In 1851 he became assistant editor of brother Orion's Hannibal *Journal and Western Union* . Although Sam Clemens left Hannibal for St. Louis in June 1853, his memories of childhood in this antebellum river town—its geographical landmarks, institutions, mores, and people—were to prove rich inspiration for much of Mark Twain's work.

Initial settlement of Hannibal was slowed by legal controversies over title to tracts of land. Much of the area fell within the unsurveyed boundaries of the Spanish land grants; many of these grants overlapped (a practice known as "shingling") and others, though filed, had never been processed. After the Louisiana Purchase (1803) the U.S. government established a land commission to evaluate grant claims; the fundamental prerequisite was that the grantee occupy and improve the land. False testimony and forged original grants, signed after the Spanish governor left office, created legal confusion, as did the fact that most of the land had never been surveyed because of interference by Fox and Sauk Indian tribes. The New Madrid earthquake (1811–1812) introduced another complication. Congress in 1815 issued earthquake certificates to 516 landowners in New Madrid County, Missouri, valid for establishing a homestead on any of the 280,000 acres the U.S. government had opened for settlement.

Only twenty bona fide earthquake victims actually redeemed their certificates; most sold them to St. Louis speculators who, in turn, resold them at profit. The appearance of counterfeit certificates made it additionally difficult to determine authenticity. A large portion of Hannibal was built on land purchased with an earthquake certificate, and court challenges left the town a log village until final determination of ownership. The first brick building appeared in 1829. As buildings succumbed to time or fire, they were replaced by brick and stone structures. After the great fire of 1852 a city ordinance forbade the erection of any wooden buildings or additions to existing buildings in downtown Hannibal.

Despite the land squabbles, Hannibal experienced steady growth—due largely to its location on the river and access to its tributaries. First to come were the fur trappers, who shipped their wares down river to New Orleans, then to Europe and Eurasia. Salt, from a mine at nearby Saverton, hemp for ropes and cables, and logs soon became additional exports and sources of employment. By the mid 1840s Hannibal had developed a major meatpacking industry. Subsidiary industries—e.g., tanneries, soap and glue factories—utilized the many by-products from the packing houses. Native yellow sandstone was quarried for construction in Hannibal, and lime was produced for agriculture and domestic use. The river yielded mussels that supplied a local pearl button factory. The great influx of ropewalk and factory workers, the men in the slaughter houses, the stock drovers, and the farmers who brought produce to the market on the square necessitated a hotel and boarding-house industry.

Livestock herds were driven to the waterfront slaughter houses from farm roads converging on Palmyra Road or on Market Street. The manure left by the hogs, cattle, and horses of the stockmen lay where it fell, smashed by hooves and carriage wheels, dried by the sun and leached by the rain until it made a strawlike mat. Not until 1911 were the streets cleaned regularly, and then by labor of men confined to the city jail. Through the nineteenth century merchants would each night scoop and sweep the day's accumulation of filth to the center of the street. These dunghills attracted insects and chickens who scavenged them daily. Some loafers had cocks that fought; other loafers fought among themselves.

The Mississippi River, which was a mile wide and its water a milky white when author Timothy Flint described it in the 1820s, was yellow when Clemens first saw it, the erosion of marble bluffs having progressed to the crumbling of clay banks. In his day the banks fell into the current along shore, carrying trees with them that grew in the river bed in the peculiar angles at which they fell. These trees were influenced by floods and changing currents, forming a trap for boatmen who could not determine the direction in which they grew. They were called "sawyers," and from them Mark Twain took the name for Tom Sawyer, his hymn to unpredictable boyhood with its joys and vagarious whims. By 1882 when Clemens returned to Hannibal to gather material for *Life on the Mississippi* (1883), the river had become a muddy brown. The Mississippi, of course, still rolls by Hannibal, its course sometimes changed in flood time by levees and dams. It is still as wide and its banks as beautiful. But the traffic on its crest is now made up of grain, coal, and cement barges, a few glorious old-style flat-bottomed steamers with paddle wheels driven by steam or motors. Scores of pleasure craft and houseboats mingle with the boats of fishermen and mussel drovers. Its waters remain polluted, not now by the offal from slaughter houses and filth from dirt roads but by poisonous chemicals and human waste.

Today Hannibal offers much to those interested in Mark Twain. There are still streets of huge wooden or brick homes from the Victorian age, carefully preserved and occupied by people who know their value. Visitors to Hannibal will find the following attractions:

The city-owned Mark Twain Visitors' Center, east of the Boyhood Home, contains rest rooms, a small theater, and an art gallery, usually showing material owned by the museum but occasionally featuring special exhibits. Ample parking is available, and the information desk provides maps and tour guides. The docents for the center, the home, and the museum are members of a volunteer organization, Jane Clemens Neighbors, who serve on a regular schedule to answer questions. They also provide guides for large groups and bus tours, by prearrangement. Services are generally free, though a fee may be assessed for large groups. The Memorial Garden nearby is planted with roses and other flowers indigenous to the regions during Mark Twain's time.

The Mark Twain Boyhood Home is one of the dwellings occupied by the Clemens family during their residence in Hannibal, originally built by John Marshall Clemens. In 1990 the house was completely renovated, after being stripped down to the foundation and restored to its original state, with contemporary furnishings of the 1840s. Donations are requested at the home to support the restoration and maintenance of all properties supervised by the Mark Twain Foundation.

The Mark Twain Museum, adjacent to the home, is a stone building housing exhibits and memorabilia. A chief attraction is the great orchestrelle that Mark Twain purchased in his old age. It can be played manually or by pedals with the music on perforated rolls. The original rolls are included. The orchestrelle has an organ keyboard, with numerous couplings for different sounds. It is on permanent loan from the Missouri State Historical Society, who received it as a gift from Albert B. Paine, Twain's official biographer. Other valuable exhibits include a facsimile manuscript of Twain's most popular writings, photos, artifacts, and a set of book illustrations by Norman Rockwell.

The John Marshall Clemens law office has been moved from its original location on Main Street to a lot on Hill Street, where visitors see it furnished as a scene for the hearings he held as justice of the peace. On the corner of Main and Hill streets is the House of Pilasters, with Dr. Grant's drug store on the first floor. The second floor apartment, where the Clemens family lived during the last illness of John, has recently had new clothing made for the mannequins in the rooms furnished with period pieces. On the grounds of the House of Pilasters is the Tom and Huck statue sculpted by Frederick Hibbard, dedicated in 1926 and its surface restored in 1984.

There are privately owned shops adjacent to this area, in a formally organized historic district. Of especial interest is the former home of the Hawkins family, whose Laura Hawkins Frazer was the inspiration for Becky Thatcher. The large frame home has the Becky Thatcher Book Store on the first floor, which carries a complete line of books by or about Mark Twain, and an assortment of gifts and souvenirs. Upstairs, a Becky Thatcher bedroom has been beautifully furnished and is open to the public.

At the Mark Twain Diner, on Hill Street, there is an outdoor "train station" where visitors may take a motorized train ride to various points of interest in Hannibal. In season, one may take a similar ride in a horse-drawn wagon, with passengers boarding at Main and Hill streets.

The Mark Twain Memorial Lighthouse, which can be seen as one looks north up Main Street, can be reached by climbing a series of steps, up the riverbank, beginning at the Tom and Huck monument. This lighthouse was built for the 1935 one-hundredth birthday celebration of Mark Twain; it provides a view of the Mississippi, its islands, and the farmland of Illinois across the river. It is not now, nor never was, a genuine Coast Guard lighthouse for the safety of traffic on the river; however, it is a beacon of Mark Twain's hometown.

Oliver Howard and Goldena Howard

BIBLIOGRAPHY

Bacon, Thomas H. *A Mirror of Hannibal, Missouri.* Hannibal, Mo.: C.P. Greene, 1905. Rev. J. Hurley and Roberta Hagood. Marceline, Mo.: Josten's, 1990.

Brashear, Minnie M. *Mark Twain: Son of Missouri.* Chapel Hill: U of North Carolina P, 1934.

Flint, Timothy. *Recollections of the Last Ten Years in the Valley of the Mississippi.* Boston: Cummings, Hilliard, 1826. Rpt. Carbondale: Southern Illinois UP, 1968.

Holcombe, R.I. *History of Marion County, Missouri.* St. Louis, Mo.: E.E. Perkins, 1884. Rpt. Marion County Historical Society, 1979.

Howard, Oliver, and Goldena Howard. *The Mark Twain Book.* New London, Mo.: Ralls County Book, 1985.

————. *Portrait and Biographical Record of Marion, Ralls, and Pike Counties, Missouri.* New London, Mo.: Ralls County Book, 1982.

Wecter, Dixon. *Sam Clemens of Hannibal.* Boston: Houghton Mifflin, 1952.

See also: Autobiography; Clemens, John Marshall; Clemens, Samuel Langhorne; Mark Twain Boyhood Home; Mississippi River

Harper and Brothers

On 15 September 1903 Frank Bliss of the American Publishing Company and Frederick A. Duneka, vice-president of the prestigious New York publisher Harper and Brothers, met with Mark Twain and Henry Huttleston Rogers to settle an ongoing dispute over the right to produce and distribute the author's work. Five weeks later, on 23 October, the three principals signed a deal that made Harper the exclusive publisher of Twain's writings and that guaranteed the author a minimum annual income of $25,000.

Although the 1903 contract with Harper completed Twain's miraculous recovery from the financial ruin of the 1890s, he never became fully satisfied that the New York firm could sell his books as effectively as Bliss or his own Charles Webster and Company had done through subscription publishing. Throughout his life, Twain had been a strong advocate of the subscription method, and he remained wary of traditional marketing strategies employed by the older houses. In 1896, after arranging to publish *Personal Recollections of Joan of Arc* (1896) and *Tom Sawyer, Detective* (1896)

with Harper, he warned Rogers that the firm typically published only "very high-class books and they go to people who are accustomed to read" (*Letters to Publishers* 7). Twain believed, with good reason, that when one of his own subscription books sold 60,000 copies, 50,000 of those went to "people who don't visit bookstores."

His dislike of Harper's marketing practices fueled Twain's general discontent with the firm and its representatives. Convinced that Duneka was cheating him out of revenues and willfully blocking publication of his work, in 1906 Twain exclaimed that the Harper executive and former friend was "slippery beyond imagination" (Hill 140). Just three years after signing his lucrative contract, the author listed what he called the "Harper treacheries" beside the crimes of his other enemies in the publishing trade—Elisha Bliss, James Osgood, Charles L. Webster, and Frank Bliss.

Henry B. Wonham

BIBLIOGRAPHY

Clemens, Samuel L. *Mark Twain in Eruption.* Ed. Bernard DeVoto. New York: Harper, 1922.

————. *Mark Twain's Letters to His Publishers, 1867–1894.* Ed. Hamlin Hill. Berkeley: U of California P, 1967.

Hill, Hamlin. *Mark Twain: God's Fool.* New York: Harper & Row, 1973.

Kaplan, Justin. *Mr. Clemens and Mark Twain.* New York: Simon & Schuster, 1966.

Paine, Albert Bigelow. *Mark Twain: A Biography.* 3 vols. New York: Harper, 1912.

Webster, Samuel Charles. *Mark Twain, Business Man.* Boston: Little, Brown, 1946.

See also: Duneka, Frederick A.; Rogers, Henry Huttleston; Subscription Publication; Webster, Charles L.

Harper's Magazine

From 1866 to 1922 Mark Twain's writings appeared with growing regularity in this periodical known for its interest in regional subjects. (Founded by the Harper publishing house to promote its books, this magazine was first titled *Harper's New Monthly Magazine* [1850–1900], then *Harper's Monthly Magazine* [1900–1925], and since 1925 it has been known as *Harper's Magazine*.) Harper and Brothers also published from 1857 until mid-1986 a weekly magazine entitled *Harper's Weekly* as a separate entity from the monthly journal.

Twain's first piece, "Forty Three Days in an Open Boat" (1866), had his name spelled as "Mark Swain," a printer's error that also occurred in the annual index. Twenty-one years later the December issue included "A Petition to the Queen of England." From 1895 through 1912 his sketches appeared every year with two exceptions. His most intensive years of contributing to the periodical came in 1895–1896 with sixteen appearances, notably *Personal Recollections of Joan of Arc* and *Tom Sawyer, Detective* (published here in August before its book publication in November 1896).

Twain's sketches in *Harper's* led to a certain fame despite his obvious efforts at using periodicals for financial advantage. An English guide in the summer of 1882 is reported to have said, "You Americans have Mark Twain and *Harper's Magazine*." The magazine seemed occasionally to be on his mind, for he wrote in reference to *Harper's* that "magazining is difficult work because every third page represents two pages that you have to put in the fire." His humor persisted with the remark that in trying to economize he considered cancelling the subscription and using a cheaper brand of toilet paper. Despite his cynicism, *Harper's* contributed significantly to the public's appetite for his books and assisted in making him a major voice in the popular culture of the time.

Thomas Bonner, Jr.

BIBLIOGRAPHY

Ferguson, DeLancey. *Mark Twain: Man and Legend.* Indianapolis: Bobbs-Merrill, 1943.

Johnson, Merle. *A Bibliography of the Works of Mark Twain.* Rev. ed. New York: Harper, 1935.

Kaplan, Justin. *Mr. Clemens and Mark Twain.* New York: Simon & Schuster, 1966.

Harris, George Washington
(1814–1869)

The best known and the most talented of the southern frontier humorists, George Washington Harris achieved fame as the creator of the character Sut Lovingood. Given to wild and extravagant metaphor, bawdy tales, and an uncontrolled penchant for engineering disastrous events, Sut is one of the most striking figures in nineteenth-century American fiction. As a reporter and contributor himself to the school of frontier humor, Mark Twain reviewed Harris's only book, *Sut Lovingood Yarns* (1867), for a California newspaper, and while he praised its humor and accurate use of dialect, he predicted that the eastern literary establishment would find it offensive and censor it. Some critics have argued that Harris's use of a first-person narrator and the American vernacular inspired Twain to attempt the same techniques in *Adventures of Huckleberry Finn* (1885) and that both Sut and Huck use subversion and anarchy in the name of a higher moral sensibility. At a minimum, they both seek freedom and independence from the expectations of society and know how to have a good time.

Harris was born in Allegheny City, Pennsylvania, but was brought as a child by his half-brother to Knoxville, Tennessee. At that time the Tennessee River made Knoxville a center for trade and industry, so the young Harris first turned to metalworking, jewelry repair, and the manufacture of machinery as vocations. Like the young Twain, he was fascinated by steamboats, and after completing his apprenticeship at age nineteen, he served as captain of the steamboat *Knoxville* for many years. Throughout the remainder of his life, Harris would follow a variety of occupations, such as farmer, surveyor, Democratic politician, Knoxville postmaster, and railroad employee.

His writing began incidentally as a series of political sketches contributed to local newspapers in the 1840s. His tales and sketches about backwoods life in Tennessee brought him national attention in the pages of New York's *Spirit of the Times,* and the first Sut Lovingood story appeared in the 4 November 1854 issue of that sporting journal. Having found a form and content best suited to his considerable literary talents, Harris published a series of widely reprinted stories and political satires using Sut as a narrator, twenty-four of which he revised and collected in *Sut Lovingood Yarns.* The manuscript for a second collection to be entitled "High Times and Hard Times" had been finished when Harris died under mysterious circumstances while returning on the train from Lynchburg, Virginia, where he had gone to arrange for its publication. The manuscript has never been found, but all of his known writings have been reprinted in modern editions, and most literary anthologies include one of his stories. Numerous writers and critics, besides Twain, have paid tribute to Harris's accomplishments, including William Faulkner, Robert Penn Warren, Flannery O'Connor, Edmund Wilson, and F.O. Matthiessen.

M. Thomas Inge

BIBLIOGRAPHY

Harris, George Washington. *High Times and Hard Times: Sketches and Tales by George Washington Harris.* Ed. M. Thomas Inge. Nashville, Tenn.: Vanderbilt UP, 1967.

————. *Sut Lovingood: Yarns Spun by a "Nat'ral Born Dum'd Fool."* New York: Dick and Fitzgerald, 1867.

Rickels, Milton. *George Washington Harris.* New York: Twayne, 1965.

Wilson, Edmund. *Patriotic Gore.* New York: Oxford UP, 1962.

See also: Southwestern Humor; Vernacular

Harris, Joel Chandler
(1848–1908)

A journalist and writer from Georgia, Harris is most widely known for his series of books containing African-American folktales narrated by Uncle Remus, beginning with *Uncle Remus, His Songs and His Sayings* (1880). No other southern writer except Twain won as much

interest and admiration from the reading public of that time.

There are at least three areas relating Joel Chandler Harris and Mark Twain. First, their lives were often remarkably similar. Harris, like Twain, began as an apprentice to a newspaper publisher, working his way up to writing short pieces for the paper. Both men turned early to writing humorous sketches. Harris, in fact, acquired a reputation for his humor as he worked for newspapers in Macon, Savannah, and finally for the Atlanta *Constitution* (1876–1900). Harris chose to continue his daily editorial work, but both men achieved international recognition primarily through their book audience. Second, the works of Harris and Twain strongly complement each other as a record of American culture. Harris's Uncle Remus and Twain's Jim are the first sensitive depictions of black characters in American literature. Harris, like Twain, contributed to the interest in and representation of American speech patterns. Uncle Remus speaks in a middle-Georgia dialect, while Daddy Jack speaks in Gullah, and other characters clearly present speech patterns from other regions of the South. Both authors were recognized for their contributions to children's (juvenile) literature and humor. Harris protested his publisher's decision to market the Uncle Remus works as humor, insisting in his introduction that the folktales and their message were to be taken seriously. He did, however, co-edit, with Andrew Lang, *The World's Wit and Humor* (1905–1906), fifteen volumes. Finally, each one's respect for the other's work ultimately led to a personal relationship, begun via correspondence (published by Julia Collier Harris and Thomas English). Twain's early inquiry to Harris about a ghost story ("The Golden Arm") led to the use of the tale by both men, although in quite different ways. The two men first met in New Orleans in 1882 (written up briefly in Twain's *Life on the Mississippi,* chapter 47), when the extremely shy Harris turned down an offer to join Twain and George Washington Cable for a lecture/reading series.

Joel Chandler Harris contributed more than any other person to an interest in American folklore and its use in literature. As a journalist and a writer, he was able to describe the South, its cultures, and some of its problems.

Eric L. Montenyohl

BIBLIOGRAPHY

Baer, Florence E. *Sources and Analogues of the Uncle Remus Tales.* Helsinki: Academie Scientiarum Fennica, 1980.

Bell, William R. "The Relationship of Joel Chandler Harris and Mark Twain." *Atlanta Historical Journal* 30.3–4 (1986–1987): 97–112.

Bickley, R. Bruce. *Joel Chandler Harris: A Reference Guide.* Boston: G.K. Hall, 1978.

————. *Joel Chandler Harris.* Athens: U of Georgia P, 1987.

Cousins, Paul M. *Joel Chandler Harris: A Biography.* Baton Rouge: Louisiana State UP, 1968.

English, Thomas H. *Mark Twain to Uncle Remus 1881–1885.* Atlanta: Emory U Library, 1953.

Harris, Julia Collier. *The Life and Letters of Joel Chandler Harris.* Boston: Houghton Mifflin, 1918. Rpt. New York: AMS P, 1973.

Montenyohl, Eric L. "The Origins of Uncle Remus." *Folklore Forum* 18.2 (Spring 1985): 136–167.

See also: Folklore

Harrison, Katharine I.
(ca. 1867–1935)

Although Mark Twain publicly gave Standard Oil magnate Henry H. Rogers full credit for helping him pay his debts and emerge from bankruptcy, it was, in fact, Rogers's administrative assistant, Miss Harrison, who handled the day-to-day financial transactions for Twain: keeping his accounts, acting as his stockbroker, and becoming one of his most trusted friends during the period from 1893 until Twain's death in 1910. It was Harrison who jubilantly wrote Twain in January 1898 to announce that she had paid off the last of his debts, with $13,000 to spare. She has been described as imposing, terrifying, severely masculine, robotlike, fascinating, a cyclopedia, a sphinx, inscrutable, unapproachable, and a pioneer female executive who knew all the secrets of Standard Oil but refused to grant interviews to the end of her life. Hamlin Hill has suggested that characters in several of Twain's later writings reflect aspects of her personality that stand in sharp contrast to the characters based upon Twain's wife, daughters, and other female friends.

Kevin Mac Donnell

BIBLIOGRAPHY

Clemens, Samuel L. *Mark Twain's Correspondence with Henry Huttleston Rogers, 1893–1909.* Berkeley: U of California P, 1969.

Hill, Hamlin. *Mark Twain: God's Fool.* New York: Harper & Row, 1973.

Paine, Albert Bigelow. *Mark Twain: A Biography.* 3 vols. New York: Harper, 1912.

Harte, Francis Bret[t]
(1836–1902)

Born in Albany, New York, Bret Harte went west with his mother, did odd jobs, mining, newspaper work, and, most importantly, wrote several stories—"The Luck of Roaring Camp" (1868) and "The Outcasts of Poker Flat," "Tennessee's Partner," and "The Idyl of Red Gulch," all in 1869—that appeared in the newly founded *Overland Monthly,* of which he was the first editor. The stories depict regional types, whose speech, attitudes, and behavior display life in the post-Civil War mining West, and so are stories of "local color," a subgenre of short fiction that Harte helped establish. His stories, usually centering around paradoxical characters—rough miners redeemed by an infant left in their midst; a gambler and prostitutes caught in a snowstorm behaving heroically to save the good and the innocent; a fallen woman giving up her young son, fathered by the town drunk, to the "good" schoolteacher, who is moved by the sound hearts of these social outcasts—were immensely popular, all the way to the East Coast. The *Atlantic Monthly* drew a contract with Harte for $10,000, in return for twelve new stories. He fulfilled his obligation, but what he wrote was inferior to the early stories. Still, Harte was a successful writer in the popular view, and Mark Twain admired him and envied his success.

If Harte had been greatly admired for his early local color stories, later criticism of the writer found much to disparage: his Dickensian sentimentality and the repeated formula of his plots, for instance. Mark Twain, however, did not object to Harte's stories on these grounds. An examination of Twain's marginalia in the first edition of *The Luck of Roaring Camp and Other Stories* (1870) shows Twain concerned principally with Harte's grammar, the accuracy of his rendition of Pike County dialect, and the factual truth of his characters' behavior (Booth 492–496). Twain admired Harte's work when it appeared. There was, then and later, talk of Mark Twain's borrowing from it. On the Harte formula of "good in the heart of an outcast," Walter Blair writes: "Twain, eager for acceptance by the literary elite, hardly would have ventured to make Huck the center of a novel if the trail had not been broken by Harte" (Blair 218).

Harte's influence on Mark Twain is more certain in *The Innocents Abroad* (1869), his first major work. Revising and augmenting his travel letters to the San Francisco *Alta California* for book publication, Twain had accumulated a "mountain of manuscript" that demanded rigorous editing, a chore from which he shrank. Half seriously he hoped Mary Mason Fairbanks would help him. In California, where he resumed his friendship with Bret Harte, he accepted Harte's offer to read the manuscript of *The Innocents Abroad*. Harte's editorial help Clemens acknowledged in letters to two persons: one to Thomas Bailey Aldrich, 28 January 1871, in which he said that "Harte trimmed and trained and schooled me patiently until he changed me from an awkward utterer of coarse grotesquenesses to a writer of paragraphs and chapters that have found a certain favor in the eyes of even some of the very decentest people in the land" (*Letters* 182); the other to Charles Henry Webb, 26 November 1870 (Library of Congress): "Harte read all the MS of the 'Innocents' &

told me what passages, paragraphs & *chapters* to leave out—& I followed orders strictly."

Some idea of the nature of Harte's editorial changes is suggested by his praise, in a review in the *Overland Monthly* (1 [1868]: 101–103) of John Franklin Swift's travel book *Going to Jericho* (1868). Harte commends Swift for avoiding the sentimentality of Lamartine and William Prime, for keeping humor restrained, for using satire sparingly, and for avoiding irreverence offensive to the devout. These qualities are all ones that Mark Twain achieved in revising his newspaper letters for book publication. Harte's editing was a real help to Twain.

Any sketch of the relation of Mark Twain and Bret Harte must mention, if only briefly, the rift that developed between the two. Twain's intemperate diatribe on Harte, appearing first in *Mark Twain in Eruption* (1940) and later in Charles Neider's edition of *The Autobiography of Mark Twain* (1959, chapter 25), is too extreme to be altogether credible. The quarrel that developed between Twain and Harte had several alleged causes. The fullest and most judicious account of the falling out is in Margaret Duckett's authoritative *Mark Twain and Bret Harte* (1964). Twain does not emerge from her careful study without blame. It is one of his most unlovely traits, the way he could turn on an old friend and destroy a valuable relationship. Will Bowen and Dan Slote suffered his reckless antagonism. And so did Bret Harte. Harte's early relation to Twain was pleasant and profitable. The later one was bitter.

Leon T. Dickinson

BIBLIOGRAPHY

Blair, Walter. *Mark Twain & Huck Finn*. Berkeley: U of California P, 1960.

Booth, Bradford. "Mark Twain's Comments on Bret Harte's Stories." *American Literature* 25 (January 1954): 492–496.

Clemens, Samuel L. *The Autobiography of Mark Twain*. Ed. Charles Neider. New York: Harper, 1959.

———. *Mark Twain in Eruption*. Ed. Bernard DeVoto. New York: Harper, 1940.

———. *Mark Twain's Letters*. Ed. Albert B. Paine. 2 vols. New York: Harper, 1917.

Duckett, Margaret. *Mark Twain and Bret Harte.* Norman: U of Oklahoma P, 1964.

Harte, Francis Bret. *The Writings of Bret Harte.* 19 vols. Boston: Houghton Mifflin, 1896–1903.

Stewart, George R., Jr. *Bret Harte: Argonaut and Exile.* Boston: Houghton Mifflin, 1931.

See also: Ah Sin: The Heathen Chinee; California; Criticism; Dialect; Local Color

Hawaii

"Hawaii" refers to a group of islands in the north Pacific Ocean, the largest island in the chain, and the fiftieth state of the United States. Sam Clemens visited Hawaii for about four months, from March to July of 1866, to write letters for the Sacramento *Union* about the business, culture, and natural scenery of the islands. The assignment would prove to be a turning point in his career because the lectures based on his experiences would greatly expand his popularity as Mark Twain.

The Sandwich Islands, as they were then called, were also at a crossroads, the basis of their economy changing from whaling to agriculture. King Kamehameha V and Dowager Queen Emma favored British ways, but their policy was actually a sign of the already immense American influence. Most of the 2,200 white immigrants counted in the 1866 census were American. Moreover, Americans occupied vital positions in politics and economics. In 1893 the monarchy was overthrown by prominent men of American descent in favor of annexation to the United States.

The cultural melange that marks society in Hawaii today was in 1866 a simple contrast between Hawaiian and American cultures, though Chinese, English, and French populations were significant. American missionaries, whose influence was everywhere evident, had established American culture two generations earlier, and they were often a lightning rod for the (mostly) private animus of Sam Clemens against his own culture. He ultimately favored Western ways, however, and publicly, as Mark Twain, praised the good accomplished by missionary efforts.

Perhaps no other topic points up the difference between Hawaiian and American cultures, and highlights the ambiguous feelings of Sam Clemens about both, than does the issue of work versus leisure. More than once Mark Twain noted with disparagement how lazy the Hawaiians were while praising the hard work of the white immigrants to Hawaii (including the missionaries) and encouraging enterprising capitalists to invest in the islands. Yet one of the longest-running jokes of Mark Twain was how lazy he was, and the tropic indolence of Hawaii brought out the truth of the joke. Clemens thought that no one enjoyed hard labor, and it is reported that he liked the natives because they admitted to laziness while white men only pretended to be industrious (Goodhue 180). Implied is the essence of Hawaii's lure: the Edenic quality of respite from work that appealed to so many Westerners who encountered Polynesian culture.

Though Mark Twain never set foot in Hawaii again, his planned stop on the world tour of 1895 foiled by cholera, he obviously retained vivid memories. In 1884 he had plans for a novel based in Hawaii, and in 1889 his famous encomium on the islands once again emphasized the absence of work and care: "that peaceful land . . . where life is one long slumberless Sabbath" (Frear 501). For Mark Twain, the "Rainbow Islands"—the name he felt was most fitting for Hawaii—imparted an enduring feeling of psychic oasis.

James E. Caron

BIBLIOGRAPHY

Clemens, Samuel L. *Mark Twain's Letters, Volume 1 (1853–1866).* Ed. Edgar M. Branch, Michael B. Frank, and Kenneth M. Sanderson. Berkeley: U of California P, 1988.

———. *Mark Twain's Notebooks & Journals, Volume I (1855–1873).* Ed. Frederick Anderson, Michael B. Frank, and Kenneth M. Sanderson. Berkeley: U of California P, 1975.

Daws, Gavin. *Shoal of Time: A History of the Hawaiian Islands.* Honolulu: U of Hawaii P, 1968.

Goodhue, E.S. "Mark Twain's Hawaiian Home." *Mid-Pacific Magazine* 12 (August 1916): 177–181.

Frear, Walter F. *Mark Twain and Hawaii.* Chicago: Lakeside P, 1947.

Kuykendall, Ralph S. *Hawaii: A History, from Polynesian Kingdom to American Commonwealth.* New York: Prentice-Hall, 1948.

See also: Letters from the Sandwich Islands

Hawaiian Gazette

The weekly *Hawaiian Gazette* succeeded the *Polynesian* in 1865 as Hawaii's political newspaper. In 1873 the *Gazette* was absorbed by Henry M. Whitney's *Pacific Commercial Advertiser* and discontinued its role as political organ. Though Clemens did not write for the paper directly, some of his Sandwich Island correspondences to the Sacramento *Union* were reprinted in the journal. The *Gazette* eventually became the Honolulu *Advertiser*.

Susan McFatter

BIBLIOGRAPHY

Frear, Walter Francis. *Mark Twain and Hawaii.* Chicago: Lakeside P, 1947.

Gregory, Winifred, ed. *American Newspapers, 1821–1836: A Union List of Files Available in the United States and Canada.* New York: Wilson, 1937.

See also: Hawaii

Hawkins, Laura

Laura Hawkins is one of the principal female characters in *The Gilded Age* (1873), which was written jointly by Mark Twain and Charles Dudley Warner. Twain wrote most of the sections dealing with Laura Hawkins, except for the material describing her false marriage (Neider xii, xiii). The name was that of a young girl Twain had known and liked in Hannibal, Missouri, when he was a boy. The story of Laura Hawkins in *The Gilded Age*, however, derived from the case of Laura Fair, a lobbyist in Washington who killed her lover and was acquitted (Neider xix).

In *The Gilded Age* Laura is adopted by the Hawkins family when her family is lost in a steamboat explosion. She grows into a beautiful young woman and is deceived into a false marriage by Colonel George Selby, a Confederate officer, who deserts her after a few months, informing her that he is already married. She returns home a bitter woman. Later she goes to Washington as the protégée of Senator Dilworthy and proves to be an effective lobbyist. Her beauty and wit, as well as the promise of great wealth, make her a power in Washington and bring her many admirers, but she is too cynical to fall in love with any of them. Then she meets Colonel Selby again and believes that she still loves him. He promises to go away with her, but she discovers that he plans to go to Europe with his wife; she follows him to New York and shoots him in a public room in a hotel. She is tried and acquitted. After the trial she attempts to go on the lecture circuit, but fails. The night after her disappointment on the lecture circuit, she dies of heart failure at the age of twenty-eight.

Laura Hawkins is one of the most effective of Twain's female characters. Along with Roxana in *Pudd'nhead Wilson* (1894), she is more fully developed than the other female characters in Twain's work: she is independent, intelligent, and possessed of a sexual nature. Twain has been criticized for having her die at the end of the novel with no other explanation for her death but as a punishment for her transgressions. William Spengemann, however, sees her death not as a punishment but as the inevitable result of her induction into a society that worships money (33).

Joyce W. Warren

BIBLIOGRAPHY

Clemens, Samuel L., and Charles Dudley Warner. *The Gilded Age.* Hartford, Conn.: American Publishing, 1873.

DeVoto, Bernard. *Mark Twain at Work.* Cambridge, Mass.: Harvard UP, 1942.

———. *Mark Twain's America.* Boston: Little, Brown, 1932.

Geismar, Maxwell. *Mark Twain: An American Prophet.* Boston: Houghton Mifflin, 1970.

Kaplan, Justin. *Mr. Clemens and Mark Twain.* New York: Simon & Schuster, 1966.

Neider, Charles. Introduction. *The Adventures of Colonel Sellers.* By Clemens. New York: Doubleday, 1965.

Paine, Albert Bigelow. *Mark Twain: A Biography.* Vol. 1. New York: Harper, 1912.

Spengemann, William C. *Mark Twain and the Backwoods Angel: The Matter of Innocence in the Works of Samuel L. Clemens.* Kent, Ohio: Kent State UP, 1966.

Walker, Franklin. "An Influence from San Francisco on Mark Twain's *The Gilded Age.*" *American Literature* 8 (March 1936): 63–66.

Warren, Joyce W. *The American Narcissus: Individualism and Women in Nineteenth-Century American Fiction.* New Brunswick, N.J.: Rutgers UP, 1984.

See also: Gilded Age, The; Roxana; Women

"Hellfire Hotchkiss"
(1967)

Written around 1897, three chapters of "Hellfire Hotchkiss" are all that Twain wrote, but they afford a glimpse of his creative attempts to reuse his successful Hannibal material. Many of the characterizations come from Hannibal citizens also worked into "Villagers of 1840–3" and the "Hannibal" or "Schoolhouse Hill" versions of *The Mysterious Stranger Manuscripts* (1969).

Oscar Carpenter is Twain's code name for his brother Orion Clemens, whose foolish inconsistencies Twain tried to form into a fictional character. Originally intended as the main character, Oscar is the subject of only chapter one. Chapters two and three shift the role of protagonist to Rachel "Hellfire" Hotchkiss, an unconventional female, strong-spirited and brave—a marked contrast to the unstable Oscar. "Hellfire" resembles Twain's favorite daughter Susy, but the description matches more closely incidents in the life of Lillie Hitchcock, a woman he knew in San Francisco (Sanborn 243–245). "Hellfire" rescues Oscar from danger that Twain had actually experienced: being trapped on the Mississippi's ice flows. His companion that

day was Tom Nash, and his description in the *Autobiography* (2:213) of Tom's sister Mary makes her another source for this composite picture, rarely drawn, of an admirable, resourceful, and heroic female protagonist.

Sandra Littleton-Uetz

BIBLIOGRAPHY

Clemens, Samuel L. "Hellfire Hotchkiss." *Huck Finn and Tom Sawyer Among the Indians, and Other Unfinished Stories.* By Clemens. Ed. Dahlia Armon and Walter Blair. Berkeley: U of California P, 1989. 109–133.

———. *Mark Twain's Autobiography.* Ed. Albert B. Paine. 2 vols. New York: Harper, 1924.

———. *Mark Twain's Mysterious Stranger Manuscripts.* Ed. William M. Gibson. Berkeley: U of California P, 1969.

———. *Mark Twain's Satires and Burlesques.* Ed. Franklin R. Rogers. Berkeley: U of California P, 1967.

Sanborn, Margaret. *Mark Twain: The Bachelor Years.* New York: Doubleday, 1990.

See also: "Autobiography of a Damned Fool"; Women

Heroism

The century in which Mark Twain lived made hero worship one of its major faiths. Its writers generated enough devout texts to constitute a bible: Thomas Carlyle's *On Heroes, Hero-Worship, and the Heroic in History* (1841), Ralph Waldo Emerson's *Representative Men* (1850), and Friedrich Nietzsche's *Thus Spake Zarathustra* (1883–1892) rank high among them. Parson Weems's *The Life of Washington the Great* (1806) and the ubiquitous Log-Cabin-to-White-House biographies of American politicians form part of its Sunday school literature. Its sacred music runs the gamut from "The Hunters of Kentucky" (celebrating Andrew Jackson's victory at New Orleans) to Richard Wagner's *Der Ring des Nibelungen* (1869–1876) and Richard Strauss's *Ein Heldenleben* (1898). Mark Twain felt the attraction of this movement, but he resisted it. The skeptical critic of Calvinism and Christian Science was reluctant to be drawn into a dangerous and undemocratic faith in heroic leadership. Yet he was through all his life sensitive to the paradox that a democratic society needs, indeed requires, heroic leadership.

We admire our heroes, "we envy them," he writes in his *Autobiography* (1924), "for great qualities we ourselves lack. Hero worship consists in that. Our heroes are the men who do things which we recognize, with regret, and sometimes with a secret shame, that we cannot do. . . . If everybody was satisfied with himself, there would be no heroes" (2:263–264).

Some critics who hold Mark Twain's masterpiece in the highest regard have seen Huckleberry Finn as a folk hero (Daniel Hoffman), even as an epic hero sharing traits with Odysseus (Andrew Jay Hoffman). There are compelling arguments for these views, and such comparisons may be illuminating; yet Huck is hardly a figure who evokes what Mark Twain means by "hero worship." Perhaps the key to Huck's universal and enduring appeal is that his inadequacies and evasions teach us to be less dissatisfied with our own. Perhaps he is even an anti-hero. If *Adventures of Huckleberry Finn* (1885) contains a figure who does things we are ashamed we cannot do, surely that figure is Colonel Sherburn (chapters 21 and 22), and he is not a character many can wholeheartedly admire. Huck does not admire him, nor does he admire any hero. In the first chapter of *Huckleberry Finn* the Widow Douglas tries to make him venerate the greatest of Hebrew heroes, Moses, but once he has found out that Moses is dead, Huck judges him "of no use to anybody, being gone. . . ." Hero worship renders the worshiper subservient to the idol and to the past—so Huck feels and so Mark Twain thought.

Mark Twain's position on the threat hero worship poses in an egalitarian society is nowhere so clearly articulated as in his treatment of Columbus in *The Innocents Abroad* (1869). He complains that American tourists in Italy "deal so much in sentiment and emotion before any relic of Columbus." He and his sidekicks the Doctor and Dan undermine every guide who tries to make them venerate the great discoverer's relics. The Doctor's stock response adumbrates Huck's response to Moses: "Christopher Colombo—pleasant name—is—is he dead?" (chapter 27).

From naming Jim Smiley's "little small bull-pup" Andrew Jackson and his celebrated jumping frog Dan'l Webster ("The Celebrated Jumping Frog of Calaveras County" [1865]) to attaching Benjamin Franklin's name to a yellow fever germ ("Three Thousand Years Among the Microbes" [written 1905]), Mark Twain's impish humor repeatedly undermines the pantheon of American political heroes. To venerate heroes, his onomastic clowning seems to suggest, is to validate heroic leadership, and heroic leadership is in essence antidemocratic. Carlyle and Nietzsche, Wagner and Strauss, these giants and their lesser followers have come to be regarded, perhaps unfairly, as protofascists; Mark Twain earned a reputation as a champion of human freedom.

The heroes of the American past were the targets of his lampoons; the heroes of his own time he treated even more harshly—although not always in works to appear while he lived. Leonard Wood he dismissed as "that sleight-of-hand major general," and to General Wood's one-time second-in-command at San Juan Hill, he devoted extended diatribes: "Mr. Roosevelt is the Tom Sawyer of the political world . . . ; in his frenzied imagination the great republic is a vast Barnum circus with him for a clown and the whole world for an audience" (*Mark Twain in Eruption* 33, 49). Yet he did make a few exceptions. He held Anson Burlingame and General Grant in the highest regard; for a time he admired Napoleon III and Czar Alexander II. He saw them, as he saw a handful of heroic figures of the past, notably Joan of Arc, Martin Luther, and Oliver Cromwell, as motivated by a moral urgency to liberate the oppressed by toppling the mighty from their seats; and all were, in his view, free from the unforgivable sin of clowning before an audience, of begging for applause, approbation, and votes.

The hero of Mark Twain's first novel, *The Gilded Age* (1873), written in collaboration with Charles Dudley Warner, is aptly named Philip Sterling. He is entirely Warner's creation; Mark Twain's contributions to the cast are ne'er-do-wells and scoundrels. His mature view of Tom Sawyer, the hero of his first independent novel, is apparent in his invoking him years later to damn President Roosevelt; but in point of fact, even before he had finished writing *The Adventures of Tom Sawyer* (1876), he had come to see his juvenile protagonist as tainted by a craving for publicity and power, by an aspiration to become a hero. The last chapters of *Tom Sawyer* are a prelude to *Huckleberry Finn* (1885), where Tom's desire to dominate Huck constitutes the most potent threat to the latter's independence and integrity. When chance dictates that Huck represent himself as Tom Sawyer in the final section of the novel, the reader should know that Huck is in trouble, for Tom is a hero worshiper, a boy befuddled and depraved by his devotion to the literature of heroism. "Why hain't you ever read any books at all?— Baron Trenck, nor Casanova, nor Benvenuto Chelleeny, nor Henry IV, nor none of them heroes?" Tom demands of Huck (chapter 25). Huck has not. In the last chapter, Huck asks Tom, "What was his idea, time of the evasion?"—the "evasion" having been Tom's labyrinthine and unfeeling plot to set Jim, the slave already freed by his mistress's last will, "free" and to accomplish the deed with a theatricality borrowed from heroic romance literature. The idea was that Jim "would be a hero, and so would we." Tom's real intent is slightly different—transparently so: it is *he* who is to be a hero. Huck will have none of it, nor will Mark Twain. At the end of *Adventures of Huckleberry Finn* Mark Twain's distaste for heroics and hero worship is manifest and unequivocal.

Yet the figure of Tom Sawyer, who was to return in *Tom Sawyer Abroad* (1894) and *Tom Sawyer, Detective* (1896) and in several unfinished stories, appealed to Mark Twain, even as he has appealed to generations of readers.

The artistic inferiority of the two published sequels to *Tom Sawyer* and *Huckleberry Finn* and the failure of other sequels to attain completion may hint at something that the ending of *Huckleberry Finn* has suggested to many critics—Huck cannot be himself in Tom Sawyer's presence; the autonomous anti-hero (Huck's typical posture is hiding out) and the Barnum clown-hero (Tom's typical posture is posturing) cannot be comfortable together. That was a hard truth for Mark Twain, for both Huck and Tom embody parts of himself. And Tom is more recognizably a portrait of young Sam Clemens than Huck is.

Tom shares many characteristics with a type of the hero called by folklorists the youngest-best or the unpromising hero (Regan). The little David who slew the giant Goliath is one; the Cinderella who won Prince Charming away from her big sisters is another. Tom slays the larger-than-life Injun Joe (not quite literally in this book, intended for readers of all ages, but effectively); he wins his princess, Becky Thatcher, and ingratiates himself to her powerful father; he emerges from his adventures "a flittering hero." Some of his townspeople believe, indeed, that "he would be president, yet, if he escaped hanging" (chapter 24). Here the last comic clause reveals that, nearing the end of the novel, Mark Twain had begun to have second thoughts about Tom, a Teddy Roosevelt-to-be. Perhaps the development of Huck into a full-fledged anti-hero in the late chapters of the novel influenced those second thoughts. Perhaps Mark Twain saw too much of himself, of his fantasies of success and power, in the boy. Whatever the explanation, Tom's days of meaningful heroics were numbered. He had become more an embarrassment than a gratification to his creator.

Mark Twain's chief artistic success in presenting youthful heroism triumphant over gigantic opposition is surely *The Prince and the Pauper*, his next novel (1882). Here he provides not one but three rags-to-riches heroes, all with hearts of gold: Tom Canty, Prince Edward, and Miles Hendon. The tale unfolds dramatically (or melodramatically) rather than satirically, as had been the case in Mark Twain's earlier fiction. As the three heroes' stories move in artfully structured parallel fashion toward their simultaneous conclusions, all of them learn to serve: Tom, the pauper constrained to play king, learns to serve the state; Miles, the swashbuckling soldier, learns to serve in feigned abjection the true king he takes to be a helpless lunatic; and little King Edward VI, in the tatters of poverty, learns to serve his people with justice and mercy. This is a political fable, as *Tom Sawyer* had been, an exposition of the formation of effective leadership; but unlike *Tom Sawyer*, it does not attempt to address an audience of all ages: *The Prince and the Pauper* is a children's book. Its lessons are clear and commendable, but its moral universe is simpler than the real universe of politics.

In the dozen years after the appearance of *Huckleberry Finn* Mark Twain published three significant novels: *A Connecticut Yankee in King Arthur's Court* (1889), *Pudd'nhead Wilson* (1894), and *Personal Recollections of Joan of Arc* (1896). All are aimed at an adult audience; all address the problem of identifying and empowering the ideal leader, the hero; and each one is in some sense a shambles—although the first two are, in spite of that, ranked high among his accomplishments both by critics and by the larger audience. Echoes of little David and Cinderella sound in all three, but they sound dissonant notes, especially so in *A Connecticut Yankee* and *Joan of Arc*. Hank Morgan slays giant after giant and becomes Sir Boss in Arthur's England, but it is not his fate to be anointed king; and where Cinderella's story begins among cinders, Joan's story, tragically, inescapably, ends among them. David Wilson, on the other hand, emerges from the action of his tale as mayor of Dawson's Landing, but to make that outcome plausible, Mark Twain had had to struggle to extricate *Pudd'nhead Wilson* from the undermining force of "Those Extraordinary Twins," as he amusingly explains in the preface to the latter. Hank, Pudd'nhead, and Joan share one significant

feature that sets them apart from Mark Twain's earlier heroes: they are outsiders. Hank comes to Camelot from another century; Pudd'nhead comes to the sleepy Missouri village from an eastern university; Joan comes to the royal court from a provincial village sleepier than Dawson's Landing and, even more significantly, enters, a mere girl, the most masculine of worlds, the army. They have more in common with the benign aliens commonly encountered in science fiction than with the youngest-best heroes of fairy tales. They introduce us to another model of the hero significant in Mark Twain's thought and art.

The Innocents Abroad had afforded an early glimpse of that figure in Wm. C. Grimes (Mark Twain's name for the well-known travel writer William C. Prime). Grimes's books rank second only to the Bible in the frequency of allusions to them in *The Innocents Abroad*. "I love to quote Grimes," Mark Twain writes, "because he is so dramatic. And because he is so romantic. And because he seems to care but little whether he tells the truth or not, so he scares the reader or excites his envy or his admiration" (chapter 50). Dwelling on his feats of arms and horsemanship, Grimes lords it over Arab brigands and overawes American readers. The heroics of Grimes, one hand always on his revolver as he rides through deserts infested with fierce Bedouins, disgusts Mark Twain; yet a reader of Mark Twain's books in their original editions cannot easily ignore the arresting similarity between the illustration of Grimes in *The Innocents Abroad* and of Hank Morgan in *A Connecticut Yankee*, both at full gallop on gallant steeds, and the illustrations are hardly the end of the resemblance between the two figures. Mark Twain's version of Teddy Roosevelt has its roots in Grimes, but so has his Connecticut Yankee.

From Grimes to Captain Ned Blakely in *Roughing It* (1872) (the first of several characters to be based on Captain Edgar Wakeman), from Captain Blakely to Colonel Sherburn, from Colonel Sherburn to the Yankee, from the Yankee to Pudd'nhead, and from Pudd'nhead to Joan, the descent is direct and unbroken. Every one of these characters comes from outside to take in hand a world mismanaged by insiders; every one performs that feat by manifesting a titanic superiority. Mark Twain's attitudes toward such promethean figures is at the outset jaundiced; it never becomes unreservedly favorable; but as he more and more despaired of democracy's dream of an enlightened electorate's choosing the best leaders, he increasingly placed before his readers fables of promethean heroism, promethean leadership—and, in the Yankee and Joan, promethean defeat.

If Mark Twain's purpose in presenting heroic figures is to suggest the character of the leader, the promethean figure is problematic: can the hero who is not *of* the people provide governance *by* and *for* the people? *The Innocents Abroad* contains another disquieting foreshadowing of later heroic figures, the figure of Jesus, "a mysterious stranger who was a god and had stood face to face with God above the clouds[,] doing strange miracles with crowds of astonished people for witnesses" (chapter 47). Is that "mysterious stranger" an adumbration of Little Satan and Forty-Four of *The Mysterious Stranger Manuscripts*? If so, he suggests an even deeper despair about democratic leadership than the promethean figure had, for these outsiders remain utterly outside our moral universe. But perhaps "the mysterious stranger" Jesus more properly foreshadows Huckleberry Finn, who becomes radically himself, who makes his world radically his own, who, even in defeat, redeems it and purifies it. Perhaps he embodies Emerson's idea of the empowered Self as hero (Johnson). Such a view allows us to see Huck as truly heroic and to place Hank and Pudd'nhead and Joan with him in Mark Twain's pantheon of heroism.

Robert Regan

BIBLIOGRAPHY

Bentley, Eric. *A Century of Hero Worship.* 2nd ed. Boston: Beacon, 1957.

Clemens, Samuel L. *A Connecticut Yankee in King Arthur's Court.* Ed. Bernard Stein. Berkeley: U of California P, 1979.

———. *The Innocents Abroad.* Hartford, Conn.: American Publishing, 1869.

———. *Mark Twain in Eruption.* Ed. Bernard DeVoto. New York: Harper, 1924.

———. *Mark Twain's Autobiography.* Vol. 2. Ed. Albert B. Paine. New York: Harper, 1924.

Hoffman, Daniel. *Form and Fable in American Fiction.* New York: Oxford UP, 1961.

Hoffman, Andrew Jay. *Twain's Heroes, Twain's Worlds.* Philadelphia: U of Pennsylvania P, 1988.

Johnson, James L. *Mark Twain and the Limits of Power: Emerson's God in Ruins.* Knoxville: U of Tennessee P, 1982.

Regan, Robert. *Unpromising Heroes: Mark Twain and His Characters.* Berkeley: U of California P, 1966.

See also: *Adventures of Huckleberry Finn*; *Adventures of Tom Sawyer, The*; Finn, Huckleberry; Joan of Arc; Morgan, Hank

Hirst, Robert H.
(1941–)

Presently general editor of the Mark Twain Project at the University of California, Berkeley, Robert Hirst assumed that position in January 1980, following the death of Frederick Anderson early in 1979 and an interim return to the editorship by Henry Nash Smith. An assistant professor of English (1976–1979) at the University of California, Los Angeles, at the time of his appointment, Hirst had been immersed in matters Twainian since his graduate studies at Berkeley. For some ten years (1966–1976) he worked with Anderson, serving successively as editor, senior editor, and principal editor for the Mark Twain Papers.

As general editor, besides many other duties, including numerous addresses to both lay and scholarly groups, Hirst is deeply involved with all of the publications of the Mark Twain Project. More specifically, he has been coeditor (with Edgar M. Branch) of *Early Tales & Sketches* (5 volumes projected) and has coauthored (with Branch) *The Grangerford-Shepherdson Feud by Mark Twain*, a discussion of the historical backgrounds of the famous episode, with facsimiles of the Darnell-Watson feud episode from the first edition of *Life on the Mississippi* (1883) and of the *Century* magazine printing of the Grangerford-Shepherdson passages. With Brandt Rowles, he has authored "William E. James's Stereoscopic Views of the Quaker City Excursion."

Hirst has also served on the Division Executive Committee on Methods of Literary Research, Modern Language Association (1985–1989); the Committee for Scholarly Editions (CSE), Modern Language Association (1985–1989); and the Advisory Board for the Writings of Charles Sanders Peirce.

Howard G. Baetzhold

BIBLIOGRAPHY

Branch, Edgar M., and Robert H. Hirst. *The Grangerford-Shepherdson Feud by Mark Twain.* Berkeley: Friends of the Bancroft Library, 1985.

Clemens, Samuel L. *The Works of Mark Twain: Early Tales & Sketches.* Ed. Edgar M. Branch and Robert H. Hirst. 2 vols. Berkeley: U of California P, 1979–1981.

Hirst, Robert H., and Brandt Rowles. "William E. James's Stereoscopic Views of the Quaker City Excursion." *Mark Twain Journal* 22 (Spring 1984): 15–33.

See also: Mark Twain Papers

History

Samuel Langhorne Clemens was no philosopher of history, nor did he think philosophically about history. The philosopher of history is much more concerned with reflecting on the nature of the historical process and on the methods by which truth can be derived from analysis of historical data. Clemens's reading of history was extremely broad, however, and like the historian he thought critically about the past and pondered its possible meanings. He was more interested in interpretation of history and what history could teach. He was attuned to the historiographical thinking of his age, which viewed history as science rather than art; he came to believe with his contemporaries that progress would develop from the acquisition of knowledge, knowledge acquired through the application of the rules of logical positivism.

Having breathed the romantic optimism of the nineteenth century, Clemens believed in the Idea of Progress. He was especially fond of the Whig interpretation of history that political liberty would be the ultimate result of a more rational grasp of the "laws of nature," which could be derived from a scientific analysis of historical facts. However, when confronted with the ugly realities of the industrial revolution and America's turn to imperialism, Clemens recanted his faith in progress and reverted to a belief in cyclical theories of history that were more consistent with his ever increasing cynicism regarding human nature.

Most sources agree that Clemens read history prodigiously, and from that reading he received a great deal of enjoyment. He believed, however, that history should do more than entertain; he believed that history could teach. Having been influenced by eighteenth-century attitudes, he came to believe that rational knowledge was a satisfactory replacement for religion. Based on his reading of Auguste Comte, he came to believe that from a scientific reading of historical facts one could derive the "laws" of history. This approach led him away from emphasis on the great men of history toward an interest in the common man. Men were, after all, only products of their environment. In "The Secret History of Eddypus" (written 1901–1902) Clemens wrote that "the sole and only history-*makers* are *circumstance* and *environment*; that these are not within the control of man, but that men are in their control, and are helpless pawns who must move as they command" (Clemens 342).

Like modern man, Clemens was caught up in paradox. While committed to the Idea of Progress, his reading of history seemed to provide confirmation for his belief in the depravity of the human race. He was also convinced that organized religion had provided little help. His anticlericalism was derived from his reading of history. Roger B. Salomon argues that Clemens saw the period from the fall of the Roman Empire to 1800 as "a single, unified epoch whose chief institutions" were the Roman Catholic Church and feudalism (Salomon 24). His attitude toward both was negative. He was "anti-Catholic, deeply influenced by Carlyle, and fascinated with violence but generally shared the Whigs' fear of mob rule and extreme democracy" (Salomon 26). For Clemens, human liberty had been born in America, which had redeemed man from "organized cruelty" and provided opportunity for human progress.

The years from 1880 to 1890 marked the apex of Clemens's faith in civilization and its inevitable progress. American contributions to this historical pageant included political and religious liberty, a more humane penal code, the reduction of pain from the use of anaesthesia, and technological progress that resulted from American inventiveness. The rise of industry in America had provided material progress, which Clemens seemed to believe was "a Prime Mover of modern civilization, on equal terms with political liberty and legal reform" (Salomon 32).

The 1880s also marked the watershed in Clemens's thinking about what history could teach. As the industrial revolution unfolded, there seemed to be no doubt in his mind that the revolution was a product of the growth of knowledge and that new knowledge had resulted in material progress. The standard of living for Americans had improved measurably. Clemens's concern with political corruption and moral decay, however, caused him to question his assumptions regarding the positive effects of the growth of knowledge. The failure of moral progress to keep pace with material prosperity and evolutionary social development made Clemens increasingly disillusioned with modern society.

The great betrayal of the American Dream was the rush to create an American empire. The Spanish-American War, resulting in the acquisition of the Philippine Islands and Puerto Rico, the annexing of Hawaii, and the announcement of the Open Door to Chinese trade, marked America's entry as an equal into the politics of world power. How could one continue to believe in the uniqueness of the American experiment? Having been steeped in the philosophy of the Enlightenment, and the Jeffersonian vision of moral man and immoral society, in which morality would triumph over oppression, Clemens began to feel a sense of personal guilt. American imperialism forced Twain "to reconcile and coalesce his theory of history with a conception of human nature that all his life had tended to be dark" (Salomon 44–45). His faith in the Whig interpretation of history was shattered.

For the Whig interpretation of history, Clemens substituted a more reactionary cyclical view of history that traced the rise of civilization from barbarism to high levels of human achievement back to barbarism. The Jeffersonian Eden of the early nineteenth century was nothing more than an illusion. When confronted with what Clemens called the facts of history, he was forced to conclude that man was damned by his own nature and an unalterable pattern of destruction built into the cosmos. Modernity had triumphed over romanticism, and the final meaning of history was that it had no meaning at all.

Stanley W. Campbell

BIBLIOGRAPHY

Baetzhold, Howard G. *Mark Twain and John Bull: The British Connection*. Bloomington: Indiana UP, 1970.

Clemens, Samuel L. "The Secret History of Eddypus, The World-Empire." *Mark Twain's Fables of Man*. By Clemens. Ed. John S. Tuckey. Berkeley: U of California P, 1972. 318–382.

Gribben, Alan. *Mark Twain's Library: A Reconstruction*. 2 vols. Boston: G.K. Hall, 1980.

Salomon, Roger B. *Twain and the Image of History*. New Haven, Conn.: Yale UP, 1961.

Williams, James D. "The Use of History in Mark Twain's *A Connecticut Yankee*." *Publications of the Modern Language Association* 80 (March 1965): 102–110.

See also: Carlyle, Thomas; *Connecticut Yankee in King Arthur's Court, A*; Evolution; Lecky, William Edward Hartpole; Philosophy

Hoax

Mark Twain's hoaxes go far beyond the usual sense of the term. Twain began, to be sure, by presenting as fact what only gradually dawned upon a reader as impossibility, and he appears to have done this for the sheer joy of the thing. As the reworkings of some of his early hoaxes show, his concern was to take in the gullible public. Soon he was exploiting the blindness and wish fantasies that accounted for that gullibility.

In his famous "Petrified Man" swindle (the hoax itself dates from October 1862; "The Petrified Man," including Twain's comments on the public's gullibility, is in *Sketches, New and Old*, 1875), as with most of the hoaxes perpetrated throughout his career, Twain achieved delight by taking in the foolish. As late as "A Double-Barreled Detective Story" (1902), with its "lilacs and laburnums . . . burning and flashing in the upper air," and various other equally beautiful and imaginary wonders of nature, Twain was still fishing for gullible consumers of mindless sentiment. And catching them. He likewise delighted in the story that gets broken off before its conclusion, after setting up the reader for some sort of conventionally sappy ending. Repeatedly, and throughout his life, he pretends to be retelling a legend or presenting a serious account, only to break off before the anticipated conclusion or else to embroil his protagonist in enormous difficulties and then to conclude—while readers gasp in disappointment—that he cannot possibly extricate the fictional victim of his ingenuity and so must move on to something else (for example, *Following the Equator* [1897], chapter 20—but examples abound).

As Twain developed his own brand of literary hoax, his target increasingly became the public's thirst for meaningless sensationalism and sentimentality. At the end of "My Bloody Massacre" (*Sketches, Old and New*, 1875—based on the "Empire City Massacre," Virginia City *Territorial Enterprise*, 28 October 1863), Twain laments the very trait that makes possible the hoax in the first place, the tendency of most readers to skim over the "dull explanatory surroundings" that would prevent their being taken in. "[W]e skip all that, and hasten to revel in the blood-curdling particulars and be happy." Were his hoaxes to succeed in their educational thrust, that is, Twain would have no more audience for them. But he rightly felt that he need have no fears on that score. To this day, readers of *Adventures of Huckleberry Finn* (1885) fully expect Tom Sawyer to free a slave. That Tom represents respectable, slaveowning society, as Huck repeatedly forces readers to see, seems to make no difference: sentimentality and other forms of wishful thinking enable people to believe in Tom's apparent rebellion. Twain's hoaxes still have willing takers.

Pascal Covici, Jr.

BIBLIOGRAPHY

Clemens, Samuel L. *Mark Twain in Eruption*. Ed. Bernard DeVoto. New York: Harper, 1940.

Covici, Pascal, Jr. *Mark Twain's Humor: The Image of a World*. Dallas: Southern Methodist UP, 1962.

Rogers, Franklin R. *Mark Twain's Burlesque Patterns as Seen in the Novels and Narratives, 1855–1885*. Dallas: Southern Methodist UP, 1960.

Smith, Henry Nash. *Mark Twain: The Development of a Writer*. Cambridge, Mass.: Harvard UP, 1962.

See also: Humor; Sentimentality

Holmes, Oliver Wendell
(1809–1894)

A minor writer and informant on the pervasive cultural climate of nineteenth-century Boston and New England and on scientific and medical issues, Oliver Wendell Holmes was not a professional man of letters. His paper on the contagiousness of puerpural fever (1843), his profession, and his writings led to his admission to the Hall of Fame of Great Americans (New York University) in 1910. His major works include *Poems* (1836), *The Autocrat of the Breakfast Table* (1858), *The Professor at the Breakfast Table* (1860), and *Elsie Venner* (1861).

Holmes was born in Cambridge, Massachusetts, graduated from Harvard, and studied medicine in Paris. He married Amelia Lee Jackson in 1840 and was appointed professor of anatomy and physiology at Harvard Medical School in 1847. Holmes's personal essays, addressed to a fictional audience, capture a still readable flavor of spontaneous talk, employing an urbane and ironical tone and offering aphoristic commentary. Acquainted with Mark Twain, Holmes generously overlooked Twain's unconscious borrowing of Holmes's dedication in his *Poems* for *Innocents Abroad* (1869).

Typical nineteenth-century criticism assesses Holmes's personal, social, and medical activities while emphasizing his anti-Calvinism and intelligent conversation. *Elsie Venner*, though not successful as fiction, credits Holmes with an attempt to originate a more liberal, a less theological, attitude toward human behavior. Critics after the 1970s begin to reappraise his view on the segregated roles of men and women and on his new treatment of the mentally ill.

Charlotte S. McClure

BIBLIOGRAPHY

Holmes, Oliver Wendell. *The Autocrat of the Breakfast Table.* Boston: Phillips, Sampson, 1858.

———. *The Complete Poetical Works of Oliver Wendell Holmes.* Cambridge ed. Boston: Houghton Mifflin, 1895.

———. *The Complete Writings of Oliver Wendell Holmes.* 13 vols. Boston: Houghton Mifflin, 1891.

———. *Elsie Venner: A Romance of Destiny.* Boston: Ticknor and Fields, 1861.

———. *The Professor at the Breakfast Table.* Boston: Ticknor and Fields, 1860.

Menikoff, Barry. "Oliver Wendell Holmes." *Fifteen American Authors Before 1900: Bibliographical Essays on Research and Criticism.* Ed. Earl N. Harbert and Robert A. Rees. Madison: U of Wisconsin P, 1984. 207–228.

Tilton, Eleanor M. *Amiable Autocrat: A Biography of Doctor Oliver Wendell Holmes.* New York: Henry Schuman, 1947.

Holmes, Sherlock

The well-known star of Arthur Conan Doyle's detective fiction, Sherlock Holmes makes a guest appearance in Mark Twain's burlesque short story "A Double-Barreled Detective Story" (1902) as the uncle of the rough and coarse Fetlock Jones. Described as "a grave and dignified foreigner of distinguished bearing and appearance" (Clemens 448), the famous detective arrives at Hope Canyon, California, to unravel the mystery of Flint Buckner's murder. He fails miserably, accusing the wrong man, Sammy Hillyer, of the crime. Hero Archy Stillman subsequently solves the case and upstages the "Extraordinary Man." Apparently Holmes makes a habit of pursuing the wrong man. A "lunatic" named James Walker appears on the scene, confessing that he has been driven witless by Holmes's dogged but misguided pursuit. Walker relates an incident in Colorado when a mob, enraged by Holmes's antics, attempted to burn the meddling detective alive only to be thwarted by the brave Sheriff Jack Fairfax. The detective's charmed life appears to end, however, when Wells-Fargo Ferguson tells the distraught Walker not to worry about Holmes any longer: "They hung him in San Bernardino last week . . . whilst he was searching around after you. Mistook him for another man. They're sorry, but they can't help it now" (Clemens 464). The reader is left uncertain of the detective's fate, however, since Ferguson is "a clever strategist" who wants to calm Walker when all attempts to do so fail; his news about Holmes may be a ruse.

Holmes is obviously an object of ridicule in this condensed novel intended to satirize by parody Arthur Conan Doyle's pompous detective. The term "Double-Barreled" in the title refers to the story's dual focus. The first installment (or barrel) is serious, replete with cruelty and sadism, as it parodies the plots of two Arthur Conan Doyle novels—*The Hound of the Baskervilles* (1901) and *A Study in Scarlet* (1887). The second installment (or barrel) seems to begin afresh on a beautiful October morning; the purple prose is so exaggerated, however, as to suggest literary parody, and the story quickly becomes a farcical burlesque of Doyle's incompetent detective (Emerson 239).

Don L.F. Nilsen

BIBLIOGRAPHY

Clemens, Samuel L. "A Double-Barreled Detective Story." *The Complete Short Stories of Mark Twain.* By Clemens. Ed. Charles Neider. Garden City, N.Y.: Hanover House, 1957. 423–469.

Emerson, Everett. *The Authentic Mark Twain: A Literary Biography of Samuel L. Clemens.* Philadelphia: U of Pennsylvania P, 1984.

Long, E. Hudson. *Mark Twain Handbook.* New York: Hendricks House, 1957.

Wilson, James D. *A Reader's Guide to the Short Stories of Mark Twain.* Boston: G.K. Hall, 1987.

See also: Detective Fiction; "Double-Barreled Detective Story, A"; Doyle, Arthur Conan

"Holy Children, The"

(1972)

Written before 1882, this story remained unpublished during Twain's lifetime, though the last half of the tale was incorporated into "The Second Advent" (written 1881), a story closely related in tone.

In "The Holy Children," three sisters—Hope, Mary, and Cecilia—through their holy living are granted immediate and definite answers to their prayers. This blessing soon leads to chaos when the many contradictory requests disrupt the weather and the lives of the townspeople. The girls' activities are restricted, but in the end the sisters are executed to preserve the natural order. Twain portrays Hope, Mary, and Cecilia as innocents whose religious qualities mature after their oppressive father's death; however, they wield their powers indiscriminately on behalf of a fickle community, a practice revealing both the sisters and the townspeople as objects of Twain's criticism.

In this ironic tale Twain shows the potential danger inherent in the Christian belief in divinely answered prayer if every petitioner is granted his request. But as a short story, "The Holy Children" remains an unrevised draft that, by relying on exaggerated incidents and an abrupt conclusion, distances the reader's sympathies from the girls' ultimate tragedy.

Charles Franklyn Beach

BIBLIOGRAPHY

Clemens, Samuel L. *Mark Twain's Fables of Man.* Ed. John S. Tuckey. Berkeley: U of California P, 1972.

Johnson, James L. *Mark Twain and the Limits of Power: Emerson's God in Ruins.* Knoxville: U of Tennessee P, 1982.

Wilson, James D. *A Reader's Guide to the Short Stories of Mark Twain.* Boston: G.K. Hall, 1987.

See also: Religion; "Second Advent, The"

Holy Land, The

On nineteenth-century maps, "Palestine" usually appeared as part of Greater Syria, which also included the Lebanon Mountains and Beirut. Though its "New Pilgrims Progress" subtitle recalls Bunyan, *The Innocents Abroad* (1869) encapsulated a wide variety of travel experiences (aside from religious pilgrimage to Jerusalem), made possible by steamships and "Thomas Cook": for example, "passionate pilgrims" to Gibraltar, Paris, Rome, and Venice; and touring "pagan" Europe and the Mediterranean. "Holy Land" is thus not a geopolitical but rather a religious concept (or a cultural "Myth"); and Mark Twain's 1869 best seller dug deep enough to be not just a journalistic mirror, but also a spiritual lamp.

In addition to *The Arabian Nights* and "the East" (James's "Asian mystery," with its romance and adventure), his primary reference was to the Promised Land of the Bible (Ensor)—and within that context, more Protestant than Catholic and perhaps more Old than New Testament. For tourists the guide was Baedeker, but for the pious there were books by Prime (satirized as "Grimes") and others. The direction was "archaeological": back through history, geography, and tradition to the medieval and ancient past.

Roughly, "The Holy Land" occupies the last twenty chapters of *The Innocents Abroad*, and Mark Twain's approach is gradual and finally dramatic. Greece and Turkey (the "Seven Churches"), the group he was with took the "long route"—that is, "out into Syria, by Baalbek to Damascus, and thence down through the full length of Palestine" (41). There is vagueness about borders in this part: of course, Damascus (44–45) was the city of St. Paul's vision; but beginning in chapter 46, we cross a line, and at Dan ("from Dan to Beersheba") "a cannonball would carry beyond the confines of Holy Land" to "profane ground three miles away." The encounter with actual Palestine requires a painful "system of reduction": "I could not conceive of a small country having so large a history." Other disillusions: "the voice of the turtle" (dove) is *not* heard by Jack; the "tombs" of Noah, Joseph (and later Adam) are not impressive; and even Jerusalem is "So small!" (end of 52).

Yet the sacred text and history have power; and after Jerusalem, they all go on to Bethany, Jericho, the Dead Sea and wilderness, Mars (sic) Saba, and Bethlehem (cf. Melville in *Clarel*). On the one hand, modern "Palestine is desolate"—and on the other, "[I]t is dreamland." For Clemens, it was associated also with Freemasonry (Solomon's Temple), the Wandering Jew of legend, Apocrypha ("Infance of Jesus"), Christmas (letter to "Mother" Fairbanks, 24 December 1868), and the poetry of religion. Mark Twain's treatment of religion was attacked as "irreverent" (Walker), but it is the *balance* between a true rhetoric of piety and the modest "some account" of a "pleasure excursion . . . with descriptions of countries, nations, incidents, and adventures as they appeared to the author" (title page) that spoke for and to Twain's generation and made *The Innocents Abroad* an American classic.

Sholom Kahn

BIBLIOGRAPHY

Clemens, Samuel L. *The Innocents Abroad*. Hartford, Conn.: American Publishing, 1869.

———. *Mark Twain to Mrs. Fairbanks*. Ed. Dixon Wecter. San Marino, Calif.: Huntington Library, 1949.

Ensor, Allison. *Mark Twain and the Bible*. Lexington: U of Kentucky P, 1969.

Handy, Robert T. *The Holy Land in American Protestant Life, 1800–1948: A Documentary History*. New York: Arno P, 1981.

Pellowe, William C.S. *Mark Twain: Pilgrim from Hannibal*. New York: Hobson Book, 1945.

Prime, William C. *Tent Life in the Holy Land*. New York: Harper, 1857.

Walker, Franklin D. *Irreverent Pilgrims: Melville, Browne and Mark Twain in the Holy Land*. Seattle: U of Washington P, 1974.

See also: Bible; *Innocents Abroad, The*; Religion

Homes and Literary Sites

Mark Twain is associated with several locations in the United States that hold interest for both visitors and scholars. The places in which he lived are Florida and Hannibal, Missouri; Hartford, Connecticut; Buffalo and Elmira, New York. His papers are housed at the Bancroft Library as part of the Mark Twain Project at the University of California at Berkeley.

Mark Twain was born in Florida, Missouri, in 1835. The town that was once Florida is now under Mark Twain Lake. Twain's log cabin birthplace is preserved within a museum open to the public that lies midway between Paris and Perry, Missouri. The museum also contains articles from other years of his life.

Probably no town in the world is more closely associated with an author than is Hannibal, Missouri, on the Mississippi River. Mark Twain's family moved approximately twenty-five miles from Florida to Hannibal, Missouri, when he was four years old in an attempt for his father, John Marshall Clemens, to increase his fortune. Twain left as a young man to become first a typesetter, to work on the river, and to endure a brief stint in the Civil War before heading for the Nevada

Territory. He returned to Hannibal sporadically during his life. His last visit to Hannibal was in 1902, but Hannibal lives forever in his writings under many names: St. Petersburg, Dawson's Landing, Hadleyburg, and others. Twain's best work reflects his childhood experience in this town near the Mississippi. The boyhood home at 208 Hill Street and its nearby museum both are open to the public, and contain many items from Mark Twain's life and work. Across the street from the boyhood home is the law office of John Marshall Clemens. The home of Twain's childhood sweetheart Laura Hawkins is next to the law office.

Mark Twain's first home as a married man was in Buffalo, New York. He and his wife, Olivia Langdon Clemens, moved into a house that was a wedding present from his father-in-law, Jervis Langdon, following their wedding in February 1870. Twain and Livy lived in this house while he worked as a newspaper editor on the Buffalo *Express*. Jervis Langdon had loaned his son-in-law the money to secure a one-third interest in this newspaper. The home in Buffalo was not a happy one for the newlyweds. Twain soon grew tired of the newspaper office. Jervis Langdon died within six months of his daughter's wedding. Twain's only son, the sickly Langdon Clemens, was born in this home, and Livy's friend Emma Nye died of typhoid there. Twain and Livy left it after living there a little over a year. Because the house later burned, visiting is no longer possible for Mark Twain enthusiasts.

Mark Twain and Livy moved to the Nook Farm area of Hartford, Connecticut, in October 1871 to be closer to Twain's publisher and Livy's friends. Twain's Nook Farm neighbors included Harriet Beecher Stowe, the author of *Uncle Tom's Cabin* (1851–1852); Isabella Beecher Hooker, the women's rights activist; Charles Dudley Warner, author and collaborator with Twain on *The Gilded Age* (1873).

At first Twain and Livy lived in a rented home. They built their three-story, high Victorian gothic style home at 351 Farmington Avenue and moved into the unfinished house

September 1874. Livy worked closely with the architect Edward Tuckerman Potter, supplying him with sketches of how she wanted the rooms laid out to overlook various parts of Nook Farm. The house resembles a riverboat, even with a third-floor "pilot's house" that overlooked a small river. Livy undertook a major redecoration of the home in 1881. The redecoration was done by Associated Artists of New York, which included Louis Comfort Tiffany. Although the expense of maintaining this home led them to live in Europe and Elmira, New York, in the summer, Twain and Livy loved the house they built and in which they raised their three daughters. In his autobiography Twain described the house as having "a heart, and a soul, and eyes." But due to financial reversals, Twain and Livy left the house in 1891 to live abroad. Livy never did enter it again. They finally sold the house in 1903, distraught and unable to live in it after Susy died there in 1896 of spinal meningitis.

The Mark Twain Memorial maintains the house today, and it is open to the public, for it has been restored to its 1881 splendor. Many papers concerning the Langdon family are part of the Stowe-Day Foundation, also located at Nook Farm. The Stowe-Day Library contains over 15,000 volumes and 100,000 manuscript items. The memorial and the foundation sponsor many educational programs from the elementary through the university level at Nook Farm, celebrating Mark Twain and his era.

Because the Hartford home was designed for entertaining, Mark Twain actually did most of his writing at the Langdon summer home of Quarry Farm in the hills above Elmira, New York. Elmira played a part in Mark Twain's life for over forty years, from 1868 when he came to visit the Langdon family until his death in 1910. Three of the Clemens children, Susy, Clara, and Jean, were born at Elmira. Twain, Livy, and their children spent many happy summers at Quarry Farm. Twain and the members of his family are buried in Elmira's Woodlawn Cemetery.

Mark Twain completed many of his best-known works—*The Adventures of Tom Sawyer* (1876), *Adventures of Huckleberry Finn* (1885), *Life on the Mississippi* (1883), and others—in an octagonal study built for him in 1874 by his sister-in-law, Sue Crane, who owned Quarry Farm. The study was 100 yards from the house. When he wrote in the study, Twain could look down on the Chemung River in the valley below. The study is now on the campus of Elmira College. The Langdon family gave Quarry Farm to Elmira College in 1982 to establish the Center for Mark Twain Studies at Quarry Farm. While not open to the public, it is a place for visiting scholars and students who wish to partake in various seminars and workshops centering on Mark Twain.

The largest deposit for Mark Twain's papers is in the Mark Twain Project at the University of California at Berkeley in the Bancroft Library. These papers include the original letters, notebooks, manuscripts, and unpublished works of Mark Twain and those close to him. Access to these materials is available through permission.

Resa Willis

BIBLIOGRAPHY

Andrews, Kenneth R. *Nook Farm: Mark Twain's Hartford Circle.* Cambridge, Mass.: Harvard UP, 1950.

Clemens, Samuel L. *Mark Twain's Autobiography.* Ed. Albert B. Paine. 2 vols. New York: Harper, 1924.

Jerome, Robert D., and Herbert A. Wisbey, Jr., eds. *Mark Twain in Elmira.* Elmira, N.Y.: Mark Twain Society, 1977.

See also: Buffalo, New York; Elmira, New York; Elmira College Center for Mark Twain Studies at Quarry Farm; Florida, Missouri; Hannibal, Missouri; Mark Twain Boyhood Home; Mark Twain Papers; Nook Farm; Quarry Farm

Hooker, Isabella Beecher
(1822–1907)

Isabella Beecher Hooker was an eccentric member of a prodigious New England family of authors and religious thinkers. Her contribution to family fame was her role as equal rights advocate and as a spiritualist who believed she was divinely appointed to govern a millenial matriarchy. She played a notable part in a major family rupture when her brother Henry Ward Beecher was accused of adultery (1872). Her works include *A Mother's Letters to Her Daughter on Women's Suffrage* (1870) and *Womanhood: Its Sanctities and Fidelities* (1873).

Isabella, "Belle," was born in Litchfield, Connecticut. She was the first living child of Lyman Beecher's second wife. She and her husband, John Hooker, founded Nook Farm in Hartford (1851). Mark Twain stayed with the Hookers when he visited Nook Farm (21 January 1868). The Clemenses rented the Hooker home (1871–1874) while their mansion in Nook Farm was built. The only Beecher to disbelieve in Henry's innocence, Isabella railed against him in a variety of embarrassing ways. This infuriated Mark Twain, a supporter of Henry Beecher. He forbade his wife Olivia ever to cross Isabella's door. Future relations were strained, understandably, and complicated in addition by the peculiarities of the Hookers' spiritualist activities.

Janet Gabler-Hover

BIBLIOGRAPHY

Andrews, Kenneth R. *Nook Farm: Mark Twain's Hartford Circle.* Cambridge, Mass.: Harvard UP, 1950.

Caskey, Marie. *Chariot of Fire: Religion and the Beecher Family.* New Haven, Conn.: Yale UP, 1977.

Hooker, Isabella Beecher. *The Isabella Beecher Hooker Project.* A Microfiche Edition of Her Papers. Millwood, N.Y.: KTO Microform, 1979. Hartford, Conn.: Stowe-Day Foundation, 1979.

Rugoff, Milton. *The Beechers: An American Family in the Nineteenth Century.* New York: Harper & Row, 1981.

See also: Beecher, Henry Ward; Hooker, John; Nook Farm

Hooker, John

(1816–1901)

Sixth in direct descent from theologian Thomas Hooker (1586–1647), John Hooker was Isabella Beecher Hooker's tolerant husband. John and Isabella bought Nook Farm (1851) and were thus the founders of the literary colony that eventually included Mark Twain (1871–1891). John's legal career missed prominence. He shared his wife's fondness for water cures and spiritualism. Although John believed with Isabella that Henry Ward Beecher was an adulterer, he loathed scandal. Hooker attempted to mend fences with the Nook Farm colony through more muted forms of accusation against Beecher. Joseph Twichell told Mark Twain in disgust that Hooker managed briefly to cast doubt on Beecher.

Janet Gabler-Hover

BIBLIOGRAPHY

Andrews, Kenneth R. *Nook Farm: Mark Twain's Hartford Circle.* Cambridge, Mass.: Harvard UP, 1950.

Caskey, Marie. *Chariot of Fire: Religion and the Beecher Family.* New Haven, Conn.: Yale UP, 1977.

Hooker, John. *Some Reminiscences of a Long Life.* Hartford, Conn.: Belknap and Warfield, 1899.

Rugoff, Milton. *The Beechers: An American Family in the Nineteenth Century.* New York: Harper & Row, 1981.

See also: Hooker, Isabella Beecher; Nook Farm

"Horse's Tale, A"

(1906)

In September 1905, when Minnie Maddern Fiske, actress and animal rights activist, asked Mark Twain to write a story that would counteract the evils of bullfighting, he agreed. "A Horse's Tale" appeared serially in the August and September 1906 issues of *Harper's Monthly.* Fiske was grateful, claiming the story would help her efforts in Mexico. A year later (1907), Harper and Brothers published "A Horse's Tale" as a slim volume of 153 pages, with illustrations by Lucius Hitchcock.

In his acknowledgments, Mark Twain confessed that his description of bullfighting [chapter 11] came straight from John Hay's *Castilian Days;* "military minutiae" was taken from three military handbooks; one bugle call was "lifted" from Delibes's "Sylvia," unplayable on the bugle but suitable when performed on the orchestrelle during Mark Twain's readings of "A Horse's Tale" to captive audiences.

Flawed by a profusion of narrators—including a talking horse, Buffalo Bill's Soldier Boy—the story centers on orphaned Cathy Alison, age nine, who has come from Europe to stay with her bachelor uncle General Tom Alison, commandant of the Seventh Cavalry at Fort Paxton. Winsome and bright, she succeeds in learning military drills, Indian languages, and the art of bugling. Eventually she returns to her native Spain with Soldier Boy, a gift from Buffalo Bill. The horse is stolen, but in the final chapter it is seen being gored during a bullfight. When Cathy rushes to embrace her horse, she is attacked by the bull. "All mangled and drenched in blood," she is taken home and later dies as a bugle sounds "Taps."

Mark Twain liked his story, especially when he finally realized the model for Cathy Alison was his deceased daughter Susy. (Cathy also resembles daughter Jean, who typed the manuscript.) To daughter Clara, Mark Twain gloated over the financial reward—an average of $700 per day for eight days' writing. Contemporaries liked the story: "Intense melodrama," with pathos, satire, and "not a little fun"; it has "a beast's eye-view of humanity," said the anonymous New York *Times* reviewer (23 November 1907). The Butte *Miner* (Montana) praised "its wonderful exposition of the workings of the mind of a child" (16 July 1911). Recent critics have called "A Horse's Tale" both overly sentimental and sadistic, uncomfortable to read.

Scholars consider this confused narrative a negligible piece of Mark Twain's later writing. Its lack of structural discipline is a serious flaw, and its gushing tone especially repelling, but here and there are peppery comments by the typical Twain, such as a horse's theory that "[man] is kind enough when he is not excited by religion." Moreover, "A Horse's Tale" is important to the study of Mark Twain's attitude toward females, including prepubescent girls.

Mary Boewe

BIBLIOGRAPHY

Clemens, Samuel L. *A Horse's Tale.* New York: Harper, 1907.

Wilson, James D. *A Reader's Guide to the Short Stories of Mark Twain.* Boston: G.K. Hall, 1987.

See also: Animals

Hotten, John Camden

(1832–1873)

English publisher, editor, and author of *The Slang Dictionary* (1859), *Handbook of Topography and Family History of England and Wales* (1863), and books reflecting diverse antiquarian interests (Welland 17), John Camden Hotten raised Twain's ire with his unauthorized publication of Twain's work. The piracies included *Innocents Abroad* in two parts in 1870 and a single-volume edition in 1871, as well as various Twain sketches in *Eye Openers* (1871) and *The Choice Humorous Works of Mark Twain* (1873), the last including Hotten's complimentary biographical sketch of Twain.

In London on 21 September 1872 Twain wrote to the *Spectator* attacking "John Camden Hottentot" for his piracies and editorial liberties. Hotten defended himself in the same forum a week later.

Though he never paid Twain directly, Hotten paradoxically helped establish the American author's reputation in England, and his memoir of Twain remained unchanged in a later edition of *The Choice Works*, one published by Chatto and Windus and approved by Twain (Ganzel 242).

After Hotten's death, Twain could mention his former adversary's name without rancor, suggesting that he felt ambivalent toward the energetic publisher (Welland 29).

Richard Gaughran

BIBLIOGRAPHY

Clemens, Samuel L. "Mark Twain's Unpublished Letters to His English Publishers." Ed. Cyril Clemens. *Mark Twain Quarterly* 4 (Summer–Fall, 1941): 1–2; 24.

Ganzel, Dewey. "Samuel Clemens and John Camden Hotten." *Library.* Fifth Series, 20 (September 1965): 230–242.

Welland, Dennis. *Mark Twain in England.* Atlantic Highlands, N.J.: Humanities P, 1978.

See also: Copyright

"How I Edited an Agricultural Paper Once"

(1870)

This sketch was first published in the *Galaxy*, July 1870. Twain describes what followed his taking over the editorship of an agricultural paper while its regular editor was away on vacation. Having had no experience either at agriculture or in editing an agricultural journal, Twain makes numerous ludicrous mistakes, imagining that turnips grow on trees, that guano is a bird, that pumpkins are berries considered very good for feeding cows even though they do not serve well as shade trees. When the editor returns, he castigates Twain for his stupidity, but Twain turns his wrath aside by pointing out numerous examples showing that knowledge of a particular field is unnecessary for writing about it in the newspaper.

Allison R. Ensor

See also: Galaxy; Journalism

"How to Tell a Story"

(1895)

In "How to Tell a Story" (*Youth's Companion*, 3 October 1895), Mark Twain became as interested in the craft of telling a story as he had been in that of piloting a steamboat. He had great capacity for taking pains in each. He knew, as he makes clear in the example of Mr.

Brown in "Old Times on the Mississippi" (1875), that too many details bury the tale and numb its auditors, but he also knew how to extract enormous humor from the very defect of unselective memory (see, among others, "His Grandfather's Ram" [1872]). Deliberate artistry lay behind the apparent spontaneity of his lazy-sounding drawl, just as the apparent ease of his written prose conceals the revisions that make the "Jumping Frog" (1865) story, for example, a sharp contrast between eastern busyness and western sociability.

His contrast between what he calls the American "humorous story"—essentially, the creation of a *persona* that becomes more important than the events that they mask or a narrator presents—and the English "comic" and the French "witty" manners of telling suggests both a clear sense of ways in which stories get told and a distorted view of his own practice. That is, he says that he scorns all but the "American" manner, which has as its end the creation of a poker-faced character too dense to see the humorous nature of his own tale. Although Twain certainly mastered this "high and delicate art," as he calls it, explicitly scorning the other modes (e.g., in his presentation of Sir Dinadan, the teller of horrendous jokes in *A Connecticut Yankee* [1889]), he frequently uses the "witty" and the "comic," too.

Twain illustrates the pause—certainly one of his own strongest technical skills—in a story that depends upon a punch line, "The Golden Arm." (This short tale has become an American favorite, appearing in print first obscurely in 1888, then in "How to Tell a Story.") Similarly, in his toast to "The Babies" (1879), again revealing absolute mastery of the pause, Twain relied upon the technique that he here maligns, the smash ending. "How to Tell a Story," however uneven as an explication of Twain's own methods, shows a master thinking insightfully about the practices of his craft. Its interest, therefore, endures.

Pascal Covici, Jr.

BIBLIOGRAPHY

Clemens, Samuel L. "How to Tell a Story." *Selected Shorter Writings of Mark Twain.* Ed. Walter Blair. Riverside ed. Boston: Houghton Mifflin, 1962. 239–245.

Covici, Pascal, Jr. *Mark Twain's Humor: The Image of a World.* Dallas: Southern Methodist UP, 1962.

Rogers, Franklin R. *Mark Twain's Burlesque Patterns as Seen in the Novels and Narratives, 1855–1885.* Dallas: Southern Methodist UP, 1960.

Smith, Henry Nash. *Mark Twain: The Development of a Writer.* Cambridge, Mass.: Harvard UP, 1962.

See also: Deadpan; Humor

Howells, William Dean
(1837–1920)

Born in Martin's Ferry, Ohio (1 March 1837), and reared in post-frontier villages, William Dean Howells rose to prominence by coming east and establishing himself in the cultural centers of Boston and, later, New York. Votary of New England's literary lights, friend and patron of contemporary writers, champion of realism as an international movement, author of more than 100 books and innumerable columns for the *Atlantic Monthly* and *Harper's Monthly*, Howells became the most influential man of letters in his generation.

Throughout a long career, Howells distinguished himself primarily as a novelist. His dozen best comprise the following: *A Foregone Conclusion* (1875), *A Modern Instance* (1882), *The Rise of Silas Lapham* (1885), *Indian Summer* (1886), *April Hopes* (1888), *Annie Kilburn* (1889), *A Hazard of New Fortunes* (1890), *The Shadow of a Dream* (1890), *The World of Chance* (1893), *The Landlord at Lion's Head* (1897), *The Son of Royal Langbrith* (1904), and *The Leatherwood God* (1916). Howells worked in nearly every other genre as well: narrative and lyric poetry, sketch, essay, critical review, short story, utopian romance, travel writing, drama, biography, and autobiography. Never widely popular as a writer, Howells was nonetheless well paid and highly respected. In 1904 he was elected to the American Academy of Arts and Letters, first among seven charter members. He served from 1908 to 1920 as the first president of the Academy, which established an award for fiction in his name.

During the 1880s especially, Howells's realism was controversial insofar as it assaulted genteel pieties and popular taste. In polemical reviews he denounced what he called the literosity and effectism of neoromantic fiction. Late in his career, however, Howells had come to seem all too benign an elder. Although he had always signed his work unpretentiously as W.D. Howells, he was now dubbed the "Dean" of American letters and lashed for posterity to a fustian, three-barreled name. At the time of his death in 1920, having outlived both his contemporaries and his disciples, Howells was condemned by the insurgent modernists as a superannuated relic of Victorian inhibition. His life and works were debunked by Van Wyck Brooks, H.L. Mencken, Sinclair Lewis, and others, and his reputation plummeted. Despite a revival of academic interest since the 1950s, Howells's currency has not fully recovered from the critical deflation of the 1920s. At present he seems, paradoxically, both to be central to Victorian American culture and to be marginal to the literary canon.

The second son in a large family, Howells was steeped in the radicalism of his father, a staunch abolitionist and Swedenborgian convert, who eked out a living as a country printer and newspaper editor. Howells was close to William Cooper Howells, a dreamy and gentle man despite his fierce opinions, but he was closer still to his mother, Mary Dean Howells, who was unfitted by temperament and background to an arduous life in the Western Reserve. Howells was profoundly affected by the marital chill that underlay the parental warmth of his family home. An anxious child, given to nightmares and phobias, he fell into nervous prostration at the age of seventeen (1854), vulnerable thereafter to mental perturbation. He suffered a subsequent breakdown in 1881, at the age of forty-four. Despite private stress, Howells, who was short and increasingly rotund, projected a public

image of calm geniality, and his career was a Franklinesque model of success in his ascent from poverty and obscurity to a state of affluence and some degree of reputation in the world.

Young Howells lacked much formal education, but he drilled himself in languages and read voraciously, turning his work in the family print shop into a writer's apprenticeship. The literary passions of his youth included Miguel de Cervantes, Heinrich Heine, William Shakespeare, Oliver Goldsmith, Jane Austen, and Alfred Tennyson, as well as the leading writers of New England. Howells began to publish poems and stories during his teens, impelled by a desire to escape the provinciality of Ohio. As a journalist in Columbus, he seized the chance to write a campaign biography of Abraham Lincoln, a fellow westerner, which was published the same year (1860) as Howells's first book, *Poems of Two Friends* (with James J. Piatt), and five poems of his accepted by James Russell Lowell for the *Atlantic Monthly*. On the strength of this entree to the East, Howells traveled to Boston, where he was ordained into the apostolic succession of the New England clerisy by such eminences as Lowell, Oliver Wendell Holmes, Henry Wadsworth Longfellow, Ralph Waldo Emerson, Nathaniel Hawthorne, and their publisher, James T. Fields.

Howells sought the patronage too of Lincoln, now president, who duly appointed him to the consulship at Venice. Here, safely removed from the Civil War, Howells got married (to Elinor Mead in 1862), explored Italy, and redoubled his literary pursuits. Dampening his poetic ambitions, he launched himself instead as a travel writer in *Venetian Life* (1866), first published to acclaim in the Boston *Advertiser*. This book and its sequel, *Italian Journeys* (1867), smoothed the way for Howells's postwar career as an assistant editor, first of the *Nation* and then of the *Atlantic* itself in 1866. Within five years he had succeeded Fields as editor-in-chief, a position that he held until 1881 and that he used strategically to enlarge the magazine's regional base to include the emergent writers, including women, of the south and west. Howells's own earliest fiction—*Suburban Sketches* (1871), *Their Wedding Journey* (1872), *A Chance Acquaintance* (1873)—also began to appear serially in the *Atlantic*.

It was in 1869, in the offices of the magazine, that Howells first met Mark Twain, who was seeking the author of an anonymous review of *The Innocents Abroad* (1869). A close and abiding friendship was forged. Throughout the next forty years, the two men's professional fortunes and personal lives were closely intertwined. Howells and Clemens shared more than western backgrounds, literary aims, and democratic principles. Their domestic circumstances were also similar: both married invalided women; both tragically lost beloved daughters; both lived peripatetically.

Before Howells's review of *The Innocents Abroad*, such subscription books had rarely been deemed worthy of notice in the lofty *Atlantic*. "Mr. Clements," as he had erroneously been called, was thrilled to find himself praised as more than a merely popular writer and set apart from the common run of California humorists. Howells's advocacy of Mark Twain, particularly of the serious dimension of his comic work, was to continue unabated in favorable reviews of *Roughing It* (1872), *Sketches, New and Old* (1875), *The Adventures of Tom Sawyer* (1876), *A Tramp Abroad* (1880), *A Connecticut Yankee in King Arthur's Court* (1889), and *Personal Recollections of Joan of Arc* (1896). Equally important was Howells's editorial midwifery of "Old Times on the Mississippi" (1875) for serialization in the *Atlantic* and his editorial surgery on *Adventures of Huckleberry Finn* (1885) and *A Connecticut Yankee*, the manuscripts of which he carefully pruned.

Some critics have indicted Howells for exerting a censorial influence on Mark Twain—as if Howells replaced the Victorian conscience that Mark Twain killed off in "Facts Concerning the Recent Carnival of Crime in Connecticut" (1876). No doubt, Howells did act at times to constrain Mark Twain's "Elizabethan breadth of parlance," as he called it in *My Mark Twain* (1910). But the idea of

Howells's playing Delilah to Mark Twain's Samson is part and parcel of the critical myths about both writers that developed in the 1920s. In Howells, Mark Twain found his most trusted literary adviser, one with an ear more keenly attuned than his own to the genteel limits on expression. If he desired to reach an audience more cultivated than the buyers of subscription books, an audience predominated by middle-class women, Mark Twain had little choice—no more than did Howells himself—but to assimilate these limits into his practice.

Despite his own compromises with refined sensitivities, Howells was imaginatively provocative in his best novels, those that reinforced his critical campaign for literary realism. Influenced by George Eliot and Ivan Turgenev, Howells admired fiction that told the unvarnished truth about the real world; and he advocated not only such American writers as Mark Twain, Henry James, Sarah Orne Jewett, Hamlin Garland, Harold Frederic, Charles W. Chesnutt, Frank Norris, and Stephen Crane, but also such Europeans as Feodor Dostoevski, Leo Tolstoy, Gustave Flaubert, Emile Zola, Bjornstjerne Bjornson, Henrik Ibsen, Giovanni Verga, and Palacio Valdes.

Realism for Howells was the fictional representation through the dramatic interactions of ordinary but complex characters and with a minimum of narrative intervention, of an unromanticized view of commonplace experience. The realistic writer is driven by a quest for moral clarity amid social and psychological complication. The ideal artist, as Howells wrote in *Criticism and Fiction* (1891), must be "robust enough to front the every-day world and catch the charm of its work-worn, care-worn, brave, kindly face." The realist stands against "the sort nurtured in the superstition of the romantic, the bizarre, the heroic, the distinguished, as the things alone worthy of painting or carving or writing."

In his own work Howells affirmed bourgeois American values while also suggesting what such values excluded. Although he was, with James, the co-inventor of the American

Girl and the international novel—in such novels as *A Foregone Conclusion, The Lady of the Aroostook* (1879), and *Indian Summer*—Howells soon abandoned Europe as a field for his fiction. After his resignation from the *Atlantic* in 1881, he turned increasingly to native themes: the erosion of New England rural life, the tensions of the modern city, the effects of industrial capitalism, and the shifting gender roles of men and women. In *A Modern Instance, The Rise of Silas Lapham*, and *A Hazard of New Fortunes*, he reached the height of his powers as a novelist. Neither so rarefied as James nor so vernacular as Mark Twain in his style, Howells adopted a middle voice that he thought was commensurate with American democracy.

After reading Tolstoy during the 1880s, Howells felt pangs of conscience over being, as he said, a theoretical socialist and a practical aristocrat. His work became preoccupied with the social crises of the Gilded Age, especially the enmity of the classes and the masses. Howells's radicalism climaxed in his public defense in 1887 of the anarchists who were charged and later executed for the Chicago Haymarket Riot. In later years he supported the cause of women's suffrage and denounced the imperialism of the Spanish-American War.

Lured from Boston to New York by a contract with Harper and Brothers, Howells became a fixture in *Harper's Monthly Magazine*, issuing columns from "The Editor's Study" (1886–1892) and later from "The Editor's Easy Chair" (1900–1920). The endurance of Howells's literary opinions attest to the shrewdness of his judgment. He had some blind spots, however, notably his ignorance of Herman Melville's fiction, his underestimation of Edith Wharton's fiction, and his distaste for Walt Whitman's poetry.

Despite his public visibility, Howells's fiction turned increasingly private after the death of his daughter Winifred in 1890. He explored the mysteries of psychic and psychological experience, and he experimented with non-realistic forms, reclaiming his filiation to Hawthorne. Howells's best late work included not only such realistic novels as *The Landlord at Lion's Head* but also *A Traveler From Altruria* (1894) and *Through the Eye of the Needle* (1907), utopian romances; *Stops of Various Quills* (1895), poems in the manner of Emily Dickinson; *Impressions and Experiences* (1896), personal essays; and *The Flight of Pony Baker* (1902), a boy book. He also published several volumes of autobiography: *A Boy's Town* (1890), *My Year in a Log Cabin* (1893), *My Literary Passions* (1895), *New Leaf Mills* (1913), and *Years of My Youth* (1916). Able to survey American literature over four generations, Howells gave his personal retrospect in *Literary Friends and Acquaintances* (1900).

Aware that Clemens had long since surpassed him in literary fame, Howells modestly recounted in *My Mark Twain* his own part in building his old friend's reputation. No one, in fact, had done more to elevate Mark Twain to the height reserved for him in the lyrical conclusion of Howells's tribute: "Emerson, Longfellow, Lowell, Holmes—I knew them all and all the rest of our sages, poets, seers, critics, humorists, they were like one another and like other literary men; but Clemens was sole, incomparable, the Lincoln of our literature."

John W. Crowley

BIBLIOGRAPHY

Arms, George, and William M. Gibson. *A Bibliography of William Dean Howells*. New York: New York Public Library, 1948.

Cady, Edwin H. *The Realist at War: The Mature Years, 1885–1920, of William Dean Howells*. Syracuse, N.Y.: Syracuse UP, 1958.

———. *The Road to Realism: The Early Years, 1837–1885, of William Dean Howells*. Syracuse, N.Y.: Syracuse UP, 1956.

Clemens, Samuel L. *Mark Twain-Howells Letters: The Correspondence of Samuel L. Clemens and William D. Howells, 1872–1910*. Ed. Henry Nash Smith, William M. Gibson, and Frederick Anderson. 2 vols. Cambridge, Mass.: Harvard UP, 1960.

Crowley, John W. *The Black Heart's Truth: The Early Career of W.D. Howells*. Chapel Hill: U of North Carolina P, 1985.

———. *The Mask of Fiction: Essays on W.D. Howells*. Amherst: U of Massachusetts P, 1989.

Eble, Kenneth B. *Old Clemens and W.D.H.: The Story of a Remarkable Friendship.* Baton Rouge: Louisiana State UP, 1985.

Howells, William Dean. *Criticism and Fiction.* New York: Harper, 1891.

———. *Life in Letters of William Dean Howells.* Ed. Mildred Howells. 2 vols. Garden City, N.Y.: Doubleday, Doran, 1928.

———. *My Mark Twain: Reminiscences and Criticisms.* New York: Harper, 1910.

———. *A Selected Edition of W.D. Howells.* Ed. David J. Nordloh, et al. 32 vols. to date. Bloomington: Indiana UP, 1968–.

———. *Selected Letters of W.D. Howells.* Ed. George Arms, Christoph K. Lohmann, et al. 6 vols. Boston: Twayne, 1979–1983.

Lynn, Kenneth S. *William Dean Howells: An American Life.* New York: Harcourt Brace Jovanovich, 1971.

Petty-Schmitt, Chapel. "Criticism of W.D. Howells: Selected Checklist." *American Literary Realism 1870–1910* 20.3 (Spring 1988): 69–92.

Woodress, James, and Stanley P. Anderson. "A Bibliography of Writing About William Dean Howells." *American Literary Realism 1870–1910* 2: special number (1969): 1–139.

See also: Atlantic Monthly; Correspondence; Realism

"Huck Finn and Tom Sawyer Among the Indians"

(1969)

A fragment of some 25,000 words, "Huck Finn and Tom Sawyer Among the Indians" was written in the 1880s, probably in 1884. It has survived not only in the original manuscript but also in galley proofs set on the Paige typesetting machine on which Mark Twain lost almost $200,000. With Huck Finn as narrator, the story picks up from the ending of *Huckleberry Finn* (1885) in which Tom Sawyer says that he and Huck and Jim should "go for howling adventures amongst the Injuns." They leave western Missouri and set out for Indian country along the north Platte, the same route that Sam and Orion Clemens took on their trip to Nevada in 1861. En route the three fall in with the Mills family—father, mother, three sons, and two daughters—who

are heading for Oregon. Presently they are joined by five Sioux braves. At first the Indians are friendly enough, but after a few days they turn hostile, kill five of the Millses, and abduct the two girls and Jim. Tom and Huck escape by hiding in the woods. Shortly the boys are joined by Brace Johnson, who is Peggy Mills's fiancé. The three follow the trail of the Indians until they come upon evidence that the Indians have tied Peggy Mills to the ground, raped, and killed her. At this point the story breaks off. Apparently, Twain's Victorian squeamishness would not allow him to explore Peggy Mills's death any further. Nor could he come up with another satisfactory way of continuing the tale. He set it aside and never went back to it.

As was his custom, the author blended material from his experience and his reading. Descriptions of the Nebraska territory undoubtedly came from his 1861 trip west, and a grudge against the Indians went back to his boyhood. The story, however, required Tom to lose a romantic illusion about Indians, and so Twain had to assemble material showing Indians both as noble Red Men and as savages. For pictures of Indians as brave and upright he turned to James Fenimore Cooper, Emerson Bennett, and Robert Montgomery Bird. For portrayals of their cruelty he consulted works by Richard Irving Dodge, Francis Parkman, William Cody (Buffalo Bill), and General George A. Custer. In fact, he used two books by Dodge so extensively that he could almost be accused of plagiarism.

Despite Huck's appealing vernacular and some fine local color sketches, the writing is by no means up to the level of *Tom Sawyer* (1876) or *Huckleberry Finn*. The story is melodramatic, and the characters two-dimensional. Huck, especially, is a disappointment because he is much too seldom the perceptive commentator on human nature that he is in the earlier books. The story has no theme that undergirds it. Walter Blair points out that Tom's disillusionment about Indians might have been such a theme, but the disillusionment occurs in the third chapter, far too soon to give cohesiveness to the entire tale. Blair also suggests that Twain might have made something of the contrast between the Christian God of the whites and the good and evil gods of the Indians, but again Twain fails to exploit the possibilities. In short, "Huck and Tom Among the Indians" falls so far short of the two great books that preceded it that Twain added to his reputation for literary judgment by not completing it.

John C. Gerber

BIBLIOGRAPHY

Clemens, Samuel L. *Mark Twain's Hannibal, Huck & Tom.* Ed. Walter Blair. Berkeley: U of California P, 1969.

See also: Finn, Huckleberry; Indians; Sawyer, Tom

Human Nature

"The last quarter century of my life has been pretty faithfully and constantly devoted to the study of the human race," Mark Twain declared in his *Autobiography* (1924). His views on the subject were influenced from the first by the Calvinist notion of innate depravity and increasingly so colored by his belief in "training" or environmental determinism that toward the end of his life he would refer derisively to the "little stinking" and "damned human race" and compare human nature to a machine. That is, the doctrine of determinism that seemed to Twain early in his career to promise a brighter future—through education and retraining both individuals and institutions might be reformed—later became the basis of his despair for the human condition.

Innocence was largely an abstract concept to Twain, who often associated it with childhood but who, even as a child, had been exposed to orthodox Calvinism. As early as 1868, in a letter to his future wife Olivia Langdon, Twain mentioned the "perversity that belongs to human nature," a point he obliquely echoed later in *The Adventures of Tom Sawyer* (1876) when Tom discovers "a great law of human action," that "in order to make a man or a boy covet a thing, it is only necessary to make the thing difficult to attain." The comment anticipates by nearly thirty years Twain's portrayal of the human animal as fundamentally self-interested in *What Is Man?* (1906). The title of the book notwithstanding, the American tourists in his travelogue *The Innocents Abroad* (1869) are pompous hypocrites or unsophisticated naifs, ironic saints, or "sinners" rather than genuinely guiltless souls.

Twain's inquiry into human nature intensified in *The Prince and the Pauper* (1882), a virtual case study in the importance of environment in the shaping of character. While Edward Tudor and the pauper Tom Canty are physically indistinguishable, they are raised under dramatically different circumstances; as a result, they are remarkably dissimilar types. (After they accidentally trade places, the prince begins to sympathize with the poor, whereas the pauper in fact becomes something of a tyrant.) In *Adventures of Huckleberry Finn* (1885) Twain also underscored the plasticity of human nature. The juvenile pariah in this novel has been only imperfectly "sivilized." He justifies his intuitively just but technically criminal decision to help the runaway slave Jim "by saying I was brung up wicked, and so I warn't so much to blame." Huck's commentary betrays the author's meliorist convictions at midcareer about training and natural goodness, views perhaps influenced by the creed of freemasonry and the theology of Horace Bushnell.

As the result of Twain's mature reading and personal reversals, these benign beliefs gradually yielded to a darker constellation of ideas that resembled a vestigial or secularized Calvinism. Not only are character traits environmentally conditioned, Twain thought, but they can also be biologically transmitted. Thus evil is ingrained and inherited and the human race inevitably damned. As Twain wrote in his notebook, "The thing in man which makes him cruel to a slave is in him permanently and will not be rooted out for a million years." The human creature, though capable of virtue, usually acts viciously. Twain repeatedly illustrated this idea in *A Connecticut Yankee in King Arthur's Court* (1889), the watershed novel he was writing at the time. "Arguments have no chance against petrified training" and "inherited ideas," as his spokesman Hank Morgan explains. "Training—training is everything; training is all there is *to* a person. We speak of nature; it is folly; there is no such thing as nature; what we call by that misleading name is merely heredity and training. We have no thoughts of our own, no opinions of our own; they are transmitted to us, trained into us." Twain still allowed for "one microscopic atom" or original or unique individuality in each character, but he had discovered the *idée fixe* that would govern his speculations on human nature over the final twenty years of his life.

His belief in the transmission of acquired characteristics permitted Twain to subscribe to a theory of racial degradation that was, at bottom, racially biased. Native Americans and African-Americans had suffered so many "decades and generations of insult and outrage" that they had become "debased" stock and deserved tolerance and compassion, the argument went. "[O]n every sin which a colored man commits, the just white man must make a considerable discount, because of the colored man's antecedents," he wrote. "The heirs of slavery cannot with any sort of justice, be required to be as clear and straight and upright as the heirs of ancient freedom." This rationalization of racial inferiority informs the novel *Pudd'nhead Wilson* (1894), particularly when the former slave Roxy attributes the criminal cowardice of her son to the fraction of black blood in his veins: "Thirty-one parts o' you is white, en on'y one part nigger, en dat po' little one part is yo' *soul*."

To be sure, Twain insisted as late as 1899, in "The Man That Corrupted Hadleyburg," that moral training must be empirical, not merely prescriptive, and that people enjoy a capacity for freedom, however limited, to exercise moral choice. In the town of Hadleyburg honesty has been taught only as an abstraction; as a result, it is an "artificial"

virtue and "weak as water when temptation comes." When Edward Richards rationalizes his dishonesty in this story by appealing to a doctrine of foreordination, his wife Mary disdainfully replies that "everything's *ordered*, when a person has to find some way out when he has been stupid." Her refusal to accept his excuse mirrors Twain's own belief at the time that people were independent moral agents responsible for their behavior.

During the final decade of his life, however, Twain would begin to describe human nature in mechanistic metaphors and his ideas would become more doggedly deterministic. As he wrote his friend Joseph Twichell in 1904, "I wish I could learn to remember that it is unjust and dishonorable to put blame upon the human race for any of its acts. For it did not make itself, it did not make its nature, it is merely a machine, it is moved wholly by outside influences, it has no hand in creating the outside influences nor in choosing which of them it will welcome or reject. Its performance is wholly automatic." Twain's fullest elaboration of this chain of determinism appeared in his privately and pseudonymously printed "gospel" *What Is Man?* (1906). "Man is a machine" fueled by desires and self-interest, the Old Man in this Socratic dialogue explains to the Young Man, a machine "made up of many mechanisms, the moral and mental ones acting automatically in accordance with the impulses of an interior Master who is built out of born-temperament and an accumulation of multitudinous outside influences and trainings; a machine whose *one* function is to secure the spiritual contentment of the Master, be his desires good or be they evil; a machine whose will is absolute and must be obeyed, and always *is* obeyed." That is, human motives are always entirely selfish. Letter VI of "Letters from the Earth" (written in 1909) contains virtually the same statement, and even in "The Turning Point of My Life" (1910), the last piece Twain wrote for publication, he declared that "I see no great difference between a man and a watch, except that the man is conscious and the watch isn't."

Elsewhere in these late papers, Twain excoriated man, the degenerate descendant of the "Higher Animals," for harboring a "Moral Sense" or conscience, the faculty "which enabled him to do wrong." As usual, Twain was not entirely free of contradiction. His determinism warred with his moralism, but, from either perspective, the human race was "damned."

Gary Scharnhorst

BIBLIOGRAPHY

Clemens, Samuel. *The Autobiography of Mark Twain.* Ed. Charles Neider. New York: Harper, 1959.

———. *Letters from the Earth.* Ed. Bernard DeVoto. Greenwich, Conn.: Fawcett, 1962.

———. *Mark Twain: Selected Writings of an American Skeptic.* Ed. Victor Doyno. Buffalo, N.Y.: Prometheus, 1983.

———. *Mark Twain's Notebook.* Ed. Albert B. Paine. New York: Harper, 1935. 187–214.

———. *Selected Letters of Mark Twain.* Ed. Charles Neider. New York: Harper & Row, 1982. 293.

———. *"What Is Man?" and Other Philosophical Writings.* Ed. Paul Baender. Berkeley: U of California P, 1973.

Long, E. Hudson. *Mark Twain Handbook.* New York: Hendricks House, 1957. 275–398.

Spengemann, William C. *Mark Twain and the Backwoods Angel: The Matter of Innocence in the Works of Samuel L. Clemens.* Kent, Ohio: Kent State UP, 1966.

See also: Calvinism; Determinism; Innocence; Philosophy; Politics

Humor

From the tall-tale hoaxes of western campfires and the simple misspellings and malapropisms dear to the "literary" comedians of his early days to the sophisticated shifts of perspective and suddenly revealed incongruities characterizing his later work, Mark Twain, even when most angered, most embittered, wrote with the pen of a humorist. He organized his stories and his meanings as if for laughs; most of the time, the jest is one that readers can share with the author, but, with increasing frequency, the joke is on us, taken in by our preconceptions and self-flattering assumptions. During his long and prolific career as a writer, Twain made at least three striking contributions to the development of American humor: he moved the source of laughter from an essentially eighteenth-century mode to a modernist perspective; he participated in altering the feelings of readers toward vernacular characters, changing those feelings from distantly bemused superiority to sympathetic identification; and he transformed the hoax from a laughter-producing gadget to a mechanism for presenting the world, and all life itself.

In the smaller techniques of generating laughter, Twain took what was ready to hand. Comic misspellings and misquotations, the easy humor in ignorant dialect and vernacular (how often the "deceased" appear as "diseased"), sudden anticlimax, incongruity, burlesque and parody, the poker-faced exaggeration of the tall tale and the hoax, understatement: in timing, contrast, finding the exactly right word, he worked on his techniques as if he had been a concert pianist. Because both his reputation and his livelihood were at stake, and because he had the temperament of an artist, he took seriously the craft of his humor, as his essays on the subject suggest. Unlike so many of his fellow journalistic humorists, however, he developed a vision that went beyond the conventions of his time.

The newspaper and journal humor of the Old Southwest familiar to young Sam Clemens as apprentice printer to his brother Orion on the Hannibal *Journal* had its roots firmly in the eighteenth century. The preface to Henry Fielding's *Joseph Andrews* (1742) makes clear that Fielding, in writing his "comic epic poem in prose," anticipated that a reader's laughter would spring from a perception of the ridiculous. Fielding proposed to display characters guilty of affected behavior, for "the only source of the true Ridiculous (as it appears to me) is Affection." Whether attempting to "purchase applause" or "to avoid censure," whether through vanity or through hypocrisy, when characters do themselves in by pretending to be what they are not, their misfortunes become fit target for laughter. The educated Easterners whose writings first presented the backwoods boors in the nineteenth-century American print found them endlessly entertaining because they so often pretended to a piety or a generosity or a gentility that they did not in truth possess. Sophisticated readers could smile with an assured superiority over pompous ignorance and pretended bravery. When "Dr." Peter Jones of Pineville, Georgia (1843), attempts to impress "the ladies" with his knowledge of the ways of the circuses, a knowledge gained through his brief sojourn in "the Philadelphia of the South," Augusta, characters and reader laugh to see Pete "audaciously tuck in" by the supposed drunk who turns out to be an accomplished equestrian and "part of the show." When Simon Suggs defrauds a camp meeting (1845), taking money under the pretenses that he has been "saved" by a minister's prayers and instruction and that he wants to start up a church of his own, now that he has seen the light, the contributors get exactly what they deserve. Author Hooper shows clearly that behind their affections of piety, humility, and generosity lurk "pride of purse," self-satisfaction, and a delight in sensual self-indulgence. People try to appear to be what they are not, and one laughs to see their pretenses, their affections, exposed.

When Mark Twain sends his king (*Adventures of Huckleberry Finn* [1885]) to Pokeville Camp meeting, on the other hand, no one is guilty of affection. Those in attendance may be ignorant—they do not question the presence of an Indian Ocean pirate in Arkansas, trying to replenish a crew "thinned out considerable" in a recent fight—but they are just as pious and generous as they appear to be. The King succeeds because the people do not know themselves any better than they know geography. Stagnating in their dull town, they thrill to the presence of the supposed pirate. "It warn't no use talking," the King concludes; "heathens don't amount to shucks alongsides of pirates to work a camp-meeting with." This is true, but the terms of its truth push a reader out of the comfortable stance of eighteenth-

century satire—comfortable, because it allowed readers to share the perspective of the superior author—and into post-Freudian and post-Einsteinian uncertainties. How well do readers know themselves? From what vantage point do readers perceive events? How can one know that the humanity of the King's fictional dupes differs in any definitive way from one's own?

Much of Twain's early humor, of course, concerns itself with the exposure of affection. Characters do stir a reader's laughter because they pretend to qualities that they do not in fact possess. But before very long, the sense of mystery outbalances the sense of certainty in Twain's work. The narrator of "The Celebrated Jumping Frog of Calaveras County" (1865) cannot be called affected. He does not pretend to qualities that he lacks. Rather, so obsessed is he with making productive use of every minute of the day that he cannot enjoy the narrative process of "garrulous old Simon Wheeler," who rambles on about a compulsive gambler named Jim Smiley, despite the narrator's stated quest for information about the Reverend Leonidas W. Smiley. In this, as in so many of Twain's stories, the fact that a narrator speaks standard English does not guarantee the reliability of his perspective, of his reaction to the life around him. As early as 1852 and the publication of "The Dandy Frightening the Squatter" in the *Carpet-Bag*, Sam Clemens—he first printed "Mark Twain" in January 1863—showed both his familiarity with the way in which humorous tales usually got told and his own allegiance to his region. Although young Sam puts vernacular words within quotation marks and tells the story in the vocabulary of an educated observer, the smooth-speaking Dandy turns out to be the affected one, while the ungrammatical squatter unpretentiously keeps his cool.

That Twain's vernacular characters become more than figures of fun took on major importance for future American writers, both humorous and not. Bookish language by a Twain narrator almost always signals hollow spots in the writing—*The Prince and the Pauper* (1882) and *Personal Recollections of Joan of Arc*

(1896), for example. When, in "Old Times on the Mississippi" (1875), Twain recounts a picture-book sunset that lingers in his memory from his pre-pilot days, the proper language, filled with painterly cliches, underscores the unreliability of the greenhorn, the newcomer, the uninitiated. The educated Easterner, who foolishly pretends to know his way around the frontier, receives the comeuppance that affection deserves. Twain gave a literary legitimacy to the social underdog that went far beyond mere regionalism, and far beyond humor, too. The language of gentility, because its assumptions have so little to do with the life lived by human beings, becomes a mark of inadequacy (e.g., the Whittier Birthday Dinner Speech of 1877) rather than an index of the socially desirable.

In his elaboration of the hoax Twain made his most marked formal contribution. Originally, the hoax was, in effect, the tall tale, the story told with a straight face around the campfire, expressing the solidarity of the group against the outsider ignorant of local conditions and ways. In print, it at first had much the same effect, bringing together the local readers in delighted scorn for gullible outsiders. The delight, as Twain came to organize it, at first allowed the reader to smile a superior smile at the mistaken narrator. Who, for example, could possibly be so foolish as not to see through the idiocy of thinking that a vacuum pump might be used to remove a vacuum? Or not to enjoy the yarns of a Simon Wheeler? In his days as reporter and editor for the Virginia City *Territorial Enterprise*, Samuel L. Clemens did the straight reporting and "Mark Twain" contributed political satire and hoaxes of the "Petrified Man" variety. The advantages of taking in the gullible reader seem to have dawned early: by *The Innocents Abroad* (1869) Twain is pulling out the rug from under those who trust him too easily, describing, for example, Marseilles in the florid cliches of conventional travel literature and then adding in brackets as the concluding sentence: "[Copyright secured according to law.]" By *The Gilded Age* (1873) it is the commentary

on a trial (chapter 58), not merely a sentence, that undercuts the conventional expectations of a nineteenth-century reader. In the ending of *Adventures of Huckleberry Finn* the issue becomes far more complicated and significant.

Just as Tom fools Huck into thinking that "respectable" Tom will actually help to free a slave, so Twain fools the reader into thinking exactly the same thing. Throughout the book, the excitements desired by the riverbank populace have been provided by various entertainers: the King and the Duke; the amateur thespian who acts out the murder of Boggs; above all, Tom Sawyer, who disappoints the members of his gang because they think they want authenticity, and he never seems to let them kill anybody or steal anything. Nowhere do these excitements conflict with the conventions of society. In the case of Tom, preserving those conventions has at least as much importance as the excitements themselves. Nevertheless, readers—including re-readers—do get pulled into Tom's nonsense at the end. "Lengthy," "tedious," no matter how harsh the words one attaches to those elaborate shenanigans, readers still expect that Tom will manage to go against his society and free a slave. When he catches his pants on that splinter and gets himself shot in the heel, one nods one's head, certain that only Tom's unconscious resistance to breaking so overtly from the respectable has led to the failure of his scheme. Then the truth comes out, and readers learn that they have been misled into assuming that theatricals, the very terms and details of which come directly from society itself, could both represent the desires of that society for sensational fun and games and also embody a serious rebellion against slavery, the society's most significant institution. Why, even "The Last Link Is Broken," the song that Jim is to play on his "juice harp" to charm the rats and snakes that Tom introduces into his prison, chains the escape—links it directly—to the Grangerfords's parlor.

This hoax is funny. Although the joke is on readers, they can still laugh. The hoax on the town of Hadleyburg is less amusing, but the structure of the story remains that of hoax, as do the structures of several of the manuscripts upon which Twain worked toward the end of his life. Was the universe itself a hoax, a pretense played upon the mind by the mind? Was life itself a dream? Was the dream real? Questions of this sort do not evoke smiles, but the energy behind them remains that of the sudden shift of perspective, the quick release of tension, bound up in the production of humor generally and the generation of hoaxes in particular. In what has come to be called the mechanisms of "bad faith," even the basic contradiction at the core both of Mark Twain's artistic problems and of his personality can be seen as central to his humor as well as to his prose. Humor, he believed, could weaken, and eventually overturn, a social injustice; anger at injustice, on the other hand, often made impossible the production of humor. Much of Twain's writing vacillates between the involved rage that interferes with humor and the observation that can distance itself from injustice in order to pillory it through laughter. One can laugh comfortably at Aunt Polly, whose desire to reform Tom conflicts with her own endless delight in finding him out in his acts of minor rebellion against her authority. No reader seems amused, however, when citizens of Hadleyburg, that totally honest town, immediately worry about the non-existent robbers who are certain to steal the bag of supposed gold that they themselves covet. Their projections perhaps remind readers of their own. As Mark Twain exposed his anger with increasing directness, he aroused less and less laughter. The forms his humor took remain the same; the charges with which he filled those forms finally became too explosive to preserve the risible fabric. As many readers have noted, the humor of Mark Twain often turns out to be no laughing matter.

Pascal Covici, Jr.

BIBLIOGRAPHY

Covici, Pascal, Jr. *Mark Twain's Humor: The Image of a World.* Dallas: Southern Methodist UP, 1962.

Cox, James M. *Mark Twain: The Fate of Humor.* Princeton, N.J.: Princeton UP, 1966.

Lynn, Kenneth S. *Mark Twain and Southwestern Humor.* Boston: Little, Brown, 1959.

Robinson, Forrest G. *In Bad Faith: The Dynamics of Deception in Mark Twain's America.* Cambridge, Mass.: Harvard UP, 1986.

Rogers, Franklin R. *Mark Twain's Burlesque Patterns as Seen in the Novels and Narratives, 1855–1885.* Dallas: Southern Methodist UP, 1960.

Sloane, David E.E. *Mark Twain as a Literary Comedian.* Baton Rouge: Louisiana State UP, 1979.

Smith, Henry Nash. *Mark Twain: The Development of a Writer.* Cambridge, Mass.: Harvard UP, 1962.

See also: Hoax; Point of View; Satire; Southwestern Humor

I

Illustrators

Illustrators and their illustrations were an integral part of Mark Twain's most important first editions from *Innocents Abroad* (1869) to *Following the Equator* (1897). Twain published most of his major works in the subscription-book market where books were sold door to door instead of over the counter. Subscription books were profusely illustrated with pictures of various types and sizes. The books were sold by agents who knocked on doors and displayed their samples, flipping through a prospectus laden with illustrations; the books themselves were seldom printed until after a substantial number had been subscribed for by customers. The pictures were used to facilitate sales through the rural and urban blue-collar neighborhoods. Thus publishers, editors, and often Mark Twain himself spent a good deal of time on design—choosing the most talented artists, directing artists in interpretation of texts, selecting from the final prints, and at times censoring drawings of material unfit for illustration.

Even in Twain's books that were not sold by subscription, illustration was still a factor—for example, *Mark Twain's (Burlesque) Autobiography* contained twelve satirical political illustrations drawn by Henry Louis Stephens. Books belonging to the twilight of Mark Twain's career—*Eve's Diary* (1906), illustrated by Lester Ralph, and *Extracts from Adam's Diary* (1904), illustrated by F. Strothmann—also exhibited profuse illustration. An understanding of the interrelation of author and illustrator, text and print, and the requirements of both subscription and trade publication contributes to our knowledge of the success or failure of Mark Twain's literary output.

Below are listed chronologically the major works of Mark Twain from 1869 to 1898 and the illustrators who did the drawings. The figure in parentheses after the publication dates indicates the total number of illustrations. Names of known illustrators follow, the first named artist being the principal illustrator. An asterisk beside the artist's name indicates that the illustrator's work was "pirated" from a previously published work:

The Innocents Abroad; or, The New Pilgrims' Progress, 1869 (234). True Williams, Roswell Morse Shurtleff

Roughing It, 1872 (300). True Williams, Roswell Morse Shurtleff, E.F. Mullen, J.C. Beard,★ J. Ross Browne,★ Henry Louis Stephens,★ A.R. Waud,★ Asa Coolidge Warren★

The Gilded Age: A Tale of To-Day (with Charles Dudley Warner), 1873 (213). Augustus Hoppin, Henry Louis Stephens, True Williams, George C. White

Mark Twain's Sketches, New and Old, 1875 (100). True Williams

The Adventures of Tom Sawyer, 1876 (160). True Williams

A Tramp Abroad, 1880 (328). Walter F. Brown, Mark Twain, True Williams, Ben Day, A.R. Waud, Joseph Twichell, J.C. Beard,★ Roswell Morse Shurtleff,★ Edward Whymper★

The Prince and the Pauper: A Tale for Young People of All Ages, 1882 (192). Frank Merrill, John Harley, L.S. Ipsen; Supervisor of Design: A.V.S. Anthony

Life on the Mississippi, 1883 (316). John Harley, Edmund Henry Garrett, A.B. Shute

Adventures of Huckleberry Finn (Tom Sawyer's Comrade), 1885 (174). Edward Windsor Kemble

A Connecticut Yankee in King Arthur's Court, 1889 (220). Daniel Carter Beard

The American Claimant, 1892 (24). Daniel Carter Beard

The Tragedy of Pudd'nhead Wilson and The Comedy Those Extraordinary Twins, 1894 (432 marginal drawings). C.H. Warren and F.M. Senior shared about equally in illustrating *Pudd'nhead Wilson*; F.M. Senior was sole illustrator of "Those Extraordinary Twins"

Tom Sawyer Abroad, 1894 (26). Daniel Carter Beard

Personal Recollections of Joan of Arc, 1896 (37). Frank Vincent DuMond

Following the Equator: A Journey Around the World, 1897 (193 illustrations and photographs). Daniel Carter Beard, A.B. Frost, B.W. Clinedinst,

Frederick Dielman, Peter Newell, F.M. Senior (misspelled F.M. Seinor in the list of illustrators, page 19), T.J. Fogarty, C.H. Warren, A.G. Reinhart, F. Berkeley Smith, C. Allan Gilbert

Illustrators of Original Works

ANTHONY, A.V.S. (1835–1906) was a talented illustrator as well as design supervisor for all James Osgood's publishing enterprises in Boston from 1865 to 1889. Anthony supervised the illustrating of *The Prince and the Pauper* and *Life on the Mississippi*.

BEARD, Daniel Carter (1850–1941). (See separate entry.)

BROWN, Walter Francis (b. 1853) was born in Providence, Rhode Island. Brown was studying with Gerome and Bonnat in Paris when Twain met the young man and commissioned him for the illustration of *A Tramp Abroad*.

CLINEDINST, Benjamin West (1859–1931) studied at the Ecole des Beaux Arts in Paris. He specialized in portraits.

DAY, Ben H. (1838–1916), son of journalist Benjamin Henry Day, was an artist, illustrator, and inventor. He worked principally for *Vanity Fair*.

DIELMAN, Frederick (1847–1935) was born in Germany but came to the United States in childhood. He illustrated the deluxe edition of both Longfellow's and Hawthorne's works. He was professor of art in the College of the City of New York and director of the Art Schools of Cooper Union in New York City. In later years he designed giant historical mosaics for public buildings.

DUMOND, Frank Vincent (1865–1951) was born in Rochester, New York. He was a pupil of Boulanger, Lefebvre, and Constant in Paris. Painter, illustrator, and teacher, he was an instructor at the Art Students League in New York. He received a silver medal for illustration at the Pan-Am Exposition in Buffalo in 1901.

FOGARTY, Thomas (1873–1938) was a pupil of Mowbray and Beckwith. He taught at the New York Art Students League, where one of his pupils was Norman Rockwell.

FROST, Arthur Burnett (1851–1928) studied with Eakins as a young man and also had some training in London. However, Frost was largely self-taught. In 1873 he drew daily cartoons for New York's the *Daily Graphic*. Later, he was one of *Harper's* greatest illustrators and was well known for his work on *Uncle Remus*. He also illustrated later editions of *Tom Sawyer*. His specialties were humorous drawings of farm and country types and animals.

GARRETT, Edmund Henry (1853–1908) studied in Paris at the Academie Julien and was a pupil of Laurens. He worked for *Life* magazine and was hired by Osgood's publishing house, where he was assigned to draw the Mississippi landscapes and street scenes in *Life on the Mississippi*.

GILBERT, Charles Allan (1873–1929) was a Hartford, Connecticut, artist who studied at the Art Students League in New York and with Constant and Laurens in Paris.

HARLEY, John (dates unknown) was commissioned in 1872 as an engraver for the monumental *Picturesque America*. Also in 1872 he worked for Appleton on James Fenimore Cooper's *The Prairie*. He became a staff artist for James R. Osgood and Company, and illustrated Harriet Beecher Stowe's *Oldtime Fireside Stories*. For *Life on the Mississippi*, Harley was assigned to do the amusing sketches and caricatures of the river folk. Earlier he had collaborated with Frank Merrill on the illustrations for *The Prince and the Pauper*.

HOPPIN, Augustus (1828–1896) graduated with degrees from Brown and Harvard Law School and practiced law for a short time. He became one of the country's leading social satirists, his shafts being aimed principally at the "high society" of the day. His talents were brought to Twain's attention through his beautiful illustrations in Howells's *Their Wedding Day*.

IPSEN, L.S. (dates unknown) was a staff illustrator for James Osgood's publishing firms. He drew thirty-five unique and elaborate "half titles" for *The Prince and the Pauper* (1882). The next year he designed similar ornate chapter headings for Sir Walter Scott's *The Lady of the Lake*.

KEMBLE, Edward Windsor (1861–1893) was born in Sacramento, California. In his early childhood he moved east with his family. He sketched at the Art Students League in New York for a brief period, which was his only formal training. His first drawings were published in *Harper's Bazaar* in September and October 1880. He then became a staff cartoonist for the *Daily Graphic*, where he drew the famous "Gold Dust" twins, a popular image for selling soap powder. In 1883 Kemble became a contributor to the new *Life* magazine, and it was one of his early *Life* drawings, "Some Uses for Electricity," that caught Mark Twain's eye. Though Kemble had no experience in book illustration, at Twain's direction, Charles Webster, Twain's nephew and publisher for *Adventures of Huckleberry Finn*, commissioned the artist to draw the illustrations for Twain's classic tale. Kemble was hired for $1,200, which was later reduced to $1,000. He drew 174 illustrations, working from approximately 17 April to early June 1884. He also illustrated *Mark Twain's Library of Humor* in 1888 and a late edition of *Pudd'nhead Wilson* in 1899. In the 1890s Kemble was cartoonist for many well-established magazines—*Colliers, Harper's Weekly*—as well as author-illustrator of his own works: *Kemble's Coons* and *A Pickaninny Calendar*. It was chiefly as a delineator of the South that he built his career as illustrator and established his early reputation. At the end of his career he was an important political cartoonist, satirizing such notables as William Howard Taft, Theodore Roosevelt, and Woodrow Wilson.

MERRILL, Frank Thayer (b. 1848) was born in Boston and studied at the Lowell Institute and the Boston Museum of Fine Arts and abroad in France and England. Early in his career he worked on the comic newspaper-magazine *Punchinello* and drew 200 pictures for Louisa May Alcott's *Little Women*. Merrill's commission as principal illustrator for *The Prince and the Pauper* marked the beginning of an impressive career as illustrator.

MULLEN, Edward F. (dates unknown) was a well-known comic illustrator. He did illustrations for A.D. Richardson's *Beyond the Mississippi*, *Artemus Ward: His Travels, Vanity Fair*, and *Harper's*. Mullen drew at least four cuts for *Roughing It* signed E.F.M. Other illustrations in that book also match his style.

NEWELL, Peter Sheaf Hersey (1862–1924) studied at the Art Students League in New York. Newell was the illustrator of *Harper's* special edition of *Alice in Wonderland* and also illustrated a book of his own entitled *Peter Newell's Pictures and Rhymes.*

REINHART, Albert Grantly (1854–1926) was born in Pittsburgh, Pennsylvania, and studied in Germany, France, and Italy. He was the brother of Charles Stanley Reinhart, also an artist of note. His specialty was portraiture, though his landscapes and figure painting won high recognition.

SHURTLEFF, Roswell Morse (1838–1915) decided to study art after graduating Dartmouth. He trained at the Lowell Institute in Boston and then moved to New York, where he worked as an illustrator on magazines and books. His specialty was landscapes and animals. He added a number of illustrations to *Innocents Abroad*, though his initials appear on only four prints (on pages 103, 132, 150, 536).

SHUTE, A.B. (dates unknown) was a staff artist for the Osgood publishing firm. Shute drew a variety of subjects for *Life on the Mississippi*, including many caricatures of Mark Twain.

SMITH, Francis Berkeley (1868–1929) studied architecture at Columbia University and practiced until 1896 when he turned to illustration, specializing in city scapes.

STEPHENS, Henry Louis (1824–1882) was originally a Philadelphian but moved to New York in 1859 and worked for Frank Leslie. He later entered the employ of Harper and Brothers. Some of his best work was in *The Cyclopedia of Wit and Humor* published in 1858. He was best known as a caricaturist and illustrator, but he also worked in water colors. His talents as a caricaturist were used in *Mark Twain's (Burlesque) Autobiography.*

TWICHELL, Joseph (1838–1918) was Mark Twain's minister, neighbor, and friend for forty years. Twichell traveled with Twain through Germany and Switzerland and added three amateur drawings to *A Tramp Abroad*. Twichell was a brigade chaplain in the Civil War and later pastor of the Asylum Hill church in Hartford. (See also separate entry.)

WHITE, George G. (d. 1898) is cited on the title page of *The Gilded Age* as one of the illustrators; however, none of the illustrations appears to bear his signature. White was a wood engraver, designer, and illustrator who

worked in Philadelphia from 1854 to 1861. He drew twenty illustrations for A.D. Richardson's *Beyond the Mississippi.*

WILLIAMS, True (dates unknown) was a well-known, free-lance illustrator of the late 1860s and 1870s who lived in Hartford, Connecticut, and often worked for the American Publishing Company. As Albert Bigelow Paine puts it in *Mark Twain: A Biography*, "Williams was a man of great talent . . . but it was necessary to lock him in a room when industry was required, with nothing more than cold water as a beverage." Williams was responsible for the majority of the illustrations in *Innocents Abroad* and *Roughing It.* He also drew all the prints in *The Adventures of Tom Sawyer* and *Mark Twain's Sketches.* A significant number of drawings in *The Gilded Age* and *A Tramp Abroad* are his as well.

Illustrators of Pirated Prints

BEARD, James Carter (1836–1913) began his career as a lawyer but soon turned to illustration. Beard drew nine illustrations for A.D. Richardson's *Beyond the Mississippi* of which two appeared in *Roughing It.* James Beard was the brother of Daniel Carter Beard, the artist who did the illustrations for *A Connecticut Yankee.*

BROWNE, John Ross (1821–1875) was an illustrator of western scenes working for *Harper's Monthly.* He was also author of several books, one of which was *Adventures in the Apache Country*, which was admired by Mark Twain. Five prints originally published in this book of Browne's, altered and recaptioned, appeared in the first edition of *Roughing It.*

STEPHENS, Henry Louis. (See Stephens's entry, above.) Stephens drew a number of prints for A.D. Richardson's *Beyond the Mississippi.* Two of these drawings appeared in *Roughing It.*

WAUD, A.R. (1828–1891) was a *Harper's Monthly* illustrator during the Civil War and combat artist for *Harper's Weekly.* He also drew forty-two illustrations for *Beyond the Mississippi.* Three of these prints, altered and recaptioned, appeared in *Roughing It.*

WARREN, Asa Coolidge (dates unknown) was a Boston artist who drew twenty-three illustrations for *Beyond the Mississippi.* One of his prints, probably pirated, appeared in *Roughing It.*

WHYMPER, Edward (dates unknown) was a London artist and engraver. He was one of the survivors of a team of climbers in the famous Matterhorn accident of 14 July 1865. Whymper wrote a book about his Alpine adventures, *Scrambling Amongst the Alps*, for which he also designed and engraved the illustrations. Seven of these illustrations were recaptioned and, in some instances, altered to appear in *A Tramp Abroad*.

Beverly David and Lester Crossman

See also: Beard, Daniel Carter; Subscription Publication; Twichell, Joseph

Imagery

Twain returned repeatedly to a core group of images in his writing, perhaps because he shaped his narratives as a series of anecdotes, each with a tableau at the center, rather than as plots and conflicts. Over the course of his career, his fiction focused on five images—the river, the journey, the outsider (or mysterious stranger), twins, and the dream. Figurative language took a back seat to these structural images, although Twain also developed characteristic figures of speech as he refined his literary style.

The myth that Clemens built his Hartford house to look like a steamboat points to the significance of the river in his imagination. Indeed, images of the river, specifically, the Mississippi River, dominate his most important fiction. As the subject of "Old Times on the Mississippi" (1875) and subsequently *Life on the Mississippi* (1883), the river defines communities and educates the narrator. But it actually controls *Adventures of Huckleberry Finn* (1885). Like some divine force the river fosters the bond between Jim and Huck, condemns the values of slaveholding society, and generates incidents of plot. The Mississippi's strong currents scuttled Twain's original plan to have Jim and Huck sail up the Ohio after passing Cairo, instead of floating down deep into slave territory. The river's strength also figures in *The Adventures of Tom Sawyer* (1876),

where it separates adult St. Petersburg from the children's island of fantasy and adventure. Discovering the river as both a symbol and a "narrative plank" (a structural device that unified a story while allowing episodic digression) was crucial to the development of the matter of Hannibal by which Twain transformed memory into art. The river and childhood often unite to represent a transcendent peace, a shield from the corruption and death of adult society on shore.

Even before Twain identified the narrative power of the river, however, he had hit upon the utility of the journey—especially the voyage. The travel narrative had great popularity among nineteenth-century readers, and as a classic image of the hero's travail, the journey not only served as a narrative plank but also as an aid to characterization. Twain barely exploited the possibilities of the device as he reworked his letters from the *Quaker City* into *The Innocents Abroad* (1869), which shows him and his unregenerate fellow Americans unchanged by their confrontation with the Old World. But he soon began putting the device to more sophisticated use in charting the development of a central character. The journey to Nevada in *Roughing It* (1872) marks what Henry Nash Smith called the "transformation of a tenderfoot." Huck's voyage down the Mississippi chronicles his increasing allegiance to Jim. In *A Connecticut Yankee in King Arthur's Court* (1889) Hank Morgan's various journeys—from the nineteenth century to the sixth and across Arthur's Britain—satirize the values of the present while excoriating the past. As late as *Following the Equator* (1897) and "An Adventure in Remote Seas" (written 1898), Twain continued to write about variations among people and places, especially the relationship between outward experience and inner life.

Among human images the lonely outsider or stranger ranks with the river in structural and symbolic importance. The outsider ranges across Twain's career from the tenderfoot and Huck Finn to Joan of Arc and Forty-Four, the Mysterious Stranger. Despite its conventional function as a plot device, the arrival of the stranger provokes deep and permanent change among the communities in *Connecticut Yankee*, "The Man That Corrupted Hadleyburg" (1899), and the various Mysterious Stranger manuscripts (written 1898–1905, pub. 1969). The outsider need not be a stranger, however. Social outcasts such as David (Pudd'nhead) Wilson and Huckleberry Finn affect Dawson's Landing and Tom Sawyer's gang in much the same ways that strangers influence Camelot, Hadleyburg, and Eseldorf: they act as instruments of ethical vision and social change.

Twins and look-alikes offer another set of symbolic contrasts, not only in *The Prince and the Pauper* (1882), "Those Extraordinary Twins" (1894), and *Pudd'nhead Wilson* (1894), but also in such tales involving disguise and multiple identities as *Huck Finn*, *Connecticut Yankee*, and *Personal Recollections of Joan of Arc* (1896). Twain's tales of twins examine the nature-nurture debate, particularly as expressed in traditions of social status and racial identity, as well as questions of agency and the self (Gillman 8–9, 68–69). As *Prince and Pauper* argues against the divine right of kings and for the role of environment in shaping character, so *Pudd'nhead Wilson* denounces hereditary bondage and privilege. The image of the twin carries over into the character double. The pattern shows most clearly in *Connecticut Yankee*, which presents the young Clarence as Hank Morgan's bureaucratic double and Morgan le Fay as his alter magician's ego.

Two narrative counterparts to the twin image amount to images in their own right: paired (i.e., parallel or doubled) episodes and questions of dream and reality. Both *Tom Sawyer* and *Huck Finn* contain a series of doubled episodes structuring the relationship between the child's world of play and the adult world of violence (Wexman). Similarly, in *Connecticut Yankee*, Morgan's journey with Arthur makes real all the dangers that, on the earlier journey with Sandy, had "vanish[ed] away like the instable fabric of a dream" (198).

As this remark suggests, dreams become increasingly important beginning with *Connecticut Yankee*, although the image is already evident in *Tom Sawyer*, where Tom describes his so-called dream of events in Aunt Polly's house on the night he sneaked back to town from his pirate escapades. The later works use dream materials more ambitiously than *Tom Sawyer*. Neither Hank's narrative nor Twain's frame ever settles whether the Connecticut Yankee has dreamed or lived his experiences in Arthur's Britain. Morgan's delirium at the end of the novel suggests that neither the material nor the mental world offers solace, and variations of this nightmare characterize many of the fragmentary later writings. "No. 44, The Mysterious Stranger" concludes with the most discouraging vision of all: "There is no God, no universe, no human race, . . . no heaven, no hell. . . . It is all a Dream, a grotesque and foolish dream" (405). Twain affirmed his own belief in Satan's sentiments in a 1904 letter to Joseph Twichell: "Time, and Life, and Death, and Joy and Sorrow and Pain [are] only a grotesque and brutal *dream*, evolved from the frantic imagination of that insane Thought" (*WWD* 24). Rather than marvel at the reality of dreams, these stories probe the very possibility of external knowledge. Indeed, the narrator of "Three Thousand Years Among the Microbes" (written 1905, pub. 1967 *WWD*) concludes that we can know little beyond our own thoughts. "It isn't safe to sit in judgment upon another person's illusion," he advises. "While you are thinking it is a dream, he may be knowing it is a planet" (492).

Augmenting these central images are several varieties of figurative language. Gladys Bellamy, an early advocate of Twain's place in America's literary pantheon, pointed out the carefully constructed similes and metaphors based on vivid physical detail—for example, a horse "whose ridgy backbone stood out . . . like the croppings of a quartz ledge" (Bellamy 121–122). Contemporary scholars have explored the psychological dimensions of his imagery. To Gillman's study of twinning imagery and sexual identity, Susan K. Harris adds other patterns: the "imagery of respite," which relieves the narrator's alienation in *Joan of Arc*,

"No. 44," *Connecticut Yankee*, and *Huck Finn*; the "imagery of release," which marks water and space images to counter anxiety in *Roughing It, Life on the Mississippi, Huck Finn*, and "Three Thousand Years"; the "imagery of unity," which reduces conflict between self and society in *Tom Sawyer, Huck Finn, The Prince and the Pauper*, and other tales of childhood. Analyses such as these reveal that the study of Twain's imagery, and its meanings for him and his work, has only just begun.

Judith Yaross Lee

BIBLIOGRAPHY

Bellamy, Gladys Carmen. *Mark Twain as a Literary Artist*. Norman: U of Oklahoma P, 1950.

Clemens, Samuel L. *Adventures of Huckleberry Finn*. Ed. Walter Blair and Victor Fischer. Berkeley: U of California P, 1985.

———. *A Connecticut Yankee in King Arthur's Court*. Ed. Bernard L. Stein. Berkeley: U of California P, 1979.

———. *Mark Twain's Mysterious Stranger Manuscripts*. Ed. William M. Gibson. Berkeley: U of California P, 1969.

———. *Mark Twain's "Which Was the Dream?" and Other Symbolic Writings of the Later Years*. Ed. John S. Tuckey. Berkeley: U of California P, 1967.

Gillman, Susan. *Dark Twins: Imposture and Identity in Mark Twain's America*. Chicago: U of Chicago P, 1989.

Harris, Susan K. *Mark Twain's Escape from Time: A Study of Patterns and Images*. Columbia: U of Missouri P, 1982.

Sewell, David R. *Mark Twain's Languages: Discourse, Dialogue, and Linguistic Variety*. Berkeley: U of California P, 1987.

Smith, Henry Nash. *Mark Twain: The Development of a Writer*. Cambridge, Mass.: Harvard UP, 1962.

Wexman, Virginia. "The Role of Structure in *Tom Sawyer* and *Huckleberry Finn*." *American Literary Realism* 6 (1973): 1–11.

See also: Angelo and Luigi (Cappello); Dreams; Mississippi River; *Mysterious Stranger, The*; Representation

Imperialism

Mark Twain lived during the "second wave" of Western imperialism, in which the civilized powers, prompted in the 1870s by the industrial revolution to seek new markets and materials, again took up "the white man's burden" as they had in the seventeenth and eighteenth centuries. By 1898 America had joined the imperialistic fray with its acquisition of the Philippines following the Spanish-American War, and debate in America began in earnest regarding this latest manifestation of imperialism. Surveying the international panorama of repression and exploitation by the great civilized powers, Mark Twain concluded that imperialism was but one more disgrace of "the damned human race."

Twain's earlier writings on imperialism evince a more cautious stance, however, than this later unequivocal position. In response to European criticism of the American war with Spain, and more particularly criticism leveled toward American citizens traveling abroad—Twain himself included—Twain wrote "A Word of Encouragement for Our Blushing Exiles" in 1898 (*Essays* 682–684). His double-edged "encouragement" consisted of pointing to the illustrious history of cruelty practiced by the great European powers, and in portraying America's actions as only the latest in a long line of imperialistic forays. Less than a vindication of American imperialism, however, Twain's is an indirect critique of the Spanish-American War as a shameful initiation into the unenviable imperialistic legacy of Europe. While permitting Americans to walk unharried among the hardly untainted Europeans, Twain implied that Americans at home should not be so morally at ease. Nevertheless, Twain's was not a blatantly scathing critique of America's role in the Spanish-American War, as he maintained that America's liberation of Cuba was rare evidence of "a righteous war" ("Welcome Home Speech," 10 October 1900) (*Speeches* 145–149). Similarly, while deploring British actions in the Boer War, Twain wrote to William Dean Howells on 25 January 1900 that he was hesitant to commit any criticisms to print, as he feared that the fall of England would result in the rise of Germany and Russia and subsequently "a sort of Middle-Age night and slavery." Given the paradox of having tacitly to support one form of imperialism in order to prevent a worse manifestation thereof, Twain despairingly asked Howells: "Why was the human race created?"

By the end of 1900 Twain posed his former ambivalence in stark terms, perhaps even creating for himself a pro-imperialist past that he could thereby wholly repudiate. Upon his return from Europe in October 1900, Twain claimed in an interview that he had left America nine years before "a red hot imperialist." He saw no argument against putting "a miniature of the American Constitution afloat in the Pacific," but only toward the end of freeing, not subjugating, the Philippines. Witnessing now the true ambitions of America, he declared himself an anti-imperialist, "opposed to having the eagle put its talons on any other land."

On 30 December 1899 the New York *Herald* published Twain's first and perhaps most succinctly trenchant attack against imperialism, a "salutation" from the nineteenth to the twentieth century. The brief statement exposed the blatant hypocrisy of exploitation in the name of Christian kindness practiced around the globe. This same criticism finds its greatest expression in Twain's essay "To the Person Sitting in Darkness" (1901), whose very title (an allusion from Matthew 4:16 to the light that Christ brought all mankind in humility and self-sacrifice) expresses the betrayal of Christ's teachings by imperialists in Christian garb (*Essays* 282–296). In his most ironic voice Twain poses the *claims* of civilization against its *acts* in the occupied nations and concludes that "the person sitting in darkness" will shortly have no choice but to "raise himself down to" the level of civilization in order to defend himself from its rapacious exploiters. The essay was subsequently published in pamphlet form by the New York Anti-Imperialism League, reaching a wide audience and stirring a grand controversy. Twain did not remove himself from the pub-

lic outcry, however, but shortly thereafter published "To My Missionary Critics" (1901), an unrelenting exposure of the underlying moral bankruptcy of the purported Christianity of Reverend William Ament and others who had responded in their own defense to Twain's earlier essay (*Essays* 296–310).

These essays remain Twain's most comprehensive criticism of imperialism, though he continued to write and occasionally publish on the subject. Among his most poignant, pathetic, and moving pieces are essays he wrote on two separate genocidal slaughters, the killing of over 10 million natives in the Belgian Congo and the slaughter of 600 Moro natives in the Philippines by American troops, described respectively in *King Leopold's Soliloquy* (1905) (*Damned Human Race* 181–193) and "Grief and Mourning for the Night" (1906) (*Pen Warmed-Up* 78–85). With journalistic realism Twain described the cruelty perpetrated by the overwhelming forces of the West on the natives of underdeveloped countries, all in the name of progress and Christianity.

As a cautionary tale for the now ascendant Occident, Twain wrote "The Fable of the Yellow Terror" (written ca. 1904–1905), a clever story of an empire of Butterflies whose superior sting gives them sway over all other insects (*Fables* 425–429). The Butterflies, through force and knowledge, introduce "civilization" throughout their empire in the form of confiscation, enforced religious piety, and the opening of new markets for their honey. Accusing the empire of the Bees of being "a yellow peril," a reference to the prevailing perception of China in the 1890s, the Butterflies conquer the Bees, but only temporarily, as the Bees learn the "great art" of civilization: "the art of how to kill and cripple and mutilate, scientifically." By describing the hypocrisy and presumption of an imaginary animal empire, Twain sought to teach a subtle lesson on man's "inhumanity," intimating that animals act cruelly toward one another only when acting "humanely." The only lesson of imperialism, Twain suggested, was that it would teach dominated nations how to dominate in turn and to use the rule of force as the legitimate rule of civilization.

Patrick Deneen

BIBLIOGRAPHY

Clemens, Samuel L. *The Complete Essays of Mark Twain*. Ed. Charles Neider. Garden City, N.Y.: Doubleday, 1963.

———. *Mark Twain on the Damned Human Race*. Ed. Janet Smith. New York: Hill and Wang, 1962.

———. *Mark Twain's Fables of Man*. Ed. John S. Tuckey. Berkeley: U of California P, 1972.

———. *Mark Twain's Speeches*. Ed. Albert B. Paine. New York: Harper, 1923.

———. *A Pen Warmed-Up in Hell: Mark Twain in Protest*. Ed. Frederick Anderson. New York: Harper & Row, 1972.

Gibson, William M. "Mark Twain and Howells: Anti-Imperialists." *New England Quarterly* 20 (1947): 435–470.

Harrington, Fred. "The Anti-Imperialist Movement in the United States." *Mississippi Valley Historical Review* 22 (1935): 211–230.

Lasch, Christopher. *The World of Nations*. New York: Knopf, 1973. 70–79.

See also: Government; *King Leopold's Soliloquy*; Missionaries; Religion; "To the Person Sitting in Darkness"

Impersonators

The first Mark Twain doubles were impostors, petty criminals who quickly moved on to their next dodge. The good-faith imitators who appeared occasionally before his death turned into a thin chain reaching the 1950s, when Hal Holbrook (1925–) began his thickening record of success. He has stirred up many competitors, who help to keep Twain's figure and personality vivid in the popular as well as the literate culture.

As early as 1868 Twain published a complaint that somebody had paraded under his identity in Cleveland before running out on hotel bills. In 1889, asked by a reporter about persons who used his pen name or claimed some of his early writings, he responded that he had not "been bothered that way so much as I have by personators," some of whom borrowed money on the strength of his name while others were merely indulging an "idiotic vanity." Before the telephone connected distant cities and the press routinely carried photography, hit-and-run imposture was feasible. However, some of the impersonators, honest or not, felt that they merely followed in Twain's steps as a showman—of the Davy Crockett–P.T. Barnum tradition—who implied a self-awareness of his theatricality and whose audiences enjoyed being hoodwinked.

During an interview in 1895 Twain complained that his "doubles," as he called them, "were around the country lecturing without giving him any of the proceeds." Though the exaggeration was meant to help promote his world lecture tour just starting, newspapers featured his whereabouts so richly by then that no such imposture could succeed. Instead, entertainers now and then included Twain among a sequence of imitations. In 1905 his secretary went to watch an impressionist do him for vaudeville in Manhattan. The fact of such performances and, much more, his seeing them (in 1877, 1889, and 1901, for instance) surely heightened not only his self-consciousness, but also that sense of a divided identity that troubled him throughout his life.

After Twain's death a flurry of impersonations on the vaudeville circuit soon quieted down. Still, memory of the charm, force, and uniqueness of his presence stayed so vivid that occasionally someone was publicized as or reverently tried to become a "look-alike." Therefore, when actors started during the 1950s to develop the one-person show, Twain emerged as an obvious choice because of his lingering image and the richness of the potential scripts. Working from the right kind of talent but also making wise decisions, Holbrook soon ranked as the dominant impersonator. Having grounded himself in the familiar and even some specialized material, such as the reviews of Twain's tour of readings in 1884–1885, Holbrook saw through the mistake of trying to improve on one of the great raconteurs. Still more wisely, he decided to resurrect Twain at age seventy-one, flaunting bushy hair and mustache and a matching white suit.

Holbrook first tried out a Twain solo in 1954. By 1959 he had accumulated enough scripts and kudos (most notably on the Ed Sullivan hour—the jewel of Sunday night television) to sustain a three-act Broadway showing in New York. Rave reviews led to other successes: later reruns on the stage, a TV special for CBS, two long-playing records, and foreign tours sponsored by the State Department as well as one-night stands throughout the United States. In fact, he began to guard against overexposure with a limit of twelve to fifteen road performances a year. Though Twain did not sport a white suit during the winter until December 1906, did not wear it regularly after that during the last three years of his life, and did not (except at one banquet) wear it while speech making, Holbrook has established it as virtually a uniform. Though Holbrook himself has granted that Twain never smoked on the platform, he features the cigar as a prop, somewhat defensibly because his performance blends the public Twain with a raconteur lolling at home (yet confiding to an audience). Likewise, under a leisurely pose Holbrook keeps alternating the famous with intriguingly fresh texts, set pieces with epigrams or quick jokes, and comic with darkly serious moods and keeps switching persona as he segues into Twain himself recreating his characters. Holbrook's act deserves the Ph.D. dissertation that analyzes the "rhetorical elements" deployed.

Holbrook has grown so closely identified with Twain that when the original returned to earth in David Carkeet's novel *I Been There Before* (1985), a hotel clerk mistook him for the impersonator. In 1989 a fictitious interview with Twain for the New York *Times* commented: "Take a few years off his face and he could pass for Hal Holbrook." Competitors often imitate Holbrook instead, adopting the white suit, the flourished cigar, and even his rendition of Twain's voice as a nasal

drawl. More broadly, they tend toward recreating a Southerner from the plantation or at least the antebellum world. During the early and mid-1980s Bill McLinn (1944–1989) performed far more authentically in black evening dress while recalling a physically sturdy Twain intent on social and political justice. As the Holbrook stereotype hardens, a few competitors have tried to market a much younger Twain or to feature his famous speeches. But the stooped white-haired figure predominates among the (probably) several hundred impersonators: in every region of the United States, of widely ranging ages under the makeup, at varied levels of talent for a matching fee (starting with none at all), from one-shot amateurs to semiprofessionals to a few who dream of a self-supporting career. By 1971 a science-fiction fantasy made an immortal Twain grumble that his impersonators had infested even heaven. The mortal Twain would doubtless have joked about the two of them who resurrected him for Charlotte, North Carolina, on the same day in 1980.

Quick-study impersonators pop up as greeters at an exhibit or sideshow or as hired strollers in a mall or at a convention. Several mechanical Twains make news (with photographs) here and there, and the cigar-smoking, drawling, computer-driven robot at Disney World has star status, if only as a marvel of technology. Twain has lasted as a popular icon evolving along a course now directed partly by media and marketing experts. They are favoring his river years over other phases of his life while, nevertheless, keeping the white suit as a logo.

Even as most canonical authors of the nineteenth century dim toward a half-life in textbooks, Twain's impersonators help to keep his fame shining and his books selling. More specifically, they are elevating a few texts above his enormous output, making his one-sentence jokes almost central to his image, and—probably the fundamental effect—shifting the spotlight to his personality, liberated from the world of print as his time knew it and simplified as somewhat testy and prone to spells of pessimism but more avuncular and tamable than the actual man meant to be.

Louis J. Budd

BIBLIOGRAPHY

Clemens, Samuel L. *Mark Twain Tonight! An Actor's Portrait.* Ed. Hal Holbrook. New York: Ives, Washburn, 1959.

Gentile, John S. "Early Examples of the Biographical One-Person Show Genre: *Emlyn Williams as Charles Dickens* and Hal Holbrook's *Mark Twain Tonight!*" *Literature in Performance* 6 (November 1985): 42–53.

Jackson, Norman Lee. "An Analysis of Hal Holbrook's Development and Performance of the Role of Mark Twain." Ph.D. diss., Brigham Young U, 1981.

See also: Barnum, Phineas Taylor; Comics; Media Interpretations

"In Defense of Harriet Shelley"

(1894)

First appearing in the *North American Review* in three installments in July, August, and September 1894, "In Defense of Harriet Shelley" was reprinted in *How to Tell a Story and Other Essays* (1897) and in several other collected editions that appeared by 1901. In this review of Edward Dowden's *The Life of Percy Bysshe Shelley* (1886) Twain angrily responds to the biographer's attempts to blame Harriet for Shelley's treatment of her. While the review deals primarily with content, it begins with a convincing attack on Dowden's pretentious style. Twain's characterization of the book as a "Frankenstein" (with its ironic reference to Shelley's second marriage) suggests the humor with which he occasionally supports his attacks. Logically and methodically, Twain refutes the points made against Harriet. This three-part review entertains and convinces the reader that Harriet Shelley was indeed wronged by both her husband and his biographer. Two letters written in 1901 to Elizabeth Aker Allen, author of the popular "Rock Me to Sleep, Mother," show Twain defending Harriet as

forcefully as he had seven years earlier in his review. He admits that "Shelley's treatment of Harriet was probably not the sole cause of her suicide, but only ninety-nine one-hundredths of the cause."

The critical response to Twain's "In Defense of Harriet Shelley" is minimal but positive, most critics finding it insightful, and Twain's anger at both style and content understandable. Sydney J. Krause finds this essay an excellent example of "Twain's inspired melancholia—his mingling of logic and absurdity, his argumentative gusto, his moral energy, and his commonsensical indictment of critics and critical prose" (103). Only Frank Baldanza finds Twain's anger inconsistent with its source.

Nancy Chinn

BIBLIOGRAPHY

Baldanza, Frank. *Mark Twain: An Introduction and Interpretation.* New York: Barnes & Noble, 1961.

Cary, Richard. "In Further Defense of Harriet Shelley: Two Unpublished Letters by Mark Twain." *Mark Twain Journal* 16.4 (Summer 1973): 13–15.

Clemens, Samuel L. "In Defense of Harriet Shelley." *How to Tell a Story and Other Essays.* By Clemens. New York: Harper, 1897. 16–77.

Krause, Sydney J. *Mark Twain as Critic.* Baltimore: Johns Hopkins UP, 1967.

Long, E. Hudson, and J.R. LeMaster. *The New Mark Twain Handbook.* New York: Garland, 1985.

Matthews, Brander. "Mark Twain and the Art of Writing." *Critical Essays on Mark Twain, 1910–1980.* Ed. Louis J. Budd. Boston: G.K. Hall, 1983. 54–65.

See also: Shelley, Harriet

India

In the course of an around-the-world lecture tour, undertaken to struggle clear of debt, Mark Twain arrived in Bombay, India, in January 1896 to an enthusiastic welcome from the city's newspapers. For the following two months he traveled extensively through the Indian subcontinent, and in *Following the Equator* (1897) he recorded observations of the country's culture and customs, addressed issues of contemporary social and political significance in India, and speculated on the use of the English language by Indians.

Twain finds the customs, colors, and sounds of India bewitching. Just as in *Life on the Mississippi* (1883) he had shown a marked interest in exploring graveyards, so Twain in Bombay is fascinated by burial customs, most specifically the special cremation method of the Parsees, which he describes in great detail. The colors and teeming life of the crowds at Jeypore in the course of a display procession virtually overwhelm him; indeed, Twain's detailed descriptions of Indian crowds, whether in railway stations or in shopping areas, are authentic and touching. Juxtaposed to the pulsating life, however, is the "melancholy" landscape on the outskirts of Benares. Here he finds "dusty sterility, decaying temples, crumbling tombs, broken mud walls, shabby huts." Contrast and paradox are inherent to India, for it is "the land . . . of fabulous wealth and fabulous poverty, of splendor and rags, of palaces and hovels." It is also unique; none of its marvels can be duplicated: "the patents cannot be infringed; imitations are not possible."

One of the Indian inimitables Twain describes with gusto is the practice of thugee: thugs traveling in packs slaughter victims to appease the goddess Bhowanee, and Twain highlights the exhilaration the frenzied thugs experience in the hunt of their prey (Gowda 22). Juxtaposed to this bloodthirsty phenomenon is the practice of suttee, which, if undertaken voluntarily, epitomizes selfless surrender and devotion. Not duplicated elsewhere, the practice of suttee prevailed in early-nineteenth-century India, and Twain provides a graphic account of an 1828 case involving a widow who defied British attempts to intervene as she willingly embraced death. The author clearly admires this heroic act, though he is perplexed as to the origins of the practice. He is also perturbed by the extravagance that frequently accompanied the custom, for in speaking of cremation in *Life on the Mississippi* he writes that the ceremonies connected

with it could be as "costly and ostentatious as a Hindu suttee."

Twain finds much less to admire in the Hindu caste system, which he claims fosters divisiveness and is thus detrimental to the growth of patriotism. After a rational assessment of the Hindu superstition in Benares, Twain becomes culturally chauvinistic, even crass: "the Hindu changed into an ass wouldn't lose anything, unless you count his religion." Indeed, he argues that the Hindu would profit greatly from such a transformation, for he would gain freedom from the innumerable gods, priests, and fakirs—as well as the Hindu hell and the Hindu heaven. At other times Twain is more tongue in cheek in his debunking of the Hindus. He reports, for example, that the Brahmans could be capricious enough occasionally to declare the Ganges unholy; when the moment was ripe, however, they would "spring something on the Indian public" which would make it clear that they were not "financially asleep" when they took "the Ganges out of the market." Twain's sarcastic treatment of Hindu customs is reminiscent of his attack on the Catholic Church in *Innocents Abroad* (1869), as it focuses on religion as an agent of repression, exploiting superstition for profit and sustaining a rigid caste system that benefits the privileged at the expense of the downtrodden masses.

Cultural chauvinism is also apparent in Twain's commentary on political issues, for there is little doubt he favors British rule of the Indian empire. He praises Warren Hastings for having saved India for England, which, in turn, was the "best service" to the Indians themselves, the "wretched heirs" of centuries of "pitiless oppression and abuse." His description of the Sepoy Mutiny of 1857 recounts only the suffering and fortitude of the British with little sensitivity to the forces and conditions that sparked the rebellion. The defense of colonialism is all the more striking, coming as it does only a few years before Twain's scathing indictment of military, economic, and cultural imperialism at the turn of the century (see entries on "To My Missionary Critics," "To the Person Sitting in Darkness," and *King Leopold's Soliloquy*).

In the chapter entitled "Babu Errors No Worse than Ours" in *Following the Equator*, Twain draws interesting parallels between the use of English by Indian and American schoolchildren. In both cases, he argues, irrational academic pressure distorts powers of expression and leads to glaring errors in language usage. Twain includes samples of letters written in English by Indians applying to the British for sundry forms of employment to demonstrate the strong ties of kinship that prevail in India. As faulty and confusing they may be in expression, the letters are moving; they show the desperate candidate seeking employment not merely for self-advancement but to support a number of dependent relations. The "language of fawning and flattery" of these letters Twain attributes to the supplicating attitude engendered by years of subjugation to native rulers. No mention is made of the more likely cause: their oppression at the hands of the British on whose favor their survival depends.

Twain's cultural biases did not prevent him from establishing rapport with the Indians during his tour. Not wanting to force a lecture on a mass audience, he staged instead a series of talks he termed "At Homes." The informality of these occasions allowed mutual exchange and encouraged his empathy with the people's joys and sorrows. The Indians, in turn, found appealing Twain's unique blend of humor and pathos (Mutalik 55–56). He was emotionally stirred by certain parts of the subcontinent (e.g., Bengal) and was invariably impressed by the gentleness of the Indian character. In short, Twain's response to India testifies to a temperament and nature more empathetic than sweepingly dismissive. He hails the country as one that "all men desire to see, and having seen once, by even a glimpse, would not give that glimpse for the shows of all the rest of the globe combined."

Srimati Mukherjee

BIBLIOGRAPHY

Clemens, Samuel L. *Following the Equator: A Journey Around the World.* 2 vols. New York: Harper, 1897.

———. *Life on the Mississippi.* Boston: James R. Osgood, 1883.

Gowda, H.H. Anniah. "Mark Twain in India." *Literary Half-Yearly* (July 1966): 17–23.

Mutalik, Keshav. *Mark Twain in India.* Bombay: Noble, 1978.

See also: England; *Following the Equator*; Imperialism

Indians

Mark Twain shared the attitude of most of his contemporaries on the western frontier toward the Indians: he despised them. As a boy in Hannibal, he was aware of only one Indian, a shiftless half-breed, the prototype of Injun Joe in *The Adventures of Tom Sawyer* (1876). When Sam Clemens rode the stagecoach west to Nevada with his brother Orion in 1861, the Sioux had attacked settlers recently enough to be something of a serious threat to passengers. The Apaches, indeed, were still interfering with travel on the southern route. Twain, however, saw no Indians until he encountered the Paiutes or Diggers in the Nevada desert. Renaming them the Goshutes in *Roughing It* (1872), Twain deprecated them as "the most wretched type of mankind I have ever seen." He claims they are more degraded than the bushmen of South Africa: subhumans, lacking manners, morals, taste, and religion.

Twain's most frequent use of the image of the Indian is as a vehicle to attack someone else's ideas. These "savages," as close to animals as to people from Twain's perspective, become a weapon in Twain's war with the romanticism of James Fenimore Cooper. Cooper's Noble Red Man is depicted both in *Roughing It* and in letters to Twain's mother as a squalid, revolting, and altogether despicable being. He contrasts the Noble Red Man of the Leatherstocking Tales with the despicable creatures he found in the deserts of Nevada.

Later in *A Tramp Abroad* (1880) he compares the French with the Comanches in their viciousness toward each other.

In the uncompleted "Huck Finn and Tom Sawyer Among the Indians" (1969) the Indians are still treacherous and ignoble, mercilessly preying on pioneers who attempt to befriend them, slaughtering the parents and kidnapping the children. Tom Sawyer, true to the character established in the earlier books, bases his concepts of the Indians on his reading of Cooper's romances, idealizes them as physically and morally superior humans in contrast to the characters as revealed through the plot. Twain's occasional positive references to Indians in subsequent years seem largely rhetorical devices to attack the current American civilization.

William McDonald

BIBLIOGRAPHY

Denton, Lynn. "Mark Twain and the American Indian." *Mark Twain Journal* 16 (1971): 1–3.

Hanson, Elizabeth. "Mark Twain's Indians Reexamined." *Mark Twain Journal* 20.4 (Summer 1981): 11–12.

See also: Cooper, James Fenimore; "Huck Finn and Tom Sawyer Among the Indians"; Racial Attitudes

"Indiantown"

(1967)

This plotless sketch is among a complex of fragments about a prosperous and happy man's nightmarish fall to disaster. Intertwining dream and reality, "Indiantown" serves as a bridge between "Which Was the Dream?" (written 1897) and "Which Was It?" (written 1899), anticipating the darker vision of the latter. Written in the summer of 1899, the sketch remained unpublished until collected by John S. Tuckey in his 1967 edition of *Mark Twain's "Which Was the Dream?" and Other Symbolic Writings of the Later Years*.

"Indiantown" opens with a description of its title village, which, like Bricksville in *Ad-*

ventures of Huckleberry Finn (1885), is modeled on Napoleon, Arkansas, and thus serves as another of Twain's sleepy southern towns whose riverbank setting suggests its precarious position on the brink of disaster. The sketch then introduces the town's inhabitants, arranged by social class; many of these recur, though with different significances attached to them, in "Which Was It?"—a related fragment begun immediately after Clemens abandoned "Indiantown." Written in the aftermath of the sudden death of Clemens's daughter Susy in 1896, "Indiantown" incorporates undisguised autobiographical elements that divert the dream-of-disaster scenario (DeVoto 117). Among parallels scholars have noted are Reverend Bailey/Joseph Twichell, George Harrison/Orion Clemens, Godkin/an osteopathic patient called "The Shadow," and the Gridleys/Samuel and Olivia Clemens. Twain drops this story before its protagonist, following his apparent blackout and time-lapse, confuses disaster with unescapable dream or happiness with unattainable dream (Tuckey 151–152). The darker implications of the later "Which Was It?" begin to intrude in "Indiantown," however, as duplicity replaces innocence.

The two central characters carry the incipient themes of the fragment. O. Lloyd Godkin's name and nicknames ("Little god," Ass-Philosopher, Ghost, Corpse) convey supernal humor and horror, suggesting the theme of tragedy-producing jokes (Gribben 190). Although denied superhuman smell when Twain decided against inserting the subsidiary fragment "A Human Bloodhound," Godkin anticipates later dream-story super characters (e.g., Philip Traum). David Gridley introduces the themes of freedom, social relationships, and duplicitous, unstable identity. He embodies Clemens's own feelings of hypocrisy and guilt resulting from his wife's editing and suppressing of his work, a capitulation to genteel propriety that generates the dichotomy of the exterior self packaged to the world and the real individual underneath, hidden and festering. The comparisons of Gridley to furniture reinforces the theme of duplicity, and phrases describing him ("sham," "bogus," "exterior Gridley," "two Davids," "humbug") reiterate his character deterioration, a theme "Which Was It?" continues to develop.

John H. Davis

BIBLIOGRAPHY

Clemens, Samuel L. "A Human Bloodhound." *Mark Twain's Hannibal, Huck & Tom.* By Clemens. Ed. Walter Blair. Berkeley: U of California P, 1969. 69–78.

———. "Indiantown." *Mark Twain's "Which Was the Dream?" and Other Symbolic Writings of the Later Years.* By Clemens. Ed. John S. Tuckey. Berkeley: U of California P, 1967. 153–176.

DeVoto, Bernard. "The Symbols of Despair." *Mark Twain at Work.* By DeVoto. Cambridge, Mass.: Harvard UP, 1942. 105–130.

Emerson, Everett. *The Authentic Mark Twain: A Literary Biography of Samuel L. Clemens.* Philadelphia: U of Pennsylvania P, 1984.

Gribben, Alan. "Those Other Thematic Patterns in Mark Twain's Writings." *Studies in American Fiction* 13.2 (Autumn 1985): 185–200.

Howell, Elmo. "Mark Twain's Indiantown." *Mark Twain Journal* 15 (January 1971): 16–19.

Messent, Peter. "Towards the Absurd: Mark Twain's *A Connecticut Yankee, Pudd'nhead Wilson,* and *The Great Dark.*" *Mark Twain: A Sumptuous Variety.* Ed. Robert Giddings. Totowa, N.J.: Barnes & Noble, 1985. 176–198.

Requa, Kenneth A. "Counterfeit Currency and Character in Mark Twain's 'Which Was It?'" *Mark Twain Journal* 17 (Winter 1974): 1–6.

See also: Dreams; "Great Dark, The"; Napoleon, Arkansas; "Which Was It?"

Ingersoll, Robert Green
(1833–1899)

As the youngest of five children, Robert G. Ingersoll, born in Dresden, New York, on 11 August 1833, was influenced by a thorough but unorthodox religious indoctrination. His father was an itinerant Calvinist preacher and his mother was a radical exponent of the abolition and temperance movements. By rejecting strict Calvinism, Ingersoll was increasingly influenced by the "free-thought" doctrines advocated by his favorite writers: Thomas Paine, Benjamin Franklin, and Voltaire. Eventually, Ingersoll discarded the tenets of organized religion while retaining his reverence for humanity (Larson 1–17).

At twenty Ingersoll began a three-year teaching career in Illinois and then Tennessee, returning in 1854 to became a member of the Illinois bar. Like Twain, Ingersoll enlisted in the Civil War. As a War Democrat, he rose to the rank of colonel of the 11th Volunteer Regiment of the cavalry. He returned to Peoria an avowed Republican. His political involvement increased as his legal practice grew. The remainder of his life was devoted to campaigning: for the Republican party, for civil rights, and most vehemently, for the Free Thought Movement (Larson 17–42).

Twain and Ingersoll were both represented on the public-speaking circuit by James Redpath of the Boston Lyceum Bureau. Like Twain, Ingersoll never failed to arouse public sentiment. Wherever he spoke, thousands crowded American arenas to hear the dynamic speaker and his heated denunciation of religious doctrines. Either shocked by his outspoken irreverence or in agreement with his sentiments, the "American Infidel's" audiences showered him with condemnation or appreciation.

According to Anderson, "the depth [of his sincerity] was unquestioned not only by his supporters but by his opponents." His supporters included Henry Ward Beecher, who believed Ingersoll was "the greatest speaker in the English language on Earth"; Walt Whitman, who "described his delivery as 'precious ointment'"; and Andrew Carnegie, who "regarded him as an American man of letters" (Anderson 31–32).

Twain and Ingersoll met only one time, on 13 November 1879. Both were in Chicago to address a banquet crowd assembled to pay tribute to Ulysses S. Grant. The men apparently spent several hours in each other's company. Later, Twain wrote to his wife: "I guess this was the memorable night of my life." Referring to Ingersoll's speech, he added: "[I]t was just the [most] supreme combination of English words that was ever put together since the world began" (Larson 235). Twain went on to elevate Ingersoll as the leader in his own field. Praising the "molten silver from [Ingersoll's] lips" that inspired 500 men to rise to their feet, Twain conceded that "the organ of human speech [was] played by a master." Later, in a letter to William Dean Howells, Twain admitted: "[N]one but the master can make them get up on their feet" (Larson 236).

Howells wrote of their relationship thirty years later, in a 1910 *Harper's Monthly* article: "[Twain] greatly admired Robert Ingersoll, whom he called an angelic orator, and regarded as an evangel of a new gospel, the gospel of Freethought" (363).

There is no evidence that they ever met again. Twain's respect and admiration for Ingersoll's free-thought doctrines survived in his public writing and his private life. Ingersoll's speeches were featured reading at Twain's "Saturday Morning Club," as were Twain's own writings (Andrews 104). Though Twain probably had access to most of the material in *The Works of Robert G. Ingersoll*, a twelve-volume set published in 1900, there is evidence that the fact was concealed by his daughter Clara.

Twain's work is filled with interesting parallels to Ingersoll's own pronouncements. Thomas D. Schwartz's article "Mark Twain and Robert Ingersoll: The Freethought Connection," discusses many of these similarities. Schwartz neglects Twain's later writings, however. Most of the writings from Twain's "dark" period show even more influence than those published in Twain's lifetime. *Letters from the Earth* (1962) and Ingersoll's *Works* bear striking similarities: the existence of hell and eternal punishment (Clemens 45, Ingersoll 11:470, 551); the earth populated by God's "pets" (Clemens 7, Ingersoll 11:241, 554). There are also parallels regarding divine Providence, God condoning man's inhumanity, atonement, God's "murder" of Christ for the sins of the innocent, and likening God to an infinite fiend.

Ingersoll died in 1899. Twain wrote to Ingersoll's niece: "Except for my daughter's I have not grieved for any death as I have grieved for his" (Wakefield 502).

Mary Minor Austin

BIBLIOGRAPHY

Anderson, David D. *Robert Ingersoll*. New York: Twayne, 1972.

Andrews, Kenneth R. *Nook Farm: Mark Twain's Hartford Circle*. Cambridge, Mass.: Harvard UP, 1950.

Clemens, Samuel L. *Letters from the Earth*. Ed. Bernard DeVoto. New York: Harper & Row, 1962.

Ingersoll, Robert G. *The Letters of Robert G. Ingersoll*. Ed. Eva Ingersoll Wakefield. New York: Philosophical Library, 1951.

———. *The Works of Robert G. Ingersoll*. 12 vols. New York: Farrell-Ingersoll, 1900.

Larson, Orvin. *American Infidel: Robert G. Ingersoll*. New York: Citadel, 1962.

Schwartz, Thomas D. "Mark Twain and Robert Ingersoll: The Freethought Connection." *American Literature* 48 (1976): 183–193.

See also: Calvinism; Free Thought

Innocence

In few instances does Mark Twain's ambivalence emerge more perplexingly than in his attitude toward the untutored and the unsophisticated. Whether innocent by virtue of their nationality, innocent by virtue of their social rank, or innocent by virtue of their youth, Mark Twain's unworldly protagonists are often shown to be superior to their elders and "betters," sometimes to be as bad or worse.

His first large published work, *The Innocents Abroad* (1869), announced the first of these contrasts between innocence and experience in its title, sounding the note of the superiority of the unsophisticated new world to the decadent old. The naive American traveler pierces the evil of received opinion, looking with his own eyes, perceiving the "realities" of Europe and the Near East behind their appearance of romance and tradition. This national contrast persists in his later travel books, *A Tramp Abroad* (1880) and *Following the Equator* (1897), and received its fictional thrust in Jim's diatribe against kings in *Adventures of Huckleberry Finn* (1885) and in Twain's frequent identification of the ills of the American South with its reverence for the trappings of English feudalism, especially in *Life on the Mississippi* (1883) and *Pudd'nhead Wilson* (1894). His most eloquent statement of the superiority of the New World to the Old was his depiction of a Connecticut Yankee who tries to bring sixth-century England up to the material and moral level of the American nineteenth century in *A Connecticut Yankee in King Arthur's Court* (1889). In posing these popular and reassuring contrasts, however, Twain unhesitatingly satirized the shortcomings of his American innocents. While they (and he) saw through the shams of Europe, they were also blind in their crass philistinism, "consummate asses" in whose equine company Twain cheerfully included himself.

As well as in his contrasting portraits of Europeans and Americans, Twain often expressed his attitude toward the virtues and shortcomings of innocence in his treatment of differing social and cultural levels. In the early sketch that made his reputation as a humorist, "The Celebrated Jumping Frog of Calaveras County" (1865), the narrator Simon Wheeler is the cultural innocent, gulling the seemingly superior eastern listener. Simon is the first of a long string of "vernacular" protagonists, cultural innocents but practical geniuses, of whom Huckleberry Finn is the supreme example. But cultural innocence has its dark side: Pap Finn and the disgusting "rednecks" of the southwestern river towns in *Adventures of Huckleberry Finn* are extreme but by no means unique examples of the depravity found in the untutored masses that, in his later pessimistic moods, Twain regarded as human "muck."

Twain's attitudes toward blacks and the American Indian provide further examples of his ambivalence toward innocence in a cultural setting. Without exception, he celebrated blacks as the embodiment of natural virtue. The young Sam Clemens got his "strong liking" for the race and his "appreciation of certain of its fine qualities" from his uncle John Quarles's slave, Uncle Dan'l, whose sensible, honest, patient affection he embodied in Jim of *Adventures of Huckleberry Finn*. The reverse side of the coin is Twain's lifelong antipathy for the most significant symbol of the cult of the noble innocent—the American Indian. He launched his bitterest literary diatribe against Cooper's portraits of the Noble Savage in "Fenimore Cooper's Literary Offenses," (1895) repeating sentiments he had expressed in "Niagara Revisited" (1869) and "The Noble Red Man," (1870) and in "Huck Finn and Tom Sawyer Among the Indians" (1969). A hero of *Adventures of Huckleberry Finn* is Jim. A villain of *The Adventures of Tom Sawyer* (1876) is Injun Joe.

While Twain regularly associated national, regional, and cultural characteristics with the virtues and shortcomings of innocence, his largest emotional involvement was often in the transnational and transcultural perspective of the youth and the child as the point of view from which to observe society. His masterpiece was concerned with the sound heart of the adolescent Huck Finn who learns to know Jim as a human being. Tom Canty in *The Prince and the Pauper* (1882) pierces the miasma of socially induced conscience, applying common sense to the problems of eighteenth-century England, while the young Prince Edward learns to see the humanity of the poor and oppressed. Twain's commitment to the values of youth shows most clearly in his depiction of Joan of Arc in *Personal Recollections of Joan of Arc* (1896). There his devotion to innocence as a cultural value and innocence as a function of unspoiled childhood coalesce in his portrait of the girl saint whose story haunted him through much of his life and whose biography he considered his best work. Joan was the embodiment of the natural virtues of innocence: in Twain's view she derived her powers from the intuitive wisdom of the common people, from her youthful freshness, and from her direct association with the forces of nature.

Here too, however, in his treatment of childhood, Twain's feelings were decidedly mixed. While he could celebrate Huck, Tom Canty, and Joan, he could also regard childhood with an unsentimental eye. From his early sketch "Those Blasted Children" (1864) to the description of the witch-stoning youngsters in "The Chronicle of Young Satan" (1969), Twain showed childhood as no better than maturity. When Hank Morgan in *A Connecticut Yankee* describes the nobles of sixth-century England as "children" and "Comanches," he means neither as a term of praise. When Twain revisited his boyhood home in *Life on the Mississippi* (1883), he found his memories crowded with guilt and terror, oppressed by a naive belief that the course of one's life was determined not by logical laws, but by "special orders . . . partly punitive . . . partly admonitory." Childhood, he had observed as early as *The Innocents Abroad*, is "no happier" than maturity: the nostalgia for it is the result of failed memory. Those who remain fixed on a stage of "sweet and sappy sixteen," he wrote to a friend, are indulgers in "mental and moral" self-abuse.

Critical controversy about Twain's attitude toward innocence is involved in paradox. On the one hand, the modernist tendency has been to emphasize and value Twain's early undercurrents of pessimism and despair about humanity, an undercurrent that grew to a flood in later years; such pessimism, of course, would run counter to a reverence for natural innocence. On the other hand, there has been the impulse to celebrate his pictures of childhood and innocence as proof of the repressiveness of civilization and the superiority of a countercultural life according to nature.

The perception of Twain's attitude toward innocence has also generated differing critical views of his attitudes toward his contemporary America. On the one hand, he has been seen as an instinctive believer in the national myth of progress based upon reliance on the natural goodness of natural man; on the other, he has been portrayed as a pessimistic believer in either the static cycle or the decline of

mankind. Modernist criticism has tended toward the latter view, making *Adventures of Huckleberry Finn* into a countercultural attack on all civilization, and has transformed Hank Morgan, the eponymous Yankee, from the "natural gentleman" that Twain intended him to be into at best a bumbler, at worst a destructive megalomaniac. A middle ground accepts Twain's ambivalences as an expression of his representativeness of an American culture that in the nineteenth century revered both primitivism and progress. While partaking of this double vision, Twain was neither uncritical of the shortcomings of American civilization nor sentimental about the virtues of innocence.

Everett Carter

Bibliography

Clemens, Samuel L. "Fenimore Cooper's Literary Offenses." *North American Review* 161 (July 1895): 1–12.

———. "Huck Finn and Tom Sawyer Among the Indians." *Mark Twain's Hannibal, Huck and Tom*. By Clemens. Ed. Walter Blair. Berkeley: U of California P, 1969. 81–140.

———. *The Innocents Abroad*. Hartford, Conn.: American Publishing, 1869.

———. "The Noble Red Man." *Contributions to "The Galaxy" 1868–1871*. By Clemens. Ed. Bruce R. McElderry, Jr. Gainesville, Fla.: Scholars' Facsimiles and Reprints, 1961. 70–73.

Emerson, Everett. *The Authentic Mark Twain: A Literary Biography of Samuel L. Clemens*. Philadelphia: U of Pennsylvania P, 1984.

Ferguson, John DeLancey. *Mark Twain: Man and Legend*. Indianapolis: Bobbs-Merrill, 1943.

Kaplan, Justin. *Mr. Clemens and Mark Twain*. New York: Simon & Schuster, 1966.

Stone, Albert E., Jr. *The Innocent Eye: Childhood in Mark Twain's Imagination*. New Haven, Conn.: Yale UP, 1961.

Wecter, Dixon. *Sam Clemens of Hannibal*. Boston: Houghton Mifflin, 1952.

See also: *Adventures of Huckleberry Finn*;
    Angel Fish and Aquarium Club;
    Childhood; Indians

Innocents Abroad, The
(1869)

Mark Twain's first full-scale work and a great popular success, *The Innocents Abroad; or, The New Pilgrim's Progress* (1869), was based on the author's letters to the San Francisco *Daily Alta California*, reporting the 163-day voyage of some seventy excursionists aboard the steamer *Quaker City* to the Mediterranean, the Black Sea, the Holy Land, Egypt, and return. The ship was a comfortable side-wheeler of 1900 tons, which under both steam and sail made some 250 miles a day.

The excursion originated in Henry Ward Beecher's Plymouth Church of the Pilgrims in Brooklyn and so from the start assumed a devotional character. This was agreeable to many passengers—three clergymen, eight physicians, and upper-middle-class retirees chiefly from the Northeast. Even Twain conducted the hymn singing and prayer meeting at least once. But mostly he found the devout ceremonies of the "pilgrims" rather too frequent and too sanctimonious. He was more comfortable with the "sinners," as he calls his card-playing, smoking and drinking companions—Slote, Jackson, Moulton, and Van Nostrand.

Besides partaking in shipboard activities, Twain busied himself writing letters to the *Alta*, which had advanced him passage money. Although an onerous task for a traveler, both on board and later ashore he found time to send dispatches regularly. Weeks later, however, he learned, probably at Alexandria, that a number of his letters had miscarried. This necessitated writing new ones to make up the loss. He relied on travel books in the ship's library, and he welcomed the help of Mrs. A.W. Fairbanks, who herself had been writing travel letters to her husband's Cleveland *Herald*. This extra work, together with the lower spirits of a return voyage, helps account for the less sprightly tone of the book's later chapters.

En route Twain had considered making a book of his travels, and once landed in New York, he headed straight for Washington, took up residence with Senator William M. Stewart

of Nevada, and began to put a book together. This involved collecting his *Alta* letters from his family and the letters of some of his fellow excursionists, cutting, rewriting, rearranging, writing new matter, and altering the tone of the whole for eastern readers. Approached by Elisha Bliss, of the American Publishing Company, about writing a book on his travels, Mark Twain visited Hartford and soon followed the advice of Henry Ward Beecher to sign with Bliss.

Progress stalled when the *Alta* people claimed ownership of the letters and announced their intention of turning them into a book of their own. A trip to San Francisco, via the Isthmus of Panama, settled the difference in Mark Twain's favor, and he worked to finish his manuscript. Bret Harte read it and suggested changes. In light of his later falling-out with Harte, one can understand Mark Twain's reluctance to credit Harte's help. But in a letter of 20 November 1870 to Charles Henry Webb, publisher of Mark Twain's first book, *The Celebrated Jumping Frog of Calaveras County and Other Sketches* (1867), the author freely acknowledged it: "Harte read all the manuscript of the 'Innocents' & told me what passages, paragraphs & *chapters* to leave out—& I followed orders strictly."

The exact nature of Harte's "orders" is impossible to determine since the manuscript has not been studied nor is it known to have survived. Some suggestion of Harte's opinion of humorous travel books, however, can be derived from the first volume of editor Harte's *Overland Monthly*. In this volume appeared an anonymous review (by Harte, Franklin Walker believes) of one such book, John Franklin Swift's *Going to Jericho: or, Sketches of Travel in Spain and the East* (1868), compiled from letters to the San Francisco *Bulletin*. The reviewer deplores excessive sentiment (citing as offenders Lamartine and William C. Prime, also mentioned in *Innocents Abroad*); he welcomes satire against such excesses, though he values satire and humor that are not strained. Finally, out of deference to the feelings of others, he likes a writer to avoid irreverence. Since study of Mark Twain's revisions shows Twain making changes in the direction of these values, they may be the best indication we have of Harte's influence.

In 1904 Mark Twain asserted that he "did not rely heavily upon the *Alta* Letters." He wrote new matter, it is true, and he pared his manuscript severely, because the *Alta* letters, he said, needed "to have some of the wind and water squeezed out of them." But in the end he used at least portions of all but one of the *Alta* letters.

Returned to Hartford, he delivered the manuscript to Bliss 30 July 1868. Several things remained to be done. One was selecting illustrations; another was choosing a title. For over a year after beginning his book Mark Twain fretted about a title, discussing it with Mrs. Fairbanks and with publisher Bliss. From the start he liked "The New Pilgrim's Progress" but was afraid that readers would "shudder at that, as taking the name of a consecrated book in vain." The solution, he concluded, was to make the Bunyan phrase less blatant by placing it in the subtitle.

Finally, there was the reading of proof, a task in which he enjoyed the help of his new fiancée, Olivia Langdon, of Elmira. He also spread his fame and publicized the forthcoming book by lecturing some fifty times as far west as Iowa.

The big book was published 20 July 1869, about a full year after Mark Twain had turned in his manuscript. It was sold by subscription, whereby agents fanned out over the country displaying a 100-page prospectus containing illustrations and samples of the text. They took orders and later retraced their steps to deliver the books and collect their money. The marketing method for *Innocents Abroad* was successful; it enjoyed, Twain wrote to a friend, "the largest sale of a *four-dollar* book . . . ever achieved in America in so short a time." Lists of all-time best-sellers usually included *Innocents Abroad*.

The book was widely reviewed. Except for religious periodicals, which could hardly be expected to appreciate Mark Twain on the Holy Land, reviewers were almost universally favorable, some enthusiastically so. All enjoyed the book's humor—satiric jibes at shipmates he dubbed the Oracle and the Poet Lariat, at know-it-all old travelers, and at sanctimonious pilgrims; personal narratives, such as buying gloves in Gibraltar and fooling the guides in Italy; and ironic passages, such as the lament at the tomb of Adam. Several reviewers valued the author's going beyond mere humor to achieve vivid word pictures of places seen. And many approved of Mark Twain's flights of what they called "eloquence"—Galilee at night and the Sphinx. The approval of William Dean Howells in the *Atlantic Monthly* was especially gratifying to Mark Twain, who called on editor Howells to thank him, thereby initiating what became one of the humorist's fondest and most durable friendships.

Still read with pleasure, *The Innocents Abroad* has come to be regarded as a definitive document in the perpetual concern of readers with the New World and the Old, and the relation between the two.

Leon T. Dickinson

BIBLIOGRAPHY

Clemens, Samuel L. *The Innocents Abroad*. Hartford, Conn.: American Publishing, 1869.

————. *Traveling with the Innocents Abroad*. Ed. Daniel M. McKeithan. Norman: U of Oklahoma P, 1958.

Dickinson, Leon T. "Marketing a Best Seller: Mark Twain's *Innocents Abroad*." *Papers of the Bibliographical Society of America* 41.2 (1947): 107–122.

————. "Mark Twain's Revisions in Writing *The Innocents Abroad*." *American Literature* 19.2 (May 1947): 139–157.

Ganzel, Dewey. *Mark Twain Abroad: The Cruise of the "Quaker City."* Chicago: U of Chicago P, 1968.

Gerber, John C. *Mark Twain*. Boston: Twayne, 1988.

Smith, Henry Nash. *Mark Twain: The Development of a Writer*. Cambridge, Mass.: Harvard UP, 1962.

See also: Europe; Harte, Francis Bret; Innocence; Pilgrims; *Quaker City*; Travel Writings

"International Lightning Trust: A Kind of Love Story, The"
(1972)

Mark Twain intended "The International Lightning Trust" for immediate publication in 1909, but the story was withdrawn from Harper and Brothers by his daughter Clara and Albert Bigelow Paine after the author's death. The satire on special providences was not published until 1972 in *Mark Twain's Fables of Man*.

Two unemployed journeyman printers, Jasper Hackett and Stephen Spaulding, become millionaires by underwriting lightning insurance: a one-dollar, lifetime premium returns a $5,000 benefit to the family of one struck by lightning. The underlying satire of the story concerns one of Mark Twain's favorite targets: special providences. Even though the cunning young men have been successful because there are only twenty-eight deaths by lightning per year and they have played on their victims' ignorance and fear, they convince themselves that they are merely instruments of God's will and must, therefore, be rewarded by God: "We are Benefactors," says Jasper. ". . . Providence sees what we are doing; Providence will recompense us."

The young entrepreneurs not only prosper but also win their true loves by a "special providence": by coincidence, Jasper is in Arkansas Flats when the estranged husbands of his and Stephen's ladyloves are struck by lightning. Jasper assists Providence by planting International Lightning Trust tickets on the deceased husbands, thereby making rich and eligible widows of Kitty and Molly. Thus Mark Twain satirizes the contemporary business trusts and the "captains of industry" who rationalize their unethical practices with arguments of greater good for society.

Unlike many of his later writings, "The International Lightning Trust" lacks the angry, pessimistic tone of other satires, perhaps, as Tuckey suggests, because Henry H. Rogers, the CEO of Standard Oil, was instrumental in saving Mark Twain from financial disaster (1893–1898).

Robert E. Lowrey

BIBLIOGRAPHY

Clemens, Samuel L. *Mark Twain's Fables of Man*. Ed. John S. Tuckey. Berkeley: U of California P, 1972.

Cox, James M. *Mark Twain: The Fate of Humor*. Princeton, N.J.: Princeton UP, 1966.

Davis, Philip E. "Mark Twain as Moral Philosopher." *San Jose Studies* 2 (1976): 83–93.

Emerson, Everett. *The Authentic Mark Twain: A Literary Biography of Samuel L. Clemens*. Philadelphia: U of Pennsylvania P, 1984.

Hill, Hamlin. *Mark Twain: God's Fool*. New York: Harper & Row, 1973.

Macnaughton, William R. *Mark Twain's Last Years as a Writer*. Columbia: U of Missouri P, 1979.

Spengemann, William C. *Mark Twain and the Backwoods Angel: The Matter of Innocence in the Works of Samuel L. Clemens*. Kent, Ohio: Kent State UP, 1966.

See also: Business; Providence; Rogers, Henry Huttleston

Interviews

Mark Twain's national career coincided roughly with the development of the newspaper interview. Though that career may have flourished even if he had avoided journalists, Twain not only welcomed publicity but exploited it richly toward selling his books, swelling his lecture audiences, and advancing his pet causes. At times he cooperated so actively with journalists as to become in effect their co-author. Alert always to mass tastes and the potentialities of a new genre, he also experimented with the interview as a form for his own writings.

Though forerunners of the interview appeared earlier, the format emerged fully after the Civil War when President Andrew Johnson outflanked his critics by holding quotable sessions with favorable and favored reporters. From partisan or other motives, Twain's first reaction was to parody the interview for lowering the standards of journalism and intruding on privacy. But, as the metropolitan dailies started using interviews with other prominent persons, Twain enjoyed being quoted by two newspapers about the walking trip he made with Joseph Twichell from Hartford to Boston in 1874. During the presidential campaign of 1876 he gave a carefully planned interview to support Rutherford B. Hayes. However, it was his return in 1879 from a seventeen-month stay abroad that showed that the press, by then using interviews regularly, would consider him an approachable yet prize subject for the rest of his life. When departing for Bermuda in January 1910, he tried, in spite of a failing heart, to oblige the reporters clustered at dockside.

Budd's listing (1977) identified 278 items, and as many as 50 more can be added though a mere total becomes deceptive because the interviews varied greatly in quality and also because, especially at Twain's homecoming of 1900 and during his trip to receive an Oxford degree in 1907, many reporters would produce essentially the same text. Still, he was probably interviewed more often than any contemporary. The other most acceptable prospects (royalty, heads of state, tycoons) were too cautious if not hostile, while he was happy to make amusing copy that would interest several levels and kinds of readers. Eventually, his interviews appeared in seven languages in fourteen countries.

Habitually spontaneous, Twain bantered with reporters toward whom, furthermore, he felt professional sympathy; they were, in turn, beguiled by his claim to once having been "one of the boys." Though usually enjoying the repartee and his always rising status as a celebrity, he had ulterior motives: to promote his books, especially *A Tramp Abroad* (1880), *A Connecticut Yankee* (1889), and *Following the Equator* (1897); to enhance his platform glitter, especially during the tour with George Washington Cable in 1884–1885 and the world tour of 1895–1896; to support personal or civic causes, especially tighter copy-right laws, the reform of New York City politics, or the campaign against atrocities in the Belgian Congo; to scotch hostile rumors about his affairs, especially during his bankruptcy or his resulting friendship with Henry Huttleston Rogers. Like all celebrities he would start to complain of being badgered, bored by the same questions, or misquoted. More relevant to his unique personality, he had to worry about spontaneity leading him into a gaffe; proud of his fame for wit, he often regretted not having risen to the occasion; justifiably, he groaned that a printed account too often smothered his superb oral gift. After 1900, planning salable autobiographical projects, he grumbled that interviews were "literary charity." But a crafty journalist could still draw him into another worthwhile interchange.

The reliability of the interviews deserves much caution. Some texts imitated, he complained, the miracle of the loaves and fishes; a few were pure fakes. Even the legitimate texts were ordinarily based on an impromptu, hurried session—without an electronic record, of course. However, perhaps surprisingly, Twain seldom clowned without a point and never misstated key facts on purpose; and reporters were typically well-meaning, even grateful. As his stature grew, they felt a matching sense of respect or at least accountability. Besides, he would probably meet their editor at some banquet or social affair.

Particularly in October 1900 and the summer of 1907, multiple versions composed a dependable record of what he said about his private life, opinions, or books. About twenty to twenty-five interviews throughout his career were prearranged and leisurely; many of those instances included the right to check the drafted text. A few times, such as during the Maxim Gorky scandal, he wrote answers to unusually sensitive questions that he expected. For his daughter Clara's wedding in 1909 he handed out typed copies (with handwritten exchanges) of a self interview. While that text is obviously accurate, even an almost slipshod interview may hold a fact or judgment that fits while enriching other sources about his career. Nagged by reporters, Twain talked about his own books far more richly through this channel than any other. Likewise, though he had always resisted analyzing his supreme talent, reporters insistently asked him about his forebears and contemporaries and about the differences in the humor preferred by various nationalities.

Beyond confirming his sense of his great popularity, the reporters' questions made him realize how the public perceived or wanted to perceive him. As the half-tone technology arrived during the 1890s and every large newspaper used more and more photographs, these helped to make him instantly recognizable anywhere. The best-known interview occurred when soon to be famous Rudyard Kipling came to pay homage in the summer of 1890. By 1902 Twain's ways of interacting with the press were so familiar that the New York *American and Journal* concocted an interview that could pass as genuine except for his convincing disclaimers.

In 1868 Twain published a burlesqued interview with President-elect Ulysses S. Grant and during the next few years toyed with the new genre condescendingly. Even so, "An Encounter with an Interviewer" (1875), a sketch apparently inconsequential (in both senses), has been reprinted and even widely translated up until the present. For the New York *Herald* in 1903 he wrote "Mark Twain, Able Yachtsman, on Why Lipton Failed to Lift the America's Cup." Unpublished manuscripts show that he tried several times to compose interviews that led some enemy into self-indictment or in which Twain himself was led into discussing touchy issues. However, Twain and the press cheerfully obligated each other for thirty-five years. Legitimately, he boasted during a speech in 1906 that the "New York papers have long known that no large question is ever really settled until I have been consulted; it is the way they feel about it, and they show it by always sending to me when they get uneasy."

Louis J. Budd

BIBLIOGRAPHY

Budd, Louis J. "Mark Twain Talks Mostly about Humor and Humorists." *Studies in American Humor* 1 (April 1974): 4–22.

———. *Our Mark Twain: The Making of His Public Personality.* Philadelphia: U of Pennsylvania P, 1983.

———, ed. "A Listing of and Selection from Newspaper and Magazine Interviews with Samuel L. Clemens: 1874–1910." *American Literary Realism 1870–1910* 10 (Winter 1977): i–xii, 1–100.

Nilsson, Nils Gunnar. "The Origin of the Interview." *Journalism Quarterly* 48 (1971): 707–713.

See also: Journalism

"Invalid's Story, The"
(1882)

The piece was apparently written in Elmira in the summer of 1877, originally intended for "Some Rambling Notes of an Idle Excursion" (1877). It was dropped on Howells's advice and first published in *The Stolen White Elephant, Etc.* in 1882. According to Everett Emerson, Clemens heard the nub of this story from Joseph Twichell, his Hartford minister and friend, with whom he had made the trip to Bermuda on which "Some Rambling Notes" is based. Twichell, his ministerial cloth notwithstanding, had long shared with Clemens a zest for rough humor. It is possible, however, that the basic anecdote was already familiar to Clemens, heard in a lecture by Artemus Ward in Virginia City in 1863 (Austin 70–71).

In this story an invalid explains how his health came to be broken by a winter railway journey undertaken to accompany the body of a friend to its place of burial. The crate with the coffin is mistakenly exchanged for a crate of rifles, which is stored in the baggage car with a package of Limburger cheese, next to a hot stove. The reader is told by the narrator of these circumstances at the outset, so the nature of the powerful smells that fill the baggage car, and so distress the narrator and the expressman, is not misunderstood. The humor of the story is in large part created by the vernacular expressman, Thompson, who rises to heights of euphemism in response to the problem. Foiled in their attempts to defeat the cheese (as we know it to be) by smoking cigars, burning feathers, and other substances, Thompson and the narrator flee to the car's platform, where they are found half frozen at trip's end.

Several elements in the story indicate its origins in frontier humor: the framing narrator, the vernacular character of Thompson, and, of course, the humor based on odors and irreverence toward death. While the vigorous humor of the frontier as an element of Mark Twain's background has long been appreciated, this story has made many readers uncomfortable. Most studies of Mark Twain's humor ignore it; Emerson calls the story unspeakable and a disaster. Only a hearty few, including Baldanza and Gibson, have praised it. There have been a few attempts to intellectualize "The Invalid's Story" as extended allegory or parody, with Horowitz discovering a covert expression of religious skepticism, and Kemper viewing it as a spoof of Poe's "Descent into the Maelstrom."

Charles L. Crow

BIBLIOGRAPHY

Austin, James C. "Artemus Ward, Mark Twain, and the Limburger Cheese." *Midcontinent American Studies Journal* 4 (Fall 1963): 70–73.

Baldanza, Frank. *Mark Twain: An Introduction and Interpretation.* New York: Barnes & Noble, 1961.

Emerson, Everett. *The Authentic Mark Twain: A Literary Biography of Samuel L. Clemens.* Philadelphia: U of Pennsylvania P, 1984.

Gibson, William. *The Art of Mark Twain.* New York: Oxford UP, 1976.

Horowitz, Floyd R. "'The Invalid's Story': An Early Mark Twain Commentary on Institutional Christianity." *Midcontinent American Studies Journal* 7 (Spring 1966): 37–44.

Kemper, Steven E. "Poe, Twain, and Limburger Cheese." *Mark Twain Journal* 21.1 (Winter 1981–1982): 13–14.

Wilson, James D. *A Reader's Guide to the Short Stories of Mark Twain.* Boston: G.K. Hall, 1987.

See also: Death; Humor

Ireland, Irish, Irishmen

While references to Ireland and the Irish occur infrequently in Mark Twain's writings, they demonstrate collectively Twain's longstanding, outspoken prejudices toward Irishmen (i.e., Irish immigrants to the United States), toward their Irish Roman Catholicism, and toward foreigners. Sharing hometown Hannibal's decidedly anti-foreigner prejudices, Twain viewed Irishmen as not quite civilized roughnecks engaged in overpopulating the United States, exerting disproportionate political clout (see his 1897 article "Concerning the Jews" in *How to Tell a Story*), and otherwise undermining white, Protestant values and traditions (Scott 131).

Such prejudice, never as pronounced as his anti-French and pro-German biases, asserts itself until as late as 1898 and reveals a sympathy for know-nothingism and intolerance for Roman Catholicism and for Irish and other immigrants. In *Roughing It* (1872) Twain typically depicts the Irishman as scapegoat and object of ridicule (Vol. 2, chapter 12) and repeats the popular phrase, "No Irish Need Apply" (Vol. 2, chapter 47; see also *The Gilded Age* [1873] Vol. 2, chapter 2). His references, however, are generally to the stereotyped Irishman and are rendered in joshing, good-natured humor, as in *Life on the Mississippi* (1883) wherein Twain quips about the dangers of mixing Irishmen and beer: "Give an Irishman lager for a month, and he's a dead man. An Irishman is lined with copper and the beer corrodes it; but whiskey polishes the copper and is the saving of him" (chapter 23).

Richard H. Cracroft

BIBLIOGRAPHY

Foner, Philip S. *Mark Twain: Social Critic.* New York: International Publishers, 1958.

Paine, Albert Bigelow. *Mark Twain: A Biography.* 3 vols. New York: Harper, 1912.

Scott, Arthur L. *Mark Twain at Large.* Chicago: Henry Regnery, 1969.

See also: Catholicism

"Is He Living or Is He Dead?"
(1893)

Written and first published in the September 1893 issue of *Cosmopolitan*, "Is He Living or Is He Dead?" later was included in *The Man That Corrupted Hadleyburg and Other Stories and Essays* (1900).

The frame of "Is He Living or Is He Dead?" takes place in a hotel in Mentone on the French Riviera in 1892. Mark Twain is engaged in conversation with a wealthy, flossy white-haired man whom he calls "Smith" to protect his real identity. Serving to foreshadow and underscore the theme and moral of the main narrative, Smith shares a Hans Christian Andersen tale with Twain in which a child's caged songbird was loved but terribly neglected until it grew weak and died. The sad and remorseful child gives the bird an elaborate funeral. In the ensuing framed narrative, Smith reveals a "curious history" about himself and three of his closest friends that has remained a well-guarded secret for many years; one of these friends was [Jean] François Millet (1814–1875), who was to become a well-known French artist of the Barbizon school. Smith presents a tale of these four starving artists whose work is of great merit but goes unrecognized until an ingenious hoax to reverse their ill fate of poverty and lack of recognition is hatched by one of the desperate artists. They decide to capitalize on "long-established facts in human history." The mastermind of the plot tells his comrades that great artists have never had the artistic merit of their works acknowledged until after their death. He proceeds to outline an elaborate plan wherein one of them must die so that "his pictures climb to high prices after his death." Millet is elected to "die," and as part of the elaborate hoax—for three months prior to his staged "death"—Millet's task is to produce and stockpile as many of his sketches and fragments of studies as possible, each with his characteristic cipher. Meanwhile, the others plot and implement brilliant marketing strategies to inflate the price of Millet's works. Indeed, human history does not let them down. Once Millet

is "dead" and the mock funeral is held, with a disguised Millet and his three friends as the pallbearers, his works command outrageous sums, thereby making them all very wealthy men. Smith boasts that society was foiled because it was unable to starve this genius and put into its pockets what was rightfully due the artist.

This satirical piece deals with society's ill treatment of artists who, during their lifetime, remain poor and unrecognized only to reap the public's appreciation from the grave. Twain satirizes the all too common tendency of art criticism to revere antiquity and dead artists. Strands of this theme—artistic hoaxes played on a duped public to turn a profit—also are evidenced in *The Innocents Abroad* (1869) and *Adventures of Huckleberry Finn* (1885).

In 1898 Clemens wrote a full-length dramatic comedy entitled *Is He Dead?* which was based on the plot of this short story. At Clemens's own urging, *Is He Dead?* was rejected by the publisher and has remained unpublished.

J.C.B. Kinch

Bibliography

Baldanza, Frank. *Mark Twain: An Introduction and Interpretation.* New York: Barnes & Noble, 1961.

Clemens, Samuel L. *The Complete Short Stories of Mark Twain.* Ed. Charles Neider. Garden City, N.Y.: Hanover House, 1957. 307–314.

Emerson, Everett. *The Authentic Mark Twain: A Literary Biography of Samuel L. Clemens.* Philadelphia: U of Pennsylvania P, 1984.

Paine, Albert Bigelow. *Mark Twain: A Biography.* 3 vols. New York: Harper, 1912.

Wilson, James D. *A Reader's Guide to the Short Stories of Mark Twain.* Boston: G.K. Hall, 1987.

See also: Art; Hoax

Is Shakespeare Dead?
(1909)

The last book of Mark Twain to be published during his life, *Is Shakespeare Dead?* (1909), presents a comic-serious reaction to the Shakespeare-Bacon controversy, a debate that began in the 1850s concerning the authorship of Shakespeare's works, one side favoring the traditional William Shakespeare of Stratford, the other favoring Francis Bacon or someone else.

Twain showed recurrent interest in the controversy. While preparing his book in the early months of 1909, he read George Greenwood's pro-Baconian *The Shakespeare Problem Restated* (1908) and early proofs of William Stone Booth's *Some Acrostic Signatures of Francis Bacon* (1909). In his book he says that his interest in the controversy was first aroused by Delia Bacon, author of *The Philosophy of the Plays of Shakespeare Unfolded* (1857), the first book on the controversy, and that he debated the issue in the 1850s as an apprentice under pilot George Ealer. In the 1880s he considered having his own company publish Ignatius Donnelly's *The Great Cryptogram* (1888).

The title of Twain's book recalls the droll response of American tourists in *Innocents Abroad* (1869) to an Old Master: "Is he dead?" With the same egalitarian humor and realism, Twain reduces Shakespeare to the known facts about his life, and these he finds too meager and crude to support an illustrious literary career. He therefore doubts Shakespeare's authorship and lists him as a fraud or "claimant" along with Satan, Louis XVII, Mary Baker Eddy, and others. By using the word "claimant," however, a favorite word of his and a likely pun on Clemens, Twain seems to include himself in this list. The subtitle of his book is "From My Autobiography," and this, along with the title, makes his book both a comic challenge to Shakespeare's greatness and a comic association of himself with Shakespeare.

Twain also uses the Shakespeare controversy to discuss environmental determinism. He transfers from Greenwood's book to his own most of a chapter about legal terminology in Shakespeare's plays, arguing that Shakespeare could not have written the plays because he was not a lawyer. To describe a profession or trade accurately, a writer must learn the terms of the trade by direct life experiences. Since Shakespeare's works are so informed and detailed on the fine points of many professions, they could not have been written by a person like Shakespeare who never held a distinguished office.

A. Berret

BIBLIOGRAPHY

Mendelsohn, Edward. "Mark Twain Confronts the Shakespeareans." *Mark Twain Journal* 17 (Winter 1973): 20–21.

Richardson, Thomas J. "Is Shakespeare Dead? Mark Twain's Irreverent Question." *Shakespeare and Southern Writers: A Study in Influence.* Ed. Philip C. Kolin. Jackson: UP of Mississippi, 1985. 63–82.

See also: Bacon, Francis; Shakespeare, William

Italy

Mark Twain's involvement with Italy spanned almost forty years and inspired two of his works, *Innocents Abroad* (1869) and *A Tramp Abroad* (1880). Twain made four European trips, all including Italy: the first in 1867 as a carefree bachelor reporter on the famous *Quaker City* excursion; the second in 1878 with the Clemens family; the third in 1892–1893 when the family lived in Florence and where Twain wrote *Pudd'nhead Wilson* (1894) and most of *Joan of Arc* (1896); and the last from October 1903 to June 1904, again to Florence, where Livy died at the Villa Quarto. These excursions not only allowed Twain to examine his middle-class Protestantism and his peculiarly American aesthetics, but also introduced him to a country rife with the contradictions in his own nature. His notebooks and journals during these periods leave little doubt that his European experiences were full of ambiguity and ambivalence; specifically, Italy's blatant contrasts of wealth and poverty, simple faith and hard-headed rationalism, breathtaking beauty and naked squalor fed Twain's ironic vision and ultimately played a crucial role in his artistic and emotional maturity.

Twain's travels in Italy took him from Milan and Lake Como in the North to Naples and Capri in the South, inspiring comments on the aesthetics, politics, and religion of a country where the three are often inextricable. The antique monuments and works of art both awed and frustrated Twain, as their dilapidated state often made it difficult to envision what they once were. His famous comments on Leonardo da Vinci's *Last Supper*, for example, illustrate his disappointment in the time-ravaged painting and his obtuse lack of understanding of those who could still admire and appreciate it. Calling Leonardo da Vinci's work a "mournful wreck," Twain was only echoing prevalent nineteenth-century iconoclasm and provinciality, but his comments show a curious imaginative gap in a writer who was elsewhere so brilliantly able to reconstruct the past. Dewey Ganzel points out the ever present conflict in Twain between his romantic idealism and his desire for realism (145). Thus, when he criticizes the Old Masters like Tintoretto or Veronese for their lack of verisimilitude, Twain is merely illustrating his American infatuation with the facts. Yet scattered among his often patently self-conscious negativisms is genuine praise for Milan's glorious cathedral, a Florentine sunset, or the simple pleasures of a native wine.

Underlying much of Twain's commentary on Italy was his attitude toward the church's absolute power. His anti-hierarchical nature rebelled at the religious and political stranglehold the church had historically exerted here. On visiting the Church of the Annunciation in Genoa, a building he admired, Twain learned that it had been built by the family presently ruling Genoa. Facing this reality of a ruling elite and its role in creating and preserving beauty tested Twain's innately democratic principles; typically, while praising the beautiful Genoan church, Twain could still berate the country—and the church—for existing parasitically off their many poor. Rome in particular excited his prejudices as the comments in his notebooks and journals clearly show. Twain, the failed businessman, describes Rome in appropriately commercial terms and seems to have regarded it as little more than a religious marketplace: "Rome seems to be a great fair of shams, humbugs & frauds. Religion is its commerce and its wealth, like dung in the Black Forest." Similarly, he satirizes the practice of saving and displaying relics, furious at what he perceived as rank exploitation of the faithful. As always, Twain admired the cathedrals' beauty while harboring suspicions about their real purpose. The hierarchical power of such an un-American institution disgusted him as much as the fake prudery of the ubiquitous fig leaf on Roman statuary.

Despite his real and feigned misgivings, Twain returned to Italy, drawn to its unhurried pace of life and stunning physical beauty. In the last decade of his life, fleeing from his American debts to the haven of Florence, a city he grew to love, Twain saw the death of his beloved wife Livy at the Villa Quarto or "Calamity House" as he called it. Yet beneath the bitterness he often unleashed on this country lies a nostalgia for the peace he found there. While Twain the stereotypical American tourist could rail at its high prices and poor service, Twain the artist could respond aesthetically to Italy's enchantments.

Mary Ann Wilson

BIBLIOGRAPHY

Clemens, Samuel L. *The Innocents Abroad.* Hartford, Conn.: American Publishing, 1869.

———. *Mark Twain's Autobiography.* Ed. Albert B. Paine. 2 vols. New York: Harper, 1924.

———. *Mark Twain's Notebooks & Journals, Volume II (1877–1883).* Ed. Frederick Anderson, Lin Salamo, and Bernard L. Stein. Berkeley: U of California P, 1975.

———. *Traveling with the Innocents Abroad.* Ed. Daniel M. McKeithan. Norman: U of Oklahoma P, 1968.

Ganzel, Dewey. *Mark Twain Abroad: The Cruise of the "Quaker City."* Chicago: U of Chicago P, 1968.

Hill, Hamlin. *Mark Twain: God's Fool.* New York: Harper & Row, 1973.

Paine, Albert Bigelow. *Mark Twain: A Biography.* 3 vols. New York: Harper, 1912.

See also: Art; Catholicism; Europe; Religion; Travel Writings

J

Jackass Hill

In the heart of the Mother Lode country, sixteen miles from Sonora and a mile past Tuttletown, Jackass Hill commemorates Mark Twain's seven-week stay with the replica of the cabin he visited in the winter of 1864–1865. The cabin belonging to Jim Gillis and partner Dick Stoker burned down in the 1890s, and to this day natives do not swear to the actual site, although a bronze plaque on California Highway 49 claims the chimney and fireplace are the originals, good enough to attract about 20,000 tourists a year. At this writing, the dozen families living in the community want the cabin moved to nearby Columbia State Park. They say Jackass Hill took its name from the congregation of jackasses in mining days. Modern tourists congregating at the cabin make more noise.

P.M. Zall

BIBLIOGRAPHY

Automobile Club of Southern California. *The Mother Lode.* Los Angeles: Automobile Club of Southern California, 1984.

Murphy, William S. "Neighbors Find Nothing Funny About Mark Twain's Cabin." Los Angeles *Times,* 30 January 1985, part 5, pp. 1, 6.

See also: Gillis, Jim

Jackson's Island

In *Adventures of Huckleberry Finn* (1885), following his faked death, Huck flees a few miles from "sivilization" to a long, narrow, wooded strip of land in the Mississippi River called Jackson's Island. In so doing, he returns to the spot where in *The Adventures of Tom Sawyer* (1876) Tom Sawyer and his gang of "pirates" had made their headquarters and where he and his companions later were when they were thought by the town to be dead.

In both novels the island is a place for growing and maturing, a sort of way station between the conventional childhood of the town and independence. There Tom's childish revolt against Aunt Polly is transformed into an initiation into manhood as he reveals his uneasiness at his aunt's worries and then rescues Becky Thatcher and Widow Douglas from Injun Joe, moving from boyish treasure hunting to manly action (Long 316–317). It is one of the few key episodes demonstrating Tom's growth (Long and LeMaster 155). And in the later book Jackson's Island is where Huck finds Jim and decides to journey with him.

Twain based Jackson's Island on Glasscock's Island near Hannibal, Missouri, which has since eroded away. For Twain it apparently represented a mythic place of asylum from the pressures of day-to-day living (Hearn 98).

Jeanne Campbell Reesman

BIBLIOGRAPHY

Clemens, Samuel L. *Adventures of Huckleberry Finn.* Ed. Walter Blair and Victor Fischer. Berkeley: U of California P, 1985.

———. *The Adventures of Tom Sawyer.* Ed. John C. Gerber and Paul Baender. Berkeley: U of California P, 1982.

———. *The Annotated Huckleberry Finn: Adventures of Huckleberry Finn by Mark Twain.* Ed. Michael Patrick Hearn. New York: Clarkson L. Potter, 1981.

Long, E. Hudson, and J.R. LeMaster. *The New Mark Twain Handbook.* New York: Garland, 1985.

See also: *Adventures of Huckleberry Finn;* *Adventures of Tom Sawyer, The*

James, Henry

(1843–1916)

Brother to the distinguished psychologist and philosopher William James, Henry James was a major nineteenth-century American author of novels, short fiction, and criticism on art, literature, and American life (*Hawthorne*, 1879; *The American Scene*, 1907). His realm is one of social privilege, and his works are distinguished by a subtle psychology of human relations and a complex style of presentation. A common theme is the relation between art and life. James is best known for his tragicomic liaisons between American and European culture (international theme) in such novels as *Daisy Miller*

(1879), *The American* (1877), *Portrait of a Lady* (1881), *The Wings of the Dove* (1902), *The Ambassadors* (1903), and *The Golden Bowl* (1904). His short fiction includes the novella *The Turn of the Screw* (1898), the introspective "The Beast in the Jungle" (1903), and "The Jolly Corner" (1909). His theory of art is developed in eighteen critical prefaces that he appended to his revised fiction in his New York Edition (1907–1909).

Henry James was born on Washington Place, New York City (1843), into a cultured New England family with strong ties to transcendentalism. Henry, Sr., was leisured through paternal inheritance; James and his siblings were shuttled back and forth between America and Europe for education and cultural enlightenment. This may have been the source of James's penchant for Europe, where he ultimately settled, as well as the source of his fictional concern with unstable childhood (*What Maisie Knew*, 1897) and with the phenomenological processes of knowing in the world from a position of innocence.

The link between Mark Twain and Henry James is great artistry. Their distinction is their diversity of treatment. Both the grandeur and disparity are observed by a contemporary reviewer (*Nation*, 1910) who elaborates that Mark Twain writes with clarity and insouciance while James is epigrammatically obscure. In addition, James writes about art while Mark Twain writes about life. These two major authors were clearly different in personality and style. Mark Twain was an expansive figure who wooed his public while James was private and guarded. Mark Twain called James Henrietta Maria. He declared that he would rather "be damned to John Bunyan's heaven" than read James's *The Bostonians* (1885). James thought that Twain's art was best reserved for the primitive mind. Nevertheless, Leon Edel suggests that James and Mark Twain had great respect for each other. They met at various times. James thought Mark Twain "a most excellent pleasant fellow . . . quaint." Edel suggests, finally, that James's hypochondriacal

Waymarsh in *The Ambassadors* was based on Mark Twain; James first called him Waymark.

The sustained reputation of these great artists may be the strongest testament to a link between them. Both have suffered temporarily from detractors, but they now stand side by side, monumentalized. Also, the narrative strategies of each pose a similar challenge to the modern critic who seeks to penetrate their vision. James's restricted point of view invites uncertain identification with his characters for the modern reader. Mark Twain's narration in *Adventures of Huckleberry Finn* (1885) obscures his view on racism for some (Booth, *Ethics of Fiction*). Both authors shared concern about truth in the world and the problematics of its accessibility.

Janet Gabler-Hover

BIBLIOGRAPHY

Anderson, Frederick, and Kenneth M. Sanderson, eds. *Mark Twain: The Critical Heritage.* New York: Barnes & Noble, 1971.

Booth, Wayne C. *The Company We Keep: An Ethics of Fiction.* Berkeley: U of California P, 1988.

Edel, Leon. *Henry James: A Life.* New York: Harper & Row, 1985.

Margolis, Anne T. *Henry James and the Problem of Audience: An International Act.* Ann Arbor, Mich.: UMI Research P, 1985.

See also: Europe; Realism

James, William

(1842–1910)

William James was a noted nineteenth-century American philosopher and psychologist whose pragmatic conceptions influenced John Dewey, Henri Bergson, Ludwig Wittgenstein, and Edmund Husserl. He also influenced Mark Twain and Henry James, his noted author brother. William James gained a medical degree from Harvard (1869), where he taught briefly as an instructor of anatomy and physiology (1873–1876) before his transfer of allegiance to Harvard's department of philosophy, where he ultimately became full professor (1885). He lectured internationally, from whence came his famous works, including *The Principles of Psychology* (1890), *The Will to Believe and Other Essays* (1897), *The Varieties of Religious Experience* (1902), *Pragmatism* (1907), and *The Meaning of Truth* (1909).

William James was the eldest in a gifted but turbulent family. William's father, Henry James, Sr., espoused reformist ideals shaped by Swedenborgian mysticism, the works of Charles Fourier, and New England transcendentalism. Of the elder Henry's famous children, Alice was beset by neurological disease, Henry was plagued with insecurity and sibling rivalry, and William seriously considered suicide. The latter affirmed his existence through his philosophy of skeptical optimism. For James, the consciousness was a process— it was a "stream"—not a container; it was creative in the sense that it was selective. The consciousness was personal and constantly changing; it selected a focus on incoming impressions through habit and self-interest, and there were always a number of incoming impressions that were peripheral or on the fringe.

James's sense that the consciousness "knows" provisionally and perforce incompletely led him to entertain the radical hypotheses of late-nineteenth-century spiritualism. He became the first American president of the British Society for Psychical Research (1896). He regarded F.W. Meyers's *Human Personality and Its Survival of Bodily Death* (1903) as a masterpiece of modern psychology, but with skepticism. Meyers's book was in Mark Twain's library, and it has been recently linked to *The Mysterious Stranger* manuscripts (Gillman). In the notebook entries to "My Platonic Sweetheart" (1898) Mark Twain credits William James. James was resonant for Mark Twain on two fronts. James's skeptical openmindedness to fringe sciences lent a certain legitimacy to mind healing and hypnosis, which Mark Twain hoped might heal the epilepsy of his youngest daughter, Jean, as it had cured a mysterious paralysis of the adolescent Olivia (Mark Twain's wife). More darkly, Mark Twain reinterpreted James's "pansychic view" of a nurturing and liberating reservoir of consciousness to be demonstrative of the dual selves of consciousness. Most often, the unconscious in Mark Twain's late writings is a region of nightmarish ambiguity that submerges the identity of the artist in a deterministic process akin to automatic writing.

Janet Gabler-Hover

BIBLIOGRAPHY

Emerson, Everett. *The Authentic Mark Twain: A Literary Biography of Samuel L. Clemens.* Philadelphia: U of Pennsylvania P, 1984.

Feinstein, Howard M. *Becoming William James.* Ithaca, N.Y.: Cornell UP, 1984.

Gillman, Susan. *Dark Twins: Imposture and Identity in Mark Twain's America.* Chicago: U of Chicago P, 1989.

James, William. *The Writings of William James: A Comprehensive Edition.* Ed. John J. McDermott. Chicago: U of Chicago P, 1977.

See also: Mental Telepathy/Extrasensory Perception; "My Platonic Sweetheart"

Jamestown, Tennessee

Jamestown is the county seat of Fentress County, on the Cumberland Plateau, described by Mark Twain as "the remote and secluded village of Jamestown, in the mountain solitudes of east Tennessee." It appears as "Obedstown" in his novel *The Gilded Age* (1873). John and Jane Clemens moved to Jamestown in 1827, following a brief residence in Gainesboro, Tennessee. John Clemens drew up specifications for the county courthouse and jail, dating them 20 March 1827, and was chosen as the first circuit court clerk of the new county. Pamela, Pleasant Hannibal, Margaret, and Benjamin Clemens were born in Jamestown. Mark Twain's autobiography has Orion born in Jamestown as well, but his birth occurred while his parents were still living in Gainesboro. Orion paid a number of visits to Jamestown in later years, both before and after the Civil War, while trying to dispose of the Tennessee Land.

The Mark Twain Park on Mark Twain Avenue in present-day Jamestown is said to be the site of the spring from which the Clemens family got its water.

Allison R. Ensor

See also: Clemens, Jane Lampton; Clemens, John Marshall; Tennessee Land

Jerusalem

The intended peak of the *Quaker City* "pilgrimage," the Jerusalem chapters of *The Innocents Abroad* (1869) are anticlimactic. Approached via Schechem, Shiloh, Beth-el, and the tomb of Nebi Samuel, the landscape seemed "tiresome to the eye." Seeing the Holy City at long last from the north, "perched on its eternal hills," with the "famed Damascus gate," "not even our pilgrims wept." How could this small "village"—and the disappointing Jordan River—have become sacred to three world religions?

Worn out physically and let down emotionally, Mark Twain fell back for two chapters on rhetoric, quotations, and historical allusions—for the most part ambivalently. He finds the view "monotonous," and the Jerusalem street balconies remind him of chicken coops: "I would not desire to live there." The rest of chapter 53 is a tour of the Church of the Holy Sepulchre, devastating in its realistic analyses and criticisms of relic worship, irrational "proofs," and fanaticisms of all kinds. After the author recalls the crusades and recent Crimean War, the final invocation of the "Prince of Peace" is grotesquely ironical.

Beginning with the Via Dolorosa, chapter 54 soon digresses into the "unhappy" wandering Jew of "song and story," who comes home every half century and "collects his rent and leaves again." Then on to the Mosque of Omar, and outside the walls to the Mount of Olives, and so forth—all adding up to very mixed emotions, with a final forced expectation of "an enchanted memory a year hence."

But here and now, alas, Jerusalem has been a city chiefly of disenchantment.

Sholom J. Kahn

BIBLIOGRAPHY

Clemens, Samuel L. *The Innocents Abroad*. Hartford, Conn.: American Publishing, 1869.

Grindea, Miron, ed. *Jerusalem: The Holy City in Literature*. London: Kahn and Averill, 1981.

Peters, F.E. *Jerusalem: The Holy City in the Eyes of Chroniclers, Visitors, Pilgrims, and Prophets from the Days of Abraham to the Beginnings of Modern Times*. Princeton, N.J.: Princeton UP, 1965.

See also: Holy Land, The; *Innocents Abroad, The*; *Quaker City*

Jews

If any Gentile may deservedly be called "philo-Semitic" in contradistinction to "anti-Semitic," it is Samuel L. Clemens, who, in both his public and private utterances and in the writings of Mark Twain, sedulously combatted anti-Jewish prejudices. Clemens first encountered Jews during his Hannibal childhood. An Alsatian Jewish family named Lesem kept a clothing store in the village after 1848, and Sam's schoolmates included the Levin brothers ("the first Jews I had ever seen"), whom the town's Christian boys derided, chased, and stoned. That young Sam was more immune to Hannibal's prejudices about Jews than he was to the town's acceptance of black slavery, as Wecter claimed, is refuted by Foner, Janet Smith, et al., who have noted instances of coarse anti-Semitic humor and stereotyping in Clemens's early (pre-Twain) writings.

When or why he shed the negative attitudes toward Jews he imbibed in his upbringing is conjectural, although Kahn has postulated some changes in Clemens's outlook and in Twain's writing about Jews after *The Innocents Abroad* (1869). It appears the cumulative experience of rabid, often violently expressed anti-Semitism during his European sojourns between 1878 and 1900 moved Clemens toward a more enlightened understanding of the plight of Jewry in the Diaspora and of the irrational bases for hostility to Jews. In March 1879 he jotted remarks about Jewish oppression in his notebook, concluding that despite 2,000 years of deprivations and persecutions Jews "are peculiarly and conspicuously the world's intellectual aristocracy," a theme upon which Twain composed many later variations.

In October 1897, for example, Clemens wrote from Vienna to the Reverend Joseph Twichell that "the difference between the brain of the average Christian and that of the average Jew . . . is about the difference between a tadpole's and an Archbishop's." A scrapbook he kept from 1889 to 1891 contains clippings of reports from European newspapers of anti-Semitic injustices and atrocities. He deplored pogroms in Russia and Poland and took an almost obsessive interest in the Dreyfus Affair in France as it unfolded after 1894, finding it a classic case of both anti-Semitism and the moral degeneracy he often alleged of the French. His story "From 'the London Times' of 1904" (1898) is a bitter satire on the second Dreyfus trial.

Nevertheless, despite a confined knowledge of the Torah (in its King James version of the Old Testament), he apparently remained uninformed about the Talmud, Jewish theology, liturgy, and religious practices, and even about Jewish life (especially ghetto and *shtetl* life) itself. He seems, moreover, to have accepted several ancient myths: of Jewish wealth, which confirmed his view that economic envy rather than Christian doctrine was the root cause of latter-day prejudice against Jews; of a Jewish propensity for cheating and shady dealing; and, until he was disabused, of the Jew's reluctance to bear arms for his adopted country. A firm assimilationist, he was unsympathetic, even derisive, toward Theodor Herzl's Zionism.

Replying to a questionnaire on causes and cures for anti-Semitism sent to some prominent Gentiles in March 1890 by the editor of a New York journal, the *American Hebrew*, Clemens (eschewing his pen name) composed a succinct statement containing several ideas he later expounded in "Concerning the Jews" (1898). If his letter was actually sent, it remained unpublished until 1972 (Appendix A to *Fables of Man*), possibly because Clemens was openly skeptical in it of any foreseeable solutions to "the rudimental Christian antipathy to the Jew."

Clemens's most painful and prolonged confrontation with anti-Semitism came during his sojourn in Vienna in 1897–1899, when he was pilloried in the city's anti-Semitic press for his socializing with prominent local Jews and even caricatured and denounced as a covert Jew himself. Although he had Jewish friends and acquaintances elsewhere, in Vienna a majority of his closest associates were either Jewish musicians and journalists or such philo-Semitic aristocrats as Princess Pauline Metternich, Countess Misa Wydenbruck-Esterhazy, Count Richard Coudonhove-Kalergi, and Baroness Bertha von Suttner. In Vienna also Clemens first observed at close range the manner in which anti-Semitism could be fomented and exploited for political purposes by demagogues like the popular mayor, Karl Lueger, and the parliamentary leader of the German nationals, Georg von Schoenerer, two of Adolf Hitler's idols.

Twain was not slow to respond to the anti-Semites' innuendos and attacks on himself, although he took no public notice of them. In 1897 or early 1898 he sketched two versions (posthumously published in *Fables of Man*) of a cautionary tale that may have had an autobiographical source and, if so, could serve to explain at least one origin of his philo-Semitism. In both sketches—the shorter, less polished "Newhouse's Jew Story," in which Twain relates an anecdote he claims to have heard from an "ancient" Mississippi pilot, George Newhouse, and the more detailed "Randall's Jew Story," where a banker, Mr. Randall, is the source—a nameless Jewish riverboat passenger rescues a Negro slave girl from the clutches of a professional gambler (in Randall's version he is also a slave trader) by killing the card sharp in a duel after the gambler wins her at poker from her profligate owner and refuses the Jew's offer of purchase (in Randall's version) or the entreaties of the owner's daughter (in Newhouse's).

Both versions are parables of Jewish compassion and munificence in the face of Gentile greed and moral cowardice even if, as Foner noted, Twain's fictional Jewish rescuer does not go the full distance by emancipating the slave girl rather than handing her back to her "rightful" owner. He may have shelved both versions in May or June 1898 when he settled upon a more direct frontal assault on anti-Semitism, using the rhetorical devices of a polemical essay rather than a narrative.

The result, after much "doctoring it and polishing it and fussing at it," was "Concerning the Jews," an article he finished in Kaltenleutgeben on 26 July 1898. "My gem of the ocean," as he called this essay of which he was inordinately proud, appeared in *Harper's Monthly Magazine* in September 1899 and was included the following year in the volume titled *Literary Essays* in his collected edition. It is one of the best organized, most cogently argued, and rhetorically effective polemics in the Twain canon despite some glaring statistical errors and, as Twain predicted to H.H. Rogers, the fact that "neither Jew nor Christian will approve of it."

Supposedly a response to an inquiring letter from an American lawyer (probably fictitious) who had read Twain's description of anti-Jewish riots in "Stirring Times in Austria" (1898), this essay traces the history of antipathy to Jews from biblical times to the present. Twain argues that religious prejudices derived from Christian doctrine have been superseded by such economic and social ones as envy of the Jew as a "better money-getter" and primordial dislike and distrust of "strangers" or outsiders as latter-day bases of anti-Semitism. There is no remedy, only a defense against this and a hope for amelioration through political organization, infiltration, and influence in the political process and a hope for assimilation into the dominant society and mainstream culture consequent on relinquishing distinctive Jewish habits and patterns of living.

While reception of "Concerning the Jews" in the British and American Jewish press, as well as the Yiddish and German Jewish press, was not altogether hostile, a typical response was that in the *Jewish Chronicle* (London): "Of all such advocates, we can but say 'Heaven save us from our friends.'" In the 1930s Nazi sympathizers and Jew-baiters in the United States wrenched portions of the article from context in a diabolical effort, quickly exposed and refuted by DeVoto, to try to make Twain appear an anti-Semite. In 1938 Sigmund Freud (1856–1939), though unable to recall its author, used a precis of Twain's essay for his own "A Comment on Anti-Semitism" in a Parisian refugee publication. Nevertheless, the article continues to perplex many Twain scholars who have dismissed it as naive and shallow.

Jewish characters are rare in Twain's fiction. Where they do occur, they are neither stereotypes nor fully developed individuals, merely nameless agents like "the Jew" in the Newhouse and Randall stories. An exception is Solomon Goldstein whose demeanor in *Extract from Captain Stormfield's Visit to Heaven* (1909) converts Ben Stormfield from his lifelong prejudices against Jews in somewhat the same way Jim confounds Huck's preconceptions about blacks. Solomon Isaacs, Jewish money lender in "The Chronicle of Young Satan" (1969) and "No. 44, The Mysterious Stranger" (1969), on the other hand, comes uncomfortably close to the Shylockian stereotype.

It is noteworthy that in October 1909, more than a decade after they first met in Vienna, Clara Clemens married the Russian Jewish pianist-conductor, Ossip Gabrilowitsch, with the unreserved blessing of her father. While one cannot expect that in the age in which he lived Clemens could have completely escaped or outgrown ethnocentrism, racism, and credal bias, there seems no conscious deceit or self-righteousness in Twain's boast in "Concerning the Jews" that he believed himself devoid of prejudices "bar one" (that, of course, being the French). "I can stand any society," he said. "All I care to know is that a man is a human being—that is enough for me: he can't be any worse."

Carl Dolmetsch

BIBLIOGRAPHY

Clemens, Samuel L. "Concerning the Jews." *Literary Essays.* By Clemens. Vol. 24 of *The Complete Works of Mark Twain.* New York: P.F. Collier & Son, 1918. 263–287.

———. *Concerning the Jews.* Philadelphia: Running Press, 1985. (This paperback single reprint contains an anonymous introduction and includes a "Postscript: The Jew as Soldier" by Clemens originally published in the English edition of the essay but not in the American.)

———. *Mark Twain on the Damned Human Race.* Ed. Janet Smith. New York: Hill and Wang, 1962. 156–180.

———. *Mark Twain's Fables of Man.* Ed. John S. Tuckey. Berkeley: U of California P, 1972. 279–289, 445–448.

DeVoto, Bernard. "Mark Twain About the Jews." *Jewish Frontier* 6 (May 1939): 7–9.

Dolmetsch, Carl. "Mark Twain and the Viennese Anti-Semites: New Light on 'Concerning the Jews.'" *Mark Twain Journal* 23.2 (Fall 1985): 10–17.

———. *"Our Famous Guest": Mark Twain in Vienna.* Athens: U of Georgia P, 1992.

Foner, Philip S. *Mark Twain: Social Critic.* New York: International Publishers, 1958.

Kahn, Sholom J. "Mark Twain's Philosemitism: 'Concerning the Jews.'" *Mark Twain Journal* 23.2 (Fall 1985): 18–25.

Richmond, Marion B. "The Lost Source in Freud's 'Comment on Anti-Semitism': Mark Twain." *Journal of the American Psychoanalytic Association* 28 (1980): 563–574.

Stewart, H.L. "Mark Twain on the Jewish Problem." *Dalhousie Review* 14 (January 1935): 455–458.

Tenney, Thomas A., ed. "Contemporary Responses to 'Concerning the Jews.'" *Mark Twain Journal* 23.2 (Fall 1985): 26–27.

See also: Austria (Austria-Hungary); *Extract from Captain Stormfield's Visit to Heaven*; Freud, Sigmund; Gabrilowitsch, Ossip; Jerusalem; Racial Attitudes

Jim

Appearing in several of Twain's works, Jim is briefly mentioned in *Life on the Mississippi* (1883), "The Morals Lecture" (1895–1896), and *Tom Sawyer, Detective* (1896); and presented as a dramatized character in *Huckleberry Finn* (1885), *Tom Sawyer Abroad* (1894), "Huck Finn and Tom Sawyer Among the Indians" (1969), and "Tom Sawyer's Conspiracy" (1969). From these works we may patch together a rather sketchy biography of the man. He is at least thirty years old when we first meet him, married with two children, Johnny and the deaf and dumb Elizabeth. He escapes from Miss Watson because Bat Bradish, the slave trader, has persuaded her to sell Jim down the river.

Jim's original plan to escape to Canada, get work, and buy his family out of slavery is diverted by the series of misadventures he has with Huck and later with Tom Sawyer. After he is freed by Miss Watson's will, he returns to St. Petersburg to work for wages for Aunt Polly. Given his subsequent adventures, it seems as though Jim is on salary. He has time, at any rate, to involve himself in the high jinx of Tom Sawyer's making and Huck's complicity—he travels west with them to the Indian territory and in a balloon with them to the Sahara, and he becomes one of the "Sons of Freedom" in "Tom Sawyer's Conspiracy," engaged in a plot to sell a blackened Tom into slavery and then steal him out again. But the plan is complicated when Jim is accused of the murder of Bat Bradish, and he is only proved innocent in last-minute courtroom disclosures.

Jim is sometimes known as "Nigger Jim," though Twain does not refer to him by that name. His proper name would be "Miss Watson's Jim"—a point Twain makes with barbed irony in *Tom Sawyer* in regard to "Bull Harbison," a dog, adding in a note that had Harbison owned a slave named Bull, his name would be "Harbison's Bull." The point is worth making because Jim is broadly and variously conceived as property in his several appearances in Twain's fiction and from several points of view—Huck fearfully reacts to Jim's desires to escape to freedom as unthinkable theft; at the end of *Huckleberry Finn* Jim's would-be lynchers change their minds because his owner might show up and make them pay for him; Jim himself brags that he is worth $800 and self-ownership will make him a rich man. Even Mark Twain playfully describes Jim as a long-suffering imaginative commodity, one whom he had "carted" around all over the globe and who had "endured it all with the patience and friendliness and loyalty which were his birthright." Unlike Huck, Jim is never a marginalized figure; he is not an outcast but chattel, whose identity is shaped by politics, geography, property values, the whims or aggravation of boys, widows, and rednecks.

As a created character, Jim owes something to Twain's acquaintance with three blacks—"Uncle Dan'l" (the Missouri slave whom Twain had known as a child); John Lewis (the handyman on the farm in Elmira); and George Griffin (the Clemenses' servant in Hartford). From the first, Twain borrowed a sense of wise counsel combined with active superstition and of broad sympathies and an admirable innocence. In John Lewis he observed a man of great strength and a certain complacency who was capable of sudden and unexpected heroism. And in George Griffin (whom Arthur Pettit believes the most important influence upon the creation of Jim) Twain found a muscular man possessed of personal charm and intellectual sophistication; Griffin was a sincerely religious man, a teetotaller, and yet extremely fond of debate and gambling.

That some or all of these qualities contributed to the imaginative creation known as Jim seems beyond dispute. Jim, however, served several purposes for Twain. He is, to be sure, a literary character, but he is as well a literary device. He may be the butt of pranks and jokes, and therefore a comic figure, but he may as well be the vehicle through whom other characters and attitudes may be satirized. He may be an image of long-suffering Christian charity and fortitude and thus the object of sympathy or, worse, pity; or he may be the dramatic occasion for testing and revealing the racist consciousness of a nation. Jim is a problem in interpretation, for his function within Twain's fiction transcends what we may determine to be the sources of his imaginative conception.

Chadwick Hansen discerned in the character of Jim a blend of several cultural types—by turns a laughable minstrel figure, a protective mammy figure, a sentimentalist, and a universal image of human dignity and reason. Jim certainly contains these and other contradictions—he is both wise and superstitious, heroic and cowardly, tolerant and bullheaded, prophetic and confused. In part, it was the very ambiguity of Jim that so appealed to Ralph Ellison, who found him one of the most fully rounded of all black characters. And it is as a black character that Jim has most concerned critics in recent years.

Because Jim is personal property, his very existence brings humanitarian values and public policy into dramatic opposition. Twain surely recognized this and often used Jim as a means to reveal hypocrisy and venality in a racist culture. It is rather more difficult to determine how completely Twain conceived of him as an actualized character. For some the distance between Jim and Uncle Tom is not great, but Louis Rubin observed in 1967 that Jim may be a good deal more canny than many have supposed. Jim does not inform Huck of Pap's death, not because he wishes to protect the boy but because he knows that he must keep Huck along if he is to have any chance at escape. Since that time (most notably in a special issue of the *Mark Twain Journal* [1984], where several black scholars addressed the question of racism in *Huckleberry Finn*, and most recently by Harold Beaver), Jim's motives and behavior have been attributed to the politics of self-preservation or the history of the black experience. This critical tendency is likely to make Jim a more intricate and probably more interesting character. Whether or not it will make him more comprehensible remains to be seen. For the most part, Jim's "qualities," and hence his identity, come out

of his reaction to extreme events. He is a valuable hostage for law-abiding Silas Phelps, a theatrical attraction for a pair of con men, a too indulgent servant to Huck and Tom in the Sahara, and a man accused of murder in "Tom Sawyer's Conspiracy." So profoundly is his life implicated in the conflicting designs and desires of a white social order that he may never acquire even the identity of a Jim Watson. However interesting a figure he may be, he is likely to remain in one way or another Miss Watson's Jim.

Tom Quirk

BIBLIOGRAPHY

Beaver, Harold. *Huckleberry Finn*. London: Unwin Hyman, 1987.

Hansen, Chadwick. "The Character of Jim and the Ending of *Huckleberry Finn*." *Massachusetts Review* 5 (Autumn 1963): 45–66.

Pettit, Arthur G. *Mark Twain and the South*. Lexington: UP of Kentucky, 1974.

Rubin, Louis D., Jr. *The Teller and the Tale*. Seattle: U of Washington P, 1967.

Smith, David L. "Huck, Jim, and American Racial Discourse." *Mark Twain Journal* 22.2 (Fall 1984): 4–12.

Weaver, Thomas, and Merline A. Williams. "Mark Twain's Jim: Identity as an Index to Cultural Studies." *American Literary Realism* 13 (Spring 1980): 19–30.

See also: *Adventures of Huckleberry Finn*; Racial Attitudes

"Jim Baker's Blue Jay Yarn"
(1880)

Along with Jim Smiley's Jumping Frog and Jim Blaine's Old Ram, the frazzled bird in "Jim Baker's Blue Jay Yarn," making its debut early in the 1880 travel book *A Tramp Abroad*, remains one of the most heralded animal acts in the Mark Twain bestiary. Its story is begun in chapter 2 through a complicated frame narrative and is itself then set forth as chapter 3 under the heading "Baker's Blue Jay Yarn"; and, as with the other stories (or, in the case of the ram, nonstories), it comes out of the classical and medieval traditions of the beast fable, now filtered distinctively by Twain through the humorous conventions of American vernacular narrative. Here, the core anecdote is relatively simple. An industrious, self-important jay finds a knothole in the roof of a Sierra cabin and undertakes the fool's errand of filling the hole with acorns. Eventually, amidst a good deal of cussing and blowing on the main actor's part, a multitude of its raucous, irreverent brethren gather around to discover, to their collective delight, that the original jay has been trying to fill the *house*. The very trees about echo with jay guffaws, then and for years after, with the only avian nonparticipant in the revelry a somber, judicious owl visiting from Nova Scotia, who said, "He couldn't see anything funny in it." The narrator concludes, "But then he was a good deal disappointed in Yo Semite, too."

In good Mark Twain fashion, then, the freshness in the humor of the beast fable comes from its connections in American storytelling. The most obvious one lies in folk legend about the creature in question: its mysterious powers of language, especially, which it manipulates almost always to devious, self-serving purposes. (American jay lore abounds, particularly in the South. Always cast as the most clever of birds, preternaturally gifted with language, they are also, invariably, the minions of the devil. In Alabama they go down to Hades on Thursdays to report on particular humans to whom they are assigned. In Arkansas they go on Friday, carrying kindling or brimstone to help with the fires.)

Here, of course, the particularly "American" humor of all this also is further extended, again in good Twainian fashion, into the particular tradition of storytelling that nourished Twain's own mysterious gifts of language, the indigenous genre of southwestern humor. In the basic model of that—initially laced, as various critics have noted, with early American implications of Whig contempt for a Jacksonian mobocracy—a frame narration by a certain kind of "literate" or "artful" narrator encloses a colorful, often crude story told at the expense of the native "originals" who figure as

its main actors and the butts of its humor. Here the basic framing, albeit in much more genial fashion, is supplied by the Baker figure. Yet here also the frame is extended in one of Twain's most ambitious uses of the device, a stretch maneuver enabling the reteller of the Baker text who is also the narrator of the larger frame text at hand—one describing him as vagrant and "foreign" in the great world of Europe—toward a complex comment on his own national and literary genealogy as well.

To be specific, the tale has arisen from the narrator's yielding himself to the enchantments of the Neckar Hills, where he muses on the "German legends and fairy tales" that have lent them "an added charm." Then, shortly in a truly Rip Van Winkle-like encounter, retranslated with some explicitude back into the original German, he falls in with some talking ravens who mock his outlandish presence. "'What a hat!' they call, and 'Oh, pull down your vest!' and that sort of thing," he says "and there is no getting around it with the fine reasoning and pretty arguments." This anecdote about clever, talking birds then naturally leads to a remembered American anecdote about talking birds. Shortly we are launched on the story of Jim Baker, which in turn launches us on the blue jay story previously recounted.

And here we see suddenly the skill that Twain, in the great middle portion of his career, could find in enlarging a basic element of his storytelling into a complex imaginative creation that has kept critics busy for more than a century since. First, he has managed to launch a Twainian entertainment, planted as an early eye-catcher, one has to suppose, in what will turn out to be a mainly pedestrian volume in every sense of that term. (Beyond the obvious pun on "tramp," as in "bum," the one-horse joke on which the book was mainly to turn involves the idea that just when the narrator is ready to walk during his journeyings in good American fashion he always finds a ride.) But it also becomes a commentary at the crucial time in Mark Twain's career (he was in the long middle of writing *Huckleberry*

Finn [1885]) about both a particular American writer and the American life of writing at large. As in his own story-within-a-story he is mocked by the German talking birds (*pace*, Irving *and* Poe), so the frustrated, feckless jay in his story-within-a-story is mocked by his raucous backwoods fellows. Abroad or at home, one simply cannot get any respect. A jay trying to fill up a house with acorns looks very like an author trying to fill up a travel book with chestnuts. (And with an unamused Nova Scotia owl in attendance, it also looks perhaps, as critics have noted, very like a southwestern entertainer who had just hideously bungled a major "literary" occasion with a miscalculated Whittier Birthday Dinner Speech.)

Finally, presiding over all this, one crucial fact of context remains. While the "Blue Jay Yarn" thus became the third of Twain's best-known animal yarns, it and the others, along with the imaginings of unforgettable cousin-beasts, were soon to fade into a long unhappiness. The prim, stupidly self-important pilgrim-bird of *The Innocents Abroad*, for instance, and the shifty, tatterdemalion coyote of *Roughing It* (1872) were already behind him, and yawning ahead was the image mainly of that vilest of the lower animals, man. Here, though, in the great middle of his career, a brilliantly original gift for humorous invention still inscribed itself into a vernacular medium that could bring it to greatness; but, as in the flat, rather long and tiresome text in which it appears, the story, like its author, proved already adrift in the uneasy parable of nationality and art into which it had been assimilated: that of the raucous entertainer who had already been cast into the increasingly long and "serious" role of being the best-known literary American of all time.

Philip D. Beidler

BIBLIOGRAPHY

Blair, Walter. *Mark Twain & Huck Finn.* Berkeley: U of California P, 1960.

Bridgman, Richard. *Traveling in Mark Twain.* Berkeley: U of California P, 1987.

Clemens, Samuel L. *A Tramp Abroad.* Hartford, Conn.: American Publishing, 1880.

Emerson, Everett. *The Authentic Mark Twain: A Literary Biography of Samuel L. Clemens.* Philadelphia: U of Pennsylvania P, 1984.

Kaplan, Justin. *Mr. Clemens and Mark Twain.* New York: Simon & Schuster, 1966.

Lynn, Kenneth S. *Mark Twain and Southwestern Humor.* Boston: Little, Brown, 1959.

Smith, Henry Nash. *Mark Twain: The Development of a Writer.* Cambridge, Mass.: Harvard UP, 1962.

Wilson, James D. *A Reader's Guide to the Short Stories of Mark Twain.* Boston: G.K. Hall, 1987.

See also: Animals; Baker, Jim; Blaine, Jim; Southwestern Humor; *Tramp Abroad, A*

"Jim Blaine and His Grandfather's Ram"
(1872)

This story is actually chapter fifty-three of Mark Twain's *Roughing It* (1872); though it is a "self-sustaining narrative" (Beidler 43) and in the twentieth century has become one of Twain's most frequently anthologized pieces, the story was never published independently during the author's lifetime. It is important to remember, therefore, that the story has a context. It is one of many splendid anecdotes and tales in *Roughing It* that capture the ambiance and character of the West and dramatize a unifying theme: the initiation of the eastern tenderfoot.

This context helps to explain the frame that encloses Jim Blaine's tale, for the frame constitutes the hoax that reinforces the book's larger theme. The "boys" goad the tenderfoot character Mark Twain into urging one Jim Blaine, a grizzled old miner, to tell the infamous story of his grandfather's ram. They pique the unsuspecting young man's interest—and that of the genteel reader he represents—by mentioning that Blaine will not tell his story to just anyone and that he must be "comfortably and socially drunk" to tell it at all. The anticipation builds as everyone awaits the appropriate moment: "I never watched a man's condition with such absorbing interest, such solicitude; I never so pined to see a man uncompromisingly drunk before" (*RI* 344). As Blaine drifts off in a drunken stupor, in the midst of his rambling, seemingly pointless discourse, the author returns to the frame: the tenderfoot, seeing the "boys" in uncontrolled laughter at his expense, confesses: "I perceived I was 'sold'" (*RI* 348).

The delight this story provides, however, lies not in the frame but in Blaine and the method of his narration. Blaine himself is modeled on a man Clemens had known in Angel's Camp, California, during his exile from San Francisco in the winter 1864–1865: one Ben Coon, who in the saloon "dozed by the stove, or told slow, endless stories, without point or application" (Paine 1:273). The slapstick anecdotes Blaine delivers and the memorable character sketches he draws are Twain's invention and have intrinsic comic appeal. Yet it is Blaine's deadpan delivery of the randomly associated reminiscences that is the focus and chief interest. Here Mark Twain captures the folk quality of oral narration, the emphasis on the telling rather than the tale. The endless digressions, the failure "to discriminate between the important and the trivial" (Covici 58), the deadpan or "poker-faced" recitation of absurdly hilarious episodes, the absence of rising action, conflict, or resolution—this is the essence of the anarchic strain of distinctively American humor that Mark Twain identifies in his essay "How to Tell a Story" (1895). The American humorous story, Twain writes, "may be spun out to great length, and may wander around as it pleases, and arrive nowhere in particular." The destination is irrelevant; the fun is in the ride. What Mark Twain describes is art that conceals art, and nowhere does he do it more effectively than in Jim Blaine's story of his grandfather's ram.

James D. Wilson

BIBLIOGRAPHY

Beidler, Philip D. "Realistic Style and the Problem of Context in *The Innocents Abroad* and *Roughing It*." *American Literature* 52 (1980–1981): 33–49.

Clemens, Samuel L. *Roughing It.* Ed. Franklin R. Rogers and Paul Baender. Berkeley: U of California P, 1972.

Covici, Pascal, Jr. *Mark Twain's Humor: The Image of a World.* Dallas: Southern Methodist UP, 1962.

Gerber, John C. "Mark Twain's Use of the Comic Pose." *Publications of the Modern Language Association* 77 (June 1962): 297–304.

Smith, Henry Nash. *Mark Twain: The Development of a Writer.* Cambridge, Mass.: Harvard UP, 1962.

Wilson, James D. *A Reader's Guide to the Short Stories of Mark Twain.* Boston: G.K. Hall, 1987.

See also: Blaine, Jim; Coon, Ben; Hoax; Humor; *Roughing It*

"Jim Wolf and the Cats"
(1867)

"Jim Wolf and the Cats" relates an incident that happened when Sam Clemens was a boy. First published in the *Californian*, 21 September 1867, it was reprinted several times and sometimes pirated. A.B. Paine included the story as "Cats and Candy" in the 1910 edition of *Mark Twain's Speeches*, but it was deleted in the 1923 edition (Johnson 229). Although Paine recounts the story in *Mark Twain: A Biography* (1:86–88), Twain himself tells it best in his *Autobiography* (135–143).

When Sam Clemens was about fifteen (dates vary), Jim Wolf(e), a shy young man of about sixteen years, came to Hannibal to learn the newspaper trade from Sam's older brother Orion and stayed in the Clemens home. Jim was especially shy of girls. One winter evening Sam's older sister Pamela was giving a taffy party for her friends, but Sam and Jim had gone to bed upstairs. While the girls in the yard below were putting their candy in the snow to cool, two tomcats on the chimney above began an outrageous quarrel. Goaded by Sam, Jim crawled out onto the comb of the roof in just his nightshirt to run the cats off. Of course, his foot slipped on the ice, and he slid down the roof and piled into the girls and hot candy in the yard below.

The next day Sam told his story to Jimmie McDaniel, a schoolmate, and thus "Jim Wolf and the Cats" is the first recorded funny story that Sam ever told (*Autobiography* 213).

Frank H. Leavell

BIBLIOGRAPHY

Clemens, Samuel L. *Mark Twain's Autobiography*. Ed. Albert B. Paine. 2 vols. New York: Harper, 1924.

———. *Mark Twain's Speeches*. New York: Harper, 1910.

Johnson, Merle. *A Bibliography of the Works of Mark Twain*. 1935. Rpt. Westport, Conn.: Greenwood P, 1972.

Paine, Albert Bigelow. *Mark Twain: A Biography*. 3 vols. New York: Harper, 1912.

Wecter, Dixon. *Sam Clemens of Hannibal*. Boston: Houghton Mifflin, 1952.

Joan of Arc

(1412?–1431)

The medieval Maid of Orleans who worked to liberate France, Joan of Arc intrigued numerous nineteenth-century writers, including Mark Twain, whose own fascination with her dates back to his Hannibal boyhood: a gust of wind blew to his feet a page from a biography describing Joan in prison. Thereafter he called her his favorite character in history, his novel *Personal Recollections of Joan of Arc* (1896) constituting (to him) the most serious and most meaningful work he had ever written. Although well received in England, *Joan of Arc* disappointed American critics and continues to spark debate. To date, the majority of critics fault the work both as history and as a realistic portrait of woman; only recently has it attracted defenders, whose renewed interest in Joan of Arc's character helps illuminate Twain's complicated attitude toward women.

Twain began writing the novel at Villa Viviani on 1 August 1892, finishing it in Paris on 8 February 1895. Publication in *Harper's Monthly Magazine* began in March 1895, and the book was published in May 1896. Twain did a great deal of research for this novel, using as sources Jules Michelet's *Jeanne d'Arc* and Janet Tuckey's *Joan of Arc*. Many critics note that Clemens based much of Joan's character on that of his daughter Susy (1872–1896); another likely source was his mother, Jane Lampton Clemens.

Critics have chastised him for sentimental-

ity, melodrama, and lack of historical understanding, as well as for his reverent but unrealistic portrait of Joan: George Bernard Shaw, accuses him of turning Joan into "an unimpeachable American school teacher in armor" (Shaw xxxix–xv). Susan Gillman believes that Twain's frequent use of the "child-women" suggests that he viewed women as essentially powerless, vulnerable, and virginal (Gillman 106). However, in "The Turning Point of My Life," Twain compares Joan's temperament to asbestos, declaring that had she instead of Eve been in the Garden, she would have foiled Satan's plot against humanity. Hamlin Hill notes Twain's interest in strong women, observing that "Hellfire Hotchkiss" (1897), written one year after *Joan of Arc* was published, has as its heroine a fiery tomboy (Hill xxi). Twain's admiration of Joan's heroic qualities are clearly stated in the novel: without her, the men are "mere dead corpses—that and nothing more; incapable of thought, hope, ambition, or motion" (322). Undoubtedly, the continuing studies of *Joan of Arc*, including the humorous "Private History of a MS That Came to Grief," will result in increasingly complex insights into Twain's views of both fictional and actual women.

Abby H.P. Werlock

BIBLIOGRAPHY

Clemens, Samuel L. *Mark Twain's Hannibal, Huck & Tom*. Ed. Walter Blair. Berkeley: U of California P, 1969.

———. *Personal Recollections of Joan of Arc*. New York: Harper, 1896.

———. "Private History of a MS That Came to Grief." *Mark Twain's Autobiography*. By Clemens. Vol. 1. Ed. Albert B. Paine. New York: Harper, 1924. 175–189.

———. *"What Is Man?" and Other Philosophical Writings*. Ed. Paul Baender. Berkeley: U of California P, 1973.

Emerson, Everett. *The Authentic Mark Twain: A Literary Biography of Samuel L. Clemens*. Philadelphia: U of Pennsylvania P, 1984.

Gillman, Susan. *Dark Twins: Imposture and Identity in Mark Twain's America*. Chicago: U of Chicago P, 1989.

Hill, Hamlin. *Mark Twain: God's Fool*. New York: Harper & Row, 1973.

Kaplan, Justin. *Mr. Clemens and Mark Twain*. New York: Simon & Schuster, 1966.

Searle, William. *The Saint and the Skeptics: Joan of Arc in the Work of Mark Twain, Anatole France, and Bernard Shaw*. Detroit: Wayne State UP, 1976.

Shaw, Bernard. Preface. *Saint Joan: A Chronicle Play in Six Scenes and an Epilogue*. By Shaw. New York: Brentano, 1924. xxvii–xli.

See also: *Personal Recollections of Joan of Arc*; Women

Joe, Injun

Injun Joe appears in *The Adventures of Tom Sawyer* (1876) as an adult vagrant of mixed Indian and white parentage. The character is based upon a historical person in Hannibal. His social status in the community is less than that of the slaves: they, at least, make an economic contribution to the town. With no familial or cultural ties to the community, Injun Joe operates outside the law, a true outlaw. As such, Injun Joe represents actual evil in the storybook world of Tom Sawyer.

Injun Joe murders Dr. Robinson in a dispute over payment for grave robbing. The real motivation, however, is vengeance. He cites his Indian blood as motivation for harboring revenge and intends to avenge himself upon the Widow Douglas by mutilating her in "Indian fashion." When McDougal's Cave is sealed off to prevent anyone else being lost within, Injun Joe is inadvertently trapped inside.

Whereas Tom and the boys played at being outlaws, romanticized like Robin Hood, Injun Joe is actually evil. Twain endows him with many of the negative characteristics of the Goshute Indians of *Roughing It*: filth, cowardice, deceit. He represents the antithesis of civilized society.

William McDonald

BIBLIOGRAPHY

Paine, Albert Bigelow. *Mark Twain: A Biography*. 3 vols. New York: Harper, 1912.

Wecter, Dixon. *Sam Clemens of Hannibal*. Boston: Houghton Mifflin, 1952.

See also: *Adventures of Tom Sawyer, The*

Johnson, John Moorman
(1804–1866)

The Reverend John Moorman Johnson was benefactor to the John Marshall Clemens family for as long as they lived in Hannibal, Missouri. Related to John Marshall Clemens on both the Johnson and Goggin sides of the family, the rural Baptist minister and farmer supplied the Clemens family with food, yarn, and handwoven clothes as it became evident that John Marshall Clemens was slowly losing the strength to support his family. The assistance continued after John Marshall's death. In his *Autobiography* Twain mentions a $500 loan from Johnson to Orion Clemens to buy the Hannibal *Journal*; he does not mention an earlier $500 loan that enabled Orion to purchase the Hannibal *Western Union*. He further claims that when Orion moved to Iowa, he relinquished the combined newspapers to Johnson, although there is no record of this transaction and none of the family recalls that Johnson ever owned a newspaper. More than likely, the loan principal and interest remained unpaid.

As children, Sam Clemens and his brother Henry spent many weekends at the Johnson farm. It was a Johnson family joke that "Henry comes to play, but Sam comes to visit the books." Indeed, Johnson owned the largest library in the area, more than 1,000 volumes, and Sam was allowed free access to them all— books of theology, geography, astronomy, poetry, fiction, mythology, and history. Since Sam was too young and his family too poor for him to have borrowing privileges at the circulating library in town, the Johnson farm furnished his first access to the world of books.

Oliver Howard and Goldena Howard

BIBLIOGRAPHY

Clemens, Samuel L. *Mark Twain's Autobiography*. Ed. Albert B. Paine. 2 vols. New York: Harper, 1924.

———. *Mark Twain's Own Autobiography: The Chapters from the "North American Review."* Ed. Michael J. Kiskis. Madison: U of Wisconsin P, 1990.

Hagood, J. Hurley, and Roberta Hagood. *The Story of Hannibal: A Bicentennial History.* Hannibal, Mo.: Hannibal Bicentennial Commission, 1976.

Howard, Oliver, and Goldena Howard. *The Mark Twain Book.* New London, Mo.: Ralls County Book, 1985.

See also: Clemens, John Marshall

Journalism

Mark Twain was a journalist for twenty-five years before he published his first novel. He was a delivery boy, printer's apprentice, editorial assistant, journeyman printer, "loculitems" reporter, feature writer, police-court reporter, hoax perpetrator, traveling correspondent, columnist, editor, humor editor, part owner of a newspaper, and free lancer for national magazines. He wrote for dailies, weeklies, and monthlies in Hannibal, Missouri; Keokuk, Iowa; Virginia City, Nevada; New Orleans; San Francisco; Sacramento; Philadelphia; Washington; New York City; and Buffalo, New York. It was as a journalist that Twain experimented with the subjects, styles, and strategies that would form the core of his most successful ventures as a writer of fiction.

From his earliest days as a printer's devil Clemens was put in intimate contact with the humorous forms of newspaper writing that were becoming increasingly popular in the nation's daily and weekly press. As he set into type skits, tall tales, anecdotes, and satires by well-known national humorists and by little-known local comics, he absorbed lessons in style and stance that would inform his finest literary creations. As a printer's devil, editorial assistant, and contributor to papers in Hannibal, New Orleans, and Keokuk, Iowa, between ages twelve and twenty-four, he began experimenting with comic personae of his own. We would probably pay no attention to the work of that feeble social critic W. Epaminondas Adrastus Blab, that obscure satirist Sergeant Fathom, or that indefatigable letter-to-the-editor-writer Thomas Jefferson Snodgrass, if we did not recognize this motley bunch as Clemens's first efforts to find a comic voice and pen name suited to his needs. Thomas Jefferson Snodgrass, a wide-eyed, semiliterate country bumpkin who travels to the nearest big city and sends ludicrously self-important letters back home to the editor of his local paper describing his travels, does not have much in common with the persona Clemens would eventually choose as his public voice, that of Mark Twain. But Snodgrass, who writes home about peanut boys "tearin' around . . . indiscriminate like" or a lecture that was "uncommon severe," speaks a variant of the famous Pike County dialect that Huck would speak. These early satires on travel letters that Clemens wrote for the Keokuk *Post* under the name "Thomas Jefferson Snodgrass" in 1856 and 1857 are a rare and early instance of an uneducated, vernacular narrator telling his own story in his own words. It was a strategy to which Clemens would return in 1874 when he published his remarkable narrative of slavery, "A True Story Repeated Word for Word as I Heard It," and it was also, of course, the strategy he would return to in *Adventures of Huckleberry Finn* (1885).

In 1862, after having tried his hand at prospecting, Clemens realized he might do better mining his own experience than he did mining silver. He took a job as a reporter on the *Territorial Enterprise* in Virginia City, Nevada. It was there that he adopted the persona and pen name of Mark Twain. And it was there, as a reporter on the Comstock Lode and in California between 1862 and 1866, that he had the chance to explore a myriad of subjects that would later find their way into his fiction: architecture, drama, politics, education, steamboat disasters, shipwrecks, racial prejudice, and a vast range of fraud, corruption, villainy, and humbug. As he would comment in later years, "Reporting is the best school in the world to get a knowledge of human beings, human nature and human ways."

Above all, Twain's apprenticeship in journalism educated his eye and ear to be suspicious. As a fellow journalist rightly observed, it was as a reporter on the Comstock that Twain first acquired "that shrewd, graceless, good-humored way of looking at things as they in fact are—unbullied by authority and indifferent to tradition." It was also there that Twain cultivated two skills that would prove to be invaluable: the first was the ability to tell a lie; the second was the ability to smell one. He would prove to be superlative at both— and both would prove to be central to his career as a novelist.

Two weeks after he was hired as a "loculitems" reporter for the *Territorial Enterprise*, for example, Twain reported (with some subtle obfuscations) that a century-old stone mummy with a wooden leg had been found winking and thumbing his nose at his excavator. Gullible editors across the country reprinted the story without comment, as did a London journal of chemistry, criticism, literature, and news.

If Twain excelled at spinning outrageous lies, he also was adept at exposing them. In Washoe and San Francisco when he smelled a financial swindle, he was quick to declare the obligation of the journalist to ferret out the facts and unmask charlatans bent on separating honest people from their money.

Financial abuses were not the only target of Twain's attacks: he went after corruption in law enforcement, abuses of justice, misuse of power, racism, and all stripes of hypocrisy as well.

In the 1860s Twain was bearing witness to a San Francisco that no one else was recording, and the truth was sometimes a pill too bitter for his editors and publishers to swallow. As a young reporter in San Francisco, Twain witnessed an incident he considered outrageous: several policemen stood idly by, apparently amused, as young white hooligans attacked a Chinese man who was going about his business. Twain wrote a straightforward report for his paper, turned it in, and looked for it. It was not there. His publishers were more concerned with not offending the paper's subscribers (who shared the police's prejudices) than with the truth. Twain quickly learned that straightforward exposure of racism in San Francisco would not be printed in newspapers

there. He responded by publishing his social criticism in his old Nevada paper and in national magazines in quasi-fictional ironic forms that allowed him to dramatize as well as report the outrages he witnessed in San Francisco. It is interesting that Twain first turned to irony to write about racism when his direct exposés were censored; a hundred years after his death he would face the prospect of being censored yet again by readers unequipped to understand his ironic style.

Twain soon lost interest in the grind of churning out news for a daily paper. "After having been hard at work from nine or ten in the morning until eleven at night scraping material together," he recalled some forty years later, "I took the pen and spread this muck out in words and phrases and made it cover as much acreage as I could. It was fearful drudgery, soulless drudgery, and almost destitute of interest." When the Sacramento *Daily Union* commissioned him in 1866 to write a series of letters from Hawaii, he jumped at the opportunity. During the next two years he would send letters as traveling correspondent to other papers as well (including the New York *Herald*) from Europe, Asia, and the Holy Land. These travel letters would eventually form the core of his first book-length coup on the literary scene, *The Innocents Abroad* (1869). In these letters Twain deconstructs the false and hackneyed images promoted by travel guidebooks, tour guides, church legends, and romantic novelists. His goal is to help his reader learn to see "with his own eyes instead of the eyes of those who travelled . . . before him." In his travel letters narrative units are strung together as beads on a necklace, united solely by the thread of the voyage. They relate to each other only by proximity and juxtaposition. Twain would return again and again to this kind of episodic structure throughout his career as a writer of fiction.

With the exception of a brief stint in the late 1860s as part owner and associate editor of the Buffalo *Express*, Twain's journalism during the last four decades of his life consisted of the wide range of articles he contributed to national magazines such as *Harper's New Monthly Magazine, Galaxy Magazine,* the *Atlantic Monthly,* and the *North American Review.* His contributions ranged from nostalgic reminiscences such as "Old Times on the Mississippi," which ran in the *Atlantic* (1875), to bitter diatribes against racism and imperialism such as "To the Person Sitting in Darkness," which ran in the *North American Review* (1901).

Twain's own extensive experience as a journalist helped him understand from the inside the press's worst flaws and foibles (see his parodies "Journalism in Tennessee" [1869] and "How I Edited an Agricultural Paper Once" [1870]), but it also gave him an abiding appreciation for the unique role the press played in our society. The press's mission, as Twain came to articulate it, "is to stand guard over a nation's liberties." As a journalist, Twain shouldered this role with characteristic courage, creativity, and wit.

Shelley Fisher Fishkin

BIBLIOGRAPHY

Branch, Edgar M. *The Literary Apprenticeship of Mark Twain.* Urbana: U of Illinois P, 1950.

Budd, Louis J. *Our Mark Twain: The Making of His Public Personality.* Philadelphia: U of Pennsylvania P, 1983.

Clemens, Samuel L. *Clemens of the "Call": Mark Twain in San Francisco.* Ed. Edgar M. Branch. Berkeley: U of California P, 1969.

———. *Mark Twain of the "Enterprise": Newspaper Articles and Other Documents, 1862–1864.* Ed. Henry Nash Smith and Frederick Anderson. Berkeley: U of California P, 1957.

———. *Mark Twain on the Damned Human Race.* Ed. Janet Smith. New York: Hill and Wang, 1962.

———. *Mark Twain's San Francisco.* Ed. Bernard Taper. New York: McGraw-Hill, 1963.

———. *The Works of Mark Twain: Early Tales & Sketches.* Ed. Edgar M. Branch and Robert H. Hirst. 2 vols. Berkeley: U of California P, 1979–1981.

Emerson, Everett. *The Authentic Mark Twain: A Literary Biography of Samuel L. Clemens.* Philadelphia: U of Pennsylvania P, 1984.

Fishkin, Shelley Fisher. *From Fact to Fiction: Journalism and Imaginative Writing in America.* New York: Oxford UP, 1988.

Foner, Philip S. *Mark Twain: Social Critic.* New York: International Publishers, 1958.

Kaplan, Justin. *Mr. Clemens and Mark Twain.* New York: Simon & Schuster, 1966.

Sloane, David E.E. *Mark Twain as a Literary Comedian.* Baton Rouge: Louisiana State UP, 1979.

See also: Humor; Nevada; Newspapers; Satire

"Journalism in Tennessee"
(1869)

In his sketch "Journalism in Tennessee," first published in the Buffalo *Express,* 4 September 1869, Twain describes his experiences when he went south to improve his health and became associate editor of a newspaper, the *Morning Glory and Johnson County War Whoop,* presumably located in the extreme northeastern corner of Tennessee. His mild article "Spirit of the Tennessee Press" is rewritten by his editor in the vigorous, insulting, "peppery" style of the newspapers of the time, a style that results in numerous physical assaults upon the new associate editor. After being shot, thrown out the window, cowhided, and scalped, Twain resigns his position, concluding that "Tennessean journalism is too stirring for me."

Allison R. Ensor

BIBLIOGRAPHY

Clemens, Samuel L. *The Complete Short Stories of Mark Twain.* Ed. Charles Neider. Garden City, N.Y.: Hanover House, 1957. 27–32.

Wilson, James D. *A Reader's Guide to the Short Stories of Mark Twain.* Boston: G.K. Hall, 1987.

See also: Doten, Alfred R.; Journalism

Journals

Established in 1936, the *Mark Twain Quarterly* was the first academic journal devoted entirely to Samuel L. Clemens. Under the editorship of Cyril Clemens, the *MTQ* changed its name in 1954 to the *Mark Twain Journal.* Since 1982 the *MTJ* has been under the editorship of Thomas A. Tenney and continues to publish scholarly articles, notes, and bibliographical information germane to Mark Twain studies. Two particular issues deserve special mention: the fall of 1984 (22.2) special number entitled "Black Writers on *Adventures of Huckleberry Finn*: 100 Years Later" and the 1985 volume, which contains the *Index to Volumes 1–21 of the Mark Twain Journal 1936–1983* (including the *MTQ*) compiled by L. Terry Oggel and William Nelles.

Another journal devoted to Mark Twain materials is the *Twainian*. Established in 1939 by George Hiram Brownell and the Mark Twain Research Foundation, the *Twainian* began a new series in 1942 when the foundation moved its headquarters from Wisconsin to Perry, Missouri, and Chester Davis assumed editorship. More recently established journals include the *Mark Twain Society Bulletin*, a semiannual publication edited by Robert D. Jerome and Herbert Wisbey for the Mark Twain Society, Elmira, New York, and the *Mark Twain Circular*. Established in 1986 as the official bimonthly newsletter of the Mark Twain Circle of America, the *MTC*, edited by James Leonard at the Citadel, is now a quarterly containing book reviews, announcements of forthcoming activities, conferences, and publication projects as well as bibliographical updates.

A continuing monograph series, *Quarry Farm Papers* is an occasional publication of the Elmira College Center for Mark Twain Studies at Quarry Farm. It is edited by the center director, Darryl Baskin. To date three volumes have appeared in the series: Henry Nash Smith, *How True Are Dreams?: The Theme of Fantasy in Mark Twain's Later Work* (foreword by Alan Gribben, 1989); John S. Tuckey, *Mark Twain: The Youth Who Lived On in the Sage* (foreword by Howard Baetzhold, 1990); and Lorraine Willing Lanmon, *Quarry Farm: A Study of the Picturesque* (1991).

Many scholarly journals regularly carry articles on Mark Twain. A few have devoted an entire issue to him: *Modern Fiction Studies* 14.1 (Spring 1968), which features a substantial checklist of Mark Twain scholarship—through 1966—compiled by Maurice Beebe and John

Feaster; *Studies in American Humor* 2.3 (January 1976) offers six articles on the general topic "Mark Twain in the 1870s," guest edited by Louis J. Budd; *Studies in American Fiction* 13.2 (Fall 1985); and *South Central Review* 5.4 (Winter 1988), a special section of six articles guest edited by James D. Wilson. Several other journals offer regular features that make them especially valuable to the Mark Twain researcher. From 1977 to 1986 *American Literary Realism* carried an annual update of Thomas A. Tenney's *Mark Twain: A Reference Guide* (1977); since 1986, that update has appeared in the *Mark Twain Circular*. The spring issue of the *Mississippi Quarterly* every year contains a section on Mark Twain in its "Checklist of Scholarship in Southern Literature." *American Literature* includes Clemens in its regular section, "A Select, Annotated List of Current Articles on American Literature," compiled by the Committee on Bibliography of the American Literature Section of the Modern Language Association. The most comprehensive listing of current Mark Twain scholarship appears in the *International Bibliography of Books and Articles on the Modern Languages and Literatures*, published annually by the Modern Language Association.

The researcher wishing to keep abreast of Mark Twain scholarship may profitably spend time perusing academic journals. In addition to the specific titles already mentioned, numerous other journals routinely carry important articles and book reviews. A sampling might include *American Quarterly*; *College Literature*; *Emerson Society Quarterly*; *English Language Notes*; *Essays in Arts and Sciences*; *New England Quarterly*; *Nineteenth-Century Literature*; *PMLA*; *South Atlantic Quarterly*; *South Atlantic Review*; *Southern Review*; *Studies in Short Fiction*; *Studies in the Novel*; *Texas Studies in Literature and Language*; and *Western American Literature*.

James D. Wilson

See also: Bibliographies; Mark Twain Research Foundation; Scholarship, Trends in Mark Twain

Keller, Helen Adams

(1880–1968)

Born normal, Helen Keller was struck by an illness in her nineteenth month that left her blind and deaf, yet she graduated with honors from Radcliffe College in 1904 and became a noted American author, lecturer, and celebrity. Being a voice for social reform, she was sympathetic to socialist and Marxist ideas. Her books were primarily autobiographies, including *The Story of My Life* (1902), *The World I Live In* (1908), *Out of the Dark* (1913), *My Religion* (1927), *Midstream: My Later Life* (1929), and *Let Us Have Faith* (1940).

When Helen was six, her parents took her to Alexander Graham Bell, who recommended she be taken to the Boston Perkins School for the Blind where a teacher could be assigned to her. On 3 March 1887 Anne Sullivan (later married to socialist writer John Macy) became Helen's teacher and was from that point onward Helen's constant companion, amanuensis, and friend. It would be an understatement

to describe their relationship as symbiotic. As Twain put it, "It took the pair of you to make and complete a perfect whole."

The long friendship of Keller and Clemens began at a party at Laurence Hutton's New York home on 31 March 1895. Keller was fourteen, the same age as Jean Clemens. She was introduced to both Twain and William Dean Howells, a meeting recalled and discussed many times after with great warmth and affection by all three. Twain told several stories that afternoon with Keller reading his lips and laughing at jokes. Keller later remembered Twain's asking her permission to swear, taking away her fingers when he did so. Keller said, "I think Mark Twain is a very appropriate nom de plume for Mr. Clemens because it has a funny and quaint sound, and goes well with his amusing writings, and its nautical significance suggests the deep and beautiful things that he has written." In turn, Twain wrote that the two most interesting figures of the nineteenth century were Napoleon and Keller. He later compared her to Joan of Arc.

Twain became a financial sponsor of Keller, watching her academic achievements at Radcliffe with great interest and pleasure. He supported her in the plagiarism suit regarding the short story "The Little King," a story Keller had apparently memorized and inadvertently plagiarized. Twain read an autographed copy of *The Story of My Life* in which Keller described her meeting with Clemens, saying, "I love Mark Twain—who does not? The gods, too, loved him and put into his heart all manner of wisdom; then, fearing lest he should become a pessimist, they spanned his mind with a rainbow of love and faith. . . . Even while he utters his cynical wisdom in an undescribably droll voice, he makes you feel that his heart is a tender island of human sympathy."

The two exchanged many letters and gifts, typically with showers of mutual compliments. Keller inscribed a copy of *The World I Live In* to her friend, saying, "Mr. Clemens, come live in my world for a little while." Twain responded on the book's inside cover, "It is a lovely book—& Helen is herself another lovely book."

Twain persuaded Henry H. Rogers to sponsor Keller. While with Rogers in Bermuda in 1908, Twain read aloud some of Keller's *Harper's Monthly Magazine* articles. After his death, Keller eulogized Twain in a number of publications, essentially retelling the story of their meeting. Twain's description of this event was published in his posthumous *Autobiography* (1924).

Wesley Britton

BIBLIOGRAPHY

Chambliss, Amy. "The Friendship of Helen Keller and Mark Twain." *Georgia Review* 24 (Fall 1970): 305–310.

Keller, Helen A. "My Friend, Mark Twain." *Mark Twain Journal* 10 (Spring-Summer 1958): 1.

———. "Our Mark Twain." *Midstream: My Later Life*. Garden City, N.Y.: Doubleday, Doran, 1929. 47–69.

———. *The Story of My Life*. New York: Doubleday, Page, 1903.

Lash, Joseph P. *Helen and Teacher: The Story of Helen Keller and Ann Sullivan Macy*. New York: Delacorte, 1980.

Kellgren, Jonas Henrik
(1837–1916)

Disdaining the use of drugs, Joseph Henrik Kellgren developed a treatment called "mechano-therapeutics" that utilized vibrations, frictions, touch, and muscular exercises. He established Kellgren Institutes in London (1875), Baden-Baden (1883), and Paris (1884), along with a health sanatorium in his native Sweden (1886).

Twain enthusiastically endorsed the work of Kellgren, which he said was akin to osteopathy. He himself participated in the treatment program while in London and believed daughter Jean's treatment in 1889–1890 cured her epilepsy.

Maverick Marvin Harris

BIBLIOGRAPHY

Clemens, Samuel L. *Mark Twain's Correspondence with Henry Huttleston Rogers, 1893–1909*. Ed. Lewis Leary. Berkeley: U of California P, 1969.

Kennan, George
(1845–1924)

Explorer, journalist, and author, George Kennan won fame for his works on Russia and Siberia. Mark Twain read his articles on the Siberian exile system as they appeared in the *Century Magazine* (1887–1889) and later heard at least one of Kennan's lectures. The articles strongly influenced Twain's antipathy toward the Russian empire and inspired some of the details in *A Connecticut Yankee* (1889) and probably in "The Czar's Soliloquy" (1905).

Howard G. Baetzhold

BIBLIOGRAPHY

Baetzhold, Howard G. "The Course of Composition of *A Connecticut Yankee*: A Reinterpretation." *American Literature* 33 (May 1961): 195–214.

Kennan, George. *Tent Life in Siberia*. New York: Arno P, 1970.

————. *Siberia and the Exile System*. 2 vols. New York: Century, 1891.

See also: "Czar's Soliloquy, The"; Russia

Keokuk, Iowa

In spring 1855 Clemens moved to Keokuk, Iowa, to work for his brother, Orion, who had just moved there with his new wife, Mollie Stotts. Orion was running the Ben Franklin book and job printing office, and he offered Clemens $5 a week to stay and help. Clemens lived there about a year and a half, using the time to read such authors as Poe and to develop a friendship with men of his own age.

However, Orion proved to be a bad manager and Clemens grew restless. He wanted to visit South America, but he did not have the money. The story goes that one day he was walking down the streets of Keokuk and found a $50 bill. Clemens claims to have advertised for the owner, but none was found. As for the visit to South America, it did not materialize.

His first writing money was made from travel letters he wrote for the Keokuk *Post*. George Rees, the editor, offered him $5 for each letter. Clemens chose the name Thomas Jefferson Snodgrass and satirized the travel genre in the letters. He also began the use of native dialect and illiterate spelling that he would develop in later writings.

Clemens would visit his family in Keokuk from time to time after his mother moved there. He suggested his brother write an autobiography, which Clemens used later as an example of the failure of the American dream.

Stuart Kenny

BIBLIOGRAPHY

Ferguson, DeLancey. *Mark Twain: Man and Legend*. Indianapolis: Bobbs-Merrill, 1943.

Paine, Albert Bigelow. *Mark Twain: A Biography*. 3 vols. New York: Harper, 1912.

See also: "Adventures of Thomas Jefferson Snodgrass, The"

Keokuk (Iowa) *Gate City*

A daily founded in 1846, the Keokuk (Iowa) *Gate City* served Clemens as an outlet for his early "letters home" from the Nevada Territory where he had accompanied his brother Orion in 1861. A version of a letter to his mother describing the Nevada desert landscape appeared in the *Gate City* on 20 November 1861, and over the following year the editors published several more of Clemens's letters, which were a combination of fact and fancy. The tone, themes, and characterizations found in these letters prefigure Clemens's later works.

Susan McFatter

BIBLIOGRAPHY

Emerson, Everett H. *The Authentic Mark Twain: A Literary Biography of Samuel L. Clemens*. Philadelphia: U of Pennsylvania P, 1984.

Lee, Robert Edson. *From West to East: Studies in the Literature of the American West*. Urbana: U of Illinois P, 1966.

See also: Journalism; Keokuk, Iowa

King, Grace
(1852–1932)

A southern writer of realist fiction, Grace King was an intimate of the Clemens family. A respected writer of short stories, novels, biographies, and historical studies, King's best-known works were her novels *Monsieur Motte* (1888) and *The Pleasant Ways of St. Medard* (1916) along with her short story "Earthlings" (1888) (which Clemens called a "masterpiece"). Most of King's works of fiction concerned women's experiences.

King was an avowed Confederate supporter and maintained a lifelong dislike of the North.

In the spring of 1887 King met the Clemenses when she came to Hartford to stay with the George Warners. Warner was her sponsor and introduced her to the literary milieu of Nook Farm. King returned during the fall of 1887 as a guest of the Clemenses and later visited the family in Florence, Italy. Both Susy and Clara regarded her as a confidant, and King and Olivia were particularly close. It was to King whom Olivia wrote asking if the family should return to Hartford after Susy's death and to King again whom Olivia confessed her doubts concerning Clara's singing career. Though King never married, she traveled widely and for a time was a literary agent for French writers who were attempting to publish in America. Of Clemens's writing abilities, King commented: "He is not critical—nor picturesque— If he were he would be a great novelist—He ought to be a great realistic novelist—but he is not" ("Impression" 4).

Laura E. Skandera

BIBLIOGRAPHY

Bush, Robert. "Grace King and Mark Twain." *American Literature* 44 (March 1972): 31–51.

King, Grace. "Mark Twain—Second Impression." Transcript. Department of Archives. Baton Rouge: Louisiana State U.

———. *Memories of a Southern Woman of Letters.* 1932. Rpt. New York: Books for Libraries P, 1971.

Taylor, Helen. *Gender, Race, and Region in the Writings of Grace King, Ruth McEnery Stuart, and Kate Chopin.* Baton Rouge: Louisiana State UP, 1989.

King Leopold's Soliloquy
(1905)

Mark Twain wrote *King Leopold's Soliloquy* (*KLS*), a satire, at the behest of Edmund Dene Morel, head of the British Congo Reform Association (C.R.A.), who visited him in New York on 17 October 1904. Finished in late February 1905, Twain submitted it to the *North American Review*, which had printed his earlier anti-imperialist articles, but the editors rejected it. The American C.R.A. then published it as a pamphlet on 28 September and brought out a second edition on 1 January 1906. Twain donated all proceeds to the association.

KLS attacks King Leopold II of Belgium, who at the Berlin Conference of 1885 got control of the Congo as his personal territory, not as a Belgian colony. In 1892 Leopold instituted a brutal system of forced labor to collect ivory and wild rubber. During his rule an estimated 3 million Congolese were killed and many more mutilated.

The form of *KLS* matches Twain's "The Czar's Soliloquy," published in the March 1905 *North American Review.* Both are dramatic monologues in which a villain gives an outrageously inadequate defense of himself. In *KLS* Leopold reads frequently from articles attacking him. Twain thus documents Leopold's crimes at the same time the king sputters feebly against his accusers.

For a period of a year-and-a-half Twain was heavily involved in Congo reform. He became a vice-president of the American C.R.A., wrote two shorter pieces, which remained unpublished, gave a lengthy newspaper interview, mentioned reform in several speeches, and made three trips to Washington to talk with President Theodore Roosevelt and high officials at the State Department. During his involvement, as in *KLS*, however, Twain made the mistake of assuming the United States had ratified the Berlin Treaty and therefore had a legal interest in the Congo. When the State Department informed him otherwise, he concluded it was useless to agitate in America.

Twain had other reasons as well for resigning from the C.R.A. on 10 February 1906. At age seventy he had neither the strength nor the desire to keep up with the demands of the movement. On a more abstract level, he was succumbing to the pessimism that filled his final years. That pessimism manifests itself even in *KLS* when Leopold, echoing Colonel Sherburn in *Huckleberry Finn* (1885), concludes the human race is too cowardly and servile ever to do anything about him.

Twain isolated himself so completely from the C.R.A. that he seems never to have learned it was ultimately successful. In December 1906, referring to enormous public pressure, President Roosevelt wrote the British foreign secretary that he was ready to move against Leopold, citing United States participation in the Declaration of Brussels of 1890 as legal basis. In 1908 Belgium finally took the Congo from Leopold. Thus Twain's humanitarian efforts bore fruit though he himself never knew it.

Hunt Hawkins

BIBLIOGRAPHY

Ascherson, Neal. *The King Incorporated: Leopold II in the Age of Trusts.* London: Allen and Unwin, 1963.

Emerson, Barbara. *Leopold II of the Belgians: King of Colonialism.* New York: St. Martins P, 1979.

Foner, Philip S. *Mark Twain: Social Critic.* New York: International Publishers, 1958.

Hawkins, Hunt. "Mark Twain's Involvement with the Congo Reform Movement: 'A Fury of Generous Indignation.'" *New England Quarterly* 51.2 (June 1978): 147–175.

Hill, Hamlin. *Mark Twain: God's Fool.* New York: Harper & Row, 1973.

Morel, Edmund D. *History of the Congo Reform Movement.* Ed. William Roger Louis and Jean Stengers. Oxford (England): Clarendon P, 1968.

See also: Belgian Congo; "Czar's Soliloquy, The"; Imperialism; Leopold II, King of the Belgians

Kingsley, Charles
(1819–1875)

A popular British novelist and social reformer, Charles Kingsley founded the Christian Socialist Movement with F.D. Maurice and J.M. Ludlow in 1848. His broad and varied career included a professorship in modern history at Cambridge University (1860) and an appointment as Canon of Westminster Abbey (1873). Kingsley was a prolific writer best known for his social-conscience novels *Yeast* (1848) and *Alton Locke* (1859) and for his historical novels *Westward Ho!* (1855) and *Hereward the Wake* (1866).

Kingsley was one of the first members of the clerical profession to advocate the theories of Charles Darwin. His recognition of Mark Twain as a talented writer did much to further Twain's reputation in England and endear him to a British audience.

Jennifer L. Rafferty

BIBLIOGRAPHY

Chitty, Susan. *The Beast and the Monk: A Life of Charles Kingsley.* New York: Mason/Charter, 1974.

Kingsley, Charles. *Life and Works of Charles Kingsley.* 19 vols. New York: Macmillan, 1901–1903.

Martin, Robert Bernard. *The Dust of Combat: A Life of Charles Kingsley.* London: Faber and Faber, 1959.

Paine, Albert Bigelow. *Mark Twain: A Biography.* Vol. 2. New York: Harper, 1912.

See also: Darwin, Charles; Evolution

Kipling, (Joseph) Rudyard
(1865–1936)

Born in Bombay, Rudyard Kipling received his primary and secondary education in England. Returning to India, from 1882 to 1889 he worked as a journalist for several newspapers and also contributed poetry and fiction that won him widespread popularity in India when his poems were collected in *Departmental Ditties* (1886) and his stories in *Plain Tales from the Hills* (1888), *Soldiers Three* (1888), *In Black and White* (1888), and *Under the Deodars* (1888). His rapid rise to world fame began in 1890 with the reissuing of his works in England and America.

After his marriage in 1892 to Caroline Balestier, an American, the Kiplings settled in Brattleboro, Vermont, for some four years before returning to England in 1896. There, except for extensive travels, they lived in Burwash, Sussex, from 1902 until Kipling's death in 1936.

Kipling's literary production was immense. By the early 1930s he had produced fourteen additional volumes of stories, including *The Jungle Books* (1894, 1895); four novels, *The*

Light that Failed (1890), *The Naulahka* (1892, with Wolcott Balestier), *Captains Courageous* (1897), and *Kim* (1901); some 800 pages of verse; and numerous volumes of travel and other nonfiction.

Recipient of many laurels during his lifetime, including an honorary degree from Oxford University in 1907 and the Nobel Prize for literature the same year, Kipling was increasingly criticized in "literary" circles for vulgarity and for excessive yielding to popular taste and by anti-imperialists for his seeming jingoism. In the latter instance, however, many of his severest critics failed to recognize his deep concern for the subject peoples and his emphasis on the responsibilities incumbent upon the colonizers. He was consistently popular with the common reader.

In 1889, during his trip from India to England by way of the United States, which he recorded in newspaper articles and his travel book *From Sea to Sea* (1899), Kipling undertook a literary pilgrimage to Elmira, New York, hoping to see Mark Twain, whose works he had long known and admired. He was thrilled by his cordial reception, and Clemens in turn was much impressed with his young visitor. But not until the following year, after a Hartford neighbor gave him a copy of a newly published New York edition of *Plain Tales From the Hills*, did Clemens realize that he had entertained a budding celebrity. From that time on he became an avid reader of Kipling's poems and stories, declaring in 1906 that he knew Kipling's writings "better than I know anybody else's books."

The friendship begun in Elmira continued for the rest of Clemens's life. The pair corresponded occasionally, met several times during Kipling's residence in the United States and for a final time in 1907 when Clemens, too, received an honorary Doctor of Letters degree from Oxford University. Clemens often alluded to Kipling in letters, speeches, and informal conversations, and especially in his later years he was fond of reading Kipling's poems to highly appreciative audiences of family or friends. *Kim* (1901) also was a favorite,

which he frequently reread. From the "incomparable" *Jungle Books* (1894, 1895) he borrowed the names of Baloo the Bear and Hathi the Elephant for "A Fable" (1909) and in "The Refuge of the Derelicts" (written in 1905, first published 1971) had Admiral Stormfield explain why he had named his beloved cat Bagheera by reading a description of Kipling's sleek black panther.

It seems clear, also, that Kipling influenced Clemens's attitudes toward British imperialism, especially as it concerned India. *Following the Equator* (1897) shows him very close to his friend's position, and although he occasionally criticized British activities in South Africa and elsewhere, Clemens obviously considered British rule superior to that of other nations. As for India, he wholeheartedly applauded the English achievement there. He would continue to praise Kipling's views even after disillusionment with American policies in the Philippines made him an active and vocal anti-imperialist.

In turn, Kipling's allusions to Mark Twain's works, and praise of their author on a number of occasions, show a considerable sense of obligation to the older writer, whom he once called "the master of us all." Allusions scattered among his essays and stories exhibit a thorough knowledge at least of *Tom Sawyer* (1876), *Life on the Mississippi* (1883), and *Huckleberry Finn* (1885). Moreover, Kipling's best novel, *Kim* (1901), though very different in some respects, bears striking resemblances to *Huckleberry Finn* (1885), especially in the journey of the boy and his mentor along India's Grand Trunk Road, a "river of life," that flows for 1,500 miles through the heart of India. For his story "The Village that Voted the Earth Was Flat" (1913)—a village that he named *Huckley*—Kipling clearly drew on "The Man That Corrupted Hadleyburg" (1899), especially for the concept of revenge upon a community for an insult and for the climactic scene and jibing song and chant that brought about the humiliation of the town and its leading citizens.

Usually reticent in his comments about fellow authors, Kipling was effusive about Mark Twain. Not only did he write to his American publisher Frank Doubleday in 1903 of his affection for "the great and godlike Clemens" whom he considered "the biggest man you have on your side of the water by a damn sight," but on the occasion of the centennial celebration of Clemens's birth in 1935, he declared that Mark Twain "was the largest man of his time; both in the direct outcome of his work, and more important still, as an indirect force in an age of iron Philistinism."

Kipling's and Clemens's mutual admiration would be important from a biographical and historical standpoint alone, but their influence on each other's works or ideas makes theirs a truly notable Anglo-American literary friendship.

Howard G. Baetzhold

BIBLIOGRAPHY

Baetzhold, Howard G. *Mark Twain and John Bull: The British Connection*. Bloomington: Indiana UP, 1970.

Carrington, Charles E. *The Life of Rudyard Kipling*. Garden City, N.Y.: Doubleday, 1955.

Eliot, T.S. "Rudyard Kipling." *A Choice of Kipling's Verse*. By Rudyard Kipling. London: Faber and Faber, 1941. 5–36.

Gribben, Alan. *Mark Twain's Library: A Reconstruction*. 2 vols. Boston: G.K. Hall, 1980.

Harrison, James. *Rudyard Kipling*. Boston: Twayne, 1982.

Kipling, Rudyard. *The Sussex Edition of the Complete Works of Rudyard Kipling*. 35 vols. London: Macmillan, 1937–1939. Rpt. *The Collected Works of Rudyard Kipling: The Burwash Edition*. 28 vols. Garden City, N.Y.: Doubleday, Doran, 1941.

Stewart, John Innes Mackintosh. *Rudyard Kipling*. New York: Dodd, Mead, 1966.

See also: England; Imperialism; Reading

L

Labor

Mark Twain enthusiastically supported the American Labor movement in its struggle to gain a foothold in the years following the Civil War. Unlike his friend William Dean Howells, he did not embrace socialism but believed that a strong labor organization would produce economic justice. His support for the movement arose from his sympathy for the underdog, his idealistic picture of what American democracy ought to be, and his almost mystical belief in the common man, "that vague, formless, inert mass, that mighty underlying force which we call 'the people'" that Sieur Louis de Conte lauds in Twain's *Personal Recollections of Joan of Arc* (1896). Twain's advocacy of the rights of workers began early in his writing career and remained firm until his death.

As early as 1867, when Twain was visiting New York City, he wrote dispatches to the *Alta California* attacking slum conditions and supporting an eight-hour day for poverty-stricken workers. Philip Foner in *Mark Twain:* *Social Critic* provides the fullest discussion of Twain's defense of labor. Although Foner is a biased source because of his pro-labor stance, nevertheless, he presents a well-documented study. He notes that Twain satirized the capitalist mentality in the manner of Swift's "Modest Proposal" in one of these dispatches when Twain suggested that working men could be "dessicated" and used to stuff sausages for trade with "natives of the Cannibal Islands." This would provide three benefits for the wealthy: a surge in exports, an increase in profits, and a salve for their consciences. William Dean Howells in *My Mark Twain* claims that Twain always sided with the labor unions in arguments but that he, Howells, was never able to convince Twain to accept socialism as the solution. Twain felt that labor unions would eventually gain enough power to bargain for the working man's fair share of the economy. He thus remained a capitalist who also wanted to see every laborer have an equal chance for economic dignity. These attitudes toward labor are most fully set forth in *Life on the Mississippi* (1883), *A Connecticut Yankee in King Arthur's Court* (1889), and "The New Dynasty" (1886).

In chapter 15 of *Life on the Mississippi*, Twain narrated the development of the Pilot's Benevolent Association into a "monopoly" or, in labor terms, "a closed shop." Through a series of well-planned tactics the association was able to force the owners into meeting their wage and labor demands in the pre–Civil War era. Twain clearly admired the pilots' success. Of course, the advent of the railroad and the start of the war ended the era of the steamboat. Twain's account of this early organization's victory was printed approvingly in several labor journals, though it was received coldly in the establishment press, which was sounding the alarm that labor unions were the tools of foreign elements such as communists, socialists, and anarchists.

The labor movement also welcomed Twain's *Connecticut Yankee*. Hank Morgan, the protagonist of the novel, calls for a "New Deal" for the economically deprived, those who do the work of society but who do not reap any of its benefits. Morgan, looking forward from the sixth century, predicts that by the nineteenth century the underdogs of society will "band themselves together" and battle their masters. "All of a sudden the wage earner" will decide that "a couple of thousand years or so is enough . . . he will rise up and take a hand at fixing his wage himself," and "a man will be his own property." Human rights will supersede the rich man's lament for property rights. So Twain had a vision of humanistic results from the labor movement. Labor leaders made sure that sections of the novel, particularly chapter 33, were read aloud at trade union meetings and labor picnics. Later, President Franklin D. Roosevelt adopted the phrase "New Deal" for his presidential campaign during the Depression.

Between the publication of *Life on the Mississippi* and *Connecticut Yankee* Twain made a speech before the Monday Evening Club of Hartford, Connecticut, on 22 March 1887, that he titled "The New Dynasty." This new dynasty was the Knights of Labor, who had gained a victory over Jay Gould in 1885 by organizing the workers of the business tycoon's southwestern rail system. Twain hailed this success as a great victory for democracy; he was particularly impressed with the Knights of Labor because the union brought together skilled and unskilled laborers, black and white Americans, and native and foreign-born citizens.

Twain pictured the movement in glowing terms, describing the confrontation of the oppressors, the king, the capitalist, and their overseers by the many. In this new dynasty all crafts will unite, a nation will rise, and those working men "who have been horses" will become the masters. There will be "fair play," "fair wages," and "fair working hours." Twain's speech was probably the most forthright pro-labor speech made by any of the writers of the period and of all the intellectuals of the time, including Henry Demerest Lloyd and William Dean Howells, who championed labor's cause, Twain alone championed labor's right to be a ruling force in society. Twain remained a capitalist, but he also stayed within the American tradition of fairness and equality that had been espoused by such men as Thomas Paine and Henry David Thoreau.

Hugo D. Johnson

BIBLIOGRAPHY

Carter, Paul J., Jr. "Mark Twain and the American Labor Movement." *New England Quarterly* 30 (September 1957): 382–388.

Clemens, Samuel L. *A Connecticut Yankee in King Arthur's Court.* Ed. Bernard Stein. Berkeley: U of California P, 1979.

———. *Life on the Mississippi.* Boston: James R. Osgood, 1883.

———. *Personal Recollections of Joan of Arc.* New York: Harper, 1896.

Foner, Philip S. *Mark Twain: Social Critic.* New York: International Publishers, 1958.

Howells, William Dean. *My Mark Twain: Reminiscences and Criticisms.* New York: Harper, 1910.

See also: Business

Lambton Family of Durham

Mark Twain's maternal ancestors descended from the Lambton family, among the most ancient nobility in northern England, whose head is the Earl of Durham. The Lambtons have been large landowners in the County Durham for more than 800 years, and the family castle still stands high above the River Wear in the English village of Chester-le-Street. Members of the family garnered honors fighting in the crusades, on Flodden Field, and at Marston Moor. Although Twain's first Lampton ancestor in the American colonies arrived in Maryland from England in 1664, Jane Lampton Clemens and most of her Lampton kinfolk considered themselves aristocrats, descendants of the noble Lambtons of Durham, England.

The Lampton family legend that Twain grew up on stated that two brothers, Samuel and William Lambton, the eldest sons of Lord Lambton, Earl of Durham, migrated around 1740 from England to the wilderness of Virginia following a fight with their father. Disgusted with what they considered the foolish fraud of hereditary aristocracy, the two were ardent colonial patriots during the Revolutionary War. While Samuel and William were exploring the wilds of the New World, their father, the Earl of Durham, died and their two younger brothers, who remained behind in England, wrongfully succeeded to the vast estates and titles. Rich seams of coal were found beneath the vast Lambton land holdings shortly after the two older brothers left for America, greatly increasing the wealth of the Lambton estates. The true Earl, Samuel lived and died in Virginia. There he reared a large family whose descendants spread out into Ohio, Indiana, and Illinois, in addition to Virginia. William, his younger brother and next in line to succession, moved to Kentucky and became progenitor of the southern branch of the Lampton family. Although the tale was full of exaggerations, the frontier Lamptons clung tightly to it, passing it on orally for generations.

The Lampton family story blew out of proportion in the 1820s after Lord John George Lambton (1792–1840) was raised to the peerage in 1828 with a barony and created First Earl of Durham and Viscount Lambton upon his retirement from the British Cabinet in 1834. "Radical Jack" Lambton, as the first earl was called, was a household word in the British realm of his day. "Radical Jack" was socially an aristocrat but politically an extreme democrat. He was an instigator of the Great Reform Bill (1832) and an influential governor general of Canada. As "Radical Jack" climbed to great prominence in British and Canadian politics, the American Lamptons, most especially the descendents of William and Samuel Lambton, began to discuss the old family legend with more intensity and concluded that the earldom and the vast Lambton holdings valued at more than $75 million had been usurped and rightfully belonged to the American Lamptons.

Family legend and Twain himself blamed the corruption of Lambton to Lampton on the idealism of the American progenitor's disdain of his noble heritage, on poor spelling of the early American Lamptons, and on their "messy hand" (handwriting) which melted the "b" into a "p" and thus Lampton.

Twain, Henry Watterson, James J. Lampton, and Jane Lampton Clemens were all obsessed with the old family story. Watterson and Twain, while in London together during the Tichborne claimant trial, investigated the claim of another Lampton cousin, Jesse Leathers, but found no legal substance to it.

The Earl of Durham legend of his Lampton kinfolk became a major theme in Twain's work. He recounted the legend in both his autobiographical dictation and his short essay "Mental Telegraphy" (1893). The legend's premise of a stolen noble heritage can be seen in *The Prince and the Pauper* (1882), *Adventures of Huckleberry Finn* (1885), *A Connecticut Yankee in King Arthur's Court* (1889), *The American Claimant* (1892), *Pudd'nhead Wilson* (1894), and the Howells-Twain collaborative play *Colonel Sellers as a Scientist* (written 1883).

Lucius M. Lampton

BIBLIOGRAPHY

Colville, Sir John. *Those Lambtons!: A Most Unusual Family*. London: Hodder and Stoughton, 1988.

Crump, Nannie-Mayes. *The Life Story of Walter M. Lampton*. Gulfport, Miss.: Dixie P, 1929.

Keith, Clayton, and Mary Lampton Reid. *Sketch of the Lampton Family in America, 1740–1914*. Magnolia, Miss.: Privately published, 1914.

Lambton, Arthur. *My Story*. London: Hurst and Blackett, 1924.

Lampton, Lucius M. "Hero in a Fool's Paradise." *Mark Twain Journal* 27.2 (Fall 1989): 1–56.

Reid, Stuart J. *Life and Letters of the First Earl of Durham*. London: Longmans, Green, 1906.

Varble, Rachel M. *Jane Clemens: The Story of Mark Twain's Mother*. Garden City, N.Y.: Doubleday, 1964.

See also: *American Claimant, The*; Lampton, James J.

Lampton, James J.
(1817–1887)

A Kentucky merchant who later became a St. Louis attorney, Major James J. Lampton was a favorite kinsman of Mark Twain and the prototype for Twain's character Colonel Mulberry Sellers of *The Gilded Age* (1873), *The American Claimant* (1892), and the play co-written with William Dean Howells, *Colonel Sellers as a Scientist* (written 1883). This first cousin of Twain's mother was born in 1817 in Adair County, Kentucky, the second of three children of Lewis and Jennie Morrison Lampton.

As a young man, Lampton moved to Hopkinsville, Kentucky, where he studied law and medicine. He married Elizabeth Webber and with her had four daughters and one son. By the early 1850s Lampton and family picked up and followed other Lampton relatives into Missouri. Upon his arrival, Lampton renewed his strong ties to Jane Lampton Clemens and her immediate family, standing in the relation of a second father to Twain.

Early in his writing career, as he contemplated ideas for his first extended work of fiction, Twain looked to Lampton, and in this tender-spirited, ever chivalrous visionary Twain perceived the essence of the American frontier of his day. Twain began secretly compiling family gossip about Lampton. In a letter written in mid-August 1870 he included a postscript to his sister Pamela Clemens Moffett, requesting all the gossip she could get out of Orion Clemens's wife Mollie about Lampton and his family, without her realizing that he wanted it. He wanted detailed information about them and proposed to make a novel around them, but not publish it for many years.

Twain did not, however, wait to publish that book but used the material in *The Gilded Age*. One of the most successful aspects of the novel was the character Colonel Sellers, directly inspired by Lampton's indestructible optimism. Twain perceived more than humor in Lampton's personality, in which he envisioned an American Don Quixote, and greatly resented any interpretation of Sellers that lacked Lampton's depth of character.

Twain's last encounter with Lampton was in January 1885 while in St. Louis on a speaking tour with George Washington Cable. The reunion left a pronounced impression on Twain, encouraging him to place the now white-headed Lampton back on paper. This culminated in the novel *The American Claimant*, in which Colonel Sellers becomes the Earl of Rossmore in the midst of other schemes.

Lampton died on 2 March 1887 due to a short bout with pneumonia. He died in such poverty that he owned no burial plot, so old friends allowed him temporary burial in theirs. More than a decade later he was moved to an unmarked grave in St. Peter's Cemetery in St. Louis, Missouri. No other blood relative, with perhaps the exception of Jane Lampton Clemens, so profoundly influenced Twain's literary development and imagination as did Lampton. As the inspiration for Colonel Sellers, Lampton provided Twain with the necessary ammunition for the creation of a memorable American fictional character.

Lucius M. Lampton

BIBLIOGRAPHY

Lampton, Lucius M. "Hero in a Fool's Paradise." *Mark Twain Journal* 27.2 (Fall 1989): 1–56.

Paine, Albert Bigelow. *Mark Twain: A Biography.* 3 vols. New York: Harper, 1912.

Turner, Arlin. "James Lampton, Mark Twain's Model for Colonel Sellers." *Modern Language Notes* 70 (December 1955): 592–594.

Watterson, Henry. *"Marse Henry": An Autobiography.* 2 vols. New York: George Doran, 1919.

See also: American Claimant, The; Colonel Sellers as a Scientist; Gilded Age, The; Sellers, Colonel

Landon, Melville D.
(1839–1910)

After nearly three decades as student, Union soldier, cotton planter, and secretary to the U.S. minister to Russia, Melville De Lancey Landon spent the remaining forty years of his life (1870–1910) as a successful journalist, lecturer, writer, and compiler of numerous anthologies.

In 1872 Landon published *Saratoga in 1901*, a collection of humorous newspaper columns by his alter ego, Eli Perkins. In his own copy, Twain wrote angry comments on twenty-seven pages, virulence underscored by his revised title: "Saratoga in 1891 or, The Droolings of an Idiot," penciled on the flyleaf. By 1891 Landon had published nine books, four of which liberally borrowed from the writings of Twain; by 1910 six more collections had been added. Although one book might appear under four different titles, this shows that Landon widely disseminated Twain's writings in various unauthorized ways.

Besides pirating lengthy selections, Landon published many other Twain remarks verbatim, thanks in part to his shorthand skills and his retentive memory. Landon also made Twain appear as a close friend, yet they only

saw each other on social occasions. In *Eli Perkins: Wit, Humor and Pathos* (1890), Landon included a spurious "How Eli Perkins Lectured in Pottsville." (From an article written by Mark Twain for *Harper's Magazine*.) If he knew about them, these eleven pages could easily have riled Twain, as could its preface, in which Twain was called one of the three greatest living American liars; Eli Perkins was the other two.

Mary Boewe

BIBLIOGRAPHY

Gribben, Alan. *Mark Twain's Library: A Reconstruction.* 2 vols. Boston: G.K. Hall, 1980.

Malone, Dumas, ed. *Dictionary of American Biography.* New York: Scribner, 1928–1937.

See also: Copyright; Literary Comedians

Lang, Andrew
(1844–1912)

A Victorian man-of-letters, Andrew Lang wrote on an extremely wide range of topics. A native Scot trained in classics, Lang won a scholarship to Oxford and was apparently destined for an academic career in that field. When he married in 1875, however, he left Oxford for London to begin a career as a journalist and critic. His interests drew him deeply into anthropology (*Magic and Religion; Myth, Ritual, and Religions*), folklore (*Custom and Myth* and many essays), and history (*History of Scotland From the Roman Occupation, The Maid of France, The Mystery of Mary Stuart, Pickle the Spy*). In addition, he wrote poetry, parody (*Old Friends, He*), translated the classics (Homer's *Illiad* and *Odyssey* and Theocritus), and edited numerous literary works (including the complete works of Sir Walter Scott, Robert Burns, and Charles Dickens). He is perhaps best remembered for his series of Christmas books, which include twelve volumes of selected fairy tales from around the world. As a critic, Lang praised several of Twain's works, especially *Huckleberry Finn* (1885). As a writer and scholar, he shared several interests with the American, including humor, Joan of Arc, and folklore. He co-edited *The World's Wit and Humor* (15 vols., 1905–1906) with Joel Chandler Harris. His research on Joan of Arc led him to publish *The Voices of Jeanne d'Arc* (1895), *The Story of Joan of Arc* (1906), and *The Maid of France* (1908). His interest in and knowledge of folklore led him to become president of a folklore society (1888–1892) and a society for psychical research (1910–1911). Lang met Twain twice in London.

Andrew Lang was one of the most influential writers and critics of the Victorian age. His support for Twain's work helped win a large audience abroad for the American.

Eric L. Montenyohl

BIBLIOGRAPHY

Dorson, Richard M. *The British Folklorists: A History.* Chicago: U of Chicago P, 1968.

Green, Roger Lancelyn. *Andrew Lang: A Critical Biography.* Leicester (England): Edmund Ward, 1946.

Lang, Andrew. "Andrew Lang on Mark Twain and Psychical Phenomena." *Illustrated London News* (7 May 1910): 684.

———. "Mark Twain and Mental Telegraphy." *Longman's Magazine* (June 1893): 185–187.

———. "Mr. Lang on the Art of Mark Twain." *Critic* 19 (25 July 1891): 45–46.

Langstaff, Eleanor de Selms. *Andrew Lang.* Boston: G.K. Hall, 1978.

Montenyohl, Eric. "Andrew Lang and the Fairy Tale." Ph.D. diss., Indiana U, 1986.

Langdon, Charles
(1849–1916)

Charles Jervis Langdon of Elmira, New York, known as "Charley," was the only son of Jervis and Olivia Lewis Langdon. As the younger brother of Olivia, he was also Mark Twain's brother-in-law.

Langdon was raised to take over his father's business interests in coal and lumber, which he did at the death of Jervis Langdon in 1870. Langdon also married Ida Clark that year. The couple had three children: Jervis, Julia, and Ida.

Upon completing his formal education, Langdon at eighteen was sent abroad by his family. He met Mark Twain aboard the *Quaker City.* Mark Twain remembered in his autobiography that he first saw his future wife's face in a miniature in her brother's stateroom. Whether Twain did or not, he first met Olivia in the flesh at the reunion of the *Quaker City* passengers at Christmastime in 1867. Mark Twain visited the Langdons in Elmira in August 1868. It was then Twain fell in love with Olivia and eventually married her in 1870.

It was through Charles Langdon that Mark Twain not only met his wife, but established his relationship with Elmira.

Resa Willis

BIBLIOGRAPHY

Jerome, Robert D., and Herbert A. Wisbey, Jr., eds. *Mark Twain in Elmira.* Elmira, N.Y.: Mark Twain Society, 1977.

See also: Elmira, New York; Langdon, Olivia Lewis; *Quaker City*

Langdon, Jervis
(1809–1870)

When Jervis Langdon died of stomach cancer on 6 August 1870, he left behind an all but inconsolable family that had recently come to include Samuel Clemens, his son-in-law of just six months. Although the two men knew each other for little more than two years, Langdon profoundly influenced the course of Clemens's early career, guiding him to what both considered a permanent position and life's work as a newspaper editor in Buffalo.

Langdon was born on 11 January 1809, the second child of Andrew and Eunice King Langdon of Vernon, New York, an upstate outpost in Oneida County. Following the early deaths of his father and his first stepfather, he was raised in the household of his mother's third husband, Jonathan Ford. In 1832 he married Olivia Lewis and subsequently worked as a storekeeper in a number of New York villages. By the time the couple moved to

Elmira in 1845 Langdon had begun to prosper in the lumber business. In Elmira that prosperity soared as he shifted to investments in coal, made his fortune, and participated prominently in abolitionist and other humanitarian causes. At his death he left his wife and three children—Susan, Olivia, and Charles—an estate valued at about $1 million.

Of his many benevolences to Clemens, none surpassed Langdon's acceptance of the Wild Humorist as his daughter Olivia's fiancé. Without ever overtly coercing him, Langdon went on to promote and finance Clemens's buying into an editorship at the Buffalo *Express*, thus establishing Mark Twain, at least for the time, as a fixture of a daily newspaper not too distant from Elmira, and he made a gift to the newlyweds of a substantial Buffalo home. Although their relationship was not without its ambivalences on both sides, Langdon provided Clemens a model of the successful, ethical man of the world, a standard against which to measure his own accomplishments and to sharpen his outrage at Gilded Age venalities. Clemens's eulogy to his father-in-law idealized him as "a very pure, and good, and noble Christian gentleman" (Buffalo *Express*, 8 August 1870).

Jeffrey Steinbrink

BIBLIOGRAPHY

Clemens, Samuel L. *Mark Twain's Autobiography.* Ed. Albert B. Paine. 2 vols. New York: Harper, 1924.

Jerome, Robert D., and Herbert A. Wisbey, Jr., eds. *Mark Twain in Elmira.* Elmira, N.Y.: Mark Twain Society, 1977.

"Jervis Langdon—His Life and Death." Buffalo *Express*, 8 August 1870.

Kaplan, Justin. *Mr. Clemens and Mark Twain.* New York: Simon & Schuster, 1966.

Paine, Albert Bigelow. *Mark Twain: A Biography.* 3 vols. New York: Harper, 1912.

See also: Buffalo, New York; Clemens, Olivia Langdon; Elmira, New York

Langdon, Olivia Lewis
(1810–1890)

The daughter of Edward and Olive Barnard Lewis, Olivia Lewis was born and grew up in Lenox, New York, and in 1832 married Jervis Langdon of nearby Vernon. The couple eventually settled in Elmira, where they raised three children, the second of whom, Olivia Louise, married Samuel Clemens in 1870.

During the provisional period of Clemens's engagement to her daughter, Mrs. Langdon expressed the family's apprehensions about his character in a letter to Mary Mason Fairbanks: ". . . What I desire is your opinion of him as a *man*; what kind of man he *has been*, and what the man he is now, or is to become" (1 December 1868; *Letters* 2:286). The Langdons went on to accept the probationer, and after her husband's death in 1870 Mrs. Langdon was a frequent presence in the Clemens's household, just as they were in hers during twenty years of summer visits to Elmira. Clemens's lifelong cordial affection for his mother-in-law was no protection against his investing $10,000 of her money in the doomed Paige typesetter.

Jeffrey Steinbrink

BIBLIOGRAPHY

Clemens, Samuel L. *Mark Twain's Letters, Volume 2 (1867–1868).* Ed. Harriet Elinor Smith and Richard Bucci. Berkeley: U of California P, 1990.

Jerome, Robert D., and Herbert A. Wisbey, Jr., eds. *Mark Twain in Elmira.* Elmira, N.Y.: Mark Twain Society, 1977.

Kaplan, Justin. *Mr. Clemens and Mark Twain.* New York: Simon & Schuster, 1966.

See also: Clemens, Olivia Langdon; Langdon, Jervis

Language

Since the 1890s most critics and readers have concurred in judging Mark Twain one of the great masters of the English language, perhaps even the inventor of the American language as a literary medium. At the same time, Twain has often paradoxically been considered a linguistic primitive, whose native language was Huck Finn's (as Van Wyck Brooks seemed to think). This uneasy dualism arises from the contrast between his evident skill *with* language and his apparent unsophistication *about* language, lacking as he did academic training in philology or classical languages. Yet Mark Twain's insight into language was complex and in many ways more modern than that of his contemporaries. Accordingly, the *theme* of language in his work rewards study equally with analysis of language as the *vehicle* of his writing.

Twain's understanding of language was at odds with the dominant philosophy of language in nineteenth-century America, which derived from the transcendentalists. For the latter, language was above all symbolic, important because it linked the individual with an object of thought. For Twain, however, language was always primarily a social phenomenon. Consider one of his rare general definitions of language: "What is the real function, the essential function, the supreme function, of language? Isn't it merely to convey ideas and emotions?" ("Spelling and Pictures" [1906]; *Writings* 28:319). The verb "convey" is the key here: language begins with a social requirement, the need to transfer inner content from one person to another. So while Emerson and Thoreau portrayed the poet as a solitary Adam naming creation anew, Twain's Adam in "Extracts from Adam's Diary" (1893) blissfully enjoys living in silence until Eve intrudes: language comes from other people. Because language is social, however, it is the site of struggles and disagreement. Twain's fiction generally reflects Talleyrand's ironic maxim that language was invented so we might conceal our thoughts. Throughout his career, in both humorous and serious works, Twain is most interested in the way language expresses differences, conflicts, and misunderstandings.

Language as a *theme* in Twain's writing develops through three roughly distinguishable modes: linguistic difference begins as comic, becomes ironic and tragic, and ends as metaphysically absurd, in a continuum that mirrors Twain's general progress from individual through social to cosmic themes. In the western writing that culminates with *Roughing It* (1872), tall tales, arguments, and clashes of dialect are used mainly for their humor. In the latter novel, for instance, the discord between fireman Scotty Briggs's dense slang and the theological jargon of the minister is wildly exaggerated for comic effect, but the conflict is playful—no one is "hurt." Likewise the western tall tale is a playful lie, part of an exuberant language game that no one takes too seriously. In the major novels of the 1880s and 1890s, however, different languages increasingly represent different ideologies and class interests, and their clash becomes deadly serious. In *A Connecticut Yankee in King Arthur's Court* (1889) Twain characterizes the mutual intolerance of democratic and feudal world views in large part through the linguistic differences between the vernacular Yankee and the courtiers whose archaic English reflects their mental inflexibility. *Pudd'nhead Wilson* (1894) focuses powerful irony on a society's failure to understand that labels like "slave" and "free" have no fixed meanings but instead are open to semantic negotiation; the novel's tragedy derives from its characters' acquiescence in what Twain elsewhere calls the "lie of silent assertion" that slavery is justifiable ("My First Lie" [1899]; *Writings* 23:161). Finally, in the fiction of Twain's last decade language itself is increasingly seen to be inherently flawed, an inadequate tool for communication in an absurd universe. Dialogue veers toward the surrealism of madhouse conversations in works like "The Refuge of the Derelicts" (1905) and *Christian Science* (1907), where characters use the same words but assign radically different meanings to them, producing mutual incomprehension. Twain even develops a theology of the Fall that depends on misunderstanding: because the word "death" was meaningless to Adam and Eve, they saw no reason to fear the thing it stood for. The Mysterious Stranger stories suggest that if humans and angels—or God—could converse, they would not understand each other.

There is no evidence that Twain took serious interest in the academic language study of his day, the Indo-European historical linguistics emanating from Germany or work in the philosophy and psychology of language by American scholars like William Dwight Whitney and William James. Four specific aspects of language, however, piqued his amateur interest and provoked a number of essays and other passages explicitly devoted to linguistic topics: the conventions of grammar and spelling; regional and historical differences in English; foreign languages; and the translanguages of dreaming and telepathy or "mental telegraphy."

Twain remained all his life a grammatical "prescriptivist," that is, one who believes that grammar should ordain and not merely describe actual usage. Most of the books about the English language that he owned were by verbal legislators like Richard Grant White and George Washington Moon, whose mission was to distinguish between correct and incorrect (or "vulgar") usage. As late as 1907 Twain would recall the grammar book by Samuel Kirkham he had studied in school, a text that summarized all of English grammar in thirty-three rules that students were expected to memorize. Twain would always claim to have forgotten the rules and to know grammar "by ear" only, and he observes in a half dozen passages that no one's grammar is perfect; nevertheless, he held himself and other writers accountable to the rules, frequently correcting grammar and usage in the margins of books he owned and condemning their authors' lapses from "good English." *Life on the Mississippi* (1883) records his scornful attack on the pilot Brown's impoverished grammar and his dismay at the "ain'ts" of even college professors in the South. When he returned to the United States in 1900 after a decade spent largely in Europe, he was struck by finding America "the ungrammatical nation" (Fatout 346). Only once was he willing to suspend the rules, when he defended General Grant against Matthew Arnold's charge that Grant's *Memoirs* were full of poor English—not because Twain disagreed with Arnold's strictures but because Grant's heroism made his shaky English a comparatively unimportant defect.

Always an excellent speller himself, Twain was more lenient toward spelling mistakes than poor grammar because the rules of English spelling seemed to him as chaotic as the rules of grammar were orderly. Off and on he would come out in favor of spelling reform; as early as 1866 he protested against the "crude, uncouth, inefficient, distressing orthography" we inherit from our ancestors (*Notebooks* 1:155). After the turn of the century, when the simplified spelling movement had gained such champions as Andrew Carnegie and Theodore Roosevelt, Twain frequently wrote and spoke on spelling reform. Like George Bernard Shaw, he ultimately came to believe that an accurately representative spelling of English would overtax the resources of the Roman alphabet, and he argued for adoption of a "phonographic" alphabet like the one Isaac Pitman had developed for shorthand ("A Simplified Alphabet" [1909]).

Twain's interest in the history of his own language rarely extended past the Renaissance; Middle and Old English were too difficult and alien to be of interest. Elizabethan diction, though, intrigued him enough that he took pages of notes on phrases he encountered in archaic books he read while working on *The Prince and the Pauper* (1882), while the bawdy dialogue of *1601* (1880) was inspired by his awareness of the much looser codes of propriety that governed familiar conversation in Shakespeare's day; he claimed that in *1601* he had "built a conversation that *could* have happened [and] used words such as *were* used at the time" (*Notebooks* 2:303). And at least one of the motives for *A Connecticut Yankee* was his desire to imitate and parody the fifteenth-century language of Malory's *Morte D'Arthur*. Twain lacked the scholarship that enabled James Russell Lowell to preface the

Biglow Papers with dauntingly learned etymologies of the Yankee vernacular, but he was an enthusiastic amateur observer of regional differences in the English of his own time. "Concerning the American Language" (1882), originally intended as a chapter for *A Tramp Abroad* (1880), contains his fullest discussion of differences in pronunciation, meaning, and idiom between British and American English, which Twain claims had evolved into different languages. His fascination and exasperation with the southern speech he rediscovered during his 1882 trip to New Orleans emerges in both his notebook entries and the passages on southern speechways in *Life on the Mississippi*.

The foreign language one immediately associates with Twain is, of course, German, his comic struggles with which are recorded in "The Awful German Language" (Appendix D of *A Tramp Abroad*) and elsewhere. (Less well known are his similar pieces on Italian, "Italian with a Grammar" [1904] and "Italian Without a Master" [1904].) But Twain's voyages from monolingual Missouri to the polyglot worlds of San Francisco, Hawaii, and Europe had a profound effect on his understanding of language. He was fascinated by the way language seemed to constrain thought: as a reporter in San Francisco he recorded as the "explanation" for the indifference of the Chinese to customs duties the lack of abstract terms for good and bad in their language, and during his 1866 trip to Hawaii he noted that the Hawaiian language had few words for virtue but many for vice. The failure of a French translator to preserve the humor of his "Jumping Frog" story suggested that world views cannot be transferred from one language to another. Twain delighted in examples of ludicrous translation, from broken English notices posted in European museums to the "Babu English" he heard from nonnative speakers of English in India; his introduction to a reissue of *The New Guide of the Conversation in Portuguese and English* (1883) celebrates the absurdity produced by a translator who was completely ignorant of his source language.

Foreign languages' power to befuddle was often funny, but it could also be frightening to Twain. "Be talking in foreign tongue & be suddenly let down by running out of words—hideous!" he writes during his German stay in 1878; there is no context that tells whether he is imagining a story idea or dreading a possible personal experience (*Notebooks* 2:98). In his later years Twain often fantasized about "foreign" languages that would have the reverse property: they would be immediately, intuitively comprehensible. The angelic characters in the Mysterious Stranger stories speak such languages among themselves; in "No 44," August is briefly allowed to experience the language of Forty-Four's world, in which spirit speaks to spirit. Likewise "My Platonic Sweetheart" (1898) imagines a dream language that speeds lovers' thoughts, with a "dream-vocabulary [that] shaves meanings finer and closer than do the world's daytime dictionaries" (*Writings* 27:296). The end point of this line of thought was Twain's sometime belief in the existence of "mental telegraphy," or telepathy. Unlike verbal language, mental telegraphy would permit "the communicating of mind with mind [to] be brought under command and reduced to certainty and system" ("Mental Telegraphy" [1891]; *Writings* 22:122). It is clear from these fantasies that Twain understood the relation between thought and language much as William James did when he postulated an undivided "stream of consciousness" underlying verbal thought: the dream language of "My Platonic Sweetheart," Twain says, allows the "vague and formless fog" of preverbal thought to be articulated infinitely faster than it ever can be by thinking conducted in ordinary language (*Writings* 27:297).

Language as a *vehicle* in Mark Twain's work has been the focus of much scholarship. Richard Bridgman, Henry Nash Smith, and Tony Tanner have all developed persuasive explanations of the connection between Twain's colloquial or vernacular voice and the values of his fiction; Tanner and Bridgman also locate Twain historically in the development of an American vernacular voice. William Gibson's chapter on Twain's style includes a superb general introduction to a variety of linguistic issues in Twain's writing.

To describe Mark Twain's "own" language is probably impossible: he was comfortable and competent in a range of styles, from western vernacular to the ceremonial, and typically he used whichever was appropriate to his circumstances. As a boy among boys he no doubt sounded like Tom Sawyer, but the letters and newspaper pieces he wrote in his teens leave no doubt that the formal standard English of the schoolroom and print shop was an idiom natural to him. Friends like William Dean Howells and Brander Matthews (the latter a professor of English at Columbia University) stressed, in their written appreciations of Twain, that his own language was always correct and eloquent; newspaper interviewers noted, sometimes in surprise, that he spoke a "very pure and literary English," in the words of a reporter for the Paris *Figaro* (Budd 49).

We do, however, have an accurate picture of Twain's written vocabulary, thanks to Frances Emberson and Robert Ramsay's extraordinarily well-documented study of his lexicon, which has not been superseded as the authoritative work in its field. "A Mark Twain Lexicon" is essential for anyone studying Twain's characteristic vocabulary, his knowledge and use of specialized jargons, and his coinages and nonce words. Like Shakespeare's, Twain's language reflects immersion in several distinct occupational dialects, particularly those of transportation and the print shop; taken altogether, Twain's language is a remarkably complete mirror of the cultural and material life of nineteenth-century America.

David R. Sewell

BIBLIOGRAPHY

Bridgman, Richard. *The Colloquial Style in America.* New York: Oxford UP, 1966.

Budd, Louis J., ed. "A Listing of and Selection from Newspaper and Magazine Interviews with Samuel L. Clemens, 1849–1910." *American Literary Realism* 10 (1977): i–xii, 1–100.

Clemens, Samuel L. *Mark Twain Speaking.* Ed. Paul Fatout. Iowa City: U of Iowa P, 1976.

———. *Mark Twain's Notebooks & Journals.* Ed. Frederick Anderson, et al. 3 vols. Berkeley: U of California P, 1975–1979.

———. *The Writings of Mark Twain.* Definitive Edition. 37 vols. New York: Gabriel Wells, 1922–1925.

Emberson, Frances Guthrie. "Mark Twain's Vocabulary: A General Survey." *University of Missouri Studies* 10.3 (1935): 1–53.

Gibson, William M. "Mark Twain's Style." *The Art of Mark Twain.* By Gibson. New York: Oxford UP, 1976. 3–32.

Ramsay, Robert L., and Frances Guthrie Emberson. "A Mark Twain Lexicon." *University of Missouri Studies* 13.1 (1938): 1–278.

Sewell, David R. *Mark Twain's Languages: Discourse, Dialogue, and Linguistic Variety.* Berkeley: U of California P, 1987.

Smith, Henry Nash. *Mark Twain: The Development of a Writer.* Cambridge Mass.: Harvard UP, 1962.

Tanner, Tony. "Mark Twain." *The Reign of Wonder: Naivety and Reality in American Literature.* By Tanner. Cambridge (England): Cambridge UP, 1965. 97–183.

See also: Dialect; French Language; German Language; Mental Telepathy/Extrasensory Perception; Style, Mark Twain's; Vernacular

Law

Early in his career Mark Twain discovered a comic and satiric staple in the law and began employing courtroom theatrics as a climactic device in his narrative fiction. His mockery of legal matters can largely be traced to his Whig-Liberal principles: as Louis Budd points out, he viewed the law as a bulwark against mob rule and encroachment upon property rights; and as Roger Salomon shows, in roughly the first half of his career he regarded legal reform as a force for long-term historical progress. Susan Gillman contends, moreover, that his earlier works are informed by an implicit trust in the law's capacity to distinguish the innocent from the guilty and to establish social, racial, and sexual identity. However, while Twain never lost his distrust of unfettered democracy, during his later years he lost faith in historical progressivism and came to perceive the law as a source of arbitrary and enslaving definitions of the self. Near the end of his life his pessimist credo included the belief that man's laws are hopelessly at odds with the laws of human nature and God.

In his western journalism of the early 1860s Twain pressed the law into comic service and ticked off legal abuses that he would excoriate for years to come. His famous "Petrified Man" hoax of October 1862 was calculated to worry a local judge with its account of an inquest on an eons-old fossilized corpse. In "A Rich Decision," a passage in his newspaper letter of 20 August 1863 (later revised as his 1870 sketch "The Facts in the Great Landslide Case"), he poked fun at an attorney whose confident prosecution of what in fact was a mock case failed to convince the judge, who pretended to find a providential dispensation in the avalanche that left, intact, one ranch on top of another. On a more serious note, in "Evidence in The Case of Smith vs. Jones" (1864) he burlesqued the testimony of perjured witnesses and sneered at trial by press and the masses' judicial sense. In addition, he scored his loss of interest in his San Francisco *Morning Call* against his editors' suppression of his story on lawless brutality against the Chinese, subject of "Disgraceful Persecution of a Boy" (1870) and "Goldsmith's Friend Abroad Again" (1870).

At the start of his eastern career Twain saw only the comic side of the dilemma posed by "Personal Habits of the Siamese Twins" (1869), a sketch in which the military, finding one twin guilty, concludes it must discharge both from custody. But in 1869 he launched his campaign against the evils of the jury system, which, he felt, empowered ignorance. In "A New Crime" (1870) and *The Gilded Age* (1873) he heaped his contempt on the insanity plea. He railed against society's sentimental coddling of felons in "Lionizing Murderers" (1872) and, later, in "Edward Mills and George Benton" (1880) and even found a place for this issue in *Tom Sawyer* (1876), where he blasts the villagers' petition for Injun Joe's

posthumous pardon. In addition, his impatience with the overcautious and dilatory ways of the law found expression in "The Judge's Spirited Woman" (1870), which applauds an act of vengeance committed in open court, and in *Roughing It* (1872), which celebrates the expeditious "justice" of Captain Ned Blakely, Brigham Young, and even the desperado Slade.

More than any other work, *The Gilded Age*, which Twain co-authored with Charles Dudley Warner, attests to his fascination with news accounts of celebrated trials, in this case the 1871–1872 prosecution of Laura D. Fair. The novel bristles with barbs directed at venal lawmakers, lowbrow jurors, the guile and theatricality of lawyers, the sentimental public, trial by newspaper, and the exploitation of the insanity plea, which sets the heroine at liberty in a sensational courtroom scene the likes of which Twain would repeat in later works, including *Tom Sawyer* and *Ah Sin*, the 1877 play on which he collaborated with Bret Harte.

Twain's explicit proposals for righting the law's wrongs lagged far behind his criticisms in number and vigor; two stand out in the 1870s. The October 1875 *Atlantic Monthly* carried his "The Curious Republic of Gondour," a description of a political utopia where voting power is proportional to a citizen's education and wealth, a reform that comes about only after a period of universal suffrage has placed power in the hands of a poor and stupid majority. Twain's concern for property rights lies at the heart of his lifelong crusade for copyright reform, begun in the 1870s and sustained by his conviction that intellectual property deserves full legal protection.

One of the clearest testimonials to his Whig principles is *The Prince and the Pauper* (1882). An embodiment of his belief that legal reform, working alongside human enlightenment, generated historical progress, the tale sends the little heir off to be schooled in the concrete effects of his country's harsh laws as it makes the usurper, Tom Canty, an agent of regal compassion and legal change. The upshot of Edward's experience is a reign characterized by its relative mildness. This vision of legal progress in Renaissance England is counterbalanced, however, by Twain's view of conditions on the home front. In *Life on the Mississippi* (1883) he recorded the lawlessness of the American South, where such antiquated customs as feuding and dueling lingered on, a consequence in part of the region's Walter Scott disease; and in his 1881 tale "The Second Advent" (1972) he presented a jury packed with religious zealots who, blind to the truth as the story's hardheaded journalists see it, find that an alleged virgin's birth is a Christ-returning miracle for Arkansas and the world.

Huckleberry Finn (1885) similarly presents the South as a legal backwater where illiterate and violent poor whites such as Pap bitterly resent "govment" interference in racial arrangements and their aristocratic brethren engage in honor-defending slaughter. Yet Huck's narrative suggests that the cowardice and conformity undergirding lawlessness are rooted deeply in human nature: as Sherburn, speaking for Twain, points out, the "average" person, northern or southern, is a coward, afraid to convict as juror, afraid not to join lynching parties. It is significant, too, that in what amounts to a trial scene in chapter 29 the villagers are balked in their effort to distinguish true from false Wilks heirs and propose at one point to drown all four claimants. Nor is Huck able to wriggle out from under his conscience, which has internalized the laws of slave property; he can work for Jim's freedom only after accepting his own damnation.

Twain taxed his Whig principles again in *A Connecticut Yankee* (1889), which takes for its premise the notion that, if the laws he transplanted from later epochs to sixth-century Britain did not in historical fact exist there, still worse forms of law occupied their place, a premise that underwrites the historical-progressivist position. Hank Morgan emerges as a self-styled agent of an accelerated legal progress, and the novel repeats the strategy of *The Prince and the Pauper* in sending the king abroad in his land to experience firsthand its laws' ef-

fects. In *Yankee*, however, Twain pins his own and his hero's hopes partly to human nature (at any rate, to the apparently inextinguishable "manhood" that repeatedly reignites the Yankee's confidence), partly to "training," the various forms of conditioning that can produce a vicious Morgan le Fay but can also create a new, improved Arthurian. While *Yankee* did give Twain opportunities to take potshots at game acts, tax inequities, protective tariff legislation, etc., it wound its way into a thematic stalemate. On the one hand, brutal laws are momentarily amended, and the large sweep of legal amelioration from medieval to modern times is underscored. On the other hand, the narrative links progress in knowledge to wholesale destruction, implies that man is recalcitrant as an object of training and cowardly in the face of the church's legal juggernaut, and moves, as Salomon notes, from darkness to darkness, adumbrating Twain's cyclical theory of history, with its periods of legal tyranny, defined in *The Secret History of Eddypus* (1972), a product of 1901–1902. Hank's dream of a republic remains a dream.

Twain's later works point to particular and generic legal problems. The balloonists' get-rich-quick scheme in *Tom Sawyer Abroad* (1893–1894) is foiled by tariff laws, while in both *Tom Sawyer, Detective* (1896) and "Tom Sawyer's Conspiracy" (1969), each with a climactic trial scene, Twain burlesques legal detection. More important, *Pudd'nhead Wilson* (1894) dramatizes the law as little more than an instrument of entrenched social prejudice. Law functions in Dawson's Landing to codify and uphold arbitrary definitions of race, blinking at the code duello (which is a higher law), and, in sorting out the innocent and the guilty, condemns the former to misery and ratifies the slaveholding status quo. Worse, "Those Extraordinary Twins" (1894) indicates that at times law cannot assign and contain guilt or avoid punishing the innocent; and as an 1897 story, "Wapping Alice" (1981), shows, it cannot always distinguish between sexes. Nor can it check the lynching frenzy he deplored in "The United States of Lyncherdom" (1901).

Due process can unjustly condemn a Dreyfus, however, and, as *Personal Recollections of Joan of Arc* (1896) recalls, it could burn a saint.

Scholars continue to debate the depth and causes of Twain's pessimism, and their disagreements are complicated by contradictions between his works' theoretical implications and his personal practice. Thus he railed in 1907 against the legal age of sexual consent and in the following year argued in "Letters from the Earth" (1962) that all of man's laws, and particularly those forbidding fornication, adultery, and polyandry, fly in the face of God-given human nature. Thus his professional life is punctuated by suits, actual or threatened, against his enemies, even when his works imply that his confidence in the law had collapsed. As Hamlin Hill aptly remarks, he was a man who sued as instinctively as he wrote; certainly his practical engagement in legal issues found its way into his writings from his career's opening to its close.

Earl F. Briden

BIBLIOGRAPHY

Budd, Louis J. *Mark Twain: Social Philosopher.* Bloomington: Indiana UP, 1962.

Foner, Philip S. *Mark Twain: Social Critic.* New York: International Publishers, 1958.

French, Bryant Morey. *Mark Twain and "The Gilded Age."* Dallas: Southern Methodist UP, 1965.

Gillman, Susan. *Dark Twins: Imposture and Identity in Mark Twain's America.* Chicago: U of Chicago P, 1989.

Hill, Hamlin. *Mark Twain: God's Fool.* New York: Harper & Row, 1973.

McKeithan, D.M. *Court Trials in Mark Twain and Other Essays.* The Hague: Martinus Nijhoff, 1958.

Salomon, Roger B. *Twain and the Image of History.* New Haven, Conn.: Yale UP, 1961.

See also: "Curious Republic of Gondour, The"; "Evidence in the Case of Smith vs. Jones, The"; "Facts in the Great Landslide Case, The"; Politics

Leary, Katy
(1856–1934)

Katy Leary's relationship to the Clemens family developed over thirty years of employment from simple, Irish maid to trusted companion. She was born Catherine Leary in Elmira, New York, on 17 March 1856. When she was twenty-four, she became Mrs. Clemens's maid. Mrs. Clemens directed her reading and a program of self-education. Katy lived with the family in Hartford, also during their summers in Elmira, and she traveled abroad with them. She was left to care for Susy and Jean Clemens when Mark Twain, Livy, and Clara went on the round-the-world lecture tour in 1895–1896. When Susy became ill, Katy opened the Hartford house and nursed her until her death. She was with Mrs. Clemens when she died in Florence in 1903 and had the responsibility of telling Mark Twain of Jean's tragic death. After Mark Twain's death in 1910 she ran a boardinghouse in New York City until she returned to Elmira, where she died on 5 October 1934.

Herbert A. Wisbey, Jr.

BIBLIOGRAPHY

Agan, Robert E. "Katie Leary: She's Always There. . . ." *Mark Twain Society Bulletin* 2.2 (June 1979).

Lawton, Mary. *A Lifetime with Mark Twain.* New York: Harcourt Brace, 1925.

Leathers, Jesse M.
(1846–1887)

Jesse Madison Leathers was a major personality influencing Mark Twain during his most productive years as a literary craftsman. Leathers and Twain thought they were third cousins, although the actual relationship was more distant. Leathers was the eldest son of the eldest son of the eldest daughter of Samuel Lampton of Culpeper County, Virginia. This Samuel Lampton was a first cousin of Twain's great grandfather, William Lampton. However, both Leathers and Twain mistakenly believed their great grandparents were brothers, scions, and heirs of the Earl of Durham.

Leathers was born in 1846 in Mercer County, Kentucky. He was the oldest son of the four children of John W. Leathers and his wife Martha. John Leathers died before his son Jesse's fourth birthday. This death forced Martha and her children to seek refuge within the Shaker Colony in Pleasant Hill, Kentucky, where "Madison" grew up.

Soon after the outbreak of the Civil War, Jesse, only fifteen years old but pretending to be eighteen, volunteered for the Kentucky 10th Infantry Company D. He fought for the Union valiantly, receiving chest wounds at the battle of Chickamauga. From these wounds he recovered. However, his contracting of tuberculosis in 1862 would alter his life forever and eventually result in his death. Throughout the rest of his life he would drift in and out of GAR (Grand Army of the Republic) hospitals, seeking recovery from the debilitating effects of this pulmonary disease.

After the war Jesse returned to Kentucky and found employment with insurance businesses in Louisville and Lexington. He soon became obsessed with the Lampton family legend about the "Durham Estate" wrongfully usurped from the Virginia Lamptons three generations earlier. In September 1875 Leathers first wrote Twain about his desire to travel to England with hopes of reclaiming the extensive Lambton estates, titles, and collieries. This letter sparked an almost immediate response from Twain in Hartford and initiated a twelve-year relationship between the two. Leathers continually sought money from Twain, pleading with him to furnish the money for the trip to England and pledging to divide the Durham Estate among the Lampton heirs.

As his tuberculosis worsened, Leathers moved to New York City, staying alternately in hotels and charity hospitals. His correspondences with Twain continued. In March 1881 Twain began encouraging Leathers to write his autobiography and submit it to publisher James R. Osgood for use in a magazine. Leathers soon forwarded Osgood a 12,000-word manuscript entitled "An American Earl,"

which told the sad story of his life to age fourteen. Although Twain believed that the autobiography "would make a cast-iron dog laugh" (Twain to Osgood, 7 March 1881), Osgood and W.D. Howells deemed the manuscript unpublishable and returned it to Leathers.

In spite of alcoholic binges and progressing consumption, Leathers was an energetic man with a dictatorial manner. He wore a sombrero with a rattlesnake skin for a hatband and carried a pair of six shooters in a leather belt. Despite attempts to keep Leathers personally at a distance, Twain was captivated by this colorful visionary. For the remainder of his life, Leathers worked off and on as a freelance reporter. In the winter of 1886–1887 his health worsened, forcing him to go to Charity Hospital on Blackwell's Island in New York. Leathers died there on 6 February 1887 of complications related to tuberculosis and was buried in Cypress Hill National Cemetery in Brooklyn, New York.

Jesse Leathers, more than any other personality, heightened Twain's fascination with the world's claimants, from Shakespeare to General Washington's favorite body servant, and made the claimant concept a central theme throughout Twain's work. Not only would the characters of the Duke of Bridgewater and the late Dauphin be directly based on his grandiose claim to the Earldom of Durham, but also the concept of Twain's *The American Claimant* (1892) and the collaborative play with Howells entitled *Colonel Sellers as a Scientist* (written 1883) were all based on Leathers's lifelong quest for that earldom. Indeed, had Leathers not left behind three daughters, Twain fully intended to use his name unchanged in his claimant novel. Liking the rhythm of the name Jesse Leathers, Twain altered it only slightly, giving his "rightful" Earl of Rossmore the name Simon Lathers. Upon learning of his death, Twain reflected, "There was something very striking, and pathetically and grotesquely picturesque (from a magazine point of view) about this long, and hopeless, and plucky, and foolish, and majestic fight of a foghorn against a fog. (Or, reverse that figure, perhaps.)" (Twain to Chapman, 15 February 1887).

Lucius M. Lampton

BIBLIOGRAPHY

Chapman, John W. "The Germ of a Book: A Footnote on Mark Twain." *Atlantic Monthly* 150 (December 1932): 720–721.

Clemens, Samuel L. *Mark Twain-Howells Letters: The Correspondence of Samuel L. Clemens and William D. Howells, 1872–1910.* Ed. Henry Nash Smith and William M. Gibson. 2 vols. Cambridge, Mass.: Harvard UP, 1960.

———. *Mark Twain's Letters to His Publishers, 1867–1894.* Ed. Hamlin Hill. Berkeley: U of California P, 1967.

Lampton, Lucius M. "Hero in a Fool's Paradise." *Mark Twain Journal* 27.2 (Fall 1989): 1–56.

Watterson, Henry. *"Marse Henry": An Autobiography.* 2 vols. New York: George Doran, 1919.

See also: American Claimant, The; Colonel Sellers; Lambton Family of Durham

Lecky, William Edward Hartpole
(1838–1903)

Historian and essayist of Scottish descent, William Edward Hartpole Lecky was born in Ireland in 1838. At the age of seventeen he entered Trinity College, Dublin, where independent private reading intensified his interest in historical research and writing. By 1861 he had published three unsuccessful volumes; undaunted, Lecky continued his research on the Middle Ages. The result was his two-volume *History of the Rise and Influence of the Spirit of Rationalism in Europe* (1865), both a critical and popular success. Four years later (1869) his two-volume *History of European Morals from Augustus to Charlemagne* appeared; considered a sequel to *Rationalism*, it was equally successful though criticized by conservative thinkers.

In 1871 Lecky married Elizabeth van Dedem, "maid of honour" to Queen Sophia of the Netherlands; London was their residence thereafter. Lecky's magnum opus, the eight-volume *A History of England in the Eigh-*

teenth Century, was published between 1878 and 1890. A discursive two-volume *Democracy and Liberty* came out in 1896. During his last years Lecky revised earlier work, published articles, lectured, and represented Dublin University in Parliament, where his very tall, thin, slightly stooped figure was well-known. His heart weakened by influenza in 1901, Lecky died suddenly in his study on 22 October 1903. His widow published a book of his essays (1908) and a lengthy life-in-letters memoir (1909).

Having doubtlessly used the 1874 edition of Lecky's *History of European Morals* (now housed at the Mark Twain Foundation in Perry, Missouri) during the seventies and even later, on 2 March 1900 Mark Twain was a dinner guest at the Lecky's home, 38 Onslow Gardens. This occasion may have rekindled Twain's interest in Lecky's writings, for the 1900 revised edition of *European Morals* became a part of the Quarry Farm library in 1902. Inscribed by Susan Crane, the first volume contains marginalia written by Mark Twain in the summer of 1903 during his Elmira visit. (That book's influence on Mark Twain's later writings, particularly "A Dog's Tale," *What Is Man?*, and *The Mysterious Stranger*, has been analyzed in scholarly detail.)

However, Twain's keen interest in Lecky began long before 1900, as suggested. Biographer Albert Bigelow Paine wrote that Mark Twain and Theodore Crane (d. 1889) read and discussed Lecky's writing "in original and unorthodox ways," but Mark Twain's marginalia was "not always quotable in the family circle," he added. In the Quarry Farm volumes now housed at Elmira College, there are numerous notes and underlinings, evidence of Mark Twain's running arguments with Lecky and of Lecky's influence on Mark Twain's thought. Of special interest is the 1884 edition of Lecky's *Rationalism*, which Mark Twain read in the summer of 1885 when his *Connecticut Yankee* (1889) was in its earliest stages. Chapters 1 and 2 of *Rationalism* discuss magic and miracle, emphasizing witchcraft, superstition, the supernatural, and their effects on the savage mind. "Terror is everywhere the beginning of religion" is the first sentence Mark Twain underlined in that book, and for *Connecticut Yankee* he borrowed illustrative details from Lecky, including descriptions of instruments of torture. *Connecticut Yankee* also contains specific material from *European Morals*, Mark Twain's acknowledged source for what he says about hermits and stylites, and Roman laws. The many large capital C's scattered in the margins of the first two volumes of Lecky's *History of England* mark portions of the text that concern the role of the Roman Catholic Church in medieval society; Mark Twain used these ideas, speaking through Yankee Hank Morgan. In fact, the Yankee is exactly the kind of power usurper described by Lecky: one who converts the terror produced by "some great calamity" (the eclipse in *Connecticut Yankee*) "into anger against an alleged sorcerer" (throwing rival Merlin in prison), and then takes "signal vengeance upon those who have offended him" (threatening to turn disgruntled citizens into horses), thereby increasing "the sense of his own importance" (by promising a second miracle after attending to "affairs of state") (*Rationalism* 1:42).

In "Thoughts on History" (1908) Lecky cautioned that novice historians make "a fatal and very common error" when they judge the past by the moral standards of their own age; this is precisely what Mark Twain did, sometimes to comic effect, in *Connecticut Yankee*. Lecky also recognized that "great events often acquire their full power over the human mind only when they have passed through the transfiguring medium of the imagination." In their different ways, both Mark Twain and Lecky succeeded in imaginatively enlivening the past from the vantage point of the prosaic present.

Mary Boewe

BIBLIOGRAPHY

Aspiz, Harold. "Lecky's Influence on Mark Twain." *Science and Society* 26 (Winter 1962): 15–25.

Baetzhold, Howard G. *Mark Twain and John Bull: The British Connection.* Bloomington: Indiana UP, 1970.

Blair, Walter. *Mark Twain & Huck Finn.* Berkeley: U of California P, 1960. 135–144.

Davis, Chester L. "Mark Twain's Religious Beliefs, as Indicated by Notations in His Books." *Twainian* 14 (May-June 1955): 1–4; (July-August 1955): 1–4; (September-October 1955): 1–4; (November-December 1955): 1–4.

Gribben, Alan. *Mark Twain's Library: A Reconstruction.* 2 vols. Boston: G.K. Hall, 1980.

Lecky, William Edward Hartpole. *Historical and Political Essays.* London: Longmans, Green, 1908.

———. *A History of England in the Eighteenth Century.* 6 vols. New York: Appleton, 1887–1888.

———. *A History of European Morals from Augustus to Charlemagne.* 2 vols. New York: Appleton, 1874.

———. *A History of the Rise and Influence of the Spirit of Rationalism in Europe.* 2 vols. New York: Appleton, 1884.

Rogers, Rodney O. "Twain, Taine, and Lecky: The Genesis of a Passage in *A Connecticut Yankee.*" *Modern Language Quarterly* 34 (December 1973): 436–447.

Salomon, Roger B. *Twain and the Image of History.* New Haven, Conn.: Yale UP, 1961. 98–102.

See also: *Connecticut Yankee in King Arthur's Court, A*; History; Medievalism; Morgan, Hank; Philosophy

Lecturer

While this article focuses on Mark Twain's career as a paid speaker, it should be noted that Twain spoke publicly on a variety of occasions and for a variety of reasons throughout his life. Sometimes he appeared as an honored guest, sometimes in honor of others, at benefits, or when some pressing cause or issue stirred his prodigious conscience. Twain appeared so often before a listening audience that it is fair to say only that our own literate bias and the material endurance of the written text lead us to characterize him more often as a writer than a speaker. Twain maintained and refined fairly exacting distinctions between oral and written delivery, and even after his major successes as an author he gave and took pleasure by personally animating his texts before crowded halls. Constituting a major source of income throughout much of his lifetime, Twain's occupation as platform speaker clearly shaped his attitudes toward language, audience, and the function of his art within the immediate social context of its production. Any assessment of Twain's standing among or reception by his contemporaries would be incomplete without a recognition of his role as speaker, for it is in this capacity that the man and his work became uniquely combined in the public mind.

Though Twain is known to have addressed an audience on a few occasions before his first organized lecture in San Francisco on 2 October 1866, this date may fairly be said to mark the beginning of his professional speaking career. The world tour undertaken in 1895 and 1896 to pay off his staggering business losses may be said to mark the end of that career. Twain ceased after this tour to look to lecturing as a source of income and undertook no more organized tours. He continued to speak publicly until less than a year before his death, but evidently refused payment or donated his services to charitable causes.

No attempt can be made here to duplicate the detailed accounts of Twain's lecture tours found in both Paul Fatout's *Mark Twain on the Lecture Circuit* (1960) and Fred W. Lorch's *The Trouble Begins at Eight: Mark Twain's Lecture Tours* (1968). However, Twain's long speaking career may be roughly divided among four phases for the purpose of discussing its general characteristics. The first phase, beginning upon his return to California from the Sandwich Islands in 1866 and ending with the tour of 1868–1869 in the Midwest and East, covers the period during which Twain established himself as a speaker, managed his own bookings and itinerary, and developed important features of the Mark Twain persona. The second phase, beginning in the fall of 1869 and continuing through the winter of 1874, includes Twain's association with James Redpath's Lyceum Bureau as well as two short but triumphant tours in Britain arranged by George Dolby, manager of Charles Dickens's earlier reading tour in the United States. This phase is marked by Twain's rise to international fame as the author of *Innocents Abroad*

(1869) and *Roughing It* (1872), a concomitant increase in demand for his services as speaker, and a synergetic interplay of these careers that resulted in a period of both financial stability and unprecedented publicity. The third phase begins roughly from the end of the second and culminates in 1884–1885 with a joint reading tour with George Washington Cable. With the exception of the Cable tour, Twain eschewed organized tours during this period, turned more and more to readings from completed works, or works-in-progress, rather than seasonally prepared lectures, and shifted energies to his writing that he had previously expended on the platform. Following the reading tour with Cable, Twain lectured only occasionally in the years leading up to the world tour, his last, undertaken from July 1895 to August 1896. This final reading tour arose out of Twain's desire to pay off his debts from the failure of the Webster Publishing Company and the ill-fated Paige typesetter as well as a number of other unsuccessful ventures.

Twain's formidable success on the platform raises old questions about the extent to which an individual may be said to be a product of his times or, conversely, an active shaper of the culture he inhabits. Certainly, precedents existed for the sort of humorous lectures Twain presented in 1866 in San Francisco and throughout the California/Nevada mining territory. Before his departure for the Sandwich Islands, Twain had heard Artemus Ward speak in Virginia City, and, certainly, Ward exerted an influence on Twain's manner of presentation, comparisons being often invoked by the press. Specifically, Ward's deadpan manner seems to have stuck with Twain; that is, the art of delivering comic material without, apparently, the least consciousness of its humorous content. Twain's use of Ward as the subject of a not uncritical lecture after Ward's death further suggests both Twain's debt to Ward and his desire to surpass this early model.

However, as important as any particular predecessor to the formation of Twain's platform identity may have been the peculiar status of the platform itself. The most frequent criticism of Twain throughout his early lecturing career, particularly in the small towns of the Midwest and East, was that while he entertained, he failed to instruct sufficiently. This may be partly accounted for by the fact that speakers like Twain were often booked by local library associations, debating clubs, and various civic improvement organizations that had their origins in the lyceum movement begun in the mid-1820s. This movement had as its original goal the dissemination of practical knowledge among the inhabitants of towns and villages and the supplementation of a public education system that was often marginal or nonexistent; and though the character of these lyceums had changed considerably over forty years, broadening its scope to include subjects ranging from phrenology to women's rights to humorous disquisitions on travel, there still lingered a culturally powerful imperative for practical and moral instruction. After the Civil War funny men like Twain, Artemus Ward, and Petroleum V. Nasby drew large crowds and filled local coffers while more staid speakers often incurred losses for their sponsors. Appearing in Keokuk, Iowa, in 1867, only a few months after Ralph Waldo Emerson, Twain was the stronger draw. But if economics reflected the fact that the public taste was turning away from instruction and toward entertainment, ambivalence toward this shift was strong, and Twain seems to have set himself above the average run of humorists by exploiting rather than dismissing this cultural schizophrenia. Despite the occasional criticism, Twain seems to have ridden the line between entertainment and instruction rather well. Certainly, Twain's own yardstick for success was his ability to incite laughter, and it may be that he wished ultimately to dissolve the distinction between pleasure and profit that seemed always to haunt the boys of his fictional creations. It appears more accurate, however, to say that the Twain persona emerged in all of its mature complexity against the backdrop of this tension.

Changes in technique and material from one engagement to the next attest to both the evolution of this persona and Twain's acute awareness of the difference between one audience and another. Those occasions in which he expounded on the art of speaking, as in "How to Tell a Story" (1895), support the conclusion that Twain's genius as a speaker lay in his ability to gauge anew on every occasion the appropriate application of past platform experience. Unpreparedness, on the one hand, or dogged loyalty to formulae, on the other, were equally inimical to platform success. In this regard, much has yet to be said about the ways in which Twain's rhetorical sensitivity on the platform may have shaped and reshaped his protean politics; made possible the degree to which, even late in life, he was able to absorb or embrace new perspectives; and informed the quality of moral contingency that pervades novels such as *Huckleberry Finn* (1885) and *Pudd'nhead Wilson* (1894).

Though he complained often of the hardships of the lecture circuit, it afforded Twain a remarkably complementary supplement to his income as a writer. He could generate cash quickly through lecturing without obligating himself for long periods of time. Both after his return from the Sandwich Islands and before his departure on the *Quaker City* excursion, lecturing supplied Twain with the funds to realize his travel ambitions. Moreover, though he never apparently stooped to explicit sales pitches, Twain enjoyed from the platform a remarkable position from which to promote his books. The reading tour with Cable in 1884 and 1885 was clearly meant to boost sales of the forthcoming *Huckleberry Finn*, a novel that Twain had a double interest in, since it would be published by his own Charles L. Webster Company. Ten years later, after the failure of this company, Twain lectured his way back to financial health (with the help of Henry Huttleston Rogers's astute money management) via an around-the-world reading tour that took him to Australia, Africa, and India and supplied the experiences for *Following the Equator* (1897). Such independence stands in contrast to the alienating drudgeries suffered by the likes of Melville and Hawthorne in their quests for financial security, and the self-reliance afforded Twain by his lecturing career, however hard-won, may have insulated him from the more onerous aspects of a literary career. It may even be conjectured that Twain's sometimes chillingly conservative social and economic views were fostered by his own unique ability to make his efforts pay on a moment's notice.

Twain's shift in the 1880s toward "readings" of passages from his published works, or works in progress, reflects the growing importance of this material to his audience as well as the increasing thinness of the didactic imperative that had haunted the earlier lyceum tours. Free of the need for preparing an advertisable lecture for a season's tour, Twain could draw on the known and growing quantity of past successes. The audience's familiarity with Twain's corpus, which had been a liability to the struggling newcomer striving for novel effect, now became an asset. Listeners anticipated and were delighted by Twain's renderings of favorite passages. Interestingly, however, Twain refined more clearly than ever before the distinction between the written and the spoken. "Readings" were not actually read, but were committed to memory and, as Twain put it, "transformed . . . into flexible talk, with all their obstructing preciseness and formalities gone out of them for good." The faces in the audience, rather than a text, supplied Twain with the vital clues that informed his timing. Working from memory, he was free to ply the ineffable links between speaker and listener. By this method he preserved even in his most studied performances an engagement with his living audience, delivering to it and gathering from it that which can only be achieved in the risky exchange of the moment.

Despite the fact that Twain's speaking career is clearly entangled with the economic, social, and professional exigencies of his life, no account of that career can overlook the sheer pleasure Twain received from his platform appearances. To be sure, he played a

risky game with his audiences, but it seems not to have been in him to play it safe. The agonies he suffered after the Whittier Birthday Dinner Speech (1877), his fear, confessed to Cable, that he was allowing himself "to be a mere buffoon,"—these and other instances of self-doubt attest that Twain's sense of platform mastery was only as strong as his last performance, as ephemeral as the human voice itself. But such contingency was the price of his oral art, and he seems to have paid it willingly, even into his old age when respect and fame might have demanded less.

David Barrow

BIBLIOGRAPHY

Budd, Louis J. *Our Mark Twain: The Making of His Public Personality*. Philadelphia: U of Pennsylvania P, 1983.

Clemens, Samuel L. *Mark Twain Speaking*. Ed. Paul Fatout. Iowa City: U of Iowa P, 1976.

Fatout, Paul. *Mark Twain on the Lecture Circuit*. Bloomington: Indiana UP, 1960.

Lorch, Fred W. *The Trouble Begins at Eight: Mark Twain's Lecture Tours*. Ames: Iowa State UP, 1968.

See also: Cable, George Washington; "How to Tell a Story"; Humor; Orality; Rhetorical Forms; Whittier Birthday Dinner Speech

Legacy

As Ernest Hemingway's oft quoted remark would have it, "All modern American literature comes from one book by Mark Twain called *Huckleberry Finn* . . . it's the best book we've had. All American writing comes from that." What Hemingway means, this writer believes, is partly that *Adventures of Huckleberry Finn* (1885) represents a clear break from the elevated British diction that had largely dominated American literature and partly that it puts a quintessentially "American" spin on the question of self vs. society.

The rub, of course, is that even a savvy claim can be so sweeping as to be virtually useless. On the other side of every coin arguing for an *all*, there is a nagging sense of a *none*; and this is doubly true for *Adventures of Huckleberry Finn*. Consider, for example, the question of southwestern humor. Critics agree that much of Twain's vision was shaped by the generation of frontier humorists who preceeded him: Joseph G. Baldwin, Augustus Baldwin Longstreet, Artemus Ward, Josh Billings. As a printer's devil, the young Samuel Clemens often set the type of their stories, "taking in" the shape and ring of native speech patterns through his fingers. The story is as old as Benjamin Franklin and, with some variations, as persistent as the would-be journalist Walter Whitman or newspapermen from Stephen Crane to Ernest Hemingway.

In short, Twain knew the central truths of southwestern humor—namely, that its art was in its poker-faced "telling" and that in its most characteristic incarnations, a good joke maimed people while a great prank killed them. Twain raised both elements to heights they had not known before, and in the process he became a national writer rather than a local colorist. But if Twain survived, one could argue that the legacy of his southwestern humor did not. Granted, a case might be made for, say, Garrison Keillor's saga of Lake Wobegon, especially if one emphasizes its darker, more satiric dimensions, or for a Roy Blount, Jr., but the larger truth is that the humor of small towns and western places largely ended when Twain did—that is, in 1910.

Not only did the hot center of American humor move to George Ade's Chicago or more impressively, to the New York of Harold Ross's *New Yorker*, but the characteristic boast of the ring-tailed roarer—namely, that he was half horse, half alligator, and that he could whup anybody in ol' Kentuck—gave way to "boasts" of a very different sort. From Charlie Chaplin's Little Tramp to Robert Benchley's Little Man, from Philip Roth's Alexander Portnoy to Woody Allen's assorted personae, the *cri de coeur* most frequently sounded was one that fused confusion, neurosis, and abject weakness into an extended *kvetch*. The effect turns the elaborate boasts so dear to the heart

of nineteenth-century humorists on their heads, and the result is a Chaplin who tilts against machinery in *Modern Times*, a Benchley who jousts (unsuccessfully) with his necktie or the directions for assembling a bicycle, a Woody Allen who worries that "the universe is merely a fleeting idea in God's mind—a pretty uncomfortable thought particularly if you've just made a down payment on a house." As Alexander Portnoy puts it in a speech that characterizes the "new steerage," the sons of immigrants must endure (Roth 117–118).

Anti-heroes thrive in the modern world, where a Leopold Bloom is more enduring (and endearing) than his classical model and where elaborate accounts of weakness play better than exaggerated sagas of strength. To be sure, in a stray episode of *Adventures of Huckleberry Finn* (published originally in *Life on the Mississippi* [1883]) Huck stumbles onto the comic battle between the Pet Child of Calamity and Sudden Death and General Desolation, and presumably he learns how cheap "tall talk" often is. Certainly, Twain himself meant to poke fun at the very traditions that had nurtured him at the beginning of his career, which is simply to point out that the days of the southwestern boast were numbered, even in 1885.

In roughly similar ways Twain's considerable talents as a travel writer—from *The Innocents Abroad* (1869) and *Roughing It* (1872) to *A Tramp Abroad* (1880) and *Following the Equator* (1897)—have not survived as an influence. For example, a piece by William Zinsser (in the 26 August 1990 New York *Times Book Review* and part of his forthcoming book on travel) acknowledges generous debts to S.J. Perelman, but it contains nary a reference to Twain. It is not merely that subscription books, with their assorted "filler" and healthy appetite for statistical tables, are no longer part of the American landscape or that we no longer have the patience required for bulky reading (no one, after all, ever accused the best-selling James Michener of writing a thin tome), but rather that Twain's characteristic posture in these books often seems dusty, altogether antique. What remains, in short, are the marvelously inventive short stories Twain folded between the covers of his "travel books": "Jim Blaine and His Grandfather's Ram" and "Bemis and the Bull" from *Roughing It*; "Jim Baker's Blue Jay Yarn" from *A Tramp Abroad*.

There are, of course, certain contemporary American fictionists who make much of donning Twain's mantle, perhaps no one more insistent about this than Kurt Vonnegut, Jr. In *Slaughterhouse-Five* (1969), for example, the narrator (who sounds suspiciously like Vonnegut himself) adopts the posture of the wise codger, a make-shift combination of Will Rogers and Mark Twain. "You can believe *me*," the framing narrator declares, and many in the Vonnegut cult of those giddy days did precisely that—including his mixture of tall tale and science fiction that was Tralfamodore, the Children's Crusade that Billy Pilgrim mounts, and the half-shrug, half-valedictory "So it goes" that becomes the novel's refrain. But like so much in Vonnegut, the result is finally sentimental, intellectually mushy, in a word, soft. At its best, Twain's vision is made of sterner, much richer stuff.

The more typical case, of course, is that of a critic out to turn juxtaposition into an instance of parallelism and then into a case of "influence." That is precisely what Cushing Strout does in his recent study of the correspondences linking Twain's *A Connecticut Yankee in King Arthur's Court* (1889) with E.L. Doctorow's *Ragtime* (1975). As Strout would have it, "if *The Connecticut Yankee* is not a close relative of *Ragtime*, it is surely at least a first cousin once removed" (Strout 118). His argument is largely given over to similarities of plot (e.g., "The climax of both stories shows an embattled hero, surrounded by a small band of youthful supporters, using modern firepower in a showdown with armed authorities" [Strout 121]) rather than to investigations of how each author used history. In fact, Strout ends his chapter by suggesting that *Ragtime* may not be the only contemporary novel strongly influenced by *A Connecticut Yankee*. After all, in Saul Bellow's *Henderson the Rain King* (1959)

"a Connecticut pig-farmer journeys to a fabulous Africa, encounters a primitive society, and becomes involved with a king" (Strout 132). The rub, of course, is that parallels of this sort can multiply endlessly, sometimes in ways that are genuinely provocative and sometimes in ways that are merely ingenious.

For these reasons and more, the focus in this analysis will be on the complicated legacy of *Adventures of Huckleberry Finn* as the work that not only has exerted the greatest "influence" on certain important American novels, but also that might avoid the trap of undue strain. Let us begin, then, with the question of *voice*. By allowing Huck to tell his own story, Twain, in the novel's opening paragraph, not only freed southwestern humor from the shackles of a high-fallutin' framing narrator, but also unleashed a powerful source of native American poetry (1). The result is to place readers entirely in what turns out to be very capable hands, for Huck describes events with a suppleness and an unsophisticated honesty that turn American speech into the very stuff of authentic poetry (consider his description of a summer storm [59–60]).

Language is one of the glories of Twain's masterpiece, but the inextricable relationship between language and experience needs to be pointed out too. Huck's narration is, after all, of a rather special sort—namely, a tale of the corruption he discovered as he and Jim floated southward. To be sure, innocence had long been a staple of the American character and of its literary protagonists; but *Adventures of Huckleberry Finn* raised the ante by sharpening the perspective. Works such as Sherwood Anderson's "I Want to Know Why" (1918), F. Scott Fitzgerald's *The Great Gatsby* (1925), Jack Kerouac's *On the Road* (1957), Robert Penn Warren's *All the King's Men* (1946), Jay McInerney's *Bright Lights, Big City* (1984), Marilynn Robinson's *Housekeeping* (1980) all spring to mind as sharing something of Huck's general condition, and no doubt others will have little trouble in adding to this admittedly short list. It must be added that it would be a mistake to imagine that *Adventures of Huckle-*

berry Finn is the only influence at work (surely the Marlow of Conrad's *Heart of Darkness* [1921] counts for something in the composition of *The Great Gatsby*) or that one means to advocate a reading in which *Adventures of Huckleberry Finn* becomes the sole "tradition" against which individual talents measure themselves and react. Still, when Hemingway singles out Twain's novel for extraordinary praise, he surely has an aspect of what is meant.

Two works, omitted from the last paragraph, are especially good illustrations of Twain's abiding presence in the contemporary American novel. Indeed, the first—J.D. Salinger's *The Catcher in the Rye* (1951)—has a long history of being linked with *Adventures of Huckleberry Finn*. After all, one need look no further than the opening lines of Salinger's novel to hear the echoes and to feel the connections: "If you really want to hear about it, the first thing you'll probably want to know is where I was born, and what my lousy childhood was like" (Salinger 1). Granted, Huck is a battered child while Holden has been spoiled rotten; Huck has no illusions about his ignorance while Holden peppers his chatter with SAT words like "ostracized"; and perhaps most important of all, Huck's experiences turn him into an estranged rebel while, many critics would argue, Holden remains the same self-indulgent sentimentalist he always was. About some similarities, however, there is little doubt.

Much the same thing can be easily observed about the penchant both protagonists have for the "stretcher." As Holden puts it, "I'm the most terrific liar you ever saw in your life. It's awful. If I'm on my way to the store to buy a magazine, even, and somebody asks me where I'm going, I'm liable to say I'm going to the opera. It's terrible" (Salinger 16). What we observe in the novel, however, are whoppers about his impending death: the "tiny little tumor" on his brain, the imaginary bullet in his gut, or the recent operation on his "clavichord." Huck, by contrast, saves up his most inventively gruesome leg-pullers for survival, but as Lionel Trilling pointed out more than forty years ago, he does not lie to himself. One could argue that Holden does precisely that, at least in most of the confrontations between the phony and the pure he reports.

What Huck and Holden share, however, aside from their respective initiations into the variety and the viciousness of adult corruption, is the mutual condition of being protagonists in death-haunted novels. Hardly a page of either book is spared the taint of mortality, whether it expresses itself in the chivalric rhetoric of the Grangerfords or in Holden's exam essay on Egyptian mummies; in the grisly specter of Buck or in the haunting memories of Allie; in Huck's conviction that "an owl, away off, who-whooing [is] about somebody that was going to die" (4); or in Holden's quick leap from a magazine article about the warning signs of cancer to the sickly certainty of the grave: "I'd had this sore on the inside of my lip for about *two weeks*. So I figured I was getting cancer" (Salinger 196).

That loneliness is an inextricable by-product of their respective broodings should hardly come as a surprise, for isolation comes with the very territory of the extended monologue. To be sure, Huck bonds with Jim in those resplendent, short-lived scenes in which man, boy, and raft merge with the river. Holden is less fortunate, for in a world where phonies vastly outnumber the pure of heart, there are only thin pockets of stasis: unspoiled, white snow, the American Museum of Natural History, Phoebe in her blue coat going round and round on the Central Park carousel. Everything else is a veritable flood tide pushing Holden toward change, toward adulthood, toward responsibility, toward abject phoniness, toward death.

The Catcher in the Rye, then, fairly aches to be read as an urban variant of *Adventures of Huckleberry Finn*, and while the generalization reduces some important distinctions, and not a few nuances, to mush, those critics who saw Twain's Mississippi refracted on Manhattan's streets were not essentially wrong. And with a stitch here, a tuck there, the same arithmetic might well be applied to Saul Bellow's *The*

Adventures of Augie March (1953). After all, Bellow's larky protagonist is to Chicago's immigrant Jewish life what Huck had been to the shore towns along the Mississippi—namely, a ball of picaresque energy rolling from one initiation experience to another.

In Bellow's pre-Augie phase his protagonists tended to be brooders, introspectively licking wounds both real and imagined. With Augie, even grim experiences roll off his back: ". . . sometimes we were chased, stoned, bitten, and beat up for Christ-killers, all of us, even Georgie, articled, whether we liked it or not, to this mysterious trade. But I never had any special grief from it, or brooded, being by and large too larky and boisterous to take it to heart" (Bellow 12). Instead, Augie appropriates the best of a Grandma Lausche or an Einhorn and moves on—often through a landscape crowded with minor characters such as Mimi, Clem, or Kayo—without much sense that one must pay for insights with suffering or that experiences per se will ever run out.

Like the Huck Finn who falls into welcomes at the Grangerfords, at the Wilkses, at the Phelpses, Augie turns out to be eminently "adoptable." But unlike Huck, Augie is on a quest for something more than a hot meal and a warm trundle bed. As Einhorn observes, there's "opposition" in him, for Augie has not only the youth that makes him suspicious of those over thirty, but also the inner conviction that he will never cross over that dreaded line himself: that is, if he holds firm to the "axial lines" and moves, ever forward, toward a "good enough fate."

In such a world, movement counts for more than commitment, and excess threatens to be all. As Augie puts it, commenting on the various jobs that Grandma Lausche would find for him: "Saying 'various jobs,' I gave out the Rosetta Stone, so to speak, to my entire life" (Bellow 28). The result is not only an endless string of jobs (everything from bookseller to clothing salesman, from assistant eagle trainer to doomed sailor), but also a motley collection of Machiavellians filled with bluster and what a future Bellow protagonist will call "re-ality instruction." Augie, however, takes the best, and worst, that urban life throws at him and, rather like Silly Putty, keeps bouncing back. To be sure, there is a decided difference between Huck's fateful decision to "light out for the Territory ahead of the rest" and Augie's bubbly paeons to his *un*-complicated fate as an American; but in terms of essential spirit, Huck and Augie seem to be cut from the same picaresque cloth.

Granted, critics continue to belabor the proposition that Mark Twain was a great writer who never wrote a great book. For them, *Adventures of Huckleberry Finn* is riddled with problems, not the least of which is the "problem" of its ending. But writers, this author would submit, could care less. Hemingway, for example, had no difficulty loving the book until the point when Huck tears up his note to Miss Watson and decides that he'll "go to hell." The rest was so much fakery and not worth his bother. What mattered was the sustained, lyrical voice of an American innocent, trying desperately to carve out an identity within or outside, below or above, the social order out to "sivilize" him.

Sanford Pinsker

BIBLIOGRAPHY

Bellow, Saul. *The Adventures of Augie March.* New York: Viking, 1953.

Clemens, Samuel L. *Adventures of Huckleberry Finn.* Ed. Walter Blair and Victor Fischer. Berkeley: U of California P, 1985.

Roth, Philip. *Portnoy's Complaint.* New York: Random House, 1969.

Salinger, J.D. *The Catcher in the Rye.* Boston: Little, Brown, 1951.

Strout, Cushing. *Making American Tradition.* New Brunswick, N.J.: Rutgers UP, 1990.

Trilling, Lionel. Introduction. *The Adventures of Huckleberry Finn.* By Clemens. New York: Rinehart, 1948. v–xviii.

See also: *Adventures of Huckleberry Finn*; Censorship; Language; South, Mark Twain and the

"Legend of the Capitoline Venus, The"

(1869)

"The Legend of the Capitoline Venus" (1869) was published in the Buffalo *Express* in which Twain had bought a one-third interest. As associate editor he published some fifty pieces in the *Express*, ending in April 1870. Of these, ten appeared in *Sketches, New and Old* (1875); one of them is "The Legend of the Capitoline Venus," the story of an artistic hoax.

Having just finished *The Innocents Abroad* (1869), Twain was still satirizing reverence for antiquity. Although it is not a burlesque of a particular novel or type of novel, like the condensed novels, "The Legend of the Capitoline Venus" is divided into six miniature chapters set in Rome. It more closely resembles a play because each chapter is a distinct scene and uses the dramatic device of indicating scenes in italicized stage directions. The fifth chapter further resembles a play because italicized identifications precede dialogue: *Chorus of Voices*; *Another Voice; All*. In chapter 1 George and Mary are unable to marry because her father refuses permission until George, a poor sculptor, has $50,000. In chapter 2 George has produced a statue of America that the Honorable Bellamy Foodle of Arkansas finds clever and a source of fame for the artist, but Mary's father insists that George must have $50,000 in six months or his daughter will marry another man. Chapter 3 finds George with a friend, John, who offers to raise the money for him. His first step is to smash the nose, two fingers, an ear, toes, and lower leg from the statue of America. Then he takes it away in a carriage. The scene in chapter 4 is six months later. When his bootmaker enters and calls him "your highness," the hungry artist learns that his position has changed. The last to enter is Mary's father offering his daughter to George. Chapter 5 explains how George was saved. The scene is set in a cafe in which an American gentleman translates an article from the newspaper telling how John Smithe bought land that he gave in payment for a debt to the artist George Arnold. Found on this property

is a remarkably ancient statue of a woman missing the same parts destroyed on the statue in chapter 3. A special commission decides that it is a Venus by a third-century B.C. artist and worth 10 million francs, half of which belongs to George, the property owner. Chapter 6 takes place ten years later, still in Rome. Now married to Mary with children, George gives John credit for their bliss. His last comment, however, indicates something less than marital bliss: "Will you never learn to take care of the children!" Perhaps rather than giving John credit for his bliss, George is blaming him for his unhappiness. Comments after the story refer to "a gigantic Petrified Man being dug up near Syracuse" and the "Barnum that buried him there." This swindle was current at the time the sketch was written. Perhaps Twain wanted to emphasize that these hoaxes take place on both sides of the Atlantic.

Little critical comment has been made on this story. Everett Emerson notes that the story is autobiographical because it was written when Twain was seeking permission to marry Olivia from her father. Frank Baldanza places it in a group of what he calls "gimmick" stories with O. Henry twists at the end.

Nancy Chinn

BIBLIOGRAPHY

Baldanza, Frank. *Mark Twain: An Introduction and Interpretation.* New York: Barnes & Noble, 1961.

Clemens, Samuel L. "The Legend of the Capitoline Venus." *Sketches, New and Old.* By Clemens. 1875. Rpt. New York: Harper, 1903. 293–300.

Emerson, Everett. *The Authentic Mark Twain: A Literary Biography of Samuel L. Clemens.* Philadelphia: U of Pennsylvania P, 1984.

See also: Art; Hoax

Leopold II, King of the Belgians

(1835–1909)

Leopold II became King of the Belgians in 1865. He founded the Congo Free State, the most inhumane colonial venture of the nineteenth century. Leopold developed the Congo

Free State without help from the Belgian government, which feared the expense. The king hired Sir Henry Morton Stanley to buy land along the Congo River eighty times the size of Belgium. Native chiefs did not comprehend these transactions. Leopold's title was recognized at the Berlin Conference in 1885.

Leopold lacked resources to exploit his acquisition. He leased large areas to private companies and exploited others through hired adventurers. Profits from rubber and ivory were the sole consideration. Villages received unrealistic rubber quotas enforced by kidnapping the women and by mass mutilations. Agents demonstrated efficiency by exhibiting a human hand for every cartridge issued.

Leopold justified his colony as a humanitarian venture to halt the slave trade. But disturbing reports circulated that were confirmed by Roger Casement's report to the British government in 1903. International outrage forced Belgium to take control from Leopold in 1908.

The Congo atrocities fascinated many writers, notably Joseph Conrad (*Heart of Darkness*, 1899) and Vachel Lindsay whose poem "The Congo" (1914) includes the lines, "Listen to the yell of Leopold's ghost, burning in Hell for his hand-maimed host/Hear how the demons chuckle and yell, cutting his hands off down in Hell."

Arthur W. White

BIBLIOGRAPHY

Anstey, Roger. *King Leopold's Legacy: The Congo Under Belgian Rule, 1908–1966*. London: Oxford UP, 1966.

Ascherson, Neal. *The King Incorporated; Leopold II in the Age of Trusts*. Garden City, N.Y.: Doubleday, 1964.

Giddings, Robert. "Mark Twain and King Leopold of the Belgians." *Mark Twain: A Sumptuous Variety*. Ed. Robert Giddings. Totowa, N.J.: Barnes & Noble, 1985. 199–221.

Lichtervelde, Louis de Comte. *Leopold of the Belgians*. Trans. Thomas H. Reed and H. Russel Reed. New York: Century, 1929.

Rappoport, Angelo S. *Leopold the Second, King of the Belgians*. New York: Sturgis and Walton, 1910.

See also: Belgian Congo; Imperialism; *King Leopold's Soliloquy*

"Letter from the Recording Angel"
(1946)

One of Mark Twain's many denunciations of hypocrisy, the "Letter from the Recording Angel" was unpublished during his lifetime, although it appeared in an early manuscript of *A Connecticut Yankee in King Arthur's Court* (1889) in different form. Apparently written in the late 1880s, the letter was edited for publication by Bernard DeVoto and first appeared in the February 1946 issue of *Harper's Magazine*, under the title "Letter from the Recording Angel." It has also appeared as "Letter to the Earth" and in *Letters from the Earth*, a volume of previously unpublished writings edited by DeVoto (1962). Twain himself did not title the work.

The letter, ostensibly from Heaven's Recording Angel to a wealthy but miserly coal dealer in Buffalo, New York, upbraids the hypocritical coal merchant (called in various editions of the letter "Abner Scofield" and "Andrew Langdon") by contrasting his "Secret Supplications of the Heart" with his "Public Prayers." While the coal dealer prays publicly for mild weather "tempered to the needs of the poor and the naked," his private wish for harsh weather that will increase the price of coal is granted, since it is his true desire. The second section of the letter calls attention to the coal dealer's rapidly rising stock in heaven, not because he has given according to his wealth, but because it is a wonder he has given at all, considering his avarice.

In this and other works Twain railed against human hypocrisy and cruelty. Like "The Man That Corrupted Hadleyburg" (1899), the "Letter From the Recording Angel" points out the distinctions between the acts and thoughts of human beings, and it does so in a way that is both humorous and honest.

Greg Garrett

BIBLIOGRAPHY

Clemens, Samuel L. "Letter from the Recording Angel." *Harper's Magazine* 192 (February 1946): 106–109.

———. "Letter to the Earth." *Letters from the Earth.* By Clemens. Ed. Bernard DeVoto. New York: Harper & Row, 1962. 117–122.

See also: *Letters from the Earth*

Letters from the Earth
(1962)

The collection of satiric letters and miscellaneous short writings *Letters from the Earth* was published in 1962 after much consideration, even censoring, of its contents. In March 1939 Bernard DeVoto, using "Letters from the Earth," the name of the first group of letters in the collection, submitted his edited collection of *Letters* to the trustees of Mark Twain's estate. However, Clara Clemens refused to allow the publication of the work because she felt that parts of it misrepresented her father. She eventually saw that her father's reputation would not be ruined by the publication of these manuscripts, and she recognized that her father's complex views on God, Satan, and mankind were being analyzed even without these writings. In September 1962 Clara Clemens agreed to the publication of *Letters* as DeVoto had submitted the collection in 1939.

The first section of the work includes the title piece, "Letters from the Earth," and two other fragments from Twain's late writings on religious themes and social conditions, "Papers of the Adam Family" and "Letter to the Earth." The second section in the volume contains DeVoto's selections from Twain's unpublished manuscripts. However, many of the works in this section had been published prior to Clara Clemens's consent for publishing the entire work. The works in the second section were written in various circumstances and with differing tones, but they have been kept together in *Letters* out of respect for DeVoto's efforts. To provide a more consistent text, DeVoto also corrected errors found in the manuscripts that Twain did not write for publication, and these corrections have also been included in the 1962 publication.

In "Letters from the Earth," eleven letters to the archangels Michael and Gabriel from Satan, who appears on earth to "see how the Human-Race experiment was coming along," Twain expresses his ideas on religion—specifically the nature of God and man's misconceptions about God, heaven, and Satan. He also expresses his ideas on human sexuality, which he seldom mentions in other works. He wrote these letters at his Redding, Connecticut, home, Stormfield, in late 1909. Twain never expected these letters to be published; in fact, he wrote to his friend Elizabeth Wallace, "This book ['Letters from the Earth'] will never be published—in fact it couldn't be . . . for it has much Holy Scripture in it of the kind that . . . can't properly be read aloud, except from the pulpit and in family worship." Critics agree that because Twain was not writing with publishing in mind, he was very candid, even playful, in writing "Letters." Indeed, because Twain spoke through Satan, who appears to have a clearer cosmic view than man, the work appears ironic rather than biting, unlike many of his critiques of man and religion. In "Letters" Twain concentrated on the contents of the first chapters of Genesis; he questioned God's judgment in allowing the Fall of man in the story of Adam and Eve and the destruction of man in the story of Noah and the ark. Despite this focus on the Old Testament, Twain managed to include a refutation of the common perception of Jesus and to propose his own, less sympathetic, view of Jesus as the inventor of hell.

"Papers of the Adam Family" contains Twain's more serious views on religious themes; however, the subject matter of this collection is the same as that of "Letters." Because Twain attacked society in "Papers," while "Letters" actually attacks the Bible, these writings could likely have been published earlier. The best-known pieces of these selections are "Extract from Methuselah's Diary," "Extract from Eve's Autobiography," and

"Extract from Shem's Diary of 920 A.C." In these three selections, as in the entire group, Twain continued with his berating of God's judgment. His accusations herein seem to center on the purpose of God's creation and the nature of a God who would create man only to watch him suffer. Using a setting prior to the Flood, Twain turned the accusations into what appear to be warnings of the direction in which society is headed. "Papers" is also seen as Twain's later attempt to concentrate and intensify his earlier works, *Adam's Diary* (1904), *Eve's Diary* (1906), and "Methuselah's Diary."

"Letter to the Earth" was first published, with the title "Letter from the Recording Angel," in 1946 in *Harper's Magazine*. Twain wrote it sometime in 1887, revised it for later use in *A Connecticut Yankee in King Arthur's Court* (1889), and then decided not to use it in the novel. The humorous letter is a response to the prayers of a coal dealer, Abner Scofield, from the Recording Angel. The letter, rather businesslike, gives Scofield an update on the actions taken after his prayers. Here Twain's cynical voice may be heard not only questioning the validity of prayers, but also the sincerity of man's meditations.

The second section in *Letters* contains many less controversial pieces, the first of which, "A Cat-Tale," Twain wrote as a bedtime story to his daughters Susy and Clara. It was first published in *Concerning Cats* in 1959, and it is a simple dialogue between Twain and his children about cats. Many of the other works in this section warrant scarce criticism. Readers apparently find little, other than humorous sketches, in "Official Report to the I.I.A.S.," "Simplified Spelling," "Something About Repentance," "From an English Notebook," and "From an Unfinished Burlesque of Books on Etiquette." The entry "Cooper's Prose Style," which DeVoto edited for *New England Quarterly*, appeared as "Fenimore Cooper's Further Literary Offenses" in the September 1946 issue. Twain criticized Cooper's use of exaggeration in this piece. "The Gorky Incident" was also published prior to the 1962 *Letters*. DeVoto edited it for the August 1944

issue of *Slavonic and East European Review*. DeVoto also included in this second section of *Letters* unpublished excerpts from Twain's manuscript of *A Tramp Abroad* (1880). And, perhaps the best-known selection in the entire *Letters*, "The Damned Human Race," follows. These writings, like many others of Twain's later writings, reflect familiar questions and quandaries on the nature of God and man. Primarily written between 1905 and 1909, "The Damned Human Race" includes thoughts similar to those Twain expressed in *What Is Man?* (1906) and *The Mysterious Stranger* (1916). The final entry in *Letters* is "The Great Dark," which Twain wrote in 1898. Twain tried to maintain a dreamlike quality in his writing here, a method which he would later use in *The Mysterious Stranger*, a work which also seems to have the same theme and subject matter of "The Great Dark." This piece was published in part in DeVoto's *Mark Twain at Work* (1942).

Although some of Twain's efforts in *Letters* are considered failures, the extracts from "Methuselah's Diary" and "Extract from Eve's Diary" for example, other selections, particularly "Letters from the Earth" and "The Damned Human Race," are successful and offer significant contributions to the understanding of Twain's satiric writings and the extent of his questioning of biblical ideas. Most readers find in this text some of the most detailed explanations of Twain's views of the Bible and the Christian religion. In fact, scholars seem to agree that Twain uses the fictional setting and the biblical allusions in most of *Letters* merely to create an opportunity to voice his own opinions. The book was well received by the general public and, despite Clara Clemens's fears, became a best seller. Critics cite the times in which the book was published as potential explanation for the book's success. Because the book seemed to embody some of the questions about God's existence and man's role in creation that society had started to ask, *Letters* proved to be an immediate success, although it helped convince some critics of Twain's misanthropy. Obviously, the publication of *Letters* has added not only to his readers' complex views of Twain, but also to the controversy over his true feelings on religious issues.

Paula Garrett

BIBLIOGRAPHY

Brodwin, Stanley. "The Theology of Mark Twain: Banished Adam and the Bible." *Mississippi Quarterly* 29 (Spring 1976): 167–189.

Clemens, Samuel L. *Letters from the Earth.* Ed. Bernard DeVoto. New York: Harper & Row, 1962.

————. *Mark Twain's Letters.* Ed. Albert B. Paine. 2 vols. New York: Harper, 1917.

Ensor, Allison. *Mark Twain and the Bible.* Lexington: U of Kentucky P, 1969.

Maxwell, D.E.S. *American Fiction: The Intellectual Background.* New York: Columbia UP, 1963.

Neider, Charles. *Mark Twain.* New York: Horizon P, 1967.

Stone, Albert E., Jr. *The Innocent Eye: Childhood in Mark Twain's Imagination.* New Haven, Conn.: Yale UP, 1961.

See also: "Damned Human Race, The"; "Eve's Diary"; "Extract from Methuselah's Diary"; God; "Letter from the Recording Angel"; Religion; "Shem's Diary"

Letters from the Sandwich Islands (1866)

Letters from the Sandwich Islands was originally a series of twenty-five letters, first published by the Sacramento *Union* in both its daily and weekly forms. Dates on the letters cannot always be trusted. Most were written while Mark Twain was in the Sandwich Islands, as Hawaii was then called, but the last eight letters were published after his return, some written in California and dated earlier. The letters next appeared in *Roughing It* (1872), though substantially rewritten. They were not reprinted as a whole until 1947.

Letters in many ways was the end of an apprenticeship, representing a culmination of the earliest version of Mark Twain, part serious reporter and part purveyor of a "west-

ern," that is, broad humor. These aspects are notably separate at times, with entire letters devoted to the whaling and sugar industries and one letter detailing the *Hornet* disaster, with hardly a joke anywhere.

The serious reporter also emerges in the scrutiny of the islands' political life, an aspect lost when *Letters* was reused for *Roughing It*. For example, the controversial Minister Harris, and the storm over Bishop Staley, especially his role in the native mourning for Princess Victoria Kamamalu, are cut completely. Material added, about natural scenery and a local liar, emphasizes this depoliticizing. *Letters from the Sandwich Islands* reveals how quickly Sam Clemens informed himself about the local scene and how surprisingly substantial his knowledge was of native history and culture. The result is a sense of detail that becomes more generalized when he later reworks the material.

The "western" brand of fun is largely byplay with Mr. Brown; for example, he bites into a proffered soapcake and provides opportunities to mention vomiting and offensive smells. The device enabled Clemens to siphon off some of the cruder elements from his Mark Twain persona. The role was sometimes filled earlier by "the Unreliable" (Clement T. Rice) and Dan De Quille (William Wright). *Roughing It* displays a notable toning down of such comic effects, where Brown is left out altogether and an incident with native women swimming naked is treated very differently, among other changes. This relative restraint, coupled with a loss of the occasionally sharp separation between the serious and the comic featured in *Letters*, creates in *The Innocents Abroad* (1869) swift and dazzling changes of tone, from the serious to the sentimental and poetic and on to the comic. This melange reveals the influence of the lecturing that falls between *Letters* and that first book-length effort. Thus *Letters from the Sandwich Islands* began another phase of Mark Twain, providing the basis for the Sandwich Islands lecture, which in turn garnered the capital—the cash, the fame, and the confidence—required to support a gamble by Sam Clemens to make it big on the East Coast.

James E. Caron

BIBLIOGRAPHY

Clemens, Samuel L. *Mark Twain's Letters, Volume 1 (1853–1866)*. Ed. Edgar M. Branch, Michael B. Frank, and Kenneth M. Sanderson. Berkeley: U of California P, 1988.

———. *Mark Twain's Letters from Hawaii*. Ed. A. Grove Day. New York: Appleton-Century, 1966.

———. *Mark Twain's Notebooks & Journals, Volume I (1855–1873)*. Ed. Frederick Anderson, Michael B. Frank, and Kenneth M. Sanderson. Berkeley: U of California P, 1975.

Frear, Walter F. *Mark Twain and Hawaii*. Chicago: Lakeside P, 1947.

See also: Hawaii; Humor; *Roughing It*; Travel Writings

Letters of Quintus Curtius Snodgrass, The

(1946)

Edited by Ernest E. Leisy, *The Letters of Quintus Curtius Snodgrass* presents a series of ten letters that appeared in the New Orleans *Crescent*, 21 January–30 March 1861. In them, Quintus Curtius relates his experiences, chiefly humorous, as a member of a Confederate militia in New Orleans, Baton Rouge, and Washington, D.C. Although Leisy makes a fairly convincing case, citing a number of resemblances to the Thomas Jefferson Snodgrass letters and other early works, Allan Bates has demonstrated that Clemens could not have been the author.

Howard G. Baetzhold

BIBLIOGRAPHY

Bates, Alan. "*The Quintus Curtius Snodgrass Letters*: A Clarification of the Mark Twain Canon." *American Literature* 36 (1964): 31–37.

Brinegar, Claude S. "Mark Twain and the Quintus Curtius Snodgrass Letters: A Statistical Test of Authorship." *Journal of the American Statistical Association* 58 (1963): 85–96.

See also: Snodgrass, Thomas Jefferson

"Letters to the Muscatine Journal"

(1853–1855)

Nine letters written by Samuel Clemens were published by his brother Orion in the Muscatine *Journal* (Iowa) between December 1853 and March 1855. These pieces, if not the very first of Clemens's efforts to appear in print, may be fairly said to constitute the beginning of his literary career. Three letters from Philadelphia and a fourth from Washington are signed with the letter "W"; the others, from St. Louis, are signed variously with the initials "S.C.," "S.L.C.," and "S.C.L."

The Philadelphia letters recount for a western audience the author's responses to historic sites and landmarks and decry the fact that such monuments as Lydia Darrah's home, the "Slate Roof House," and Carpenter's Hall have been allowed to deteriorate. One of the letters (3 February 1854) makes reference to the obituary poetry published regularly in the Philadelphia *Public Ledger*—"most villainous doggerel"—and hence, as Branch points out (3), introduces a subject Mark Twain will exploit with humorous effect in a later sketch for the *Galaxy* (November 1870) and, most adroitly, in the "tributes" of Emmeline Grangerford as recounted by the deadpan Huck in *Adventures of Huckleberry Finn* (1885). The Washington letter details visits to both houses of Congress and to the Smithsonian. Clemens reserves his greatest enthusiasm for the Patent Office museum, "the largest collection of oddities in the United States"; of particular interest is the printing press that Ben Franklin used in London. In general, the St. Louis letters are more reportorial, much of the information coming from news accounts Clemens read in the St. Louis *Missouri Republican* and the *Daily Evening News*. In the letter of 24 February 1855, for example, on city crime reports, there is an account of a Negro girl who attempted to pass as a slave "to avoid the consequences of this breach of the law" and a rather provocative mention of an Indian raid in New Mexico in which "fourteen men were butchered." These are interspersed with agricultural and livestock prices and complaints about mail service. On occasion there is satire, as in the first St. Louis letter that comments pointedly on a destitute widow in a city whose churches contribute generously to the abstract poor abroad. Apparently xenophobic comments in these letters reflect Clemens's sympathy at the time with Know-Nothing aims and nativism.

Humor and artistry are at a premium in these early "travel" letters. Nevertheless, they may be seen as early experiments in a genre to which Clemens will return when a decade or so later, as Mark Twain, he will write letters from New York, Europe, and the Holy Land for the *Alta California*.

Jarrell A. O'Kelley

BIBLIOGRAPHY

Branch, Edgar M. "Three New Letters by Samuel Clemens in the *Muscatine Journal*." *Mark Twain Journal* 22.1 (Spring 1984): 2–7.

Clemens, Samuel L. *Mark Twain's Letters in the Muscatine Journal*. Ed. Edgar M. Branch. Chicago: Mark Twain Association of America, 1942.

———. *Mark Twain's Notebooks & Journals, Volume I (1855–1873)*. Ed. Frederick Anderson, Michael B. Frank, and Kenneth M. Sanderson. Berkeley: U of California P, 1975.

Long, E. Hudson, and J.R. LeMaster. *The New Mark Twain Handbook*. New York: Garland, 1985.

See also: Correspondence; Muscatine, Iowa; Travel Writings

Lewis, John T.
(1835–1906)

John T. Lewis's association with Mark Twain was the result of an act of heroism in 1877 at Quarry Farm in Elmira. Mark Twain described the incident in a letter to William Dean Howells, declining to have it published. Lewis, who worked at the farm, was driving a manure wagon up the steep hill below the house. Tearing down the hill was a run-away horse and carriage containing Livy Langdon, Clemens's sister-in-law, her child, and nurse.

At the risk of his own life, Lewis stopped the horse and saved their lives. He was suitably rewarded and became a local celebrity, befriended by Mark Twain and the Langdon family for the rest of his life.

Lewis was born a freeman in Maryland in 1835. He joined the Church of the Brethren there and was the only Dunkard in Elmira after he came to New York State in 1862. He was eulogized after his death in 1906 as one of the "best citizens of his race."

Herbert A. Wisbey, Jr.

BIBLIOGRAPHY

Clemens, Samuel L. *Mark Twain's Letters*. Vol. 1. Ed. Albert B. Paine. New York: Harper, 1917. 304–309.

See also: Quarry Farm

Life on the Mississippi
(1883)

In this volume Mark Twain combined "Old Times on the Mississippi," the amusing, fictionalized account of his experiences as a cub pilot that was written in Hartford in the winter of 1874–1875 and published in the *Atlantic Monthly*, with a description of the great river as he had found it during a month-long trip undertaken in the spring of 1882 specifically to collect information for the book. The chapters written early are masterful; the others are uneven, for the author found the writing difficult and resorted to padding and using borrowed sources. The later chapters were begun in Hartford during May and June 1882, continued at Quarry Farm in Elmira during July, August, and September, and finished in Hartford during the period October 1882–January 1883. The book was published by James R. Osgood on 12 May 1883, as a subscription book, after considerable cutting. The holograph is in the J.P. Morgan Library, New York City.

"Old Times on the Mississippi" was written as the result of a request by William Dean Howells on behalf of the *Atlantic* that Clemens provide a sequel to "A True Story" (1874). The notion of writing about Mississippi River piloting came to Clemens while walking with Joseph Twichell, though the writer had intended as early as 1866 to write a book on the great river. (His original plan was to begin on the Missouri River in Montana, then go to New Orleans.) Soon Clemens decided that he could write a whole series on piloting, and seven installments in all appeared in the *Atlantic*. By common consent these chapters, either in their original form or in the lightly revised form in which they appear in *Life on the Mississippi*, are among Mark Twain's masterpieces.

In "Old Times on the Mississippi" Mark Twain chose to limit himself largely to the story of the education of a pilot cub, which he describes in terms no doubt influenced by his audience, for he describes learning the river as analogous to book learning. But mostly it is an account of embarrassments and humiliations, comically told. Although he was an adult who had traveled a good deal before he attempted to become a riverboat pilot, the author portrays his former self as an innocent boy who suffers painfully at the hands of the master pilot Horace Bixby. Although the emphasis is very much on humor, the account ends on a serious note—a strong sense of loss—when ignorance and innocence yield to knowledge and experience.

Soon after he began "Old Times," Clemens decided that it was time to write a book on the river; he hoped that his friend W.D. Howells would go with him to gather materials. (Canadian pirates made a book out of the *Atlantic* chapters: Belfast Brothers of Toronto published *Old Times on the Mississippi* in 1876.) It was not, however, until the spring of 1882 that the trip was made, by which time Clemens had signed a contract with James R. Osgood; he agreed to have the book finished by 1 October of the same year. Traveling with Osgood himself and a stenographer, Roswell Phelps, Clemens went from St. Louis to New Orleans by ship. He expected to interview steamboatmen during the voyage but was distracted by socializing. Afterward, he went back up the river to St. Louis and Hannibal, and after a visit to his boyhood home he continued up the river to St. Paul, Minnesota.

Turning to his task in Hartford, Clemens first added to the chapter on his cub piloting an account of his experiences with the pilot Brown and the death of his brother Henry. His original plan was to continue the book with more stories of himself as an innocent victim. On his return to the river, however, the author's attempt to travel incognito failed early, and thereafter, without a fictional narrator the report is on the whole sober. The narrator is not the familiar Mark Twain but the middle-aged gentleman that Clemens was at that time. Feeling at a loss for materials, he sought from Osgood's books on the river and its towns. Osgood supplied twenty-five, and Clemens used many, though he later dropped from the book some of the derived material.

Perhaps because he was uncertain about his identity in the second part of the book, he included an account, generally thought to be false, concerning how he obtained his name "Mark Twain." He alleges that the most venerable pilot on the Mississippi was Captain Isaiah Sellers, who used the pen name before he did in articles for the New Orleans *Picayune*. But Sellers appears never to have used that name.

Highlights of the book as it was published are the chapter from the manuscript of the then unfinished *Huckleberry Finn* concerning Huck's visit to a raft; "The House Beautiful," a satire of contemporary taste in interior decoration; and the discussion of how Sir Walter Scott's brand of romanticism was "in great measure responsible" for the Civil War. The theme of mutability and change has been identified as the organizing principle of the latter part of the book. In contrast to some severe social criticism of the South, Clemens made much of the signs of progress he saw from St. Louis northward, though he was also nostalgic about his lost past. He was unable, however, to give the chapters based on his trip any sense of continuity. He improvised: he inserted "The Professor's Yarn," left over from

A Tramp Abroad (1880), and he wrote an introduction largely derived from Francis Parkman's histories. Still he was unable to meet his October deadline and was disgusted with the effort to finish the book. Even before he was finished, he gave what he had written to Osgood to edit. It was not until 28 December that he was able to write the final chapters and respond to Osgood's suggestions, which, unfortunately, involved making many deletions. The whole complicated story is well told by Horst Kruse in *Mark Twain and "Life on the Mississippi."* The book was published on 12 May 1883 and sold *"by subscription only."*

Despite its weaknesses, notably its formlessness, *Life on the Mississippi* has some virtues. First, it satisfies one's curiosity about the successful author's return in his forties to his humble beginnings in Hannibal that was familiar to readers of *Tom Sawyer* (1876) and *Huckleberry Finn.* To enjoy all that Mark Twain wrote for this book about his return, one must have access to the Penguin American Library edition, which contains both the so-called "suppressed passages" including one about Hannibal (earlier available only in the Heritage Press edition of *Life on the Mississippi*) and another passage about Hannibal published by Penguin for the first time. The whole book provides one with a sense of the growth of the man, who by the time of his return had wider horizons and conducted himself with authority.

The book also presents the author's views on many subjects and thus serves well as a commentary on topics Mark Twain rendered in fiction in *Huckleberry Finn.* Especially interesting in this connection are Mark Twain's comments on emancipation's not yet having reached white Southerners and his statements that in the South single "ruffians" and "lynchers" "with masks on" were acting on behalf of "public justice," witnesses were "corrected," and murderers went unpunished. (See the Penguin or Heritage Press edition for this discussion, found between chapters 47 and 48.)

Readers looking for the familiar humor of Mark Twain are usually disappointed with the reportage; the original manuscript included much that was entertaining, deleted because the author thought of himself as creating "a standard work." The deleted passages appear in the 1944 Limited Editions Club text. On May 1908 the author returned to the book to begin the task of revision, presumably for a revised edition of his works, but he did not complete the task. The revisions are preserved in a copy of the book in the Alderman Library, University of Virginia.

Life on the Mississippi is one of Mark Twain's most important books, since it contains the masterful "Old Times on the Mississippi." It usefully supplements Mark Twain's fictional works about the river and includes much else of value, especially when read in an edition that restores from the manuscript valuable passages deleted from the first edition.

Everett Emerson

BIBLIOGRAPHY

Brodwin, Stanley. "The Useful and the Useless River: *Life on the Mississippi* Revisited." *Studies in American Humor* 2 (1976): 196–208.

Cardwell, Guy A. "*Life on the Mississippi*: Vulgar Facts and Learned Errors." *Emerson Society Quarterly* 19 (4th quarter 1973): 283–293.

———. "Samuel Clemens's Magical Pseudonym." *New England Quarterly* 48 (1975): 175–193.

———. "A Self-Emasculated Hero." *Emerson Society Quarterly* 23 (1977): 173–187.

Clemens, Samuel L. *Life on the Mississippi.* New York: Limited Editions Club, 1944.

———. *Life on the Mississippi.* Ed. James M. Cox. New York: Penguin, 1984.

Cox, James M. *Mark Twain: The Fate of Humor.* Princeton, N.J.: Princeton UP, 1966.

Fatout, Paul. "Mark Twain's *Nom de Plume.*" *American Literature* 34 (March 1962): 1–7.

Ganzel, Dewey. "Twain, Travel Books, and *Life on the Mississippi.*" *American Literature* 34 (1962): 405–416.

Kruse, Horst H. *Mark Twain and "Life on the Mississippi."* Amherst: U of Massachusetts P, 1981.

Salomon, Roger B. *Twain and the Image of History.* New Haven, Conn.: Yale UP, 1961.

See also: Autobiography; Mississippi River; "Old Times on the Mississippi"; South, Mark Twain and the

Literary Comedians

During the last half of the nineteenth century the "literary comedians" were prominent on the American literary and lecture scene. These writers published humorous books, wrote for regional and national newspapers and magazines, and delivered their comic lectures throughout the United States, the western territory, and Canada.

Literary comedians numbered in the dozens, but the major ones were as follows (their popular pseudonyms in parentheses): Charles Farrar Browne (Artemus Ward, 1834–1837), George Horatio Derby (John Phoenix or Squibob, 1823–1861), Henry Wheeler Shaw (Josh Billings, 1818–1895), David Ross Locke (Petroleum V. Nasby, 1833–1888), Robert H. Newell (Orpheus C. Kerr, 1836–1901), Charles H. Smith (Bill Arp, 1826–1903), Edgar Wilson Nye (Bill Nye, 1850–1896), Melville D. Landon (Eli Perkins, 1839–1910), James M. Bailey (the Danbury *News* Man, 1841–1894), Charles Heber Clark (Max Adeler, 1841–1914), Marietta Holley (Samantha Allen, 1836–1926), and Finley Peter Dunne (Mr. Dooley, 1868–1936). Like "Mark Twain" itself, the pen names, often the most widely recognized names used by these people, provided each writer with an alter ego, a disguise that freed the author to assume a personality different from his or her own. One of the best examples of this "split personality" is found in Charles Farrar Browne, whose Artemus Ward, the congenial, bald showman parading his wax museum from coast to coast, was far removed from the quiet, dapper, sophisticated Browne himself.

Though usually referred to as a group or even "school" of humorists, the literary comedians were far from being homogeneous in their talents, tastes, and outlooks. Too often they have been viewed as mere literary funnymen who toyed with writing and lecturing while engaged more seriously in their "real" vocations of journalism, politics, business, teaching, etc. Currently, thanks to the work of such critics as Walter Blair, Hamlin Hill, Jesse Bier, James C. Austin, David E.E.

Sloane, and Brom Weber, the literary comedians are seen as more distinctive and serious-minded professional writers who worked hard to perfect their trade and became masters of the language of humor.

The literary comedians differ sharply from another major nineteenth-century type of humorists, those of the old Southwest, in that they focused on the contemporary scene, did less with the oral tradition of the tall tale, and tended (with exceptions) to be egalitarian politically. Essays and lectures often addressed current social, political, and cultural issues such as the Civil War, reconstruction, life in the newly settled West, women's rights, Chinese labor, and law and order. They have even been labeled some of the first realists in American literature, not only because of their contemporary focus but because they often reflected on the darker side of the human condition. The literary comedians, then, were not simply funny men; they shared Mark Twain's sobering insights into the complexities of life.

They were a colorful lot on stage, and their carefully rehearsed eccentricities and stage tricks were adopted and personalized by Mark Twain, with his unlit cigars, white suit, and the apparently rambling structure of his lectures. The stage tricks, indeed, were a major part of the evening's entertainment when a literary comedian lectured. Josh Billings, for example, wore his dark hair in a heavy mane, refused to wear a tie, entered the stage without introduction, sat down to lecture, and often had as his only prop an untouched pitcher of milk on a table in front of him. Bill Nye—tall, angular, and bald—mastered the blank expression and emotionless monotone that contrasted sharply with the humorous subjects he addressed. Charles Farrar Browne was also noted for the deadpan expression. The lectures of the literary comedians often appeared disjointed, another ruse to incite humor. In actuality, much work and hours of memorization went into these comic stage appearances. The best of the platform humorists rivaled, in popularity and financial gain, the most highly acclaimed serious lecturers of the day, often earning $100 per night.

Tricks on the stage were echoed by tricks on the page. Among the stylistic devices used by many of the literary comedians were intentional misspellings (cacography), flawed grammar, inverted syntax, and the use of such language play as puns, understatement, anticlimax, and antiproverbialism. Striking imagery abounded. Critic Max Eastman has even referred to Josh Billings as the father of imagism. The verbal trickery, especially misspelling, was designed to evoke humor out of the very appearance of words on a page. Its comic value has been disputed by critics and general readers, but in the nineteenth century it generally succeeded with readers. Josh Billings got nowhere with his "Essay on the Mule" until he published it as "Essa on the Muel" and loaded it with misspellings, incorrect grammar, and exaggerated images.

Mark Twain owed much to the literary comedians. He knew many of these writers personally, traveled with them on the circuit (e.g., Billings and Nasby), and adapted some of their stage and literary techniques for his own use. Indeed, it was Artemus Ward who helped Twain get "The Celebrated Jumping Frog of Calaveras County" in print and who urged Twain to begin lecturing. Critics such as Walter Blair and David E.E. Sloane have especially charted Twain's indebtedness to the literary comedians, Sloane feeling that they were the major formative influence in the growth of Twain as humorist. The tendencies of the literary comedians to extol egalitarian and democratic principles was a strong influence on the developing young Clemens. A major path of departure, of course, was that Twain wrote novels, a genre undertaken by few of the literary comedians. In fact, their writings were more in the line of humorous essays, sketches, aphorisms, and burlesques rather than fiction. They left us no major characters other than their own pseudonyms, no Tom Sawyers or Colonel Sellers.

In short, the literary comedians were early American comic literary realists, masters of satire, and clever manipulators of the language for humorous effect. They were also stage luminaries in their own right, drawing large crowds on the lecture circuit. Many of them were journalists and wrote popular columns for leading newspapers. Above all, contrary to their image, they were well-read, enlightened men and women who commented on the human condition in some of the most effective satirical writings of the nineteenth century. Lincoln, as we know, read from the likes of Ward and Nasby to his cabinet. In many ways they were the forerunners of Will Rogers, Dave Barry, Andy Rooney, and Garrison Keillor—the popular philosophers and critics who echo the basic attitudes and beliefs of so many of us.

David B. Kesterson

BIBLIOGRAPHY

Bier, Jesse. "'Literary Comedians': The Civil War and Reconstruction." *The Rise and Fall of American Humor.* New York: Holt, Rinehart and Winston, 1968. 77–116.

Blair, Walter. "Burlesques in Nineteenth-Century American Humor." *American Literature* 2 (1930): 236–247.

———. *Horse Sense in American Humor.* Chicago: U of Chicago P, 1942.

———. *Native American Humor.* New York: American Book, 1937. Rpt. San Francisco: Chandler, 1960.

———. "The Popularity of Nineteenth-Century American Humorists." *American Literature* 3 (1931): 175–194.

Kesterson, David B. "The Literary Comedians: A Review of Modern Scholarship." *Amerikastudien* (*American Studies*) 30 (1985): 167–175.

———. "The Literary Comedians and the Language of Humor." *Studies in American Humor* 1 (June 1982): 44–51.

———. "Mark Twain and the Humorist Tradition." *Samuel Clemens: A Mysterious Stranger.* Ed. Hans Borchers and Daniel E. Williams. New York: Peter Lang, 1986. 55–69.

———. "Those *Literary* Comedians." *Critical Essays on American Humor.* Ed. William Bedford Clark and W. Craig Turner. Boston: G.K. Hall, 1984. 167–183.

Sloane, David E.E. *The Literary Humor of the Urban Northeast, 1830–1890.* Baton Rouge: Louisiana State UP, 1983.

————. *Mark Twain as a Literary Comedian.* Baton Rouge: Louisiana State UP, 1979.

Tandy, Jennette. *Crackerbox Philosophers in American Humor and Satire.* New York: Columbia UP, 1925.

Weber, Brom. "The Misspellers." *The Comic Imagination in American Literature.* Ed. Louis D. Rubin, Jr. New Brunswick, N.J.: Rutgers UP, 1973. 127–137.

See also: Billings, Josh; Humor; Lecturer; Nye, Bill; Orality; Southwestern Humor; Ward, Artemus

"Little Bessie"
(1972)

The six "Little Bessie" chapters were written during 1908 and 1909, the time when Mark Twain was also working on *The Mysterious Stranger.* Ironically, the most disheartening of the chapters, "Little Bessie Would Assist Providence," in which Bessie questions the harsh disciplinary tactics of divine justice, was written while Twain was yachting. Albert Bigelow Paine included much of this chapter in an appendix to his biography (1912). The whole of the piece remained among the unpublished works in the Mark Twain Papers until 1972, when they were included in *Mark Twain's Fables of Man.* The editor of this compilation, John S. Tuckey, arranged the order of the chapters and included them in the section titled "The Myth of Providence."

Continuing Twain's theological writing, the "Little Bessie" chapters explore this "myth" of Providence. An incredibly precocious three-year-old searching for order in the universe, Bessie questions her mother about God's fairness in creating an innately depraved race and then punishing it for its depravity. She cannot understand her mother's belief that man deserves his fate; Mr. Hollister's theory of the creator's responsibility for human behavior makes more sense to her. Through Bessie and Mr. Hollister, Twain also satirizes people's insistence on the virginity of Mary, and he notes the similarity between the virgin birth of the Christian God and that of other gods.

The tone of these chapters is much less bitter than those dealing with the reason for evil in the world. Mr. Hollister points out that Mary would have a difficult time convincing people in the present that God was the father of her child. Similarly, Twain shows in these chapters that man no longer expects miracles from Providence to ease his sufferings; rather, he sees his hardships as punishments from God for some failure in following His commandments.

Twain referred to the "Little Bessie" chapters as "moral ideas." The work further develops Twain's dark view of "the damned human race" and pessimistic attitude regarding expectations of help from an apathetic, if not malicious, God. It also reflects his tendency to satirize man's acceptance of the goodness of his God, regardless of the evil in the world. In spite of its continuation of these themes, this piece has received little critical attention.

Margaret D. Bauer

BIBLIOGRAPHY
Clemens, Samuel L. *Mark Twain's Fables of Man.* Ed. John S. Tuckey. Berkeley: U of California P, 1972. 33–44.

Paine, Albert Bigelow. *Mark Twain: A Biography.* Vol. 3. New York: Harper, 1912. 1671–1673.

Wilson, James D. *A Reader's Guide to the Short Stories of Mark Twain.* Boston: G.K. Hall, 1987.

See also: God; Religion

Local Color

The local-color movement in literature, which flourished in America after the Civil War, is characterized by careful descriptions of the topography and climate of a given region, by an emphasis on the particularities of dress, behavior, mental habits, and customs of people native to the region, and by skillful use of dialect as a vehicle for pathos and humor. Influenced by British and French romanticism and by such antebellum American authors as Washington Irving, James Russell Lowell, and the southwestern humorists, the local-color movement was particularly strong in New

England, the South, and the West, as exemplified in the short fiction of Sarah Orne Jewett, Joel Chandler Harris, and Bret Harte. The traditions of local color, which persisted after the movement waned, affected novelists ranging from Mark Twain and George Washington Cable to Robert Penn Warren and Eudora Welty.

Among the many sociocultural influences conducive to the development of local color were an interest in sectionalism arising in the early nineteenth century and intensified by the Civil War; the desire of northern readers for idealized depictions of the antebellum South; the willingness of southern authors to supply such depictions; and the appetite of the mass reading public for romantic visions of a vanished past. Increasing competitiveness among the sections stimulated patriotic portrayals of regional distinctiveness, while the rapid industrialization of America and western Europe whetted nostalgic interest in rural as distinct from urban life. Although local-color novels and poems exist (Lowell's *Biglow Papers* [1848] an example of the latter), postbellum publishing conditions, particularly the prestige and commercial success of northern magazines like *Scribner's*, encouraged the use of short fictional forms, the story and the sketch, in which local-color authors excelled.

Local color is usually described as one strand of literary realism, but it has ties to romantic writing as well. The influence of Walter Scott and Maria Edgeworth in Britain and of the tradition of *coleur locale* exhibited by such authors as Victor Hugo in France encouraged the use of exotic settings and unusual customs in American local-color fiction; romantic traditions also lie behind that fiction's moral cast and the preference of its authors for happy endings. The influence of realism appears in the efforts of writers to portray character and setting with great fidelity of detail. Local color differs from realism, however, in its neglect of significant philosophical or sociological issues and its avoidance of such matters as human sexuality, psychological problems, and sordid living conditions.

The movement is one of several literary traditions that exercised great influence upon the writing of Mark Twain. According to some scholars, Twain began his career as a local colorist with pieces like "The Celebrated Jumping Frog of Calaveras County" (1864) that emanate from his experiences in the Far West. Local-color elements pervade his later writing, though their presence is often disguised by his inventive humor and darkly sardonic vision. Twain's detailed descriptions of such natural phenomena as the Mississippi River, his careful depictions of rural communities, his often satiric emphasis upon the eccentricities of rural people, and his clever use of dialect for comic and sinister effects connect him with the local-color movement. As he would do with another great influence upon him, that of southwestern humor, Twain in his genius transformed the elements of local color into the material of high and memorable art.

Mary Ann Wimsatt

BIBLIOGRAPHY

Hart, James D. *The Oxford Companion to American Literature.* 5th ed. New York: Oxford UP, 1983.

Holman, C. Hugh. *A Handbook to Literature.* 4th ed. Indianapolis: Bobbs-Merrill, 1980.

Skaggs, Merrill Maguire. *The Folk of Southern Fiction.* Athens: U of Georgia P, 1972.

Warfel, Harry A., and G. Harrison Orians, eds. *American Local-Color Stories.* New York: American Book, 1941.

See also: Realism; Regionalism; Southwestern Humor

Loftus, Mrs.

At the end of chapter 10 of *Adventures of Huckleberry Finn* (1885), Huck, disguised as a girl and seeking news of his "murder" and Jim's disappearance, peeps into a window and spies a woman of about forty. To his relief, he does not recognize her and believes his disguise will work. Chapter 11 opens with this woman, Mrs. Judith Loftus, inviting him inside; Huck introduces himself as Sarah Williams.

Though new to St. Petersburg, Mrs. Loftus does indeed provide Huck with the information he wants. The latest theory about Huck's murder has, in fact, linked the two events: people are conjecturing that Jim killed Huck. The $300 bounty on Jim's head has motivated men such as Mr. Loftus into searching for the runaway, while people are no longer very interested in accusing Huck's father of the "murder."

Huck tries to hide his anxiety by concentrating on threading a needle. Her suspicions aroused by his clumsy attempt, Mrs. Loftus tricks him into admitting that he is a boy. When she asks if he is a runaway apprentice, Huck immediately creates another fanciful tale of his identity to satisfy her, exhibiting his ability to think quickly under pressure. Mrs. Loftus accepts this story, cautions him about dressing as a girl, and sends him on his way, offering her services if he should need them in the future.

Margaret D. Bauer

BIBLIOGRAPHY

Clemens, Samuel L. *Adventures of Huckleberry Finn.* Ed. Walter Blair and Victor Fischer. Berkeley: U of California P, 1985.

See also: *Adventures of Huckleberry Finn*

Longfellow, Henry Wadsworth
(1897–1882)

Mark Twain was ambivalent in his attitude toward Henry Wadsworth Longfellow, the most honored American poet of his time. As an example of his playful quoting of Longfellow's poetry, in a letter of 21 November 1860 to his brother Orion, Twain used a stanza from "Psalm of Life" in an irreverent way; on the other hand, in 1875 he and his wife showed their respect as guests at Longfellow's Craigie House, and in 1880 he enlisted Longfellow to join him in petitioning the secretary of state regarding an international copyright treaty.

Interpreting Mark Twain's speech at the dinner for John Greenleaf Whittier's seventieth birthday (17 December 1877), Henry Nash Smith sees it as revealing unconscious antagonism toward New England literary titans. Edward Wagenknecht disagrees and says that Smith was led astray by an unfounded observation on the part of Edmund Wilson. In the speech, Mark Twain parodied Emerson, Holmes, and Longfellow in a story that included a bogus Longfellow who was "built like a prize-fighter" and who sprouted forth lines of Longfellow's poetry in absurd contexts. Distressed by what he later perceived as disrespect toward men whom he said he reverenced, Mark Twain sent Longfellow, Emerson, and Holmes abject letters of apology. Longfellow replied graciously that he did not believe anybody was much hurt and encouraged Mark Twain to dismiss the matter from his mind without further remorse.

Two years later, Clemens had an opportunity to redeem himself at a breakfast given to Dr. Holmes at which Longfellow was present.

Richard Dilworth Rust

BIBLIOGRAPHY

Clemens, Samuel L. *Mark Twain Speaking.* Ed. Paul Fatout. Iowa City: U of Iowa P, 1976.

———. *Mark Twain's Letters, Volume 1 (1853–1866).* Ed. Edgar M. Branch, Michael B. Frank, and Kenneth M. Sanderson. Berkeley: U of California P, 1988.

Smith, Henry Nash. *Mark Twain: The Development of a Writer.* Cambridge, Mass.: Harvard UP, 1962.

Wagenknecht, Edward. *Mark Twain: The Man and His Work.* Rev. ed. Norman: U of Oklahoma P, 1967.

See also: Whittier Birthday Dinner Speech

"Loves of Alonzo Fitz Clarence and Rosannah Ethelton, The"
(1878)

A burlesque love story, "The Loves of Alonzo Fitz Clarence and Rosannah Ethelton" was written in 1877 and was first published in the *Atlantic Monthly* in March 1878. The story is probably most notable for containing the first significant use of the telephone in a work of fiction.

The plot concerns Alonzo Fitz Clarence, a bored Maine aristocrat, and his courtship of Rosannah Ethelton, a beauty from San Francisco, as well as the interventions of a villainous rival, Sidney Algernon Burley. The courtship and the plot are conventional in that the two fall in love, the dastardly Burley causes them to have a falling-out, then they reunite and marry, while the chatty narrator makes deflating comments about the whole enterprise. What may have been merely a burlesque of love fiction and popular melodrama is altered by the introduction of a telephone as the means of courtship, breakup, and marriage. The narrator conceals this at first, having the snowbound Alonzo speak mysteriously into a cabinet to his aunt, who talks about her tropical weather and a three-and-a-half hour time difference. These discrepancies make the story seem absurd, almost surreal, until the narrator reveals that the characters have been talking into a telephone—and a transcontinental telephone at that. This is not the least of the technological wonders: later, telephones seemingly lurk in every convenient spot, and at one point Alonzo embarks on a trip with a *portable* phone.

One can certainly understand W.D. Howells's apparent lack of enthusiasm for the piece, but to modern eyes the story seems strangely prophetic. In this slight but interesting story, Mark Twain captures some of the odd disjointedness of modern life—the telephone brings people closer together, but also cuts them off from one another; it makes both communication and misunderstanding more likely. If nothing else, "Loves" served Mark Twain as a kind of rehearsal for the telephone sequences in *A Connecticut Yankee in King Arthur's Court* (1889), a more extended and central use of the telephone in a fictional work. This early use of the telephone in fiction, written the same year as the introduction of the first commercial model, reveals yet again not only Mark Twain's fascination with gadgets, inventions, and technology, but also his ongoing ambivalence, if not downright distrust, of some of civilization's progress.

John Bird

BIBLIOGRAPHY

Clemens, Samuel L. *The Science Fiction of Mark Twain.* Ed. David Ketterer. Hamden, Conn.: Archon, 1984.

———. *Selected Mark Twain-Howells Letters, 1872–1910.* Ed. Frederick Anderson, William M. Gibson, and Henry Nash Smith. Cambridge, Mass.: Harvard UP, 1967.

———. *The Stolen White Elephant, Etc.* Boston: James R. Osgood, 1882. 278–306.

———. *Tom Sawyer Abroad.* Vol. 14 of *The Complete Works of Mark Twain.* New York: Harper, 1917.

Horowitz, Floyd R. "Mark Twain's Belle Lettre in 'The Loves of Alonzo Fitz Clarence and Rosannah Ethelton.'" *Mark Twain Journal* 13 (Winter 1965): 16.

See also: Burlesque; "Stolen White Elephant, The"; Technology, Mark Twain and

Lowell, James Russell
(1819–1891)

A poet, a Harvard professor, an editor, an essayist, and a public servant, James Russell Lowell acted out the nineteenth-century concept of a man of letters whose accomplishments and influence are revealed as much through a reference to his biography and the historical context of an evolving nation as to his writings. His key poetic works, written in midlife, are *A Fable for Critics* (1848) and *The Biglow Papers*, First and Second Series (1848, 1867); they indicate a new literature with local-color elements and satirical passages that attracted a larger audience and predated the writings of William Dean Howells and Mark Twain. These are the same local-color elements, however, that would inform such early pieces as "The Celebrated Jumping Frog of Calaveras County" (1864) as well as many of the Mississippi River scenes of description;

and these are the same satirical passages that would become equally pronounced in their influence on his use of satire in such works as *Adventures of Huckleberry Finn* (1885).

Born in Cambridge and educated at Harvard, Lowell engaged in abolitionist crusades, encouraged by his abolitionist wife, Maria White. He served as minister to Spain (1877–1880) and to England (1880–1885).

Recent historical biographies, one by Edward Wagenknecht, and reassessment of Lowell's place in the history of American poetry by Marjorie R. Kaufman and of his literary criticism by Herbert F. Smith point out a righting of previous mixed and misdirected critical praise and lament as to his importance in American literature.

Charlotte S. McClure

BIBLIOGRAPHY

Lowell, James Russell. *The Biglow Papers (First Series): A Critical Edition*. Ed. Thomas Wortham. DeKalb: Northern Illinois UP, 1977.

————. *Literary Criticism of James Russell Lowell*. Ed. Herbert F. Smith. Lincoln: U of Nebraska P, 1969.

————. *The Poetical Works of James Russell Lowell*. Rev. with Intro. Marjorie R. Kaufman. Boston: Houghton Mifflin, 1978.

Rees, Robert A. "James Russell Lowell." *Fifteen American Authors Before 1900: Bibliographical Essays on Research and Criticism*. Ed. Earl N. Harbert and Robert A. Rees. Madison: U of Wisconsin P, 1971. 285–305.

Wagenknecht, Edward. *James Russell Lowell: Portrait of a Many-sided Man*. New York: Oxford UP, 1971.

See also: Local Color

"Lowest Animal, The"

(1962)

Originally published in 1962 in *Letters from the Earth* as "The Lowest Animal," a title supplied by Bernard DeVoto, the essay was given its present tentative title ("Man's Place in the Animal World") by Paul Baender when it was republished in *"What Is Man?" and Other Philosophical Writings* in 1973. Baender based his title on the discovery of an envelope in the Mark Twain Papers on which Twain had written, "Lower Animals/*not* the lower animals/Man's Place in the Animal World." Since the first page of the original manuscript is missing, certainty as to Twain's intended title is not finally established. Baender bases the date of composition (1896) on the appearance in London newspapers during 10–13 August 1896 of accounts of atrocities, referred to in the essay, inflicted on monks in Crete.

Characteristic of the increasing pessimism of Twain's older age, the essay explores the idea that man is not simply an animal, but an inferior animal. Assuming the role of a scientist who has been conducting behavioral experiments, Twain concludes that man is the only animal possessed of the qualities of greed, selfishness, malice, vindictiveness, indecency, and obscenity, and he attributes man's despicable character to his singular possession of a Moral Sense.

Twain's conception of man as an animal and his idea that the Moral Sense is responsible for man's degenerate character are, at least in part, his response to the age of Darwin. He read widely in current science. Alan Gribben lists two hundred science titles in Twain's library, including heavily notated volumes of Darwin's *Origin of Species*, *Decent of Man*, and *Expression of Emotions in Man and Animals*. Twain also read extensively in astronomy, geology, biology, and paleontology, which tend to diminish man's significance in the scheme of creation. His own experiences with and observations of humans must also have had their influence.

The ideas in this essay—that man is one of the lower animals and that he is degraded by his Moral Sense—reappear in later works such as *What Is Man?* (1906).

Susan Matthewson

BIBLIOGRAPHY

Baender, Paul. "The Date of Mark Twain's 'The Lowest Animal.'" *American Literature* 36 (May 1964): 174–179.

Clemens, Samuel L. *Letters from the Earth*. Ed. Bernard DeVoto. New York: Harper & Row, 1962. 175–184.

———. *Mark Twain's Fables of Man*. Ed. John S. Tuckey. Berkeley: U of California P, 1972.

———. *"What Is Man?" and Other Philosophical Writings*. Ed. Paul Baender. Berkeley: U of California P, 1973. 80–89.

Cummings, Sherwood. *Mark Twain and Science: Adventures of a Mind*. Baton Rouge: Louisiana State UP, 1988.

Gribben, Alan. *Mark Twain's Library: A Reconstruction*. 2 vols. Boston: G.K. Hall, 1980.

Tuckey, John S. *Mark Twain and Little Satan: The Writing of "The Mysterious Stranger."* West Lafayette, Ind.: Purdue U Studies, 1963.

See also: Science

times humorous role played by chance in the lives and reputations of the famous.

Craig Albin

BIBLIOGRAPHY

Clemens, Samuel L. *Mark Twain in Eruption*. Ed. Bernard DeVoto. New York: Harper, 1940. 209–210.

———. *Mark Twain's Notebooks & Journals, Volume III (1883–1891)*. Ed. Robert Pack Browning, Michael B. Frank, and Lin Salamo. Berkeley: U of California P, 1979.

Long, E. Hudson. *Mark Twain Handbook*. New York: Hendricks House, 1957.

Wagenknecht, Edward. *Mark Twain: The Man and His Work*. Rev. ed. Norman: U of Oklahoma P, 1967.

"Luck"

(1891)

"Luck" is a brief sketch that, though written in April 1886, did not appear in print until August 1891 when it was published in *Harper's Monthly Magazine*. Mark Twain's tenuous financial situation resulting from the failure of the Paige typesetter seems to have been a motivating factor in his choice to market this sketch.

"Luck" concerns the remarkable good fortune in the career of an English military officer whose fame is predicated upon a series of blunders—blunders that his superiors have inevitably interpreted as the unorthodox actions of a military genius. Because of this unerring good fortune, the officer eventually achieves the rank of lieutenant-general.

Twain claimed he did not invent this story but rather heard it from a clergyman who had once been an instructor at the officer's military school and who had been an eyewitness to the officer's remarkable rise. He also claimed that on his 1891 trip through Europe two separate Englishmen told him that the real identity in "Luck" of Lieutenant-General Lord Arthur Scoresby was actually Lord Wolsely.

"Luck" is a minor work that reveals, with typical Twainian insight, the ironic and some-

"Lucretia Smith's Soldier"

(1864)

Clemens wrote "Lucretia Smith's Soldier" in 1864; it was published in the *Californian* on 3 December of the same year. Written in the popular genre of a "condensed novel," the story was reprinted a number of times just after its first appearance. Clemens included it in *The Celebrated Jumping Frog of Calaveras County and Other Sketches* (1867).

Set in Massachusetts in 1861, "LSS" opens with grocery and dry goods clerk Reginald de Whittaker optimistically anticipating the moment when he will tell Lucretia Smith that he has enlisted. Before he has the chance, however, Lucretia sends him away, offended by his common job. Ironically, while Lucretia pines for what could have been if only he were a soldier, Reginald joins his company. Lucretia hears of her mistake and, dismayed that she has no one "representing" her in the army, follows the news of Reginald from the letters her friends receive from their beaux. Learning that an R.D. Whittaker lies wounded in a Washington hospital, Lucretia rushes to the bedside of a soldier whose wounded jaw has left him mute and his face wrapped in bandages. When the bandages are removed, Lucretia is horrified to discover she has "gone and fooled away three mortal weeks here, snuffling and slobbering over the wrong soldier!"

The story's plot and style burlesque romantic war stories and sentimental novels, three in particular that have been identified as the sources for this story's satire by the editors of the Iowa-California edition of *Early Tales & Sketches*, in which "LSS" is included: "An Exchange of Prisoners," a war story published in *Harper's Weekly* 3 January 1863; Pierce Egan's sentimental novel *Such Is Life*, published serially throughout 1864 in the *Golden Era*; and Mary Elizabeth Braddon's sentimental novel *The Trail of the Serpent*, also published serially from 1863 to 1864 in the *Era*. Such satirizing of high sentimentality prevails throughout Clemens's work; perhaps the most famous example is the poetry of Emmeline Grangerford in *Adventures of Huckleberry Finn* (1885). Following the tradition of the sentimental novel, Clemens includes a "Note from the Author," who is identified as M.T., in which the story's "truthfulness" is established.

Margaret D. Bauer

BIBLIOGRAPHY

Clemens, Samuel L. "Lucretia Smith's Soldier." *The Works of Mark Twain: Early Tales & Sketches, Volume 2 (1864–1865)*. By Clemens. Ed. Edgar M. Branch and Robert H. Hirst. Berkeley: U of California P, 1981. 125–133.

Wilson, James D. *A Reader's Guide to the Short Stories of Mark Twain*. Boston: G.K. Hall, 1987.

See also: Condensed Novels; Sentimentality

Lyon, Isabel

(1863–1958)

Samuel Clemens hired Miss Lyon in November 1902 to serve as his social secretary, bookkeeper, and letter-writer. As Olivia's health declined, Isabel became increasingly important in the family circle. Until 1909 she carried out the duties of business manager, social secretary, nurse for Jean Clemens, supervisor of the building of Stormfield, and personal audience for much of Mark Twain's writing of the last few years of his life.

High-strung and of a sensitive and emotional temperament, Lyon was a mixture of sycophant, idolator, and "Boswell" for Mark Twain in the last years of his life, pouring out her responses to his personality in notes, diaries, daybooks, journals, and snapshots of her subject.

In 1909 Clara Clemens became suspicious and perhaps jealous of Lyon's influence over her father, and she began insinuating that Lyon and Ralph Ashcroft were guilty of embezzling money from the humorist. Lyon married Ashcroft, "without loving him," as she later claimed. On 15 April 1909 Clemens fired Lyon, evicted her from her cottage, "The Lobster Pot," on the grounds of Stormfield, filed lawsuits against her and Ashcroft, and claimed that she had hypnotized him into "the enslaved condition that I had been in for the past two or three years." On 7 September 1909, an out-of-court agreement removed the Ashcrofts, physically at least, from the scene. Isabel, however, became the subject of the "Ashcroft-Lyon Manuscript" and the target of Clara Clemens's vindictiveness for literally decades.

The Ashcrofts divorced in the early 1920s, and Isabel worked for the Home Title Company in Brooklyn until her death, at age 95, in 1958. She stipulated that none of her commentaries about Mark Twain should be made available for scholarly study until after Clara's death. Those comments provide an intimate, perhaps overly devoted, glimpse into the daily life of Mark Twain more voluminously than any other record.

Hamlin Hill

BIBLIOGRAPHY

Hill, Hamlin. *Mark Twain: God's Fool*. New York: Harper, 1973.

See also: Ashcroft, Ralph; "Ashcroft-Lyon Manuscript"; Samossoud, Clara Clemens

M

Macaulay, Thomas Babington, Lord
(1800–1859)

British historian and politician, Thomas Macaulay was one of the most popular literary figures of the nineteenth century. He graduated from Cambridge and was called to the bar, but it was his essay for the *Edinburgh Review* on Milton (1825) that won acclaim. Everything he wrote, from reviews to verse to his well-known *History of England*, was phenomenally successful. In addition, he served in Parliament at various times and on the British Supreme Council of India from 1834 to 1838.

Mark Twain was probably familiar with Macaulay from boyhood—American schoolchildren knew "Horatius at the Bridge" from *Lays of Ancient Rome* (1842), and the poem is alluded to in *A Connecticut Yankee in King Arthur's Court* (1889). Twain used William E.H. Lecky's books on English history in writing *A Connecticut Yankee*; Lecky, in turn, was indebted to Macaulay. Twain admired Macaulay's brilliant and elegant writing; as he noted in *The Innocents Abroad* (1869), "Macaulay is present when we follow the march of his stately sentences" (2:220). In *A Connecticut Yankee*, and his other historical novels, Twain strove to emulate Macaulay's vivid depiction of life in past times.

Twain mentions Macaulay in many of his essays, from his 1870 hoax review of *The Innocents Abroad* to his long essay, *Is Shakespeare Dead?* (1909), where he quotes extensively from Macaulay's essay "Lord Bacon" (1837). Twain wrote his poem "The Derelict" (1893) after he had read Macaulay's essays on Clive and Hastings to his wife and his daughter Susy. Macaulay's writings on India influenced Twain's *Following the Equator* (1897), and Twain referred to the essays on Clive and Hastings again in his speech "Edmund Burke on Croker and Tammany" (1901).

When Albert Bigelow Paine went to Bermuda in 1910 to bring Twain home for the last time, Twain had been rereading Macaulay's *History of England*; he read it numerous times throughout his life. Twain commented negatively on Macaulay in his *Autobiography*, elevating the monkey over Macaulay for an "Ignorant . . . trivial and jejune" (280) speech he made in Parliament regarding a great thorn in Twain's side, the copyright laws.

Patricia Hunt

BIBLIOGRAPHY

Clemens, Samuel L. *Mark Twain Speaking*. Ed. Paul Fatout. Iowa City: U of Iowa P, 1976.

Krause, Sydney J. *Mark Twain as Critic*. Baltimore: Johns Hopkins UP, 1967.

Long, E. Hudson. *Mark Twain Handbook*. New York: Hendricks House, 1957.

Macaulay, Thomas Babington. *Lord Macaulay's Essays and Lays of Ancient Rome*. London: Longmans, Green, 1886.

———. *Macaulay's Life of Johnson*. Ed. Stewart Lee Garrison. New York: F.M. Ambrose, 1928.

Paine, Albert Bigelow. *Mark Twain: A Biography*. 3 vols. New York: Harper, 1912.

See also: Copyright; Lecky, William Edward Hartpole

McDougal's Cave

The vast limestone cavern that provides a setting for melodrama in *The Adventures of Tom Sawyer* (1876), McDougal's Cave is a fictional representation of what was Hannibal's premier tourist attraction during the early nineteenth century. Curious visitors traveled long distances to explore Simms Cave—later renamed Saltpeter Cave, later still McDowell's Cave—a "tangled wilderness of narrow and lofty clefts and passages" located two miles south of town, where Sam Clemens and his friends played often as children (Clemens, *Autobiography* 104).

According to Mark Twain's recollection, the cave was the scene of events even more melodramatic than the gradual starvation of Injun Joe at the end of *Tom Sawyer*. Several

local inhabitants, including "General" Gaines, Hannibal's first town drunk, survived for days after becoming lost inside by living off the endless supply of bats. Throughout Clemens's boyhood, the cave was owned by an eccentric doctor, E.D. McDowell, who stored armaments for an invasion of Mexico in one of its secret chambers. McDowell apparently also entombed within the cave the cadaver of a young girl—rumored to be his own daughter—which he placed in a copper cylinder filled with alcohol as an experiment in petrification. These and other bizarre stories associated with Hannibal's mysterious cavern, stories that Twain's biographers generally regard as true, must have excited Sam Clemens's imagination during the mid-1840s and may in part explain why cave imagery figures importantly in some of Mark Twain's best fiction, including *Tom Sawyer*, *Adventures of Huckleberry Finn* (1885), and *A Connecticut Yankee in King Arthur's Court* (1889).

Henry B. Wonham

BIBLIOGRAPHY

Clemens, Samuel L. *The Adventures of Tom Sawyer*. Ed. John C. Gerber and Paul Baender. Berkeley: U of California P, 1982.

———. *Life on the Mississippi*. Boston: James R. Osgood, 1883.

———. *Mark Twain's Autobiography*. Ed. Albert B. Paine. 2 vols. New York: Harper, 1924.

Paine, Albert Bigelow. *Mark Twain: A Biography*. 3 vols. New York: Harper, 1912.

Sanborn, Margaret. *Mark Twain: The Bachelor Years*. New York: Doubleday, 1990.

Wecter, Dixon. *Sam Clemens of Hannibal*. Boston: Houghton Mifflin, 1952.

See also: *Adventures of Tom Sawyer, The*

Macfarlane

A section of *Mark Twain's Autobiography* (1924) under the heading "Macfarlane" recounts the exposure of young Samuel Clemens to the pessimistic evolutionary ideas of a dour Scotchman in Cincinnati, Ohio, during the winter of 1857. Although no other trace of

Macfarlane has appeared, Twain's biographers since Albert Bigelow Paine cite the encounter between Clemens and Macfarlane as significant in the development of the author's views on humankind.

According to Twain, Macfarlane, an amateur philosopher and expert on both the dictionary and the Bible, spent the evenings at their boardinghouse propounding a theory of evolution antedating that of Darwin. He proposed that man passed through stages originating in a seed germ. Instead of being the apex of evolution, however, man, because of his propensity to vice and violence, is morally worse than the lesser forms. Worst of all, man used what should have been the crowning achievement of evolution, his reasoning power, not to gain moral stature but to control other people.

The negative ideas that Twain attributes to Macfarlane here are inseparable from Twain's own bitter concepts about the general state of humankind as expressed in such works as *What Is Man?* (1906) and "The Damned Human Race," especially the section "The Lowest Animal" (written ca. 1896), which is largely an amplification of these ideas. The similarity between Twain's own ideas and those of Macfarlane, together with the lack of any other evidence in support of the existence, has led Paul Baender and Howard Baetzhold to question the actuality of a Macfarlane. They propose that he is one of the masks Twain wore to express many of his more controversial ideas.

William McDonald

BIBLIOGRAPHY

Baender, Paul. "Alias Macfarlane: A Revision of Mark Twain Biography." *American Literature* 38 (1966): 187–197.

Baetzhold, Howard G. *Mark Twain and John Bull: The British Connection.* Bloomington: Indiana UP, 1970.

Clemens, Samuel L. *Letters from the Earth.* Ed. Bernard DeVoto. New York: Harper & Row, 1962.

———. *Mark Twain's Autobiography.* Ed. Albert B. Paine. 2 vols. New York: Harper, 1924.

———. *A Pen Warmed-Up in Hell: Mark Twain in Protest.* Ed. Frederick Anderson. New York: Harper & Row, 1972.

See also: Cincinnati, Ohio; "Damned Human Race, The"; Darwin, Charles; "Lowest Animal, The"; *What Is Man?*

Machiavelli, Niccolò
(1469–1527)

A Florentine political theorist and the author of *The Prince* and the *Discourses on Livy,* Niccolò Machiavelli is regarded as the founder of modern political philosophy and political science. Machiavelli rejected the view that the standard for politics is set by nature, the political ideal, or the best regime, holding that government's title to rule derives from "the effectual truth" and the ability to get results, through technical skill and the command over force.

As early as 1878, Twain listed Machiavelli among the "celebrated" Florentines who are "familiar to every schoolboy in the Christian world" (*Notebooks & Journals* 2:227–228). Later, in his essay "William Dean Howells," (1906) Twain lauded Howells's "paper on Machiavelli" (a review of Louis Dyer's *Machiavelli and the Modern State,* 1904), singling out for special praise Howells's description of Machiavelli as "an idealist immersed in realities" who "involuntarily transmutes the events under his eye into something like the visionary issues of reverie"—an "airy thought," Twain wrote, expressed with remarkable brevity and subtlety ("William Dean Howells" 402). Twain applauded, in other words, Howells's view that Machiavellian "realism" is really a kind of dreamy idealism, one that underrated the real constraints of practice. It is this error, for Twain as for Howells, that led the republican Machiavelli, confronted with civic corruption, to imagine that republicanism could be restored by a cunning and forceful prince.

In *A Connecticut Yankee in King Arthur's Court* (1889) Hank Morgan resembles a version of Machiavelli's prince, a man eager to rule, inclined to commerce, but whose "real trade" was learned in the Colt arms factory, paralleling Machiavelli's prescription that the prince "take nothing else as his art but the art of war." The Yankee, like Machiavelli, hopes to revive a people's political imagination and create a republic by technique and—in the last analysis—by force and fear. That he fails indicates Twain's verdict on Machiavellianism. By contrast, Twain believed that civic virtue must be nurtured by humor and story, beguiling human beings out of fearful self-interest, as in Howells's description of *Connecticut Yankee* as a fable that calls attention to and draws us into our own times.

Wilson Carey McWilliams

BIBLIOGRAPHY

Clemens, Samuel L. *A Connecticut Yankee in King Arthur's Court.* Ed. Bernard Stein. Berkeley: U of California P, 1979.

———. *Mark Twain's Notebooks & Journals.* Ed. Frederick Anderson, et al. 3 vols. Berkeley: U of California P, 1975–1979.

———. "William Dean Howells." *The Complete Essays of Mark Twain.* Ed. Charles Neider. Garden City, N.Y.: Doubleday, 1963. 400–407.

Howells, William Dean. "The Editor's Study." *Harper's New Monthly Magazine* 80 (January 1890): 318–323.

Mansfield, Harvey C., Jr. *Machiavelli's New Modes and Orders: A Study of The Discourses on Livy.* Ithaca, N.Y.: Cornell UP, 1979.

Smith, Bruce James. *Politics and Remembrance: Republican Themes In Machiavelli, Burke, and Tocqueville.* Princeton, N.J.: Princeton UP, 1985.

Strauss, Leo. *Thoughts on Machiavelli.* Glencoe, Ill.: Free P, 1958.

See also: Connecticut Yankee in King Arthur's Court, A; Morgan, Hank

McWilliams, Mortimer and Caroline (Evangeline)

Mr. and Mrs. McWilliams appear in three short works: "Experience of the McWilliamses with Membranous Croup" (1875), "Mrs. McWilliams and the Lightning" (1880), and "The McWilliamses and the Burglar Alarm" (1882). In the first story Mrs. McWilliams is named Caroline, but in the second story her name is Evangeline. The McWilliamses are a married couple, the parents of at least two children.

In the comic pieces on the McWilliams family, Mortimer McWilliams is the narrator, telling the stories to Mark Twain on the train. The tone is one of male camaraderie, with the characters sharing an awareness of the foibles of women. The humor turns on the portrayal of the long-suffering husband's attempts to satisfy a demanding and rather silly wife. At the end of each story the husband is vindicated. In the "Membranous Croup" story Mr. McWilliams suggests that it might be dangerous for their young child to chew on a piece of pine stick. Mrs. McWilliams argues with him, and Mr. McWilliams notes that "women cannot receive even the most palpably judicious suggestion without arguing it; that is married women" (7:85). When the child coughs, Mrs. McWilliams becomes convinced that the child is dangerously ill with the croup. After keeping her husband awake all night running unnecessary errands to administer to the "sick" child, she learns from the doctor in the morning that the child's cough was caused by bits of pine stick that were caught in her throat. McWilliams implies that this incident is useful to hold over his wife's head to avoid marital friction, and Twain concludes the story with a postscript suggesting that other married men might enjoy reading a story in which a husband's experience has such a satisfying conclusion.

The humor in "Mrs. McWilliams and the Lightning" derives from Mrs. McWilliams's fear of lightning, a fear that, the narrator says, is "mostly confined to women" (19:330). Believing that there is a severe electrical storm, Mrs. McWilliams makes Mr. McWilliams take a series of ridiculous precautions to protect himself from the lightning. In the morning the McWilliamses find that there was no electrical storm at all; the noise and flashes were caused by the cannon celebrating a political victory. In "The McWilliamses and the Burglar Alarm" the humor revolves around the family's experiences with the burglar alarm (its malfunctioning, the expense, the burglars it fails to keep out) rather than the ridiculous demands of Mrs. McWilliams. However, the burglar alarm was Mrs. McWilliams's idea. By the end of the story, after nine years of harassment caused by problems with the alarm, Mr. McWilliams has the "full consent" of Mrs. McWilliams to take out the alarm system (27:324).

For the most part, the critics have tended to ignore the McWilliams stories, which are not regarded as examples of Twain's best humor (Budd 52; DeVoto 56). However, some critics have praised them for the ironies of their domestic humor (Baldanza 128; Covici 45–46), and the stories have been said to reflect Twain's own domestic life at the time (Gibson 80; Baldanza 99; Emerson 88). James Wilson finds value in Mr. McWilliams as a figure with whom the middle class can identify (80), but Alfred Habegger points out that the McWilliams stories generate sympathy for the husband at the expense of the wife (888). Certainly, Twain's generalizations about women in these stories and his portrayal of Mrs. McWilliams in stereotypical terms are consistent with the limited view of women in much of his writing and with his failure throughout his fiction to portray women as fully developed characters.

Joyce W. Warren

BIBLIOGRAPHY

Baldanza, Frank. *Mark Twain: An Introduction and Interpretation.* New York: Barnes & Noble, 1961.

Budd, Louis J. *Our Mark Twain: The Making of His Public Personality.* Philadelphia: U of Pennsylvania P, 1983.

Clemens, Samuel L. *The Writings of Mark Twain.* Stormfield Ed. Vols. 7, 19, 27. New York: Harper, 1929.

Covici, Pascal, Jr. *Mark Twain's Humor: The Image of a World.* Dallas: Southern Methodist UP, 1962.

DeVoto, Bernard. *Mark Twain at Work.* Cambridge, Mass.: Harvard UP, 1942.

Emerson, Everett. *The Authentic Mark Twain: A Literary Biography of Samuel L. Clemens.* Philadelphia: U of Pennsylvania P, 1984.

Gibson, William M. *The Art of Mark Twain.* New York: Oxford UP, 1976.

Habegger, Alfred. "Nineteenth-Century American Humor: Easygoing Males, Anxious Ladies, and Penelope Lapham." *Publications of the Modern Language Association* 91 (October 1976): 884–899.

Wilson, James D. *A Reader's Guide to the Short Stories of Mark Twain.* Boston: G.K. Hall, 1987.

See also: "Experience of the McWilliamses with Membranous Croup"; Humor; "McWilliamses and the Burglar Alarm, The"; "Mrs. McWilliams and the Lightning"; Women

"McWilliamses and the Burglar Alarm, The"
(1882)

The last and funniest of three domestic comedies about the McWilliams family, "The McWilliamses and the Burglar Alarm," written June 1882 for the Title Club, appeared in *Harper's Christmas, 1882,* an illustrated supplement to *Harper's Monthly* edited by club members (Emerson 118). The story is reprinted in the 1922 edition of *The Mysterious Stranger and Other Stories.* Just as "The McWilliamses and the Burglar Alarm" specifically derives from an episode involving wife Olivia and Clemens's home alarm, the entire McWilliams series generally derives from Clemens's domestic life. Twain's fondness and identification are indicated by his use of "McWilliams" as a substitute autograph.

The loose derivation of the story from Clemens's personal life has spawned diverse critical responses. As portraits of male reason subjugated to female ill logic and as comic mirrors of Clemens's marital interchanges, the three McWilliams stories seem to form a unit with the later Adam-Eve diaries. William Dean Howells reads the McWilliams stories as Mark Twain's continuing marital joke; Everett Emerson calls them the author's "subtle revenge." Van Wyck Brooks and Alfred Habegger are harsher: for the former, the stories provide evidence of Twain's artistic and creative decline under Olivia's guidance into middle-class life and values; the latter sees sexist assumptions underlying the series. In "The McWilliamses and the Burglar Alarm," the final story in the series, focus shifts from distress with nature, from disease in the home and lightning outside, and from family confrontations, to intrusion of the home faced together. Although it is Evangeline who insists that they buy the alarm system, and Mortimer assumes his customary role as henpecked husband (explaining compromise as doing what the wife wants), emphasis in the story quickly centers on their mutual difficulties and suffering at the hands of an alien mechanical system.

Twain's well-known fascination with new gadgets here develops into a metaphor for the pursuit of outlets for new, middle-class affluence. The McWilliamses's affluence is sorely tested, however, because burglaries occur on successive floors even after the initial $325 first-floor installation and subsequent $300 investments for second- and third-floor installations. Money, however, is only the beginning of the aggravation with a mechanical system that never works properly. The cook sets off the alarm when she enters the house each morning at five. To remedy this glitch, the confused butler switches the alarm off every night, then back on the next morning, just in time for the arriving cook to trip it off again and awaken the family. Desperate for a night's unbroken sleep, the family rigs the system so that the opened kitchen door will shut down the system; this response, however, allows burglars quiet access to the house. The McWilliamses suffer numerous false alarms and have to replace the system every three months with clocks that invariably switch on and off at the wrong time. After false alarms cause Mortimer to shoot a nurse, and the coachman to shoot him, the distraught master of the house systematically disconnects all faulty alarms and burglars begin to occupy his rooms as havens from the police.

Gently satirizing middle-class use of prosperity, Twain places in perspective human flaws and frustrations by reducing them to burlesque amusement replete with exaggeration and irony. Beginning in medias res, like the previous stories in the series and employing the same frame of traveler McWilliams's relating his family's recent misadventures to fellow passenger Twain, "The McWilliamses and the Burglar Alarm" has less marital conflict and more marital togetherness. In fact, the movement of the three stories has been toward mutual involvement. The uncontrollable alarm machinery is as incomprehensible as the German safety instructions for thunderstorms they together mistranslate in the "Lightning" story. The wife, like Mortimer, is at the mercy of the device as much as he, the reasonable forebearing male, is at the mercy of her female whims. Universality stems from familiar domesticity, though exaggerated, and human inadequacy before machinery.

Enduring humiliation, discouragement, and financial loss, Mortimer, spirit unbroken, wins reader sympathy and respect by confronting his problems with resignation, self-awareness, irony, and deadpan humor. The first-person narrative framework permits him distance from his acknowledged ludicrousness and the reader's smiling identification with Mortimer's futile fight against life's irrationalities.

John H. Davis

BIBLIOGRAPHY

Baldanza, Frank. *Mark Twain: An Introduction and Interpretation.* New York: Barnes & Noble, 1961.

Brooks, Van Wyck. *The Ordeal of Mark Twain.* Rev. ed. New York: Dutton, 1933.

Clemens, Samuel L. *Mark Twain-Howells Letters: The Correspondence of Samuel L. Clemens and William D. Howells.* Vol. 2. Ed. Henry Nash Smith and William M. Gibson. Cambridge, Mass.: Harvard UP, 1960.

———. *The Mysterious Stranger and Other Stories.* New York: Harper, 1922. 315–324.

Covici, Pascal, Jr. *Mark Twain's Humor: The Image of a World.* Dallas: Southern Methodist UP, 1962.

Emerson, Everett. *The Authentic Mark Twain: A Literary Biography of Samuel L. Clemens.* Philadelphia: U of Pennsylvania P, 1984.

Gibson, William M. *The Art of Mark Twain.* New York: Oxford UP, 1976.

Habegger, Alfred. "Nineteenth-Century American Humor: Easygoing Males, Anxious Ladies, and Penelope Lapham." *Publications of the Modern Language Association* 91 (October 1976): 884–899.

Howells, William Dean. *My Mark Twain: Reminiscences and Criticisms.* New York: Harper, 1910.

Wilson, James D. *A Reader's Guide to the Short Stories of Mark Twain.* Boston: G.K. Hall, 1987.

See also: "Experience of the McWilliamses with Membranous Croup"; Family Life; McWilliams, Mortimer and Caroline (Evangeline); "Mrs. McWilliams and the Lightning"

Malory, Sir Thomas
(1400?–1471)

Sir Thomas Malory was an English writer, famous as the author of *Le Morte D'Arthur*. The identity of Malory (or "Maleore," as he spelled his name in the colophon of the *Morte D'Arthur*) remains uncertain, but it is probable that he was a Warwickshire knight who spent much of his adult life in prison and may have died there.

According to Twain's account, he bought a copy of *Morte D'Arthur* (in Sir Edward Strachey's edition) on the recommendation of George Washington Cable in December 1884. From the beginning, then, the book helped to inspire and shape *A Connecticut Yankee in King Arthur's Court* (1889), and Twain refers to Malory's tales in other writings, such as *Pudd'nhead Wilson* (1894). Twain regarded Malory's storytelling as magisterial and spoke of Sir Ector de Maris's eulogy for Launcelot as "perfect," an example of rhetoric equal to the Gettysburg Address, and he used it as a model when composing his own eulogy for General Grant (*Notebooks & Journals* 3:159).

A Connecticut Yankee makes frequent allusions to Malory, and long quotations from *Morte D'Arthur* are included in the text, the "Word of Explanation" as well as the Stranger's "Tale of the Lost Land." The archaic quality of Malory's prose allowed Twain to convey a sense of time past as well as the sound and flavor of antiquity. However, Twain also used *Morte D'Arthur* as a subtext, a design hinted at by his early plan to include a cheap edition of Malory with each copy of *A Connecticut Yankee*.

The Yankee's manuscript, Twain told his readers, proved to be a palimpsest, written over an older account (implicitly Malory's), only part of which survives in Twain's book. In every case but one, there are significant omissions from Malory in Twain's long excerpts (and the exception, Merlin's Tale, itself omits critical elements of an earlier version of the story in *Morte D'Arthur*). In chapter 19 of *A Connecticut Yankee* Twain followed the conclusion of Sandy's tale with a footnote: "The story is borrowed, language and all, from *Morte D'Arthur*," but an important part of the tale has been left out, and to emphasize the point, the Yankee refers to the omitted materials at the end of the chapter. Many other allusions to Malory in *A Connecticut Yankee* involve errors or half-truths. The effect of all these omissions and mistakes is to call attention to the fact that the Yankee either lacks or suppresses Malory's appreciation of the fragility of fraternity and honor when confronted with old resentments and dreams of revenge, the desire for dominion, and—above all—sexual passion. The comparison with Malory underlines the Yankee's shortcomings, the shallowness of his view of human nature and his exaggeration of the possibilities of political change, foreshadowing and helping to explain his failure and fate.

Wilson Carey McWilliams

BIBLIOGRAPHY

Clemens, Samuel L. *A Connecticut Yankee in King Arthur's Court.* Ed. Bernard Stein. Berkeley: U of California P, 1979.

———. *Mark Twain's Notebooks & Journals.* 3 vols. Ed. Frederick Anderson, et al. Berkeley: U of California P, 1975–1979.

Gribben, Alan. "The Master Hand of Old Malory: Mark Twain's Acquaintance with the *Morte D'Arthur*." *English Language Notes* 16 (1978): 32–40.

Malory, Sir Thomas. *Morte D'Arthur*. Ed. Sir Edward Strachey. Globe Edition. London: Macmillan, 1876.

Vinaver, Eugiene. *The Rise of Romance*. New York: Oxford UP, 1971.

Wilson, Robert H. "Malory in *The Connecticut Yankee*." *Texas Studies in English* 27 (1948): 185–205.

See also: *Connecticut Yankee in King Arthur's Court, A*

"Mammoth Cod, The"

(written ca. 1902)

A short bawdy piece attributed to Mark Twain, "The Mammoth Cod" may have been written in the first weeks of March 1902 (Legman 14); it was discovered in a typewritten book, Henry N. Cary's *A Treasury of Erotic and Facetious Memorabilia* (Chicago, 1901–1915). Blanck lists a New York publication, circa 1920. In the Cary book the piece is attributed to Petroleum V. Nasby, but scholars generally accept Mark Twain's authorship. The most accessible version is G. Legman's limited edition.

"The Mammoth Cod" is in the form of a letter from a supposedly prudish man refusing the company of a club of men because he disapproves of their pride in thinking themselves well endowed. The centerpiece of the letter is a poem that celebrates the size and works of various animals' penises. The letter goes on, full of puns and double entendres, making humorous, satiric points about male pride, masturbation, social diseases, and God's plan. Although he claims to be a moral, religious man, above the wicked practices of the Mammoth Cod Club, the letter writer's tone is clearly ironic, revealing him to be just as pleasure seeking as the men he supposedly berates.

Although Legman sees the short piece as proof that Mark Twain was impotent (5), probably its only real importance is as an example of Twain's bawdy.

John Bird

BIBLIOGRAPHY

Clemens, Samuel L. *The Mammoth Cod*. Ed. G. Legman. Milwaukee: Maledicta, 1976.

See also: Scatology; *1601*; "Some Thoughts on the Science of Onanism"

"Man That Corrupted Hadleyburg, The"

(1899)

Written in Vienna in December 1898, "The Man That Corrupted Hadleyburg" was first published in *Harper's New Monthly Magazine* for December 1899.

In this story Mark Twain explores the psychological basis of the two ills that in his judgment beset late-nineteenth-century America: money fever and slavish social, intellectual, and moral conformity. The story reveals that these ills are manifestations of a psychology that Twain explicitly developed in other works of his pessimist period. Above all, its characters are embodiments of his contention in *What Is Man?* (the first draft of which was completed in 1898) that man-the-machine is activated, in all his various motions, by one master passion, the absolute need for self-approval; this imperative, Twain's "gospel" contends, propels man's physical, intellectual, and moral faculties, which operate automatically.

In "Hadleyburg" self-approval has the two primary sources identified in "Corn-Pone Opinions" (1901): the approval of others, whose opinion is thus a powerful force for conformity; and wealth, the individualist pursuit of which can also result in a paradoxically conformist behavior. In addition, the story pushes to its bleak conclusions Twain's attack, launched in "The Character of Man" (1885), upon the common-sense belief in undetermined selfhood, a personal identity not fabricated by heredity and environmental "training." In this essay and *A Connecticut Yankee* (1889), however, Twain left open the possibility of a microscopic original self worth saving, the derivative remainder of what passes for personal identity beneath serious notice;

in "Hadleyburg" he denies even this microscopic self.

The opening section of the story establishes the hold these two varieties of self-contentment have upon the town and its consequent vulnerability to temptation. Hadleyburg's smug complacency is a product of its reputation for honesty, i.e., of the image of itself it finds reflected in the eyes of neighboring towns. Communal self-approval is thus founded in large measure upon the approval of other communities. Its citizens are susceptible to the corrupting influence of the satanic stranger, however, in part because they value their contentment-breeding reputation more than the practice of honesty itself, in part because of the weakness in their training program, which shields Hadleyburgian honesty from the toughening test of exposure to temptation.

The eroded self-esteem of the central characters points to other areas of vulnerability. In the past old Edward and Mary Richards gained their "good name," the self-gratifying personal equivalent of the town's reputation, by knuckling under to a tyrannical public opinion, even when, as in the case of Reverend Burgess, that opinion was cruelly wrongheaded. Yet Edward's self-regard is damaged by his cowardice, which prevented outright defiance of the collective judgment, as it is further weakened by his poverty. His dejection upon his homecoming indicates that in Hadleyburg self-satisfaction is in fact a function of economic status. The ironic stranger's sack of gilded lead disks fully activates the Richardses's already felt need for the pocketbook variety of self-approval.

In the first half of the narrative Twain chronicles the gradual collapse of the moral identity of the town's leading citizens, the "Nineteeners." As the Richardses and their equals give in to temptation, however, what is ironically revealed is a society not of distinct individuals but instead of people who are essentially duplicates, in thought and action, of one another. In chasing frantically after money, the village oligarchs resemble puppets whose intricate movements are identical. The initial distraction and greedy decision of the Richardses are duplicated by the Coxes. The old couple's subsequent scenes of guesswork, rationalization, and self-deceiving fabrication of a personal history that establishes their eligibility for the gold are repeated, as "plagiarisms," by all of their equals in social caste. As their pattern unfolds, an image emerges of man the mass-produced, standardized machine powered by a single motive force. Even the Nineteeners' similar-sounding names suggest this uniformity: this is a community of Billsons, Wilsons, Wilcoxes, and Coxes.

In the second half Twain enlarges the scale of duplication. At the eventful town meeting he blurs individualizing details, describing the audience as a single entity that rises in a body, holds its collective breath, is "stricken with a paralysis," and so forth. All Hadleyburgians are transfixed by the sack of gold. When commoners are individualized, Twain discloses that they are aspirants to membership in the elite class, indicating the uniformity of interest and character of the two groups. A pathetic final instance of duplication involves the fate of the Richardses, who make identical remarks even in their delirium; thus it is no surprise that they die on the same day.

In the singularity of their destruction, the Richardses are individualized; in this respect they are aligned with other characters who stand outside the communal identity. There is Barclay Goodson, the non-native. There is Jack Halliday, the "no-account" loafer who has offered the town his illusion-dispelling perspective of laughter, a gift that, until the truth-revealing town meeting, it has refused. There is Burgess, whose long-standing grievance makes him a logical choice as an agent of the town's chastening and whose acceptability as master of ceremonies attests to the community's unconscious wish to be punished. But the unshared destiny of the Richardses is a further instance of Twainian determinism, a dramatic working out of the theory presented in "The Chronicle of Young Satan," written between 1897 and 1900, that a person's life is a chain of linked events, each determined by its predecessor and determining, in turn, the event that follows. The old couple's fate thus stretches back through a sequence of inexorable events to their initial entanglement with Burgess, which amounts to the crucial turning point in their lives.

There is considerable scholarly disagreement about the consequences for good or ill of Hadleyburg's fall and the role of Twain's pessimist philosophy in the story. His ironic concluding paragraph is decisive, however, in its indication that, having been afforded a basis for redemption, the town has in fact reverted to its proud self-sufficiency and gained only a suspicious wariness of ruses such as the stranger's. Moreover, the story's predominant image of undifferentiated selfhood and mechanized action indicates that it is of a thematic piece with other determinist works of Twain's bleakly skeptical period. There is widespread agreement, however, that with its resonant echoes of Dante and Milton, its narrative economy and objectivity, and its ironic vitality, "The Man That Corrupted Hadleyburg" ranks among the finest of Mark Twain's short stories.

Earl F. Briden

BIBLIOGRAPHY

Clemens, Samuel L. *The Man That Corrupted Hadleyburg and Other Stories and Essays.* New York: Harper, 1900.

———. *Mark Twain's Mysterious Stranger Manuscripts.* Ed. William M. Gibson. Berkeley: U of California P, 1969.

———. *"What Is Man?" and Other Philosophical Writings.* Ed. Paul Baender. Berkeley: U of California P, 1973.

Covici, Pascal, Jr. *Mark Twain's Humor: The Image of a World.* Dallas: Southern Methodist UP, 1962.

Emerson, Everett. *The Authentic Mark Twain: A Literary Biography of Samuel L. Clemens.* Philadelphia: U of Pennsylvania P, 1984.

Wilson, James D. *A Reader's Guide to the Short Stories of Mark Twain.* Boston: G.K. Hall, 1987.

See also: Determinism; Richards, Edward and Mary; *What Is Man?*

"Man Who Put Up at Gadsby's, The"
(1880)

The earliest version of this story appeared in a letter to the Virginia City *Territorial Enterprise* for 8 February 1868. In early 1879, while Twain was traveling in Europe, he reminded himself of it briefly in his notebook and then included an expanded version in chapter 26 of *A Tramp Abroad* (1880). Like "Jim Baker's Blue Jay Yarn" (1880), "The Man Who Put Up at Gadsby's" is a blatantly irrelevant American digression in the middle of Twain's account of an European walking tour: the sight of patient but unsuccessful fishermen in Lucerne reminds him of a patient but unsuccessful office seeker in Washington, D.C.

The story draws on Twain's experience in Washington during the winter of 1867–1868, when Twain and James H. Riley were working there. When he and his friend Riley meet a San Francisco schoolteacher, Lykins, who is waiting for an imminent postmastership, Riley corners him with a long story about a man from Tennessee who came to Washington in 1834 to settle a claim, put up at Gadsby's Hotel, gradually sold off his possessions, and was still waiting optimistically for his settlement. When Lykins does not get the point, Riley advises him to put up at Gadsby's. Twain notes that Lykins "never got that post-office."

In its use of frame narration and in the victimization of an innocent outsider by a deadpan storyteller, "Gadsby's" is reminiscent of stories like "The Celebrated Jumping Frog of Calaveras County" (1865) and "Grandfather's Old Ram" (1872). It differs from them, however, in that the frame narrator here is not the victim; the greenhorn in this case is the unsophisticated Westerner who has not yet learned how the government works.

As a satire on Washington, "Gadsby's" is more closely related to *The Gilded Age* (1873)— and to contemporary political fiction such as Henry Adams's *Democracy* (1880)—than to the rest of *A Tramp Abroad*. Among Twain's own shorter works James D. Wilson points out similarities to "Facts Concerning the Recent Resignation" (1868), "The Facts in the Great Beef Contract" (1869), and "The Belated Russian Passport" (1902). As a satire on the spoils system in particular, "Gadsby's" also echoes contemporary pieces such as Artemus Ward's "Interview with President Lincoln" (1862) and Petroleum V. Nasby's "The Reward of Virtue" (1867).

Paul Witkowsky

BIBLIOGRAPHY

Clemens, Samuel L. *The Complete Short Stories of Mark Twain.* Ed. Charles Neider. Garden City, N.Y.: Hanover House, 1957. 149–153.

————. *A Tramp Abroad.* Hartford, Conn.: American Publishing, 1880.

Emerson, Everett. *The Authentic Mark Twain: A Literary Biography of Samuel L. Clemens.* Philadelphia: U of Pennsylvania P, 1984.

Kaplan, Justin. *Mr. Clemens and Mark Twain.* New York: Simon & Schuster, 1966.

Wilson, James D. *A Reader's Guide to the Short Stories of Mark Twain.* Boston: G.K. Hall, 1987.

See also: *Tramp Abroad, A*; Washington, D.C.

Manuscript Collections

Of the hundreds of universities, museums, historical societies, and private collections known to have manuscripts by Mark Twain, most contain letters only. Manuscripts still exist for the vast majority of more than 11,500 letters, only a portion of Clemens's output, and new manuscript letters are regularly being discovered. Although most of these have been donated to private and public institutions, others, kept by their recipients' families or sold at auction to private collectors, are inaccessible or known only through auction catalog listings. The only comprehensive guide to the location of manuscript letters is the *Union Catalog of Clemens Letters* (1986), edited by Paul Machlis.

There is, unfortunately, no comparable comprehensive listing of Clemens's literary manuscripts or private papers. The best available sources of information are the *Library of Congress National Union Catalog of Manuscripts* (published serially since 1959) and *American Literary Manuscripts* (1977). The best guide to the location of books with Clemens marginalia is *Mark Twain's Library: A Reconstruction* (1980), by Alan Gribben. The largest manuscript collections are in the eight institutions listed below. Literary manuscripts continue to be discovered, but at a much less rapid rate than letters. The printers and publishers of Clemens's journalism and literary work from the 1860s and early 1870s usually destroyed manuscripts after typesetting. Much that survives from this time is therefore rejected material or working notes. The manuscripts and typescripts of later works, however, were more often preserved, either by Clemens or his publishers, but their accessibility varies. Clemens himself evidently gave the second half of his *Adventures of Huckleberry Finn* (1885) manuscript to the library of the Young Men's Association of Buffalo in 1885. It survives today in the Buffalo and Erie County Library. The first half, though lost for a hundred years, was in 1990 discovered in a California attic. It is now inaccessible to scholars while title is under litigation. Clemens's publisher, the American Publishing Company, broke up the manuscripts of *The Gilded Age* (1873) and *A Tramp Abroad* (1880) by tipping individual pages into volumes of a special edition of Mark Twain's works and by further selling off individual chapters. A scholar can now be reasonably sure of seeing all of the *Huck Finn* manuscript reunited. However, bits and chunks of *The Gilded Age* and *A Tramp Abroad* not only are known to be in more than fifteen institutions, but are also, though uncatalogued and inaccessible, in countless private and public collections worldwide.

A list of the eight major archives of letters and papers follows:

1. *Houghton Library, Harvard University, Cambridge, Massachusetts 02138.* The Houghton contains mainly letters: well

over 200 to William Dean Howells and many to Thomas Bailey Aldrich, James R. Osgood, and James Redpath, among others.

2. *Huntington Library, 1151 Oxford Road, San Marino, California 91108.* The Huntington includes a large collection of letters to Mary Mason Fairbanks, Frances Nunnally, William W. Phelps, Elizabeth Wallace, and others. Literary manuscripts include "A Private History of the Jumping Frog Story," *Meisterschaft*, *The Prince and the Pauper* (1882), and various pages from *The Gilded Age* and *A Tramp Abroad*. Although holdings are indexed separately by collection, the Rare Book Room provides access to all. The Huntington publishes a *Guide for Readers*.

3. *Mark Twain Memorial, 351 Farmington Ave.*, and *Stowe-Day Foundation, 77 Forest Street, Hartford, Connecticut 06105.* The Memorial's manuscript collection (as of 1991 on deposit at Trinity College in Hartford) contains letters to and by Clemens, Olivia Langdon Clemens, and their three daughters, as well as letters to Charles J. and Ida Langdon, Jervis and Olivia Lewis Langdon, and friends and associates such as Charles E. Perkins, John T. Raymond, Henry H. Rogers, George H. Warner, and Franklin G. and Harriet E. Whitmore. Other manuscript holdings include an outline of *The Gilded Age*, a family reminiscence, and an unpublished story, "The Shakespeare Mulberry." Access to the collection is in the Watkinson Library of Trinity College (Hartford, Connecticut 06016) and may be granted by applying directly to the Watkinson. The Stowe-Day collection includes letters to Joseph H. Twichell and papers of many of Clemens's Nook Farm neighbors. Access is in the Stowe-Day Library. A lavishly illustrated but now incomplete bibliography of the Mark Twain collection, published in 1984 by William McBride, may be available in some libraries.

4. *Mark Twain Papers, The Bancroft Library, University of California, Berkeley, California 94720.* Although a few of Mark Twain's letters are housed in separate Bancroft Library collections, most are in the Mark Twain Papers. They include letters of Clemens, Olivia Langdon Clemens, and their three daughters to and from relatives in the Clemens, Moffett, Webster, Langdon, and Crane families; and a large and diverse collection of Clemens's personal and business letters to friends and associates. Some 17,000 letters to Clemens or his associates, the majority in manuscript, are also part of the collection. Among the literary manuscripts are *The American Claimant* (1892), *Tom Sawyer, Detective* (1896), portions of *The Gilded Age*, *A Tramp Abroad*, the *Mysterious Stranger* manuscripts, autobiographical dictations, short pieces, plays, notebooks, working notes, and fragments. Access is either through the Mark Twain Papers offices or the Bancroft reading room. A brief general guide, *The Mark Twain Papers*, is available. A microfilm of the manuscript collection can be borrowed, two reels at a time, through the Interlibrary Loan Department, 307 Doe Library, University of California, Berkeley 94720; copies of the index are available from the Mark Twain Papers at the user's cost.

5. *The Research Libraries, New York Public Library, Fifth Avenue and 42nd Street, New York, New York 10018.* Several collections, separately housed, make up these holdings, the largest of which, the Henry W. and Albert A. Berg Collection, contains letters to Elisha and Frank Bliss, Chatto and Windus, Frederick Duneka, Frederick J. Hall, William Dean Howells, James B. Pond, Henry Rogers, and Charles L. Webster and Company, among others. Literary manuscripts (or partial manuscripts) include *A Connecticut Yankee in King Arthur's Court* (1889), *Pudd'nhead Wilson* (1894), *Tom Sawyer Abroad* (1894), *Personal Recollections of Joan of Arc* (1896), and *Following the Equator* (1897). Other letters and manuscripts are housed in the Rare Books and Manuscripts Division and the smaller Arents Collections. Large research libraries

will likely have the Berg Collection *Dictionary Catalog* (1969), which lists much of the manuscript collection.

6. *The Library, Vassar College, Poughkeepsie, New York 12601.* The Jean Webster McKinney Family Papers, Francis Fitz Randolph Rare Book Room, contain letters to Clemens family members including Jane Lampton Clemens, Orion and Mollie Clemens, Pamela Moffett, Annie Moffett Webster, and an extraordinary number to Charles L. Webster. Several hundred pages of manuscripts include two versions of the Jumping Frog Story, "Taming the Bicycle," and fragments of *The Innocents Abroad* (1869) and *A Tramp Abroad.* A keepsake describing the collection, *Mark Twain Goes Back to Vassar* by Alan Simpson, was published in 1977.

7. *Special Collections/Manuscripts, Alderman Library, University of Virginia, Charlottesville, Virginia 22903.* The Clifton Waller Barrett collection contains a large and diverse body of letters, including some to Clemens's family, to his publishers (Elisha Bliss, Chatto and Windus, Frederick J. Hall, and James R. Osgood), and to friends Edward H. House and John Y. MacAlister. Literary holdings include "Concerning the Jews," "The Great Revolution in Pitcairn," "The Jumping Frog. In English. Then in French . . .," "A True Story," draft prefaces for *The Innocents Abroad,* and pages from *The Gilded Age* and *A Tramp Abroad.*

8. *Beinecke Rare Book and Manuscript Library, 1603A Yale Station, Yale University, New Haven, Connecticut 06520.* The Collection of American Literature in the Beinecke contains numerous letters, in particular to Connecticut friends, associates, and business connections such as Elisha Bliss, James Hammond Trumbull, and Joseph Twichell. Literary holdings include "A Telephonic Conversation," "My Debut as a Literary Person," "Struwwelpeter," and pages of the ubiquitous *Gilded Age* and *Tramp Abroad.*

Other institutions with notable collections of letters include the Columbia University Library, with over a hundred letters to the likes of Moncure Conway, Brander Matthews, and Henry H. Rogers; and the Library of Congress, with letters to Andrew Carnegie, Whitelaw Reid, and John Russell Young. Libraries with notable literary manuscripts include that of Georgetown University, with *The Adventures of Tom Sawyer* (1876); the Pierpont Morgan Library, with *Life on the Mississippi* (1883) and *Pudd'nhead Wilson*; and the Claremont Colleges' Honnold Library, with still more chapters from *A Tramp Abroad.* Although private collections are largely unavailable, some collectors have placed manuscripts or photocopies on deposit at various institutions, often with restrictions.

A few archives, like the Huntington Library, the Mark Twain Memorial, and the New York Public Library, have museum cases where manuscript is regularly on display for the general public. Likewise, the Mark Twain Papers maintains a small display in the Bancroft Library offices. Otherwise, archives are open to scholars only. Though each has slightly different rules, a few general guidelines apply for access to manuscript materials. It is always advisable to write first, explaining the nature of the research, the materials desired, and the projected span of time needed for working in the collection. Proper identification is often required before a reader's card is issued. The use of ink for note taking is generally forbidden, and there may be formal procedures for signing in and out. Some reading rooms allow use of laptop computers.

To quote from unpublished manuscripts, two kinds of permission are necessary: that of the document holder and that of the copyright holder. All institutions that hold documents require submission of a form or letter of request. When permission is granted, each usually provides a preferred form of citation. To gain permission of the copyright holder, however, application to the General Editor of the Mark Twain Project is necessary. As a condition, a copyright notice must accompany the quoted words. Such notices indicate in part that previously unpublished words are copyrighted by Edward J. Willi and Manufacturers Hanover Trust Company as trustees of the Mark Twain Foundation, and that quotation is made with the permission of the University of California Press and Robert H. Hirst, General Editor of the Mark Twain Project. Fees, often waived for nonprofit work, are usually required for commercial work—both by the document holder and the copyright holder.

Victor Fischer

BIBLIOGRAPHY

Berg Collection. *Dictionary Catalog of the Henry W. and Albert A. Berg Collection of English and American Literature.* 5 vols. Boston: G.K. Hall, 1969. 2 supps., 1975, 1983.

Congress, Library of. *The National Union Catalog of Manuscript Collections.* Washington, D.C.: The Library, 1959–1987.

Gribben, Alan. *Mark Twain's Library: A Reconstruction.* 2 vols. Boston: G.K. Hall, 1980.

McBride, William M., comp. *Mark Twain: A Bibliography of the Collections of the Mark Twain Memorial and the Stowe-Day Foundation.* Hartford, Conn: McBride, 1984.

Robbins, J. Albert, et al., comps. *American Literary Manuscripts.* 2nd ed. Athens: U of Georgia P, 1977.

Simpson, Alan. *Mark Twain Goes Back to Vassar: An Introduction to the Jean Webster McKinney Family Papers.* Published for the dedication of the Francis Fitz Randolph Rare Book Room, 1977.

See also: Auctions; Bibliographies; Homes and Literary Sites; Mark Twain Papers

"Marjorie Fleming, the Wonder Child"

(1909)

Twain apparently compiled "Marjorie Fleming, the Wonder Child" while in Bermuda in 1909 and published it in *Harper's Bazaar* for December 1909. It consists mostly of extracts from the writings of Marjorie Fleming (1803–1811), taken from L.

MacBean's book, *Marjorie Fleming*, along with comments by Twain. Dr. John Brown, Marjorie's biographer, introduced Twain to her writings during Twain's brief stay in Edinburgh in 1873.

Twain calls Marjorie, who began keeping journals when she was six, "tender," "loving," "free," "honest," and "precious" and "the bewitchingest speller and punctuator in all Christendom." He says that she is "a quaint and charming and free-spoken little thinker and philosopher" and finds her "frank" views on religion and morality and her occasional mild profanity especially refreshing. Her poem about the death of three young turkeys delights him, especially the final couplet: "But she was more than usual calm, / She did not give a single dam[*sic*]."

In this essay Twain displays his skeptical attitude concerning religion. Simultaneously, he is at his most sentimental, lamenting the loss to the world of Marjorie, who died before she reached the age of nine.

Richard Tuerk

BIBLIOGRAPHY

Brown, John. *Rab and His Friends, Marjorie Fleming and Other Papers.* Philadelphia: Altemus, 1893.

Clemens, Samuel L. "Marjorie Fleming, the Wonder Child." *Harper's Bazaar* 43 (December 1909): 1182–1183.

Hill, Hamlin. *Mark Twain: God's Fool.* New York: Harper & Row, 1973.

MacBean, L. *Marjorie Fleming: The Story of Pet Marjorie Fleming Together with her Journals and her Letters to Which is Added Marjorie Fleming: A Story of Child-Life Fifty Years Ago by John Brown, M.D.* American ed. New York: Putnam, 1904.

Sidgwick, Frank, ed. *The Complete Marjorie Fleming: Her Journals, Letters, and Verses.* New York: Oxford UP, 1935.

See also: Angel Fish and Aquarium Club; Brown, John, M.D.; Childhood

Mark Twain Boyhood Home

The small frame house that was home to the Clemens family when Samuel L. Clemens was a child is preserved in Hannibal, Missouri. The house is immortalized as the residence of Aunt Polly, Tom, Mary, and Sid in *The Adventures of Tom Sawyer* (1876). It also provides the setting for "Jim Wolfe and the Cats" (1867), another story of Jim Wolfe and wasps, and many short recollections in Mark Twain's writings.

The early history of the Mark Twain Boyhood Home remains uncertain. John Marshall Clemens moved his family to Hannibal in late 1839 and purchased a lot of land, including the site of the home. In October 1843 the lot was subdivided and sold. A cousin from St. Louis, James Clemens, Jr., purchased the parcel of land where the boyhood home is located. In his *Autobiography*, Mark Twain writes that in 1849, "We were still living in . . . the new 'frame' house built by my father five years before [i.e., 1844]. That is, some of us lived in the new part, the rest in the old part back of it and attached to it" (1:125). No other references to the construction of the house have been located. During the 1990–1991 restoration of the home evidence surfaced to indicate that the house was originally two stories in front and one story in back, the rear upstairs rooms having been added later. It is impossible, however, to determine precisely when the original edifice was constructed or when the additions were made to it. We do know that the Clemens family lived in the house from late 1843 or early 1844 (when Sam was eight years old) until 1853 (when Sam was seventeen), except for a brief period of time in 1846–1847.

Following the Clemens family's departure from Hannibal in 1853, the house became rental property. City directories reveal that it was very transient property and that occasionally two families shared the premises. In 1911 plans for new construction were announced that included demolition of the boyhood home. The Hannibal Commercial Club, forerunner of the Hannibal Chamber of Commerce, attempted a public subscription to raise funds to save the house. Progress was slow until a local attorney, George A. Mahan, pur-

chased the property, restored the house during the winter 1911–1912, and donated the Mark Twain Boyhood Home to the city of Hannibal on 15 May 1912. A caretaker then lived upstairs in the house and used the kitchen on the first floor; the front room, or parlor, was opened to the public and contained a modest collection of Mark Twain memorabilia.

During the 1935 Mark Twain Centennial, the Mark Twain Museum opened in temporary quarters in the city. The museum proved popular, and in 1937 moved into a permanent structure built by the Works Progress Administration (WPA) adjacent to the Mark Twain Boyhood Home. The caretaker moved into living quarters above the museum, and the remaining rooms of the house were opened to the public. The WPA repaired the house, replaced flooring on the first level, and added heating ducts from the new museum. In the mid 1930s the city of Hannibal established a commission to maintain and operate the home. This commission became the Mark Twain Home Board. In January 1990 the home and related properties were leased to the Mark Twain Home Foundation, a nonprofit organization. The city of Hannibal retains ownership, but daily operation and maintenance are the responsibilities of the foundation.

Heavy tourist traffic through the house from 1912 to 1984 took its toll on the aged frame construction. After 1984 visitors were not allowed in the house; rather, they were routed along an adjacent viewing platform from which they peered through windows. As plans were drawn for a complete renovation of the structure, it was discovered from an 1883 photograph that the house preserved since 1912 was incomplete. The photograph revealed that there had been other rooms both upstairs and downstairs at the rear of the house and that changes had occurred in chimneys and windows. Archaeological studies and careful inspection of the structure verified these changes; the speculation is that at some time in the 1880s a chimney between the back rooms collapsed and resulted in the demise of the rear portion of the house. A complete restoration of the home was completed between March 1990 and May 1991. The structure was dismantled to the interior timbers, then strengthened and restored as closely as possible to its appearance at the time of the Clemens family's residence there. Visitors are now allowed to tour the inside of the house.

Henry H. Sweets III

BIBLIOGRAPHY

Clemens, Samuel L. *Mark Twain's Autobiography.* Ed. Albert B. Paine. 2 vols. New York: Harper, 1924.

Sweets, Henry H., III. "History of Mark Twain Boyhood Home." Hannibal *Courier-Post,* 15 May 1991, supplement.

Wecter, Dixon. *Sam Clemens of Hannibal.* Boston: Houghton Mifflin, 1952.

See also: Clemens, John Marshall; Hannibal, Missouri; Homes and Literary Sites

Mark Twain Circle of America

The Mark Twain Circle of America was founded in 1986. Though college-level teachers are its most active members, it welcomes all admirers of Twain's writings. It publishes a bimonthly newsletter and meets at least once annually.

In 1984 Everett Emerson, professor of English and American Studies at the University of North Carolina at Chapel Hill, acted on his perception that the career, personality, and writings of Mark Twain were continuing to attract so much interest on both popular and scholarly levels, both in the United States and abroad, that a widely based group would be useful. He also perceived that such a group should, appropriate to Twain's own aims, reach beyond college teachers of literature, cultivate a spirit of appreciation rather than an exclusivity claiming expertise, and consider informal exchange among members as one of its key purposes. In that spirit, discussion led to settling on "Circle" as a meaningful sign.

Emerson invited Louis J. Budd, of nearby Duke University, and Alan Gribben, of the University of Texas, to join him in a call for support. Preferring to function as the secretary-treasurer, Emerson invited Budd to chair a meeting of about twenty-five members of the Modern Language Association during its 1986 convention in New York City. That meeting elected Budd as president, Gribben as vice-president, and Emerson as executive coordinator (a title that, the group felt, would better describe his role). An interim executive committee was appointed along with committees on membership and on bylaws. David Tomlinson, then chair of the Department of English at the U.S. Naval Academy, served as the driving force to write a set of bylaws—required by the state of North Carolina before any group can be issued a charter, which is in turn required for nonprofit tax-exempt status. Emerson arranged for the legal incorporation of the circle in 1987. Thomas A. Tenney, first at his own expense, established the *Mark Twain Circular* as "A Newsletter of the *Mark Twain Journal* Published in Association with the Mark Twain Circle of America." Also, he persuaded Bill Watterson, not yet famous as the creator of "Calvin and Hobbes," to draw the bust logo of Twain for the *Circular,* which appeared promptly in January 1987. With the February issue, James S. Leonard, of The Citadel, became editor.

Without changing its goal of a broader base than academia, the circle first worked toward status as an allied organization with the MLA because this would provide an annual, predictable, and convenient gathering point for some of its members. At the 1986 MLA convention the circle-to-be presented a panel, chaired by Alan Gribben, on "Mark Twain and Women." During the 1987 convention in San Francisco the circle presented a panel on "Mark Twain and the West." At its first business meeting, where Emerson announced a paid ($5.00) membership of 175, the circle ratified a set of bylaws designed to encourage democratic procedures; most notably, the bylaws stipulate a rotation of officers (with a pattern of staggered two-year terms to provide continuity). Pascal Covici, Jr., of Southern Methodist University, was elected vice-president and Gribben, president. At the 1988 MLA convention in New Orleans the circle held a dinner meeting followed by two papers on Twain's river years; it also arranged a cruise on the paddlewheel *Creole Queen*. Finishing his term as the first executive coordinator, Emerson could announce a paid membership of 225. He was succeeded by James D. Wilson, of the University of Southwestern Louisiana, who had served vigorously as chair of the membership committee. With the January 1989 issue the *Circular* asserted its greater autonomy; its masthead now states that it is "Published in Association with the *Mark Twain Journal*."

For the dinner meeting at the National Press Club during the 1989 MLA convention in Washington, D.C., Budd discussed Twain's few weeks as a Capitol reporter in 1867–1868. By that time the circle clearly felt well-established, and its *Circular* was a bimonthly carrying the latest news of interest to members, notes and queries, and bibliographical surveys. The circle achieved allied status with the MLA in 1991 and has also developed ties with the new American Literature Association. Its membership reaches to South America, Europe, the Near East, and the Far East and hopes eventually to hold its own, independent meetings.

Louis J. Budd

Mark Twain Company

(1908–)

Registered in New York on 23 December 1908, with capital of $5,000 divided into fifty shares (all owned by Clemens), the Mark Twain Company was part of his final scheme to secure perpetual copyright, at least for himself and his children. Three days after registration, Clemens assigned it all of his literary property, including his present and future copyrights, as well as his pseudonym, already registered as a trade mark. Clemens credited

Ralph W. Ashcroft with the idea of incorporation—"a stroke of genius" that "may supersede copyright-law someday" (Clemens to Clara Clemens, 11 March 1909). The plan was to block unwanted publication of his works after their copyrights expired by licensing the right to use the name "Mark Twain." This strategy had some success when Clemens's executors and the directors of the company (usually one and the same) closed ranks with Harper and Brothers, his official publishers. In its first year the company's directors were Clemens himself, Jean Clemens, Clara Clemens, Isabel V. Lyon, and Ashcroft. By August 1909 all but Clemens had been replaced by Edward Eugene Loomis (1864–1937), Jervis Langdon II (1875–1952), and Zoheth Sparrow Freeman (b. 1875), who were also his executors, and Albert Bigelow Paine, his official biographer. By August 1910 Charles Tressler Lark (1870–1946) replaced Freeman as director, and in August 1913 Paine resigned and was not replaced. Loomis, Langdon, and Lark served as the directors until Loomis's death in 1937; Lark and Langdon served as sole directors until 1943 when, having quarreled with Clara, they resigned both as executors of her father's estate and as directors of the company. Thomas G. Chamberlain (1896–1978) and the Central Hanover Bank & Trust Company were then appointed successor trustees, becoming directors of the company as well. Chamberlain was succeeded by his partner Edward J. Willi. When Clara's trust was closed on 17 November 1978, all of its assets, including the company, became the property of the Mark Twain Foundation. Willi, Robert D. Ouchterloney, Richard A. Watson, John J. Kindred III, and Charles Grimes are the current directors.

J.R. LeMaster and James D. Wilson

BIBLIOGRAPHY

"Certificate of Incorporation of Mark Twain Company." Department of State, Albany, New York.

Hill, Hamlin. *Mark Twain: God's Fool*. New York: Harper & Row, 1973.

"Mark Twain Turns into a Corporation." *New York Times*, 24 December 1908, 2.

See also: Ashcroft, Ralph; Estate of Samuel
L. Clemens; Harper and Brothers;
Lyon, Isabel

Mark Twain Papers
(1910–)

The Mark Twain Papers consist of those manuscripts and documents that Mark Twain made available to Albert Bigelow Paine for the official biography and from which Paine published several highly selective editions. The papers contain more than 300 literary manuscripts, including the autobiographical dictations; 45 notebooks; some 10,000 letters to Clemens; about 3,000 letters by him; roughly 100 books from his library; as well as uncounted clippings, contracts, bills, checks, photographs, scrapbooks, and other family artifacts. The precise contents of the papers have never been entirely stable; as early as February 1911, Paine authorized the sale of several hundred books with pages of manuscript inserted to enhance their market value. And still other documents that were evidently stolen or lost even before Clemens's death in 1910, from time to time, have been replevied by the estate or voluntarily returned to the papers.

Permission to see the papers rested with the trustees of Clemens's estate, who were obliged by Clemens's will to follow the advice of Paine and of Clara Clemens Samossoud. Until Paine's death in 1937 access of any kind was consistently denied to all applicants—a policy that drew the fire of Bernard DeVoto, who said in his preface to *Mark Twain's America* (1932) that because only Paine had seen the manuscripts, "they must some day be accounted for. Public benevolence constrains me to offer the Estate my services" (xiii). In a 1935 edition of *Mark Twain: A Biography*, Paine called this offer "the only humor in an entire book" about Mark Twain, but in the spring of 1938 the editors at Harper and Brothers persuaded the estate to accept it: DeVoto was asked to read through the papers and to recommend further publication (if any), which he accomplished between March and May 1938. In consequence, he was formally appointed to finish the task of organizing and cataloguing the papers, which Paine had left in some disarray, and to prepare editions of what it was agreed should be published from them. DeVoto thus replaced Paine as "literary editor," but not as "literary executor," since Clara survived until 1962 and she eventually opposed most of what DeVoto thought should be published. In the summer of 1938 the papers were moved from the Lincoln Warehouse in New York (where Paine had stored most of them) to number 98 Widener Library at Harvard, where DeVoto began to organize and transcribe them. Within a year Clara found and returned a trunk of some 100 additional manuscripts that Paine, for lack of space, had sent her for safekeeping. DeVoto and his chief assistant, Rosamond Hart Chapman, arranged, transcribed, and catalogued nearly 300 manuscripts, while also searching for missing items such as Orion's autobiography (never found) as well as for manuscripts never owned by the estate, such as those for Mark Twain's major books, not to mention literally thousands of personal and business letters. DeVoto eventually published some of these papers in *Mark Twain in Eruption* (1940), *Mark Twain at Work* (1942), and *The Portable Mark Twain* (1946), but Clara prevented publication of *Letters from the Earth* until 1962, almost twenty-five years after DeVoto had prepared it in 1939.

DeVoto also permitted limited access to the papers by independent scholars. In 1946, however, he resigned in favor of Dixon Wecter, who was planning a full-scale biography of Mark Twain and whom the estate formally appointed literary editor in November 1946. The estate agreed to a long-term loan of the papers to the Henry E. Huntington Library in San Marino, California, where Wecter was chairman of the research group. They arrived in San Marino in January 1947, but before Wecter had published any significant portion of them, he was appointed Byrne Professor of American History at the University of California in Berkeley. He soon persuaded Clara not only to let him move the papers to Berkeley, but also to change her will, bequeathing them to the university rather than to Yale, as she had originally intended. Wecter died suddenly on 24 June 1950. He was not replaced until 1953, when Henry Nash Smith came to Berkeley from the University of Minnesota. Smith and William M. Gibson published the *Mark Twain-Howells Letters* (1960), and Smith and Frederick Anderson published *Mark Twain of the "Enterprise"* (1957), both of which drew on the papers for documentation but left most of the manuscripts unpublished. Smith resigned as literary editor in 1964 in favor of his assistant, Frederick Anderson. With the creation of editorial subsidies from the National Endowment for the Humanities in 1966, Anderson began systematic publication of the Mark Twain Papers through the University of California Press, a series that is still in progress.

J.R. LeMaster and James D. Wilson

BIBLIOGRAPHY

DeVoto, Bernard. *Mark Twain's America.* Boston: Little, Brown, 1932.

Paine, Albert Bigelow. *Mark Twain: A Biography.* Centenary ed. New York: Harper, 1935.

Various documents in the Mark Twain Papers (Subject File), Mark Twain Project, The Bancroft Library, University of California, Berkeley.

See also: Anderson, Frederick; DeVoto, Bernard; Estate of Samuel L. Clemens; Hirst, Robert H.; Paine, Albert Bigelow; Samossoud, Clara Clemens; Smith, Henry Nash; Wecter, Dixon

Mark Twain Project

(1980–)

Created in 1980 at the Bancroft Library in Berkeley after the appointment of Robert H. Hirst as general editor of the Mark Twain Papers, the Mark Twain Project united two formerly distinct editorial projects: the Mark Twain Papers based at the University of California in Berkeley and the Works of Mark Twain founded and based originally at the University of Iowa in Iowa City. The second Mark Twain Papers project was begun in 1962 by Henry Nash Smith, then literary editor of the Clemens estate. It was designed to publish scholarly editions of Clemens's unpublished literary manuscripts, notebooks, and letters under an agreement signed in January 1962 between the University of California Press and the trustees of the Clemens estate, granting the press "an exclusive license to publish" these materials, many of them in the author's own papers at Berkeley (contract in the Mark Twain Papers archives). In 1964 Frederick Anderson succeeded Smith as literary editor and soon became series editor of the Mark Twain Papers project, assigning editors to the various volumes planned and, following the creation of editorial subsidies from the Center for Editions of American Authors (CEAA) in 1966, assembling an editorial staff in Berkeley, some of whom are still with the Mark Twain Project. Between 1967 and 1979 ten volumes of the papers were issued by the University of California Press: *Letters to His Publishers, 1867–1894* (1967), edited by Hamlin Hill; *Satires & Burlesques* (1967), edited by Franklin R. Rogers; *"Which Was the Dream?" and Other Symbolic Writings of the Later Years* (1967), edited by John S. Tuckey; *Hannibal, Huck & Tom* (1969), edited by Walter Blair; *Mysterious Stranger Manuscripts* (1969), edited by William M. Gibson; *Correspondence with Henry Huttleston Rogers, 1893–1909* (1969), edited by Lewis Leary; *Fables of Man* (1972), edited by John S. Tuckey, Kenneth M. Sanderson, and Bernard L. Stein; *Notebooks & Journals, Volume I (1855–1873)* (1975), edited by Frederick Anderson, Michael B. Frank, and Kenneth M. Sanderson; *Notebooks & Journals, Volume II (1877–1883)* (1975), edited by Frederick Anderson, Lin Salamo, and Bernard L. Stein; and *Notebooks & Journals, Volume III (1883–1891)* (1979), edited by Robert Pack Browning, Michael B. Frank, and Lin Salamo.

The Works of Mark Twain was conceived by John C. Gerber in Iowa City in 1961. It was designed to publish authoritative texts of all Mark Twain's published works, in an estimated twenty-five volumes, to be issued by Harper & Row. By 1965 Gerber had assembled and assigned twenty-two Mark Twain experts as volume editors, secured four years of funding from the U.S. Office of Education, and established a Center for Textual Study at Iowa. In 1967 Harper & Row withdrew as publishers but, within a year, had been replaced by the University of California Press. In 1972 responsibility for establishing the text was given to Anderson, who became series editor of the Works of Mark Twain as well as the Mark Twain Papers and who thereafter secured funding for both from the National Endowment for the Humanities (NEH). Between 1972 and 1980 the Works of Mark Twain (known as the Iowa-California edition) published six volumes: *Roughing It* (1972), edited by Franklin R. Rogers and Paul Baender; *"What Is Man?" and Other Philosophical Writings* (1973), edited by Paul Baender; *A Connecticut Yankee in King Arthur's Court* (1979), edited by Bernard L. Stein and Henry Nash Smith; *The Prince and the Pauper* (1979), edited by Victor Fischer and Lin Salamo, with Mary Jane Jones; *Early Tales & Sketches, Volume 1 (1851–1864)* (1979), edited by Edgar M. Branch and Robert H. Hirst, with Harriet Elinor Smith; and *The Adventures of Tom Sawyer; Tom Sawyer Abroad; Tom Sawyer Detective* (1980), edited by John C. Gerber, Paul Baender, and Terry Firkins.

Since the establishment of the Mark Twain Project, both series have been continuously funded by NEH and private donations raised by Friends of The Bancroft Library. The following volumes have been published in the Mark Twain Papers series since 1980: *Letters, Volume 1 (1853–1866)* (1988), edited by Edgar M. Branch, Michael B. Frank, Kenneth M. Sanderson, Harriet Elinor Smith, Lin Salamo, and Richard Bucci; *Letters, Volume 2 (1867–1868)* (1990), edited by Harriet Elinor Smith, Richard Bucci, and Lin Salamo; *Letters, Volume 3 (1869)* (1992), edited by Victor Fischer, Michael B. Frank, and Dahlia Armon. At least twenty more volumes of the letters are planned,

along with the *Autobiography*, one further volume of literary manuscripts, and two more volumes of *Notebooks & Journals*. The following volumes in the works have been published since 1980: *Early Tales & Sketches, Volume 2 (1864–1865)* (1981), edited by Edgar M. Branch and Robert H. Hirst, with Harriet Elinor Smith; and *Adventures of Huckleberry Finn* (1988), edited by Walter Blair and Victor Fischer, with Dahlia Armon and Harriet Elinor Smith. A revised edition of *Roughing It*, including all the original illustrations, and three more volumes of *Early Tales & Sketches* are scheduled to be published. The following are in active preparation: *Middle Tales & Sketches, 1872–1895*; *The Innocents Abroad*; *Life on the Mississippi*; *Late Tales & Sketches, 1896–1910* (including *The American Claimant*); *Early Travel Writings, 1858–1868*; *Social & Political Writings, 1852–1871*; *The Tragedy of Pudd'nhead Wilson*; *The Gilded Age*; *Following the Equator*; *Joan of Arc*; and *A Tramp Abroad*. Tentative plans have been made to revise *Huckleberry Finn* in light of the discovery of the first half of the manuscript.

In 1982 the Mark Twain Project began a third series of books called the Mark Twain Library, designed for the general trade. Drawn from the edited texts published in the Mark Twain Papers and the Works of Mark Twain, but lacking the technical apparatus of those two series, Mark Twain Library volumes often include corrections to the edited text and substantial new annotation, and they always include the original illustrations. Books in this series appear simultaneously in cloth and paper covers. Published to date are the following: *No. 44, The Mysterious Stranger* (1982), edited by John S. Tuckey and William M. Gibson; *The Adventures of Tom Sawyer* (1982), edited by John C. Gerber and Paul Baender; *Tom Sawyer Abroad, Tom Sawyer, Detective* (1982), edited by John C. Gerber and Terry Firkins; *The Prince and the Pauper* (1983), edited by Victor Fischer and Michael B. Frank; *A Connecticut Yankee in King Arthur's Court* (1983), edited by Bernard L. Stein; *Adventures of Huckleberry Finn* (1985), edited by Walter

Blair and Victor Fischer; and *Huck Finn and Tom Sawyer Among the Indians and Other Unfinished Stories* (1989), edited by Dahlia Armon and Walter Blair, with text established by Armon and Blair as well as Paul Baender, William M. Gibson, and Franklin R. Rogers. Other Mark Twain Project publications include *The Devil's Race-Track: Mark Twain's Great Dark Writings* (1980), edited by John S. Tuckey; and the *Union Catalog of Clemens Letters* (1986), edited by Paul Machlis. Currently in preparation is the *Union Catalog of Letters to Clemens*, which lists all known letters to Clemens and his associates.

Victor Fischer

BIBLIOGRAPHY

Mark Twain Papers archives. Contracts and documents in the Mark Twain Papers, The Bancroft Library, University of California, Berkeley, relating to the formation of the Mark Twain Papers, the Works of Mark Twain, and the Mark Twain Project.

See also: Estate of Samuel L. Clemens; Mark Twain Company; Mark Twain Papers

Mark Twain Research Foundation

(1939–)

This organization began in 1938 as the Mark Twain Society of Chicago. A group of scholars and writers interested in Mark Twain, the society held initial meetings in the home of founder George Ade (1866–1944), a newspaper columnist who also wrote comic opera librettos and movie scripts. Because of widening interest, the group quickly changed its name to the Mark Twain Association of America. The secretary and director of research of the fledgling organization was George Hiram Brownell (1875–1950), a newspaperman who had amassed a major collection of Twain manuscript materials, letters, and books. Under Brownell's leadership the organization moved to Wisconsin, where in 1939 it was incorporated as the Mark Twain Research Foundation. In the same year Brownell sent out the first issue of the *Twainian*, a bimonthly, four-page publication that contained news of interest to the organization's more than 200 members as well as notes, brief scholarly articles, bibliographical information, and previously unpublished Twain materials.

After Brownell's death in 1950 the Mark Twain Research Foundation moved its collections and offices to Perry, Missouri, home of the organization's new executive secretary, Chester L. Davis (1903–1987). Under Davis's direction the organization actively began to acquire Twain artifacts and memorabilia. Mr. and Mrs. Lorenzo D. Norris and Mrs. B.L. Fishback of Perry, Missouri, represented the foundation at a public auction held in Hollywood, California, at the home of Clara Clemens Samossoud on 9 April 1951. The foundation acquired the large oil-over-photo of Samuel Clemens by Thomas Marr, as painted by Isaac Rader in 1903, reputedly the author's favorite portrait of himself. In addition, the foundation purchased furniture that Clemens had acquired in Italy for his Hartford home, other portraits of Clemens family members, books from the author's library, and personal belongings. These are all currently on display at the Mark Twain Birthplace Museum in Florida, Missouri.

After the death of the senior Davis, 6 December 1987, Chester L. Davis, Jr., of Detroit, Michigan, became executive secretary of the foundation, and Davis's widow, Nina (of Perry, Missouri), became editor of the *Twainian*.

Oliver Howard and Goldena Howard

See also: Brownell, George Hiram; Journals; *Twainian, The*

Mark Twain's Study

The original site of Mark Twain's octagonal study was Quarry Farm, the residence on East Hill in Elmira, New York, of Theodore and Susan Langdon Crane. During most of the summers in the 1870s, 1880s, and 1890s Twain and his family spent some of their happiest times together at Quarry Farm visiting with his wife Olivia's relatives.

In 1874 Susan Crane, Olivia's sister, had a study built as a surprise for her brother-in-law. It was located on a rise about one hundred yards behind the Crane residence and overlooked the Chemung River valley and the city of Elmira. Twain was delighted with the study, which resembled a steamboat's pilothouse. But more important, it afforded him a quiet and private place where he could write undisturbed. He did some of his most productive work there and composed the first half of *The Adventures of Tom Sawyer* (1876), *Adventures of Huckleberry Finn* (1885), *The Prince and the Pauper* (1882), several chapters of *A Tramp Abroad* (1880), *Life on the Mississippi* (1883), and a major portion of *A Connecticut Yankee in King Arthur's Court* (1889) (Jerome and Wisbey 234).

In 1952 Jervis Langdon, Sr., Twain's nephew, presented the study to Elmira College. It was moved to the campus, just below Cowles Hall, on 7 May of that year and was completely restored. The study, furnished with a few chairs, a table, and an old sofa, also contains a changing exhibit of historical photographs. The study is open to the public.

Joan V. Lindquist

BIBLIOGRAPHY

Clemens, Clara. *My Father, Mark Twain*. New York: Harper, 1931.

Clemens, Samuel L. *Mark Twain's Letters*. Ed. Albert B. Paine. 2 vols. New York: Harper, 1917.

Jerome, Robert D., and Herbert A. Wisbey, Jr., eds. *Mark Twain in Elmira*. Elmira, N.Y.: Mark Twain Society, 1977.

Kaplan, Justin. *Mr. Clemens and Mark Twain*. New York: Simon & Schuster, 1966.

Lindquist, Joan V. "A Room of His Own: Mark Twain at Elmira." *Mark Twain Journal* 21.3 (Spring 1983): 40.

See also: Quarry Farm

Mark Twain's Travels with Mr. Brown
(1940)

A series of travel letters originally published in the San Francisco *Alta California* in 1866–1867 was collected and edited by Franklin Walker and G. Ezra Dane in 1940 as *Mark Twain's Travels with Mr. Brown*. This series provides a transition between the Sandwich Island letters of 1866 and the 1867 European/Holy Land letters that would form the basis of *The Innocents Abroad* (1869).

The character Mr. William Brown appears in these letters as a disreputable, unpoetic, vernacular man with an earthy, realistic view of life and human motivation. A "Caliban," Mr. Brown accompanies Mark Twain on his 1866–1867 voyage from San Francisco to New York via the Isthmus of Panama; en route they travel through Nicaragua and along the coast of Florida. The function of Mr. Brown is to act as the alter ego of Mark Twain. The letters alternate chapters of straight description with chapters of exchanges between Twain and Brown. Whereas Twain is refined, genteel, restrained, and uses formal, sophisticated language, Brown is vulgar, spontaneous, and uses vernacular dialect peppered with crude slang. Brown's realistic, though often coarse and vulgar, perspective serves to undercut Twain's romantic, genteel vision. E. Hudson Long suggests that before Clemens had created Mr. Brown, his persona Mark Twain had been the realist; once Brown was created to assume that role, Mark Twain could represent a more refined perspective on life. In revising the *Alta* letters for *The Innocents Abroad*, Clemens eliminated Brown as an alternative narrative voice, and the point of view becomes totally that of Mark Twain—a "sinner" among the sickeningly pious pilgrims. Subsidiary characters are allowed an occasional vulgar or crude remark, but on the whole *The Innocents Abroad* is less highly seasoned with slang than were the original *Alta* letters because of Brown's absence. Sydney Krause suggests that Clemens got rid of the earthy Mr.

Brown in order to appeal to a wider, primarily eastern, audience.

Mr. Brown may have been inspired by William Brown, a riverboat pilot under whose supervision Clemens served briefly as a cub in November 1857. If so, then Robert Gale may be correct to assume that the Mr. Brown of the *Alta* letters is the same character as the Mr. Brown who later appears in the Mississippi River narratives. He is briefly mentioned in "Old Times on the Mississippi" (1875) as a man who, like Jim Blaine in *Roughing It* (1872), is a victim of total recall. In *Life on the Mississippi* (1883), however, Brown assumes a more sinister coloring. As the pilot of the *Pennsylvania*, Brown is an evil tyrant, like Pap in *Huckleberry Finn* (1885), who administers frequent tongue lashings to humiliate his cub pilot. When Brown physically assaults the cub's younger brother, Henry, the cub rebels and attacks Brown with a stool, thoroughly thrashing him. Because of the incident, the cub transfers to the *A. T. Lacey* and watches as the *Pennsylvania*—with his brother still on board—leaves New Orleans on its way to St. Louis. Unfortunately Brown's boat never reaches its destination because of an explosion near Memphis that claims Henry's life.

Don L. F. Nilsen

BIBLIOGRAPHY

Clemens, Samuel. *Life on the Mississippi*. Boston: James R. Osgood, 1883.

————. *Mark Twain's Own Autobiography: The Chapters from the "North American Review."* Ed. Michael J. Kiskis. Madison: U of Wisconsin P, 1990.

————. *Mark Twain's Travels with Mr. Brown*. Ed. Franklin Walker and G. Ezra Dane. New York: Knopf, 1940.

Cox, James M. *Mark Twain: The Fate of Humor*. Princeton, N.J.: Princeton UP, 1966.

Gale, Robert L. *Plots and Characters in the Works of Mark Twain*. New York: Archon, 1973.

Krause, Sydney J. *Mark Twain as Critic*. Baltimore: Johns Hopkins UP, 1967.

Long, E. Hudson. *Mark Twain Handbook*. New York: Hendricks House, 1957.

See also: Comic Poses; *Innocents Abroad, The*; Travel Writings

Matthews, J. Brander
(1852–1929)

One of the first academics to recognize the excellence of Clemens's writing, Brander Matthews, an English professor at Columbia University, was the person to whom Clemens confided the famous statement that his books wrote themselves. Spanning over forty years, in more than a dozen reviews and essays, Matthews wrote astute criticism about Clemens's work, drawing attention to the effectiveness of the first-person point of view in *Adventures of Huckleberry Finn* (1885), elucidating Clemens's skill at reproducing colloquial language, and praising Clemens's artistry as a storyteller and speaker. Matthews observed that though Clemens was a master of prose, humorous writers—and Clemens ranked with Chaucer, Cervantes, and Molière—are often penalized by not being taken seriously; so Clemens, having more humor than most, had to pay a higher penalty. Clemens thought well of Matthews as a literary critic, though he disagreed strongly with him about Scott and Cooper and was not averse to using Matthews's reputation as a foil, as in his "Fenimore Cooper's Literary Offenses." The long personal friendship between the two men cooled briefly in the late 1880s when Clemens excoriated Matthews in print about Matthews's public criticism of English copyright laws over American ones.

L. Terry Oggel

BIBLIOGRAPHY

Clemens, Samuel L. "American Authors and British Pirates I. A Private Letter and a Public Postscript." *New Princeton Review* 5 (January 1888): 46–54.

Matthews, J. Brander. "American Authors and British Pirates." *New Princeton Review* 4 (September 1887): 201–212.

————. "American Authors and British Pirates II. An Open Letter to Close a Correspondence." *New Princeton Review* (London) 5 (January 1888): 54–65.

————. "Mark Twain and the Art of Writing." *Harper's Monthly* 141 (October 1920): 635–643.

————. "Mark Twain as Speech Maker and Story Teller." *The Mentor* 12 (May 1924): 24–28.

———. "Memories of Mark Twain." *Saturday Evening Post* 192 (6 March 1920): 14–15, 77–81.

———. "The Penalty of Humor." *Harper's Monthly* 92 (May 1896): 897–900.

———. *These Many Years: Recollections of a New Yorker.* New York: Scribner, 1917.

See also: Copyright; "Fenimore Cooper's Literary Offenses"

Media Interpretations of Mark Twain's Life and Works

Twain's friend Thomas Edison first captured Mark Twain on audio-visual media when Twain visited Edison's New York laboratory in 1909 and recited stories for Edison's wax cylinders. These recordings were lost in a 1914 fire. Also in 1909 Edison visited Twain at his Stormfield home and made a "home movie" of Clemens and daughter Jean. This short film is still extant and can be seen in PBS's *The History of English* series. Also in 1909 Edison filmed a production of *The Prince and the Pauper*, the first media adaptation of a Twain work.

Many hours of film, tape, and vinyl recordings have been devoted to the life and works of Mark Twain. In 1944 Twain himself became a character on screen, played by Fredric March in Warner Brothers's *The Adventures of Mark Twain*. In 1983 Twain (with the voice of James Whitmore) became a Claymation character along with Huck, Tom, and Becky Thatcher in another *Adventures* film. Whitmore hosted his own television series, *Mark Twain's America*, and served as narrator or introducer to big-screen adaptations of Twain's works, many of which the author would not have recognized in their media form.

The first novels to be produced for film were those most often redone: *Adventures of Huckleberry Finn*, *The Adventures of Tom Sawyer*, *A Connecticut Yankee in King Arthur's Court*, and *The Prince and the Pauper* all first appeared as silent films, then were reworked by various Hollywood studios in the 1930s and 1940s. Animations followed in the 1970s. MGM/United Artists and Paramount studios each produced a series of recycled Twain material. Most commercial versions—especially those with children as central characters—were innocuous, intentionally juvenile fare, although many educational producers occasionally attempted adaptations close to the spirit and letter of the original works. The most notable of these tended first to appear on Public Broadcast television, most notably the productions of the Great Amwell Company and the American Playhouse series of the 1970s (see list below).

Movies and T.V.

All discussions of movies and T.V. versions below are listed by work in alphabetical order except those done for Public Television. They are covered in a separate section.

A Connecticut Yankee in King Arthur's Court. A story often repeated, imitated, and bowdlerized beyond resemblance to the original story, *A Connecticut Yankee* has been a musical (1949) with Bing Crosby, a vehicle for Will Rogers (1931), and a Disney cartoon with a robot accompanying the time traveler. Probably the oddest version to date is the December 1989 T.V. movie reversing the traveler's age, sex, race, and time frame. The most useful version for educators is the 1978 one-hour production made for television by WQED.

Releases: 1921, Fox; 1931, Fox; 1949, Paramount; 1970, MGM/UA/Home Video; 1973, Disney; 1978, WQED (Pittsburgh/Master Vision Video); 1989, NBC.

Adventures of Huckleberry Finn. Of the many adaptations of this novel, perhaps the most noteworthy is Georgian director Georgi Danelia's *Hopelessly Lost* (1973), filmed in Moscow, in which a naturalistic ending has Huck and Jim still on the raft under the thumb of the King and Duke. PBS aired a four-part series in 1985 that considerably shortened the ending, restored the "Raftsmen's Passage" to the story, and added the raftsman's painting Huck blue for spying on them.

MGM has made three versions, the most touted being the 1960 edition starring ex-boxer

Archie Moore as Jim and Tony Randall as the King. In 1965 Britannica Educational Corporation released *Huck Finn and the American Experience* for the classroom, which illustrated how the novel fulfilled basic essentials of classic literature, especially universality; and in November 1990 the Disney channel aired *Return to Hannibal: The New Adventures of Huckleberry Finn and Tom Sawyer.*

Releases: 1919, Morosco-Lasky; 1931, Paramount; 1939, MGM/Loewes; 1946, MGM/Custodians; 1956, Syracuse University/NET Film Service; 1960, MGM; 1965, Britannica Educational Corporation; 1974, United Artists (Musical); 1980, ABC/Circle Films; 1981, television movie; 1981, New Hope Productions (cartoon); 1984, Embassy Home Entertainment (cartoon); 1985, American Playhouse Productions; 1985, *The Raft Adventures of Huck and Jim* (animated).

The Adventures of Tom Sawyer. *Mark Twain and Tom Sawyer* was released in 1952, now available on video, from the International Film Bureau for use in the classroom. Most efforts to put Tom Sawyer on film were more characteristically escapes from the classroom, especially in the *Adventures of Tom Sawyer* T.V. series aired in 1979 on the Showtime cable channel.

In 1938 Paramount issued a faithful and entertaining adaptation of *Tom Sawyer, Detective*. It starred Billy Cook and Donald O'Connor, was directed by Louis King with a Twain-flavored screenplay by Lewis Foster, Stuart Anthony, and Robert Yost. Because of the light nature of the original text, the story and characters made an easy transition to the screen.

In 1981 Disney's *Rascals and Robbers: The Secret Adventures of Tom Sawyer and Huckleberry Finn* starred Ed Begley, Jr., Michael Hall, and Anthony Zerbe in the most modern recreation of Twain's boys to date.

Releases: 1912, Morosco-Lasky (silent); 1930, Paramount Pictures; 1938, Selznick/United Artists; 1973, Reader's Digest; 1973, United Artists.

The Prince and the Pauper. Another often repeated and wildly adapted story, *The Prince and the Pauper*'s tale of reversed roles has been parodied, borrowed, and revised in a plethora of entertainment films. The version closest to the text—and the most popular—was Warner Brothers's highly touted 1937 star-studded vehicle starring Bobby and Billy Marsh (twin brothers), Errol Flynn, Claude Rains, and Alan Hale.

Releases: 1909, Edison (silent); 1915, Famous Players-Paramount (silent); 1923, produced in Austria; 1937, Warner Brothers; 1954, *Crossed Swords*; 1962, Disney; 1977, Fox; 1977, MGM/UA/Home Video (animated); 1978, Warner Brothers.

The Great Amwell Company and Public Television. Among the many interesting adaptations of Twain's short stories, Alexander Korda's "Thousand [Million] Pound Bank Note" was probably the first. (Korda also directed the 1923 Austrian silent *The Prince and the Pauper*.) But not until 1980 was a serious effort made to make credible productions of Twain's works, both short stories and novels. In 1980 the Great Amwell Company began its series of outstanding filmed Twain works choosing *Life on the Mississippi* for its first critically acclaimed effort. Made for Public Broadcasting, these films featured fine production, writing, and casting: *Life on the Mississippi* was directed by veteran William Perry and starred Robert Lansing as the irresistible Horace Bixby. Kurt Vonnegut, Jr., introduced the film, briefly noting the importance of the book and Twain's influence on his own writing. (A German version is available on video tape, and both versions run just under two hours.) In 1956 *Kasrilevka on the Mississippi* was released by the Jewish Theological Seminary of America and NBC for the Academy for Adult Jewish Studies.

Also in 1980 the *American Short Story* Public Television series issued *The Man That Corrupted Hadleyburg* starring Robert Preston and Fred Gwynne, Preston as narrator/stranger. *Hadleyburg* is one of the most discussed Twain media projects in print: Calvin Skaggs, the show's producer, has collected the stories, filmscript, selections, interviews with screenwriters, and comments by scholars in *The American Short Story* (Dell, 1980; *Hadleyburg* is discussed in Vol. 2).

In 1981 the Great Amwell Company released "The Private History of a Campaign That Failed," adding a rendering of "The War Prayer" as a coda to the title story. As with all Great Amwell projects, the script was close to the original text although some variations in characterization are noticeable.

In 1982 the company released *Innocents Abroad*. Many of the more memorable scenes and descriptions from the work come realistically to life, the screenplay candidly reflecting Sam Clemens's youth and immaturity in 1867. Among the noted stars of this production was David Ogden Stiers of "M.A.S.H." fame as the doctor.

The Mysterious Stranger also appeared in 1982, directed by Peter H. Hunt and produced by William Perry. It was based on the more credible "No. 44" version of the story but toned down the darker aspects. Christopher Makepeace and Fred Gwynne starred, Gwynne as the magician, one variation from the "44" text.

Pudd'nhead Wilson, first produced as a silent movie in 1916 by the Famous Players/Paramount Studio, was the next title adapted by the Great Amwell Company/American Playhouse Presentations. In 1983 Amwell's *Wilson* starred Ken Howard as David Wilson, and Lise Hilboldt as a determined and passionate Roxy. Filmed at Harper's Ferry, West Virginia, this production is among the very best adaptations available on video or film. All Great Amwell productions are now available on MCA Home Video.

Other notable Twain T.V. projects include Hal Holbrook's "Mark Twain Tonight" (aired on CBS) and the 1978 series *Mark Twain's America* by Schik Sun Productions. Created by Charles F. Sellier, Jr., and James L. Conway, the series presented fictional biographies of famous Americans introduced by Mark Twain (played by Walker Edmiston). In 1989 David

Birney adapted and starred in "Extracts from the Diaries of Adam and Eve" with his wife Meredith Baxter-Birney; the couple toured the United States in spring and summer 1989, airing the show on PBS in the fall. Birney's attempt to capture and reflect the letter and spirit of Twain was above average and stands beside the Great Amwell's *Pudd'nhead Wilson* as among the best media adaptations of Twain.

Biography

The life of Mark Twain is as much legend as his stories, and filmmakers have had varying success at contributing to an understanding of Mark Twain as a man and writer. *The Adventures of Mark Twain* (Warner Brothers, 1944) featured a fanciful script sanctioned by Clara Clemens Samossoud that was far more myth than fact. Perhaps the most useful filmed biographies of Twain were the 1960s *Mark Twain's America* (not to be confused with the Disney series of the same name) and the 1980s *Mark Twain: Beneath the Laughter*, a candid look into Twain's final unhappy years. Certainly the most memorable and appealing look at Twain and his works was the 1986 Claymation *Adventures of Mark Twain*, which included witticisms and adaptations of Twain's work that illustrate his popular and private sides for an audience of all ages and education. Most recent is the 1990 Arts and Entertainment broadcast *Mark Twain and Will Rogers*, introduced by Peter Graves, combined from two thirty-minute segments previously broadcast on CBS and narrated by Mike Wallace.

Releases: 1944, Warner Brothers, *The Adventures of Mark Twain*; 1946, Academic Film Company/Almanac Film, *Mark Twain*; 1953, Group Film Productions (United Kingdom), *Man in a Million*; 1957, Coronet Instructional Films, *Mark Twain: Background for His Works*; 1960, NBC, *Mark Twain's America*; 1961, Coronet Instructional Films, *Mark Twain Gives an Interview*; 1969, ABC News/Benchmark Productions, *The Legend of Mark Twain*; 1972, Rophel Association/West Hartford, Conn. Fenwick Productions, *The House That Mark Built*; 1977, National Geographic Society, *Mark*

Twain: "When I Was a Boy"; 1978, Coronet Films, *Mark Twain: Background for His Works*; 1978, Commercial Union Leasing Corporation, made by Wingstar Film Production, Inc., *Mark Twain and His Automated Office*; 1980, Pyramid Film and Video, *Mark Twain: Beneath the Laughter*; 1981, Comco Productions/ AIMS, *Mark Twain: Hartford's Home*; 1982, Great Amwell Company/MGM Home Video, *Mark Twain Classics*; 1986, *Adventures of Mark Twain* (Claymation); 1990, Arts and Entertainment (*Biography* series), *Mark Twain and Will Rogers*.

Radio

In radio drama's heyday, adaptations of literary works were common and often well done if greatly abridged renderings of the "classics." *CBS Radio Theatre*'s *Roughing It* was one of the more imaginative in which Sam Clemens advised Hollywood screenwriters to read and refer to his book for authenticity in big screen westerns. To demonstrate the "realism" in his book, Clemens recounts some of the most memorable episodes in *Roughing It*.

Life on the Mississippi, from the *Cavalcade of Stars* radio series, starred Raymond Massey as Clemens in a fine adaptation of the first half of the original text. *Huckleberry Finn* and *A Connecticut Yankee in King Arthur's Court* were adapted in 1948 by the NBC *Radio Theatre* into one-hour dramas.

In 1979 the CBS *Mystery Theatre*, reviving the idea of radio drama, broadcast a meandering adaptation of "The Stolen White Elephant," and KERA, 90 FM in Dallas, Texas, broadcast a three-part "Mark Twain in the Morning" series which featured biography and short passages from Twain's writing. On 1 December 1990, PBS broadcast Garrison Keillor's "American Radio Theatre of the Air" from Twain's Hartford home featuring dramatizations, readings, a tour of the house, and a pool game between Keillor and humorist Roy Blount. The show was rebroadcast on 3 August 1991.

Filmstrip

A common tool for classroom use in the 1950s, 1960s, and 1970s, filmstrips of single-frame slides with accompanying scripts are now often replaced by more modern films and videos. Still, many filmstrips have been made on the life and works of Mark Twain and can still be useful for educational purposes. A list of available titles follows.

Releases: 1946, "Tom Sawyer Whitewashes the Fence," William P. Gottlieb Co./Encyclopedia Britannica Films; 1958, "Mark Twain," Curriculum Materials Corp.; 1961, "Three Great Writers," Eye Gate House; 1965, "Mark Twain's America 1835–1910," Wolper Productions, Filmstrip of the Month Club; 1966, "Mark Twain—More a Man Than a Legend," RMI Film Productions; 1967, "Mark Twain," Wolper Prod., Filmstrip of the Month Club; 1967, "Mark Twain: A Biography," Wolper Prod., Filmstrip of the Month Club; 1967, "Mark Twain Part One: Mississippi Days," EMC/Ginn and Co.; 1967, "Mark Twain Part Two: Out West," EMC/Ginn and Co.; 1968, "The World of Mark Twain," Guidance Association of Pleasantville, N.Y.; 1968, "The Adventures of Huckleberry Finn," Educational Dimensions Corp.; 1968, "The Adventures of Huckleberry Finn," Popular Science Pub. Co., Audio-Visual Div.; 1969, "Mark Twain: The Hannibal Years," Perfectia Form Co.; 1969, "Mark Twain: The Man and His Works," Society for Visual Education; 1969, "The Adventures of Tom Sawyer: Analysis and Evaluation," Society for Visual Education; 1969, "A Connecticut Yankee in King Arthur's Court," Popular Science Pub., Audio-Visual Div.; 1969, "Mark Twain's Mississippi," Educational Audio-Visual; 1970, "Uncle Mark," Thomas S. Klise Co.; 1971, "Mark Twain," Eye Gate House; 1972, "The Mississippi of Tom Sawyer and Huckleberry Finn," Brunswick Prod.; 1974, "Mark Twain: The Man," Coronet Instructional Media; 1974, "Mark Twain: The Humorist," Coronet Instructional Media; 1974, "Mark Twain: The Social Critic," Coronet Instructional Media; 1977, "Mark Twain: Mississippi Renaissance Man," South Yarmouth, Mass.–Aids of Cape Cod; 1978, "The Adventures of Huckleberry Finn," Educational Dimensions Group; 1980, "Great American Holiday Stories," Spoken Arts Inc.

Musical Treatments

Mark Twain as a figure as well as his works have inspired some composers to attempt adapting his work for musical settings. In addition to the list below, some interesting musicals are available on audio media: Elmira College's *Mark Twain*, a musical focused on Twain's connections with Elmira, New York, is available on cassette tape. Roger Miller's 1985 *Big River*, the first successful adaptation of *Huckleberry Finn* on Broadway, is available on cassette, l.p., and compact disc. Lucas Foss's odd operetta of "The Celebrated Jumping Frog" is also available on record, but has inspired little interest.

Releases: 1956, *Mark Twain: Portrait for Orchestra*, Jerome Kern, Columbia Records; 1985, *Big River*, album produced by Jimmy Bowen for Lynwood Productions.

Audio Recordings (Spoken Word)

Audio adaptations of Mark Twain's words have been recorded as educational tools, entertainment cassettes for easy reading, and releases of Twain impersonators' one-man shows. Many radio shows were subsequently released on record or cassette tape. The most useful source is the Caedmon Records catalogue of spoken word recordings of Twain's works including Will Geer reading from the *Autobiography* on a two-record set, Walter Brennan reading "The Celebrated Jumping Frog," and a wealth of lesser-known professional voices reading a variety of passages from Twain's works. Most of these recordings are available in public and school libraries.

Huckleberry Finn has been adapted for cassette tape by Cram Cassettes, Comprehensive Communications Inc., Audio Language Studios, Listen for Pleasure, Audio Books on Cassette, Distributors Recorded Books Inc., and Spoken Arts Inc. *Tom Sawyer* has also been recorded on tape by Cram Cassettes, Audio Books on Cassette, Audio Language Studios, Books in Motion, Spoken Arts, Books on Tape, and Listen for Pleasure. Many of these abridged renderings are available in book stores.

Modern impersonators of Twain have also been recorded on audio media: Columbia Records issued three Hal Holbrook as Mark Twain record albums: *Mark Twain Tonight* (1959), *More Mark Twain Tonight* (1960), and *Mark Twain Tonight* (highlights from the CBS television special). The Molin/Clemens Corporation has issued a series of Bill Molin as Twain cassette tapes including Molin's "Mark Twain for President" 1988 campaign for the "Anti-Doughnut Party."

Releases: 1955, "The Best of Mark Twain: Seventeen Stories and Sketches," St. Joseph's, Michigan Audio Book Club; 1956, "Stories of Mark Twain," Caedmon Records.

Wesley Britton

BIBLIOGRAPHY

Enser, A.G.S. *Filmed Books and Plays: A List of Books and Plays From Which Movies Have Been Made. 1928–1974*. London: Andre Deutsch, 1975.

Peary, Gerald, and Roger Shatzkin, eds. *The Classic American Novel and the Movies*. New York: Frederick Ungar, 1977.

Sinyard, Neil. *Filming Literature: The Art of Screen Adaptation*. New York: St. Martin's, 1986.

See also: Comics; Impersonators

"Medieval Romance, A"
(1870)

This piece was written in the unsettled period between *Innocents Abroad* (1869) and Clemens's marriage to Olivia Langdon. First published as "An Awful Terrible Medieval Romance" in the Buffalo *Express* (1 January 1870), "A Medieval Romance" was issued as a separate book by Sheldon and Company in 1871, but, due to a contractual conflict with Elisha Bliss, Clemens obtained and destroyed the plates. In 1872 the story was collected in a British volume of Mark Twain's work, and it appeared under its present title in *Mark Twain's Sketches, New and Old* (1875).

The plot is artfully improbable and self-destructing. Lord Klugenstein hopes to win the succession of his line from his brother, the Duke of Brandenburg. The succession will go to the male heir or, failing that, to the female heir of unblemished reputation. Klugenstein raises his daughter as a son, Conrad; he also sends a handsome nobleman to seduce the Brandenburg heir, Lady Constance. When Brandenburg's health declines, young Conrad is sent to assume his (her) duties as eventual heir. However, Klugenstein's plot ensnares itself when the unmarried Lady Constance gives birth to a child. Conrad is forced to ascend the premier's chair to judge Lady Constance; no uncrowned female may sit in the chair on penalty of death. When Lady Constance accuses Conrad of fathering her child, the young judge is trapped. To reveal her gender would bring death for sitting on the forbidden chair; not to reveal it also would mean death as the seducer of Lady Constance. At this overheated moment Mark Twain intervenes to announce his inability to resolve the tangle or conclude the tale, leaving readers to pocket their frustration as best they can.

"A Medieval Romance" combines two popular nineteenth-century types, the burlesque condensed novel and the literary hoax. As Franklin Rogers explains, the condensed novel had been made popular by Thackeray and Bret Harte and had its own tightly drawn conventions, including the division into miniature chapters used in "A Medieval Romance." Mark Twain had written seven condensed novels while in San Francisco, in the time of his closest association with Harte, of which the most familiar are "The Story of the Bad Little Boy" and "The Story of the Good Little Boy" (although these two do not have the conventional division into chapters). The literary hoax, the imposition of a joke upon the unsuspecting reader, had been practiced by Defoe, Poe, and others. Mark Twain had polished his hoaxing skills in friendly rivalry with Dan De Quille during his Virginia City days; well-known instances are his Petrified Man, and the Solitary Esophagus passage of "A Double-Barrelled Detective Story."

"A Medieval Romance" burlesques the nineteenth-century love of historical romances in the tradition of Scott, as well as the emotionally manipulative plots favored by Victorians, but it also stands at the beginning of Mark Twain's long and ambiguous fascination with medievalism, which would produce works as diverse as *The Prince and the Pauper* (1882) and *The Mysterious Stranger* (1916).

Charles L. Crow

BIBLIOGRAPHY

Baldanza, Frank. *Mark Twain: An Introduction and Interpretation.* New York: Barnes & Noble, 1961.

Covici, Pascal, Jr. *Mark Twain's Humor: The Image of a World.* Dallas: Southern Methodist UP, 1962.

Rogers, Franklin. *Mark Twain's Burlesque Patterns as Seen in the Novels and Narratives, 1855–1885.* Dallas: Southern Methodist UP, 1960.

Wilson, James D. *A Reader's Guide to the Short Stories of Mark Twain.* Boston: G.K. Hall, 1987.

See also: Burlesque; Condensed Novels; Medievalism

Medievalism

The nineteenth century's fascination with the Middle Ages was a response to sweeping and disorienting change, an appeal to the ideals of a largely imagined era of simplicity and grace. This impulse was felt on both sides of the Atlantic and in every level of culture, from Walter Scott and Victor Hugo at the beginning of the century to Alfred Tennyson's *The Idylls of the King* at the end, and from bestsellers like Charles Major's *When Knighthood Was in Flower* (1898) to the scholarly investigations of medieval architecture by Henry Adams, Clemens's contemporary. So deeply steeped in medievalism was the popular imagination during Clemens's lifetime that the great public debates of the age often drew upon medieval imagery. In the antebellum South the planter class could pretend itself ennobled by a code of medieval chivalry; and later, businessmen of the Gilded Age could cloak their pursuits with references to knights and crusaders, while one of the nation's early organizations for industrial workers called itself the Knights of Labor.

Samuel Clemens responded deeply to the popular culture of his age—the persona Mark Twain was, after all, one of its significant icons—while he was at the same time a critic of its excesses. As might be predicted, his reaction to medievalism was complex and ambiguous.

One strain of Clemens's thought is easily charted. He was reared, as Kenneth Lynn reminds us, in a Whig tradition (his father was a Whig politician) that valued reason, common sense, and progress. His reading of Thomas Paine and other Enlightenment thinkers as a young man reinforced these values. The Middle Ages, and this way of thinking, was associated with superstition, antidemocratic feudal values, and the Catholic Church, all of which stood in the way of social advancement toward rational politics, a free and educated public, and scientific knowledge. Thus medievalism—the nostalgic celebration of the Middle Ages—is a dangerous regression, subversive of the best American traditions. This is the logic of Mark Twain's celebrated jab against Walter Scott (in *Life on the Mississippi*, 1883) as the cause of the Civil War. *A Connecticut Yankee in King Arthur's Court* (1889), however one reads the completed novel, was clearly begun as a satire against medievalism and those institutions in the present, especially in Britain, which perpetuate medieval, anti-progressive thinking.

Of course, it is not that simple; it never is with the many-sided Clemens. There was always an idealist in him to clash with the realist, and in his idealistic moods he could respond, like the rest of his age, to medievalism. He would sometimes claim that his ambition to be a writer began on the boyhood day he found a page of a book about Joan of Arc in the streets of Hannibal (Paine 1:81–83; 3:1261). His own book on the Maid, *Personal Recollections of Joan of Arc* (1896), certainly displays medievalism, as does *The Prince and the Pauper* (1882), the work by Mark Twain most admired by his family and which he sometimes believed to be his best, even better than *Huckleberry Finn*.

Moreover, Clemens's faith in modern progress, the basis for his satire of medievalism, eroded in his later life. Some critics, led by Henry Nash Smith, have argued that this crisis occurred while writing *A Connecticut Yankee*, so that what started as a critique of the Middle Ages and medievalism ended with bitter disillusionment about modern values. This is a point still disputed by scholars, but it seems certain that as Clemens aged and suffered the humiliating failure of the Paige typesetting machine, and consequent bankruptcy (1894), he could no longer believe in the promises of technology or that mechanical progress was necessarily linked to moral and social progress. The object of his satire became the entire Damned Human Race, its universal flaws, rather than the follies of particular times. *The Mysterious Stranger* (1916) is set in St. Petersburg (Hannibal) in some of its versions, in medieval Austria in others: both settings must have seemed the lost and remote past to the aging Clemens, equally appropriate for exposing the foolish daydreams of humanity. Both celebration and satire of the Middle Ages had become by then irrelevant.

Charles L. Crow

BIBLIOGRAPHY

Baetzhold, Howard G. *Mark Twain and John Bull: The British Connection*. Bloomington: Indiana UP, 1970.

Cummings, Sherwood. *Mark Twain and Science: Adventures of a Mind*. Baton Rouge: Louisiana State UP, 1988.

Lynn, Kenneth S. *Mark Twain and Southwestern Humor*. Boston: Little, Brown, 1959.

Martin, Jay. *Harvests of Change: American Literature 1865–1914*. Englewood Cliffs, N.J.: Prentice-Hall, 1967.

Paine, Albert Bigelow. *Mark Twain: A Biography*. 3 vols. New York: Harper, 1912.

Smith, Henry Nash. *Mark Twain's Fable of Progress: Political and Economic Ideas in "A Connecticut Yankee."* New Brunswick, N.J.: Rutgers UP, 1964.

See also: Catholicism; *Connecticut Yankee in King Arthur's Court, A*; *Personal Recollections of Joan of Arc*; *Prince and the Pauper, The*; Scott, Walter; South, Mark Twain and the

Meine, Franklin J.
(1896–1968)

An authority on American humor and folklore, compiler of an extensive collection of books and materials on these subjects, Franklin Julius Meine was also a teacher and editor. His major books are *Tall Tales of the Southwest* (1930), *Mike Fink, King of the Mississippi Keelboatmen* (1933, with Walter Blair), *Mark Twain's First Story* (1952), *The Crockett Almanacs* (1955), and *Half Horse-Half Alligator: The Growth of the Mike Fink Legend* (1956, with Walter Blair). He also edited the *American People's Encyclopedia* (20 vols., 1953).

Born in Chicago to Frank Henry C. and Theresa (Salomon) Meine, young Meine was educated at the University of Chicago, the Carnegie Institute of Technology, and Harvard University. He served in the U.S. Army in World War I, married Helen Lomax in 1926, and had two sons. Meine's scholarly efforts were an important contribution to Twain studies. Among other things, he discovered and edited the text of Twain's first story, "The Dandy Frightening the Squatter," and edited Twain's ribald *1601*.

David B. Kesterson

BIBLIOGRAPHY

Clemens, Samuel L. *Mark Twain's First Story*. Ed. Franklin Meine. Iowa City: Prairie P, 1952.

Meine, Franklin J. *Tall Tales of the Southwest*. New York: Knopf, 1930.

See also: Blair, Walter; Southwestern Humor

Meisterschaft
(1888)

Meisterschaft: In Three Acts is a bilingual play first published in 1888 in *Century Magazine*. In it Mark Twain humorously criticizes language as a mode of communication and proves that, especially among lovers, language often serves only as an obstacle to true understanding. The unfamiliar language must deal with sense and emotion, but difficulties arise. Accordingly, those not involved in the lovemaking lack comprehension.

To dramatize the irrelevance of language itself—in this play which he calls the "Patent Universally-Applicable Automatically-Adjustable Language Drama"—Twain at the outset points out that German could easily be replaced by French or any other foreign tongue. Paradoxically, the piece requires solid command of German in order to appreciate fully its humor.

The setting of the play is the parlor of a small house in a presumably German village (although Twain never clearly spells that out). Conflict arises when two sisters, Margaret and Annie, are sent there by their father, partially to separate them from two young admirers but primarily to practice their German. Supposedly by chance they find out that their beaus, George and William, will also stay nearby under the same conditions. Both the girls and the young men may receive visitors but are restricted to conversation in the hated and as yet unmastered language. What seemed initially an insurmountable task becomes child's play once they know of the beaus' need to speak in German.

The couples develop their courtship by using inappropriate phrases from their primers, *Meisterschaft* and *Ollendorf*, in order to find a way to communicate with each other. (It is noteworthy that Sam and Livy Clemens's daughters studied German from the same handbooks.)

Although initial verbal exchanges by the two girls appear nonsensical and simply ridiculous to the casual observer, interaction does take place in that they achieve a completely different message that, amazingly, is understood by the other.

Twain also mocks the standard method of learning a foreign language by repetition of supposedly useful irrelevant phrases. Outwardly the couples seem to employ this method, but by misusing the sentences and subverting the conventional rules of language, words take on different meanings and values, resulting in a more natural and spontaneous way of communication. Annie's joyful exclamation that learning German is "getting as easy as nine times seven equals forty-six" (with an allusion to *Huckleberry Finn*) suggests that the lovers have invented their own language. An inappropriate rote phrasing, like "If at all possible, I would like to arrive this forenoon, since I am interested in meeting one of my business acquaintances," acts as a metaphor for the desire to meet the potential sweetheart. Misuse of the word *umsteigen*, commonly used only in the context of changing a vehicle, implies a change is taking place.

Interestingly, once the lovers have mastered the German grammar and vocabulary, and after the young men resort to conventional declarations of love by passing a sentimental Heinrich Heine love poem off as their own creation, the new language breaks down. Language can be borrowed or plagiarized, but once it is understood on the obvious level, it ends in "failure to communicate." Twain insinuates that language in itself is ambiguous and untrustworthy; perhaps this difficulty is true of the language of love, and certainly it is true of pragmatic language. Only the language of heart and soul contains honesty and truth. When Gretchen, the chaperon, and Mrs. Blumenthal constantly misinterpret the four lovers' conversation and actions, Twain proves that this language, which transcends any linguistic barrier is limited to those in love.

From the American perspective, Heine's poem, *Meisterschaft*, *Ollendorf*, and the awful German language, which Twain so successfully mocks in this uniquely innovative play,

represent the superficiality and restriction of European culture and values.

As a character, Stephenson takes the place of Twain himself, who manipulates the action, the characters, and the audience from the start. One is left with the opinion that from the beginning Stephenson had no doubt about the outcome of this plot.

Doris Gelencser

See also: "Awful German Language, The";
    Dramatist, Mark Twain as; German
    Language; Language

Melodrama

The word *melodrama* literally means music drama, a drama or story accompanied by music. The connotations of the word, however, include a story of strong emotional sentiment, an idealization of human experience, maudlin sentimentality, and a contrived plot. The plot is usually developed sensationally with little regard for convincing motivation. Generally, the characters in a melodrama tend to be stereotyped into good or bad, heroic or villainous, and are rewarded or punished at the end of the drama. Furthermore, in melodrama characterization is usually flat, subordinated to the necessities of plot. The dialogue contains strong emotional appeal and usually follows a predictable pattern.

Although Mark Twain constantly spoke out against sentimentality in fiction, he produced a number of pieces that make excessive appeal to the emotions of his audience as in "The Death Disk" (1901) and in his sentimental stance about the unfortunate fate of animals in "A Horse's Tale" (1906) and "A Dog's Tale" (1903). Some of his stories, such as "A Horse's Tale" and "Was It Heaven? or Hell?" (1902), seem also to contain poignant autobiographical references to the medical problems of Olivia and Jean, and to the death of Susy (Cox 265). Albert B. Paine refers to the latter story as one of Mark Twain's finest fictional sermons (Paine 177). In "The Californian's Tale" (1893)

Twain also plays upon the reader's emotions in his pathetic account of the old miner who over a period of nineteen years keeps alive the memory of his dead bride. Of course, some of Mark Twain's melodramatic excesses, such as Emmeline Grangerford's poetry and Sherlock Holmes's farfetched deductions in "A Double-Barreled Detective Story" (1902), are attempts at parody.

Andy J. Moore

BIBLIOGRAPHY

Dickinson, Thomas H. *The Contemporary Drama of England*. Boston: Little, Brown, 1931.

Heilman, Robert B. *Tragedy and Melodrama*. Seattle: U of Washington P, 1968.

Holman, C. Hugh, and William Harmon. *A Handbook to Literature*. 5th ed. New York: Macmillan, 1986.

Paine, Albert Bigelow. *Mark Twain: A Biography*. Vol. 1. New York: Harper, 1912.

See also: Sentimentality

"Memorable Midnight Experience, A"

(1874)

Capitalizing on an exclusive tour through Westminster Abbey (a favor shown him by Charles Kingsley late in 1873), Mark Twain wrote "A Memorable Midnight Experience" to open his *Number One: Mark Twain's Sketches* (1874). The account of a nocturnal visit fuses traditional as well as Twainian themes and techniques (graveyard poetry, gothic fiction, international theme, irreverent persona, travel companion) that hinge on the museum motif for their texture. Groping his way in the dark, the narrator feels a cold monument and, simultaneously, is being touched by a cat. As in an epiphany, he becomes aware of death and life, past and present, stasis and flux. An emblematic scene—the cat curled up at the feet of Queen Elizabeth's statue—specifies the lesson of his flash of recognition: he is led to muse upon human pride and transitoriness (subtly also upon female nature). His thoughts end on a conciliatory note that still cannot

obliterate the impact of a "museum of moldering vanities." The aesthetics of death creates horror, the guide fails to provide true meaning, the narrator evades an elective affinity and resorts to moral judgment. Thus, though duly impressed, he preserves his identity. Deliberately crafted, "Memorable Midnight Experience" survives as the most elaborate piece from the author's plans for a book on England.

Karl-Otto Strohmidel

BIBLIOGRAPHY

Clemens, Samuel L. *The Complete Essays of Mark Twain*. Ed. Charles Neider. Garden City, N.Y.: Doubleday, 1963. 28–36.

———. *Number One: Mark Twain's Sketches*. New York: American News, 1874. 3–8.

Kruse, Horst H. "The Museum Motif in English and American Fiction of the Nineteenth Century." *Amerkastudien (American Studies)* 31 (1986): 71–79.

Stahl, John Daniel. "Mark Twain and Female Power: Public and Private." *Studies in American Fiction* 16.1 (1988): 51–63.

See also: England; Gothic

Memphis, Tennessee

County seat of Shelby County, Memphis is the largest city in Tennessee. Located on the Mississippi River, it was visited by Sam Clemens numerous times during his years on the river, 1857–1861. At an improvised hospital in the Memphis Cotton Exchange, Henry Clemens, Sam's younger brother, died on 21 June 1858, following the explosion of the *Pennsylvania* near Ship Island, some seventy miles below the city, on 13 June. Moved by the city's kindness to Henry and other victims, Sam called it at the time "the noblest city on the face of the earth" and later "the Good Samaritan City of the Mississippi." Clemens briefly visited the city on 23 April 1882 during the trip down the river that he describes in *Life on the Mississippi* (1883) and was there again in May as he returned up the river.

Allison R. Ensor

BIBLIOGRAPHY

Clemens, Samuel L. *Life On the Mississippi*. Boston: James R. Osgood, 1883.

———. *Mark Twain's Autobiography*. Ed. Albert B. Paine. 2 vols. New York: Harper, 1924.

See also: Clemens, Henry; *Life on the Mississippi*; Mississippi River

"Mental Telegraphy"
(1891)

and

"Mental Telegraphy Again"
(1895)

In a preface to "Mental Telegraphy," written in 1878 but first published in *Harper's Magazine* (December 1891), Mark Twain outlined the genesis of his article. Although the preface contains inaccuracies regarding the dating of several episodes, it generally records the beginnings of his lifelong interest in mental phenomena as well as provides some curious episodes.

Twain explains that he made his discovery about "mental telegraphy" (what we would today call telepathy) in 1874 or 1875 as a result of circumstances surrounding the writing of "the Great Bonanza book"—a book by William H. Wright (Dan De Quille) detailing the richest silver strike in American history in the Comstock Lode of Nevada. From that time he frequently recorded instances in which minds "telegraphed" thoughts to each other, several of which are included in his article. During his trip to Germany in 1878 he wrote up some of them for inclusion in *A Tramp Abroad* (1880), but he later removed the passages for fear that the public would take the subject seriously in a book devoted to humor. Then in either 1881 or 1883 he tried to publish the article anonymously in the *North American Review*, but it was rejected because it dealt with coincidences. Since then the world has grown more receptive, partly because of the work of the English Society for Psychical Research.

In "Mental Telegraphy Again," first published in *Harper's Magazine* (September 1895), Twain adds additional incidents of mental telegraphy that he discovered after he wrote his original essay seventeen years earlier.

Both essays have a direct bearing on the theme of instantaneous communication, and both provide evidence of Twain's concern with psychic possibilities, telepathy, extrasensory phenomena, and spiritualism. Twain concludes that there are instances in which he actually read people's minds. There are simply too many instances of thought transference and events of people simultaneously having the same thoughts to dismiss each as mere coincidence.

In "Mental Telegraphy" Twain posits that a good invention would be the "phrenophone," which might communicate thoughts instantaneously, just as the telephone communicates the spoken word.

Joseph B. McCullough

BIBLIOGRAPHY

Clemens, Samuel L. *The Science Fiction of Mark Twain*. Ed. David Ketterer. Hamden, Conn.: Archon, 1984.

Hill, Hamlin. *Mark Twain and Elisha Bliss*. Columbia: U of Missouri P, 1964.

See also: Mental Telepathy/Extrasensory Perception; Occult; Spiritualism

Mental Telepathy/Extrasensory Perception

While hesitant to display his beliefs publicly, Twain was long interested in psychic phenomena. According to Alan Gribben in "'When Other Amusements Fail': Mark Twain and the Occult," Twain was a member of the English Society for Psychical Research between 1884 and 1902 (Lester M. Hirsch, in "Mark Twain and ESP," records Twain's membership as 1884–1894). Twain's notebooks from the 1870s forward record telepathic experiences; and in 1898, in a letter to Richard Watson Gilder, he averred, "Some people do not believe in mental telepathy, but

I have had twenty-one years of experience of it and have written a novel with that as *motif* (don't be alarmed—I burned it) and I know considerable about it" (Clemens to Richard Watson Gilder, 6 November 1898, Mark Twain Papers). His most extended written explication of his experiences and the beliefs they inspired occurs in "Mental Telegraphy" and "Mental Telegraphy Again" (*In Defense of Harriet Shelley*, 1925). The former was, according to Twain, originally written in 1878 for inclusion in *A Tramp Abroad* (1880) but was excluded from that manuscript because Twain "feared that the public would treat the thing as a joke and throw it aside, whereas I was in earnest." Twain later offered it to *North American Review* on the condition that it be published anonymously; the journal refused, and Twain withdrew the article. The author's hesitation, Susan Gillman notes in *Dark Twins: Imposture and Identity in Mark Twain's America*, indicates Twain's doubts that, as a humorist, he would ever be taken seriously.

Twain's theories about what he calls "mental telegraphy" begin in the commonplace experiences of crossed letters and premonitions. Often, he explains, he will begin thinking about someone with whom he has had no contact for years, write him or her a letter, only to receive a letter in return that was begun on the day he wrote his or even before. One of the most startling incidents he records is his experience of waking early one morning and suddenly conceiving the idea for a book about the Nevada silver mines, to be written by an old Nevada friend whom he had neither seen nor heard from for over a decade. Twain immediately wrote to this friend, outlining the project and the reasons why his friend should undertake it, but pigeonholed the letter—after sealing it—hoping to find an interested publisher before sending it on to his friend. A week later he received a letter from the friend, written the same hour and day that he had conceived his idea for the book, suggesting the same project. From this and other similar incidents Twain concludes that "I could not doubt—there was no tenable reason for

doubting—that Mr. Wright's mind and mine had been in close and crystal-clear communication with each other across three thousand miles of mountain and desert . . ." (119). Moreover, he continues, "I am forced to believe that one human mind (still inhabiting the flesh) can communicate with another, over any sort of distance, and without any *artificial* preparation of 'sympathetic conditions' to act as a transmitting agent" (122). In other words, Twain is, publicly at least, dubious about messages from the spirit world but convinced that messages could pass from the mind of one living person to another.

Inanimate objects also came under his scrutiny as the bearers, or stimulators, of telepathic messages. Sometimes, he claims, "inanimate objects do not confine their activities to helping the clairvoyant, but do now and then give the mental telegraphist a lift" (132). The most frequent example he cites is the experience of thinking about someone, or some subject, not generally thought about and then having a letter from the person or about the subject delivered within a day or two. Here, he says, the proximity of the as-yet-undelivered letter "influences" the mind of its intended recipient, and in "Mental Telegraphy Again" he claims that "[l]etters often act like that. Instead of the *thought* coming to you in an instant . . . the (apparently) unsentient letter imparts it to you as it glides invisibly past your elbow in the mail-bag" (142). In 1882 he told Rutherford Hayes that a letter from Hayes had arrived minutes after the family had discussed both him and mental telegraphy, evidence, Twain felt, that the letter itself had communicated to them (Clemens to Rutherford Hayes, 10 April 1882, Mark Twain Papers). In these essays Twain also records incidents in which he decided that he had seen apparitions.

Twain's interest in mental telepathy, phrenology, spiritualism, dreams, and even fingerprinting are best viewed, first, within the context of his culture's fascination with all forms of parapsychology and, second, within his own quest for the sources of his creative powers.

R. Laurence Moore's *In Search of White Crows: Spiritualism, Parapsychology, and American Culture* (1977) is one of many works to explore the widespread interest in all forms of extrasensory perception during the latter half of the nineteenth century. As many of these secondary works point out, William James's *Principles of Psychology* (1890) studied mesmerists and mediums as well as schizophrenics, an indication that the nascent field of psychology had not yet clarified its definitions of what constituted appropriate areas of investigation. Within this cultural framework, Twain's idiosyncratic search for the sources of creativity took into account telepathic experiences as well as dreams. In "Mental Telegraphy" he is most concerned to determine which of several minds originated ideas, using as examples both his own experiences (as in the Nevada silver mines episode), and other histories of simultaneous inventions and discoveries, such as the Darwin-Wallace controversy. In 1897 Twain wrote to Sir John Adams that he had decided that the mind "originates nothing, creates nothing, gathers all its materials from the outside, and weaves them into combination automatically, and without anybody's help" (reprinted in Sir John Adams, *Everyman's Psychology*, 1929). Most often cited as evidence of Twain's determinism, this letter also illustrates one of the bases for his interest in mental telepathy. Minds that do not originate obtain their materials from somewhere else; in Twain's view that "somewhere" can be communication with another mind across vast geographical spaces.

Susan K. Harris

BIBLIOGRAPHY

Clemens, Samuel L. *In Defense of Harriet Shelley*. New York: Harper, 1925.

Ebon, Martin. *They Knew the Unknown*. New York: World, 1971.

Gillman, Susan. *Dark Twins: Imposture and Identity in Mark Twain's America*. Chicago: U of Chicago P, 1989.

Gribben, Alan. "'When Other Amusements Fail': Mark Twain and the Occult." *The Haunted Dusk: American Supernatural Fiction, 1820–1920.* Ed. Howard Kerr, John W. Crowley, and Charles L. Crow. Athens: U of Georgia P, 1983. 171–189.

Harris, Susan K. *Mark Twain's Escape from Time: A Study of Patterns and Images*. Columbia: U of Missouri P, 1982.

Hirsch, Lester M. "Mark Twain and ESP." *Mark Twain Journal* 21.3 (Spring 1983): 35–36.

Kerr, Howard. *Mediums, and Spirit-Rappers, and Roaring Radicals*. Urbana: U of Illinois P, 1972.

Paine, Albert Bigelow. *Mark Twain: A Biography*. 3 vols. New York: Harper, 1912.

See also: Determinism; Dreams; James, William; "Mental Telegraphy" and "Mental Telegraphy Again"; Occult; Spiritualism

Merlin

A colorful figure in Welsh folklore and medieval romance (both English and French), the bard Merlin was a necromancer whose supernatural powers shaped historical events; he was both human and mystical, bold and baffling. In Malory's *Morte D'Arthur* (1485), Merlin, ageless and shadowy, could not prevent the destruction of King Arthur's world even by Celtic magic.

In *A Connecticut Yankee in King Arthur's Court* (1889) Mark Twain made extensive use of Sir Edward Strachey's Globe Edition of Malory, a modernized text faithful to the original; however, *his* Merlin is a caricature in the garb of a stereotypical wizard: "a flowing black gown" decorated with occult symbols by illustrator Daniel Beard. This Merlin, a mumbling, bumbling old man, represents "the magic of folderol" and its superstitions, whereas the Yankee typifies "the magic of science," a superior force and the basis for an enlightened civilization.

After the miracle of the solar eclipse, when the Yankee is named second to the king, the jealous Merlin becomes his enemy. During the struggle between "the two master enchanters of the age" that follows, the continually defeated Merlin is a foil for the Yankee's successes. Merlin is "that cheap old humbug, that maundering old ass," says the disdainful Yankee; he is "Brer Merlin," "a very passable artist, but only in the parlour-magic line"—typical examples of Twain's denunciation by epithet.

At the end of *Connecticut Yankee* a disguised Merlin casts a spell upon the sleeping Yankee that eventually returns him to the nineteenth century. (This act and that physical blow that catapulted the Yankee into the sixth century are the book's only true miracles because they cannot be explained by science.) In return for his miracle of charity, Merlin becomes impaled on one of the Yankee's electric fences; "that petrified laugh" on the dead Merlin's face mocks the pretensions of science in Mark Twain's world and in our own.

Mary Boewe

BIBLIOGRAPHY

Clemens, Samuel L. *A Connecticut Yankee in King Arthur's Court.* Ed. Bernard L. Stein. Berkeley: U of California P, 1979.

Gardiner, Jane. "'A More Splendid Necromancy': Mark Twain's *Connecticut Yankee* and the Electrical Revolution." *Studies in the Novel* 19 (Winter 1987): 448–458.

Scudder, Vida D. *Le Morte Darthur of Sir Thomas Malory: A Study of the Book and Its Sources.* New York: Haskell House, 1965.

Strachey, Sir Edward. *Morte Darthur.* Globe Edition. Philadelphia: Lippincott, 1868.

Wilson, Robert H. "Malory in the *Connecticut Yankee.*" *Texas Studies in English* 27 (June 1948): 185–206.

See also: Beard, Daniel Carter; *Connecticut Yankee in King Arthur's Court, A*; Illustrators; Malory, Sir Thomas

"Mexican Plug, The"
(1872)

The story of the Genuine Mexican Plug appears as chapter 24 in *Roughing It* (1872). The account of young Sam Clemens's purchase of a rambunctious horse shortly after his arrival in Carson City, Nevada, is a combination initiation story, horse-swapping joke, and southwestern tall tale.

The narrator of the story adopts an extremely naive point of view for the telling of this story, claiming that he learned the difference between horses and cows only since coming west. Prompted by the tenderfoot's desire to emulate the cowboys and prodded by a skillful shill, who identifies the animal as a genuine Mexican plug and a great bucker, Sam buys at auction an uncontrollable horse. Unable to ride it himself, the tenderfoot lends the horse to local politicians. Nobody wants to ride the horse twice, however. In typical tall-tale fashion the exploits of the horse become increasingly unrealistic. Having been initiated into local business practice, Sam foists the horse off upon an even more gullible tenderfoot.

Whether or not the incident of the Mexican plug has any basis in fact is questionable. Twain's biographers do not comment on it, and its generic patterns are so overt as to arouse the reader's skepticism about the narration of the story itself. Twain concludes his tale with the suggestion that it was merely a "fanciful sketch."

William McDonald

BIBLIOGRAPHY

Blair, Walter. *Horse Sense in American Humor.* Chicago: U of Chicago P, 1942.

———. *Native American Humor.* New York: American, 1937.

Gerber, John C. "Mark Twain's Use of the Comic Pose." *Publications of the Modern Language Association* 77 (1962): 297–304.

Smith, Henry Nash. "Mark Twain as an Interpreter of the Far West: The Structure of *Roughing It.*" *The Frontier Perspective.* Ed. Walker D. Wyman and Clifton B. Kroeber. Madison: U of Wisconsin P, 1957. 205–208.

See also: Roughing It

Millet, Francis Davis
(1846–1912)

Born in Mattapoisett, Massachusetts, Francis Millet was a painter, architect, and journalist with a distinguished career in public service.

After graduation from Harvard University, Millet studied art at the Royal Academy in Antwerp, Belgium. He soon became a portraitist of some distinction; his painting of a young girl in an inglenook by sunlight, entitled "The Cozy Corner," hangs in New York City's Metropolitan Museum of Art. Later he turned to decorating federal buildings and county court houses and to painting murals for business buildings around the world. Millet was appointed by the President of the United States to several civic commissions and had an office in Washington. He helped to stage the Chicago Columbian Exposition and was inspector for the U.S. pavilion and member of the International Jury of Awards at the Paris Universal International Exposition of 1900. Millet was director of the American Academy of Art in Rome at the time of his death aboard the *Titanic* in 1912.

Friends of Olivia Langdon Clemens recommended Millet to her when in 1876 she urged her husband to sit for his first oil portrait. The thirty-year-old Millet was in New England at the time, staying with his parents prior to leaving the country to serve as a correspondent during the Russo-Turkish war. Invited to stay with the Clemens family as a house guest, Millet brought with him a single piece of canvas, as it was his intention to make his sketches and complete the portrait later in his home studio. Olivia admired the preliminary sketch and asked to keep it; wanting to oblige her, Millet went with Clemens to town to purchase another canvas. Clemens left Millet in the art shop to run an errand. When he returned, Millet was aghast: Clemens had been to a barber shop and had had his tumbling auburn curls styled into waves. With this impish prank began a lifelong friendship.

The Millet portrait captures a relaxed, middle-aged Clemens with piercing blue eyes, ears with almost no lobes tapering to the proper place in the jawline, heavy dark red hair with noticeable waves. The subject is comfortably seated in a velvet chair, his jaunty little tie askew. Although the painting is more than 115 years old, the flesh tones of Clemens's face and hands are clear. The portrait has been hanging over the fireplace mantel in the Hannibal library reading room since November 1935, at which time it was presented by Twain's daughter Clara at the observance of the one hundredth anniversary of her father's birth.

When Millet married Lily Merrell of Boston in a civil ceremony in Paris in 1879, Twain was one of the required official witnesses. At the reception Olivia gave the newlyweds a set of china; Twain gave them a stick of firewood, to which the Millets tied a big ribbon and hung it on the wall of their sitting room. The Twain-Millet friendship no doubt inspired "Is He Living or Is He Dead?" (1893), Mark Twain's *Cosmopolitan* sketch about a group of four starving artists who perpetrate a hoax by claiming one of them, a "François Millet," has died. The ruse is enormously successful. The four capitalize on the inflated value of Millet's work to a public that patronizes only dead artists, and Millet can still paint to satisfy an ever increasing demand.

A twist on the Millet-Mark Twain relationship surfaced many years after both men were dead. In the 1940s the Missouri State Legislature purchased a copy of an original manuscript of *Tom Sawyer*, which is, of course, in the author's handwriting. It was placed in a case in the museum on the first floor of the state capitol at Jefferson City. Two influential gentlemen from Perry, Missouri, thought the capitol building should also have a portrait of Mark Twain, and they asked the dealer who had discovered the manuscript to find a suitable portrait for them, preferably the first one painted. After a few weeks, the dealer offered them a large canvas with the name "F.D. Millet" across the top in large black letters, and this portrait was placed in the capitol. When the Mark Twain Birthplace Memorial Shrine, in the state park at Florida, Missouri, was ready for dedication, the two-room cottage in which Twain was born and other of his objects were moved into this shrine building. The manuscript and portrait arrived from Jefferson City; hundreds of people viewed this large garish profile of an old man with almost straight gray hair, pendulous fat earlobes, and a face that did not much resemble other Twain portraits in the museum's glass-lined walls. Some sensed fraud; avid scholars recalled that Twain was in his mid-forties when he sat for the Millet portrait. Many were puzzled at the black letters across the top of the picture, when most artists sign their work in a lower corner. But the work stayed on exhibit for almost forty years.

When plans were under way for the observance of Mark Twain's hundred and fiftieth, two books appeared that proved conclusively that the "F.D. Millet" portrait was fraudulent: one, a biography of her grandfather, *Soldier of Fortune*, by Millet's granddaughter, Joyce Sharper-Shafer of Penzance, England; the other, the *Mark Twain Book* (1985), by Oliver and Goldena Howard. This second bogus Millet then disappeared; its whereabouts are unknown.

Oliver Howard and Goldena Howard

BIBLIOGRAPHY

Howard, Oliver, and Goldena Howard. *The Mark Twain Book*. New London, Mo.: Ralls County Book, 1985.

Howells, William Dean. *William Dean Howells, Life in Letters*. Ed. Mildred Howells. 2 vols. Garden City, N.Y.: Doubleday, 1928.

Paine, Albert Bigelow. *Mark Twain: A Biography*. 3 vols. New York: Harper, 1912.

Sharper-Shafer, Joyce A. *Soldier of Fortune, F.D. Millet (1846–1912)*. Utica, N.Y.: n.p., 1984.

"£1,000,000 Bank-Note, The"
(1893)

This short story was written in the summer or fall of 1892, as Clemens worked strenuously to evade financial ruin. It was first published in the January 1893 *Century Magazine*, then reprinted the following month by Charles L. Webster and Company in *The £1,000,000 Bank-Note and Other New Stories*.

The story combines a number of enduring popular stereotypes and formulas. The hero,

Henry Adams, a young, successful broker in San Francisco, is swept out to sea in his sailboat, forced to work as a deck hand on a merchant ship that discharges him, nearly penniless, in London; he is loaned the fabulous, and unspendable, bank note by two brothers, who have a bet on its effect upon a poor but intelligent man; in the month of the experiment he becomes a lion of London society, earns a fortune for himself and a San Francisco friend he meets in London; and wins the hand of an English society belle, who turns out to be the stepdaughter of one of the eccentric brothers who lent him the bank note.

The twists and turns of the plot and its triumph of ingenuity and virtue (suggesting perhaps the work of O. Henry and of Horatio Alger, respectively), its saccharine love story, and its neatly contrived resolution, all indicate a careful calculation of the popular audience of the 1890s. So does its satire of English society life, amusing and flattering to American sensibilities, but mild enough to offend few British readers. Certainly the story reflects little of the increasingly cynical and deterministic thinking of Clemens in the period. In "Bank-Note" there is a moment, perhaps, when this darker vision is suggested, as the starving Adams seems about to grovel for a pear discarded in the street by a child; but it is at this point that he is called into the home of the two brothers, who have selected him because of the intelligence and moral qualities evident in his face. Thus we are left with the comfortable assurance that character, at least for a self-reliant American, is stronger than misfortune.

Beneath what seems a cynical manipulation of formulas, the story reveals issues of urgent importance to Clemens. The hero, coming from San Francisco to Europe and fame, obviously outlines Clemens's own career; his sense of being an impostor or prankster echoes the author's own occasional sense of the dreamlike improbability of his career, a sense that grew as bankruptcy threatened. The million-pound note itself is a particularly evocative emblem. It can be seen, most obviously, as a hopeful fantasy at a time when the author was searching for credit to save his publishing company and the Paige typesetter scheme. Less apparently, it may serve as a symbol of the author's own greatest capital, his artistic talent. Further, the issues raised by the note, which represents wealth but paradoxically cannot be spent, were vigorously debated by Americans of the period. Can paper be "real" money? What is the appropriate basis of credit? The bank-note story, in other words, can be read as a kind of allegory of the monetary concerns of the Populist era.

Finally, the name of the hero, Henry Adams, suggests that the impish, playful side of Mark Twain was subversively at work in the piece. The name offered an opportunity for one of Twain's descent from Adam jokes, a source of continuing delight to the author. But Clemens's selection of the name of his exact contemporary, the distinguished editor, journalist, historian, and Harvard professor, could not have been innocent. Clemens must have drawn some malicious glee from imagining this scion of America's most distinguished family walking in rags through London.

Charles L. Crow

BIBLIOGRAPHY

Cox, James M. *Mark Twain: The Fate of Humor.* Princeton, N.J.: Princeton UP, 1966.

Emerson, Everett. *The Authentic Mark Twain: A Literary Biography of Samuel L. Clemens.* Philadelphia: U of Pennsylvania P, 1984.

Wilson, James D. *A Reader's Guide to the Short Stories of Mark Twain.* Boston: G.K. Hall, 1987.

See also: Bankruptcy; England; Paige Typesetting Machine

Miscegenation

Twain grew up in a slaveholding society in which the sexual abuse of black women by males of the white master caste was endemic, though hardly sanctioned by the public mores, religious and secular, of the day. Still, the presence of increasing numbers of light-skinned blacks—mulattos, quadroons, octoroons—among the slave population served to convict white Southerners of frequent and flagrant transgressions of the color line. Since the offspring of slave women were themselves chattel, subject to being bought and sold, documented cases of a slaveholder trafficking in his own flesh and blood did arise, and the undeniable fact of widespread miscegenation in the South became one of the most effective moral weapons in the abolitionists' crusade against the "peculiar institution" as a whole. Fugitive slave narratives and anti-slavery fiction from the 1830s on often featured the plight of the "tragic mulatto," a walking embodiment of the South's collective sin. In turn, southern writers from the Civil War to the present have been obsessed with the theme of miscegenation, and Twain's *Pudd'nhead Wilson* (1894) must be regarded as a major outgrowth of this tradition.

Like all sexual vices, illicit miscegenation provided tempting material for smutty humor, and in the earlier stages of his career Twain, not yet the vocal champion of racial justice he would become, tended to approach the subject of interracial liaisons with a measure of virile bawdry that on at least one occasion put him in peril. It was a crude suggestion that the proceeds of the ladies' charity ball were to be used to fund a "Miscegenation Society" that nearly led him to fight a duel with a fellow journalist in Virginia City and precipitated his hasty departure for California in 1864. Ideologically fastidious commentators point to this episode as an example of Twain's crass insensitivity toward blacks, but it is possible to read his admittedly tasteless joke in a more positive light—as evidence of his iconoclastic willingness to satirize the most inviolable of taboos. Twain recognized that the purported sexual mystique of blacks might appeal to more than just the *male* members of the white race. Just such a touchy assumption provided the basis for a newspaper burlesque of *Othello* he would write in 1869, and in a private communication Twain once waggishly likened his relief over William Dean Howells's positive reaction to *Roughing It* (1872) to that of a woman who had "given birth to a white baby" when she feared it might be "a mulatto." Twain had seen enough of the world to know that the sexual bridge that spanned the color line ran both ways.

Whether or not Twain's later sense of the South's communal guilt with regard to slavery and his shift toward a more compassionate portrayal of black characters can be traced to his association with George W. Cable in the early 1880s remains a matter of speculation. What is certain is that Cable had addressed the theme of miscegenation in his fiction to a degree unprecedented for a southern writer in the post-Reconstruction era, emphasizing the tragic dimensions of the mulatto character's marginalized status. When Twain came to write *Pudd'nhead Wilson*, he may have had the pioneering example of Cable in mind. But characteristically, Twain wove his own set of comic variations on the somber theme of miscegenation. He might (with whatever measure of irony) call *Pudd'nhead Wilson* a "Tragedy," but what he created was a novel of an altogether different order.

Apart from the antics of the Italian twins and the amateur sleuthing of the title character, *Pudd'nhead Wilson* clearly contains all the elements associated with the tale of miscegenation. Roxana, a beautiful slave girl with only the slightest trace of African ancestry, bears the child of a southern gentleman of "formidable calibre." In time—and in the course of a convoluted plot involving, among other things, Twain's obsessive theme of switched identities—this child, and emblem of the South's shame, emerges as a type of the mulatto avenger. Ultimately, he murders his surrogate father, Judge Driscoll, himself an avatar of the southern chivalric ideal. Like Cable, and like the generations of southern novelists who would follow him, Twain uses miscegenation metaphorically to illustrate how slavery and a system of racial caste tend to pollute every aspect of a society. He presents an even more radical suggestion. Since Roxana's son, legally a "Negro and slave," grows up undetected as the spoiled heir of the town's leading family, Twain implies that the very

notion of race may be little more than a social fiction, thus anticipating a work like Faulkner's *Light in August* (1932) and innumerable Afro-American novels dealing with the phenomenon of "passing." Yet what sets *Pudd'nhead Wilson* apart is its author's insistence upon subjecting the intrinsically tragic aspects of the the theme of miscegenation to a sardonic, at times bitter, irony. The result is a kind of cosmic farce, in which the problem of evil is reduced to a matter of perverse human folly and characters and events alike become the material of an immense sarcastic joke.

Given the extent to which humor was for Twain a defense mechanism, a way of exorcising realities that might otherwise prove too painful, *Pudd'nhead Wilson* can be regarded as Twain's attempt to ease his stricken southern conscience by resorting to laughter, since miscegenation provided the most readily available symbol for the South's legacy of racial injustice. If so, the exorcism was only temporary. In "Which Was It?"—an unfinished fragment written at the turn of the century—Twain felt again compelled to take up the archetypal theme of miscegenation. In that truncated narrative, the intrusive presence of the mulatto-avenger Jasper comes to subvert what began as yet another botched attempt by Twain to capitalize once more on the Matter of Hannibal late in his life. Clearly, the ghosts of the South's sexual misdeeds lived on in Twain's troubled imagination. *Pudd'nhead Wilson* had not done its office.

William Bedford Clark

BIBLIOGRAPHY

Clark, William Bedford. "The Serpent of Lust in the Southern Garden." *Southern Review* NS 10 (1974): 809–822.

———. "Twain and Faulkner: Miscegenation and the Comic Muse." *Faulkner and Humor*. Ed. Doreen Fowler and Ann J. Abadie. Jackson: UP of Mississippi, 1986. 97–109.

Gillman, Susan. *Dark Twins: Imposture and Identity in Mark Twain's America*. Chicago: U of Chicago P, 1989.

Pettit, Arthur G. *Mark Twain and the South*. Lexington: UP of Kentucky, 1974.

Williamson, Joel. *New People: Miscegenation and Mulattoes in the United States.* New York: Free P, 1980.

See also: Abolition; *Pudd'nhead Wilson, The Tragedy of*; Racial Attitudes; South, Mark Twain and the

Missionaries

In his letters from the Sandwich Islands (1866) Clemens reflected a typical American attitude toward Christian missionaries when he described the ones he found there as self-sacrificing and devoted to the well-being of the natives. Even then, however, he could not help but write that the missionaries were also bigoted, puritanical, and unforgiving. This darker view of missionaries was confirmed during Clemens's travels in the Holy Land (1867) when he discovered that the missionaries there, far from being martyrs who sacrificed their own material comfort for the spiritual good of others, lived in luxury amid the overwhelming poverty of the natives. Later, when he came to view missionaries as the agents of imperialists, Clemens's attitude became unrelentingly critical, reaching its greatest intensity in 1901 in "To the Person Sitting in Darkness" and "To My Missionary Critics," in which he satirized the American Board of Commissioners of Foreign Missions for its ruthlessness and hypocrisy in China.

L. Terry Oggel

BIBLIOGRAPHY

Clemens, Samuel L. *Mark Twain's Letters from Hawaii.* Ed. A. Grove Day. New York: Appleton-Century, 1966.

Foner, Philip S. *Mark Twain: Social Critic.* New York: International Publishers, 1958.

Ganzel, Dewey. *Mark Twain Abroad: The Cruise of the "Quaker City."* Chicago: U of Chicago P, 1968.

Lorch, Fred W. *The Trouble Begins at Eight: Mark Twain's Lecture Tours.* Ames: Iowa State UP, 1968.

See also: American Board of Foreign Missions; "To My Missionary Critics"; "To the Person Sitting in Darkness"

Mississippi River

Except for brief stays in Cincinnati and the East, Mark Twain lived in Hannibal and other small towns on the banks of the Mississippi from 1838 to 1857. In 1857 he began to "learn the river" as a cub pilot, continuing as a pilot after he had earned his license on 9 April 1859. When he left for Nevada in 1861, he had experienced the Mississippi River in all of its aspects but was far from realizing the meaning and the significance of the store of such experiences and the river's potential as a literary subject. Although the river had appeared in his journalistic juvenilia, interests in what to him were more exotic and more newsworthy subjects intervened until, in 1874, he discovered what had come to be called the "Matter of the River" (Henry Nash Smith), a discovery that enabled him to replace set phrases like "the turbid waters" ("The Dandy Frightening the Squatter" [1852]) and "the crystal waters of the proud Mississippi" ("Hannibal, Missouri" [1852]) with what are perhaps the best-known words in all of his writings—"the great Mississippi, the majestic, the magnificent Mississippi, rolling its mile-wide tide along, shining in the sun." An early reference of 1866 to a projected book about the river and the exploratory use of the matter in chapter 4 of *The Gilded Age* (1873) notwithstanding, it did take the suggestions of William Dean Howells and Joseph H. Twichell to make Mark Twain see the enormous literary potential inherent in his personal familiarity with all phases of the river's life. In addition to recording Sam Clemens's process of learning the river, the installments of "Old Times on the Mississippi" (1875) present that river in manifold contexts and frames of reference. The Mississippi emerges in its physical shape and its particular geography, its "towns, 'points,' bars, islands, bends, reaches, etc.," in its particular technical terminology ("the language of this water"), in its atmospheric aspects (such as different kinds of moonlight) and its seasonal aspects (such as its June rise and its December rise), in the changing shape of its banks and of its channel, in its commercial and its social function as a great waterway, and as an ever present challenge to the "cub" and even the experienced pilot. The central lesson, which gives the account its unity as well as its lasting significance, is the gradual but inevitable replacement of a view that focuses on the aesthetic values of the river by a view that focuses on pragmatic values and questions of usefulness, lending the protagonist to speculate whether he has gained more or lost more by becoming the expert that he now is.

"Old Times," the first of his so-called Mississippi Writings to be published, was written during the composition of *The Adventures of Tom Sawyer* (1876), but it does not seem to have affected the novel's portrayal of the river much. The Mississippi remains wholly subservient to the author's conception of his book as "simply a hymn, put into prose form to give it a worldly air": it provides idyllic Jackson's Island an easy current to facilitate the boys' crossing over to it, plenty of delicious fish, a channel narrow enough for a swimmer to return at will. "The mighty river lay like an ocean at rest," and St. Petersburg is seen, "peacefully sleeping, beyond the vague vast sweep of star-gemmed water"; a thunderstorm produces a "billowy river, white with foam," but quickly passes, and only a criminal is found to drown in it.

Like that of *Tom Sawyer*, the protracted composition of *Adventures of Huckleberry Finn* (1885), begun immediately after the completion of the manuscript of the earlier novel, was interrupted by the writing of nonfiction material about the Mississippi, but in this case the intervening work did influence the presentation of the river in the novel. Even when Twain conceived his book about the Mississippi in 1866, he felt that he first needed to return there to collect materials for it. The trip, undertaken in 1882, provided him with such materials and also with a narrative structure for what came to be *Life on the Mississippi* (1883). Not a continuation of "Old Times" but rather a more comprehensive work on the river designed to incorporate the earlier series, the book extends the scope of the per-

spective on the Mississippi well beyond that of Mark Twain's personal experiences and the time span covered by them. In addition to presenting the river's history and to providing statistics and data concerning its role in the commerce and the economy of the Mississippi valley past and present, the work becomes an instrument in his deliberate attempt to fight southern backwardness and to further progress, republicanism, and reconstruction along the lines of the motto taken from Abraham Lincoln's Annual Message to Congress of 1 December 1862, which proclaims the basin of the Mississippi to be the "Body of the Nation."

The implications of such a view together with the revival of old memories, as well as his earlier decision to have Huck Finn tell his own adventures in his own idiom, in the vernacular, facilitate a totally different presentation of the river, preclude, in fact, all traditional rhetoric. But even before his return to the Mississippi, and even without resorting to the narrative strategy he had devised for *Huckleberry Finn*, the author was able to break the mood of *Tom Sawyer* as well as to improve on the realism of "Old Times" in his description of the disastrous effects of the semiannual overflow of the river on a fatalistic Arkansas village in a sketch editorially titled "Tupperville-Dobbsville" (written between 1876 and 1880), parts of which he revived in the novel. In *Huckleberry Finn* the river fully comes into its own, Mark Twain's firsthand knowledge of Jim's escape from slavery into a different kind of story in which the Mississippi becomes both the locus as well as the symbol of freedom. This is reinforced by the use of what is the most natural and therefore the most appropriate of all watercraft on the great river—the raft. It is on a raft, "a sliding down the river," that Huck and Jim feel "free," "easy," and "safe," and it is the raft in its exposure to the currents and the conditions of the river that provides and accounts for a natural and a realistic view of the Mississippi. Moreover, unlike that of the older narrator in "Old Times," Huck's perspective precludes all sentimentality; it is naive in the true sense of the word in that it shows him to be in perfect harmony with and even a part of nature. Thus there is no dichotomy between an aesthetic and a pragmatic view of the world waiting to be resolved in favor of the latter. From the beginning the Mississippi emerges as beautiful as well as dangerous, and even what purports to be a general account of the river experience in the first third of chapter 19 is both detailed and particularized, an array of different sense impressions, any summary of which would counteract its very purpose, to take the reader as close as possible to experiencing the reality of river—as close as he will ever come in the work of Mark Twain.

Pudd'nhead Wilson (1894) is the last novel counted among the Mississippi Writings. A survey of the types of steamboats stopping at or gliding by Dawson's Landing is used to provide a list of tributaries suggesting the importance and the magnitude of the river, and so does a reference to its communities, "from the frosty Falls of St. Anthony down through nine climates to torrid New Orleans." As in previous works, the river facilitates the comings and goings of the characters and determines the life of the village. It is important to note, however, that the aesthetic qualities of the Mississippi are never stressed. After the initial statement that "the hamlet's front was washed by the clear waters of the great river," the characters are, much like the widow Cooper in chapter 5, "gazing with unseeing eyes upon the shining reaches of the mighty Mississippi." When they do regard it, as Roxy does in chapter 16, it is with a "practised eye" to read the tell-tale break on a snag that informs her that she is "sole down de river." Indeed, the abiding presence of the Mississippi in the text is established first and foremost through the phrase "to be sold down the river." It is the white man's threat and the black people's fear and doom throughout. Even the black woman's counterpart of the white boy's dream of becoming a steamboatman—to "go chambermaiding on a steamboat, the darling ambition of her race and sex"—fails Roxy in

the end. As in *Huckleberry Finn*, life on the river cannot be lived independently of life ashore: the money she earns during her eight years as a chambermaid is lost when her bank in New Orleans goes bankrupt. But then she learns "that if there was anything better in this world than steamboating, it was the glory to be got by telling about it." The statement can well be read as reflecting the author's very own experience once he had discovered the matter of the Mississippi, but it should be noted that the theme of *Pudd'nhead Wilson*—as well as those of his later writings—afforded him as few opportunities to indulge in such pleasure as it did Roxy after her return to Dawson's Landing.

Taking for a subject a river that in itself occupies a prominent place in the imagination of Americans and choosing for himself a pseudonym directly related to this subject contribute significantly to the stature of Mark Twain and the abiding appeal of his works.

Horst H. Kruse

BIBLIOGRAPHY

Bates, Alan. "Mark Twain and the Mississippi River." Ph.D. diss., U of Chicago, 1968.

Blair, Walter. *Mark Twain & Huck Finn.* Berkeley: U of California P, 1960.

Kruse, Horst H. *Mark Twain and "Life on the Mississippi."* Amherst: U of Massachusetts P, 1981.

Marx, Leo. "The Pilot and the Passenger: Landscape Conventions and the Style of *Huckleberry Finn*." *American Literature* 28 (May 1956): 129–146.

Smith, Henry Nash. *Mark Twain: The Development of a Writer.* Cambridge, Mass.: Harvard UP, 1962.

See also: Adventures of Huckleberry Finn; Bixby, Horace E.; *Life on the Mississippi;* "Old Times on the Mississippi"; Piloting

Moffett, Pamela
(1827–1904)

The second child and only surviving daughter of Jane (Lampton) and John Marshall Clemens, Pamela Moffett was born in Tennessee on 13 September 1827; named Pamela Ann Clemens, she was called "Pa-mee´la" or simply "Mee´la." In 1851 she married William A. Moffett, described by brother Samuel as "a fine man in every way." The Moffetts had two children: Annie (b. 1852) and Samuel (b. 1860). Widowed in 1865, P.A.M., as she signed her letters, shared a home with her mother in St. Louis and later in Fredonia, New York. She died 31 August 1904, a date Mark Twain mistakenly recorded as September first.

In *Tom Sawyer* P.A.M. appears as Cousin Mary, who brought "song and sunshine" into the house and acted as a buffer between the mischievous Tom and an often provoked Aunt Polly. In his autobiography Mark Twain identified his sister as the mother of Samuel E. Moffett and a lifelong invalid, in that order. It is only in her correspondence that P.A.M. comes to life. There, she is not merely the earliest of Mark Twain's censors, as described by grandson Samuel C. Webster, nor is she a grim blend of piety and melancholy, as recently depicted; instead, she is revealed as proud, sensitive, witty, intense, shrewd, thoughtful, with interests ranging from family matters to world affairs, all reported in meticulous detail. When writing to relatives, she sometimes transcribed portions of her brother's letters, thus preserving a record otherwise lost.

Only twenty-four letters from P.A.M. to Mark Twain exist today. The oldest surviving Mark Twain holograph is a letter to his sister dated 8 October 1853. In all, there are eighty-one extant Mark Twain letters written solely to P.A.M. and forty-three others addressed jointly to her and mother Jane Clemens. Mark Twain's last known communication with his sister is dated 21 July 1904. In it widower Sam Clemens wrote that he still grieved too much to leave his Massachusetts home; in nearby Connecticut, P.A.M., ill in a sanitarium, was soon to die.

Mary Boewe

BIBLIOGRAPHY

Clemens, Samuel L. *Mark Twain's Letters, Volume 1 (1853–1866)*. Ed. Edgar M. Branch, Michael B. Frank, and Kenneth M. Sanderson. Berkeley: U of California P, 1988.

Moffett Correspondence, Mark Twain Papers, U of California, Berkeley.

Webster, Samuel Charles. *Mark Twain, Business Man*. Boston: Little, Brown, 1946.

See also: *Adventures of Tom Sawyer, The*; Autobiography; Correspondence; St. Louis, Missouri; Webster, Annie Moffett

Monday Evening Club of Hartford

Founded in the 1860s by Horace Bushnell, Calvin E. Stowe, and James Hammond Trumbull, the Monday Evening Club provided an intellectual forum for leading Hartford citizens. The club met on alternate Mondays between October and May; at each meeting a member presented a paper and discussion followed.

Mark Twain was elected to the Monday Evening Club in February 1873; Joseph Twichell and Charles Dudley Warner were also members. Twain presented several notable papers to the club, including "The Facts Concerning the Recent Carnival of Crime in Connecticut" (1876), expressing his interest in duality and conscience; "What Is Happiness?" (1882), which eventually became *What Is Man?* (1906); and "Consistency" (1884), which questioned blind allegiance to a political party. "The New Dynasty" (1886), presented the year he began *A Connecticut Yankee in King Arthur's Court* (1889), expressed Twain's support of labor unions, and "Universal Suffrage" (1875) championed women's right to vote.

Twain was an active member of the Monday Evening Club while he lived in Hartford, until 1895, and remained a nominal member until the end of his life.

Patricia Hunt

BIBLIOGRAPHY

Andrews, Kenneth R. *Nook Farm: Mark Twain's Hartford Circle*. Cambridge, Mass.: Harvard UP, 1950.

Kaplan, Justin. *Mr. Clemens and Mark Twain*. New York: Simon & Schuster, 1966.

Paine, Albert Bigelow. *Mark Twain: A Biography*. 3 vols. New York: Harper, 1912.

Smith, Henry Nash. *Mark Twain: The Development of a Writer*. Cambridge, Mass.: Harvard UP, 1962.

See also: Nook Farm

"Monument to Adam, A"

(1905)

In "A Monument to Adam," first published in *Harper's Weekly* (15 July 1905), Mark Twain reminisced about a project that had captured his attention in 1879. Citing a New York *Tribune* report that he had since proposed to the Reverend Thomas K. Beecher of Elmira, New York, a plan to memorialize the Father of the Human Race with a suitable monument, he went on to describe the ensuing developments. An example of the sort of brief pieces Twain often wrote in response to items in the news, the sketch has additional implications.

Begun as a joke, the monument project surprisingly gained support of a number of businessmen who saw commercial advantages in the idea. To keep the joke going, Clemens prepared a florid petition, ultimately signed by ninety-four of Elmira's leading citizens (with his own name conspicuously absent), requesting Congress to grant Elmira exclusive right to construct the monument. General Joseph Hawley, a congressman friend even agreed to present the petition to the House of Representatives, but subsequently had sober second thoughts about the possible repercussions.

To conclude the article, Mark Twain cited the *Tribune's* mention of "this forgotten jest of thirty years ago" as a case of mental telegraphy, since he had recently been working on a story that included one of its character's connection with such a project. That story was "The Refuge of the Derelicts," (q.v.) in which the "Adam Monument" subplot implicitly satirized both the idea itself and the natural selfishness that causes man to resist contributing to subscriptions for worthy tributes.

Obviously, Clemens had continued to be intrigued by the humorous and satiric implications of this monument project. In May 1883 he had commented and expanded upon it in some detail in a speech entitled "On Adam." Some six months later, having been solicited for a letter to be raffled off for a fund to complete a pedestal for the Statue of Liberty, his reply, including a check, argued—tongue-in-cheek—that a monument to Adam would be a far worthier memorial than the current one. Again in the early 1900s, inspired by news that "the Presbytery" had refused to admit two young men applying for places in the ministry because they believed Adam to be a myth, he drafted a brief "Proposal for the Renewal of the Adam Monument Petition," satirically citing Adam's intellectual superiority to such giants as Socrates, Aristotle, Shakespeare, Darwin, Herbert Spencer, and others.

Especially when seen in the light of the related documents, "A Monument to Adam" helps illustrate Mark Twain's abiding fascination with Adam and the Genesis story as a vehicle for commenting on the fables and follies of the human race, an interest that he treated most fully in "Extracts from Adam's Diary" (1893), the "Autobiography of Eve" (written early 1900s, published in part in *Letters from the Earth*, 1962), "Eve's Diary" (1905), and "Letters from the Earth" (written 1909).

Howard G. Baetzhold

BIBLIOGRAPHY

Clemens, Samuel L. "Adam Monument Proposal—Documents." Appendix B of *Mark Twain's Fables of Man*. Ed. John S. Tuckey. Berkeley: U of California P, 1972. 449–452.

———. "On Adam." *Mark Twain Speaking*. Ed. Paul Fatout. Iowa City: U of Iowa P, 1976. 178–180.

———. "Mark Twain Aggrieved." New York *Times*, 4 December 1883. Rpt. in *Mark Twain Speaks for Himself*. Ed. Paul Fatout. Lafayette, Ind.: Purdue UP, 1978. 135–136.

Jerome, Robert D., and Herbert A. Wisbey, Jr., eds. *Mark Twain in Elmira*. Elmira, N.Y.: Mark Twain Society, 1977. 61–62, 83–91, 195.

See also: "Eve's Diary"; "Extracts from Adam's Diary"; *Letters from the Earth*; "Mental Telegraphy" and "Mental Telegraphy Again"

Moore, Julia A.
(1847–1920)

Julia A. Moore is an American poetess known as "The Sweet Singer of Michigan" from the title of her first book, *The Sweet Singer of Michigan Salutes the Public* (1876). An "obituary poet," Moore is generally thought to be the model for Emmeline Grangerford in *Adventures of Huckleberry Finn* (1885).

Both Blair and Michaelson point to several such poets in the 1870s whom Clemens knew and labeled "mortuary songsters," but they concede that Moore is the most likely model for the author of "Ode to Stephen Dowling Bots, Dec'd." In *Following the Equator* (1897) Clemens admits reading Moore's poetry over a period of twenty years and credits her with "the touch that makes an intentionally humorous episode pathetic, and an intentionally pathetic one, funny" (339).

Mary Ann Wilson

BIBLIOGRAPHY

Blair, Walter. *Mark Twain & Huck Finn*. Berkeley: U of California P, 1960.

Clemens, Samuel L. *Adventures of Huckleberry Finn*. Ed. Walter Blair and Victor Fischer. Berkeley: U of California P, 1985.

———. *Following the Equator*. Hartford, Conn.: American Publishing, 1897.

Michaelson, L.W. "Four Emmeline Grangerfords." *Mark Twain Journal* 11.3 (Fall 1961): 10–12.

See also: Grangerfords, The; Sentimentality

Morgan, Hank

The protagonist and principal narrator of *A Connecticut Yankee in King Arthur's Court* (1889),

Hank Morgan remains one of Mark Twain's most controversial major characters. An erstwhile horse doctor and the son of a country blacksmith, Hank has worked and learned his way up through the ranks of industry to become a "head superintendent" in the Colt arms factory in Bridgeport, Connecticut. A crowbar blow to his skull sends him back somehow to the legendary Camelot of the sixth century. Through most of the novel Hank combats the squalor and backwardness constituting the truth behind Malory's and Tennyson's Arthurian dreams. As "The Boss" of Arthur's kingdom he acquires immense power and lays the foundations of a modern technological republic; in the final three chapters he destroys his new civilization and the massed chivalry of England, trapping himself and fifty loyal boys in a circle of death and destruction. A spell brings Hank back through the ages to the late nineteenth century, and he dies in a hotel near Warwick Castle, after passing his "Tale of the Lost Land" manuscript to Mark Twain.

As a modern pragmatist and a representative of the new technological world, Hank Morgan may be partially based on James W. Paige, the Colt employee whose typesetting machine was still firing Mark Twain's enthusiasm as principal investor and sapping his funds, and on James Welsh, a Philadelphia topographer and union leader who Mark Twain heard testify eloquently before Congress in January 1886 and who he praised to the Hartford Monday Evening Club as a new and "rightful sovereign of this world." For much of the novel, Hank seems to stand for American common sense, ingenuity, and democratic values, set off against the pretenses, oppressions, technological stasis, and ignorance fostered by a caste system, an established church, and an hereditary aristocracy. The narrative and Daniel Beard's lavish satiric illustrations make clear that the target of *CY* is the social system and literary scene in modern England. Interpretive problems flourish, however, because Hank is also a killer—first sporadically and then with great deliberateness and relish: in the climactic "Battle of the Sand Belt" he wipes out thousands of English knights with mines, gatling guns, and electrified wire and dynamites by remote control the modern culture he has brought to the Middle Ages. He also shows no qualms about slaughtering uncooperative customers for his new business and hanging bad musicians and jokesters. Hank's attitudes toward women are also hard to overlook or satisfactorily explain: one of the shocks of the novel for modern readers is that Hank finds perfect marital and sentimental bliss with "Sandy," the Demoiselle Alisande la Carteloise, who Hank has previously described as a "perfect blatherskite," an ignorant girl with no sense of the differences between fantasy and truth.

By the middle of this century it was conventional to read Hank's final holocaust as dictated by some process of discovery Mark Twain underwent as he wrote the novel, his gradual recognition of the dark side of the protagonist he had unleashed on medieval England. By this line of interpretation Hank can be a tragic hero of a "fable of progress," a cautionary tale of the ruthlessness inherent in the industrial age, of the merciless side of modern demagogues and all-out reformers, or of a civilization whose new energies are accelerating out of control. Readings of *Yankee* on such allegorical terms, however, have difficulties with certain facts about its composition. An early version of Hank Morgan, a "Sir Robert Smith of Camelot" whom Twain introduced in a reading at Governor's Island, New York City, in 1886, when the *Yankee* project was far from completion, features automated mass murder in a sketch that delights unsatirically in power and sheer invention; and Mark Twain's working notes, letters, and notebook entries from those years frequently suggest a melding of Hank's social and political anger with Mark Twain's own—to the extent that a case for Hank Morgan, either as a distinct entity from his creator or a figure whose mentality is intended to appall, is difficult to sustain.

Bruce Michelson

BIBLIOGRAPHY

Carter, Everett. "The Meaning of *A Connecticut Yankee.*" *American Literature* 50 (1978): 418–440.

Cox, James M. "*A Connecticut Yankee in King Arthur's Court*: The Machinery of Self-Preservation." *Yale Review* 50 (Autumn 1960): 89–102.

Griffith, Clark. "Merlin's Grin: From 'Tom' to 'Huck' in *A Connecticut Yankee.*" *The New England Quarterly* 48.1 (March 1975): 28–46.

Smith, Henry Nash. *Mark Twain's Fable of Progress: Political and Economic Ideas in "A Connecticut Yankee."* New Brunswick, N.J.: Rutgers UP, 1964.

———. "Object Lesson in Democracy." *Mark Twain: The Development of a Writer.* By Smith. Cambridge, Mass.: Harvard UP, 1962. 138–170.

See also: Connecticut Yankee in King Arthur's Court, A; Point of View; Technology, Mark Twain and

Mormons

Expelled from Missouri under threat of extermination in 1838, the main body of Mormons (members of the Church of Jesus Christ of Latter-day Saints) settled in Nauvoo, Illinois, some fifty miles upstream from Samuel Clemens's childhood home in Hannibal. As Richard Cracroft points out, living this close to them, young Sam must have heard a great deal about the Mormons throughout his youth. He also would have known of the Mormon migration westward that began in 1846.

Mark Twain has some humorous one-liners about Brigham Young, Mormons, and Mormonism in *The Innocents Abroad* (1869) and in his columns in the Buffalo *Express* (1869–1870). For example, in "Favors from Correspondents" (1870) he quotes a Mormon wedding announcement listing the various names of women Brigham Young is marrying.

Mark Twain's most extensive comments about Mormons are recorded in chapters 12 through 17 in *Roughing It* (1872). Twain visited the Mormons in Salt Lake City en route to Carson City in 1862. Stirred by popular accounts of Mormons and their "peculiar institution," he was intensely curious about polygamy. As Herman Nibbelink points out, Twain did not indulge, however, in the self-righteous condemnation of Mormons found in other travelers' accounts; rather, he gave a humorous parody of those accounts. Cracroft affirms that Twain's anecdotes about Mormon folkways are enduring, classic examples of his genius for exaggeration and the tall tale.

Accompanying his brother Orion, secretary of Nevada Territory, Twain was taken to visit the "King," Brigham Young. He found him to be "a quiet, kindly, easy-mannered, dignified, self-possessed old gentleman" who did not give Twain the attention he had hoped for.

With an eye to the entertainment of his eastern audience, Twain further in *Roughing It* recounts Gentile tales about Brigham Young's problems with his large family, such as a visitor's gift of a whistle to one child—which required whistles to be given to all. He purports to "analyze" the *Book of Mormon*, considering that if the ubiquitous phrase "And it came to pass" were removed, the book "would have been only a pamphlet." Still, he finds much to admire in the industrious Mormons, recognizing that for their faith they were "mobbed, beaten, and shot down; cursed, despised, expatriated; banished to a remote desert."

Richard Dilworth Rust

BIBLIOGRAPHY

Clemens, Samuel L. *Roughing It*. Ed. Franklin R. Rogers and Paul Baender. Berkeley: U of California P, 1972.

Cracroft, Richard H. "The Gentle Blasphemer: Mark Twain, Holy Scripture, and the *Book of Mormon*." *Brigham Young University Studies* 11 (Winter 1971): 119–140.

Nibbelink, Herman. "Mark Twain and the Mormons." *Mark Twain Journal* 17 (Winter 1973): 1–5.

See also: Innocents Abroad, The; Roughing It

"Mrs. McWilliams and the Lightning"
(1880)

The second of three domestic comedies about the McWilliams family, this story appeared in the *Atlantic Monthly* in September 1880 and was first reprinted in *The Stolen White Elephant, Etc.* (1882). Like the other two stories in the series, "Lightning" begins with a digression by a traveler, Mortimer McWilliams, to the author Mark Twain. All three stories are loosely derived from spousal interplay and domestic situations in the Clemens household as described by Clemens to William Dean Howells.

Typically, Mortimer responds to his wife's phobias and superstitions with irony and resignation; in this story, however, he descends to absurd rationalization and digression from her faulty premises, creating comic inverse instructions for attracting and repelling the lightning. Fearing flashes and booms, Evangeline awakens Mortimer and, from her closet hiding place, scolds him for his actions, which she claims have brought this storm upon them. "One of the most appealing husbands of all time" (Covici 46), Mortimer responds with reason—then profanity, irony, and sarcasm. His eventual acquiescence and digressions make him a spectacle and aggravate her obsessions. After humoring Evangeline by helping her to mistranslate a German book outlining safety precautions one should take during thunderstorms, Mortimer becomes fully involved, adding to her list of preventative measures only to learn from the laughing neighbors his clanging dinner bell attracts that the "thunderstorm" is actually cannon fire announcing Garfield's presidential nomination.

Mortimer's pompous digressions and hyperbolic responses render him more complicitous in the action than he appeared in "Experience of the McWilliamses with Membranous Croup" (1875), complicity all the more damning if the stories reflect, as many critics argue, Olivia's real-life editing of Clemens's initiation into middle-class, genteel America (Gibson 82). Such complicity, coupled with Mortimer's irony and self-deprecating humor, serves to deflect the charges of sexism these stories have generated from some readers. Like Twain in his letters to Howells, Mortimer is aware of his own ludicrousness; he views himself humorously, and readers, allowed by the author's narrative method to see through Mortimer's eyes, identify with his ineffectiveness against irrationality. Called "uncommon good" by Howells (*Letters* 1:317), neglected (Emerson 277), universally applicable (Wilson 76), "subtle artistry" (Covici 47), "Mrs. McWilliams and the Lightning" pictures the unbroken spirit of a put-upon man accepting domestic tribulation with insight and deadpan humor (Covici 46).

The key to all three stories is not Mrs. McWilliams's actions but Mortimer's reactions. Just as in the first story in the series, she worries that Providence punishes the family because they have not lived as they should, so here Mrs. McWilliams scolds Mortimer for causing the lightning by neglecting his prayers. Mortimer's defensive responses to his wife's accusations build climactically, endearing him to the reader and illustrating Twain's satiric method; Evangeline is unfair, Mortimer pleads, because at the time of his neglect of holy duties the sky was cloudless, because he does not neglect them often, and because he has not missed his prayers since he caused an earthquake four years earlier. In comically exaggerating human follies so that they amuse rather than frustrate, Mark Twain permits Mortimer to triumph, and through his self-awareness and the distance afforded by the first-person narrative framework, he permits the reader to join him as part of a vulnerable community striving to understand a puzzling world.

John H. Davis

BIBLIOGRAPHY

Baldanza, Frank. *Mark Twain: An Introduction and Interpretation.* New York: Barnes & Noble, 1961.

Clemens, Samuel L. *The American Claimant and Other Stories and Sketches.* New York: Harper, 1899. 330–340.

———. *Mark Twain–Howells Letters: The Correspondence of Samuel L. Clemens and William D. Howells,* 1872–1910. Ed. Henry Nash Smith and William M. Gibson. 2 vols. Cambridge, Mass.: Harvard UP, 1960.

Covici, Pascal, Jr. *Mark Twain's Humor: The Image of a World.* Dallas: Southern Methodist UP, 1962.

Emerson, Everett. *The Authentic Mark Twain: A Literary Biography of Samuel L. Clemens.* Philadelphia: U of Pennsylvania P, 1984.

Gibson, William M. *The Art of Mark Twain.* New York: Oxford UP, 1976.

Habegger, Alfred. "Nineteenth-Century American Humor: Easygoing Males, Anxious Ladies, and Penelope Lapham." *Publications of the Modern Language Association* 91 (October 1976): 884–899.

Wilson, James D. *A Reader's Guide to the Short Stories of Mark Twain.* Boston: G.K. Hall, 1987.

See also: "Experience of the McWilliamses with Membranous Croup"; McWilliams, Mortimer and Caroline (Evangeline); "McWilliamses and the Burglar Alarm, The"

"Murder, a Mystery, and a Marriage, A"

This is the proposed title of a series of "Blindfold Novelettes" or "Skeleton Novelettes" that Mark Twain and William Dean Howells tried unsuccessfully to arrange for serialization in the *Atlantic Monthly* in 1876. A plot outline, furnished by Twain, was to be provided to twelve authors, each of whom would write his or her version of the story without knowing what the others were doing, and the stories would run in consecutive issues of the magazine. In addition to writing their own versions, Howells and Twain hoped to secure contributions from writers whom Twain considered "big literary fish," such as Charles Dudley Warner, Bret Harte, Henry James, Oliver Wendell Holmes, James Russell Lowell, and Thomas Bailey Aldrich.

The project was never completed, although Mark Twain attempted periodically to revive it as late as 1893. His version of the story, approximately 8,600 words long, is a burlesque tale of intrigue that begins when a Frenchman in a balloon drops into a small town in south-western Missouri. It was not published in Twain's lifetime and still remains generally inaccessible, although a version was privately printed in 1945.

Robert Sattelmeyer

BIBLIOGRAPHY

Clemens, Samuel L. *Mark Twain-Howells Letters: The Correspondence of Samuel L. Clemens and William D. Howells, 1872–1910.* Ed. Henry Nash Smith and William M. Gibson. 2 vols. Cambridge, Mass.: Harvard UP, 1960.

Muscatine, Iowa

Located on the eastern border of Iowa across the Mississippi River from Illinois, Muscatine housed the Clemens family and Orion Clemens's *Journal* from the late fall of 1853 until the move to Keokuk in 1855. Samuel Clemens came to Muscatine in the summer of 1854 and worked briefly for his brother, probably staying until the fall when he moved to St. Louis (Paine 1:92–104). Shortly after the move to Muscatine, Orion Clemens asked his brother for letter contributions to the *Journal*, and Samuel Clemens obliged with nine letters composed between 26 October 1853 and 1 March 1855 (Branch, *Mark Twain's Letters* 2).

Ginger Thornton

BIBLIOGRAPHY

Branch, Edgar M. "Three New Letters by Samuel Clemens in the Muscatine *Journal*." *Mark Twain Journal* 22.1 (Spring 1984): 2–7.

Clemens, Samuel L. *Mark Twain's Letters in the "Muscatine Journal."* Ed. Edgar M. Branch. Chicago: Mark Twain Association of America, 1942.

Lorch, Fred W. "Mark Twain in Iowa." *Iowa Journal of History and Politics* 27 (July 1929): 408–456.

———. "Mark Twain's Philadelphia Letters in the Muscatine *Journal*." *American Literature* 17 (Jan. 1946): 348–352.

Paine, Albert Bigelow. *Mark Twain: A Biography.* 3 vols. New York: Harper, 1912.

See also: "Letters to the Muscatine *Journal*"

Music

Mark Twain's interest in many different kinds of music manifested itself early and appears again and again in his writing. His earliest musical knowledge was of hymns and gospel songs that he heard at church, the songs of the slaves at his Uncle John Quarles's plantation, the songs of the various minstrel troupes that visited Hannibal, and the popular songs of the time. Twain seems always to have had an affinity for black spirituals, Scottish ballads, and German folk songs, at the same time loathing excessively sentimental songs such as "The Last Link Is Broken" and "Old Dog Tray" and striving in vain to like such classical forms as the opera.

Twain himself had some ability as a musician, and his daughter Clara recalled his sitting down at the piano to play and sing his favorite black spirituals. His playing was, according to her, done entirely by ear, as he was not able to read music. Twain maintained a lifelong aversion to the piano and was especially irritated by the playing of such virtuoso piano pieces as Franz Kotzwara's "The Battle of Prague."

In Geneva, in 1878, Twain obtained for $400 an elaborate music box capable of playing ten tunes. As the years went on, his knowledge would expand to the Italian opera, particularly Verdi's *Il Trovatore*, which he burlesqued, and to Wagner, whose *Tannhäuser* ("the only operatic favorite I have ever had"), *Lohengrin*, and *Parsifal* he would hear at the Festspielhaus in Bayreuth, as described in "At the Shrine of St. Wagner" (1891).

In 1904 Twain obtained a $3,000 Aeolian orchestrelle, a kind of player organ, along with a large number of rolls of music. At one time his secretary, Isabel Lyon, played for him nightly, sometimes for two or three hours. Through the music of the orchestrelle Twain came to appreciate such composers as Beethoven, Schubert, Chopin, and Wagner, though he had earlier declared his intense dislike of classical music and claimed to be truly excited only by what many termed "low-grade" music. It was on the orchestrelle that Albert Bigelow Paine played at Twain's request three pieces as Jean Clemens's body was taken from Stormfield in 1909: Schubert's "Impromptu" for Jean, the "Intermezzo" from Mascagni's *Cavalleria Rusticana* for Susy, and Handel's "Largo" for Livy.

Twain disliked concerts and according to his daughter Clara never stayed to the end of any except one or two of hers. (She studied both piano and voice and married Ossip Gabrilowitsch, a pianist and symphony conductor.)

When Livy lay dying, one of the last things she heard was her husband singing some of the black spirituals he loved. Clara recalled that her father's last request was that she sing for him; she complied by humming a favorite Scottish song of his, "Flow Gently, Sweet Afton."

There have been numerous musical adaptations of the works of Mark Twain, most notably the Richard Rodgers and Lorenz Hart *Connecticut Yankee* (1927, revised 1943) and Roger Miller's *Big River: The Adventures of Huckleberry Finn* (1985). Jerome Kern composed *Portrait for Orchestra: Mark Twain* (1942), with sections bearing such titles as "Hannibal Days," "Georgeous Pilot House," and "Wanderings Westward," ending with "Mark in Eruption." An earlier "Mark Twain Waltz" (1880), said to have been written while the composer was smoking Mark Twain cigars, was considerably less distinguished. William Perry provided both music and lyrics for *The Mark Twain Musical Drama* (1987), an annual summer production at the Elmira College Domes, Elmira, New York.

Allison R. Ensor

BIBLIOGRAPHY

Flack, Frank Morgan. "Mark Twain and Music." *Twainian* 2.1 (1942): 1–4; 2.2 (1942): 1–4.

Holmes, Ralph. "Mark Twain and Music." *Century Illustrated Monthly Magazine* 104 (October 1922): 844–850.

Meador, Roy. "Mark Twain Takes on Classical Music." *Ovation* 2 (August 1981): 8–11.

Richards, James Howard. "Music and the Reed Organ in the Life of Mark Twain." *American Music* 1.3 (1983): 38–47.

Slater, Joseph. "Music at Colonel Grangerford's: A Footnote to *Huckleberry Finn*." *American Literature* 21 (1949–1950): 108–111.

See also: Austria; Family Life; Gabrilowitsch, Ossip; Media Interpretations; Samossoud, Clara Clemens

"My Boyhood Dreams"
(1900)

Written in Sanna, Sweden, in July–October 1899 while Clemens's daughter Jean underwent osteopathic treatments for epilepsy, "My Boyhood Dreams" appeared in the January 1900 issue of *McClure's Magazine*. Clemens initially hoped to receive $500 for the essay and was angered when the publisher offered only $300; even after Robert McClure increased Harper's offer to $400, Clemens railed against the publisher's one-sided contracts, cheapness, disorganization, and failure to advertise and market his books. The essay was reprinted in *The Man That Corrupted Hadleyburg and Other Stories and Essays* (1900), a volume Clemens had threatened to withdraw from scheduled publication until placated by a $100 post-publication check for "My Boyhood Dreams" he received from S.S. McClure on 11 January.

Despite its title, "My Boyhood Dreams" examines not Mark Twain's dreams but those of his friends. Its subject is aging; and as Baetzhold reports, the author's concern about Jean's illness, lingering grief over Susy's death, and continuing dissatisfaction with humanity undercut with melancholy the seeming jokes about the disappointments and indignities that accompany old age (Baetzhold 210–214). Insisting that "dream-failures" be measured by the dreamers' disappointments, Twain contrasts the youthful career ambitions of his dreamers with their old-age realities: W.D. Howells (auctioneer, editor); John Hay (steamboat mate, secretary of state); T.B. Aldrich (horse doctor, poet); Brander Matthews (cowboy, professor); Frank Stockton (barkeeper, author); George W. Cable (circus ringmaster, theologian, and novelist); Joel Chandler Harris (bucaneer, storyteller). With all the dreamers, a "descent" is involved, for they are all now old and ill fitted for their dream jobs.

Mourning lost youth, old-age infirmities, and beckoning death "To the Above Old People," "My Boyhood Dreams" recalls Edward FitzGerald's *Rubáiyát*. Twain jovially concludes "My Boyhood Dreams" by repudiating his friends' denials of their dreams; he appeals to his truthful memory of their 1830 confessional meeting—which occurred before any participant's birth.

John H. Davis

BIBLIOGRAPHY

Baetzhold, Howard G. *Mark Twain and John Bull: The British Connection.* Bloomington: Indiana UP, 1970.

Clemens, Samuel L. *The Man That Corrupted Hadleyburg and Other Stories and Essays.* 1900. Rpt. New York: Harper, 1917. 254–262.

————. *Mark Twain's Correspondence with Henry Huttleston Rogers, 1893–1909.* Ed. Lewis Leary. Berkeley: U of California P, 1969.

Emerson, Everett. *The Authentic Mark Twain: A Literary Biography of Samuel L. Clemens.* Philadelphia: U of Pennsylvania P, 1984.

See also: "Lowest Animal, The"; "Three Thousand Years Among the Microbes"

"My Debut as a Literary Person"

(1889)

Variously printed, "My Debut as a Literary Person" first appeared in *Century Magazine*, November 1889. At core a rehash of "Forty-Three Days in an Open Boat" (1866), its frame recounts the events leading to Twain's first article published in an eastern magazine.

A correspondent to the Sandwich Islands for the Sacramento *Union*, Twain heard that fifteen survivors of a burned San Francisco-

bound clipper, the *Hornet*, had arrived in Hilo after forty-three days at sea. Anson Burlingame interviewed the seamen while Twain took notes. Twain worked through the night preparing the letter, and by his effort the *Union* scooped the *Hornet* story.

Returning to California, Twain traveled with *Hornet* Captain Josiah Mitchell and two surviving passengers, Henry and Samuel Ferguson. He copied their journals and transformed them into "Forty-Three Days," published unsigned in *Harper's New Monthly Magazine*, December 1866. The yearly index credited this "debut" to "Mark Swain." An abbreviated *Hornet* tale also appeared as "Short and Singular Rations" in *The Celebrated Jumping Frog of Calaveras County and Other Sketches* (1867).

Andrew Jay Hoffman

BIBLIOGRAPHY

Branch, Edgar M. *The Literary Apprenticeship of Mark Twain.* Urbana: U of Illinois P, 1950.

Clemens, Samuel L. "Forty-Three Days in an Open Boat." *Harper's New Monthly Magazine* 34 (December 1866): 104–113.

————. "My Debut as a Literary Person." *Century Magazine* 59 (November 1899): 76–88.

Frear, Walter Francis. *Mark Twain and Hawaii.* Chicago: Lakeside P, 1947.

"My First Lie, and How I Got Out of It"

(1899)

"My First Lie, and How I Got Out of It" appeared on 10 December 1899 in the New York *World* and was reprinted in *The Man That Corrupted Hadleyburg and Other Stories and Essays* (1900).

The sketch begins on a light note, as Twain claims that when he was nine days old, he pretended to have been stuck by a diaper pin in order to gain attention. As is characteristic of Twain's later writings, however, the humor quickly gives way to anger. Twain damns the human race for being liars. He contends that the worst form of lying is "silent assertion"—the failure to oppose the "colossal National Lies" responsible for such evils as American slavery, British imperialism in South Africa, and the French persecution of Alfred Dreyfus.

Twain's satire is biting, but his remark in the closing passage that he will be judicious and allow others to lead the fight against National Lies has aroused controversy, some critics charging that the comment implicates Twain in the silent assertion he condemns.

Lawrence J. Oliver

BIBLIOGRAPHY

Budd, Louis J. *Our Mark Twain: The Making of His Public Personality.* Philadelphia: U of Pennsylvania P, 1983.

Clemens, Samuel L. *Mark Twain on the Damned Human Race.* Ed. Janet Smith. New York: Hill and Wang, 1962.

———. *Mark Twain's Correspondence with Henry Huttleston Rogers, 1893–1909.* Ed. Lewis Leary. Berkeley: U of California P, 1969.

Emerson, Everett. *The Authentic Mark Twain: A Literary Biography of Samuel L. Clemens.* Philadelphia: U of Pennsylvania P, 1984.

Robinson, Forrest G. *In Bad Faith: The Dynamics of Deception in Mark Twain's America.* Cambridge, Mass.: Harvard UP, 1986.

"My Platonic Sweetheart"
(1912)

Originally "My Lost Sweetheart" (written 1898), Twain withdrew it from circulation after three publisher's rejections. Paine published an abbreviated version of it in 1912 in *Harper's* (Emerson 219–220). It later appeared in *The Mysterious Stranger and Other Stories* (1922). Like Twain's Mysterious Stranger character and other dream-disaster ideas of the late 1890s, the theme suggests the possibility and identity of a "dream self." Considerable attention has been given to identifying the sweetheart. Twain met, fell in love, and lost contact with Laura M. Wright when he was a young riverboat pilot. The idea of a lost sweetheart can be traced through a number of his works, early and late, and thus shows how important

this experience was to him (Baetzhold 414–429). But the concept, developed late in life, of an alternate self is ultimately more revealing about Twain's psychological bent and his delight in paranormal experiences.

Sandra Littleton-Uetz

BIBLIOGRAPHY

Baetzhold, Howard G. "Found: Mark Twain's 'Lost Sweetheart.'" *American Literature* 44.3 (November 1972): 414–429.

Clemens, Samuel L. "My Platonic Sweetheart." *The Mysterious Stranger and Other Stories.* By Clemens. New York: Harper, 1922. 287–304.

Emerson, Everett. *The Authentic Mark Twain: A Literary Biography of Samuel L. Clemens.* Philadelphia: U of Pennsylvania P, 1984.

Tuckey, John S. "Mark Twain's Later Dialogue: The 'Me' and the Machine." *American Literature* 41.1 (January 1970): 532–542.

See also: Dreams; *Mysterious Stranger, The*; "Which Was the Dream?"

Mysterious Stranger, The
(1916)

This discussion must take into consideration both a specific "bad text" (*The Mysterious Stranger, A Romance*, 1916; reprinted in *The Mysterious Stranger and Other Stories*, 1922, and much anthologized), *and* the manuscript writings from which it was derived (written 1897–1908), with the many problems these present. Thus, for half a century critics and scholars wrote at length about "an editorial fraud perpetrated" by Albert B. Paine and Frederick A. Duneka (Harper editor); this anomaly was finally corrected by John S. Tuckey's monograph (1963) and by William M. Gibson's edition (1969). Tuckey first established with almost perfect accuracy facts on which others could build; he was also a perceptive critic in editing and arranging texts and writing introductions, commentaries, and essays—most notably in *Mark Twain's "The Mysterious Stranger" and the Critics* (1968), an excellent summation of all the pre-Gibson developments.

Since 1969 awareness has grown of Twain's very complex achievement, with two chief questions still moot: (1) To Tuckey's query: ". . . does the Paine-Duneka edition . . . deserve to perish, to endure, or to prevail?" (*Critics* 90), James M. Cox and others have replied that as the "closest thing to Twain's intention that we shall ever have" (*Fate* 272), it should and will prevail. Kahn later argued that "No. 44" in fact was completed and expressed Twain's intention beautifully and therefore should prevail and that the 1916 version, an unsuccessful hybrid, may unfortunately endure (like Tate's improved version of *Lear*) as a historical curiosity. (2) Putting aside Paine-Duneka, what are the relative values of the newly discovered "Young Satan" and "No. 44"? Stages of rehabilitation may be traced in studies by Kahn (1978), Macnaughton (1979), and Emerson (1984). Practically, publication of *No. 44, The Mysterious Stranger* (1982) in the Mark Twain Library as the authentic version has permanently settled the scholarly question; problems of further analysis and evaluation of course remain.

"The Chronicle of Young Satan" (written 1897–1900)

This first substantial version of "The Mysterious Stranger" was begun in Vienna (September 1897), incorporating a brief "St. Petersburg Fragment" in which American setting a Mr. Black appeared (in Austria: Father Peter, a good priest). It was written in three stages and left incomplete (chapter numbers below refer to the 1969 edition).

Through January 1898: Twain wrote chapters 1–2, the beginning of chapter 3, and part of 10. Emphasizing conflict between a good priest and an evil one (Adolf), and the appearance of a handsome stranger called Satan (the familiar one being his uncle), these sections are set in an Austrian village called Eseldorf, which means "Donkeytown" or "Assville" in English. Peter finds gold and is falsely accused of theft, leading to a trial. This initial hesitation between America and Europe found fuller expression (November–December 1898) in

"Schoolhouse Hill," a Hannibal-St. Petersburg version (see below).

Between May (Vienna) and October (London) 1899: chapters 3–5. These include "Socratic dialogues" (Gibson) on the Moral Sense and episodes involving love and witchcraft. A summary early in chapter 6 begins: "What a lot of dismal haps had befallen the village"—there are *two pairs* of baffled lovers—"and certainly Satan seemed to be the father of the whole of them. . . ."

In London and Dollis Hill, June–August 1900: chapters 6–11. These are many scattered episodes; for example, changes of life plans (only the angel can bring "freedom"—from outside) illustrate Clemens's determinism and the fallibility of human judgments. Finally, Father Peter is exonerated, with the help of Satan (10), and achieves happiness by going mad: "No sane man can be happy, for to him life is real. . . ." Of course, Satan here is "referring to the extreme cases." "Chronicle" (11) "peters out" with a Rajah in India.

In its 1916 version "Young Satan" has powerful passages familiar to many readers; for example, the angel's oft quoted statements (9–10) about civilization and *humor*: "Against the assault of laughter nothing can stand." Narrated by a boy, Theodor Fischer, who has two companions, Seppi and Nikolaus, it may remind us of Tom Sawyer and his gang. Satan is known to the villagers as Philip Traum ("Dream"), and the basic plot-action is of alternation between the angel-with-the-boys and Traum-with-the-villagers. In the second half he takes Theodor on trips in Europe and Asia; wars at the turn of the century (especially against the Boers, and later Cuba and the Philippines) were angering Clemens. More important, Philip Traum is indeed a stranger—but *not* mysterious to the boys, who know his true identity. However, there are elements of mystery (in other senses) in his working miracles and other transcendent behavior.

"Schoolhouse Hill" (written 1898)

That this Hannibal version, however brief, was Twain's breakthrough into satire is evident from the brilliant notebook summary beginning: "Story of little Satan, Jr" (Gibson, ed. 8), plans for love between the angel and "Hellfire Hotchkiss," and an "Anti-Moral-Sense" Sunday school—all humorous conceptions. Also, the developing Dreyfus Affair (Zola's "*J'accuse*" in January) helps explain the emergence of "No. 44" with a *French* name: "Quarante-quatre." Clemens's tank was running over.

A transitional digression in the writing of the Austrian "No. 44," "Schoolhouse" shows also the simultaneous pull toward autobiography, especially its Missouri phase (see "Villagers of 1840–3," written in Switzerland, 1897). The very complex character Forty-Four, however, needed more scope than was provided by Hannibal-St. Petersburg. Huck Finn had escaped to the river, and now Eseldorf in 1490 was to become the focus of a world historical science fiction.

Brimful with vital variety, "Schoolhouse" lacks a unifying narrative voice. Twain as omniscient author, however, worked successfully toward definition of his emerging character, in terms chiefly of a distinction between miracles and mysteries. Basing Forty-Four on an actual historical prodigy (the "Admirable Crichton") implied a sort of naturalism; but the miscellaneous pulls beyond involved magic (Negro bewitchments), "Hellfire" and sex, and time and space travel—with no destination in view, however. The Vienna influences brought Twain back to the character Satan in May 1899.

"No. 44, The Mysterious Stranger" (written 1902–1908)

This final and authentic version (linked to "Young Satan," chiefly by the opening chapter) took Twain back to his own apprenticeship in the Hannibal print shop; and Forty-Four developed into a full-fledged character in a richly diversified situation and plot, enabling Clemens to work out themes relating especially to religion and the soul. The genuine problem of Forty-Four's identity justified the title; and the education in self-understand-

ing of an adolescent narrator (August Feldner) was related to that complex mystery. "No. 44" was written in three chief stages: 1902–1903, chapters 1–7; 1904, 8–25, plus 34; and 1905, 26–32, with a final link (33) added in 1908. Thus the major middle chapters and projected end were all written in Florence while Mrs. Clemens was on her deathbed.

That frequent rereading of "No. 44" reveals ever new delights does not imply initially difficult obscurities, but it may suggest analogies with works by such writers as Rabelais, Cervantes, Joyce—even U. Eco. An organic weave of many interacting levels moves coherently (not without digressions) toward the well-known appalling conclusion. This version's practiced storyteller entertains, dramatizes, poeticizes, ponders various puzzles—and withal creates a sort of spiritual autobiography. The blend of lightness with profundity, potential tragedy with comic treatment, and high with low styles seems effortless—but could only have been achieved by the author of *Huckleberry Finn* (1885) and *Connecticut Yankee* (1889).

Twain's choice of period and place was inspired. The year 1490 is poised historically in the relatively quiet (but quarrelsome) center of an expanding world: the emergence of printing (Gutenberg), Columbus and other voyages of discovery, Renaissance and Reformation, sleepy complacency and subversive enlightenment. As Tuckey put it in his foreword to *No. 44, The Mysterious Stranger:* "Psychologically considered," Eseldorf is "the world" (x).

Twain begins with social realism, depicting an Austrian village and its neighboring castle in which most of the story will be concentrated; from the start, fifteenth-century Europe is also present (cities mentioned: London, Paris, Frankfort, Venice, Vienna). The play with time (present and historical) and the cosmos (reaching to distant planets and outer space) is remarkably effective. As in *Connecticut Yankee*, the American scene is frequently recalled (backwards)—most obviously when, for example, the medieval printers' guild becomes a modern union on strike, duplicates are rescued from *The American Claimant* (and the *Colonel Sellers as a Scientist* play), "corn-pone" and saccharin and "darky" minstrel songs are evoked, and satire on prophecy enables Twain to bring in Christian Science via a 1905 newspaper. Thus, towers of fantasy and clouds of psychology are being built on solid foundations. Somewhat as in "Young Satan" the social setting and its problems are a backdrop for the central motion of August's relations with Forty-Four—two outsiders in the print-shop world, with its mixed family of richly varied characters. Throughout their meetings, conversations, and ever wilder adventures, August and we the readers are made to wonder about the mysterious stranger with the peculiar name. Beginning around chapter 18, but especially in 23–25, a series of carefully contrived situations (beginning with August's invisibility, going on to dreams, sleep walking, split personalities, and so forth) enabled Clemens to explore "the complex self" (Kahn, chapter 9). With extraordinary insights gained from wide life-experience and much reading, this text (more than *What Is Man?* [1906] certainly) established Twain's claim to have been (for a pre-Freudian psychologist) a profound and original thinker (in parables and fables). Animals (dogs and cats), love, women, and miracles are among other themes in this Rabelaisian profusion.

Who (or what) is Forty-Four? In some sense created by the mind of August (or Twain), he is also objectively an angel of God, sent to teach August this truth: "But I your poor servant have revealed you to yourself and set you free. Dream other dreams, and better!" Writing this final masterwork of fiction while she was dying was the truest tribute Clemens could pay to his beloved Livy.

Sholom J. Kahn

BIBLIOGRAPHY

Brooks, Van Wyck. *The Ordeal of Mark Twain.* Rev. ed. New York: Dutton, 1933.

Clemens, Samuel L. *Mark Twain's Mysterious Stranger Manuscripts.* Ed. William M. Gibson. Berkeley: U of California P, 1969.

————. *No. 44, The Mysterious Stranger.* Foreword and Notes by John S. Tuckey. Berkeley: U of California P, 1982.

Cox, James M. *Mark Twain: The Fate of Humor.* Princeton, N.J.: Princeton UP, 1966.

Emerson, Everett. *The Authentic Mark Twain: A Literary Biography of Samuel L. Clemens.* Philadelphia: U of Pennsylvania P, 1984.

Kahn, Sholom J. *Mark Twain's Mysterious Stranger: A Study of the Manuscript Texts.* Columbia: U of Missouri P, 1978.

Macnaughton, William R. *Mark Twain's Last Years as a Writer.* Columbia: U of Missouri P, 1979.

Tuckey, John S. *Mark Twain and Little Satan: The Writing of "The Mysterious Stranger."* West Lafayette, Ind.: Purdue UP, 1963.

————. *Mark Twain's "The Mysterious Stranger" and the Critics.* Belmont, Calif.: Wadsworth, 1968.

See also: Eseldorf; Fischer, Theodor; Forty-Four; Traum, Philip

Napoleon, Arkansas

Situated at the confluence of the Arkansas and the Mississippi rivers, Napoleon was one of the stops regularly made by riverboats during Samuel Clemens's days as a pilot. It is mentioned in *Life on the Mississippi* (1883) as the place where, in 1858, he first saw a newspaper account of the explosion of the *Pennsylvania*, which fatally injured his brother Henry.

Napoleon appears again in the second part of the book. Here it affords an opportunity for the author to insert into the account of his nostalgic trip down the river a gothic tale in the manner of E.T.A. Hoffmann. Charged by the dying Karl Ritter in Munich to find $10,000 concealed in Napoleon and to give it to Adam Kruger, whose father Ritter had wrongfully slain, the narrator and his companions are on the verge of being corrupted by greed when they discover that Napoleon has been destroyed by a flood.

Jarrell A. O'Kelley

BIBLIOGRAPHY

Clemens, Samuel L. *Life on the Mississippi*. Boston: James R. Osgood, 1883.

See also: Clemens, Henry; *Life on the Mississippi*

Naturalism

As a literary movement naturalism is generally defined in relation to realism. While it shares a certain basic orientation with realism, it also possesses a number of important additional characteristics that distinguish it significantly from its antecedent.

Naturalism follows on realism in its fundamental adherence to the doctrine of truthfulness and the faithful depiction of common life as the essence of art. A German theoretician of naturalism, Arno Holz, pushed this idea to its extreme by asserting that art = nature − x, "x" representing the deficiency in the artist's ability to copy with total fidelity. So the naturalists' ideal was to present a slice of raw life, a human document, that did not shun the vulgar or the ugly, that was nonjudgmental, and that conveyed an exact image of both settings and scenes.

Upon this intrinsically mimetic view of art the naturalists grafted certain elements derived from the dominant scientific and philosophical beliefs of the mid-nineteenth century. The crucial impact came from Darwin, whose *On the Origin of Species By Means of Natural Selection, or the Preservation of Favoured Races in the Struggle for Life* appeared in 1859 and profoundly altered human beings' perception of themselves and of their relationship to the world around them. Basing his hypothesis on scientific observations carried out over many years, Darwin argued that the human species had evolved gradually through a process of adaptation to the environment in which it was the fittest who survived. The naturalists applied this Darwinian theory of evolution to the present in their central belief that human character and action are determined by three closely interrelated factors: heredity, environment, and the pressure of the moment. Given certain genetic tendencies (e.g., alcoholism, avarice) and conditioned by the environment in which they were raised, people were seen as bound to react in specific ways under the pressure of circumstances. This vision of human behavior is known as determinism. Since it largely deprives people of free will and moral choice, it has been attacked as pessimistic and reductive.

The naturalists were also formed, though to a lesser extent, by the philosophy of positivism put forward by the French thinker Auguste Comte in his *Course on Positivist Philosophy* (1836; 2nd rev. ed. 1864). Comte asserted that science provided the model for the only kind of knowledge attainable with certainty. He advocated meticulous observation and dispassionate recording as the appropriate method for discerning the constant, inherent laws of life. The physician Claude Bernard in his *Introduction to the Experimental Study of Medicine* (1865) offered a practical example of positivism in action.

"Experimental" is a key term for naturalism. It is used by Emile Zola, the French novelist and leading figure of the movement, in his theoretical treatise *The Experimental Novel* (1879). Drawing directly on Bernard, Comte, and Darwin, Zola envisages the writer as an "experimenter" whose work parallels that of scientists and philosophers in its rigorous methodology and its logical analysis of human existence. In his cycle of twenty novels, *The Rougon-Macquarts* (1871–1893), Zola traces, under the subtitle "The Natural and Social History of a Family under the Second Empire," the careers of five generations of a large and diverse family, showing how heredity, environment, and circumstances shape their lives. In the family's varied occupations Zola gives a vivid portrayal of the social and economic situation in France between 1850 and 1870. However, through his abounding poetic imagination Zola far transcends the rather limited doctrines of naturalism to create powerful and haunting works of art, especially in *L'Assommoir* (1877; English translation, 1954). The outstanding writers among the naturalists were to follow the same pattern, starting from a positivistic, scientifically colored creed, yet rising to heights of symbolical imagination.

Naturalism in the United States was influenced by Zola first through Frank Norris after his stay in Paris (1887–1889) and later through James T. Farrell, who aspired to give an integrated panorama of American life in his *Studs Lonigan* trilogy (1932–1935) reminiscent of Zola's endeavor with *The Rougon-Macquarts*. But the native tradition of local-color regionalist writing, represented by Hamlin Garland and Sherwood Anderson, proved an even stronger formative factor. Naturalism emerged later in the United States than in Europe and was less doctrinaire and more pragmatic. Much greater emphasis was placed on environment, and correspondingly less on heredity, in determining behavior, while the pressure of circumstances frequently assumed the form of financial exigency. This is evident in works as diverse as Norris's *McTeague* (1899), Stephen Crane's *Maggie: A Girl of the Streets* (1893), Theodore Dreiser's *An American Tragedy* (1925), and John Steinbeck's *The Grapes of Wrath* (1939). All these novels closely link to native social and economic conditions in their analysis of the protagonists' struggle against the adverse situation into which forces beyond their control have driven them. Like their European predecessors, the American naturalists sympathize with the "have-nots," showing how they are exploited by the "haves."

Dreiser's *An American Tragedy*, which is often considered the most completely naturalistic of all American works, follows the life of Clyde Griffiths through more than 800 pages from the deprivations of his childhood to his efforts to make good in the world and to achieve the American dream of success and money. A pleasant but weak character, Clyde finds himself thwarted by his lack of status and funds. Seeing his big opportunity when he is taken up by Sondra, one of his rich cousin's circle, he gets rid of his pregnant working-class girl friend in a manipulated boating accident. Is he guilty of her death? To what extent can he be held responsible for his action? By pleading "you didn't make yourself," his defense lawyer shifts the blame onto society and Clyde's environment.

Such a view opens the writings of the American naturalists to political interpretation as an indictment of capitalism. But many American naturalists also tempered their work with quite other elements, notably romance and mythology. This becomes apparent in Norris, Steinbeck, and Jack London among the novelists and in Eugene O'Neill, the foremost dramatist associated with American naturalism. In the finest examples of naturalism a balance is achieved between scientific documentation and poetic imagination.

One finds elements of naturalism throughout much of Twain's work, especially the late work, but for overwhelming evidence of his interest in naturalism one can do no better than read "The Damned Human Race" as it

appears in *Letters from the Earth* (1962). The titles alone of the five divisions making up this section of *Letters from the Earth* are revealing: "Was the World Made for Man?" "In the Animals' Court," "Zola's *La Terre*," "The Intelligence of God," and "The Lowest Animal." As Sherwood Cummings suggests, however, Twain reacted to science on different levels at different times in his career. The determinism of *What Is Man?* (1906) is sometimes transformed in Twain's late preoccupation with what he called the "dream-self."

Lilian R. Furst

BIBLIOGRAPHY

Ahnebrink, Lars. *The Beginnings of Naturalism in American Fiction.* Cambridge, Mass.: Harvard UP, 1950.

Beer, Gillian. *Darwin's Plots: Evolutionary Narrative in Darwin, George Eliot and Nineteenth Century Fiction.* London: Routledge & Kegan Paul, 1983.

Block, Haskell M. *Naturalistic Triptych: The Fictive and the Real in Zola, Mann, and Dreiser.* New York: Random House, 1970.

Furst, Lilian R. *"L'Assommoir": A Working Woman's Life.* Boston: Twayne, 1990.

———, and Peter N. Skrine. *Naturalism.* London: Methuen, 1971.

Howard, June. *Form and History in American Literary Naturalism.* Chapel Hill: U of North Carolina P, 1985.

Kohn, David, ed. *The Darwinian Heritage.* Princeton, N.J.: Princeton UP, 1985.

Larkin, Maurice. *Man and Society in Nineteenth Century Realism: Determinism and Literature.* Totowa, N.J.: Rowman and Littlefield, 1977.

Pizer, Donald. *Realism and Naturalism in Nineteenth Century American Literature.* Rev. ed. Carbondale: Southern Illinois UP, 1984.

Walcutt, Charles Child. *American Literary Naturalism.* Minneapolis: U of Minnesota P, 1956.

See also: Darwin, Charles; Realism; Science

Nevada

Samuel Clemens ripened his talents for his distinctive kind of humor and found his true calling as a writer in Nevada. That is where Samuel Clemens became Mark Twain.

Twain arrived in the Nevada Territory in August 1861, unseasoned and unknown, a clerk to his older brother Orion, who had been appointed territorial secretary. He left the territory in May 1864, well-known, a seasoned journalist, and a humorist of note. What happened in those less than three years to so change him and start him on the path of his career as an author Twain told inimitably in *Roughing It* (1872), but that book is so heavily fictionalized as to be biographically unreliable.

When Twain arrived in Nevada, it was a booming and boisterous territory in the grip of silver fever. Just two years before the first silver and gold discoveries had been made on what became the Comstock Lode, the richest concentration of precious metals in history. Prospectors and miners poured into the territory from California and the East. Soon, other silver and gold strikes were found in many parts of western Nevada, and the dream of getting rich quickly and easily affected Twain as it did many others.

He filed a timber claim on the shore of Lake Tahoe, visited mining sites in Aurora, Esmeralda County, and Unionville, Humboldt County, and decided to become a miner in Aurora, where a friend gave him shares in a developing mine. From April to September 1862 he tried prospecting and mining, and laboring in a quartz mill. He discovered he was not interested in hard work and did not have the capital to pay others to do it for him. Although he came close, once, to making a small fortune in a mining property, and believed he came close to making money in the "beggars' revel" of the frantic trading and buying and selling of mining shares that often substituted for both physical labor and cash among prospectors, he was never close enough.

During this time, however, Twain wrote travel letters for the *Gate City* (Keokuk, Iowa), and began to send humorous letters signed with the pen name of "Josh" to the *Territorial Enterprise* of Virginia City. Joseph Goodman, one of the *Enterprise* owners and the editor-in-chief, was aware that Orion was influential in the awarding of printing contracts, but he offered the young writer a job on the strength

of his talent. Early in 1862 the new employee dropped Josh as a pen name and became Mark Twain.

Goodman was a superb editor and quickly attracted some of the best journalistic talent on the West Coast to the *Enterprise*. He did so by offering high wages, encouraging talent, and allowing his reporters free rein, only provided that they take responsibility for what they wrote. As a consequence, the *Enterprise* soon became one of the largest and most important newspapers west of the Mississippi. Besides Twain, other outstanding *Enterprise* staffers included Dan De Quille, C.C. Goodwin, Rollin M. Daggett, Jim Townsend, Steve Gillis, and Alf Doten, most of whom went on to distinction or significant achievement later in their lives. As writers, these men were equally at home with vernacular dialogue or formal, elegant style. Tough-minded and cynical about most things, they had a sentimental side for things they held noble. Their personal lives were a curious mixture of Bohemian profligacy, integrity, fearlessness, and idealism. The congeniality Twain felt with these men was profound and thereafter shaped his values as well as his literary style.

Virginia City in its early years was one of the most exciting journalistic environments in America. It was a place of twenty-four-hour activity, both above and below ground; of constant turmoil; of gambling, drinking, and prostitution openly countenanced; of lawlessness and corruption; and of ubiquitous economic and political opportunity. Just to describe this scene would have been stimulating in itself, but the Comstock journalists also attempted to shape public opinion by accurate reporting and, occasionally, their approbation or criticism.

Twain was inclined toward biting, and often the difference between his good-humored satire and irony and his serious attacks was just the degree of bite. Twain's coverage of the meetings of the territory legislature earned him praise and respect. His blend of accuracy and wit was so popular with both his readers and the legislators that he was elected "Governor" of the Third House—a takeoff on the two houses of the legislature (much like today's "roasts")—whose members were mostly journalists and legislators. But when Twain criticized a public official or exposed a swindle, he was less witty and more vituperative. He engaged in friendly feuds with some of his colleagues, especially Dan De Quille and Clement T. Rice ("the Unreliable"), in which he extravagantly insulted them, and they him, but when he turned his attentions to other journalists, they were not so easygoing or forgiving. His coverage of social events also struck more than a few Nevadans as being closer to ridicule than good-natured humor.

Twain's penchant for imaginative and outlandish humor early found expression in several hoaxes he wrote. The first, "Petrified Man," was published in October 1862, only a month after he joined the *Enterprise*. Twain later said that he intended it as a double satire on a local coroner and a current literary fad of stories about petrification, but the piece was appreciated as a work of skill and humor and was widely reprinted. He was not so lucky with a second hoax, "A Bloody Massacre near Carson," which he wrote in October 1863. It is hard today, once the facts of the matter are known, to understand why it was not instantly recognized as a clever hoax and enjoyed, but such was not the case. It was instead misinterpreted and resented. The animus that had been building against Twain for his brash, condescending, and cutting attitudes was focused on this piece, and he was widely criticized and insulted.

There were a number of reasons for disliking Twain. In addition to the attitudinal reasons just cited, he had a violent temper and did not control it well. He was seen by some journalists as being somewhat opportunistic, abandoning old friends when someone more influential came on the horizon. There is some truth to this, for Twain did look out for his own interests and actively promoted his career. He was resented for "stealing" from other writers: taking their ideas and material and never acknowledging his debts. Dan De Quille

was named by many, and Jim Townsend by at least one, as having been thus taken advantage of. Finally, Twain was fond of playing practical jokes on others—but was notoriously intolerant of such jokes being played on him. Twain's last visit to the Comstock in November 1866 was spoiled by his outrage at a practical joke arranged by some of his friends. For all these reasons, at no time in his life was Twain ever the most popular writer on the Comstock.

This does not mean, however, that Twain did not have good times and good friends. In addition to the creative opportunities his job gave him, he was appreciated by his fellow *Enterprise* staffers and joined them in their frequent parties and drinking bouts. He attended many of the plays that came to Virginia City. The famous actress Adah Isaacs Menken was impressed by him when he reviewed one of her plays, and she invited him to a private party in her room. Most importantly, he met Artemus Ward on his memorable week-long visit to Virginia City in December 1863. Ward impressed Twain mightily and may well have had an important literary influence on him. Ward also gave him critical advice and support and encouraged him to leave Virginia City for the wider world.

Twain was, in fact, growing restive in Virginia City. He had begun in 1863 to publish humorous pieces in the *Golden Era*, a San Francisco literary journal, and was ambitious to be more widely known in California and the East. When the draft of a satirical article was mistakenly printed by the *Enterprise* in May 1864, it affronted many Nevadans, and he again fell out of favor on the Comstock. Humiliated and frustrated, Twain unwisely exchanged insults in print with another editor and challenged him to a duel. Twain's recollection of the affair in the *Autobiography* was faulty; the principals never met. But Twain did leave Nevada for California abruptly and angrily on 29 May 1864.

This unfortunate exit from the Comstock and the other disagreeable experiences he had in Nevada were exceptions to the general fact that he thrived in Nevada. Dan De Quille later characterized Twain's years there as his "salad days." In any event, Twain benefitted enormously from the practical instruction he received there. He learned the trick of the hoax, which became one of his characteristic literary techniques. He mastered the use of vernacular, another hallmark of his style, and perfected the ability to mingle different writing styles in the same work. He became adept at the tall tale and the art of humorous exaggeration. Although some of his lessons were hard ones, he did learn a great deal about satire and how far he could push a joke. He learned timing, and he learned how to advance a main point while seeming to ramble. A moralist at heart, he also learned how to sugar coat his moralizing with wit and humor.

Although *Roughing It* is unreliable for factual details of Twain's life in Nevada, the book itself is the best possible testimony of what he learned there. Its superb humor, presented in a variety of forms with dazzling virtuosity, and its serious purposes beneath that humor could hardly have been possible without the experiences and training he acquired in Nevada. It is difficult to overestimate the importance of the Nevada years on Twain.

Lawrence I. Berkove

BIBLIOGRAPHY

Angel, Myron. *History of Nevada*. Oakland, Calif.: Thompson and West, 1881. Rpt. Berkeley: Howell-North, 1958.

Benson, Ivan. *Mark Twain's Western Years*. Stanford, Calif.: Stanford UP, 1938.

Branch, Edgar M. *The Literary Apprenticeship of Mark Twain*. Urbana: U of Illinois P, 1950.

Clemens, Samuel L. *Mark Twain of the "Enterprise": Newspaper Articles and Other Documents, 1862–1864*. Ed. Henry Nash Smith and Frederick Anderson. Berkeley: U of California P, 1957.

———. *Mark Twain's Letters, Volume 1 (1853–1866)*. Ed. Edgar M. Branch, Michael B. Frank, and Kenneth M. Sanderson. Berkeley: U of California P, 1988.

———. *Roughing It*. Ed. Franklin R. Rogers and Paul Baender. Berkeley: U of California P, 1972.

———. *The Works of Mark Twain: Early Tales & Sketches, Volume 1 (1851–1864)*. Ed. Edgar M.

Branch and Robert H. Hirst. Berkeley: U of California P, 1979.

Drury, Wells. *An Editor on the Comstock Lode*. Reno: U of Nevada P, 1984.

Fatout, Paul. *Mark Twain in Virginia City*. Bloomington: Indiana UP, 1964.

Moss, George. "Silver Frolic: Popular Entertainment in Virginia City, Nevada, 1859–1863." *Journal of Popular Culture* 22.2 (Fall 1988): 1–31.

See also: Daggett, Rollin Mallory; De Quille, Dan; Goodman, Joseph Thompson; Goodwin, Charles Carroll; *Roughing It*; Townsend, James; Virginia City *Territorial Enterprise*; Washoe Wits

New Orleans, Louisiana

Mark Twain's experience in New Orleans, an economic and cultural center and the South's major port at the mouth of the Mississippi River, comes from two periods of direct contact, from 1857 to 1861 when he was training and working as a river-boat pilot and from spring 1882 to when he came to the city to see George Washington Cable and Joel Chandler Harris. Most of what is known of his experience in this river city comes from Twain himself in *Life on the Mississippi* (1883).

As a young man, Twain had been to New York City, but he had never traveled abroad. When he went to New Orleans in his early twenties, he did so with the idea of the city's being on the edge of an exotic world, a convenient and exciting place from which to depart to foreign lands across the seas. His first objective was to reach Brazil, as he points out in *Life on the Mississippi*: "It was only about fifteen hundred miles from Cincinnati to New Orleans, where I could doubtless get a ship. I had thirty dollars left; I would go and complete the exploration of the Amazon." By the time he had passed Louisville on the Mississippi River, this river had captured his fancy for the next four years. During this period he also wrote anecdotal humor (a possible source for his pseudonym) for New Orleans newspapers; later he criticized local journalists for romantic views of the city and the South.

His observations of New Orleans reveal a careful eye for detail expected of a boat pilot, which his memory filtered through the near present, and the metaphorical tendency of a storyteller: "The old brick salt warehouses clustered at the upper end of the city looked as they had always looked: warehouses which had a kind of Aladdin's lamp experience . . . for when the war broke out the proprietor went to bed one night leaving them packed with thousands of bags of vulgar salt, worth a couple of dollars a sack, and got up in the morning and found his mountain of salt turned into a mountain of gold." The city appeared an almost willing subject for his scrutiny as he observed its contrasts: dusty, litter-filled streets with standing water in the gutters as well as the "five miles of electric lights" along the riverfront. In matters of architecture he found merit only in the raised tombs of the cemeteries.

Although his appreciation of New Orleans was mixed, he did give his mother a trip to the city in 1859 and related a story of a $10 dinner at a French restaurant. His own return in the early 1880s had the character of a tour as well, for Cable personally led him throughout the entire urban area, nearby suburbs, and rural recreational spots. Food was obviously a highlight: Twain records having dined on pompano, crayfish, shrimp, and soft-shelled crabs. In a letter to his wife he describes his visit as a "whirlpool of hospitality."

Finally, Twain's experiences in New Orleans emerge in fiction through *Adventures of Huckleberry Finn* (1885). A youthful rendering of *Romeo and Juliet* at a party contributes to the Duke and the King's Shakespearean sequence. His seeing the old slave market in the French Quarter and his holding negative views of the city's newspapers inspired him to include the passage about advertising for Jim in the New Orleans newspapers.

Thomas Bonner, Jr.

BIBLIOGRAPHY

Clemens, Samuel L. *Life on the Mississippi*. Boston: James R. Osgood, 1883.

——. *The Love Letters of Mark Twain*. Ed. Dixon Wecter. New York: Harper, 1949.

——. *Mark Twain's Autobiography*. Ed. Albert B. Paine. 2 vols. New York: Harper, 1924.

DeVoto, Bernard. *Mark Twain's America*. Boston: Little, Brown, 1932.

Ferguson, DeLancey. *Mark Twain: Man and Legend*. Indianapolis: Bobbs-Merrill, 1943.

Kaplan, Justin. *Mr. Clemens and Mark Twain*. New York: Simon & Schuster, 1966.

Turner, Frederick. *Spirit of Place: The Making of an American Literary Landscape*. San Francisco: Sierra Club Books, 1989.

See also: Cable, George Washington; *Life on the Mississippi*

New York, New York

New York attracted Clemens for both business and pleasure throughout his life, but his permanent residences in the city can be distinctly divided into five periods.

Clemens first lived in New York during the fifteen-month period of 1853–1854 that Albert B. Paine labels Twain's "*Wanderjahr*" (Paine 1:102). The Crystal Palace Fair, then under way in the city, symbolized for Clemens the immensity of the city itself. He wrote home that every day the visitors to the fair alone were "double the population of Hannibal" (Paine 1:95). Clemens worked setting type for John A. Gray and Green Company and lived in a boardinghouse for mechanics before he returned to Missouri in 1854.

Not until 1867 did Clemens again spend a significant amount of time in New York. That year saw Charles Henry Webb's publication of Twain's first book, *The Celebrated Jumping Frog of Calaveras County*, on 1 May; Twain's first eastern speaking engagement at the Cooper Institute on 6 May; the voyage on the *Quaker City* that would provide the material for Twain's *Innocents Abroad* (1869) from 8 June to 19 November; and Clemens's first meeting of his future wife, Olivia, in New York at Christmas time.

Clemens also settled in New York during the months of late 1893 and early 1894 when he was overseeing his faltering investment in the Paige typesetting machine. These months were a time of such frenzied social activity for the writer that a friend dubbed him "The Belle of New York" (Paine 3:972). Clemens first met Henry H. Rogers during this time. In April 1894, when Charles L. Webster and Company went bankrupt, Clemens joined his family in Europe.

After the world speaking tour Clemens took to repay his creditors, the Clemens family settled at 14 W. 10th St. in the fall of 1900. Clemens spoke to numerous groups during the following months about his opinions of such contemporary issues as the Boxer Rebellion, Cuba, the Philippines, South Africa, and Tammany Hall. In February 1901 Clemens wrote the controversial "To the Person Sitting in Darkness" for the *North American Review* to articulate his views on imperialism. The Clemenses left New York in the summer of 1901.

Clemens's longest residence in New York began in the fall of the year his wife died, 1904. He lived with his daughter Jean in an ornate establishment on the corner of Ninth Street and Fifth Avenue. The period was a time of great productivity for Twain's later and more notably cynical works. The following major works were published during this period: *King Leopold's Soliloquy* and "Eve's Diary" (1905); *The $30,000 Bequest and Other Stories* and *What Is Man?* (1906); selections from the *Autobiography* in the *North American Review* (1906–1907); *Christian Science* (1907); and "Extract from Captain Stormfield's Visit to Heaven" in *Harper's Magazine* (December 1907 and January 1908). Clemens moved permanently to Redding, Connecticut, in June 1908.

Although Clemens is usually thought of as residing in such places as Missouri or Connecticut, New York was the cosmopolitan center that afforded him the business opportunities and social interaction that were so necessary to the man who became a cultural hero. Nowhere in America provided Clemens with either the visibility or the stimulation that New York did.

Roberta Seelinger Trites

BIBLIOGRAPHY

Hill, Hamlin. *Mark Twain: God's Fool*. New York: Harper & Row, 1973.

Paine, Albert Bigelow. *Mark Twain: A Biography*. 4 vols. New York: Harper, 1912.

See also: Riverdale, New York

New York *Saturday Press*

The weekly New York *Saturday Press*, edited by Henry Clapp, was a short-lived literary magazine. By circuitous route, Clemens's jumping frog story appeared in the *Press* on 18 November 1865. The story, later called "The Celebrated Jumping Frog of Calaveras County," appeared in the journal under the title of "Jim Smiley and His Jumping Frog." The story was turned over to Clapp by publisher George W. Carleton, who was either unable or unwilling to include it in a collection of Artemus Ward's tales for which it was intended. After the story appeared in the *Saturday Press*, it was reprinted in a number of journals, winning Clemens national acclaim as a humorist. The tale appeared in Clemens's first book, a collection of stories entitled *The Celebrated Jumping Frog of Calaveras County and Other Sketches* (1867).

Susan McFatter

BIBLIOGRAPHY

Branch, Edgar M. *The Literary Apprenticeship of Mark Twain*. Urbana: U of Illinois P, 1950.

Emerson, Everett H. *The Authentic Mark Twain: A Literary Biography of Samuel L. Clemens*. Philadelphia: U of Pennsylvania P, 1984.

Kaplan, Justin. *Mr. Clemens and Mark Twain*. New York: Simon & Schuster, 1966.

See also: "Celebrated Jumping Frog of Calaveras County, The"

New Zealand

Perhaps one of the least known and loneliest of any civilized country of importance is New Zealand. Lying some 1,200 miles east-southeast of Australia, this group of islands approximately 1,000 miles long and 180 miles at the widest point accommodates a population today of about 3 million. In 1840 Britain subjugated the Maoris and brought the islands under British rule; today it is a self-governing member of the Commonwealth of Nations.

For about six weeks in late 1895 Twain toured New Zealand as part of a year-long lecture tour to pay off debts incurred from lost investments in the failed Paige typesetting machine and his publishing business, Charles L. Webster and Company. Twain recorded the trip in chapters 30–35 of *Following the Equator* (1897), the literary result of his travels to Australia, New Zealand, India, and South Africa. The pattern had long before been set when, as a cub reporter and later as an established writer, his extensive travels formed the basis of articles in newspapers or for such well-received books as *The Innocents Abroad* (1869), *Roughing It* (1872), *A Tramp Abroad* (1880), and *A Connecticut Yankee in King Arthur's Court* (1889).

In early November he landed at Bluff on the south end of South Island and from there proceeded to Invercargill, Dunedin, Omoru, Tamaru, Christchurch, Nelson, New Plymouth, Auckland, Gisborne, Napier, Palmerston North, Wanganui, Hawera, and Wellington. What he found there impressed him: a rabbit plague at Bluff; the Maori chiefs, whom he compared to Roman patricians; Maori art and antiquities in museums at Dunedin and Christchurch; Maori taboos, love of war, and patriotism; efficient trains; dogs in the lecture hall; suffrage for New Zealand women; the infamous story of a merciless murder in Nelson in 1866; and the lush vegetation of the island, which he termed Junior England—"in fact, just a garden."

Maverick Marvin Harris

BIBLIOGRAPHY

Fatout, Paul. *Mark Twain on the Lecture Circuit.* Bloomington: Indiana UP, 1960.

Long, E. Hudson. *Mark Twain Handbook.* New York: Hendricks House, 1957.

See also: Following the Equator; Travel Writings

Newspapers

"News is history in its first and best form, its vivid and fascinating form, and history is the pale and tranquil reflection of it," wrote Mark Twain. He knew journalism from the inside, having worked as a reporter, correspondent, and editor before turning to fiction. He knew the press's flaws and he knew its strengths; he was as capable of vilifying the press as the debaser of the nation's morals as he was of championing it as the protector of the nation's liberties. He revered the press as a fertile source of information about his world and reviled it as just plain fertilizer. In either case, he was addicted to it: Twain was a passionately devoted reader of the daily papers all his life.

Twain as an author and public personality was as happy to "use" the press as it was to "use" him. The relationship, for the most part symbiotic, was forged by their shared recognition of a common enemy: dullness. The same hunger that produced an insatiable appetite for anecdotes about Mark Twain, however, also produces an unending stream of drivel, as Twain well knew.

Twain's favorite paper was the New York *Evening Post*, a paper that catered to New York's WASP upper-middle class and eschewed sensationalism in favor of such serious issues as crusades for civil service reform, a subject close to Twain's heart. But Twain consumed a rich and varied diet of daily and weekly papers at home and throughout his travels, often reading several papers, front to back, in a morning.

Twain's personal enjoyment of the press never stopped him from lambasting newspapers for being proud, arrogant, ill-informed.

In "Journalism in Tennessee" (1869) Twain satirized the duels of violent vituperation in which rival newspapers sometimes engaged. In "How I Edited an Agricultural Paper Once" (1870) his target was ignorance and arrogance in the city room. Twain respected newspapers that disdained flashy bombast and stuck to news. His otherwise high opinion of a paper was likely to plummet, however, if it published a bad review of one of his books.

Long after journalism ceased to be his principal source of income, Twain enjoyed making news as much as he enjoyed consuming it. Despite his disdain for his interviewers' inaccuracies and distortions ("They put words into my mouth. I'd rather they had put street sweepings"), Twain was one of the most popular and sought-after interview subjects of his time. Newspapers published more letters to the editor from Twain than from any other writer. And his efforts to influence and shape the press's reactions to his books, lectures, business ventures, and public persona are legendary. Whether he was reading about his world, or reading about himself, whether he was writing stories, clipping stories, or planting stories, Twain found newspapers illuminating, infuriating, and, above all, indispensable.

Shelley Fisher Fishkin

BIBLIOGRAPHY

Budd, Louis J. "Color Him Curious About Yellow Journalism: Mark Twain and the New York City Press." *Journal of Popular Culture* 15.2 (Fall 1981): 25–33.

———. *Our Mark Twain: The Making of His Public Personality.* Philadelphia: U of Pennsylvania P, 1983.

———, ed. *Listing of and Selection from Newspaper and Magazine Interviews with Samuel L. Clemens.* Arlington, Tex.: ALRP, 1977.

Fishkin, Shelley Fisher. *From Fact to Fiction: Journalism and Imaginative Writing in America.* New York: Oxford UP, 1988.

Kaplan, Justin. *Mr. Clemens and Mark Twain.* New York: Simon & Schuster, 1966.

See also: "How I Edited an Agricultural Paper Once"; Interviews; Journalism; "Journalism in Tennessee"

Nook Farm

From 1871 to 1891 Twain made his home at Nook Farm, a 140-acre residential community on the western boundary of Hartford, Connecticut. Here Twain raised his family, established enduring friendships, and published *Roughing It* (1872), *The Gilded Age* (1873), *The Adventures of Tom Sawyer* (1876), *A Tramp Abroad* (1880), *The Prince and the Pauper* (1882), *Life on the Mississippi* (1883), *Personal Memoirs of U.S. Grant* (1885), *Adventures of Huckleberry Finn* (1885), and *A Connecticut Yankee in King Arthur's Court* (1889).

Granted in the seventeenth century to John Haynes, Connecticut colony's first governor, the farm was owned by Hartford merchant William Imlay in 1853 when John Hooker (1816–1901) and his brother-in-law Francis Gillette (1807–1879) bought it and began to sell building lots to their relatives and business associates. Twain, who had admired Nook Farm during his first visit to Hartford in January 1868, was not related directly to John and Isabella (Beecher) Hooker (1822–1907). He met them through his future mother-in-law, who was an intimate friend of Isabella Hooker. In 1871 Twain moved to Nook Farm renting the Hooker's house for $300 a quarter. Later, Twain supported Isabella's feminism by contributing money for speakers who championed women's rights. From trips to Washington, D.C., he brought her news about legislation of interest to women. When John Hooker's law partner put his Nook Farm house up for sale, Twain tried to persuade William Dean Howells (1837–1920) to buy it.

Francis Gillette, husband of John Hooker's sister Elisabeth (1813–1893), was a founder of the Asylum Hill Church attended by Twain and his family. A room in the basement of his barn was a station on the underground railroad. Twain arranged stage parts and contributed money for the acting lessons of Gillette's son William (1853–1937), who adapted for stage and performed in the character of Sherlock Holmes.

In 1864 Harriet Beecher Stowe (1811–1896), Isabella Hooker's sister, and her husband Calvin Ellis (1792–1886) built Oakholm, a large house on the southern edge of Nook Farm. When it proved too expensive to maintain, they moved to a smaller home on Forest Avenue. Calvin Ellis Stowe helped establish the Monday Evening Club, of which Twain was a member. The community's most successful writers, Harriet Beecher Stowe and Twain enhanced their earnings by encouraging favorable publicity from their literary and publishing associates in Hartford and in Boston. Sharing a property line with Twain, Stowe was a frequent visitor to his house and gardens.

Francis and Elisabeth Gillette's daughter Elisabeth (1838–1915) married George H. Warner (1833–1919). They built the Nook Farm house later purchased by George's brother, Charles Dudley Warner (1829–1900). Charles Dudley Warner was co-author with Twain of *The Gilded Age*. He was also Twain's close friend and a favorite hiking companion. His wife, Susan Lee (1838–1921), was a talented amateur pianist and a patron of the arts. Susan and Olivia Clemens became lifelong friends. The Warners later built their own house, sharing property boundaries with both the Stowes and Mark Twain.

In October 1874, when his own house was completed on the five and a half acres he had purchased in 1873, Twain moved to 351 Farmington Avenue, on the northern boundary of Nook Farm. From its 800 foot frontage Twain's property sloped back to Park River. Designed by architect Edward Tuckerman Potter, Twain's slate-roofed, brick Victorian gothic house sparked comment. William Dean Howells described it as in the English Violet style, probably in reference to the French architect Eugene Viollet-le-Duc. Often compared to a Mississippi riverboat, the outside of the house reminded others of a Navajo blanket because of the bright red paint on alternate bands of bricks. Porches and balconies in the wooden "sticks" and "brackets" style reminded some of a cuckoo clock. Outbuildings included a brick barn, coachman's quarters, and a greenhouse. In the *Traveller's Record*,

January 1877, Twain said he was "author, architect, humorist," writing

> In his cozy, sunny and snug retreat,
> At once both city and country seat,
> Made up of bricks of various hue
> And shape and position, straight and askew,
> With its nooks and angles and gables too,
> The curious house that Mark built.

The entrance foyer of the Twain house consisted of marble floors, carved woodwork, and stenciled ceilings. A third-floor billiard room was the setting for frequent contests with friends and occasional middle-of-the-night games between Twain and his butler. A bed imported from Venice now stands in the master bedroom, complete with the detachable wooden angels Twain's daughters played with. An early telephone, intercom, and shower head recall Twain's interest in inventions as does a bedroom frequently occupied by visiting inventors. In the basement a small museum houses the Paige typesetting machine.

After his daughter Olivia Susan (Susy) died in 1896, Twain never returned to the Nook Farm house. First he rented it to John Calvin Day; in 1903 he sold it to the owner of the Hartford Fire Insurance Company, who later leased it to the Kingswood School for boys. When sold again, it was converted to a warehouse and then to apartments before being purchased and renovated by the Mark Twain Memorial Committee. This group was organized by the Friends of Hartford and directed by Katharine Seymour Day (1870–1964), daughter of Calvin Day and grandniece of Harriet Beecher Stowe.

Today Hartford business and apartment buildings and a high school have replaced several of the Nook Farm houses. The original Hooker residence has been converted into apartments. Another of the original homes, located at 77 Forest Street, contains the Nook Farm Research Library. The homes of Harriet Beecher Stowe and Mark Twain, their restorations completed in 1968 and 1974, respectively, are maintained jointly by the Stowe-Day Foundation and the Mark Twain Library and Memorial Commission. Foundations, contributions, and tour fees fund a continually updated collection of the papers of the original Nook Farm residents, many first editions, relevant historical documents, and hundreds of letters.

While many critics and biographers suggest that Twain found the community's sophistication and propriety stifling, most agree that its intellectual stimulation and social cohesion enhanced his art.

Mary S. Comfort

BIBLIOGRAPHY

Andrews, Kenneth R. *Nook Farm: Mark Twain's Hartford Circle*. Cambridge, Mass.: Harvard UP, 1950.

Chafee, Richard. "Edward Tuckerman and Samuel Clemens: An Architect and His Client." Ph.D. diss. Yale U, 1966.

Emerson, Everett. "Mark Twain's Move to Hartford." *Mark Twain Journal* 32.1 (Spring 1985): 18–20.

Faude, William H. *The Renaissance of Mark Twain's House: Handbook for Restoration*. Intro. Oliver Jensen. Larchmont, N.Y.: Queens House, 1978.

Lawton, Mary. *A Lifetime with Mark Twain*. New York: Harcourt, 1925.

Mark Twain Library and Memorial Commission. *Mark Twain in Hartford*. 2nd ed. Hartford, Conn.: Finlay Brothers, 1966.

See also: Hooker, Isabella Beecher; Stowe, Harriet Beecher; Twichell, Joseph; Women's Rights

Mark Twain's late phase as political commentator and social critic matched the *NAR*'s own evolution into a national voice on contemporary events. His connection to the *NAR*, and especially his relationship with George M. Harvey (1864–1928), who purchased the operation in 1899, was pivotal to his literary work during his last decade. Besides the twenty five installments of "Chapters from My Autobiography," published during 1906 and 1907, several of Twain's more influential anti-imperialist essays also appeared in the *NAR*: "To the Person Sitting in Darkness" and "To My Missionary Critics" (1901), "A Defense of General Funston" (1902), and "The Czar's Soliloquy" (1905).

Michael J. Kiskis

BIBLIOGRAPHY

Clemens, Samuel L. *Mark Twain's Correspondence with Henry Huttleston Rogers, 1893–1909*. Ed. Lewis Leary. Berkeley: U of California P, 1969.

———. *Mark Twain's Letters to His Publishers, 1867–1894*. Ed. Hamlin Hill. Berkeley: U of California P, 1967.

———. *Mark Twain's Own Autobiography: The Chapters from the "North American Review."* Ed. Michael J. Kiskis. Madison: U of Wisconsin P, 1990.

Paine, Albert Bigelow. *Mark Twain: A Biography*. 3 vols. New York: Harper, 1912.

See also: Autobiography; "Chapters from My Autobiography"; Imperialism

North American Review

The *North American Review* (*NAR*) began in Boston in 1815 as a quarterly devoted to literary, critical, and historical writing; it was moved to New York City in 1878. Its early reputation was tied to New England literary culture, but it adopted new emphases as it evolved: its initial focus on belles lettres shifted to commentary on contemporary social and political issues. The journal ceased publication in 1939; however, it was resurrected in 1963 as a quarterly published through the University of Northern Iowa.

Notebooks and Journals

During most of his adult life, from 1855 to 1910 and with only occasional breaks, Mark Twain kept a notebook or journal to write down details he thought he might later wish to recall. Although primarily of interest to literary scholars, the resulting forty-nine journals reveal as much about Samuel Clemens as they do Mark Twain; that is, they contain great stores of material Twain used in his writing, but they also tell us about Clemens's social life, his feelings for his family, and his business dealings. The notebooks were first compiled and published in abridged form by

Albert Bigelow Paine in 1935 as *Mark Twain's Notebook*. The complete *Notebooks & Journals* is in the process of being issued by the University of California Press; three of the four volumes have been published, with the first appearing in 1975.

The original notebooks varied in form and size from the accounting ledger Twain used as his first journal to memorandum books and appointment books. The entries were usually made by Twain himself except in those cases where he engaged a secretary to take dictation from him. Given the diversity of Twain's interests, the diversity of the notebook entries is not surprising. In his first journal, begun when he was nineteen, Twain includes, among other things, French lessons, phrenology, chess problems, promissory notes, furniture inventories, and laundry lists. Later journals detail his close study of the Mississippi River as he studied to gain his pilot's license, his travels to Europe, the Sandwich Islands, and the Holy Land, his business dealings, and his thoughts on political, religious, artistic, and social matters.

Because of their eclectic and shorthand nature, the journals are not good reading in and of themselves. They often contain cryptic notations (such as "Beautiful sky, view—and Indian summer" or "He was as dirty as Adam"), which reveal little to the reader but which Twain would later flesh out in his fiction, essays, or travel writing. Sometimes he consciously prepared to write using the journals, as when he recorded the details of a Mississippi cruise just prior to writing *Life on the Mississippi* (1883) and *Adventures of Huckleberry Finn* (1885). In addition to their use as an aid to recall, Twain also employed his journals as a literary device, often pretending to quote from them in *Roughing It* (1872), even though the passages he cites bear little or no resemblance to material actually in the notebooks.

Despite the fact that these journals are occasionally cryptic, and certainly not as interesting as the works that evolved from them, they provide unrivaled insight into the artistic methods of Mark Twain and into the private life of Samuel Clemens. As such, they are important records of an extraordinary life.

Greg Garrett

BIBLIOGRAPHY

Clemens, Samuel L. *Mark Twain's Notebook*. Ed. Albert B. Paine. New York: Harper, 1935.

———. *Mark Twain's Notebooks & Journals, Volume I (1855–1873)*. Ed. Frederick Anderson, Michael B. Frank, and Kenneth M. Sanderson; *Volume II (1877–1883)*. Ed. Frederick Anderson, Lin Salamo, and Bernard L. Stein; *Volume III (1883–1891)*. Ed. Robert Pack Browning, Michael B. Frank, and Lin Salamo. Berkeley: U of California P, 1975–1979.

Long, E. Hudson, and J.R. LeMaster. *The New Mark Twain Handbook*. New York: Garland, 1985.

See also: Mark Twain Project; Paine, Albert Bigelow

Novel

That Mark Twain significantly influenced the progress of the American novel seems ironic considering that he neither appreciated other novelists of his time nor considered himself a novelist. So many of Twain's writings, though clearly fiction, are not considered novels because of their lack of the conventional traits—characterization and plot. In fact, even those works that are classified as novels by most Twain scholars still maintain a slight rebellion from the traditional American novel; that is, most of his novels, with their humorous tangents and lack of structure, secure his position as a humorist, while relaxing the rules to which a novel must subscribe.

However, Twain is often cited for making contributions to the status of American fiction, even the status of the novel. Twain's employment of autobiographical material, his travels and his boyhood, provided the necessary plots and characters for many of his works to be considered novels. Twain used his past to produce a mixture of romance and realism. Because the strains of realism overshadow the romance most often, and because this realistic approach allowed Twain to use dialect more authentically than many of his peers, it is his leadership in the trend toward realism in American fiction for which Twain is most often credited.

Twain's personal opinions of other novelists and his view of the value of novels make the credit he is given somewhat ironic. Before he even tried to write his own novels, Twain satirized other attempts at American fiction because of their artificiality. Although he supposedly appreciated few novels, Twain did enjoy reading the works of Charles Dickens. He apparently tolerated the works of William Dean Howells, which their friendship may explain. He clearly disliked Jane Austen's novels as well as the works of Edgar Allan Poe and George Eliot, and he referred to these writers often in letters to Howells, who did not share Twain's sentiments. Twain's criticism of these writers' works seems to be centered most often on their lack of adventure, the very thing that Twain's works had in excess. On the other hand, Twain disliked Sir Walter Scott's writings, and even attacked them in *Life on the Mississippi* (1883), for their overuse of adventure and overemphasis on chivalry.

Twain's own progress as a novelist deserves attention because it seems to have occurred despite Twain's attempts to prevent it. Starting his writing career as a journalist, he always held nonfiction in higher esteem than fiction. Also, he considered himself incapable of writing novels. He said repeatedly that he detested novels; yet in a letter to Howells, he stated, "I can't write a novel for I lack the faculty." Still, in many of his other writings he called his own books novels, and in the essay "What Paul Bourget Thinks of Us," which he wrote in 1894, he discussed the novel's attributes. Few comments on the impact of Twain's novels summarize the general feeling toward Twain's works as well as Ernest Hemingway's remark, "[A]ll modern American literature comes from one book by Mark Twain called *Huckleberry Finn.*"

Paula Garrett

BIBLIOGRAPHY

Brooks, Van Wyck. *The Ordeal of Mark Twain.* Rev. ed. New York: Dutton, 1933.

Cowie, Alexander. *The Rise of the American Novel.* New York: American Book, 1948.

Leary, Lewis, ed. *A Casebook on Mark Twain's Wound.* New York: Crowell, 1962.

Maxwell, D.E.S. *American Fiction: The Intellectual Background.* New York: Columbia UP, 1963.

Neider, Charles. *Mark Twain.* New York: Horizon P, 1967.

Quinn, Arthur Hobson. *American Fiction: An Historical and Survey.* New York: Appleton-Century-Crofts, 1964.

See also: Legacy; Realism; "What Paul Bourget Thinks of Us"

Nye, Bill
(1850–1896)

Bill Nye (pseudonym for Edgar Wilson Nye) was one of the "literary comedians," a well-known journalist, humorist, essayist, and comic lecturer. His rise to fame began with his founding editorship of the Laramie, Wyoming, *Boomerang* (1881–1883), a newspaper for which he wrote humorous and satirical columns. Nye's major books of essays and sketches are *Bill Nye and Boomerang* (1881), *Forty Liars, and Other Lies* (1882), *Baled Hay* (1884), *Remarks* (1887), and *A Guest at the Ludlow* (1897). He co-authored two books with Hoosier poet James Whitcomb Riley: *Nye and Riley's Railway Guide* (1888) and *Nye and Riley's Wit and Humor* (1901), collections of Nye's witty essays and sketches and Riley's dialect poems. He also wrote two popular burlesque histories: *Bill Nye's History of the United States* (1894) and *Bill Nye's History of England* (1896). Nye first used the name "Bill" Nye in 1876 while assistant editor for the Laramie *Sentinel*.

Nye was born in Maine, spent his early years in Wisconsin, and then lived in Wyoming and Colorado before returning to the East, residing in New York and North Carolina. He married Clara Frances Smith (1877), with whom he had seven children. Starting with the western years, Nye became an important newspaper columnist and platform lecturer, his published satires and humorous speeches attracting audiences across the United

States and in Canada. The prestigious New York *World* featured him as Sunday columnist from 1887 until his death in 1896. The column was syndicated in over eighty newspapers. On the lecture circuit Nye's popularity rivaled Mark Twain's, both as a solo act and when in tandem with James Whitcomb Riley—the two billed as the "Twins of Genius."

The subject matter of Nye's writings and lectures was broad, ranging from western topics—not unlike many of Twain's in *Roughing It* (1872) and other western sketches—to the comical antics of politicos in Washington, D.C. Nye's wit could be both genial and caustic, and the darker strains are similar to Twain's more somber reflections. Twain met Nye while on the lecture circuit and praised him in his autobiography as a true humorist.

Though Nye's name is not a household term currently, his humor bears reading, not only as an index to nineteenth-century humorous style and popular topics, but for its treatment of more universal subjects too, the tone and treatment of which are often surprisingly modern. Of pleasurable relief to the modern reader is the fact that Nye avoided the comical misspellings and various grammatical tricks practiced by many of the literary comedians.

David B. Kesterson

BIBLIOGRAPHY

Blair, Walter. "The Background of Bill Nye in American Humor." Ph.D. diss., U of Chicago, 1931.

Kesterson, David B. *Bill Nye: The Western Writings.* Boise, Ida.: Boise State U, 1976.

———. *Bill Nye.* Boston: G.K. Hall (Twayne), 1981.

Nye, Frank Wilson. *Bill Nye: His Own Life Story.* New York: Century, 1926.

See also: Literary Comedians

Nye, Emma
(1846–1870)

The death of Emma Nye in September 1870, in the Clemenses' home in Buffalo, New York, was one of several devastating events that year that influenced Mark Twain's feelings about that city.

Emma M. Nye, born in January 1846, was almost the same age as Olivia Langdon Clemens, and the two girls grew up together in Elmira attending the same school and the same church. Livy felt guilty, comparing her own good fortune with that of her friend, when Emma's family moved to Aiken, South Carolina. On her way to a teaching position in Detroit, Emma stopped in Buffalo and came down with typhoid fever and died. She was brought back to Elmira for burial.

Herbert A. Wisbey, Jr.

BIBLIOGRAPHY

Clemens, Samuel L. *Mark Twain's Letters.* Ed. Albert B. Paine. Vol. 1. New York: Harper, 1917. 176–177.

See also: Buffalo, New York

Occult

Throughout his life, Mark Twain was fascinated by the mysteries of occult sciences. Frequently, Twain's ridicule of occult beliefs and their practitioners plays a central role in his humor. However, Alan Gribben suggests that, despite his outspoken public criticism of the paranormal, Twain was torn between belief and skepticism. He often conducted private experiments to determine the validity of occult practices and observed phenomena.

Among the few occult practices to earn Twain's open and consistent ridicule was witchcraft, which he considered the product of superstitious minds. An example of Twain's attitude appears in chapter 2 of *Huckleberry Finn* (1885), when Jim creates an elaborate tale of being tormented by witches in order to explain his hat's moving from his head to a tree branch while he was asleep—with the result that only other uneducated slaves believe Jim's story.

Although he maintained a skeptical attitude toward spiritualism, Twain was intrigued by the attempts of psychics to contact the spirits of the dead. From 1884 to 1902 Twain was a member of the English Society for Psychical Research, an organization committed to exploring claims of life after death and spiritual apparitions. However, his direct involvement with this practice was minimal until he and his wife tried unsuccessfully to contact their daughter Susy through a spiritualist.

Twain made the two occult sciences of phrenology and palmistry a part of his personal life. His interest in phrenology, the belief that a person's skull can predict character traits, continued virtually his entire adult life, during which time he had regular readings of his skull. His primary objection to the science arose out of the exaggerated claims of professional phrenologists, claims that, like the Duke's in *Huckleberry Finn*, eventually undermined the credibility of the practice. Likewise, from his own experiences Twain developed respect for palmistry. During the 1890s, while he was facing financial difficulties, Twain had his palm read several times by Louis Hamon (whose professional name was Cheiro). Hamon foretold that by Twain's sixty-eighth birthday the humorist's finances would have fully recovered, a prediction fulfilled by Twain's new contract with Harper and Brothers in October 1903. Twain shows his extensive knowledge of palmistry through his description of David Wilson's practices in *Pudd'nhead Wilson* (1894).

Twain was also fascinated with claims of unusual and paranormal mental powers, including mental telepathy, prophetic dreams, and hypnotism. His essay "Mental Telegraphy" presents evidence suggesting that mental telepathy involves actual extrasensory powers and not just coincidences. This power is demonstrated by Satan in *The Mysterious Stranger* (1916). For Twain, dreams had a prophetic power, especially after one of his dreams accurately predicted his brother Henry's death in 1858. In addition, Twain considered hypnotism a valid option in his attempts to find a cure for Jean Clemens's epilepsy, even though as a young man he had discovered the fraudulent nature of some mesmerists.

Although he frequently reiterated his skeptical attitude toward the beliefs and practices of his day, Twain dabbled in the occult during his adult life, and his writings contain numerous examples of ghosts, gothic horror, *doppelgängers*, and other incidents associated with occult phenomena. Despite the frequency of such references, however, the supernatural never replaces Twain's primary emphasis on the natural functions of mental and physical existence.

Charles Franklyn Beach

BIBLIOGRAPHY

Cummings, Sherwood. *Mark Twain and Science: Adventures of a Mind*. Baton Rouge: Louisiana State UP, 1988.

Gillman, Susan. *Dark Twins: Imposture and Identity in Mark Twain's America*. Chicago: U of Chicago P, 1989.

Gribben, Alan. "Mark Twain, Phrenology, and the 'Temperaments': A Study of Pseudoscientific Influence." *American Quarterly* 24 (1972): 45–68.

————. "'When Other Amusements Fail': Mark Twain and the Occult." *The Haunted Dusk: American Supernatural Fiction, 1820–1920*. Ed. Howard Kerr, John W. Crowley, and Charles L. Crow. Athens: U of Georgia P, 1983. 169–189.

Kerr, Howard H. *Mediums, Spirit-Rappers, and Roaring Radicals: Spiritualism in American Literature, 1850–1890*. Urbana: U of Illinois P, 1972.

See also: Dreams; "Mental Telegraphy" and "Mental Telegraphy Again"; Mental Telepathy/Extrasensory Perception; Phrenology; Spiritualism

"Old Times on the Mississippi"
(1875)

Published in the *Atlantic Monthly* between January and August of 1875, the seven articles of "Old Times on the Mississippi" became the basis for chapters 4 through 17 of *Life on the Mississippi* (1883). William Dean Howells, editor of the *Atlantic Monthly*, asked Twain for a contribution to the publication. Originally Twain declined, claiming lack of inspiration. Later, however, Joseph Hopkins Twichell convinced Twain that the stories of his days as a Mississippi cub pilot would make great serial articles. This began the seven sketches that became what has been called the best and most interesting part of *Life on the Mississippi*. The articles so delighted Howells that he printed them without modification.

The narrator of "Old Times" recounts his education as a Mississippi steamboat pilot. Twain begins the story with the narrator's reminiscences of his childhood days, when the steamboats came to the docks, announced by the Negro drayman's cry, "S-t-e-a-m-boat a-comin'!" The narrator remembers the town's excitement and the children's awe of the riverboat's crew. He tells of his struggles as a boy trying to attain "the permanent ambition" of all the boys in the village, to become a steamboatman. In the eyes of the children, "Pilot was the grandest position of all." The narrator relates how he, as a boy, set out to achieve this grand position.

The narrator first plans to join a government expedition to the mouth of the Amazon. However, he learns that the expedition plans to sail much later, and his pitiful finances prohibit his waiting. The youth convinces the pilot of the steamboat *Paul Jones* to "learn him the river." He sets off, starry-eyed, to become a conqueror of the river, a steamboat pilot. Under the instruction of his chief, "Mr. B.——," the cub begins to realize how much he must learn about the river in order to pilot a steamboat through its often treacherous waters. He ceases to see the river as a mysterious beauty when he learns to read the water's surface for information about currents, snags, and other watery dangers. The Mississippi, although still marvelous, exchanges its romantic mysteries for scientific ones.

The cub also loses his idealism about the people who run the riverboats. Early in the story he describes himself, with his boyhood friends, watching and listening to the steamboat workers with amazement and envy. He has nothing but admiration for their colorful language. He even comments, "I wished I could talk like that." Later, when he suffers a torrent of expletives at the hands of his pilot/teacher, he wonders at the force involved in issuing a simple command.

Despite his loss of romanticism, one part of the Mississippi never loses its wonder for him—the pilots who fearlessly run it, night and day. The greater part of "Old Times" is a tribute to the former pilots of the Mississippi and to the incredible amounts of information their minds process daily. Twain compares the Mississippi to a street; a pilot must be able to identify every inch. To further complicate matters, the street mixes up its signs twice a week, but the pilot must still perfectly navigate it. Twain stresses that the pilots knew the entire river as it changed with the currents, the weather, and the seasons. By the end of his education, the cub marvels that both he and the other pilots remember these massive amounts of detail.

By the end of article four the cub's education concludes. The remaining three articles contain Twain's closing thoughts. Twain devotes an article to a brief history of the foundation and success of the Pilots' Benevolent Association. This organization, although at first enduring ridicule and rejection at the hands of those whose rights it tried to protect, eventually established an occupational monopoly of riverboat pilots. Twain praises the efforts of these pilots to establish a process for licensing new pilots. Twain's love of the Mississippi and its pilots shines above everything else in "Old Times." The real regret he feels when railroads and tugboats replace his beloved steamboats is evident as he describes the association and the science of piloting as "things of the dead and pathetic past."

In the seventh and final article Twain describes the custom of racing the steamboats up the river from New Orleans. He points out that the fastest times did not necessarily imply the fastest speeds, since the river continually shortened itself by cutting through the "horseshoe banks." In these final three articles Twain betrays the fascination that both the Mississippi and piloting still held for him. "Old Times" is Mark Twain's tribute to the Mississippi and its pilots.

J.R. LeMaster and Kathryn Kalin Lee

BIBLIOGRAPHY

Clemens, Samuel L. *Mark Twain's Letters*. Ed. Albert B. Paine. 2 vols. New York: Harper, 1917.

Davis, Sara deSaussure, and Philip D. Beidler, eds. *The Mythologizing of Mark Twain*. Tuscaloosa: U of Alabama P, 1984.

Kruse, Horst H. *Mark Twain and "Life on the Mississippi."* Amherst: U of Massachusetts P, 1981.

Mills, Barriss. "'Old Times on the Mississippi' as an Initiation Story." *College English* 25 (1964): 283–289.

Spengemann, William C. *Mark Twain and the Backwoods Angel: The Matter of Innocence in the Works of Samuel L. Clemens*. Kent, Ohio: Kent State UP, 1966.

See also: Bixby, Horace E.; *Life on the Mississippi*; Mississippi River; Piloting

Ollendorff and Mr. Ballou

In *Roughing It* (1872) Twain, Ollendorff, and Mr. Ballou leave the Humboldt silver mines to return to Carson City. Ollendorff is "a Prussian" (232), and Ballou a kind-hearted elderly blacksmith who inappropriately uses "big words *for their own sakes*" (217).

Ballou, Ollendorff, and Twain set out in a snowstorm, and then are trapped by a flood at "Honey Lake Smith's," an inn on the Carson River. After eight days, they leave, unable to tolerate the barbaric conditions. Ollendorff upends their canoe when they try to cross the river, but their attempt the next day is successful. The three are hampered by a second snowstorm and, on Ollendorff's insistence that "his instinct was as sensitive as any compass" (241), they circle, following their own tracks for two hours. Mr. Ballou describes the situation as "perfectly hydraulic" and calls Ollendorff "a logarithm" (242). Assuming they will die, they make peace with one another, and renounce their vices. They wake up in the morning "not fifteen steps" (249) from the stage station. Twain returns to his vice, his pipe, in secret, but in doing so he discovers Ollendorff with whiskey bottle to his lips and Mr. Ballou with his greasy deck of cards.

Ballou was based on a Mr. Tillou, a blacksmith who was with Clemens at the Humboldt mines. Twain's companions on the trip to Carson City were Benjamin B. Bunker, Colonel Onstein, and Captain Pfersdorff, on whom the character of Ollendorff is based. Onstein was the card player.

Patricia Hunt

BIBLIOGRAPHY

Clemens, Samuel L. *Roughing It.* Ed. Franklin R. Rogers and Paul Baender. Berkeley: U of California P, 1972.

Paine, Albert Bigelow. *Mark Twain: A Biography.* 3 vols. New York: Harper, 1912.

See also: Roughing It

"Open Letter to the American People, An"
(1866)

This early sketch was written in San Francisco in January 1866 and first published in the New York *Weekly Review* on 17 February 1866. An abbreviated version (apparently without authorial revision) entitled "A Complaint About Correspondents" was reprinted in the San Francisco *Californian* on 24 March 1866 and then (again without the author's consent) included by C.H. Webb in *The Celebrated Jumping Frog of Calaveras County and Other Stories* (1867), with "Dated in San Francisco" added to its title. After further unauthorized reprintings Mark Twain eventually called it "rubbish" and had it deleted from the first authorized reissue of *The Choice Humorous Works of Mark Twain* (London: Chatto and Windus, 1874). Modern reprintings (in Charles Neider, ed., *The Complete Humorous Sketches and Tales of Mark Twain* [1961] and Bernard Taper, ed., *Mark Twain's San Francisco* [1963]) make use of the abbreviated version. The full text will become available as item 181 in the Iowa-California edition of *The Works of Mark Twain: Early Tales & Sketches, Volume 3 (1866–1868)* to be published in the 1990s.

"An Open Letter to the American People" is Mark Twain's "complaint about correspondents" in which he decries the lack of useful and interesting information contained in the letters he receives from relatives and friends "east of the Rocky Mountains." To illustrate his point, he presents a few such purported letters: from his "Aunt Nancy," from "a young dry goods clerk whom I knew well in New Orleans," from a friend, "Miss Althea Blathers," from his "venerable uncle Balaam," and from his "venerable mother"; all of these fail obviously to discuss "things and people" the recipient "takes a living interest in." Mark Twain then effectively contrasts all this useless verbiage with a letter from a small girl, leading him to conclude that "the most useful and interesting letters we get here from home are from children seven or eight years old." They have nothing to talk about but home, neighbors, and family, they write simply and naturally, they do not strain for effect, and they seldom deal in abstractions or moral homilies.

Mark Twain's real correspondence (letter to Jane Lampton Clemens and Pamela A. Moffett, 20 January 1866, and letter to Jane Lampton Clemens and Family, 21 February 1868) as well as other circumstantial evidence indicates that while the fictitious letters from adults are partly based on letters from his mother and his sister Pamela, the model letter is based on one received from his niece Annie Moffett. In touching up the original text and in preparing his comment on the specific qualities inherent in letters written by children, Mark Twain clearly saw the literary and critical advantages of combining first-person narration with the innocent-eye perspective, an insight that was to serve him in *Adventures of Huckleberry Finn* (1885). An interesting aspect of the subsequent publication history would seem to corroborate this, for while Twain eventually dismissed the sketch in its entirety as "rubbish" and had it deleted from his *Choice Humorous Works*, Annie's letter along with his commentary was reprinted in the Buffalo *Express* of 10 November 1869.

Horst H. Kruse

BIBLIOGRAPHY

Kruse, Horst H. "Annie and Huck: A Note on the *Adventures of Huckleberry Finn*." *American Literature* 39 (May 1967): 207–214.

See also: Childhood; Webster, Annie Moffett

Orality

Orality studies have had an important impact in recent years on disciplines ranging from anthropology to literary criticism. They may be said in general to focus on the differences between literate and oral cognition and the implications of such differences with respect to questions of interpretation, representation, and the domination of Western civilizations by print culture. Such an approach might find its point of departure in one or more of several relevant features of the life and works of Mark Twain. His career as a platform lecturer and reader, his exploitation of the oral folktale, the rapid evolution of print technology during his lifetime, and the collision of oral and literate cultures recorded in his writings all suggest fruitful application of this perspective.

Whereas structuralist and deconstructive accounts of language tend to collapse the distinction between oral and written discourses, subsuming them within a contiguous system of arbitrary signification, orality studies emphasize a range of differences between speech and text, including the extent to which spoken words may be said to be active and experiential rather than representational and the impact on the mind of aural vs. visual stimuli. Pointing to the existence of contemporary cultures that do not have recourse to the technology of writing as well as ancient cultures that preceded that technology, orality studies seek not so much to escape the hegemony of print culture as they do to posit an "other" to that print culture that has radically different dynamics and can function to change and condition print culture. The extent to which one is convinced that such an extratextual other persists residually and ineradicably in print culture can be invoked by writing or, conversely, the extent to which one sees the oral as simply an ingenious variation of Derridean logocentrism, that is, the trope of presence by which writing conceals its arbitrary nature, will determine one's attitude toward orality as an investigative assumption. The arguments for both sides being beyond the scope of the present discussion, the remainder of the article assumes the viability of orality as an investigative concept.

Little need be said of the extent to which Twain drew upon the ear as the primary organ of sense in the rhetoric of his fiction. From his earliest successes as writer and professional speaker, it was manner rather than matter that took precedence. Twain's relationship to the oral is perhaps less obvious than it might seem through a simple cataloguing of his prodigious representations of the speaking voice.

Treatments of the vernacular perspective in Twain's writing, pioneered and epitomized by Henry Nash Smith's *Mark Twain: The Development of a Writer* (1962), break important ground in revealing a clash between radically different modes of discourse in his major works, and the examination of this clash as between the oral and the literate consciousness may be profitably seen as a complementary extension of the vernacular argument. The result of this recharacterization of the vernacular argument might take a number of forms. Diachronically, it suggests that Twain's work be situated in the historical shift from orality to literacy that characterizes the evolution of Western thought. From the perspective of this long view, Twain might be said to represent the imaginative adaptation of literacy to orality, a possibility emerging from the successful dissemination of literacy in America during the last half of the nineteenth century and the consequent rupture between relatively concrete local values and the abstract institutional values made possible *by* the technology of writing.

Synchronically, it suggests an examination of the communities in Twain's works. In *Huckleberry Finn* (1885), for instance, much may be gained by an investigation of Pap and Jim as primarily oral types. Bereft of a community of interlocutors by which to sustain and adapt his knowledge of the world, the former is lead inevitably toward extinction. Ironically, on the other hand, Jim is sustained by a viable oral community that exists by dint of its forced separation from the literate economy.

Biographically and psychologically, Twain's own development from oral childhood to literate adulthood, the conditions under which his literacy was acquired, and the extent to which he might be said to have participated in or resisted the dominance of the written over the oral, either in his own time or with an eye toward some future "territory" of human interaction, constitute a rich constellation of research possibilities. Moreover, the interrelatedness of Twain's speaking and writing careers might be seen in yet a more revealing light.

Finally, and perhaps most controversially, orality studies may remind us that Twain can yet *speak* to us, with all of the immediacy and force that might imply.

David Barrow

BIBLIOGRAPHY

Clemens, Samuel L. *Adventures of Huckleberry Finn.* Ed. Walter Blair and Victor Fischer. Berkeley: U of California P, 1985.

Ong, Walter. *Orality and Literacy: The Technologizing of the Word.* London: Methuen, 1982.

Smith, Henry Nash. *Mark Twain: The Development of a Writer.* Cambridge, Mass.: Harvard UP, 1962.

Tyler, Stephen. *The Unspeakable.* Madison: U of Wisconsin P, 1987.

See also: Language; Lecturer; Representation; Rhetorical Forms; Vernacular

Osgood, James Ripley
(1836–1892)

In 1881 James Ripley Osgood, of Boston, succeeded Elisha Bliss as Twain's publisher, though he appears to have served as little more than an unsuccessful literary agent (Kaplan 238).

Twain's partnership with Osgood lasted through *The Prince and the Pauper* (1882), *The Stolen White Elephant* (1882), and *Life on the Mississippi* (1883), all relative failures financially. According to Twain, he and Osgood neglected publishing duties in favor of billiard playing and "a good time" (*Autobiography* 228), though the careless and inexperienced Osgood would receive the blame for the commercial blunders. Clients and associates—Bret Harte, Harriet Beecher Stowe, and James T. Fields— also complained about Osgood's inattentiveness to business (Kaplan 237).

Twain ended the working relationship with Osgood in 1883 in favor of Charles L. Webster and Company. Osgood's firm collapsed in 1885. Twain, happy to be free from the publisher's inexperienced hand (Hill 164–165; 183), nevertheless, valued Osgood, in later years calling him "one of the dearest and sweetest and loveliest human beings to be found on the planet anywhere" (*Autobiography* 228).

Richard Gaughran

BIBLIOGRAPHY

Clemens, Samuel L. *The Autobiography of Mark Twain.* Ed. Charles Neider. New York: Harper, 1959.

————. *Mark Twain's Letters to His Publishers, 1867–1894.* Ed. Hamlin Hill. Berkeley: U of California P, 1967.

Kaplan, Justin. *Mr. Clemens and Mark Twain.* New York: Simon & Schuster, 1966.

Weber, Carl J. *The Rise and Fall of James Ripley Osgood: A Biography.* Waterville, Me.: Colby College P, 1959.

P

Page, Thomas Nelson
(1853–1922)

A chauvinistic Virginian who is generally regarded as the preeminent champion of the
Old South in fiction, Thomas Nelson Page is
best remembered today for *In Ole Virginia*
(1887) or *Marsechan and Other Stories* (1887), a
collection of short stories, and *Red Rock* (1898),
a novel dealing with Reconstruction. Page
depicted the pre-Civil War plantation South
as a romantic prelapsarian world peopled by
virtuous ladies, knightly gentlemen, and childlike slaves devoted to their white folks. Conversely, he portrayed the defeat of the Confederacy and the alleged horrors of Reconstruction as nothing less than an apocalyptic
dismantling of the highest civilization ever
attained by mankind. Though Page was a thoroughly unreconstructed Southerner, the patently racist assumptions on which his writing
rests are relatively benign when compared with
the views of a rabid Negrophobe like Thomas
Dixon, Jr. A lawyer by training, Page maintained an active interest in the political scene
and entered the diplomatic service toward the
end of his life.

Mark Twain regarded with undisguised
scorn many of the southern "virtues" Page
sought to celebrate: aristocratic pretensions
(especially among Virginians); the cult of sentimental medievalism (with its often bloody
code of honor); and the supposedly benign
paternalism of chattel slavery. Still, the two
men seem to have shared a relatively cordial,
if casual, acquaintanceship. They were among
the distinguished group of public figures, including William Dean Howells and George
W. Cable, who were awarded honorary degrees from Yale in 1901. Page's later novels
reveal him to be a critic of capitalist materialism in a way that parallels Twain and Howells,
and in this respect he can be regarded as anticipating the insights of the later southern
agrarians.

William Bedford Clark

BIBLIOGRAPHY

Gross, Theodore L. *Thomas Nelson Page*. New York: Twayne, 1967.

Longest, George C. *Three Virginia Writers: A Reference Guide*. Boston: G.K. Hall, 1978.

Page, Rosewell. *Thomas Nelson Page: A Memoir of a Virginia Gentleman*. New York: Scribner, 1923.

See also: *Life on the Mississippi*; South, Mark Twain and the

Paige, James W.

An inventor in the Yankee tradition, James W. Paige worked for more than twenty years to perfect his mechanical typesetting machine, the Paige typesetter. Mark Twain invested much money and faith in both the invention and the inventor; ultimately, however, the intricate typesetter proved too delicate to operate reliably for extended periods of time, and its failure contributed greatly to Twain's bankruptcy in the 1890s.

Paige got the idea for his typesetter in 1872 in his native Rochester, New York, received a patent in 1874, then in 1875, after acquiring a wife and a new wardrobe, moved to Hartford, Connecticut, where he listed himself in the city directory as a patentee and began work on the machine at the Colt arms factory. Mark Twain met Paige in 1880 after having already invested $5,000. Evidently, Twain fell under the spell not only of Paige's wondrous machine but also of the smooth-talking visionary inventor, as did a number of other investors; Twain once said Paige could talk a fish into leaving the water and going for a walk with him. Twain's comments on Paige exhibit an interesting mixture of attitudes: in his *Autobiography*, he calls Paige a poet (*I*:72), but he also says if he had Paige in a steel trap, he would cut off all food and water and "watch that trap till he died" (*I*:78). After the failure of the machine in 1894 in tests at the Chicago *Herald*, Paige remained in Chicago working on other inventions, including a pneumatic tire and an improved corn-husking machine, none of which were commercially successful.

Mark Twain soon after embarked on his around-the-world lecture tour in an attempt to pay back his creditors, his bankruptcy brought on in large part because of his faith in Paige and his typesetter.

John Bird

BIBLIOGRAPHY

Burlingame, Roger. *Engines of Democracy: Inventions and Society in Mature America*. New York: Scribner, 1940.

Clemens, Samuel L. *Mark Twain's Autobiography*. Ed. Albert B. Paine. 2 vols. New York: Harper, 1924.

———. *Mark Twain's Correspondence with Henry Huttleston Rogers, 1893–1909*. Ed. Lewis Leary. Berkeley: U of California P, 1969.

———. *Mark Twain's Letters*. Ed. Albert B. Paine. 2 vols. New York: Harper, 1917.

Kaplan, Justin. *Mr. Clemens and Mark Twain*. New York: Simon & Schuster, 1966.

See also: Bankruptcy; Business; Paige Typesetting Machine; Technology, Mark Twain and

Paige Typesetting Machine

In 1880 Samuel Clemens began investing in the development of a machine invented by James W. Paige that would automatically set, justify, and distribute movable type. Clemens believed the machine would revolutionize the printing industry and bring its backers immense wealth, and he gradually increased his investments and involvement until he owned a controlling interest in the enterprise. His expenses rose accordingly, however, as delay followed delay and the complex machine required more and more refinement, running to further investment of more than $3,000 per month at one point and finally to a cost totaling over $200,000. The typesetter was finally too complicated to work reliably or even to manufacture, and its failure was the chief cause of Clemens's bankruptcy in 1894.

In the history of technology the Paige typesetter is an example of the failure of the "human analogy," the design of machines to accomplish a task by mechanically replicating the way a human would perform it. Its competitor, the Linotype machine, invented by Ottmar Merganthaler, succeeded by bypassing the human analogy and casting lines of metal type that could simply be melted down and reused. This human analogy, unfortunately, was probably what attracted Clemens in the first place: he had spent his youth setting type by hand for newspapers, and the apparent wizardry of the Paige machine in performing (on those rare occasions when it was operational) with incredible rapidity the painstaking operations of setting, justifying, and distributing (restoring) type cast a kind of spell over him that blinded him to its impracticality.

In the overall trajectory of his career, Samuel Clemens's involvement with the Paige typesetter not only marks his failure as a businessman, but also demonstrates the extent to which his literary and entrepreneurial impulses were inextricably intertwined. As a best-selling author Clemens formed a publishing company to market and sell his own books, and he sought through the typesetter to make a vast fortune that would free him from the necessity to write. The failure of this scheme, in turn, forced him back to writing and lecturing to pay off his debts. His involvement with the machine was especially close during the composition of *A Connecticut Yankee in King Arthur's Court* (1889), and that novel demonstrates more than any other his ambivalence toward technology. Its hero, Hank Morgan, a mechanical genius like Paige, transforms sixth-century Britain into a nineteenth-century industrial society, only to end up using his technological advances to destroy the entire civilization.

Robert Sattelmeyer

BIBLIOGRAPHY

Burlingame, Roger. *Engines of Democracy: Inventions and Society in Mature America.* New York: Scribner, 1940. 145–148.

Burnham, Tom. "Mark Twain and the Paige Typesetter: A Background for Despair." *Western Humanities Review* 6 (1951): 29–36.

Kaplan, Justin. *Mr. Clemens and Mark Twain.* New York: Simon & Schuster, 1966.

Kasson, John F. *Civilizing the Machine: Technology and Republican Values in America 1776–1900.* New York: Grossman, 1976.

Paine, Albert Bigelow. *Mark Twain: A Biography.* 3 vols. New York: Harper, 1912.

See also: Bankruptcy; Business; Paige, James W.; Technology, Mark Twain and

Paine, Albert Bigelow
(1861–1937)

Albert Bigelow Paine was born on 10 July 1861 in New Bedford, Massachusetts. When the family moved to the Midwest, he received his only formal education, eight years of grammar school. Young Paine became a photographer and dealer in photographic supplies and also had occasional stories and poems published in *Harper's Weekly.* He went to New York in 1895 to become a writer and subsequently landed a job as an editor for *St. Nicholas* magazine, a post he held for about ten years. One critic described him as dignified-appearing and "a bit pompous." Another remarked that his writing had "a touch of condescension." During his lifetime Paine would write or edit over forty books, nearly one-fifth of them concerned with Mark Twain.

At a fateful Players Club dinner on 5 January 1906, Albert Bigelow Paine sat across from Mark Twain. Seated next to Paine was Charles Harvey Genung, who whispered, "You should write his life." Paine had already written a well-regarded biography of Thomas Nast, published two years before. At the dinner Paine engaged Twain in a conversation that eventually led to his monumental three-volume *Mark Twain: A Biography.* On 7 October 1912 Paine affectionately inscribed a first edition of the Twain biography to his friend Genung: "Not only did you officiate in the union which produced this book, but the actual labor of its delivery. . . my *best-loved* offspring" (Karanovich collection).

From January 1906 until Mark Twain's death in 1910 Paine became Twain's closest companion, continuous billiard competitor, general editorial assistant, and business manager. Together they strolled, discussed, worked, and traveled. Toward the end of the author's life Paine and his family became members of Mark Twain's household. Twain's only surviving daughter, Clara, came to regard Paine as the officially chosen guardian of Twain's public image (see Hamlin Hill, *Mark Twain: God's Fool*, 1973).

Isabel V. Lyon, Twain's secretary, wrote in January 1906 that Paine had begun classifying the autobiographical and biographical papers. She said Paine, a "worshipping creature," was bringing order to the mass of papers. That same month Paine referred to Twain as "King—distinguished above all others." Paine in January also hired Josephine S. Hobby as Twain's stenographer. During the next three years she took over a half-million words of autobiographical dictation. Paine included about half of them in editing *Mark Twain's Autobiography* in 1924.

Paine published *The Boy's Life of Mark Twain* in 1916 and *A Short Life of Mark Twain* in 1920. In editing *The Mysterious Stranger* in 1916, he pruned, bowdlerized, amplified, and reordered Twain's original manuscripts. Likewise his two-volume edition of *Mark Twain's Letters*, published in 1917, censored and willingly suppressed facts. Paine also assembled Mark Twain's essays in *Europe and Elsewhere* in 1923. On the centenary of Mark Twain's birth in 1935, Paine edited *Mark Twain's Notebook*, using only about one-fourth of the words found in the nearly fifty notebooks kept by the renowned author.

As the first literary executor of Mark Twain's estate, Albert Bigelow Paine signed the certificates of authenticity placed in each of 483 books from Mark Twain's library sold at auction on 7–8 February 1911. That sale began the posthumous control of the celebrated author's literary affairs and image by Paine and Clara. This influence lasted until Paine's death on 9 April 1937.

The Paine Estate auction in New York City on 11 December 1937 contained about 100 choice Mark Twain letters and manuscripts and almost 3,000 letters to Paine from late-nineteenth-century and early-twentieth-century literati, celebrities, and political figures. Included were letters from Dan Beard, Horatio Alger, H.L. Mencken, Andrew Carnegie, William Dean Howells, Rudyard Kipling, and Theodore Roosevelt. Paine had been understandably proud of his acquaintances. Over 290 of the letters pertained to Mark Twain. Included in the sale were also about 135 letters from Mark Twain's daughter Clara.

Albert Bigelow Paine's portrayal of Mark Twain is viewed by some scholars as comprehensive and surprisingly fair. Others say that Paine suppressed the tragedy of Twain's closing years when he was a tormented and faltering imaginative genius. In 1926 Paine wrote to Twain's publisher concerning the potential depreciation of Mark Twain property and warned that if other people wrote about Twain the tradition might "fade and change." Paine's portrayal of Twain as an authentic American hero and a warm, beloved, and genial family author has seemingly had a lasting effect.

Nick Karanovich

BIBLIOGRAPHY

Clemens, Samuel L. *Mark Twain's Notebooks & Journals, Volume III (1883–1891).* Ed. Robert Pack Browning, Michael B. Frank, and Lin Salamo. Berkeley: U of California P, 1979.

Cushman, Bigelow Paine. Letter to Nick Karanovich. Deer Isle, Maine. 7 March 1990.

Hill, Hamlin. *Mark Twain: God's Fool.* New York: Harper & Row, 1973.

Kaplan, Justin. *Mark Twain and His World.* New York: Simon & Schuster, 1974.

Kunitz, Stanley J., and Howard Haycraft. *Twentieth Century Authors.* New York: H.W. Wilson, 1961.

See also: Biographers

Paine, Thomas
(1737–1809)

Born in England, Thomas Paine became an important pamphleteer and advocate for the

American and French revolutions. Paine, who called himself the "Great Commoner of Mankind," until he was thirty-seven lived an unsettled life, which included a variety of homes and occupations and two unhappy marriages. He was twice fired from an excise man position where he developed his social philosophy sympathetic to those oppressed by taxes. He was forced into bankruptcy after publishing *The Case of the Officers of Excise* (1772), a plea for higher wages.

By 1774 Paine was ready for a fresh start. In London he met and impressed Benjamin Franklin, who liked his interests and learning. Franklin guardedly sponsored Paine's fresh start in Philadelphia, where Paine arrived at the end of November. A frequent contributor to the *Pennsylvania Magazine* and *Pennsylvania Journal*, he first earned wide recognition as author of *Common Sense* (10 January 1776) when he called for a "Declaration of Independence." While a soldier in the Revolutionary Army, Paine continued his political writings in the *Pennsylvania Packet* and notably in his series of pamphlets *The American Crisis* (December 1776–April 1783), supporting the independence cause. After the war Paine spent time in England and France advocating the French Revolution until the French jailed him for exposing the Reign of Terror. In jail, and finally in James Monroe's ambassadorial home in Paris, Paine wrote *The Age of Reason* (1794–1795), his deistic treatise for rational religion. Because of his "atheistic" views, his last years were spent in neglect and obscurity until his death in 1809. His gravesite is still unknown.

As for Paine's influence on Twain, it is commonly accepted that Paine, along with John Clemens, John Quarles, and Macfarlane, are responsible for Twain's religious skepticism and deterministic ideas. Clemens admired Paine's writings most of his life, at least by 1853 when he first mentions *The Crisis* in correspondence. Twain reread *The Age of Reason* in 1908, saying, "I read it first when I was a cub pilot, read it with fear and hesitation, but marveling at its fearlessness and power. I read it again a year or two ago . . . and was amazed to see how tame it had become." Twain's own thinking had gone beyond Paine's "heresies" by his last decade when he wrote propagandist essays in the fashion of Paine's pamphlets.

Twain's strong feeling for Paine's work is evident in both his private notes and published works. In marginal notes in FitzGerald's *Rubáiyát of Omar Kháyyam*, Twain compared Paine favorably with Kháyyam, defending Paine's irreverent thinking. He attacked those "who call it a sin to respect Tom Paine or know of his great service to his race." He used Paine as a symbol of contrast in the first chapter of "Those Extraordinary Twins" (1894). Luigi reads Paine's *The Age of Reason* while his brother Angelo reads a devotional work.

Wesley Britton

BIBLIOGRAPHY

Aldridge, Alfred O. *Man of Reason: The Life of Thomas Paine*. Philadelphia: Lippincott, 1959.

Britton, Wesley A. "Mark Twain and Tom Paine: 'Common Sense' as Source for 'The War Prayer.'" *Conference of College Teachers of English Studies* 54 (September 1989): 13–19.

Conway, Moncure D. *The Life of Thomas Paine*. 2 vols. New York: Putnam, 1892.

See also: Philosophy

Pall Mall, Tennessee

Pall Mall is a village in Fentress County, principally noted as the home of World War I hero Sergeant Alvin C. York. John Marshall Clemens served as postmaster of Pall Mall, 1832–1835. The Clemens family lived for several years in the village prior to their departure for Missouri in 1835.

Allison R. Ensor

See also: Clemens, John Marshall; Jamestown, Tennessee; Tennessee Land

Paris, France

Mark Twain first encountered Paris, France, in 1867 during his trip with the other "pilgrims" of the ship *Quaker City*. After landing in Marseilles, he traveled by rail to Paris. His first impression of the grand European capital was one of delight and admiration. There he saw the regular tourist fare: the "Old Masters" at the Louvre, Napoleon Bonaparte's tomb, the Tuileries, the Pantheon, Notre Dame, the opera, the morgue, the poor section of Faubourg, St. Antoine, Versailles, and the can-can. His humorously embellished impressions are recorded in *The Innocents Abroad* (1869), where he unmercifully pokes fun at Parisian barbers, poor-quality billiard tables, and hotel accommodations, yet comments on the beauty and history of the city. He also briefly visited the Paris International Exhibition and, coincidentally, saw Napoleon III entertain the sultan of Turkey in a Grand Military Review on the Champs Élysées. Although initially he considered Napoleon III "the greatest man in the world today," he later became gravely disillusioned with both the man and his policies. Twain ridiculed and mocked military strategies and the popular maps of the Franco-Prussian War found in big-city newspapers with his deliberately childish, primitively engraved, reversed-image "Map of Paris," which was first published in the Buffalo *Express* (17 September 1870). Throughout his life he periodically visited Paris; during the unseasonably cold spring of 1879 the Clemens family lived in Paris. Twain's claim that "France has neither winter nor summer nor morals—apart from those drawbacks it is a fine country" (*Mark Twain's Notebook* 153) can be traced, in part, to his dreadful experiences that spring. Despite her father's growing dislike of France, Clara Clemens studied music in Paris.

J.C.B. Kinch

BIBLIOGRAPHY

Clemens, Samuel L. *The Innocents Abroad.* Hartford, Conn.: American Publishing, 1869.

———. *Mark Twain's Notebook.* Ed. Albert B. Paine. New York: Harper, 1935.

———. *Tom Sawyer Abroad, Tom Sawyer, Detective, and Other Stories, Etc., Etc.* New York: Harper, 1896. 377–379, 435.

———. *Traveling with the Innocents Abroad.* Ed. Daniel M. McKeithan. Norman: U of Oklahoma P, 1958.

Ganzel, Dewey. *Mark Twain Abroad: The Cruise of the "Quaker City."* Chicago: U of Chicago P, 1968.

Kaplan, Justin. *Mr. Clemens and Mark Twain.* New York: Simon & Schuster, 1966.

Sanborn, Margaret. *Mark Twain: The Bachelor Years.* New York: Doubleday, 1990.

Scott, Arthur L. *Mark Twain at Large.* Chicago: Henry Regnery, 1969.

See also: Europe; France; *Innocents Abroad, The*

Park Church, The

On the National Register of Historic Places, The Park Church in Elmira, New York, is listed as a landmark for its anti-slavery heritage, unique building, Beecher history, and Twain connections. It was founded in 1846 as an Independent Congregational Church after a split within the Presbyterian Church over the slavery issue. Jervis and Olivia Lewis Langdon were among its charter members. The Langdon family were contributors to the construction of the present building (1871–1876). Their home was directly across the street from the church and a favorite resting place for its pastor, Thomas K. Beecher, and his wife Julia. Olivia Clemens attended the Sunday school as a girl and was a church member. In a recollection written in the 1920s Olivia's friend, Anna Beecher Holden, said that during his summers in Elmira Twain was a "faithful attendant at Park Church" (*The Mark Twain Society Bulletin* 6.2 [July 1983]: 2). During Twain's last visit to Elmira he attended and spoke at an organ recital honoring Thomas K. Beecher at Park Church on 3 April 1907.

A massive structure combining classical, Byzantine, and gothic architectural features, Park Church was designed to be a "church home," central to the daily lives of its members. The building plan, conceived by Beecher and a committee including Susan Crane and Charles Langdon, called for an auditorium to seat 800, a kitchen equipped for 200, parlors, play areas with a stage for theater, space for dancing and games, a billiard table, and a public library. Twain endorsed and drew attention to the plan with his exaggerated description, "The New Beecher Church," in the *American Publisher*, July 1871.

In the tradition of the early church and Beecher's ecumenical leadership, Park Church maintains its independent spirit while belonging to the United Church of Christ and affiliating with county, state, national, and world councils of churches. Much of the building has been preserved, particularly the parlors, which now contain some original furniture and a mirror from the Langdon home. An adjacent meeting room, which was Elmira's only lending library for twenty years, has a conference table incorporating the base of the Beecher billiard table and such displays of memorabilia as a "Jabberwok," so named by Twain. The working archive contains the Thomas Kinnicut Beecher Collection with Beecher's appointment book noting the Clemens's wedding, membership rolls with marriage and death records from 1845, sermons, Sunday school liturgy, board of trustee minutes, photographs, and several association Twain books.

Gretchen E. Sharlow

BIBLIOGRAPHY

Rugoff, Milton. *The Beechers: An American Family in the Nineteenth Century.* New York: Harper & Row, 1981.

Stowe, Lyman Beecher. *Saints, Sinners and Beechers.* New York: Blue Ribbon Books, 1934.

Taylor, Eva. *A History of The Park Church.* Elmira, N.Y.: The Park Church, 1946.

See also: Beecher, Julia Jones; Beecher, Thomas Kinnicut; Elmira, New York

Parker, Edwin P.
(1836–1920)

One of Hartford's three most admired religious leaders, Edwin P. Parker (like the other two leaders) was a close friend of Mark Twain. Twain and the three clergymen all belonged to the Monday Evening Club, a forum composed of Hartford's keenest minds. All four were widely acquainted, highly popular, well read, tolerant, devoted to the pleasure of the company, politically conservative, and theologically liberal. Coming down from Maine in 1860 to minister to the Second Church for sixty years, one of Parker's first acts was to celebrate Christmas, a first in a New England Congregational Church. Parker suggested to Twain that he write a work of sober character and permanent value. The result was *The Prince and the Pauper* (1882). Despite their theological differences, Twain numbered Parker among his dozen closest friends.

Mark Draper

BIBLIOGRAPHY

Andrews, Kenneth R. *Nook Farm: Mark Twain's Hartford Circle.* Cambridge, Mass.: Harvard UP, 1950.

Clemens, Samuel L. *Mark Twain's Autobiography.* Vol. 1. Ed. Albert B. Paine. New York: Harper, 1924.

Dole, Nathan, Forrest Morgan, and Caroline Ticknor. *The Bibliophile Library of Literature, Art, and Rare Manuscripts.* New York: International Bibliophile Society, 1904.

See also: Nook Farm

Pastoralism

As a distinct genre, the pastoral became obsolete around 1800. Its attitudes, concepts, and topics, however, continued to be alive: the dialects of country vs. city, naiveté vs. corruption, natural vs. artificial, as well as the yearning for a place of freedom from worldly affairs and leisure for artistic activity, be it paradise, heaven, some exotic Happy Isles, or any spiritual Arcadia. This longing for peace, harmony, contentment, and happiness is usually expressed by someone exiled from such a state (cf. Virgil's "First Eclogue") and wandering the world—responding to his loss with elegiac reminiscences and to a restoration with ecstatic exultation.

Such were Mark Twain's reactions to his sense of alienation in the 1870s, which brought forth evocative recollections of his boyhood and established the themes of childhood and innocence. *The Adventures of Tom Sawyer* (1876) celebrates a carefree world of child's play in a prelapsarian, pre-Civil War America; its author felt it to be "simply a hymn put into prose form." *Adventures of Huckleberry Finn* (1885), however, shows the child in conflict with the same society. The clash of the innate goodness of a backwoods youth with the inhumane rules of civilization leads to exile, avoidance, and retreat; still the author felt a "sound heart" had won over a "deformed conscience." Sequels to these novels, published and unpublished, as well as *The Prince and the Pauper* (1882) and the Mysterious Stranger manuscripts (written 1897–1908) testify to Mark Twain's abiding interest in these themes as well as in child protagonists who tend to appear as possible saviors of a corrupt world.

Another touchstone of Mark Twain's pastoralism is the dualism of "pilot" and "passenger" ("Old Times on the Mississippi," 1875). The pilot deals expertly with the challenges of reality whereas the passenger reacts innocently to the beauty of the visible world and fails to perceive its dangers. His spontaneous enjoyment of the beautiful along with his sense of wonder and awe are the hallmark of many lyrical descriptions of landscapes, sights, and scenery throughout Mark Twain's writings, public and private. In these idylls (the erroneous, though long-accepted etymology is "small pictures"), where personal associations merge with pastoral topics, the author made the most varied and ample use of pastoralism. In fact, he seems to have entertained an idiosyncratic pattern, a genotype that spawned many phenotypes in the visual and aural descriptions,

especially of the travel books. Formulaic in its wording, the elevated style betrays an automatic writing suggestive of Mark Twain's improvisational working habits. At best, the mood is one of "tranquil ecstasy" (cf. the rafting episode in *A Tramp Abroad*, 1880, or, as a different benchmark, the "prose poem" on Hawaii, 1889), and the soul is found in happy accord with its surroundings. At worst, a single false note or a bitter punch line dissociates the soul from its happy state. More typically, authorial humor, irony, and sarcasm counterbalance the pastoral moment.

The growth of his pessimism notwithstanding, Mark Twain's pastoralism survives in the passenger's impressionist aesthetics (*Following the Equator*, 1897), though exultation frequently gives way to despair. Yet, the author cherishes his impulse all the more by denying reality its power over him and denouncing it as a bad dream, inventing better ones for himself: writing itself becomes a pastoral activity exploring death as the ultimate retreat ("My Platonic Sweetheart," *Extract from Captain Stormfield's Visit to Heaven*, 1909). The psychic root of all pastoralism, the quest for a home and for peace, must have held particular meaning for Mark Twain during his last years.

He shared much of his era's watered-down romanticism, nostalgia, and sentimentalism, but at the core of his own version is a distinct pastoral impulse. To be sure, he wrote no idylls of small-town country life as criticism of nineteenth-century industrialization and progress. His attitude toward either remained ambiguous. Nevertheless, he pursued the passenger's ideal of an aesthetically rewarding world by celebrating its wonders with ever more stylistic virtuosity. The majority of critics have analyzed the nexus between writer and pilot to evaluate Mark Twain's literary maturing, but it is worth noting that he never disavowed his affiliation with the passenger. Both, pilot and passenger, continue to serve as alter egos of the writer, take part in his development, and have their share in his authority.

Karl-Otto Strohmidel

BIBLIOGRAPHY

Harris, Susan K. *Mark Twain's Escape from Time: A Study of Patterns and Images.* Columbia: U of Missouri P, 1982.

Kruse, Horst H. "Realismus und Idylle: Zu einem Stilproblem Mark Twains." *Studien zur Englischen Philologie: Edgar Mertner zum 70. Geburtstag.* Ed. Herbert Mainusch and Dietrich Rolle. Frankfurt A.M., Bern, and Cirencester: Lang, 1979. 189–201.

Marx, Leo. "The Pilot and the Passenger: Landscape Conventions and the Style of *Huckleberry Finn.*" *American Literature* 28 (1956): 129–146.

Salomon, Roger B. *Twain and the Image of History.* New Haven, Conn.: Yale UP, 1961.

Smith, Henry Nash. *Mark Twain: The Development of a Writer.* Cambridge, Mass.: Harvard UP, 1962.

———. "Mark Twain's Images of Hannibal: From St. Petersburg to Eseldorf." *Texas Studies in English* 37 (1958): 3–23.

Spengemann, William C. *Mark Twain and the Backwoods Angel: The Matter of Innocence in the Works of Samuel L. Clemens.* Kent, Ohio: Kent State UP, 1966.

Stone, Albert E. *The Innocent Eye: Childhood in Mark Twain's Imagination.* New Haven, Conn.: Yale UP, 1961.

Strohmidel, Karl-Otto. *"Tranquil Ecstasy": Mark Twains pastorale Neigung und ihre literarische Gestaltung.* Amsterdam: Gruner, 1986.

See also: Childhood; Innocence

Pepys, Samuel
(1633–1703)

The famous English diarist Samuel Pepys was educated at Cambridge. He became a civil servant with the Admiralty until the Revolution of 1688 ended his career. He was twice elected to Parliament, was a fellow and once president of the Royal Society (1684), and was an accomplished amateur musician. His only publication is *Memoirs of the Navy* (1690). His *Diary*, which covers the period from 1660 to 1669, was written in various forms of cipher; it was first decoded and published in 1819.

According to A.B. Paine, Pepys's *Diary* was a perennial favorite of Mark Twain's, a work he read regularly and often, especially toward the end of his life. Two editions were found in his reconstructed library. Pepys's influence is apparent in Mark Twain's fictionalized diary pieces, e.g., "Shem's Diary" and "Methuselah's Diary." Baetzhold (80–87) demonstrates Pepys's influence on *Adventures of Huckleberry Finn* (1885) and other works. In view of Mark Twain's special interest in the *Diary*, surprisingly little critical attention has been given to the subject.

Fred Weldon

BIBLIOGRAPHY

Baetzhold, Howard G. *Mark Twain and John Bull: The British Connection.* Bloomington: Indiana UP, 1970.

Gribben, Alan. *Mark Twain's Library: A Reconstruction.* 2 vols. Boston: G.K. Hall, 1980.

Paine, Albert Bigelow. *Mark Twain: A Biography.* 3 vols. New York: Harper, 1912.

Personal Memoirs of U.S. Grant
(1885)

Ulysses Simpson Grant (1822–1885), graduate of West Point, officer in the Mexican War, officer and ultimately General in Chief of the Union armies in the Civil War, and eighteenth President of the United States (1869–1877), was also the author of a notable memoir that covers his background and youth, military education and earlier career, and his leadership in the Civil War. Mark Twain secured the contract for its publication, encouraged Grant during the composition of the work, oversaw the printing and binding of the book, and designed and guided a massive and successful sales campaign.

Twain interviewed Grant as early as 1868 and had intermittent contact with him over the next sixteen years. During a visit in 1881 Twain "tried hard . . . to get General Grant to agree to write his personal memoirs for publication" (*Mark Twain's Autobiography* 2:26). Grant, doubtful of his ability to write and sure such a work would have little appeal, would not agree. In November 1884 Twain discovered quite by accident that Grant had at last decided to turn author. Without delay, Twain visited Grant and discovered that *Century Magazine* had contracted for several articles and had offered a contract for a book. On the spot Twain offered much better terms for publication with Charles L. Webster, the publishing firm Twain had organized and still controlled. After consultation with several concerned people, Grant accepted Twain's terms and began work in February 1885.

By this time Grant was seriously ill with cancer of the throat and clearly had but a few months to live. Working steadily, sometimes writing and sometimes dictating, Grant completed the massive manuscript a few days before his death on 23 July 1885.

During the composition of the memoirs Mark Twain was deeply involved in all aspects of the project. He visited Grant frequently, dealt with the press, and supervised the preparations for printing, binding, and organizing a large network of canvassers to sell the books on the subscription plan. Twain predicted (with astonishing accuracy, as it turned out) that sales would amount to 300,000 two-volume sets. Suppliers of paper, print shops, and binderies had to be put under contract to complete the massive task within less than six months. Twain's notebooks of the time are full of complaints about the performance of Charles L. Webster, manager of the firm that bore his name, who was no doubt somewhat inept, was certainly not in robust health, and apparently was not competent to meet all the demands that Twain constantly showered upon him. Twain's notebooks also contain repeated calculations of the great profits to be expected, with a rising note of exultation as the returns came in from the far-flung crew of solicitors.

During the writing of the work and indeed for long after its issuance, insinuations in the press suggested that Twain "had taken an unfair advantage of the *Century* people and got the book away from them . . ." (*Mark Twain's Autobiography* 1:55). Twain prepared a reply, but did not succeed in having it published. In addition, the New York *World* claimed that

Grant was not actually writing the work, but had prepared notes to be written up by General Adam Badeau, Grant's wartime secretary, who had already written his own work, *Military History of U.S. Grant*. Grant wrote a refutation, which the *World* published.

Throughout the printing and binding process Twain feared that individual sheets or an entire set would be stolen and published or that rival biographies would diminish the sales of the finished volumes. This fear was not realized, nor did sales suffer from the appearance of competing biographies.

Ultimately, all obstacles were overcome; the first volume was issued on the scheduled date of 1 December 1885, the second on 1 March 1886. On 7 February 1886 Mrs. Julia Grant received an initial royalty check for $200,000, a figure that for many years stood as the largest single royalty amount ever paid. The total paid to Mrs. Grant was between $420,000 and $450,000.

The *Personal Memoirs of U.S. Grant* is a significant and durable contribution to the documentation of American history and to American literature. It has often and properly been praised for its straightforward, simple style. In addition, it is made vivid by Grant's remarkable recollection of detail and by his ability to order the narrative of complex events through a vision that mediates between the large framework of history and the telling local scene. It is a standard source for historians and a rewarding work for the general reader.

Lynn Altenbernd

BIBLIOGRAPHY

Badeau, Adam. *The Military History of Ulysses S. Grant.* 3 vols. New York: Appleton, 1868–1881.

Catton, Bruce. *Grant Moves South.* Boston: Little, Brown, 1960.

———. *Grant Takes Command.* Boston: Little, Brown, 1969.

The Civil War. Public Broadcasting Service television documentary. Prod. Ken Burns. 1990.

Clemens, Samuel L. *Mark Twain's Autobiography.* Ed. Albert B. Paine. 2 vols. New York: Harper, 1924.

Grant, Ulysses Simpson. *The Papers of U.S. Grant*. Ed. John Y. Simon. Carbondale: Southern Illinois UP, 1967-present.

———. *Personal Memoirs of U.S. Grant*. 2 vols. New York: Charles L. Webster, 1885–1886.

Lewis, Lloyd. *Captain Sam Grant*. Boston: Little, Brown, 1950.

McFeely, William S. *Grant: A Biography*. New York: Norton, 1981.

McPherson, James M. *Battle Cry of Freedom: The Civil War Era*. Vol. 6 of *The Oxford History of the United States*. New York: Oxford UP, 1988.

Williams, Kenneth P. *Lincoln Finds a General: A Military Study of the Civil War*. 5 vols. New York: Macmillan, 1949–1959.

Wilson, Edmund. "Northern Soldiers: Ulysses S. Grant." *Patriotic Gore: Studies in the Literature of the American Civil War*. By Wilson. New York: Oxford UP, 1962. 131–173.

See also: Civil War; Grant, Ulysses Simpson; Webster and Company, Charles L.

Personal Recollections of Joan of Arc
(1896)

One of Twain's longest works, *Personal Recollections of Joan of Arc* (1896) is the one he personally considered his best (Paine 2:1034). This next-to-last full-length publication by Twain covers the life of Joan from shortly after her birth in Domremy, France, in 1412 through her execution by burning at the stake in 1431. Unlike many of Twain's works that are based on personal experiences (the Matter of Hannibal), this work involved extensive research: reading histories, biographies, historical romances, and teaching himself the French language. In Twain's only full-length work to focus on a female, Joan of Arc—modeled after his favorite daughter, Susy—is characterized as capable, defiant, independent, dynamic, and courageous (Emerson 200).

Like many of Twain's works, the gestation period between the idea of *Joan of Arc* and actual publication date is lengthy. An apocryphal story has it that Twain's fascination with Joan of Arc began during his printing apprenticeship period (1848–1853) in Hannibal when a page from a history of Joan of Arc blew into his hands at age thirteen (Wecter 211). Not until 1892, after books by German, French, British, and American writers had established Joan of Arc as a cult figure, did Twain begin work on his manuscript (Emerson 195). From August 1892 when he began the work in Florence, Italy, until March 1893, Twain wrote feverishly and completed the first twenty-two chapters, approximately half of the final composition. Having covered Joan's life from her early years through the victorious siege of Orleans, he considered the work complete (Salomon 168). Pressing financial concerns necessitated several trips to the United States, and Twain did not return to the manuscript until August 1894 and only then after urging by his editors. In Paris in March 1895 he finally completed the manuscript (Stone 205–211). Regarding this as a "serious" work and not wanting to disappoint readers who expected humorous material, Twain insisted on anonymous publication. Thus monthly installments in *Harper's Magazine* that began in April 1895 and continued through April 1896 did not bear Twain's name. On 18 March 1896 Twain copyrighted the book version, and in May 1896 *Personal Recollections of Joan of Arc* was published simultaneously in England by Chatto and Windus and in the United States by Harper and Brothers with Twain's name on the spine and front cover but not on the title page. Instead, the title page cited as author Sieur Louis de Conte, the narrator with initials identical to Samuel L. Clemens (Emerson 197).

Told in 1492 by the eighty-two-year-old Conte, former secretary to Joan of Arc, the narrative employs the technique reminiscent of "Old Times on the Mississippi" (1875) and *Roughing It* (1872), other works that treat youthful experiences from an older, more mature perspective. Like other Twain works, *Joan of Arc* exemplifies both democratic and Protestant characteristics (Spengemann 117). Although born and raised in Catholic France, Joan is symbolic of Protestant ideals: a protestor of authority and government, an individual who champions democratic ideals, one devoted to the concept of work and the work ethic. She exemplifies her democratic inclinations by her compassion for common people and her sympathy for the oppressed. She rebels against tyranny and injustice. This work also exemplifies the tension between the innocent, idyllic youthful world and the ominous, hypocritical adult world, another theme characteristic of Twain's best fiction. For one critic, Joan of Arc is the living embodiment of the ideas of the fictional Huck Finn (Wiggins 112–113). Beyond these thematic parallels with other Twain fiction is his unique perception of Joan of Arc, a female deviating from such models as Aunt Polly, Widow Douglas, and prepubescent females of earlier fiction.

Although themes reminiscent of Twain's classic material suggest the importance of this work to the author, Twain's scholarship extends the importance (Stone 209–211). More than fourteen books in his library deal specifically either with this figure or with the historical period. From marginal notes in his copies of *La Vierge Lorraine, Jeanne d'Arc son histoire au point de vue de l'heroisme, de la sainteté et du martyre* by Armand de Chabannes; *Joan of Arc* by Ronald Gower; *History of the English People* by John Richard Green; *Jeanne d'Arc* by Jules Michelet; *Joan of Arc* by John O'Hagan; *Jeanne d'Arc* by Marius Sepet; and *Joan of Arc, The Maid* by Janet Tuckey, Twain's interest in the figure is evident. Of these seven works, Twain, in fact, was influenced most by two: the French historian Michelet and the British writer Janet Tuckey. Although reliant on his sources for factual details and accuracy of Joan's life, Twain in *Joan of Arc* moves beyond his sources to do what he does best: invent characters, modify details, develop setting and embellish situations, and interpret character. Twain's Joan, for example, with her courage, energy, individuality, conviction, and drive is more in keeping with the Protestant American than with the medieval Catholic of Michelet's portrayal. In her defiance of rank and status she is different from Tuckey's Joan.

As the least known and least read of all Twain's major writings (Stone 204), *Joan of Arc* has been regarded by twentieth-century critics as lacking imagination, being sentimental and too derivative—in short, an aberration. In 1896, however, when three works on *Joan of Arc* were published, Twain's was singled out for its scholarship, truthful treatment, and merits of handling source material, style, character invention, detail, and seriousness. More positive critical attention in this century has focused on the charisma, compassion, defiant yet gentle nature, and tragic death: in short, Joan of Arc as Christlike or the divine child (Mott 251). In its portrayal of idealism, hope for the downtrodden and oppressed, contempt for pretense, and fierce conviction of the basic goodness of common people, *Joan of Arc* stands outside the critical perception of Twain's despair and pessimism in the 1890s. For its focus on and treatment of a female (Zwarg 60–62) and for its essential optimism and idealism regarding human potential in a period when many of his other works reflect pessimism and despair, Twain's *Joan of Arc* deserves wider attention, reexamination, and reappraisal.

Thomas A. Maik

BIBLIOGRAPHY

Clemens, Samuel L. *Personal Recollections of Joan of Arc.* Westport, Conn.: Greenwood P, 1980.

Cox, James M. *Mark Twain: The Fate of Humor.* Princeton, N.J.: Princeton UP, 1966.

Emerson, Everett. *The Authentic Mark Twain: A Literary Biography of Samuel L. Clemens.* Philadelphia: U of Pennsylvania P, 1984.

Gribben, Alan. *Mark Twain's Library: A Reconstruction.* 2 vols. Boston: G.K. Hall, 1980.

Mott, Bertram, Jr. "Twain's Joan: A Divine Anomaly." *Études Anglaises* 23 (1970): 246–255.

Paine, Albert Bigelow. *Mark Twain: A Biography.* 3 vols. New York: Harper, 1912.

Salomon, Roger B. *Twain and the Image of History.* New Haven, Conn.: Yale UP, 1961.

Spengemann, William C. *Mark Twain and the Backwoods Angel: The Matter of Innocence in the Works of Samuel L. Clemens.* Kent, Ohio: Kent State UP, 1966.

Stone, Albert E., Jr. *The Innocent Eye: Childhood in Mark Twain's Imagination.* New Haven, Conn.: Yale UP, 1961.

Wecter, Dixon. *Sam Clemens of Hannibal.* Boston: Houghton Mifflin, 1952.

Wiggins, Robert A. *Mark Twain: Jackleg Novelist.* Seattle: U of Washington P, 1964.

Zwarg, Christina. "Woman as Force in Twain's *Joan of Arc:* The Unwordable Fascination." *Criticism* 27 (1985): 57–72.

See also: Catholicism; Joan of Arc; Women

"Petrified Man, The"
(1862)

Mark Twain wrote the hoax of "The Petrified Man" soon after he joined the *Territorial Enterprise* in Virginia City, Nevada, in 1862. Although no extant copy of the original printing exists, two other newspapers attribute the story to the 4 October 1862 issue of the *Enterprise* (*ET&S* 155). Twelve papers in California and Nevada printed it, but only four of these recognized its humor (*ET&S* 158).

The discovery of a preserved prehistoric man could easily fool a reader who overlooked the implausibility of the physical facts and the judge's actions or jest intended in the stony finger crooked over the stony nose. Twain's joke on Sewall, a local figure of authority in both mining and law, and the gullibility of the newspapers pleased the Westerners and spread the reputation of both the *Enterprise* and the author. In commenting on the events surrounding the satire in 1870, Twain recalls his delight in sending Sewall marked newspapers from all over the world concerning the Petrified Man (*Sketches, New and Old* 319–320).

"A Washoe Joke," as the piece was titled by the San Francisco *Daily Evening Bulletin*, demonstrates Twain's early ability to blend fact and foolishness. Such humorous works helped establish his growing reputation and foreshadowed his later social satires (Branch 83).

Sandra Gravitt

BIBLIOGRAPHY

Benson, Ivan. *Mark Twain's Western Years.* Stanford, Calif.: Stanford UP, 1938.

Branch, Edgar M. *The Literary Apprenticeship of Mark Twain.* Urbana: U of Illinois P, 1950.

Clemens, Samuel L. *Mark Twain's Sketches, New and Old.* Hartford, Conn.: American Publishing, 1875.

———. *The Works of Mark Twain: Early Tales & Sketches, Volume 1 (1851–1864).* Ed. Edgar M. Branch and Robert H. Hirst. Berkeley: U of California P, 1979. 155–159.

Paine, Albert Bigelow. *Mark Twain: A Biography.* 3 vols. New York: Harper, 1912.

See also: De Quille, Dan; Hoax; Virginia City *Territorial Enterprise*

Phelps, Elizabeth Stuart (Ward)
(1844–1911)

(Married Herbert Dickinson Ward, 1888. Pseudonyms: E.S. Phelps, Mary Adams, Elizabeth Stuart Phelps.) Phelps was christened Mary Gray Phelps, but she took her mother's name (Elizabeth Wooster Stuart Phelps was also a writer) sometime after the mother's death. Growing up in Andover, Massachusetts, Phelps began publishing in the early 1860s. Her first publications were "Sunday school books"—didactic literature designed to teach correct behavior and instill Christian values. *The Gates Ajar* (1868) and its sequel, *The Gates Between* (1887), were long the best known of Phelps's works; popular best-sellers, these works also inspired contempt among secular critics, contemporary and later. Only recently has feminist criticism provided the means for understanding Phelps's Christian radicalism: in these texts Phelps provides emotional power to women, whose concerns official Christianity did not, she felt, reflect. Best known of Phelps's works today are *The Silent Partner* (1871), *The Story of Avis* (1877), and *Doctor Zay* (1882), all secular, feminist, texts.

Mark Twain was one of the secular contemporaries who satirized *The Gates Ajar.* There is no record of his having read it; if he did, he refused to process it as Phelps intended. In 1897 and again in 1906 Twain claimed that "Captain Stormfield's Visit to Heaven" (*Harper's Magazine*, December 1907–January 1908) was intended as a satire on *The Gates Ajar*. Robert Rees and Franklin R. Rogers suggest, rightly, in this writer's opinion, that Twain confused "Captain Stormfield" with another early manuscript, "The Story of Mamie Grant, the Child-Missionary" (*Notebooks & Journals* I:499–506), which is much more clearly a parody of *The Gates Ajar*.

Susan K. Harris

BIBLIOGRAPHY

Clemens, Samuel L. *Mark Twain's Notebooks & Journals, Volume I (1855–1873)*. Ed. Frederick Anderson, Michael B. Frank, and Kenneth M. Sanderson. Berkeley: U of California P, 1975.

———. *Mark Twain's Satires & Burlesques*. Ed. Franklin R. Rogers. Berkeley: U of California P, 1967.

Gribben, Alan. *Mark Twain's Library: A Reconstruction*. 2 vols. Boston: G.K. Hall, 1980.

Kessler, Carol Farley. *Elizabeth Stuart Phelps*. Boston: Twayne, 1982.

Rees, Robert. "*Captain Stormfield's Visit to Heaven* and *The Gates Ajar*." *English Language Notes* 7.3 (March 1970): 197–202.

See also: Condensed Novels; *Extract from Captain Stormfield's Visit to Heaven*; Providence; Religion; "Story of Mamie Grant, the Child-Missionary, The"

Phelps, Silas

Although Tom Sawyer's absent-minded uncle Silas Phelps preaches "the bladedest jumbledest idiotic sermons" (*Tom Sawyer, Detective* 415), his main trait is decency. He first appears in *Adventures of Huckleberry Finn* (1885) as an Arkansas preacher who owns the small cotton farm and sawmill where Huck and Tom plot Jim's escape from slavery. Phelps returns as Parson Silas, charged with the murder of Jubiter Dunlap, in *Tom Sawyer, Detective* (1896). Silas is also mentioned in "Huck Finn and Tom Sawyer Among the Indians" (written 1884)

and "Tom Sawyer's Conspiracy" (written 1897).

Phelps demonstrates that some southern masters treated slaves kindly (Howell 9), yet both *Huck Finn* and *Tom Sawyer, Detective*, engage him mainly as a foil to Tom Sawyer. When Tom and Huck exploit his absent-mindedness by plugging up rat holes and playing with the contents of his pockets, among other pranks, they deflect interest from uncomfortable issues about Jim's enslavement to simple enjoyment of Tom's jokes. Phelps's sermon on Acts 17 debunks the ideal of the good slaveholder (Arner 12); so does the conflict between his conscientious search for Jim's master and his blindness to the boys' rescue efforts. He remains a victim of his own conscientiousness in *Tom Sawyer, Detective*, but his concession that he probably did murder Jubiter makes Tom's solution of the mystery—and the courtroom "effects" that go with it—all the more spectacular.

Judith Yaross Lee

BIBLIOGRAPHY

Arner, Robert D. "Acts Seventeen and *Huckleberry Finn*: A Note on Silas Phelps' Sermon." *Mark Twain Journal* 16.2 (1972): 12.

Clemens, Samuel L. *The Adventures of Tom Sawyer, Tom Sawyer Abroad, Tom Sawyer, Detective*. Ed. John C. Gerber, Paul Baender, and Terry Firkins. Berkeley: U of California P, 1980.

Howell, Elmo. "Uncle Silas Phelps: A Note on Mark Twain's Characterization." *Mark Twain Journal* 14.2 (1968): 8–12.

See also: *Adventures of Huckleberry Finn*; *Tom Sawyer, Detective*

Philosophy

Mark Twain's earliest philosophical ideas, like those of many American writers in the nineteenth century, were shaped by the Christian teachings of his mother and the church. Scholars have disagreed about the extent to which Jane Clemens's frontier Calvinism shaped Twain's philosophy, but his early religious instruction certainly impressed upon him the notion that human nature is evil and a corresponding sense of personal guilt. The stern Calvinistic creed, however, was diluted by his mother's tolerant spirit and his father's skepticism. John Clemens held his own strict moral convictions, but as a freethinker, he remained aloof from the church and its doctrines.

Given these conflicting religious values, it is not surprising that, as a young man in his early twenties, Twain was open to the skeptical ideas he encountered in Thomas Paine's *The Age of Reason* (1794). Based on Newtonian science, Paine's deistic philosophy was rather old-fashioned by the 1850s, but as a cub pilot on the Mississippi River, Twain read it "with fear and hesitation," shocked by the "fearlessness and wonderful power" with which Paine challenged accepted truths (Paine 3:1445). The "deist's bible" armed him with the intellectual weapons to attack the Calvinistic theology he had already begun to question. In an 1870 manuscript articulating his personal philosophy, Twain contrasted the "irascible, vindictive" God of the Bible to the "true God," whom he described as benevolent, rational, just, and changeless (Paine 1:412). Twain also adopted the deistic reverence for science with its sense of an expansive and well-ordered universe. Writing to Olivia Langdon shortly before their marriage in 1870, he contrasted the "pigmy little world" of the earth with the "millions & millions of worlds that hold their majestic courses above our heads" (*Love Letters* 133). Humanity's false sense of importance in relation to the immensity of the universe became one of Twain's favorite themes, dramatized in such late pieces as "Was the World Made for Man?" (1903) and the microcosmic fantasy, "Three Thousand Years Among the Microbes" (1905).

By the 1870s, however, science itself was struggling with new evidence that replaced the fixed absolutes of Newton with a random process of evolution. Twain read Darwin's *The Descent of Man* (1871), and although marginal notations in his copy of the book indicate that he responded favorably, it was years before he assimilated its most radical implica-

tions. What he immediately grasped was Darwin's claim that human efforts to relieve the suffering of others originate not from altruistic motives but from the impulse to relieve one's own feelings of pain aroused by contact with suffering. Twain's developing theory of morality was further influenced by his reading of W.E.H. Lecky's *History of European Morals* (1869). Besides the record of atrocities committed in the name of church and crown to perpetuate the power structures of feudal Europe, the book introduced Twain to the contemporary debate between utilitarian and intuitionist moral philosophers. An advocate of intuitionism, Lecky argued that the innate ability to distinguish between right and wrong revealed the imprint of God upon every individual. Utilitarians denied such innate perceptions, arguing instead that morality is based entirely upon human experience. Despite his admiration for Lecky, Twain found utilitarian philosophy more attractive; the claim that moral behavior is based on self-interest confirmed his suspicion that excessive piety and moralism often masked an underlying selfishness and hypocrisy. Still, Twain found some of Lecky's intuitionist arguments convincing, particularly his claim that conscience and moral intuitions are not identical, since the intuitive sense of right and wrong can be overshadowed by training in society's values. Lecky's considerable influence upon Twain has been traced in "The Facts Concerning the Recent Carnival of Crime in Connecticut" (1876), *The Prince and the Pauper* (1882), and other works. As Walter Blair has shown, Twain's ambivalence toward Lecky also shapes the central action of *Adventures of Huckleberry Finn* (1885), where Huck's response to the central moral dilemma reflects both utilitarian and intuitionist ideas.

By the time *Huckleberry Finn* was published, the well-ordered machinery of Twain's deistic universe had begun to seem less benign. In a speech titled "What Is Happiness?" (February 1883) he argued that the individual is "merely a machine automatically functioning." His short essay on "The Character of Man"

(1885) went even further, describing man as "the tail-end of a tape-worm eternity of ancestors" reaching back to "our source in the monkeys" (*What Is Man?* 61). The Darwinian ideas and images he had pondered in the early 1870s and written about privately in the 1880s also turned up in his next novel, *A Connecticut Yankee in King Arthur's Court* (1889). Frustrated by his unsuccessful efforts to break the power of the church in medieval England, Hank Morgan declares that "[t]raining is all there is *to* a person . . . there is no such thing as nature; what we call by that misleading name is merely heredity and training" (208). In the last of the great Mississippi Writings, *Pudd'nhead Wilson* (1894), Twain developed these same themes in the context of a devastating critique of the South's obsessions about racial identity and social class.

Twain's growing pessimism was reinforced by a series of personal misfortunes in the mid-1890s. The most traumatic of these, the death of his oldest daughter, Susy, in 1896, provoked a bitter Twain to blame his loss on the cruel designs of a malevolent deity. Until this point Twain's philosophical ideas had deepened and enriched his storytelling; afterward, they dominated his work.

In *What Is Man?* (1906), Twain's most ambitious attempt to construct a systematic philosophy, he developed more fully the ideas he had been contemplating for several years: that man is a machine; that instinct and training rigidly determine an individual's destiny; that free will is an illusion; that good deeds are motivated by the instinct for self-preservation; and that the Moral Sense, far from elevating man above the other animals, degrades him because it takes away his innocence. Yet, in the context of this profoundly pessimistic philosophy, Twain insists that the only appropriate response is to "train your ideals *upward*" in order to gain happiness through conduct that benefits "your neighbor and the community" (169).

This contradiction between Twain's mechanistic philosophy and his moral idealism runs through much of his late work. In "The Victims" (written early 1900s) and "Refuge of the Derelicts" (written 1905–1906), for example, Twain structures his fictional environment on the theory of natural selection, with human beings taking their place alongside other species in a grim competition for survival. But unlike social Darwinists, who believed that the rigors of competition improved the species, Twain could never reconcile the cruelty of the evolutionary process with his humane values. Though he found in Darwinism a powerful expression of the greed and injustice that dominated his world, he was never content with that world, and he clung to the hope of solidarity and human community as an alternative to the actuality of Darwinian individualism.

One of the curiosities of Twain's late career is that the growth of his philosophical determinism did not extinguish his efforts to bring about political and social change. Always fond of the underdog, Twain had celebrated the energy and wit of his vernacular characters, often at the expense of the wealthy and educated. Nothing drew more fire from him than the inherited privileges and artificial class distinctions of aristocratic societies. Louis Budd has pointed out, however, that as a property owner in the affluent Nook Farm community, Twain shared his neighbors' complacent, upper-middle-class political values. His sympathy for the poor could be intense, but it never led him seriously to question the institutions of private ownership and free enterprise. He maintained friendships with wealthy capitalists like Andrew Carnegie and Henry H. Rogers, the Standard Oil executive who became his financial adviser in the 1890s. Still, his hatred of injustice made him increasingly uncomfortable with the abuses of unrestrained capitalism and prompted his scathing attacks upon Western imperialism in "To the Person Sitting in Darkness" (1901), *King Leopold's Soliloquy* (1905), and other political satires of the late period. His strongest condemnation was directed toward the so-called Christian nations, including his own, who rationalized their exploitation of colonial peoples by claiming to bring them "the blessings of civilization." At times Twain's disillusionment took the form of solipsistic fantasies, most of them unfinished, in which dream and reality become indistinguishable. In one of the Mysterious Stranger manuscripts (*Mark Twain's Mysterious Stranger Manuscripts*, 1969) the title character declares, that "Nothing exists but You. And You are but a *Thought* . . . wandering forlorn among the empty eternities!" (405). The philosophical nihilism of these moods takes place among other ideas Twain explored, not as a final, conclusive truth, but as an indication of the range of ideas that stimulated his imagination. Though he never came to rest in a permanent philosophical homeland, his quest for truth kept him actively engaged in a fight against ignorance, superstition, and cruelty long after his artistic powers had begun to decline.

Stan Poole

BIBLIOGRAPHY

Baetzhold, Howard G. *Mark Twain and John Bull: The British Connection.* Bloomington: Indiana UP, 1970.

Blair, Walter. *Mark Twain & Huck Finn.* Berkeley: U of California P, 1960.

Budd, Louis J. *Mark Twain: Social Philosopher.* Bloomington: Indiana UP, 1962.

Clemens, Samuel L. *A Connecticut Yankee in King Arthur's Court.* Ed. Bernard L. Stein. Berkeley: U of California P, 1979.

———. *The Love Letters of Mark Twain.* Ed. Dixon Wecter. New York: Harper, 1949.

———. *Mark Twain on the Damned Human Race.* Ed. Janet Smith. New York: Hill and Wang, 1962.

———. *Mark Twain's Autobiography.* Ed. Albert B. Paine. 2 vols. New York: Harper, 1924.

———. *Mark Twain's Fables of Man.* Ed. John S. Tuckey. Berkeley: U of California P, 1972.

———. *Mark Twain's Mysterious Stranger Manuscripts.* Ed. William M. Gibson. Berkeley: U of California P, 1969.

———. *"What Is Man?" and Other Philosophical Writings.* Ed. Paul Baender. Berkeley: U of California P, 1973.

Cummings, Sherwood. *Mark Twain and Science: Adventures of a Mind.* Baton Rouge: Louisiana State UP, 1988.

Hill, Hamlin. *Mark Twain: God's Fool.* New York: Harper & Row, 1973.

Macnaughton, William R. *Mark Twain's Last Years As a Writer.* Columbia: U of Missouri P, 1979.

Paine, Albert Bigelow. *Mark Twain: A Biography.* 3 vols. New York: Harper, 1912.

See also: Calvinism; Darwin, Charles; Determinism; Imperialism; Lecky, William Edward Hartpole; Paine, Thomas; Religion; Science

Photographs

"Just Stunning" is how Mark Twain described himself in a letter dated 5 March 1907 to his daughter Clara. He had dressed in white broadcloth full evening wear at Robert Collier's dinner with "a lot of people" in attendance. His first public appearance in a dazzling white suit, out of season, had occurred in December 1906 as he removed his dark overcoat in a dimly lit congressional committee room in Washington. Twain appeared there, white from his feet to his silvery head, to lobby on behalf of copyright laws. The effect was electric. That image of the author endures in photographs.

Mark Twain was theatrical and viewed his life as a series of dramatic events. The first photograph of him was a daguerreotype taken in 1851 at age fifteen when he was a printer's devil. He coyly holds a compositor's stick to look like his belt buckle, spelling out in large type his first name, "Sam." This first photograph was made five years after Abraham Lincoln had his first photographic image made. The last film record of Twain was exposed as he lay in state in his casket in 1910 at the Brick Church in New York City; he was dressed in his white suit. The number of photographs between his first and last is quite large—approximately 650. Yet Twain is seldom seen smiling. He said to Elizabeth Wallace, "I think a photograph is a most important document; and there is nothing more damning to go down to posterity than a smile caught and fixed forever."

The recognition of the appeal of Twain's image began in the early 1870s. His portraits were used to advertise a number of commercial products and services: a scrap book, dry goods, a restaurant, tobacco premiums, a pharmacy, plumbers—and of course, cigars. By the time *Life on the Mississippi* appeared in 1883 he was universally recognized. Most of the advertisements of these two decades used etchings, engravings, and chromolithographs. The photographs taken during this period were generally "studio sittings" that produced *carte-de-visite* and cabinet-size poses. One 1874 stereopticon card shows him at work writing. Twain detested a studio portrait taken in 1880 by Sarony because he complained it made him look like a "gorilla in an overcoat." A daring pose in the 1880s shows him shirtless. In 1885 he appeared in a white serge suit with his still auburn hair—not quite the flamboyant "all white" costume of his later years.

"Kodaking," or snapshot taking, increased in the 1890s. Mark Twain was photographed over forty times in a series of more than 120 pictures taken by Major James B. Pond on a trip in the summer of 1895. Twain and his party traveled across North America on his famous world tour to recover from the great American sin—bankruptcy.

One of the most picturesque figures in nineteenth-century literature, he began to appear in photographs during the latter part of its final decade in *McClure's*, *Ladies Home Journal*, and *St. Nicholas* magazines. His image as the people's author grew.

Twain writes facetiously about the history of photography in a 1901 unfinished manuscript describing the imaginary world of Eddypus. He discusses the supposedly forgotten "Dagger, Dugger, or Dagueerre," whose sun pictures disappeared from tin plates due to witchcraft. In the historian's muddled version, several people with black cats were put on trial and the witch madness ended. Dagger then fixed images on the plates with silver nitrate, followed by a Turkish bath and a collodion skin. He patented the process and, guesses the historian, subsequently produced paper photographs, electrical pictures, tele-

scopic photographs of stars, and photographs of the wandering spirits of the departed.

Half-tone photographs of Twain began to appear in newspapers at the turn of the century. The New York *World*, the *Herald*, and Hearst's *Journal* covered him at everything from the Yale-Princeton game to celebrity dinners and a 1902 visit at his Hannibal boyhood home. A portrait of Twain appeared on the front cover of the 1901 book *Famous Authors and Their Books*. Harper and Brothers produced a souvenir photographic booklet to commemorate his seventieth birthday dinner in New York. A new peak of celebrity was established as the New York *Times* in 1906 printed a photograph of Twain in bed, bedecked in his white nightgown. America's most famous humorist posed in academic robes, a bathing suit, a motor car, with cats, young girls, Woodrow Wilson, Nicola Tesla, and Helen Keller.

The first literary biography using photographs was *Mark Twain* by Archibald Henderson in 1911, with pictures by Alvin Langdon Coburn. Albert Bigelow Paine followed in 1912 with *Mark Twain: A Biography*, a three-volume authorized biography, containing many photographs taken by Paine. In 1960 Milton Meltzer employed over 600 photographs and illustrations in *Mark Twain Himself*. The hundreds of preserved images of this immortal literary master differ so very widely in their effect that they could support almost any theory about Twain's character and spirit. The photographs in Hamlin Hill's book, *Mark Twain: God's Fool* (1973), supported his portrayal of a vain, domineering "king." Likewise, John Seelye's *Mark Twain in the Movies* (1977) reinforced Hill's work and provided fresh views of Twain. Louis Budd's well-illustrated *Our Mark Twain* (1983) demonstrated how Twain's posturing worked and also probed the meanings of his white-suited public personality.

Mark Twain in the camera's eye is discussed in "Visions and Revisions," a study in progress by James Waller. More than 600 images of Twain photographs are located in the Mark Twain Project at The Bancroft Library, University of California at Berkeley. The Mark Twain Memorial in Hartford has approximately 450 images, and the Mark Twain Boyhood Home in Hannibal possesses at least twenty-five photographs. The Clifton Waller Barrett Collection in the Alderman Library at the University of Virginia includes 135 images, and the Beinecke Library at Yale holds 330 images of Twain. Vassar has about 25, and the New York Public Library lists approximately 45 images.

Mark Twain's immortal charisma and endearing chutzpah are both captured on photographs. A colored photograph of him in his white suit and Oxford robes taken by Alvin Langdon Coburn especially catches this charming combination. The image of the gleaming white suit and the white head is dramatic. One photo that Twain particularly liked was the "Tapestry" photo taken by Frederic B. Hyde in 1908. The mottling of the background was caused by adding menthol late in the developing process. Twain admired the eerie photograph so much that he made postcards of it. To the very end Twain rearranged his visual image to take advantage of one of the most revolutionary technological developments of his time. In one portrait sitting when asked to hold a book, Twain said, "I suppose the book looks better, but a cigar would be more like me."

Nick Karanovich

BIBLIOGRAPHY

Budd, Louis J. *Our Mark Twain: The Making of His Public Personality*. Philadelphia: U of Pennsylvania P, 1983.

Henderson, Archibald. *Mark Twain*. London: Duckworth, 1911.

Hill, Hamlin. *Mark Twain: God's Fool*. New York: Harper & Row, 1973.

Howells, William Dean. *My Mark Twain: Reminiscences and Criticisms*. New York: Harper, 1910.

Meltzer, Milton. *Mark Twain Himself: A Pictoral Biography*. New York: Crowell, 1960.

Paine, Albert Bigelow. *Mark Twain: A Biography*. 3 vols. New York: Harper, 1912.

Seelye, John. *Mark Twain in the Movies*. New York: Viking P, 1977.

Phrenology

Mark Twain's interest in phrenology as a predictor of character and an object of satire lasted all his adult life. This crude faculty psychology was invented in the 1790s by the Viennese anatomist Franz Joseph Gall, who located some thirty putative faculties of animal drives, emotions, intellect, perception, and spirituality in specific areas of the brain's hemispheres and postulated that the development of each of the brain's faculties was measurable by its protuberance on the skull's surface. Thus a well-developed faculty of amativeness would create a measurable "bump" near the nape of the neck. By calibrating the size and contours of the skull, and observing physical traits, phrenological examiners could develop personality profiles.

From the 1830s onward phrenology had a vogue among the American masses and such devotees as Henry Ward Beecher and Horace Mann as an analytical methodology and a social panacea. As a pseudoscientific catchall, the phrenological "system" incorporated ideas from the temperaments (the four "humors"), physiognomy, eugenics, and health and social reforms. By mid-century tens of thousands had been phrenologized or had read manuals of phrenological self-analysis. The phrenological parlors of Fowler and Wells were a great tourist attraction when Clemens visited New York City in 1853. In the 1850s Fowler and Wells books were available in Hannibal, and at least one of their phrenologists is known to have visited there. In 1855 Clemens read a phrenological manual by George Sumner Weaver, copied out passages on the temperaments, and partially formulated a favorable self-analysis of his traits. (Similarly, Edgar Allan Poe and Walt Whitman advertised their phrenological traits to prove their artistic mettle.) An 1872 phrenological examination in London by the renowned phrenologist Lorenzo N. Fowler prompted Twain's autobiographical comment that this examination "gave me a prejudice against phrenology that has lasted until now" (Neider 69). "The Secret History of Eddypus" (written 1901–1902), belittling the pretensions of phrenologists to analyze the human mind and character, calls them "damned asses" (61). According to Twain's autobiography, not recognizing Twain, Fowler had found his organ of mirthfulness to be deficient (a "cavity"). Reexamined later, when Fowler knew his identity, Clemens's mirthfulness was declared to be a "Mount Everest" (Neider 69–73). In view of Fowler's expertise in mnemonics, says Stern (183), the story is questionable. Clemens may have been "phrenologized" again in 1885. An astute 1901 analysis by Jessie A. Fowler probed close to Clemens's tragic nature; no record exists of his reaction.

Although his library contained several phrenological volumes, Clemens never mastered the technics of phrenology or sympathized with its eugenic or reformist tendencies. And phrenology played no major role in the fiction despite some satirical allusions. Best known are "a phrenologist and a mesmerist" who come to town in *The Adventures of Tom Sawyer* (1876) (chapter 22) and the scoundrelly Duke in *Adventures of Huckleberry Finn* (1885) who "take[s] a turn at phrenology and mesmerism" (chapter 19).

Harold Aspiz

BIBLIOGRAPHY

Clemens, Samuel L. *The Autobiography of Mark Twain.* Ed. Charles Neider. New York: Harper, 1959.

———. "The Secret History of Eddypus." *Mark Twain's Fables of Man.* By Clemens. Ed. John S. Tuckey. Berkeley: U of California P, 1972. 348–353.

Gribben, Alan. "Mark Twain, Phrenology, and the 'Temperaments': A Study of Pseudoscientific Influence." *American Quarterly* 24 (1972): 44–68.

———. *Mark Twain's Library: A Reconstruction.* 2 vols. Boston: G.K. Hall, 1980.

Stern, Madeleine B. *Heads & Headlines: The Phrenological Fowlers.* Norman: U of Oklahoma P, 1971.

See also: Mental Telepathy/Extrasensory Perception; Occult; Science

Picaresque

As applied to literature, the term "picaresque" is usually defined in one of three ways: (1) a specifically Spanish prose genre, i.e., novels written for the most part in the sixteenth and seventeenth centuries, centered around the adventures of a *picaro* (a low-life, often criminal character), set in realistically plebian social contexts, and narrated episodically in plain, broad, frequently satirical style; (2) novels directly influenced by and sometimes patterned after the Spanish tales just mentioned, again usually structured episodically; and (3) fiction produced at any time in recorded history that recounts, in episodic form, the adventures of a rascally hero (or heroine): the earliest example cited is Apuleius's *The Golden Ass* (second century A.D.).

Lazarillo de Tormes (1554) begins the specifically Spanish genre, followed by the first fully picaresque novel, Mateo Aleman's *Guzman de Alfarache* (1599–1604, translated in 1622 under the revealing title *The Rogue*). The height of the genre was reached in Francisco de Quevedo's *El Buscon* (*The Swindler* 1626, though probably written roughly twenty years earlier). Cervantes's *Don Quixote* (1605 and 1615) is related to but not part of the genre.

Many European and American novels show the clear influence of the genre, from Johann Jakob Grimmelshausen's *Simplicissimus* (1669), Alain-René Lesage's *Gil Blas* (1715–1735), Daniel Defoe's *Moll Flanders* (1722), Tobias Smollett's *Roderick Random* (1748), Henry Fielding's *Tom Jones* (1749), and *Les Mémoires de Vidocq* (1828) to Saul Bellow's *The Adventures of Augie March* (1953) and Thomas Mann's *The Confessions of Felix Krull, Confidence Man* (1954).

In its third and loosest usage, picaresque need not characterize the whole of a novel but may also be applied to an aspect or to only a part of the whole, or to a tendency, as in "a flavor of the picaresque" or even "a whiff of the picaresque." First used in English in 1810, picaresque has for the last hundred years been used in nonliterary contexts to mean "having an affection for the roguish." It is in this loosest sense that one views Twain and the picaresque. He was fascinated by Cervantes's *Don Quixote*, but for his uses of the picaresque tradition one can most profitably examine *The Prince and the Pauper* (1882) and *Connecticut Yankee* (1889). The trip downriver in *Adventures of Huckleberry Finn* (1885) also contains characteristics of the picaresque as loosely defined.

Burton Raffel

BIBLIOGRAPHY

Blackburn, Alexander. *The Myth of the Picaro: Continuity and Transformation of the Picaresque Novel, 1554–1954*. Chapel Hill: U of North Carolina P, 1979.

Dunn, Peter N. *The Spanish Picaresque Novel*. Boston: Twayne, 1979.

Parker, Alexander Augustine. *Literature and the Delinquent: The Picaresque Novel in Spain and Europe, 1599–1753*. Edinburgh: U of Edinburgh P, 1967.

Sieber, Harry. *The Picaresque*. London: Methuen, 1977.

See also: Cervantes, Saveedra, Miguel de; Rabelais, François

Pilgrims

"Pilgrims" in *The Innocents Abroad* (1869) is what Mark Twain calls the officiously pious members of the *Quaker City* excursion, often the butt of his ridicule and satire. The term is also connotative of the Pilgrim Fathers, who in 1620 landed at Plymouth, whence the name of the Brooklyn church—"Plymouth Church of the Pilgrims"—where the excursion originated. The hymnal used aboard by the *Quaker City* believers at prayer meetings was *The Plymouth Collection of Hymns and Tunes: For the Use of Christian Congregations* (1856). The author's close comrades—the "night-hawks," given to smoking, cards, whiskey, and late hours—Mark Twain, in mock acceptance of the pilgrims' judgment, calls the "sinners." Henry Nash Smith's study shows that the opposition of pilgrim and sinner runs through much of *Innocents Abroad*.

At the zoo in Marseilles Twain and his fellow sinners are vastly amused at a "preposterously uncomely bird," with "close-fitting wings like the tails of a dress-coat," under which he appears to be hiding his hands. He exudes "gravity, . . . self-righteousness, and . . . self-complacency." They dub him "The Pilgrim."

Later, Twain's treatment goes beyond such light-hearted ridicule. During the trip through Palestine on horseback, Twain and three fellow sinners are thrown in with several pilgrims, whose behavior they find contemptible. These zealous horsemen drive their mounts hard one day to avoid having to travel the next day, the Sabbath. Wishing to boat on Galilee, they haggle with a boatman over the fare until he sails off without them. They then berate one another for their foolish failure.

A pilgrim especially obnoxious to Twain was Captain Charles C. Duncan, prime mover of the expedition at Plymouth Church and during the voyage. Years later Twain's antipathy to Duncan erupted into a verbal feud in the newspapers. Twain called Duncan a "canting hypocrite," full of "sham godliness" and "dripping false piety and pharisaical prayers." Walter Blair has shown Duncan to be a prototype of the King in *Adventures of Huckleberry Finn* (1885).

Leon T. Dickinson

BIBLIOGRAPHY

Blair, Walter. *Mark Twain & Huck Finn*. Berkeley: U of California P, 1960.

Clemens, Samuel L. *The Innocents Abroad*. Hartford, Conn.: American Publishing, 1869.

Ganzel, Dewey. *Mark Twain Abroad: The Cruise of the "Quaker City."* Chicago: U of Chicago P, 1968.

Smith, Henry Nash. *Mark Twain: The Development of a Writer*. Cambridge, Mass.: Harvard UP, 1962.

See also: Duncan, Charles C.; Holy Land, The; *Innocents Abroad, The*; *Quaker City*

Piloting

The importance of Mark Twain's four-year stint (1857–1861) as apprentice and then licensed pilot on the Mississippi River can scarcely be exaggerated. Not only did it provide him with his famous pseudonym (signifying two fathoms or twelve feet of water), but also with his first professional success and most important, a store of experiences and memories that would help provide the imaginative core of his most famous books and figure prominently in many others. Paradoxically, however, the very richness and detail of Twain's autobiographical writings about his years on the river tend to mask the sparseness of what is actually known about this period in his life. His accounts, like all autobiographical writing, employ various strategies of selection, evasion, and embellishment that make them more satisfying as imaginative writing than reliable as fact.

Mark Twain's tendency to fictionalize himself is obvious in his account of starting his career on the river. Unlike the inexperienced boy with the romantic yearning to become a steamboatman of "Old Times on the Mississippi" (1875), Samuel Clemens in 1857 was a twenty-one-year-old printer who had lived and worked in St. Louis, Cincinnati, Philadelphia, and New York and who had already published humorous sketches and travel letters. He was probably more interested in economic opportunities offered by the trade than in its glamour (although that doubtless appealed to him), for as a pilot he could expect to earn $250 to $500 a month, whereas the average worker might not earn that much in a year. But there were risks and disadvantages as well: the long, difficult, and unpaid period of learning; periods of inactivity caused by low water, ice, competition for places, and the volatile economy of the western rivers; and the significant dangers of the trade itself. The life expectancy of the Mississippi steamboat, before it burned, sank, or exploded, was four to five years.

Nevertheless, in April 1857 on board the *Paul Jones*, bound from Cincinnati to New Orleans and then into the New Orleans-St. Louis trade, Samuel Clemens reached an agreement to pay Horace Bixby $500 to become his "cub." He began the arduous task of learning the river, and the first year of his apprenticeship passed uneventfully enough. By the early summer of 1858 he was no longer steering for Bixby, who had temporarily gone into the Missouri River trade, but he had a good berth on the *Pennsylvania* under pilot William Brown, and he had managed to get his younger brother Henry on board as an apprentice or "mud" clerk. An altercation with Brown, however, led to Samuel's being left ashore in New Orleans when the *Pennsylvania* left for St. Louis on 9 June. On 13 June she exploded with great loss of life, and Clemens, coming upriver on the *Alfred T. Lacey*, found his brother, fatally injured, in Memphis, where the survivors had been taken. Henry died on 21 June.

This tragedy, movingly described in *Life on the Mississippi* (1883) and the *Autobiography* (1924), profoundly affected Mark Twain for the rest of his life, but it did not deter him from pursuing his career as a pilot. By August at the latest he was back on the river, and the following April he received his pilot's license. For the next two years, he had regular berths as pilot on some of the largest and best-known boats on the river. His last assignment, from September 1859 until May 1861, was on the *Alonzo Child*, where his co-pilots were his Hannibal friend Will Bowen and his former chief Horace Bixby. Despite various stories that have circulated about his deficiencies as a pilot, his record of employment in itself is ample evidence that he was skilled and careful.

When the Civil War broke out in the spring of 1861, regular trade halted and Clemens left the river, despite the fact that experienced pilots were in demand by both Union and Confederate forces. Following his abortive enlistment in the Confederate militia that summer, he left for Nevada with his brother Orion, never again to follow the profession he said he loved better than any other. On the river the war accelerated changes already underway that would spell the end of the steamboat era. Even during Mark Twain's years behind the pilot wheel, networks of railroads were advancing—both from east to west and up and down the Mississippi valley—that would put an end to the profitability of steamboats as passenger carriers, reduce their role to freight haulers, and eventually lead to their conversion to or replacement by barge towboats. These changes had all taken effect by the time Mark Twain returned to the river in 1882 to gather material for *Life on the Mississippi*.

While he was learning the river, Mark Twain had little time for the journalistic sketches he had been accustomed to publishing, but after he became a pilot, he began writing again intermittently. His most significant piece from this period is "River Intelligence," a skillful burlesque of the old pilot Isaiah Sellers's columns of river news that was published in the New Orleans *Crescent* on 17 May 1859. In the same vein he published a burlesque "Pilot's Memorandum" in the St. Louis *Missouri Republican* on 30 August 1860, and he may have contributed other articles pseudonymously to newspapers. He also wrote two stories during his pilot years, neither one published during his life. One, titled by its editors "The Mysterious Murders in Risse," was composed in 1859 and is a brief gothic tale of love and murder with a few incongruous comic touches. The longer and more skillful "Ghost Life on the Mississippi" is a supernatural tale set on a steamboat, a literary treatment of river lore and legend that anticipates the story of the haunted barrel in chapter 3 of *Life on the Mississippi* (*Early Tales & Sketches* 1:126–151).

One of the most lasting legacies of Mark Twain's piloting experience was the "brief, sharp schooling" in human nature that he got during these years, which doubtless helped equip him for his career as a writer. And the vibrancy and richness of the portrayal of the Mississippi valley and its culture in *Adventures of Huckleberry Finn* (1885), *The Adventures of Tom Sawyer* (1876), and *Pudd'nhead Wilson*

(1894) clearly owed much to his experiences on the river. But most important of all is the indelible portrait of piloting itself that he created in the series of sketches titled "Old Times on the Mississippi" in 1875 and expanded in *Life on the Mississippi* in 1883. "Old Times" was the first extended portrayal of piloting, and it has dominated all later portraits. Although rivermen were already part of American folklore in the mid-nineteenth century, the special place of the steamboat pilot in American popular culture has its origins and its most eloquent expression in Mark Twain's account of his brief apprenticeship during the waning years of the "flush times" before the Civil War.

Robert Sattelmeyer

BIBLIOGRAPHY

Bates, Allan. "Mark Twain and the Mississippi River." Ph.D. diss., U of Chicago, 1968.

————. "Sam Clemens, Pilot-Humorist of a Tramp Steamboat." *American Literature* 39 (1967): 102–109.

Branch, Edgar M. "Mark Twain: The Pilot and the Writer." *Mark Twain Journal* 23.2 (1985): 28–43.

————. *Men Call Me Lucky: Mark Twain and the "Pennsylvania."* Oxford, Ohio: Friends of the Library Society, Miami U, 1985.

————. "A New Clemens Footprint: Soleather Steps Forward." *American Literature* 54 (1982): 497–510.

————. "A Proposed Calendar of Samuel Clemens's Steamboats, 15 April 1857 to 8 May 1861, with Commentary." *Mark Twain Journal* 24.2 (1986): 2–24.

Burde, Edgar J. "Mark Twain: The Writer as Pilot." *Publications of the Modern Language Association* 93 (1978): 878–892.

Clemens, Samuel L. *Life on the Mississippi*. Boston: James R. Osgood, 1883.

————. *Mark Twain's Letters, Volume 1 (1853–1866)*. Ed. Edgar M. Branch, Michael B. Frank, and Kenneth M. Sanderson. Berkeley: U of California P, 1988.

————. *Mark Twain's Notebooks & Journals, Volume I (1855–1873)*. Ed. Frederick Anderson, Michael B. Frank, and Kenneth M. Sanderson. Berkeley: U of California P, 1975.

————. *The Works of Mark Twain: Early Tales & Sketches*. 2 vols. Ed. Edgar M. Branch and Robert H. Hirst. Berkeley: U of California P, 1979–1981.

Hutcherson, Dudley R. "Mark Twain as a Pilot." *American Literature* 12 (1940): 353–355.

See also: *Life on the Mississippi*; Mississippi River; "Old Times on the Mississippi"

Pinkerton, Allan
(1819–1884)

Detective and author of quasi-fictional crime narratives, Allan Pinkerton was born in Glasgow, Scotland, but immigrated to the Chicago area in 1842. In 1850 he organized the Pinkerton's National Detective Agency and became one of the most famous detectives of his day. Among other successes, he achieved national notoriety in uncovering and aborting an 1861 plot to assassinate President-elect Abraham Lincoln (*National Cyclopedia* 208). Also, in 1861, he organized an intricate system for acquiring military information from the southern states; from this success he later is given credit for developing and organizing the Federal Secret Service (*National Cyclopedia* 209). Based on the work of his detectives, he wrote and published sixteen books, notably *The Molly Maguires and the Detectives* (1877), *The Spy and the Rebellion* (1883), and *Thirty Years a Detective* (1884).

Mark Twain's play *Cap'n Simon Wheeler, the Amateur Detective* (written 1877) had obvious allusions to Pinkerton. Wheeler introduces his alliterated detectives Baxter, Billings, and Bullet as members of "Inspector Flathead's celebrated St. Louis Detective Agency" and the Inspector as the one "that writes the wonderful detective tales, you know" (Baetzhold 191). Also, Twain's story "The Stolen White Elephant" (1882) is another burlesque of the Pinkerton Detective Agency and its pretensions of infallibility (Baldanza 100). Twain was to go on and satirize other writers of detective fiction, notably Arthur Conan Doyle.

Andy J. Moore

BIBLIOGRAPHY

Baetzhold, Howard G. "Of Detectives and Their Derring-Do: The Genesis of Mark Twain's 'The Stolen White Elephant.'" *Studies in American Humor* 2 (January 1976): 183–195.

Baldanza, Frank. *Mark Twain: An Introduction and Interpretation*. New York: Barnes & Noble, 1961.

The National Cyclopedia of American Biographies. Vol. 3. New York: James T. White, 1893.

Paine, Albert Bigelow. *Mark Twain: A Biography*. 3 vols. New York: Harper, 1912.

See also: Detective Fiction; "Stolen White Elephant, The"

Plasmon

Twain viewed plasmon, a health food made from dried milk, both as a solution to world hunger and as a miracle cure to restore his ailing wife to health.

According to a letter he wrote Henry Huttleston Rogers, Twain first noticed plasmon in Vienna in 1898. He invested 5,000 pounds sterling in a syndicate to market the product in 1900, becoming a director on 19 April 1900. The investment, made without the knowledge or consent of Rogers, the man who had managed Twain's business affairs since his bankruptcy, proved an unwise one. Of course, the initial amount was followed by other, larger commitments.

The American branch of the company, originally headed by Henry A. Butters, caused Twain the most difficulty, and Butters himself received the recriminations Twain meted out for loss of capital and the failure of his dreams.

Plasmon never gained the worldwide popularity Twain had envisioned for it, nor did it alter Livy's condition. While in the blush of infatuation with the product, Twain could send Howells instructions on how to prepare it for consumption and could brag to Rogers that his family substituted plasmon for beef, a quarter of a pound for four pounds of the red meat.

The plasmon investment bedeviled Twain until 1909.

David O. Tomlinson

BIBLIOGRAPHY

Clemens, Samuel L. *Mark Twain–Howells Letters: The Correspondence of Samuel L. Clemens and William D. Howells, 1872–1910.* Ed. Henry Nash Smith and William Gibson. 2 vols. Cambridge, Mass.: Harvard UP, 1960.

———. *Mark Twain's Correspondence with Henry Huttleston Rogers, 1893–1909.* Ed. Lewis Leary. Berkeley: U of California P, 1969.

Lauber, John. *The Inventions of Mark Twain.* New York: Hill and Wang, 1990.

See also: Business; Butters, Henry A.

"Playing Courier"
(1891)

This relatively obscure later piece by Twain was originally written as part of a series of six letters for the McClure Syndicate while the Clemenses were traveling in Europe during 1891–1892. It first appeared in the *Illustrated London News* on 19 and 26 December 1891. Twain later revised the letter into story form and included it in an 1893 collection, *The £1,000,000 Bank-Note and Other New Stories.*

While Twain was in Europe during the nineties, he was gathering material for a new book that he intended to write. In many ways this short story is similar to the travel literature that Twain began in *Innocents Abroad* (1869). The story is a light comic piece in which the first person narrator forgets to hire a courier to guide his party from Aix-les-Bains to Bayreuth. The multiplicity of details and the narrator's own faulty memory soon spell disaster. Many of Twain's travel themes are here, including the difficulty with French and pressing travel schedules.

David G. Miller

BIBLIOGRAPHY

Clemens, Samuel L. *The Complete Short Stories of Mark Twain.* Ed. Charles Neider. Garden City, N.Y.: Hanover House, 1957. 253–265.

———. *Mark Twain's Letters.* Ed. Albert B. Paine. 2 vols. New York: Harper, 1917.

———. *Mark Twain's Notebooks & Journals, Volume III (1883–1891).* Ed. Robert Pack Browning, Michael B. Frank, and Lin Salamo. Berkeley: U of California P, 1979.

Point of View

Mark Twain experimented freely with point of view during his nearly fifty-year career as a professional writer, though one attitude remained constant throughout and guided his experimentation: Twain never accepted narrative omniscience as a legitimate storytelling technique. The teller, he believed, is always an interested participant in the narrative performance, regardless of whether that performance takes place in person or in print. His well-known broadsides against James Fenimore Cooper's fiction were really directed at the concept of omniscience itself, which in Twain's view constituted a sort of literary fraud aimed at disguising the author-narrator behind an implausible mask of neutrality. In "Cooper's Prose Style" (1895) he quotes a scene from *The Last of the Mohicans* in which a band of Indians prepares a venison dinner "[w]ithout any aid from the science of cookery." Cooper explains that "Magua alone sat apart, without participating in the revolting meal, and apparently buried in the deepest thought." Twain observes that Cooper "does not say who it is that is revolted by the meal. It is really Cooper himself," for "Magua is an Indian and likes raw meat" (*Letters from the Earth* 117–120). The teller's presence in the narrative, according to Twain, is inevitable; Cooper errs not in expressing his opinion but in attempting to conceal the author-narrator's presence by foisting his own emotions upon his characters, thus confusing Magua's angle of vision with his own.

Twain's dislike of omniscient narration emerged as a natural consequence of his journalistic apprenticeship in Nevada and California, where he learned to entertain readers by juxtaposing radically opposed points of view. Henry Nash Smith begins his classic account of Mark Twain's development as a writer with a chapter titled "Two Ways of Viewing the World," a phrase that appropriately identifies the importance of perspective in Twain's humorous writing during his western years. In hundreds of sketches from "The Dandy Frightening the Squatter" (1852) to "Jim Smiley and His Jumping Frog" (1865), many of which he adapted from oral tales, Twain earned rich comic dividends by dramatizing the sometimes violent confrontation between genteel and vernacular points of view. The narrator of these sketches, unlike Cooper's romancer, always participates self-consciously in the conflict of perspectives, as when "Mark Twain" of the Virginia City *Territorial Enterprise* assumes the pose of a dandified reporter in order to trade exaggerated insults with another local journalist, Clement T. Rice, dubbed by Twain "the Unreliable." In 1866, by then a celebrated humorist and traveling correspondent for several papers in San Francisco, Twain replaced "the Unreliable" with an imaginary vernacular antagonist, Mr. Brown, whose rough and practical point of view provided an ideal foil for "Mr. Mark Twain's" exaggerated romantic fulminations. Neither character in the comic exchanges between "Mr. Twain" and Mr. Brown offers a competent critique of the other, yet the implied author never intervenes to settle their dispute; rather, the humor of the Twain/Brown confrontation lies in the unmediated juxtaposition of two irreconcilable angles of vision. In the most important of his western sketches, "The Jumping Frog," Twain again dramatizes a conflict between two ways of viewing the world, that of a pedantic Easterner named "Mark Twain" and his storytelling host, Simon Wheeler, both of whom vie for the reader's identification in a verbal test of narrative authority. Wheeler's vernacular point of view, as embodied in his pictorial style of narration ("his under-jaw'd begin to stick out like the fo'castle of a steamboat"), presents a subtle challenge to "Mark Twain's" purported omniscience, which, as it turns out, amounts to nothing more than naive overconfidence in the presence of a skilled yarn spinner (*Early Tales* 284).

The traditional frame structure of southwestern humor offered a convenient and effective method for dramatizing the conflict of perspectives in "The Jumping Frog" and other short sketches; yet with his decision to write longer narratives Twain recognized the need for a more flexible structure. At first, he strained to enact the contest of perspectives at the expense of effective characterization in *The Innocents Abroad* (1869). The narrator of that book is another newspaper correspondent, but unlike his prototypes in the early sketches, this "Mark Twain" alternates unpredictably between and among a variety of comic poses. Instead of challenging rival speakers with his basic colloquialism, the letter writer attempts to combine the personalities of the yarn spinner, the pedant, the satirist, and the amiable idiot within a single narrative point of view. Twain achieves some memorable comic effects in each of these roles, but the correspondent's almost wild profusion of styles does more to confuse the narrative persona than to enact a sustained contest between different ways of viewing the world.

In *Roughing It* (1872) and "Old Times on the Mississippi" (1875) Twain discovered a new device, memory, through which he was able to revive the old game of counterpoint. By reflecting on past innocence from an experienced perspective, the adult narrators of those stories encompass opposing points of view more logically and economically than the roving correspondent of *IA*. In what are ostensibly autobiographical accounts, the old-timer of *RI* mocks his formerly romantic attitude toward the West and the experienced narrator of "Old Times" describes his humiliating initiation to the piloting profession. Twain deliberately exaggerates the actual contrast of perspectives in both stories, setting his age at around sixteen in "Old Times," for example, when in fact Samuel Clemens was a worldly twenty-one-year-old at the time he began his apprenticeship in the pilot house of a Mississippi steamboat. Twain already possessed a wide reputation in the West by virtue of his artful juxtaposition of competing perspectives in countless humorous sketches; during the early 1870s, writing for a new audience in the East, he learned to use the same principle of exaggerated contrast as a means of structuring longer narratives. Not coincidentally, his writing in both *RI* and "Old Times" is most effective when the distance that separates the narrator from his past is greatest—that is, when the man's point of view is most clearly distinguishable from that of the boy's. As the contrasting perspectives begin to merge in the second half of *RI* and in the continuation of "OT," *Life on the Mississippi* (1883), the disappearance of counterpoint marks a noticeable disappearance of vigor in Twain's style.

In "OT" Twain developed a subtle juxtaposition of perspectives—a version of the old Twain/Brown confrontation—by viewing youth through the filter of experience. In *Adventures of Huckleberry Finn* (1885) he reverses this structure by viewing adult society through the filter of innocence. As the solemn narrator of his own adventures, Huck presents the world as experienced through an innocent eye, and his innocence constantly stimulates the reader's mature understanding in order to enact a contrast of perspectives that Huck himself can never fully appreciate. In effect, Twain removes the experienced point of view—the "pilot's perspective" of "OT"—from the text of *HF*, so that the novel's satire becomes indirect and its use of counterpoint implicit. When, in a typical passage, Huck declares enthusiastically that Silas Phelps "never charged nothing for his preaching, and it was worth it, too," Twain invites his reader to appreciate an irony that escapes the narrator's own comprehension (285). The reader, in other words, performs the role that usually belongs to the old-timers of Twain's writing by bringing to the text a certain way of "viewing the world." Huck's innocence and the reader's experience function together to produce the novel's powerfully ironic juxtapositions.

In *A Connecticut Yankee in King Arthur's Court* (1889) Twain intended to reproduce the narrative strategy that had worked so well in *HF* by allowing another vernacular character to narrate his adventures in a strange and hostile land. But the outspoken satirist in Mark Twain became impatient with the limitations imposed by Hank Morgan's point of view.

After the opening chapters Hank begins to sound more like a liberal polemicist than a machinist from Connecticut, and by the end of the novel his political diatribes make him virtually indistinguishable from the author, whose direct participation in the narrative point of view discourages the lyrical and ironic effect Twain had achieved with first person narration in *HF*. Hank's story remains technically restricted to a single point of view, but his patchwork style, like that of the letter-writing narrator of *IA*, prevents Twain from representing Hank's world as experienced from a particular angle of vision. Much as Twain noticed Cooper's voice intruding upon Magua's consciousness in *The Last of the Mohicans*, the reader of *CY* struggles to distinguish between Hank's point of view and the author's own.

In his seminal essay on point of view in Mark Twain's fiction, John Gerber notes that Twain was at his best when he had someone else tell a story—that is, when he dramatized the event of narrative performance by allowing a character to narrate for him ("Point of View" 155). Twain seems to have sensed the truth of what came to be Gerber's position, for even in works narrated from an ostensibly omniscient point of view, like *The Adventures of Tom Sawyer* (1876) and *Pudd'nhead Wilson* (1894), he never places his faith entirely in omniscience. Characters in each of these novels effectively undermine the narrator's claims to authority, much as Simon Wheeler undermines "Mark Twain's" omniscient authority in "Jumping Frog." Twain's best writing, as Gerber implies, constantly enacts a struggle between competing points of view. Whether he represents the struggle as a contest between the pilot and the passenger, or between "Mr. Twain" and Mr. Brown, or between the tenderfoot and the old-timer, Twain depicts every act of narration as a form of challenge that demands a response. Omniscience remained in his thinking an illegitimate point of view, a literary artifice, for Mark Twain's storyteller, whether he speaks in the first or third person, is always a character in the drama initiated by his own performance.

Henry B. Wonham

BIBLIOGRAPHY

Clemens, Samuel L. *Adventures of Huckleberry Finn.* Ed. Walter Blair and Victor Fischer. Berkeley: U of California P, 1985.

————. *Letters from the Earth.* Ed. Bernard DeVoto. New York: Harper & Row, 1962.

————. *The Works of Mark Twain: Early Tales & Sketches.* Ed. Edgar M. Branch and Robert H. Hirst. 2 vols. Berkeley: U of California P, 1979–1981.

Cox, James M. *Mark Twain: The Fate of Humor.* Princeton, N.J.: Princeton UP, 1966.

Emerson, Everett. *The Authentic Mark Twain: A Literary Biography of Samuel L. Clemens.* Philadelphia: U of Pennsylvania P, 1984.

Gerber, John C. "Mark Twain's Use of the Comic Pose." *Publications of the Modern Language Association* 77 (1962): 297–304.

————. "The Relation between Style and Point of View in the Works of Mark Twain." *Style in Prose Fiction.* Vol. 1 of English Institute Essays. Ed. Harold C. Martin. New York: Columbia UP, 1959. 142–171.

Kolb, Harold H., Jr. *The Illusion of Life: American Realism as a Literary Form.* Charlottesville: UP of Virginia, 1969.

McKay, Janet Holmgren. *Narration and Discourse in American Realistic Fiction.* Philadelphia: U of Pennsylvania P, 1982.

Marx, Leo. "The Pilot and the Passenger: Landscape Conventions and the Style of *Huckleberry Finn.*" *American Literature* 28 (May 1956): 129–146.

Rogers, Franklin R. *Mark Twain's Burlesque Patterns as Seen in the Novels and Narratives, 1855–1885.* Dallas: Southern Methodist UP, 1960.

Smith, Henry Nash. *Mark Twain: The Development of a Writer.* Cambridge, Mass.: Harvard UP, 1962.

See also: Comic Poses; Humor; Style, Mark Twain's; Vernacular

"Political Economy"

(1870)

From May 1870 to April 1871 Mark Twain wrote a humorous column called "Memoranda" for *Galaxy* magazine. His short story "Political Economy" appeared in the September 1870 issue and is preserved in *Sketches, New and Old* (1875). Twain's introductory contribution to "Memoranda" announces that the department will carry ample dissertations upon political economy (Neider 92). Thus he sets the stage for this farce and identifies the persona as a vain, loquacious bore.

As the story goes, the persona is composing an eloquent treatise on political economy when he is interrupted by a lightning-rod salesman. The writer is so annoyed both by the interruption and by the tradesman's superior rhetoric that he dismisses the intruder with an order for abundant rods of the most expensive quality. The salesman, however, continues to interrupt the writer until the house, kitchen, and barn bristle with more than 1,600 rods. Although the residence becomes the attraction for all the neighbors from miles around, it is even more the attraction for the next thunderstorm, which rains 764 bolts of lightning upon the house. The writer now offers a forest of lightning rods for sale, but he has not yet found the courage to return to his essay on political economy.

The story is an explosion of grandiloquence and exaggeration. It is, furthermore, a satiric attack on flamboyant language used to describe trivial subjects. The irony is that the tradesman inundates his customer with both his superior rhetoric and business skill, exposing the writer as the world's most inept political economist.

Frank H. Leavell

BIBLIOGRAPHY

Clemens, Samuel L. *Mark Twain: Life as I Find It.* Ed. Charles Neider. New York: Harper & Row, 1977.

————. *Mark Twain's Sketches, New and Old.* Hartford, Conn.: American Publishing, 1875.

See also: Galaxy

Politics

At the end of his life it was common for Americans to regard Mark Twain as a "statesman without salary," a teacher and exemplar of civic virtue, and, to that extent, a political man. His politics, however, elude conventional definitions.

Twain was a shrewd political observer, his perceptions sharpened by his early term as a reporter covering Congress. With the years, his political activity grew more visible and his tone more strident, so that Twain was increasingly identified with an irreverent, but still respectable, version of nineteenth-century liberalism. A self-identified Mugwump, "pure from the marrow out," Twain broke with the Republican Party (and many of his friends, William Dean Howells included) to support Grover Cleveland in 1884, and he was a frequent critic of machine politics and of party loyalty in general. He was an early advocate of civil service reform and he became a supporter of free trade (although he defended the protective tariff as late as 1880), a position for which Hank Morgan is a spokesman in *A Connecticut Yankee in King Arthur's Court* (1889). A ferocious opponent of imperialism, Twain also ranged himself against lynching and the death penalty, calling the latter an "anachronism" and the "opposite of a deterrent" (*Notebooks & Journals* 3:347). Yet while Twain was a matchless satirist of hereditary aristocracies and religious establishments, he regarded economic inequality as relatively justified, and he defended the pursuit of gain when it led to a "contribution to the world's wealth" (*Notebooks & Journals* 3:520–521). Twain did support regulations and limits on wealth, such as taxation based on the ability to pay, but Louis J. Budd's balanced treatment is superior to that of critics, like Philip S. Foner, who attempt to claim Twain for the left. Twain crossed the line to radicalism only in his sometimes ambivalent sympathy for trade unions and his support for laws enforcing the eight-hour day.

As Twain often observed, however, the alternatives in political practice are matters of better and worse—and often, of bad and worse—defined by prevailing "circumstances," including the habits of mind-entrenched cul-

ture. Twain's stance in relation to the issues of the time, consequently, only hints at his political theorizing, his ideas of the nature of politics and the best political regime.

In Twain's teaching human nature is a constant, the basis and limit of all political societies. All human beings begin as children of the Old Adam, moved by the self-centered desire to do as they please, the root of the taste for dominion that Twain regarded as an ineradicable element of the human spirit. At the same time human beings feel a craving for security and reassurance, which underlies their willingness to conform and their often desperate pretensions. Yet the human's yearning to "stand well with his fellows" ("Corn-Pone Opinions"), the race's itch for approval and esteem, also leads human beings beyond themselves and can shape and even override self-interest, narrowly defined. Civil society cannot transform human beings, but it can elevate them.

Laws and social norms rest on implicit distinctions between the excellent and the base, attempting to reward virtue and punish vice and to establish social standards of attraction and aversion. When in an optimistic mood in 1888 Twain praised the United States as the only society "not founded in cold hard selfishness," the only one that "does not degrade many to exalt the few," he was not advocating a rigid economic or social equality: he was contending that in the United States the *purpose* of legal and social distinction was the elevation of the many, a stimulus to aspiration rather than a citadel of privilege (*Notebooks & Journals* 3:400–401). For Twain, politics was at bottom educational, the nurture and discipline of souls.

Yet despite the exalted role he saw for politics, Twain regarded the state as subject to fundamental, practical constraints. He held that all rule, whether democratic or not, rests and depends on majority opinion and credence. No government, consequently, can be much better than the people it rules. As the Connecticut Yankee's failure makes clear, even very revolutionary changes in institutions do not imply a new modeling of civic character, except perhaps in the very long term. Moreover, it is part of the paradox of democratic politics that the public is asked to set the standards for its own emulation, like pupils asked to prescribe their own schooling.

Twain's doubts about the capacity of the American electorate were reflected in *The Gilded Age* (co-authored with Charles Dudley Warner, 1873) and nurtured by his genteel circle at Nook Farm. In 1875 Twain's unsigned essay in the *Atlantic Monthly*, "The Curious Republic of Gondour," argued that the wealthy and educated should receive more than one vote, representing their greater contribution to the commonweal. Since Twain contended that the learned would outnumber and outvote the wealthy in such a scheme, his fanciful story mirrored Twain's conviction that mass opinion needed the guidance of an educated gentry, able to counteract the influence of demagogues and plutocrats. (His proposal for a "casting-vote party," in 1905, returned to this notion in a somewhat different form.) That Twain took a more democratic stance in his later years indicates a loss of faith in the redemptive qualities of gentility more than any new confidence in the judgment of the many.

Republicanism, Twain observed in 1908, is always relatively fragile, since it depends on civic fraternity and public spirit and, hence, runs counter to what is low and universal in human nature. Following Montesquieu and ancient Greek political philosophy, Twain held that republican rule can be relatively durable only in politics that are small (hence, within the compass of a citizen's feelings and personal relationships) and relatively poor. A political society that is large and affluent—the regime designed by the framers of the American Constitution—will suffer civic fragmentation and be tempted by power, inevitably sliding toward monarchy. This decline, Twain thought, was virtually complete in the United States, in which centralized government was dominated by an imperial presidency, personified by

Theodore Roosevelt, "the worst President we have ever had" (*Mark Twain in Eruption* 34).

The degeneration of the republic, Twain observed, was the work of "circumstance" rather than conscious choice, especially the growth in scale, wealth, and power associated with technology. Henry Nash Smith may have exaggerated Twain's doubts and understated the extent to which Twain appreciated technology and admired its capacity for alleviating drudgery and misery. Yet Smith and other critics are right to observe that Twain regarded material progress as inherently dangerous, since the possibility of great and sudden wealth was a standing temptation to humanity's worst impulses. As Twain indicated in "The Man That Corrupted Hadleyburg" (1899), moral restraint is ordinarily unable to resist such enticements for long, especially where society and its laws exaggerate human self-sufficiency.

America, as Twain saw it, was increasingly inclined to a shallow understanding of human nature, and individualistic utilitarianism blind, as *The Connecticut Yankee* hints, to the force and significance of human passion and religious yearning, and preoccupied with appearances, externalities like race and gender as well as respectability. In *Huckleberry Finn* (1885) Jim's nobility is clear to Huck and even to Tom, in his not so fantastic vision of Jim as an imprisoned king, but these are boys, still outsiders to adult society. In *Pudd'nhead Wilson* (1894) Roxy's natural regality is recognized by nobody, not even by Wilson, for all of his mensurative and empirical science. (More than once Twain imagined a future America in which whites got their comeuppance, being subordinated to Jim Crow rules imposed by blacks, just as he supported "any methods" necessary to win women's suffrage.)

As Twain saw it, the decay of the American republic was too deeply rooted to be arrested through the state or even by appeals to the public at the conscious level. Although impelled by urgency, he was willing to try both. His prescription for political health required a shaping of the public's most basic images and ideas, unlikely but possible only by an address to that "mighty mass of the uncultivates," who, as Twain wrote Andrew Lang in 1889, were his special audience (*Mark Twain's Letters* 3:525–528). In Twain's political teaching it is storytellers who lay the foundations of politics—and especially of republican political life and virtue.

Wilson Carey McWilliams

BIBLIOGRAPHY

Andrews, Kenneth R. *Nook Farm: Mark Twain's Hartford Circle.* Cambridge, Mass.: Harvard UP, 1950.

Blues, Thomas. *Mark Twain & the Community.* Lexington: UP of Kentucky, 1970.

Budd, Louis J. *Mark Twain: Social Philosopher.* Bloomington: Indiana UP, 1962.

Clemens, Samuel L. *Adventures of Huckleberry Finn.* Ed. Walter Blair and Victor Fischer. Berkeley: U of California P, 1985.

———. *A Connecticut Yankee in King Arthur's Court.* Ed. Bernard Stein. Berkeley: U of California P, 1979.

———. *Mark Twain in Eruption.* Ed. Bernard DeVoto. New York: Harper, 1940.

———. *Mark Twain's Letters.* Ed. Albert B. Paine. 2 vols. New York: Harper, 1917.

———. *Mark Twain's Notebooks & Journals.* Ed. Frederick Anderson, et al. 3 vols. Berkeley: U of California P, 1975–1979.

———. *Pudd'nhead Wilson and Those Extraordinary Twins.* Ed. Sidney E. Berger. Norton Crit. Ed. New York: Norton, 1980.

Clemens, Samuel L., and Charles Dudley Warner. *The Gilded Age.* Hartford, Conn.: American Publishing, 1873–1874.

Foner, Philip S. *Mark Twain: Social Critic.* New York: International Publishers, 1958.

McWilliams, Wilson Carey. *The Idea of Fraternity in America.* Berkeley: U of California P, 1973.

Smith, Henry Nash. *Mark Twain's Fable of Progress: Political and Economic Ideas in "A Connecticut Yankee in King Arthur's Court."* New Brunswick, N.J.: Rutgers UP, 1964.

Zuckert, Catherine H. *Natural Right and the American Imagination: Political Philosophy in Novel Form.* Savage, Md.: Rowman and Littlefield, 1990.

See also: Government; Human Nature; Law; Washington, D.C.

Polly, Aunt

Tom Sawyer's Aunt Polly appears in *The Adventures of Tom Sawyer* (1876), *Adventures of Huckleberry Finn* (1885), and *Tom Sawyer Abroad* (1894). Although the elderly aunt has only brief roles outside of *Tom Sawyer*, her characterization is consistent throughout Twain's works. She spends most of her time mothering Tom and his half-brother, Sid. Her caring, meddling disposition characterizes her attitude toward Tom; she wants him to look nice, behave, and be "a good little boy."

Aunt Polly generally introduces humor into the episodes in which she appears. Tom's incessant pranks, especially when they go unsuspected, illustrate her gullibility and pathetic naiveté. However, Aunt Polly can evoke the reader's sympathy. For example, when she erroneously believes Tom to have been drowned in the river, the reader briefly pities her grief. But before one can develop a lasting sympathy for her, Tom reenters, adding levity to the scene.

Critics have suggested that Twain modeled Aunt Polly in part on his mother, Jane Clemens. An illustration of Aunt Polly in the first edition of *Tom Sawyer* bears a striking similarity to Mrs. Clemens. Supposedly, that portrait is made to resemble Ruth Partington, the aunt of another "bad boy" named Ike, found in Benjamin Penhallow Shillaber's 1854 book. Twain also credited his mother with performing actions like those of Ruth Partington. The similarities are too exact to be merely coincidental. Some have suggested that Twain and his mother shared a secret joke and found such imitations couched in the character of Aunt Polly humorous.

J.R. LeMaster and David Haines, Jr.

BIBLIOGRAPHY

Baldanza, Frank. *Mark Twain: An Introduction and Interpretation.* New York: Barnes & Noble, 1961.

Long, E. Hudson, and J.R. LeMaster. *The New Mark Twain Handbook.* New York: Garland, 1985.

Norton, Charles A. *Writing "Tom Sawyer": The Adventures of a Classic.* Jefferson, N.C.: McFarland, 1983.

See also: *Adventures of Tom Sawyer, The*;
Clemens, Jane Lampton

Pond, James
(1838–1903)

James Pond was a printer and newspaperman
who had served as a major in the Civil War.
In 1874 he joined James Redpath's Boston
Lyceum Bureau. The next year Pond was a
partner in buying out Redpath, and in 1879
he established an agency of his own in New
York. In 1884 Clemens, who toured only
when he needed money desperately, contacted
Major Pond to arrange a joint tour for himself
and George Washington Cable. Billed by Pond
as "Twins of Genius," the two toured portions of the United States and Canada from
November 1884 to February 1885, performing over 100 times in about 80 cities. Using
chiefly *Huckleberry Finn* (1885), which was
being serialized in *Century Magazine*, Clemens
followed the example of Charles Dickens by
reading from his works rather than lecturing.
Though it netted less than $150 per perfor-
mance, Clemens's tour enhanced the sales of
his novel considerably. In 1895, needing
money worse than ever, Clemens again contacted Pond, this time to be agent for his last
trip across America, the first portion of his
1895–1896 world tour. From July to August
Clemens read 23 times in 22 cities, netting
about $230 for each performance. Later, as
Pond noted in his *Eccentricities of Genius*,
Clemens urged Howells to have Pond as agent
for his lecture tour of 1899.

L. Terry Oggel

BIBLIOGRAPHY

Cardwell, Guy. *Twins of Genius*. East Lansing: Michi-
gan State College P, 1953.
Fatout, Paul. *Mark Twain on the Lecture Circuit*.
Bloomington: Indiana UP, 1960.
Lorch, Fred W. *The Trouble Begins at Eight: Mark
Twain's Lecture Tours*. Ames: Iowa State UP,
1968.
Pond, James B. *Eccentricities of Genius*. New York:
Dillingham [1900].

Rubin, Louis D., Jr. *George W. Cable: The Life and
Times of a Southern Heretic*. New York: Pegasus,
1969.

See also: Lecturer

Potter, Muff

In *The Adventures of Tom Sawyer* (1876) Muff
Potter appears as the drunkard who helps Injun
Joe and Dr. Robinson rob a grave. When
Potter threatens the doctor with a knife at the
grave site, Dr. Robinson knocks Potter unconscious with the tombstone. While Potter
is unconscious, Injun Joe struggles with the
doctor and kills him with Potter's knife. When
Potter regains consciousness, he is holding his
bloody knife and Dr. Robinson lies dead beside him. Potter is confused and does not remember stabbing the doctor, but since he had
had too much whiskey that night, Potter is
easily convinced by Injun Joe that he is guilty
of the crime. He is put on trial for the murder,
but he is eventually exonerated in court by
Tom Sawyer who witnessed Injun Joe's crime.
Muff Potter also appears in *Tom Sawyer: A
Play* as the town drunk who loves children.

Donna Onebane

BIBLIOGRAPHY

Clemens, Samuel L. *The Adventures of Tom Sawyer*.
Ed. John C. Gerber and Paul Baender. Berkeley:
U of California P, 1982.

See also: *Adventures of Tom Sawyer, The*

Prime, William C.
(1825–1905)

Usually called "Grimes" in *The Innocents Abroad*
(1869), William C. Prime was the author of
Tent Life in the Holy Land (1865), which Mark
Twain called "representative of a *class* of Palestine books" (*IA* 2:271). Besides overidealiz-
ing their descriptions of scenery, the writers
of these books, Prime especially, were over-
emotional in recording their feelings upon
seeing places of holy associations. Twain found

Prime's sentimentality ludicrous when coupled with his habit of brandishing a revolver to keep the natives in line. Writes Twain, "Always, when he [Prime, or "Grimes"] was not on the point of crying over a holy place, he was on the point of killing an Arab" (*IA* 2:267). Mark Twain included further ridiculing of excessive sentimentality in a letter to the *Alta California* (McKeithan 265), deleted from *IA*.

Leon T. Dickinson

BIBLIOGRAPHY

Clemens, Samuel L. *The Innocents Abroad.* 2 vols. in 1. New York: Harper, 1911.

———. *Traveling with the Innocents Abroad.* Ed. Daniel M. McKeithan. Norman: U of Oklahoma P, 1958.

Dickinson, Leon T. "Mark Twain's Revisions in Writing *The Innocents Abroad.*" *American Literature* 19 (May 1947): 136–157.

See also: Innocents Abroad, The; Sentimentality

Prince and the Pauper: A Tale for Young People of All Ages, The
(1882)

Written between 1876 and 1881, *The Prince and the Pauper* is the historical romance about the exchange of identities with which Mark Twain sought to establish his capacity as an author of serious fiction. Loosely incorporating varied historical details of sixteenth-century Britain, such as Tudor speech, clothing, and court customs, *The Prince and the Pauper*, nonetheless, shares the themes of searching for freedom, identity, and surrogate fathers with *Adventures of Huckleberry Finn* (1885), which Mark Twain wrote during roughly the same period. Though it was influenced by Charlotte M. Yonge's *The Little Duke* (1854), and generally remained within the bounds of the genteel historical romance, *The Prince and the Pauper* reveals Mark Twain's delight in picaresque elements and develops a strand of social satire that points forward to stronger doses of the same in *A Connecticut Yankee* (1889). The novel, which Mark Twain's fam-

ily and friends almost unanimously praised as his best, was also adapted into a play. Mark Twain took pleasure in acting the role of Miles Hendon for audiences at home.

For several years, while he was writing the book, Mark Twain considered publishing *The Prince and the Pauper* anonymously to avoid evoking his reputation as a humorist. He researched the historical background widely, primarily in Shakespeare's plays (for expressions characteristic of the times) and in Sir Walter Scott's novels, but he was not careful to limit his choice of diction and other details to the time period he set his novel in. He lifted lengthy passages of description of court ceremonies from other sources for verbatim use, giving some of the book a rather wooden effect. However, he was at least equally interested in the fictional possibilities of the exchange of identities between two boys, one royal and the other impoverished, and the psychological and social consequences of that exchange. On one level, the story is, like so many of Mark Twain's, an exploration of the artificial nature of our social identity and a contrast between social extremes. On another level, however, the story touches on some of the deepest existential anxieties Mark Twain sets forth through his fiction: the fears and guilts of orphanhood, the search of a lost child for his legitimate father or for a surrogate father figure, and the loneliness of the outcast and oppressed. The novel is implicitly, and at times explicitly, critical of British laws and customs, particularly aristocratic privilege, superstition, and the corruption of justice. Nonetheless, it is first and foremost a romantic adventure story, full of the glamor, suspense, and exotic flavor of a distant time and an exciting boys' adventure.

When *Prince and the Pauper* first appeared, reviews were almost uniformly positive. The novel was praised for its purity and refinement, its morality and artistry. William Dean Howells, in an anonymous review, suggested that the book would surprise those who expected only humor from Mark Twain by its "artistic sense" and the "strain of deep earnestness" beneath the comedy. The novel conformed to Victorian expectations of children's fiction and was welcomed by those who valued propriety and didacticism in books for the young. It was less enthusiastically received by those who wished for more contemporary American fare from Mark Twain and by some British critics who did not take kindly to an American author's criticism of British history and law. Mark Twain dismissed the latter critics with the remark that they would not praise the Holy Scriptures if an American had written them.

More recently, critics have been divided about the merits of *The Prince and the Pauper*. Van Wyck Brooks saw Olivia Clemens's preference for *The Prince and the Pauper*, a book that he thought almost anybody could have written, "equally respectable in its tendency and infantile in its appeal," as symptomatic of her censorial and repressive influence on Mark Twain's work. Later critics often echo the charge that the book is childish, either in its implausible plot or in its implied view of the world as a place that can be readily improved through the social reforms of a good boy in a position of power. James M. Cox recognizes that Mark Twain was addressing an adult audience as much as a child audience, and he acknowledges the importance of the social criticism in the novel to the history of Mark Twain's thought on the subject. He ultimately judges the book a failure, however, because it lacks humor. A few critics assert that its merits need not be measured in comparison with *Huckleberry Finn* or *Tom Sawyer* (1876) but that it has value both in relation to Mark Twain's development as a literary artist and as a work in the genre that its author was consciously writing in: the juvenile romance.

The novel features three orphaned sons, each searching for his father or for a father substitute. Each son has a benevolent and a malevolent father figure, and each son—Tom Canty, Edward, and Miles Hendon—must find his way through adventures and misadventures to claim as his own the father figure who can grant him an identity and a productive

place in society. This male quest myth is underlined by the superficiality of the portraits of women in the book: the most vivid female figures are the kindly Baptist prisoners who are burnt at the stake in a harrowingly brutal scene. They are characteristically Victorian stereotypes: self-sacrificing, angelic women. Mark Twain criticizes the cruelty of patriarchal law and privilege, but offers in its stead only the weak hope that humanity can be reeducated through experience and innate kindheartedness. Nevertheless, the scenes of threatened or actual violence, such as the mad hermit's brandishing of a knife over the bound boy, suggest the depth of the terrors about human nature and about mis-trained imaginations that haunted Mark Twain.

The Prince and the Pauper is surely not a masterpiece, but it has been underrated in its reaction against the tenets of nineteenth-century genteel children's fiction. Its flaws include the overly contrived plot, excessively long and dull passages of description, and a sometimes facile and ahistorical attack on customs and superstitions of an imagined past. Its lasting value, however, stems from its compassionate and imaginative play with the vagaries of identity, its hunger for fathering, a satirical yet ambivalent attraction to ritual and power, and a keen sense of injustice. As a work that stands between the lighthearted satire of *Innocents Abroad* (1869) and the full-fledged historical criticisms of *A Connecticut Yankee*, *The Prince and the Pauper* represents a significant step in the evolution of Mark Twain's thought and literary art.

John Daniel Stahl

BIBLIOGRAPHY

Andrews, Kenneth R. *Nook Farm: Mark Twain's Hartford Circle*. Cambridge, Mass.: Harvard UP, 1950.

Blair, Walter. *Mark Twain & Huck Finn*. Berkeley: U of California P, 1960.

Clemens, Samuel L. *The Prince and the Pauper*. Ed. Victor Fischer and Lin Salamo. Berkeley: U of California P, 1979.

Cox, James M. *Mark Twain: The Fate of Humor*. Princeton, N.J.: Princeton UP, 1966.

Dickinson, Leon T. "The Sources of *The Prince and the Pauper.*" *Modern Language Notes* 64 (1949): 103–106.

Regan, Robert. *Unpromising Heroes: Mark Twain and His Characters.* Berkeley: U of California P, 1966.

Stahl, John Daniel. "American Myth in European Disguise: Fathers and Sons in *The Prince and the Pauper.*" *American Literature* 58.2 (1986): 203–216.

Stone, Albert E., Jr. *The Innocent Eye: Childhood in Mark Twain's Imagination.* New Haven, Conn.: Yale UP, 1961.

Towers, Tom H. "*The Prince and the Pauper:* Mark Twain's Once and Future King." *Studies in American Fiction* 6 (1978): 193–202.

Vogelback, Arthur L. "*The Prince and the Pauper:* A Study in Critical Standards." *American Literature* 14 (1942): 48–54.

See also: Boy Books; England; Picaresque

Profanity

Considerable distinction exists between Mark Twain's profanity in speech and that in print. Profanity was an essential element of his rages, and according to his contemporaries, to hear him made all the difference. In his writing the tendency toward profanity appears descriptive but somewhat restrained.

A letter to William Dean Howells reveals a close connection to Twain's oral performances as this phrasing nearly sounds off from the page: "quadrilateral astronomical incandescent son of a bitch." A letter to an editor complaining about a proofreader's errors includes a common "damned bastard" and the exotic "damn half developed foetus." In his letters to Mary Mason Fairbanks Twain shows remarkable restraint with italics and exclamation points being the most extreme form of emphasis.

His published works also reflect an awareness of form and audience. In *Life on the Mississippi* (1883) Twain disguises profanity with the dash following or between the key letters. The frequency of these devices indicates his interest in defying convention and in being aware of the orthodoxy of his readers.

Most people were not offended by his use of profanity. Charles Major, whom Twain greeted enthusiastically with a "damn," felt friendship rather than displeasure. Katy Leary observed that it was "part of him . . . not like real swearing." But Robertson Nicoll thought it "disgusting." Simply put, Twain's characteristic irreverence reinforced his tendency toward profanity.

Thomas Bonner, Jr.

BIBLIOGRAPHY

Clemens, Samuel L. *Mark Twain-Howells Letters: The Correspondence of Samuel L. Clemens and William D. Howells, 1872–1910.* Ed. Henry Nash Smith and William M. Gibson. 2 vols. Cambridge, Mass.: Harvard UP, 1960.

———. *Mark Twain to Mrs. Fairbanks.* Ed. Dixon Wecter. San Marino, Calif.: Huntington Library, 1949.

Wagenknecht, Edward. *Mark Twain: The Man and His Work.* Rev. ed. Norman: U of Oklahoma P, 1967.

See also: Language

"Professor's Yarn, The"
(1883)

Although Mark Twain wrote "The Professor's Yarn" in the 1870s, he did not include it in *A Tramp Abroad* (1880). James R. Osgood published the short narrative in *Life on the Mississippi* in 1883. When Twain contracted to write the book about the Mississippi River, he planned to use the serialized articles from the *Atlantic Monthly* and add his more recent impressions after revisiting the river. As the deadline approached, he lacked sufficient material to finish the book and, consequently, included "The Professor's Yarn" along with several other sections that had not been written originally for the book (Wilson 61–62). Osgood suggested shortening the piece or moving the setting to the Mississippi, but Twain made no changes (Kruse 116–117). He introduces chapter 26 in *Life on the Mississippi*, however, by admitting that he includes the yarn not because it "belongs" there but because "it is a good story."

The "good story" concerns professional gamblers duping each other and the reader. The author successfully disguises the truth until the end when the dissembler flaunts his trickery. Reminiscent of his earlier western humor, Twain's expertise in contriving a believable hoax teases the reader with the differences between appearance and reality.

Sandra Gravitt

BIBLIOGRAPHY

Clemens, Samuel L. *The Complete Short Stories of Mark Twain.* Ed. Charles Neider. Garden City, N.Y.: Hanover House, 1957. 239–244.

———. *Life on the Mississippi.* Boston: James R. Osgood, 1883.

Kruse, Horst H. *Mark Twain and "Life on the Mississippi."* Amherst: U of Massachusetts P, 1981.

Wilson, James D. *A Reader's Guide to the Short Stories of Mark Twain.* Boston: G.K. Hall, 1987.

See also: Hoax; *Life on the Mississippi*

Providence

In Mark Twain's work Providence stands metaphorically for *God*, in the broadest sense, but especially for God as orderer of the earth, humanity, and human destiny. In his *Autobiography* (1924) Twain accentuates the scars seared into his consciousness by the Providence of an awesome frontier Protestantism, largely an Old Testament-dominated religion emphasizing original sin and dirty-rag righteousness; a stern and jealous God who in his Providence saw every sin and spared none of his powers to gain retribution and who was reported to protect the obedient but who could as often subject them to unfathomable tests; and a sentimentalized heaven and torturous hell as reward and punishment eternal. The effect, Twain says, left him and the rest of the race "never quite sane in the night" (*Autobiography* 46).

The effect of his religious upbringing also left Twain with Providence as a major theme, one integral to all his social criticism. Twain treats Providence in a variety of literary and discursive modes, ranging from comedy to comic satire to satire verging on tragedy and ending in serious speculation on the nature of a manifestly improvident God. Generally, Twain's progression toward bitter satire parallels his chronologically progressive religious skepticism.

In his simplest treatment of Providence Twain speaks in merely facetious terms, as in the *Autobiography* where he begins a chapter (his twenty-sixth, on rutted bowling alleys and crooked cues) with the declaration that Providence protects children and idiots, but no satiric point is made. Similarly, in the *Autobiography* (chapter 24) he burlesques his dismissal from the San Francisco *Morning Call* (which he claimed resulted in the San Francisco earthquake) but the object of the parody in this case is himself, and Providence is only a straight man to Twain's clown.

At one step beyond the merely humorous, Twain adds a barbed point to his comments on Providence, many of which are aphoristic in origin. In a March 1866 newspaper piece, "Reflections on the Sabbath," he observes that no man can "meddle with the exclusive affairs" of Providence, that we must "take things as we find them," though it "goes against the grain . . . sometimes" (*Early Tales & Sketches*). More pointedly, Pudd'nhead Wilson's calendar entry beginning chapter 4 points up a problem with special providences—it's difficult to identify the "intended . . . beneficiary." In longer pieces of this mode Twain burlesques special providences, though somewhat short of direct attack. In *Roughing It* (1872, chapter 53), for example, Twain tells of an Irish hod carrier falling from a ladder to land on a passing stranger and knock the "everlasting aspirations" out of him. Providence, Twain says, put the stranger there to save the life of the Irishman, with Uncle Lem and his dog present. Later, in the *Autobiography* (chapter 35), Twain explains, pretending to respond to a scoffer at Providence, that the stranger was required to serve Providence because the dog was "too indifferent to pious restraints" and too sensitive to his own safety to be depended on in an emergency, even when the orders "come from on high." Finally, through the guise of Huck Finn, Twain carefully examines two types of morality, one—selfless—the result of the Widow Douglas's concept of Providence, the other—selfish—Miss Watson's. For Widow Douglas's Providence both Huck and Twain had some sympathy. Of Miss Watson's, the one more common to Twain's Missouri Presbyterianism, Huck can only say that "there warn't no help for a [poor chap] any more" (*Huck Finn*, chapter 3); and Twain admits that when he repented, he did so "in his own interest" (*Autobiography*, chapter 9).

During the last two decades of his life Twain mounts an intense attack on the whole concept of Providence and "sentimental justice" (*Notebook* 360), declaring his belief that both Old and New Testaments were "imagined and written by man" (*Biography* 3:1538). Twain dramatizes his belief that Providence "cares not a rap for us" (*Notebook* 360) in "The Chronicle of Young Satan" (chapter 2) when Satan—the truthspeaker (Gibson 14–15)—creates and destroys a castle community and (chapters 6 and 7) when Satan demonstrates human destinies with Nikolaus and Lisa as examples: following humans' first acts, only "circumstance and environment" order their fates; God does not. Giving the full lie, Twain takes the last measure of a tragically improvident God: angels and gods care no more for humans than the elephant for the red spider ("Chronicle," chapter 6) or the sun for rushlight ("No. 44, The Mysterious Stranger," chapter 19).

Finally during his later years especially, Twain speculates on the "true God." Against the "irascible, vindictive, fierce and ever fickle" God of the Old Testament, he contrasts his God as "steadfast" to his unknown purposes (*Biography* 1:412). In Whitmanesque tone and detail he describes God as the maker of "suns and planets of a billion billion solar systems" (*Biography* 3:1538), the "perfect artisan" whose creations are "utterly and minutely perfect," who is not ignorant enough to mistake his "myriad great sums" for mere tallow candles

to light "this forgotten potato . . . Earth," and who reveals himself and "His law" in "His real Bible, which is Nature and her history" (*Notebook* 360).

Donald R. Holliday

BIBLIOGRAPHY

Clemens, Samuel L. *Mark Twain's Autobiography*. Ed. Albert B. Paine. 2 vols. New York: Harper, 1924.

———. *Mark Twain's Notebook*. Ed. Albert B. Paine. New York: Harper, 1935. Rpt. New York: Cooper Square, 1972.

Gibson, William M. Introduction. *Mark Twain's Mysterious Stranger Manuscripts*. By Clemens. Ed. William M. Gibson. Berkeley: U of California P, 1969. 1–34.

Paine, Albert Bigelow. *Mark Twain: A Biography*. 3 vols. New York: Harper, 1912.

Tuckey, John S. *Mark Twain and Little Satan: The Writing of "The Mysterious Stranger."* West Lafayette, Ind.: Purdue UP, 1963.

See also: Calvinism; God; Religion

Pudd'nhead Wilson, The Tragedy of (1894)

By his own admission, Mark Twain was not "born with the novel-writing gift," and indeed *Pudd'nhead Wilson* may stand as a major example of a work plagued by compositional difficulties stemming from his seemingly contradictory purposes and subsequent revisions. Begun in 1892, while Twain suffered financial pressures, this problematic work was initially conceived as a "howling farce" involving his long-standing fascination with Siamese twins and questions of psychological identity. Twain's original manuscript contained the minor characters of Dave Wilson, the mulatto Roxana, and Tom Driscoll, as well as the more complex but undeveloped themes of miscegenation, slavery, and criminal detection through fingerprinting, a dramatic device stimulated by Twain's reading of Sir Francis Galton's *Finger Prints* (1892). Obviously unhappy with his initial conception, Twain tells us that the work "changed itself" radically "from a farce to a tragedy" and so required "a kind of literary Caesarian operation" in order to create not only a publishable narrative but also, we may infer, to express his profoundest concerns about American culture and the effects of environmental determinism or "training" that had consistently engaged him as an explanation for human behavior. Although we may be disarmed, mystified, or critically irritated by Twain's methods of patching, cutting, and in other ways tying up "loose ends," one of the most crucial problems about the book's composition remains: what were the aesthetic and psychological forces that effected the transition from farce to tragedy? This problem embodies and points to many of the thematic and tonal tensions in *Pudd'nhead Wilson* and reveals, in its unrelenting ironies, a more trenchant, paradoxical dualism in Twain's imaginative processes than the traditional fictional devices of twins, doubling, and role reversals ostensibly suggest. Indeed, farce and tragedy are perhaps the intrinsic aesthetic "twins" in this novel and the grounds of its troubled thematic unity.

By 1893 Twain had completed his "operation" separating *Pudd'nhead Wilson* from "Those Extraordinary Twins," which he would publish with the novel in the first American edition (1894). In an important statement to Fred J. Hall, Twain insisted that the new work was a shortened "reconstruction" in "divergence or side-play" to inhibit (presumably) a story shaped by a deterministic philosophy and melodramatically imaged by his favored themes and techniques of changelings, reversals, a slave, and a slavish humanity; Tom Sawyer "effects" of courtroom revelation; and, finally, the ironic ways of fate or Providence itself. Serialized in *Century Magazine* in seven installments from December 1893 to June 1894, *Pudd'nhead Wilson* the book was published in the United States and in England in November 1894. The reviews immediately reflected a range of opinion that acknowledged both the book's artistic unity and power as well as its plot confusions or difficulties in weaving together a story of miscegenation, role reversals, and modern scientific detection. Also praised was Twain's satiric narrative style teasingly glossed by Pudd'nhead's remarkable calendar headings, aphorisms, mordant (even Calvinistically hopeless on human nature) or satirically cautionary by turns. Surely, as modern critics have noted, these aphorisms point to a darker, revised Twainian version of Poor Richard's wisdom geared to another America. In 1895 an anonymous reviewer, while praising the book's power and language, still wondered whether, in contrast to other national humorists like Aristophanes, Cervantes, Molière, or Swift, Twain created a work of "literature." Other critics cited flaws such as the unrealistic appearance of the Italian twins, Angelo and Luigi, in a southern, antebellum Mississippi river town, the "shadowy" presence of Pudd'nhead himself in the action, and the "irrelevance" of Wilson's election to mayor while acknowledging the strong characterization of Roxy and the "realistic picture of that phase of American life with which the author is most familiar." Indeed, most twentieth-century criticism, from a variety of theoretical positions, has centered on the problematics of the book's genre and on the issue of Twain's attitudes toward slavery and race, particularly exacerbated by the character of Tom Driscoll, Roxy's mulatto son, whose vicious nature can be attributed either to his race or to "training" or to some mixture of both.

Essays by Leslie Fiedler (1955) and F.R. Leavis (1956), without ignoring the book's weaknesses, helped elevate it to a high level in Twain's canon, stressing its moral and tragic power, a position that it still maintains, although Hershel Parker's analysis of the holographs and revisions (1984) warns against assuming any internal thematic coherence and "intentionality" on Twain's part. *Pudd'nhead Wilson*'s provocative subject matter and form continue to attract critical attention to the extent that a conference held at the University of California at Santa Cruz in 1987 was devoted entirely to the novel.

The narrative line of *The Tragedy of Pudd'nhead Wilson* (as it is also titled) is deceptively simple and direct, masking many underlying complex issues of race, character, and American culture. Yet another of Twain's "strangers," the young "college-bred" lawyer, Dave Wilson, comes into the slaveholding river town of Dawson's Landing dominated by the F.F.V.s (First Families of Virginia) and there quickly alienates himself from the townsfolk by his sharp ironic humor and symbolically suggestive joke that if he owned half of the howling dog then disturbing everyone, he would kill it. Now labeled a "pudd'nhead," Wilson is forced to retreat into his private world of "freethinking" and his hobbies of palmistry and fingerprinting, signaling his (and Twain's) preoccupation with the often futile role of satiric humor in an obtuse society and questions of an identity that must always remain lurking beneath the masks or disguises culture necessarily imposes on humanity. But Wilson's arrival is coincident that February 1830 with the birth of a son to one of the town's leading aristocrats, Percy Northumberland Driscoll, whose wife dies within the week, as well as a son to his one-sixteenth black mulatto slave, Roxana, who must take care of both babies. When, shortly after, Percy threatens to sell some slaves "down the river" for petty theft, Roxy, a recently new-born Christian, in a sinfully parodic act with tragic implications, acts as an agent of a Calvinistic "free grace" in order to protect her child, Valet de Chambre (or Chambers), from this dread fate and switches the infants in their cradles. In this way the stage is set for a deterministic and ironic providential drama in which Wilson's penchant for the detection of identity and character is fatefully bound to the national sin of slavery and its cruelties.

The burden of the narrative is to explore the truly inevitable psychological and social consequences of these two events as Wilson fingerprints the infants and again at later stages of their growth, the actions that Roxy regards with suspicion and alarm, although Wilson himself does not suspect the truth. The slave child, now Thomas à Beckett Driscoll, a white child to all appearances, grows into a vicious, pampered child, embodying all the vices of the stock aristocratic villain: cruel, treacherous, a gambler, a thief, and finally a murderer of his "uncle," Judge York Leicester Driscoll, with whom he comes to live after the death of his "father." Percy Driscoll's real son, Chambers, grows into a long-suffering, humble slave. It is this basic, if skeletal, pattern that dominates the novel's action, ending, as it must, in the revelation at the court trial in the final scenes where truth, reward, and punishment ironically triumph even as the force of training and the values of a materialistic slave society are exposed. Instead of being punished as a murderer, Tom, now a valuable slave, is "sold down the river" to pay off debts, thus completing a pattern of a dehumanized ideological necessity Roxy had tried to prevent but which she is instrumental in bringing about, truly making her, in her own words, a "sinner" in the "fallen" world of which she is a part. Pudd'nhead's final calendar entry encapsulates the satiric-tragic idea: "*October 12, the Discovery. It was wonderful to find America, but it would have been more wonderful to miss it.*"

Within this skeletal but rigid structure, and fleshing out its pattern of iron necessity, are Twain's incisive if troubling analyses of how Roxy's maternal feelings are alternately humiliated and then transformed into the need for revenge and self-justification as she becomes a deferential slave to her own child and the racist ideology of her oppressors. Also included is Twain's analysis of her son's cowardly nature in refusing to duel Luigi, who had humiliated him, and the fixed elements of his character that cannot change even when Tom learns from Roxy that his now dead father was the aristocrat Cecil Burleigh Essex, thus giving him a redeeming chance to understand what it means to be black in a white slave culture but that, instead, incites him later to the further outrages of selling his mother "down the river" and killing his "uncle," ostensibly for money. Further analysis reveals the provincial, fawning attitudes of the townspeople toward the exotic Italian twins, Luigi and Angelo, one of whom, Luigi, has also killed a man, a fact Wilson discovers registered in the lines of his palm. Also included are the events leading to the inconclusive duel between Judge Driscoll and Luigi, Wilson's subsequent election, the judge's murder, the trial of falsely accused Luigi, and finally, Twain's typical courtroom scene of melodramatic suspense in which Wilson's scientific "magic" reveals the truth of the changelings and the sexual abuse of slavery lying behind it. His remark (in the full philosophic and moral voice of Mark Twain) that whoever switched the infants did so for "selfish" reasons, is a principle informing, in one guise or another, the social world of the novel.

Pudd'nhead Wilson may well be flawed by Twain's emphasis on and extended use of "stock" melodramatic situations and stereotypes, but at the same time Twain's taut realistic and satiric language offers a counterbalancing aesthetic dimension that distances the reader from the exaggerated emotionalism such situations normally evoke. The conventional is thus translated into credible action rich in symbolic suggestion. All of the book's major images—beginning with Wilson's initial joke, the calendar headings that often relate directly to the action as well as to Wilson's vision of life, the fingerprintings, palmistry, twins, changelings, the social training and economic needs that define the world of Dawson's Landing—create a compelling vision of pessimistic determinism. This determinism also springs from humanity's inherent character defined by selfishness, greed, the manipulation of sexual and political power, and the need for social esteem affecting victims and victimizers alike, as several of Pudd'nhead's maxims state. We see the irresistible compulsions of a culture that can be interpreted as the workings of an avenging Providence or social destiny. Unquestionably, the book's most powerful image or metaphor lies in the concept that our identities and therefore our destinies are literally embodied in flesh, a concept fraught with theological as well as secular behavioral meaning about human nature.

In the development of Mark Twain's work as a whole, *Pudd'nhead Wilson* is a kind of summation in novel form of his views on determinism, training, and the social and moral duplicities of racism and slavery. A bitter commentary on antebellum and, by extension, of late nineteenth-century America, the novel reflects the best and worst artistic aspects of Twain's primarily folk imagination and appropriation of his culture's taste for popular melodrama and extravagant situation. In its despairing, certainly skeptical, view about human freedom and possibilities of redemption from slavery, the novel helps us understand, in part, Twain's artistic attempts soon to follow in *The Mysterious Stranger* complex (written 1897–1908) where he sought some salvational ideal or release from this entrapment in "dream philosophy" subsuming the problems of determinism and the images of the Adamic myth with which he had long been imaginatively involved and that he was exploring in "Extracts from Adam's Diary" (1893) even while working on *Pudd'nhead Wilson*. Indeed, that influence appears in several of Pudd'nhead's maxims about Adam and Eve, "special providences," death, and the necessity of the Fall, for the "mistake was in forbidding the serpent; then [Adam] would have eaten the serpent." And when Tom Driscoll, on learning that he is Roxy's son, cries, "What crime did the uncreated first nigger commit that the curse of birth was decreed for him?" we see the tragic link between a fallen world and slavery. Perhaps, as some critics have indicated, by raising such issues, however problematically, the novel can be viewed as a precursor to similar themes in writers such as William Faulkner and Richard Wright.

In an attempt to capitalize on the relative success of *Pudd'nhead Wilson* and interest in the new science of fingerprinting, Twain allowed the novel to be dramatized in 1895 by Frank Mayo, a popular actor, who played Wilson. He also continued Pudd'nhead's maxims in a "New Calendar" for *Following the Equator* (1897), the most significant being:

"Everything human is pathetic. The secret source of Humor itself is not joy but sorrow." In 1985 the Public Broadcasting System presented a made-for-television movie based on the novel in the *American Playhouse* series, starring Ken Howard and Lise Hilboldt, which was well received.

Stanley Brodwin

BIBLIOGRAPHY

Anderson, Frederick. Introduction. *Pudd'nhead Wilson*. Facsimile of the first American edition. By Clemens. San Francisco: Chandler, 1968. vii–xxxii.

Brodwin, Stanley. "Blackness and the Adamic Myth in Mark Twain's *Pudd'nhead Wilson*." *Texas Studies in Literature and Language* 15 (1973–1974): 167–176.

Budd, Louis J. "Mark Twain's Fingerprints in *Pudd'nhead Wilson*." *Études Anglaises* 40 (1987): 385–399.

Butcher, Philip. "Mark Twain Sells Roxy Down the River." *College Language Association Journal* 8 (1965): 225–233.

Chellis, Barbara A. "Those Extraordinary Twins: Negroes and Whites." *American Quarterly* 21 (1969): 100–112.

Clemens, Samuel L. *Pudd'nhead Wilson and Those Extraordinary Twins*. Ed. Sidney E. Berger. Norton crit. ed. New York: Norton, 1980.

Cox, James M. *Mark Twain: The Fate of Humor*. Princeton, N.J.: Princeton UP, 1966.

Fiedler, Leslie. "As Free as Any Cretur. . . ." *The New Republic* 133 (15 August 1955): 17–18; (22 August 1955): 16–18.

Gerber, John C. "*Pudd'nhead Wilson* as Fabulation." *Studies in American Humor* 2 (1975): 21–31.

Gillman, Susan, and Forrest G. Robinson, eds. *Mark Twain's Pudd'nhead Wilson: Race, Conflict, and Culture*. Durham, N.C.: Duke UP, 1990.

Griffith, Clark. "*Pudd'nhead Wilson* as Dark Comedy." *Journal of English Literary History* 43.2 (1976): 209–226.

McKeithan, Daniel M. *The Morgan Manuscript of Mark Twain's "Pudd'nhead Wilson."* Essays and Studies on American Language and Literature. Vol. 12. Cambridge, Mass.: Harvard UP, 1961. 1–64.

Parker, Hershel. "*Pudd'nhead Wilson*: Jack-Leg Author, Unreadable Text, and Sense-Making Critics." *Flawed Texts and Verbal Icons: Literary Authority in American Fiction*. Evanston, Ind.: Northwestern UP, 1984. 115–145.

Pettit, Arthur G. *Mark Twain and the South*. Lexington: UP of Kentucky, 1974.

Rowlette, Robert. *Twain's* Pudd'nhead Wilson: *The Development and Design*. Bowling Green, Ohio: Bowling Green U Popular P, 1971.

Spangler, George M. "*Pudd'nhead Wilson*: A Parable of Property." *American Literature* 42 (1970): 28–37.

Wigger, Anne P. "The Composition of Mark Twain's *Pudd'nhead Wilson and Those Extraordinary Twins*: Chronology and Development." *Modern Philology* 55 (1957): 93–102.

See also: Angelo and Luigi (Cappello); Dawson's Landing; Miscegenation; Roxana; South, Mark Twain and the; Wilson, David

Punch, Brothers, Punch!
(1878)

Published by Mark Twain's friend and business associate Dan Slote, *Punch, Brothers, Punch! and Other Sketches* includes nine reprinted sketches. The title piece, "Punch, Brothers, Punch!," originally appeared in 1876 as "A Literary Nightmare" in the *Atlantic Monthly*. The sketch, based on a newspaper jingle written by Isaac H. Bromley and Noah Brooks, with an added chorus by W.C. Wycoff and Moses P. Handy, proved enormously popular, and the jingle was even set to music.

Twain reads the verse that begins "Punch, brothers, punch" in the newspaper. The jingle swirls about in his head, driving out all other thoughts until he is left "a tottering wreck." Relief comes days later, when he recites it to a companion, who then takes on the obsession.

Though one of Twain's slighter works, he used its enormous popularity to launch the collection of sketches, which included substantial advertising of his self-pasting scrapbook, another Slote, Woodman and Company product. The success of *Punch, Brothers, Punch!* reveals a Mark Twain who was attuned to popular culture and was able to create a fad as well as profit by it. A version of the sketch became a standard in Twain's lecture programs.

Nancy Cook

BIBLIOGRAPHY

Blanck, Jacob. *Bibliography of American Literature, Vol. 2, George W. Cable to Timothy Dwight.* New Haven, Conn.: Yale UP, 1957.

Clemens, Samuel L. *The Comic Mark Twain Reader.* Ed. Charles Neider. Garden City, N.Y.: Doubleday, 1977.

————. *Mark Twain Speaking.* Ed. Paul Fatout. Iowa City: U of Iowa P, 1976.

————. *Punch, Brothers, Punch! and Other Sketches.* New York: Slote, Woodman, 1878.

Paine, Albert Bigelow. *Mark Twain: A Biography.* 3 vols. New York: Harper, 1912.

See also: Slote, Daniel

Putnam & Sons, G. P.

Putnams, a venerable publishing house founded by George P. Putnam, had distributed *Putnam's Magazine* trans-America during Twain's boyhood, and by Twain's Hartford days had published numerous authors, known as the Putnam Phalanx of Hartford. George Haven Putnam, Putnam president during Twain's later years, whom Twain included in a "gang . . . of nice publishers and nice literary folk" (Smith and Gibson 804), was notable for his association with William Dean Howells and Twain in their struggle for international copyrights.

Donald R. Holliday

BIBLIOGRAPHY

Clemens, Samuel L. *Mark Twain-Howells Letters: The Correspondence of Samuel L. Clemens and William D. Howells, 1872–1910.* Ed. Henry Nash Smith and William M. Gibson. 2 vols. Cambridge, Mass.: Harvard UP, 1960.

Cox, James M. *Mark Twain: The Fate of Humor.* Princeton, N.J.: Princeton UP, 1966.

Quaker City

The *Quaker City* was the steamship that carried Mark Twain and over seventy other passengers on an excursion to Europe, the Holy Land, and Egypt in 1867. In order to fulfill his contractual obligation, Twain reported to the *Daily Alta California* in fifty letters upon the events of the excursion; he transformed his reports into *The Innocents Abroad* (1869), a travel book in which the *Quaker City* figures prominently. The *Quaker City* set out from New York on 8 June 1867 and it returned from the excursion on 19 November of the same year.

The ship itself, which Twain described as "sumptuously fitted up," was quite adequate for the excursion to Europe and the Holy Land. It was nineteen hundred tons and thirteen years old at the time of the 1867 voyage. A paddle-wheel steamer that relied upon both steam engines and sails for propulsion, the *Quaker City* had been used for North Atlantic service, running between New York and Liverpool; however, during the Civil War it was used as a supply ship. At the time of the excursion, publicity for the voyage reported that the ship had been newly refurbished, but such renovation consisted mostly of fresh paint. Captain C.C. Duncan was the ship's commander during Twain's 1867 excursion.

Trevor J. Morgan

BIBLIOGRAPHY

Budd, Louis J. *Mark Twain: Social Philosopher.* Bloomington: Indiana UP, 1962.

Clemens, Samuel L. *Traveling with the Innocents Abroad.* Ed. Daniel M. McKeithan. Norman: U of Oklahoma P, 1958.

Ganzel, Dewey. *Mark Twain Abroad: The Cruise of the "Quaker City."* Chicago: U of Chicago P, 1968.

Long, E. Hudson. *Mark Twain Handbook.* New York: Hendricks House, 1957.

See also: Innocents Abroad, The

Quarles, John Adams

(1801–1876)

Married in June 1824 to Martha Ann "Patsy" Lampton (1807–1850), younger sister of Jane Lampton Clemens, John Quarles moved his family to Florida, Missouri, in 1834. Quarles opened a general store on Main Street before the John Marshall Clemens family arrived in 1835. Although he was a successful merchant, Quarles soon sold his store and moved to his seventy-acre farm northwest of town. He was relatively prosperous and became an active force in the development of Monroe County; in 1851 he was installed as a justice of the county court and named a justice of the peace. Two years after the death of his wife in 1850, Quarles sold the farm and moved to Paris, Missouri, where he was proprietor of a hotel. Visits from the Clemens family ceased after his remarriage, although the Clemens children continued to correspond with their uncle until his death in 1876 at age seventy-five.

Quarles may well have been the first hearty, robust man his young nephew Sam Clemens knew intimately. Whereas Sam's austere father was a frail introvert, suffering real and imagined diseases in silence, more given to reading than to romping with his children, Quarles was well-liked, warm, and vivacious. At his store he offered smiles, affectionate concern, and good humor. Loafers were welcome; a pan of ashes by the stove served lingering tobacco chewers and cats. Provided no ladies were present, ribaldry was acceptable. Old yarns received the same receptive ear they had enjoyed in various versions during previous visits.

The same affectionate warmth, good humor, and ambiance of freedom characterized the Quarles farm, where Sam was a frequent visitor and, at his uncle's insistence, would always bring his favorite cat. At home the children of John and Jane Clemens were restricted by rules of decorum and eternal vigilance; on the farm they and the ten children of John and Patsy Quarles tumbled in joyful abandon in and out of doors, ate and slept well. A "freethinker," or more specifically, a Universalist, Quarles is often cited as a formative influence on Sam Clemens's later religious beliefs. Certainly, he gave the boy time and a sympathetic ear, encouraged free and open discourse, and counterbalanced Sam's formal religious training in the Hannibal Presbyterian Church. Yet the most lasting impression was the man's deep-seated humanity, infectious good humor, and the teeming life and uninhibited vitality of the farm over which he presided.

Oliver Howard and Goldena Howard

BIBLIOGRAPHY

Paine, Albert Bigelow. *Mark Twain: A Biography.* 3 vols. New York: Harper, 1912.

See also: Quarles Farm

Quarles Farm

A favorite retreat of young Sam Clemens, his uncle John Quarles's farm was a seventy-acre homestead located three-and-a-half miles northwest of Florida, Missouri. The main part of the farmhouse consisted of two square two-story log cabins, standing twenty feet apart with one wall of each parallel to the other. The log sills of each cabin rested firmly on large flat limestone rocks. Each one of these "towers" had a single large room downstairs with a huge stone fireplace. The upper room was probably partitioned. The twenty-foot space between the two cabins was floored at the same level with the rooms on either side, and roofed—forming a breezeway perfect for outdoor dining, sleeping dogs, or storing ricks of wood in winter. The kitchen was a third cabin in the rear, one-story high and joined to the main house by an outdoor floor that extended along the back of the living room. Covered by a roof, the walkway also served as a porch.

The Quarles farm was productive and teeming with life. A large apple orchard ranged on a sloping hill at the side of the main house, and Quarles sent hundreds of barrels of apples to market by freight boat in the early days before apple orchards covered the hillsides and there were special "Missouri Apple Boats" that stopped at the commission houses in Hannibal. His grain served two markets: much of it went to the grist mills at Florida; from the rest he made whiskey to be shipped in barrels made at the many cooper shops that once flourished in the area. His flax, wool, and hemp were also profitable, and his woodlands furnished his table with abundant game.

John Marshall Clemens's sons were allowed no guns; after their father's death, Sam and Henry pled with older brother Orion to buy them a gun for hunting, but he replied with a dreary recital of expenses and unpaid accounts and refused. Nevertheless, on the Quarles farm the boys, with their cousins and uncle, could hunt abundant deer, pheasant, prairie chickens, wild turkey, quail, and pigeons.

Slaves furnished much of the labor on the farm. At one time there were twelve whites in the family and thirty black slaves—all to be fed, quartered, and clothed. From the meager information about slave ownership revealed in the census, it appears that Quarles and his wife kept every slave they ever owned. Unlike most white Missourians of his time, Quarles did not sell his slaves as they reached maturity; neither would he separate them from their families. Each slave family was permitted to build its own cabin and live in it.

The frequent visits to his uncle's farm thus furnished the boy Sam Clemens his first, and certainly crucial, sustained contact with blacks. Black and white children played together in the pasture, creek, and orchard. The white children attended a subscription school in summer. Since it was against Missouri law to teach a slave to read or write, the black children tended to chores assigned to them for the day. Their mothers worked at the farmhouse as cooks, laundresses, weavers, wet nurses, and baby tenders; the black men were field hands. But in the evenings and on weekends all would gather to share stories. Uncle Dan'l, a shaping force on the conception of the character Jim in *Adventures of Huckleberry Finn* (1885), was the favorite raconteur, but there were others.

An ancient black woman lived alone in a cabin near the main house. The boy Sam Clemens was enthralled by her story of her hair turning white with fright as she and her people escaped from the Egyptians hundreds of thousands of years previously. He and the other children, black and white, were in awe of her extended age and gathered at her cabin to listen to her repertoire of adventures.

The Quarles farm is now privately owned and not open to the public. There are no original buildings on it to be examined and few landmarks to indicate its location.

Oliver Howard and Goldena Howard

BIBLIOGRAPHY

Clemens, Samuel L. *Mark Twain's Autobiography*. Ed. Albert B. Paine. 2 vols. New York: Harper, 1924.

See also: Dan'l, Uncle; Quarles, John Adams

Quarry Farm

Perched almost atop East Hill on the outskirts of Elmira, New York, Quarry Farm was by his own reckoning Mark Twain's favorite and most productive workplace. It was there that Samuel Clemens and his family spent almost twenty summers between 1871 and 1889 and there that he drafted substantial portions of his most famous books, including *Roughing It* (1872), *Tom Sawyer* (1876), *Huckleberry Finn* (1885), and *A Connecticut Yankee* (1889).

Jervis Langdon, Clemens's father-in-law, bought the property in 1869 as a family summer retreat. The initial purchase included about seven acres of land, outbuildings, and a farmhouse that had formerly been a stonecutter's cottage. The name "Quarry Farm" was suggested by the Langdon's friend and minister, Thomas K. Beecher, in acknowledgment of an abandoned stone quarry on the property. The Langdons's East Hill neighbors included Beecher himself and Doctors Silas O. and Rachel Brooks Gleason, who operated a renowned water cure nearby.

At his death in 1870 Langdon left the property to his adopted daughter, Susan Langdon Crane, who, together with her husband Theodore, eventually moved there and made additions to both house and property, at one point owning more than 250 acres and operating a successful dairy farm on the premises. Even before the Cranes took up residence, however, the Clemenses made their first summer-long visit to Elmira in 1871, and Clemens began the practice of resorting to the farm's quiet solitude in order to write without interruption or distraction. In 1874, with the Crane and Clemens families having taken over Quarry Farm for the summer, Susan Crane surprised her brother-in-law with the gift of a small octagonal study on a crest of a hill a short distance from the main house. There he was able to maintain the privacy that had initially drawn him to the spot and that enabled him to do much of his best work.

The Clemenses lived in Hartford, Connecticut, during the two decades whose summers they spent at Quarry Farm. In their elaborate Hartford home the demands of a growing family and the frequent arrival of visitors left Clemens few periods of sustained quiet in which to write. In his study on the farm, contrastingly, he spoke of working "in complete isolation" in the "cosy nest" Susan Crane had built for him as he looked out over Elmira and the Chemung River valley below and the "distant blue hills" of Pennsylvania. His custom was to work without interruption in the study from about ten in the morning to five in the afternoon, often reading the days' production aloud to a family gathering on the Quarry Farm porch in the evening.

There was for Clemens a kind of meditative, summertime ease and contentment about Quarry Farm that he sometimes attributed to such places of his own creation as St. Petersburg. With the deaths of Theodore Crane in 1899 and of Clemens's mother-in-law, Olivia Lewis Langdon, in 1890, though, the family broke its custom of gathering annually in Elmira, and the Clemenses spent just two more summers, those of 1895 and 1903, at the farm.

During that last summer Clemens wrote "A Dog's Tale," probably the last piece of work he did at Quarry Farm. In 1983 Jervis Langdon, Jr., Clemens's grand-nephew, made a gift of the farm and surrounding land to Elmira College, which has since established the Center for Mark Twain Studies at Quarry Farm on the site.

Jeffrey Steinbrink

BIBLIOGRAPHY

Jerome, Robert D., and Herbert A. Wisbey, Jr., eds. *Mark Twain in Elmira.* Elmira, N.Y.: Mark Twain Society, 1977.

Paine, Albert Bigelow. *Mark Twain: A Biography.* 3 vols. New York: Harper, 1912.

See also: Crane, Susan; Elmira, New York; Elmira College Center for Mark Twain Studies at Quarry Farm

"Queen Victoria's Jubilee"
(1897)

In this article Mark Twain describes the parade in London on 22 June 1897 that celebrated sixty years of Queen Victoria's rule. The article was first published in the New York *Journal* on 22–23 June 1897, syndicated to other American newspapers at the time, and subsequently reprinted in the volume *Europe and Elsewhere* (1923).

The article falls into a genre that Twain loved, the catalogue—and more specifically, the catalogue of a procession. The chief interest of the article is Twain's imaginary comparison of Queen Victoria's parade with the pageant of 1415 to celebrate Henry V's victory at Agincourt. A "spirit correspondent" provides the description of the earlier procession. Twain's account of the later event offers an occasion for him to meditate on the material and moral progress of England and of humanity generally. As in *A Connecticut Yankee in King Arthur's Court* (1889) Twain thinks the progress has been positive and immense, but also as in *CY* Twain betrays a not altogether conscious ambivalence. He calls modern life both "easy and difficult, convenient and awkward, happy and horrible." Twain does not elaborate on the negative side of his equation though he does note the absence from the procession of the arch-imperialist Cecil Rhodes.

In the canon of Mark Twain's work this piece is minor but interesting for its revelation of Twain as a somewhat singed apostle of progress.

Hunt Hawkins

BIBLIOGRAPHY

Baetzhold, Howard G. *Mark Twain and John Bull: The British Connection.* Bloomington: Indiana UP, 1970.

Budd, Louis J. *Mark Twain: Social Philosopher.* Bloomington: Indiana UP, 1962.

Salomon, Roger B. *Twain and the Image of History.* New Haven, Conn.: Yale UP, 1961.

Scott, Arthur L. *Mark Twain at Large.* Chicago: Henry Regnery, 1969.

See also: England; Rhodes, Cecil

R

Rabelais, François
(1494?–1553)

Little is known about François Rabelais, including his exact date of birth. His father was a successful provincial lawyer and a rich landowner in Tourraine, France. By 1520 young Rabelais was a Franciscan monk. As an ordained priest, he took a medical degree in 1530 and became a practicing doctor. Adept in humanist letters and law, he was personal physician and a close confidant of the powerful, politically liberal du Bellays, first serving Cardinal Jean du Bellay and then his brother, Guillaume. Rabelais was also an accomplished linguist and folklorist and deeply concerned with developments in almost all the fields of knowledge known in his day. This rich background, seasoned and supplemented by his travels across France and in Italy, provided the sources for his great pioneering novel, *Gargantua and Pantagruel*, the first four books of which were published from 1533 to 1552. The fifth and doubtfully authentic book appeared posthumously in 1558. Never married, Rabelais is known to have lived with a woman who bore him a son; the child died young.

Begun as a kind of extended joke—half parody of a popular book on the giant Gargantua that had appeared in 1532, half vehicle for Rabelais's sprawling sense of humor and his well-ripened wisdom—the novel quickly became a huge success. (*Gargantua* appeared in 1534; it is invariably printed as if it were the first book and *Pantagruel* the second, since in the fictional chronology Gargantua, the father, obviously comes before Pantagruel, his son.) By the time *Gargantua* appeared, what had started as a high-spirited pleasantry was already deepening into a profound examination of the human spirit. Because Rabelais never abandoned his sense of fun, there are riotous episodes from start to finish, embellished with slashing satire and immense learning. (Rabelais, who had himself edited Greek and Latin medical and legal texts, was much influenced by the great humanist scholar Erasmus, with whom he corresponded.) But for all its splendid spoofing and much-celebrated earthiness, *Gargantua and Pantagruel* had almost from the start turned into a moving exploration of human existence.

Rabelais is neither a popular writer nor an easy one to read. He makes heavy use of the classical references common to humanist thinkers; he draws freely and continuously on printed and oral sources of the most diverse kind (at one point Gargantua and his newfound companion, Panurge, converse in thirteen different languages, three of them invented); and his vast, all-embracing enthusiasm draws the characters in his book, like the readers of that book, into the most wonderfully far-flung highways and byways.

And he writes magnificently, one moment spinning long, dense, multitoned sentences, the next capturing the easy, excited flow of contemporary speech—then turning to concise, taut narration or hilariously extravagant fables and tales of any and every sort (including a good deal of highly allusive verse, some of it almost impossible to understand today). The joy of Rabelais's writing always carries the book, no matter where the narrative takes it—or whether the narrative decides simply to dawdle. He puns, he plays, he piles up mocking catalogues and lists, he weaves utopian fantasies and excrement-drowned fables. The novel is profoundly spiritual, and in the highest, but not always the orthodox, sense religious. The church was not always happy with Rabelais: it burned one of his friends at the stake and Rabelais himself was frequently in danger. Regardless, he remained deeply Christian.

Twain knew both Rabelais and his reputation as an iconoclastic and sometimes scandalous writer. In public, at least, Twain rejected attempts to label his own work Rabelaisian. But the largess and the freedom of Rabelais, the immense gusto and the intense love of good people and their deeds, the excited zest for good things and their use and consumption, plainly inspired and abetted Twain throughout his career.

Burton Raffel

BIBLIOGRAPHY

Bakhtin, Mikhail. *Rabelais and His World*. Trans. Helene Iswolsky. Bloomington: Indiana UP, 1984.

Rabelais, François. *Gargantua and Pantagruel*. Trans. Burton Raffel. New York: Norton, 1990.

Screech, Michael Andrew. *Rabelais*. Ithaca, N.Y.: Cornell UP, 1979.

Weinberg, Florence M. *The Wine and the Will: Rabelais's Bacchic Christianity*. Detroit: Wayne State UP, 1972.

See also: Picaresque; Scatology

Rachel, Aunt

Modeled on Mary Ann Cord, Susan Crane's cook and domestic servant at Quarry Farm, Aunt Rachel is the central character in Mark Twain's "A True Story Repeated Word for Word as I Heard It," published in the November 1874 issue of the *Atlantic Monthly*. A woman "of mighty frame and stature . . . her eye . . . undimmed and her strength unbated," Rachel is one of the most compelling and heroic characters in all of Mark Twain's fiction. Like Mark Twain's two other complex and fully developed black characters (Jim in *Huckleberry Finn*, 1885, and Roxana in *Pudd'nhead Wilson*, 1894), Rachel is realistic, human, and vibrant. Her suffering at the hands of a white social order that denies her humanity affords Mark Twain an opportunity to deflate racist misconceptions including, ironically, his own.

Within the confined social world of the white, genteel household, Rachel appears to occupy a subservient position, "sitting respectfully below our level . . . for she was colored." When she rises to tell her story of the slave auction that splintered her family, however, Rachel assumes her natural dignity and voice; she "towered above us, black against the stars." Sparked by the character Mark Twain's racist

assumptions that her cheerful disposition testifies to the absence of suffering in her life, her
tale is at once a harrowing indictment of chattel slavery and a commentary on the customs,
behavior, and psychology of African-Americans in the antebellum South.

Rachel explodes the character Mark
Twain's complacent assumptions of superiority by poignantly reinforcing their common
humanity. She too had a loving spouse and
seven children: "an' we loved dem chil'en jist
de same as you loves yo' chil'en." Her tale of
persecution, her faith in the face of profound
adversity, and her remarkable spiritual resiliency leave "Misto C—," and no doubt the
nineteenth-century genteel class he represents,
stunned and speechless.

Mark Twain the author gives Rachel dignity and humanity through the realistic depiction of her character. There is no minstrel
stereotyping here. Rachel has her petty vanities that individualize her. She is proud of her
Maryland ancestry, that she is "one o' de old
Blue Hen's chickens." She reigns like a tyrant
over her kitchen in a humorous but ultimately
pathetic attempt to exercise control over her
life in a social order that grants her precious
little. Mark Twain reinforces the realism of
his character depiction with meticulous attention to Rachel's language. He informed William Dean Howells that he polished Rachel's
speech by reading it aloud from galleys. Auntie
Cord, on whom Rachel was modeled, had
pronounced the same word variously depending upon its location in a sentence, and he
sought to capture the same effect through spelling (Gibson 19). The attention to details of
language to make his black characters authentic and human anticipates the author's concern with Jim's speech in *Adventures of Huckleberry Finn*.

James D. Wilson

BIBLIOGRAPHY

Clemens, Samuel L. "A True Story." *Atlantic Monthly*
4 (November 1874): 591–594.

———. *A True Story and the Recent Carnival of Crime.*
Boston: James R. Osgood, 1877.

Gibson, William M. *The Art of Mark Twain*. New
York: Oxford UP, 1976.

Kellner, Robert Scott. "Mark Twain and the Mental
Cripple: The Challenge of Myth." *Mark Twain
Journal* 21.4 (Fall 1983): 18–20.

Wilson, James D. *A Reader's Guide to the Short Stories
of Mark Twain*. Boston: G.K. Hall, 1987.

See also: Abolition; *Adventures of Huckleberry
Finn*; Cord, Mary Ann ("Auntie");
Racial Attitudes; "True Story, A"

Racial Attitudes

For the first thirty years or so of his life, Mark
Twain, author of what is arguably one of the
greatest anti-racist works of fiction written by
an American, was a racist.

In his "schoolboy days," Twain recalled in
his autobiography, he "had no aversion to
slavery." He was "not aware that there was
anything wrong about it." No one around
him challenged the institution; local churches
taught that "God approved it, that it was a
holy thing." Childhood memories of the sad
faces of slaves chained together on a chain
gang, "lying on the pavement, awaiting ship-
ment to the Southern slave market," or of an
overseer fatally flinging "a lump of iron-ore at
a slave-man in anger, for merely doing something awkwardly," stayed with Twain all his
life, as did other memories of hauntingly beautiful spirituals (always Twain's favorite form
of music), of spirited cakewalks, of sly humor,
of a rich vernacular language, and of individual slaves whose lives had touched Twain's
in positive ways.

Contact with former abolitionists in the
East after the Civil War and his marriage into
Olivia Langdon's abolitionist family helped
prompt Twain to reexamine his views in the
late 1860s. An editorial he wrote for the Buffalo *Express* condemning a lynching, "Only a
Nigger" (1869), marked some of the changes
in his sensitivity on this subject. In "A True
Story" (1874), published in the *Atlantic
Monthly*, an ex-slave, in her own powerful
and eloquent language, told of being sepa-

rated from her child on the auction block and of being reunited years later; the sketch won Twain critical acclaim for his dramatic evocation of "Aunt Rachel's" pain and joy.

Twain's subsequent major imaginative works focusing on the issue of race—*Adventures of Huckleberry Finn* (1885) and *The Tragedy of Pudd'nhead Wilson* (1894)—explored the subject of racism through satire and irony, a strategy that has often led readers to miss the point entirely or to take as Twain's message the opposite of what he intended to convey. While readers' misreading of his irony has helped prompt recent moves to ban *Huckleberry Finn* as "racist," it is interesting that Twain originally developed this strategy when a direct exposé of racism that he wrote was censored.

As a young reporter in San Francisco in the mid-1860s, Twain witnessed an incident he considered outrageous: several policemen stood idly by, apparently amused, as young white hooligans attacked a Chinese man who was going about his business. Twain's publishers refused to run the account he wrote of the incident, caring more about not offending the paper's subscribers (who shared the police's prejudices) than about the truth. Twain quickly learned that exposés of racism in San Francisco would not be printed in newspapers there. So he started writing a different kind of story, one with the same subject but an alternate strategy, and published it in a paper in the next state and in a national magazine. He had already published satires on travel letters, society balls, and corporate stock prospectuses. Now he turned his skill as an ironist on its thorniest target yet—racism.

These satires were told from the perspective of an invented character too innocent or bigoted to see anything wrong with the injustices he related. In "What Have the Police Been Doing?" (1866), for example, the narrator, posing as the policemen's most loyal friend and defender, paints a devastating portrait of corrupt and brutal police officers who constantly victimize the local Chinese population. In "Disgraceful Persecution of a Boy"

(1870) Twain focuses on a community that collects unlawful mining taxes from the Chinese not once but twice, whose courts convict the Chinese not just when guilty but always, whose police stand idly by when the Chinese are mugged by gangs—all occurrences he had witnessed in San Francisco. A young boy who has been taught by his elders that it was "a high and holy thing" to abuse the Chinese answers the call by stoning "a Chinaman" on his way to Sunday school. When the boy is arrested, the narrator decries the injustice of the fact that the boy "no sooner attempts to do his duty than he is punished for it."

When Twain took up the subject of racism in *Adventures of Huckleberry Finn*, the time, the place, and the race would be different. But the central question would be much the same: how can a society that debases human lives on a mass scale consider itself civilized? In *Huckleberry Finn*, as in earlier works, Twain used irony to shame his countrymen into recognizing the gap between their images of themselves and reality, as he portrays a racist society through the eyes of a boy too innocent to challenge that society's norms.

Readers who are not misled by Twain's irony find his attack on racism in *Huckleberry Finn* to be effective and memorable. Consider the exchange between Huck and Aunt Sally regarding a steamboat accident Huck has invented to make conversation. "Good gracious! anybody hurt?" Aunt Sally asks. Huck answers, "No'm. Killed a nigger." Aunt Sally responds, "Well, it's lucky, because sometimes people do get hurt" (chapter 32). Huck, of course, knows that at least one "nigger"—Jim—is certainly a person; but he also knows that if he is to play his role convincingly (he has undertaken it in order to rescue Jim), he has to assent to Aunt Sally's assumption that the two words refer to two different orders of being. A further irony stems from the fact that despite his love for Jim and his commitment to "stealing him" into freedom, Huck never achieves a larger awareness that black people in general are human and that the laws that define them as property are wrong. If Huck never reaches this awareness, the reader, however, certainly does.

Efforts to ban *Huckleberry Finn* as racist have surfaced periodically since 1957, when the New York City Board of Education, citing "some passages derogatory to Negroes," removed it from the approved textbook lists of elementary and junior high schools. Challenges to this novel have been mounted in Pennsylvania, Washington, Florida, Texas, Virginia, Illinois, Canada, and elsewhere, and they will probably continue.

Those who charge the book with being racist say that the term "nigger" (used close to 200 times in the book) retains the power to hurt more strongly than ever; that the presence of demeaning minstrel stereotypes in Twain's characterization of Jim is painful in a society in which negative stereotypes of black people have not disappeared, and that the transformation of the quest for freedom into a series of farcical escapades trivializes the moral impact of the story.

Twain's defenders note that if one wants to satirize racists, one must first show them as they are—and "nigger" is the term they would have used. They acknowledge that the minstrel mask is there but emphasize that Jim's and Twain's humanity and complexity emerge from behind that mask. (Ralph Ellison made this point in his historic essay "Change the Joke and Slip the Yoke.") As for the novel's burlesque ending, critics have recently begun to understand this problematical element in the context of events happening in the South during the period Twain was composing the novel, the late 1870s and early 1880s, suggesting that it may reflect the ways in which American culture itself was making a farce of the idea of freedom and equality for black Americans.

Sometimes a work of art can be a prism through which a historical moment becomes refracted into its constituent parts in stunning clarity and brilliant color. *Huckleberry Finn* may well perform that function for American race relations in the period 1876 through the early 1880s, just as *Pudd'nhead Wilson* may be thought to play that role for American race relations in the 1890s.

Twain began and abandoned *Huckleberry Finn* in the summer of 1876, during the greatest formal celebration of freedom the country had ever mounted, the centennial of the Declaration of Independence. But, like the charade of chivalry that prevented the Grangerford family from seeing the barbarity of their way of life, the rhetoric of freedom that dominated the national discourse that summer tended to blind people to the fact that the fate of free black Americans was about to be dealt a near fatal blow. The summer of 1876 brought not only the centennial celebrations, but also the death throes of Reconstruction. With the Hayes-Tilden compromise and the withdrawal of federal troops from the South, America was about to enter the period historians refer to as the "nadir," the all-time low point in American race relations.

Our contemporary sense of how far off freedom was that summer of 1876 may help explain why Twain decided to smash the raft and shelve the manuscript; and the confirmation of these fears during the next seven years may well have induced him to use the unsatisfying, burlesque, artificial ending that he eventually chose for his book. Twain's failure to resolve the moral conflicts set in motion in the first part of the book underlines the troublesome complexity of those issues and the difficulty of settling them even now, more than a hundred years later, which may be one reason why the ending continues to perplex us. Like America itself, *Huckleberry Finn* is castigated for its shortcomings precisely because of the boldness and daring of the challenge it took on from its start. It occupies the unique niche we have reserved for it in part because it dramatizes, as only a work of art can, both the dream and the denial of the dream, both the spectacular boldness of our national experiment (premised on the idea that "all men are created equal") and our spectacular failure to fulfill our promise.

In an analogous manner, *Pudd'nhead Wil-*

son (1894) illuminates the confusing and ironic social, legal, cultural, and political history of American race relations in the 1890s. The late 1880s through the turn of the century was a period when white America made unprecedented moves to consolidate its power: it repeatedly stripped black Americans—legally and illegally—of hard-won rights and took a myriad of steps, often violent ones, to ensure that the canvas on which black Americans could paint their lives was as constricted as possible. The most common forms that hatred took were the rise of Jim Crow laws and lynchings, both of which increased dramatically in the 1890s. During this time, while black America produced writers, artists, composers, athletes, businessmen, and educators of the first rank, white America grew increasingly obsessed with asserting black inferiority and with ensuring, legally and extralegally, the separation of the races. (*Plessy v. Ferguson*, 1896, which made "separate but equal" the law of the land, was handed down two years after *Pudd'nhead Wilson* appeared.) And as the project of ensuring the separation of the races was elaborated meticulously in a Byzantine code of laws, the possibility of actually delineating sharp lines between black and white grew more and more elusive: for despite white America's obsession with racial "purity," America was becoming an increasingly mulatto nation.

These highly discordant elements produced a confused culture at war against itself, a society ready to sacrifice its ideals, its rational self-interest, and its prospects for a nonviolent future on a shaky altar of bigotry, hatred, and racial pride. Some white fiction writers, such as Thomas Nelson Page, responded to these conflicts by avoiding them altogether and writing "plantation-school" romances of antebellum life; others, like Thomas Dixon, produced virulent, hugely popular, racist manifestos that unabashedly fueled the fires of racial prejudice.

Mark Twain, like the "plantation-school" writers, sets his novel *Pudd'nhead Wilson* in antebellum days. But his antebellum tale is shot through with the acid irony, numbing pain, and crippling despair that so many African-Americans must have found themselves struggling to overcome in the 1880s and 1890s in the face of lynchings, political intimidation, and social and cultural isolation and ostracism.

By a "fiction of law and custom" Roxana, who to all appearances is white, is deemed black, due to the "one-drop rule" that shaped race relations in American legal history (in which a person with any known degree of black ancestry was considered black). It is precisely this "fiction of law and custom" that Twain's novel explores so pointedly, raising serious challenges to the legitimacy of the entire enterprise of dividing American society into simple categories of "white" and "black."

David Wilson's absurd comment that he would "kill his half" of the dog makes him a marked fool in his community. But his fellow citizens are engaged in just such a proposition: as they systematically degrade and destroy that "half" of the people in their land whose skin is the "wrong" color, they destroy their own community as well. (If they do not within the confines of the novel, for the book ends before the Civil War, one may be sure that this sleepy, comfortable, contented slaveholding town will be violently jarred quite shortly.) Just as slavery had dehumanized slaveholders as well as slaves in the antebellum era, postwar racism took its moral and psychological toll on whites as well as blacks. When Twain's white contemporaries passed new Jim Crow laws, revoked rights, ostracized, reviled, insulted, abused, and lynched in the 1890s, they thought they were simply killing "half a dog." The project was, of course, absurd: what they were really killing off were their own illegitimate children, the fruits of their own illegitimate power, a part of themselves, their fellow citizens, their country's future.

The sickness of racism—designed to denigrate one group and elevate another—would send an entire nation, not half a nation, into painful, drawn-out convulsions. The violence and destruction of the race riots of the 1890s and at the turn of the century would be followed in the 1960s by the murder of civil rights workers, the blowing up of children in church, the assassination of Martin Luther King, Jr., and the uprisings that wracked so many cities; the legacy of the black underclass shaped by Jim Crow laws at the end of the nineteenth century remains clearly in place.

Twain's two major novels that address problems of race relations are both extraordinarily powerful books—and also powerfully flawed books. Twain limns a subversive indictment of racism in both of these books but retreats before he is through. The problems Twain could not solve as an artist, however, are the problems America still cannot solve as a nation—and thus his failures, reflecting as they do the complex times in which he wrote, and in which we live, are provocative and instructive.

"We have ground the manhood out of them," Twain wrote on Christmas Eve in 1885, referring to black people. "The shame is ours, not theirs and we should pay for it." His brutally succinct comment on racism in this letter is a rare nonironic statement of the personal anguish he felt regarding the destructive legacy of slavery. From the 1880s until his death Twain employed a variety of methods to "pay for it." He paid with money, supporting a black student, Warner McGuinn, at the Yale Law School, and another, A.W. Jones, at Lincoln University, and funding the Paris apprenticeship of the black painter Charles Ethan Porter. He paid with service, performing gratis in black churches whenever asked. He paid with his influence, writing publicity blurbs for the Fisk Jubilee Singers' international tour or interceding with President Garfield when Frederick Douglass was about to be dismissed from a federal post. And he also endeavored to pay with his work. For all its flaws, that work continues to spark debate, stimulate discussion, and push Americans to probe the gaps between the ideals they celebrate and the realities they tolerate.

Never as outspoken on the condition of African-Americans as his friend George Washington Cable, whose widely known views on the subject made travel to certain parts of the South hazardous to his health, Mark Twain always wanted to be able to "go home again." He had planned to write a book on lynchings but then changed his mind. "I shouldn't have even half a dozen friends left after it issued from the press," he wrote his publisher.

He maintained great affection for a number of African-Americans he had known well, such as "Uncle Dan'l," a slave at his uncle John Quarles's farm, near Florida, Missouri; Mary Ann Cord, an ex-slave who was the cook at Twain's summer home, Quarry Farm, in Elmira, New York; John Lewis, the coachman there; and George Griffin, his butler in Hartford. But with the exception of his friendship with Frederick Douglass (which he cited when he intervened with President Garfield on his behalf), there is no evidence that Twain maintained relationships with educated African-Americans who might have been his social and intellectual equals. Twain's library contained only a handful of books by African-American writers. This "desouthernized Southerner" (as Howells called him) never completely eradicated all remnants of his racist past: occasional "nigger" jokes appear in his later journals, a range of racist stereotypes continue to surface in his work, and his stance toward individual blacks was often condescending and paternalistic.

Twain's appreciation of the power of African-American vernacular speech, his recognition of the moral challenge that racism posed to the American experiment, and his understanding of the power of irony to shame Americans into a clearer understanding of their failings helped inspire twentieth-century African-American writers over three generations, including Langston Hughes, Ralph Ellison, and David Bradley.

Sadly, Twain manifested wildly inconsistent attitudes toward racism directed against other groups. A series of works—"Randall's Jew Story," "Newhouse's Jew Story," and, most importantly, "Concerning the Jews" (1899)—represent his three-pronged attack on anti-Semitism, an attack that is clearly well-meaning, if limited, in its effectiveness. In *Following the Equator* (1897) he satirized the white man's treatment of Australian aborigines, as well as African blacks. Yet despite the sensitivity he often manifested regarding racism directed against the Chinese, African-Americans, Jews, and aborigines, Twain remained rabidly hostile to Native Americans throughout his life and is responsible for reinforcing a number of negative stereotypes. His early writing on the Sandwich Islands reveals a mixed set of attitudes toward native Hawaiians.

In other works, however, such as "To the Person Sitting in Darkness" (1901) and "Grief and Mourning for the Night" (1906), Twain raged at the gall of a race that claimed to have a monopoly on civilization while exporting the most heinous brutality around the globe. To his credit, Twain published these anti-racist diatribes despite the fact that friends like Joseph Twichell warned him that speaking out on this subject would harm his reputation.

Mark Twain never managed to transcend completely the limits of his time, his place, and his race. Yet both his published work and the fragments that remained unpublished at his death attest to his continuing interest in the social, political, and moral complexities of living in a "civilized" society that was built upon, and that still tolerated, racism. A number of the issues Twain tried, and failed, to address would become some of the central themes animating African-American writing in the twentieth century. The fecundity of these subjects and themes for African-American writers confirms one's sense that Twain was on the right track even if he was doomed to be derailed.

In an unpublished plot outline of a novel about "passing" set in the post-Reconstruction North that he wrote some time between 1883 and 1889 (["The Man With Negro Blood"]), he follows the fortunes of a light-skinned black who has no desire to deny his black blood but who finds that his "blackness" constantly stands in the way of opportu-

nities and advancement; Twain demonstrates his sensitivity to the kinds of anguished choices that would later form a major strain in fiction by African-American writers, including Frances E.W. Harper's *Iola Leroy* (1892), James Weldon Johnson's *Autobiography of an Ex-Colored Man* (1912), and Nella Larsen's *Passing* (1929). In portions of *Pudd'nhead Wilson* that Twain cut before publishing the novel in 1894 (Morgan Manuscript) he demonstrated his awareness of the social roots of problems in African-American life—an insight that prefigures the sociological analyses W.E.B. Du Bois would begin to publish several years later in *The Philadelphia Negro* and his Atlanta University studies. In fragments of unfinished fiction, like the novel "Which Was It?," Twain showed a prescient awareness of some of the forms that pent-up rage could take if the degradations of racism went unchecked. That stark tale of psychological violence, unleashed anger, and revenge for centuries of racial injustice that Twain began and abandoned between 1899 and 1903, anticipates some of the searing protest literature African-American writers would produce in the 1960s.

Mark Twain's disgust with his race was deep-seated and profound, and his prognosis for America was not good. There was a long road to travel before any real change or progress could take place, and he knew it would not happen in his lifetime. "The shame," as he put it in 1885, "is ours."

Shelley Fisher Fishkin

BIBLIOGRAPHY

Budd, Louis J. *Mark Twain: Social Philosopher.* Bloomington: Indiana UP, 1962.

———. "Southward Currents Under Huck Finn's Raft." *Mississippi Valley Historical Review* 46.2 (September 1959): 222–237.

Cardwell, Guy. *The Man Who Was Mark Twain: Images and Ideologies.* New Haven, Conn.: Yale UP, 1991.

Cummings, Sherwood. *Mark Twain and Science: Adventures of a Mind.* Baton Rouge: Louisiana State UP, 1988.

Davis, Thadious, James S. Leonard, and Thomas A. Tenney. *Satire or Evasion?: Black Perspectives on Huckleberry Finn.* Durham, N.C.: Duke UP, 1991.

Doyno, Victor. *Writing "Huck Finn": Mark Twain's Creative Process.* Philadelphia: U of Pennsylvania P, 1991.

Ellison, Ralph. *Shadow and Act.* New York: Random House, 1964.

Frederickson, George M. *The Black Image in the White Mind.* New York: Harper & Row, 1972.

Foner, Philip S. *Mark Twain: Social Critic.* New York: International Publishers, 1958.

Gillman, Susan. *Dark Twins: Imposture and Identity in Mark Twain's America.* Chicago: U of Chicago P, 1989.

Gillman, Susan, and Forrest G. Robinson, eds. *Mark Twain's Pudd'nhead Wilson: Race, Conflict, and Culture.* Durham, N.C.: Duke UP, 1990.

Gross, Seymour L., and John Edward Hardy, eds. *Images of the Negro in American Literature.* Chicago: U of Chicago P, 1966.

Kaplan, Justin. *Mr. Clemens and Mark Twain.* New York: Simon & Schuster, 1966.

Logan, Rayford. *The Betrayal of the Negro from Rutherford B. Hayes to Woodrow Wilson.* New York: Macmillan, 1970.

Pettit, Arthur G. *Mark Twain and the South.* Lexington: UP of Kentucky, 1974.

Robinson, Forrest. *In Bad Faith: The Dynamics of Deception in Mark Twain's America.* Cambridge, Mass.: Harvard UP, 1986.

Salomon, Roger B. *Twain and the Image of History.* New Haven, Conn.: Yale UP, 1961.

Sumida, Stephen H. "Reevaluating Mark Twain's Novel of Hawaii." *American Literature* 61.4 (December 1989): 586–609.

See also: Abolition; *Adventures of Huckleberry Finn;* Indians; Jews; Miscegenation; *Pudd'nhead Wilson, The Tragedy of;* Rachel, Aunt; Slavery

Raftsmen's Passage, The (in *Huckleberry Finn*)

When Mark Twain sent the manuscript of *Adventures of Huckleberry Finn* (1885) to his publisher, it included near the start of chapter 16 a fifteen-page passage describing Huck's visit to a large raft to see if he could eavesdrop to learn how far they were from Cairo. Twain's publisher, Charles Webster, however, talked Twain into letting him remove the passage from the published first edition of the novel.

Webster gave two reasons for the excision: (1) the passage had already been published in *Life on the Mississippi* (1883) and so might be thought of as "old" by readers, and (2) including it would make *Huck Finn* too long to be an obvious companion novel to *The Adventures of Tom Sawyer* (1876).

Most of the early editions of Twain's most famous work have followed the first edition in leaving out the passage, which Twain himself, in correspondence with Webster, called "the raft episode" in letters to Webster and to William Dean Howells. Increasingly, however, modern editors are reinserting the passage and publishing the novel with the passage in place after the second paragraph of chapter 16.

Their reasons for doing so are as follows: (1) it was clearly Twain's original intention to publish the passage in *Huck Finn,* and he agreed to omit it only at the last minute and at the urging of a publisher whose only interest was making the book shorter; (2) Huck learns by listening to the raftsmen information that he later uses in making decisions about his trip—information that is curiously and obviously absent if the passage is omitted; (3) including the passage provides information to the reader that Huck himself does not learn and so increases the dramatic irony of the novel; (4) the passage reveals important information about Huck's psychological state as he reacts to the story that one of the raftsmen tells about a drowned and abandoned baby. For more information about this passage, see Beidler, "Raft Episode," and Blair and Fischer, 394–398, 446–448, and 498–499.

Peter G. Beidler

BIBLIOGRAPHY

Beidler, Peter G. "The Raft Episode in *Huckleberry Finn.*" *Modern Fiction Studies* 14 (Spring 1968): 11–20.

Clemens, Samuel L. *Adventures of Huckleberry Finn.* Ed. Walter Blair and Victor Fischer. Berkeley: U of California P, 1985.

See also: Adventures of Huckleberry Finn

Ragsdale, Bill

Mark Twain met Bill or "Billy" Ragsdale while in Hawaii. Twain was attracted to the story of this "half-white" parliamentary interpreter who contracted leprosy. When Billy discovered he had the early stages of the disease, he broke off his engagement and retired to one of the island's leper colonies where he later died. Twain apparently intended to use the story as the basis for a novel about the Sandwich Islands. He includes the outline of Billy's story in *Following the Equator* (1897) where he comments briefly on Billy's self-sacrifice.

Twain suggested to William Dean Howells that Billy's story would illustrate "that the religious folly you are born in you will die in." Apparently the book was to develop further Twain's comments on religion. Twain claimed to have finished the novel, but all that survives are seventeen fragmentary pages. He also discussed with Howells the possibility of dramatizing the story, but if it was written, the play is no longer extant.

David G. Miller

BIBLIOGRAPHY

Clemens, Samuel L. *Following the Equator*. Hartford, Conn.: American Publishing, 1897.

———. *Mark Twain-Howells Letters: The Correspondence of Samuel L. Clemens and William D. Howells, 1872–1910*. Ed. Henry Nash Smith and William M. Gibson. 2 vols. Cambridge, Mass.: Harvard UP, 1960.

———. *Mark Twain's Notebooks & Journals*. Ed. Frederick Anderson, et al. 3 vols. Berkeley: U of California P, 1975–1979.

See also: *Following the Equator*

Rare Books

Evidence of interest in Mark Twain's books as collectors' items can be found at least as early as 1885 when the New York bookselling firm of Leon and Brothers published a catalogue that included all thirteen books Twain had written by that time, including *The Celebrated Jumping Frog* (1867) at $1.25, *The Adventures of Tom Sawyer* at $2.00, and *Adventures of Huckleberry Finn* (published only months earlier) at $2.75.

In 1893 Herbert Stone published the first comprehensive guide to collecting American first editions and included a checklist of Twain's published works. By 1898 Twain was well aware of his value as a "collected" author, and he wrote to the publishing firm of Chatto and Windus in November about a poem he had written, urging them to "try a new thing. Make a rare book for collectors—limited edition: 500 copies at $50 a copy; or thirty copies at $1,000 a copy. . . ." It is reported that Twain discovered his autograph signature for sale in an autograph dealer's catalogue for $5 and thereafter would sign books on the inside front cover rather than the free end paper, so that collectors could not remove his autograph and sell it.

In 1910, shortly after Twain's death, Merle Johnson published the first bibliography devoted to Twain's works. It was published in a deluxe format in an edition of 500 copies and found a ready market among early collectors like DeWitt Miller (an early American book collector), Irving S. Underhill (a New York publisher), James Tufts (a San Francisco newspaper editor), and Willard Morse (collection now at Yale University). Still, Twain was ignored by the previous generation of collectors such as Frank Maier, Stephen H. Wakeman, William Harris Arnold, and Jacob Chester Chamberlain. About 1913 Johnson, a bookseller, published a sale catalogue of Twain's works that stimulated further interest; and by 1931, when Underhill's collection was sold at auction, interest and prices were strong (*Celebrated Jumping Frog*, $350; *Tom Sawyer*, $910). Despite the Depression, interest in collecting increased and Johnson brought out a revised edition of his *Bibliography* in 1935. Three years later a Philip Duschnes sales catalogue reflected that prices had stabilized somewhat (*Celebrated Jumping Frog*, $225; *Tom Sawyer*, $500).

Collecting interest in Twain's works has steadily grown due to three factors: his continuing popularity with each generation of readers, the variety of formats and attractiveness of the first editions of his works (many were issued in colorful pictorial bindings and heavily illustrated), and the relative availability and affordability of his first editions. Because of his huge popularity, most of his first editions were published in large editions and have a good survival rate today, keeping prices reasonable compared to other nineteenth-century authors. In 1980 bookseller Alan Fox issued a sales catalogue with 765 items (*Celebrated Jumping Frog*, $4,500; *Tom Sawyer*, $5,250). Such prices were a bit ahead of their time, and only 16 percent of the catalogue sold before another bookseller took over the sale of the collection and slashed the prices to sell the material. While collecting interest in Twain continues to grow, auction prices for H. Bradley Martin's handful of Twain first editions (*Celebrated Jumping Frog*, $15,400; *Tom Sawyer*, $18,700) are double and triple, respectively, what these books generally sell at.

Besides first editions, books from Twain's library have become much sought after in recent years. Once neglected by collectors despite Twain's 1911 estate sale and the 1951 estate sale of Twain's daughter, these important association books that could often be bought for less than $100 in the 1970s now fetch eight to ten times as much, and those with good annotations can bring several thousand dollars. Alan Gribben's *Mark Twain's Library: A Reconstruction* is the standard reference for collectors and scholars.

And yet, for the collector of moderate means it is still possible to assemble, with patience and caution, a representative collection of Twain first editions. Prices vary widely, depending on "issue points" and condition, but many first editions are readily available in the $100 range in correct bibliographical state and in well-preserved original bindings. *Adventures of Huckleberry Finn* (1885), in the correct early state of the first edition and in original cloth, can range in price from $300 to $3,000, depending solely on condition. The best bibliographical guide for the collector or scholar is *The Bibliography of American Literature* (Volume 2), known as *BAL*. Although no comprehensive descriptive bibliography of Twain yet exists, *BAL*, Johnson, and McBride's colorfully illustrated checklist of the Mark Twain Memorial Collection are useful references.

Kevin Mac Donnell

BIBLIOGRAPHY

American Art Association. *Hawthorne, Melville, Clemens, Burroughs, Whitman*. New York: Anderson Galleries, 1931. Lots 35–126.

Anderson Auction Company. *Catalogue of the Library and Manuscripts of Samuel L. Clemens*. New York: Anderson Auction, 1911.

Blanck, Jacob, ed. *Bibliography of American Literature*. New Haven, Conn.: Yale UP, 1955 to date.

Christie, Manson, and Woods International, Inc. *The Estelle Doheny Collection*. New York: Christie, Manson and Woods, 1987.

Duschnes, Philip C. *Mark Twain, Catalogue 30*. New York: Philip C. Duschnes, 1938.

Fox, Alan C. *Mark Twain, Catalogue One*. Sherman Oaks, Calif.: Alan C. Fox, 1980.

Gabrilowitsch, Clara Clemens. *Mark Twain Library Auction*. Los Angeles: E.F. Whitman and F.B. O'Connor, 1951.

Gribben, Alan. *Mark Twain's Library: A Reconstruction*. 2 vols. Boston: G.K. Hall, 1980.

Gribben, Alan, and Kevin Mac Donnell, eds. *Mark Twain's Rubáiyát*. Austin, Tex.: Jenkins Publishing, 1983.

Johnson, Merle. *A Bibliography of the Works of Mark Twain*. New York: Harper, 1910.

Leab, Katharine, and Daniel Leab, eds. *American Book Prices Current*. New York: Bancroft-Parkman, 1895–1990.

Leon and Brother. *First Editions of American Authors*. New York: Leon and Brother, 1885.

McBride, William M. *Mark Twain: A Bibliography of the Collections of the Mark Twain Memorial and the Stowe-Day Foundation*. Hartford, Conn.: McBride, 1984.

Stone, Herbert S. *First Editions of American Authors*. Cambridge, Mass.: Stone and Kimball, 1893.

See also: Auctions; Manuscript Collections

Raymond, John T.
(1836–1887)

A comic actor noted for his deadpan manner, John T. Raymond played the role of Colonel

Mulberry Sellers in Mark Twain's dramatization of *The Gilded Age* (1873). He was born John O'Brien on 5 April 1836 in Buffalo, New York, the son of illiterate Irish immigrants. His first appearance on the stage was in nearby Rochester on 27 June 1853, and soon he made his way to Boston. The Know-Nothing party was asserting itself strongly at this time, and Raymond, seeking not to garner the anti-Irish wrath of the party, changed his stage name from O'Brien to Raymond, and by this professional name he became universally known.

Raymond's association with Twain's character Colonel Sellers began in April 1874, after Gilbert B. Densmore, drama critic of the San Francisco *Golden Era*, submitted to him an unauthorized stage adaptation of the best-selling novel *The Gilded Age*. Despite Densmore's shabby dramatization, Raymond's comedic skill brought the play instant popularity. Charles Dudley Warner, co-author of the novel, first learned of Densmore's piracy and immediately contacted Twain. The two authors owned a dramatic copyright on the novel; however, since Densmore's play was largely based on Twain's creation, Sellers, Twain convinced Warner to renounce any claim upon the novel's characters created by Twain. Then Twain telegraphed and enjoined the play's performance before beginning a correspondence with Densmore and Raymond. Twain paid Densmore a total of $400 for his script and made some use of Densmore's plot as a skeleton in his three rewritings of the final version, which he copyrighted in July 1874. Although Twain wanted either Edwin Booth or Lawrence Barrett in the title role, he settled reluctantly on Raymond, who had already proved himself a success playing Sellers.

Raymond's production of *The Gilded Age* first opened at the Park Theatre, New York, 16 September 1874. The play drew overflow crowds and eventually became one of the most successful plays on the American stage in the 1870s and 1880s. The play succeeded financially from the start and made a fortune for both the actor and author. However, when Raymond took the play to London, it failed miserably, like several other American plays of the day.

Despite Raymond's ability to captivate his audiences, Twain grew to detest him. Some of this resentment can be attributed to Twain's feeling that Raymond presented an inappropriate representation of his beloved cousin, Major James Lampton, the man who was Sellers in Twain's mind. However, Twain's resentment goes deeper. Raymond had hinted to Twain that his acting ability, rather than Twain's pen, had created the great character Sellers, and the writer's ego and proprietary feeling matched the actor's. For the rest of his life in letters, conversations, and autobiographical dictations, Twain maintained that the finer points in Sellers's character were above Raymond's acting ability.

After Twain and William D. Howells co-authored a dramatic revival of Sellers in *Colonel Sellers as as Scientist* (written 1883), Raymond refused to play the lead role because he felt the two authors had corrupted the character Sellers, presenting a lunatic rather than the stage-worthy visionary he had played before. His rejection of the Sellers role prevented the bizarre play from ever reaching the stage.

Raymond continued playing comic roles until his sudden death in a hotel in Evansville, Indiana, on 10 April 1887 during one of his midwestern tours. Almost two decades later, Twain's bitterness toward the actor remained unassuaged. In the first section of his autobiography published in the *North American Review* (7 September 1906), Twain slammed Raymond as wholly destitute of manliness, honor, and honesty, and called him empty, selfish, and vulgar. Raymond's only son responded to these attacks with a personal letter to Twain dated 19 November 1906. In the letter, Raymond's son cited peers' published accounts of his father's generosity and kindness, and he entreated Twain not to besmirch further the name of a man long dead. Twain's proprietary jealousy for his creation Sellers did not negate the reality that Raymond had a claim on the character. The comedian had shaped and helped make popular among contemporary audiences Twain's immortal character Sellers and his famous cry, "There's millions in it!" Raymond had performed a most pivotal role in Twain's first experience as a dramatist.

Lucius M. Lampton

BIBLIOGRAPHY

Clemens, Samuel L. *Mark Twain-Howells Letters: The Correspondence of Samuel L. Clemens and William D. Howells 1872–1910.* Ed. Henry Nash Smith and William M. Gibson. 2 vols. Cambridge, Mass.: Harvard UP, 1960.

French, Bryant Morey. *Mark Twain and "The Gilded Age."* Dallas: Southern Methodist UP, 1965.

Kendall, John S. *The Golden Age of the New Orleans Theater.* Baton Rouge: Louisiana State UP, 1952.

Lampton, Lucius M. "Hero in a Fool's Paradise." *Mark Twain Journal* 27.2 (Fall 1989): 1–56.

Matthews, Brander, and Laurence Hutton. *The Life and Art of Edwin Booth and His Contemporaries.* Boston: L.C. Page, 1886.

Odell, George C.D. *Annals of the New York Stage.* New York: Columbia UP, 1939.

See also: Colonel Sellers; Dramatist, Mark Twain as; Sellers, Colonel; Lampton, James J.

Reading

Like Ernest Hemingway and other American authors who lacked a college education or for whom strong claims of originality are made, Mark Twain has persistently been viewed as a relatively "unread" individual, someone who essentially lacked literary sophistication. In part this erroneous impression was a result of William Dean Howells's offhand observations about Twain's eager, almost childlike campaigns at reading on a certain topic of passing interest (*My Mark Twain*, 1910). Albert Bigelow Paine, Twain's designated biographer, reinforced that opinion by emphasizing the narrow range of Twain's reading, his strong affection for history, biography, and personal memoirs and his tendency to read out of a curiosity about celebrated people (Paine 1:510–512, 3:1536–1540, 3:1576).

Twain himself seemed pleased with his image as a world-famous author who read but little, and that only for entertainment or diversion—reading as a "lazy" pastime pictured in his posing for photographs in chair or bed. This was another part of the casual, untutored literary artist pose he created; probably he initially had found it an advisable mask for an author whose audience would for decades be reached by door-to-door canvassers approaching the homes and businesses of those for whom reading was still viewed as a luxury and literacy itself was never taken for granted.

In fact, Mark Twain was a voracious, insightful, and often systematic reader. Hundreds of volumes from his library bear marks—in the form of underlinings, brackets, and annotations—of his careful perusal. The marginal jottings are often witty, as when he complained of one translator of Suetonius that "he reels from tense to tense like a Scot going home from a Burns banquet." Mocking the French missionaries' tactic of converting the Algonquins by warning them that God burns his enemies, just as they themselves sometimes do, Twain wrote disgustedly across the page of Parkman's *Jesuits in North America*, "Therefore God is an Algonquin." In a copy of H.G. Wells's *The Future of America* Twain opined: "We have a bastard Patriotism, a sarcasm, a burlesque; but we have no such thing as a public conscience." A page of Saint-Simon's *Memoirs* received this blast: "These low scoundrels, these shams, these play-acting sentimental pukes. How French it all is!" In a preface written by Lew Wallace for an edition of *Ben Hur*, Twain could not resist a sarcasm about Wallace's description of his religious awakening: "In this fairy tale we have a curiously grotesque situation: God, ambushed in a Pullman sleeper, surreptitiously & unfairly betraying an unsuspecting good & honest infidel [Robert G. Ingersoll] into converting Lew Wallace. To what trivial uses may we come at last." Reading Greville's *Memoirs*, Twain noted, "What a man sees in the human race is merely himself in the deep and honest privacy of his own heart."

Among favorite, oft-read titles in Clemens's library must be numbered the writings of W.E.H. Lecky (especially *History of European Morals*), the Bible, *The Arabian Nights*, Malory's *Morte D'Arthur*, Benvenuto Cellini's *Life*, Swift's *Gulliver's Travels*, Cervantes's *Don Quixote*, Defoe's *Robinson Crusoe*, Samuel Pepys's *Diary*, Shakespeare's works, Richard Henry Dana's *Two Years Before the Mast*, Suetonius's *Lives of the Caesars*, FitzGerald's *Rubáiyát of Omar Khayyám*, Rudyard Kipling's works, and Carlyle's *French Revolution*, among others. Some of these volumes are now missing. Depredations to his private library that once contained at least 2,500 titles have left less than a third of its contents extant; these losses primarily resulted form his early travels, his decision to leave the Hartford house, and his gifts to public libraries. Today the surviving volumes, when they make their infrequent appearances on the rare book auction block, command thousands of dollars in prices.

One of Twain's greatest pleasures lay in reading history, particularly English history, and he was familiar with, and often annotated the works of Taine, Carlyle, Froude, Hume, Macaulay, and others. But he was also more current in the literature of his time than many literary critics have assumed. Robert Louis Stevenson, Joel Chandler Harris, James Whitcomb Riley, Joseph C. Lincoln (*Cape Cod Ballads*), John Kendrick Bangs, and other popular authors had their place on his bookshelves. Even the literary fads such as John Habberton's *Helen's Babies* (1876) and *The Jericho Road* (1877) and Sarah Grand's *The Heavenly Twins* (1893) received his careful attention. He was an assiduous reader of George Washington Cable's fiction. Edgar Watson Howe's disturbing tale, *The Story of a Country Town* (1883), gained Clemens's notice and praise. He certainly knew by heart the literary materials he burlesqued, from Alexandre Dumas's prison romances to Felicia Hemans's "Casabianca" to Arthur Conan Doyle's Sherlock Holmes series. The novels and stories he sometimes disparaged—those by Jane Austen, Sir Walter Scott, James Fenimore Cooper, George Eliot, Bret Harte, Henry James, George Meredith, for example—nevertheless, were well represented, and often well marked, in his or his family's personal library. His relationship with Charles Dickens became that of a jealous later rival to some extent, but he knew and respected Dickens's works. Robert Browning developed into a full-fledged avocation for Twain, and he even led discussion groups devoted to Browning's poetry; a large number of meticulously marked volumes from these public readings survive. Juvenile fiction formed a sizeable part of Twain's library and family-circle reading, and it ranged from Jacob Abbott's Beechnut, Rodolphus, Ellen Linn, and Rollo stories to Lewis Carroll's *Alice's Adventures in Wonderland* and *Through the Looking-Glass*. Twain also shared the conventional veneration for Tennyson, Longfellow, Emerson, Lowell, Holmes, and other lionized authors of his period.

For literary effusions of truly little merit Clemens developed an absorbing, compulsive appetite. Two or three dozen works of poetry and prose earned inclusion in his hypothetical "Library of Literary Hogwash," relished for their exquisite badness. Julia A Moore's *Sentimental Song Book*, Samuel Watson Royston's *The Enemy Conquered or, Love Triumphant*, S.O. Stedman's *Allen Bay, A Story*, Levi Bishop's *Poetical Works*, Edward Payson Hammond's *Sketches of Palestine*, James Milne's *The Romance of Pro-Consul*, and Belton O. Townsend's *Plantation Lays and Other Poems* were among the gems that earned Twain's lambasting comments. Learning of his insatiable search for such examples of literary efforts gone awry, Twain's friends and acquaintances sent him occasional additions to his cherished "Hogwash" collection.

A field of science that particularly interested Twain was astronomy; he devoured and marked a dozen books on that subject. He heavily annotated works of Charles Darwin and examined various books on geology and geography. The nascent discipline of psychology—represented, for instance, by John Adams's *Herbartian Psychology*—fascinated Mark Twain, as did books about the social nature of insects and animals, such as Sir John Lubbock's *Ants, Bees, and Wasps.*

Guidebooks accompanied Twain on virtually all of his many travels, and frequently they were either cited or scoffed at in the narrative that resulted from a journey. Foreign-language dictionaries and grammars were staples of the library collection of Clemens and his entire family, and a surprising percentage of volumes testify to his willingness to attempt foreign-language editions of literary works in French, Italian, and German, rather than translation.

Clemens's reading tastes were hardly inerrant. A massive portion of his library shelves was given over to the now nearly forgotten prose and poetry of Thomas Bailey Aldrich. Presumably Clemens's repeated praise of Aldrich's idealistic verse was the result of their friendship and of Aldrich's exalted standing among his contemporaries. The books and essays of Hartford neighbor Charles Dudley Warner understandably had regular claims upon Clemens's time. Clemens likewise knew most of his friend William Dean Howells's writing by heart, and though Howells's literary reputation has fared better than Aldrich's or Warner's, he is still studied far less today than several of his then less eminent fellow authors. Less predictably, Clemens knew and liked the work of many women writers from various eras, including Wilhemine (*Memoirs*), Lady Duff-Gordon, Harriet Beecher Stowe, Sarah Orne Jewett, Grace King, Sarah P. McLean Greene (*Cape Cod Folks, Flood-tide*), and Mariia Bashkirtseva (*The Journal of a Young Artist*). Frances Trollope's travel narrative about the United States earned his strong admiration, for example.

A few commentators have expressed disappointment in Twain's limited acquaintance with ethnic authors, aside from his awareness of a few African-American slave narratives and several other works, including the poetry of Paul Lawrence Dunbar. At the same time, scholars should remind themselves before reaching conclusions about the contents of Clemens's library that it underwent various losses and that, for this reason, our knowledge of the books he owned and read must remain tentative and incomplete. His reading can be better documented than that of some American authors, such as Stephen Crane, whose libraries have vanished almost completely or, as in the case of Herman Melville, writers whose surviving collections display obvious gaps. But we do possess enough indications of Twain's wide-ranging inquisitiveness in the form of allusions (in his books, notebooks, and letters, as well as bookstore receipts and other records and the testimony of his acquaintances) to grant him respect as a dedicated, intrepid reader. Although evidence seems to suggest that Twain somehow missed three major influences of the age that succeeded his—Herman Melville, Karl Marx, and Sigmund Freud—he was otherwise very much an advanced reader for his times and perspicacious in his selection of material for study. Any notion of him as an indolent, casual reader is unjustified.

Alan Gribben

BIBLIOGRAPHY

Gribben, Alan. *Mark Twain's Library: A Reconstruction.* 2 vols. Boston: G.K. Hall, 1980.

Howells, William Dean. *My Mark Twain: Reminiscences and Criticisms.* New York: Harper, 1910.

Paine, Albert Bigelow. *Mark Twain: A Biography.* 3 vols. New York: Harper, 1912.

See also: Clemens, Samuel Langhorne

Realism

In considering realism it is important to differentiate between the basic attitude to life that can be deemed "realistic" and the literary movement that bears this name. The two are interconnected, stemming from the same root, but as a literary mode realism operates in a more complex manner than is generally thought.

The term "realism" derives from the Latin word, *res*, meaning "thing." Realism therefore denotes a fundamental attachment to the things of this world without any transcendence. In philosophy it has commonly been associated with materialism. Those who are realists by temperament or belief cling to the positive aspect of things within their reach, in contrast to those of romantic disposition who always yearn precisely for what is beyond reach as the most ardently desirable objective.

In literary criticism, too, realism is often envisaged in opposition to romanticism. The term was first applied to literature in a French journal of 1826 to describe a type of writing that sought to imitate directly and originally from nature rather than from previous artistic models, as had been customary. The word and the issue, however, became popular only after the middle of the century. In 1855 the French painter Gustave Courbet exhibited his paintings of peasant life and work under the collective title "Le Réalisme." *Réalisme* was also the name of a review that appeared July 1856–May 1857; it proclaimed that art should give a truthful representation of the real world, that it should study contemporary life meticulously in order to give an exact, complete, and sincere reproduction of the social milieu, and that it should do so dispassionately, impersonally, and objectively. Gustave Flaubert's masterpiece, *Madame Bovary* (1857), is a landmark in the evolution of realism because of its portrayal of commonplace people in a dreary provincial environment and the prominence it accords to the humble details of everyday life.

This conceptualization of realism was for long upheld, in part because it stemmed from the testimony of the writers themselves. Their major emphasis was on the truthfulness and faithfulness of the reproduction of ordinary life close at hand (again in antithesis to the exoticism favored by the romantics). The self-image of ingenuousness that the realists fostered is most succinctly summarized in the contention "*All is true*" uttered by the narrator at the beginning of *Old Goriot* by the French novelist Balzac. The phrase is highlighted through its appearance in a foreign language and in italics. It is actually an allusion to Shakespeare's *Henry V*, whose initial subtitle was "All is true." The irony of grounding the claim to the fiction's truthfulness to life by means of a citation of another literary work seems to have escaped nineteenth-century readers entirely. The metaphor of the mirror was also frequently invoked (e.g., by Dickens, George Eliot, and the French novelist Stendhal) to express the essential mission of realist narrative in representing an unembellished reflection of surrounding life.

This rather naive view of realism persisted well into the twentieth century and led to an underestimation of the literary interest of realism as compared to more obviously complicated modes of writing such as romanticism, surrealism, or self-conscious fiction. However, realism became the major focus of the Marxist critics, notably Georg (Gyorgy) Lukács, whose various studies of European realism, written in the 1920s and 1930s, became available in English translation some twenty to thirty years later. Relying on an emphatically referential model of the realist novel, Lukács sees it as giving a terrifyingly accurate and typical picture of the social reality of capitalist society.

This referential perception of realism was not seriously challenged until the revolution in literary criticism wrought in the late 1960s by the advent of structuralism and post-structuralism. Although most of the structuralists were not particularly drawn to realism, their close attention to the linguistic texture of the text suggested a new approach to realism through study of its figuration. The outstanding example of such an innovative reading is Roland Barthes's highly idiosyncratic analysis of Balzac's story *Sarrasine*, in *S/Z* (1970). Proceeding by his own admission "in the manner of a minor earthquake," Barthes breaks the text up into small segments, in which he traces the five "codes that constitute it: the hermeneutic, the semantic, the symbolic, the proairetic (concerning action), and the cultural." The importance of Barthes's work lies less in its specific methodology than in its overall vision of the realist text as a largely self-contained web of words governed by its own internal codes and systems of reference. This represents the diametric opposite to the traditional understanding of realism as an imitation of life. Disturbing and perhaps overstated though *S/Z* is, it has, nonetheless, helped to stimulate a renewal of interest in realism as a mode of writing worth serious scrutiny.

Most recent studies of realism aim to probe its literary convention. The task is so difficult precisely because realism takes such great care to conceal its artifices under the pretense of simple imitation. Many of the old myths and platitudes have now been discredited. For instance, sustaining patterns of recurrent imagery have been uncovered in a novel such as George Eliot's *Middlemarch*. Also, acceptance of the writer's claims to objectivity have been disproven through identification of a distinctive narrating voice that projects an ironic, a comic, or a satirical image of the protagonists and their actions. Such insights have been facilitated by the increasing subtlety in the techniques of narrative analysis that have cumulatively revealed a picture of realism as a far more intricate and finely crafted mode of writing than used to be assumed. Nowadays it is widely conceded that a shaping artistic imagination is as intrinsic to realism as to any other literary mode.

William Dean Howells, to whom Twain often turned for advice and criticism, led the reaction to early nineteenth-century romanticism in the United States. Howells insisted on verisimilitude, calling for the artist to portray life as it was. From the 1870s on, Twain was a willing follower, although his range would not allow him to become "merely" a realist. Nor would he refer to himself as a realist. Besides such pieces as *The Prince and the Pauper* (1882) and *Pudd'nhead Wilson* (1894), one needs to examine *Adventures of Huckleberry Finn* (1885), in which the various attempts to reproduce dialect, attention to details with almost scientific accuracy, and descriptions of the Mississippi River environs surely pleased Howells as models of "sticking to the facts."

Lilian R. Furst

BIBLIOGRAPHY

Barthes, Roland. "The Reality Effect." *French Literary Theory Today.* Trans. R. Carter. Ed. Tzvetan Todorov. New York: Cambridge UP, 1982. 11–17.

———. *S/Z.* Trans. Richard Miller. New York: Hill and Wang, 1974.

Becker, George J., ed. *Documents of Modern Literary Realism.* Princeton, N.J.: Princeton UP, 1963.

Ermarth, Elizabeth D. *Realism and Consensus in the English Novel.* Princeton, N.J.: Princeton UP, 1983.

Furst, Lilian R. "Realism and Its 'Code of Accreditation.'" *Comparative Literature Studies* 25.2 (1988): 101–126.

Hemmings, F.W.J., ed. *The Age of Realism.* Harmondsworth, England: Penguin Books, 1974.

Levin, Harry T. *The Gates of Horn. A Study of Five French Realists.* New York: Oxford UP, 1963.

Levine, George Lewis. *The Realistic Imagination.* Chicago: U of Chicago P, 1981.

Lukács, Georg. *Studies in European Realism.* Trans. Edith Bone. London: Hillway, 1950.

Stern, J.P. *On Realism.* London: Routledge & Kegan Paul, 1973.

Williams, D.A., ed. *The Monster in the Mirror.* London: Oxford UP, 1978.

Wellek, René. "The Concept of Realism." *Concepts of Criticism.* Ed. Stephen G. Nichols, Jr. New Haven, Conn.: Yale UP, 1963. 222–255.

See also: Howells, William Dean; Naturalism; Regionalism; Science; Sentimentality

Redpath, James
(1833–1891)

A journalist and author, James Redpath established the Boston Lyceum Bureau in 1869 at a time when local lyceums were failing because, he was convinced, they did not include humorous lectures and concerts in addition to the traditional didactic lectures on philosophical, literary, and religious subjects (by such speakers as Emerson, Phillips, and Dickinson). To provide variety, Redpath signed contracts with Mark Twain as well as such other humorists as Nasby, Billings, and Nye. Twain lectured two full seasons with Redpath as his agent. During 1869–1870 he gave forty-seven performances of "Our Fellow Savages of the Sandwich Islands" over twelve weeks; during the 1871–1872 season he lectured seventy-six times over sixteen weeks, mainly using his "Roughing It" lecture. Though Twain thought highly of Redpath, he disliked lecturing. He performed chiefly because he was paid well, earning $100–$150 for each performance (with 10 percent going to Redpath). Years later (in 1885) Redpath, who had learned shorthand in his native Scotland, served as Twain's amanuensis in preparing Twain's autobiographical dictations concerning Grant's *Memoirs*.

L. Terry Oggel

BIBLIOGRAPHY

Fatout, Paul. *Mark Twain on the Lecture Circuit.* Bloomington: Indiana UP, 1960.

Lorch, Fred W. *The Trouble Begins at Eight: Mark Twain's Lecture Tours.* Ames: Iowa State UP, 1968.

See also: Lecturer

"Reflections on Religion"
(1963)

Dictated to stenographer Josephine Hobby on June 1906, as a portion of his autobiography, Mark Twain's five chapters on religion, later titled "Reflections on Religion" by Charles Neider, were first published in the *Hudson Review* (Autumn 1963), after having been suppressed for fifty-seven years. The savagely irreverent chapters were suppressed first by Twain himself, then by biographer and literary executor Albert Bigelow Paine, and finally by Twain's daughter Clara Clemens Samossoud. Paine's edition of *Mark Twain's Autobiography* (1924) cites bits and fragments from the chapters but does not identify them. At Mrs. Samossoud's insistence, Bernard DeVoto omitted the chapters from *Mark Twain in Eruption* (1940). In 1960, after discussions with Neider, Mrs. Samossoud changed her mind about permitting publication of the manuscript, and Neider published the chap-

ters in the *Hudson Review* as "Reflections on Religion." In 1987 Neider published the chapters for the first time in book form in *The Outrageous Mark Twain* (Doubleday).

Twain wrote William Dean Howells (17 June 1906): "Tomorrow I mean to dictate a chapter which will get my heirs and assigns burnt alive if they venture to print it on this side of A.D. 2006—which I judge they won't" (Neider 6). Twain would finish dictating his five "Reflections on Religion" chapters on 25 June, writing to Howells, "I have been dictating some fearful things, for four successive mornings for no eye but yours to see until I have been dead a century—if then. But I got them out of my system, where they had been festering for years—and that was the main thing. I feel better now" (Neider 6).

In "Reflections on Religion" a vitrolic Twain ("the dead are the only human beings who are really well off," 32) lashes out with such savage vehemence and abandon that he seems to sputter. His very rage seems to sweep him beyond mere agnosticism, atheism, or nihilism to wreak an Ahab-like vengeance upon an inscrutable and malicious Deity. For the modern reader, Twain's vehement and irrational eruptions may seem somewhat embarrassing and puzzling—like observing the tantrums of a friend. Still, Twain's very rage seems to affirm that, beneath it all, he is "a profoundly religious man" (Neider 2) bent on attacking a real, though indifferent or even malicious Deity.

Venting a terrible rage, Twain cannot focus his lightning bolts; rather he fires them in all directions. At the base of his argument is what he insists is a two-faced, unloving Father, "vindictive, unjust, ungenerous, pitiless and vengeful," who inflicts untold miseries on His children. Raging suddenly in another direction, Twain attacks the Bible as full of falsehoods, from Noah's Flood to the Immaculate Conception (he means the Virgin Birth) and assails the book as a soiler of Christian youth. He then reverses his direction to attack the murders undertaken over two millenia in the name of Christianity, then thrusts in yet another direction to take comfort in assuring that Christianity, like all other religions, will not long endure. Regardless of how burningly Twain believes his arguments and assertions, the sheer uncontrolled aggregate of these impassioned mudslingings suggests that Mark Twain was raging like a shunned and disappointed lover at a real but former object of his affection.

In chapter 4 the still sputtering Twain returns to the subject of a God who cannot engage in such trivialities as listening to human prayers. Twain fumes, slapping yet another sacred cow, "There is nothing resembling proof that" God has ever listened to or answered prayers. Indeed, no one can get God's attention, much less move Him to pity (45), for He is busy "ingeniously" fashioning and implementing "the ten-thousandfold law of punishment" (46), by which every creature must suffer pain and misery and "stand astonished at God's all-comprehensive malice" (45). Twain scoffs at a clergy who teach that this cruel Father commits these crimes to "purify" the sufferer, to "train him for the society of the Deity" (46). We should, he shudders, use such technique with our own children.

Twain fumes over the promise of God's reward of a nonexistent heaven. After all, what kind of heaven can mankind expect from a malicious God? "It is not likely," he muses, "that there will be a Heaven hereafter." In fact, given the nature of Deity, "It is exceedingly likely that there will be a Hell—and it is nearly dead certain that nobody is going to escape it" (49).

Twain concludes his five bitter essays by returning to a favorite theme, an attack on the "Damned Human Race," "the poorest of all [God's] inventions" (50). But Twain's deterministic theology is sometimes contradictory and confusing, and he hastens to point out that pitiful man is, after all, a determined creature of fate, not responsible for any of it—and thus free from responsibility for sin, save for the sin of creating a God who makes us responsible. Man "didn't make himself. He has no control over himself . . .; he has no will.

He is as purely a piece of automatic mechanism as is a watch" and is certainly not obligated, Twain insists, "to the unknown Power that inflicted this outrage upon him." Concludes Twain, in this confused and frenzied psychic scream, the echoes of which resonate through the dark writings of his last years, "God, and God alone, is responsible for every act and word of a human being's life between cradle and grave" (51).

Richard H. Cracroft

BIBLIOGRAPHY

Clemens, Samuel L. *The Outrageous Mark Twain.* Ed. Charles Neider. New York: Doubleday, 1987.

See also: "Damned Human Race, The"; Determinism; God; Philosophy; Religion

"Refuge of the Derelicts, The" (1972)

Mark Twain worked on his incomplete and unpublished novel "The Refuge of the Derelicts" during the spring of 1905 and summer of 1906. His notes suggest that its original working title was "The House of Tragedies," but the title it bears in *Mark Twain's Fables of Man* (1972) is what Twain said he would "probably entitle" the work when he referred to it in an autobiographical dictation in August 1906.

The novel's plot is slight. George Sterling, an artist-poet, visits the blustery Admiral Stormfield (one of Twain's many characters based on Ned Wakefield) to request his support for a proposed monument to Adam. Taking lodgings with the admiral, he meets the household's servants and hangers-on, most of them "derelicts," victims of tragedy caused by ill luck or their own overscrupulous morals. The story's main interest comes from its character sketches and development of philosophical themes. Only apparently does it center on the striking Admiral Stormfield, who evolves from an incomprehensible old salt to a spokesman for Twain's own revisionary theology

(Adam was not responsible for the Fall because he could not possibly have understood what kind of a punishment "death" would be). Instead, the story's unity depends on Sterling, who falls from innocence into an awareness of human suffering and universal injustice. And the bitterly ironic ending, which juxtaposes the Reverend Lo-what-God-hath-Wrought's praise of a beneficent nature with a slide show featuring grisly parasitism and predation, is anomalous; Twain's dominant tone in portraying "those pathetic figures," the derelicts, is a gentle, sentimental irony that recalls Nathaniel Hawthorne's allegorical tale "The Christmas Banquet" (1844), about an annual feast for the ten most miserable persons who can be found.

"Refuge" has received sparse critical attention. John Tuckey, Sholom Kahn, and William Macnaughton discuss the tale in the context of other late works presenting the "Satanic" view of the human condition, where God is the author of an ultimate injustice against which human fellowship is the sole weak defense. Maria Marotti sees "Refuge" as Twain's rewriting of the myth of the fall. While its generic mixture of comic and pathetic realism lacks the symbolic power of Twain's late cosmic fantasies, it strikingly depicts the human consequences of an unkind Providence.

David R. Sewell

BIBLIOGRAPHY

Clemens, Samuel L. "The Refuge of the Derelicts." *Mark Twain's Fables of Man.* By Clemens. Ed. John S. Tuckey. Berkeley: U of California P, 1972. 157–248.

Kahn, Sholom J. "New Mark Twain Materials: Fresh Perspectives." *Amerikastudien (American Studies)* 19 (1974): 375–386.

Macnaughton, William R. *Mark Twain's Last Years as a Writer.* Columbia: U of Missouri P, 1979.

Marotti, Maria Ornella. *The Duplicating Imagination: Twain and the Twain Papers.* University Park: Pennsylvania State UP, 1990.

See also: "Monument to Adam, A"; Providence; Religion

Regionalism

Too often regionalism has been considered a somewhat derogatory term in the sense that a regional writer is sometimes thought of as a provincial writer, delimited by his or her geographical area and given over to a detailed portraiture containing little but local color.

In actuality, regionalism can well be viewed as being at the very heart of American literature, with the best regional writing emphasizing the universal as well as the particular. Though regionalism is usually associated with such later nineteenth-century writers as Bret Harte in the West, Sarah Orne Jewett in New England, and George Washington Cable in the South, it is just as pertinent to speak of Nathaniel Hawthorne as a New England regionalist, Herman Melville as a writer of the region of the sea, and James Fenimore Cooper as depictor of New York State. In a country as large and diverse as the United States it was inevitable that regional writing would become a mainstay of the nation's literary output. Most good writers, it could be said, write *out of* a region at the same time they write *about* it. The best writers all enjoy a sense of place, though that place does not have to be geographical. It can be said, for example, that Emily Dickenson's "place" is not Amherst, Massachusetts, but the imaginative reaches of the mind or that Henry James's "place" is not Boston, London, Paris, or Rome, but the psychological realm of consciousness and experience.

Generally speaking, however, regionalism pertains to a particular geographical area, the writer attempting to capture the rhythms, customs, speech, and manners of the locale. Region gives the writer a home base, a sense of location, from which to branch forth much broader thematic context. The local colorist often stops at a more superficial level of coverage, while the true regionalist pushes beyond those bounds to imbue the characters, events, and themes of the work with elements characteristic of all persons and places.

Although the beginnings of regionalism in America are usually associated with the post-

Civil War era, with the likes of Harte, Jewett, Cable, Harriet Beecher Stowe, Edward Eggleston, James Lane Allen, Mary E. Wilkins Freeman, and many others, the movement can be traced to much earlier origins. It perhaps began with the fervent literary nationalism that sprang up in America after the Revolutionary War and the War of 1812, a glorifying of nationhood that, as the country grew and spread out, devolved upon particular regions. More assuredly, regionalism found its roots in the Old Southwest frontier humor during the three decades before the Civil War. Works such as A.B. Longstreet's *Georgia Scenes* (1835), W.T. Thompson's *Major Jones' Courtship* (1843), J.J. Hooper's *Some Adventures of Captain Simon Suggs* (1845), and J.G. Baldwin's *Flush Times of Alabama and Mississippi* (1853) focused on particular rural areas in the Old South, emphasizing colloquial speech, local mores, provincial manners, and customs of the region. Though there was much exaggeration and boisterous humor in Old Southwest literature, there was also an attempt to record many aspects of frontier life accurately. Thus the regional literature of the Old Southwest also contributed to the rise of realism later in the century.

The Civil War, along with growth west of the Mississippi, brought a newly heightened sensitivity to regionalism, even though officially, or politically, the country was reunited after the war. The sectionalism that existed concomitant with the war survived as legitimate regionalism, giving rise to the local-color movement first and then more mature and genuine regional literature. The growth of regionalism constituted the very decentralization of American literature that William Dean Howells and especially Hamlin Garland called for. By 1868, when Bret Harte's stories portraying life in the California mining camps became popular, regionalism in the United States was emerging in the four major geographical areas of the Northeast, South, West, and Midwest. The high peak of regional literature, from 1875 to 1900, influenced most of the writers of the last quarter of the nineteenth century and indeed had a bearing on early twentieth-century literature.

Mark Twain, born in 1835 of southern parents, grew up in the period that was rife with Old Southwest frontier humor. Thus he was grounded in a literary regionalism that stressed vernacular speech, exaggerated incidents and tall tales, and colorful, largely rural characters. The influence on Twain of the Old South was both strong and permanent, as is seen in the Mississippi River settings of the Hannibal books and *Life on the Mississippi* (1883). Twain's regionalism, however, embraces far more than the South. Given his wide-ranging travels and sojourns in various quarters of the country, Twain became a western regionalist (*Roughing It* [1872], "The Celebrated Jumping Frog" [1865]), an eastern regionalist (he was heavily influenced by the northeastern humorists and literary comedians), and a midwestern regionalist. Like Walt Whitman, Twain was "large" and "contained multitudes" and could not be confined to one specific region of the country.

Twain is a regionalist in the best sense of the term, avoiding the dangerous trap of provincialism that ensnared many of the local colorists. He knew several geographical regions thoroughly and wrote not just *about* them, but *of* them. Moreover, he transcends the boundaries of locale. *Adventures of Huckleberry Finn* (1885), with all its regional settings and local-color appointments (rustic characters, vernacular speech, graphic description of the river and its adjacent small towns), rises above being a provincial novel about manners in the Mississippi valley before the Civil War. The novel is regional in its mooring but catholic in its thematic implications on such subjects as race, human understanding, and responsibility and on the narrowness and cruelty of human beings. The same can be said for Twain's other works set in particular regions. Twain knew well the importance of having a region from and about which to write. In the classic sense of the term, regionalism provided the home ground, the familiar territory upon which he could base novels and stories that realistically and convincingly address universal issues.

David B. Kesterson

BIBLIOGRAPHY

Berry, Wendell. "Writer and Region." *Hudson Review* 40 (Spring 1987): 15–30.

Krauth, Leland. "Mark Twain: A Man for All Regions." *Studies in American Fiction* 13.2 (Autumn 1985): 239–246.

McDowell, Tremaine. "Regionalism in American Literature." *Minnesota History* 20 (June 1939): 105–118.

Petry, Alice Hall. "Universal and Particular: The Local-Color Phenomenon Reconsidered." *American Literary Realism* 12 (Spring 1979): 111–126.

Spencer, Benjamin T. *The Quest for Nationality: An American Literary Campaign.* Syracuse, N.Y.: Syracuse UP, 1951. 252–289.

———. "Regionalism in American Literature." *Regionalism in America.* Ed. Merrill Jensen. Madison: U of Wisconsin P, 1951. 219–260.

Steiner, Michael. "Literature." *Region and Regionalism in the United States: A Source Book for the Humanities and Social Sciences.* Ed. Michael Steiner and Clarence Mondale. New York: Garland, 1988. 333–335.

Weathers, Winston. "The Writer and His Region." *Southwestern American Literature* 2 (Spring 1972): 25–32.

See also: Baldwin, Joseph Glover; Cable, George Washington; Harte, Francis Bret; Local Color; Realism; Southwestern Humor; Thompson, William Tappan

Reid, Whitelaw

(1837–1912)

Journalist, editor, and diplomat, Whitelaw Reid became managing editor of the powerful New York *Tribune* in 1869 and editor in 1872. As early as 1869 Clemens sought to have Reid use his position at the *Tribune* for Clemens's advantage. At first Reid complied, but in 1873 he refused to allow Edward House to review *The Gilded Age* because House was collaborating with Clemens in a dramatization of the book. For this, Clemens called

Reid a "contemptible cur." In October 1881, with Reid out of the country, Clemens succeeded in having *The Prince and the Pauper* (1882) reviewed in the paper by William Dean Howells. Reid was predictably displeased. When rumors reached Clemens that the *Tribune* was engaged in a crusade against him, he spent weeks filling his notebook with derogations like "ennuch" and "missing link" that were to become part of a "revenge" biography of Reid, discarded only when Clemens discovered that the rumors were unfounded. In 1886 Reid converted the *Tribune* to the Mergenthaler Linotype, a machine whose development he had backed financially for years. Clemens's hatred for Reid probably contributed to his unreasonable support of the inferior Paige typesetter. Ironically, it was Reid, as U.S. ambassador to Great Britain (1905–1912), who, in 1907, officially invited Clemens to receive an honorary degree from Oxford and hosted a banquet in Clemens's honor. Clemens's attitude persisted, however, and he filled his autobiographical dictation for 27 August 1907 with vituperation against Reid.

L. Terry Oggel

BIBLIOGRAPHY

Clemens, Samuel L. *Mark Twain–Howells Letters: The Correspondence of Samuel L. Clemens and William D. Howells, 1872–1910.* Ed. Henry Nash Smith and William M. Gibson. 2 vols. Cambridge, Mass.: Harvard UP, 1960.

———. *Mark Twain's Letters to His Publishers 1867–1894.* Ed. Hamlin Hill. Berkeley: U of California P, 1967.

———. *Mark Twain's Notebook's & Journals, Volume II (1877–1883).* Ed. Frederick Anderson, Lin Salamo, and Bernard L. Stein. Berkeley: U of California P, 1975.

Cortissoz, Royal. *The Life of Whitelaw Reid.* 2 vols. New York: Scribner, 1921.

Kaplan, Justin. *Mr. Clemens and Mark Twain.* New York: Simon & Schuster, 1966.

Lauber, John. *The Inventions of Mark Twain.* New York: Hill and Wang, 1990.

Montiero, George. "A Note on the Mark Twain–Whitelaw Reid Relationship." *Emerson Society Quarterly* 19 (1960): 20–21.

Religion

Throughout his life, Mark Twain had a continuing interest in religion that was sometimes a preoccupation. Brought up as a Protestant, he became a deist in his late teens, and in his early western sketches he made gentility, including some varieties of Christianity, the butt of his humor. At the time of his marriage he attempted briefly to become a believer and a churchgoer, only to return to deism and an admiration for contemporary science, which he felt was in strong opposition to religion. In his later years he was highly critical of Christianity and in some of his autobiographical dictations even attacked the God that he believed ruled the universe.

As a small boy, Clemens attended Sunday school, first at a Methodist church, then a Presbyterian church that his mother had joined. Although his father made a point of staying away from church, young Sam, like Tom Sawyer, was soon obliged to attend services and hear sermons. He learned as well about revivals, which were an important part of religious life in Hannibal; he was to remember them in *Huckleberry Finn* (1885). Spiritualism too was part of life in Hannibal; later Clemens described in "Schoolhouse Hill" a seance that took place in the fictional town that resembles Hannibal.

Four important results of Clemens's religious upbringing can be identified:

1. His continuing interest in the Bible. Albert Bigelow Paine quotes him as having said that in his early teens his mother made him read through "an unexpurgated Bible." Some of the Bibles that Clemens owned or used in his adult years are heavily annotated, and he wrote many works that are derived from the Bible, such as "Adam's Diary."

2. His continuing supposition that all Christians are fundamentalists. He was to write at the end of his life in "Letters from the Earth" that "the Christian thinks every word of it [the Bible] was dictated by God."

3. His association of hell-fire and damnation with Christianity. The two were closely identified in the thinking of Hannibal. Perhaps for this reason he eventually attacked Jesus Christ as the inventor of hell.

4. His identification of religion with the socializing process. Clemens always remembered that in his youth religion was associated, as in *Tom Sawyer* (1876), with discipline and rigid adult ways.

Clemens's questioning of the validity of religious belief may have begun with the discovery that his first schoolteacher had misled him. She had told him, according to one of his autobiographical dictations (published in *Mark Twain in Eruption*), that if he prayed earnestly, his prayers would be answered. But his prayer was not answered, to his shock and astonishment. He thought that perhaps his later conviction that Christianity and all religions are "lies and swindles" may have derived from that experience. More systematic questioning came in Clemens's years as a cub pilot, when he read Thomas Paine's *The Age of Reason* "with fear and hesitation," as Albert Bigelow Paine reports. He marveled "at its fearlessness and wonderful power." For a time Clemens became, like Tom Paine, a deist.

Religious concerns began to be an important aspect of Clemens's writing as early as his years in California. In his role as critic of the dominant genteel culture, Clemens satirized religion and the clergy, as in his imaginary "Important Correspondence" concerning the vacant high-paying position at the Episcopal cathedral in San Francisco that, according to his sketches, such eminent candidates as the Reverend Phillips Brooks were seeking.

More important and clearly a powerful influence in Clemens's life were his experiences with what he called "the pilgrims" on his trip to Europe and the Holy Land on board the *Quaker City* in 1867. He was offended by the hypocrisy of his companions who identified themselves as pious Christians. Though he revealed his attitude in his subsequent book *The Innocents Abroad* (1869), one gets a better sense of his unvarnished attitude in the original pieces he wrote for newspaper readers, collected in *Traveling with the Innocents Abroad* (1958). There he makes clear that very little he saw in the Holy Land met his expectations as a reader of the Bible.

Living in an age when scientific discoveries were profoundly influencing attitudes toward physical reality, Clemens in the 1870s was much struck by the immensity of the universe. In a letter to the woman he was courting, Olivia Langdon, he cited a writer who noted that telescopes could see stars the light of which took fifty thousand years to reach earth, apparently in opposition to the account of the creation in Genesis. At the same time, he was under an obligation to be more accepting of the attitudes of the dominant culture since he hoped to marry Miss Langdon, daughter of a wealthy industrialist. He recognized that Protestant Christianity was a dominant force in his culture. He wrote to his friend Mrs. Fairbanks that he intended to become a Christian, and to Olivia he explained that at times he felt very near to the Savior. He tried to pray and finally was able to write to his future mother-in-law that he now claimed to be a Christian.

After their marriage the Clemenses for a time went to church together and read the Bible. But soon they gave up both practices. The change began when Clemens found offensive the notion that he should read the Bible, especially the Old Testament, for the improvement of his soul. In 1878 Clemens wrote to his brother that he did not believe in hell or the divinity of Christ, though he still thought of Jesus as "the saviour . . . a sacred Personage." At this time Clemens was not attacking God but the attitude of Christians toward God and the kinds of God he supposed Christians believed in. Thus he distinguished the "true God" from the God of the Bible; the former he found "beneficent, exact, . . . steadfast." Particularly repulsive to Clemens was the concept of special providences, the belief that God intervened in response to prayer, which he satirized in his sketch "The Holy Children" (1972). His objection was based on his sense that science and

religion were incompatible and that only scientific truths were valid.

Such statements were not for publication. Several of them appeared for the first time as "Three Statements of the Eighties" in *"What Is Man?" and Other Philosophical Writings* (1973). Here Clemens acknowledged the existence of God but denied that he had ever communicated with humanity or intervened in human affairs. He blamed the Bible as the authority for "religious atrocities" of the Middle Ages but identified the book as not God's work but the work of men, and not very remarkable men at that.

Much concerned not to offend his audience, Clemens hid his heterodox opinions, though in *A Connecticut Yankee in King Arthur's Court* (1889) he clearly expressed his determinism in a famous passage on the importance of training and in "Pudd'nhead Wilson's Calendar" a good deal of his pessimism. One person who may have encountered Clemens's distaste for Christian piety was George Washington Cable, with whom he traveled on a lecture tour. Clemens was offended by Cable's strict observation of the Sabbath.

How Clemens felt about his growing skepticism is suggested by a letter to his old friend Charles Warren Stoddard, who wrote that he had become a Catholic and thereby achieved peace of mind. Clemens responded that he had found "perfect peace" in "absolute unbelief." He went so far as to report that he was horrified that he had ever been a believer.

Despite his doubts, Clemens was able to admire Joan of Arc, a deeply religious person, and to make her in the 1890s the heroine of a book, perhaps because there was a side of him that needed to believe in godly innocence. Otherwise, all of the evidence from the mid 1880s on is that Clemens was becoming more hostile toward both Christianity and the Deity. His attitudes were reinforced by his personal misfortunes, but it seems clear that such events as his bankruptcy and the death of first his daughter Susy and then his wife were not the sources of his philosophic point of view. The first clear exposition of what might be called his theology appears in a portion of *What Is Man?* entitled "God," written in 1898 but not published till the 1973 volume *"What Is Man?" and Other Philosophical Writings*. Here, in the continuing dialogue between an old man, representing Clemens, and a young man, representing perhaps the man in the street, the old man declares that he believes that God exists and that "He is not a bunch of Laws but a personality." This personality, according to the old man, has revealed himself to man by his deeds and works. Man's experience of God begins with his birth when innocent babes are made to suffer. Thereafter humanity's daily experience is pain in each portion of the body. These he calls "wanton tortures" and holds that the God who made the laws of nature, man, and man's nature is responsible for man's sinful nature and his eagerness to break God's laws. Man murders and tortures, is avaricious, indecent, vulgar, and obscene because he is what God made him.

In his dialogue the old man is usually a dispassionate philosopher. Clemens was much more personal in the series of autobiographical dictations made in the summer of 1906, first published in the *Hudson Review* (Autumn 1963) and appearing later as "Reflections on Religion" in *The Outrageous Mark Twain*, edited by Charles Neider. After dictating these statements, Clemens wrote to Howells that "some fearful things" he had been writing were not to be published for a century; later he extended the proposed date of publication to 2406.

It is important to note that in these dictations Clemens did not seek to characterize what others believed about God but rather what he himself believed, or, as he would have said, what he knew about "the real God, the genuine God, the Maker of the mighty universe." God's only interest in people is to entertain himself and prevent boredom by torturing and killing them. Despite the clarity of his statement, Clemens was even in his last years inconsistent, as John Tuckey has effectively shown. As late as 1907 he told Albert Bigelow Paine that he had seen absolutely no

proof that there is life after death but was still "strongly inclined to expect one."

Mark Twain did find one outlet for his need to attack religious belief. He judged that he would not offend too many of his readers if he satirized Christian Science—and in the process took a few swipes at traditional Christianity. Writing in two periods, in 1898–1899 and in 1902–1903, he put together a disorderly collection of writings that are largely an attack on Mary Baker Eddy, whom he called both "an old swindler" and "in several ways the most interesting woman that ever lived." At the same time he fully recognized that many illnesses can be cured by faith healing. Also included is a discussion of man's inability to recognize the validity of any opinions but his own and an amusing exploration of the disagreements among Protestants on the issue of whether Jesus claimed to be God. The book is both a revelation of Clemens's contradictory attitudes toward religious questions and a display of the author's eager fondness for making fun of what some regard as sacred.

Clemens's last extended statements on his religious views appear in *Letters from the Earth* (1962), but here two elements interfere with one's accepting the views presented as Clemens's. First, they appear in a work that is fictional, with Clemens using Satan, an archangel familiar with heaven, as his spokesman, and second, the work is intended to be humorous and entertaining. Nevertheless, one must confront not only a long and witty denunciation of God as the source of all men's pains and diseases, but also a denunciation of Jesus Christ, who has been mistakenly characterized as gentle and forgiving when in fact he was far more severe than the Old Testament God, for he had "devised hell and proclaimed it!" Here Clemens seems to be recalling what he had been taught about God and religion in his Hannibal days of revivals and hell-fire preaching.

The subject of Mark Twain's religious thought has been taken up repeatedly and is the theme of a number of books. None of them is wholly satisfactory, in part because the subject needs to be treated contextually, in terms of both Clemens's life and the religious (or anti-religious) spirit of the times in which he lived. Though much has been made of his friendliness with clergymen, notably his Hartford friend the Reverend Joseph Twichell, Clemens shared with many of his contemporaries a belief that recent scientific discoveries had undercut completely traditional religious beliefs. One might associate Clemens's thinking with that of other skeptical thinkers of the times, such as Henry Adams.

Everett Emerson

BIBLIOGRAPHY

Cummings, Sherwood. *Mark Twain and Science: Adventures of a Mind.* Baton Rouge: Louisiana State UP, 1988.

Emerson, Everett. "Mark Twain's Quarrel with God." *Order in Variety: Essays and Poems in Honor of Donald E. Stanford.* Ed. R.W. Crump. Newark: U of Delaware P, 1991. 32–48.

Ensor, Allison. *Mark Twain and the Bible.* Lexington: U of Kentucky P, 1969.

Frederick, John T. *The Darkened Sky: Nineteenth-Century Novelists and Religion.* Notre Dame, Ind.: U of Notre Dame P, 1969.

Gribben, Alan. *Mark Twain's Library: A Reconstruction.* 2 vols. Boston: G.K. Hall, 1980.

Harnsberger, Caroline. *Mark Twain's Views of Religion.* Evanston, Ill.: Schori P, 1961.

Hays, John Q. *Mark Twain and Religion: A Mirror of American Eclecticism.* Ed. Fred A. Rodewald. New York: Peter Lang, 1989.

Jones, Howard Mumford. *Belief and Disbelief in American Literature.* Chicago: U of Chicago P, 1967.

Paine, Albert Bigelow. *Mark Twain: A Biography.* 3 vols. New York: Harper, 1912.

Tuckey, John S. "Mark Twain's Later Dialogue: The 'Me' and the Machine." *On Mark Twain.* Ed. Louis J. Budd and Edwin H. Cady. Durham, N.C.: Duke UP, 1987. 127–137.

Wecter, Dixon. *Sam Clemens of Hannibal.* Boston: Houghton Mifflin, 1952.

See also: Bible; Calvinism; Catholicism; Clergy; Determinism; "Extracts from Adam's Diary"; God; *Letters from the Earth*; Philosophy; Science; *What Is Man?*

Representation

In literary usage, "representation" refers to a shared world an author portrays, partially and illusorily, in his or her language, characters, plot, and images. Mark Twain, increasingly in his later years, would likely have contested the assumption of a shared world behind the term. To Twain, what we share is the language, the characters, the plots, and the images; the world beyond is partial and illusory.

In Twain's world angels walk, animals talk, and ship captains commandeer comets across the cosmos. A transcendence of reality empowers even Twain's more realistic creations. Huck Finn dies and is reborn. Aunt Rachel of "A True Story" (1874) rises with her history, becoming larger and more luminous as she finds her freedom and her family. The pedestrian David Wilson of *Pudd'nhead Wilson* (1894) has vision that allows him to "track a bird at night."

And yet, as Sherwood Cummings has shown in his excellent *Mark Twain and Science: Adventures of a Mind*, Twain drew his texts from the world around him. The increasing authority of science swept away Twain's native Calvinism and youthful deism, and he constructed his literature from scientific perception: an index of particulars, the weight of evidence, and tentative theories about the workings of the world.

These two views seem impossible to blend, yet both seem true. How can Twain present a scientific vision of reality peopled with ghosts, myths, and fantasies? How did Twain choose to represent the world, in its dreams *and* in its detail?

In his huge corpus Twain repeats plots, characters, and images; they are the repertoire of the literary artist. With repetition, these subjects embody the imagined world we think of as Twain's; taken together, they define it. An index of Twain's most oft used images, characters, and plots helps to resolve the conflict between his fantastic imagination and his realistic presentation.

The *plots* in his longer works are frequently haphazard. Twain often began them in a flood of experience with, memory of, or passion for his subject, and they grew in bursts. While the larger plots vary considerably, the plots of the burst—incidents, groups of chapters, and short stories as well—have strong similarities.

At root we find a contest of mastery. Two people, or groups, find themselves in opposition: the King and Duke against the Wilks clan in *Adventures of Huckleberry Finn* (1885); the narrator and Simon Wheeler in "The Celebrated Jumping Frog" (1865); the twins and the F.F.V. aristocracy in the duel and after in *Pudd'nhead Wilson* (1894). In each case, and in most of the short stories and book segments, characters contend not only with one another, but also with a hidden hierarchy of excellence. The King and Duke play bereaved English relatives in order to bilk the Wilks clan, and when the deceit works, they play for the entire estate. By selling it off piecemeal, though, they lose the sympathy of the Wilks girls. The appearance of new pretenders to the fortune only seals their loss. Huck's actions have already assured the Wilks girls victory in what is actually a battle of sympathy, not wits.

The same pattern repeats in Twain: a conflict over some apparent matter is in fact a conflict over something else entirely. Success results from meeting criteria hidden at the start. Even that success, however, is partial. In the Wilks episode the King and Duke escape unscathed; Huck, the instrument of victory, loses. In "The Recent Carnival of Crime" (1876) the narrator defeats his conscience, but he becomes an irredeemable villain. Apparent terms of conflict give way to other criteria, and the impression remains that the second criteria might give way too. The terms of virtue in the world are hence unknowable. In Twain's literary world one can only assert an ethic, not know one.

Twain's *characters* are particularized types. Almost always male and typically strangers, the types he used most are developed most thoroughly as title characters in *Huck Finn*, *A Connecticut Yankee in King Arthur's Court* (1889), and *Pudd'nhead Wilson*. Huck Finn is the In-nocent. Hank Morgan is the Competent Fool. David Wilson is the Wise Fool.

These typified characters appear frequently in Twain's work. Most of his children, the McWilliamses, and most secondary characters, are Innocents. Their concerns are immediate. If larger currents swirl around them, they do not notice. If they find they have been had, they accept it. Their innocence, their unknowingness, has no limit.

The Competent Fool asserts his mastery, only to be overthrown, often by his own machinations. (Tom Sawyer in *The Adventures of Tom Sawyer* [1876] is a variation of this character who does not lose; possibly, his childhood defends him.) Roxy and Tom in *Pudd'nhead Wilson*, Jim Smiley, and most of Twain's liars and technicians are Competent Fools. They dominate their worlds as they circumscribe them, but beyond their range they become Innocents, and they react with rage at having been fooled.

The Wise Fool appears most often in Twain's later work. David Wilson, Joan of Arc, and Reverend Burgess in "The Man That Corrupted Hadleyburg" (1899) are of the type, secure in the rightness of their knowledge and unwilling to relinquish that integrity for worldly comfort, approval, or survival. Their knowledge is often only faith and of little value to anyone but themselves. The truth value of their knowledge in their literary context is that readers share it.

In his authorial voice Mark Twain played all these types. They were of a piece with him, and pieces of them often mingled, as when Huck arranges his escape from Pap's cabin or when Hank Morgan grasps Arthur's bravery in the small-pox hut. Knowledge and their relationship to it defines these types; all are fools, in that they pursue questionable goals, but possession of knowledge, real or otherwise, distinguishes them from one another.

Twain's *images* do not categorize easily. His figures of speech personify animals, mechanize humans, and allegorize objects, often in service of humor. He does rely on certain imagistic touchstones, though they were often disguised by his linguistic manipulation. Nature, history, dreams, and duality or twinness reside in the center of Twain's imagistic cosmology. Though these topics appear to cover most of the known world, in Twain's writing they circumscribe much more limited spheres: nature is the world free of human beings; history is the physical and inescapable pattern of human behavior; and dreams are the capacity of humans to see what is not there. Images of duality are Twain's response to the impossibility of these spheres intersecting: If humans cannot escape history, at least they can project themselves into nature or out of it completely, into dreams, where nothing matches the world we know.

We can see, then, that knowledge—or more properly, epistemology—lies at the root of Mark Twain's imagined worlds. Two human forces can contend with one another, but the terms of their struggle will always remain obscure to them. Whether the characters are Innocents, Competent Fools, or Wise Fools depends on their recognition of the limit of their own knowledge. The images Twain uses to represent his world depict in concrete terms the impossibility of a secure human environment; even the most restful domestic bliss can be suddenly invaded by dreams, history, or nature.

Knowledge or questions about the knowable bridge Mark Twain's detailed and realistic presentation of his worlds and the fantastic creatures and improbable events that comprise them. The world's unknowability cannot dissuade human attempts at knowledge, which must begin with particulars. In "An Encounter with an Interviewer" (1878) Twain presents himself as a man entirely devoid of knowledge. Imagination takes its place, confusing the interviewer by the absence of shared reality, until he eventually adjusts. Mark Twain's humor points out that humans require knowledge, even uncertain knowledge, and that imagination "makes up the deffisit." His later work implies we are machines with the liberating capacity to imagine, and his life-

time of writing represents our position in the world in just those terms.

Andrew Jay Hoffman

BIBLIOGRAPHY

Covici, Pascal, Jr. *Mark Twain's Humor: The Image of a World*. Dallas: Southern Methodist UP, 1962.

Cox, James M. *Mark Twain: The Fate of Humor*. Princeton, N.J.: Princeton UP, 1966.

Cummings, Sherwood. *Mark Twain and Science: Adventures of a Mind*. Baton Rouge: Louisiana State UP, 1988.

Gillman, Susan. *Dark Twins: Imposture and Identity in Mark Twain's America*. Chicago: U of Chicago P, 1989.

Harris, Susan K. *Mark Twain's Escape from Time: A Study of Patterns and Images*. Columbia: U of Missouri P, 1982.

Johnson, James L. *Mark Twain and the Limits of Power: Emerson's God in Ruins*. Knoxville: U of Tennessee P, 1982.

Sloane, David E.E. *Mark Twain as a Literary Comedian*. Baton Rouge: Louisiana State UP, 1979.

See also: Conscience; Dreams; Imagery; Language; Philosophy; Realism

Rhetorical Forms

Rhetorical use of language involves strategies directed at exercising power over audiences. Anticipating the emergence of modern reader-oriented critical theories, Mark Twain throughout his writing and lecturing career evinced a clear awareness of his audiences and the challenges they presented. A manifestation of this concern with the audience is the dazzling array of rhetorical forms in both travel writing and fiction: audience-oriented devices like imperative and interrogative sentence structures, "we" and "you" pronouns used to include the reader, direct address of the reader as "reader" and otherwise, and larger forms like speeches and polemic pieces.

Pervasive and varied, these rhetorical forms appear throughout the Mark Twain canon, but the greatest concentration of them is in the travel narrative *The Innocents Abroad* (1869). Other of his travel books through *Life on the*

Mississippi (1883) employ the devices but with a declining frequency, while the fictional works tend to be more understated and sophisticated in their use of these forms.

The preface of *The Innocents Abroad* gives as its aim "to suggest to the reader how *he* would be likely to see Europe and the East if he looked at them with his own eyes" (1:xxxvii). Imperative statements in the book further this aim by inviting the reader to participate vicariously in the speaker's adventures; referring to the historically resonant terrain near Ephesus, the narrator declaims: "Go where you will about these broad plains, you will find the most exquisitely-sculpted marble fragments scattered thick among the dust and weeds . . ." (2:161). Still more obtrusive in the text are numerous interrogatives, involving the reader as an implied interlocutor. Rhetorical questions as well as ones designed to be answered appear throughout the book, again often leading the reader to imagine sharing experiences of the traveler. The exciting difficulty of deciding where to go first upon arriving in an admired city emerges through: "What would one naturally wish to see first in Venice?" This question comes complete with an answer: "The Bridge of Sighs, of course—and next the Church and the Great Square of St. Mark" (2:284). Providing answers may enhance the involvement of the reader as a kind of interlocutor-construct, but it also leaves the way open for him to decline the invitation, to resist rhetorical control, simply by embracing a different answer.

Personal pronouns can likewise operate to locate some version of the reader within the text. Most first-person plural pronouns refer to the speaker and his fellow travelers, but some are more inclusive. These locutions tend to convey general observations about human nature: "We all like to see people seasick when we are not, ourselves" (2:63). The second-person pronoun as well is at times employed impersonally, but often it points directly at the reader. The narrator playfully defends his use of emphatic diction against a tedious Gibraltar legend: "If you had been bored so,

when you had the noble panorama of Spain and Africa and the blue Mediterranean spread at your feet . . . you might have burst into stronger language than I did" (1:102).

The reader himself appears in many contexts of *The Innocents Abroad*. Conceding playfully that he will not recount any of the city of Jaffa's history, the narrator offers an alternative: "If the reader will call at the circulating library and mention my name, he will be furnished with books which will afford him the fullest information concerning Jaffa" (2:391). Elsewhere pretentious behavior of Americans traveling abroad provides an eccentric occasion for invoking the familiar "gentle reader": "The gentle reader will never know what a consummate ass he can become until he goes abroad" (1:299). Later, while discussing the writings of the very productive "Poet Lariat," who has been favoring fellow passengers on the *Quaker City* with doggerel, Mark Twain suggests: "Perhaps the savage reader would like a specimen of his style" (2:133). He defends this usage as a refreshing variant of the overworked "gentle reader," but the device also conveys some ideology along with its novelty. Since the "gentle reader" is conventionally read as a compliment to the reader's social status rather than to his temperament, this playfully offered antonym changes the sense in which we must understand the original term "gentle." Rather than the reverse of "common," it signifies the reverse of "savage," thereby excising the implicit social class discrimination.

On a larger scale, two polemic details in *Adventures of Huckleberry Finn* (1885) demonstrate a contrast in the rhetorical implications of the ethos, or character, of the speaker. Pap Finn's outraged snarl "Call this a govment!" (33–34) repels the reader in part because of the profoundly unsympathetic ethos of the addresser, a bigoted, illiterate, drunken child abuser. Notwithstanding his failure to convince that his rights to custody of Huck and control of Huck's $6,000 have been compromised, Finn is technically correct in his complaint. Huck's point of view (a well-founded fear of his father) so dominates the reader's experience here that few notice Pap's defensible claim. In a more complex operation of a speaker's ethos, Colonel Sherburn contemptuously defies a mob proposing to lynch him for killing the intoxicated Boggs. He presents his case with the evident authority of a *raisonneur*. This speech is entirely successful in its dramatic context. The townspeople retreat in disorder, showing how precise Sherburn's assessment of them as cowards has been, and the reader's assent follows. The rhetorical impact of Sherburn's speech is thus further reinforced by a second demonstration: the shooting of the hapless Boggs has it seems done little to undermine the colonel's ethos or to lead the reader to question this killer's evaluation of his fellowman.

A characteristic rhetorical strategy in *A Connecticut Yankee in King Arthur's Court* (1889) is Hank Morgan's repeated use of "you see" and similar locutions. Morgan begins an account of plans to overthrow the Catholic Church and establish universal suffrage: "You see, I had two schemes in my head, which were the vastest of all my projects" (444). In one sense, this language may be read as nudging the audience toward continued attentiveness or as an indicator of conversational informality. However, Morgan's difficulties in sixth-century England arose in his view from a rhetorical failure, from an inability to convince the populace that supporting his position would serve their interests. Moreover, early in the novel communication falters, even at the semantic level between sixth-century and nineteenth-century speakers. These factors and the heavy concentration of "you see" in ideological sections of the book suggest that they reflect an implicit plea for the modern reader's understanding and assent.

A final rhetorical strategy Mark Twain employed was to impart interpretive information, uniting the narrator and reader on a level above that of the characters. When Judge Driscoll in *The Tragedy of Pudd'nhead Wilson* (1894) optimistically shows some clever mottoes from Wilson's calendar to citizens of Dawson's Landing, the results are not what he expected: ". . . irony was not for those people; their mental vision was not focussed for it. They read those playful trifles in the solidest earnest" (52). Beyond alerting the audience, if necessary, to an appropriate reading of the mottoes, this information serves yet another rhetorical purpose, guiding the reader's evaluation of Wilson's eventual triumph in this intellectually limited community.

Mark Twain's preoccupation with rhetorical features of writing intersects several other aspects of his career: the publication by subscription of most major works, his years as a platform speaker before live and responding audiences, and his disposition to see authorship as a commercial endeavor (placing the reader in the critical role of customer). Finally, rhetorical forms may demonstrate a degree of endorsement of egalitarian ideology: prominence of the reader in a work suggests that the author is declining some of the privilege of his position, effacing a measure of his authority in favor of an enhanced significance for the reader.

Eileen Nixon Meredith

BIBLIOGRAPHY

Budd, Louis J. *Our Mark Twain: The Making of His Public Personality.* Philadelphia: U of Pennsylvania P, 1983.

Clemens, Samuel L. *Adventures of Huckleberry Finn.* Ed. Walter Blair and Victor Fischer. Berkeley: U of California P, 1985.

———. *A Connecticut Yankee in King Arthur's Court.* Ed. Bernard Stein. Berkeley: U of California P, 1979.

———. *The Innocents Abroad.* Hartford, Conn.: American Publishing, 1869.

———. *Pudd'nhead Wilson and Those Extraordinary Twins.* Ed. Sidney E. Berger. Norton crit. ed. New York: Norton, 1980.

Gerber, John C. "The Relation Between Point of View and Style in the Works of Mark Twain." *Style in Prose Fiction.* Ed. Harold C. Martin. New York: Columbia UP, 1959. 142–171.

Mailloux, Steven. *Rhetorical Power.* Ithaca, N.Y.: Cornell UP, 1989.

Sewell, David R. *Mark Twain's Languages: Discourse, Dialogue, and Linguistic Variety.* Berkeley: U of California P, 1987.

See also: Language; Sentimentality; Style, Mark Twain's

Rhodes, Cecil
(1853–1902)

The British financier and colonial politician known best to Americans as the founder of the Rhodes Scholarship Trust, Cecil Rhodes is featured recurrently in Twain's *Following the Equator* (1897) as the great apostle of nineteenth-century empire. By the time of the book's publication, Rhodes had attained a combination of international fame and notoriety ironically not unlike Twain's own. As a financial speculator, he had amalgamated the diamond-mining operations in South Africa into the De Beers Corporation. As prime minister of the Cape Colony, he had instigated the Jameson Raid as a way of justifying aggressive British consolidation of the Boer Republic into its South African holdings.

In *Following the Equator*, Rhodes figures initially through a spurious anecdote about his early career as a professional shark murderer collecting bounty from the Australian government. In that capacity, we are told, he discovers in the belly of one of his fast-swimming victims a communication from London giving him advance information sufficient to corner the sheep wool market.

Rhodes's most important role in the text, however, comes in concluding sections of the second volume, which, we know with certainty, were required at the last minute to pad out an already "finished" work. Of these, Twain wrote to Henry Huttleston Rogers, his publisher, "I have added 30,000 words. Part of it has been most enjoyable work to me—chaffing Rhodes and making fun of his Jameson raid." And in the text itself, albeit after a rather dubious late justification of the relative benefits of law and stability promised by colonial rule around the globe, Rhodes's own imperial person finally gets both anti-colonialist barrels. Despite his geopolitical raiding, robbing, and intriguing, observes Twain,

"there he stands, to this day, upon his dizzy summit under the dome of the sky, an apparent permanency, the marvel of the time, the mystery of the age, an Archangel with wings to half the world, Satan with a tail to the other half." He concludes: "I admire him, I frankly confess it; and when his time comes I shall buy a piece of the rope for a keepsake."

Philip D. Beidler

BIBLIOGRAPHY

Clemens, Samuel L. *Following the Equator*. Hartford, Conn.: American Publishing, 1897.

———. *Mark Twain's Correspondence with Henry Huttleston Rogers, 1893–1909*. Ed. Lewis Leary. Berkeley: U of California P, 1969.

Lee, Sir Sidney, ed. *The Dictionary of National Biography*. Supplement, January 1901–December 1911. Vol. 3. London: Oxford UP, 1912.

Macnaughton, William R. *Mark Twain's Last Years as a Writer*. Columbia: U of Missouri P, 1979.

Shillingsburg, Miriam Jones. *At Home Abroad: Mark Twain in Australasia*. Jackson: UP of Mississippi, 1988.

See also: Boer War; "Cecil Rhodes and the Shark"; *Following the Equator*; Imperialism

Richards, Edward and Mary

The protagonists of "The Man That Corrupted Hadleyburg" (1899), Edward and Mary Richards are a poor and childless old couple whose lives are destroyed by the events triggered by the stranger's hoax. He is a bank cashier, she a housewife. Together they epitomize the communal character.

The Richardses function primarily as the representative consciousness of the town, providing the story with its psychological emphasis. In their reaction to the sack of gold, for example, they reveal not only their society's money hunger, but also the self-deception inherent in Hadleyburgian honesty: she projects her urge to steal upon imaginary, and improbable, robbers, while he rationalizes his as a romantic fantasy. The idiom of confession and repentance in their discussion of Reverend Burgess establishes that in Hadleyburg public opinion is a godlike force for slavish conformity. His rush to publish the stranger's message dramatizes the town's smug pride in its reputation for an honesty that, as the entire town is to discover, is "artificial," never having been put to the test of temptation before the advent of the ironic stranger.

The first half of the story unfolds as a series of paired scenes in which Mark Twain first closely analyzes the old couple's hypocritical maneuvers and then briefly recapitulates each of their scenes as they are enacted, in precisely duplicated form, by their fellows among the village elite. Twain's implication is that self-seeking ironically reveals the drearily undifferentiated identity of people produced by a radically conformist, money-hungry culture. Indeed, even in their uneasy preeminence following the town meeting, where they are elected symbols of incorruptibility, the Richardses serve to dramatize the undercurrent of suspicion and cynicism that runs deeply in the communal consciousness.

Scholars disagree about the Richardses' typicality and latitude for moral choice. Yet Twain's revelation of mass man's collective identity underscores the paradigmatic nature of his protagonists, just as his choreographic presentation of his cast's exactly duplicated machinations points to the illusoriness of moral freedom in this parable of man the machine.

Earl F. Briden

BIBLIOGRAPHY

Covici, Pascal, Jr. *Mark Twain's Humor: The Image of a World.* Dallas: Southern Methodist UP, 1962.

See also: Determinism; Hadleyburg; Halliday, Jack; Hoax; "Man That Corrupted Hadleyburg, The"

"Riley—Newspaper Correspondent"

(1870)

"Riley—Newspaper Correspondent" first appeared in the Buffalo *Express* on 29 October 1870 and was reprinted in the *Galaxy* 10 (November 1870): 726–727. Twain later included it in *Sketches, New and Old* (1875).

Twain had met James Henry Riley when the two were San Francisco newspapermen. They had remarkably similar personalities and interests. Thus Twain's flattering portrait of his old friend (who would die in 1872 of blood poisoning contracted after Twain had sent him to South Africa to gather material for a book that Twain planned to write) emphasizes the same traits that Twain prided himself on possessing: sense of humor, ready wit, "unfailing vein of irony," genuine charity, loyalty to friends. Twain marvels at Riley's ability to maintain a serious countenance when telling a humorous story. As illustration, Twain recalls the time that Riley's tearful landlady asked him to suggest an epitaph for a faithful black woman who had accidentally burned to death by falling onto a red-hot stove: "Put it, '*Well done*, good and faithful servant,'" Riley solemnly replied. Twain made profitable use of such deadpan humor in his own writings and speeches.

Though having scant literary merit, the sketch is significant because it reveals what traits the early Twain most valued in a story and in a friend.

Lawrence J. Oliver

BIBLIOGRAPHY

Brownell, George Hiram. "Whence Came 'Well Done, Good and Faithful Servant.'" *Twainian* 5 (January-February 1946): 3–4.

Clemens, Samuel L. *Sketches, New and Old.* Hartford, Conn.: American Publishing, 1875.

Kaplan, Justin. *Mr. Clemens and Mark Twain.* New York: Simon & Schuster, 1966.

Riverdale, New York

Riverdale, New York, or Riverdale-on-the-Hudson, lies in the borough of the Bronx, just inside the New York City limits. The Clemens family rented a home there from the fall of 1901 to the summer of 1903. In Clemens's time the three-story fieldstone house at 645 West 252nd Street was known as Holbrook Hall; it subsequently became known as Wave Hill, now designated a New York landmark. Besides Mark Twain, it was home to many celebrated persons, including Theodore Roosevelt, Thomas Appleton, and, later, Arturo Toscanini.

Nancy Cook

BIBLIOGRAPHY

The Heritage of New York. New York: Fordham UP, 1970.

Hill, Hamlin. *Mark Twain: God's Fool*. New York: Harper & Row, 1973.

Paine, Albert Bigelow. *Mark Twain: A Biography*. 3 vols. New York: Harper, 1912.

See also: New York, New York

Rogers, Ben and Billy

Ben Rogers appears in both *The Adventures of Tom Sawyer* (1876) and *Adventures of Huckleberry Finn* (1885) as one of Tom Sawyer's school-age friends. In chapter 2 of *Tom Sawyer* Rogers becomes the first boy to accept Sawyer's enticement to whitewash Aunt Polly's fence. Rogers appears only once more, in the book-tearing scene of chapter 20, yet is mentioned in chapters 6, 7, 22, 25, 28, and 33. Rogers has a larger role in *Huckleberry Finn* as a member of Sawyer's gang, and as point-by-point critic of Sawyer's scheme. Rogers challenges Sawyer's book-fed chivalry on practical grounds, saying, "Mighty soon we'll have the cave so cluttered up with women, and fellows waiting to be ransomed, that there won't be no place for the robbers."

Critics see Rogers's brief appearance in *Tom Sawyer* as a mere device supporting Sawyer's role as a ringleader of boys his age (Norton 149). But Rogers's challenge of Sawyer in the later work suggests that Twain revised his early view: though Sawyer remains popular, his romantic ideas will not be accepted without challenge. Although Rogers's character remains a device, his sense of the practical mirrors Huck's own.

Billy Rogers is the self-conscious hero of "Boy's Manuscript" (written ca. 1868), Twain's first attempt to describe his boyhood. Rogers, though a burlesque figure, shares many of the author's prankish characteristics: playing hooky, lazing around (*Autobiography* 2:91–92), and suffering from the throes of first love. Some scholars view Rogers as the earliest Tom Sawyer though without the nostalgia, charm, and dimension of the later character.

Susan Schneider

BIBLIOGRAPHY

Clemens, Samuel L. *Adventures of Huckleberry Finn*. Ed. Walter Blair and Victor Fischer. Berkeley: U of California P, 1985.

———. *The Adventures of Tom Sawyer*. New York: Harper, 1903.

———. *Mark Twain's Autobiography*. Ed. Albert B. Paine. 2 vols. New York: Harper, 1924.

DeVoto, Bernard. *Mark Twain at Work*. Cambridge, Mass.: Harvard UP, 1942.

Norton, Charles A. *Writing "Tom Sawyer": The Adventures of a Classic*. Jefferson, N.C.: McFarland, 1983.

See also: *Adventures of Huckleberry Finn*; *Adventures of Tom Sawyer, The*; "Boy's Manuscript"

Rogers, Henry Huttleston
(1840–1909)

"He is," wrote Clemens, "not only the best friend I ever had, but is the best man I have known." Clemens added, he is "the only man I would give a *damn* for." Although Henry Huttleston Rogers entered Clemens's life late (in 1892 after both men had passed the mid-century mark), the influence of Rogers on Clemens's financial affairs was significant. In return Clemens served Rogers by playing the jester in Rogers's social life. Each man served the other's needs.

Rogers's business and financial career exemplified the Horatio Alger theme of rags to riches through discipline and hard work, although his critics, especially the muckrakers who attacked him in his later years, pointed out that mercilessness and tyranny probably contributed more to his success than did mere determination. His ruthlessness and rapacity were balanced by commitment to his friends, a charming personality, and generous contributions to Booker T. Washington and Helen Keller.

Rogers was born on 29 January 1840, in Mattapoisett, Massachusetts, but he grew up in nearby Fairhaven, a city that profited immensely from his philanthropic largesse. He worked at a series of low-paying jobs, including clerking in a grocery store, peddling newspapers, and as a brakeman on a local railroad. By the age of twenty-one, he had saved $600, which he invested in the newly opened oil fields of Pennsylvania. In 1866 he was invited to join Charles Pratt and Company, which owned one of the largest refineries of crude oil in the Allegheny valley. And in 1874, when the Standard Oil Company was being formed, he became a major figure in the alliance. After the reorganization of 1890 Rogers was named a vice-president and director, virtually controlling the wide business interests of Standard Oil.

For sixteen years, from 1893 to 1909, Rogers befriended Clemens, assisting and advising him, working to untangle Clemens's scrambled business affairs. In September 1893 Clemens returned from Europe, hoping that his large investments in the Paige typesetting machine would pay off. Introduced to Rogers by Dr. Clarence C. Rice, Clemens entertained Rogers with his humorous tales, and a genuine and almost instantaneous, but also public, friendship developed. Both men enjoyed masculine and sporting company. Cruises on Rogers's yacht, the *Kanawha*, included late card games, heavy drinking, and playful exchanges of insults. Rogers tried to set the business affairs of the Paige machine in order, but not even he could save that ill-fated venture. When the publishing firm of Charles Webster and Company declared bankruptcy in 1894, Rogers helped to steer Clemens to Harper and Brothers. After the death of daughter Susy in 1896, Clemens left most of his financial affairs in Rogers's hands. It was Rogers who marketed Clemens's pieces and supervised his investments, enabling Clemens to repay the debts of Charles Webster and Company by March 1898.

Until his death in 1909, Rogers worked assiduously to relieve Clemens of financial worries—as Clemens said, rescuing him from "leather-headed business snarls." And Clemens seemed not to be bothered by the heavy burden he placed on Rogers and his staff. Rogers was precise, consistent, and clear-headed, and he provided Clemens with much-needed business advice. Curiously, although the men were very close and although Clemens was a frequent guest in the Rogers's home, the Clemens family and the Rogers family saw little of each other. Following the death of wife Olivia in Italy in 1904, Clemens returned to the United States where he continued his close ties with the Rogers family. After Rogers suffered a stroke in 1907, from which he never fully recovered, Clemens and Rogers traveled together, even taking a cruise to Bermuda. Both men were ill when, just two months before Rogers's death, they journeyed to Norfolk, Virginia, to celebrate the opening of the Virginian Railway, nearly 500 miles of track that Rogers had built primarily with his own capital, perhaps accounting for the estimated $50 million depreciation of his personal wealth. On 19 May 1909 Clemens arrived in New York City's Grand Central Station en route to see Rogers, but he was met with the news that his friend had died that morning. His grief became public when reporters recorded Clemens's comment: "This is terrible, terrible, and I cannot talk about it."

James E. Barcus

BIBLIOGRAPHY

Clemens, Samuel L. *Mark Twain's Correspondence with Henry Huttleston Rogers, 1893–1909*. Ed. Lewis Leary. Berkeley: U of California P, 1969.

Hill, Hamlin. *Mark Twain: God's Fool*. New York: Harper & Row, 1973.

Kaplan, Justin. *Mark Twain and His World*. New York: Simon & Schuster, 1974.

———. *Mr. Clemens and Mark Twain*. New York: Simon & Schuster, 1966.

See also: Bankruptcy; Business; Paige Typesetting Machine

Roughing It
(1872)

Mark Twain wrote *Roughing It* during what for him was a turbulent transitional period. Having moved to Hartford from Buffalo to build a house (a "mansion," one could call it) in the high-toned Nook Farm literary community, Twain found himself caring for a wife worn out from nursing her dying father. At the same time he was concerned about a sickly son, and another child was on the way. Through all of this, he was struggling to meet his obligations to provide copy of a humorous nature for newspaper columns. In addition, he was trying to fit in with the conventional proprieties of eastern gentility as well as to measure up to the financial demands of the lifestyle to which he was trying to become accustomed. The reckless abandonment to the lazy pleasures of the moment that Twain evokes in the book's opening pages takes on even greater charm in contrast to the author's personal preoccupations at the time of writing.

The Civil War having interrupted his life as a Mississippi riverboat pilot, a life that Twain had apparently settled into for good (see "Old Times on the Mississippi," 1875), and the soldiering career of a Confederate volunteer (see "The Private History of a Campaign That Failed," 1874) proving distasteful both in fact and in principle, twenty-six-year-old Sam had gone west with brother Orion, newly appointed Secretary to the Governor of the Nevada Territory. Celebrating, lamenting, and castigating life in the territory and in California as he had known it during the 1860s, *Roughing It* vividly documents various aspects of the boom-and-bust American West while reflecting the increasing confidence of the author in his ability to go beyond the recording of impressions to the exploration of meaning.

Roughing It purports to be an account of Twain's experience west of the river, but from the opening paragraph the creative writer rather than the data-bound reporter holds sway. Instead of the experienced and independent traveler that he had in truth been, Twain presents himself as a youngster (of indeterminable age) who "had never been away from home," suffering from severe envy of a big brother who was going to "have all kinds of adventures and maybe get hanged or scalped, and have ever such a fine time." It is this naive narrator, this greenhorn, whose initiation into the realities of the West supplies a skeleton for the book. Through him, Twain presents the important ambivalences toward civilization and its opposites that will inform so much of his work for the rest of his career.

Dressed like a renegade, the narrator feels "bully." But he comes to see the romance of silver mining as drudgery; the random shooting of citizens by gun slingers eager to make names for themselves becomes, finally, the reverse of glorious: in a society where the highest status is accorded a bartender who had "killed his man," narrator and author find themselves increasingly in sympathy with conventional respectability, with law and order. When, halfway through the book, the narrator follows Sam Clemens's example and gives up silver mining to go to work as city editor of the Virginia City *Daily Territorial Enterprise*, he pointedly changes his clothes—"I secured a more Christian costume," as he so elegantly puts it—along with his perspective. The admirable lawlessness and the delights of uncouth profanity and of vernacular speech in general provide distraction and contrast—but not the raw materials for a permanent way of life.

Most particularly, the delights of vernacular speech mark the narrator's western experience, shaping it and also revealing the nature of its attraction and the limits of its worth. A friendly but loquacious fellow passenger on the stagecoach first pleases and then almost drowns the narrator in a "tossing waste of dislocated grammar and decomposed pronunciation!" The unprepossessing coyote of chapter 5, discussed at length by Henry Nash Smith, leads the town-bred eastern dog of the narrator's imagination to stoop to vernacular in order to express his chagrin at having been taken in so thoroughly by the scruffy western speedster. Western vulgarity and competence amuse, amaze, and then depress the representative of civilization. His response culminates in anger at the brutal western treatment of the Chinese.

Even the delightful stories reflect ambivalence: "Buck Fanshaw's Funeral" pits the vernacular honesty of Scotty Briggs against the elegant eastern density of a pompous minister. The cultivated reverend absolutely refuses to allow vernacular phrasing to communicate Scotty's wish for a good send-off for the dead Buck. Scotty's manly grief and sincerity win a reader's delighted sympathy, in part because of fresh western slang and leaky grammar. But then the narrator asserts that Scotty later turned to religion himself, teaching Sunday school and telling "the beautiful story of Joseph and his brethren" to "his little learners" in a version "riddled with slang," both teacher and pupils "unconscious . . . that any violence was being done to the sacred proprieties!" The genteel condescension shows how far the narrator has finally withdrawn from his initial desire to be "one of the boys."

Yet there is pure pleasure in vernacular narrative, too, just as in the western experience: as Simon Wheeler earlier had "wasted" the time of a greenhorn impatient for information, so Jim Blaine, in his drunken effort to tell the story of "His Grandfather's Ram," delights all but the narrator as he rambles through the thickets of memory, unable to interrupt the flow of his own associations with any statement pertinent to either grandfather or ram.

The final verdict, implicit in a variety of episodes—among them, an account of a visit to New York City by two ignorant nabobs of the gold fields; parodies of Horace Greeley's letters and of Horace Greeley in the West—comes down against western lawlessness and confusion. To go west does not have much to do with growing up with the country, or with growing up at all. In his western-most excursion, Twain shows us the Sandwich Islands (Hawaii) through eyes both offended by and attracted to the innocent promiscuity and nudity of natives for whom Christianity seems both a necessary process toward refinement and a cruel imposition. Ambivalence, perhaps the most prominent characteristic revealed by Twain's humor from beginning to end, here becomes a deliberate part of the writer's strategy. Setting himself up as experienced, or perceptive, or appreciative, or naively trusting, the narrator can be counted upon to put himself in a contradicting light sooner rather than later. The scenery at Lake Tahoe fills him with awed delight; here is heaven on earth, total relaxation, beauty and quiet to repair the soul. Then the narrator starts a campfire that quickly gets out of control, destroying thousands of acres and turning paradise into desolation. Returned from Hawaii, the narrator begins the lecture career of Mark Twain: "Doors open at 7 1/2. The trouble will begin at 8." But the lecture is to be more than funny: the narrator, here indistinguishable from Mark Twain, wants pathos as well as humor. Uneasy lest his humor misfire, he signals certain trusted members of the audience when to laugh. And they do, and that is good. One of them, however, mistakes his signal, and what Twain intends as pathos turns to humor. He is glad to have made a hit, but sorry to have been misunderstood.

Roughing It, though certainly popular when it first came out, sold less well than *The Innocents Abroad* (1869). Today, readers see it as a richer book than its predecessor, less dependent on daily journalism, more thorough in its evocation of shades of feeling, of aspiration, of evaluation. With its greater distance between the writer and his experience than was the case in *Innocents*, the book suggests the talents and conflicts that Twain will use so effectively in the major work that lies ahead.

Pascal Covici, Jr.

BIBLIOGRAPHY

Fatout, Paul. *Mark Twain in Virginia City.* Bloomington: Indiana UP, 1964.

Mack, Effie Mona. *Mark Twain in Nevada.* New York: Scribner, 1947.

Rogers, Franklin R. *Mark Twain's Burlesque Patterns as Seen in the Novels and Narratives, 1855–1885.* Dallas: Southern Methodist UP, 1960.

Sloane, David E.E. *Mark Twain as a Literary Comedian.* Baton Rouge: Louisiana State UP, 1979.

Smith, Henry Nash. *Mark Twain: The Development of a Writer.* Cambridge, Mass.: Harvard UP, 1962.

See also: "Buck Fanshaw's Funeral"; Humor; "Jim Blaine and His Grandfather's Ram"; Travel Writings; Vernacular

Routledge and Sons, George

Founded by George Routledge (1812–1888) in 1843 as Routledge, Warne, and Routledge, this publishing firm was famous for its inexpensive editions of classic books. In 1872 Twain had Routledge and Sons publish *Roughing It* in advance of the American edition in order to protect the book under English copyright law from the piracy his earlier works had suffered. The publisher also handled the authorized English editions of *Innocents at Home* (1872), *A Curious Dream and Other Sketches* (1872), and *Information Wanted and Other Sketches* (1876).

Charles Franklyn Beach

BIBLIOGRAPHY

McBride, William M. *Mark Twain: A Bibliography of the Collections of the Mark Twain Memorial and the Stowe-Day Foundation.* Hartford, Conn.: McBride, 1984.

Paine, Albert Bigelow. *Mark Twain: A Biography.* 3 vols. New York: Harper, 1912.

See also: Copyright

Roxana

In Mark Twain's *Pudd'nhead Wilson* (1894), twenty-year-old Roxana is a slave of Percy Northumberland Driscoll. Roxy, who is one-sixteenth black, looks Caucasian. As a young woman, Roxy is tall and majestic, with a fair complexion, brown eyes, and brown hair. Her only Negro characteristic is the black dialect she speaks. When among the slaves, her vivacious personality emerges, and she is full of fire and life.

Roxy gives birth to the deceased Colonel Essex's illegitimate son on the same day Percy Driscoll's son is born: 1 February 1830. Mrs. Driscoll dies within a week after giving birth, and Roxy assumes responsibility for both babies. Thinking the name sounds aristocratic, Roxy names her son Valet de Chambre. Although the child is one thirty-second black, he is a slave just like his mother. "Chambers" is practically indistinguishable from Tom. Even Percy Driscoll cannot tell the two apart.

Roxy is painfully aware of the life her "black" baby will lead in Dawson's Landing. She plans to spare Chambers from his fate by drowning herself and him. Suddenly she has a plan: if she switches the babies, her son will grow up with all the privileges white people have, especially as a son in a First Family of Virginia (F.F.V.) household. She changes the babies' clothing and places her child in Tom's cradle. Unwittingly, Roxy has sealed his doom. The training "Tom" undergoes as one of the "elect" damages his character more than being a slave would have done. In releasing her child from his fate, she has effectively secured hers.

When Roxy is thirty-five, she is freed and becomes a chambermaid on a Cincinnati boat in the New Orleans trade. She stays there for eight years and becomes head chambermaid. Eventually, she develops rheumatism in her arms and retires. She has saved $400 from her work; however, the bank in which her money is deposited fails, leaving her penniless. Desperate, Roxy returns to Dawson's Landing and asks Tom for money. At last, outraged by the humiliating and cruel rebuffs that meet her appeal, she confronts him with his true identity. Immediately, their roles reverse, and Roxy is Tom's "master." She completely subjects him to her will. She forces him to give her his pension, constructs a plan to regain his gambling losses, and tells him how to act toward his uncle. Later, when Tom heatedly threatens to injure Roxy, she tells him, falsely, that the secret to his heritage is written down and delivered into safe hands. She also tells Tom that the holder has instructions to expose the papers should anything happen to her. Tom believes her and withdraws. This is an important victory for Roxy, for the word of a slave would never be taken over that of an F.F.V.

In order to pay Tom's gambling debts, Roxy suggests that Tom sell her up the river, and buy her back within a year. However, Tom sells her down the river to a master in Arkansas, where slaves are treated much more harshly. She escapes and returns to Dawson's Landing, infuriated with Tom. She is convinced it is the black part of Tom that causes him to do these evil deeds. She tells Tom to confess his deeds to his uncle and ask for money to buy Roxy's freedom. Tom plans to steal the money, but he murders his uncle instead.

While Roxy strictly adheres to the white social code, Tom adheres to no code at all. Roxy attributes these flaws to the "black blood" in him; she does not adhere to Mark Twain's tenet that training is everything. Ironically, Tom's malice toward Roxy is a direct result of the way she had indulged him as a child.

Roxy's character, the tragic Mulatto, or tragic Octoroon, was not Twain's original creation. The character was tragic precisely because he or she appeared white but was forced by society into slavery. The tragic Mulatto could "pass" for a white person but usually was forced back across the color line in shame and degradation. Cable, Melville, Stowe, and Howells also explored this stereotype.

Through Roxy, Twain blurs the lines between black and white. Roxy is one vehicle through which Twain demonstrates his "training is all" theory. For Twain, Roxy is an exemplification of the tragedy of slaveholding society.

J.R. LeMaster and Carolyn Gay

BIBLIOGRAPHY

Allen, Jerry. *The Adventures of Mark Twain*. Boston: Little, Brown, 1954.

Baldanza, Frank. *Mark Twain: An Introduction and Interpretation*. New York: Barnes & Noble, 1961.

Brashear, Minnie M., and Robert M. Rodney. *The Art, Humor, and Humanity of Mark Twain*. Norman: U of Oklahoma P, 1959.

Budd, Louis J. *Critical Essays on Mark Twain 1867–1910*. Boston: G.K. Hall, 1982.

———. *Our Mark Twain: The Making of His Public Personality*. Philadelphia: U of Pennsylvania P, 1983.

DeVoto, Bernard. *Mark Twain's America*. Boston: Little, Brown, 1932.

Geismar, Maxwell. *Mark Twain: An American Prophet*. Boston: Houghton Mifflin, 1970.

Kaplan, Justin. *Mark Twain and His World*. New York: Simon & Schuster, 1974.

Pettit, Arthur G. *Mark Twain and the South*. Lexington: UP of Kentucky, 1974.

See also: Miscegenation; *Pudd'nhead Wilson, The Tragedy of*; "Those Extraordinary Twins, The Comedy"; Women

"Royal Nonesuch, The"

Also called "The King's Camelopard," "The Royal Nonesuch" is the skit that the King and the Duke stage in chapters 22 and 23 of *Adventures of Huckleberry Finn* (1885), when Shakespeare proves too much for the Arkansas "lunkheads." The King prances around like an animal with stripes of many colors painted all over his naked body.

This skit follows the tradition of the "Guyuscutus" hoax, in which the exhibit of a ferocious beast is advertised and people pay to see it. Roars and pounding are heard backstage, but when screams announce that the beast has escaped, the audience dashes for the doors and the tricksters disappear with the money. Apparently, however, Mark Twain had planned more. His original title for the skit, "The Burning Shame," refers to a story that Jim Gillis had told him in California in 1865 that he thought too obscene to include in his novel. It may have involved a lighted candle stuck in the naked man's posterior. This could be what Huck does not mention about "the rest of his outfit." There is also a possible allusion here to Edgar Allan Poe's story, "Four Beasts in One/The Homo-Camelopard."

A. Berret

BIBLIOGRAPHY

Graves, Wallace. "Mark Twain's 'Burning Shame.'" *Nineteenth-Century Fiction* 23 (June 1968): 93–98.

Whiting, B.J. "Guyuscutus, Royal Nonesuch and Other Hoaxes." *Southern Folklore Quarterly* 8 (December 1944): 251–275.

See also: *Adventures of Huckleberry Finn*; "Burning Shame, The"; Gillis, James H.; Hoax

Russia

Mark Twain's single visit to Russia occurred in 1867 on the *Quaker City* cruise that became the basis for *The Innocents Abroad* (1869). He and the other *Quaker City* pilgrims stopped at Sebastopol, where Twain noted the extreme devastation resulting from the Crimean War (1854–1856) and at Odessa, which seemed to him much like an American city. Then, minus several passengers who refused to participate, the group sailed to Yalta specifically for the purpose of soliciting an audience with Czar Alexander II. Twain, not yet exhibiting his later anti-czarist fervor, chaired a committee to prepare an address to the czar, and, by his own account, ended up writing the whole address—as fawning and yet rhetorically pompous a document as any monarchist could desire. Twain's various reports of the meeting found little objectionable in the behavior of either the czar or the czar-seeking pilgrims.

However, Russia later became for Twain a symbol of oppression of the suffering many by the undeserving few. He showed himself generally sympathetic toward the Russian people, signing an 1891 circular establishing the Society of American Friends of Russian Freedom, and he attacked czarist government in *A Connecticut Yankee in King Arthur's Court* (1889) and *The American Claimant* (1892). Despite an embarrassing episode in which he had to dissociate himself from writer and revolutionist Maxim Gorky after Gorky was found to be traveling with a woman who was not his wife, Twain participated in fund-raising activities and efforts to arouse American public support for the anti-czarist movement. He also expressed extreme impatience, however, with the popular submission to czarist oppression—as in "The Czar's Soliloquy" (1905), in which Czar Nicholas II soliloquizes, at times convincingly, about the spinelessness of the Russian people and in the unpublished "Flies & Russians," which compares its two subjects in a manner not advantageous to the latter.

Since the first Russian translation of Twain's work, an 1872 rendering of "The Celebrated Jumping Frog of Calaveras County," his popularity in Russia has been rivaled among American authors only by Jack London. While not, like London, perceived as a socialist (except perhaps unknowingly), he was praised by Soviet critics for his assaults on both monarchy and, more importantly, American capitalism. The number of editions of his work published in Russia has been exceeded only in the United States, Great Britain, and Germany.

James S. Leonard

BIBLIOGRAPHY

Budd, Louis J. *Mark Twain: Social Philosopher.* Bloomington: Indiana UP, 1962.

Clemens, Samuel L. *The Innocents Abroad.* Hartford, Conn.: American Publishing, 1869.

Ganzel, Dewey. *Mark Twain Abroad: The Cruise of the "Quaker City."* Chicago: U of Chicago P, 1968.

Neider, Charles. *Mark Twain and the Russians: An Exchange of Views.* New York: Hill and Wang, 1960.

Parry, Albert. "Mark Twain in Russia." *Books Abroad* 15 (April 1941): 168–175.

Rodney, Robert M., ed. *Mark Twain International: A Bibliography and Interpretation of His Worldwide Popularity.* Westport, Conn.: Greenwood P, 1982.

Scott, Arthur L. *Mark Twain at Large.* New York: Henry Regnery, 1969.

See also: "Czar's Soliloquy, The"; *Innocents Abroad, The*

S

St. Louis, Missouri

Established in 1764 by the French provincial government headquartered in New Orleans, this Mississippi River town had a population of 8,000 when John Marshall Clemens arrived there from Tennessee with his family in 1835. The elder Clemens had relatives in St. Louis, and he intended to practice law there. He soon saw better opportunity awaiting in the Salt River country near Hannibal, and in June he moved his family to Florida, Missouri. Jane Lampton Clemens was delighted, for she was pregnant with her sixth child in an alien city; in Florida she would at least be near her sister. The child, Samuel Langhorne Clemens, was born in Florida in November 1835.

Sam Clemens made his way to St. Louis in 1853, after serving his apprenticeship to printer Joseph Ament and working for a brief spell with brother Orion's Hannibal newspapers. He roomed in a boardinghouse on the corner of Fourth and Washington streets owned by a former Hannibal resident, Mrs. Napoleon Pavey. The eighteen-year-old Sam Clemens worked briefly as a journeyman printer in St. Louis to earn money to travel and soon left the city for Cincinnati, Philadelphia, New York, and Washington, D.C. But the river beckoned, and Sam returned to St. Louis—this time planning to train to become a steamboat pilot on the lower Mississippi. He lived with his sister Pamela and her husband, William A. Moffett, from whom he borrowed the $100 down payment required for his training as a cub pilot. Although much of his time in the late 1850s was spent on the river, Clemens's home base was St. Louis. He attended the Christian Church there, whose pastor, Barton Stone, was the grandfather of Clemens's childhood friend Will Bowen. He also joined the Polar Star Masonic Lodge, where he rose to the rank of master mason.

St. Louis was Clemens's first exposure to a major metropolitan area. By 1860 its population had swollen to more than 160,000. The town had twenty-one newspapers and twelve magazines, and its ethnic diversity provided a rich cultural ambiance. The city also had its problems, specifically crime and urban poverty. The influx of immigrants from Germany, Italy, and Ireland brought with it heterodox customs, and St. Louis was never homogenized. Differences in religion and languages spoken in homes kept the sectors of the city discrete. Moreover, the large concentrations of immigrants, primarily poor and Catholic, fed the phobias of the Know-Nothing party, generating resentment and distrust. Many of young Sam Clemens's prejudices, as they surface in his journals and travel letters in the 1860s, may stem in part from his experiences in this volatile environment.

Oliver Howard and Goldena Howard

BIBLIOGRAPHY

Clemens, Samuel L. *Mark Twain's Autobiography*. Ed. Albert B. Paine. 2 vols. New York: Harper, 1924.

————. *Mark Twain's Notebooks & Journals, Volume I (1855–1973)*. Ed. Frederick Anderson, Michael B. Frank, and Kenneth M. Sanderson. Berkeley: U of California P, 1975.

Howard, Oliver, and Goldena Howard. *The Mark Twain Book*. New London, Mo.: Ralls County Book, 1985.

See also: Clemens, John Marshall; Florida, Missouri; Hannibal, Missouri

St. Petersburg

The fictional setting of *The Adventures of Tom Sawyer* (1876), St. Petersburg is heavily modeled on Clemens's recollections of his childhood home in Hannibal, Missouri. Like Hannibal, St. Petersburg is a small town on the west bank of the Missouri River. Clemens attempts to recreate a boyhood Eden in which everything is seen through the eyes of a young boy: the house, the school, the church all loom over the young Tom Sawyer; he is drawn by the woods and caves beyond the town; the heart of darkness in the town is hidden in the slave quarters, the jailhouse, and courthouse.

The setting is essential to the understanding of the novel. The name St. Petersburg

reminds the reader that this is, in a sense, heaven, and yet it is also the place where Tom learns the meaning of betrayal and death. Clemens takes each scene from reality but draws it larger than life; for instance, the final scene in the cave is based on an incident in Hannibal in which some children get lost, but Clemens transforms the cave into an anteroom for adulthood in which the children are given a new awareness of human existence. The town is not so much a recreation of the historic Hannibal as it is a sketch drawn from Clemens's memory of his boyhood.

Stuart Kenny

BIBLIOGRAPHY

Gerber, John C. *Mark Twain*. Boston: Twayne, 1988.

Kaplan, Justin. *Mr. Clemens and Mark Twain*. New York: Simon & Schuster, 1966.

See also: *Adventures of Tom Sawyer, The*; Childhood; Hannibal, Missouri

"Salutation Speech from the Nineteenth Century to the Twentieth, A"

(1900)

"A Salutation Speech from the Nineteenth Century to the Twentieth" appeared in the New York *Herald* on 30 December 1900 under the headline "New Century Greeting Which Mark Twain Recalled." It was composed as a toast to be read at Red Cross Watch meetings on New Year's Eve, but the Red Cross manager returned the piece because Twain was dissatisfied with the meeting announcement. Twain then sent the text to the New York *Herald*.

The statement's fifty-four words indict Christendom's actions toward populations in Africa, China, and the Philippines through its involvement in South Africa's Boer War, China's Boxer Rebellion, and the United States's war with Spain for control of the Philippines. The greeting was later published on thousands of small cards that were distributed nationwide by the American Anti-Imperialist League.

This was Twain's first truly unambiguous, public statement that identified him with the anti-imperialist movement. It can be considered a preamble for "To the Person Sitting in Darkness" (1901).

Michael J. Kiskis

BIBLIOGRAPHY

Budd, Louis J. *Our Mark Twain: The Making of His Public Personality.* Philadelphia: U of Pennsylvania P, 1983.

Clemens, Samuel L. *Mark Twain–Howells Letters: The Correspondence of Samuel L. Clemens and William D. Howells, 1872–1910.* Ed. Henry Nash Smith and William M. Gibson. 2 vols. Cambridge, Mass.: Harvard UP, 1960.

———. "New Century Greeting Which Mark Twain Recalled." New York *Herald*, 30 December 1900, sec. 1, p. 7.

Foner, Philip S. *Mark Twain: Social Critic.* New York: International Publishers, 1958.

Paine, Albert Bigelow. *Mark Twain: A Biography.* 3 vols. New York: Harper, 1912.

See also: Imperialism; "To the Person Sitting in Darkness"

Samossoud, Clara Clemens
(1874–1962)

Clara Clemens was born on 8 June 1874 at Quarry Farm, Elmira, New York. The middle of three girls, Clara was closest to her sister Susy, the "spiritual one." When Clara was four months old, the family moved into their Hartford, Connecticut, home. There, in the second-floor schoolroom, Clara and her sisters were taught by their college-educated mother, Olivia Langdon Clemens, a German governess, and private tutors. Clara's home education included such subjects as math, history, literature, philosophy, English, and German. Clara remained under private tutelage until age fourteen, when she entered Hartford Public School for one year. The family moved to Europe in 1891, and Clara attended the private American School for Girls in Berlin, graduating in 1893.

When Clara was six, she developed a love for the piano. Her parents bought a small upright around which many recitals and plays were centered. When the question of serious musical training was raised, the family moved to Vienna (1898) so Clara could study under the renowned master Theodor Leschetizky. Here her fluency in German allowed her a robust social and educational life, and in 1898 she met fellow musician-student Ossip Gabrilowitsch. Clara married Gabrilowitsch in 1909.

Frustrated by her limited reach across the piano keys, Clara, now in her early twenties, switched to singing. Her vocal training started in Vienna, continued in Munich, and eventually brought her back to the United States, where she studied at New York's Metropolitan Opera under Freida Ashforth. A contralto, in 1906 at age thirty-two, Clara made her American singing debut in Norwalk, Connecticut. She subsequently performed in Boston, Philadelphia, Chicago, and St. Louis and returned to Europe singing in Munich and Florence. Clara's major achievement in music consisted of composing a series of seven historical programs titled "The Development of Song." The work traced the chronological evolution of song from early folk music to contemporary composers. Clara's last professional appearance was in 1934.

Though described by her father as practical, earthy, and businesslike, Clara would soon adopt her sister Susy's interests in metaphysics and mental science. Drawn to a variety of Eastern religions and philosophies, she practiced meditation, energy (or rhythmic) breathing, and the principles of Yoga. Eventually she focused on Christian Science, which she practiced throughout her adult life. Her book *Awake to a Perfect Day* (1956) is devoted to the subject.

Clara authored five books and numerous articles. She also wrote several unpublished manuscripts and essays, many on spiritual subjects. In addition to her singing and writing, Clara enjoyed acting. As a member of two Detroit theater groups, the Theater Arts Club and Civic Theater, Clara had roles in Bernard Shaw's *Saint Joan*, John Galsworthy's *Escape*, Sutton Vane's *Outward Bound*, Edward Sheldon's *Romance*, and Noel Coward's *The Marquise*. Her most notable role was that of Joan in the play *Joan of Arc*, based on her father's book. Due to her frequent bouts with aphasia, however, her acting days soon ended.

Clara married Gabrilowitsch on 6 October 1909 at Stormfield, Clemens's Redding, Connecticut, home. Immediately following their wedding, the couple moved to Nymphenburg, Germany. Clara returned to Stormfield shortly before her father died. Four months later she gave birth to Clemens's only grandchild, Nina, on 18 August 1910. The family returned to Europe, but the onset of World War I forced their return to America. During the war years they lived in Philadelphia and summered in Maine. In 1918 Ossip accepted the position of conductor/director of the Detroit Symphony Orchestra where he remained until his death from cancer in 1936. Clara's marriage to Gabrilowitsch lasted twenty-seven years.

Eight years later Clara was engaged to another Russian musician/composer, an old friend of Ossip's, Jacques Samossoud. They first met while she was acting at the Civic Theater in Detroit. Years later they met again in Hollywood, California, where Clara had moved after Ossip's death and where Samossoud was conducting and directing a local opera company. The two married on 11 May 1944; Clara was seventy years old. For seven years the couple lived at Clara's Hollywood home, Casa Allegra. In 1951 the house was sold at public auction, along with many of Twain's valuable manuscripts and books. Clara's marriage to Samossoud lasted until her death on 20 November 1962. At eighty-eight, she had outlived her parents and siblings. Samossoud died in 1966, followed within months by Clara's daughter, Nina.

*Laura E. Skandera and
Deborah O'Connell-Brown*

BIBLIOGRAPHY

Clemens, Clara. *Awake to a Perfect Day: My Experiences with Christian Science.* New York: Citadel P, 1956.

———. "How I Got Rid of Nervousness in Public." *Étude* 41 (May 1923): 295–296.

———. *My Father, Mark Twain.* New York: Harper, 1931.

———. *My Husband, Gabrilowitsch.* New York: Harper, 1938.

Harnsberger, Caroline Thomas. *Mark Twain, Family Man.* New York: Citadel P, 1960.

See also: Austria (Austria-Hungary); Family Life; Gabrilowitsch, Nina Clemens; Gabrilowitsch, Ossip

San Andreas *Independent*

The San Andreas *Independent*, a weekly newspaper owned by Armor Clayes and Benjamin Parke Kooser, was established in San Andreas, California, on 24 September 1856. The paper, edited first by Kooser and later by Samuel Seabough, was dedicated to the social and intellectual refinement of the citizens of Calaveras County. The *Independent* published an unfavorable review of Samuel Clemens and Charles Warner's *The Gilded Age* (1873), finding the work to be both too bitterly satiric and too critical of America.

Susan McFatter

BIBLIOGRAPHY

Kaplan, Justin. *Mr. Clemens and Mark Twain.* New York: Simon & Schuster, 1966.

Kemble, Edward C. *A History of California Newspapers, 1846–1858.* Ed. Helen Harding Bretnor. Los Gatos, Calif.: Talisman, 1962.

San Francisco, California

Mark Twain first visited San Francisco in early May 1863 on a three-month vacation; he moved to this metropolis seeking fame, fortune, and fun exactly a year later. By the time he left for New York in mid-December 1866, he had won regional acclaim as comical columnist, humorous lecturer, and promising travel writer, a pretty good achievement considering the competition in a city with twelve daily newspapers in a time of prosperity attracting literati on the order of Sir Richard Burton.

The city catered to cosmopolitan tastes with dance halls for sailors, bullfights across the bay advertised in bilingual handbills, dramas in Spanish, German, French, and Chinese, plus opera in English. Maguire's Opera House offered large gambling rooms along with a stock exchange for the favorite sport of speculating in silver-mine stocks. The Lyceum offered ballet; the Eureka, minstrel shows; a museum and an anatomical exhibition gave different kinds of shows; and there was even a park with gardens for sabbatarian strolls. The city never closed.

Putting up at the lush Occidental Hotel at $2.50 a day, Twain found San Francisco living "heaven on the half-shell," yet he soon moved to the more opulent Lick House that could match New York's best. In a population estimated at 115,000 with 41 churches and 105 schools, he found 231 barrooms. The fanciest, called "The Stock Exchange," put out a luxurious free lunch along with its twenty-five-cent drinks plus the use of a full library of current newspapers and periodicals from back east and abroad, *Punch* and *Illustrated London News* among them. Most barrooms had billiard rooms. None admitted ladies.

This was Twain's beat as general assignment reporter for the *Morning Call*. The *Call* being a morning paper meant Twain worked nights. He stood it four months, then tried subsisting on a $300 annual salary from an agricultural society in Nevada along with whatever he could make as correspondent for Virginia City and Sacramento newspapers or as contributor to the local literary weeklies *Golden Era* and the brand new *Californian*. His reputation as comical hoaxer had preceded him from Nevada. The Virginia City *Territorial Enterprise*, for which Twain had written, was in fact a spinoff of the *Golden Era*, and he had little trouble connecting at the *Era*, since he had been its Virginia City correspondent.

The advantage of the *Golden Era* was its reputation for serious literature. In its columns the novels of Charles Dickens appeared freshly serialized alongside the then avant-garde verse of Samuel Taylor Coleridge. Its editorial office attracted young writers like Bret Harte and Joaquin Miller who would there meet such celebrities as Adah Isaacs Menken or the painter Albert Bierstadt and his effete companion Fitzhugh Ludlow, whose presence cast a spell of Bohemianism over the city's youth.

The *Californian* began publishing at the time Twain settled in the city. Between September and mid-November, he published nine humorous pieces in its columns. Widely reprinted in the East, they won him fame as the funniest of the California humorists even before the jumping frog story appeared in November 1865. By this time the term "Californian" was being identified with the new literary weekly, especially for its mixture of "California cleverness, Nevada naiveté, and New York naughtiness." Twain's contributions after returning from the Mother Lode evolved a modification of that style that would one day be all his own.

This evolving style profited from the career change that followed Twain's return to the city after four months in the Sandwich Islands (Hawaii). In lecturing he found it easier to apply the techniques of timing and pacing learned in Nevada from Artemus Ward who had perfected the art of rambling storytelling Twain had enjoyed in Angel's Camp. More important, Ward offered him a model satirist completely different from the *Californian*'s mean-spirited Charles H. Webb, for Ward believed he could accomplish more "through good-humored raillery than envenomed wit."

Finally, Twain's lecturing encouraged him to depart from the practice of Ward and other "phunny phellows" by writing for the ear rather than the eye, reading aloud as he wrote, adjusting the music as well as the words to form the style of his own as "the wild humorist of the Pacific Slope."

P.M. Zall

BIBLIOGRAPHY

Hingston, Edward P. *The Genial Showman: Being the Reminiscences of the Life of Ward.* Intro. Walter Muir Whitehill. Barre, Mass.: Imprint Society, 1971.

Walker, Franklin. *San Francisco's Literary Frontier.* New York: Knopf, 1939.

Wecter, Dixon. "Mark Twain and the West." *Huntington Library Quarterly* 8 (1945): 359–377.

See also: California; Harte, Francis Bret; Ward, Artemus

San Francisco *Alta California*

Founded in San Francisco in 1849 by Edward Gilbert, Edward Kemble, and G.C. Hubbard, the *Alta* became the first California daily newspaper in 1850. The paper flourished until 1891.

Samuel Clemens's connection with the *Alta* began in 1866 when he arranged with his friend and editor of the paper, Colonel John McComb, to contribute a series of weekly travel letters describing his journey to New York and later his tour of Europe, Egypt, and Palestine. In compensation for the letters, modeled after his Sandwich Island (Hawaiian) correspondence to the Sacramento *Union*, Clemens received his passage on the steamship *Quaker City*, bound for an excursion to the Holy Land, and $20 for each contribution. From 25 August 1867 to 17 May 1868 the *Alta* published fifty of Clemens's "Holy Land Excursion Letters."

Clemens's experience as a roving reporter for the *Alta* proved to be significant for the developing writer. During the first leg of his voyage from California to New York City, he met Ned Wakeman, the ebullient captain of the steamer *America*, who later appeared in his fiction under the pseudonyms of Ned Blakely, Captain Stormfield, and Hurricane Jones. While on board the *Quaker City*, Clemens made the acquaintance of Mary Mason Fairbanks, wife of the owner of the Cleveland *Herald*, herself a practicing travel journalist. Mrs. Fairbanks served as Clemens's eastern conscience, acting as critic and censor of his writing.

Upon Clemens's return to New York in November 1867 after the Holy Land excursion, publisher Elisha Bliss contracted with him to write a work based upon his travel letters. After a successful battle with *Alta* owner Frederick MacCrellish over the ownership rights of the letters, Clemens fulfilled the contract with Bliss, publishing *Innocents Abroad* in 1869. It was not until 1940 that the *Alta* letters were collected and published in a volume titled *Mark Twain's Travel's with Mr. Brown*.

Susan McFatter

BIBLIOGRAPHY

Clemens, Samuel L. *Traveling with the Innocents Abroad.* Ed. Daniel M. McKeithan. Norman: U of Oklahoma P, 1958.

Emerson, Everett. *The Authentic Mark Twain: A Literary Biography of Samuel L. Clemens.* Philadelphia: U of Pennsylvania P, 1984.

Ferguson, DeLancey. *Mark Twain: Man and Legend.* Indianapolis: Bobbs-Merrill, 1943.

Kaplan, Justin. *Mr. Clemens and Mark Twain.* New York: Simon & Schuster, 1966.

Kemble, Edward C. *A History of California Newspapers, 1846–1858.* Ed. Helen Harding Bretnor. Los Gatos, Calif.: Talisman, 1962.

See also: *Mark Twain's Travels with Mr. Brown*

San Francisco *Call*

Five printers bought the San Francisco *Herald* on 1 December 1856, renaming the paper the *Call*. In 1857 George Barnes bought an interest in the paper, and he and fellow proprietor James J. Ayers acted as controlling partners of the conservative morning daily.

During the summer of 1863 Samuel Clemens, who held a position on the Virginia City *Territorial Enterprise* at the time, contracted with the *Call* to write a series of letters reporting the Nevada news. These letters appear in the *Call* from August through December 1863.

In June 1864 Barnes hired Clemens as a city editor on the *Call*. His duties included a wide variety of assignments. He reported on local daily developments, sensational events, public meetings, and even the local theater productions. In addition, he covered crime and court reports as well as local politics. Clemens's hours on the *Call* were long and irregular, and his writing assignments proved unrewarding. His candid articles on racial and social injustices and police corruption in San Francisco were regularly censored and often scrapped by the paper's conservative editor.

Until he was joined by William McGrew in September 1864, it appears that Clemens served as the *Call*'s only reporter. McGrew is likely the Smiggy McGlural alluded to in Clemens's *Autobiography* (1904). The new reporter willingly worked long hours and enthusiastically covered assignments that Clemens found to be routine. In October 1864, fewer than five months after hiring him, Barnes dismissed Clemens.

Although Clemens's work in the *Call* appears without by-lines, his distinctive style is recognizable in many of the local articles appearing between 7 June and 11 October 1864.

Susan McFatter

BIBLIOGRAPHY

Branch, Edgar M. *The Literary Apprenticeship of Mark Twain*. Urbana: U of Illinois P, 1950.

Clemens, Samuel L. *Clemens of the "Call": Mark Twain in San Francisco*. Ed. Edgar M. Branch. Berkeley: U of California P, 1969.

Emerson, Everett. *The Authentic Mark Twain: A Literary Biography of Samuel L. Clemens*. Philadelphia: U of Pennsylvania P, 1984.

Mott, Frank L. *American Journalism: A History, 1690–1960*. 3rd ed. New York: Macmillan, 1962.

See also: Journalism; San Francisco, California

Sandy

Demoiselle Alisande la Carteloise of the land of Moder first appears in chapter 11 of *A Connecticut Yankee in King Arthur's Court* (1889) as "a comely enough creature" who "didn't know as much as a lady's watch," according to the supercilious Yankee Hank Morgan.

Near the end of chapter 12 this "perfect blatherskite" is called Sandy; her only connection with Malory's *Morte D'Arthur* (1485) is the similarity of her name to Alisaunder le Orphelin, young knight and courtly lover.

In *Connecticut Yankee* Sandy serves her Yankee liege as traveling companion, nurse, adviser, protector, and as a raconteur, whose tales come directly from Strachey's Globe Edition of Malory's *Morte D'Arthur*. When in chapter 20 Sandy has the "curious delusion" of seeing pigs as princesses, the Yankee chivalrously claims that *he* is the enchanted one and helps corral the royalty—an example of a knight's devotion to his lady. Soon after, in an emotionally explosive scene in chapter 22, midway through the book, the Yankee taunts Sandy for her failure to understand his vernacular; Sandy then delivers her 304-word soliloquy, a one-sentence paragraph of petition, praise, apology, and the turning point in their relationship, for the Yankee then admits his "mysterious and shuddery reverence" for Sandy, whom he dubs "Mother of the German language."

Casual mention of the wedding of Sandy and the Yankee is an afterthought in chapter 41, for the illness of their baby, Hello-Central, was featured in the previous chapter. Sandy, like Twain's wife Livy was "flawless," and a worshipful husband soon declared theirs "the dearest and perfectest comradeship that ever was." However, the Connecticut Yankee's impulsive return to England from France, causing permanent separation from Sandy, violated a knight's chivalric pledge of loyalty to his lady. Only in illustrator Beard's last drawing were Hank, Sandy, and their child reunited at the end.

Mary Boewe

BIBLIOGRAPHY

Clemens, Samuel L. *A Connecticut Yankee in King Arthur's Court*. Ed. Bernard L. Stein. Berkeley: U of California P, 1979.

Hoffman, Andrew Jay. *Twain's Heroes, Twain's Worlds*. Philadelphia: U of Pennsylvania P, 1988.

See also: *Connecticut Yankee in King Arthur's
        Court, A*; England; Malory, Sir
        Thomas; Morgan, Hank

Sanitary Commission

Headed in 1864 by a Unitarian clergyman,
the Reverend Dr. Henry Bellows, the United
States Sanitary Commission (also called the
Sanitary Fund) was a philanthropic organization whose purpose was to raise money for
wounded Union soldiers. Friendly with Bellows, who admired his newspaper pieces,
Samuel Clemens praised the commission's
fund-raising efforts, as well as those of the
similar United States Christian Commission,
in articles written for the San Francisco *Morning Call*. His support of the organization was
shared by his friend Ruel Gridley. Yet it had
been a scandal Clemens created regarding the
fund that forced him, in 1863, to leave Virginia City. Two pieces that he wrote for the
Territorial Enterprise (and which were perhaps
not really intended for publication) provoked
heated controversy. One, alleging that money
raised for the fund by Virginia City women
had been given to a "Miscegenation Society,"
was probably a heavy-handed satiric answer
to the charge that opponents of slavery endorsed racial intermarriage.

Jarrell A. O'Kelley

BIBLIOGRAPHY

Clemens, Samuel L. *Clemens of the "Call": Mark
    Twain in San Francisco*. Ed. Edgar M. Branch.
    Berkeley: U of California P, 1969.

———. *Mark Twain's Autobiography*. Ed. Albert B.
    Paine. 2 vols. New York: Harper, 1924.

Satire

If we accept the idea of satire's traditional location in a shared confidence, on the part of
certain writers, about the relationship between
humorous literary expression and the correction of social error, we must conclude that
Mark Twain was never really a satirist in the
broad cultural sense, for example, in the sense
that Aristophanes or Fielding were satirists.
Perhaps in a most general sense, like Swift, he
could be said to have written relentless satires
of folly. Or we might say that he often wrote
incidental satire of an extremely high order
but that he never possessed the comprehensive vision of satire. (On the other hand, one
might deal straight from etymology and suggest that if there were ever a banquet of dishes
of mixed fruits conjured up by a comical wizard of the outlandish, it is Twain's.) There
are, of course, conventional explanations for
this: that America even after its great
technopolitical coming of age was too thin a
culture for a satirist to understand what *it* was;
or that Mark Twain's deep confusions about
his own role as literary person and an American person also prevented him from understanding who *he* was.

We are always warned with justice to trust
the text and not the author. In the case of
Twain and satire, however, this particular author really seems to have been the authority
on his particular problem. "A man can't write
successful satire unless he be in a calm judicial
good humor," he wrote to Howells in 1879.
"I don't ever seem to be in a good enough
humor with ANYthing to *satirize* it; no, I
want to stand up before it and curse it, and
foam at the mouth—or take a club and pound
it to rags and pulp."

Those sentences, written in the great middle
passage of Twain's career, aptly describe what
the reader looking across that career locates as
a crisis of satire in what can further be seen as
a long evolution. The key lies in the phrase
"calm judicial good humor." To this day,
works in which Twain made his entrance on
the American scene such as *The Innocents Abroad*
(1869) and *Roughing It* (1872) contain in large
sections some of the funniest specific commentary on American pieties, pomposities, and
plain idiocies ever recorded. Here Mark Twain
had the sense of humor, of comic celebration,
that could make affirmative satire possible. He
was still working, however, on a "judicial"
confidence of broad cultural perspective suffi-

cient to render it not effective social critique. Then, about the time of the letter to Howells cited above, he clearly had begun to take himself seriously as a critic of culture. But by now, as Twain rightly noted, things were no longer funny in a way that could support a *comic* sense of humor that might still make satire possible. Instead, humor had become the constant bedmate of anger. This accounts surely for the almost maddening satirical ambivalence (the word almost seems made for Twain) of disparate "middle" works, including *Tom Sawyer* (1876), *The Prince and the Pauper* (1882), *Life on the Mississippi* (1883), *A Tramp Abroad* (1880), and *Huckleberry Finn* (1885), the latter of which, especially, seems composed almost in equal part of comic *joie de vivre* and tragic yearning for a world of human social possibility not remotely within human reach. In many ways, indeed, one might say that, with the abandonment of search for a moral center, the notorious beginning of the end in *Huckleberry Finn* is truly the beginning of the end for Mark Twain the satirist. The ashen, absurd parody of fun acted out by Tom, Huck, Jim, and all the others in that section becomes the point of departure for what James Cox has called more generally in Twain "the fate of humor." In works such as *A Connecticut Yankee* (1889), *Pudd'nhead Wilson* (1894), "The Man That Corrupted Hadleyburg" (1899), the "Mysterious Stranger" fragments (written 1897–1908), and the incredible hoard of other projects begun and aborted, where satire is even attempted, that which is uproariously laugh provoking often seems so without being remotely funny or without being remotely humorous. Apace, an index of the displacement of humor by black fulmination lies in the tendency of such works to self-destruct on the ground of interpretive debate. Entire books have been devoted to the manic ambivalences of *A Connecticut Yankee*. A recent symposium *and* volume of proceedings on *Pudd'nhead Wilson* have enshrined that enigmatic textual collocation as a storehouse of postmodern indeterminacies. What one is talking about here, in fact, ultimately eludes any discussion even of a sat-

ire of modes. (To borrow classical categories, Twain really never practices the geniality of a Horatian. And by the time he begins to take himself seriously as a satirist, as he himself acknowledges, he has already passed beyond the acerbity of a Juvenalian.) What is funny in these works has a relentless P.T. Barnum (or Tom Sawyer) quality of callous showmanship, of the cruel delight in human discomfort, say, of southwestern humor raised to the level of metaphysical slapstick. Or, to make an analogy probably closer to Twain's own sense of his late project, the author-god of these texts had become a kind of cosmic practical joker, trying to make manic hilarity out of a uniform horror. Cruelty, contempt, and derision become the expressions of a tortured heart trying to make a prayer for suffering humanity.

In conclusion, if there is a single literary term that might help us focus on issues of satire in Mark Twain from beginning *to* end, it is probably that identifying a *kind* of satire we would call "burlesque." An appropriately "low" mode of humor, it differs from formal satire essentially in that satire makes fun of that which is not funny for the sake of moral amendment, while burlesque makes fun of that which is not funny for the fun of making fun. While the fun was there in Mark Twain, *through burlesque* he wrote some of the funniest incidental satire ever recorded by an American. We see this as "early" as that wonderful lampoon *The Innocents Abroad*, in the great "middle" masterworks *Huckleberry Finn* and *A Connecticut Yankee*, and as "late" as that tortured fantasy *Pudd'nhead Wilson*. Increasingly, however, the fun of making fun was gone, and nothing was funny enough to deem susceptible to amendment or even the expense of laughter.

Philip D. Beidler

BIBLIOGRAPHY

Budd, Louis J. *Mark Twain: Social Philosopher.* Bloomington: Indiana UP, 1962.

Clemens, Samuel L. *Mark Twain–Howells Letters: The Correspondence of Samuel L. Clemens and William D. Howells, 1872–1910.* Ed. Henry Nash Smith and William M. Gibson. 2 vols. Cambridge, Mass.: Harvard UP, 1960.

Covici, Pascal, Jr. *Mark Twain's Humor: The Image of a World.* Dallas: Southern Methodist UP, 1962.

Cox, James M. *Mark Twain: The Fate of Humor.* Princeton, N.J.: Princeton UP, 1966.

Kaplan, Justin. *Mr. Clemens and Mark Twain.* New York: Simon & Schuster, 1966.

Krause, Sydney J. *Mark Twain as Critic.* Baltimore: Johns Hopkins UP, 1967.

Lynn, Kenneth S. *Mark Twain and Southwestern Humor.* Boston: Little, Brown, 1959.

Rogers, Franklin R. *Mark Twain's Burlesque Patterns as Seen in the Novels and Narratives, 1855–1885.* Dallas: Southern Methodist UP, 1960.

Sloane, David E.E. *Mark Twain as a Literary Comedian.* Baton Rouge: Louisiana State UP, 1979.

Smith, Henry Nash. *Mark Twain: The Development of a Writer.* Cambridge, Mass.: Harvard UP, 1962.

See also: Burlesque; Humor; Southwestern Humor

Sawyer, Sid

Tom's younger brother in *The Adventures of Tom Sawyer* (1876), Sid is loosely modeled after Twain's younger brother Henry. An orphan like Tom, he stands as one model of the "good boy" and defines Tom's badness as his foil. Sid may appear mannerly, but underneath his obedient exterior lies the heart of a tattler and scoundrel, whose intentions are self-aggrandizement and exposure of Tom's well-intentioned rascality.

The reader understands that Sid has some unforgivable character flaw because of the difference between his external appearance and internal motivation; any boy who likes Sunday school is suspect. His name suggests insidiousness and treachery. His final drubbing at Tom's hands at the end of the novel is long awaited and eminently satisfying, both to Tom and the reader. Tom's badness is thereby defined as ingenuous goodheartedness temporarily misguided, as measured by Sid's goodness, which is strictly appearance, masking villainy.

Ruth K. MacDonald

BIBLIOGRAPHY

Clemens, Samuel L. *The Adventures of Tom Sawyer.* Ed. John C. Gerber and Paul Baender. Berkeley: U of California P, 1982.

See also: Adventures of Tom Sawyer, The; Sawyer, Tom

Sawyer, Tom

Tom Sawyer is the youthful leader of children's adventures in St. Petersburg, the fictionalized Hannibal, Missouri. An orphan of deliberately uncertain age living with his brother Sid and Aunt Polly, Tom is full of romantic enthusiasms from reading Sir Walter Scott and James Fenimore Cooper. He first appeared in *The Adventures of Tom Sawyer* (1876) and continued to engineer wild escapades through half a dozen sequels. Of these, only *Adventures of Huckleberry Finn* (1885), *Tom Sawyer Abroad* (1894), and *Tom Sawyer, Detective* (1896) saw publication, although Twain secured a copyright on *Tom Sawyer: A Drama* in 1875 and completed the script in 1884 (Gerber 25, n. 54). Written between 1884 and 1902, the other sequels remained fragments: "Huck Finn and Tom Sawyer Among the Indians," "Tom Sawyer's Gang Plans a Naval Battle," "Tom Sawyer's Conspiracy," and "Doughface" were first published in *Mark Twain's Hannibal, Huck & Tom* (1969); "Schoolhouse Hill" (written, 1898) appeared in *Mark Twain's Mysterious Stranger Manuscripts* (1969). The stories never formed an ongoing series, despite Twain's interest in replicating the success of the Oliver Optic and Horatio Alger books (Gerber 246).

In characterizing Tom, Twain drew not only on memories of himself and childhood friends Will Bowen, John Briggs, and John Garth, but also on the basically good bad boys of nineteenth-century American fiction, most notably Tom Bailey of Aldrich's *The Story of a Bad Boy* (1869). Like his fictional predecessors, Tom steals, avoids school, evades chores, taunts the family pet, engages in wild games, defrauds his buddies, and generally exasperates adults, but in the benign world of *TS* such pranks lack serious consequences—especially when compared to the violence of Injun Joe or (in *HF*) the threats to Huck and Jim. Furthermore, Tom's mischief goes hand in hand with often admirable behavior—testifying in court, accepting Becky's punishment, or kissing Aunt Polly as she sleeps. The combination of naughtiness and goodness makes Tom a realistic character and helps structure *TS* as a tale of the hero's induction into the adult world. Whether one sees this process as maturation or the end of rebellion (Fetterley, "Sanctioned Rebel"), it explains why the quintessential Tom appears only in the third-person narrative of *TS*, and it raises disturbing questions about his character in the sequels, which Huck narrates.

Twain realized on finishing *TS* that Tom "would not be a good character" for the first-person narratives to come (*Twain-Howells Letters* 92). Tom is indeed a different person in Huck's eyes than in Twain's, but point of view accounts only in part for why Tom changes from an exuberant mischief-maker to a self-centered tyrant (almost a caricature of his earlier self) after *TS*. The shift reinforces *TS*'s implication that Tom is becoming a typical St. Petersburg adult, hypocritical and pro-slavery (Blair 88). It also hints at Twain's waning affection for Tom beginning near the end of *TS*, where Twain discovered Huck's narrative voice ("Rebel" 303), and deepening in *HF*, which opens with Tom's unkindness to his comrades and climaxes with his cruelty to Jim ("Disenchantment" 71). Disaffection does not, however, explain why Twain explored the violent consequences of Tom's imagination in two fragmentary sequels: his fantasies lead to massacre and rape in "Huck Finn and Tom Sawyer Among the Indians," and they threaten Jim with the gallows in "Tom Sawyer's Conspiracy." The sequels, though less apocalyptic, likewise fail to resurrect the hero's original ebullience. In *Tom Sawyer, Detective*, Tom's bold talk gets his uncle, Silas Phelps, arrested for murder. Even the comparatively tame *Tom Sawyer Abroad*, which alternately burlesques Tom's pedantry and ridicules Huck and Jim's ignorance, owes its adventure to Tom's insistence on besting an opponent.

Twain's continuing effort to explore Tom's heroism underscores the author's deep investment in the boy and his imagination, despite his increasing flatness. The investment explains some of the conflicts among the Tom Sawyer stories: why they appear sequential but lack a clear chronology of events, why they contradict one another on such significant details as whether Miss Watson is alive or dead or whether Jim—or Tom—is an adult or a child. Tom's flatness, while damaging to *HF*'s sequels, would have enhanced a juvenile series of Tom and Huck adventures by providing a properly formulaic character. Even this incarnation, however, shows the centrality of Tom Sawyer to Twain's conceptions of boyhood, burlesque, and the Matter of Hannibal.

Judith Yaross Lee

BIBLIOGRAPHY

Blair, Walter. "On the Structure of *Tom Sawyer*." *Modern Philology* 37 (1939): 75–88.

Clemens, Samuel L. *The Adventures of Tom Sawyer, Tom Sawyer Abroad, Tom Sawyer, Detective.* Ed. John C. Gerber, Paul Baender, and Terry Firkins. Berkeley: U of California P, 1980.

———. *Mark Twain–Howells Letters: The Correspondence of Samuel L. Clemens and William D. Howells, 1872–1910.* Ed. Henry Nash Smith and William M. Gibson. 2 vols. Cambridge, Mass.: Harvard UP, 1960.

———. *Mark Twain's Hannibal, Huck & Tom.* Ed. Walter Blair. Berkeley: U of California P, 1969.

———. *Mark Twain's Mysterious Stranger Manuscripts.* Ed. William Gibson. Berkeley: U of California P, 1969.

Fetterley, Judith. "Disenchantment: Tom Sawyer in *Huckleberry Finn*." *Publications of the Modern Language Association* 87.1 (1972): 69–72.

———. "The Sanctioned Rebel." *Studies in the Novel* 3 (1971): 293–304.

Hill, Hamlin. "The Composition and the Structure of *Tom Sawyer*." *American Literature* 32 (1961): 379–392.

Norton, Charles A. *Writing "Tom Sawyer": The Adventures of a Classic.* Jefferson, N.C.: McFarland, 1983.

Stone, Albert E., Jr. *The Innocent Eye: Childhood in Mark Twain's Imagination.* New Haven, Conn.: Yale UP, 1961.

See also: Adventures of Huckleberry Finn; Adventures of Tom Sawyer, The; Boy Books; Tom Sawyer Abroad; Tom Sawyer, Detective; "Tom Sawyer's Conspiracy"

Scatology

In literary terms, scatology is the study of references to human waste and excretions and to body parts involved in those operations (Rollfinke 1117). For various reasons and purposes many literary artists have made use of scatology in their writings, Mark Twain among them. Despite the relatively small number of scatological references in the Twain canon, these uses are important for what they reveal about the works, about Mark Twain and his attitudes, and about the times in which he lived.

Artists have used scatology for satire, for light humor, for shock value in breaking a societal taboo, or for a combination of these reasons (Rollfinke 1117–1118). Scatology has proven an especially potent weapon in the hands of artists who wish to subvert, shake up, or attack their societies, as can be seen by considering a selective list of notable authors throughout history who have used the device: Aristophanes, Martial, Juvenal, Dante, Boccaccio, Chaucer, Luther, Rabelais, Shakespeare, and Swift.

Mark Twain's attitudes toward scatology can best be gauged by examining his works, dividing them into two categories: works not intended for publication containing overt scatology and works intended for publication containing more muted references. The best and most extended example of the first category is *1601* (written 1876), a short satirical, scatological, and bawdy piece that Twain wrote for the amusement of a few male friends, which has been privately printed in limited editions a number of times since 1880. Using the most

graphic and taboo language, Twain describes Queen Elizabeth's search for the "author" of an anonymous breaking of wind, the suspects including Shakespeare, Bacon, Sir Walter Raleigh, and Francis Beaumont; upon finding that Raleigh is the culprit, the august group moves on to a frank discussion of sexual and bodily manners, again in the most graphic of language. Two other pieces not intended for publication—"Some Thoughts on the Science of Onanism" (1879) and "The Mammoth Cod" (ca. 1902)—are not principally scatological, centering as they do on masturbation and male sexual organs, but both contain scatological references, and both share the crude male "locker-room" mentality of *1601*. The common point in all of these is that they were written for the amusement of men, and only men, and they all had some sort of satirical thrust.

Scatological references in Mark Twain's published work are much more muted. In his early hoax "Petrified Man" (1862), the alleged curiosity is frozen in the position of thumbing his nose, an entreaty to engage in a scatological act, although this posture is purposely obscured somewhat by Twain's description. Loosely speaking, "The Invalid's Story" (1882) could be considered scatological since its grim humor centers around the stench of rotting corpses. The "nub" of "Jim Wolf and His Tom-Cats" (1867) depends on the title character burning his posterior in hot candy and scampering nearly naked before the girls at the taffy pull, a situation with affinities to Chaucer's fabliaux. In *The Adventures of Tom Sawyer* (1876) Tom catches Becky Thatcher looking at an engraving of a naked man in an anatomy book, which so flusters Becky that she tears the page. Mark Twain's most famous and important work, *Adventures of Huckleberry Finn* (1885), contains several scatological references, chief among these the play put on by the King and Duke, "The Royal Nonesuch," which involves a painted up but otherwise naked King prancing before an all-male audience; Huck demurs from describing the performance in greater detail, but Mark Twain later made autobiographical comments relating the show to Jim Gillis's "The Burning Shame," saying he had to water down the scene for propriety (*Eruption* 361). Wallace Graves has speculated that the actual show involved a lit candle strategically placed in the posterior (98).

What these works reveal is a man who clearly enjoys scatological humor, especially for its shock value, its coarseness, and its satirical uses, but only before a private, male audience; Mark Twain repeatedly made it clear that he was trying to shield women and children from such humor. Readers today might accuse Twain of hypocrisy and perhaps even of discrimination (certainly of being patronizing), but he clearly was being quite Victorian in his public/private split. Indeed, this and other splits have been centerpieces of Mark Twain criticism almost from the start; scatology itself has been cited as one proof of Mark Twain's emasculation by his general society (Brooks 227), although other critics have used it as evidence of his robust, lively, exuberant nature.

Three influencing factors help explain Mark Twain's attitudes toward scatology: reading, personal association, and cultural forces. From his voracious reading Twain knew a long line of scatological writings, including the classic authors cited earlier, but also very obscure scatological and bawdy writers, which one can best see by consulting Alan Gribben's *Mark Twain's Library: A Reconstruction*. His personal associations also exerted an influence, and also reveal a split and possible conflict. On the one hand are the coarse, western, predominantly masculine influences from the first half of Twain's life—boyhood in a river town, jobs as a jour printer, a steamboat man, a miner, a western journalist, and associations with male friends—all of which would have exposed Twain to scatological humor. On the other hand are his more refined, eastern, "feminine" influences: Mary Mason Fairbanks, his wife Olivia, the Nook Farm Community, the eastern literary establishment.

Such a delineation is reductive, of course, but it does contain some truth, in that these personal associations highlight the larger cultural forces at work on Mark Twain: the shaping influence of a western, predominantly male society and the refining influence of an eastern, Victorian society. Mark Twain forged his own identity in the midst of these conflicting forces; and since that split, Mark Twain's handling of it, and his creation of self remain at the center of Twain criticism, scatology maintains some kind of importance in showing a very clear delineation of the split. If nothing else, scatology reveals another facet of Mark Twain's humor: shocking, outrageous, satirical but also funny, even if the humor is of a very low order.

John Bird

BIBLIOGRAPHY

Brooks, Van Wyck. *The Ordeal of Mark Twain*. Rev. ed. New York: Dutton, 1933.

Clemens, Samuel L. *Mark Twain in Eruption*. Ed. Bernard DeVoto. New York: Harper, 1940.

Graves, Wallace. "Mark Twain's 'Burning Shame.'" *Nineteenth-Century Fiction* 23 (June 1968): 93–98.

Gribben, Alan. *Mark Twain's Library: A Reconstruction*. 2 vols. Boston: G.K. Hall, 1980.

Rollfinke, Dieter J. "Scatology." *Dictionary of Literary Themes and Motifs*. Ed. Jean-Charles Seigneuret. Vol. 2. Westport, Conn.: Greenwood P, 1988. 1117–1126.

See also: Brooks, Van Wyck; "Invalid's Story, The"; "Mammoth Cod, The"; "Petrified Man, The"; "Royal Nonesuch, The"; Satire; *1601*; "Some Thoughts on the Science of Onanism"; "Wapping Alice"

Scholarship, Trends in Mark Twain

The first stages of scholarship examining the life and works of Samuel L. Clemens followed a pattern recognizable as the inevitable natural order of preliminary investigations of most authors: first an intimate, personal memoir by a close friend (William Dean Howells's, in 1910), then a comprehensive, defining biography (Albert Bigelow Paine's, in 1912), then an edition of the selected letters (1917), next an extensive bibliography of the writer's publications (Merle Johnson's, in 1935), combined with a major, sweeping commentary on Twain's mind and writings (Edward Wagenknecht's, also in 1935). During the latter part of this same period, it might be noted, Walter Blair was performing much the same sort of groundbreaking work on the entire field of American literary humor, culminating in his epochal *Native American Humor* (1937), whose contributions paralleled the tasks of classification, analysis, and synthesis being undertaken by scholars focusing their attention on Mark Twain.

A tremendous impetus for Twain studies turned out to be a book by Van Wyck Brooks (*The Ordeal of Mark Twain*, 1920, 1933) that was so deeply critical of Twain's alleged yielding to internal and environmental pressures as to seem, initially, to have the potential to erase or at least diminish the expanding admiration for his work within academic circles. In the long run, however, Brooks's charges instead inspired such a legion of worthy books and articles defending Mark Twain's achievements and environmental influences that Brooks's original criticisms were all but buried in the countervailing praise; the direct and indirect rebuttals included Bernard DeVoto's *Mark Twain's America* (1932), Minnie M. Brashear's *Mark Twain: Son of Missouri* (1934), and Gladys Carmen Bellamy's *Mark Twain as a Literary Artist* (1950). Brooks's attack, on the other hand, established a powerful precedent that would be reinvoked in nearly every succeeding decade, whenever exasperated commentators, turning cynical about the public worship and classroom adulation of an author who became as much an icon in the second half of the twentieth century as he was a popular celebrity in his own day, sought to balance the record by emphasizing Mark Twain's limitations.

That urge to challenge prevailing views animated, for example, William Van O'Connor's immensely controversial "Why *Huckleberry Finn* Is Not the Great American Novel" (*College English* 17 [October 1955]: 6–10). Sound if provocative scholarship often dominates the studies in this dissenting tradition, as Hamlin Hill's important, iconoclastic *Mark Twain: God's Fool* (1973) illustrates. More recently, Forrest G. Robinson's *In Bad Faith: The Dynamics of Deception in Mark Twain's America* (1986) and Susan Gillman's *Dark Twins: Imposture and Identity in Mark Twain's America* (1989) seem to imply, and Guy Cardwell's *The Man Who Was Mark Twain: Images and Ideologies* (1991) to assert, that Twain was a writer controlled far too often by unhealthy psychological impulses and by race, class, and gender prejudices all too apparent in his society. "The Mark Twain to come," prophesies Professor Cardwell, "will be less suitable than the Mark Twain that is now being displaced for inflating America's self-esteem." Other, even more rebuking, books and articles are promised about Twain's purported shortcomings as an opponent of racism, classism, and sexism in the nineteenth-century literary scene. If history repeats itself, these criticisms will prompt an answering series of publications that justify, explain, and redeem Twain's stature in any reevaluated canon of eminent American authors.

Other trends have been at work within this field of scholarship, of course, and some of these have been nearly as fertile in promoting valuable studies of Mark Twain. A predictable movement toward increasingly specialized research followed the pioneering general commentaries. But first, three seminal studies in the 1960s formed a crucial, intermediate stage between the earliest scholars and the legions of specializing studies that would ensue. Walter Blair's *Mark Twain & Huck Finn* (1962) analyzed the origins, composition, and reception of Twain's masterpiece in such detail as to provide the starting point for virtually every subsequent examination of Twain's book. Henry Nash Smith's *Mark Twain: The Devel-*

opment of a Writer (1962) became for three decades the most essential, often cited exploration of Twain's artistry, particularly his search for an authentic voice within the American idiom; Smith, twice chosen as literary editor of the Mark Twain Papers, attained a degree of influence on the next generations of scholars that is difficult to calculate today because of its very pervasiveness. Yet it was James M. Cox's *Mark Twain: The Fate of Humor* (1966) that proved to possess a strong appeal for the scholars who began to feel an affinity for the tenets of poststructuralist theory and "progressive" political commentary from the 1970s onward, and Cox's work endowed them with a vital sense of participating in a "tradition" within the field of Twain studies itself.

Flowing from these enormously esteemed studies by Blair, Smith, and Cox came a torrent of much more specialized books and articles. Howard G. Baetzhold's *Mark Twain and John Bull: The British Connection* (1970), to take an example, summarized Twain's many and sometimes ambivalent links with English history, literature, and culture, and Dennis Welland's *Mark Twain in England* (1978) deepened our understanding of certain features of that relationship, especially Twain's attitudes toward his British publishers. Sholom J. Kahn's *Mark Twain's Mysterious Stranger: A Study of the Manuscript Texts* (1978) and William R. Macnaughton's *Mark Twain's Last Years as a Writer* (1979) helped focus attention on the final decade of the author's life. David E.E. Sloane's *Mark Twain as a Literary Comedian* (1979) reminded scholars of the vigorous comedic tradition from which Twain sprang. Susan K. Harris's *Mark Twain's Escape from Time: A Study of Patterns and Images* (1982) initiated similar discussions by other commentators. David R. Sewell's *Mark Twain's Languages: Discourse, Dialogue, and Linguistic Variety* (1987) answered some of the questions that have surrounded the linguistic achievements in Twain's fiction.

There were other fine books in the 1960s that exerted only slightly less influence than those of the Blair-Smith-Cox triumvirate.

Louis J. Budd's *Mark Twain: Social Philosopher* (1962) began an assessment of Twain's political and philosophical assumptions that continues today in a variety of studies. Pascal Covici, Jr.'s *Mark Twain's Humor: The Image of a World* (1962) rewards every reader with insights that linger in a scholar's mind. Albert E. Stone, Jr.'s *The Innocent Eye: Childhood in Mark Twain's Imagination* (1961) gave new readings of certain aspects of Twain's obsession with youthfulness, and William C. Spengemann's *Mark Twain and the Backwoods Angel: The Matter of Innocence in the Works of Samuel L. Clemens* (1966) added other observations. Robert Regan's *Unpromising Heroes: Mark Twain and His Characters* (1966) looked at certain folk motifs in a deft, helpful manner. Henry Nash Smith and William M. Gibson's edition of *Mark Twain–Howells Letters: The Correspondence of Samuel L. Clemens and William D. Howells, 1872–1910* (1960) announced a new standard in textual editing of American documents and revealed the depth of a friendship that encouraged Twain to confide his inmost thoughts about books, authors, politics, and philosophy. Sydney J. Krause's *Mark Twain as Critic* (1967) was in many ways never surpassed in its analysis of Twain's tendencies as a commentator on art and life.

Biographical studies, too, have probed more and more fully into selected areas of Twain's life. Edgar M. Branch's *The Literary Apprenticeship of Mark Twain* (1950) began the trend toward isolating certain periods for close scrutiny. Margaret Sanborn has written *Mark Twain: The Bachelor Years* (1990), making ample use of Twain's own accounts. Jeffrey Steinbrink's *Getting To Be Mark Twain* (1991) makes detailed reference to primary materials in tracking the emergence of "Mark Twain" in the years 1867 to 1871. Several books— such as *Mark Twain's Aquarium: The Samuel Clemens–Angelfish Correspondence, 1905–1910* (1991), which elucidates the subject of one of Hamlin Hill's most scandalous insinuations— have gathered and presented Twain's previously unpublished works to fill out the picture of a decade. Doubtless these kinds of specialized studies will continue to offer glimpses into specific areas of Twain's life—into his relationship with Olivia Langdon Clemens, for instance, and with women in general. Indeed, Samuel Clemens's wife is receiving her own measure of full attention at last and is being accorded due credit for her contributions to his success as an author and prominent citizen. A few biographies have taken the opposite tack, however, essaying comprehensiveness. Justin Kaplan's *Mr. Clemens and Mark Twain: A Biography* (1966) became the standard biography despite its controversial psychological conclusions (about a divided personality) by surveying the main contours of Twain's entire life after 1866. Quite a different life appeared in 1984, Everett Emerson's *The Authentic Mark Twain: A Literary Biography of Samuel L. Clemens*, which provided a context for even his minor writings.

These and other biographical studies depended heavily upon the manuscript collections in the Mark Twain Project, Bancroft Library, University of California at Berkeley, as well as in the Mark Twain Memorial at Hartford, the McKinney Papers of Vassar College, the Pierpont Morgan Library (New York City), the Beinecke Rare Books and Library at Yale University, and other institutions. But the gradually unfolding volumes in the Mark Twain Papers series—such as *Mark Twain's Letters, Volume 1 (1853–1866)*, edited by Edgar M. Branch et al. (1988), and *Mark Twain's Letters, Volume 2 (1867–1868)*, edited by Harriet Elinor Smith et al. (1990)—and in the Works of Mark Twain series—including *Early Tales & Sketches, Volume 1 (1851–1864)* and *Early Tales & Sketches, Volume 2 (1864–1865)*, edited by Edgar M. Branch and Robert H. Hirst (1979, 1981)—make available such extensively annotated and unrestricted primary materials as to enable every scholar to act as his own editor. This access to nearly all of Twain's documentary records, including his notebooks, journals, and correspondence, as well as various drafts of his literary manuscripts, will be the most significant determinant of future trends in Mark Twain scholar-

ship. What the earliest scholars were initially denied—permission to inspect—by the administrators of a squeamish, profit-minded literary estate, and what subsequent scholars have perused only at the expense of costly travel and hotel arrangements, can now gradually be leafed through in the comfort of one's school library or home. The opportunity to second-guess previous commentators will be irresistible, but there will likewise be the chance to perceive altogether new relationships and parallels because of the advantage of reviewing materials so frequently and easily. The field of Mark Twain studies, then, stands at the threshold of an era that Frederick Anderson, John C. Gerber, and others foresaw when they obtained funding for the inaugural phases of what became known as the Mark Twain Project at Berkeley. The ultimate release of all texts comprising the Dead Sea Scrolls resembled a veritable cornucopia in the eyes of a majority of the world's biblical scholars, and so, in a far humbler sense, the publication of the Mark Twain materials by the University of California Press opens up new vistas for all students of Twain, American literature, American history, and American studies. The consequence is that every perspective on Mark Twain is likely to be challenged and possibly altered to some extent. Even a scholar at a remote college with miniscule travel funds, or an independent scholar without any institutional affiliation, will soon have equal access to authoritative editions of Twain's writings.

One of the later but essential stages in an author's transformation into a full-fledged academic industry is the accumulation of reference books devoted solely to that person's career and literary productions. Research tools to aid Mark Twain scholars have been numerous and well-designed. E. Hudson Long prepared one of the first, a long-used *Mark Twain Handbook* in 1957, revised by Long and J.R. LeMaster as *The New Mark Twain Handbook* (1985). John C. Gerber's *Mark Twain* (1988) offered another introductory guide. Robert L. Gale's *Plots and Characters in the Works of Mark Twain* (1973) allowed readers to review the basic features of any work at a glance. Even more monumental was Thomas Asa Tenney's *Mark Twain: A Reference Guide* (1977), supplemented by annual reports in *American Literary Realism* beginning in 1977. Tenney's annotated bibliography afforded the working scholar some hope of staying atop the mounting mass of Twain studies, and of finding and grouping together studies on related topics. A modest number of Mark Twain books and articles in the 1950s and 1960s had mushroomed, along with a proliferation of scholarly journals and publishing houses, into an awesome situation in which literally hundreds of informative studies competed for a scholar's notice. Several other reference books also contributed to this goal of assisting the working scholar. William M. McBride's *Mark Twain: A Bibliography of the Collections of the Mark Twain Memorial and the Stowe-Day Foundation* (1984) listed the books, pamphlets, and articles collected in one important archive. Alan Gribben's two-volume *Mark Twain's Library: A Reconstruction* (1980), together with a series of related articles, reported on Mark Twain's reading and his family's private library collection. Louis J. Budd's "A Listing of and Selection from the Newspaper and Magazine Interviews with Samuel L. Clemens" (*American Literary Realism* 10 [1977]: i–100) rescued many long-forgotten responses of the humorist to reporters' questions. James D. Wilson's *A Reader's Guide to the Short Stories of Mark Twain* (1987) drew attention to the craftsmanship in Twain's short fiction and noted thematic parallels.

Shifting directions as well as cyclical patterns in Mark Twain scholarship are discernible, perhaps, in five suggestive titles published in the 1980s and 1990s. Andrew Jay Hoffman, in *Twain's Heroes, Twain's Worlds: Mark Twain's Adventures of Huckleberry Finn, A Connecticut Yankee in King Arthur's Court, and Pudd'nhead Wilson* (1988), acknowledges James M. Cox as an "important" influence. Louis J. Budd's *Our Mark Twain: The Making of His Public Personality* (1983) finally confronts the issue of how much Mark Twain created his own im-

age and how much the press, public, and readers have assisted in this phenomenon. Victor A. Doyno's *Writing "Huck Finn": Mark Twain's Creative Process* (1991) demonstrates the innovative scholarship possible in a genetic textual study concentrating on a single work. Miriam Jones Shillingsburg, in *At Home Abroad: Mark Twain in Australasia* (1988), recounts her research done among neglected first-hand accounts of Twain's tour of Australia and New Zealand in 1895. Sherwood Cummings's revelatory *Mark Twain and Science: Adventures of a Mind* (1988) ponders Twain's intellectual background and how his fiction reflects his views of social and moral issues. If the unceasing publication of innovative scholarly books and articles is the measure of an author's enduring power to tantalize and challenge, then Twain's status, like that of the scholarship enshrining and critiquing him, is secure for the foreseeable future.

Alan Gribben

See also: Bibliographies; Biographers; Editions; Manuscript Collections; Smith, Henry Nash

Schultz, Christian, Jr.
(1770?–1814?)

Christian Schultz, Jr., was an early traveler to and writer about the Mississippi valley. Of German ancestry, Schultz made a long "inland voyage" in 1807–1808. He traveled up the Hudson River, through two of the Great Lakes, then down the Allegheny, the Ohio, and the Mississippi rivers to New Orleans. He wrote a series of detailed descriptions home to "a particular friend." The letters were later edited and published in 1810 as *Travels on an Inland Voyage.*

There is no incontrovertible evidence that Twain had read this book, and he never referred either to it or to Schultz. Still, as Alan Gribben has pointed out, it is known that Twain read thousands of books. Twain himself admitted that he particularly liked to read travel books. It is also known that he took pains to consult them, especially when working on *Life on the Mississippi* (1883) and *Adventures of Huckleberry Finn* (1885).

Schultz's *Travels* is particularly likely to have been known to Twain because it offers a number of descriptions that parallel those found in *HF*: the blinding fog, the house perched on the edge of a river bank being gnawed at by the shifting river, bragging riverboat men, the properties of muddy river water.

Peter G. Beidler

BIBLIOGRAPHY

Beidler, Peter G. "Christian Schultz's *Travels*: A New Source for *Huckleberry Finn?*" *English Language Notes* 28 (1990): 51–61.

Gribben, Alan. *Mark Twain's Library: A Reconstruction.* 2 vols. Boston: G.K. Hall, 1980.

Schultz, Christian, Jr. *Travels on an Inland Voyage.* New York: Isaac Riley, 1810. Rpt. Ridgewood, N.J.: Gregg P, 1968.

See also: Adventures of Huckleberry Finn; Life on the Mississippi

Science

Mark Twain's interest in science, his biographer Albert Bigelow Paine (1861–1937) tells us, "amounted to a passion." It was an emotion entirely appropriate to someone living through and trying to understand an era when science was revolutionizing the way people thought and felt. In coping with the revolution Twain lacked formal education in science, but he repaired that deficiency through lifelong reading in science. He had, besides, early training in two sciences.

Twain read in and strongly reacted to science from the time he as an adolescent pored over astronomies through his last decade when, for example, he responded to Marie Curie's "Radium and Radioactivity" (1904) with his "Sold to Satan" (1923), in which he envisioned an atomic explosion that would destroy the earth and turn the moon into a "snow-shower of gray ashes." His favorite sciences, judging from the 160 science titles in

Alan Gribben's *Mark Twain's Library* (1980), were astronomy, anthropology, archaeology, geology, and biology. His library included John George Wood's *The Uncivilized Races, or Natural History of Man* (1870), John Tyndall's *Sound* (1876), Amedee Guillemin's *The Heavens* (1878), Nathaniel S. Shaler's *Aspects of the Earth* (1890), Thomas Huxley's *Evolution and Ethics* (1894), Andrew Dickenson White's *A History of the Warfare of Science with Theology* (1901), and a twelve-volume set of Charles Darwin's work.

During his four years (1857–1861) on Mississippi River steamboats Twain learned and practiced what he repeatedly called "the science of piloting"; and his detailed description of the process, beginning with memorizing data, deriving from them the "shape" of the river, and finally getting that shape in his head, is a lesson in the scientific method of inducing concept and theory from countless particulars. His next endeavor (1861–1862) was to prospect for silver ore in Nevada. In that activity he developed a fairly sophisticated interest in geology, which is here and there reflected in his work, especially in his travel books.

Mark Twain reacted to science on several different levels. As citizen of his time of stunning progress, he gloried in the scientific and technical achievements he witnessed. At seventeen he described New York's Croton aqueduct as "the greatest wonder yet," and six years later he joined in "the wave of jubilation and astonishment that swept the planet" when the first message was sent via the transatlantic cable. In like manner he greeted other of his century's technological miracles: the telephone, the sewing machine, the electric-powered elevator, the skyscrapers that followed, and, in 1907, the Marconi Company's first transatlantic wireless message. He honored scientists, inventors, and engineers. In *A Connecticut Yankee* (1889) he called Johannes Gutenberg, James Watt, Richard Arkwright, Samuel Morse, George Stephenson, and Alexander Graham Bell "the creators of this world—after God" and later added Thomas Edison. The inventor he knew best—James W. Paige, whose typesetter Twain financed—was "a most great and genuine poet, whose sublime creations are written in steel." Inventors in his fiction generally received (Colonel Sellers is an exception) similar praise: the "genius" who invented the flying machine in *Tom Sawyer Abroad* (1894) was "one of the men that lifts up nations and makes civilizations," and Hank Morgan, the Connecticut Yankee, could make "anything in the world." He honored inventors through more than praise. He claimed he was the first private user of the telephone and the "first person in the world to apply the type-machine to literature" in typewriting the manuscript to *Tom Sawyer* (1876). He may have been the first author to use phonographic dictation in composing *American Claimant* in 1891. He was one of the first users of the fountain pen, the high-wheeled bicycle, and the telharmonium, which transmitted music by wire from a microphone to an amplifier.

He was himself an inventor of, it is true, simple devices or games for family use—a bed clamp to keep baby's covers on, a perpetual-calendar watch-charm, a way to suspend trousers from waistcoats, a history game played with a board and cards, and the Mark Twain Scrap-Book, which required no pastepot. The last three he had patented, and he not only had the Mark Twain Scrap-Book produced but realized a profit from its sale as well. He also financed the development of other people's inventions—a steam generator, a steam pulley, a new method of marine telegraphy, the Kaolotype process of printing colored illustrations, and the Paige typesetter—and lost several hundred thousand dollars in the process.

When he turned from investing in science to investing his imagination in science fiction, he was more successful. David Ketterer as editor of *Mark Twain's Science Fiction* (1984) puts Twain in the company of such "seminal" science-fiction authors as Jonathan Swift, Jules Verne, and H.G. Wells, with whose work Twain was familiar. Twain's signal achievement in the field is *A Connecticut Yankee* (1889), but there are numerous other fascinating examples of the genre from his "Petrified Man"

(1862) to "Three Thousand Years Among the Microbes" (1905), and they exploit such engaging ideas as traveling by comet ("A Curious Pleasure Excursion," 1874), the "reality of a dream person" ("My Platonic Sweetheart," 1898), and a miniaturized family's voyaging across a waterdrop under a microscope ("The Great Dark," 1898).

At quite another level, Twain persistently sought through science to understand the whole meaning of life. This deeper level seems an anomaly in a person who spent so much of his talent and energy in creating a public image. We begin to understand the dimensions of his genius when we realize that as well as being a great showman, he was deeply philosophical.

Raised in Hannibal, Missouri, where the prevailing religious view was Protestant and fundamentalist, he was made to "fear God and dread the Sunday school." Escaping Hannibal at age seventeen, and supporting himself as journeyman printer in St. Louis, Philadelphia, New York, Cincinnati, and Keokuk, he broadened his horizons through a program of self-education. He read Thomas Paine's "deist's bible," the *Age of Reason* (1794), as a cub pilot, and by 1861, as evidenced in his joining the Polar Star Masonic Lodge of St. Louis, he had become a full-fledged deist. His current world view would be based on the science of the eighteenth century, principally that of Isaac Newton. That science, in emphasizing the regularity and dependability of universal law, had encouraged certain Western thinkers to see the world as in the charge of a purposeful, benevolent, and intelligible deity. That Twain was one of those thinkers is amply evidenced in two private credos that he composed, one around 1870 and the second perhaps ten years later. In those credos, which run to some thousands of words, he rejected "the God of the Bible" in favor of the "true God . . . whose beneficent, exact & changeless ordering of the machinery of his colossal universe" proves that he is "steadfast, . . . just and fair."

Twain remained a deist for some thirty years, but his faith was not without challenges and erosion. It was strained by the absurdity of his western experience (1861–1866)—his "drifting about the outskirts of the world"; it was temporarily overlain in 1868 and 1869 with the evangelical Congregationalism of his fiancée and of his friend, the Reverend Joseph Twichell, when his conversion to Christianity was made a condition of his engagement to Olivia Langdon; and it was challenged in 1871 by his reading Charles Darwin's *Descent of Man* (1871). Darwin's world view, unlike Newton's, was agnostic. The heartless process of natural selection, requiring the constant elimination of "unfit" individual lives, coupled with the science's unimaginable expansions of geologic time and astronomical distance, bespoke for many thinkers a remote and uncaring God. Twain became one of them. He resisted the implications of Darwinism for about a decade, but by the end of another ten years—in 1891—he came to regard all religions, including his deism, as "lies and swindles."

He salvaged from his deistic belief the conviction that natural law did indeed prevail, but he went beyond Paine, who declared that men were "free agents" and insisted that such law controlled people's thoughts and actions, that men's responses were automatic, that they had no will of their own. Such is the philosophy that he worked out in *What Is Man?* (1906). In continuing to apply Darwinian ideas to human society he further concluded that "there is no such thing as morality," that men in their wars, conquests, and competitiveness lived by the same law "animals follow." Such dire statements, though often enough repeated, were not, however, his only old-age expressions. In total contradiction to his determinism, for example, is the amazing "dream-self" fantasy toward the end of "No. 44, The Mysterious Stranger" (written c. 1904). It is a hymn to the freedom of the imagination.

At still another level of Twain's response to science is his accommodation to realism. Realism was a self-conscious literary movement led in the United States by Twain's good friend William Dean Howells. Its emergence on the American scene was a signal that the idealism and romanticism of such standard American authors as Longfellow, Whittier, Poe, Emerson, and Holmes was at an end. In its place, Howells insisted, should be literature that portrayed life as it actually was, one that paid attention not to romance and ideals but to the homely details of everyday existence. As such, realism was an accommodation to nineteenth-century science, which in its particularity was undermining the elegant abstractions of Newtonian science. Twain was Howells's willing disciple in the early 1870s, heeding such admonitions of Howells as, "stick to actual fact . . . and give things in *detail*," and in 1878 he wrote gratefully to Howells that he owed as much to Howells's training "as the rude country job printer owes to the city boss." Twain was, finally, too ranging a writer to be classified simply as a realist; indeed, he never called himself a realist or used the term "realism." Nevertheless, much of his major work, notably the *Prince and the Pauper* (1882), *Huckleberry Finn* (1885), and especially *Pudd'nhead Wilson* (1894), displays the scientific objectivity and attention to detail that characterize literary realism.

Sherwood Cummings

BIBLIOGRAPHY

Clemens, Samuel L. *The Science Fiction of Mark Twain.* Ed. David Ketterer. Hamden, Conn.: Archon, 1984.

———. *"What Is Man?" and Other Philosophical Writings.* Ed. Paul Baender. Berkeley: U of California P, 1973.

Cummings, Sherwood. *Mark Twain and Science: Adventures of a Mind.* Baton Rouge: Louisiana State UP, 1988.

Gribben, Alan. *Mark Twain's Library: A Reconstruction.* 2 vols. Boston: G.K. Hall, 1980.

Poole, Stan. "In Search of the Missing Link: Mark Twain and Darwinism." *Studies in American Fiction* 13.2 (1985): 201–215.

Waggoner, Hyatt Howe. "Science in the Thought of Mark Twain." *American Literature* 8 (1937): 357–370.

See also: Darwin, Charles; Determinism; Evolution; "Great Dark, The"; Howells, William Dean; Paine,

Thomas; Realism; Religion; "Sold to Satan"; "Three Thousand Years Among the Microbes"; *What Is Man?*

Scott, Walter
(1771–1832)

Scottish novelist and poet Sir Walter Scott was immensely popular in the American South during the early and middle nineteenth century. Mark Twain read Scott extensively and owned a number of volumes of his work, including a complete twelve-volume set of *The Waverly Novels* (Abbotsford Edition), yet he was often critical of both Scott's writing and his influence. The most notorious instance is his flamboyant contention in *Life on the Mississippi* (1883) (chapters 40, 45, and 46) that Scott was the source of a deluded romanticism—"the Sir Walter disease"—significantly hindering southern progress and that Scott may have been "in great measure responsible" for the Civil War. This "wild proposition," as Twain called it, has often been rebutted, but it has also found defenders among subsequent critics and historians. Elsewhere Twain complained that Scott's novels are "juvenile," "artificial," and "shoddy," marred by a "poverty of invention" and inhabited by characters who are "bloodless shams" and "mild-and-water humbugs"; the one novel that he professed to admire was *Quentin Durward*. He made Scott's novels, especially those with medieval settings, a frequent target for satirical treatment, playing off Scott in such works as *The Prince and the Pauper* (1882), *Adventures of Huckleberry Finn* (1885), and *A Connecticut Yankee in King Arthur's Court* (1889). The wrecked steamboat *Walter Scott* in *Huckleberry Finn* can be seen as an emblem of the no-longer-visible romantic ideals Twain associated with Scott.

James S. Leonard

BIBLIOGRAPHY

Clemens, Samuel L. *Life on the Mississippi*. Boston: James R. Osgood, 1883.

————. *Mark Twain's Letters*. Ed. Albert B. Paine. 2 vols. New York: Harper, 1917. 737–739.

Gribben, Alan. *Mark Twain's Library: A Reconstruction*. 2 vols. Boston: G.K. Hall, 1980. 612–618.

Krause, Sydney J. *Mark Twain as Critic*. Baltimore: Johns Hopkins UP, 1967.

————. "Twain and Scott: Experience Versus Adventures." *Modern Philology* 62 (February 1965): 227–236.

See also: *Life on the Mississippi*; South, Mark Twain and the; *Walter Scott*

"Second Advent, The"
(1972)

Written in 1881, "The Second Advent" was first published in *Mark Twain's Fables of Man* (1972). Mark Twain borrowed materials from "The Holy Children" to flesh out the second half of his satire on immaculate conception and special providences. An 1883 notebook entry (3:17) suggests that he planned to extend the story and replace St. Talmage (perhaps Reverend Thomas DeWitt Talmage, 1832–1874) with Paddy Ryan and "lots of Irish disciples."

Mark Twain satirizes the gullibility of people who blindly accept the authority of the Bible and religious enthusiasts who lack a healthy skepticism. However, he also recognizes the paradox, suggested by Herman Melville in *The Confidence Man* (1857), that without faith you cannot have faith.

Nancy Hopkins claims to be carrying God's child. The town loafers delight in ribbing her fiancé, Jackson Barnes, about this supposed miracle; but, in fact, there IS a second coming and the scoffers are shown up. The Barnes family remains in Black Jack, Arkansas, to raise the supernatural child.

The focus shifts, thirty years later, to the human disciples, with typical human weaknesses for power, who disrupt the natural order of things by exploiting the new Christ's supernatural powers according to their own inferior abilities to understand the universal significance of their acts. The inhabitants of the sleepy village learn from their experiences with these inept disciples and form resolutions (perhaps representing the power of democracy) that prayers must be sincere expressions of concern but without expectation of fulfillment; that if prayers were routinely answered the world would be in chaos and destructive confusion forever; that anyone expressing a belief in a special providence would be judged insane; that anyone in Arkansas attempting to help God run the world would be put to death; and that all prayers in Arkansas henceforth shall end with "Lord, Thy will, not mine, be done." But the new Savior and his disciples could not stay out of the miracle business and were eventually crucified—except for St. Talmage, the informer, who was paid thirty pieces of silver.

"The Second Advent" is another of Mark Twain's satires on the destructiveness of human misconceptions of piety and divinity, based on human pride and ignorance. It does not, however, deny the supernatural or faith.

Robert Lowrey

BIBLIOGRAPHY

Brodwin, Stanley. "The Theology of Mark Twain: Banished Adam and the Bible." *Mississippi Quarterly* 29.2 (1976): 167–189.

Clemens, Samuel L. *Mark Twain's Fables of Man.* Ed. John S. Tuckey. Berkeley: U of California P, 1972.

———. *Mark Twain's Notebooks & Journals, Volume III (1883–1891).* Ed. Robert Pack Browning, Michael B. Frank, and Lin Salamo. Berkeley: U of California P, 1979.

Emerson, Everett. *The Authentic Mark Twain: A Literary Biography of Samuel L. Clemens.* Philadelphia: U of Pennsylvania P, 1984.

Wilson, James D. "Religious and Esthetic Vision in Mark Twain's Early Career." *Canadian Review of American Studies* 17 (1986): 155–72.

See also: "Holy Children, The"; Religion

Sellers, Colonel

Mark Twain's first extended work of fiction, *The Gilded Age* (1873), presented the memorable male character Colonel Eschol Sellers, a middle-aged visionary deluded not only by his own money-making schemes and inventions, but also by his ardent belief that he was the rightful heir to an English earldom. Twain based three other works around Colonel Sellers: the novel *The American Claimant* (1892) and two plays, *The Gilded Age* (1874; also known as *Colonel Sellers*) and *Colonel Sellers as a Scientist* (written 1883).

Twain based Sellers directly on his beloved cousin Major James J. Lampton, although the character's speculative nature and cravings for the English earldom can be seen in others, including Orion Clemens, John Marshall Clemens, Jesse Leathers, and Mark Twain himself. But Sellers is more than just Lampton's breezy qualities put on paper. In Sellers Twain had captured a distinctive American personality, representative of that post-Civil War era of unbridled and unscrupulous speculation. Sellers was so identifiable as an American type and his traits so broadly recognizable that both Twain and comedian John T. Raymond were often accosted by men and women who believed that Sellers was based either on them or on someone they knew.

In *The Gilded Age*, his biting satire on American democracy, Twain introduces Eschol Sellers, who after the first edition becomes Beriah Sellers due to the complaints of a living Eschol Sellers in Bowlesville, Illinois. In the novel Sellers goes to Washington to represent the poverty-stricken Hawkins family, who desperately cling to their inheritance of 75,000 acres of land in the Knobs of East Tennessee. In Washington he helps lobby for the passage of the Tennessee Land bill and stands by Laura Hawkins during her trial for murdering Colonel Selby. After the trial and the defeat of the land bill, Sellers returns home to practice law in the primitive village of Hawkeye, Missouri, aspiring to become eventually Chief Justice of the Supreme Court. Although he is an honorable and honest man, he is completely at ease among the corruptions of his day. Finding himself hard up for cash following the Civil War, Sellers, a southern gentleman of good blood who had served as a Confederate captain in Missouri, has no reservations about dealing with the Unionists and carpetbaggers now in power. He maintains always his courtly manner and generous affability in spite of his continuous financial difficulties. Inviting his friends to share his blissful dreams of enormous wealth, he is a spellbinding and enthusiastic promoter whose tireless tongue catapults trading in magic eye water, corn, hogs, and mules to astral levels. He is constantly talking of grand schemes and millions of dollars. However, he never seems to have ready money and feeds his family raw turnips and water for dinner.

The character Colonel Sellers was largely responsible for the success of *The Gilded Age*, and within a year of its publication Twain had successfully dramatized the novel in a popular play starring John Raymond. In this drama Twain changed the character's name to its final form, Mulberry Sellers.

Almost a decade later, Twain collaborated with his talented friend William Dean Howells to bring Sellers back to the stage in what they considered "the Great American comedy." Originally referred to by its authors as *The Steam Generator* and *Orme's Motor*, this new play was finally called *Colonel Sellers as a Scientist*. The play picks up Sellers thirty years after the main action of *The Gilded Age*. Believing he is an heir to the Earldom of Dover, Sellers is an older version of the original character, plotting schemes involving billions of dollars as creditors are taking cheap chromos from the wall of his "mansion" to settle $1.50 debts. However, he is a corrupted Sellers, more silly and ridiculous than the original. Not only is he preoccupied with the materialization of departed spirits, but he also wears a fire extinguisher all day long. His daughter Mary has feelings toward her father bordering on bitterness, and he is strikingly unlike the earlier Sellers, who was worshiped by his family. Although Howells and Twain had great fun in writing the play, this Sellers is less convincing than the Sellers of *The Gilded Age*.

Lampton's influence seems less direct, and Twain infuses elements from Orion Clemens's outlandish invention schemes, Jesse Leathers's claims to the Lambton estates in England, and Raymond's comedic stage portrayal of Sellers.

Twain had not seen Lampton for many years when he co-authored this later play. When Howells and Twain wrote *Colonel Sellers as a Scientist*, they did so in late 1883, more than a year before Twain's final and poignant visit with the now elderly Lampton at the Southern Hotel in St. Louis in early 1885. The visit and Lampton's still bubbling indestructable optimism apparently brought Twain back to his original affectionately serious image of Sellers. The Sellers in *The American Claimant* is the James Lampton whom Twain and George W. Cable met at the Southern Hotel.

The plot of *The American Claimant* is largely a rehashed version of the play *Colonel Sellers as a Scientist*. Although the white-headed Sellers is still "as young, alert, buoyant, visionary, and enterprising as ever," he becomes a peripheral character in the adventures of Viscount Berkeley, the young heir to the Earldom of Rossmore. Twain had failed to build a worthy plot for one of his favorite creations.

Twain never abandoned the hope of casting Sellers in another play or novel. In "Three Thousand Years Among the Microbes" (1905) one of the narrator's microbic friends is named Colonel Mulberry Sellers. As late as 1906 Twain and his friend Henry Watterson were discussing "the Sellers motif" in an "altogether" new play. In Twain's eyes, his character Colonel Sellers, a tender-spirited, ever chivalrous optimist, embodied the essence of the American frontier. Twain brought humorous triumph to the disasters that beset Sellers by delving into the beautiful spirit with which Sellers soars above calamity; in the same breath that he confronts failure, Sellers enters into a new and more fantastic speculation that, as he talks about it, becomes a side interest, a mere trifle to keep his capital from lying idle, as he contemplates an even more fantastic scheme. Twain intended on repeating Sellers several more times and establishing him as "the American character," to be used by future generations of authors and actors in any number of different plots, in the manner of Pantalone, Arlecchino, and other stock characters of the Italian commedia dell'arte.

Lucius M. Lampton

BIBLIOGRAPHY

French, Bryant Morey. *Mark Twain and "The Gilded Age."* Dallas: Southern Methodist UP, 1965.

Howells, William Dean. *The Complete Plays of W.D. Howells.* Ed. Walter J. Meserve, William J. Gibson, and George Arns. New York: New York UP, 1960.

Kaplan, Justin. *Mr. Clemens and Mark Twain.* New York: Simon & Schuster, 1966.

Lampton, Lucius M. "Hero in a Fool's Paradise." *Mark Twain Journal* 27.2 (Fall 1989): 1–56.

See also: American Claimant, The; Business; Colonel Sellers as a Scientist; Dramatist, Mark Twain as; *Gilded Age, The;* Lampton, James J.

Sentimentality

The role of sentimentality in Mark Twain's life and writings has been very little considered, other than the occasional, generally disapproving, comment by critics that Twain demonstrated his mastery of sentimental style even as he parodied it. In *Mark Twain's Languages* (1987) David Sewell does not even discuss sentimentality. But sentimentality was an important linguistic mode for Twain, and it served many functions in his work, life, and environment.

Twain simultaneously affirmed and exploited sentimentality, both as sentiment (i.e., feeling) and as the language that evokes it. In *Sacred Tears: Sentimentality in Victorian Literature* Fred Kaplan demonstrates the development of British sentimentality out of the eighteenth-century valuation of feeling, showing how it originally valorized moral action and hence the moral worth of those experiencing it. Coming to the eastern establishment as a "funny man," Twain may have initially felt that demonstration of sentiment—and its expression in lyric prose—would help certify him as a serious writer. Certainly passages in *The Innocents Abroad* (1869) and *Roughing It* (1872) display the author's own. But Twain also satirized sentimental discourse, in large part because his function as vernacular humorist was precisely to critique such collective modes. Throughout his writings Twain parodies sentimental style and the false perceptions he feels it evokes—the "effusive" compositions of the girls at the schoolhouse ceremonies in *The Adventures of Tom Sawyer* (1876) being one of the best-known examples. The evidence presents us with a major and fascinating contradiction in Twain's work and psychology, passages of parody existing side by side with "straight" sentimentality.

One explanation for the contradiction exists in the possibility that for Twain, sentimentality evolved from its initial function as a legitimizing agent to a major psychological release, becoming one of the means Twain used to escape from what can be termed "the anxiety of realism." In Twain's writing sentimentality became a linguistic pattern capable of triggering an imaginative alternative to life as he usually found it and as he increasingly portrayed it in his "dark" fiction and his deterministic essays, that is, random and ultimately tragic. Certain words, phrases, or images would precipitate outbursts of writing that have often been labeled as sentimental or escapist (critics tend to use these terms interchangeably): images of drifting, for instance, that preface lyrical passages in works from *Roughing It* through *Adventures of Huckleberry Finn* (1885) to the late "dark" manuscripts; certain images of childhood, especially in country villages during the summer; images of good wives and mothers. Since similar images appear in works by other nineteenth-century writers, from Harriet Beecher Stowe through Donald Grant Mitchell, twentieth-century critics have tended to assume that Twain was parodying these earlier, "popular" writers. But as Susan Gillman has shown in other contexts, rather than seeing Twain as opposed to (and relentlessly critical of) his society, it is useful to examine the elements he shared with his contemporaries. Contrary to modern critics' reductive notions of his sentimentality, in Twain's time (even late in the nineteenth century) it was still a significant cultural concept. Its durability is a key to its functionality: sentimental language and iconography provided imaginative release for a society increasingly aware of its own degeneration. As analysts of comedy from Freud and Jung to Bakhtin have noted, much vernacular humor provides collective and individual freedom from the official culture's authoritarian strictures. Similarly, sentimentality provided a group ideal that represented a collective longing for the good in a society where official ideologies rarely effected social cohesion. Sentimental passages demonstrate writers' responses to both their own and their society's need for ideal landscapes, human and geographical, that would provide alternatives to the moral fragmentation their "real" environment demonstrated. Seen intertextually, the high incidences of sentimental language and the characters, themes, and rhetorical structures that it generates suggest that it had become a culturally approved alternative to the release that comedy (never quite respectable in nineteenth-century bourgeois society) also provided. For Twain, then, this presented a double temptation: personally, it provided emotional escape from the pressure of competition and manipulation that his class and gender mandated, suggested ideal goals and relationships, and implied that the universe was run according to a benevolent plan rather than being the endless series of amoral incidents that he posited in pieces like "The Turning Point of My Life" (1901). Professionally, it provided him with a means of appealing to a marketplace fastidious about the "bodily lower stratum" (see Mikhail Bakhtin, *Rabelais and His World*, 1984) on which the humorous traditions in which Twain did his apprenticeship tended to focus. In addition—and paradoxically—it also gave him yet more material for parody. Both as a writer and as an individual then, Twain used sentimental language and values in a complex variety of ways, telling us much about both

himself and the culture that generated these possibilities.

Susan K. Harris

BIBLIOGRAPHY

Clemens, Samuel L. "The Turning Point of My Life." *Great Short Works of Mark Twain*. Ed. Justin Kaplan. New York: Harper & Row, 1967. 222–230.

Harris, Susan K. *Mark Twain's Escape from Time: A Study of Patterns and Images*. Columbia: U of Missouri P, 1982.

Kaplan, Fred. *Sacred Tears: Sentimentality in Victorian Literature*. Princeton, N.J.: Princeton UP, 1987.

See also: Language; Realism; Rhetorical Forms

Sexuality

The major themes of Mark Twain's preoccupation with sexuality can be summarized as follows: intense, guilty, hidden pleasure in sexuality; idealization and rarification of "virtuous women," whom Twain saw as chaste, angelic, and asexual (the penultimate example is Joan of Arc, the child-woman in *Joan of Arc*, 1896); ambivalent anxiety about the aggressive nature of male sexuality; fear of powerful, sexual women, especially of female sexual voracity; the association of illicit sexuality, and, in fact, of the violation of all kinds of social boundaries, with miscegenation; and a lifelong and intensifying interest in stories of exchanges of identity between male and female, stories that play with the gender signification of clothing, speech, and mental and emotional habits. Male camaraderie often is a more important experience in his fiction than romance, which is generally represented through cliches.

Samuel Clemens's attitude toward sexuality was divided in characteristic male Victorian fashion. He reveled in private bawdry, which he jotted down in his notebooks and journals and composed for exclusively male audiences. But he was extremely reticent about sexual innuendo in his commercial fiction, censorious about sexual explicitness in works of art, and disapproving of "irregular unions" in life. However, this duality is not merely the expression of sexual hypocrisy. Instead, it is indicative of a confused, sometimes tormented, ambivalence about sexuality that was rooted in the Presbyterian legacy of his upbringing and in his anxieties about his identity as a man and as a public figure.

In his childhood in Hannibal, and in his young manhood on the Mississippi River and in California and Nevada, Sam Clemens witnessed or heard about all kinds of sexual behavior. Though he later idealized Hannibal as a place of innocence and propriety, his reminiscences in "Villagers of 1840–3" show that he was aware early of adultery, forced marriage, prostitution, rape, child marriage, and diverse forms of romantic passion. He claimed that no unmarried girl was seduced or even gossiped about in Hannibal, but he did so in the context of contrasting a lost era of "sentimentality and romance" with the hard, cynical, money-hungry turn of the century. *Tom Sawyer* (1876) reflects a fictionalized version of his own romances with several girls in his hometown, at least one of whom, Annie Laurie Hawkins, called Laura by most, he remembered affectionately all his life.

Throughout his life Sam Clemens had a recurrent dream of ideal romance. In "My Platonic Sweetheart" (1898) he described dream encounters, experienced at irregular intervals over a period of forty-four years, dreams in which he is always seventeen and his beloved is always fifteen. He kisses and caresses his sweetheart, but the dominant emotions he feels in these dreams are comfort, affection, and contentment, not the fire of erotic passion. He describes their feeling as closer than that of brother and sister. The blissful serenity of these dream fancies is accompanied by periodic feelings of loss, since in many of these dreams the girl dies. However, his grief is transformed by the knowledge that she will always reappear.

This idyllic if somewhat melancholy vision has an interesting counterpart in a dream vision of an encounter with a black woman,

eating a mushy pie, who offered him her spoon to eat with. Though he notes the physical details of her appearance with great precision, in a way that suggests his attraction to the young woman, he turns away in revulsion from a "disgusting proposition" she makes, which yet seems quite natural to him. Both dreams reveal sexual imagery, but "My Platonic Sweetheart" is a vision of "pure," refined love, in which he is the active partner and she the more passive recipient of his affections, while the dream of the "Negro wench" makes visible Clemens's disgust at his own attraction to physical sexuality and his fear of female sexual initiative.

Nevada Territory and California in the 1860s were rough and tumble places. There Sam Clemens lived among journalists, miners, and gamblers, generally men not known for their restraint in drinking or sexual affairs. How far Sam Clemens ventured in the latter will always be a matter of speculation, but it is fair to assume that he had a thorough education in worldly matters, whether as an observer or as a participant. During this period he developed his taste for raunchy jokes, and his newspaper sketches frequently have a lurid, sexually allusive cast to them.

As he moved east, and as he courted Olivia Langdon and her family, Sam Clemens repressed some of his earlier freedom of expression about matters sexual and erotic; instead he became concerned with the proper degree of genteel "purity." With the help of Mary Mason Fairbanks, his adopted "Mother," he edited some of the coarseness out of his account of his travels to Europe and the "Holy Lands," and it was to her that he made his famous statement that he would not marry a girl he was worthy of because she would not be respectable enough. Nevertheless, in *The Innocents Abroad* (1869) he displayed conflicts about sexuality that haunted him, in one form or another, all his life. He covered his face with his hands when the cancan dancers in the Jardin Mabille kicked up their legs—but he peered through his fingers, thus acknowledging comically both his interest and his sense of guilt. He lambasted Abelard as Heloise's "seducer," preferring to think of the woman as the victim of sexuality rather than acknowledging her independent sexual drive. In *A Tramp Abroad* (1880) he attacked the double standard that permitted nudity in art but censored frank description in literature, but he also condemned Titian's *Venus* as lascivious because of her sexually explicit pose. In general, "good" women in his fiction are portrayed as asexual, while sexuality is associated with women in positions of exceptional power who become quasi-masculine in Clemens's imagination (such as Queen Elizabeth in *1601* or Morgan le Fay in *A Connecticut Yankee*) or with slave women and "fallen" women who become social outcasts, such as Laura Hawkins in *The Gilded Age* (1873).

Men are not free from sexual guilt for Mark Twain either. Dixon Wecter noted that for Sam Clemens sex was something polluting and degrading from an early age onward, surely in part because of the influence of his Presbyterian upbringing. Clemens believed that men were the seducers, women always the seduced, a theme that he explored obsessively in his "Wapping Alice" manuscripts and in "Why Not Abolish It?", "It" being the age of consent (see Gillman, chapter 4).

However, within the boundaries of marriage, Clemens had an active, affectionate, and apparently fulfilling sexual life. His letters to Livy from London in 1873, after several weeks of separation, reflect his passionate longing for her and his vivid pleasures in fantasies of their reunion ("then to bed, and—everything happy and jolly as it should be"). Sexual intercourse was the one earthly pleasure human beings value above all others combined, he argued in "Letters from the Earth." Yet sexuality was for him closely circumscribed by social and psychological constraints, and Clemens was painfully observant of the limits set by propriety, male privilege, and his conception of female virtue.

As a young man he allowed himself the freedom of frankly erotic interest in women, often in the form of rather juvenile humorous anecdotes, as in his fascination with the nudity of bathing women or in a joke about peering up women's skirts as they climb the pyramids. Many of these jokes, such as the story about a sausage used by a masturbating girl, remained in the privacy of his notebooks. In his middle years he wrote bawdy sketches and speeches (*1601*, a tale about flatulence and ribaldry among Queen Elizabeth's court; "The Science of Onanism"; and his Stomach Club Speech are the primary examples) exclusively for male audiences such as private men's clubs, but he rigorously suppressed sexual allusions in his public writings. He tended to equate chastity with moral virtue in his fiction. When Maxim Gorky registered at an American hotel with his mistress, Clemens's enthusiastic endorsement of the Russian revolutionary's ideas turned into embarrassed withdrawal. His fear of condemnation by conventional morality in the sexual realm was greater than his moral courage in the political realm. In old age he acted out his fascination with prepubescent female "innocence" through his friendships with the girls of a Lewis Carroll–like circle of admirers, whom he dubbed the Angel Fish Club. He also expressed himself more explicitly and extensively than before about sexuality, but in statements meant to be published only after his death.

Roxana, the light-skinned slave woman in *Pudd'nhead Wilson* (1894), is often named by critics as the most convincingly active and complex woman in Mark Twain's writings, but she is virtually alone as a sympathetically portrayed sexually alive woman. Most of Mark Twain's female characters are girls, matrons, or "spinsters," and most of these are seen from the limitations of a boyish perspective. Huck undoubtedly has a crush on Mary Jane Wilks, but it is a comically idealizing adolescent passion. He resents the authority the "spinster" Miss Watson and the Widow Douglas attempt to exercise over him, also in typically adolescent fashion.

The matron is another story. Judith Loftus is a sympathetically portrayed mother figure in *Huckleberry Finn* (1885), and she illustrates

Sam Clemens's respect for the tough-minded, quick-witted, and affectionate mother whom he experienced in Jane Lampton Clemens and whom he adopted in Mary Mason Fairbanks. Yet such influential mother figures are rare and marginal in his fiction, and the limits of his respect for matriarchal power are illustrated in his hostility toward strong, ambitious women such as Mary Baker Eddy, whom he vilified for many of the qualities he himself possessed; Queen Elizabeth, whom he ambivalently portrayed as an historical icon in the British pantheon but whom he characterized as ominously vengeful, dissolute, and mannish in the closed sketch *1601*; and Morgan le Fay in *A Connecticut Yankee*, who mirrors Hank Morgan's cruelty and desire for power but is represented as cold-bloodedly villainous.

Thus it becomes clear that, in Samuel Clemens's conception of sexual roles, female virtue is circumscribed by its dependence on male power and protection. Consonant with that insight is Clemens's oppressively over-protective attitude toward his daughters, whose social relations with young men he sought to control to a tyrannical though typically Victorian degree. Similarly, in his fiction motherhood is frequently associated with victimization and even martyrdom. The mother torn from her child and burned at the stake is one of his recurrent images, of such emotional power to Clemens that it even sometimes, as in *A Connecticut Yankee*, has undercurrents of erotic feeling. The faithful wife and mother who suffers for her virtue is one of the most evocative sources of emotion for Twain, though not necessarily for his readers. Conversely, adultery aroused Clemens's ire, in part because it signified the woman's violation of the laws of patriarchy and a nation that, to him, sanctioned adultery, France, which elicited from him a lifelong stream of invective and vituperation. The French attitude toward sexual liaisons flew in the face of his belief in female identity as defined by the masculine conventions of marriage, prostitution, and chastity. He was quite willing to make allow-ances for the male sex drive, as when he urged that "clean," healthy prostitutes be furnished for British troops in India, but the double standard clearly obtained in his reasoning that the men would return to marry "fresh young English girls." He desired for himself, in his private writings, the freedom of expression of a Rabelais, but he censored *Don Quixote* for his fiancée and considered *Tom Jones* utterly unsuitable for her "purity." The white heat of his outrage at a God who could permit torture and massacre among human beings revealingly took the form of recounting rape and female sexual mutilation by American Indians (in "Huck Finn and Tom Sawyer Among the Indians"), displaying the nexus of his anger against the cruel side of patriarchal authority (a God he did not believe in, yet rallied against), fear of savagery (displaced onto images of "inferior" races), and horrified fascination with male sexual aggression and female victimization. His careful adherence to the sexual and gender conventions of his time provided him with only partial protections against the fears and traumas sexuality evoked for him.

Mark Twain, like many of his central male characters, experienced a struggle between a power-hungry ego and a fierce sense of guilt, arising from or extending itself into the realm of sexuality. This struggle is revealed in the streak of male exhibitionism of some of his characters and in Sam Clemens himself. Hank Morgan in *CY* deplores the British court's lack of shame about undress, but he appears for battle in a skin-tight outfit that simulates nudity. Clemens envied the gaudiness of female dress and reveled in the bright plumage of his Oxford robes.

In his "Mysterious Stranger" manuscripts, and in other late writings, Mark Twain indulged in fictional play with the question of what constitutes gender through multiple exchanges of clothes, bodies, and personalities. In *Following the Equator* (1897), for example, he explored the gender ambiguity of dress and appearance of a Ceylonese servant.

For Mark Twain, sexuality evoked the split between ideals and reality, between the possibilities of the spirit and the actualities of the body. In stories such as his fantasies about Adam and Eve he dreamed of a pure, idyllic, joyful sensuality, but the social and psychological reality of sexuality remained for him "besmirched" by guilt and the abuse of power in a fallen world.

John Daniel Stahl

BIBLIOGRAPHY

Bridgman, Richard. "Mark Twain and Dan Beard's Clarence: An Anatomy." *Centennial Review* 31 (1987): 212–227.

Clemens, Samuel L. *Letters from the Earth.* Ed. Bernard DeVoto. New York: Harper & Row, 1962.

———. "Why Not Abolish It?" *Harper's Weekly* 47 (2 May 1903). Rpt. *Mark Twain Speaks for Himself.* By Clemens. Ed. Paul Fatout. West Lafayette, Ind.: Purdue UP, 1978. 180–185.

Garcia, Wilma. *Mothers and Others: Myths of the Female in the Works of Melville, Twain, and Hemingway.* New York: Peter Lang, 1984.

Gillman, Susan. *Dark Twins: Imposture and Identity in Mark Twain's America.* Chicago: U of Chicago P, 1989.

Harris, Susan K. "Mark Twain's Bad Women." *Studies in American Fiction* 13 (1985): 157–168.

———. *Mark Twain's Escape from Time: A Study of Patterns and Images.* Columbia: U of Missouri P, 1982.

Hill, Hamlin. *Mark Twain: God's Fool.* New York: Harper & Row, 1973.

Jones, Alexander E. "Mark Twain and Sexuality." *Publications of the Modern Language Association* 71 (1956): 595–616.

Kaplan, Justin. *Mr. Clemens and Mark Twain.* New York: Simon & Schuster, 1966.

Karpowitz, Steven. "Tom Sawyer and Mark Twain: Fictional Women and Real in the the Play of Conscience with the Imagination." *Literature and Psychology* 23 (1973): 5–12.

May, Charles E. "Literary Masters and Masturbators: Sexuality, Fantasy, and Reality in *Huckleberry Finn.*" *Literature and Psychology* 28 (1978): 85–92.

Meine, Franklin J. Introduction. *Date 1601, Conversation, As It Was by the Social Fireside in the Time of the Tudors.* By Clemens. New York: Lyle Stuart, 1938. 9–29.

Pettit, Arthur G. *Mark Twain and the South.* Lexington: UP of Kentucky, 1974.

Stahl, John Daniel. "Mark Twain and Female Power." *Studies in American Fiction* 16 (1988): 51–63.

Wecter, Dixon. *Sam Clemens of Hannibal.* Boston: Houghton Mifflin, 1952.

See also: Genteel Tradition; *Pudd'nhead Wilson, The Tragedy of*; Scatology; Sentimentality; "Wapping Alice"; Women

Shakespeare, William
(1564–1616)

References to most of Shakespeare's works appear in Mark Twain's sketches, stories, letters, and notebooks, showing a broad and active familiarity. Twain read Shakespeare frequently, saw Edwin Forrest's Othello and Edwin Booth's Hamlet, and conducted home performances of the plays with his family and friends. As a writer and humorist, however, he utilized Shakespeare in more creative and significant ways, and these can be divided into four categories: burlesque, history and archaic language, plot and character analogues, and biography.

Viewing Shakespeare as the symbol of high culture, Twain scattered scenes and quotations of Shakespeare through his writings to dramatize class and regional differences and to satirize the "highfalutin'" and pretentious. In this he followed a popular tradition of Shakespeare burlesque in newspapers, comic lectures, circuses, and minstrel shows. In one of his reports to the *Territorial Enterprise*, for example, a speaker in the Nevada legislature opposes a bill with lines from *Hamlet*: "Let it go hence to that undiscovered country from whose bourne no traveler returns." In another sketch a refined minister from the East uses the same lines to refer to Buck Fanshaw's death in contrast to the Westerner Scotty Briggs's "kicked the bucket." In a longer piece, "The Killing of Julius Caesar *Localized*," Twain rendered Caesar's assassination in the terms of a big city newspaper controlled by ward politicians. He also planned and began a complete *Hamlet* with the addition of a subscription-book agent interrupting the poetic speeches with his mundane sales pitch. Perhaps his most widely read burlesque is in *Adventures of Huckleberry Finn* (1885) where the King and the Duke present scenes from *Romeo and Juliet* and *Richard III* and rehearse a botched version of Hamlet's soliloquy. They force Shakespeare on small-town yokels and expose their own cultural and aristocratic pretensions.

But Twain used Shakespeare for more than just burlesque and satire. In preparation for *The Prince and the Pauper* (1882) he read history and studied geography. He also compiled a list of "Middle-Age phrases for a historical story," and many of the words and phrases on this list come from Shakespeare. Although he practiced using these phrases in a comic exercise, *1601. Conversation, As It Was by the Social Fireside, in the Time of the Tudors* (written 1876), he considered *The Prince and the Pauper* a "grave and stately work," and the critics found in it artistic depth, historical fact, and moral purpose. It represents a turn from comic to serious in Twain's writing and in his use of Shakespeare. Now he appealed to Shakespeare for historical setting and classical stature, and he joined other authors who did the same: Sir Walter Scott, for example, whose name and phrases also appear on Twain's list. *A Connecticut Yankee in King Arthur's Court* (1889) and *Personal Recollections of Joan of Arc* (1896) are other novels that draw both language and historical ambience from Shakespeare.

Plot and character analogues to Shakespeare further contribute to Twain's classical aspirations. In *The Prince and the Pauper* Prince Edward is locked out of his palace and forced to suffer the elements like King Lear, learning through this ordeal to pity the poor and wretched. King Arthur's wanderings in disguise with Hank Morgan in *CY* reflect the same episodes from *King Lear*, and Hank's magic displays and efforts at social reform are described in terms that associate him with Prospero in *The Tempest*. Several traits and deeds of Edmund Aubrey in *Joan of Arc* resemble those of Falstaff. Especially surprising are the Shakespeare analogues in *HF* because they are not needed there as historical props.

The Grangerford-Shepherdson feud and the Boggs-Sherburn duel are echoed and amplified by the King and the Duke in their scenes from *Romeo and Juliet* and *Richard III*. Similarly, Huck and Jim experience conflicts and changes on the raft like Lear's on the heath, and Huck's personal dilemmas, his hesitations and qualms of conscience about helping Jim escape, gain intensity and universality by clear associations with *Hamlet*. Shakespeare analogues in *HF*, and in the historical novels, give classical paradigms to the immediate actions and raise those actions to the heights of tragic grandeur.

Finally, Twain studied the life of Shakespeare in connection with the Shakespeare-Bacon controversy, which he treated both seriously and humorously in his last book, *Is Shakespeare Dead?* (1909). The lack of verifiable details about Shakespeare's life, especially those relating to professional training and noteworthy experiences, led Twain to doubt his authorship and comically to present himself as superior to Shakespeare because of his own notoriety and expert training.

A. Berret

BIBLIOGRAPHY

Baetzhold, Howard G. *Mark Twain and John Bull: The British Connection.* Bloomington: Indiana UP, 1970.

Berret, Anthony J. "The Influence of *Hamlet* on *Huckleberry Finn*." *American Literary Realism* 18 (Spring and Autumn 1985): 196–207.

Gale, Robert L. "*The Prince and the Pauper* and *King Lear*." *Mark Twain Journal* 12 (Spring 1963): 14–17.

Gribben, Alan. *Mark Twain's Library: A Reconstruction.* 2 vols. Boston: G.K. Hall, 1980. 623–636.

Kirkham, E. Bruce. "Huck and Hamlet: An Examination of Twain's Use of Shakespeare." *Mark Twain Journal* 14 (Summer 1969): 17–19.

Richardson, Thomas J. "Is Shakespeare Dead? Mark Twain's Irreverent Question." *Shakespeare and Southern Writers: A Study of Influence.* Ed. Philip C. Kolin. UP of Mississippi, 1985. 63–82.

See also: Bacon, Francis; England; *Is Shakespeare Dead?*

Shaw, George Bernard
(1856–1950)

With similar outlooks on life, Samuel Clemens and George Bernard Shaw were writers of roughly the same period. They both agreed, for instance, in the overthrow of conventional morality and dogma. In his notebooks Clemens defended Shaw's right to discuss sexual intercourse frankly, and after reading one of Shaw's lectures on atheism in which Shaw said that no dogma could be accepted without reservation, Clemens replied: "Certainly not—the reservation is that he is a d——d fool to accept it at all."

Clemens met Shaw on a trip to London in 1907 where Clemens was to accept a degree from Oxford. While sharing lunch and admiration for each other's work, Shaw called him an American genius. Later in a letter, Shaw said, "I am persuaded that the future historians of America will find your works as indispensable . . . as a French historian finds the political tracts of Voltaire."

Both authors had a fascination for Joan of Arc and both wrote works in honor of her, Clemens's appearing in 1896. Shaw says in his introduction to his play on Joan that Clemens's Joan "remains a credible human goodygoody in spite of her creator's infatuation."

Stuart Kenny

BIBLIOGRAPHY

Geismar, Maxwell. *Mark Twain: An American Prophet.* Boston: Houghton Mifflin, 1970.

Kaplan, Justin. *Mr. Clemens and Mark Twain.* New York: Simon & Schuster, 1966.

Shaw, Bernard. *Saint Joan: A Chronicle Play in Six Scenes and an Epilogue.* London: Constable, 1924.

See also: Joan of Arc; *Personal Recollections of Joan of Arc*

Shelley, Harriet
(1795–1816)

Born in London to John and Ann (Elliot) Westbrook, Harriet Westbrook was the youngest of four daughters in an upper-middle-class family. She attended Mrs. Fenning's School with Mary and Hellen Shelley, whose brother Percy she eloped with on 29 August 1811. As a freethinker, Percy Bysshe refused to recognize such a social convention as monogamy. Harriet made valiant efforts to maintain a stable relationship, even remarrying him on 24 March 1814 after one of his affairs. In July of that year he abandoned her permanently, eloping with Mary Wollstonecraft Godwin. There was no need for divorce in his opinion. For her objections and refusal to become only a friend, Harriet received his scorn, was subjected to privation and public abuse. She had borne Shelley two children: Ianthe in 1813 and Charles in 1814. Her death in 1816 was suspected to be a suicide.

Edward Dowden published Shelley's biography in 1886. The false accusations concerning Harriet and the abominable literary style stirred a critical response from Twain, who wrote "In Defense of Harriet Shelley" (*North American Review*, 1894), collected in the 1897 *How to Tell a Story and Other Essays*. Twain was, and still is, one of the few to present the case without whitewashing Shelley's character in deference to his stature as a poet.

Sandra Littleton-Uetz

BIBLIOGRAPHY

Boas, Louise S. *Harriet Shelley: Five Long Years.* London: Greenwood P, 1979.

Emerson, Everett. *The Authentic Mark Twain: A Literary Biography of Samuel L. Clemens.* Philadelphia: U of Pennsylvania P, 1984.

See also: "In Defense of Harriet Shelley"; Shelley, Mary Godwin

Shelley, Mary Godwin
(1797–1851)

Daughter of Mary Wollstonecraft and William Godwin, and second wife of Percy Bysshe Shelley, Mary Godwin Shelley is the author of *Frankenstein* (1818). She is mentioned in one of Mark Twain's literary essays, "In Defense of Harriet Shelley" (1897), which critiques Edward Dowden's *Life of Shelley* (1886) for its factual and interpretive errors. Specifically, Mark Twain attacks Dowden for blaming Shelley's wife Harriet for the poet's infidelities. Instead, Twain contends, the wiles of women like Mary Godwin ensnared Shelley and caused Harriet's suicide.

Twain's essay describes Shelley's wooing sixteen-year-old Mary, who became his child bride. Twain goes on to call Mary Godwin a "rapacious mendicant" and "concubine" who used Shelley's money to rescue her indigent father while she enjoyed the luxuries of a kept woman. Maxwell Geismar calls this essay strange and perplexing, and he attributes its tone to Twain's sympathy with Shelley's radicalism and with William Godwin's financial woes (358). Twain ends his "In Defense of Harriet Shelley" by quoting from a letter Shelley wrote to his dead wife's sister Eliza, in which he admits his taking up with Mary Godwin might be regarded as the cause of Harriet's ruin.

Mary Ann Wilson

BIBLIOGRAPHY

Clemens, Samuel L. "In Defense of Harriet Shelley." *How to Tell a Story and Other Essays.* By Clemens. New York: Harper, 1897. 16–77

Dowden, Edward. *The Life of Percy Bysshe Shelley.* 2 vols. 1886. Rpt. New York: Barnes & Noble, 1969.

Geismar, Maxwell. *Mark Twain: An American Prophet.* Boston: Houghton Mifflin, 1970.

Shelley, Mary Godwin. *Frankenstein; or The Modern Prometheus.* London: Oxford UP, 1969.

White, Newman Ivey. *Shelley.* 2 vols. New York: Knopf, 1940.

See also: "In Defense of Harriet Shelley"; Shelley, Harriet

"Shem's Diary"

The extant portions of Mark Twain's diary of Shem consist of two fragments, one written in the early 1870s, the other in late 1908 or early 1909. Twain first attempted to tell Shem's story during the late 1860s, but that manuscript, some seventy or eighty pages long, must have been lost or destroyed. The segments remaining in the Mark Twain Papers, doubtless a new start, total only eight pages. In 1870 Twain was planning a "Noah's Ark book," which was to include the diaries of Shem and his brothers, and a few years later he began a diary of Methuselah.

The Noah's Ark book never came into being, but in late 1908 or early 1909 Twain undertook a new version of Shem's diary, slightly longer than the earlier one. That piece was first published, along with the two remaining fragments of Methuselah's diary, in *Letters from the Earth* (1962). The 1870s segments of "Shem's Diary" have remained unpublished, except for several paragraphs quoted by Albert Bigelow Paine in *Mark Twain: A Biography* (1912), and one in "Found: Mark Twain's 'Lost Sweetheart.'"

The early version briefly records the rush and wrangling in the shipyard during construction of the ark and notes vitrolic criticisms by Methuselah, who still refers to the diarist as "Shemmy," though he and his brothers are past their hundredth year and married. Shem partly excuses Methuselah's bitterness, however, explaining that the patriarch had been disappointed in love during his youth and even after nine centuries still dreamed of the girl.

The later diary describes the populace carousing on the Sabbath, poking fun at the ark, and scoffing at the idea of a flood. Methuselah, though venerated because of his great age, remains sharp-tongued, but now Twain emphasizes his vanity and his jealousy of Noah's prominence and further develops his sneering at the youthfulness of Shem and his brothers.

The dates of the two attempts at "Shem's Diary" vividly illustrate the temporal extent of Twain's interest in the Genesis stories, which he expressed more fully in "Extracts from Adam's Diary" (1893), "Eve's Autobiography," "That Day in Eden," "Eve Speaks" (all written in the early 1900s), and "Eve's Diary" (1905). Moreover, Shem's reference to Methuselah's dreams of a lost love reflects Clemens's own repeated dreams of Laura Wright, a sweetheart from his piloting days, an experience that also inspired "My Platonic Sweetheart" (published in part in 1912).

Howard G. Baetzhold

BIBLIOGRAPHY

Baetzhold, Howard G. "Found: Mark Twain's 'Lost Sweetheart.'" *American Literature* 44.3 (November 1972): 414–429.

Clemens, Samuel L. "Extract from Shem's Diary of 920 A.C." *Letters from the Earth.* By Clemens. Ed. Bernard DeVoto. New York: Harper & Row, 1962. 111–114.

Ensor, Allison. *Mark Twain and the Bible.* Lexington: U of Kentucky P, 1969.

Paine, Albert Bigelow. *Mark Twain: A Biography.* 3 vols. New York: Harper, 1912.

See also: Bible; Religion

Shepherdson Family

In chapter 17 of *Huckleberry Finn* (1885) Huck swims ashore when his raft is rammed by a paddleboat. He happens upon the Grangerford family's farmhouse and is introduced to a bloody feud between the Grangerfords and the Shepherdsons. Huck learns that the two families have feuded for thirty years but have long forgotten why.

Huck learns that Baldy Shepherdson killed young Bud Grangerford three months earlier and then was killed less than a week later. Buck's brutal slaying at the end of chapter 18 is instigated by Harney Shepherdson's eloping with Sophia Grangerford. Buck Grangerford tells Huck, "There a'int a coward amongst them Shepherdsons. . . ."

Several critics believe the Shepherdson-Grangerford episode has little to do with the overall thesis of *Huckleberry Finn.* However, examination of the Shepherdson family reveals several themes prevalent in Mark Twain's other novels.

Twain also uses feuding in *Life on the Mississippi* (1883), which he worked on concurrently with *Huckleberry Finn.* Consequently, the two passages are very similar. The Shepherdsons and the Grangerfords, like the Darnells and the Watsons of *Life on the Mississippi*, feud over a forgotten issue; in both stories the families attend the same church, sitting on opposite sides of the congregation with weapons in hand; and both sets kill their enemies mercilessly.

Southern aristocracy is another Twainian theme related to the Shepherdsons. The Shepherdsons think themselves of aristocratic stock, when in reality they may be only a family with a small farm. Twain, by elevating their social standing and their debased form of feuding, satirizes the landed southern aristocrat. Tangent to this theme is Twain's disgust over the romantic, antebellum ideals of southern culture. Twain felt such misconceptions were perpetuated by the writings of authors like Sir Walter Scott. Just as Scott's knights had to adapt to changes brought about by the Renaissance, Twain requires the southern aristocrats to relinquish their antiquated way of life in the face of an evolving world.

Huck sees the slander, strife, and murder committed by those families for what it actually is: barbarism. Huck watches as his friend Buck Grangerford and Buck's cousin are shot down—like game—from their perches in a tree. As Buck and his cousin swim toward safety, the Shepherdsons run along the bank yelling, "Kill them, kill them!" Huck says that the scene makes him sick, and he declines to narrate the details. Because he encounters such violent acts every time he comes ashore, it is no wonder Huck develops a strong dislike for civilization. Nor is Huck's enthusiasm surprising when he is reunited with Jim and they depart on the raft heading once more downriver.

J.R. LeMaster and David Haines, Jr.

BIBLIOGRAPHY

Baldanza, Frank. *Mark Twain: An Introduction and Interpretation.* New York: Barnes & Noble, 1961.

Blair, Walter. *Mark Twain & Huck Finn.* Berkeley: U of California P, 1960.

DeVoto, Bernard. *Mark Twain's America.* Boston: Little, Brown, 1932.

Leary, Lewis, ed. *A Casebook on Mark Twain's Wound.* New York: Crowell, 1962.

See also: Dueling; Scott, Walter; South

Sherburn, Colonel

"A proud-looking man about fifty-five [and] . . . a heap the best-dressed man" in the town of Bricksville, Arkansas, Colonel Sherburn appears in chapters 21–22 of *Adventures of Huckleberry Finn* (1885), where he murders the town drunk, Boggs, for insulting him. Sherburn is an imposing figure; his scornful denunciation of his neighbors, who form a mob to lynch him following Boggs's murder, attacks the entire social system of the South, but Twain also satirizes his adherence to a rigid code of "honor." Significantly, Sherburn's appearance follows a detailed description of Bricksville's oafish town bullies and precedes the sly bullying of the Wilks family by the Duke and the King, which Huck says "make[s] a body ashamed of the human race" (chapter 33). Sherburn's description of the low character of the townspeople rings true, but in his laugh, "not the pleasant kind, but the kind that makes you feel like when you are eating bread that's got sand in it" (chapter 22), he too embodies southern violence.

Twain recreated in the Sherburn-Boggs episode a disturbing incident from his childhood in Hannibal, Missouri: the first murder in the town's history. William Owsley, a prosperous merchant, had been repeatedly insulted by a drunken "Uncle Sam" Smarr, who told anyone who would listen that Owsley was "a damned son of a bitch" whom he would kill for swindling some friends. According to depositions taken by Judge John M. Clemens, the two men confronted each other on 24 Janu-ary 1845, only a few steps from the Clemens home. Owsley drew a pistol, and, despite Smarr's pleas of "don't fire," shot Smarr twice and then walked away. Smarr was taken into a store, where he died (*Mark Twain's Hannibal, Huck & Tom* 36; Wecter 106–109; Hearn 212). Twain was troubled long after by "the grotesque closing picture—the great family Bible spread open on the profane old man's breast by some thoughtful idiot" (*Autobiography* chapter 9). Owsley was apparently not faced with a lynch mob and was acquitted, but Twain recalled that after the acquittal "there was a cloud upon him—a social chill—and he presently moved away" (*Mark Twain's Hannibal, Huck & Tom* 36).

In the rendering of Sherburn's speech the narrator, Huck, seems to be replaced by Twain's own idiom, for the speech reflects Twain's condemnation of southern violence, as also expressed in the suppressed chapter of *Life on the Mississippi* (Hearn 122–123, 217–218) and in "The United States of Lyncherdom" (*A Pen Warmed-Up in Hell* 180–190). Twain clearly admires the strong man who is able to defeat the mob; Sherburn's speech is comparable to Dr. Robinson's righteous denunciation of the King and the Duke soon thereafter. Yet Twain desired to portray as broad a picture of the southern social system as possible (Ferguson 228). Accordingly, the incident as retold in *Adventures of Huckleberry Finn* reflects a dark cynicism. Not only is the mob stupid and cowardly and Sherburn a cold tyrant, but Huck too is swept along in the excitement and joins the lynching party on its way to Sherburn's house, though he remains a spectator only. Huck afterward heads for the circus, perhaps as relief from what he has just witnessed.

Jeanne Campbell Reesman

BIBLIOGRAPHY

Clemens, Samuel L. *Adventures of Huckleberry Finn.* Ed. Walter Blair and Victor Fischer. Berkeley: U of California P, 1985.

———. *The Annotated Huckleberry Finn: Adventures of Huckleberry Finn by Mark Twain.* Ed. Michael

Patrick Hearn. New York: Clarkson N. Potter, 1981.

———. *Life on the Mississippi*. Boston: James R. Osgood, 1883.

———. *Mark Twain's Autobiography*. 2 vols. Ed. Albert B. Paine. New York: Harper, 1924.

———. *Mark Twain's Hannibal, Huck & Tom*. Ed. Walter Blair. Berkeley: U of California P, 1969.

———. *A Pen Warmed-Up in Hell: Mark Twain in Protest*. Ed. Frederick Anderson. New York: Harper & Row, 1972.

Wecter, Dixon. *Sam Clemens of Hannibal*. Boston: Houghton Mifflin, 1952.

See also: *Adventures of Huckleberry Finn*;
Smarr, Sam

Sherman, William Tecumseh
(1820–1891)

Union army general and leader of the famous "march to the sea," William T. Sherman and Clemens were first linked in 1867 when Sherman was widely announced as one of the celebrities to go on the *Quaker City* excursion, though in the end he did not go on the trip. The two men first met in 1879 when, with many others, they shared the lecture platform at the reunion of the Army of Tennessee in Chicago to honor U.S. Grant. On other occasions they met, and Clemens enjoyed the association with Sherman, whom he spoke of as a military figure second only to Grant. In 1885 Sherman, who had published his own *Memoirs* ten years earlier, wished to take advantage of the success of Grant's *Personal Memoirs*, published by Clemens's Webster and Company, and sent Clemens the manuscript of a travel book. Clemens promptly rejected it, but in 1890 he was instrumental in getting Webster and Company to reprint Sherman's *Memoirs* as one of the company's "Great War Library" of volumes by and about former military leaders of the Civil War. The next year, just after Sherman's death, Clemens had the book brought up to date through an "appendix" by Sherman's son about the general's final years and had it republished by Webster and Company.

L. *Terry Oggel*

BIBLIOGRAPHY

Clemens, Samuel L. *The Innocents Abroad*. Hartford, Conn.: American Publishing, 1869.

Paine, Albert Bigelow. *Mark Twain: A Biography*. 3 vols. New York: Harper, 1912.

Short Story

Mark Twain came closest to artistic perfection and conscious craftsmanship in his shorter works. His short stories range from the anecdote, hoax, and burlesque to the philosophical fable, sentimental tale, and domestic farce. Twain's first short story was titled "The Dandy Frightening the Squatter" (1852), but he is best known for works like "Jim Smiley and His Jumping Frog" (1865), "Buck Fanshaw's Funeral" (1872), "Jim Blaine and His Grandfather's Ram" (1872), "A True Story" (1874), "Facts Concerning the Recent Carnival of Crime in Connecticut" (1876), "Jim Baker's Blue Jay Yarn" (1880), and "The Man That Corrupted Hadleyburg" (1899). His achievements in the short story genre include a mastery of voice and dialect in the development of the vernacular character and an ability to get at the moral and ethical issues concerning America through the agency of the humorous tale.

Mark Twain placed his original stamp on an evolving tradition of humorous short fiction. His early years as a printer's devil and journeyman printer gave him considerable knowledge of American humor in the southwestern tradition. To this was added his exposure to the literary comedians of the 1850s and the Civil War period. Bret Harte, Charles Webb, and Artemus Ward schooled Mark Twain during his frontier years in both technique and theme. It was during the years in the West (1861–1866) that Mark Twain recognized the importance of choosing the "right" word rather than an "approximate" substitution. From this time Twain also moved away from the simplistic humorist techniques of misspellings and malapropisms to a more sophisticated use of metaphor and hyperbole. Twain transferred the pose of the oral storyteller and platform lecturer into his narrative stance, enabling him to manage subtle mood changes, ironic reversals, and an informal style. Unlike Poe or James, Twain lacks a theory of the short story as a genre; instead he focuses his energies on marking his written stories with the strategies of oral performance. Twain creates the illusion that his stories are being heard rather than read. Elements of style flow naturally from the voice of the vernacular character. Twain's careful artistry with the deadpan monologue and aimless digression are his trademarks in stories like the "Jumping Frog" and "Grandfather's Ram."

A consideration of Twain's evolving opinions necessarily begins with his short fiction. In the early short fiction Twain achieves a pure, colloquial style that reflects a commitment to democratic values. His stories frequently depend on the structure of the frame tale and on a shift in point of view from a detached witness to the vernacular narrator. The western tales wed a naive innocent with a man of experience as a means of generating a conflict between eastern and western American values. The ways in which Twain's narrators are alternately duped by and initiated into a culture are part of the author's process of celebrating difference while delineating commonality and fellowship in the American experience. Twain's humor in the early short stories depends on the consistent balance of his materials. The inane is weighed equally with the important in the ultimate democratization of his subject.

The short stories composed in the middle and latter part of Twain's career suffer in voice and style for what they gain in moral and psychological complexity. As a result, his personal obsessions and concerns begin to surface. Twain's interest in human drives and motivations, his fascination with tests of con-

science, and his indictment of the "damned human race" are all brought to bear on stories like the "Recent Carnival of Crime" (1876) and "The Man That Corrupted Hadleyburg." Through these and other fables of human experience, Twain makes a moral sounding of American self-confidence. In other stories he undertakes a studied, naturalistic analysis of human motivations and choices under prescribed conditions. In "Edward Mills and George Benton: A Tale" (1880) he considers the importance of nature as opposed to nurture in human development and in stories concerning windfall profits and inheritances like "Hadleyburg," "The £1,000,000 Bank-Note" (1893), and "The $30,000 Bequest" (1904) he studies the limits of moral virtue. Twain continues to develop certain structural patterns from his western years. Into the world of cloistered social order represented by the town, village, or family, he brings the figure of the outsider or stranger who either annihilates the community with his volcanic energies or leaves its inhabitants with a shattering recognition of their own failings. While in the early stories Twain's humor evokes the chaotic energy of the frontier, this energy brings him at mid and late career to consider the absurd as the basis of human existence.

In keeping with Twain's assertion that he could perfect a story by rehearsing it as "talk," his best short fiction is that in which plot, theme, and style emerge from voice. Yet in the large store of other tales where Twain explores psychological and philosophical issues, certain of his internal battles with his persona, profession, and audience are most evident.

Jennifer L. Rafferty

BIBLIOGRAPHY

Clemens, Samuel L. *The Complete Short Stories of Mark Twain.* Ed. Charles Neider. Garden City, N.Y.: Hanover House, 1957.

———. *Great Short Stories of Mark Twain.* Ed. Justin Kaplan. New York: Harper & Row, 1967.

———. *Selected Shorter Writings of Mark Twain.* Ed. Walter Blair. Boston: Houghton Mifflin, 1962.

———. *The Works of Mark Twain: Early Tales & Sketches, Volume 1 (1851–1864).* Ed. Edgar M. Branch and Robert H. Hirst. Berkeley: U of California P, 1979.

———. *The Works of Mark Twain: Early Tales & Sketches, Volume 2 (1864–1865).* Ed. Edgar M. Branch and Robert H. Hirst. Berkeley: U of California P, 1981.

Covici, Pascal, Jr. *Mark Twain's Humor: The Image of a World.* Dallas: Southern Methodist UP, 1962.

Cox, James M. *Mark Twain: The Fate of Humor.* Princeton, N.J.: Princeton UP, 1966.

Emerson, Everett. *The Authentic Mark Twain: A Literary Biography of Samuel L. Clemens.* Philadelphia: U of Pennsylvania P, 1984.

Gibson, William M. *The Art of Mark Twain.* New York: Oxford UP, 1976.

Male, Roy R. "The Story of the Mysterious Stranger in American Fiction." *Criticism* 3 (Fall 1961): 281–294.

Rogers, Franklin R. *Mark Twain's Burlesque Patterns as Seen in the Novels and Narratives, 1855–1885.* Dallas: Southern Methodist UP, 1960.

Sloane, David E.E. *Mark Twain as a Literary Comedian.* Baton Rouge: Louisiana State UP, 1979.

Wilson, James D. *A Reader's Guide to the Short Stories of Mark Twain.* Boston: G.K. Hall, 1987.

See also: Harte, Francis Bret; Humor; Vernacular; Ward, Artemus

"Singular Episode, A"
(1970)

Written the winter of 1891–1892 in Berlin, and published in 1970 (*Mark Twain's Quarrel with Heaven*), "A Singular Episode" satirizes Christian notions of heaven and those who believe only themselves worthy of it. Despite frequent after-dinner readings, expressed delight, and desire to publish, Twain considered "A Singular Episode" religiously offensive (stopping a German printing) and wrote atop the holograph, "Not published—forbidden by Mrs. Clemens" (*Love Letters* 305; "Mental" 119; Paine 1431). Holographically altered from "A Singular Episode in Heaven," "Singular Episode" became "The Late Reverend Sam Jones's Reception in Heaven." Specific inspirations are a dream and Samuel Porter Jones,

a fiery contemporary evangelist (Paine 1430; Browne 30).

Though these titles reveal thematic origins in "Captain Stormfield's Visit to Heaven," critics consider "Singular Episode" contemporaneously "singular," high amid minor achievements (Emerson 178; Browne 31), and canonically microcosmic of Twain as moralist excluded from higher realms because of being a humorist (Brodwin 138–140).

Sheol-bound, Twain exchanges tickets with the Archbishop of Canterbury; St. Peter, reluctantly admitting Jones and Twain, offers the pompous prelate another opportunity; Canterbury, indignant about Jones, happily declines. Heavenly democracy is ambivalent: rules admitting preachers bar humorists; a class system preferring pomp and scorning commonality equates vernacular humor and preaching and identifies Twain—exposed by language and mannerisms—with Jones. "Singular Episode" emphasizes this connection; artist-moralists find flaws, even there. Fulfilling the injunction to preach, Jones drives everyone from heaven, thereby calling to question notions of election. Applying democratic guidelines paradoxically to exclude others, God's creations—earthly and heavenly—ironically find agreeable society in hell.

Parodying religious humorlessness (symbolized by Twain's exclusion) and quasi-democracy, "A Singular Episode" restores humor, a democratic necessity. Merging preacher and humorist, the sketch epitomizes Twain's career.

John H. Davis

BIBLIOGRAPHY

Brodwin, Stanley. "Mark Twain and the Myth of the Daring Jest." *The Mythologizing of Mark Twain.* Ed. Sara deSaussure Davis and Philip D. Beidler. Tuscaloosa: U of Alabama P, 1984. 136–157.

Clemens, Samuel L. "The Late Rev. Sam Jones's Reception into Heaven." *Mark Twain's Quarrel with Heaven.* By Clemens. Ed. Ray B. Browne. New Haven, Conn.: College and UP, 1970. 111–116.

———. *The Love Letters of Mark Twain.* Ed. Dixon Wecter. New York: Harper, 1949. 304–305.

———. "Mental Telegraphy." *Mark Twain's Quarrel with Heaven*. By Clemens. Ed. Ray B. Browne. New Haven: College and UP, 1970. 117–119.

Emerson, Everett. *The Authentic Mark Twain: A Literary Biography of Samuel L. Clemens*. Philadelphia: U of Pennsylvania P, 1984.

Paine, Albert Bigelow. *Mark Twain: A Biography*. 3 vols. New York: Harper, 1912.

See also: Satire

1601

(written 1876)

In the summer of 1876 at Quarry Farm, Mark Twain wrote a short bawdy piece entitled *1601 . . . Conversation as It Was by the Social Fireside in the Time of the Tudors*. Although Twain originally sent the piece only to his friend the Reverend Joseph Twichell, it was soon widely distributed, author anonymous, then printed in a limited edition of fifty copies at West Point (1882) as *Date 1601. Conversation, As It Was by the Social Fireside, in the Time of the Tudors. . . .* Since then *1601* has often served as a surreptitious exercise in the printer's art, with over fifty editions appearing in private printings, usually in small numbers. The most accessible edition is that of Franklin Meine; Martha Anne Turner has compiled a bibliography of the piece's checkered printing history.

1601 takes the form of a diary entry by Queen Elizabeth's cup-bearer, recording a meeting of the queen and such notables as Francis Bacon, Sir Walter Raleigh, Ben Jonson, William Shakespeare, Francis Beaumont, and several ladies. As the story begins, someone breaks wind and Queen Elizabeth attempts to find the "author." After discovering that Raleigh is the culprit, talk turns to graphic discussions of sexual prowess. In dealing with this graphic subject matter, the characters use graphic vernacular language, one of Twain's points being that the figures we now hold in such high regard habitually used extremely coarse language. In addition, he tries to make the language seem authentic through archaic

spelling and syntax, mainly by the addition of an unneccessary final -*e*, final -*th*, and through inversion of normal word order. The "diary entry" itself is at once narrative, drama, interpretation, and a long dirty joke. Twain wrote in his *Autobiography* (1924) that he found the bulk of the humor in the cup-bearer narrator's squeamish discomfort at having to be present in such company (Neider 268–269). Walter Blair suggests several sources for the various anecdotes in books Twain was reading to prepare himself for writing *The Prince and the Pauper* (1882), including D'Urfey's *Wit and Mirth, or Pills to Purge Melancholy* (1719) (Blair 96–97).

Mark Twain's friends proclaimed *1601* a classic on the order of Rabelais; critical reaction to *1601* has included total absence of any comment, dismissal of the piece as an interesting but ultimately unimportant work, censure on the grounds of bad taste, praise on the grounds of its humor, and psychoanalytic scrutiny for what it reveals about Mark Twain. Van Wyck Brooks saw *1601* as a rebellion against the Victorian repression of his wife, Olivia, and his editor, William Dean Howells, thus using *1601* as proof of his thesis that Mark Twain abdicated his role as an artist (227). Almost all succeeding criticism has either been a defense or a refutation of Brooks's stand, with most recent critics seeing *1601* as a basically harmless humorous sketch. One might argue, however, that this short piece, written at the height of Mark Twain's powers, and containing as it does frank, satiric attacks on several of the author's favorite targets—royalty, religion, romanticism, and hypocrisy—deserves a higher place than that of a minor curiosity. At any rate, *1601* serves as the best and most extended example of Twain's body of scatological and bawdy writings.

John Bird

BIBLIOGRAPHY

Blair, Walter. *Mark Twain & Huck Finn*. Berkeley: U of California P, 1960.

Brooks, Van Wyck. *The Ordeal of Mark Twain*. Rev. ed. New York: Dutton, 1933.

Clemens, Samuel L. *The Autobiography of Mark Twain.* Ed. Charles Neider. New York: Harper, 1959.

————. *Date 1601, Conversation as it Was by the Social Fireside in the Time of the Tudors.* Ed. Franklin J. Meine. Chicago: n.p., 1939. Rpt. New York: Lyle Stuart, 1961.

Turner, Martha Anne. "Mark Twain's *1601* Through Fifty Editions." *Mark Twain Journal* 12 (1965): 10–15, 21.

See also: Rabelais; Scatology

Sketches, New and Old
(1875)

Sketches, New and Old gathered about sixty-five writings and originally sold by subscription for $3 to $6. Because these "sketches" ranged in length from half a page to about fifteen pages, nothing in this well-illustrated volume would exhaust the subscription buyer's powers of endurance in reading. Moreover, the volume offered a dazzling variety of subjects, from time to tourism to taxes, from national prejudices to politics, from mock romance to domestic comedy. Readers of the book found a surprising diversity of humor, with little pretension, and with great tonal variety.

The persona of Mark Twain speaks in his own inimitable way, with mockery, with self-deprecation, with deadpan humor, with systematic exaggeration. In "My Watch" several well-intentioned adjustments make the timepiece misbehave in every possible way; in "Political Economy" the bumbling narrator is attempting to write an essay in a polysyllabic abstract style, while a lightning rod salesman interrupts and festoons the home with enough lightning attracters to make the home frighteningly unlivable. Exaggeration and comic contrasts would certainly be apparent if a subscribing purchaser read aloud one sketch an evening to a family or an assembled group. However, "The Jumping Frog" story appears in its metafictional form, first in English, then translated into French, then "clawed back" by

a literalist, inept translator into the most clumsy, awkward semi-English imaginable.

The volume creates a sense of madcap humor. What target will occur next? An innocent tourist at Niagara Falls addresses trinket sellers with the overblown language of literary Indians only to be cursed and abused by them in solid Irish fashion.

Occasionally Twain sounds a serious note. In "A True Story" the dialect of Aunt Rachel precisely and powerfully conveys her sorrow and her endurance. In "A Learned Fable for Good Old Boys and Girls" fantasy rules—with several philosophical points. Important thematic concerns are evident, as in the parodic "Good Little Boy" and "Bad Little Boy" stories. Twain includes several other literary burlesques.

Overall, this volume includes enough humor, satire, social criticism, and philosophy to engage any reader and to increase the growth of Mark Twain's reputation. Any reader of this sampler might be eager to buy another book by Twain, eager to enjoy more of Twain's variety.

Victor Doyno

BIBLIOGRAPHY

Clemens, Samuel L. *Mark Twain's Sketches, New and Old.* Hartford, Conn.: American Publishing, 1875.

See also: Subscription Publication

Slade, Joseph A. ("Jack")
(ca. 1842–1864)

Slade was a notorious gunman and line superintendent for the Central Overland California and Pike's Peak Express Company. Mark Twain met him in 1861 and recorded his impression in *Roughing It* (1872); Slade was "so friendly and so gentle-spoken that I warmed to him in spite of his awful history." Slade's future would be no less "awful."

Born in Carlyle, Illinois, Slade served in the Mexican War and, according to legend, was for a time a schoolteacher before moving west and finding employment with the Overland around 1858. Ordered by his general superintendent to investigate charges that one Jules Bene, located near Julesburg, Colorado, had been stealing company stock and harboring other thieves, Slade set out to resolve the difficulty. Bene, however, managed to ambush Slade, shooting him several times and then firing both barrels of a shotgun into what he believed to be Slade's lifeless corpse. Miraculously, Slade survived, nursed back to health by his wife Virginia, a famous beauty. Bene fled eastward but later returned. At this point, Slade exacted the revenge that established his reputation. Capturing Bene, he tied him up and proceeded to shoot him to death by inches while enjoying drinks with his men. Finally, he killed Bene and cut off his ears, wearing one for a watch fob. Depredations in his area of responsibility were curtailed by reason of his justly gained notoriety.

Like many other western badmen, Slade succumbed to strong drink. Fired by Overland in 1862 for shooting up the Fort Halleck post canteen while drunk, Slade moved to Montana at the behest of his wife. There he operated a small ranch near Virginia City, but his sprees of drinking and violence continued. Ultimately, he was arrested by the Virginia City vigilantes and hanged. His behavior was unexpected in that he begged for his life and wept repeatedly, but to no avail.

Arriving late, Virginia Slade cursed the vigilantes and vowed that her husband would not be buried in Montana. She ordered a specially constructed tin-lined coffin and had his body immersed in alcohol within it, planning to return it to Illinois for burial. The travel was too arduous, however, and Slade was interred in the Mormon cemetery in Salt Lake City, Utah, on 20 July 1864.

Herbert V. Fackler

BIBLIOGRAPHY

Dimsdale, Thomas. *The Vigilantes of Montana.* Norman: U of Oklahoma P, 1951.

Long, James A. "Old Julesburg—Wickedest City on the Plains." *Frontier Times* 38 (February-March 1964): 24–26, 61–62.

Morton, J. Sterling. *Illustrated History of Nebraska.* Lincoln, Nebr.: North, 1907.

Parkhill, Forbes. *The Law Goes West.* Denver: Sage Books, 1956.

Rosa, Joseph G. *The Gunfighter: Man or Myth?* Norman: U of Oklahoma P, 1969.

See also: Law; *Roughing It*

Slavery

Opposition to slavery, anywhere, in any form, is a fundamental element of Mark Twain's value system and a distinguishing characteristic of his literature. No other major American author of the nineteenth century fought slavery as long, on so broad a front, in such depth, and with such passionate commitment as Mark Twain, nor did any of his contemporaries match his agonized involvement with the issue. For Twain, slavery was not an entity that affected only the Negro race; regarded as a state of involuntary servitude to a malicious power, it was the human condition.

Twain did not grow up with this attitude. He, of course, was familiar with the institution of slavery as it existed in the American South prior to the Civil War. Missouri was a slave state, and young Sam Clemens saw slavery in action. His father once owned slaves. As a child, Sam had played with slave children; saw black slaves at work in fields, on the wharves, and in homes; saw them bought and sold; and was familiar with the arguments taught in the schools, preached in the churches, and upheld by the courts of law that justified slavery. He grew to manhood generally accepting the mores of the South. Although he later claimed that his father, before he died, recognized slavery as a great wrong, and although he described his mother as being uncommonly tender toward slave children, there is no reason to believe Sam Clemens the Missourian was a sympathizer of abolition.

On the contrary, when the Civil War broke out in 1861 and brought his career as a pilot to an end, Clemens aligned himself with the Confederacy. According to his autobiographical sketch, "The Private History of a Campaign That Failed," he joined a company of military irregulars called the Marion Rangers. Its sole experience with war consisted of ambushing and killing a stranger. Soon afterward Sam Clemens decided he was not cut out for bloodletting and deserted the Confederacy. His brother Orion, a Union sympathizer who had been appointed secretary of the Nevada Territory, offered him a clerical job. Sam accepted immediately and left the South behind. That was the last time he put himself in the position of defending slavery.

Nevada Territory had many Southerners but it was aggressively dominated by Union men. Pro-Confederate or pro-slavery sentiments were unpopular to the point of being risky, but Twain, as he was now known, had changed his sentiments and now supported the Union. Just as Twain began his literary career in Virginia City so did his experience with the free-hearted miners and fellow journalists on the *Territorial Enterprise* convince him of new values and attitudes that he subsequently internalized.

With the end of the Civil War slavery also came to an end. As regards literature, the institution of slavery became a dead target; henceforth, defenses or criticisms of slavery were either nostalgic or "academic"; no one was prepared to go to war again to bring it back. It is important to recognize this fact because it means that all works by Twain that touch on the subject of slavery, *Huckleberry Finn* (1885) and *Pudd'nhead Wilson* (1894), for example, are not literally concerned with slavery but use it as a vehicle to convey other themes and values.

Twain was encouraged to develop the ideas by his contact with George Washington Cable. Cable was also a Southerner, from New Orleans, but one who had fought in the Confederate army. After the war Cable came to the realization that slavery was immoral and that

he had fought for the wrong cause. When he saw, therefore, unreconstructed rebels resurrecting the racist values of the antebellum South in the Jim Crow laws of the post-Reconstruction era, Cable immediately exposed the process. *The Grandissimes* (1880), his most important novel, uses the motif of the free man of color (F.M.C.) in the Louisiana of 1803–1804, which was just entering the Union, as an allegorical parallel to the freed slaves of the southern states that had just had their sovereignty returned to them. Cable's purpose was to show that just as the liberty of the F.M.C.s had been hollow, so was the liberty of the new freedmen; that the blacks of the South had been returned to a state of practical slavery despite their technically legal freedom.

The intention of *The Grandissimes* was quickly recognized and attacked across the South. Cable had few southern defenders, but among them was Mark Twain, who praised him in *Life on the Mississippi* (1883) for being a "masterly delineator of its [the South's] interior life and its history." Twain went beyond praising Cable to following his lead. A brief look at *Huckleberry Finn* (1885) shows both how much Twain incorporated from Cable and also how much more deeply he carried Cable's treatment of slavery.

Like the earlier novel, *Huckleberry Finn* is also set in the South, deals seriously with its interior life and history, and makes central use of the motif of the F.M.C. What is expressed directly in *The Grandissimes*, however, is represented more subtly in *Huckleberry Finn*. The term "F.M.C." does not appear in Twain's novel, although Jim became one as soon as he was manumitted by Miss Watson. But that Twain was fully aware of F.M.C.s and their precarious status is unmistakably evident in the unfinished sequel, "Huck Finn and Tom Sawyer Among the Indians." The same tragic irony that Cable directs toward the illusionary freedom of F.M.C.s Twain applies to Jim, but whereas Cable spells it out in the unhappy end of the dark Honoré, Twain leaves it implied for Jim.

But where Cable restricted himself in his novel to attacking the practical reenslavement of blacks on political and moral grounds, Twain deepened and extended the notion of slavery. Part of the South's strategy to reduce blacks to practical slaves, for example, was the enactment of convict-lease laws that empowered courts to convict offenders (especially blacks) for trifling offenses, sentence them to very long terms, and then lease them out as laborers so that they brought revenue to the state. Cable was also an opponent of this system but had not incorporated it into his 1880 novel. Tom Sawyer's control of Jim in the evasion chapters of *Huckleberry Finn*, however, can be easily seen as Twain's attack on this viciously clever reintroduction of involuntary servitude. *Pudd'nhead Wilson* (1894) extends Twain's attack on this immoral system in its conclusion, where the true Valet de Chambre is pardoned from the gallows so that his economic value as a slave might be realized by his sale.

On a yet deeper level, Twain considered that status of the F.M.C. to be a true representation of all men for, according to his heretically Calvinistic perspective, no man could be anything but a slave, given a God who predestined everybody and everything. Slavery could be opposed and corrected in its human forms and consequences—political, legal, and economic—but it was invulnerable if divinely ordained. By subtly but ironically making Jim the type of humanity when Tom Sawyer proclaims him as free as any creature that "walks this earth," *Huckleberry Finn* opens up bleak new depths to an understanding of slavery.

Twain's major novels, *Huckleberry Finn*, *Connecticut Yankee* (1889), and *Pudd'nhead Wilson*, all deal ironically with the notion of freedom and show human beings—regardless of race, gender, or class—to be not ultimately free. No one is as free as he thinks on political, economic, or psychological levels; on the theological level, all humans are slaves of a tyrant God.

Twain's opposition to slavery became increasingly overt. He regarded Western imperialism as imposing a de facto political and economic slavery on colonial peoples and therefore attacked its manifestation in China, South Africa, the Congo, and the Philippines. He hated the oppression of the Russian serfs by the czarist government and he took seriously the phrase "wage slave" as it applied to American society. But in such grim and gloomy literary works of his last years as the *Mysterious Stranger* manuscripts, *Letters from the Earth*, *What Is Man?* and "The Great Dark," Twain reveals the depth of his obsession with slavery in its ultimate form: the subjugation of human beings by a deceitful God who toys with them cruelly and whimsically, who creates them imperfect and then punishes them for their limitation.

Alone of America's greatest authors in his personal familiarity with slavery, Twain was definitely shaped by that experience and by his lifelong brooding over it. A masterly delineation of his interior life might see a battleground upon which raged a Civil War between the forces of slavery and freedom. If that battle seemed to give the edge to the forces of slavery, it is to Twain's eternal credit that he never conceded defeat, that he remained an unreconstructed rebel—but on the side of freedom.

Lawrence I. Berkove

Bibliography

Berkove, Lawrence I. "The Free Man of Color in *The Grandissimes* and Works by Harris and Mark Twain." *Southern Quarterly* 18:4 (Summer 1980): 60–73.

———. "The 'Poor Players' of *Huckleberry Finn*." *Papers of the Michigan Academy of Science, Arts and Letters* 53 (1968): 18–26.

Budd, Louis J. *Mark Twain: Social Philosopher.* Bloomington: Indiana UP, 1962.

Cummings, Sherwood. *Mark Twain and Science: Adventures of a Mind.* Baton Rouge: Louisiana State UP, 1988.

Doyno, Victor. *Writing "Huck Finn": Mark Twain's Creative Process.* Philadelphia: U of Pennsylvania P, 1991.

Foner, Philip S. *Mark Twain: Social Critic.* New York: International Publishers, 1958.

Hill, Hamlin. *Mark Twain: God's Fool.* New York: Harper & Row, 1973.

Kaplan, Justin. *Mr. Clemens and Mark Twain.* New York: Simon & Schuster, 1966.

Smith, Henry Nash. *Mark Twain: The Development of a Writer.* Cambridge, Mass.: Harvard UP, 1962.

Wecter, Dixon. *Sam Clemens of Hannibal.* Boston: Houghton Mifflin, 1952.

See also: *Adventures of Huckleberry Finn*; Cable, George Washington; *Connecticut Yankee in King Arthur's Court, A*; Free Man of Color; Freedom; Imperialism; Jim; *Pudd'nhead Wilson, The Tragedy of*; Racial Attitudes; South, Mark Twain and the

Slote, Daniel
(d. 1882)

Slote was a close associate and cabin mate of Samuel Clemens aboard the *Quaker City*; he was characterized by the author as "a splendid . . . roommate who is as good . . . and right-minded a man as ever lived." The Slote-Clemens friendship outlasted the voyage, and they became associated in a number of business ventures. Notably, Slote contracted to manufacture and distribute Clemens's patented self-pasting scrapbook. A dispute over money matters ended their fourteen-year friendship in 1881. When Slote died (1882) Clemens complained to Mrs. A.W. Fairbanks that Slote had swindled him—adding, "I came . . . near sending him to the penitentiary." Dan Slote's portrait appears in the first edition of *The Innocents Abroad* (1869, 288).

Beverly David

BIBLIOGRAPHY

Clemens, Samuel L. *The Innocents Abroad.* Hartford, Conn.: American Publishing, 1869.

———. *Mark Twain to Mrs. Fairbanks.* Ed. Dixon Wecter. San Marino, Calif.: Huntington Library, 1949.

Ganzel, Dewey. *Mark Twain Abroad: The Cruise of the "Quaker City."* Chicago: U of Chicago P, 1968.

Meltzer, Milton. *Mark Twain Himself.* New York: Crowell, 1960.

See also: *Innocents Abroad, The*

Smarr, Sam
(d. 1845)

Sam Smarr was a farmer who lived near Hannibal and was given to excesses when on his frequent drinking sprees in Hannibal. According to depositions taken by Clemens's father, John M. Clemens, J.P., and recounted by Dixon Wecter (*Sam Clemens of Hannibal*, 1952), on several occasions Smarr publicly accused a prosperous merchant, William Owsley, of having cheated two of Smarr's friends. On 24 January 1845, when Smarr returned to town and repeated his accusations, Owsley shot him dead in the street a few steps from the Clemens home. The event, recaptured vividly in the Sherburn-Boggs episode in *Huckleberry Finn* (1885) with embellishments, is discussed by Clemens himself (*Mark Twain's Autobiography*, 1924).

L. Terry Oggel

BIBLIOGRAPHY

Clemens, Samuel L. *Mark Twain's Autobiography.* Ed. Albert B. Paine. 2 vols. New York: Harper, 1924.

Wecter, Dixon. *Sam Clemens of Hannibal.* Boston: Houghton Mifflin, 1952.

See also: Sherburn, Colonel

Smiley, Jim

Jim Smiley is the optimistic frog trainer and owner from Twain's "The Celebrated Jumping Frog of Calaveras County," originally called "Jim Smiley and His Jumping Frog" (1865) and written in the form of a letter to Artemus Ward.

To say that Smiley is one of Twain's characters is misleading, however, or at least too simple. Simon Wheeler, narrating within the story's frame, is Smiley's creator. Twain's narrator asks Wheeler instead for news of Reverend Leonidas W. Smiley, whom he concludes is a "myth." The story's richness derives not from character per se but from the manner of telling, S.J. Krause having identified eight levels of story within the story (563–546).

The two narrators, Wheeler and "Twain," interpret Smiley differently. According to Wheeler, Smiley, who bets on anything, regardless of the likelihood of success, is "lucky, uncommon lucky," "the curiousest man," "the dangdest feller." Narrator "Twain" decides that Smiley is less interesting, calling his story "tedious" and "useless." He refers also to "the infamous Jim Smiley" and wryly to "the enterprising vagabond." The last description is typical of the deadpan style of both narrators (see Rodgers). Through both characterizations Smiley comes across as single-minded, optimistic, and persistent.

In naming his bull pup Andrew Jackson and his frog Dan'l Webster, Smiley is most likely being superstitious (Krause 567), thinking that the names of two heroes of his recent past will enoble his enterprises, though Twain's purpose in using the names was undoubtedly more satirical (Krause 567–576).

The original for Smiley was "Coleman," the frog owner in the story that Twain heard Ben Coon tell at Angel's Camp, California, in 1864 (Paine 271). Twain later would offer the information that the original Jim Smiley was a Boethian from two thousand years ago ("Private History"). The name Smiley suggests frontier optimism, as do Smiley's betting habits, and various commentators have noted that the story pits western single-mindedness and simplicity, in Smiley, against the genteel tradition, in the stranger who loads the frog with lead (Cox, Krause, Lynn).

Although George Hiram Brownell has conjectured that Twain may have been thinking of Horace Greeley in Jim Smiley, it is more likely that Twain remembered the case of the adventurer Thomas J.L. Smiley, indicted in 1864 for appropriating some of the treasure from the ship *Golden Gate*, which sunk off the coast of Mexico in 1862 (Branch 596–597). The name logically fits a character dedicated to chance and a belief in his impending good fortune, like forty-niners of a few years earlier. As for the name Leonidas, Branch points out that Twain had been getting some comic mileage out of it for a couple of years, espe-

cially in his literary bouts with Albert S. Evans of the San Francisco *Alta California* (596).

Richard Gaughran

BIBLIOGRAPHY

Branch, Edgar M. "'My Voice Is Still for Setchell': A Background Study of 'Jim Smiley and His Jumping Frog.'" *Publications of the Modern Language Association* 82 (1967): 591–601.

Brownell, George Hiram. "The Mystery of 'Jim Greenley.'" *Twainian* 2 (December 1942): 4–5.

Clemens, Samuel L. *The Complete Short Stories of Mark Twain.* Ed. Charles Neider. Garden City, N.Y.: Hanover House, 1957.

————. "Private History of the 'Jumping Frog' Story." *Literary Essays.* New York: Harper, 1918.

Cox, James M. *Mark Twain: The Fate of Humor.* Princeton, N.J.: Princeton UP, 1966.

Krause, S.J. "The Art and Satire of Twain's 'Jumping Frog' Story." *American Quarterly* 16.4 (Winter 1964): 562–576.

Lynn, Kenneth S. *Mark Twain and Southwestern Humor.* Boston: Little, Brown, 1959.

Paine, Albert Bigelow. *Mark Twain: A Biography.* 3 vols. New York: Harper, 1912.

Rodgers, Paul C., Jr. "Artemus Ward and Mark Twain's 'Jumping Frog.'" *Nineteenth Century Fiction* 28 (December 1973): 273–286.

See also: "Celebrated Jumping Frog of Calaveras County, The"; Southwestern Humor; Wheeler, Simon

Smith, Henry Nash
(1906–1986)

Born and reared in Dallas, Texas, Henry Nash Smith began his teaching career at Southern Methodist University; during the same period (1927–1941) he served on the editorial staff of the *Southwest Review*. Later he held posts at the University of Texas and the University of Minnesota before going to the University of California, Berkeley, in 1952. When he retired at Berkeley in 1974, he concluded an eminent career of forty-seven years in the classroom but until his death in 1986 continued a multifaceted career as critic, scholar, and editor, in no area so prominently as in that of Mark Twain studies. The year before he died, in fact, he lectured at Elmira College on "The Theme of Fantasy in Mark Twain's Later Work," consulted about the plans being made for the Elmira College Center for Mark Twain Studies, and accepted an invitation to serve on a national advisory board for the center. Unfortunately, the Elmira visit put an end to the interest that had long since led to Smith's recognition as the central figure in Mark Twain scholarship and criticism. The author of *Mark Twain: The Development of a Writer* (1962), an indispensable work of interpretation; co-editor of the *Mark Twain–Howells Letters* (1960), a definitive resource for biographical and historical inquiry; and editor of the Mark Twain Papers at the University of California, Berkeley (1953–1954, 1979–1980), Smith was also the author of *Mark Twain's Fable of Progress: Political and Economic Ideas in "A Connecticut Yankee"* (1964) and the editor of *Mark Twain of the "Enterprise"* (1957), *Mark Twain: San Francisco Correspondent* (1957), and the Rinehart Edition (with an introduction) of *Adventures of Huckleberry Finn* (1958).

Smith's dedication to Mark Twain studies cannot be understood without reference to its broad context. As revealed in *Virgin Land: The American West as Symbol and Myth* (1950), *Democracy and the Novel: Resistance to Classic American Writers* (1978), and (an edited volume) *Popular Culture and Industrialism, 1865–1890* (1967), the elements of this contextual frame of interests may be identified as a concern with certain underlying interconnected historical issues in American cultural history, including the relationship between regionalism and literary expression; the impact of industrialism on the representation of American life; the connection between literary styles and culture; the vocation of the writer; and, always a fundamental concern, the shaping influence of "symbol" and "myth," terms that Smith thought of as designating "larger or smaller units of the same kind of thing, namely an intellectual construction that fuses concept and emotion into an image."

All of Smith's thought was informed by the self-conscious cultural environment of the city

where he was born and reared and where he continued to live until he was in his mid-thirties. Located in the north central part of a state that, although it became a part of the Confederacy, had been at the time of the Civil War, like Missouri, a borderland area in the extension of the slave system—and, even more than Missouri, an area impinging on the frontier—Dallas is situated just beyond the bounds of East Texas, the only section of Texas that had been distinctly attached to the Old South, or to speak more precisely, to the Old Southwest (Tennessee, Georgia, Alabama, Arkansas, and Louisiana). Dallas was to find its destiny as the populous and affluent center of a New Southwest (Texas, Oklahoma, and New Mexico), a world distinctly different in tone from that of the Old Southwest. How different may be judged by the fate of an effort made in the 1930s by Louisiana State University and Southern Methodist University to join in the publication of the *Southwest Review*. For a brief time the names of Cleanth Brooks and Robert Penn Warren appeared on the masthead of the magazine along with those of John H. McGinnis and Henry Nash Smith, but the venture in the literary unification of Dallas and Baton Rouge soon ended. The philosophical differences that made such a union impossible were later succinctly summed up by Smith when he pointed out that the natural gravitation of the Dallas men of letters—and their allies, a number of writers and scholars at the University of Texas in Austin—was toward Albuquerque and Norman rather than toward Baton Rouge and Chapel Hill.

Enjoying both editorial and personal contact with J. Frank Dobie, Walter Prescott Webb, and Mody C. Boatright in Austin as well as with John McGinnis, Lon Tinkle, and others in Dallas, Smith participated in an intellectual community that (sharing the conviction, as he put it, that "Texas really belongs to the West rather than to the South") found a strong common interest in interpreting the meaning of the concept of the West in American history. One notable product of this interest was Webb's landmark study, *The Great*

Plains (1931), a major revisionary study of the theory of the settlement of the American West set forth in Frederick Jackson Turner's famous essay on "The Significance of the Frontier in American History" (1893). Following a methodology suggested by the new program of interdisciplinary American studies being fostered at Harvard in the 1930s by Howard Mumford Jones and others, Smith undertook what was in effect a more comprehensive and more fundamental investigation of the motives of the westward movement than Webb's. Making a brilliant assimilation of political, economic, social, literary, and subliterary materials, he wrote a doctoral dissertation that eventually became another landmark study. Analyzing the confused but powerful drama of the contradictory interpretative duality implicit in the interpretation of the West in terms of "the idea of nature" on the one hand and "the opposing idea of civilization" on the other, Smith discovered in *Virgin Land* a crucial contradiction in the Turnerian interpretation of the agrarian motive in the settlement and expansion of the American nation. Disclosing Turner's thesis to be essentially mythic, he concluded that "a new intellectual system was requisite before the West could be adequately dealt with in literature or its social development fully understood."

The quest to establish the new system for interpreting the meaning of the West in American history Smith had announced in *Virgin Land* may be discerned as a central motive in his study of Mark Twain's development as a writer. In this work, which largely assumes that Mark Twain is a Westerner, not a Southerner, the inherent conflict between the idea of nature and the idea of civilization is seen to assume the form of a struggle in Twain's mind and heart. Searching for his vocation as a writer, Twain experienced deeply the division between the American devotion to English and European style and taste (or to what Santayana called the "genteel tradition") and a usurping and subverting "vernacular culture" that had begun to evolve even before the culture of a colonial people took on the aspect of a revo-

lutionary and nationalistic difference from the "old" culture on the other side of the Atlantic. Thinking as an artist in "presentational," not as a critic does, in "discursive," terms, Mark Twain, in Smith's interpretation, intuitively perceived the "ideality" of the genteel mode as a falsification of the genuinely ideal values to be found in the American democratic commonplace. In a careful, sensitive, altogether masterly series of readings of Mark Twain's chief writings—with the heaviest emphasis on *The Innocents Abroad* (1869), *Roughing It* (1872), *The Adventures of Tom Sawyer* (1876), *Adventures of Huckleberry Finn* (1885), *A Connecticut Yankee in King Arthur's Court* (1889), and the fragmentary manuscripts known as *The Mysterious Stranger Manuscripts* (published after Smith's book was written as edited by William Gibson, 1969)—Smith progressively exposes the subtle ironies involved in Mark Twain's efforts to find his identity as a serious writer in the face of the tyranny of a tradition that "apparently obliged him either to conform to the priestly role of the man of letters" or "be content with the humble function of providing comic relief from higher concerns." The moment of triumph in his search came when Mark Twain, conceiving of allowing the vernacular voice to take over completely in *Huckleberry Finn*, identified himself with Huck. As the author of and chief actor in his own story, Huck Finn was a persona of unmatched possibilities, and in relating his adventures as a thirteen-year-old youth with a "sound heart and a deformed conscience" creates a work that has its flaws yet "approaches perfection as an embodiment of American experience in a new and appropriate literary mode." But Huck obviously had strict limitations as a narrator, and seeking to discover the capacities of another vernacular persona, the Yankee in his next book, *A Connecticut Yankee in King Arthur's Court*, Mark Twain subjected the "vernacular perspective to a test that destroyed it" when he "tried not merely to transform the vernacular value system into a political ideology, but to make the novel a conceptual framework for a novel embodying his philosophy of history." Unable again to create a persona who could fill the role of detached observer like Huck, Mark Twain, having nothing more to say, said as much by desperately trying to identify himself with a supernatural observer, Satan in *The Mysterious Stranger*, "for whom mankind is but a race of vermin, hardly worth even contempt." By implication Smith in *Democracy and the Novel* may be said to suggest that some American writers who were more sophisticated than the Westerner Mark Twain—especially Hawthorne, Melville, and James—did transcend the genteel tradition, though not the achievement of Mark Twain in his finest novel.

Lewis P. Simpson

BIBLIOGRAPHY

Clemens, Samuel L. *Mark Twain–Howells Letters: The Correspondence of Samuel L. Clemens and William D. Howells, 1872–1910*. Ed. Henry Nash Smith and William M. Gibson. 2 vols. Cambridge, Mass.: Harvard UP, 1960.

Smith, Henry Nash. *Democracy and the Novel: Resistance to Classic American Writers*. New York: Oxford UP, 1978.

———. *Mark Twain: The Development of a Writer*. Cambridge, Mass.: Harvard UP, 1962.

———. *Mark Twain's Fable of Progress: Political and Economic Ideas in "A Connecticut Yankee."* New Brunswick, N.J.: Rutgers UP, 1964.

———. *Virgin Land: The American West as Symbol and Myth*. Cambridge, Mass.: Harvard UP, 1950.

See also: Language; Mark Twain Papers; Scholarship, Trends in Mark Twain; South, Mark Twain and the; Vernacular

Smoking

When he was seven years old, peer pressure induced Samuel Clemens to try chewing tobacco. It made him sick and he never acquired the habit, but in a society where tobacco was cheap and widely used by members of both sexes, he had become a smoker by the age of nine. He continued to smoke the rest of his life; Olivia's opposition to smoking, along with other vices, had little effect.

In Twain's works references to tobacco afford opportunities for humor at his own expense, and attacks on hypocrisy or affectations of taste. Such references are usually anecdotal. He reveals that the privilege of wearing a red merino sash, as Cadet of Temperance, once kept him smokeless for three months. Twain suspects that his discriminating friends would like his cheap cigars if they bore "the red and gold bands" of expensive brands. Perhaps his best-known jab at hypocrisy relating to tobacco is Huck Finn's observation that Miss Watson, who opposed smoking, uses snuff herself.

Jarrell A. O'Kelley

BIBLIOGRAPHY

Clemens, Samuel L. *Life as I Find It*. Cutchogue, N.Y.: Buccaneer Books, 1989.

———. *Mark Twain's Autobiography*. Ed. Albert B. Paine. 2 vols. New York: Harper, 1924.

Kaplan, Justin. *Mr. Clemens and Mark Twain*. New York: Simon & Schuster, 1966.

Smythe, Carlyle and R.S.

In order to recover from his financial disasters with the Charles L. Webster publishing firm and the Paige typesetter, Mark Twain agreed in April 1895 to embark upon a lecturing tour of Australia, New Zealand, and various parts of Asia and Africa. R.S. Smythe, a Melbourne-based Australian manager of many notable speakers, contacted Twain and offered him a lucrative opportunity for the tour. Livy and Clara accompanied Twain to Australia; Smythe's son, Carlyle, met Twain and his family when they arrived and traveled with them throughout the duration of the Australian tour. In a letter to Henry H. Rogers, Twain insisted that his initial contact with R.S. Smythe was due to mental telegraphy, for only nine days after Twain wrote to Smythe, he received a letter from him answering his questions.

Trevor J. Morgan

BIBLIOGRAPHY

Clemens, Samuel L. *Mark Twain's Correspondence with Henry Huttleston Rogers, 1893–1909*. Ed. Lewis Leary. Berkeley: U of California P, 1969.

Emerson, Everett. *The Authentic Mark Twain: A Literary Biography of Samuel L. Clemens*. Philadelphia: U of Pennsylvania P, 1984.

Fatout, Paul. *Mark Twain on the Lecture Circuit*. Bloomington: Indiana UP, 1960.

Long, E. Hudson. *Mark Twain Handbook*. New York: Hendricks House, 1957.

Paine, Albert Bigelow. *Mark Twain: A Biography*. 3 vols. New York: Harper, 1912.

Parsons, Coleman O. "Mark Twain in Australia." *Antioch Review* 21 (Winter 1961): 455–468.

Scott, Arthur L. *Mark Twain at Large*. Chicago: Henry Regnery, 1969.

See also: Mental Telepathy/Extrasensory Perception

Snodgrass, Quintus Curtius

This Snodgrass was once thought to be one of Samuel Clemens's early pseudonyms, like Thomas Jefferson Snodgrass. Scholars have shown, however, that the attribution was inaccurate. See *The Letters of Quintus Curtius Snodgrass*.

Howard G. Baetzhold

BIBLIOGRAPHY

Leisy, Ernest E., ed. *The Letters of Quintus Curtius Snodgrass*. Dallas: Southern Methodist UP, 1946.

See also: Snodgrass, Thomas Jefferson

Snodgrass, Thomas Jefferson

Thomas Jefferson Snodgrass is the outspoken rustic who chronicles his travels in three travel letters Twain wrote for the Keokuk *Post*. The letters appeared in the *Post* on 1 November 1856, 29 November 1856, and 10 April 1857 and are now collected under the title *The Adventures of Thomas Jefferson Snodgrass* (1928).

The letters reveal an uneducated, unsophisticated man as he first encounters the wonders of modern city life and the unfamiliar types who populate those cities. The humor in these letters is at the expense of the unfortunate Snodgrass; his unfamiliarity with the theater, train travel, and the more worldly city folks produces humorous situations in which the country bumpkin comes up short. As Snodgrass recounts his impressions of city life in his letters to the editor, the dialect and grammatical/spelling errors of those letters contribute to character development; Snodgrass is an outsider geographically and linguistically.

This early creation of Twain's exhibits traits and strategies that appear in his later works. Throughout his career Twain used dialect to define character. Another strategy he adapted to achieve both humorous and serious effects in works such as *The Innocents Abroad* (1869), *A Connecticut Yankee in King Arthur's Court* (1889), *Adventures of Huckleberry Finn* (1885), and the unfinished "Little Satan" manuscripts is the juxtaposition of inherently opposite types, or the placement of an outsider in an unfamiliar situation, to reveal weaknesses or flaws in people, institutions, or beliefs.

Janet L. Abshire

BIBLIOGRAPHY

Clemens, Samuel L. *The Adventures of Thomas Jefferson Snodgrass*. Ed. Charles Honce. Chicago: Pascal Covici, 1928.

See also: "Adventures of Thomas Jefferson Snodgrass, The"; Keokuk, Iowa; Travel Writings

Social Philosophy

Critical preoccupation with Mark Twain's humor has led to a paucity of serious examination of his social philosophy. Now recognized as an important social commentator, Twain is called by one writer "America's greatest sociologist in letters" (Foner 53). Though always intrigued by society, a fascination derived mostly from his newspaper background, Twain never held a consistent view on society. "More than most men," writes Louis Budd, "Twain is hard to pin down neatly; he had the habit of dropping an opinion for several years and then suddenly taking it on again." The careful observer of Twain, then, must read his social philosophy as something developmental and evolutionary. For tied always to his views on politics, religion, and history, Twain's social philosophy remains equivocal and problematic.

For example, Twain had to overcome early prejudice against Irish-Americans, Chinese-Americans, the Native Americans, and Catholics. He also had to shed early anti-Semitic feelings and gender discrimination and had to grow to appreciate the strong moral protestations against slavery from his brother and intimate friends. As ambiguous are Twain's views on government and labor and his attitude to money. Still one can detect patterns in his views on society.

Much of what exists in Twain's protean corpus pertains to his views of and attitude toward society. Some one quarter of what he published before 1866 (most of it as topical columns in newspapers) concerns social matters, and his subsequent lectures and significant writings often countenance social causes, leaving, one critic observes, a "long, rich trail already proving his concern with public affairs" (Budd 17).

Dominating Twain's social philosophy are his views on ethnic groups. Regarding the construction of the California side of the Pacific Railroad, for example, Twain felt that it should be built not by whites who were paid $3 a day but by the Chinese who were paid $1. However, in this he was concerned not so much with the exploitation of the Chinese as with Irish squabbles over working conditions and wages. On his trip to the Sandwich Islands—that "paradise for an indolent man"—he appears unsympathetic to the working conditions of the Chinese, more impressed instead by the fact that they were working, and that such labor benefits society. This trip, and his extended ones through Europe (1891–1900), also reveals Twain's anti-Catholic sentiments. He blamed the poverty he saw in the Azores and in Italy on the Catholic Church,

whose dogma and politics were, he felt, hostile to social progress. Twain also despised the Indians, dwelling unfairly on what he saw as uncivil in them, and advocated in the face of much opposition their continued extinction by the army. In *Roughing It* (1872) he was particularly contemptuous of the Goshoot tribe, calling them "the wretchedest type of mankind." In that trip west Twain lost all of the influence that James Fenimore Cooper's glorification of the Indians had on him. With the glitter gone, Twain now felt that the Indian tribes in general were merely environmentally modified Goshutes. Thus his portrait of Injun Joe in *Tom Sawyer* (1876) remains equivocal; much of what surfaces is Joe's cold cruelty.

Twain's views on democracy are likewise equivocal, often questioning some of the privileges available within its system. For instance, he did not endorse one man, one vote, for he maintained that because the uneducated mass cannot vote intelligently, the vote of an educated individual was worth more than that of one unable to differentiate good from evil. Because of this he not so facetiously favored a system of extra votes for the educated and propertied. He felt similarly about woman suffrage. He questioned in "The Temperance Crusade and Women's Rights" (1873) a true democracy that leaves half of its citizens "voiceless . . . their tongues tied and their hands fettered." And in "Votes for Women" (1901), an address to a Hebrew technical school for women in New York City, he anticipated the time when women would participate in making the laws, when that "whip-lash, the ballot, in the hands of women" would correct current social evils. Educated women, he believed, should not be denied certain rights, including the right to vote.

It appears that approaching his 1872 trip to England, Twain felt little regard for individuals on the periphery of an industrial society, so tied to results and the profit motive was his philosophy. However, his social philosophy underwent a gradual evolution. He attacked the Unionist who felt that the black was not a potential equal to the white. And in reaction to the lynching and rampage of blacks in Pierce City, Missouri, Twain wrote "The United States of Lyncherdom" (written 1901). In it he warned against the mania of lynching and the thirst for spectacle, and called for moral bravery and sound principles. So exercised was Twain over the event that he suggested that American missionaries from China be recalled to labor in the fruitful lynch fields of the South. In *Huckleberry Finn* (1885) Twain came around to the stance taken by his friend George Washington Cable, the Christian opponent of Jim Crow laws in the South, that legal and political rights should be granted to blacks; this is a view earlier shared by Orion Clemens, whose strong stand on slavery cost him his job. Later in *Pudd'nhead Wilson* (1894) Twain expressed, among other concerns, the view that the profit motive perpetuated slavery. When he finally became convinced that blacks should be granted citizenship, Twain opened up to the idea of citizenship for Chinese-Americans.

Twain also warmed up to Jewish rights. However, his patronizing comments and excesses in "Concerning the Jews" (1899)—which characterize the Jew as a "well-behaved citizen" who is no rioter or loafer; who if plans to be a physician, becomes the best; if a farmer, then other farmers should pursue some other occupation and that failing to do so can be saved from poverty only by the law—is so laced with stereotypes that the essay might appear more anti-Semitic than a defense. One gets the same impression when Twain comments on how disproportionate the Jew's physical stature is when compared to his accomplishments and when he concludes by questioning the secret to the Jew's "immortality"—"All things are mortal but the Jew; all other forces pass, but he remains." A similar stereotype of the Chinese appears in *Roughing It*, in spite of Twain's appeal from the population for the same moral fortitude he solicited when blacks were being lynched. Evident in spite of these indiscreet comments, however, is the feeling that Twain genuinely sought the welfare of these groups, but his racist upbring-

ing and culture from which he was seeking to dissociate himself continued, nevertheless, to influence the language used to decry the social injustices he wished to expose. By 1901, however, he would claim in a mature response that a man is a human being—"that is enough for me; he can't be worse."

Twain's notions on race and religion, nonetheless, remain less ambivalent than his economic views. He followed politics closely and had an animus for congressmen whom he saw driven by economic self-interest. Though critical of the very economic system that permitted graft, Twain also was attracted to materialism and pursued enormous wealth. William Dean Howells once described him as both a theoretical socialist and a practical aristocrat. Twain despised the growth of large capital, and he felt that the nation becomes defenseless when its welfare is managed by selfish industrialists. He also abhorred eastern monetary principles and resented the poverty he witnessed in New York City, blaming it on meager wages and poor working conditions. Yet when Twain journeyed east, he immersed himself in its materialism and was part of the acquisitive spirit of the Gilded Age obsessed with fame and wealth.

In *The Gilded Age* (1873), the novel that alerted the public to the social immorality of the rich whom Twain held responsible for the nation's moral and social decay, Twain embraced a laissez-faire economic policy, believing that government should refrain from any involvement in the economic affairs of the cities and its citizens. In his words, "the mania for giving the Government power to meddle with the private affairs of cities or citizens is likely to cause trouble." But his faith in the profit motive tied to technology often compromised his social agenda and conscience, even to the point where he despised private charities. While Twain championed the cause of labor, once calling it "the new dynasty," he was also a strong advocate of the machine, which, ironically, made redundant the very labor force he praised.

Twain's mechanistic doctrine, what he called his "Private Philosophy," is best articulated in *What Is Man?*—a work he began writing in 1885 and completed in 1898. Livy bristled at the work's pessimistic tone and possibly at its "infernal philosophy." Twain's response, however, was that the truth "always has that effect on people." *What Is Man?* demonstrates that Twain, especially the late Twain, became less of a humorist and more of a critical and pessimistic observer of humans and their behavior. In the words of the Old Man, Twain advocated a mechanistic view of society and apparently saw society as damned because it was driven by radical self-interest. Two years later this view was played out in "The Man That Corrupted Hadleyburg" (1899), Twain's satire on a society driven by greed, hypocrisy, deception, and selfishness. Ironically, *What Is Man?* is also Twain's defense of his materialistic philosophy. In the work he contends that money is a symbol whose real value is spiritual and not material, for the material value in itself renders money worthless.

Believing that the "maudlin Middle-Age romanticism" of the novels of Sir Walter Scott influenced not only the "caste" system in the South, but actually caused the Civil War and made the South less advanced—positions for which he was charged with intellectual shallowness—Twain would later take to task the British monarchial system, what he called "that worm-eaten and dilapidated social structure in England." *A Connecticut Yankee in King Arthur's Court* (1889), a masterpiece of social criticism, indicts the British governmental system with possessing an outworn chivalric code, a code that denied legitimate democratic rights to its citizens.

Twain's literary career shows him always engaged with political, social, and economic questions. In 1904 when he met the Fabian Socialist George Bernard Shaw on the platform at London's St. Pancras station, Shaw noted their similarities, pointing especially to their shared satirical temperament. But Twain's social philosophy resists neat codification. It should not be thought of as Marxist or capitalist, democratic or republican. Rather, it is best seen as a liquefied blend of several systems. Twain believed as much in human community as in the individual, as much in the individual right to vote as in restrictions on that right. Thus he remains not so much a "Curious Republican" as an evasive theorist, a philosopher, and a keen observer of the human in society.

Jude Nixon

BIBLIOGRAPHY

Blues, Thomas. *Mark Twain & the Community.* Lexington: UP of Kentucky, 1970.

Budd, Louis J. *Mark Twain: Social Philosopher.* Bloomington: Indiana UP, 1962.

Clemens, Samuel L. *The Complete Essays of Mark Twain.* Ed. Charles Neider. Garden City, N.Y.: Doubleday, 1963.

———. *A Connecticut Yankee in King Arthur's Court.* Ed. Bernard Stein. Berkeley: U of California P, 1979.

———. *Mark Twain and the Government.* Comp. Svend Peterson. Caldwell, Idaho: Caxton, 1960.

———. *Mark Twain's Letters.* Ed. Albert B. Paine. 2 vols. New York: Harper, 1917.

———. *Mark Twain's Speeches.* New York: Harper, 1923.

Clemens, Samuel L., and Charles Dudley Warner. *The Gilded Age.* Hartford, Conn.: American Publishing, 1873.

Foner, Philip S. *Mark Twain: Social Critic.* New York: International Publishers, 1958.

French, Bryant Morey. *Mark Twain and "The Gilded Age."* Dallas: Southern Methodist UP, 1965.

Paine, Albert Bigelow. *Mark Twain: A Biography.* 3 vols. New York: Harper, 1912.

Salomon, Roger B. *Twain and the Image of History.* New Haven, Conn.: Yale UP, 1961.

See also: Abolition; Business; Civil War; Government; Jews; Philosophy; Politics; Racial Attitudes; Women's Rights

Social Reform

Mark Twain wrote extensively on a number of social issues: women's suffrage, imperialism and colonialism, party politics, war, and prejudice. His earliest writings as sub-editor on his brother Orion's Hannibal newspaper showed a concern with morality in terms of the community, and Charles Henry Webb, who published "The Celebrated Jumping Fog of Calaveras County" in 1867, asserted from the outset that Twain was more moralist than humorist. For Twain, the product of individual morality was always seen in terms of the culture and society in which the individual was trained.

The moral dilemma perhaps most familiar to Twain's readers occurs in *Adventures of Huckleberry Finn* (1885). Huck is going to turn Jim in as a runaway slave; all his cultural training as a boy from the slave state of Missouri tells him it is the right thing to do. But Huck reflects on Jim's goodness and human dignity and decides he will go to hell before he will betray his beloved friend. Here, and in many of his other works, Twain reveals his belief that civilization does not always make people civilized and that cultures that boast the most "civilization" may, in fact, contain the least humanity. In *HF* cultural forces are of dubious morality and Huck's ability and willingness to use his rational mind in making the decision is aided by his isolation from society; Huck is able to make his own moral decision because he is *away from* the social context that approves slavery. However, Twain generally saw rational individual morality as unable to rectify institutions (or human nature).

Twain particularly despised nineteenth-century medievalism, a widespread fascination with medieval times. Thomas Carlyle in England and the architect Ralph Adams Cram in America, among others, propounded the idea that life in the Middle Ages had been more fulfilling than life in modern times. Twain attacked the chivalric ideals portrayed in the novels of Sir Walter Scott in *Life on the Mississippi* (1883) and continued to satirize the class system integral to chivalry in *A Connecticut Yankee in King Arthur's Court* (1889). He was not merely critiquing past civilizations, but expressing disgust at a cultural paradigm that encouraged the South's commitment to slavery.

William Dean Howells called his friend "the most serious, the most humane, the most conscientious of men" (*My Mark Twain* 34). Three figures were most influential in Twain's development: his mother, Jane Lampton Clemens; his father, John Marshall Clemens; and his favorite uncle, John A. Quarles. Twain wrote of his mother's compassion for "people and other animals," her interest in "the whole world and everything and everybody in it" ("Jane Lampton Clemens" 83), and her eloquence and wit. Twain's father seems to have had less fire than his mother, but he was known for his morality and fairness. John Quarles was a humorous, kind, and strong man, who questioned the religious doctrines of his day.

In his later years, after he had suffered overwhelming personal tragedies and survived financial disaster, Twain wrote a number of works that gave rise to the labels "pessimist" and "misanthrope," such as *What Is Man?* (1906), "Was It Heaven? Or Hell?" (1902), and *The Mysterious Stranger* (1916). However, these labels become hard to justify when we consider that until the end of his life Twain was writing strongly against social injustice and cruelty, which means in favor of humanity and human dignity. In 1870 he had written "Disgraceful Persecution of a Boy," a caustic essay in which he argues that a boy whose culture teaches him that persecution of Chinese people is laudable can hardly be punished for acting on his training. In "The United States of Lyncherdom," written in 1901 and published after his death, Twain begged missionaries in China to "come home and convert these Christians!" who were torturing and lynching African-Americans in the South. "To the Person Sitting in Darkness" (1901) decries imperialism that is masked as educational and religious enlightenment. During his last visit with William Dean Howells, he was still talking with great hope that labor unions might unite "the weak against the strong" (*My Mark Twain* 100).

Patricia Hunt

BIBLIOGRAPHY

Andrews, Kenneth R. *Nook Farm: Mark Twain's Hartford Circle*. Cambridge, Mass.: Harvard UP, 1950.

Brashear, Minnie M. *Mark Twain: Son of Missouri*. Chapel Hill: U of North Carolina P, 1934.

Emerson, Everett. *The Authentic Mark Twain: A Literary Biography of Samuel L. Clemens*. Philadelphia: U of Pennsylvania P, 1984.

Foner, Philip S. *Mark Twain: Social Critic*. New York: International Publishers, 1958.

Howells, William Dean. *My Mark Twain: Reminiscences and Criticisms*. New York: Harper, 1910.

Kaplan, Justin. *Mr. Clemens and Mark Twain*. New York: Simon & Schuster, 1966.

Paine, Albert Bigelow. *Mark Twain: A Biography*. 3 vols. New York: Harper, 1912.

See also: Racial Attitudes; Social Philosophy; Women's Rights

"Sold to Satan"
(1923)

Early in January 1904 Mark Twain notified Frederick Duneka, his editor at Harper and Brothers, that he had written and revised a sketch entitled "Sold to Satan." The sketch was not published, however, until Albert Bigelow Paine included it in *Europe and Elsewhere* (1923).

"Sold to Satan" updates the story of Mephistopheles by setting up negotiations between Satan and Mark Twain, who intends to sell his soul in order to raise funds for speculating in the stock market. Satan comes to the interview clothed in radium, the radioactive element recently discovered by Madame Curie, and promises to give Twain secrets that will help him reap tremendous profits from atomic power. The tone darkens as Satan mentions that he has the power to destroy the world "in a flash of flame and a puff of smoke," leaving "a mere snow-shower of gray ashes" floating through space.

With subtle irony this sketch brings into focus an ominous future shaped by the dynamics of personal greed, big-business tactics, and scientific knowledge. "Sold to Satan" has been recognized not only as an example of Twain's burlesque humor, but a remarkably prophetic glimpse of the dilemmas of life in a postatomic world.

Stan Poole

BIBLIOGRAPHY

Baetzhold, Howard G. *Mark Twain and John Bull: The British Connection*. Bloomington: Indiana UP, 1970.

Brodwin, Stanley. "Mark Twain's Masks of Satan: The Final Phase." *American Literature* 45 (May 1973): 206–227.

Clemens, Samuel L. "Sold to Satan." *Europe and Elsewhere*. By Clemens. Ed. Albert B. Paine. New York: Harper, 1923. 326–338.

Cummings, Sherwood. *Mark Twain and Science: Adventures of a Mind*. Baton Rouge: Louisiana State UP, 1988.

Hill, Hamlin. *Mark Twain: God's Fool*. New York: Harper & Row, 1973.

See also: Business; Science

"Some Learned Fables for Good Old Boys and Girls"
(1875)

Written in 1874, this fable was sent to William Dean Howells for possible publication in the *Atlantic Monthly*. It was rejected by Howells so Twain included it as one of the new sketches in his 1875 publication of *Mark Twain's Sketches, New and Old*. The original was revised and a new title assigned: "Some Fables for Good Old Boys and Girls: Part First, Part Second, Part Third."

"Learned Fables" is a satiric account of scientific investigation in the late nineteenth century. By reducing men of science to insects and animals (Professor Mud Turtle, Dr. Bull Frog, Chief Engineer Spider, Sir Grass Hopper), Twain burlesques both scientists and the general public who too willingly accept the conclusions of scientific investigation based on questionable methodology and evidence. Albert Paine and later Howard Baetzhold point out the Swiftian style of this fable, and Baetzhold details the contemporary allusions to events and people Twain most likely targeted. Gibson shows how Twain's characters use a nonsensical jargon ("perlustration and perscontation") to further deride the savants of the scientific community (14).

James D. Wilson notes that the animal and insect characters of this fable represent three classes of the nineteenth century: the scientists, the aristocracy, and the common laborers (242). As they set out into "the great Unknown World," they misinterpret every observation they make. Professor Mud Turtle declares a passing locomotive as the Vernal Equinox, while Lord Grand-Daddy-Longlegs pronounces the passing of a second locomotive as the transit of Venus. Chief Engineer Spider deduces that a telegraph wire is a web hung by "some colossal member of his own species."

The lowly laborer Tumble-Bug, as Sherwood Cummings points out, is the hero of this fable (13). His common-sense speculations are declared ludicrous by the learned men of science, yet his conclusions are more accurate than any other account. In fact, it is Tumble-Bug who voices the moral of this tale: "He said that all he had learned by his travels was that science only needed a spoonful of supposition to build a mountain of demonstrated fact out of; and that for the future he meant to be content with the knowledge that nature had made free to all creatures and not go prying into the august secrets of the Deity" (121).

A subject of debate stimulated by "Learned Fables" is whether this burlesque of the scientific community faithfully represents Twain's view of science. That Twain was very interested in science has been documented in detail by Cummings and others before him. In the nineteenth-century debate between religion and science, Twain was undoubtedly on the side of science. Why then would he present the scientific intelligentsia in such a ludicrous

manner? Wilson documents other works by Twain in which he casts serious doubt on scientific investigation. One such example is the series of articles Twain wrote for the Buffalo *Express* in 1871 which targeted paleontology because of its lack of hard evidence on which to base its conclusions (243).

Stan Poole investigated the effect of Darwinism on Twain, concluding that Darwin's theories provided an apt metaphor for Twain's own philosophy of the nature of man. However, Twain recognized the many flaws in the new sciences and, according to Poole, concluded that there is no theory that is unified and complete. It can be said with certainty that Twain found in the new sciences a limitless source for comedy.

Donna Onebane

BIBLIOGRAPHY

Baetzhold, Howard. "Mark Twain on Scientific Investigation: Contemporary Allusions in 'Some Learned Fables for Good Old Boys and Girls.'" *Literature and Ideas in America: Essays in Memory of Harry Hayden Clark.* Ed. Robert Falk. Athens: Ohio UP, 1975. 128–154.

Clemens, Samuel L. *Mark Twain's Sketches, New and Old.* Hartford, Conn.: American Publishing, 1875.

Cummings, Sherwood. *Mark Twain and Science: Adventures of a Mind.* Baton Rouge: Louisiana State UP, 1988.

Gibson, William M. *The Art of Mark Twain.* New York: Oxford UP, 1976.

Paine, Albert Bigelow. *Mark Twain: A Biography.* Vol. 2. New York: Harper, 1912.

Poole, Stan. "In Search of the Missing Link: Mark Twain and Darwinism." *Studies in American Fiction* 13.2 (August 1985): 201–215.

Wilson, James D. *A Reader's Guide to the Short Stories of Mark Twain.* Boston: G.K. Hall, 1987.

See also: Science

"Some Rambling Notes of an Idle Excursion"
(1877–1878)

Struggling with getting *Ah Sin* on stage, Mark Twain abruptly sailed on a ten-day trip to

Bermuda in May 1877 with his good friend the Reverend Joseph Twichell. It was his first vacation to Bermuda (he would return often between 1907 and 1910) and his first extended sojourn with Twichell, who would be his companion for the European trip the following year, described in *A Tramp Abroad* (1880).

The voyage appealed because it "suggested a novelty, namely a trip for pure recreation, the bread-and-butter element left out." Typically, however, Twain turned the experience into literary and profitable ends. Notebook entries of the trip reveal the imagination of a writer already at work, and the result was "Some Rambling Notes of an Idle Excursion." It first appeared in the *Atlantic Monthly* October 1877 through January 1878 and then in *Punch, Brothers, Punch!* (1878) with the title "Random Notes of an Idle Excursion." Reprinting it in *The Stolen White Elephant* (1882), Twain added "The Invalid's Story" as a tale told on the return trip.

About half the piece is given to the voyage to Bermuda; the other to the four-day visit there. The first part features the yarns of whaling captains and Clemens's own anecdotes about Captain "Hurricane" Jones, in reality Captain Edgar M. (Ned) Wakeman, and his version of the story of Isaac and the prophets of Baal. A favorite character type in Clemens's travel sketches is the Bore. Here he is called "the Ass," a "grave, pale young man" who confounds sociable talk with inappropriate questions and observations, although "there was no harm in him."

In Bermuda Clemens admired the vivid whiteness of the homes made of whitewashed native coral surrounded by luxuriant flowers and foliage and the cleanliness and simple happiness of life there generally. "Nowhere is there dirt or stench, puddle or hog-wallow, neglect, disorder, or lack of trimness and neatness." As for the famous Bermuda onion, Clemens wrote humorously that it provided a metaphor for perfection, and the highest praise a native could give of someone is that "He was an onion!" Observing that dogs were "ab-stemious" on the island provided the opportunity to spin an elaborate comic story on cats with such august names as Hector G. Yelverton and To-Be-Or-Not-To-Be-That-Is-The-Question-Jackson. Typical of Samuel Clemens's travel pieces, "Some Rambling Notes" merges events from the trip itself with anecdotes from many sources and interests of many kinds.

Cameron C. Nickels

BIBLIOGRAPHY

Clemens, Samuel L. *The Stolen White Elephant, Etc.* Boston: James R. Osgood, 1882. 36–105.

Emerson, Everett. *The Authentic Mark Twain: A Literary Biography of Samuel L. Clemens.* Philadelphia: U of Pennsylvania P, 1984.

See also: "Invalid's Story, The"

"Some Thoughts on the Science of Onanism"

In spring 1879, Mark Twain delivered a ribald speech, "Some Thoughts on the Science of Onanism," at the Stomach Club in Paris. The speech has been printed privately several times since the 1950s; Fatout includes it along with notes and textual information, in *Mark Twain Speaking* (125–127).

Speaking before a group of men who met occasionally in Paris to enjoy bawdy entertainment, Twain takes as his subject the evils of masturbation. The speech opens with bowdlerized and out-of-context quotations on the subject from a succession of "authorities," including Homer, Caesar, Robinson Crusoe, Queen Elizabeth, Michelangelo, and Solomon. The humor of the piece derives not only from the taboo subject matter, but also from Twain's elevated tone, which creates nearly constant incongruity. As in the best of Twain's speeches, the piece builds to several characteristic, climactic "snappers."

Although certainly a slight piece, "Some Thoughts on the Science of Onanism" serves as a good example of Mark Twain's bawdy humor as well as testament to his ability to entertain the tastes of the Victorian gentlemen of his day.

John Bird

BIBLIOGRAPHY

Clemens, Samuel L. *Mark Twain Speaking.* Ed. Paul Fatout. Iowa City: U of Iowa P, 1976.

See also: Burlesque; "Mammoth Cod, The"; Scatology; *1601*

South, Mark Twain and the

The affinity Americans display for Mark Twain is illuminated by the insistent emphasis some of his students (including Arlin Turner, Louis D. Rubin, Jr., and Arthur G. Pettit) have placed on the shaping influence of the South in his representation of life in America. It is a notable aspect of American literary history that, except for Thomas Jefferson and Edgar Allan Poe, Mark Twain is the only indisputably major American writer who derived his consciousness of slavery from being reared in a southern slaveholding community. It was a small community, moreover, in which the intimate details of the chattel slavery system were more graphically evident than in the society of its derivation, that of the southern seaboard. With the extension of the southern slave society into Kentucky and Tennessee toward its ultimate boundaries in Arkansas, Texas, and Missouri, it tended to exhibit something like the rigidity of a colonial society. "Missouri was Western," William Dean Howells observed in an essay on Mark Twain in the *North American Review* (1901), "but it was also Southern not only in the institution of slavery, to the custom and acceptance of which Mark Twain was born and bred without any applied doubts of its divinity, but in the peculiar social civilization of the older South from which his native State was settled."

Growing up in the semifrontier world of the middle Mississippi valley before the Civil War, Mark Twain accepted the ways of a slaveholding society—his own family was a part of it—in which the best people, like the Grangerfords in *Adventures of Huckleberry Finn* (1885), lived in houses tended by slaves whose owners proudly displayed emblems of American freedom, like pictures called "Signing the Declaration" and oilcloth table covers emblazoned with red and blue spread eagles. With a simple, powerful intensity, this society dramatized the complicated ironies of American life: a life dedicated at once to the idea of America as the unfolding revolutionary redemption of human history and to the somewhat counter idea of America as in fact an already accomplished and superior arrangement of existence, a nation capable of dealing expediently with the occasions of history.

The circumstances of his birth, boyhood, and young manhood, in short, offered Mark Twain the most fertile education nineteenth-century America afforded in the dilemma of being an American. In his well-known remark in *My Mark Twain* (1910) that Mark Twain freed himself from his early environment so completely that he became "the most desouthernized Southerner I ever knew," Howells badly underestimated the complexity of his friend's mind. Mark Twain ironically never transcended his origin in a southern slaveholding family and the world that the slaveholders made in a republic invented and put into operation by a singularly remarkable generation of colonial revolutionaries, a few of whom, like James Madison, were still alive when he was born in 1835. In struggling with the tensions inherent in the situation of being at once an American and a southern writer, Mark Twain created in his greatest works a relationship between the South and the inmost American imagination of things we scarcely find in writers we may more assuredly call "southern," not even in William Faulkner.

When he says in the second part of *Life on the Mississippi* (1883) that in his friend George Washington Cable the "South has found" not only "a masterly delineator of its interior life and its history," but the author of books in which "the untrained eye and vacant mind can inspect" the South "and learn of and judge of it" even "more clearly and profitably . . . than by personal contact," Mark Twain undoubtedly implies a comment on his own evolving literary motive. With his discovery in the mid 1870s of what Henry Nash Smith labeled as "the Matter of Hannibal" and "the Matter of the South," Mark Twain had, in fact, begun to sketch a more penetrating portrayal of the South than his friend Cable would achieve. Having published "Old Times on the Mississippi," which became the first part of *Life on the Mississippi*, in the *Atlantic* in 1875, he had seen *The Adventures of Tom Sawyer* into print in 1876 and in the same year had conceived and begun writing *Huckleberry Finn*. In 1882, following his return to the Mississippi River after a twenty-year absence from the South, Mark Twain wrote the second part of *Life on the Mississippi*. By the time this book had been published in late 1883, Mark Twain had once again applied himself to the saga of Huck Finn. The task of writing it had suddenly become transformational. A compulsive and expansive act of memory had metamorphosed the personal recollection of the South as known to a boy coming of age in the little world of Hannibal, Missouri, in the 1830s and 1840s and later to a steamboat pilot moving up and down the river between St. Louis and New Orleans. Remembrance had assumed the scope and power of a vision of the inner life and history of the whole Mississippi valley society as this had existed in the two decades before the Civil War. Mark Twain now applied himself to the composition of *Huckleberry Finn* with such vigor that, although he still had the bulk of the story to write, it was ready for publication by late 1884.

The rapidity with which he finally finished his most famous and most important book, and more significantly, in contrast to *Tom Sawyer*, the breadth and depth of the historical dimension of *Huckleberry Finn*, indicate that in the six-year interval between its inception and publication the tale of the adventures of the semiliterate waif who was "Tom Sawyer's Comrade" had not languished in neglect. It

had been undergoing a process of germination, which came to a sudden flowering after Mark Twain's revisitation of the scenes of his boyhood and young manhood.

The germinating process is nowhere more essentially evident than in the chapter in the second part of *Life on the Mississippi* in which Mark Twain records his return to the river metropolis a decade and a half after New Orleans had seen the departure of the occupying forces of the notorious General Benjamin F. Butler. Whereas in social conversation in the North, he remarks, one seldom hears the war mentioned, in the South the war is "what A.D. is elsewhere; they date from it." So did the displaced Southerner Mark Twain. The humorous account in *Life on the Mississippi* of how New Orleanians talk about things happening "du'in the waw; or befo' the waw; or right aftah the waw" registers the profound effect the mighty struggle that was called in the North the "War of the Rebellion" and in the South the "War for Southern Independence" on his own consciousness of time and history. Before he became Mark Twain, twenty-five-year-old Sam Clemens had separated himself from the South when he withdrew from (or, to speak less politely, deserted from) a rag-tag volunteer company of Missouri Confederates to go adventuring on the new frontiers of Nevada and California. While in Nevada as a reporter for the *Territorial Enterprise*, he adopted as his literary name the familiar cry of the leadsman on Mississippi River steamboats he had piloted for three years prior to the war. It was as Mark Twain that after the war Sam Clemens went to live in the North, and later, always increasing in fame and having become a world traveler, to reside at times in Europe. But he was always haunted by a troubling sense of his fundamental identity. The relationship between his difficulty in knowing himself and his permanent absence without leave from the Confederate Army (though under the informal circumstances of his service, he can hardly be said to have gone "AWOL" in a legal sense) is of course conjectural. A good deal has been made of his semifictitious apologia, "The Private History of a Campaign That Failed," but it may be more significant to see how in *Life on the Mississippi* Mark Twain—whether in love or hate, or at times both—writes out of a persistent, deeply empathic relationship with the South. It is in his identity as a postbellum Southerner that the author speaks when he says that to grasp the significance of the war the stranger to the South must realize "how intimately every individual" Southerner was involved in it. Ostensibly quoting a gentleman he had met at a New Orleans club, Mark Twain observes that the calamity of the war was so intense and encompassing in the South that each Southerner, "in his own person," seems to have been "visited . . . by that tremendous episode," and "in his own person . . . to have sampled all the different varieties of human experience." In *Life on the Mississippi* Mark Twain implies his understanding that the four years of civil slaughter and destruction had altered the American sense of the very structure of time, history, and memory; that Americans—Southerners more self-consciously so than the victors in the war—now live in two republics. One is the "Old Republic" of nostalgic remembrance: the republic of the constitutional federation of self-liberated colonies that had freed themselves from imperial rule in that distant time "befo' the waw"; the other republic, the actual republic, is the present one: the "Second American Republic," the integral union of states, the "nation state" that came into existence "aftah the waw."

Mark Twain also understood that for Southerners, the defeated citizens of the aborted Confederate States of America (a republic they had founded in the belief that it represented and would preserve the truth of the original republic), the sense of a displacement of history was expressed in a more particular terminology, the "Old South" and the "New South." In contrast to southern romanticists like Thomas Nelson Page or the later George Washington Cable, Mark Twain, envisioning the individual life as existing always in an intimately ironic tension with the displacing force

of history, anticipated the novelists of the twentieth-century "Southern Renascence"—William Faulkner, Robert Penn Warren, Allen Tate, Andrew Lytle, Caroline Gordon—by creating a novel in which memory and history coalesce in the imagination of a literary genius who at times seemingly despised the South and yet could not at all spurn it. In his response to the drama of the quarrel in his imagination about the South, Twain discovered a way to project the quarrel through the vernacular language of a homeless, scarcely literate, "po' white" boy who becomes involved in the effort of a slave to escape to freedom. In the climatic moment of the story Huck defies the dictate of his "conscience" and decides that he will "go to hell" rather than betray his friendship with Jim, only in the next moment—declaring that he will "go to work and steal Jim out of slavery again," having been "brung up to wickedness"—to reveal that his transcendence of the morality of his society is more apparent than real. In its full dimensions the historical context of Huck's moral situation is larger, however, than his involvement in the southern slave society. As Mark Twain is in a sense the author of his own autobiography in the book he had published two years earlier, *Life on the Mississippi*, Huck, as Mark Twain could not, reveals the coalescence of the inner history of the South and the inner history of the nation. Following his writing of a story set in the frontier microcosm of a slave society that referred its origin to a document proclaiming the innate sovereignty of the self—a manifesto heralding a "Great Experiment" in the human capacity for rational governance—Mark Twain, as *Pudd'nhead Wilson* (1894) so tellingly indicates, increasingly saw the South as a symbol of a national history that had become a bitter tragicomedy.

Lewis P. Simpson

BIBLIOGRAPHY

Howells, William Dean. *My Mark Twain: Reminiscences and Criticisms.* New York: Harper, 1910.

Pettit, Arthur G. *Mark Twain and the South.* Lexington: UP of Kentucky, 1974.

Rubin, Louis D., Jr. *The Writer in the South: Studies in a Literary Community.* Athens: U of Georgia P, 1972.

Smith, Henry Nash. *Mark Twain: The Development of a Writer.* Cambridge, Mass.: Harvard UP, 1962.

———. *Virgin Land: The American West as Symbol and Myth.* Cambridge, Mass.: Harvard UP, 1950.

Tate, Allen. "A Southern Mode of the Imagination." *Essays of Four Decades.* By Tate. Chicago: Swallow, 1968. 577–592.

Turner, Arlin. "Mark Twain and the South: An Affair of Love and Anger." *Southern Review* n.s. 4 (Spring 1968): 493–519.

See also: Abolition; Civil War; *Pudd'nhead Wilson, The Tragedy of*; Slavery; Smith, Henry Nash

Southwestern Humor

(ca. 1830–ca. 1860)

Southwestern humor was a self-conscious form of comedy that flourished in Georgia, Alabama, Mississippi, Louisiana, Tennessee, Arkansas, and parts of Kentucky and Missouri from approximately 1830 to the Civil War. It is the humor from which Mark Twain learned his basic comic techniques and the school of nineteenth-century humor that has exerted the greatest influence on subsequent American literature.

The southwestern frontier at the beginning of the nineteenth century was characterized by physical hardships, brutality, and violence. It was a world of variety and contrast in which effete offspring of Virginia aristocrats mingled with experienced hardened backwoodsmen and plantation owners and professionals routinely rubbed shoulders with dirt farmers and gamblers. Its inhabitants valued physical abilities such as shooting prowess, horseback riding, and fistfighting as practical skills sometimes necessary to survive; but they also valued good storytellers who could relieve them of the boredom of a long winter's night by regaling them with oral tales that converted the violent, the grotesque, and the ugly aspects of their world into comic folk art.

The advent of a newspaper market for such humorous sketches aimed at lower- and middle-class audiences, the rise of Jacksonian democracy, and the desire to create an accurate depiction of the rough and ready morals and manners of the region led to the rapid blossoming of a literary southwestern humor in the late 1820s and early 1830s that culminated with the publication of Augustus Baldwin Longstreet's *Georgia Scenes* (1835) as the first major collection of southwest humor. The humorists themselves were typically educated, genteel, conservative professional men who seemed simultaneously to revel in and look down upon the exuberant, colorful lifestyles of the lower social groups surrounding them. Their essential genius was the ability to convey authentically the frontier experience with its local folklore, legends, and tall tales, especially through their use of the tradition of oral storytelling. The dichotomy between these gentlemanly writers educated in the best tradition of eighteenth-century British essayists and the escapades, language, and wit of their backwoods protagonists almost naturally led to a most ingenious method for telling their stories: the frame narrative. In the frame narrative the literate storyteller maintains the guise of an overly refined sophisticate condescending to the subjects he introduces, while the heroes of the fiction are allowed to speak in their own vernacular and dialect, thus bringing the energy and zest of life on the southwestern frontier directly into the experience of the stories.

And the southwestern humorists did, indeed, ground these stories firmly in their geographical place setting: they made fiction from the complex life about them and thus led the way for the development of realism in American literature. Among their primary purposes in writing was to record the speech, manners, and characters peculiar to the region—to interpret the region and its denizens to the larger outside world. A sampling of some titles of the best of their works reveals their focus on the local: Longstreet's *Georgia Scenes*, William

Tappan Thompson's *Chronicle of Pineville* [Georgia] (1845), Henry Clay Lewis's *Odd Leaves from the Life of a Louisiana Swamp Doctor* (1850), and Joseph Glover Baldwin's *The Flush Times of Alabama and Mississippi* (1853).

These humorists drew not only on the tangible local color of the area, but also on the spirit that pervaded the region: the Old Southwest was an unsettled, unsure region in the process of defining itself, of becoming southern rather than of celebrating an established identity. Consequently, the typical conflict that emerged was between the civilizing, stabilizing forces in the community, frequently represented in the frame narrator, and the more individualistic frontier spirit, usually embodied in the protagonist of the story. These contradictory claims of self versus the larger community became the informing factor in much southwestern humor.

The significant result of this rhetorical strategy is that the laughter arises from irony, not satire. The frame narrator becomes something of a displaced person (in, but not of, the culture he is celebrating) and therefore gains an objective insider's perspective that affords a valuable sense of aesthetic distance. These genteel chroniclers of the southwestern frontier typically turned away from didacticism in favor of vernacular realism and imaginative balance—the corrective spirit yielded to the genuinely comic. As they cultivated their abilities to see and present the multiplicity of life on the frontier, they seemed also to develop a broader acceptance of a wide variety of experience and a deeper appreciation of the dualities of human life—the heart of the true comic spirit. Their humorous fiction thus stands as a celebration of the human spirit in its quest for freedom and opportunity in a new country.

The mood that governs their work, however, is one of general irreverence. Their exploitation of the comedy of physical discomfort, of procreative and bodily functions, of the violent and the grotesque is a further extension of their humorous realism. Such graphic comic realism is, according to Mikhail Bakhtin, an essential element of the culture of folk humor in its attempt to capture the tenuous state of becoming by representing simultaneously that which is being born and that which is dying away. Again, the predominant spirit is ironic, not satiric.

Another basic folk element in southwestern humor is its use of animals and animal imagery. The southwestern humorists frequently gave human characteristics to the animals in their stories and animal characteristics to the human beings: thus, they employed conscious symbolism and artistic distancing in forms familiar to their readers and appropriate to their subjects. The deliberate choice to develop such conscious representation was a critical step in the advancement from the oral folk tale to the written literary story: they lifted anecdotes into the realm of narrative art by investing them with pathos, humanity, and even mythic stature. Such art achieves its highest level in the most famous of the southwestern stories, "The Big Bear of Arkansas" (1841) by Thomas Bangs Thorpe. In this classic frame narrative story backwoodsman Jim Doggett tells the interior tale of an unhuntable bear who is unexpectedly killed by Doggett as the hunter defecates in the woods. Doggett's wistful conclusion is that the bear "died when his time come," and the story takes on mythic proportions as Thorpe's representation of the death of a piece of the frontier that has become civilized.

Doggett also illustrates one of the typical characters that developed in southwestern humor stories: the backwoods alazon—a character who claimed more for himself than was his due. Such tall-tale-telling southwestern characters as frontiersman Davy Crockett, keelboatman Mike Fink, and bear hunter Jim Doggett raised the brag to the level of art in proclaiming their physical skills with vivid and imaginative hyperbole. Another popular southwestern character was the picaro, a roughish vagabond of low degree who lives off wits and cunning. This character type reached its apex in Simon Suggs (*Adventures of Simon Suggs*, 1845) and Sut Lovingood (*Sut Lovingood Yarns*, 1867), the creations of Alabamian Johnson J.

Hooper and Tennessean George W. Harris, respectively. Suggs's motto—"It's good to be shifty in a new country"—epitomizes their approach to frontier survival.

In spite of the remarkable accomplishments of these frontier comedians, the culmination of this humor as art did not occur until Mark Twain returned to his southwestern literary progenitors and began to incorporate their techniques into his own writing. Adding to this foundation his apprenticeship in western burlesque, his experience as a literary comedian, his reverence for highbrow eastern literature, and his native abilities as a local colorist, Twain built a career that both sums up and surpasses the achievements of the antebellum southwestern humorists. While Twain obviously wrote for different audiences and from different geographical areas at different points in his career, his roots in the Mississippi River valley imbued him with the dialect and vernacular, the tall tales and the local lore, and the appreciation for exuberant, rough humor that became the hallmarks of his reputation as America's greatest literary humorist.

W. Craig Turner

BIBLIOGRAPHY

Bakhtin, Mikhail. *Rabelais and His World*. Trans. Helene Iswolsky. Cambridge, Mass.: Massachusetts Institute of Technology P, 1968.

Beir, Jesse. *The Rise and Fall of American Humor*. New York: Holt, 1968.

Blair, Walter. *Native American Humor*. San Francisco: Chandler, 1960.

Blair, Walter, and Hamlin Hill. *America's Humor: From Poor Richard to Doonesbury*. New York: Oxford UP, 1978.

Clark, William Bedford, and W. Craig Turner, eds. *Critical Essays on American Humor*. Boston: G.K. Hall, 1984.

Cox, James M. *Mark Twain: The Fate of Humor*. Princeton, N.J.: Princeton UP, 1966.

Inge, M. Thomas, ed. *The Frontier Humorists: Critical Views*. Hamden, Conn.: Archon, 1975.

Lynn, Kenneth S. *Mark Twain and Southwestern Humor*. Boston: Little, Brown, 1959.

Rubin, Louis D., Jr. *The Comic Imagination in American Literature*. New Brunswick, N.J.: Rutgers UP, 1973.

See also: Animals; Baldwin, Joseph Glover; Literary Comedians; Local Color; Orality; Regionalism; Thorpe, Thomas Bangs; Vernacular

Spanish-American War, The (April–August 1898)

Mark Twain favored the brief Spanish-American War, but he turned strongly against the subsequent war in the Philippines in which the United States took over, rather than liberated, the former Spanish colony. That war elicited Twain's best anti-imperialist writing.

In 1895 an insurrection against Spanish rule began in Cuba that the yellow press urged the United States to support, especially after the sinking of the *Maine* in Havana harbor. Even though Spain capitulated to all American demands, the United States declared war on 25 April 1898, and quickly defeated Spain on 12 August. According to the Treaty of Paris in December, Cuba became free, but Puerto Rico and Guam were ceded and for $20 million the Philippines was sold to the United States. The Filipinos, who had started a revolt against Spain in 1896 led by Emilio Aguinaldo, now began fighting the Americans. This war lasted over two years until Aguinaldo was captured by General Frederick Funston in March 1901. Sporadic fighting continued until 1913.

Mark Twain applauded the Spanish-American War since he thought its purpose was to liberate Spain's colonies. When he read the Treaty of Paris, though, he began to protest. Affiliating himself with the Anti-Imperialist League, Twain wrote letters, gave newspaper interviews, and made speeches against the Philippine war. His published articles were the short "A Salutation Speech from the Nineteenth Century to the Twentieth" (1900), his major effort "To the Person Sitting in Darkness" (1901), and the bitter "A Defense of General Funston" (1902). Between 1902 and 1906 Twain started more articles on the lingering war but broke them off in despair over the doomed cause. In 1906 he refused any further involvement. The triumph of the imperialists became a major factor in the pessimism that overwhelmed Twain at the end of his life.

Hunt Hawkins

BIBLIOGRAPHY

Bain, David H. *Sitting in Darkness: Americans in the Philippines*. Boston: Houghton Mifflin, 1984.

Budd, Louis J. *Mark Twain: Social Philosopher*. Bloomington: Indiana UP, 1962.

Foner, Philip S. *Mark Twain: Social Critic*. New York: International Publishers, 1958.

Gibson, William M. "Mark Twain and Howells: Anti-Imperialists." *New England Quarterly* 20 (1947): 435–470.

Tompkins, E. Berkeley. *Anti-Imperialism in the United States: The Great Debate, 1890–1920*. Philadelphia: U of Pennsylvania P, 1970.

Welch, Richard E. *Response to Imperialism: The United States and the Philippine-American War, 1899–1902*. Chapel Hill: U of North Carolina P, 1979.

See also: "Defense of General Funston, A"; Imperialism; "To the Person Sitting in Darkness"; War

Spencer, Herbert
(1820–1903)

English philosopher and sociologist Herbert Spencer is best known for his theory, set forth in his *Synthetic Philosophy* (1896), that evolution from simple to complex forms is a fundamental law of nature. More a popularizer and less a scientist than Charles Darwin (1809–1882), his theory differs from Darwin's in his belief that attitudes and intuitions can be inherited. It was, however, he who coined the phrase "survival of the fittest," and Darwin who adopted it as descriptive of his own theory.

Mark Twain met Spencer in England in 1873 and thereafter referred to him several times in complimentary but general terms; e.g., Spencer's is one of "certain splendid names." Alan Gribben's *Mark Twain's Library* (1980) includes no Spencer titles. Spencer's influence may be discernible in *A Connecticut Yankee*

(1889) where the Boss entertains the idea that opinions and attitudes can be genetically transmitted.

Patricia Sexton and Sherwood Cummings

BIBLIOGRAPHY

Cummings, Sherwood. *Mark Twain and Science: Adventures of a Mind*. Baton Rouge: Louisiana State UP, 1988.

Spencer, Herbert. *An Autobiography*. London: Williams and Norgate, 1904.

See also: Darwin, Charles; Evolution; Science

Sphinx

The Great Sphinx of Gizeh is located near the Pyramid of Khafra in Egypt. The high-flown language of the piece on the Sphinx in *The Innocents Abroad* (1869, Vol. 2, chap. 31) is what Mark Twain often ridiculed in the writing of others and in his own. Here there is no deflation of the elevated expression. Is it therefore a sincere statement of his feelings? Was he truly moved by the Sphinx? Possibly. Although often the iconoclast, he is not always so. At times he can be as moved by a renowned sight as any conventional tourist. Possibly he was moved by the Sphinx.

But there is reason to doubt his sincerity. The writings of his fellow excursionists do not celebrate the great statue. Some mention it not at all (Nesbit, Moulton, Duncan); some barely mention it (Newell, Jackson); one mentions only the dilapidated nose (Beach); and Mrs. Fairbanks, in her letter to the Cleveland *Herald*, admits that she "experienced not the least symptom of rhapsody" over the Sphinx. Replying to a letter from Mrs. Fairbanks (17 June 1868), Twain says he is writing to her "instead of going on moralizing over the Sphinx," hardly the expression of one who takes his panegyric seriously.

In what he wrote, however, he sounds to have been genuinely moved by the ancient monument. The passage was new writing, done eight months after the experience. He had no notes written on the spot. In reading up on the Sphinx he may have been influenced to adopt a philosophical tone for his piece, for, as Henry Nash Smith has shown, several of Twain's details are close to those in books he most likely read at the time. But the rhetorical embellishments—lofty diction, studied parallelism, personification of the statue, references to time—are Twain's. What precedes the Sphinx passage is foolishness; what follows is satire. It is likely, therefore, that Twain felt that a pure paean to the Sphinx would be his most telling treatment of the monument.

If later readers have found the set piece on the Sphinx overwrought and unconvincing, Twain's contemporaries admired it greatly. It appeared, together with a full-page engraving of the Sphinx, in the prospectus that agents showed to customers for *IA*. Reviewers were pleasantly surprised to find an acknowledged humorist capable also of impressive rhetorical flights. Twain's biographer, Albert Bigelow Paine (*Mark Twain's Notebook*, 1935), thought the Sphinx passage "probably the high spot of [Twain's] book."

Leon T. Dickinson

BIBLIOGRAPHY

Clemens, Samuel L. *Mark Twain to Mrs. Fairbanks*. Ed. Dixon Wecter. San Marino, Calif.: Huntington Library, 1949.

————. *Mark Twain's Notebook*. Ed. Albert B. Paine. New York: Harper, 1935.

Dickinson, Leon T. "Mark Twain's Revisions in Writing *The Innocents Abroad*." *American Literature* 19 (May 1947): 139–157.

Gerber, John C. *Mark Twain*. Boston: Twayne, 1988.

Smith, Henry Nash. *Mark Twain: The Development of a Writer*. Cambridge, Mass.: Harvard UP, 1962.

See also: Egypt; *Innocents Abroad, The*

Spiritualism

Mark Twain was a great debunker of spiritualistic humbug, attacking superstition relentlessly in novels (*A Connecticut Yankee in King Arthur's Court*, 1889), essays, and sketches. But his exposure of spiritualistic fraud seems to have been driven by a deeper desire to uncover, by tough-minded means, solid psychic principles that would revolutionize the relation between conscious life and immaterial forces. Twain was for many years a member of the English Society for Psychical Research, professing to "read their pamphlets with avidity as fast as they arrived"; and he avowed certain knowledge of the truth of mental telepathy, which he labeled "mental telegraphy" in recognition of its analogical relation to the hard technological reality of the telegraph. He also believed in prophetic dream experience (as a result of his dream vision preceding his brother Henry's death), resorted to seances in company with his wife Livy to contact their daughter Susy after her death at age twenty-four, and investigated hypnosis as a possible treatment for daughter Jean's epilepsy. Spiritualism is a particularly prevalent issue in Twain's later writings, which satirize and otherwise attack belief in witchcraft and other superstitions and make fun of the conventional Christian vision of afterlife (*Extract from Captain Stormfield's Visit to Heaven*, 1909), but also ponder at length—as in *The Mysterious Stranger* and "Which Was the Dream?"—the problematic relation of dream to reality.

James S. Leonard

BIBLIOGRAPHY

Clemens, Samuel L. *Christian Science, with Notes Containing Corrections to Date*. New York: Harper, 1907.

————. *Extract from Captain Stormfield's Visit to Heaven*. New York: Harper, 1909.

————. *Mark Twain's "Which Was the Dream" and Other Symbolic Writings of the Later Years*. Ed. John S. Tuckey. Berkeley: U of California P, 1967.

Ebon, Martin. *They Knew the Unknown*. New York: World, 1971.

Gribben, Alan. "'When Other Amusements Fail': Mark Twain and the Occult." *The Haunted Dusk: American Supernatural Fiction, 1820–1920*. Ed. Howard Kerr, John W. Crowley, and Charles L. Crow. Athens: U of Georgia P, 1983. 169–189.

Kerr, Howard. *Mediums, and Spirit-Rappers, and Roaring Radicals: Spiritualism in American Literature, 1850–1900.* Urbana: U of Illinois P, 1972.

Ketterer, David. *The Science Fiction of Mark Twain.* Hamden, Conn.: Archon, 1984.

See also: Dreams; "Mental Telegraphy" and "Mental Telegraphy Again"; Mental Telepathy/Extrasensory Perception; Occult

Springfield *Republican*

Samuel Bowles II founded the politically oriented weekly *Massachusetts Republican* in 1824, which, under the direction of his son Samuel Bowles III, became the daily Springfield *Republican* in 1844. The paper became less political and more concerned with the coverage of local and telegraph news, which it set forth in a succinct, direct style. Bowles had a significant influence in the world of journalism as Samuel Clemens discovered in February 1869 when he approached Hartford *Courant* owners General Joseph Hawley and Charles Dudley Warner with the prospect of buying into their partnership. After consulting with Bowles on the matter, the *Courant* owners rejected Twain's proposition. Instead, Clemens bought a partnership in the Buffalo *Express.* Several years later, the conservative *Republican* harshly criticized the speech delivered by Clemens at a commemorative dinner held for John Greenleaf Whittier on his seventieth birthday, 17 December 1877. Comments censuring the vulgarity of the speech appeared on 19 December and again on 24 December, and a long, unsigned letter to the editor excoriating Clemens personally for his impropriety appeared on 27 December.

Susan McFatter

BIBLIOGRAPHY

Kaplan, Justin. *Mr. Clemens and Mark Twain.* New York: Simon & Schuster, 1966.

McKerns, Joseph P., ed. *Biographical Dictionary of American Journalism.* Westport, Conn.: Greenwood P, 1989.

Mott, Frank L. *American Journalism: A History, (1690–1960).* 3rd ed. New York: Macmillan, 1962.

Smith, Henry Nash. *Mark Twain: The Development of a Writer.* Cambridge, Mass.: Harvard UP, 1962.

See also: Whittier Birthday Dinner Speech

Stedman, Arthur
(1859–1908)

Arthur Stedman, son of Edmund Clarence Stedman, was an editor for Charles L. Webster and Company, Mark Twain's publishing company. Stedman held an M.A. degree from Yale. He was the general editor of the "Fiction, Fact, and Fancy Series" and editor of Walt Whitman's *Autobiography* for the Webster Company.

In a letter to Fred J. Hall on 30 June 1890, Twain, annoyed with Edmund Clarence Stedman, characterized both father and son by declaring that "idiotcy [*sic*] runs in the family" and advised Hall to ignore letters from both men, "that pair of quite too wonderful people" (*Letters to His Publishers* 261). In an 1893 letter to Hall, Twain proposed but never published an "inexpensive" magazine to be edited by Arthur Stedman and his father (*Letters to His Publishers* 352). Arthur Stedman published Twain's "The Californian's Tale" in *The First Book of the Authors Club, Liber Scriptorum* in 1893.

Sandra Gravitt

BIBLIOGRAPHY

Clemens, Samuel L. *Mark Twain in Eruption.* Ed. Bernard DeVoto. New York: Harper, 1940.

———. *Mark Twain's Letters to His Publishers, 1867–1894.* Ed. Hamlin Hill. Berkeley: U of California P, 1967.

Emerson, Everett. *The Authentic Mark Twain: A Literary Biography of Samuel L. Clemens.* Philadelphia: U of Pennsylvania P, 1984.

Paine, Albert Bigelow. *Mark Twain, A Biography.* 3 vols. New York: Harper, 1912.

See also: Webster and Company, Charles L.

Stevenson, Robert Louis
(1850–1894)

Scottish-born author Robert Louis Stevenson waged a forty-four year battle against tuberculosis—which was long enough to win international acclaim as a poet, essayist, writer of travel narratives, and novelist (especially *Treasure Island*, 1883; *Kidnapped*, 1886; and *The Strange Case of Dr. Jekyll and Mr. Hyde*, 1866).

Stevenson and Twain met only once, during Stevenson's 1888 visit to New York City, when the two authors spent a memorable afternoon together on a bench in Washington Square, talking, Stevenson later recalled, "like a couple of characters out of a story by Henry James" (Stevenson to Clemens, 16 April 1893). In 1904 Twain recollected the afternoon very warmly, pointing out that Stevenson's emaciated frame heightened the "special distinction" of his "splendid eyes," which burned with a "smoldering rich fire under the penthouse of his brows, and they made him beautiful" (*Autobiography* 1:247; Paine 3:794, 859–860). After Stevenson became established in Samoa (1889), the two corresponded, and Stevenson fleetingly explored the possibility of publishing with Charles L. Webster and Company.

Twain was fascinated by the implications of the Jeckyll-Hyde *Doppelgänger*-dualism for his own ideas about the mystery of personality and the "dream self," insisting that Stevenson came "nearer, yes, but not near enough to the truth" (Kaplan 169–171).

Richard H. Cracroft

BIBLIOGRAPHY

Baetzhold, Howard G. *Mark Twain and John Bull: The British Connection*. Bloomington: Indiana UP, 1970.

Clemens, Samuel L. *Mark Twain's Autobiography*. Ed. Albert B. Paine. 2 vols. New York: Harper, 1924.

———. *Mark Twain's Notebooks & Journals, Volume III (1883–1891)*. Ed. Robert Pack Browning, Michael B. Frank, and Lin Salamo. Berkeley: U of California P, 1979.

Kaplan, Justin. *Mark Twain and His World*. New York: Simon & Schuster, 1974.

Paine, Albert Bigelow. *Mark Twain: A Biography*. 3 vols. New York: Harper, 1912.

Stevenson, Robert Louis. "Letter From Robert Louis Stevenson to Mark Twain." *Twainian* 9 (September-October 1950): 1, 4.

See also: Dreams

Stewart, William M.
(1825–1909)

A frontier lawyer and politician, William M. Stewart served two terms as United States senator from Nevada, 1864–1875 and 1887–1905.

Twain labeled Stewart "Bullyragging Bill" in the Virginia City *Territorial Enterprise* because Stewart would ruthlessly drive his cases through the courts. Twain complained that Stewart was always "construing something" and suggested that Stewart would even "climb out of his coffin and construe the burial service" (Smith 97). Stewart's opposition to taxation on miners provided Twain with further satiric material.

The relationship between Twain and Stewart became strained when Stewart asked Twain to serve as his private secretary in Washington, D.C., in 1867. Although Twain expected to make the most of the appointment, he and Stewart parted ways after only two months. Speculation has arisen concerning the origin of the falling out between Twain and Stewart. Twain may have had some vestiges of southern political sympathy that brought him into conflict with Stewart, a radical republican, on the eve of the Johnson impeachment. Twain left the post with little regret and proceeded "to burlesque the whole business in print" in his essay "My Late Senatorial Secretaryship" (1868).

Stewart, however, introduced Twain to President Ulysses S. Grant in July 1870. The minor quarrel between the two gained added fuel through Twain's satiric portrait of Stewart in *Roughing It* (1872) and the somewhat bitter rebuttals from Stewart in public statements and in his memoirs.

Jennifer L. Rafferty

BIBLIOGRAPHY

Clemens, Samuel L. *Mark Twain of the "Enterprise": Newspaper Articles and Other Documents 1862–1864.* Ed. Henry Nash Smith and Frederick Anderson. Berkeley: U of California P, 1957.

———. "My Late Senatorial Secretaryship." *Sketches New and Old.* By Clemens. Hartford, Conn.: American Publishing, 1899. 141–147.

———. *Roughing It.* Ed. Paul Baender. Berkeley: U of California P, 1972.

Kaplan, Justin. *Mr. Clemens and Mark Twain.* New York: Simon & Schuster, 1966.

Mack, Effie Mona. *Mark Twain in Nevada.* New York: Scribner, 1947.

Rogers, Franklin R. "'Clemens' Political Affiliations Bearing on 'L'Homme Qui Rit.'" *Mark Twain's Satires & Burlesques.* By Clemens. Ed. Rogers. Berkeley: U of California P, 1967. 460–464.

See also: Washington, D.C.

Stoddard, Charles Warren
(1843–1909)

Charles Warren Stoddard was poet, newspaper correspondent, novelist, college professor, and personal secretary to Mark Twain. His main works are *Poems* (1867); *South Sea Idyls* (1873), probably his best book; *Mashallah: A Flight into Egypt* (1881); *The Lepers of Molokai* (1885); *A Troubled Heart* (1885), autobiographical; and *For the Pleasure of His Company* (1903), his only novel.

Stoddard was born in New York City to Samuel Burr and Harriet Abigail (Freeman) Stoddard. Educated in California and New York, he taught English literature at Notre Dame (1885–1886) and Catholic University of America (1889–1902). His personal charm and popularity among the literati prompted Mark Twain to hire him as his personal secretary while in London in 1873. Known for his wit and sociability, Stoddard was as much companion as secretary to Twain.

Literarily, Stoddard is chiefly remembered for his South Sea Island books, especially *South Sea Idyls*.

David B. Kesterson

BIBLIOGRAPHY

Longtin, Ray C. *Three Writers of the Far West: A Reference Guide.* Boston: G.K. Hall, 1980. 121–182.

Stoddard, Charles Warren. *Poems of Charles Warren Stoddard.* Ed. Ina Coolbrith. New York: John Lane, 1917.

Stroven, Carl G. "A Life of Charles Warren Stoddard." Ph.D. diss., Duke U, 1939.

"Stolen White Elephant, The"
(1882)

Twain originally planned "The Stolen White Elephant," written in November or December 1878, as a chapter in *A Tramp Abroad* (1880), but he deleted it from that volume and made it the title piece of a collection of short fiction published in 1882. Later, it was again published in *Tom Sawyer Abroad* (1896).

Twain drew upon sensational newspaper accounts of the hapless efforts of New York detectives to recover the corpse of Alexander T. Stewart, whose body had been stolen from the family tomb on 7 November 1878. However, the object of the detectives' search in Twain's story—a white elephant—is perhaps even more bizarre than its real-life counterpart. Nevertheless, the ineffectual antics of the detectives are equally absurd in both the factual and the fictitious accounts.

"The Stolen White Elephant" commences with a stock narrative device—a tale related by another to the listener/narrator, who can then retire from the scene and permit the tale to be told in the first person. The "narrator" is a former Siamese civil servant whose task it was to deliver the gift of a white elephant from the King of Siam to the Queen of England. While the ship transporting the elephant to England is docked in Jersey City, the elephant is apparently stolen. The civil servant rushes to New York City to enlist the help of the chief of detectives, Inspector Blunt, "a person of no common order," and from that point the madness begins.

When the narrator relates his incredible dilemma to the inspector, Blunt is utterly unmoved and treats the affair as if it were any other case of theft that might come under his jurisdiction. He solicits from the narrator a physical description of the white elephant, as well as a photograph, and astonishingly detailed information regarding what the elephant eats, drinks, and his various other habits—as if such information would be necessary to locate a white elephant on the loose in New York. Subsequently, Inspector Blunt sends his massive corps of detectives in search of the elephant, and the telegraphic reports they send back raise the level of comic incongruity to the breaking point. Of course, the detectives are unable to apprehend thieves (the primary suspects turn out to have been dead for some time) or the elephant, which finally turns up dead in the detectives' quarters of the police station—literally under their noses. Throughout this burlesque the narrator never loses respect for Blunt or his methods. In fact, these ludicrous misadventures only seem to make him rise in the narrator's esteem until it becomes difficult to tell who is the more thick and naive one, Inspector Blunt or the narrator (Wilson 249).

Twain's story is a relentless lampoon of the detective and his often absurdly extravagant methods, which frequently produce few, if any, results. In particular, Twain had in mind Allan Pinkerton and his detective agency, whom Twain had previously made the object of his ridicule in *Cap'n Simon Wheeler, the Amateur Detective*, written in 1877. "The Stolen White Elephant" is arguably a light-hearted burlesque in the tradition of Twain's earlier work (Wilson 248). Yet, it is still possible to see the seeds of his later pessimism and disdain for humanity in his treatment of the detectives and in his recognition of the tendency of law enforcement agencies to concentrate on the punishment rather than the prevention of crime.

Tim Poland

BIBLIOGRAPHY

Baetzhold, Howard G. "Of Detectives and Their Derring-Do: The Genesis of Mark Twain's 'The Stolen White Elephant.'" *Studies in American Humor* 2 (January 1976): 183–195.

Baldanza, Frank. *Mark Twain: An Introduction and Interpretation.* New York: Barnes & Noble, 1961.

Bellamy, Gladys Carmen. *Mark Twain as a Literary Artist.* Norman: U of Oklahoma P, 1950.

Clemens, Samuel L. *The Complete Short Stories of Mark Twain.* Ed. Charles Neider. Garden City, N.Y.: Hanover House, 1957. 199–216.

———. *Mark Twain–Howells Letters: The Correspondence of Samuel L. Clemens and William D. Howells, 1872–1910.* Ed. Henry Nash Smith and William M. Gibson. Vol. 1. Cambridge, Mass.: Harvard UP, 1960.

Paine, Albert Bigelow. *Mark Twain: A Biography.* Vol 2. New York: Harper, 1912.

Wilson, James D. *A Reader's Guide to the Short Stories of Mark Twain.* Boston: G.K. Hall, 1987.

See also: Burlesque; Detective Fiction; Pinkerton, Allan

Stormfield, Captain

The fictitious character Captain Stormfield is based loosely on Captain Edgar Wakeman, on whose vessel, the steamship *America*, Twain sailed from San Francisco to the Isthmus of Panama on 15 December 1866. On his return to California in 1868 Twain sailed again with Wakeman. In the course of the voyages, Twain came to admire Wakeman. Many years later he published two works involving Captain Stormfield, "Extract from Captain Stormfield's Visit to Heaven" (*Harper's*, December 1907 and January 1908) and the longer book with the same title (1909). This is the last book of Twain's published before his death.

The figure of Captain Stormfield has a long genesis. He appears as Captain Ned Blakely in *Roughing It* (1872) and as Captain Hurricane Jones in "Some Rambling Notes of an Idle Excursion" (1877–1878). He appears in many of Twain's manuscript fragments from as early as the 1870s under the name of Captain Ben

Stormfield and Captain Eli Stormfield. Twain was especially interested in Wakeman's account of a dream in which he had visited heaven. To Wakeman, the visit seemed extremely real. Twain started to work the material into a story, he writes, in the early 1870s. In this version Twain initially called the captain Hurricane Jones but crossed out that name and put Stormfield in its place. Stormfield also appears in an unfinished novel that involves erecting a monument to Adam, the first man. Like Wakeman as Twain describes him, Stormfield is a straight-talking, clear-sighted, fearless sinner, unsure of his ultimate destination until he reaches heaven. Even then, he finds he has reached the wrong port of entry because of his determination on the way to race a comet bearing a cargo to the nether regions. Twain apparently found the captain very likeable since he named his house in Redding, Connecticut, Stormfield.

Many scholars find Captain Stormfield one of Twain's most attractive characters. Through him Twain satirizes the inadequacy of human religion and especially of human attempts to picture heaven in material terms. Simultaneously, Captain Stormfield is a sympathetic, wholly human, highly fallible character.

Richard Tuerk

BIBLIOGRAPHY

Clemens, Samuel L. *Extract from Captain Stormfield's Visit to Heaven.* New York: Harper, 1909.

Hill, Hamlin. *Mark Twain: God's Fool.* New York: Harper & Row, 1973.

Wecter, Dixon. Introduction. *Report from Paradise.* By Clemens. New York: Harper, 1952.

See also: Blakely, Captain Ned; *Extract from Captain Stormfield's Visit to Heaven*; Wakeman, Edgar

"Story of Mamie Grant, the Child-Missionary, The"

(1967)

Written in 1868 during Mark Twain's journey between San Francisco and New York and collected in *Mark Twain's Satires & Burlesques* (1967), this condensed burlesque relates the tale of Mamie Grant, a precocious nine-year-old religious enthusiast visiting her aunt and uncle. Fervent to the point of propelling any conversational remarks into fire-and-brimstone messages about the fate of mankind, Mamie becomes so concerned about the fortune of several strangers who visit her aunt and uncle's house that she ultimately destroys her uncle, leaving him destitute.

Speaking in highly inflated language, Mamie expresses her concern for mankind and its folly to her aunt and uncle, the census taker, newspaper collector, mortgage foreclosure agent, and a man owing her uncle a thousand dollars by paraphrasing the sermons of Sunday school pamphlets and temperance preachers. She incites each of them to forsake their present jobs and deliver religious tracts, while convincing them of the folly of their present errand. After she takes off to deliver her tracts to the poor and destitute, she returns to find that her uncle has been marked delinquent on his newspaper, which has been cancelled, has a black mark next to his name from the tax-collecting census, has failed to retrieve the thousand dollars he loaned, and is homeless as his mortgage has been foreclosed. Nevertheless, Mamie rests easily that night, saying "I have saved a paper carrier, a census bureau, a creditor and a debtor, and they will bless me forever. I have done a noble work today. I may yet see my poor little name in a beautiful Sunday school book . . ." (39).

Franklin Rogers notes that "Mamie Grant" bears striking resemblance to Elizabeth Stuart Phelps's book *The Gates Ajar* (1868), which consists of discussions about Christianity, death, and the nature of heaven between Mamie Grant and her "Auntie" Winifred Forceythe (*Satires & Burlesques* 31–32). Like Twain's Mamie, Phelps's character acts upon every feasible opportunity to launch into pontifications on religious matters. In an autobiographical dictation in 1906, however, Twain attributes a burlesque of Phelps's book to a draft of "Captain Stormfield's Visit to

Heaven." Rogers concludes that either Twain wrote two burlesques of *The Gates Ajar* or he confused "Mamie Grant" with an early version of "Captain Stormfield" (*Satires & Burlesques* 32).

Mamie's fanatical recitation of her Sunday school tracts affords Twain the opportunity to experiment with a twofold burlesque or, as Franklin Rogers explains, to work numerous condensed burlesques into the basic narrative (*Satires & Burlesques* 32). The central tale presents an unflattering view of religious fanaticism, illustrating the folly of rejecting fundamental needs in favor of grandiose words and ideas of missionaries. Mamie's summaries of her various Sunday school pamphlets and temperance ministers afford Twain the opportunity to burlesque specific ideas presented by such pamphlets and by leaders of the religious temperance movement, including Timothy Shay Arthur and John Ballantine Gough.

Christie Graves Hamric

BIBLIOGRAPHY

Clemens, Samuel L. *Mark Twain's Satires & Burlesques.* Ed. Franklin R. Rogers. Berkeley: U of California P, 1967. 31–39.

Rogers, Franklin R. *Mark Twain's Burlesque Patterns as Seen in the Novels and Narratives, 1855–1885.* Dallas: Southern Methodist UP, 1960.

See also: Burlesque; Condensed Novels; Phelps, Elizabeth Stuart

"Story of the Bad Little Boy Who Didn't Come to Grief, The"

(1865)

First published in the *Californian*, 23 December 1865, this story is an early criticism of simple-minded Sunday school morality and the coincidence of its plotting and moral retribution. Jim is a bad boy who gets away with schoolboy pranks, which, in Sunday school books, are summarily punished. At the end of his life he is "the infernalist wickedest scoundrel" and a legislator as a reward for his evil deeds, having ax-murdered his large family along the way.

The plotting here is neither subtle nor sophisticated, befitting the rough frontier audience of its original publication, but not the *Atlantic*, which refused to accept it. As Stone points out, the story is simply an extended joke with no effort to develop character or plot.

Ruth K. MacDonald

BIBLIOGRAPHY

Clemens, Samuel L. "The Story of the Bad Little Boy." *The Complete Short Stories of Mark Twain.* Ed. Charles Neider. Garden City, N.Y.: Doubleday, 1957. 6–9.

Stone, Albert E., Jr. *The Innocent Eye: Childhood in Mark Twain.* New Haven, Conn.: Yale UP, 1961.

See also: Boy Books; "Story of the Good Little Boy Who Did Not Prosper, The"

"Story of the Good Little Boy Who Did Not Prosper, The"

(1870)

Another exploration of the misleading, implausible plotting and consequences in Sunday school books, this story was more acceptable to eastern audiences than its companion "Story of the Bad Little Boy Who Didn't Come to Grief." It was reprinted in *Piccadilly Annual* (1870) and *Nast's Almanac* (1873), having first appeared in *Galaxy* (1870). The good boy tries to live right, according to the books, but finds that stray dogs, abused blind men, and recalcitrant schoolboys do not appreciate his ministrations and retaliate against him.

He dies, as do the good boys in his guide books, but unfortunately, he is blown up, rather than dying of consumption, and so gets neither the opportunity to deliver his parting words nor the funeral befitting such an exemplary life. An extended joke, featuring an incredible hero believing implausible literature, the good boy prefigures the prodigy in *Tom*

Sawyer (1876) who memorizes so many Bible verses that he loses his mind.

Ruth K. Macdonald

BIBLIOGRAPHY

Clemens, Samuel L. "The Story of the Good Little Boy." *The Complete Short Stories of Mark Twain.* Ed. Charles Neider. Garden City, N.Y.: Doubleday, 1957. 67–70.

Stone, Albert E., Jr. *The Innocent Eye: Childhood in Mark Twain's Imagination.* New Haven, Conn.: Yale UP, 1961.

See also: Boy Books; "Story of the Bad Little Boy Who Didn't Come to Grief, The"

"Story Without an End, A"
(1897)

Untitled by Mark Twain, "A Story Without an End" appeared during the author's lifetime only in *Following the Equator* (1897). Sometimes referred to as "A Delicately Improper Tale" (Emerson 206), the sketch, written probably in 1896, is a hoax Twain calls a "storiette." The anticlimactic joke resembling "Grandfather's Old Ram" victimizes readers, satirizing unrealistic expectations for happy endings and romantic forms inherently flawed (Covici 144). Readers from the beginning are asked to conclude it under rules given *after* the anticlimax.

Circumstances place shy John Brown—clothed above, naked below—in a buggy surrounded by four proper ladies, including his fiancée's mother, whom he must impress, reaching, as "Story Without an End" stops, for his lap robe. Its rules-restrictive sexual dilemma akin to "A Medieval Romance" (Baldanza 100), "Story Without an End" traps readers with a game (Wilson 28–29), warning of the nonending, teasing with sexual suggestions, enticing expectations of solution. Its fourth word announcing the game, "Story" is a humorous story (stressing storytelling manner) about writing stories (Charters and Sheidley 19), building resolved miniclimaxes

(threats to Brown's laprobe) to the unsolvable anticlimax.

Recalling Brown's impending exposure in the final paragraph, Twain merges joke, game, dilemma, storytelling, and sexual innuendo in the last-sentence challenge "to determine . . . how the thing came out." The reader-player-given rules (character consistency, happy ending) hinder resolution. Left dangling by the story and a train wreck curtailing its first telling, the reader faces a Brownian dilemma. The only option is to stop reading, leaving "Story" a storiette.

John H. Davis

BIBLIOGRAPHY

Baldanza, Frank. *Mark Twain: An Introduction and Interpretation.* New York: Barnes & Noble, 1961.

Charters, Ann, and William E. Sheidley. *Instructor's Manual to Accompany The Story and Its Writer: An Introduction to Short Fiction.* New York: St. Martin's, 1983. 19–20.

Clemens, Samuel L. *The Complete Short Stories of Mark Twain.* Ed. Charles Neider. Garden City, N.Y.: Hanover House, 1957. 343–349.

Covici, Pascal, Jr. *Mark Twain's Humor: The Image of a World.* Dallas: Southern Methodist UP, 1962.

Emerson, Everett. *The Authentic Mark Twain: A Literary Biography of Samuel L. Clemens.* Philadelphia: U of Pennsylvania P, 1984.

Wilson, James D. *A Reader's Guide to the Short Stories of Mark Twain.* Boston: G.K. Hall, 1987.

See also: Hoax; "Medieval Romance, A"

Stowe, Harriet Beecher
(1811–1896)

For years, Harriet Beecher Stowe was best known for *Uncle Tom's Cabin* (1852). Many readers, however, have also known and admired her other work, especially *The Minister's Wooing* (1859), *The Pearl of Orr's Island* (1862), and *Oldtown Folks* (1869). These have long been recognized as excellent studies in the psychology of the Calvinist legacy; with Stowe's other writings, they are now recognized as important for the study of nineteenth-century feminism as well.

Harriet and Calvin Stowe were neighbors of Olivia and Samuel Clemens in Hartford, and though Harriet Stowe's mind was slipping during this period, the Clemenses were appreciative of their neighbor's accomplishments. The family owned a variety of Stowe's works. According to Paul Baender's "Mark Twain and the Byron Scandal," prior to their move to Nook Farm, Twain had burlesqued Stowe's initial articles exposing Lord Byron's affair with his sister in a series of editorials for the Buffalo *Express*. Generally in favor of Stowe's stance, Twain, nonetheless, tried to exploit the situation for its humorous possibilities.

In *Mark Twain's Library* Alan Gribben has shown that Twain was interested in *Uncle Tom's Cabin* not only for its content, but also for its popularity, noting its many dramatic performances and comparing its tales to his own works. Twain also used Stowe's copyright problems about the book in his testimony to a congressional committee on copyright reform in 1906. References to "Sam Lawson," a character from Stowe's *Oldtown Folks*, appear in notes Twain made about English and American authors in 1888 and in his 1899 story "The Man That Corrupted Hadleyburg."

Susan K. Harris

BIBLIOGRAPHY

Andrews, Kenneth R. *Nook Farm: Mark Twain's Hartford Circle.* Cambridge, Mass.: Harvard UP, 1950.

Baender, Paul. "Mark Twain and the Byron Scandal." *American Literature* 30.4 (January 1959): 467–485.

Gerson, Noel B. *Harriet Beecher Stowe: A Biography.* New York: Praeger, 1976.

Gribben, Alan. *Mark Twain's Library: A Reconstruction.* 2 vols. Boston: G.K. Hall, 1980.

Jakoubek, Robert E. *Harriet Beecher Stowe.* New York: Chelsea House, 1989.

"Strange Dream, A"
(1866)

"A Strange Dream" first appeared in the New York *Saturday Press* (2 June 1866). About a year later it appeared in Mark Twain's first book, *The Celebrated Jumping Frog of Calaveras County and Other Sketches* (1 May 1867). Inspired by stories about secret burial sites of Hawaiian kings, Twain's first dream story is a hoax, written in Hawaii (April 1866) and published the day before Twain arrived at Kilauea Volcano, its setting. Distrusting conflicting stories (*Hawaii* 278), Twain ridicules native, tourist, narrator, and reader gullibility about stories and dreams. Hearing Kamehameha I's body will reappear when certain conditions occur, reading about dream revelations, then dreaming that he follows a mysterious figure beneath Kilauea to an easily moved boulder covering the warrior king's bones, the narrator decides he has been appointed to solve the mystery. Finding all as in his recurring dream, he believes it a revelation. Suggesting the hoax are his stiff syntactical exclamation, his labor in moving the boulder, and anticlimactically positioned "awe," "sank," "darkness . . . spirit" in his first utterance after rolling it aside and finding no bones. The joke becomes obvious as he switches to humorous colloquialisms and exaggeration, concluding, after implying otherwise, that dreams are undependable.

John H. Davis

BIBLIOGRAPHY

Clemens, Samuel L. *Mark Twain's Letters from Hawaii.* Ed. A. Grove Day. New York: Appleton-Century, 1966.

———. *Mark Twain's Letters, Volume 1 (1853–1866).* Ed. Edgar M. Branch, Michael B. Frank, and Kenneth M. Sanderson. Berkeley: U of California P, 1988.

———. *Mark Twain's Notebooks & Journals, Volume I (1855–1873).* Ed. Frederick Anderson, Michael B. Frank, and Kenneth M. Sanderson. Berkeley: U of California P, 1975.

———. "A Strange Dream." *The Celebrated Jumping Frog of Calaveras County, and Other Sketches.* Ed. John Paul. New York: Webb, 1867. 182–193.

―――. *The Works of Mark Twain: Early Tales & Sketches, Volume 1 (1851–1864)*. Ed. Edgar M. Branch and Robert H. Hirst. Berkeley: U of California P, 1979. 33–53, 501–546.

Paine, Albert Bigelow. *Mark Twain: A Biography*. 3 vols. 1912. Rpt. New York: Chelsea House, 1980. 318–320.

See also: Dreams; Hoax

"Stupendous Procession, The"
(1972)

This short work, written in 1901, is essentially a letter written to the new century modeled on Queen Victoria's funeral procession. As such, it marks the end of an era. Clemens describes a series of allegorical parade groups marching past. Each image reflects the nature of what is described. For instance, "Christendom" is seen as a "majestic matron in flowing robes and drenched with blood." Her honor guards are "Missionaries and German, French, Russian, and British soldiers laden with loot." She is followed by a long procession of American symbols such as the American Eagle, "ashamed, bedraggled, moulting, one foot chained," and the Statue of Liberty, "enlightening the world, torch extinguished and reversed."

Stuart Kenny

BIBLIOGRAPHY

Clemens, Samuel L. *Mark Twain's Fables of Man*. Ed. John S. Tuckey. Berkeley: U of California P, 1972. 403–419.

Style, Mark Twain's

Mark Twain's style deserves credit for a significant portion of his position in American letters. His innovative word use, relative syntactical simplicity, and sensitive depiction of conversation pioneered new standards of literary excellence. In addition, his faithfulness to detail, his aptness of metaphor, and his literary humor distinguish his style.

Twain believed the key to style was vocabulary. In his own writing, he wrestled vocabulary away from the British idiom that dominated American literature before him and penned his own. In *A Mark Twain Lexicon* Ramsay and Emberson assert Twain used over 5,000 Americanisms in his writings (viii). They also find more than 4,000 words Twain appears to have been the first to use in print (lvii). Many of these word choices reflect Twain's special interests in sports and games, piloting and mining, business and printing. Many others come from spoken American English. But Twain also coined new uses for old words by using articles, prepositions, conjunctions, and auxiliaries in a distinctively American way; for example, "the most anxious for to hang a nigger" (*Adventures of Huckleberry Finn*, 1885). He also added adverbs to our language by adding -*ly* to verbals and adjectives and by using traditional adjectives as adverbs, as we do in common speech.

Hybrid and action verbs form another strain in Twain's style. These verb uses have two distinct effects on Twain's style. First, they create figures of speech, giving the prose opportunities for more concrete expression by transforming conventional nouns into unconventional verbs. They personify animals more effectively and offer greater opportunity for alliteration. They also assist Twain in constructing metaphors; for example, the denouement to "The Man That Corrupted Hadleyburg" (1899) begins "suspicion flamed up into conviction," giving weight to Twain's implication that the tempting bag of gold has demonic power. Second, these verbs simplify his syntax. Avoiding passive constructions and verbal qualifications allows Twain to bring his subject and verb into close proximity. The engine of his sentence thus becomes an integral unit and more easily supports longer sentences and more complex constructions.

Twain's style, however, is not simply the product of new word uses. His syntactical habits include parallelism, sentence fragments, and eternally varying construction. Twain rarely used similarly constructed sentences consecutively without clear purpose. He does repeat his syntax in single sentences broken into similar parts with semicolons, a technique he uses often in the way he uses lists: to leave a photographic record of a scene. He also uses these serial sentences to pivot a change in perception. When in "Old Times on the Mississippi" (1875) another cub outsmarts Twain for some female's attention, he writes "That girl couldn't seem to have enough of that pitiful 'herp' . . . ; but little I cared; I loathed her, anyway." His sentences, even his long and complicated ones, have a sleek power derived from his judicious use of qualifying phrases.

This power finds its best use in incident and description. Twain's paragraphs about nature, seen to best advantage in *Roughing It* (1872) and *HF*, have a compact drive. Rather than recounting scenes as they pass or as the eye wanders over them, Twain captures in these passages an instantaneous flash of nature, as though the scene simply exists and is not perceived and recorded.

Seldom, however, does he employ a paragraph of description in the recounting of an incident. Incident is Twain's most certain narrative block, and he constructs the vast majority of his incidents out of the same fodder. One person will best another because of a superior knowledge of the hidden rules of the game being played. Tom Sawyer's whitewashing, the Connecticut Yankee's dinner with Marco and company, Roxy's confession to Tom in *Pudd'nhead Wilson* (1894)—in these typical and memorable incidents the favored characters either win or lose based on the accuracy of their perception, not on their power or skill.

This relative sameness of incident contributes to Twain's well-documented difficulty in sustaining a book-length narrative. Twain's early experience with and later stage use of what he termed "the humorous story" ("How to Tell a Story," 1895) no doubt trained him in shorter narrative. To him, these stories remain at essence oral, even after they are written down. He learned how to tell stories by listening carefully to how others spoke. Though this limited him in his efforts at sustained narrative, his attention paid dividends in his incomparable ability to render dialogue.

Dialogue is one of Twain's greatest stylistic accomplishments. In a departure from the techniques of storytellers preceding him, Twain creates dialect by word choice and cadence rather than by peculiar spelling and syntax. *Huckleberry Finn* appears to most readers to be written in dialect, but a random review shows the majority of the novel is grammatically and orthographically correct. A comparison with the gossips' talk in chapter 41 shows what Twain could have done throughout the book, and what his predecessors did. Instead, by faithfully rendering slang and by manipulating prepositions, articles, and verb endings to adjust the rhythm of the book's language, Twain creates the impression of dialect without resorting to techniques that present dialect as substandard English.

Twain's faithfulness to detail has earned him an undeserved reputation as a practitioner of realism. Much of his work, in fact, falls closer to fantasy, more so in his later years, though his early penchant for exaggeration shows a lifelong disinterest in the bounds of lived existence. His attention to detail, though, is such that his worlds seem real, even in pure fantasy. This detail even appears in his metaphors, which tend to the concrete rather than the abstract, such as his observation that "Cauliflower is nothing but cabbage with a college education" (*PW*).

His humor adds to this sense, springing more from an incongruity of detail than from absurdity, from the homeliness of the rendition rather than in the situation itself. This is, in fact, the peculiar strength in Twain's humor: the absurd situation, Jim's prolonged captivity, for example, becomes pathos, while skillful language portrays it in a way that makes us laugh. Twain's mastery of style, the surface of literature, reveals the undisturbed core of literature—its passion, drama, and insight.

Andrew Jay Hoffman

BIBLIOGRAPHY

Covici, Pascal, Jr. *Mark Twain's Humor: The Image of a World*. Dallas: Southern Methodist UP, 1962.

Gibson, William M. *The Art of Mark Twain*. New York: Oxford UP, 1976.

Krause, Sydney J. *Mark Twain as Critic*. Baltimore: Johns Hopkins UP, 1967.

Lynn, Kenneth S. *Mark Twain and Southwestern Humor*. Boston: Little, Brown, 1959.

McKay, Janet Holmgren. *Narration and Discourse in American Realistic Fiction*. Philadelphia: U of Pennsylvania P, 1982.

Ramsay, Robert L., and Frances G. Emberson. *A Mark Twain Lexicon*. New York: Russell and Russell, 1963.

Sewell, David R. *Mark Twain's Languages: Discourse, Dialogue, and Linguistic Variety*. Berkeley: U of California P, 1987.

Sloane, David E.E. *Mark Twain as a Literary Comedian*. Baton Rouge: Louisiana State UP, 1979.

Smith, Henry Nash. *Mark Twain: The Development of a Writer*. Cambridge, Mass.: Harvard UP, 1962.

Wiggins, Robert A. *Mark Twain: Jackleg Novelist*. Seattle: U of Washington P, 1964.

See also: Dialect; Language; Point of View; Rhetorical Forms

Subscription Publication

Although it had antecedents in the pre-Civil War period, the heyday of subscription publishing in the United States occurred during the last third of the nineteenth century. An army of Civil War veterans, and others, made their way into small towns and rural areas, armed with a prospectus, a sample showing the cover, some illustrations, and some sample pages from a book being offered for sale "by subscription only." Prospective buyers signed the prospectus, indicating which binding they preferred and agreeing to pay the subscription agent when he returned on a second visit to deliver the book. Predominantly, the books were Civil War histories, biblical commentaries, and legal and medical self-help books, those, as Huck Finn says, "which told you all about what to do if a body was sick or dead." Expensive by comparison with typical trade-publication books, subscription volumes tended to be large, profusely illustrated with poor woodcuts, and cheaply bound: they needed to appear to be a bargain value to the "farmers and mechanics" who purchased them.

In addition, legal cases established that subscription books could not be sold in bookstores, insuring a captive audience and producing a hostile and antagonistic response from trade publishers and bookstores. Nevertheless, the mechanics of subscription publishing included "dumping" books into bookstores once the subscription market had been exhausted. As a result of the antagonism, authors of subscription books suffered the ridicule of the literary establishment for the commercialization of their works.

Mark Twain published all of his major nineteenth-century titles by subscription. The American Publishing Company printed *The Innocents Abroad* (1869), *Roughing It* (1872), *The Gilded Age* (1873), *Sketches, New and Old* (1875), *The Adventures of Tom Sawyer* (1876), *A Tramp Abroad* (1880), and in the 1890s *Pudd'nhead Wilson* (1894) and *Following the Equator* (1897). A subscription branch of James R. Osgood marketed *The Prince and the Pauper* (1882) and *Life on the Mississippi* (1883); and Mark Twain's own subscription house, Charles L. Webster and Company, published *Adventures of Huckleberry Finn* (1885) and *A Connecticut Yankee in King Arthur's Court* (1889). The failure of the last house contributed to Mark Twain's own personal bankruptcy in 1894.

As he became more experienced in the details of subscription publishing, Twain took a commanding role in the advertising and marketing of his subscription volumes, choosing passages and illustrations to go in the prospectuses, recommending the appropriate timing for publication and "dumping," and nominating other authors and titles for consideration. His commercial instincts, for better or worse, conditioned his decisions about subject matter, appropriate illustrations, and the propriety of material for his audience. He was to become the spokesman for "the masses," but he was also formed and constrained by his remarkable instinct for what that audience desired in its literature.

It is impossible to guess what Mark Twain's literary reputation would now be had he not, fortuitously, decided to accept Elisha Bliss's invitation to publish the volume that would become *The Innocents Abroad* by subscription only. It is certain, however, that his instantaneous popularity with what is now called mass culture would never have been achieved, and that his folk-legend status would undoubtedly be smaller than it is. He created a popular-culture audience, and it, in turn, contributed to the creation of Mark Twain.

Hamlin Hill

BIBLIOGRAPHY

Clemens, Samuel L. *Mark Twain's Letters to His Publishers, 1867–1894.* Ed. Hamlin Hill. Berkeley: U of California P, 1967.

See also: American Publishing Company; Bankruptcy; Bliss, Elisha; Business; Illustrators; Webster and Company, Charles L.

Swift, Jonathan
(1667–1745)

A clergyman, pamphleteer, and satirist, born in Dublin of English parents, Jonathan Swift was educated at Trinity college, Dublin, and at Oxford. His interests were politics and literature, but circumstances forced him into a career in the church, and his appointment in 1713 as dean of St. Patrick's in Dublin, a Tory political prize, bound him to Ireland. Swift was not popular among the Irish and preferred life in London where, until the 1720s, he spent much of his time enjoying the company of his literary friends Pope, Addison, and Steele. In 1724 Swift published the "Drapier Letters" wherein he sided with Irish nationalists on a political issue and gained sudden popularity. This helped him to make his peace with Ireland and eventually accept it as home. It was during this period of transition to Ireland

that he wrote *Gulliver's Travels* (1726) and "A Modest Proposal" (1729), the two works most relevant to Mark Twain studies.

In 1869 Mark Twain wrote his wife Olivia Langdon Clemens that he was rereading *Gulliver's Travels*, a book he had first read in his youth. The direct influence of that work on Mark Twain's writing has been amply demonstrated by several studies that have combed his works for references to Lilliputian names, places, and themes. Alan Gribben's *Mark Twain's Library: A Reconstruction* lists some twenty specific references to *Gulliver's Travels* found in Mark Twain's works.

The influence of *Gulliver's Travels* on Mark Twain's satire is frequently mentioned by Mark Twain scholars and critics who have compared Twain's and Swift's use of such literary devices as irony, parody, allegory, burlesque, ingenue traveler-narrator, and the like; some compare them as social critics and reformers, and still others compare their capacities for strong feeling and their relative degrees of cynicism and disillusionment.

Fred Weldon

BIBLIOGRAPHY

Baetzhold, Howard G. *Mark Twain and John Bull: The British Connection.* Bloomington: Indiana UP, 1970.

Brooks, Van Wyck. *The Ordeal of Mark Twain.* Rev. ed. New York: Dutton, 1933.

Fatout, Paul. *Mark Twain on the Lecture Circuit.* Bloomington: Indiana UP, 1960.

Ferguson, DeLancey. *Mark Twain: Man and Legend.* Indianapolis: Bobbs-Merrill, 1943.

Gribben, Alan. *Mark Twain's Library: A Reconstruction.* 2 vols. Boston: G.K. Hall, 1980.

Paine, Albert Bigelow. *Mark Twain: A Biography.* 3 vols. New York: Harper, 1912.

Passon, Richard H. "Twain and 18th Century Satire: The Ingenu Narrator in *Huckleberry Finn.*" *Mark Twain Journal* 21.4 (Fall 1983): 33–36.

Rogers, Franklin R. *Mark Twain's Burlesque Patterns as Seen in the Novels and Narratives, 1855–1885.* Dallas: Southern Methodist UP, 1960.

Taylor, Coley B. *Mark Twain's Margins on Thackeray's "Swift."* Norwood, Penn.: Norwood, 1976.

Walsh, Kathleen. "Rude Awakenings and Swift Recoveries: The Problem of Reality in Mark Twain's

'The Great Dark' and 'Three Thousand Years Among the Microbes.'" *American Literary Realism 1870–1910* 21.1 (Fall 1988): 19–28.

See also: Satire

Switzerland

The Confederatio Helvetica (Switzerland), especially its German-speaking cantons, comprised one of Samuel L. Clemens's favorite lands. He first went there 1 August 1878, traversing the alpine country from Schaffhausen in the north to the central canton of Luzern, thence to Zermatt in the south, and to Lausanne and Geneva in the southwest on a month-long excursion with the Reverend Joseph Twichell and, during the tour's final weeks, with Olivia Clemens and their three daughters. Together with his sojourn in Germany in 1878–1879, this Swiss odyssey was immortalized in *A Tramp Abroad* (1880), one of Mark Twain's best travel books and still his most popular work in that genre in Europe today.

Clemens returned for three weeks in September 1891, spending several days each in Interlaken, Weggis, and Vitznau en route to a ten-day boat trip he took down the Rhône River from Lac Léman (Lake Geneva). This journey resulted in a 174-page abortive travelogue, "The Innocents Adrift," and a humorous article, "Switzerland, The Cradle of Liberty," one of six travel letters Twain wrote in 1891 for the New York *Sun* and McClure's Syndicate. This article concludes with a humorous anecdote about a vulgar German-American tourist who encounters the King of Greece in a Swiss railway car and, not recognizing the monarch, offers him a "better" job as foreman in a brewery back home. Both pieces (the former in an attenuated version) were posthumously published in *Europe and Elsewhere* (1923).

Clemens was briefly again in Luzern (Lucerne) in late June and early July 1892 en route to Italy. Five years later, on 18 July 1897, the entire Clemens family with Katy

Leary, their housekeeper, began a two-month sojourn at Villa Brühlegg in the picturesque village of Weggis on the northeast shore of the Vierwaldstättersee (Lake Lucerne) at the foot of the 6,000-foot Rigi-Kulm with snow-capped Pilatus looming in the distance across the lake. Still mourning the death of Susy a year earlier, the family lived quietly here until 19 September 1897, when they entrained for their twenty-month residence in Austria. In an effort to resume his normal summer work habits, Twain engaged a room in the Villa Tannen, about a mile along the lakeshore from the Villa Brühlegg, where he secluded himself from family activities while writing.

Most of what he commenced writing in Weggis, however, was left unfinished or put aside until later. An exception was the poem "In Memoriam Olivia Susan Clemens," written on the first anniversary of Susy's death and published in *Harper's Monthly*. But the four chapters he wrote in Weggis of "Tom Sawyer's Conspiracy," a novelette of some 30,000 words on which he also worked sporadically in Vienna, the opening chapters of a novel to be called "Which Was the Dream?" reworked into the somewhat longer fragment, "The Great Dark" the following summer in Kaltenleutgeben, and another fictional fragment, "Hellfire Hotchkiss," remained for posthumous collections published by the Mark Twain Project in Berkeley, California, between 1962 and 1973. The despondency that blocked the writer's creative imagination and sapped his energy during his stay in Weggis may be glimpsed from the brief confessional piece he completed there, "In My Bitterness," in which Twain rails at a Deity who "gives you a wife and children you adore, only that through the spectacle of the wanton shame and miseries which He will inflict upon them He may tear the palpitating heart out of your breast and slap you in the face with it."

From Twain's published notebook of his first Swiss sojourn (1878) and the still unpublished one of his Weggis summer, it is clear Twain greatly appreciated Switzerland's scenic beauties—its lofty peaks with their breathtaking prospects, its verdurous countryside, its myriad glacial lakes, and its cuckoo-clock architecture—but he regarded the Swiss as stolid, unimaginative, almost humorless though nonetheless "happy contented animals" who seemed oblivious to their Edenlike surroundings. In sum, however, it must be said that Twain's experiences in Switzerland, no matter how pleasant or diverting, did not exercise a formative influence on his creative mind or intellectual development of the kind and extent he derived from such other European countries as Great Britain, France, and, above all, Germany and Austria-Hungary.

Carl Dolmetsch

BIBLIOGRAPHY

Clemens, Samuel L. "The Innocents Adrift." *Europe and Elsewhere*. By Clemens. Ed. Albert B. Paine. New York: Harper, 1923. 129–174.

———. *Mark Twain's Notebooks & Journals, Volume II (1877–1883)*. Ed. Frederick Anderson, Lin Salamo, and Bernard L. Stein. Berkeley: U of California P, 1975.

———. "Switzerland, The Cradle of Liberty." *"What Is Man?" and Other Essays*. By Clemens. Ed. Albert B. Paine. New York: Harper, 1917. 193–208.

———. *A Tramp Abroad*. Vols. 13–14 of *The Writings of Mark Twain*. New York: Collier, 1918.

Dolmetsch, Carl. *"Our Famous Guest": Mark Twain in Vienna*. Athens: U of Georgia P, 1992.

Scott, Arthur L. *"The Innocents Adrift* Edited by Mark Twain's Official Biographer." *Publications of the Modern Language Association* 78 (June 1963): 230–227.

———. *Mark Twain at Large*. Chicago: Henry Regnery, 1969.

See also: Europe; Germany; *Tramp Abroad, A*

T

Taine, Hippolyte
(1828–1893)

Called "one of the most original thinkers of the nineteenth century," France's Hippolyte Taine was a major force in directing the literature of his time, in the United States as well as in Europe, toward realism and naturalism. As a philosopher, he was convinced that truth could be approached only inductively, that is, through the careful consideration of particular facts. As a historian of France's ancient regime, he filled his pages with countless examples of the poverty and oppression suffered by the underclass and the extravagant excesses of the ruling class. As a critic, he insisted that literature must concern itself with exact representation "of all those appearances by which man manifests himself," for only through homely details could a reader's "sympathetic imagination" be touched. By the same token, he regarded the literature of the previous century, with its romantic and idealistic blurrings of reality, as unhealthy.

The profound and pervasive influence of Taine on Mark Twain's thought and writing is perhaps obscured by the fact that Twain did not call himself a realist or even use the term realism. That fact is especially curious when we consider that Twain was the friend and protégé of William Dean Howells (1837–1920) during the early 1870s when Howells, through his reading of Taine, completed his doctrine of realism and began a lifetime of advocating it. Twain's avoidance of the term cannot be attributed to ignorance of Taine's work. He, too, read Taine in the early 1870s, discussed him with Howells, and gratefully accepted Howells's Tainean editorial advice (e.g., "Stick to actual fact and character . . . and give things in *detail*"). Certainly Twain *practiced* realism in much of his work, and in "What Paul Bourget Thinks of Us" (1895) he wrote a lucid and penetrating discussion of realism without using the term. Twain's declining to call himself a realist—or to nestle within the confines of any literary category—was the act of an exploratory spirit.

His debt to Taine, nevertheless, can be judged by the way that the stratified society of Taine's *Ancient Regime* (1876) is reflected in *The Prince and the Pauper* (1882) and *A Connecticut Yankee* (1889) and particularly by the many borrowings of detail and incident. In *The Prince and the Pauper*, for example, the royal court of England is drawn from Taine's description of the court of the Louis, and Twain's menacing English vagrants are closely akin to Taine's "refractory" French beggars. Moreover, the deterministic philosophy that Twain developed in his last decades, along with his growing conviction that man, along with the other animals, was a creature of nature, echoes Taine's philosophy, at the same time expressing major tenets of literary naturalism.

Sherwood Cummings

BIBLIOGRAPHY

Cummings, Sherwood. *Mark Twain and Science: Adventures of a Mind.* Baton Rouge: Louisiana State UP, 1988.

Gribben, Alan. *Mark Twain's Library: A Reconstruction.* 2 vols. Boston: G.K. Hall, 1980.

Weinstein, Leo. *Hippolyte Taine.* New York: Twayne, 1972.

See also: Naturalism; Realism

Talmage, T[homas] DeWitt
(1832–1902)

Thomas DeWitt Talmage was an American clergyman and lecturer who achieved fame because of his flamboyant style of preaching. As minister of the Central Presbyterian Church of Brooklyn, New York (1869–1894), he drew larger crowds than any other minister in America. *Crumbs Swept Up* (1870) and *Everyday Religion* (1875) are notable collections of his sermons.

In 1870 Talmage sparked the ire of Mark Twain by suggesting that working men, because they emitted strong, distasteful smells,

should not be allowed to worship with the "uncommon" congregations. Twain's caustic response was "About Smells" (1870), a piece for the *Galaxy* magazine in which he suggested that Talmage would not have associated with Christ's original apostles because some of them would have been tainted by the odor of fish.

Twain often satirized Talmage as an example of religious hypocrisy. In "The Second Advent" (written 1881), the most bitter satire, a "St. Talmage" betrays the Savior for thirty pieces of silver and his own life.

Craig Albin

BIBLIOGRAPHY

Kaplan, Justin. *Mr. Clemens and Mark Twain.* New York: Simon & Schuster, 1966.

Long, E. Hudson. *Mark Twain Handbook.* New York: Hendricks House, 1957.

Meltzer, Milton. *Mark Twain Himself: A Pictorial Biography Produced by Milton Meltzer.* New York: Crowell, 1960.

"Talmage, Thomas DeWitt." *Dictionary of American Biography.* Vol. 18. New York: Scribner, 1936. 287–288.

See also: "Second Advent, The"

Taylor, Bayard
(1825–1878)

Globe-trotter, novelist, translator, diplomat, dramatist, journalist, lecturer, bon vivant, raconteur—Bayard Taylor was all of these in his fifty-three years. At nineteen he published his first book of poems and began a two-year jaunt about Europe. The result was *Views Afoot* (1846), the first of a dozen books of travel. The peak of his literary reputation came with his translation of Goethe's *Faust* (2 vols., 1870–1871), then widely regarded as the best English rendering.

Taylor and Twain were casual friends and fellow passengers when Taylor sailed in 1878 to take up his post as U.S. minister to Germany. He died in Berlin after eight months in office. In his notebook Twain recorded recollections of Taylor on the voyage, noting his geniality, his remarkable memory, and his facility in a variety of foreign languages, concluding, "He was a very lovable man."

Lynn Altenbernd

BIBLIOGRAPHY

Beatty, Richard Croom. *Bayard Taylor: Laureate of the Gilded Age.* Norman: U of Oklahoma P, 1936.

Cary, Richard. *The Genteel Circle: Bayard Taylor and His New York Friends.* Cornell Studies in American History, Literature, and Folklore, No. 5. Ithaca, N.Y.: Cornell UP, 1952.

Krumpelmann, John T. *Bayard Taylor and German Letters.* Hamburg: Cram, de Gruyter, 1959.

Schultz, John Richie. *The Unpublished Letters of Bayard Taylor In the Huntington Library.* San Marino, Calif.: Huntington Library, 1937.

Taylor, Bayard. *Life and Letters of Bayard Taylor.* Ed. Marie Hanson-Taylor and Horace E. Scudder. 2 vols. Boston: Houghton-Mifflin, 1884.

Wermuth, Paul Charles. *Bayard Taylor.* New York: Twayne, 1973.

Technology, Mark Twain and

Mark Twain's attitude toward technology can best be described as ambivalent. However, he seemed to understand that its power came from human sources and was cumulative in nature. In a rejected speech for a "Typothetae" dinner in 1886 Twain tied the development of science and its accompanying technology to the invention of movable type, that is, the ability of man to communicate more readily and conserve his ideas more effectively. This ability to share collectively in learning became a "star-sun" from which "divergent threads of light stretch down through the centuries . . . to each and every precious and wonderful achievement of man's inventive genius which goes to make up today the sum of what we rightly call the most extraordinary age the world has ever seen." He did not doubt the ability of technology to enhance man's life through increased convenience; he merely held out that the moral cost of some of the advancements might be too high.

In his personal life Twain showed a continual fascination with technology's machines.

When he had his new Hartford home built on Farmington Avenue in 1874, it had a central gas furnace and a telephone, among other modern items. He claimed that each was a first. Even though Twain lauded these inventions, the gas company was the recipient of his heat when they failed to deliver adequate fuel, and he kept a "grade card" (which was sent in at the end of each month) on "how [the phone company] was doing" in his phone booth off the entry hall.

He was a prolific investor in the new inventions that were dumped upon the public by the scientific frenzy of the age. A short list of speculations include a steam generator, a steam pulley, an envelope maker, a machine telegraph, an engraver, a carpet pattern machine, a special telescope, plasmon (a food additive), and an advanced cash register. His own inventions included a history game, the self-pasting scrapbook (which did make a profit), a spiral hatpin, a calendar watch fob, and a self-adjusting vest strap.

The most obvious expression of Twain's interest in technology was his investment of some $300,000 in the infamous Paige typesetter. The prospect of participating in the first advancement related to movable type for four centuries certainly intrigued him. Moreover, the prospect of receiving some of the "millions" he believed the machine would generate made him ecstatic. Had it been successful, two of his greatest desires could have been satisfied simultaneously. From 1885 through 1894 he averaged putting between $3,000 and $4,000 per month into new machines.

Even more significant than Twain's personal interest in technology, however, was his use of it literarily. Many of his works are enhanced by his abundant readings of technological research and shaped by his feelings toward machines and the progress they produced.

The earliest incorporation of technology reveals a somewhat benign attitude; primarily the machine provides transportation without serious challenges to the environment or to the social milieu. The steamer *Quaker City* of *The Innocents Abroad* (1869) provides the means for the excursion to the old world but does not threaten its order or historicity.

The Gilded Age (1873), a burlesque of corruption in politics and business, presents the steamboat differently. Here the machine becomes a means of death and destruction, personally and economically. When the *Amaranth* blows up, it destroys both human life and life savings. Railroads, which join the steamboats as symbols of progress, also produce as much disappointment as they do hope. Railroad companies become the progenitors of land speculation gone amuck and the political corruption that accompanies it. Later, *Adventures of Huckleberry Finn* (1885) extends this sense of danger produced by machines. As Huck and Jim float naturally down the Mississippi, they are run over by a steamboat, escaping somewhat miraculously with their lives, though the raft is destroyed.

No work depicts the potential horror of technology more poignantly than *A Connecticut Yankee in King Arthur's Court* (1889). Electricity, a power capable of driving seemingly limitless technology, portends a devastation that is truly appalling. Hank's role as gunsmith for the Colt firearms factory at the beginning of the novel sets a fearful tone from the outset. His later appropriation of electrical power as a weapon of war predicts technology's greatest danger. Already rifles, a sometimes beneficent machine, had been adapted for war purposes with horrific results. But when Hank becomes boss in a primitive world without any technology, he is free to use all of his scientific knowledge, regardless of its initial innocent application, as a weapon of destruction. The results are revulsive, and the fear of such applications becomes haunting.

Pudd'nhead Wilson (1894) offers another example of Twain's use of technology, but one less frightening. The ability to "read" fingerprints captured Twain's imagination when he first discovered it. His use of the technique, therefore, as the hinge upon which to turn the plot of *Pudd'nhead* is not surprising. This capability is a perfect response to the problem of mistaken identity and provides protection against the foibles of man's cruelty.

Twain attempted other works that dealt more specifically with the idea of scientific experimentation; presenting attempts to both produce and use the benefits of technology. In the play *Colonel Sellers* (written 1874) the Colonel relies upon knowledge he supposedly gained reading "European Scientific Magazines" to cover his lack of funds to provide heat for his family. When the door falls from his stove accidentally, a lit candle is discovered in the middle of it. "What one wants is the appearance of heat," he explains, citing the magazines as evidence. In order to capitalize upon the Colonel's profitability and popularity, Twain worked on a new play for him with William Dean Howells sporadically from 1880 through 1883 and under different titles that suggest his interest in science and technology: *Orme's Motor* and *The Steam Generator*. The finished version became *Colonel Sellers as a Scientist* (1883).

One of the sequels to *Tom Sawyer* conceives of Tom as a detective (1896), and one of the earlier plays was *Cap'n Simon Wheeler, the Amateur Detective* (written 1877). Both pieces exploit ideas of science assisting in detective work, similar to, but much less successful than, Sherlock Holmes.

As Twain approached the twentieth century, a century that surely faced an ever increasing dependence upon a technology and its concomitant evil of dehumanization, he became increasingly pessimistic toward the machine age. As expressed in the subtitle to *What Is Man?* (1906), he became fearful that such forces could lead to "Man the Machine." Perhaps an even greater insight into his sense of fright of this new era is to be found in two late science-fiction stories. Both pieces present the protagonist as a microcosm awash in a miniature world. "The Great Dark" (written 1898, published 1962) presents man's life as it exists while trapped in a drop of water. "Three Thousand Years Among the Microbes" (written 1905, published 1967) presents a miniaturized narrator encapsulated in the body of a diseased tramp.

Twain ultimately joined ranks with those who came to believe that technology proffered a greater potential for destruction than it did for benefit.

Jerry W. Thomason

BIBLIOGRAPHY

Clemens, Samuel L. *The Science Fiction of Mark Twain.* Ed. David Ketterer. Hamden, Conn.: Archon, 1984.

Cummings, Sherwood. *Mark Twain and Science: Adventures of a Mind.* Baton Rouge: Louisiana State UP, 1988.

Foner, Philip S. *Mark Twain: Social Critic.* New York: International Publishers, 1958.

Lauber, John. *The Inventions of Mark Twain.* New York: Hill and Wang, 1990.

Marx, Leo. *The Machine in the Garden: Technology and the Pastoral Ideal in America.* New York: Oxford UP, 1964.

Smith, Henry Nash. *Mark Twain: The Development of a Writer.* Cambridge, Mass.: Harvard UP, 1962.

See also: Business; *Connecticut Yankee in King Arthur's Court, A*; Science

Teller, Charlotte

(b. 1876)

Clemens corresponded briefly with Charlotte Teller (née Charlotte Teller Johnson) after learning at a meeting in 1906 for the support of Russian revolutionaries that she was writing a play about Joan of Arc. Teller, living in a rooming house for political writers at 3 Fifth Avenue in New York City, was a close neighbor when Clemens later moved back to 21 Fifth Avenue. Gossip of romance, possibly started by Teller or Clemens's secretary, Isabel Lyon, prompted Clemens to ask Teller to move. She refused.

Teller wrote a novel, *The Cage* (1907), about the labor movement among emigrants. Later as Mrs. Charlotte Hirsch, she published *Higginbotham* (a play, 1916) and *The Diary of an Expectant Mother* (1917). Under the name of John Brangwyn, she wrote two books,

Everybody's Paris (1935) and *Reasons for France* (1939).

Ira Royals, Jr.

BIBLIOGRAPHY

Hill, Hamlin. *Mark Twain: God's Fool.* New York: Harper & Row, 1973.

See also: Lyon, Isabel

Tennessee Land

This tract of land was located in Fentress County, Tennessee, consisting of around 75,000 acres. Its purchase and disposition forms a major plot element in *The Gilded Age* (1873) and was a concern of the Clemens family for much of the nineteenth century.

John Marshall Clemens's most significant act while living in East Tennessee was his purchase of some 75,000 (the figure in *The Gilded Age*) to 100,000 acres (the figure stated in a footnote to *Mark Twain's Autobiography*) of Fentress County land in the belief that it would eventually make his heirs fabulously wealthy. Purchased over a period of about twelve years in parcels seldom larger than 5,000 acres, the land was bought for about $400–$500.

In the novel Jamestown becomes "Obedstown" and Si Hawkins goes through the elder Clemens's experience of buying 75,000 acres of land before moving to Missouri. Hawkins dreams that the land will eventually sell at $1,000 per acre, a total of $75 million, and in his last words cautions his family never to lose sight of "the Tennessee Land." Later a bill is introduced in Congress calling for the government to purchase 65,000 acres of the land at a price of $3 million, so that Knobs Industrial University, a school for training blacks in the sciences, might be established there—despite the fact that Fentress County was almost 100 percent white. The bill fails to pass, and Si Hawkins's son Washington lets the land be sold for taxes, declaring that he is "done with that [land] forever and forever."

Over the years the Clemens family made numerous attempts to sell the real Tennessee Land, a matter that Sam could hardly speak of without becoming intemperate. "It is Orion's duty to sell that land," he once declared, adding that "if he lets it be sold for taxes, all his religion will not wipe out the sin." Later Sam would tell Orion never to ask his "advice, opinion, or consent about that hated property." Orion made various trips to Fentress County to see about the land.

The Fentress County property was mostly disposed of in the 1870s and 1880s by Jane and Orion Clemens, who received from ten to fifty cents an acre for it. Ultimately, the only one making much money from the Tennessee Land was Samuel Clemens, and his profit was largely literary, earned from *The Gilded Age* and the play based on it. From the former he received $15,000–$20,000 and from the latter, $75,000–$80,000: as he remarked, "just about a dollar an acre."

Allison R. Ensor

BIBLIOGRAPHY

Ensor, Allison R. "The 'Tennessee Land' of *The Gilded Age*: Fiction and Reality." *Tennessee Studies in Literature* 15 (1970): 15–23.

Wecter, Dixon. "The Tennessee Land." *Sam Clemens of Hannibal*. By Wecter. Boston: Houghton Mifflin, 1952. 28–38

See also: Clemens, John Marshall; *Gilded Age, The*

"That Day in Eden"
(1923)

Written sometime during the early 1900s, "That Day in Eden" was first published in *Europe and Elsewhere* (1923) by Albert Bigelow Paine, who demoted Mark Twain's own designation, "Passage from Satan's Diary," to a subtitle. Along with its companion piece, "Eve Speaks" (also Paine's title), it was originally intended for inclusion in a longer work, parts of which Bernard DeVoto published as "Papers of the Adam Family" in *Letters from the Earth* (1962). Details in the manuscript show that it was probably meant to precede the segment that DeVoto titled "Passage from Eve's Autobiography, Year of the World 920" (89), and was itself to be followed by "Eve Speaks" (Twain's title, "Passage from Eve's Diary").

"That Day in Eden" presents Satan's observations of the Fall—how Adam and Eve, puzzled by God's command and unable to understand the meaning of good and evil, the Moral Sense, and death, cannot comprehend Satan's attempts to explain because those matters were beyond the range of their experiences. Finally, though Satan tells Eve that she is much better off not knowing, she decides to eat the apple simply to see what these mysterious things might be like, whereupon Adam "loyally and bravely" follows her lead.

In this, as in the longer work that would have included it, Mark Twain was dealing with much more serious ideas than he had in "Extracts from Adam's Diary" (1893) and would in "Eve's Diary" (1905). If he considered publication at the time, he doubtless decided that the contemporary reading public was not ready for the blasphemous implication that the Fall of man resulted from God's stupidity in issuing a command that Adam and Eve could not possibly comprehend. He would criticize the biblical story even more severely in autobiographical dictations of June 1906 (see "Reflections on Religion") and in "Letters from the Earth" (written 1909), but these, too, would not be published until long after his death.

Howard G. Baetzhold

BIBLIOGRAPHY

Baetzhold, Howard G., Joseph M. McCullough, and Donald Malcolm. "Mark Twain's Eden/Flood Parable: 'The Autobiography of Eve.'" *American Literary Realism 1870–1910* 24.1 (Fall 1991): 23–38.

Clemens, Samuel L. "Letters from the Earth." *Letters from the Earth*. By Clemens. Ed. Bernard DeVoto. New York: Harper & Row, 1962. 1–55.

———. "Reflections on Religion." Ed. Charles Neider. *Hudson Review* 16.3 (Autumn 1963): 329–352.

———. "That Day in Eden." *Europe and Elsewhere.* By Clemens. New York: Harper, 1923. 339–346.

Ensor, Allison. *Mark Twain and the Bible.* Lexington: U of Kentucky P, 1969.

See also: "Eve Speaks"; "Eve's Diary"; "Extracts from Adam's Diary"; Religion

Thatcher, Becky

Tom Sawyer's young girlfriend in *The Adventures of Tom Sawyer* (1876) and the same age as Tom, Becky Thatcher is a schoolgirl from a wealthy family recently moved to St. Petersburg from Constantinople, Missouri. She was modeled after Laura Hawkins, an acquaintance, though not necessarily a love interest, in Twain's youth.

Blonde, blue-eyed, well-to-do, innocent, and desirable, she stands for the idealized, untouchable sentimental heroine. Her relationship with Tom is barely sexual; their idea of engagement to be married has little relationship to the actualities of married life. Tom and Becky are bolder than most couples in juvenile fiction of the period; they actually kiss each other rather than remaining apart at a discreet, adoring distance.

Becky's presence causes Tom to show off to get her attention, her absence causes deep, nearly suicidal despair, and the gap between the two states is so extreme that neither can be taken seriously. The rapid turns of emotion point to the fickleness of youthful alliances and the whimsical changeability of youth, though the depth of feeling points to their utter importance while in such extremes.

Becky herself models her emotions after those of sentimental heroines in popular nineteenth-century fiction, being prepared to die when lost in the cave, conducting herself as a flirtatious tease when Tom is out of her good graces. Herself a good girl, she defines Tom's conventionality in his traditionally courtly relationship with her and his own bad-boy ethos—daring but not iconoclastic. The theme of marriage points to Tom's eventual incorporation into the social fabric via marriage.

Ruth K. MacDonald

BIBLIOGRAPHY

Clemens, Samuel L. *The Adventures of Tom Sawyer.* Ed. John C. Gerber and Paul Baender. Berkeley: U of California P, 1982.

See also: Adventures of Tom Sawyer, The; Boy Books; Sentimentality; Women

Thatcher, Judge

First introduced as a minor character in Mark Twain's *The Adventures of Tom Sawyer* (1876), Judge Thatcher reappears briefly in *Adventures of Huckleberry Finn* (1885). As the county judge living in Constantinople, Missouri, Thatcher initially travels the twelve miles to St. Petersburg in *Tom Sawyer* to visit his brother, the town lawyer. A part of Thatcher's importance in *Tom Sawyer* is his role in bringing his daughter, Becky Thatcher, to St. Petersburg, where she becomes the focus of Sawyer's amorous attentions. In *Tom Sawyer* Thatcher invests Tom Sawyer's half of the treasure that Tom and Huck Finn discovered. His involvement with the two boys continues in *Huck Finn,* where he attempts without success to gain custody of Huck Finn to protect him from his father, Pap. Judge Thatcher is Twain's stock "good guy" who sees the essential character of others despite their surface appearance. In the larger scheme of Twain's work, Judge Thatcher represents the best qualities of that civilization against which both Tom Sawyer and Huck Finn rebel.

Ginger Thornton

BIBLIOGRAPHY

Clemens, Samuel L. *Adventures of Huckleberry Finn.* Ed. Walter Blair and Victor Fischer. Berkeley: U of California P, 1985.

———. *The Adventures of Tom Sawyer.* Ed. John C. Gerber and Paul Baender. Berkeley: U of California P, 1982.

See also: Adventures of Huckleberry Finn; Adventures of Tom Sawyer, The

"$30,000 Bequest, The"
(1904)

Written during the winter of 1903–1904, "The $30,000 Bequest" first appeared in *Harper's Weekly* for 10 December 1904.

The story dramatizes the psychological and moral displacements produced by an American money culture. Saladin and Electra Foster are started on their ruinous course by a relative whose promise of an inheritance energizes their dreams of wealth and social advancement and initiates a pattern of reversals. Their simple daily lives are displaced by obsessive fantasies of speculating and spending. As their imaginary fortune multiplies, they lose friends, turn their daughters into commodities on the marriage market, and compromise their religious principles. The reversed sex roles implied by their names—she is Aleck, he is Sally—are played fully. She becomes an investment tycoon and celebrated philanthropist, dealing in spiritual as well as earthly futures. He submits to her domination, contributing nothing to their economic success and indulging in extravagant forms of consumption. Finally they go insane; and, before their death, Sally proposes that their lives serve as a lesson in the dangers of sudden riches.

As a dramatic integration of Mark Twain's psychological theories the story points to a more complex conclusion. The pessimism and determinism of *What Is Man?* (1906) are at work in this narrative. The Fosters are driven by the single motive Twain found at the root of all action, the imperative of self-satisfaction. Moreover, they have an "inheritance" of a "romance-tinge" in their blood; thus their disposition to dream of comradeship with royalty is inborn. The bequest hoax sets this disposition in wilder motion and triggers their imagination "machines," which operate automatically. Their imaginations also undergo investment "training," Twain's word for the various forms of circumstantial conditioning that further shape the self.

Twain fuses this mechanistic psychology with a theory first explored in a journal entry dated 7 January 1897 in the Paine edition of the *Notebook* but probably recorded a year later. Twain's contention is that man has multiple selves, including a virtually autonomous dream-self. The Fosters are so immersed in dream identities that they cannot clearly distinguish waking from dream experiences, and the entanglement of the two forms of experience serves, as Pascal Covici notes, to underscore the moral unreality of their topsy-turvy money-chasing civilization.

Thus the Fosters are products and victims of an absolute drive, of hereditary temperaments, and of environmental conditioning. Their story, a grimly funny determinist fable, achieves its dramatic inevitability and tonal and thematic richness through an economy of language and episode characteristic of the best published work of Mark Twain's troubled last years as a writer.

Earl F. Briden

BIBLIOGRAPHY

Clemens, Samuel L. *Mark Twain's Notebook*. Ed. Albert B. Paine. New York: Harper, 1935.

——. *"What Is Man?" and Other Philosophical Writings*. Ed. Paul Baender. Berkeley: U of California P, 1973.

Covici, Pascal, Jr. *Mark Twain's Humor: The Image of a World*. Dallas: Southern Methodist UP, 1962.

Geismar, Maxwell. *Mark Twain: An American Prophet*. Boston: Houghton Mifflin, 1970.

Wilson, James D. *A Reader's Guide to the Short Stories of Mark Twain*. Boston: G.K. Hall, 1987.

See also: Business; Determinism; Dreams; Foster, Saladin and Electra

Thompson, William Tappan
(1812–1882)

In addition to being a prominent southern humorist and playwright, journalist, printer, law student, soldier, and public servant, William Tappan Thompson was one of the most notable of the Old Southwest humorists. He made his literary fame with the "Major Jones" letters. His chief works are *Major Jones's Courtship* (1843), *Chronicles of Pineville* (1845), *John's Alive; or, The Bride of a Ghost* (1846), *Major*

Jones's Sketches of Travel (1848), and *Rancy Cottem's Courtship* (1879).

Although identified with the South, Thompson was born in Ravenna, Ohio, son of David and Catherine (Kerney) Thompson. Thompson married Carolina A. Carrie in 1837, a marriage that produced ten children. He tried his hand at many vocations, but he always came back to journalism. Indeed, it was while editing the *Family Companion and Ladies' Mirror* (1842) of Macon, Georgia, and the *Southern Miscellany* (1842–1844) of Madison, Georgia, that he began publishing his "Major Jones letters" in their columns.

Thompson's reputation rides mainly on these humorous letters of Major Joseph Jones, the comical farmer of Pineville, Georgia; secondarily on the depiction of Georgia life in *Chronicles of Pineville* (reminiscent of Augustus Baldwin Longstreet's *Georgia Scenes* [1835]). Jones is one of the earliest of the Georgia "Crackers," whose homespun wit and wisdom, offered up in atrocious grammar and country dialect, spoke to the realities of life in the antebellum South. The humor is often rough and extravagant, inspired by the boisterous oral tradition of the tall tale. Thompson's use of dialect and realistic, unsentimental tone influenced Twain. Further, *Major Jones's Sketches of Travel* may have exerted a direct influence on Twain's Snodgrass letters. Undoubtedly, certain specific scenes in Twain's works owe allegiance to Thompson, such as a farcical circus scene in *Major Jones's Courtship* that resembles an incident at the circus attended by Huckleberry Finn.

Never a writer of the first order, Thompson is now obscure; but his Major Jones and Pineville sketches can still be enjoyed for their own sake and appreciated for their role in establishing a distinctive American literature and offering historically realistic glimpses of an important segment of nineteenth-century American life.

David B. Kesterson

BIBLIOGRAPHY

Miller, Henry Prentice. "The Background and Significance of *Major Jones's Courtship*." *Georgia Historical Quarterly* 30 (December 1946): 267–296.

———. "The Life and Works of William Tappan Thompson." Ph.D. diss., U of Chicago, 1942.

Shippey, Herbert. "William Tappan Thompson (1812–1882)." *Fifty Southern Writers Before 1900*. Ed. Robert Bain and Joseph M. Flora. Westport, Conn.: Greenwood P, 1987. 440–451.

See also: "Adventures of Thomas Jefferson Snodgrass, The"; Southwestern Humor

Thorpe, Thomas Bangs
(1815–1878)

A painter, editor, and journalist, Thomas Bangs Thorpe is noted for his humorous and sporting narratives of life in antebellum Arkansas and Louisiana. These narratives were collected in two volumes, *The Mysteries of the Backwoods* (1846) and *The Hive of "The Bee-Hunter"* (1854), the latter an expansion of *Mysteries*. Thorpe also wrote two books about the Mexican War, *Our Army on the Rio Grande* (1846) and *Our Army at Monterey* (1847). His other books included *The Taylor Anecdote Book* (1848), containing material about Zachary Taylor, and *The Master's House* (1854), one of several antebellum southern responses to *Uncle Tom's Cabin*.

Thorpe was born in Massachusetts but spent much of his early life in New York City. In 1837 he moved to Louisiana, where he remained for seventeen years, editing newspapers and holding various political offices in the state. While in Louisiana, he became a correspondent for William T. Porter's sporting and humorous weekly, the *Spirit of the Times*, in which "The Big Bear of Arkansas" appeared in 1841. The deservedly high reputation of this story has obscured Thorpe's achievement in other humorous works, notably "Bob Herring, the Arkansas Bear Hunter" and the masterful satire of travel literature entitled "Letters from the Far West."

Despite the excellence of these pieces, Thorpe was not primarily a humorist; the bulk of his work is sentimental, nostalgic, and genteel. But the prominence of "The Big Bear" has earned him a place among the major humorists of the Old Southwest. As a candid observer of rural life and a clever depictor of backwoods character, he belongs to a literary tradition that exercised a major influence on the writing of Mark Twain.

Mary Ann Wimsatt

BIBLIOGRAPHY

Blair, Walter, and Hamlin Hill. *America's Humor: From Poor Richard to Doonesbury.* New York: Oxford UP, 1978.

Cox, Leland H., Jr. "T.B. Thorpe's Far West Letters." *Gyascutus: Studies in Antebellum Southern Humorous and Sporting Writing.* Ed. James L.W. West III. Atlantic Highlands, N.J.: Humanities P, 1978. 115–157.

Current-Garcia, Eugene. "Thomas Bangs Thorpe (1815–1878)." *Fifty Southern Writers Before 1900: A Bio-bibliographical Sourcebook.* Ed. Robert Bain and Joseph M. Flora. Westport, Conn.: Greenwood P, 1987. 452–463.

Garner, Stanton. "Thomas Bangs Thorpe in the Gilded Age: Shifty in a New Country." *Mississippi Quarterly* 36 (Winter 1982–1983): 35–52.

Lemay, J.A. Leo. "The Text, Tradition, and Themes of 'The Big Bear of Arkansas.'" *American Literature* 47 (November 1975): 321–342.

Rickles, Milton. *Thomas Bangs Thorpe: Humorist of the Old Southwest.* Baton Rouge: Louisiana State UP, 1962.

Thorpe, Thomas Bangs. *A New Collection of Thomas Bangs Thorpe's Sketches of the Old Southwest.* Ed. David C. Estes. Baton Rouge: Louisiana State UP, 1989.

See also: Southwestern Humor

"Those Annual Bills"

(written 1875)

In his short poem "Those Annual Bills," written in January 1875 and modeled on Thomas Moore's "Those Evening Bells," which described the joyous emotions inspired by the bells, Mark Twain vented the very different emotions inspired by his review of family expenses during the preceding year. Though his complaint primarily bemoans the costs of food, a major contributing factor was certainly the huge expense that year of constructing the new house in Hartford.

On 7 January 1875 he sent the original draft of the poem to publisher James T. Fields, mistakenly dated 1874 (Twain was in England during early January 1874). Later in 1875 under the title "A Couple of Poems by Twain and Moore," he included "Those Evening Bells" and his own piece in *Sketches, New and Old* (1875).

In thus parodying a popular poem, Mark Twain employed a device common among humorists of his own day and earlier and one he himself had often used ever since his apprenticeship on the Hannibal *Journal.*

Howard G. Baetzhold

BIBLIOGRAPHY

Baetzhold, Howard G. *Mark Twain and John Bull: The British Connection.* Bloomington: Indiana UP, 1970.

Gribben, Alan. *Mark Twain's Library: A Reconstruction.* 2 vols. Boston: G.K. Hall, 1980.

Scott, Arthur L. *On the Poetry of Mark Twain.* Urbana: U of Illinois P, 1966.

"Those Blasted Children"

(written 1864)

Written during the night of 9–10 January 1864 from a draft begun a few months earlier, this sketch was published in the *Sunday Mercury* on 21 February. "Those Blasted Children" was the second of Twain's writings (following "Doings in Nevada") on his experiences in the West to be printed by an eastern magazine.

Set in Twain's lodgings at Lick House, the first-person narrative is interrupted by the household's children, whose antics are described in military terminology. In response to the children's assault, the narrator details several extreme (and obviously fatal) remedies parents might use to cure their children of illnesses and ill manners. Additionally, the story relies on inside jokes: the children's names are those of prominent San Franciscans and the testimonial that supports Twain's remedies is attributed to his friend Zeb Leavenworth, the Mississippi pilot.

Charles Franklyn Beach

BIBLIOGRAPHY

Clemens, Samuel L. "Those Blasted Children." *The Works of Mark Twain: Early Tales & Sketches, Volume 1 (1851–1864).* Ed. Edgar M. Branch and Robert H. Hirst. Berkeley: U of California P, 1979. 347–356.

"Those Extraordinary Twins, The Comedy"

(1894)

The title of the "suppressed farce" represents both the original inspiration for and the left-over product of Mark Twain's novel *The Tragedy of Pudd'nhead Wilson* (1894). Fascinated by twinship and doubling all his literary life (as early as 1869 he wrote a sketch titled "Personal Habits of the Siamese Twins"), Twain began in 1892 a burlesque story about the Siamese twins Luigi and Angelo Cappello, who share a body and a pair of legs but possess two heads and four arms. Each has a distinct personality and is temperamentally opposed to the other. The dark Luigi is a somewhat cynical and dissipated freethinker, while the blonde Angelo is a pious teetotaler, who, like Twain's brother Orion, frequently changes his religious affiliations. They are introduced into the society of a small Mississippi River town, and absurd complications follow, chief among which is that they are charged with assault and battery for kicking Tom Driscoll but acquitted when it cannot be proved which twin was in command of the legs when the kick was administered. Pudd'nhead Wilson, given his first case in twenty years, is the successful defense lawyer. Following their acquittal, each twin runs separately for alderman; Luigi is elected but cannot take his place because his brother is not allowed to be present at meetings. To solve this legal and political impasse, and to end the story, the townspeople hang Luigi. According to Twain's account of the composition of *Pudd'nhead Wilson*, this story

was superseded by the emergence of Roxy, Tom Driscoll, Pudd'nhead Wilson, and the race-centered plot generated by Roxy's switching of the slave and white babies, so he removed the Siamese twins from the novel. Traces of the original plot and characters remain, however, in the non-Siamese twins Luigi and Angelo of *Pudd'nhead Wilson*. Ostensibly to illustrate his difficulties as a "jackleg" novelist, Twain published "Those Extraordinary Twins," along with an account of the genesis of the novel, as a supplement to *Pudd'nhead Wilson*. The suppressed farce, however, shares in a comic mode many of the concerns of the published novel, legal determination of truth, and the behavior and morality of ordinary people in small towns.

Robert Sattelmeyer

BIBLIOGRAPHY

Clemens, Samuel L. *Pudd'nhead Wilson and Those Extraordinary Twins.* Ed. Sidney E. Berger. Norton crit. ed. New York: Norton, 1980.

Fredricks, Nancy. "Twain's Indelible Twins." *Nineteenth Century Literature* 43.4 (March 1989): 484–499.

Gillman, Susan. *Dark Twins: Imposture and Identity in Mark Twain's America.* Chicago: U of Chicago P, 1989.

Parker, Hershel. "Pudd'nhead Wilson: Jack-leg Author, Unreadable Text, and Sense Making Critics." *Flawed Texts and Verbal Icons: Literary Authority in American Fiction.* Evanston, Ill.: Northwestern UP, 1984. 115–145.

See also: Angelo and Luigi (Cappello);
Pudd'nhead Wilson, The Tragedy of

"Three Thousand Years Among the Microbes"

(1967)

Mark Twain undertook the writing of "Three Thousand Years Among the Microbes" in spring 1905 as a kind of therapeutic distraction from the sorrow and loneliness that followed the death of his wife in Florence, Italy, the previous spring. The long but unfinished fantasy, based on an idea for a satire Twain had been pondering for more than twenty years, was written at Upton House near Dublin, New Hampshire. It was begun on 20 May and abandoned on 23 June. Referred to by Twain as "The Adventures of a Microbe During Three Thousand Years—by a Microbe," the work, running to some 40,000 words, was not published in its entirety until John S. Tuckey's *Mark Twain's "Which Was the Dream?" and Other Symbolic Writings of the Later Years* (1967). A 5,000-word segment had appeared in Albert Bigelow Paine's *Mark Twain: A Biography* (1912).

His fantasy, a "translation" of a history recorded by a microbe living in the "blood of a hoary and mouldering old bald-headed tramp," permitted Twain to address painful subjects as if he were an observer from another world. Indeed, the microbe narrator, named B.b. Bkshp and nicknamed "Huck," claims he is an earthly man who, either by a magician's trick gone awry or his own choosing (the narrative suggests both) is turned into a cholera germ. Through Huck's consciousness of two parallel but opposing realities—one his human past, which survives as memory, and the other the microbic present, which he is living—Twain manipulates time and space perspectives to speculate about philosophical dilemmas.

As in other symbolic writings of his later years, Twain wrestles in "Three Thousand Years" with philosophical and cosmological problems. His representation of the microbic universe as in actuality the body of a stinking, repulsive tramp called Blitzowski deflated mankind's arbitrary egocentricity. In Huck's discourse on pantheism the possibility of a soul that survives the body's demise is explored, and in considering the Darwinian view that all life destroys other life, Huck "reached down to comfort . . . and an easy conscience." Other episodes confirm Hippolyte Taine's determinism. The ideas of Charles Darwin, William James, C.W. Saleeby, W.H. Conn, Henry Adams, and C.T. Stockwell among others find room in the narrative as well, as do satires on imperialism, Christian Science, Walter Scottism, silver coinage, America's greed, and the corrupting influence of fame. In addition to philosophical and theological discussions, links to Twain's boyhood enrich "Three Thousand Years." Huck, who like Huckleberry Finn is based on Twain's boyhood friend Tom Blankenship, adventures down veins and arteries that make "the Mississippi . . . trifling . . . by comparison."

"Three Thousand Years," admired by Paine as superb Swiftian satire, has come to be regarded as a noteworthy, albeit minor, indicator of Twain's persistent grappling with mammoth questions concerning the nature of existence. Along with most of the other dark writings of Twain's later years, "Three Thousand Years" has been categorized as an oddity and relegated to the background of Twain scholarship. Occasionally, however, an idea in "Three Thousand Years" will strike the chord of contemporary concerns and arouse a critic's comment in a reference or article or chapter. Then "Three Thousand Years" enters the literary fray still provoking confusion, still biting at philistine philosophies, and somehow still strangely satisfying.

Virginia Starrett

BIBLIOGRAPHY

Clemens, Samuel L. *Mark Twain's "Which Was the Dream?" and Other Symbolic Writings of the Later Years.* Ed. John S. Tuckey. Berkeley: U of California P, 1967. 430–553.

——. *The Science Fiction of Mark Twain.* Ed. David Ketterer. Hamden, Conn.: Archon, 1984.

Cummings, Sherwood. *Mark Twain and Science: Adventures of a Mind.* Baton Rouge: Louisiana State UP, 1988.

Lindborg, Henry J. "A Cosmic Tramp: Samuel Clemens's *Three Thousand Years Among the Microbes.*" *American Literature* 44 (1973): 652–657.

Tuckey, John S. "Mark Twain's Later Dialogue: The 'Me' and the Machine." *American Literature* 41 (1970): 532–542.

Walsh, Kathleen. "Rude Awakenings and Swift Recoveries: The Problem of Reality in Mark Twain's 'The Great Dark' and 'Three Thousand Years among the Microbes.'" *American Literary Realism 1870–1910* 21 (1988): 19–28.

See also: Determinism; Philosophy; "Reflections on Religion"; Science

Ticknor, Caroline
(1866–1937)

As the daughter of Benjamin Holt Ticknor, Caroline Ticknor had many occasions to meet her father's friend, Mark Twain. Though she published short fiction and magazine articles, she is better known for her biographies and reminiscences of American authors, including *Glimpses of Authors* (1922). Her chapter on Twain's *Life on the Mississippi* and an earlier article in *The Bookman* (1914) were the first to describe the suppression of one chapter, and they have provided important information about illustrations, expurgations, revisions, and publication history. In his introduction to the only edition of *Life on the Mississippi* (1944) to include suppressed material, Edward Wagenknecht comments on Ticknor's work and provides a few factual corrections.

Nancy Cook

BIBLIOGRAPHY

Clemens, Samuel L. *Life on the Mississippi.* Ed. Edward Wagenknecht. New York: Heritage P, 1944.

Kruse, Horst H. *Mark Twain and "Life on the Mississippi."* Amherst: U of Massachusetts P, 1981.

Mainiero, Lina, ed. *American Women Writers, Volume 4 (S to Z).* New York: Frederick Ungar, 1979–1982.

Ticknor, Caroline. *Glimpses of Authors.* Boston: Houghton Mifflin, 1922.

———. "Mark Twain's Missing Chapter." *Bookman* 39 (1914): 298–309.

"To My Missionary Critics"
(1901)

Though it was not intended as a sequel, "To My Missionary Critics" (*North American Review*, April 1901) has the effect of one; it is a shadow of the more substantial, masterful anti-imperialist polemic "To the Person Sitting in Darkness" (*NAR*, February 1901). In the latter Mark Twain had expressed sardonic outrage at several blatant instances of American and European aggression in the name of the "blessings of civilization" conferred, or rather inflicted, on Africans, Filipinos, and Chinese.

His suggestion that missionaries actually aided and abetted imperialism, exemplified by the activities of the American Board of Foreign Missions in China, elicited indignant responses from various champions of the missions, including the Reverend Dr. Judson Smith, corresponding secretary of the board, who demanded an apology. "To My Missionary Critics" is Twain's justification for his attack on the missionary William Ament, to whom he does not apologize.

Smith believed that Twain's case against Ament was based on a cable error. In "To the Person" Twain had quoted Ament's letter in which he boasted having collected from the Chinese peasants an indemnity thirteen times the worth of property destroyed by Boxers. The money was used in "the propagation of the Gospels." After Ament assured Smith of the cable error—the fines were one-third, not thirteen times, the damages—Smith exculpated Ament and demanded an apology from Twain. Ament further insisted that the money was used to assist the widows and orphans of missionaries killed by the Boxers.

Twain accepted the correction of the cable error, which, however, changed nothing in his view—blood money is blood money, regardless of the amount. The gist of his argument was that the Board of Foreign Missions in China, through Ament, extorted the money from innocent Chinese; none of the peasants from whom it was collected was tried by any "Christian code of morals and law." On the contrary, Ament justified the "theft and extortion" by assuring Smith that it was "approved by the Chinese officials." Such a cavalier "do-as-the-Romans-do" attitude made Ament an easy target for Twain's irony. Christians rationalize unchristian behavior (i.e., revenge) by adopting "pagan morals and justice." The only way they could justify the fines was by "revising the Ten Commandments," adding an exception to "Thou shalt not steal": theft is permissible if it is "the custom of the country."

Although the overall effect of "To My Missionary Critics" is that of redundancy (perhaps even of beating a dead horse), in his relentless attempts to expose the board's hypocrisy Twain effectively uses Swiftean irony, concise parable, and persuasive analogy (especially in the sections entitled "The Tale of the King and his Treasurer" and "The Watermelons"). But then he concludes with an assurance that though missionaries mean well, they tend to be "all heart"; they do not often think straight. By suggesting that Ament and the board had their hearts in the right place but made "errors in judgment," he softened the satirical blows he had inflicted. The result is a bit anticlimactic.

Joseph Andriano

BIBLIOGRAPHY

Clemens, Samuel L. "To My Missionary Critics." *The Complete Essays of Mark Twain.* Ed. Charles Neider. Garden City, N.Y.: Doubleday, 1963. 296–311.

———. "To the Person Sitting in Darkness." *The Complete Essays of Mark Twain.* Ed. Charles Neider. Garden City, N.Y.: Doubleday, 1963. 275–296.

Emerson, Everett H. *The Authentic Mark Twain: A Literary Biography of Samuel L. Clemens.* Philadelphia: U of Pennsylvania P, 1984.

Foner, Philip S. *Mark Twain: Social Critic.* New York: International Publishers, 1958.

Hill, Hamlin. *Mark Twain: God's Fool.* New York: Harper & Row, 1973.

Macnaughton, William R. *Mark Twain's Last Years as a Writer.* Columbia: U of Missouri P, 1979.

See also: Ament, Joseph; American Board of Foreign Missions; Boxer Rebellion, The; China; Imperialism; Politics; "To the Person Sitting in Darkness"

"To the Person Sitting in Darkness"

(1901)

This essay, Mark Twain's most significant anti-imperialist work, was written in January 1901 and published the following month in the *North American Review.* It was also distributed at that time as a pamphlet in an edition of 125,000 copies by the Anti-Imperialist League. Later it was reprinted in the collection *Europe and Elsewhere* (1923). Since then it has been reprinted often when it has seemed to have an almost uncanny relevance to more recent political events; for example, in Frederick Anderson's edition *A Pen Warmed-Up in Hell* which appeared in 1972 during the Vietnam War.

In the essay Twain attacked all the imperialist wars going on at the turn of the century: the English fighting the Boers in South Africa, the Germans fighting the Chinese in Shantung, the Russians seizing Port Arthur and Manchuria, and the United States taking the Philippines. This concatenation shows Twain had developed a unitary concept of imperialism. Since his method of attack is ironic, however, the exact basis of his criticism is unclear. Philip Foner in *Mark Twain: Social Critic* has argued that Twain saw imperialism as the consequence of the "robber barons" and thus was leftist in outlook. Louis Budd in *Mark Twain: Social Philosopher*, though, has convincingly replied that Twain did not conceive Lenin's notion that surplus finance capital caused imperialism; rather Twain simply saw innate human greed expressing itself in taking over other people's territories. Twain's criticism, then, was democratic and humanitarian.

Twain's ironic attack starts with the premise that in the past imperialist powers have justified themselves by claiming they were spreading the "blessings of civilization" to backward areas. While Twain makes no explicit reference, he may have been thinking here of Rudyard Kipling's poem published two years earlier, "The White Man's Burden," subtitled "The United States and the Philippine Islands." Twain goes on to say that in recent years the imperialists dropped their altruistic pretext, thereby ceasing to fool "the people sitting in darkness" (the phrase comes from Matthew 4:16). He sarcastically recommends that the empire builders go back to their pretext so "we can resume Business at the old stand."

Twain does make one exception for the United States helping to liberate Cuba in the Spanish-American War. He sees this act as genuinely altruistic and calls it the "American game." In the Philippines, though, he asserts that the United States took up the "European game" of professing benevolence while only intending to conquer, and he believes the same may still happen in Cuba as well.

As the strongest anti-imperialist statement by any American author of the period, "To the Person" has contributed to Twain's worldwide popularity, especially in the former colonies. It established Twain as a champion of democracy and humanitarianism notwithstanding the pessimism he may have expressed about their viability in *What Is Man?* (1906) and the other dark writings of his final years.

Hunt Hawkins

BIBLIOGRAPHY

Budd, Louis J. *Mark Twain: Social Philosopher.* Bloomington: Indiana UP, 1962.

Clemens, Samuel L. *A Pen Warmed-Up in Hell: Mark Twain in Protest.* Ed. Frederick Anderson. New York: Harper & Row, 1972.

Foner, Philip S. *Mark Twain: Social Critic.* New York: International Publishers, 1958.

Geismar, Maxwell. *Mark Twain: An American Prophet.* Boston: Houghton Mifflin, 1970.

Gibson, William M. "Mark Twain and Howells: Anti-Imperialists." *New England Quarterly* 20 (1947): 435–470.

Hill, Hamlin. *Mark Twain: God's Fool.* New York: Harper & Row, 1973.

See also: Boer War; Imperialism; Spanish-American War, The; "To My Missionary Critics"

Tom Sawyer Abroad
(1894)

One of the earliest American attempts at science fiction, *Tom Sawyer Abroad* tells in Huck Finn's vernacular how Tom Sawyer, Huck, and the ex-slave Jim take over a power-driven balloon and navigate it across the Atlantic Ocean and the Sahara Desert to Egypt and Palestine. Mark Twain wrote the story in August 1892 while he and his family were in Bad Nauheim. Originally, he intended it to

be the first of a series of stories about travels of his famous threesome to foreign lands, but he never carried the plan beyond this first volume. After editing the first draft extensively, he sold it to Mrs. Mabel Mapes Dodge for $4,000. Mrs. Dodge then published it as a six-part serial in her *St. Nicholas Magazine,* November 1893 to April 1894. Unfortunately, Mrs. Dodge considered herself an arbiter of taste for her young readers and bowdlerized the text outrageously. Subsequently it was published as a book in the United States by Charles L. Webster and Company, Twain's own company, and in England by Chatto and Windus. Both publishers issued the book in the spring of 1894. To Mark Twain's great embarrassment the first nine chapters of the American edition were set from the *St. Nicholas* bowdlerized text though the remaining four chapters and all of the English edition were set from authoritative typescripts. A still further embarrassment for the author was that the American edition was filed for copyright on the very day that Charles L. Webster and Company went bankrupt.

Like Twain's travel books, *TSA* is in structure a picaresque account controlled by the nature and course of the journey. This journey, however, is imaginary and purposeless, and its episodes are too often copied from such sources as Jules Verne's *Five Weeks in a Balloon* (1887) and his *Dick Sands* (1878), Sir Walter Scott's *The Talisman* (1825), the Bible, and *The Arabian Nights* (1885–1888). The author borrows, also, from his own *Innocents Abroad* (1869) and *Roughing It* (1872), not only for particulars but more generally for the combination of satire and sentiment in describing foreign lands. In addition, as in *A Connecticut Yankee* (1889) Twain maneuvers occasional conversations so that they deal with current political and economic happenings that irritate him. In fact, Tom Sawyer in his interests and manner seems closer to the Yankee than to the earlier Tom Sawyer. Although Tom and Huck and Jim do keep something of the natures they possess in the last fifth of *Huckleberry Finn* (1885), they also resemble the chief characters in *Five Weeks in a Balloon.* Tom is much like Verne's knowledgeable and imaginative Dr. Samuel Fergusson, Huck like the practical-minded Dick Kennedy, and Jim like Joe, the faithful manservant.

Most interesting for many readers is the talk of the main characters. Tom is constantly disgusted at what he thinks to be the obtuseness of the other two, and Huck and Jim are just as constantly irked because Tom does not recognize the point in Huck's common sense or in Jim's literalness. Bernard DeVoto has praised the book for being a deliberate exploration of three stages of the provincial mind caused by variations in prejudices, ignorances, assumptions, wisdom, and cunning. Even so, despite these perceptions and Huck's appealing vernacular and a few passages of a topnotch humor, *TSA* is too artificially contrived to be one of Mark Twain's major works.

John C. Gerber

BIBLIOGRAPHY

Brack, O.M., Jr. "Mark Twain in Kneepants: The Expurgation of *Tom Sawyer Abroad.*" *Proof* 2 (1972): 143–151.

Budd, Louis J. *Mark Twain: Social Philosopher.* Bloomington: Indiana UP, 1962.

Clemens, Samuel L. *The Adventures of Tom Sawyer, Tom Sawyer Abroad, Tom Sawyer, Detective.* Ed. John C. Gerber, Paul Baender, and Terry Firkins. Berkeley: U of California P, 1980.

———. *The Portable Mark Twain.* Ed. Bernard DeVoto. New York: Viking, 1946. 31–32.

Emerson, Everett. *The Authentic Mark Twain: A Literary Biography of Samuel L. Clemens.* Philadelphia: U of Pennsylvania P, 1984.

See also: Finn, Huckleberry; Sawyer, Tom

Tom Sawyer, Detective

(1896)

The third and last complete Tom Sawyer narrative, *Tom Sawyer, Detective,* was frankly cobbled together by Mark Twain to bring in badly needed income. The story rests primarily on an 1829 Danish novel entitled (in English) *The Minister of Veilby* and written by Steen Steensen Blicher. Twain heard the story summarized by the American wife of a Danish diplomat in Paris late in December 1894. The novel, in turn, had been based on the unhappy life of Soren Jensen Quist, a seventeenth-century Danish pastor who was executed for a murder he did not commit. Twain became so excited by the novel's possibilities for an American story that he interrupted his work on *Joan of Arc* (1896) and set to work on *TSD.* He wrote it in three weeks in January 1895—all 28,000 words of it—and sold it to Harper and Brothers, who serialized it in the August and September 1896 issues of *Harper's New Monthly Magazine.* Subsequently Harpers published it in a collection entitled *Tom Sawyer Abroad, Tom Sawyer, Detective, and Other Stories* (November 1896). In London, Chatto and Windus issued the English edition as *Tom Sawyer, Detective as Told by Huck Finn and Other Stories* (December 1896—though the title page carries 1897).

Before writing *TSD* Twain had been experimenting with the detective story and had even started one called *Tom Sawyer's Mystery* though he had not found a satisfactory plot for it. The Blicher story, he felt, supplied the complication he needed. He transferred many of the main incidents from Denmark to the Phelps farm in Arkansas that he had used in the last part of *Huckleberry Finn* (1885). He turned Reverend Silas Phelps (now quite dotty) into an accused murderer and used the neighboring Dunlap twins as villains. Tom and Huck, newly arrived from St. Petersburg, he made into boyish imitations of Sherlock Holmes and Dr. Watson. To complicate the narrative still further, he added elements from *Tom Sawyer's Mystery.* Also he inserted such favorite devices as sleepwalking, Halloween-type disguises, male twins, a phony deaf mute, and a trial at which Tom Sawyer shows once more his extraordinary powers of reasoning. Enmeshed in such happenings, the characters lose reality: the minor characters are pasteboard, and Tom and Huck are such exaggerated versions of Holmes and Watson that they become ridiculous. Even Huck's vernacular is not so appealing as it once was, and the use of the Phelps farm (in real life the farm of the author's Uncle John Quarles) for murder and near madness reveals a sad indifference to a spot that Twain once had viewed with uncommon affection. In short, Twain seems to have lost almost all respect for the setting and for his favorite boys, and the story suffers accordingly. A modest amount of suspense and several farcical scenes provide such appeal as the narrative has.

John C. Gerber

BIBLIOGRAPHY

Bay, J. Christian. *"Tom Sawyer, Detective*: The Origin of the Plot." *Essays Offered to Herbert Putnam by his Colleagues and Friends on His Thirtieth Anniversary as Librarian of Congress, 5 April 1929.* Ed. William Warner Bishop and Andrew Keogh. New Haven, Conn.: Yale UP, 1929. 80–88.

Clemens, Samuel L. *The Adventures of Tom Sawyer, Tom Sawyer Abroad, Tom Sawyer, Detective.* Ed. John C. Gerber, Paul Baender, and Terry Firkins. Berkeley: U of California P, 1980.

Emerson, Everett. *The Authentic Mark Twain: A Literary Biography of Samuel L. Clemens.* Philadelphia: U of Pennsylvania P, 1984.

McKeithan, Daniel M. *Court Trials in Mark Twain and Other Essays.* The Hague: Martinus Nijhoff, 1958.

See also: Adventures of Tom Sawyer, The; Detective Fiction; Sawyer, Tom

"Tom Sawyer's Conspiracy"
(1969)

"Tom Sawyer's Conspiracy" is a fragment of about 28,000 words that Mark Twain began in Weggis, Switzerland, in 1897; he returned to it several times before dropping it finally in 1899 or 1900. Huckleberry Finn is the narrator, and the locale is the area in and around St. Petersburg (Hannibal) during the days of slavery when abolitionists were especially unpopular. The conspiracy is that Tom is to disguise himself as a slave, be sold to a slave trader, and then discard his disguise in order to help search for the "escaped" slave. But before all this takes place, Twain drops the story (at the end of chapter 4). When he re-

turns to it, he changes the conspiracy plot into a detective plot. Just as Tom has meant to do, another white man passes himself off as a slave, and in the events that follow the slave trader is killed. Subsequently Jim is picked up as the murderer, and Tom, after many absurd twists and turns in the plot, seems about to convince a jury that Jim is innocent when the story suddenly stops. It would seem that the murderers are the King and the Duke, who have been pulled out of *Huckleberry Finn* (1885)! Even Twain must have become embarrassed by all of the preposterous coincidences. Certainly, the reader grows weary of them. There are high spots, however, in some of Huck's observations and the argument of Tom with Huck and Jim about the nature of Providence. In fact, satiric allusions to orthodox beliefs in Providence serve as a leit motif in the story and relate it slightly to *The Mysterious Stranger,* which Twain was also working on. Taken as a whole, however, "TSC" is the work of a great writer whose power of invention has deteriorated into mechanical tinkering with used materials.

John C. Gerber

BIBLIOGRAPHY

Clemens, Samuel L. *Mark Twain's Hannibal, Huck & Tom.* Ed. Walter Blair. Berkeley: U of California P, 1969.

See also: Abolition; Detective Fiction; Sawyer, Tom

"Tournament in A.D. 1870, The"
(1870)

In March 1870 Mark Twain informed his publisher, Elisha Bliss, of his "vague half-notion" to spend the summer in England collecting material on British manners and customs for a sequel to *The Innocents Abroad* (1869). Two years elapsed before he actually made the journey, but later that year Twain did experiment with the idea of a burlesque treatment of British customs in a brief sketch titled

"The Tournament in A.D. 1870," which appeared in the July issue of *Galaxy* magazine. Although the projected sequel to *IA* never materialized, Twain's burlesque treatment of British chivalry is remembered today for its anticipation of the theme and mood of a much later work, *A Connecticut Yankee in King Arthur's Court* (1889).

Twain's 1870 sketch employs an inverted version of the burlesque formula that he later developed far more extensively in *Connecticut Yankee*. Instead of a nineteenth-century Yankee in King Arthur's Camelot, the *Galaxy* sketch describes a medieval tournament in contemporary Brooklyn, New York. By focusing on the incongruous image of knights jousting and butchering one another amid "the refinement and dignity of a carefully-developed modern civilization," Twain intends to expose the celebrated "mock-heroics of our ancestors" as evidence of "absurdity gone crazy." Anticipating *Connecticut Yankee*, "The Tournament" relentlessly burlesques the "chivalrous absurdities" of Arthur's court, though the sketch does not, like the novel, include a counterindictment of modern civilization as part of its theme.

Henry B. Wonham

BIBLIOGRAPHY

Baetzhold, Howard G. *Mark Twain and John Bull: The British Connection.* Bloomington: Indiana UP, 1970.

Clemens, Samuel L. *Contributions to "The Galaxy" 1869–1871.* Ed. Bruce R. McElderry, Jr. Gainesville, Fla.: Scholars' Facsimiles & Reprints, 1961.

See also: Connecticut Yankee in King Arthur's Court, A

Townsend, James William Emery
(1838–1900)

Even in his own time James William Emery Townsend was a semilegendary itinerant journalist and confidence man on the eastern slope of the Sierra Nevada Mountains. Variously known as "Captain Jim" and "Lying Jim," he was famous for his colorful personality and his irrepressible mendacity, especially his talent for creating artistic tall tales on the spur of the moment.

In an environment of practical jokers, swindlers, frauds, and tall-tale tellers, Townsend kept up with the competition. He is generally believed to have been the model for "Truthful James" in Bret Harte's "Plain Language from Truthful James" (1870). Sam Davis slightly fictionalized Townsend's part in an audacious international swindle in a charming story, "My Friend, The Editor" (1889). Dan De Quille included him as a regular character in a series of newspaper columns devoted to tall tales. And Twain, in chapter 35 of *Roughing It* (1872), humorously recalled how Townsend recognized and exposed a tunnel fraud scheme.

Townsend was one of the many unjustly neglected newspapermen and authors of the Old West who helped create the milieu and rich stock of western humor that nurtured Twain.

Lawrence I. Berkove

BIBLIOGRAPHY

Drury, Wells. *An Editor on the Comstock Lode.* Reno: U of Nevada P, 1984.

Dwyer, Richard A., and Richard E. Lingenfelter. *Lying on the Eastern Slope: James Townsend's Comic Journalism on the Mining Frontier.* Miami: Florida International UP, 1984.

See also: De Quille, Dan; *Roughing It*

Tramp Abroad, A
(1880)

Section one of the contract concluded on 8 March 1878 between Mark Twain and his publisher Francis E. Bliss for what became *A Tramp Abroad* indicates that the author "proposes to visit Europe very soon" and agrees "during his sojourn there to prepare Manuscript of original matter in quantity sufficient to make a volume when published of size suitable to sell by agents as a subscription book." Different from *The Innocents Abroad* (1869) and *Roughing It* (1872), the plan for Mark Twain's third travel book thus preceded the journey it was to be about and also affected his itinerary and his procedure. As well as planning to rent workrooms for himself (and actually renting such rooms during his stays in Heidelberg and in Munich), Mark Twain invited his friend Joseph H. Twichell to Europe for walking tours in the Black Forest and in Switzerland, rejecting criticism of the fact that a humorist was paying a clergyman's expenses by pointing out that actually it was Twichell who was bestowing money on him. Considering the space that is given to their excursions in the published book (as compared to the author's overall experiences in Germany, Switzerland, Italy, France, and England between April 1878 and August 1879), as well as the role Twichell played in helping Mark Twain conceive the persona of a traveling companion named Harris, his statement was certainly correct. But Twain had begun to write independent portions of the book even before Twichell's arrival in Baden-Baden on 1 August 1878, and making these and further extraneous items part of an evolving narrative structure proved exceedingly difficult. Despite the impetus provided by Twichell's visit and despite the author's note taking and writing throughout his European tour, the manuscript was not completed when he and his family returned to New York on 3 September 1879. It took Twain until January to finish writing and revising, and contrary to his expectations *A Tramp Abroad* did not get published before 13 March 1880.

Although Mark Twain was still a long way from finishing the work, his characterization of it given in an interview on 25 April 1879 in Paris (and printed in the New York *Times* of 11 May) describes the final product even then: "It is a gossipy volume of travel, and will be similar to the 'Innocents Abroad' in size, and similarly illustrated. I shall draw some of the pictures for it myself. However, that need not frighten anybody, for I shall draw only a few. . . . I call it a gossipy volume, and that is what

it is. It talks about anything and everything, and always drops a subject the moment my interest in it begins to slacken. . . . I have been drifting around on an idle, easy-going tramp—so to speak—for a year, stopping when I pleased, moving on when I got ready. My book has caught the complexion of that trip. In a word, it is a book written by one loafer for a brother loafer to read." Whatever criticism the loose structure of the work has invited, it can thus hardly be said to have fallen short of the author's own intentions in writing it. Its immediate commercial success, moreover, goes to show that by 1880 Mark Twain's readers were prepared to appreciate his humor regardless of the kind of vehicle he chose for it.

Both the tramp metaphor (which was to provide the title for the work) and the gossip metaphor are apt to describe what little structure the book has, and both metaphors are in fact combined in a letter of 9 September 1878 from Mark Twain to Twichell in which he bewails the fact that their "pleasant tramping and talking" had ended. Tramping, however, suggests walking (as an unused preface specifies), but it was to be the very plan of the author to have his two trampers resort to every possible mode of travel rather than actually walk: "I am in pedestrian costume, as a general thing, & *start* on pedestrian tours, but mount the first conveyance that offers, making but slight explanation or excuse, & endeavoring to seem unconscious that this is not legitimate pedestrianizing" (letter to W.D. Howells, 30 January 1879). This intention of burlesque regarding what serves as the basic structuring principle of the account also extends to the two supporting structural devices introduced in its very opening—"to study art" and "to learn the German language." These stated plans were of necessity at odds with much of the actual experience of Mark Twain, who for the most part of his stay had not been free to tramp but had been burdened, as it were, with his family (and other people in his traveling party) as well as with the task of writing a book. The ensuing need to extend the walking tour with Twichell beyond the confines of actual experience and to assign or to reassign individual incidents is reflected in his notebooks and his correspondence. In a letter of 26 January 1879 to Twichell he relates how he hunted for a sock in the dark room of his pension and concludes by saying that he "transferred the adventure to our big room in the hotel at Heilbronn, and got it on paper a good deal to my satisfaction." However, such satisfaction did not always result; and, all in all, neither pedestrianizing with "Harris" nor the study of art and the process of learning the German language, nor even the burlesque stance, are kept before the reader consistently enough to maintain a narrative thread or even to keep alive his interest in the two characters and their responses to European scenery, manners, and institutions. Despite the significant role that Twichell played in the genesis of the book, his fictive counterpart does not become a person in his own right, let alone a kind of vernacular presence like the Mr. Brown of earlier writings. In fact, the generalized "we" of both the opening and the closing chapters seems to refer to Mark Twain and his family rather than to the author and his traveling companion (who, in terms of the actual experience of the trip, had not yet arrived on the scene or had long since returned to the United States).

The extent to which biographical experience and the fictionalized account of it are at odds is particularly obvious in chapter 1. The "short halt" in Frankfurt, inspired by the 1878 itinerary of Mark Twain and his party en route to Heidelberg, does not further either the pedestrian tour nor the study of art or of the German language: in the final event it turns out to have been made solely in the interest of accommodating the legend of "The Knave of Bergen," borrowed from *The Legends of the Rhine from Basle to Rotterdam,* a book by one F.J. Kiefer that charmed Mark Twain "nearly to death" and was to serve him several times to provide copy for his manuscript. Digressions of this sort, serious as well as burlesque, occur throughout the narrative, and frequently

the relation of such material has commanded more interest than the matter of the pedestrian tour itself. "Jim Baker's Blue Jay Yarn" (also known as "What Stumped the Blue Jays") in particular, but also "The Great French Duel," "Nicodemus Dodge and the Skeleton," and "The Man Who Put Up at Gadsby's" have frequently been reprinted and interpreted independently of their immediate context in *A Tramp Abroad.* The same has happened to material that belongs to the actual matter of the book, such as passages about Heidelberg and its student life, the author's observations on "The Awful German Language" (Appendix D of the work), the "Legend of the 'Spectacular Ruin,'" and the account of the ascent of the Riffelberg.

Indeed, as a travel book *A Tramp Abroad* in its entirety today makes for somewhat tedious reading. If, however, the work is taken up for what it tells us about Mark Twain in 1878–1879 and for its occasional glimpses of the author's thematic concerns in earlier and later works, reading it will be found to be a rewarding experience: the rafting episode on the Neckar (largely fictitious in its details) contains many of the constituents of Huck Finn's rafting down the Mississippi; Sir Wissenschaft in the "Legend of the 'Spectacular Ruin'" foreshadows Hank Morgan in *A Connecticut Yankee in King Arthur's Court* (1889); the discussion of the Old Masters implicitly and explicitly harks back to *The Innocents Abroad,* as does the Riffelberg expedition to "Some Learned Fables for Good Old Boys and Girls" (1875); and the statement that "tastes are made, not born" can readily be related to Pudd'nhead Wilson's idea that "training is everything." But descriptions like that of the American porterhouse steak (presented in the next to the last chapter of the book) are still waiting to be discovered and savored for their own sakes.

Horst H. Kruse

BIBLIOGRAPHY

Blair, Walter. *Mark Twain & Huck Finn.* Berkeley: U of California P, 1960.

Bridgman, Richard. *Traveling in Mark Twain.* Berkeley: U of California P, 1987.

Clemens, Samuel L. *Mark Twain's Notebooks & Journals, Volume II (1877–1883).* Ed. Frederick Anderson, Lin Salamo, and Bernard L. Stein. Berkeley: U of California P, 1975.

Neider, Charles. Introduction. *A Tramp Abroad.* By Clemens. Ed. Neider. New York: Harper & Row, 1977. ix–xxiv.

See also: "Awful German Language, The"; Europe; "Jim Baker's Blue Jay Yarn"; "Man Who Put Up at Gadsby's, The"; Travel Writings; Twichell, Joseph

Traum, Philip

Philip Traum is the name Young Satan uses in the company of the villagers in the "Chronicle of Young Satan" (*The Mysterious Stranger Manuscripts* [1969], edited by William M. Gibson). No one in the story knows the mysterious youth by his celestial name except the boys, Theodor Fischer, Nikolaus Baumann, and Seppi Wohlmeyer.

The name Traum, German for "dream," suggests connections with the dream visions Theodor experiences, under the influence of Satan, and his frequent suspicions that Satan's revelations must be dreams rather than reality. It also begs comparison with similar reactions of other Mark Twain characters (Hank Morgan, Tom Canty, Pudd'nhead Wilson, Sieur Louis de Conte, and others) and stories such as "Which Was the Dream?" (written 1897), "The Great Dark" (written 1898), "My Platonic Sweetheart" (written 1898, published 1912), "My Boyhood Dreams" (1900), "A Curious Dream" (1870), and "A Strange Dream" (1867).

Robert E. Lowrey

BIBLIOGRAPHY

Brodwin, Stanley. "Mark Twain's Masks of Satan: The Final Phase." *American Literature* 45 (May 1973): 206–227.

Clemens, Samuel L. *Mark Twain's Mysterious Stranger Manuscripts.* Ed. William M. Gibson. Berkeley: U of California P, 1969.

Kahn, Sholom J. *Mark Twain's Mysterious Stranger: A Study of the Manuscript Texts.* Columbia: U of Missouri P, 1978.

May, John R. "The Gospel According to Philip Traum: Structural Unity in *The Mysterious Stranger.*" *Studies in Short Fiction* 8 (Summer 1971): 411–422.

Tuckey, John S. *Mark Twain and Little Satan: The Writing of "The Mysterious Stranger."* West Lafayette, Ind.: Purdue UP, 1963.

See also: Dreams; *Mysterious Stranger, The*

Travel Writings
(1869–1897)

During his lifetime, Mark Twain published three book-length accounts of foreign travels: *The Innocents Abroad; or, The New Pilgrim's Progress* (1869), *A Tramp Abroad* (1880), and *Following the Equator: Journey Around the World* (1897). In addition, two of his most popular and durable nonfiction volumes, *Roughing It* (1872) and *Life on the Mississippi* (1883) include substantial accounts of Mark Twain's travels in the American West. *Roughing It* also incorporates sixteen chapters on the Sandwich Islands (Hawaii), which began as letters Mark Twain had written in 1866 as a correspondent for the Sacramento *Union*. Twain's literary executor, Albert B. Paine, compiled a miscellaneous volume, *Europe and Elsewhere* (1923), from Mark Twain's uncollected essays and unpublished papers, including an extensive fragment written and revised in the early 1890s, about a trip afloat down the Rhône River in the vicinity of Arles in the summer of 1891. Tentatively titled *The Innocents Adrift*, this fragment was renamed "Down the Rhône" by Paine. Nearly twenty years later, Franklin Walker and G. Ezra Dane compiled *Mark Twain's Travels with Mr. Brown* (New York: Knopf, 1940), a volume that includes travel letters and lectures written about Hawaii, Central America, and Twain's ocean passage to New York in the company of Brown, a fictitious gruff sidekick. Mark Twain eventually abandoned this literary device as he composed his letters home from the *Quaker City* voyage and revised them into *The Innocents Abroad*. The Sacramento *Union* letters from the Sandwich Islands are gathered in *Mark Twain's Letters from Hawaii*, edited by A. Grove Day. However, the first three volumes listed above comprise the travel books completed and published as such during Mark Twain's lifetime, and the heart of his contribution to this genre.

The first and most famous of these books, *The Innocents Abroad*, grew from letters Mark Twain was commissioned to write for a newspaper, the San Francisco *Daily Alta California* as a passenger on the steamship *Quaker City* for its voyage to Europe and the Holy Land from June to November 1867. The book also includes voyage reports originally published in the New York *Tribune* and the New York *Herald*. Extensively refitted for the first American luxury cruise to these storified locations, the *Quaker City* was the vanguard for what has since become an immense industry, and in its early chapters Mark Twain's account makes much of the novelty, paradoxes, and scope of the idea, a monied "expedition" for both pilgrimage and pleasure. The unprecedented nature of the trip, the much publicized Paris Exposition of that year, and the American hunger for reconnection to the larger world after the long period of the Civil War, promised a large audience for a lively, detailed book.

Travel books, however, were hardly a new entertainment idea when Mark Twain set about writing these letters; nor were all previous American accounts of European travel fueled by sentimentality. Though American writers like Washington Irving, Henry Wadsworth Longfellow, and Bayard Taylor had spread the romantic habit of reverence and awe among foreign vistas and experiences, there were works in print by other writers (e.g., Samuel Fiske, John W. De Forest, and James De Mill) that either expressed disillusionment at Europe's ruins, poverty, and filth or poked common-sense Yankee fun at the pretenses of guides and worshipful visitors. This is the pattern Mark Twain followed in *The Innocents Abroad*: insofar as there is a plot

in this tale of comfortable wanderings, it involves the efforts of Mark Twain and the "boys" (as he calls a handful of like-minded fellow travelers) to evade or frustrate false piety and sham connoisseurship wherever they find it and enjoy instead spontaneous reactions and imaginings as people at play and as Americans with values grounded in a different cultural milieu.

Certain motifs, therefore, recur in *The Innocents Abroad*, providing some narrative continuity. Mark Twain and his chosen few often escape like wayward schoolchildren from the established tour routes; they mutter or proclaim their suspicions about the broken statues, cracked and discolored paintings by officially sanctioned Old Masters, the stiff poses and stylizations of medieval and early Renaissance art, as well as the sanctimonious guides who call for reverence before such artifacts. Thanks in part to the impact of John Ruskin's criticism, the color, exuberance, opulence, and drama of much High Renaissance art had moved out of favor, and in France and Italy Mark Twain satirizes his fellow voyagers' pseudo-Ruskinian scorn for work that appealed immediately to both the senses and common sense. The continuing adversary, in these mildly agonistic European chapters, is anything that threatens dogmatic control over intuitions, imagination, or pragmatic American habits of thought. Mark Twain lampoons or vilifies poorly plotted or morally confused local legends and fables, uncomfortable and overrated fashions emulated by the American bourgeoisie, certain ballyhooed natural wonders that are surpassed by American scenery, and various artifacts and practices of Roman Catholicism, a faith that a mid-century American writer could chide with safety and with a strong chance of pleasing readers at home.

Satire and Yankee derision, however, are balanced in *The Innocents Abroad* by moments of enthusiasm, of high feeling achieved in ventures off the tourist track, either physically or imaginatively. Delighting in the exotic back streets of Tangier, in Notre Dame and the Bois de Boulogne in Paris, in dungeons and other sights associated with romantic fiction and sensibilities, in the Blue Grotto, Lake Como, and the ruins of Pompeii, Mark Twain at times offers purple passages to rival the sentimental travel accounts. Several of these passages work well in context because their moods are not worked to exhaustion, and their brevity may reflect certain time limits inherent in American-style emotional response. These cadenzas are often relieved and conserved by comedy and sharp, refreshing returns to the prosaic. Thirty-two years old, Mark Twain had a solid layman's familiarity with European history, and he waxes eloquent about the antiquity of walls, statues, and great shrines and about what dramatic events these artifacts had witnessed. The sentimental or romantic side of Mark Twain's account and his interest in human history sometimes carry the book into a morbidity familiar in nineteenth-century travel literature. Especially in France and Italy, Mark Twain shows, by modern standards, excessive interest in decayed corpses, morgues, mass graves, cemeteries, and convents full of bones and skeletons. Sometimes the theme seems to be the macabre side of Roman Catholic religious practice; on other occasions Mark Twain seems to try for *momento mori* high seriousness or indulge in the open-grave voyeurism sometimes found in Hawthorne, Emerson, and other Anglo-American Protestant writers of the time.

The lasting popularity and pleasure of *The Innocents Abroad* may stem in part from exuberant digressions, refusal to stay "on tour" as a narrative, and willingness to wander like its protagonist and create fun where it is not readily found. Mark Twain concocts preposterous legends, gladiator playbills and sports-page reports, and ancient Wall Street style slave-market summaries; at Lake Como he waxes eloquent about the clear water and good trout fishing at Lake Tahoe and then rails for several paragraphs about its dreadful Indian name. Chapters 29 and 30, supposedly about the group's ascent of Mt. Vesuvius, are a running gag about not being able to stay on the announced subject. Though Mark Twain pad-

ded all of his travel books for the sake of the subscription trade, which sought massive volumes for door-to-door sales, such "padding" in *The Innocents Abroad* includes much of the lively and original material in the volume and seems central to one of its major principles—vigorous, improvising resistance to travel as somber, genteel, worshipful, singleminded pilgrimage.

Readers often express disappointment at tonal and thematic changes that set in when Mark Twain's account shifts to the Holy Land. Here the overwhelming solemnity of the major attractions, the hostility of the climate, and the unpleasantness (to American sensibilities) of local customs seem to thwart the capricious digressions, the improvised myths and legends, and the social and religious satire. Compared to what has gone before, many of the last twenty chapters seem encumbered or fatigued, as if both the trip and the account have gone on for too long. Fashioning a straw-man adversary of "William C. Grimes," (actually W.C. Prime, author of *Tent Life in the Holy Land*), Mark Twain grumbles about melodramatic and self-aggrandizing accounts of adventures in the region and about the sordid realities he finds: the unheroic Bedouins, the urban poverty and endless begging, and the gaudy profanation, by competing Christian sects, of the holiest shrines of Christendom. Nonetheless, there are moments in which Mark Twain takes chances with the material he must work with: his comic cadenza on the Tomb of Adam, which he finds in the Church of the Holy Sepulchre, satirizes not only his own capacity for sentimentality, but also the whole spectacle around him, of believers prostrated at dubious material relics and stone slabs and marked-out spots on the earth—the idolatrous perils of religious practice.

Because of the commercial success of *The Innocents Abroad*, Mark Twain returned to travel writing about ten years later while wandering with his family through Germany, Italy, France, Belgium, Holland, and England from April to November 1878. Mark Twain had come to Europe to do sustained writing and to control expenses, since he had been running up debts living the high life of a famous author at home. His close friend Joseph Twichell joined him for a six-week ramble through Bavaria and Switzerland, and from this excursion Mark Twain fashioned most of *A Tramp Abroad*.

If the name of the book suggests a potboiler, *Tramp* is more liable to that charge than *Innocents*. When Mark Twain relies on a continuing joke for very long in a narrative, the result can be imaginative constriction and labored humor. In *Tramp* the recurring joke is about Mark Twain's style of tramping: elaborate preparations for rugged expeditions on foot, scrapped at the last minute in favor of coach rides, train rides, couriers, afternoons on hotel verandas, and "travelling" by telescope. Adventure-by-proxy is also a narrative strategy in *Tramp*, as Mark Twain borrows lavishly from accounts of mountaineers and of disasters on the Matterhorn and Mont Blanc, most notably from Edward Whymper's 1871 volume *Scrambles Amongst the Alps*; in addition, Beverly David has discovered that seven illustrations in the 1880 edition were adapted (to put it gently) from Whymper's book and another from a lithograph by Gustave Doré.

For continuing interest, therefore, *Tramp* depends more heavily on digressions and incongruous inclusions than does *Innocents*. Much of the oddest, most diverting material occurs in the first half of the book and in six appendices. Ostensibly triggered by an encounter with a raven in the Heidelberg woods, "What Stumped the Blue Jays," the satiric short story, spreads over chapters 2 and 3 of *Tramp*, and the rambling tale of Nicodemus Dodge, the Hannibal print shop, and Jimmy Finn's skeleton is but a part of a drifting conversation between Harris (Twichell) and Mark Twain as they stroll through the Black Forest from Baden-Baden to Oppenau. The most famous of the six appendices is "The Awful German Language," a comic lesson often reprinted by itself. Amusing as these units may be in themselves, they suggest little connection to the business at hand, not even as refusal or relief.

Of the three travel books, *Tramp* is the only one to have been abridged in modern editions, a decision that may itself reflect the diffuseness and occasional low temperature of the book as a whole.

Fifteen years later, Mark Twain was bankrupt, having lost hundreds of thousands of dollars on the disastrous Paige typesetter and the failure of the Charles Webster Publishing Company. To pay his debts and recover financially, he, accompanied by Olivia and Clara Clemens, embarked in August 1895 on a lecture trip around the world. When the tour ended in Europe in July 1896, Mark Twain had accumulated the material that yielded *Following the Equator* in 1897.

Of the three travel books, *Following the Equator* is known the least: no popular-priced edition of it is now in print, and it has received comparatively little critical attention. Its obscurity is unfortunate, for though the book lacks the broadly funny agonistic structures of *The Innocents Abroad* and the extractable narrative gems of *A Tramp Abroad*, *Following the Equator* has virtues of other kinds. This sprawling, final travel account seems more consistently focused on the world as observed and less on Mark Twain himself as the hero or jester in the exotic landscape. The centers of interest in *Following* are three: Hawaii as a place returned to after a thirty-year absence; Australia as a new white culture, with money and energy of the sort that Mark Twain could immediately understand; and India as an alien culture that awakened his taste for the gory, spectacular *gestes* of British colonial history. Sights and people in New Zealand and South Africa are also described, but more quickly and with less gusto.

"Following" is an apt watchword for the book, for throughout *Following the Equator* Mark Twain seems uncommonly at peace with himself as an international personage and with the rituals of the Grand Tour. With no pretenses here about striking out on his own, he seems contented with the comforts of organized travel: guides, flattering customs agents, obsequious Indian "bearers," admiring local dignitaries, the unhurried cadences of a trip planned and scheduled by others, and what he calls the "irresponsible trade" of the "Unbiased Traveler Seeking Information." His diary entries provide the cue to many of the chapters, which often seem to roll easily away, in unpredictable directions, from the events of the given day. Mark Twain the social critic is nonetheless in evidence. The Hawaii chapters include accounts of the enslavement of natives in plantation labor; the Australia and New Zealand visits review the decimation of the aboriginal and Maori populations; in India Twain meditates on the ancient and religiously founded injustices of the caste system; and in Africa he musters some respect for the Boers as doughty and skillful native resisters of British imperial rule. Yet in most of these passages Mark Twain's response to injustice seems muted, when compared to "King Leopold's Soliloquy" (1905), "To the Person Sitting in Darkness" (1901), and other of his late writings, or to Hank Morgan's rage in *A Connecticut Yankee* (1889), and the dry wit and easy self-deprecation in the narrative voice seem to encompass and mollify Mark Twain's severity as an aging Yankee moralist. Also contrasting to the social criticism, and disconcerting some readers, is his apparent delight in recounting tales of massacre involving innocent people and in telling of the bloody heroics of the British army, specifically Clive's revenge for the atrocities of the Black Hole and Colin Campbell's vast slaughters in raising the siege of Lucknow and suppressing the great Sepoy Mutiny of 1857–1858. Substantial space is also given over to narratives of the thuggee murders of the early century. Throughout his life, some side of Mark Twain took boyish pleasure in fantasies of carnage and tales of military mayhem. The evidence of that fascination is clear in *Following the Equator*, and it might be fittingly recalled when one develops thematic readings of violence in the major novels.

Readers of *Following the Equator* may also find some tonal confusion in Mark Twain's references to certain unscrupulous movers and shakers on the new worldwide stage, notably Cecil Rhodes and Mark Twain's late friend P.T. Barnum. Manufacturing a legend about a young, penniless Rhodes using a newspaper from a shark's stomach to make a fortune on the Australian wool crop, Mark Twain introduces him to the book as neither monstrous nor magnificent, but only as "extraordinary," in his luck and opportunism. Similar ambivalence toward Rhodes turns up again in the late chapters on South Africa. Barnum is likewise presented as a man notable for the scale of his schemes and success rather than as either wonderful or horrific as an American entrepreneur. Toward the end of volume one, in a playful footnote, Mark Twain defines the marsupial as a creature "whose specialty is its pocket" and lists himself as the "latest marsupial" in a succession that includes Cecil Rhodes and John Jacob Astor. Standing apart from some of the other late writings, *Following the Equator* does not portray mankind as basically contemplative and villainous, for the human species in this book seems enigmatic and largely beyond the reach of fierce or final moral judgment.

Each chapter of *Following the Equator* is headed with an aphorism from *Pudd'nhead Wilson's New Calendar*, an unpublished trove of mordant proverbs, which Mark Twain apparently continued to churn out after the completion of *Pudd'nhead Wilson* (1894). The new witticisms seem less bitter, as a group, than their forbearers in the novel; there are very few wholesale indictments here of religious belief or human nature per se and no celebrations of death as release from worldly pain. Instead, there are wry comments on social and political life, on cuckoo clocks, on the natural world, on humor and faith, on the hard business of making maxims, and on the complex art of telling lies. Like much of the narrative, these maxims avoid severe and self-cornering indictments of the human condition. The mild fun that they occasionally poke at Mark Twain himself as a champion American liar telling the truth (or something like it) about civil adventures in faraway places enhances *Following the Equator* as a broad, provocative exposition of Mark Twain's temperament in his later years, as a view of the mores of luxurious tourism in the 1890s, and as a glimpse of how the waning century and a powerful Anglo-American culture contemplated the mark they had made.

Bruce Michelson

BIBLIOGRAPHY

Bridgman, Richard. *Traveling in Mark Twain.* Berkeley: U of California P, 1987.

Clemens, Samuel L. *Traveling with the Innocents Abroad.* Ed. Daniel M. McKeithan. Norman: U of Oklahoma P, 1958.

Ganzel, Dewey. *Mark Twain Abroad: The Cruise of the "Quaker City."* Chicago: U of Chicago P, 1968.

Scott, Arthur L. *Mark Twain at Large.* Chicago: Henry Regnery, 1969.

See also: Europe; *Following the Equator;* Holy Land, The; India; *Innocents Abroad, The;* Sentimentality; *Tramp Abroad, A*

verdict and then carries out the hanging, pausing to read four chapters of the Book of Genesis to the condemned. The narrator's conclusion that the anecdote enhanced Captain Ned's reputation in California satirizes the anarchic system of frontier justice.

J. Mark Baggett

BIBLIOGRAPHY

Benson, Ivan. *Mark Twain's Western Years.* Stanford, Calif.: Stanford UP, 1966.

Clemens, Samuel L. *The Complete Short Stories of Mark Twain.* Ed. Charles Neider. Garden City, N.Y.: Hanover House, 1957. 84–89.

———. *Roughing It.* Ed. Franklin R. Rogers and Paul Baender. Berkeley: U of California P, 1972. 318–324, 591–592.

Fatout, Paul. *Mark Twain in Virginia City.* Bloomington: Indiana UP, 1964.

Wilson, James D. *A Reader's Guide to the Short Stories of Mark Twain.* Boston: G.K. Hall, 1987.

See also: Blakely, Captain Ned; Law; *Roughing It*

"Trial, A"

(1872)

The short story "A Trial" is the name given to chapter 50 of *Roughing It* (1872), one of a handful of independent stories in the book (*RI* 318–324). First published in the 1872 volume, the story has been anthologized in *Complete Short Stories* (1957).

"A Trial" recalls an incident of frontier justice involving Captain Ned Blakely, a fictitious name for Captain Edgar (Ned) Wakeman whom Mark Twain met on a voyage from San Francisco to Nicaragua in 1866. However, Wakeman's biography makes no mention of the events that take place in "A Trial" (*RI* 591–592) in which Captain Ned avenges the murder of his mate by hanging the killer, bully Bill Noakes.

Set in the remote Chincha Islands of Peru, Captain Ned, who particularly distrusts the law, captures the criminal himself and finally agrees to conduct a perfunctory trial. He intimidates the jury into rendering a "guilty"

Trollope, Frances

(1780–1863)

The mother of English novelist Anthony Trollope, Frances Trollope wrote travel books on Belgium, Paris, Vienna, and America. She began her literary career writing novels, her two best being *The Vicar of Wrexhill* (1837) and *The Widow Barnaby* (1838). She wrote over a period of thirty years and died in Florence, Italy. After a visit to America (1827–1830), she wrote *Domestic Manners of the Americans* (1832), a critique that provoked many angry responses from its American readers.

Samuel Clemens quotes from her travel book on America in chapter 27 of his *Life on the Mississippi* (1883). The passage relates Trollope's "emotions" evoked by her viewing of the "utterly desolate" but "mighty river" in 1827. Twain found the comments of several foreign critics, like Trollope's, to be accurate and fair, in spite of the typically hostile American response. In an unpublished passage deleted from *Life on the Mississippi*, Twain praises Trollope for her courage and plain talk and attacks the Americans who wrongfully "cursed" her for telling the truth. In his notebook entry for 2 April 1889, Clemens lists Lepel Griffin, Matthew Arnold, Charles Dickens, and Trollope (Anthony or Frances?) as "Englishmen on America."

Kevin Hadduck

BIBLIOGRAPHY

Clemens, Samuel L. *Mark Twain's Notebooks & Journals, Volume III (1883–1891).* Ed. Robert Pack Browning, Michael B. Frank, and Lin Salamo. Berkeley: U of California P, 1979.

Kruse, Horst H. *Mark Twain and "Life on the Mississippi."* Amherst: U of Massachusetts P, 1981.

Lynn, Kenneth S. *Mark Twain and Southwestern Humor.* Boston: Little, Brown, 1959.

Pettit, Arthur G. *Mark Twain and the South.* Lexington: UP of Kentucky, 1974.

See also: England; *Life on the Mississippi*

"True Story, A"

(1874)

One of Twain's finest dialect tales, "A True Story Repeated Word for Word as I Heard It" was composed in the summer of 1874 (Emerson 77) and first appeared in the *Atlantic Monthly* (November 1874). The magazine paid its highest rate, $20 a page (*MHTL* 25); Clemens's pleasure over his first acceptance from the *Atlantic* offset his disappointment at receiving only $60 (Kaplan 181). The sketch remained one of his favorites, republished in *Sketches, New and Old* (1875), mentioned repeatedly in his notebooks, and featured on his 1895 Australian lecture tour. The qualities that William Dean Howells admired in 1875 are still the tale's virtues: realistic African-American dialect, skillful frame-narrative technique, powerful first-person characterization, and subtle social history and criticism.

Clemens based the story on an apparently historical incident involving his sister-in-law's Quarry Farm cook, "Auntie" Mary Ann Cord (1798–1888) (Wisbey 1, 3–4). A more serious literary effort than the title suggests, "A True Story" features the dramatic monologue of a former slave now working for "Misto C—," the frame narrator, who reveals his own insensitivity while introducing "our servant" (*Sketches* 265). The first detail he relates about "Aunt Rachel," pointing to the pseudonym with quotation marks, is particularly telling: despite her implied family ties, she sits "respectfully below our level" on the porch because of her rank and her race. The narrator's sentimental commentary soon reveals a racist condescension not very different from a slaveholder's, an implication reinforced by the name "Misto C—." Aunt Rachel, like many another mammy, is "a cheerful, hearty soul" with a "mighty frame and stature" who "let[s] off peal after peal of laughter" (*Sketches* 265); like many another white master, Misto C— takes her appearance and behavior as evidence that she "*can't* have had any trouble" (*Skteches* 266).

Aunt Rachel's dialect narrative shows just how superficial and self-serving that judgment is. This former slave, named after the biblical mother searching for her children (Gibson 77), endured the indignity of chains and physical inspections on the auction block, the sale of her husband and all her seven children, and the difficulties of the Civil War and its aftermath, when she and other slaves abandoned by their masters had to fend for themselves. She bore all these troubles with dignity, taking pride in the high status of her Maryland birth by asserting, "I want you niggers to understan' dat I wa'nt bawn in de mash to be fool' by trash! i's one o' de old Blue Hen's Chickens, I is!" (*Sketches* 267, 271). In this context, her unexpected reunion with her youngest child, Henry, amounts to high poetic justice. Having somehow managed to escape to the North, he reappears as a Union soldier dancing in her kitchen. In a discovery scene of classical symmetry, he recognizes her by her trope of self-assertion, and she recognizes him by marks on his forehead and wrist. So she justly concludes her narrative, and "A True Story" as a whole, with a sarcastic, "Oh, no, Misto C——, *I* hain't had no trouble. An' no *joy!*" (*Sketches* 272), said while standing above her listener, in an inversion of the opening frame. The absence of a closing frame by Misto C— (a convention of the genre) scorns him further by giving Aunt Rachel the last word.

"A True Story" has won praise for its faithful rendering of dialect, which Twain edited painstakingly (*MTHL* 24–26), its sensitive portrait of black families in the Civil War era, including the role of black soldiers in the Union Army (Foner 265–266), and its anticipation of *Huckleberry Finn's* narrative techniques and themes (Kaplan 180–181). "A True Story" also shows very sophisticated use of comic techniques mastered a decade earlier in "The Celebrated Jumping Frog of Calaveras County" (1865). "A True Story" has the frame narrator undergo an initiation worth the embarrassment while the dialect speaker reveals secrets worth knowing. In this sense, the story represents a significant turning point in Twain's career.

Judith Yaross Lee

BIBLIOGRAPHY

Clemens, Samuel L. *Mark Twain-Howells Letters: The Correspondence of Samuel L. Clemens and William D. Howells, 1872–1910.* Ed. Henry Nash Smith and William M. Gibson. 2 vols. Cambridge, Mass.: Harvard UP, 1960

———. *Mark Twain's Notebooks & Journals, Volume III (1883–1891).* Ed. Robert Pack Browning, Michael B. Frank, and Lin Salamo. Berkeley: U of California P, 1979.

———. "A True Story, Repeated Word for Word as I Heard It." *Atlantic Monthly* 34.205 (1874): 591–594. Rpt. *Sketches, New and Old.* Author's National Edition. Vol 19. New York: Harper, 1903. 265–272.

Emerson, Everett. *The Authentic Mark Twain: A Literary Biography of Samuel L. Clemens.* Philadelphia: U of Pennsylvania P, 1984.

Foner, Philip S. *Mark Twain: Social Critic.* 2nd ed. New York: International Publishers, 1966.

Gibson, William M. *The Art of Mark Twain.* New York: Oxford UP, 1976.

Kaplan, Justin. *Mr. Clemens and Mark Twain.* New York: Simon & Schuster, 1966.

McMahan, Elizabeth, ed. *Critical Approaches to Mark Twain's Short Stories.* Port Washington, N.Y.: Kennikat, 1981.

Shillingsburg, Miriam Jones. *At Home Abroad: Mark Twain in Australasia.* Jackson: UP of Mississippi, 1988.

Wisbey, Herbert A., Jr. "The True Story of Auntie Cord." *Mark Twain Society Bulletin* 4.2 (1981): 1, 3–5.

See also: Cord, Mary Ann ("Auntie"); Rachel, Aunt; Racial Attitudes

Trumbull, James Hammond (1821–1897)

Hartford historian, philologist, and bibliographer, James Hammond Trumbull wrote numerous scholarly works including *The Memorial History of Hartford Connecticut 1633–1884* (1886) and *The True-Blue Laws of Connecticut* (1876). Twain owned and read both these volumes. Twain referred to Trumbull, his friend and Nook Farm neighbor, as "the most learned man in Hartford."

Born in Stonington, Connecticut, Trumbull attended Yale University in 1838 but withdrew due to ill health. He helped James Harvey Linsley catalogue Connecticut wildlife (1842–1843), then served two terms as Connecticut assistant secretary of state. After service as state librarian and registrar, he was elected secretary of state (1861–1866).

When Clemens and Warner completed *The Gilded Age*, they asked Trumbull to write chapter-head quotations in a variety of languages, including Chinese, Sanskrit, and Sioux Indian. For the novel Trumbull wrote mottoes parodying the common overuse of gimmicky chapter headings while adding a running commentary on the novel's plot. An appendix of translations was added in 1890 that prolonged the novel's copyright.

According to Twain's citations and "General Note," Trumbull's *The True-Blue Laws of Connecticut* was a source for chapters 15, 23, and 27 in *The Prince and the Pauper* (1882). Twain made many marginal comments and annotations in his copy of Trumbull's study, making comments on fifty-nine pages. In an 1889 projected appendix for *A Connecticut*

Yankee, Twain cited *Blue Laws* as his source for "Boil in Oil." In 1897 Twain wrote an obituary on Trumbull whom he said "could swear in 27 different languages."

Wesley Britton

BIBLIOGRAPHY

Dickinson, Leon T. "The Sources of *The Prince and the Pauper.*" *Modern Language Notes* 64 (February 1949): 103–106.

French, Bryant Morey. "James Hammond Trumbull's Alternative Chapter Headings for *The Gilded Age.*" *Philological Quarterly* 50 (April 1971): 271–280.

Tuckey, John S[utton]
(1921–1987)

Educated entirely at the University of Notre Dame (A.B., 1943; M.A., 1949; Ph.D., 1953), editor and scholar John S. Tuckey joined the English department at the Calumet Campus of Purdue University in Hammond, Indiana, in 1953 and taught there until his death. For more than a decade (beginning in 1972) he served as head of his department and also (after 1974) as assistant dean of the graduate school. In 1981 he became Frederick L. Hovde Distinguished Professor of English, the first faculty member to be thus honored at a regional Purdue campus.

A genial man, Professor Tuckey was known for his generosity in assisting other scholars, particularly younger ones. In the field of Mark Twain studies he edited a series of volumes of Twain's writings with exemplary thoroughness and historical appreciation and also made valuable discoveries involving the work known as *The Mysterious Stranger.* Inspecting the manuscript collection of the Mark Twain Papers at the University of California, Berkeley, in 1961 on a grant from the Purdue Research Foundation, Professor John Tuckey was the first scholar to grasp the full extent of the misrepresentation practiced in the publication of Albert Bigelow Paine and Frederick Duneka's edition of Twain's *The Mysterious Stranger* (1916). Tuckey's findings, presented in *Mark Twain and Little Satan: The Writing of "The Mysterious Stranger"* (1963), set the stage for William M. Gibson's edition of *Mark Twain's Mysterious Stranger Manuscripts* (1969). Never again would it be possible for informed readers to assume that there are fewer than three *Mysterious Stranger* manuscripts or that Twain ever intended to conflate them in the manner that Paine and Duneka did.

Tuckey subsequently developed an interest in the deterministic views Twain manifested in his later period and became an authority on Twain's thought and writings after 1895. His article "Mark Twain's Later Dialogue: The 'Me' and the Machine" (*American Literature* 1970), for example, helped begin the reevaluation of Twain as elder commentator on human nature, and Tuckey's inquiry contributed new respectability to Twain's intellectual theories. Tuckey's edition of *Mark Twain's "Which Was the Dream?" and Other Symbolic Writings of the Later Years* (1967) was followed by an edition of *Mark Twain's Fables of Man* (1972)—and selections from both were excerpted for Tuckey's edition of *The Devil's Race-Track: Mark Twain's Great Dark Writings* (1980). He also edited *Mark Twain's "Mysterious Stranger" and the Critics* (1968) and *No. 44, The Mysterious Stranger* (1982). In a rare show of public disagreement he disputed in two notable book reviews some implications of Hamlin Hill's *Mark Twain: God's Fool* (1973), questioning whether a caricatured image of Mark Twain emerges from the iconoclastic biography. At the time of his death, in 1987, Tuckey was engaged in a study of Twain's concepts of dreams and dream-life.

Alan Gribben

BIBLIOGRAPHY

Baetzhold, Howard G. "John Sutton Tuckey." *Mark Twain Circular* 1 (November 1987): 1–2.

Clemens, Samuel L. *The Devil's Race-Track: Mark Twain's Great Dark Writings.* Ed. John S. Tuckey. Berkeley: U of California P, 1980.

———. *Mark Twain's Fables of Man.* Ed. John S. Tuckey. Berkeley: U of California P, 1972.

———. *Mark Twain's "Which Was the Dream?" and Other Symbolic Writings of the Later Years.* Ed.

John S. Tuckey. Berkeley: U of California P, 1967.

———. *No. 44, The Mysterious Stranger.* Foreword and Notes by John S. Tuckey. Berkeley: U of California P, 1982.

Tuckey, John S. *Mark Twain and Little Satan: The Writing of "The Mysterious Stranger."* West Lafayette, Ind.: Purdue UP, 1963.

———. "Mark Twain's Later Dialogue: The 'Me' and the Machine." *American Literature* 41 (January 1970): 532–542.

———. Review of *Mark Twain: God's Fool.* By Hamlin Hill. *American Literature* 46 (1974): 117.

———, ed. *Mark Twain's "The Mysterious Stranger" and the Critics.* New York: Wadsworth, 1968.

See also: Mark Twain Project; *Mysterious Stranger, The*; Scholarship, Trends in Mark Twain

"Turning Point of My Life, The"

(1910)

Twain wrote "The Turning Point of My Life" in response to a request from *Harper's Bazaar.* Published in the February 1910 issue, this essay is an exposition of Twain's ideas on determinism. Twain shatters the notion that each human life has a meaningful goal that is achieved through rational human decisions. Rather than understanding human events as an orderly progression of cause-and-effect reactions designed to benefit mankind, Twain sees human life as determined by chance interactions between circumstance and temperament, forces that are indifferent to the lives of humans.

The essay is divided into three sections. In part 1 Twain repeats words such as "appointed" and "scheme" and symbolizes human life as an orderly "chain" of cause-and-effect "links," thus ironically establishing that each human life has a goal toward which it logically progresses. He then undermines this idea that he ostensibly supports. Twain subtly conveys that it was neither the "omens of the gods" nor human rationality that prompted the famous crossing of the Rubicon; rather it was the unplanned outburst of a nearby trumpeteer.

He then mocks cause-and-effect reasoning, the supposed "links" in this orderly chain of life, through exaggeration.

In part 2 Twain abandons the fairy-tale narrative voice and realistically portrays his own life. Obviously not a rational progression toward the "literary feature" of his identity, Twain's actions have been dictated by circumstance and his own uncontrollable temperament. In this section Twain elevates circumstance through personification while reducing humans to the subhuman—animals and objects. Finally, through repeating the phrase "to help or hurt," Twain portrays circumstance and temperament as indifferent toward the needs of humans.

Part 3 is a concise explanation of Twain's determinism. He reduces human actions to circumstance and human beings to their uncontrollable temperaments. This last section is the most realistic in voice. Throughout the essay Twain's developing realism in his language is a symbol for the growing truth of his words. In part 1 he uses a fairy-tale voice when espousing an idea in which he does not believe. In part 3 he states that he took his false idea of man as an "intellectual marvel" from "out of books," echoing the ridiculous ideas that Tom Sawyer takes from books in the Tom and Huck novels. The last paragraph of the essay denies any benevolence in the determinism that rules mankind. Twain cynically presents his literary career as an inevitable result of the Fall of Adam and Eve. It is thus that Twain portrays humankind as subject to a haphazard form of determinism.

Christina Linenfelser

BIBLIOGRAPHY

Clemens, Samuel L. *Mark Twain-Howells Letters: The Correspondence of Samuel L. Clemens and William D. Howells, 1872–1910.* Ed. Henry Nash Smith and William M. Gibson. 2 vols. Cambridge, Mass.: Harvard UP, 1960.

———. "The Turning Point of My Life." *Harper's Bazaar* (February 1910): 118–119.

Hill, Hamlin. *Mark Twain: God's Fool.* New York: Harper & Row, 1973.

See also: Determinism; Naturalism

Twainian, The

The Twainian is the second oldest American journal devoted to one author, and from 1939 to 1951 it was a valuable organ of camaraderie and scholarship, an exchange of questions and new information. The Mark Twain Society of Chicago, with about thirty members, began it as a typed mimeographed newsletter; regular type and printing would come in January 1945. The editor was George Hiram Brownell.

Publication ceased in 1941 and resumed in 1942 as a new series under the auspices of the Mark Twain Association of America, still in Chicago. Officers were the humorist George Ade as president, Franklin J. Meine as vice president, and Brownell as editor and executive secretary. *Twainian* changed its mailing address to Elkhorn, Wisconsin, in May. In June 1944 Brownell reported the death of Ade and described the past history of the Mark Twain Association. Plans had been to create an endowed foundation, but appeals to the Rockefeller and Guggenheim foundations for support were unsuccessful. The Edison Institute (founded by Henry Ford at Dearborn, Michigan) expressed interest for a time, but the institution chiefly wanted a house associated with Twain's early years to dismantle and move to their Greenfield Village; none was available, and the group lost interest.

For a time only Brownell's name appeared, as "Editor and Publisher," until the first 1947 issue, which listed the Mark Twain Research Foundation as publisher. There were no further changes until the death of Brownell in early June 1950. During his tenure as editor *The Twainian* grew and matured as a newsletter for scholars and enthusiasts and as a small but useful academic journal. It contained articles still cited in Mark Twain scholarship, useful bibliographies, and reprinted material (such as the late 1867 travel letters) still most readily accessible.

The May–June 1948 *Twainian* listed Brownell only as secretary to a board of governors that included Dixon Wecter, with Samuel C. Webster as president. When the May–June 1950 issue reported the deaths of Brownell and Wecter, the new secretary was Chester Davis and the new place of publication was Perry, Missouri; Davis later reported (May–June 1970) that moving the *Twainian* and the "files and materials of the Mark Twain Research Foundation from Wisconsin to Missouri" had required "several cars and trucks."

Davis set as a priority the development of a center for Twain studies—a major goal of the old Mark Twain Association of America—and took satisfaction in seeing the opening of the Mark Twain Birthplace Museum, in Stoutsville, Missouri. Today, a modern building encloses the small house where Samuel Clemens was born and a small manuscript library; there are useful holdings there, but it is not a major research library, and it is not under the control of the Mark Twain Research Foundation.

Davis confessed himself inexperienced as an editor, but for a time *The Twainian* coasted along on material that had been sent to Brownell or to Davis as his successor. When the flow slackened, Davis filled the pages any way he could. There were articles reprinted from such standard journals as *American Literature* "to make them more accessible to our members" (chiefly college libraries) and "Mark Twain Items Published Elsewhere," reprintings from *Abstracts of English Studies*; often these were items of tangential relation to Twain or items that themselves had appeared in the *Twainian* (but never abstracts of articles in the *Mark Twain Journal*). Sometimes whole issues were filled with these abstracts, already available in any good research collection. Another space filler was the small collection of books from Twain's personal library, often with extensive reprinting of the texts themselves, but scant mention of annotations. For example, the seventeenth-century *Letters of Madame De Sévigné* occupied considerable space in issues of *The Twainian* from November–December 1971 through September–October 1974. Davis said (May–June 1972) that he had enough material in the files to fill the *Twainian* for another fifty years, but refused to provide any sort of catalogue or to allow scholars to examine material he had not already published.

Still, there was no way of knowing whether he had anything more of value. After the University of California had published editions edited by Hill, Rogers, and Tuckey, he said that "the Foundation has many unpublished letters, some of which would certainly have been of value to the authors of those books" (November–December 1967).

Davis was always the cordial host, ready to show visiting scholars a few things they knew about already, frequently *one* new item, his collection of old automobiles, and the Mark Twain State Park, but he refused to allow scholars to work in the files of his "Research Foundation." The exasperation he created over two decades can be imagined, however. Hamlin Hill, for example, referred in print to "the anal-retentive Chester Davis, who is saving the revelations in the Mark Twain Research Foundation, Pizza Parlor, and Used-Car lot in Perry, Missouri, until he thinks the world is ready for them" (*American Literary Realism* [Autumn 1980]: 298).

Chester Davis died 6 December 1987. He was succeeded as executive secretary by his son, Chester L. Davis, Jr., a Detroit lawyer. There were a few more issues of *The Twainian* in 1988 and 1989, with what appears to have been the last one edited by his widow, Nina Davis, for April–May–June 1989. What will become of the holdings of the Mark Twain Research Foundation is uncertain. Chester Davis had purchased some material out of his own pocket, and refused to give a public accounting of what the foundation held. Chester Davis, Jr., has sold some items belonging to his late father at auction, and he says there are plans for holdings of the Mark Twain Research Foundation to go to an academic library, presumably in Missouri.

Thomas A. Tenney

See also: Clemens, Cyril Coniston; Mark Twain Research Foundation

Tweed, William Marcy ("Boss")
(1823–1878)

William M. Tweed led the Democratic party organization of Tammany Hall in New York City during its most corrupt era in the 1860s. Tweed's significant role in dictating Democratic nominations for mayor of New York City and governor of New York, and in directing city finances and graft into his own friends' private accounts, earned him the title "Boss," the attention of numerous reformers including Thomas Nast, and eventually several jail terms.

As a mugwump and reviler of political—and particularly partisan—corruption, Twain invoked Tweed repeatedly as a symbol of the times. Twain criticized Tweed's electoral manipulations and the rampant patronage system of the day throughout his editorial tenure in the 1860s and 1870s, and he eventually incorporated aspects of Tweed's character in his portrayal of political corruption in *The Gilded Age* (1873). Some of Hank Morgan's ambiguous political characteristics in *A Connecticut Yankee in King Arthur's Court* (1889) are evinced in his title "Boss," a reference in part to Tweed and the ultimate failure of democracy when imposed by leaders from above.

Patrick Deneen

BIBLIOGRAPHY

Callow, Alexander. *The Tweed Ring*. New York: Oxford UP, 1966.

Clemens, Samuel L. "Municipal Corruption." *Mark Twain's Speeches*. By Clemens. Ed. Albert B. Paine. New York: Harper, 1923. 218–221.

———. "The Stupendous Procession." *Mark Twain's Fables of Man*. By Clemens. Ed. John S. Tuckey. Berkeley: U of California P, 1972. 403–419.

Mandelbaum, Seymour J. *Boss Tweed's New York*. New York: John Wiley, 1965.

See also: Gilded Age, The; Politics

Twichell, Joseph Hopkins
(1838–1918)

Affectionately known as "Mark Twain's pastor," Joseph (Joe) Hopkins Twichell was a central figure in the Nook Farm community of Hartford, Connecticut, and, with the possible exception of William Dean Howells, the closest and most loyal friend Samuel Clemens ever had.

Twichell was born in Southington, Connecticut, where he attended the Lewis Academy. He entered Yale University at age seventeen; he was a popular, gregarious, and ruggedly athletic young man who distinguished himself in English composition. After graduating from Yale, Twichell attended Union Theological Seminary before joining the Union Army at the outbreak of the Civil War. His experiences as a chaplain to a rowdy and largely Roman Catholic New York regiment were both broadening and sobering, and they are recorded in touching detail in his war journals. To the suffering and devastation of war Twichell responded concretely rather than with theological or patriotic abstraction: "his concerns," Andrews writes, "were more for their [his men] lives than for their souls" (12). After the war, in November 1865, Twichell married Julia Harmony Cushman, and within a month assumed the position of associate pastor of the Asylum Hill Congregational Church in Hartford, where he would remain for the rest of his life.

Handsome, vigorous with a lively and earthy sense of humor, Twichell charmed his parishoners as he pastored a church less interested in doctrinal debate than in the practical application of genteel humanitarianism. The rigors of Calvinism had given way to a social gospel administered and encouraged by literate men—Nathaniel Burton, Edwin Parker, Twichell—who emphasized love, brotherhood, and toleration. Like Thomas K. Beecher's Park Church in Olivia Clemens's hometown of Elmira, New York, the Asylum Hill Congregational Church was a center of community social life, sponsoring spelling bees, lectures on the arts, charitable functions, and addresses by national celebrities on issues of political, economic, and ethical concern. The environment was perfect for Twichell, who, though a highly principled man particularly adverse to drunkenness and sexual misconduct, rarely brooded over complex theological issues. Though he did write a book on John Winthrop, Twichell was "more important as a man than as a minister" (Andrews 45).

Samuel Clemens found the religious climate at Twichell's church congenial with the comfortable deism into which he had settled in the decade after his 1870 marriage to Olivia. Though never officially joining Twichell's congregation (he and Olivia were registered tithing members of Park Church in Elmira until 1891), Clemens rented a family pew and attended services regularly at Asylum Hill. Twichell not only tolerated Clemens's irreverence, profanity, and occasionally salacious humor; he enjoyed them. As Charles Dudley Warner said of Twichell, he had "a liberal and receptive mind." He accompanied Clemens on a walking tour of Bermuda in May 1877, the experience providing the basis of "Some Rambling Notes of an Idle Excursion" (1877), and in 1878 he joined Clemens in Europe, where their walks proved the starting point for *A Tramp Abroad* (1880).

Twichell served as Clemens's confidant, adviser, and responsive ear. More importantly, Clemens trusted, respected, and loved him. When Clemens felt dejected after the Whittier Birthday Dinner fiasco (November 1877), and alienated from William Dean Howells, Twichell went with him to Europe, boosted his spirits and confidence, and helped to restore his good humor. In the 1890s when bankruptcy, Olivia's illness, and Susy's death (1896) devastated Clemens, Twichell encouraged Clemens to vent his anger in their personal correspondence. He in turn responded with patient understanding and, in appropriately muted but never condescending terms, reaffirmed a benevolently ordered universe. Twichell even good-naturedly chided his bitter friend that he had become quite "orthodox on the doctrine of Total Human Depravity." From most others Clemens had no patience for homiletic reassurances, for by the turn of the century his vision of man and God had darkened into an implacable determinism rigged by a malevolent deity. Yet to Twichell, Clemens writes: "You have a something divine in you that is not in other men. You have the touch that heals, not lacerates" (*Letters* 2:640–641).

James D. Wilson

BIBLIOGRAPHY

Andrews, Kenneth R. *Nook Farm: Mark Twain's Hartford Circle*. Cambridge, Mass.: Harvard UP, 1950.

Clemens, Samuel L. *Mark Twain's Letters*. Ed. Albert B. Paine. 2 vols. New York: Harper, 1917.

Strong, Leah A. *Joseph Hopkins Twichell: Mark Twain's Friend and Pastor*. Athens: U of Georgia P, 1966.

Twichell, Joseph H. *John Winthrop, First Governor of the Massachusetts Colony*. New York: Dodd, Mead, 1891.

———. "Mark Twain." *Harper's Monthly* 92 (May 1896): 816–827.

See also: Clergy; Nook Farm; *Tramp Abroad, A*

"Two Little Tales"

(1901)

"Two Little Tales" was first published in November 1901 in *Century Magazine*. According to Albert Bigelow Paine, the story was inspired by J.Y.M. MacAlister's complaint to Clemens about the medical director general of the British Army. MacAlister wanted the army to adopt plasmon, a skimmed-milk product in which he and Clemens had interests, but the director general refused to see MacAlister. Clemens advised his friend to approach the director general through a close friend; MacAlister did, and the army adopted the product (Paine 3:1098–1099).

Clemens transformed the incident into "Two Little Tales." Set in London in 1900, the story begins with a friend of the narrator who complains that he cannot gain the ear of a certain public official. The narrator, proclaiming himself to be "very old and very wise," offers advice to his friend in the form of a tall tale, "How the Chimney Sweep Got the Ear of the Emperor."

In the tall tale Jimmy, a chimney sweep, knows a cure for the emperor's dysentery. Tommy, an assistant cess-pool cleaner, advises Jimmy to get the emperor's attention through a chain of twenty-five friends that range from the cat-meat's man to the emperor's page. The plot of the framing tale parallels the tall tale: Jimmy corresponds to the narrator's friend, Tommy to the Twain narrator figure, and the emperor to the director general.

The story advances democratic principles in that a member of the lower class is more capable of counseling the emperor than his advisers are. Moreover, the cesspool cleaner's interest in having the emperor's dysentery cured provides a scatological commentary on Twain's opinion of politicians.

Roberta Seelinger Trites

BIBLIOGRAPHY

Clemens, Samuel L. "Two Little Tales." *The Man That Corrupted Hadleyburg and Other Stories and Essays*. New York: Harper, 1906. 186–201.

Paine, Albert Bigelow. *Mark Twain: A Biography*. 4 vols. New York: Harper, 1912.

See also: Business; Plasmon

U & V

"Unbiased Criticism, An"

(1865)

This short piece, written by Twain, first appeared in the *Californian* (number 100) on 18 March 1865. Later Twain shortened, revised, and renamed the piece "Literature in the Dry Diggings." He included it under this title in his first collection, *The Celebrated Jumping Frog of Calaveras County and Other Sketches* (1867), and he apparently also intended to include it in *Sketches, Old and New* (1875), although he deleted it before publication.

In its original form the piece begins and ends with a report of an art exhibit in the California Art Union. The references to the exhibit frame a central narrative by a second narrator, Coon, about the reading habits of miners in a remote camp. This center section, especially an election day speech in Calaveras County, is all that remains in the shortened version.

In addition to its humor, its main attraction today is the figure of Coon, the central narra-

tor, as a forerunner of Simon Wheeler.

David G. Miller

BIBLIOGRAPHY

Clemens, Samuel L. *The Works of Mark Twain: Early Tales & Sketches, Volume 2 (1864–1865)*. Ed. Edgar M. Branch and Robert H. Hirst. Berkeley: U of California P, 1981. 134–143.

See also: Coon, Ben; Wheeler, Simon

"United States of Lyncherdom, The"

(1923)

Written in 1901, "The United States of Lyncherdom" was never published during Twain's lifetime but appeared in 1923, heavily edited by Albert Bigelow Paine, in *Europe and Elsewhere*. The essay is a direct attack on lynching and the mentality of mob violence and an indirect attack on American missionaries. In early 1901 Twain had contributed two articles about the American missionary to *North American Review*, and "The United States of Lyncherdom" may have been conceived as a continuation of that discussion (Anderson, *A Pen Warmed-Up in Hell* 209–210).

Though the essay was never published and Twain clearly would vacillate on the issues of race and violence, he reacted powerfully to the prevalence of lynching, particularly in the South, and was publicly outspoken on the issue. Twain briefly planned an extensive study of the phenomenon of lynching, tentatively to be entitled "History of Lynching" or "Rise and Progress of Lynching" and sold as a subscription book. However, he quickly backed off from the project for fear of social ostracism and poor sales of a book on such a topic (Emerson 238). Twain's choice not to pursue the project is ironic and telling, for one of the major reasons he gives for the persistence of lynching is people's fear of taking a stand in opposition to popular opinion. Furthermore, despite the forcefulness of Twain's attack, his approach to the problem of racial violence remains facile. He persists in addressing lynching only in terms of mob violence and fails to recognize the premise of racial hatred and subjugation, which is the basis for lynching.

"The United States of Lyncherdom" is typical of the cynical, deterministic tone of Twain's later work. The principal point of literary interest regarding the essay is how specifically it is anticipated in the encounter between Colonel Sherburn and the lynch mob in *Adventures of Huckleberry Finn* (1885). Sherburn is decidedly a prototype for the "man known to be splendidly brave" that Twain calls for, perhaps naively, perhaps cynically, as the requisite for stopping the practice of lynching.

Tim Poland

BIBLIOGRAPHY

Budd, Louis J. *Mark Twain: Social Philosopher.* Bloomington: Indiana UP, 1962.

Clemens, Samuel L. *Europe and Elsewhere.* New York: Harper, 1923. 239–249.

———. *Mark Twain's Notebooks & Journals, Volume II (1877–1883).* Ed. Frederick Anderson, Lin Salamo, and Bernard L. Stein. Berkeley: U of California P, 1975.

———. *A Pen Warmed-Up in Hell: Mark Twain in Protest.* Ed. Frederick Anderson. New York: Harper & Row, 1972.

Emerson, Everett. *The Authentic Mark Twain: A Literary Biography of Samuel L. Clemens.* Philadelphia: U of Pennsylvania P, 1984.

See also: Law; Racial Attitudes; Sherburn, Colonel; "Trial, A"

Vanderbilt, Cornelius
(1794–1877)

Born on Staten Island, New York, Cornelius Vanderbilt served as commodore in the U.S. Navy, bought the ferry lines on the New York and New Jersey coasts, on Long Island, and on the Hudson River, opened a shipping line from New York to California and Europe, and bought the New York Central Railroad. Vanderbilt built his empire ruthlessly, his battles with Daniel Drew for the Erie Railroad providing some of our most eventful financial history. He was also an art collector. In his will he left nearly all of his fortune to his eldest son, William Henry. Beginning in 1877, the second son and the two daughters contested the will unsuccessfully, although William eventually gave them larger portions. The Vanderbilt will case drew great publicity.

Samuel Clemens introduced the idea of writing a bogus account of the will during his Pittsburgh lecture of 29 December 1884, and Parker L. Water of the Pittsburgh *Chronicle Telegraph* told Clemens in a letter of 17 November 1887 that he had written the story. In "The Esquimau Maiden's Romance" (1893) Clemens portrays a "polar Vanderbilt" who uses a fortune of fish hooks to gain prestige in his tribe. In "Various Literary People" he calls the Vanderbilts "professional grafters," and in his "Open Letter to Commodore Vanderbilt" (1869) he denounces the tycoon's lawlessness and vulgarity. Clemens spoke out strongly against abuses perpetrated by various wealthy Americans.

Kevin Hadduck

BIBLIOGRAPHY

Budd, Louis J. *Mark Twain: Social Philosopher.* Bloomington: Indiana UP, 1962.

Clemens, Samuel L. *Mark Twain in Eruption.* Ed. Bernard DeVoto. New York: Harper, 1940.

———. *Mark Twain's Notebooks & Journals, Volume III (1883–1891).* Ed. Robert Pack Browning, Michael B. Frank, and Lin Salamo. Berkeley: U of California P, 1979.

See also: Business; Carnegie, Andrew; "Esquimau Maiden's Romance, The"; Social Philosophy

Vernacular

In writing what has come to be called the humor of the Old Southwest, Mark Twain's predecessors used the common speech of the uneducated and unrefined to signal inferiority to the educated narrator and the refined reader. Vernacular characters might exhibit the enviable gusto of a Sut Lovingood, or the successful swindling techniques of a Simon Suggs, but they and their vernacular victims were not to be taken seriously. In any given story the speaker—usually the writer—of standard English had the trustworthy perspective. Educated in the East, the men (women may have read, but did not write, this particular genre) composing the sketches and yarns found the customs and the speech of the backwoods both fascinating and threatening to social order. Their efforts to report and to entertain, which appeared in William T. Porter's weekly *The Spirit of the Times* (New York, 1831–1861) and in many other weekly or monthly or quarterly journals, rapidly accustomed readers to distinguish between "the self-controlled gentleman" and the boorish hick from the sticks.

From its very beginning, Mark Twain's use of the vernacular reevaluated that familiar pattern. In "The Dandy Frightening the Squatter" (1852) young Sam Clemens writes as if he himself were the conventional gentleman, but it is the rough-speaking squatter who gets the better of the standard-speaking dandy. In "The Celebrated Jumping Frog of Calaveras County" (1865) Twain's educated narrator, complete with a "friend in the East" who sends him after information concerning "the Reverend Leonidas W. Smiley," cannot enjoy the deliciously vernacular ramblings of "garrulous old Simon Wheeler": the foolish, although certainly well-spoken, narrator wants a useful product—straight talk—and has no patience with aesthetic process.

Peaking in *Adventures of Huckleberry Finn* (1885), the first full-length novel to be told in a character's speaking voice, Twain developed the vernacular into a richly precise instrument of moral analysis as well as of pictorial elegance. Beyond the evocation of sunrise on the river (discussed most tellingly by Leo Marx), and other similarly lyrical passages, Twain's Huck unconsciously reveals the moral poverty of the society from which he flees by echoing with approval the pro-slavery cliches of standard speech in his own far more direct language. The effect is to force readers to contrast empty, and distancing, theory with the intimate knowledge of Huck's experience with Jim. Huck's moral stance in action totally contradicts Huck's verbal prescriptions (that is, the prescriptions of educated society) so that although Twain still uses vernacular for comic effects, he forces it to transcend the strictly comic.

Even by implication, Twain's predecessors managed to do this only fleetingly. When George Washington Harris's "George" tries to tell a story in genteel lingo, sentimentalizing over the "graveyard" and "forbidden walnut-trees" of his happy, carefree youth, Sut rudely interrupts him with a vernacular explosion—"Oh, komplicated durnashun! that haint hit"—and then tells the yarn in his own uncouth style. Sut's telling gives immediacy and importance to scatological fundamentals usually ignored by polite society, but more by way of temporary relaxation from the suppressive rigors of civilization than as egalitarian principal. Twain, on the other hand, retained his vernacular perspective, despite even his own efforts to come to terms with eastern standards. On occasion the tension between the two got him into trouble, as with the Whittier Birthday Dinner Speech (1877), but his work marks the beginning of the triumph of what we now take for granted: the vernacular voice in American prose fiction.

Pascal Covici, Jr.

BIBLIOGRAPHY

Bridgman, Richard. *The Colloquial Style in America.* New York: Oxford UP, 1966.

Covici, Pascal, Jr. *Mark Twain's Humor: The Image of a World.* Dallas: Southern Methodist UP, 1962.

Lynn, Kenneth S. *Mark Twain and Southwestern Humor.* Boston: Little, Brown, 1959.

Marx, Leo. *The Pilot and the Passenger: Essays on Literature, Technology, and Culture in the United States.* New York: Oxford UP, 1988.

Smith, Henry Nash. *Mark Twain: The Development of a Writer.* Cambridge, Mass.: Harvard UP, 1962.

See also: "Buck Fanshaw's Funeral"; Dialect; Humor; Language; Legacy; Southwestern Humor

"Victims, The"

(1972)

An incomplete sketch, though clear in its vigorous outline, "The Victims" was first published by John S. Tuckey in *Mark Twain's Fables of Man* (1972). Albert Bigelow Paine, first editor of the Mark Twain Papers, believed it was composed in 1902, at about the time of "The Five Boons of Life." Everett Emerson accepts Paine's dating, but Tuckey, studying ink and handwriting, places it only somewhere between 1900 and 1905.

There is a "picnic" to which all young creatures, great and small, are invited. Little Johnny Microbe begs to go and is allowed to do so by his mother, who evokes the "good spirit" to protect him from harm; then Mamma Microbe goes and kills little Willie Molecule, a second picnicker, as supper for her son. Johnny is killed for another's supper, and so it

goes up the scale to Jumbo Jackson, who is killed by the Gem-of-the-creation, Man. The sketch ends with Mamma Molecule's grief and despairing rejection of the "good spirit."

The sketch presents a savage, Darwinian world and ridicules, by implication, any belief in a benevolent Creator. There is also a jab against Western imperialism: the Man uses jumbo's tusks to buy slaves. These values are consistent with Clemens's political opinions after the Spanish-American War and the Boxer Rebellion and with his rage against the unfeeling universe that had taken his daughter Susy.

Charles L. Crow

BIBLIOGRAPHY

Clemens, Samuel L. *Mark Twain's Fables of Man.* Ed. John S. Tuckey. Berkeley: U of California P, 1972. 133–140.

Emerson, Everett. *The Authentic Mark Twain: A Literary Biography of Samuel L. Clemens.* Philadelphia: U of Pennsylvania P, 1984.

Hill, Hamlin. *Mark Twain: God's Fool.* New York: Harper & Row, 1973.

See also: Darwin, Charles; Determinism; Imperialism

Virginia City *Territorial Enterprise*

Chapters 42–55 of *Roughing It* (1872) recapture much of the brilliant, brawling, and halcyon atmosphere of the early Comstock Lode that Twain experienced as a reporter on the Virginia City *Territorial Enterprise.* The position was Mark Twain's first job as a professional writer.

The *Enterprise* had been purchased in March 1861 by Joseph T. Goodman and Denis McCarthy. The new owners quickly converted a struggling weekly into a profitable daily that was the most respected newspaper on the Comstock and in the West. Goodman and McCarthy attracted to the paper an outstanding staff of writers and printers with high pay, emphasis on interesting and authoritative writing, and the guarantee of editorial freedom.

Among the notable men who worked on it in its early years were Dan De Quille, Rollin Daggett, C.C. Goodwin, Steve Gillis, Jim Townsend, and Alf Doten.

Clemens joined the paper in September 1862 and soon adopted the pen name of "Josh," which he changed to Mark Twain in February 1863. Under the guidance of De Quille, Twain learned to write news copy, but he was not interested in routine or detailed items. He needed no direction to be inventive and to write humor; his "Petrified Man" hoax was published in October 1862. Even some of his regular news stories provided him with an opportunity to be creative. He found targets for burlesque and social satire when he covered the legislature, reviewed plays, and reported on gunplay and court cases.

Twain reveled in the camaraderie of the *Enterprise* staff and honed his wit by engaging in mock-serious journalistic feuds with Clement T. Rice ("the Unreliable"), of the Virginia City *Union*, and Dan De Quille. But he also earned a certain unpopularity because of his excessive sarcasm and because some of his humor backfired.

Twain quit the *Enterprise* abruptly in May 1864, probably because of embarrassment over a failed joke that alienated many Nevadans. He continued to send the *Enterprise* copy from San Francisco, however, particularly from October 1865 to March 1868.

Twain's *Enterprise* years were formative. They gave him invaluable lessons about his capacities in the craft of writing and fixed in him the irreverent but ethical habit of mind that characterizes his literature.

Lawrence I. Berkove

BIBLIOGRAPHY

Branch, Edgar M. *The Literary Apprenticeship of Mark Twain.* Urbana: U of Illinois P, 1950.

Clemens, Samuel L. *Mark Twain of the "Enterprise": Newspaper Articles and Other Documents, 1862–1864.* Ed. Henry Nash Smith and Frederick Anderson. Berkeley: U of California P, 1957.

Cummins, Ella Sterling. *The Story of the Files: A Review of Californian Writers and Literature.* San Francisco: World's Fair Commission of California, 1893.

Lewis, Oscar, ed. *The Life and Times of the Virginia City Territorial Enterprise.* Ashland: Lewis Osborne, 1971.

See also: Daggett, Rollin Malory; De Quille, Dan; Goodman, Joseph Thompson; Hoax; Journalism; Nevada

Wakeman, Edgar

(1817–1875)

Edgar ("Ned") Wakeman had a long and adventurous career as a sailor in the Pacific, rising from ordinary seaman to command various steamships, including the *America*, which carried Mark Twain from San Francisco to Nicaragua in December 1866. A gifted storyteller, he made an immediate impression on Twain, who wrote during the voyage, "I had rather travel with that old Ned Wakeman than with any other man I ever ran across" (*N&J* 1:253). He is Captain Waxman in Mark Twain's letters to the *Alta California* about the trip.

Wakeman continued to occupy a prominent place in Mark Twain's imagination. He appears as the heroic Captain Ned Blakely in chapter 50 of *Roughing It* (1872), in a story based on an incident Wakeman related to Twain on the 1866 voyage but whose details Twain altered significantly: Wakeman's story had been of "hanging the negro in the Chinchas [Islands]" (*N&J* 1:253), but in *Roughing It* Blakely hangs a white man who has murdered the Negro mate of Blakely's ship. Wakeman next appears as Captain Hurricane Jones in "Some Rambling Notes of an Idle Excursion" (1877). Mark Twain also drew on Wakeman for the title character in an unpublished play, *Cap'n Simon Wheeler, the Amateur Detective*, also written in 1877. Finally, Wakeman's character and a dream he related to Twain during the 1866 voyage are the source of a series of stories about Captain Stormfield's visit to heaven, which Mark Twain worked on periodically from the late 1860s until the last decade of his life and which he finally published as "Extract from Captain Stormfield's Visit to Heaven" in *Harper's Monthly Magazine*, 1907 and 1908.

Twain saw Wakeman again only briefly in 1868, but he wrote a letter to assist his family, then in financial difficulties, in 1872. In 1874, shortly before his death, Wakeman asked Twain to assist him in writing his memoirs.

Twain declined, although he attempted to interest his brother Orion in the project. Wakeman's reminiscences were eventually edited by his daughter and published in 1878 as *The Log of an Ancient Mariner*.

Robert Sattelmeyer

BIBLIOGRAPHY

Browne, Ray B. "Mark Twain and Captain Wakeman." *American Literature* 33 (1961): 320–329.

Clemens, Samuel L. *Mark Twain's Letters, Volume 1 (1853–1866)*. Ed. Edgar M. Branch, Michael B. Frank, and Kenneth M. Sanderson. Berkeley: U of California P, 1988.

———. *Mark Twain's Notebooks & Journals, Volume I (1855–1873)*. Ed. Frederick Anderson, Michael B. Frank, and Kenneth M. Sanderson. Berkeley: U of California P, 1975.

See also: Cap'n Simon Wheeler, the Amateur Detective; Extract from Captain Stormfield's Visit to Heaven; "Some Rambling Notes of an Idle Excursion"; Stormfield, Captain; "Trial, A"

Wallace, Elizabeth

(1866–1960)

A professor of Romance languages at the University of Chicago, Elizabeth Wallace was born in Bogotá, Colombia, of missionary parents. She attended Wellesley College, the University of Minnesota, and the University of Chicago. Her academic specializations were in Latin American culture and French literature.

Wallace met Clemens in 1908 while they were both vacationing in Bermuda. At that time she observed his friendships with the young girls he called "Angel Fish." After Clemens's death, Wallace wrote *The Happy Island* (1913), which documents her friendship with him and describes both his fascination with the Angel Fish and their attraction to him.

Roberta Seelinger Trites

BIBLIOGRAPHY

Wallace, Elizabeth. *Mark Twain and the Happy Island*. Chicago: McClurg, 1913.

———. *The Unending Journey*. Minneapolis: U of Minnesota P, 1952.

See also: Angel Fish and Aquarium Club; Bermuda

Walter Scott

Twain named the wrecked steamboat in chapter 13 of *Adventures of Huckleberry Finn* (1885) after Sir Walter Scott (1771–1832), British author of romantic historical novels including *Ivanhoe, Rob Roy*, and *The Heart of Midlothian*. A steamboat called the *Walter Scott* traveled the Mississippi River from 1829 until 1838. Several others were named for Scott's characters during the nineteenth century, including the *Ivanhoe* and the *Lady of the Lake* (Hearn 139).

Twain's choice of names was another in a series of jibes he made against Scott. Scott's books were wildly popular in the antebellum South. According to Twain, "the Sir Walter disease" practically caused the American Civil War by filling the South with "sham grandeurs, sham gauds, and sham chivalries." Scott did "measureless harm" with his "sillinesses and emptinesses . . . of a brainless and worthless long-vanished society" (*Life on the Mississippi*, chapter 46). As he tended to seek a personal villain for a social ill, Twain saw Scott as the father of all he disliked in unrealistic literature (Ferguson 213). As a political and literary realist, Twain felt that the romances of Scott and James Fenimore Cooper as well as the antebellum culture Huck encounters in his journey downriver had foundered like a broken-down steamboat (*Adventures of Huckleberry Finn* 62).

The *Walter Scott* incident functions as an example of how Huck's desire to emulate Tom Sawyer's adventuring creates difficulties for Huck and Jim. Following their escape from the criminals on board the wreck, among Huck and Jim's booty are "a lot of books," from which Huck reads to Jim "about kings, and dukes, and earls, and such, and how gaudy they dressed, and how much style they put on." The ironic argument about "King Sollermun" follows (*Adventures of Huckleberry Finn*, chapter 14). The *Walter Scott* episode prefigures the rascality of the King and Duke in general, thus powerfully contrasting the good life of the raft with the venality of life on the land (Emerson 141).

In *The American Claimant* (1892) Twain invented Rowena-Ivanhoe College, "the selectest and most aristocratic seat of learning for young ladies in our country," where the girls "don't learn a blessed thing . . . but showy rubbish and un-American pretentiousness" (chapter 4). In 1900 Twain responded to a professor's charge that Scott would outlive all his critics by remarking that one could either read Scott as a child or as a very old man and that a literary critic would have to be exceptionally "well-regulated" to attain the necessary old age ("The Disappearance of Literature" 359). In 1904 Twain returned to his foe with blunted scorn. After confessing that in Scott's *Guy Mannering* he could find no literary or stylistic merit, he reasons that because "nothing is eternal in this world," literature as much as any other intellectual manifestation is "subject to the character of the times." Twain puts Dickens and Thackeray in the same category as Scott, concluding that "it's like when they show us some weird old picture and say it's wonderful. I dare say it's wonderful for its time; but its time is past" ("Mark Twain to Reform the Language of Italy" 190).

Jeanne Campbell Reesman

BIBLIOGRAPHY

Clemens, Samuel L. *Adventures of Huckleberry Finn.* Ed. Walter Blair and Victor Fischer. Berkeley: U of California P, 1985.

———. *The American Claimant.* New York: Charles L. Webster, 1892.

———. "The Disappearance of Literature." *Mark Twain Speaking.* By Clemens. Ed. Paul Fatout. Iowa City: U of Iowa P, 1976. 358–360.

———. "Mark Twain to Reform the Language of Italy." *Mark Twain Speaks for Himself.* By Clemens.

Ed. Paul Fatout. West Lafayette, Ind.: Purdue UP, 1978. 189–191.

Emerson, Everett. *The Authentic Mark Twain: A Literary Biography of Samuel L. Clemens.* Philadelphia: U of Pennsylvania P, 1984.

Ferguson, DeLancey. *Mark Twain: Man and Legend.* Indianapolis: Bobbs-Merrill, 1943.

See also: Criticism; *Life on the Mississippi*; Scott, Walter

"Wapping Alice"
(1981)

A manuscript on which Mark Twain worked, in various forms, for three decades, "Wapping Alice" tells the story of a maid in the Clemens household who tripped the burglar alarm in 1877 in the Hartford house. An innocuous version, "The McWilliamses and the Burglar Alarm," was published in the book *Harper's Christmas* (1882). Intrigued with the seduction motif that the story contained—the maid confessed to opening the basement door to allow her lover to enter, claimed that she was pregnant, and after an elaborate and melodramatic confrontation scene staged by Clemens, accepted her seducer's proposal of marriage—Mark Twain returned to it in 1897 or 1898, writing a factual account of the story. In November 1898 he changed all the names of the principals to fictional ones. Startlingly, after the marriage ceremony was performed, Wapping Alice turns out to be a male transvestite.

On 10 April 1907 Mark Twain again returned to the plot of the story, this time including it in his autobiographical dictation for that day. In this version the author admits that Alice (actually named Lizzie) was in fact female and explains that the switch in gender was "non-essential" and that "for delicacy's sake I was obliged to make the change."

"Wapping Alice" is probably the most blatantly sexual of the long lists of plots in which Mark Twain explored the murky area of changelings, look-alikes, gender shifts, and cross-dressing. Clearly, he was aware of the homosexual level in the story; nevertheless, he claimed that the all-male marriage was intended to "soften the little drama sufficiently to enable me to exploit it in a magazine without risk of overshocking the magazine's readers." In all its variant versions "Wapping Alice" was first printed by the University of California for the Friends of the Bancroft Library in 1981.

Hamlin Hill

BIBLIOGRAPHY

Hill, Hamlin. *Mark Twain: God's Fool.* New York: Harper & Row, 1973.

Macnaughton, William R. *Mark Twain's Last Years as a Writer.* Columbia: U of Missouri P, 1979.

See also: "McWilliamses and the Burglar Alarm, The"; Scatology; Sexuality

War

In *The Mysterious Stranger* (1916) Mark Twain's surrogate, Satan, or Philip Traum, tells young Theodor Fischer and Theodor's young cronies from the medieval Austrian village of Eseldorf that there has never been a just or honorable war. According to Satan, wars are fought either for "the private interest of royal families" or "to crush a weak nation." In his earlier novel, *A Connecticut Yankee in King Arthur's Court* (1889), Twain's alter ego, Hank Morgan, proclaims to the reader that "no people in the world" have ever achieved "their fortune by goody-good talk and moral suasion," but only by bloody revolution. Hence, Twain was obviously not a pacifist; rather, he opposed wars that were instigated by the powerful against the weak while he supported revolutions in which the oppressed overthrew their oppressors. He was incensed by wars of imperialism, which became commonplace in the late nineteenth and early twentieth centuries, even those wars conducted by his own country.

While he was very vocal about imperialistic wars, Twain had largely maintained silence about the Civil War, except for a few references in *Life on the Mississippi* (1883). As a young man he had chosen to avoid direct involvement in the war and had spent the war years in the West. However, in 1885 he published the biographical yarn "The Private History of a Campaign That Failed" in *Century Magazine.* For the most part, this story has been viewed as an apology for his desertion as a rebel soldier; it can, nevertheless, be seen as a satire on war. That *Century* published the account in the midst of an edition meant to praise men's heroism in the war presents a delicious irony that Twain must have enjoyed, for he depicts himself and his fellow warriors in this misadventure as anything but heroic and as a result makes a strong antiwar statement. In a disarming, straightforward, and often understated manner, Twain pictures the "Marion Rangers" as raw youth playing at the romance of war. They roam the countryside trying to avoid contact with the enemy, sponging off the farmers, and fleeing from rumors that Union soldiers are abroad looking for rebels to hang. What begins as a lark turns grim when the boys, while cowering in a corncrib with the rats, kill a stranger whom they mistake as the vanguard of that rumored Union force said to be led by a young colonel by the name of Ulysses S. Grant. Grant's place in the story, and perhaps the killing, are probably apocryphal, but Twain is more concerned about making a point than with being historically accurate. This point is that "the epitome of war" is "the killing of strangers against whom you feel no personal animosity" and "whom you might otherwise help if you found them in trouble." Seventeen years later, Thomas Hardy echoed Twain's words in his short poem "The Man He Killed," by noting that war is "curious" because "you shoot a fellow down" whom you might treat to a drink or "help to half a crown" in normal circumstances. Both Twain and Hardy had deep concern for the way the powerful used the common folk in war. And Twain in this short episode, "The Campaign That Failed," shows the pointlessness of war while at the same time excusing his own behavior. He concludes that even at twenty-four he is "not rightly" equipped for this "awful business," and "that war is intended for men" while "he is only suitable as a child's nurse." He and half of his friends desert, but he notes that some of the boys remain behind and learn the "grim trade," learn "to obey like machines," and thus become "valuable soldiers." With this comment Twain makes it clear that he does not view soldiering as heroic work but as training to be a mere mechanical man.

Hank Morgan, the mechanical man in Twain's 1889 novel, *A Connecticut Yankee*, leads us into a darker picture of war when he slaughters English knighthood in the "Battle of the Sand Belt" by blowing them into "homogeneous protoplasm with alloys of iron and buttons." And this darker vision of war became more pronounced as Twain confronted the imperialism of America and western Europe in the final two decades of his life. Though he initially supported the Spanish-American War in 1898 because he believed that the United States had entered it with the noble purpose of freeing Cuba from Spanish rule, he came to a very different conclusion about the nation's occupation of the Philippines a few years later. He was especially scathing in his attack on General Funston for his massacre of several hundred defenseless Moros in that imperialistic venture. Twain believed that such imperialism resulted from an unholy alliance between greed and religion with wealthy industrialists looking for profit, on the one hand, and the institutionalized church looking for proselytes, on the other. For their own gain, this alliance would bring light to "the people sitting in darkness." In this context Twain defined the true patriot as one who refused to accept blindly the blind dictum of "my country right or wrong."

His final condemnation of such wars, "The War Prayer," was not printed until thirteen years after his death because he feared it was too truthful for people to hear. Here Twain shows how wars get started when blind patriotism is wedded to ardent institutionalized religion. A stranger is sent as a messenger from God to a war-fevered congregation to reveal the true meaning of praying for the defeat of the enemy: the "tearing" of young men "to bloody shreds"; the "laying" to "waste" of people's homes; the "wringing" of the "hearts of grieving widows"; and the making homeless of "little children to wander in the wastes of a desolated land." All of this the congregation has prayed for in "the spirit of love" to the "God who is the source of love."

Thus Twain, in his last years, had reached the pessimistic conclusion that humans were bent on killing each other in ever more destructive and oppressive wars. That Christian civilization had become especially competent at killing in the name of the "God of love" he found especially ironic.

Hugo D. Johnson

BIBLIOGRAPHY

Clemens, Samuel L. *A Connecticut Yankee in King Arthur's Court.* Ed. Bernard Stein. Berkeley: U of California P, 1979.

———. *Mark Twain on the Damned Human Race.* Ed. Janet Smith. New York: Hill and Wang, 1962.

———. *Mark Twain's Autobiography.* Ed. Albert B. Paine. 2 vols. New York: Harper, 1924.

Foner, Philip S. *Mark Twain: Social Critic.* New York: International Publishers, 1958.

Geismar, Maxwell. *Mark Twain: An American Prophet.* Boston: Houghton Mifflin, 1970.

See also: Civil War; *Connecticut Yankee in King Arthur's Court, A*; Imperialism; Spanish-American War, The; "War Prayer, The"

"War Prayer, The"
(1923)

One of several essays Twain wrote on the dangers of unthinking patriotism, "The War Prayer" was composed in 1905 in response to Twain's growing disaffection with global bloodletting and American policies, but he considered it too damaging to the illusions and traditions of mankind to consider publication. The essay was not published until after Twain's death, appearing in 1923 in *Europe and Elsewhere*.

Like Twain's "Letters from the Earth," "The War Prayer" forces readers to look more closely at unquestioned human practices, in this case a prayer for victory over an enemy, and as in the "Letter from the Recording Angel" (1946), Twain points out that the private desire and the public prayer often differ. After a minister delivers a stirring prayer invoking aid for the nation's soldiers—"None could remember the like of it for passionate pleading and moving and beautiful language"—a mysterious stranger interrupts the church service. He calls himself a "messenger from the Throne" and tells the congregation that their prayer for victory actually asks a merciful God to "help us to tear their soldiers to bloody shred with our shells," to bring desolation to their countryside, to make widows and orphans of their wives and children. Unfortunately, the congregation cannot grasp his message through their patriotic fervor, and they conclude "[T]here was no sense in what he said."

Elsewhere, Twain condemns "the damned human race" for being the only animal who kills wantonly; in "The War Prayer" he shows the reader that even piety and patriotism may play their part in this wanton destruction.

Greg Garrett

Bibliography

Britton, Wesley. "Tom Paine and Mark Twain: 'Common Sense' as Source for 'The War Prayer.'" *Conference of College Teachers of English Studies* 54 (1989): 13–19.

Clemens, Samuel L. *Europe and Elsewhere*. New York: Harper, 1923.

See also: War

Ward, Artemus (Charles Farrar Browne)
(1834–1867)

Artemus Ward, born Charles Farrar Brown (the "e" was added in 1861 by Ward), was America's chief literary comedian in the 1860s. Ward's humorous letters and travel pieces project some of the important themes and mannerisms of Twain's humor and social commentary, making him especially significant in the study of Twain's writing. In addition, Ward's career as a lecturer established the humorous lecture as American entertainment and paved the way for Twain's later success in this field. Ward's early death prevented him from taking the exaggerated pragmatic Americanism of the "Old Showman" around the globe, as Twain was to do in 1895.

Charles Farrar Brown was born in Waterford, Maine. His father died when Brown was thirteen, leading to his early apprenticeship as a printer. By 1852 he was an office boy in B.P. Shillaber's comic newspaper *The Carpet-Bag*, in which he published a number of pieces, one on the same date as Clemens's publication of "The Dandy Frightening the Squatter." After various wanderings, his comic pieces for the Cleveland *Plain Dealer*, burlesquing P.T. Barnum under the guise of an "old showman" named Artemus Ward, brought him to national attention and the editorship of the New York comic paper *Vanity Fair*, the most brilliant comic paper of the day in 1860. The old showman letters were burlesques of vulgar self-interest that actually supported American patriotic and humane ideals, although Ward was not in favor of abolition at the cost of the Union. By 1861 he began lecturing in a much more sophisticated voice than the writings of the old showman would suggest, offering audiences witty non sequiturs and an hour of fooling on topics as diverse as "The Babes in the Wood" and "Africa." *Artemus Ward, His Book*, a collection of his newspaper pieces, comic letters, literary burlesques, and comic interviews with Mormons, Shakers, and various politicians, including Lincoln and Prince Albert Edward, was a major success in 1862. As the Civil War progressed, Ward became staunchly pro-Union, but humanitarian attempts to benefit Confederate war widows in the South led to much criticism of him in the North.

Ward attempted to broaden his humor by traveling to the Mormon West, following up an earlier letter burlesquing Brigham Young.

On that trip, in 1863–1864, he met Mark Twain, caroused with him, presented comic lectures in the Virginia City area, and attempted to get the young humorist to accompany him east, an offer that Twain declined. Ward survived a serious illness in Utah to return and publish *Artemus Ward, His Travels Among the Mormons* in 1865, without Twain's "Notorious Jumping Frog of Calaveras County," which arrived in response to Ward's solicitation too late to be included and went instead into a New York newspaper and instant national success. After lecturing on the Mormons, Ward decided in 1866 to follow in Barnum's footsteps to England; he arrived there in early 1867 to wide acclaim, instant popularity, packed houses for his lectures, and an invitation to write travel letters for *Punch*, later published as *Artemus Ward in London* in 1867. Some of the letters for this magazine were among his best, including the "Is he dead?" joke that Twain borrowed for *Innocents Abroad* (1869) and other literary humor that took a more thoughtful historical perspective than had other comedians before him. Tragically, he died of pneumonia in March 1867, leaving his style, manner, and mantle to be adopted by others, including especially Mark Twain.

Ward's query to Prince Napoleon about his father, "I want to know how he stands as a man," sets the tone for Ward's canon, with its insistent burlesquing of political rhetoric, religious fanaticism, and moral stereotyping. His irreverently breezy, colloquial letters were written in an exaggerated vulgar dialect, as well as featuring misspelling (cacography) that has lowered him in the eyes of serious critics and caused him to be lumped with lesser newspaper humorists of his time. Yet, British recognition of the broader toleration and hostility to fraud, pretense, and humbuggery, even when seen at the British Museum or the Tower of London, caused Ward to be recognized as having some significance. Ward, Charles G. Leland, Bret Harte, and Twain all shared the wider recognition of Britains for American ideals as expressed in comic literature. At the time of his death, Ward's voice was becoming increasingly sophisticated, he was recognized as having popularized the comic lecture, and his financial success had demonstrated that a career could be based on the writing of serious humor. Although Twain took pains to disassociate himself from the "phunny" humor of the literary comedians, the attitudes and persona of Ward were influential on Twain's literary comedy in both general and specific ways.

David E.E. Sloane

BIBLIOGRAPHY

Abram, Robert E. "Charles Farrar Browne." *American Humorists: 1800–1950.* Vol. 1. Ed. J. Stanley Trachtenberg. Detroit: Gale Research, 1982. 60–68.

Austin, James C. *Artemus Ward.* New York: Twayne, 1964.

Blair, Walter. *Native American Humor.* New York: American Book, 1937.

Branch, Edgar M. "'The Babes in the Woods': Artemus Ward's 'Double Health' to Mark Twain." *Publications of the Modern Language Association* 93 (October 1978): 955–972.

Hingston, Edward Peron. *The Genial Showman.* New York: Harper, 1870.

Pullen, John J. *Comic Relief: The Life and Laughter of Artemus Ward, 1834–1867.* Hamden, Conn.: Archon, 1983.

Seitz, Don Carlos. *Artemus Ward (Charles Farrar Browne): A Biography and Bibliography.* New York: Harper, 1919.

Sloane, David E.E. *Mark Twain as a Literary Comedian.* Baton Rouge: Louisiana State UP, 1979.

Ward, Artemus. *The Complete Works of Artemus Ward.* London: Chatto and Windus, 1922.

See also: Lecturer; Literary Comedians

Warner, Charles Dudley
(1829–1900)

Born in Massachusetts and reared in western New York, Charles Dudley Warner spent most of his adult life in Hartford, Connecticut. Though educated for the bar (B.A. Hamilton College, 1851; LL.B. University of Pennsylvania, 1858), he worked for nearly forty years as a man of letters. In 1860 he left law practice in Chicago to join a former Hamilton classmate, Joseph R. Hawley (1826–1905), in the management of the recently founded *Evening Press* in Hartford. In 1867 the partners bought the Hartford *Courant*, for which Warner served as manager or contributor during the following thirty-three years.

Soon after turning journalist, Warner began to write charming and amusing personal essays for the paper and for magazines, and from time to time he gathered them for book publication. With growing prosperity he made frequent trips to Europe and the Middle East, or within North America, once again producing pleasant sketches that also appeared eventually in book form. In the nineties, now editing "The Editor's Study" of *Harper's New Monthly Magazine*, he turned to literary criticism and also wrote a trilogy of substantial novels dealing with the morally corrosive effect of excessive wealth.

As early settlers in the Nook Farm neighborhood, Charley and Susan Warner became close and enduring friends of the Clemenses. The relationship between the men was never as warm as those of Twain with Joseph Twichell or William Dean Howells and was occasionally marred by a sense of rivalry. Nevertheless, the friendship must be counted as one of the most important of Twain's life.

Despite the high regard in which he was held during his lifetime, Warner is now chiefly remembered as the co-author, with Twain, of *The Gilded Age* (1873).

Lynn Altenbernd

BIBLIOGRAPHY

Andrews, Kenneth R. *Nook Farm: Mark Twain's Hartford Circle*. Cambridge, Mass.: Harvard UP, 1950.

French, Bryant Morey. *Mark Twain and "The Gilded Age."* Dallas: Southern Methodist UP, 1965.

Lounsbury, Thomas R. Bibliographical Sketch. *The Complete Writings of Charles Dudley Warner*. By Warner. Vol. 15. Hartford, Conn.: American Publishing, 1904. i–xxxviii.

See also: Gilded Age, The; Nook Farm

"Was It Heaven? Or Hell?"
(1902)

Twain wrote "Was It Heaven? Or Hell?" in the summer of 1902, at York Harbor, Maine, while wife Olivia was ill after suffering a heart attack (Ferguson 292). The story, based on an incident related to Twain by W.D. Howells (Emerson 243), appeared in the December issue of *Harper's Monthly* that year.

"WHH" resembles "The Man That Corrupted Hadleyburg" (1899) in its exposure of rigid, literal Christianity. The family doctor functions, as does Howard L. Stephenson in "Hadleyburg," to illustrate the inevitable hypocrisy of the self-righteous. In "WHH" the doctor forces two maiden aunts to admit that they have habitually lied to avoid unpleasantness; then, on doctor's orders, the two train themselves as liars, shielding their dying Margaret from the news of her daughter's illness and eventual death.

The story also reworks the "You Can't Pray a Lie" chapter of *Huckleberry Finn* (1885). As Huck risks his soul, choosing hell in order to save Jim, so the aunts accept their fate as sinners in order to comfort a dying woman. In both *HF* and in this story the protagonists ironically continue to accept the terms of literal Christianity, though allying themselves with "the enemy" for admirably humane reasons. Readers who answer the question of the story's title before rephrasing it find themselves in a similar paradox.

Albert Bigelow Paine praises the story for its psychological depth (1177), but as Everett Emerson suggests (244), "WHH" may be more sentimental than heartbreaking. The maiden aunts are too pathetic to be objects of satire, too trusting and naive to elicit either blame or praise. More complex are the enigmatic doctor and the narrator's ambivalent tone toward him. Although the doctor champions a practical Christianity that lacks sanctimony, he also relishes an argument for its own sake and proudly considers himself the only sound Christian.

After "WHH" appeared, Twain received a letter from a man who claimed that the story almost represented his own situation, down to the author's use of the name Helen—a coincidence that involved Twain's own household. Within a few months of its writing, "WHH" was literally reenacted after Twain's daughter Jean contracted pneumonia, for throughout the various deceptions by the Twain family the news was kept from the girl's bedridden mother (Paine 1190).

Richard Gaughran

BIBLIOGRAPHY

Clemens, Samuel L. *Adventures of Huckleberry Finn.* Ed. Walter Blair and Victor Fischer. Berkeley: U of California P, 1985.

———. *The Complete Short Stories of Mark Twain.* Ed. Charles Neider. Garden City, N.Y.: Hanover House, 1957. 472–488.

Emerson, Everett. *The Authentic Mark Twain: A Literary Biography of Samuel L. Clemens.* Philadelphia: U of Pennsylvania P, 1984.

Ferguson, DeLancey. *Mark Twain: Man and Legend.* Indianapolis: Bobbs-Merrill, 1943.

Paine, Albert Bigelow. *Mark Twain: A Biography.* 3 vols. New York: Harper, 1912.

"Was the World Made for Man?"

(1962)

Mark Twain composed "Was the World Made for Man?" in 1903, in response to Alfred Russel Wallace's widely discussed essay "Man's Place in the Universe" (February 1903). An influential scientist and early proponent of evolution, Wallace claimed that the earth lay at the center of the universe and was the only habitable body in it. Twain's parody of these theories, first published in *Letters from the Earth* (1962), also appeared in *"What Is Man?" and Other Philosophical Writings* (1973). Portions of it, in a different form, were included in Albert Bigelow Paine's 1912 biography.

Adopting the persona of a bemused scientist pondering Wallace's conclusions, Twain traces the long history of evolution from the invertebrates to the appearance of humans. According to Wallace's absurd logic, Twain

suggests, a hundred million years elapsed and hundreds of species both came into existence and suffered extinction only to prepare the world for man.

"Was the World Made for Man?" has received little critical attention, perhaps because Twain treated the theme of humanity's false sense of self-importance in so many other works. In selecting it for inclusion in *Letters from the Earth,* Bernard DeVoto judged it to be one of the best of Twain's late philosophical sketches.

Stan Poole

BIBLIOGRAPHY

Clemens, Samuel L. *Letters from the Earth.* Ed. Bernard DeVoto. New York: Harper & Row, 1962.

———. *"What Is Man?" and Other Philosophical Writings.* Ed. Paul Baender. Berkeley: U of California P, 1973.

Frederick, John T. *The Darkened Sky: Nineteenth-Century American Novelists and Religion.* Notre Dame, Ind.: U of Notre Dame P, 1969.

Paine, Albert Bigelow. *Mark Twain: A Biography.* 3 vols. New York: Harper, 1912.

See also: Darwin, Charles; Evolution; *Letters from the Earth*; Philosophy; Science

Washington, D.C.

In *Mark Twain's Autobiography* (1924) Samuel Clemens recalls his first trip to Washington, D.C., as part of an 1853 sight-seeing excursion to the East Coast. Though he returned to the nation's capital several times between the ages of eighteen and seventy-one, this initial visit seems to have been the only one he undertook purely for amusement. Post-Civil War Washington became what historian Vernon Parrington called a "great barbecue" of money, influence, and raw material for satire, and thereafter Clemens kept a practical eye on all three courses of the feast.

From a literary perspective, Clemens's most productive days in Washington were during his brief stint as a secretary to Nevada Senator William Stewart in 1867–1868 and a short foray on behalf of his father-in-law in 1870.

Though in his career he was to write enough humorous and critical material about government to fill a fair-size volume, these early visits furnished his funniest and most scathing material on the capital and its denizens. "My Late Senatorial Secretaryship" (1867), "Cannibalism in the Cars" (1868), "The Man Who Put Up at Gadsby's" (1868), and "The Facts in the Case of the Great Beef Contract" (1869) all burlesque official Washington's penchant for cutthroat parliamentary procedure, unrelenting avarice, and endless red tape. Although he would continue using short stories to rail at bureaucracy as late as 1902 (in "The Belated Russian Passport") and conclude his book-length discourse *Christian Science* (1907) with an involved joke at the expense of Congress, *The Gilded Age* (1873), written with Charles Dudley Warner, is Clemens's anti-Washington masterpiece.

The narrator of *Gilded Age*, an extremely acerbic version of the Mark Twain persona, abandons in chapter 24 the rather melodramatic plot of the novel to complain of Washington's transportation facilities (carriages should be taken "out of service and put . . . in the museum; we have few enough antiquities") and its accommodations ("a hundred and eighteen bad hotels, and only one good one"). The city's climate irritates him ("to view the city . . . take an umbrella, an overcoat, and a fan"), and its unique architecture leaves him cold (the White House "is ugly enough outside, but . . . [d]reariness, flimsiness, bad taste reduced to mathematical completeness is what the inside offers to the eye . . ."). He is particularly caustic about national monuments: the Washington Monument "has the aspect of a factory chimney with the top broken off. . . . You might take [Lincoln's] marble emancipation proclamation, which he holds out in his hand and contemplates, for a folded napkin; and you might conceive from his expression and his attitude, that he is finding fault with the washing."

But Clemens always aimed his most violent satire at Washington's swarm of government officials and hangers-on. Later he would call Congress "America's only distinctly native criminal class" and deem Washington "the place to get a low opinion of everybody in." Chapter 24 of *Gilded Age* sets the tone for these ruminations: to illustrate one point, he begins one sentence with "If you are a member of Congress . . ." but feels obliged to put the words "no offense" in parentheses before completing the supposition. He reports that the reputation of the nation's lawmakers for chicanery and outright thievery is so well-known that local landladies will not rent them space in the dingiest rooming house unless they submit a substantial advance deposit.

Yet these oft homeless scoundrels are not to be pitied, for their conduct has its remuneration. Every jobholder in post–Civil War Washington, from the highest officer to "the darkey boy who purifies the Department spittoons," is subject to the political influence of elected officials, and political influence is a brisk commodity on the local market. Nepotism and featherbedding also abound; the capital is a haven for officeholders' friends and family members—the vast majority of whom, according to our narrator, are lazy, incompetent, and/or idiotic. Twain concludes: "There is something good and motherly about Washington, the grand old benevolent National Asylum for the Helpless."

In view of his wholesale condemnation of Washington's spoils, influence, and patronage systems, it is interesting that Clemens usually went to Washington in order to exploit that system and pursue government largesse for himself and his family. His "secretaryship" to Senator Stewart was a sinecure bestowed as a public relations move by the senator in order to attach the fame of a rising writer and lecturer; few actual duties were required to collect the taxpayer-furnished salary. Clemens, nonetheless, became disenchanted with the position (or was fired with the threat of "a thrashing," depending on whose account of the facts one accepts). Upon notice of his unemployment, various Washington officials, impressed with his brilliant after-dinner speeches, were quick to assure him that, although he reported no experience in diplomacy or mail management, they could arrange a consulate or postmastership for his eventual occupation. He also spent two months promoting a civil service career for his brother Orion, and he made the 1870 trip, in which he gathered what he called a "goldmine" of dirt on Washington, in order to lobby for a redistricting bill that would benefit the railroad interests of his in-laws. Most of his Washington excursions over the next thirty-five years were undertaken for specific material gain, usually either to give testimony on proposed amendments in the copyright laws (which would garner him more income from his books) or to promote the various inventions in which he had invested.

Of note to those concerned with the trappings of the "Mark Twain Legend" is the use Clemens made of his last official trip to the capital. On 12 December 1906, during testimony before a committee considering the extension of copyright from twenty-eight to forty-two years, he unveiled what was to become his trademark all-white suit. He may have been more interested in the impression made by his outfit than that made by his congressional testimony, for he began his press conference afterward explaining that he was wearing "the uniform of the American Association of Purity and Perfection, of which I am . . . the only man in the United States eligible to membership" (Fatout 530).

Regarding Clemens's political relationship with Washington, it is well to view a man's outlook in the context of his era. Although he did support several Republican candidates, Clemens considered himself a Mugwump, one of a group of political freethinkers who swore allegiance to no political party. This attitude seems tame enough now, but in the late nineteenth century voting the "straight ticket" was a mark of decency in a man, even when one's party proffered frauds, thieves, and hypocrites on the ballot.

Keeping relatively aloof from "the swag" in Washington was no small accomplishment for a man of Mark Twain's influence and popularity; certainly temptation to become a demagogue was ever present, but Twain laughed off such opportunity. Not overly mindful of "where he got his corn pone," he targeted Democrats and Republicans alike in his humorous and too-barbed-to-be-humorous attacks. Although he did take an occasional dip in Washington's murky pools of influence, he reserved the right to speak his mind. He attacked such earmarks of the gilded age status quo as U.S. intervention in the Philippines and government complicity with "Robber Baron" capitalists. He also supported women's suffrage, higher education for blacks, and other "progressive" positions of his day—and he did so without benefit of the popular assent to those causes enjoyed by late-twentieth-century critics who would sniff at his (by current standards) sometimes suspicious deportment.

Washington, for all its annoyances, provided a steady source of material for Samuel Clemens's sensibility as well as his sense of humor. He managed to touch on something serious, silly, or both about the government in most of his books; the capital as city and system served as a perfect all-purpose example of the puffery, sham, and mindless greed he detested in others and resisted reasonably well in his own life. Clemens the self-deprecator might disagree, but if we were to measure the average level of integrity (whether in the Great Barbecue milieu he loved to satirize or our present Gilded Age), Mark Twain—and even somewhat seedy young Sam Clemens—could emerge as a viable candidate for an "American Association of Purity and Perfection."

Richard Hill

BIBLIOGRAPHY

Clemens, Samuel L. *The Complete Short Stories of Mark Twain*. Ed. Charles Neider. Garden City, N.Y.: Hanover House, 1957.

———. *Mark Twain and the Government*. Comp. Svend Petersen. Caldwell, Idaho: Caxton, 1960.

———. *Mark Twain Speaking*. Ed. Paul Fatout. Iowa City: U of Iowa P, 1976.

———. *Mark Twain's Autobiography*. Ed. Albert B. Paine. 2 vols. New York: Harper, 1924.

———. "To the Person Sitting in Darkness." *Selected Shorter Writings of Mark Twain*. By Clemens. Ed.

Walter Blair. Boston: Houghton Mifflin, 1962. 290–305.

Clemens, Samuel L., and Charles Dudley Warner. *The Gilded Age.* 2 vols. Hartford, Conn.: American Publishing, 1873–1874.

Foner, Philip S. *Mark Twain: Social Critic.* New York: International Publishers, 1958.

Kaplan, Justin. *Mr. Clemens and Mark Twain.* New York: Simon & Schuster, 1966.

Paine, Albert Bigelow. *Mark Twain: A Biography.* 3 vols. New York: Harper, 1912.

Parrington, Vernon. *Main Currents in American Thought.* 3 vols. New York: Harcourt, Brace and World, 1928.

Wilson, James D. *A Reader's Guide to the Short Stories of Mark Twain.* Boston: G.K. Hall, 1987.

See also: "Cannibalism in the Cars"; *Gilded Age, The*; Government; "Man Who Put Up at Gadsby's, The"; Politics; Satire

Washoe Wits

The Washoe Wits were a group of humorists writing in the early 1860s for recently established newspapers in the Nevada territory, then known unofficially as Washoe. When Samuel Clemens took a job with the *Territorial Enterprise* in September 1862 in Virginia City, he became associated with one of the most talented of these writers, Dan De Quille (William Wright). During this phase of his apprenticeship Clemens worked closely with De Quille, developing a comic style to suit the brashness of the Washoe mining district during its flush times.

Washoe wit, also known as sagebrush humor, embroidered journalistic fact with humorous exaggeration in such native forms as the tall tale, the burlesque, and the hoax. Like the southwestern humorists, the Washoe Wits exploited contrasts between the genteel culture of the East and the crude manners of the western frontier, but they abandoned the stereotype of the illiterate backwoodsman and the verbal tricks of eye dialect and cacography favored by the earlier humorists (Branch 103). They often satirized attempts to impose eastern cultural forms—elaborate weddings, fu-

nerals, formal parties—upon a rugged, uncivilized West (Fender 743–744).

The influence of Washoe wit upon Twain's writing is evident in the comic extravagance of *Roughing It* (1872). Though his Washoe material lacks the control and subtlety of his mature comic style (Branch 110), it anticipates the level of energy, the sophisticated social critique, and the range of comic voice typical of Twain's best work.

Stan Poole

BIBLIOGRAPHY

Branch, Edgar M. *The Literary Apprenticeship of Mark Twain.* Urbana: U of Illinois P, 1950.

Clemens, Samuel L. *The Works of Mark Twain: Early Tales & Sketches, Volume 1 (1851–1864).* Ed. Edgar M. Branch and Robert H. Hirst. Berkeley: U of California P, 1979.

Fatout, Paul. *Mark Twain in Virginia City.* Bloomington: Indiana UP, 1964.

Fender, Stephen. "'The Prodigal in a Far Country Chawing of Husks': Mark Twain's Search for a Style in the West." *Modern Language Review* 71 (1976): 737–756.

Sloane, David E.E. *Mark Twain as a Literary Comedian.* Baton Rouge: Louisiana State UP, 1979.

Smith, Henry Nash. *Mark Twain: The Development of a Writer.* Cambridge, Mass.: Harvard UP, 1962.

See also: De Quille, Dan; Nevada; Virginia City *Territorial Enterprise*

Watson, Miss

A spinster of uncertain age, this stern, rigidly pious Miss Watson, bespectacled sister of Widow Douglas, joins the widow's household on Cardiff Hill in St. Petersburg at the beginning of *Adventures of Huckleberry Finn* (1885), where she is introduced to provide a contrast to the widow's gentleness and generosity and to serve the purpose of Twain's criticism of the religious hypocrisy of one aspect of the slaveholding South. She makes life miserable for Huck, "pecking" at him until it gets "tiresome and lonesome" for him, and she treats Jim "pooty rough." Her plan to sell Jim down to the plantation hells is one of the principal motivations for the flight of Jim and

Huck to freedom. The contrast between her and her benevolent sister is emphasized when Jim says the "widder she try to get her to say she wouldn't" sell him down the river. Tom Sawyer tells of her deathbed repentance when she frees Jim in her will, a report apparently authenticated by Jim's reappearance as a freed Negro in the sequels, published and unpublished, of the Tom Sawyer–Huck Finn stories. Miss Watson is mentioned briefly as Jim's former owner in "Huck Finn and Tom Sawyer Among the Indians" (1969), and, strangely enough, she is apparently alive in "Tom Sawyer's Conspiracy" (1969), where Huck reports that he and Tom "was back home . . . at the Widow Douglas's . . . getting civilized along of her and old Miss Watson." Huck rejects Miss Watson's religion of hellfire and retribution, seeing that if Miss Watson's Providence got hold of him, "there warn't no help for him" but that "a poor chap would stand considerable show with the widow's Providence."

Everett Carter

BIBLIOGRAPHY

Branch, Edgar M. "The Two Providences: Thematic Form in Huckleberry Finn." *College English* 11 (January 1950): 188–195.

Clemens, Samuel L. *Adventures of Huckleberry Finn.* Ed. Walter Blair and Victor Fischer. Berkeley: U of California P, 1985.

———. *Mark Twain's Hannibal, Huck & Tom.* Ed. Walter Blair. Berkeley: U of California P, 1969.

Pettit, Arthur G. *Mark Twain and the South.* Lexington: UP of Kentucky, 1974.

See also: *Adventures of Huckleberry Finn*; Douglas, Widow; Providence

Watterson, Henry

(1840–1921)

Often called the last of the old-time journalists, Henry Watterson began his newspaper career in 1856; in 1868 he became editor of Louisville's newly merged *Courier-Journal* and remained in that post until his retirement in 1919. He died two years later while wintering in Florida.

A Kentuckian by adoption, "Marse Henry" became nationally known through his editorials, lectures, and books. Among his famous friends was Mark Twain, to whom he was "connected by a domestic tie"; however, "this apart, we were lifetime cronies." The two men corresponded and were infrequently together in London or New York and in Louisville during the Twain-Cable lecture of 1885.

At New York's Carnegie Hall on 11 February 1901, at a Lincoln Birthday celebration, Mark Twain introduced Watterson, the featured speaker, referring to them both as "two Confederates, one-time rebels"; later Albert Bigelow Paine called this introduction "one of the choicest of Mark Twain's speeches." Again at Carnegie Hall, during the Mark Twain commemoration of 30 November 1910, Watterson compared Mark Twain and Lincoln, two geniuses "who possessed a kinship" based on hardships and handicaps. For Mark Twain and Watterson, kinship meant the sharing of two cousins, the originals of Colonel Sellers and the Earl of Durham.

Mary Boewe

BIBLIOGRAPHY

Clemens, Samuel L. *Mark Twain Speaking.* Ed. Paul Fatout. Iowa City: U of Iowa P, 1976.

Wall, Joseph Frazier. *Henry Watterson: Reconstructed Rebel.* New York: Oxford UP, 1956.

Watterson, Henry. "Mark Twain—An Intimate Memory." *American Magazine* 70 (July 1910): 372–375.

———. *"Marse Henry": An Autobiography.* Vol. 1. New York: George H. Doran, 1919. 119–133.

See also: South, Mark Twain and the

Watts-Dunton, Theodore

(1832–1914)

An English poet and novelist, Theodore Watts-Dunton became one of the most important critical voices of the *Athenaeum* between the years of 1876 and 1898, serving for much of that time as its chief reviewer of poetry. Although he achieved popular success with *Aylwin*, his 1899 novel of gypsy life, most of his work aside from the largely anonymous *Athenaeum* contributions is of minor importance. Watts-Dunton, who until 1897 was known merely as Theodore Watts, added in that year Dunton, his mother's maiden name.

Twain's treatment at the hands of the *Athenaeum* during Watts-Dunton's tenure there indicates that, for the most part, Twain was considered an amusing humorist possessed of a distinctly American voice. The reviewers, while perceptive in sensing his serious literary aspirations, often seemed reluctant to concede that his abilities could fulfill those aspirations. He was for them a notable American wag—but not a fully polished artist.

Craig Albin

BIBLIOGRAPHY

Anderson, Frederick, and Kenneth M. Sanderson, eds. *Mark Twain: The Critical Heritage*. New York: Barnes & Noble, 1971.

Kunitz, Stanley J., ed. *British Authors of the Nineteenth Century*. New York: H.W. Wilson, 1936.

Marchand, Leslie A. *The Athenaeum: A Mirror of Victorian Culture*. Chapel Hill: U of North Carolina P, 1941.

Welland, Dennis. *Mark Twain in England*. London: Chatto and Windus, 1978.

See also: England

Webb, Charles Henry
(1834–1905)

Best known as a California humorist, Charles Henry Webb spent only three years out west in a journalism career spanning half a century. Born in Rouses Point, New York, on 24 January 1834, he spent his youth on a whaling schooner and working in the family feed store in Illinois before paragraphs he contributed to Chicago and New York newspapers led to his joining the New York *Times*. He served as city editor of the San Francisco *Bulletin* and then edited the *Golden Era* until founding the *Californian* and becoming the West Coast's most influential editor.

Losing money in Mexican mining stocks sent Webb back to New York in 1866. This time his columns by "John Paul" for the New York *Tribune* would make him a national favorite. He issued several collections of his parodies in verse and prose, among them *John Paul's Book* (1874) and *Along Varying Shores* (1901). At the same time he dabbled in the New York Stock Exchange (1872–1873) until the panic of 1873 drove him to live abroad for a few years, during which time he continued contributing to the American press. He also dabbled in inventions, the best one an adding machine that took eight years to perfect, until his company went broke in the panic of 1893. Webb continued contributing to *Harper's Monthly* and the Springfield *Republican* from his home in Nantucket. He died in New York City after a short illness on 24 May 1905.

Webb's influence on Twain's career has been overshadowed by that of their mutual friend Artemus Ward, whose encouragement is supposed to have turned Twain's head toward the eastern seaboard, or Bret Harte, who is supposed to have taught him the tricks of their trade. It was Webb, however, who assured both Harte and Twain of a warm welcome back east and then acquired a publisher for Twain's first book with his own pseudonym, John Paul, on the title page as editor. Through his editorial assistance in this, as on the *Golden Era* and the *Californian*, Webb also offered access to these newer writers through a network of literati on both coasts.

On first going to New York he had joined the round table at Pfaff's Tavern, the center of the city's pseudo-Bohemian life, as well as the watering place for writers from the literary weekly *Round Table* and the humorous *Vanity Fair*, then edited by Ward. When he began the *Californian* in San Francisco a few years later (28 May 1864), Webb imitated the *Round Table* with eight nicely printed pages every Saturday selling at $5 a year. Twain signed on to do an article a week at $50 a month because it offered him the chance to do a higher class of literature. Instead he published sketches not much distinguished from those of the other writers—Harte, Prentice Mulford, Webb as "Inigo," and later Ambrose Bierce.

Webb imitated the *Round Table*'s tone, too. At first he aimed to promote regional literature. While he did republish the jumping frog story after its appearance in the *Saturday Press* and changed, for instance, the name of the fictional setting to "Angel's Camp," the bulk of his material was, like the *Round Table*'s, most catholic in scope. He did, however, reshape its tone from the New Yorkers' slick sophistication to a distinctively bittersweet satire sometimes slipping into acidity and invective, later characteristic of Bierce and the elder Twain.

This was a function of writing his weekly columns about happenings in San Francisco, attacking the city government and civic stupidity at large. So long as Webb balanced that kind of satire with lively parodies of fashionable novels or plays, the mixture proved attractive. Under pressure, both the local columns and the burlesques began attacking traditional values of the region, even the luster of the California pioneers and the gold miners, along with such basic assumptions as "Virtue is its own reward." The satire limited its circulation, and the weekly barely survived Webb's departure, welcomed by San Franciscans tired of his constant carping.

Back in more congenial surroundings, Webb assumed the more pleasing conviviality that had earlier charmed his readers on the East Coast and settled down to his lifetime of parody and burlesque. When Mark Twain arrived in New York, January 1867, he looked up Webb, who not only helped him find a publisher but introduced him to people in the newspaper world able to put him to work and to make sure his work received a favorable press when it appeared.

P.M. Zall

BIBLIOGRAPHY

Stewart, George R., Jr. *Bret Harte, Argonaut and Exile.* Boston: Houghton Mifflin, 1931.

Walker, Franklin D. *San Francisco's Literary Frontier.* New York: Knopf, 1939.

See also: San Francisco, California

Webster, Annie Moffett
(1852–1950)

Annie Moffett, born on 1 July 1852 in St. Louis, Missouri, died on 24 March 1950 in New York City, New York, was the daughter of Pamela Clemens Moffett, Mark Twain's sister, and William Anderson Moffett, a St. Louis businessman. In 1870 the Moffett family (which had been joined by Jane Lampton Clemens, Mark Twain's mother) moved from St. Louis to Fredonia, New York, where on 28 September 1875 Annie married Charles Luther Webster (1851–1891), who later became the manager of the firm of Charles L. Webster and Company that published many of Twain's works. Of her three children, Alice Jane (writing as Jean Webster) became famous as the author of *Daddy Long Legs* (1912), while Samuel Charles eventually published *Mark Twain, Business Man* (1946) to correct the impression given by Mark Twain that it was chiefly his father who was to be blamed for the failure of the publishing house.

During his years as a pilot on the Mississippi River, Mark Twain made the Moffett house in St. Louis his home; thus Annie Moffett grew up under the same roof with Twain and was considered "his pet." In 1862 he insisted on naming a claim to a Nevada ledge for her. Through this close association she was later able to furnish information on those years, most notably in chapter 5, "As His Niece Remembers Him," of *Mark Twain, Business Man*, which is entirely in her words. The account given here and information provided throughout the book correspond in many of their details to her "Family Chronicle Written for Jean Webster McKinney by Her Grandmother," dated 26 October 1918, a forty-four page typescript on deposit at Vassar College.

More important, it was a letter from her

written as a child and addressed to Mark Twain while he was in the West that served the author to demonstrate the qualities of an exemplary informative letter in a humorous sketch entitled "An Open Letter to the American People" (1866). In touching up the original and in preparing his comment on it, the author saw what could be done with the combination of first-person narrator and the child perspective in terms of humor as well as social and moral criticism.

All in all, seventeen letters from Mark Twain to Annie (covering the period from ca. 2 November 1866 to 25 December 1909) and ten letters from Annie to Mark Twain (covering the period from 29 August 1882 to 24 December 1909), as well as 212 letters from her to other correspondents, survive, chiefly in the Mark Twain papers at Vassar and at the Mark Twain Memorial in Hartford.

Horst H. Kruse

BIBLIOGRAPHY

Webster, Annie Moffett. "Family Chronicle Written for Jean Webster McKinney by Her Grandmother." [26 October 1918], TS. Jean Webster McKinney Family Papers. Vassar College Library, Poughkeepsie, New York.

Webster, Samuel Charles. *Mark Twain, Business Man.* Boston: Little, Brown, 1946.

See also: "Open Letter to the American People, An"

Webster, Charles L.
(1851–1891)

A civil engineer from Fredonia, New York, Charles L. Webster married Mark Twain's niece, Annie Moffett, in 1875. One of their three children, Samuel Charles Webster, attempted to vindicate his father's reputation by publishing *Mark Twain, Business Man* in 1946. Charles Webster began to work for Mark Twain in 1881, supervising the Kaolatype Company, then acting as his general business manager.

By 1882 they had formed a publishing company, Charles L. Webster and Company, with

Webster as partner and manager. Although the firm benefitted from the success of *Adventures of Huckleberry Finn* (1885) and U.S. Grant's *Memoirs*, sold by subscription, they had few other triumphs. Among the failures, Webster promoted a biography of Pope Leo XIII, earning him a papal knighthood but no profits for the company. Twain accused Webster of stupidity and mismanagement, and Webster in turn found Twain to be an erratic and interfering partner. Webster's health declined, and he sold his interest in 1888 with the company in distress. By 1894 the company was bankrupt.

Twain's account of the disaster appears in *Mark Twain in Eruption* (1940), with Samuel Webster responding in 1946. Hamlin Hill has written about it in his introduction to *Mark Twain's Letters to his Publishers, 1867–1894* (1967).

Nancy Cook

BIBLIOGRAPHY

Clemens, Samuel L. *Mark Twain in Eruption.* Ed. Bernard DeVoto. New York: Harper, 1940.

———. *Mark Twain's Letters to his Publishers, 1867–1894.* Ed. Hamlin Hill. Berkeley: U of California P, 1967.

Paine, Albert Bigelow. *Mark Twain: A Biography.* 3 vols. New York: Harper, 1912.

Webster, Samuel Charles. *Mark Twain, Business Man.* Boston: Little, Brown, 1946.

See also: Business; Webster and Company, Charles L.

Webster, Jean
(1876–1916)

Named Alice Jane Chandler Webster by her parents, Annie (Moffett) and Charles L. Webster, Mark Twain's publisher and business manager, she was known as Jean Webster; her grandmother, Pamela Moffett, was Twain's sister. Webster married Glenn Ford McKinney in September 1915 and the following June, at age thirty-nine, she died after giving birth to a daughter.

Novelist Webster published eight books, including the popular *Daddy Long Legs* (1912). In an undated note to Livy, Twain called his grandniece's first book, *When Patty Went to College* (1903), "limpid, bright, sometimes brilliant" and praised its "genuine" humor, "not often overstrained." Webster remembered her great-uncle as "the smokiest man" she had known in childhood, "a human furnace."

Although a large Spiridon portrait of Twain hung over her desk, Webster kept publicly aloof of him, maintaining a silence that has been attributed either to dismay over his harsh treatment of her father or determination to succeed on her own. It is also possible that Webster did not want her girlish and often gushy prose compared unfavorably with that of her famous relative.

Mary Boewe

BIBLIOGRAPHY

Clemens, Clara. *My Father, Mark Twain.* New York: Harper, 1931.

Simpson, Alan. *Mark Twain Goes Back to Vassar: An Introduction to the Jean Webster McKinney Family Papers.* Poughkeepsie, N.Y.: Vassar College, 1977.

Simpson, Alan, and Mary Simpson, with Ralph Connor. *Jean Webster, Story-teller.* Poughkeepsie, N.Y.: Tymor Associates, 1984.

See also: Webster, Annie Moffett; Webster, Charles L.

Webster and Company, Charles L.

In 1884, unhappy with the wasteful business practices of his publisher, James R. Osgood, Mark Twain invited Charles Webster, his niece's ambitious young husband, to become titular director of the author's own subscription publishing firm.

Charles Webster and Company enjoyed meteoric success with its first publication, *Adventures of Huckleberry Finn,* which had sold over 40,000 copies by the time distribution began in February 1885. The company followed that triumph by publishing Ulysses S. Grant's *Memoirs* in a two-volume set that immediately sold over 300,000 copies and paid more than $450,000 to the former president's impoverished estate, both figures unprecedented in nineteenth-century American publishing records. With hopes running high at the end of 1885, Webster contracted to publish a number of expensive volumes, including *The Life of Pope Leo XIII* (1887), which Twain predicted would outsell the Koran and the Bible. The pope's book earned only a modest profit, however, and a long list of subsequent publications, primarily the memoirs of ex-military officers, also failed to live up to expectations. Although Twain's own work continued to earn profits, steadily rising expenses and a declining economic climate soon forced the firm to borrow heavily to sustain its operations. Overworked and in failing health, Webster sold his interest in the company to Fred Hall in 1888, and on 18 April 1894 Charles Webster and Company met with its creditors to arrange liquidation of the firm's assets. The company owed over $160,000 at the time, all of which Twain eventually repaid by undertaking a grueling lecture tour in 1895 and 1896.

Henry B. Wonham

BIBLIOGRAPHY

Clemens, Samuel L. *Mark Twain in Eruption.* Ed. Bernard DeVoto. New York: Harper, 1940.

———. *Mark Twain's Letters to His Publishers, 1867–1894.* Ed. Hamlin Hill. Berkeley: U of California P, 1967.

Hill, Hamlin. *Mark Twain: God's Fool.* New York: Harper & Row, 1973.

Kaplan, Justin. *Mr. Clemens and Mark Twain.* New York: Simon & Schuster, 1966.

Paine, Albert Bigelow. *Mark Twain: A Biography.* 3 vols. New York: Harper, 1912.

Webster, Samuel Charles. *Mark Twain, Business Man.* Boston: Little, Brown, 1946.

See also: Business; Webster, Charles L.

Wecter, Dixon
(1906–1950)

Margaret Byrne Professor of American History at the University of California, Berkeley, at the time of his death, Dixon Wecter was a brilliant historian. A noted Mark Twain scholar, Wecter became literary executor of the Twain estate in 1946; his predecessors were Albert Bigelow Paine and Bernard DeVoto. Wecter wrote and edited various authoritative books of "Twainiana," along with the definitive biography of Samuel Clemens's youth.

Wecter was born in Houston, Texas, on 12 January 1906. In 1925 he graduated from Baylor University, which later gave him an honorary degree. After acquiring his master of science degree from Yale in 1926, Wecter became a Rhodes Scholar at Merton College, Oxford, where he received his bachelor of literature degree in 1930. Wecter held a variety of academic positions. He was an instructor of English at the University of Texas (1930), assistant professor of English at the University of Denver (1933–1934) and also at the University of Colorado (1934), where he became associate professor. He received his Ph.D. from Yale in 1936. In 1939 he became professor of history at the University of California at Los Angeles. Wecter was a John Simon Guggenheim Memorial Fellow (1942–1943) and was the first American professor to teach American history at the University of Sydney, Australia (1945).

Wecter wrote of the Great Depression and the Civil War in *The Saga of American Society* (1937), *The Hero in America* (1941), and *When Johnny Comes Marching Home* (1944). He compiled a book entitled *Mark Twain* (1947) listing the thousands of documents, papers, and letters from the Twain estate that were on loan to the Huntington Library at San Marino, California. He intended to use these papers for a two-volume biography of Twain but died after completing the first volume. His widow, Elizabeth, published the manuscript under the title *Sam Clemens of Hannibal* (1952). The book chronicles the author's life from early boyhood to his journalistic achievements in St. Louis. Because Wecter used much previously unpublished material, this biography is essential to Twain scholars.

In the preface to *Sam Clemens of Hannibal*, Elizabeth Wecter explains her husband's plan to publish all of the material found in Twain's estate. Wecter began by compiling and editing *Mark Twain to Mrs. Fairbanks* (1948) and *The Love Letters of Mark Twain* (1949). While working on these, Wecter received help from Clara Clemens Samossoud (Twain's only surviving daughter) and others who had known Twain and Olivia.

In 1950 Wecter addressed the California Library Association on "One Hundred Years of California Writing." In this speech he spoke of Twain's valuable role in creating a western, and ultimately American, humor. Shortly afterward (24 June 1950), Wecter died of a heart attack at age forty-four.

J.R. LeMaster and Lisa Asher

BIBLIOGRAPHY

Clemens, Samuel L. *The Love Letters of Mark Twain.* Ed. Dixon Wecter. New York: Harper, 1949.

———. *Mark Twain to Mrs. Fairbanks.* Ed. Dixon Wecter. San Marino, Calif.: Huntington Library, 1949.

Warren, Robert Penn. "Dixon Wecter (1906–1950)." *American Oxonian* 38.1 (January 1951): 37–40.

Wecter, Dixon. *Mark Twain.* Los Angeles: Anderson & Ritchie, 1947.

———. *Mark Twain in Three Moods.* Boston: Little, Brown, 1943.

———. *Sam Clemens of Hannibal.* Boston: Houghton Mifflin, 1952.

See also: Mark Twain Papers; Scholarship, Trends in Mark Twain

Welsh, James

James Welsh was president of the Philadelphia Typographical Union, No. 2, affiliated with the Knights of Labor. In January 1886 he testified before a joint congressional committee on international copyright. Another witness was Mark Twain.

Twain heard in Welsh's testimony the authentic voice of American workers. That March he presented an essay to the Monday Evening Club, "Knights of Labor—The New Dynasty," in which he vigorously championed organized labor. Twain also began writing *A Connecticut Yankee in King Arthur's Court* (1889) at this time, and Welsh became a part of Hank Morgan, the practical, technologically sophisticated democrat who nearly rids the human race of ignorance and poverty.

Patricia Hunt

BIBLIOGRAPHY

Clemens, Samuel L. *A Connecticut Yankee in King Arthur's Court*. Ed. Bernard L. Stein. Berkeley: U of California P, 1979.

———. *Mark Twain Speaking*. Ed. Paul Fatout. Iowa City: U of Iowa P, 1976.

Foner, Philip S. *Mark Twain: Social Critic*. New York: International Publishers, 1958.

Smith, Henry Nash. *Mark Twain: The Development of a Writer*. Cambridge, Mass.: Harvard UP, 1962.

"What Is Happiness?"

Presented before the Hartford Monday Evening Club on 19 February 1883, "What Is Happiness?" marked an important stage in the development of Clemens's deterministic philosophy. The piece, which he later described as partly "a skeleton sketch" but mostly "talk," argued that man is a machine, functioning automatically, controlled by outside forces, and therefore entitled to neither praise nor blame for his actions. Denying the existence of free will or of true self-sacrifice, it further asserted that no one does a duty for duty's sake, but only to achieve the satisfaction one might derive therefrom or to avoid the discomfort one would feel if he shirked the duty. The presentation thus set forth some of the principal ideas that Mark Twain would develop much more fully in *What Is Man?* (1906).

Howard G. Baetzhold

BIBLIOGRAPHY

Baetzhold, Howard G. *Mark Twain and John Bull: The British Connection*. Bloomington: Indiana UP, 1970.

Blair, Walter. *Mark Twain & Huck Finn*. Berkeley: U of California P, 1960.

Clemens, Samuel L. *Mark Twain In Eruption*. Ed. Bernard DeVoto. New York: Harper, 1940. 239–243.

See also: Determinism; Monday Evening Club of Hartford; *What Is Man?*

What Is Man?
(1906)

Mark Twain's *What Is Man?* has had a varied critical history. Scholars have tried to both suppress its existence and make it central to readings of Twain's last quarter century. For some readers the conversation between the Old Man and the Young Man embodies Twain's bitter wisdom; for others it reflects the cynicism of his depressive temperament.

Twain spent more than eight years on the text, adding and deleting sections, making changes both large and small. (In his preface to the 1906 edition, he claims that the studies for the essay were "begun twenty-five or twenty-seven years ago," and James Hart says the essay's genesis was Twain's 1893 paper, "What Is Happiness?" delivered for the Monday Evening Club of Hartford.) The first draft (of nearly half the published essay) was written between April and July 1898 in Vienna. Some segments that Twain thought belonged in the text were later cut (i.e., "The Quality of Man"); many others were added. The whole was reorganized. The 1898 version, known as "the Vienna typescript," is the basis for the second, typed in 1902. It differs appreciably from the first, as does the third in 1905.

Because Twain had been discussing this work with friends, sometimes reading it aloud to them, he felt that it was ready to see print—but secretly. In 1906 he had 250 copies of *What Is Man?* printed by De Vinne Press, anonymously and privately. In August the work was sent out with a letter signed by J.W. Bothwell, the superintendent of De Vinne (the work being copyrighted in the name of Bothwell also).

While Twain saw the 1906 publication as a convenience to himself, in that he would not need to discuss his ideas personally, in 1908 he said that *What Is Man?* had had so little effect that he wished he had not printed it. The few newspapers that reviewed it found little new and compared the philosophy with that of Ibsen, Nietzsche, and Shaw. As Twain said, the people he wanted to reach were the busy professionals and intellectuals, who would have responded with more interest to something that carried his name. The work received very little attention until two days after Twain's death in 1910 when the New York *Tribune* published a feature article about *What Is Man?* Most of the commentary then focused on the fact that the greatest of America's humorists had had such dark, and in some views antireligious, sentiments. After the initial flurry of publicity, later critics have seen the work as an integral part of Twain's late prose.

What Is Man? is, in fact, an assemblage of dialogues, with the character of the Old Man questioning the comparatively naive, and usually affirmative, Young Man. The long work is divided into seven numbered sections, many of these subdivided into titled segments as well. Headings include "Man the Machine," "Personal Merit," "Man's Sole Impulse—The Securing of His Own Approval," "Training," "Admonition," "Instinct and Thought," "Free Will," and "The Master-Passion." Scattered in the dialogues are set pieces of illustration, titled "A Little Story," "A Parable," and "Further Instances." Structured as a debate, with the protagonists circling back to what they consider their premier arguments, the dialogue moves like a narrative—and it was undoubtedly this structural rhythm Twain was working hardest toward as he added, changed order, or deleted.

The Old Man's argument is that human kind is a machine, incapable of creating anything, motivated only by the deepest self-interest. That self-interest Twain defines as "the impulse to content his own spirit . . . and win its approval." In the illustrations that pepper the text the Old Man shows repeatedly that

people's so-called selfless acts have as their first motivation making the doer feel content. The Old Man calls this the "Master Impulse" and shows that people behave to win their own comfort both instinctively and because their consciences are trained to respond in such a manner. The Young Man worries, questions, and finally attacks the Old Man for this "Gospel of Self-Approval," but the Old Man remains assured and confident in his principles. Parts one through three comprise this dialogue.

Part four focuses on the "training" the Old Man defines as any outside influences, cultural as well as educational. Every person is the result of a complex of forces, for he is a "chameleon; by a law of his nature he takes the color of his place of resort." After many examples of the powerlessness of the human mind to avoid this training, the dialogue returns to the initial paradigm, that man is a machine, incapable of creating, formed only to respond. The human thought process is compared with acquiring information as a machine might— the mind observes, infers, finds, adds, concludes. The Old Man contends that thinking is a mechanical process and that "reasoning" cannot exist independently; it too results from cultural process. The notion of free will is also suspect because the mind trained to respond as it has been cannot upset those mechanical patterns to make choices: even personal life choices are the result of training. Therefore, free will is a misnomer.

Here the Young Man attacks, charging the Old Man with "elusive terminology." From this pivotal point they resume discussion of the "Master-Passion," the conscience, defined as another manifestation of "the hunger of Self-Approval." The circling structure reinforces the thematic circling to the matter of the first two books. As the dialogue concludes, the Old Man assumes that he has won (the discussion has become so arduous that the Young Man has taken a holiday, a week-long mountain tramp) and spends the last few paragraphs consoling the younger man. He points out that even though he has adopted this belief system, which in itself is dehumanizing and cheerless, he is himself cheerful. When the Young Man points out that such an attitude is the result of his temperament, the Old Man replies, "If a Man is born with an unhappy temperament, nothing can make him happy; if he is born with a happy temperament, nothing can make him unhappy."

When the Young Man questions his belief in the dominance of temperament, asking what "a degrading and heart-chilling system of beliefs" might accomplish, the Old Man assures him that the philosophical undertaking they have just experienced has little effect on inherited temperament. And the dialogue concludes with his admonishing the Young Man "not to be troubled." Whether his assurance is sophistry or compassion, Twain does not identify.

What Is Man? is a continuation of the strain of questioning disillusion that first appeared in Twain's 1889 novel *A Connecticut Yankee in King Arthur's Court*, a work Philip Fisher calls "a parable of cultural arrogance and its self-destructive naivete." Twain's pessimism was even more apparent in the late stories, *The Mysterious Stranger* (written 1897–1908, published 1916) and "The Man That Corrupted Hadleyburg" (1899). It should be no surprise that the disillusion of an aging writer, who sees the human condition worsening rather than improving despite material advantages and sophisticated technology, suffuses both his fiction and his essays as he realizes that all the gentle moralizing of his earlier much acclaimed works has had little effect.

Linda Wagner-Martin

BIBLIOGRAPHY

Baender, Paul. Introduction. *"What Is Man?" and Other Philosophical Writings*. By Clemens. Ed. Baender. Berkeley: U of California P, 1973. 1–34.

Bridgman, Richard. *Traveling in Mark Twain*. Berkeley: U of California P, 1987.

Fisher, Philip. "Mark Twain." *Columbia Literary History of the United States*. Ed. Emory Elliott. New York: Columbia UP, 1988. 627–644.

Gillman, Susan. *Dark Twins: Imposture and Identity in Mark Twain's America*. Chicago: U of Chicago P, 1989.

Hart, James D. *"What Is Man?" The Oxford Companion to American Literature*. 5th ed. New York: Oxford UP, 1983. 814.

See also: Conscience; Determinism; Philosophy; "What Is Happiness?"

"What Paul Bourget Thinks of Us"
(1895)

Twain published his essay "What Paul Bourget Thinks of Us" in the *North American Review* in 1895 as a response to Bourget's publication of *Outre-Mer*, the author's impressions of the United States. Bourget was a French novelist, critic, poet, journalist, and member of the French Academy. In his essay Twain roundly disputes Bourget's findings and broadly satirizes his European perspective of America life.

Journeying back and forth to visit his family in France, Twain began his reply at first as a pleasant means of putting some time to use. But he worked for weeks before mailing the essay; when Paul Blouet (as "Max O'Rell") attacked Twain's essay in the pages of the *North American Review*, Twain penned "A Little Note to M. Paul Bourget," mistakenly supposing that Bourget had rebutted through Blouet. Though Bourget had been as severe on the United States in print as Twain had previously been on Europe, Twain retaliated in grand style against the critical Frenchman (Emerson 194).

Twain felt Bourget could not apply the term "American" to kinds of behavior exhibited across a country of millions. He particularly attacks Bourget's notions of social deportment learned at Newport, Rhode Island, and his view of the American woman. He gleefully takes up and redirects a joke of Bourget's—that if one asks an American who his grandfather is he will not know—with a jibe directed at the French: a Frenchman can overcome his own boredom by inquiring as to who his father is. Twain recommends that Bourget read American novels: "Observation? Of what real value is it? One learns peoples through the heart, not the eyes or the intellect" ("What Paul Bourget Thinks of Us" 145).

Jeanne Campbell Reesman

BIBLIOGRAPHY

Bourget, Paul. *Outre-Mer: Impressions of America.* London: T. Fisher Unwin, 1895.

Clemens, Samuel L. "A Little Note to Paul Bourget." *How to Tell a Story and Other Essays.* By Clemens. New York: Harper, 1897. 165–181.

———. "What Paul Bourget Thinks of Us." *How to Tell a Story and Other Essays.* By Clemens. New York: Harper, 1897. 141–164.

Emerson, Everett. *The Authentic Mark Twain: A Literary Biography of Samuel L. Clemens.* Philadelphia: U of Pennsylvania P, 1984.

See also: France; *North American Review*

Wheeler, Simon

Modeled on Ben Coon, a wizened derelict Clemens encountered during the winter of 1864–1865 at Angel's Camp, California, Simon Wheeler is the good-natured garrulous old miner who tells the story of Jim Smiley and his menagerie of pet animals in "The Celebrated Jumping Frog of Calaveras County" (1865). James M. Cox contends that it is the voice of Simon Wheeler that enables Clemens to transform the story he had heard from Coon of Smiley and his frog into enduring art, for in Wheeler he finds the perfect vehicle to capture the method of oral delivery he considered the essence of American humor.

There are actually two narrators in "The Celebrated Jumping Frog of Calaveras County": one is a conspicuously genteel Mark Twain, an ambassador from the East who uses formal, literary, written language in inquiring about the imposing sounding Reverend Leonidas W. Smiley; the other is Simon Wheeler, who responds in nonliterary vernacular dialect with the unwelcomed tale of the infamous gambler Jim Smiley. Cox contrasts "The Jumping Frog" with Thomas Bangs

Thorpe's "The Big Bear of Arkansas" (1841). The formal narrator in Thorpe's tale constantly interrupts his vernacular counterpart; the genteel character Mark Twain, however, never interrupts Wheeler once he begins his seemingly random and pointless account of Smiley's adventures with his pet animals. Furthermore, during the telling Wheeler never smiles, never frowns, never changes his voice, never shows a trace of enthusiasm; Wheeler finds nothing funny or ridiculous in an absurd story rendered with total earnestness and sincerity. It is of course Wheeler's deadpan delivery that makes the story hilarious (Cox 26–28), but the butt of the joke is Mark Twain, the self-important narrator who frames the tale.

Wheeler's total self-absorption and obliviousness to everything except his story defines his character. He is so focused that he forgets not a single detail, and even when he absent-mindedly digresses, his mind does not miss a thing: an example is his detailed description of Smiley's dog who, though incidental to the main thrust of the story, is nevertheless fully rendered, characterized, and humanized. Cox compares the grave, pained, earnest style of Simon Wheeler to Mark Twain's subsequent deadpan delivery on the lecture platform. The seriousness provides a backdrop to highlight the humor (Cox 29–32).

Paul Schmidt argues that Wheeler is the western con man outwitting a supercilious Easterner; indeed, the story marks an early example of the genteel-vernacular confrontation that was to become Twain's recurrent humorous strategy. Yet, as Paul Baender points out, the "Jumping Frog" is more than a clash of western and eastern ideologies. Indeed, the development of Simon Wheeler as the deadpan narrator of the "Jumping Frog" story proved one of the most significant events in Samuel Clemens's writing career, for Wheeler transported Clemens's mind from the real world to the world of fantasy in general, and of burlesque in particular. On 19 October 1865, just after he had finished writing "Jim Smiley and His Jumping Frog," Clemens wrote to his brother Orion, claiming he finally felt like a writer. He said that when he was young he had wanted to become a preacher, but now he had a different "calling." Instead of having a call to develop sermons about the higher order, he had a call to literature of a low order—namely, humor.

Samuel Clemens tried to resurrect Simon Wheeler on a number of different occasions, most notably in *Cap'n Simon Wheeler, the Amateur Detective* (written 1877) and in a fragmentary novelistic adaptation of that unproduced play *Simon Wheeler, Detective* (written 1877–1898). But he was never quite successful. Cox suggests a reason. Clemens had developed Simon Wheeler as a long-winded, endlessly digressive character, but he had done so with great compression and economy of writing style: in the "Jumping Frog" story Wheeler seems to go on in his ramblings even after Clemens stops writing about him. When a decade later or so Clemens tried to resurrect Wheeler, he found that he could only keep rambling on. He had already said all that he was able to say (Cox 32).

Don L.F. Nilsen

BIBLIOGRAPHY

Baender, Paul. "The Jumping Frog as a Comedian's First Virtue." *Modern Philology* 60 (February 1963): 192–200.

Branch, Edgar M. *The Literary Apprenticeship of Mark Twain.* Urbana: U of Illinois P, 1950.

Clemens, Samuel L. "The Simon Wheeler Sequence." *Mark Twain's Satires & Burlesques.* By Clemens. Ed. Franklin R. Rogers. Berkeley: U of California P, 1967. 205–454.

Cox, James M. *Mark Twain: The Fate of Humor.* Princeton, N.J.: Princeton UP, 1966.

Emerson, Everett. *The Authentic Mark Twain: A Literary Biography of Samuel L. Clemens.* Philadelphia: U of Pennsylvania P, 1984.

Schmidt, Paul. "The Deadpan on Simon Wheeler." *Southwestern Review* 41 (Summer 1956): 270–277.

See also: *Cap'n Simon Wheeler, the Amateur Detective*; "Celebrated Jumping Frog of Calaveras County, The"; Coon, Ben; Deadpan; Humor; Vernacular

"Which Was It?"
(1967)

Mark Twain began "Which Was It?"—the longest and the least humorous of his dream-story fragments—in the summer-fall of 1899 while he was in London and then Sweden seeking treatment for his daughter Jean's epilepsy. He initially titled the piece "Which Was Which?" but when he returned to work on the manuscript in 1900–1902 he retitled it "Which Was It?" By May 1903 Twain had almost finished the fragment; he prepared two typescripts, considered publication, but then in the summer of 1906 he finally decided against completing the story and abandoned it. John S. Tuckey first published the story in his edition of *"Which Was the Dream?" and Other Symbolic Writings of the Later Years* (1967).

This version of the familiar dream-disaster scenario deviates from "Which Was the Dream?" and "Indiantown" in that it emphasizes the effects of failure on the conscience of a guilty victim who pleads blamelessness (DeVoto 119–120; Emerson 239–240). The protagonist—prosperous, happily married George Harrison—falls asleep and has a nightmarish dream in which his essentially selfish and brutal nature surfaces. Fearing financial ruin, Harrison intends to burn his mill for insurance; however, overhearing the Bleekers plotting to rob Squire Fairfax to avenge his horsewhipping of one of their own, Harrison decides instead that he will rob Fairfax, who had earlier threatened to expose his father as a counterfeit money passer. Interrupted in the process of the robbery, Harrison murders Jake Bleeker with Fairfax's cane. The innocent Fairfax is arrested and accused of Jake's murder, thus continuing a series of crimes for which Harrison, in his greed, is responsible. The central conflict is posed by a free mulatto, Jasper, who torments and blackmails conscience-stricken Harrison—silent following Fairfax's arrest—with the handkerchief mask Harrison had discarded during his witnessed murder and flight.

Like the other dream-disaster fragments, "Which Was It?" contains recurring autobiographical elements, specifically Twain's guilt over his bankruptcy, Susy's death, and his deteriorating family life (DeVoto 118). The setting, the small southern village of Indiantown, recalls Hannibal and, as DeVoto suggests, reflects Twain's nostalgia for the secure, fulfilling life that had eluded him (115). The story, however, has wider cultural implications as well. The themes of duplicity, cowardice, pettiness, and greed link Indiantown not to Hannibal so much as to Hadleyburg or Bricksville—a village polluted by slavery, racial fear, prejudice, and guilt (Pettit 167–168; Robinson 218). The story continues the attack on southern mores characteristic of "Indiantown" (Requa 2). Harrison's wife Alison uses superlatives, clichés, joyful references, and excessive exclamation points in descriptions of her daughters, which recall the romantic sentimentalism Twain thought pervasive and destructive in southern culture. They give an illusory cast to the supposedly real "waking" world (Tuerk 28). More disturbingly realistic is the nightmare in which Jasper switches master and slave roles, punishing Harrison, who represents the sins and guilt of white America. Forced to buy freedom thrice, Jasper is Harrison's cousin-become-conscience, illustrating the thin barrier separating free man and slave: family, community, and conscience enslave; all people, all races, are potentially masters and slaves (Pettit 171–172).

A weak, hypocritical man suffering guilt, Harrison is too ashamed to tell his own story—or to face its darker implications. Hence there is a shift from first-person narration in the opening dream frame to impersonal omniscient narration of the main story in which George Harrison becomes merely a character objectively delineated. The setting (winter) and imagery (lighting, mirrors, fire) reflect psychological states. Although ostensibly incomplete, "Which Was It?" achieves the resolution *Huckleberry Finn* (1885) avoided. It evades a darker conclusion by permanently deferring an ending, but it implies no racial reconciliation (Pettit 173). White man eter-

nally confronts a nightmare retribution lurking on the edge of waking reality (Robinson 218).

John H. Davis

BIBLIOGRAPHY

Clemens, Samuel L. *Mark Twain's "Which Was the Dream?" and Other Symbolic Writings of the Later Years.* Ed. John S. Tuckey. Berkeley: U of California P, 1967. 179–429.

DeVoto, Bernard. "The Symbols of Despair." *Mark Twain at Work.* By DeVoto. 1942. Rpt. Boston: Houghton Mifflin, 1967. 105–130.

Emerson, Everett. *The Authentic Mark Twain: A Literary Biography of Samuel L. Clemens.* Philadelphia: U of Pennsylvania P, 1984.

Pettit, Arthur G. *Mark Twain and the South.* Lexington: UP of Kentucky, 1974.

Requa, Kenneth A. "Counterfeit Currency and Character in Mark Twain's 'Which Was It?'" *Mark Twain Journal* 17 (Winter 1974): 1–6.

Robinson, Forrest G. *In Bad Faith: The Dynamics of Deception in Mark Twain's America.* Cambridge, Mass.: Harvard UP, 1986.

Tuerk, Richard. "Appearance and Reality in Mark Twain's 'Which Was the Dream?' 'The Great Dark' and 'Which Was It?'" *Illinois Quarterly* 40 (Spring 1978): 23–34.

See also: Conscience; Dreams; Slavery; "Which Was the Dream?"

"Which Was the Dream?"
(1967)

Planned in early 1895, written in 1897, and apparently abandoned in August of that year around the first anniversary of Susy's death, the fragmentary "Which Was the Dream?" remained unpublished until John S. Tuckey's edition in 1967. The story employs common dream-fiction techniques—frame, prominent man's fall, questioning of the nature of reality, voyage of disaster—as it explores unconscious powers that in 1898 notebook entries Mark Twain describes as "dream-selves" (*Notebook* 348–352).

Autobiographical elements permeate "WWD?" The piece merges Twain's metaphor for his daughter Susy's death (a burned house) with recurring motifs illustrative of the author's personal struggles in the 1890s: bankruptcy, infamy, a disconsolate hearth, the suspicion (or hope) life may be a dream illusion. Wife Alice, as she awaits her daughters' play party, sees husband Tom doze off while writing his autobiography for Bessie and Jessie. Abruptly, their house burns. Learning he is uninsured, penniless, indebted, and cheated by Alice's cousin Jeff, Tom loses consciousness. He awakens eighteen months later in unfamiliar surroundings with the same family but with a new name and a different life. The voyage of disaster story operates on the theme of sudden, inexplicable reversal, with Tom at the end questioning his identity and the value of existence. The happy life that appears real may in fact be the illusion; the nightmarish series of catastrophes, seemingly a dream, may be the ultimate reality. Protagonist Tom X, who is thirty-four (the age Mark Twain began to gain national acclaim), doubts the reality of his lost good fortune and, like Mark Twain the artist, approaches madness as a refuge from guilt, responsibility, and despair (Gribben 190; Harris 160; DeVoto 105–130).

In choosing fantasy in lieu of realism as his approach to truth, Twain minimizes distinctions separating dream and reality (Tuerk 24) or art and life (DeVoto 109). As he revealed in a letter to William D. Howells, Twain structures "WWD?" as comedy to draw unsuspecting readers into a "tragedy-trap" (*Letters* 2:675–676) in which the apparent reality—sentimental, romantic happiness—becomes the illusion and the apparent nightmare becomes the final reality of the author's late life. In the process Twain constructs an absurd but unfunny universe (Messent 185) that forces the reader to question both the nature of existence and the possibility of knowledge. Intrusive family memories, more tedious than amusing, call attention to the illusion through hyperbole: children are too good, wife too perfect and loving, husband too successful, heroic, admired. This is the stuff of romance, escapist and destructive. The dream of disaster, on the other hand, is all too real. "WWD?" develops themes and a characteristic tone that dominated Mark Twain's writing during the last decade of his life.

John H. Davis

BIBLIOGRAPHY

Clemens, Samuel L. *Mark Twain–Howells Letters: The Correspondence of Samuel L. Clemens and William D. Howells, 1872–1910.* Vol. 2. Ed. Henry Nash Smith and William M. Gibson. Cambridge, Mass.: Harvard UP, 1960.

———. *Mark Twain's Notebook.* Ed. Albert B. Paine. New York: Harper, 1935.

———. *Mark Twain's "Which Was the Dream?" and Other Symbolic Writings of the Later Years.* Ed. John S. Tuckey. Berkeley: U of California P, 1967. 33–73.

DeVoto, Bernard. "The Symbols of Despair." *Mark Twain at Work.* By DeVoto. Cambridge, Mass.: Harvard UP, 1942. 105–130.

Duncan, Jeffrey L. "The Empirical and the Ideal in Mark Twain." *Publications of the Modern Language Association* 95 (March 1980): 201–212.

Emerson, Everett. *The Authentic Mark Twain: A Literary Biography of Samuel L. Clemens.* Philadelphia: U of Pennsylvania P, 1984.

Gribben, Alan. "Those Other Thematic Patterns in Mark Twain's Writings." *Studies in American Fiction* 13.2 (Autumn 1985): 185–200.

Harris, Susan K. "Mark Twain's Bad Women." *Studies in American Fiction* 13.2 (Autumn 1985): 157–168.

Messent, Peter. "Towards the Absurd: Mark Twain's *A Connecticut Yankee, Pudd'nhead Wilson,* and *The Great Dark.*" *Mark Twain: A Sumptuous Variety.* Ed. Robert Giddings. Totowa, N.J.: Barnes & Noble, 1985. 176–198.

Tuckey, John S. "Mark Twain's Later Dialogue: The 'Me' and the Machine." *American Literature* 41 (January 1970): 532–542.

Tuerk, Richard. "Appearance and Reality in Mark Twain's 'Which Was the Dream?' 'The Great Dark' and 'Which Was It?'" *Illinois Quarterly* 40 (Spring 1978): 23–34.

See also: Dreams; Family Life; "Great Dark, The"; "Which Was It?"

Whitmore, Franklin Gray
(1846–1926)

Franklin Whitmore, a Hartford real estate and insurance man, began acting as a business agent for Mark Twain by 1886 and continued in that capacity until the sale of the Hartford house in 1903. Whitmore was also a part of the Clemenses's social circle, including the "Friday Evening Club," a group of Twain's billiard-playing friends.

As with nearly all of his business associates, Twain's relationship with Whitmore was uneven. Despite criticism of him found in Twain's correspondence during the period, Whitmore made efforts to protect Twain's business interests, particularly with regard to the Paige typesetter.

Nancy Cook

BIBLIOGRAPHY

Andrews, Kenneth R. *Nook Farm: Mark Twain's Hartford Circle*. Cambridge, Mass.: Harvard UP, 1950.

Clemens, Samuel L. *Mark Twain's Correspondence with Henry Huttleston Rogers, 1893–1909*. Ed. Lewis Leary. Berkeley: U of California P, 1969.

———. *Mark Twain's Notebooks & Journals, Volume III (1883–1891)*. Ed. Robert Pack Browning, Michael B. Frank, and Lin Salamo. Berkeley: U of California P, 1979.

———. *Mark Twain's "Which Was the Dream?" and Other Symbolic Writings of the Later Years*. Ed. John S. Tuckey. Berkeley: U of California P, 1967.

Paine, Albert Bigelow. *Mark Twain: A Biography*. 3 vols. New York: Harper, 1912.

See also: Business; Paige Typesetting Machine

Whittier, John Greenleaf
(1807–1892)

Essayist, poet, journalist, and writer of letters and abolitionist tracts, John Greenleaf Whittier became a legend in his own time, a reputation that in turn was repudiated. Born in Haverhill, Massachusetts, into a Quaker farm family and influenced by his reading of Byron and Burns, he thought of the New England past and the land around him as the proper subject of poetry. Unmarried, he was torn by a deep inner conflict between wanting a Quaker-like peace and gaining fame from his political and writing activities; yet he revealed his life as a whole man in extensive correspondence. Beginning

his career in abolition with William Garrison in 1833, Whittier used his facility in verse as a device for editorial and propagandistic success.

Because of Whittier's personality, his moral emphasis, and his strong abolitionist stance, it was difficult in the nineteenth century to assess his work aesthetically, but once he moved beyond his "poetical" notion of poetry, in Robert Penn Warren's estimate, Whittier ground his poetry in experience. He fused a deep personal and dramatic impulse with his politics in "Ichabod" (1850), and wove his nostalgia for a childhood past into his best poems such as "Telling the Bees" (1858) and "Snow-Bound: A Winter Idyl" (1866). Whittier's well-attended seventieth birthday dinner, at which Mark Twain's famous blundering parody of three New England poets— Henry Wadsworth Longfellow, Ralph Waldo Emerson, and Oliver Wendell Holmes—occurred, gives evidence of Whittier's high literary esteem among his peers.

Twentieth-century criticism of Whittier's work, moving beyond the dual attitude of the nineteenth, is concerned with placing the poet in perspective as a working journalist for thirty years and as a minor but not obscure writer.

Charlotte S. McClure

BIBLIOGRAPHY

Keller, Karl. "John Greenleaf Whittier." *Fifteen American Authors Before 1900: Bibliographical Essays on Research and Criticism*. Ed. Earl N. Harbert and Robert A. Rees. Madison: U of Wisconsin P, 1984. 468–499.

Whittier, John Greenleaf. *John Greenleaf Whittier's Poetry: An Appraisal and a Selection*. Intro. Robert Penn Warren. Minneapolis: U of Minnesota P, 1971.

———. *Letters of John Greenleaf Whittier*. Ed. John B. Pickard. 3 vols. Cambridge, Mass.: Harvard UP, 1975.

———. *Whittier on Writers and Writing: The Uncollected Critical Writings of John Greenleaf Whittier*. Ed. Edwin H. Cady and Harry Hayden Clark. Syracuse, N.Y.: Syracuse UP, 1950.

———. *The Writings of John Greenleaf Whittier*. Riverside ed. Ed. Horace E. Scudder. 7 vols. Boston: Houghton Mifflin, 1888, 1904.

See also: Whittier Birthday Dinner Speech

Whittier Birthday Dinner Speech

At the invitation of William Dean Howells, Mark Twain spoke at the Brunswick Hotel in Boston on the evening of 17 December 1877 after a formal dinner hosted by the staff of the *Atlantic Monthly* in honor of John Greenleaf Whittier's seventieth birthday. Howells, as toastmaster, introduced Twain to the audience, which included fifty-eight distinguished men of letters, as "a humorist who never makes you blush to have enjoyed his joke" and "whose generous wit has no meanness in it." He "had been particularly fortunate in his notion for the speech," as Howells later recalled, and "had worked it out in joyous self-reliance." In the speech Twain related an episode that had ostensibly occurred in the foothills of the California Sierras some fifteen years earlier. He had visited the cabin of a "jaded, melancholy" miner who had recently been victimized by three hoboes who answered to the names Ralph Waldo Emerson, Oliver Wendell Holmes, and Henry Wadsworth Longfellow. "Mr. Emerson was a seedy little bit of a chap, red-headed," this miner had explained. "Mr. Holmes was as fat as a balloon; he weighed as much as three hundred, and had double chins all the way down to his stomach. Mr. Longfellow was built like a prize fighter. His head was cropped and bristly, like as if he had a wig made of hairbrushes." These "littery people" had cheated at cards and drank the miner's whiskey, all the while misquoting the verse of the authors they impersonated and misidentifying titles of their work, and finally they had stolen his only pair of boots on their way out the door.

Unfortunately, as Twain noted in his autobiographical dictation years later, many faces in the audience "turned to a sort of black frost" in the course of this address. While contemporary news accounts suggest the speech was reasonably well received, Howells also remembered that the silence in the room weighed "many tons to the square inch" and was finally broken "by the hysterical and blood-curdling laughter of a single guest, whose name shall not be handed down to infamy." In a word, the joke failed utterly because, according to Howells, Twain failed to gauge accurately "the species of religious veneration" in which Emerson and the Brahmins were held, and he underestimated the difficulty of poking even good-natured fun at these men in their presence "and expecting them to enter into the delight of it." The senile Emerson listened "with a sort of Jovian oblivion of this nether world"; Longfellow regarded the speaker "with an air of pensive puzzle"; and Holmes jotted notes on his menu "with a well-feigned effect of preoccupation." While they took no offense, and though Twain offered each of them an immediate sincere apology, the address soon became a cause célèbre. The speaker was so roundly censured by custodians of genteel culture from Boston to Chicago and Cincinnati that he feared the appearance of his work in its pages would "hurt the *Atlantic*," and he offered to "retire from before the public at present." The controversy may also have been a factor in his decision a few months later to move with his family to Europe for two years.

Twain was ambivalent about the address to the end of his life, sometimes dismissing it as "coarse" or "detestable," at other times admiring it as "smart" and "saturated with humor." In any event, he considered repeating the speech at a dinner for journalists as late as 1906.

Gary Scharnhorst

BIBLIOGRAPHY

Clemens, Samuel L. *Mark Twain's Autobiography*. Ed. Albert B. Paine. 2 vols. New York: Harper, 1924.

———. *Selected Shorter Writings of Mark Twain*. Ed. Walter Blair. Boston: Houghton Mifflin, 1962.

Duckett, Margaret. *Mark Twain and Bret Harte*. Norman: U of Oklahoma P, 1964.

Howells, William Dean. *My Mark Twain: Reminiscences and Criticisms*. New York: Harper, 1910.

L[athrop], G[eorge] P[arsons]. "The Whittier Dinner." New York *Evening Post*, 19 December 1877, 1.

Paine, Albert Bigelow. *Mark Twain: A Biography*. 3 vols. New York: Harper, 1912.

Smith, Henry Nash. *Mark Twain: The Development of a Writer.* Cambridge, Mass.: Harvard UP, 1962.

See also: Emerson, Ralph Waldo; Whittier, John Greenleaf

Wilde, Oscar
(1854–1900)

Dublin-born writer of criticism, fiction, poems, and plays, Oscar Wilde was noted for his satirical wit and flamboyant demeanor.

After distinguishing himself in the classics at Trinity College, Wilde attended Magdalen College in 1874. He became known for his "effeminate" disdain for sports, wearing his hair long, and decorating his quarters with peacock feathers and flowers. He became an apostle of J.M. Whistler's "art for art's sake" doctrine. In 1884 he married Constance Lloyd, with whom he had two sons. He published a series of short-story collections beginning with *The Happy Prince and Other Tales* (1888). His blank verse tragedy, *The Duchess of Padua* (1891), was produced in New York, but popular success eluded him until *Lady Windermere's Fan* (1892), *A Woman of No Importance* (1893), and *The Importance of Being Earnest* (1895).

In 1893 the licenser of plays refused to license *Salome*, the first of Wilde's troubles with English authorities. In 1895 Wilde brought a libel suit against the Marquis of Queensbury, which he lost. He was sentenced to two years hard labor in Reading Gaol. Leaving prison in 1897, Wilde was bankrupt and moved to the Continent under the name Sebastian Melmoth. In 1898 he wrote "The Ballad of Reading Gaol." He died in Paris in 1900.

Twain called on the Wildes in London in the late 1880s, signing Constance's autograph book. According to Clara Clemens, Twain and Wilde met in a hotel in Bad Nauheim, Germany. Wilde wore a "carnation as large as a baby sunflower" and created great excitement for the Clemens women.

George Bernard Shaw thought Wilde's humor resembled Twain's, principally because of their similar quips. Wilde first said, "I never put off till to-morrow what I can possibly do the day after," a phrase reworked by Twain. Wilde told his wife "divine providence" provided "nice, plump missionaries" for starving cannibals, echoing Twain's comment: "Christianity? We understand it very well, we have eaten the missionaries."

In an unfinished essay written about 1880, "The Walt Whitman Controversy," Twain grouped Wilde with Whitman and Swinburne as poets of "new bad books" and said he owned none of their works. Wilde's enthusiastic review of Twain's "English as She Is Taught" in the *Century* (1887) was a precursor to Wilde's use of children in "The Happy Prince" and other stories. Wilde said much could be learned from the voice of Twain's American children. In an April 1887 letter Wilde called Twain's article "amazing and amusing."

Wesley Britton

BIBLIOGRAPHY

Hart-Davis, Rupert. *More Letters of Oscar Wilde.* New York: Vanguard, 1985.

Morley, Sheridan. *Oscar Wilde.* New York: Holt, Rinehart, 1976.

Shewan, Rodney. *Oscar Wilde: Art and Egotism.* New York: Barnes & Noble, 1977.

Wilks Family

The Wilks family appears in *Adventures of Huckleberry Finn* (1885) in chapters 24 through 29. The King and the Duke (and Huck and Jim) learn the lowdown on the monied Wilkses in a little "Arkansaw" town as these facts are naively related by a flathead on his way to "Ryo Janeero." There were two local Wilks brothers: George, a carpenter, married with three daughters; and Peter, a tanner. George died the year previously; Peter had just died, survived by three nieces, Mary Jane (nineteen), Susan (fifteen), and Joanna, "the harelip," as Huck will call her (about fourteen)— survived also by the money that he has hidden for his successors in lieu of a will. The flathead thought the King was Harvey Wilks, a "dissentering" minister from England, brother to George and Peter. There is also William Wilks, who is "the deaf and dumb one" (thirty or thirty-five); he lives with Harvey in England. The King is told about a letter Peter sent to Harvey when Peter became ill. Harvey was to come to America to unearth the hidden money and take care of George's girls.

This information invites one of the King and Duke's most ludicrous impersonations as Harvey and William Wilks. In this sequence Mark Twain extends his satiric view of false religious piety and sentiment. The King's distorted version of bereavement in his impersonation of minister Harvey Wilks—he refers to Peter's funeral obsequies as "orgies"—exploits the townspeople's hedonistic desire for sentiment and sententiousness. But it is in this sequence also that Huck, for the first time, morally condemns this exploitation, in response to Mary Jane Wilks's admirable qualities. Scholars find moral significance in the subsequent actions of the episode. Increasingly, the moral question is formulated in terms of Mark Twain's view on truthful language. For many, Huck's decision to undeceive Mary Jane about the Duke and King's scam suggests an unusual instance when truth transcends falsity in the novel. The basis for this truth is kindness; Huck transcends his fear of truth with Mary Jane in response to her empathy. One scholar even suggests that Mark Twain risks sentimentalism when he morally invests provincial Mary Jane with the sanction of standard idiom. In chapter 28 she even navigates "the moral waters of 'shall' and 'will'" (Sewell). In an opposing view, however, the Wilks episode has been judged by some to complicate language. An additional set of Wilks brothers does not settle false identity. The person whom Huck calls the "real" William has broken his writing arm: scientific evidence cannot be used to detect fraud. The scene dramatizes that systems and signs break down.

Scholars have also suggested some tentative sources for the Wilks episode. Mary Jane originates from, although she transcends, the stereotype of the pious Victorian woman (Sloane; Walker). The scene with the real brothers re-

sembles one in Horace Fuller's *Noted French Trials: Imposters and Adventurers* (1882), although it surpasses it (Emerson). The scene with the disrupted sermon and the explanatory "He had a rat" resembles a story circulating in Hartford about the Reverend Joseph Twichell (Sloane).

Janet Gabler-Hover

BIBLIOGRAPHY

Clemens, Samuel L. *Adventures of Huckleberry Finn.* Ed. Walter Blair and Victor Fischer. Berkeley: U of California P, 1985.

Emerson, Everett. *The Authentic Mark Twain: A Literary Biography of Samuel L. Clemens.* Philadelphia: U of Pennsylvania P, 1984.

Gabler-Hover, Janet. *Truth in American Fiction: The Legacy of Rhetorical Idealism.* Athens: U of Georgia P, 1990.

Sewell, David R. *Mark Twain's Languages: Discourse, Dialogue, and Linguistic Variety.* Berkeley: U of California P, 1987.

Sloane, David E.E. *Adventures of Huckleberry Finn: American Comic Vision.* Boston: G.K. Hall, 1988.

Thomas, Brook. "Language and Identity in *Adventures of Huckleberry Finn.*" *Mark Twain Journal* 20.3 (Winter 1980–1981): 17–21.

Walker, Nancy. "Reformers and Young Maidens: Women and Virtue in *Huckleberry Finn.*" *Huck Finn.* Ed. Harold Bloom. New York: Chelsea House, 1990. 139–154.

See also: Adventures of Huckleberry Finn; Language

Wilson, David

David Wilson is the given name of the title character of *Pudd'nhead Wilson*, which appeared first as a *Century Magazine* serial (1893–1894). Of Scotch parentage, a native of New York and graduate of an eastern law school, David Wilson arrived at Dawson's Landing, Missouri, in 1830 to seek his fortune at age twenty-five. On his first day in town, upon hearing a dog causing a ruckus, he remarked to a group of townspeople, "I wish I owned half of that dog." Asked why, he responded, "Because, I would kill my half." Unable to understand the joke, the citizens deemed him a fool, and within a week his first name had been replaced with "Pudd'nhead." The designation stuck for over twenty years, and although it "soon ceased to carry any harsh or unfriendly feeling" with it, "no one took on his services as a lawyer, and so he turned to surveying and keeping books" for making a living. His hobbies included palmistry, collecting and studying the fingerprints of his townspeople, and composing a "calendar with a little dab of ostensible philosophy, usually in ironic form," for amusement—activities that reaffirmed the town's judgment of him as a pudd'nhead. He "was liked, he was welcomed enough all around, but he simply didn't account for anything." His fortunes began to change quickly, however, after the Italian twins, Counts Luigi and Angelo Cappello, came to town. David Wilson and the twins became good friends, and when Tom Driscoll took Luigi to court for assault, Wilson represented the Italian, his first court case. Although he lost, the Democratic Party asked him to run for mayor, "a recognition of his debut into the town's life and activities at last." He did run and was elected the first mayor of a town that was soon to be a chartered city. Wilson came again to Luigi's defense when he was brought to trial for murdering Judge Driscoll. In a climactic and dramatic court scene, Wilson's use of the science of fingerprinting proved the Count innocent but revealed as well not only that Tom Driscoll was the murderer, but also that he was Roxy's mulatto child whom she had switched with the child of her white master some twenty years earlier. As the story ends, David Wilson's "long fight against hard luck and prejudice was ended; he was a made man for good."

About Wilson as a literary character, Twain wrote to his wife, "I have never thought of Pudd'nhead as a character but only as a piece of machinery—a button, or crank, or lever with a useful function to perform in a machine, but with no dignity above that." True, Wilson is not deeply aware of or concerned with the thematic issues of the book—slavery, miscegenation, antebellum southern mores generally—but most literary critics see him as more than a plot device although not necessarily favorably as a literary character. Given his ambition and his flair for theatrics, David Wilson is often compared with Tom Sawyer. Some see him as another manifestation of Twain's interest in the private detective characterization of popular fiction. Others see Wilson as a version of Twain's transcendent figure, given that he is a rather emotionally detached outsider with a superior, almost supernatural, intelligence, a characterization that also has parallels to Twain's interest in the detective figure.

Any understanding of Wilson's character must take into account to some degree "Pudd'nhead Wilson's Calendar," the aphorisms that appear at the beginning of each chapter, such as "If you pick up a starving dog and make him prosperous, he will not bite you. This is the principal difference between a dog and a man" and "Training is everything. The peach was once a bitter almond; the cauliflower is nothing but cabbage with a college education." For the most part, the humorous, usually satirical aphorisms have little bearing on the plot of the story, but they do reveal a character very different from the accommodating, ambitious hero of that plot. Representing the deeper, private thoughts that lie behind the mask of the Pudd'nhead, the sardonic irony that his townspeople cannot understand, the calendar entries have much in common with Mark Twain's commentary on the damned human race.

Cameron C. Nickels

BIBLIOGRAPHY

Alsen, Eberhard. "Pudd'nhead Wilson's Fight for Popularity and Power." *Western American Literature* 7 (1972): 135–143.

Brand, John M. "The Incipient Wilderness: A Study of *Pudd'nhead Wilson*." *Western American Literature* 7 (1972): 125–134.

Cox, James M. *Mark Twain: The Fate of Humor.* Princeton, N.J.: Princeton UP, 1966.

Fiedler, Leslie. "As Free as Any Cretur. . . ." *New Republic* 133 (15 August 1955): 17–18; (22 August 1955): 16–18.

Fisher, Marvin, and Michael Elliott. "*Pudd'nhead Wilson*: Half a Dog Is Worse than None." *Southern Review* 8 (July 1972): 533–537.

Regan, Robert. *Unpromising Heroes: Mark Twain and His Characters*. Berkeley: U of California P, 1966.

Smith, Henry Nash. *Mark Twain: The Development of a Writer*. Cambridge, Mass.: Harvard UP, 1962.

Spangler, George M. "*Pudd'nhead Wilson*: A Parable of Property." *American Literature* 42 (1970): 28–37.

See also: Aphorisms; *Pudd'nhead Wilson, The Tragedy of*

Women (Characters in Mark Twain's Fiction)

In *Roughing It* (1872) Mark Twain tells of how when he was in the mining territory he stood in line to see a "genuine, live woman" through a crack in a cabin wall (*Works* 6: 2:133–135 [two volumes in one]). This story, whether true or apocryphal, provides a metaphor for the way in which Twain portrayed women throughout most of his fiction: from the outside, from a distance, as one would look at a picture. For the most part, he does not view women as persons to be interacted with; the woman is an image, not a person.

Twain's female characters fall into two general categories. In *Tom Sawyer* (1876) Tom tells Huck that he is going to marry a "girl," not a "gal" (*Works* 1:204), and this differentiation can be used to understand the two categories of women in Twain's fiction. The "girl" is Twain's ideal woman: modest, unassertive, and innocent. In Twain's fiction the ideal woman is a girl—prepubescent and asexual. Even if she is a wife and a mother, she is expected to be as innocent and ignorant as a child. The other type of woman, the "gal," is assertive and sexually experienced. The difference between these two concepts of women is suggested by two dreams that Twain reported. One was the recurring dream that he described in the essay "My Platonic Sweetheart." Twain tells of how he met a young girl in his dreams (always the same sweet, earnest girl of fifteen). But each dream ended before the relationship was consummated (*Works* 8:287–304). In another dream that Twain described in his notebook in 1897, he was pursued by a "negro wench," who disgusted him with her sexual advances (*Works* 22:351–352). In Twain's fiction the "girl" is pure, even asexual, and lacking in substance and individuality. The "gal" is more fully developed and possesses a sexual identity, but her low social status, her sexuality, and her self-assertion win her the author's disapproval.

These two categories of female characters derive from the stereotyped images of women that were common during Twain's lifetime: the genteel lady and the whore. Tom Sawyer's ideal "girl" is Becky Thatcher, the judge's daughter. She is as pretty as an angel, Tom thinks, even though she is a "fool" (*Works* 1:22, 172). Tom's cousin Mary is even less interesting than Becky. Twain portrays her as the embodiment of the female civilizing influence, which is a characteristic he associates with most of his women characters, particularly his older women: Aunt Polly, Aunt Sally, the Widow Douglas. The "girls" in *Huckleberry Finn* (1885), *The Prince and the Pauper* (1882), and *A Connecticut Yankee in King Arthur's Court* (1889) are peripheral and uninteresting. Mary Jane Wilks in *Huckleberry Finn* has "sand" or grit, but she is no more than an image. Peggy Mills in "Huck Finn and Tom Sawyer Among the Indians" is ingenuous to the point of stupidity. Twain himself was not much interested in his female characters. He sometimes even forgot their names. He was more interested in the male adventurer.

For Twain, the ideal woman was a perpetual maiden. Twain's own favorite of this type was his portrayal of Joan in *Joan of Arc* (1896). Joan embodies all of the characteristics of Twain's ideal woman. He describes her as "wholly noble, pure, truthful, brave, compassionate, generous, pious, unselfish, modest, blameless as the very flowers in the fields" (*Works* 2:200). To Twain, Joan was not a strapping peasant woman but a girl. He called her "the most innocent, the most lovely, the most adorable child the ages have produced" (Paine 3:1030).

Twain's most believable female character is Roxana in *Pudd'nhead Wilson* (1894), but she is a "gal" not a "girl." Apparently, it is her social status that permits Twain to endow Roxy with the strength of character and individuality that is lacking in his genteel women. Roxy is a slave, and as such does not count since Twain does not perceive her as a marriage candidate. The other female character in Twain's fiction who is portrayed with individuality also does not count: Laura Hawkins, who was Twain's creation in *The Gilded Age* (1873), written in collaboration with Charles Dudley Warner, is of questionable background. In both cases, however, Twain short-circuited the development of the strong female character. Roxy's possibilities as a protagonist are buried under a mountain of dialect while her tragic situation is obscured by the plot, which moves in the opposite direction. Laura Hawkins, like other morally transgressing women in nineteenth-century American fiction, is punished for her deviance: Twain kills her. Twain, who became famous for his realistic portrayal of the nongenteel male protagonist, held very rigid expectations for women.

Twain's excessive concern for female purity focused on the genteel lady, either the "girl" who was eligible for marriage or the wife. There is more to Twain's insistence on sexual purity than Victorian prudishness, however. The woman who repelled him was not only sexually aware; she was independent, aggressive, and selfish—the opposite of all the qualities he associated with ideal womanhood. That Twain associated sexual experience with independence and aggressiveness is apparent from the fact that, except for Eve, the only two women in his fiction who have a sexual identity are also aggressive and dominant. Laura Hawkins in *The Gilded Age* is manipulative and selfish. Roxy in *Pudd'nhead Wilson* is strong and shrewd, with "aggressive and commanding ways" (*Works* 3:79). In Twain's mind the sexually experienced woman (like the concu-

bines he criticized in his diatribes against French immorality) was a threat to male autonomy (*Notebooks & Journals* 2:323). The innocent "girl," whether wife or maid, was selfless and dependent and posed no threat.

It was this fear of female self-assertion that was behind Twain's insistence on female purity and passivity. As Susan Gillman points out, although Twain unequivocally condemned racial stereotypes and discrimination, he associated the breakdown of gender stereotypes with moral disorder (102). In fragments like "Hellfire Hotchkiss" (1897) and "Wapping Alice" (1898), which deal with sexual role reversal, Twain was unable to bring the stories to closure because he was uncomfortable with the idea that women could be "masculine"; aggressive, clever women were too much of a threat.

The one female character in Twain's fiction that cannot be easily classified in either of the two categories is Eve, who appears in several works written between 1893 and 1906. She is portrayed with the feminine prettiness of the "good girls," but with more of the independence and substance of the "gals." Twain also suggests that she has a sexual identity. The only female character in Twain's fiction who speaks in her own voice, Eve has more individuality than the other good women in Twain's fiction. Moreover, Twain gives her more credence than he does his other female characters; in the posthumously published "Eve's Autobiography" and "Eve Speaks" she voices Twain's own controversial ideas. Part of the explanation for Eve's greater individuality is her relationship to Twain's wife Olivia. In "Eve's Diary," which Twain wrote around the time of Livy's death in 1904, Adam has inscribed on Eve's grave, "Wheresoever she was *there* was Eden" (*Works* 18:381). Eve reflects Twain's recognition of his dependence upon his wife, her cheerfulness, her common sense, and her emotional strength. Whether consciously or unconsciously, in his creation of Eve, Twain acknowledged that a person who provided such strength could not be the passive nonentity of his genteel ideal. As Susan K. Harris points out, Eve and the wives in the nightmare fragments ("The Great Dark" and "Which Was the Dream?") represent the concept of women as possessing the stability that Twain arrived at later in his career, when he himself was floundering in uncertainty (123–128).

Although this image of women gives Twain's female character more strength, nevertheless, it is still an *image*, an image of woman as viewed by and in relation to man; she is not seen as a person in her own right. Eve says of Adam, "I wish to learn to like everything he is interested in" (*Works* 18:379). Twain's ideal woman existed for him. After Livy died, he surrounded himself with very young girls; his Angel Fish he called them. They were like playthings who amused him and brought him pleasure. They were no threat to the self. He insisted that they be very young and unspoiled—the symbol of girlish innocence and selflessness that characterized his portrayal of women throughout his fiction.

Joyce W. Warren

BIBLIOGRAPHY

Clemens, Samuel L. *The Complete Works of Mark Twain.* 24 vols. New York: Harper, 1923.

———. *Letters from the Earth.* Ed. Bernard DeVoto. New York: Harper, 1962.

———. *Mark Twain's Notebooks & Journals.* Ed. Frederick Anderson, et al. 3 vols. Berkeley: U of California P, 1975–1979.

Gillman, Susan. *Dark Twins: Imposture and Identity in Mark Twain's America.* Chicago: U of Chicago P, 1989.

Goad, Mary Ellen. *The Image and the Woman in the Life and Writings of Mark Twain.* Emporia: Kansas State Teachers College, 1971.

Harris, Susan K. *Mark Twain's Escape from Time: A Study of Patterns and Images.* Columbia: U of Missouri P, 1982.

Paine, Albert Bigelow. *Mark Twain: A Biography.* 3 vols. New York: Harper, 1912.

Warren, Joyce W. *The American Narcissus: Individualism and Women in Nineteenth-Century American Fiction.* New Brunswick, N.J.: Rutgers UP, 1984.

See also: Eve; Hawkins, Laura; Roxana; Thatcher, Becky; Women's Rights

Women's Rights

The first Women's Rights Convention in the United States was held at Seneca Falls, New York, in 1848, and after the Civil War the movement intensified. Although Mark Twain at times seemed to express support for women's suffrage, his comments on the subject reveal ambivalence about the goals of the women's rights movement: the goals of social, political, or economic equality.

His position on women's rights derived from his attitude toward women. In a speech in Washington, D.C., early in 1868, Twain summarized his conception of woman: "Woman," he said, "is lovable, gracious, kind of heart, beautiful; worthy of all respect, of all esteem, of all deference" (*Works* 24:33). In a speech in Scotland in 1872 he stressed the elevated position of women and emphasized that woman was important only in relation to other people (*Works* 24:42–45). These two ideas about women determined Twain's position on women's rights. Emphasizing women's purity, Twain was not comfortable with ideas that in his view would threaten the innocence and childlike ignorance that he liked in women; he associated the independent action of women with sexual experience, which to him represented the threat of female power. Moreover, since he believed that woman was important only in relation to other people, rather than for herself, he could not conceive of ideas that projected an independent life for woman or assumed her individuality.

Twain's attitude toward women is apparent in his portrayal of women in his fiction as well as in his relationship with the real women in his life. With the exception of Roxy in *Pudd'nhead Wilson* (1894) and Laura Hawkins in *The Gilded Age* (1873) (who because of race or sexual experience are not regarded as marriage candidates), Twain's female characters are sexless and lifeless, idealized abstractions rather than real people. Twain also created idealized images for real women. He censored his wife's reading and cast her in the role of reformer. Writing to her before their marriage, he made clear what his image of her was: "You are as pure as snow, & I would have you always so—untainted, untouched even by the impure thoughts of others" (*Love Letters* 76).

When Twain addressed the issue of women's suffrage, his attitude varied, particularly in his early works. In a humorous piece in 1867 he ridiculed middle-aged, unattractive women who fought shrilly for the vote, but he was sympathetic to young pretty women who spoke in favor of women's rights gently and with "feminine" modesty (*Life* 10–21). Twain shared the opinion of many Americans during a period of mass immigration that an educated, intelligent, native-born woman might well vote if "every ignorant whiskey-drinking foreign-born savage in the land" had that privilege (*Works* 20:24–30). Also, his belief in women's elevated status included the common belief that women were morally superior to men, and in an 1873 essay on the temperance crusade he noted that for this reason women might be valuable in the electoral process (*Works* 20:24–30).

Later in his career, Twain was occasionally explicit in his support of women's suffrage. In a speech at a girl's school in 1901, Twain concluded that there would be less corruption in government if women had the vote (*Works* 24:222–224). In *Following the Equator* (1897) he noted that women in New Zealand, both white and Maori women, were able to vote. He observed that the women voted in large numbers and that they were not molested at the polls—the fear of which was a major reason given by Americans for denying women the vote. Although the New Zealand women were not able to serve in the legislature, Twain said (without commenting on this restriction), they were able to vote. He observed that the law stated specifically that the word "person" included women. Twain expressed annoyance at the average American man who refused to recognize that women were intelligent enough to vote (*Works* 1:284–285). In an interview just four months before he died, Twain said that he supported any methods women might choose to accomplish their aims (Budd 188).

And in the posthumous *Letters from the Earth* (1962) he listed among the failures of mankind the fact that "woman's equality with man has never been conceded by any people" (176).

In theory, Twain believed that it was "just" that women should vote, and he advocated equality of the sexes (*Mark Twain and the Three R's* 196). But he did not think that it was "right." The idea of women's entering the political arena repulsed him. He was distressed by the thought of seeing these "earthly angels" at the polls or out electioneering (*Life* 10–21).

Joyce W. Warren

BIBLIOGRAPHY

Budd, Louis J. *Our Mark Twain: The Making of His Public Personality*. Philadelphia: U of Pennsylvania P, 1983.

Clemens, Samuel L. *The Complete Works of Mark Twain*. American Artists Edition. 24 vols. New York: Harper, 1923.

———. *Letters from the Earth*. Ed. Bernard DeVoto. New York: Harper & Row, 1962.

———. *Life as I Find It*. Ed. Charles Neider. Garden City, N.Y.: Hanover House, 1961.

———. *The Love Letters of Mark Twain*. Ed. Dixon Wecter. New York: Harper, 1949.

———. *Mark Twain and the Three R's: Race, Religion, Revolution—and Related Matters*. Ed. Maxwell Geismar. Indianapolis, Ind.: Bobbs-Merrill, 1973.

Foner, Philip S. *Mark Twain: Social Critic*. New York: International Publishers, 1958.

Goad, Mary Ellen. *The Image and the Woman in the Life and Writings of Mark Twain*. Emporia: Kansas State Teachers College, 1971.

Warren, Joyce W. *The American Narcissus: Individualism and Women in Nineteenth-Century American Fiction*. New Brunswick, N.J.: Rutgers UP, 1984.

See also: Clemens, Olivia Langdon; Family Life; Politics; Sexuality; Women

"Word of Encouragement for Our Blushing Exiles, A"
(1923)

First published in 1923 in *Europe and Elsewhere*, this short essay of less than a 1,000 words was written, according to Albert B. Paine, in 1898. It has seldom been republished.

In response to a heated letter from a member of the American colony in Paris who felt ashamed of America's involvement in the Cuba-Spain confrontation, Twain assumed that the writer must be ashamed because he believed his country was meddling in another nation's internal affairs under a sham humanitarian pretext but actually to filch Cuba. Satirically, Twain points out that the United States would not lose respect in Europe—certainly not in Russia because of its episodes in Manchuria, Siberia, and Port Arthur; nor in France, which had deserted its young female savior, had experienced Bartholomew's Day and the Reign of Terror, had imprisoned Dreyfus and insulted Emile Zola, and had sent Maximillian to Mexico; nor definitely in Spain, which had chained Columbus, enslaved or killed West Indians, robbed and slaughtered the Incas, drenched the New World in blood, driven the Jews out of Spain, perpetrated the Inquisition, and committed many other ingnominies.

Maverick Marvin Harris

BIBLIOGRAPHY

Clemens, Samuel L. *Europe and Elsewhere*. New York: Harper, 1923.

See also: Europe

Wright, Laura M.

Clemens first met Laura M. Wright, an early love, in May 1858, aboard the *John J. Roe* in New Orleans, where she was visiting her uncle, William C. Youngblood, a pilot friend of Clemens. Daughter of Judge Foster P. Wright of Warsaw, Missouri (about 150 miles west of St. Louis), she was not yet fifteen at the time. Though Clemens later claimed that the first meeting and parting was the only one, the pair corresponded over some period of time, and Clemens also visited Warsaw at least once. There was a falling-out, however, and Laura some years later married a Mr. Dake.

Although Clemens never saw her again, his memory and dreams of her remained remarkably persistent. Scholars have found echoes of the relationship in an unpublished fragment from "Shem's Diary" (written early 1870s), *The Gilded Age* (1873), *Tom Sawyer* (1876), *A Connecticut Yankee* (1889), and an unpublished portion of "Eve's Autobiography" (written early 1900s), "Eve's Diary" (1905), "The Refuge of the Derelicts" (written 1905–1906), "Three Thousand Years Among the Microbes" (written 1905), and particularly in "My Platonic Sweetheart" (written 1898), first published, slightly abridged, in *Harper's Monthly*, December 1912.

Howard G. Baetzhold

BIBLIOGRAPHY

Baetzhold, Howard G. "Found: Mark Twain's 'Lost Sweetheart.'" *American Literature* 44.3 (November 1972): 414–429.

Clemens, Samuel L. *Mark Twain's Letters, Volume 1 (1853–1866)*. Ed. Edgar M. Branch, Michael B. Frank, and Kenneth M. Sanderson. Berkeley: U of California P, 1988.

See also: "My Platonic Sweetheart"

York Harbor, Maine

During the summer of 1902 the Clemens family stayed at the Pines, a cottage overlooking the York River at York Harbor, Maine. What began as a peaceful interlude with Olivia Langdon Clemens resting and Mark Twain spending hours with William Dean Howells or writing in a neighbor's cottage changed abruptly on 12 August when Olivia Clemens suffered a severe heart attack. Despite his wife's ill health, he did write "The Belated Russian Passport" (1902) and "Was It Heaven? Or Hell?" (1902) and finished his last poem during the summer. Although Henry H. Rogers offered his yacht, Twain arranged for his wife to travel by invalid car back to Riverdale, New York, on 16 September 1902.

Sandra Gravitt

BIBLIOGRAPHY

Clemens, Clara. *My Father, Mark Twain*. New York: Harper, 1931.

Hill, Hamlin. *Mark Twain: God's Fool*. New York: Harper & Row, 1973.

Howells, William Dean. *My Mark Twain: Reminiscences and Criticisms*. New York: Harper, 1910.

Paine, Albert Bigelow. *Mark Twain: A Biography*. 3 vols. New York: Harper, 1912.

"You've Been a Dam Fool, Mary. You Always Was!"
(1972)

"You've Been a Dam Fool, Mary. You Always Was!" is an originally unpublished story that Mark Twain wrote in December 1903, in Florence, Italy, and that he submitted to Harper and Brothers in February 1904. The publisher seems to have been hesitant about the title, and Twain responded by suggesting the less controversial "You're a Jackass, Mary." Still another possible title was "The Honest Rebel," but the story remained unpublished until collected in Tuckey's edition of *Mark Twain's Fables of Man* (1972).

Twain found inspiration for the story in the real-life friendship and business partnership that existed between New Englander Daniel Hand and South Carolinian George W. Williams. Like their fictional counterparts Thomas Hill and James Marsh, these two men were forced to part company because of the Civil War, but eventually they were able to continue their friendship and to settle their business affairs with such courtesy and grace that the story was told in New England for many years thereafter.

"You've Been a Dam Fool, Mary" is a somewhat lengthy story that explores dual themes of honor and friendship. In particular, the question of southern honor arises when Thomas Hill, the Connecticut blacksmith who returns to the North with the outbreak of the Civil War, announces his confidence in his southern business partner James Marsh and is told by his neighbors that Southerners do not pay northern debts. Hill maintains his faith throughout the story and is predictably rewarded with great wealth, while Marsh is showered with praises for his integrity.

Twain cynically counterpoints the friendship and trust existing between the two men through the character of Mary Lester, who is Thomas Hill's fiancée and the Mary mentioned in the title of the story. Mary breaks her engagement with Hill in order to marry a wealthier suitor and to avoid being excluded from her uncle's will. Her actions are motivated by self-interest and clearly contrast with those of Marsh, who goes to great lengths in order to keep his promise of loyalty and friendship to Hill.

Yet the moral texture of the story is deepened somewhat by the fact that both main characters practice forms of deception. Hill, whose business success is continuously ruined by his timidity in demanding payment from customers, does not hesitate to fake his own death when the opportunity arises. The deception enables him to escape his debts and to start life anew. Similarly, Marsh disguises his identity and his economic station by dressing as a tramp and by occasionally affecting drunkenness. The ruse enables him to collect valuable information from the villagers and to be taken much less seriously than his true intentions would warrant.

"You've Been a Dam Fool, Mary" is more laden with mawkish sentiment than is customary in Twain's fiction, but the story does possess an undercurrent of cynicism that lends needed ambiguity to its strongly moralistic theme. In addition, the final moments of the story reverberate with irony. Mary, who chooses wealth rather than Hill, unwittingly rejects wealth.

Craig Albin

BIBLIOGRAPHY

Clemens, Samuel L. *Mark Twain's Correspondence with Henry Huttleston Rogers, 1893–1909.* Ed. Lewis Leary. Berkeley: U of California P, 1969.

———. "You've Been a Dam Fool, Mary. You Always Was!" *Mark Twain's Fables of Man.* By Clemens. Ed. John S. Tuckey. Berkeley: U of California P, 1972. 249–278.

Macnaughton, William R. *Mark Twain's Last Years as a Writer.* Columbia: U of Missouri P, 1979.

Appendix

GENEALOGY

LAMPTON ANCESTORS OF MARK TWAIN

VII.   **Marke (also Mark) Lampton**   married   Elizabeth.
        b. 1648   d. 1696
        d. 1701

In 1664, sixteen-year-old Mark Lampton arrived in the Colony of Maryland as the first Lampton (Lambton) in America. A recusant Catholic from Durham, England, he became a successful tobacco planter in Charles County, Maryland.

VI.   **William Lampton (1)** married three times.
        b. 29 April 1682
        d. 1 December 1722

After his death, his third wife, Hester Davis Lampton, married James Jones, and by Jones had three more children. One of these, daughter Elizabeth Jones, married a Spence Monroe, and they had a son whom they named James. James Monroe was elected to be the fifth president of the United States. William (1) and his first wife, name unknown, were the parents of Twain's great-great-grandfather, William Lampton (2). William (1) and his third wife, Hester, were the parents of Joshua Lampton (1720–1774), who was the great-great-grandfather of the Lambton claimant, Jesse Madison Leathers.

V.   **William Lampton (2)**   married   Sarah.
        b. 1708
        d. 1760

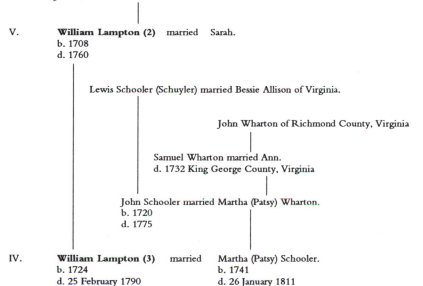

Lewis Schooler (Schuyler) married Bessie Allison of Virginia.

John Wharton of Richmond County, Virginia

Samuel Wharton married Ann.
d. 1732 King George County, Virginia

John Schooler married Martha (Patsy) Wharton.
b. 1720
d. 1775

IV.   **William Lampton (3)**   married   Martha (Patsy) Schooler.
        b. 1724   b. 1741
        d. 25 February 1790   d. 26 January 1811

Known as "William the Pioneer," he had served in the militia of the Colony of Virginia from 1755–1760 and was probably with the group that made the abortive attempt led by young George Washington to capture Fort Duquesne from the French. He married Patsy Schooler in Spotsylvania County, Virginia, in 1763, and they raised a family of eight sons and three daughters. He proved his military service before the Spotsylvania County Court in February 1780 and received a bounty of fifty acres of land in what was to become Kentucky. He soon moved his family to the Clark and Bourbon County areas of Kentucky, where he died in 1790, aged sixty-six years, and was buried near Winchester, Kentucky. He was believed by his great-grandson Twain to be a son of the Earl of Durham.

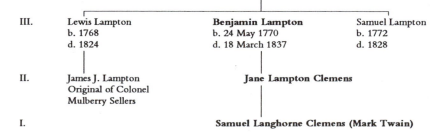

III.   Lewis Lampton   **Benjamin Lampton**   Samuel Lampton
        b. 1768   b. 24 May 1770   b. 1772
        d. 1824   d. 18 March 1837   d. 1828

II.   James J. Lampton   **Jane Lampton Clemens**
        Original of Colonel
        Mulberry Sellers

I.   **Samuel Langhorne Clemens (Mark Twain)**

CASEY AND MONTGOMERY ANCESTORS OF MARK TWAIN

V.   **William Montgomery** married Jane (Jean) Patterson in 1747.
            b. 1727 in County Tyrone, Ireland
            d. 18 March 1780, twelve miles from St. Asaph's, Kentucky

The parents of William Montgomery were Alexander and Mary Montgomery, and the parents of Jane Patterson (his wife) were Peter Patterson and Eleanor Lytle. William Montgomery came from Ireland by way of Pennsylvania to Virginia. In 1779, he journeyed with his family into Kentucky. He and his son John were killed by Indians on the Green River near Logan's Fort, Kentucky.

Captain Benjamin Casey married Julia Carson.
b. 21 January 1731
d. 4 April 1779

Benjamin Casey was born in Anne Arundel County, Maryland. He was a captain in the Virginia Line (12th and 8th Virginia regiments; became captain 1 September 1777). He was killed in battle (Frederick County, Virginia) in 1779.

IV.   **Jane Montgomery**   married   Colonel William Casey in 1779.
            b. 1761   b. 1754
            d. 30 January 1844   d. 1 December 1816

Colonel William Casey, a native of Frederick County, Virginia, was a noted Indian fighter and Revolutionary War hero. He served as a sergeant in Captain Logan's Company during the Revolutionary War (See *D.A.R. Lineage Book* 99 page 187). In 1806, Casey County, Kentucky, was named in his honor. Near Russell's Creek, Kentucky, he was buried sitting bolt upright—as he had died while suffering from arthritis. Living almost thirty years after her husband's death, Jane Montgomery was buried in West Point, Iowa.

III.   Benjamin Lampton   married   (1) **Margaret (Peggy) Casey** on 19 March 1801.
            b. 24 May 1770   b. 31 March 1783
            d. 18 March 1837   d. 6 October 1818

                                            (2) Mary Margaret (Polly) Hays on 2 February 1819.
                                                b. 27 May 1788
                                                d. 26 March 1842

II.   **Jane Lampton**

I.   **Samuel Langhorne Clemens**

CLEMENS ANCESTORS OF MARK TWAIN

XI.   **Richard Clements (1)**   married   Elizabeth in 1535.
            b. 1506 in Leicestershire, England
            d. February 1571 in Croft, England

X.   **Robert Clements (1)**   married   (1) Alice in 1561.
            b. 1536 in England   (2) Margaret.
            d. June 1606 in Croft, England

IX.   **Richard Clements (2)**   married   Agnes Fellows on 2 March 1595 in Cosby, England.
            b. 1570 in Croft
            d. July 1617 in Cosby   d. 1619

VIII.   **Robert Clements (2)**   married   Lydia.
            b. December 1595 in England
            d. 29 September 1658 in Haverhill, Massachusetts

In May 1642, two months after the death of his wife Lydia in Warwickshire, England, Robert Clements sailed for the American colonies. Purchasing land from the Indians, he helped found Haverhill, Massachusetts. He was an active leader in the community, serving as a judge from 1647 to 1654.

> John Fawne married Elizabeth; settled in Ipswich, Massachusetts, in 1732.

VII.   **Robert Clements (3)** married Elizabeth Fawne in 1652 in Massachusetts.
b. 1634 in England
d. 1714 in Massachusetts

> Edward Gove married Hannah Partridge.
> d. July 1691

VI.   **Abraham Clements**   married   Hannah Gove on 10 May 1683.
b. 14 July 1657 in Massachusetts   b. March 1664
d. 1716 in Bucks County, Pennsylvania

Around 1701 Abraham moved with his wife and children from Salisbury, Massachusetts, to Bristol, Pennsylvania, a growing town in this new colony.

V.   **Ezekiel Clemens** married Christina Castell in 1725.
b. 1 February 1696
d. 1778

Ezekiel experienced financial difficulties his entire life and died in Virginia still owing debts.

> Edward Howell
>
> Rev. John Moore married Margaret Howell.
> b. 1615   b. 1622
> d. 13 October 1657 in Massachusetts
>
> Gershom Moore (1) married Mary Fish.
> d. 1691 in Newton, Massachusetts
>
> Josiah Furman married Sarah Strickland
>
> Gershom Moore (2) married Mercy Furman.
> d. 1722 in Massachusetts
>
> Gershom Moore (3)
> b. 1713

IV.   **Jeremiah Clemens**   married   Elizabeth Moore in 1763.
b. 1732 in New Jersey
d. 17 November 1811 in Virginia

III.   **Samuel B. Clemens**   married   Pamela Goggin on 29 October 1797 in Bedford County, Virginia.
b. 1770 in Virginia
d. 1805 in Mason County, West Virginia

According to family tradition, Samuel Clemens, Mark Twain's grandfather, was "killed by a falling log at a house raising at Point Pleasant" in Mason County, West Virginia. Twain gave the same fate to Simon Lathers in *The American Claimant* (1892), who was "crushed by a log at a smoke-house raising" in the similarly remote hamlet of Duffy's Corners, Arkansas.

II.   **John Marshall Clemens** married Jane Lampton.
b. 11 August 1798 in Campbell County, Virginia.
d. 24 March 1847 in Hannibal, Missouri.

I.   **Samuel Langhorne Clemens**

GOGGIN ANCESTORS OF MARK TWAIN

V.   **Stephen Goggin, Sr.**

In 1742, Stephen as a young man came to Bedford County, Virginia, from Queen's County, Ireland. The name of his first wife is unknown; however, she was the mother of his son Stephen, Jr., (great-grandfather of Mark Twain). Stephen, Sr., married a second time to Susannah Terry of Bedford County, Virginia, 5 September 1772. Stephen, Sr., was a member of the Anglican Church.

Thomas Moorman married Rachel Clark.

IV.   **Stephen Goggin, Jr.,**   married   Rachel Moorman on 15 June 1773.
         b. 1752 in Virginia   b. 1754
         d. 1802 in Virginia   d. 1833

Stephen, Jr., was a first lieutenant in the Bedford County militia during the Revolutionary War. Stephen and Rachel were married in 1773 in Bedford County, Virginia. For Rachel Moorman's ancestors, see Moorman ancestors of Mark Twain.

III.   **Pamela (also Parmelia and Pamelia) Goggin**   married   (1) Samuel B. Clemens,
         29 October 1797 in Bedford County, Virginia.
         b. 31 October 1775 Virginia
         d. 1844 Kentucky

After Samuel's accidental death at a house raising in 1805, Pamela married (2) Simon Hancock (1774–1856) on 21 May 1809, by whom she had four more children.

II.   **John Marshall Clemens**

I.   **Samuel Langhorne Clemens (Mark Twain)**

MOORMAN ANCESTORS OF MARK TWAIN

VIII.   **Zachariah Moorman** married Candler.
               b. 1620 England

In 1669, Zachariah immigrated with his family from Southampton, England, in the *Glasgow* to Barbados in the West Indies and later to Charleston, South Carolina. He and his son Thomas settled in the Green Springs section of Louisa County, Virginia, in 1670 and later in Nansemond County, Virginia. The Moormans were Quakers. Family legend contends that Zachariah was a captain in Cromwell's army, but that he and his family were exiled because they were against the beheading of Charles I.

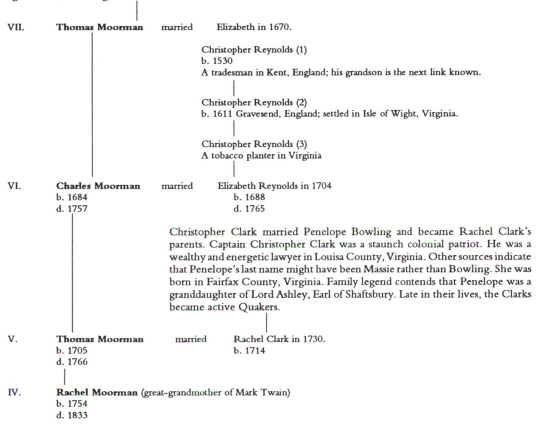

VII.   **Thomas Moorman**   married   Elizabeth in 1670.

                                      Christopher Reynolds (1)
                                        b. 1530
                                        A tradesman in Kent, England; his grandson is the next link known.

                                        Christopher Reynolds (2)
                                        b. 1611 Gravesend, England; settled in Isle of Wight, Virginia.

                                        Christopher Reynolds (3)
                                        A tobacco planter in Virginia

VI.   **Charles Moorman**   married   Elizabeth Reynolds in 1704
               b. 1684   b. 1688
               d. 1757   d. 1765

                                        Christopher Clark married Penelope Bowling and became Rachel Clark's parents. Captain Christopher Clark was a staunch colonial patriot. He was a wealthy and energetic lawyer in Louisa County, Virginia. Other sources indicate that Penelope's last name might have been Massie rather than Bowling. She was born in Fairfax County, Virginia. Family legend contends that Penelope was a granddaughter of Lord Ashley, Earl of Shaftsbury. Late in their lives, the Clarks became active Quakers.

V.   **Thomas Moorman**   married   Rachel Clark in 1730.
               b. 1705   b. 1714
               d. 1766

IV.   **Rachel Moorman** (great-grandmother of Mark Twain)
               b. 1754
                d. 1833

(see Goggin ancestors of Mark Twain)

FAMILY OF JOHN MARSHALL AND JANE LAMPTON CLEMENS

John Marshall Clemens married **Jane Lampton** on 6 May 1823.
b. 11 August 1798   b. 18 June 1803
d. 24 March 1847   d. 27 October 1890

Issue

1.   Orion Clemens married   Mary Eleanor (Mollie) Stotts on 19 December 1854.
     b. 17 July 1825   b. 4 April 1834
     d. 11 December 1897   d. 15 January 1904

2.   Pamela Ann Clemens   married   William Anderson Moffett on 20 September 1851.
     b. 13 September 1827   b. 13 July 1816
     d. 31 August 1904   d. 4 August 1865

3.   Pleasant Hannibal Clemens
     b. 1828 or 1829
     d. at 3 months of age

4.   Margaret Lampton Clemens
     b. 31 May 1830
     d. 17 August 1839

5.   Benjamin Lampton Clemens
     b. 8 June 1832
     d. 12 May 1842

6.   **Samuel Langhorne Clemens** married Olivia Louise Langdon on 2 February 1870.
     b. 30 November 1835   b. 27 November 1845
     d. 21 April 1910   d. 5 June 1904

7.   Henry Clemens
     b. 13 July 1838
     d. 21 June 1858

FAMILY OF SAMUEL LANGHORNE CLEMENS AND OLIVIA LOUISE LANGDON

Samuel Langhorne Clemens   married   Olivia Louise (Livy) Langdon (daughter of Jervis Langdon [1809–1870] and Olivia Lewis [1810–1890]) on 2 February 1870.

     b. 30 November 1835   b. 27 November 1845
     d. 21 April 1910   d. 5 June 1904

Issue

1.   Langdon Clemens
     b. 7 November 1870
     d. 2 June 1872

2.   Olivia Susan (Susy) Clemens
     b. 19 March 1872
     d. 18 August 1896

3.   Clara Langdon Clemens   married   (1) Ossip Solomonovitch Gabrilowitsch on 6 October 1909.
     b. 8 June 1874   b. 8 February 1878
     d. 19 November 1962   d. 14 September 1936

                                      (2) Jacques Alexander Samossoud on 11 May 1944.
                                      b. 8 September 1894
                                      d. 13 June 1966

4.   Jane Lampton (Jean) Clemens
     b. 26 July 1880
     d. 24 December 1909

FAMILY OF CLARA LANGDON CLEMENS AND
OSSIP SOLOMONOVITCH GABRILOWITSCH

Clara Langdon Clemens   married   (1) Ossip Solomonovitch Gabrilowitsch (son of Solomon Gabrilowitsch and Rosa Segal of St. Petersburg, Russia) on 6 October 1909.

b. 8 June 1874	b. 8 February 1878
d. 19 November 1962	d. 14 September 1936

                                            (2) Jacques Alexander Samossoud on 11 May 1944.
                                            b. 8 September 1894
                                            d. 13 June 1966

Issue (by Gabrilowitsch)

1.   Nina Clemens Gabrilowitsch   married   Carl Roters in 1934.
                 b. 18 August 1910
                 d. 16 January 1966

Note: Carl Roters lived with Nina in her New York apartment from around 1932–1935, much to the chagrin of her parents. Although Nina once told a reporter during a newspaper interview that she had been married to Roters, no record of the marriage has been found (see pages 208–226 in Caroline Thomas Harnsberger's *Mark Twain's Clara*). I have seen Roters's name spelled "Rutgers" and "Rogers," but in letters between Nina and Clara of the period, "Roters" seems to be correct. Soon after her father's death and her separation from Roters, Nina changed her name from Gabrilowitsch and with the court's permission became Nina Clemens. She was the last descendant of Mark Twain.

Lucius M. Lampton

Index

The editor's have tried to generate a usable index for this volume, and largely by doing two things: by listing only those items that might facilitate research and by placing in bold type inclusive page numbers for those items that also appear as entry titles in the text. For titles of works by Mark Twain, look under Samuel Langhorne Clemens.

A

Abbott, Jacob, 620
Abbey (character), 211
A.B. Chambers (steamboat), 93
Abel, 262, 263, 264
abolition, **3–4**, 65, 114, 156, 189, 371, 441, 474, 516, 564, 609, 686, 790
aborigines, 614
Abstracts of English Studies, 755
absurdism, 326, 442
absurdity, 213
Academie Julien (Paris), 383
Academy of Design (New York), 40
Academy of Music (San Francisco), xii
Acorns (society), 106
Acropolis, 44
Adair County, Kentucky, 152, 438
Adam, 5, 29–30, 74, 75–76, 119, 120, 157, 167, 177, 181, 261, 263–265, 273–275, 323, 327, 344, 442, 461, 516, 522, 598, 625–626, 714, 730
Adams, Henry, 505
    Democracy, 486
Adams, Henry (character), 111, 515–516
Adams, (Sir) John, 512
    Everyman's Psychology, 512; *Herbartian Psychology*, 621
Adams, Lucille
    "Huckleberry Finn": A Descriptive Bibliography of the "Huckleberry Finn" Collections at the Buffalo Public Library, 78
Adams Colony, 245
Ade, George, 137, 455, 497, 755
adolescence, 94–96, 104
Adolf, Father, 290
adultery, 65, 674
Adventures of Huckleberry Finn (book) (see Clemens, Samuel Langhorne)
Adventures of Huckleberry Finn (comic strip), 168
Adventures of Huckleberry Finn (video), 500–501
Adventures of Mark Twain (video), 500, 502
Adventures of Tom Sawyer, The (book) (see Clemens, Samuel Langhorne)
Adventures of Tom Sawyer, The (video), 500, 501
advice column, 15–16, 34, 46–47

Aesop's fables, 223
Agincourt, Battle of, 604
Aguinaldo, Emilio, 211, 707
Aix-les-Bains, France, 18, **19**, 583
Alabama, University of, 173
Alabama Symposium on English and American Literature, 173
Alaska, 115
Albany, New York, 165, 319, 351
Albert, Prince Consort, 244–245
Alcott, Louisa May, **19–20**, 95
    Jo's Boys, 19; *Little Men*, 19, 20; *Little Women*, 19, 95, 383; *Work: A Story of Experience*, 19
Alden, Henry M., 265
Alderman Library (University of Virginia), 186, 467, 489, 577
Aldrich, Thomas Bailey, **20–21**, 352, 488, 526, 528, 621
    "Ballad of Babie Bell," 20; "Marjorie Daw," 20; *Story of a Bad Boy, The*, 13, 20, 94–95, 172, 652
Aleman, Mateo
    Guzman de Alfarache, 578
Alexander II, Czar of Russia, 356, 645
Alexander III, Czar of Russia, 18
Alexandra, Queen of England, 245
Alexandria (Egypt), 245
Alfred T. Lacey (steamboat), 93, 580
Alger, Horatio, 95, 128, 562, 656
Alighieri, Dante (see Dante)
Alisande la Carteloise (see Sandy)
Alison, Cathy (character), 368
Allbright, Dick (character), 209, 332
allegory, 180
Allen, Elizabeth Aker, 391
    "Rock Me to Sleep, Mother," 391
Allen, Helen, **21**, 28
Allen, James Lane, 627
Allen, William H., 21, 72
Allen, Woody, 455
Allminax, 81, 82
Alonzo Child (steamboat), 93, 580
Altangi, Lien Chi (character), 330
Ament, Joseph P., xi, **22**, 345, 647
Ament, Reverend William S., 23, 142, 388, 737–738
America (steamship), 713, 765
American Academy of Art (Rome, Italy), 514
American Academy of Arts and Letters, **370–371**
American Bible Society, **22**
American Board of Foreign Missions, **23**, 142, 261, 518, 737
American Copyright League, 183
American folklore, 350–351
American Folklore Society, 294
American Hebrew, The, 413
American Humor Association, 174
American Literary Realism, 78, 426
American Literary Scholarship: An Annual, 78, 82, 242

American Literature, 78, 88, 426, 755
American Literature Association, 173, 493
American Museum (New York), 63
American Playhouse series, 500, 501–502, 598
American Publisher, 67, 565
American Publishing Company, 13, **25**, 29, 90, 91, 160, 240–241, 348, 384, 399, 487, 720
American Quarterly, 426
"American Radio Theatre of the Air, The," 503
American Revolution, 563
American School for Girls (Berlin), 649
American Studies Association, 173
anarchy, 349
Anderson, David D., 395
Anderson, Frederick, **26**, 186, 359, 495, 496, 662, 738
Anderson, Sherwood, 536
    "I Want to Know Why," 456
Andrews, Kenneth R., 314
    Nook Farm: Mark Twain's Hartford Circle, 325
Andreyeva, Maria, 331
Angel Fish (see Angel Fish and Aquarium Club)
Angel Fish and Aquarium Club, 21, **28**, 72, 141, 158, 211, 284, 309, 673, 766, 797
Angel's Camp, California, xii, **26–27**, 60, 108, 116, 117, 134, 181, 321, 420, 651, 690, 779, 786
Angelo and Luigi (Cappello) (characters), **28–31**, 232, 563, 596–598, 735, 794
animals, 27, **31–34**, 48, 49, 60, 116, 134–135, 153, 202, 216, 223–224, 251, 277, 296, 368–369, 388, 417–419, 508, 513, 533, 699–700, 706, 786
Anthony, A.V.S., 382
Anthony, Stuart, 501
Anthony, Susan B., **35**, 322
anti-hero, 357, 455
anti-imperialism (see imperialism)
Anti-Imperialist League (New York), 388, 649, 707, 738
anti-Semitism, 52, 234, 272, 413–414, 613, 695
Antoinette, Marie, 127, 205, 307
Apaches, 393
aphorisms, **35–36**, 80, 82, 213, 237, 297, 363, 594, 596, 597, 749, 794
Appleton, Thomas, 639
Apuleius
    Golden Ass, The, 578
Aquarium Club (see Angel Fish and Aquarium Club)
Arac, Jonathan, 173
Argonaut, 80

Esmeralda County, Nevada, 538
essay, 162, 223
Essays in Arts and Sciences, 426
Essex, Colonel Cecil Burleigh (character), 597, 643
Estate of Samuel L. Clemens, 149, 168, **256–257**, 494, 562
Estelle Doheny Collection, 298
Ethelton, Rosannah (character), 473
ethics, 290
Étretat, France, 300
Europe, xii, 49–53, 55, 70, 89, 131, 160, 161, 167, 214, 251–252, 254, **257–260**, 260–261, 315, 373, 387, 396–397, 406–407, 410–411, 413, 507, 532, 564, 583, 722–723, 742–744, 746–748, 785, 799
European travels (*see* travels)
Eve, 5, 75–76, 119, 120, 181, 261, **262–263**, 263–265, 274, 327, 421, 442, 461, 730, 796
Everett, Edward, 115
Every Saturday, 233
evil, 29–31, 275, 422, 517
evolution, 67, 121, 202, 204–205, 216, **267–268**, 361, 474, 478–479, 536, 574, 666, 708, 773
exaggeration, 40, 106, 178, 213, **268–269**, 270, 280, 287, 319, 377, 462, 482, 525, 540, 584, 586, 682, 685
"Extracts from the Diaries of Adam and Eve" (video), 502
extrasensory perception, 443, 444, **510–512**, 552, 709

F

F.F.V. (First Families of Virginia), 231, 232, 234, 597, 643
fable, 388, 417–419, 682, 699–700
Fago, John Norwood, 170
Fair, Laura, 354, 446
Fairbanks, Abel W., 281
Fairbanks, Mary Mason, 75, 101, 103, 136, 186, 249, **281–282**, 309, 316, 352, 399–400, 441, 488, 593, 630, 652, 659, 672, 674, 689, 708
Fairfax, Jack (character), 226, 363
Fairfax, Squire (character), 787
faith, 121, 667
faith healing, 143, 153, 234, 238–239, 411, 631
Fall (of man), 75, 76, 121, 181, 261, 262–263, 264, 265–266, 274–275, 343, 442, 626, 730, 754
family life, 52, 70, 82, 84, 103–104, 155–158, 189, 246–247, 269–270, **282–284**, 292, 315, 338–339, 366–367, 480–483, 527–528, 544–545, 649, 673–674, 788–789
Famous Authors and Their Books, 576
Fanshaw, Buck, **285**, 675

fantasy, 300, 533, 632–633, 685, 719, 736, 789
farce, 29, 124–125, 280, 595, 735
Farmer, Philip Jose, 272
  Dark Design, The, 272; *Fabulous Riverboat, The*, 272
Farr, Naunerle, 170
Farrell, James T., 536
  Studs Lonigan, 536
Fathom, Sergeant (character), 423
Fatout, Paul
  Mark Twain in Virginia City, 84; *Mark Twain on the Lecture Circuit*, 452
Faubourg, St. Antoine (Paris), 564
Faulkner, William, 9, 350, 598, 702, 704
  Light in August, 517
Faux, William, **285**
  Memorable Days in America, 285
Fawkes, William (*see* Faux, William)
Fay, Morgan le, 209, **285–286**, 386, 674
Feaster, John, 426
Feldman, Scott, 169
Feldner, August (character), 177, 180, 230–231, 279, 290, 298–299, 444, 532–533
feminism, 221
Fenians, **286**
Fentress County, Tennessee, 153, 312, 412, 729
Ferdinand, Franz, 50
Ferguson, DeLancey, 77
  Mark Twain: Man and Legend, 83
Ferguson, Henry, 529
Ferguson, Samuel, 529
Fernseher, 51
feudalism, 175, 252, 361, 397, 442, 506
feuds, 125, 205, 209, 336, 447, 676, 679
Fiedler, Leslie, 131, 173, 309, 596
Field, Eugene, II, 298
Field, Stephen J., 339
Fielding, Henry, 140, 253, 654
  Joseph Andrews, 377; *Tom Jones*, 578, 674
Fields, James T., 45, **288**, 371, 556, 734
  Yesterdays with Authors, 288
films (*see* media interpretations)
filmstrips, 503–504
fingerprinting, 215, 511, 595, 597–598, 728, 794
Fink, Mike, 706
Finn, Huckleberry, 6–11, 13, 15, 75, 90, 93, 120, 162, 176, 180, 209, 227, 234–235, **288–289**, 349, 356, 357, 359, 362, 374–375, 379, 385, 397, 416, 456, 457, 471–472, 500, 519, 615, 633, 635–636, 657, 676, 679, 692, 693, 698, 704, 731, 739–740, 741, 761
Finn, Jimmy, 288, 289

Finn, Pap, 7, 197, **289–290**, 397, 447, 556, 635
Firkins, Terry, 496
First Book of the Author's Club, Liber Scriptorum, The, 117, 710
First Church of Christ, Scientist, 143, 239
first-person narration (*see* point of view)
Fischer, Theodor, 180, 279, **290–291**, 531, 745, 768
Fischer, Victor, 88, 496
Fisher, Isaac, 61
Fisher, Philip, 785
Fiske, Harrison Grey, 291
  Hester Crewe, 291
Fiske, Minnie Maddern, 233, **291**, 368
FitzGerald, Edward, 16, **291–292**
  Rubáiyát of Omar Khayyám, The, 16, 253, 291, 529, 563, 620
Fitzgerald, F. Scott
  Great Gatsby, The, 456, 457
Flaubert, Gustave, 372, 622
  Madame Bovary, 622
Fleming, Marjorie, 100, 239, 240
Flint, Timothy, 346
Florence, Italy, 49, 53, 55, 157, 223, 247, 258, 406–407, 430, 532, 569, 735, 750, 801
Florida, Missouri, 151, 154, 159, 174, **293**, 328, 345, 365, 497, 514, 602, 603, 613, 647
Flynn, Errol, 501
Foard, J. Macdonough, 329
Fogarty, Thomas, 382
folklore, 27, 74, 135, 218, 274, **293–295**, 328–329, 350–351, 418, 439–440, 507, 512, 581, 705, 706
folktales, 274, 332, 350, 555
Foner, Philip S., 199, 211, 320, 413, 414, 587
  Mark Twain: Social Critic, 435, 738
Foote, Mary Hallock, 101
Ford, Darius R., 38–39
forgeries, **297–298**, 514–515
Forrest, Edwin, 675
Forty-Four, 176, 177, 180, **298–299**, 359, 385, 532–533
Forum, The (magazine), 36, 51, **299**
Foss, Lucas, 504
Foster, Electra (Aleck) (character), 300
Foster, Lewis, 501
Foster, Saladin (Sally) (character), 111, 300
Foster, Saladin and Electra, **300**, 732
Fowler, Jessie A., 578
Fowler, Lorenzo Niles, 577
Fowler and Wells, phrenologists, 577
Fox, Alan, 617
fragmentation, 671
frame device, 123, 134, 176, 255, 270, 404, 418–420, 482, 486, 584, 682, 705, 712, 751–752, 788
France, xiv, 89, 126–128, 132, 258, **300–301**, 306, 307, 334, 421, 536,